Mozart's enduring popularity, among music lovers as a composer and among music historians as a subject for continued study, lies at the heart of *The Cambridge Mozart Encyclopedia*. This reference book functions both as a starting point for information on specific works, people, places and concepts as well as a summation of current thinking about Mozart. The extended articles on genres reflect the latest in scholarship and new ways of thinking about the works while the articles on people and places provide a historical framework, as well as interpretation. The book also includes a series of thematic articles that cast a wide net over the eighteenth century and Mozart's relationship to it: these include Austria, Germany, aesthetics, travel, Enlightenment, Mozart as a reader, and contemporaneous medicine, among others. Many of the topics covered have never been written about before in English-language Mozart publications or in such detail, and represent today's greater interest in previously unexplored aspects of Mozart's life, context and reception. The worklist provides the most up-to-date account in English of the authenticity and chronology of Mozart's compositions.

CLIFF EISEN is Reader in Historical Musicology at King's College London. He has published numerous articles on Mozart and late eighteenth-century music, and is currently working on an annotated translation of Hermann Abert's classic *W. A. Mozart* as well as an edition of selected Mozart letters.

SIMON P. KEEFE is Professor and Head of Music at City University London. He is the author of *Mozart's Piano Concertos: Dramatic Dialogue in the Age of Enlightenment* (2001) and editor of *The Cambridge Companion to Mozart* (2003) and *The Cambridge Companion to the Concerto* (2005).

The Cambridge Mozart Encyclopedia

Edited by CLIFF EISEN and SIMON P. KEEFE

CAMBRIDGE
UNIVERSITY PRESS

CAMBRIDGE UNIVERSITY PRESS
Cambridge, New York, Melbourne, Madrid, Cape Town, Singapore, São Paulo

Cambridge University Press
The Edinburgh Building, Cambridge CB2 2RU, UK

Published in the United States of America by Cambridge University Press, New York

www.cambridge.org
Information on this title: www.cambridge.org/9780521856591

First published 2006

Printed in the United Kingdom at the University Press, Cambridge

A catalogue record for this publication is available from the British Library

Library of Congress Cataloguing in Publication data
The Cambridge Mozart encyclopedia / edited by Cliff Eisen and Simon P. Keefe.
p. cm.
Includes bibliographical references.
ISBN 0-521-85659-0 (hardback)
1. Mozart, Wolfgang Amadeus, 1756–1791 – Encyclopedias. I. Eisen, Cliff,
1952– II. Keefe, Simon P., 1968– III. Title.
ML410.M9C257 2006
780′.92–dc22 2005012509

ISBN-13 978-0-521-85659-1 hardback
ISBN-10 0-521-85659-0 hardback

To Katy, Sam, Celia, Abraham and Madeleine

Contents

Contributors

SARAH ADAMS
Isham Memorial Library, Harvard University

RUDOLPH ANGERMÜLLER
Internationale Stiftung Mozarteum, Salzburg

DEREK BEALES
University of Cambridge

RACHEL BECKLES WILLSON
Royal Holloway, University of London

PETER BRANSCOMBE
University of St Andrews

BRUCE ALAN BROWN
University of Southern California

†A. PETER BROWN

TIM CARTER
University of North Carolina

SHARON CHOA
University of East Anglia

PAUL CORNEILSON
Carl Philipp Emanuel Bach Edition, Cambridge, MA

TIA DENORA
University of Exeter

SERGIO DURANTE
University of Padua

CLIFF EISEN
King's College London

FAYE FERGUSON
Neue Mozart-Ausgabe, Salzburg

GENEVIEVE GEFFRAY
Biblioteca Mozartiana, Internationale Stiftung Mozarteum, Salzburg

RUTH HALLIWELL
Independent scholar

ROGER HELLYER
Independent scholar

MARY HUNTER
Bowdoin College

THOMAS IRVINE
Cornell University

JOHN IRVING
University of Bristol

FRIEDL JARY
Independent scholar

DAVID WYN JONES
University of Wales, Cardiff

SIMON P. KEEFE
City University London

ULRICH KONRAD
University of Würzburg

ANDREA LINDMAYR-BRANDL
University of Salzburg

DOROTHEA LINK
University of Georgia

BRUCE C. MACINTYRE
Brooklyn College, Conservatory of Music

SIMON MCVEIGH
Goldsmiths College, University of London

NICHOLAS MATHEW
University of Oxford

MARY SUE MORROW
University of Cincinnati

ROBERT MÜNSTER
Bayerische Staatsbibliothek, Munich

DON NEVILLE
University of Western Ontario

MICHEL NOIRAY
Institut de recherche sur le patrimoine musical en France, Paris

PAMELA L. POULIN
Johns Hopkins University

MICHAEL QUINN
King's College London

WOLFGANG REHM
Neue Mozart-Ausgabe, Salzburg

JOHN A. RICE
Independent scholar

JULIAN RUSHTON
University of Leeds

†STANLEY SADIE

DAVID SCHROEDER
Dalhousie University

ÁINE SHEIL
Royal Opera House, London

JAN SMACZNY
Queen's University Belfast

JOHN SPITZER
San Francisco Conservatory of Music

WILLIAM STAFFORD
University of Huddersfield

YO TOMITA
Queen's University of Belfast

LINDA L. TYLER
Princeton University

JESSICA WALDOFF
College of the Holy Cross, Worcester, MA

HARRY WHITE
University College Dublin

NEAL ZASLAW
Cornell University

Preface

Mozart's enduring popularity, among music lovers as a composer and among music historians as a subject for continued study, lies at the heart of this book: even now, 250 years after his birth, Mozart remains an iconic figure in western society. One fortunate result of this – fortunate for both the music lover and the musicologist – is that new 'facts' about his life, new sources for his music, and new interpretations of his works are a regular feature of Mozart performance and the Mozart literature. As much as for any other composer, then, we constantly renew our relationship with Mozart, through listening and reading and thinking.

There have been some distinguished Mozart compendia in the past: H. C. Robbins Landon and Donald Mitchell's *Mozart Companion* of 1956 springs immediately to mind; so too does Landon's *Mozart Compendium* of 1990. The first of these coincided with the two hundredth anniversary of Mozart's birth, the second with the two hundredth anniversary of his death. The *Cambridge Mozart Encyclopedia* celebrates Mozart's two hundred and fiftieth birthday but it differs from those two volumes in significant ways. *The Mozart Companion* was a collection of extended, often brilliant, essays, organized by genre; it was not the volume's intention to give an account of Mozart's life or the contexts in which he worked. *The Mozart Compendium*, on the other hand, paid much more attention to Mozart's life and times but included much shorter essays on the music itself.

It is not the case, however, that we have merely attempted to bridge the gap. On the contrary, this book attempts to bring together the complex of Mozart's life and works in the form of a dictionary that is full of implicit and explicit cross-references and that can be read bit by bit or even, by the brave, all at once: that is to say, it functions both as a starting point for information on specific works, people, places and concepts as well as a summation of current thinking about Mozart. The extended articles on genres reflect the latest in scholarship and new ways of thinking about the works while the articles on people and places provide the necessary historical framework, as well as interpretation. At the same time, we have included a series of thematic articles that cast a wide net over the eighteenth century and Mozart's relationship to it: these include Austria, Germany, aesthetics, travel, Enlightenment, Mozart as a reader and contemporaneous medicine, among others.

The volume is organized in dictionary format, with individual articles, long or short, ranging from A to Z. This hardly solves the problem of finding specific information on people, places and works, though: not every place, or every person, or even every work has its own entry. But they are here somewhere and we encourage the reader to consult the index, which we have tried to make as comprehensive as possible.

In addition, we include several appendices. The most important, perhaps, is the worklist, which provides the most up-to-date account in English of the authenticity and chronology of Mozart's compositions; it supersedes a similar worklist in the revised edition of *The New Grove Dictionary of Music and Musicians* (London, 2001) and *The New Grove Mozart* (London, 2002). Other appendices include lists of theatrically released Mozart biopics (an area ripe for further study), commercially released videos of the operas, important Mozart institutions and Mozart websites.

In general, we have relied on some standard Mozart texts for basic information. They are not cited in individual lists of 'further reading' but they contributed significantly (if tacitly) to virtually every article in this volume: Otto Erich Deutsch, *Mozart: die Dokumente seines Lebens* (Kassel, 1961; English trans. Eric Blom, Peter Branscombe and Jeremy Noble as *Mozart: A Documentary Biography* (London, 1965)); Wilhelm A. Bauer, Otto Erich Deutsch and Joseph Heinz Eibl, eds., *Mozart: Briefe und Aufzeichnungen* (Kassel, 1962–75; for a partial translation of the Mozart letters, see Emily Anderson, ed., *The Letters of Mozart and his Family* (London, 1985) and Cliff Eisen, ed., *Mozart. A Life in Letters* (London, 2006)); Peter Clive, *Mozart and his Circle* (New Haven, 1993). We encourage readers to consult these volumes as well.

Works are identified by their numbers in the standard catalogue of Mozart's works by Ludwig Köchel (see Appendix 1: Worklist for full details). Pitches are identified by the Helmholtz system, where middle C is identified as c′, the c above as c″ and the c above that as c‴; similarly the c below middle c is identified as c, the c below that as C. All pitches within any particular ascending octave are similarly identified.

Finally, we want to thank all of the contributors both for their hard work and for their patience; Cambridge University Press, and in particular Vicki Cooper, for taking on this volume; and especially Ruth Halliwell, who contributed significantly to shaping the book in its early stage, providing constant good advice.

CLIFF EISEN and SIMON P. KEEFE

A

Abduction, The. See ENTFÜHRUNG AUS DEM SERAIL, DIE

Abel, Carl Friedrich (b. Cöthen 22 Dec. 1723; d. London 20 June 1787). German composer and viola da gamba player, resident mainly in LONDON. Abel's father was a court musician at Cöthen alongside J. S. BACH, and Carl Friedrich may subsequently have studied with Bach in Leipzig. He left a post at the Dresden court as a result of the Seven Years War, travelling to London, where he gave his first concert on 5 April 1759. Arriving at the very start of a vogue for the latest German symphonies, Abel quickly became a major figure in London's concert life, both as instrumentalist and composer. Though the viola da gamba was regarded as outdated, even an eccentricity, his playing was so deeply expressive that his solos were constantly in demand for over twenty years (his Adagio became a byword for heartfelt performance and a model for string players). He was also successful in nurturing the patronage of aristocrats such as the Earl of Thanet (at whose house in 1764 LEOPOLD MOZART became seriously ill); and probably in 1763 he was appointed chamber musician to the Queen. So too was J. C. BACH (whom he may have known from Germany), and on 29 February 1764 they gave their first concert together. In 1765 they joined forces in what became known as the Bach–Abel concerts, a series that ran until Bach's death in 1782. Though closer to J. C. BACH, Mozart must have worked alongside Abel; he even copied out his symphony Op. 7 No. 6 (mistakenly attributed to Mozart in the first edition of the Köchel catalogue, K18). In E flat major, it unusually features trios for two clarinets and bassoon, a sonority Mozart favoured later in life. Abel was mainly known for his symphonies and string quartets: though not perhaps as compelling as those of J. C. BACH (Burney found a certain languor in Abel's refinement and learning), they tap a richer vein of counterpoint and chromaticism, with slow movements often exploiting a sonorous four-part string texture.

Mozart seems to have lost contact with Abel, whose career was largely tied up with London's concert life for the next twenty years. A close friend of Gainsborough, Abel outlived Bach and ran the concerts in 1782; after a visit to Germany he was appointed principal composer to the Professional Concert in 1785. Mozart did not forget him entirely, however: shortly after Abel's death in 1787, he refashioned a moto perpetuo theme from Abel's early trio Op. 5 No. 5 in the finale of the violin sonata K526. SIMON MCVEIGH

Adamberger, Johann Valentin (b. Rohr, Bavaria, 22 Feb. 1740; d. Vienna, 24 Aug. 1804). German tenor. Adamberger's early career took him to Italy in 1762, where he sang under the name Adamonti, and LONDON in 1777, where he sang the title role in J. C. BACH's *La clemenza di Scipione*. He was engaged at VIENNA in 1780, first at the German opera and later at the Italian opera. His roles included Orfeo in GLUCK's *Orfeo ed Euridice* (1781) and Ruggiero in Sacchini's *La contadina in corte* (1782); Adamberger was the original Belmonte in Mozart's DIE ENTFÜHRUNG AUS DEM SERAIL (also 1782). Mozart thought highly of Adamberger while the dramatist Gebler described him as combining 'great artistry with a marvellous voice'. In addition to Belmonte in *Die Entführung*, Mozart also composed for Adamberger the part of Monsieur Vogelsang in DER SCHAUSPIELDIREKTOR as well as the aria 'Per pietà, non ricercate', K420, the recitative and aria *Misero! O sogno . . . Aura, che intorno spiri*, K431, the aria 'A te, fra tanti affanni', K469 and possibly the tenor part in the cantata *Die Maurerfreude*, K471. No doubt Adamberger and Mozart were good friends: they socialized frequently and both were Freemasons and members of the lodge 'Zur neugekrönten Hoffnung' ('New Crowned Hope'). Adamberger retired from the stage in 1792.

CLIFF EISEN

'Adelaide Concerto'. A spurious violin concerto by H. Casadesus. See APPENDIX 1, WORKLIST

Adlgasser, Anton Cajetan (b. Inzell, Bavaria, 1 Oct. 1729; d. Salzburg, 21/2 Dec. 1777). Organist and composer. Adlgasser, who from 1744 studied at the SALZBURG Cathedral chapel house, was appointed court and cathedral organist in 1750; from 1760 he also served as organist at the Dreifaltigkeitskirche. Chiefly a composer of sacred music, Adlgasser collaborated with MICHAEL HAYDN and Mozart on the oratorio *Die Schuldigkeit des ersten Gebots* (1767). A friend of the Mozart family – Leopold was a witness at all three of his weddings – Adlgasser died after suffering a stroke while performing at the cathedral. Leopold described the event in a letter of 22 December 1777. Mozart succeeded Adlgasser as court and cathedral organist in 1779.

CLIFF EISEN

aesthetics. Composers since the eighteenth century often have had much to say about their own compositional principles, philosophical inclinations, the influences on them, or relationships with their listeners; these matters, when added together, could provide a composite view of their aesthetics. It would be desirable, of course, to have such declarations from major eighteenth-century composers as well, and we generally believe we have this kind of statement from Mozart in his letters to his father about the composition of DIE ENTFÜHRUNG AUS DEM SERAIL. These letters include, among other comments, his famous remark (in a letter of 13 Oct. 1781) that 'in an opera the poetry must absolutely be the obedient daughter of the music', in apparent contradiction to GLUCK's equally famous dictum that the role of music must be subordinate to poetry.

To take this and some of Mozart's other pronouncements about *Die Entführung* at face value would involve a much too naive reading of his letters. At this point in 1782 Mozart had good reason to write things that his father LEOPOLD MOZART wanted to hear. The two of them had just had a highly rancorous exchange of letters over Mozart's departure from service in Salzburg, and possibly anticipating an even more fractious correspondence over his impending marriage plans, Mozart may have written these letters as a kind of peace offering, reviving Leopold's long-standing enthusiasm for hearing about his son's works. For a number of reasons these remarks about opera appear to have more to do with strategies in dealing with an overbearing father than true sentiments about composition; in fact, the time for frankness in such matters had in all probability elapsed.

Both Mozart and his father could readily recognize that Gluck held a pre-eminent position among opera composers, but Leopold had an old grudge against Gluck dating back to the early 1760s, involving imagined plots against himself and his children, supposedly instigated by Gluck. Leopold rekindled this animosity now that Mozart lived in Vienna, and Mozart's statement on music and poetry, contrary to Gluck's view, could have been intended to give Leopold satisfaction. Leopold also expected Mozart to repay his financial debt to him, and a number of Mozart's views about composition seem designed to demonstrate the soundness of his compositional principles, which would allow him to appeal to an audience and make more money than he could in Salzburg.

In the early 1780s, JOSEPH VON SONNENFELS still exerted considerable influence on the cultural life of VIENNA, advancing a sober, moralistic approach in the old style of the ENLIGHTENMENT which undoubtedly appealed to Leopold Mozart, banishing HANSWURST from the stage and showing a strong preference for serious works devoid of comic features. One of Mozart's first statements to his father on composing opera in Vienna accounted directly for Sonnenfels's reforms: 'do you really believe that I would write an opéra comique the same way as an opera seria? In an opera seria there should be less frivolity and more erudition and sensibility, as in an opera buffa there should be less of the learned and all the more frivolity and merriment . . . here [in Vienna] they correctly differentiate on this point. I definitely find in music that Hanswurst has not yet been eradicated, and in this case the French are right' (letter of 16 June 1781). In the end these views had little bearing on *Die Entführung*, which not only mixed the comic and serious equally but also gave rise to another form of Hanswurst, this time in Turkish garb in the role of Osmin.

Leopold Mozart held strong views on aesthetics, which he tried valiantly to inculcate in his son, approaches adapted not only from the leading writers of music treatises such as Johann Mattheson, C. P. E. BACH and Friedrich Wilhelm Marpurg, but from his favourite literary figures as well, including Johann Christoph Gottsched, CHRISTIAN FÜRCHTEGOTT GELLERT and CHRISTOPH MARTIN WIELAND. Following the lead of these writers, Leopold argued the need to adjust to the taste of the audience in any particular locale, to maintain simplicity and clarity, to serve moral goals in the old enlightened sense of promoting refinement, and to secure approbation before attempting anything more complex or challenging.

As the gulf between father and son became greater – probably by the end of the sojourn in Paris in January 1779 it had expanded to an unbridgeable distance – Mozart became much less inclined to take any of this advice seriously. Already before reaching the age of fourteen Mozart had expressed his derision for Gellert, Leopold's ultimate aesthetic model and one-time correspondent, with his cheeky commentary to his sister (including a pun on Gellert and *gelehrt*, or learned) on the poet's death: 'I have nothing new except that Herr gelehrt, the poet from Leipzig, died and since his death has composed no more poetry' (letter of 26 Jan. 1770). Both siblings were no doubt relieved to be spared more moralizing from that quarter.

Identifying the old aesthetic approaches that Mozart rejected may very well be easier than placing him within an aesthetic outlook to which he subscribed. In fact, finding the parallels between aesthetics, a branch of philosophy concerned with such things as beauty and taste or the study of the principles of art, and the products of the creative mind, can be challenging. While composers of the Enlightenment frequently saw themselves on a mission of morality or intelligibility that could be defined in specific aesthetic terms, Mozart in many respects defied that type of identification, often subverting those principles in both vocal and instrumental works.

Aesthetic opinion in the second half of the eighteenth century had not always been kind to instrumental music, regarding vocal music as superior because of its potential to sustain rhetoric and achieve intelligibility. Even JOSEPH HAYDN took that into account when describing his own achievements in 1776, singling out his various vocal works while referring only casually to his instrumental output. We have no reason to believe that Mozart would have been interested in or bothered by this distinction.

Similarly, some of the lively debates among certain prominent aestheticians, including Diderot, d'Alembert, Rousseau, Kant and Lessing, appear to have been of no particular interest to Mozart. In developing a theory of language, Rousseau generally confined music to a role of expressing feelings, something melody could do especially well; this relegated harmony and counterpoint to a place of insignificance since rationality lay beyond the reach of music. D'Alembert pegged music even lower in a comparison with the other arts, and Kant dropped it to the very bottom, entirely lacking, in his view, any rational or cognitive potential. Frustrated by these arguments, Lessing countered that the contrasting properties of the different arts rendered any such comparison useless. Diderot placed music highest among the arts because, he believed, the imagination can grasp and work the material of music most directly, not requiring conventional language as an intermediary. Diderot surely came closest to describing the origin and effect of Mozart's music, and Mozart, through his friendship with Diderot's colleague Louise d'Epinay, had perhaps even learned principles from Diderot, such as the workings of irony, which could be transferred into musical language.

As philosophers, aestheticians do not necessarily concern themselves with the actual workings of an art such as music when formulating principles that apply to it. Kant's categories appear to have arisen from a personal dislike of music, an annoyance that at times prevented his concentration on the serious business of philosophy. Rousseau as a practising musician stood in a better position, although that did not translate into a greater appreciation. Diderot, the most generous in his rating of music, anticipated the views of the *Frühromantiker*, who preferred abstraction to the definite nature of language; in the end this spoke more directly to poetry than to music. Various aspects of Mozart's musical language, with its topoi related to dance, liturgy, carnival or nationality – to say nothing of a host of other ways in which his music could define its own contexts and associations – escaped the grasp of the philosophical writers. Even Diderot would have been astounded to discover that irony, so fundamental to his own literary style, could be generated by Mozart through purely musical means. Here the apparatus of aesthetics dissipates, as the discussion of beauty, taste, the sublime and other facets of aesthetics must give way to the same interpretative considerations as language. Mozart undoubtedly knew that statements about such things as the weighting of music and poetry in opera were pointless, and perhaps even mischievous, and therefore made them only to someone like his father for specific strategic purposes. DAVID SCHROEDER

B. Hosler, *Changing Aesthetic Views of Instrumental Music in 18th-Century Germany* (Ann Arbor, 1981)
P. le Huray and J. Day, eds., *Music and Aesthetics in the Eighteenth and Early-Nineteenth Centuries* (Cambridge, 1981)
D. Schroeder, *Mozart in Revolt: Strategies of Resistance, Mischief and Deception* (New Haven and London, 1999)
'Mozart and Late Eighteenth-Century Aesthetics', in *The Cambridge Companion to Mozart*, ed. S. P. Keefe (Cambridge, 2003), 48–58

Affligio, Giuseppe (b. Naples, 16 Mar. 1722; d. Portoferraio, Elba, 23 June 1788). Theatrical impresario. Described by Casanova as having the 'face of a gallows bird', Affligio travelled throughout Europe as an adventurer before signing a ten-year contract, in 1767, as theatrical impresario in VIENNA. Financial crises forced him to share management of the theatres under his direction, first with Baron Bender, then with GLUCK, before he was obliged in 1770 to transfer control to a Hungarian nobleman, Count Kohary. In 1778 Affligio was arrested for forgery and in 1779 condemned to life imprisonment. It was during his tenure of the Viennese theatres in 1768 that Leopold Mozart tried unsuccessfully to secure a performance of Wolfgang's opera LA FINTA SEMPLICE.

CLIFF EISEN

G. Affligio, *Vita di Giuseppe Affligio*, ed. G. Croll and H. Wagner (Kassel, 1977)
Casanova, *Mémoires*, ed. R. Abirached (Paris, 1958–60)
J.-G. Prod'homme, 'Deux collaborateurs italiens de Gluck. II: Giuseppe d'Affligio', *Rivista Musicale Italiana* 23 (1916), 210–18

Albertarelli, Francesco (fl. 1782–99), Italian bass. He sang the title role of Don Giovanni in the first Viennese production of the opera, under the composer's direction, on 7 May 1788. Mozart also contributed an aria for him (K541) as Don Pompeo in Anfossi's *Le gelosie fortunate* (1788). Albertarelli sang in VIENNA only for the 1788–9 season; most of his career was spent in Italy, although he also visited LONDON (1791), Madrid (1792) and St Petersburg (1799). Benedetto Frizzi described him as an expressive actor and stylish singer.

DOROTHEA LINK

J. Rice, 'Benedetto Frizzi on Singers, Composers and Opera in Late Eighteenth-Century Italy', *Studi musicali* 23 (1994), 367–93

Albrechtsberger, Johann Georg (b. Klosterneuburg, 3 Feb. 1736; d. Vienna, 7 Mar. 1809), German organist and theorist and prolific composer of both church and instrumental music. Educated at Melk Abbey and in VIENNA, Albrechtsberger was appointed second court organist in 1772 and first court organist in

1791. In 1791 he succeeded Mozart as assistant music director at St Stephen's Cathedral; in 1793 he became Kapellmeister following the death of LEOPOLD HOFMANN. Highly regarded as a contrapuntist, Albrechtsberger was also renowned as a theorist and teacher; his pupils included HUMMEL (who had earlier studied with Mozart), BEETHOVEN and Mozart's son, FRANZ XAVER MOZART. Mozart held Albrechtsberger in high esteem. In a letter of 16 April 1789 he wrote with reference to Johann Wilhelm Hässler: 'He is incapable of executing a fugue properly, and does not possess a sound technique. He is thus far from being another Albrechtsberger.' Albrechtsberger may also have counted among Mozart's closest friends; he was probably among the few mourners to accompany the composer's remains to the city gates on 6 December 1791. CLIFF EISEN

Amicis, Anna Lucia de (b. Naples, c.1733; d. Naples, 1816). Italian soprano. Amicis's brilliant career as a singer of opera seria included performances in her native Italy, in PARIS, Dublin, Brussels and in 1762 at the King's Theatre, LONDON. She first met Mozart in Mainz in August 1763 and again in Naples in May 1770. Mozart wrote to his sister on 29 May 1770 that 'De Amicis sings incomparably' and LEOPOLD MOZART wrote to his wife on 26 December 1772 that 'She sings and acts like an angel'. Amicis created the role of Giunia in *Lucio Silla* (Milan, 1772). Her last public performance was in 1779; thereafter she sang privately for several years at Naples. CLIFF EISEN

André, Johann Anton (b. Offenbach, 6 Oct. 1775; d. Offenbach, 6 Apr. 1842). GERMAN composer and music publisher. Johann Anton's father, also Johann and also a composer, mainly of singspiel, had founded a publishing house in 1774 where his son worked at least from 1795. In 1799, Johann Anton visited VIENNA, where on 8 November he signed a contract with CONSTANZE MOZART to purchase Mozart's musical estate; most of the manuscripts were shipped to Offenbach where they were catalogued and studied. André subsequently published 'authentic' editions of many of Mozart's works as well as an edition of Mozart's own thematic catalogue. His study of the manuscripts was a landmark of early musicological endeavour, an attempt to order chronologically the manuscripts according to the characteristics of their handwriting; his pioneering methodology became a mainstay of Mozart scholarship for nearly two hundred years. CLIFF EISEN

A. H. André, *Zur Geschichte der Familie André* (Garmisch, 1963)
U.-M. and J.-J. André, *Festschrift André zum 225. Firmenjubiläum* (Offenbach, 1999)
W. Matthäus, *Johann André Musikverlag zu Offenbach am Main: Verlagsgeschichte und Bibliographie 1772–1800* (Tutzing, 1973)

Antretter family. Members of SALZBURG's minor nobility. Johann Ernst von Antretter (b. Grabenstätt, Chiemsee, 9 Jan. 1718; d. Salzburg, 15 Jan. 1791) was *Landschaftskanzler*. His second wife was Maria Anna Elisabeth Baumgartner (b. 1730; d. 1796). Several of their children were musical, and MARIA ANNA ('NANNERL') MOZART was teacher to one of their daughters.

There are two Mozart works with Antretter connections. The first is the so-called 'Antretter-Serenade', K185, with its march K189. It is believed to have been written as *Finalmusik* in 1773, at the request of the Antretters' son Judas Thaddäus (b. 1753). *Finalmusik* was a genre peculiar to Salzburg, performed by university students to honour and thank their professors in August. The other work cannot be identified with certainty, but since a letter by LEOPOLD MOZART of 25 September 1777 refers to the 'Antretterin Musik' (feminine ending), it must have been written for a woman. It has been suggested that the divertimento K205 (with the march K290), was meant, and that it was written in 1773 to celebrate Antretter's wife's name day (Anne) on 26 July. RUTH HALLIWELL

H. Schuler, *Mozarts Salzburger Freunde und Bekannte* (Wilhelmshaven, 1995), 202–10

Apollo et Hyacinthus, K38. By 1767, the precocious talents of the eleven-year-old Mozart were well known to the small musical community of SALZBURG. Between the return of the Mozart family to Salzburg in December 1766, following three and a half years of travel around the courts of Europe, and Wolfgang's second trip to Vienna with his father in the following September, Mozart composed a series of compositions on a remarkable scale for one so young. They included the Passion cantata known as the *Grabmusik* and Mozart's first dramatic composition, the oratorio *Die Schuldigkeit des ersten Gebots*, performed at the Salzburg *Residenz* on Ash Wednesday. *Apollo et Hyacinthus* was another such composition from this time.

Music historians in search of biographical milestones may be inclined to call *Apollo et Hyacinthus* Mozart's first 'operatic composition' – and with some justification. It is, after all, a secular drama made up of five arias, two duets, a chorus and a trio, all connected with recitatives. That said, a modern score gives the rather misleading impression of a continuous and self-contained stage work. *Apollo et Hyacinthus* was in fact a contribution to a much larger theatrical spectacle – the end-of-term Latin 'final comoedia' staged at the grammar school of the Benedictine University in Salzburg. The custom on such school occasions was to perform short musical dramas known as 'intermedia' between the acts of the principal play, a convention that seems to have evolved from the earlier tradition of concluding each act with musical 'choruses'. Thus, Mozart's piece, interspersed between the acts of a spoken drama, was from one point of view not really an independent composition at all. On 13 May 1767, it shared the stage with a five-act tragedy by the Benedictine monk and philosophy professor Rufinius Widl (1731–98) entitled *Clementia Croesi* – a somewhat long-winded staging of an episode from Herodotus. Indeed, even the title of Mozart's contribution to the entertainment (also written by Father Rufinius) – whose three parts are simply called Prologus, Chorus I and Chorus II – remained unknown until after the composer's death, when his sister NANNERL MOZART entered a piece called 'Apollo und Hyacinth' into LEOPOLD MOZART's 'catalogue' of his son's early works. Until this time, it was not even necessary for Mozart's composition to have a distinguishing title of its own.

The two interlocking dramas by Widl were clearly designed to share general themes and literary motifs. The main tragedy dealt with the accidental death of the son of Croesus, King of Lydia, who was killed by a wayward spear throw by Adrastus, son of Midas, King of Phrygia. Mozart's parallel musical 'comedy' (based on a story first recounted by Euripides) also concerned a tragic accidental killing, although the victim was in this case the object of Apollo's amorous attention, the beautiful youth Hyacinth who was killed by one of Apollo's stray discus throws (albeit with an unhelpful nudge from Apollo's jealous rival Zephyr, the West Wind). Eventually, the grief-stricken Apollo causes a flower of incomparable beauty to grow from Hyacinth's grave.

Although Father Rufinius retained the outlines of this story, he evidently wanted to remove the central theme of sexual love between a man and a boy. The resulting plot is rather more convoluted, featuring two new characters: Hyacinth's father Oebalus and his sister Melia, who is now the principal object of Apollo's affections and Zephyr's jealousy. After Mozart's short D major intrada, the prologue opens with a brief exchange between Zephyr and Hyacinth confirming the youth's attachment to Apollo and Zephyr's envy. Soon after, King Oebalus and Melia appear, preparing a sacrifice to Apollo. The ceremony appears to take a turn for the worse, however, when a violent storm brews up, eventually destroying the altar with lightning. Oebalus fears the worst, but his son reassures him that they have done nothing to incur the wrath of Apollo. At the end of the prologue, Apollo himself appears to confirm Hyacinth's words; he asks for evidence of Melia's love for him and it emerges that it is only Zephyr who aroused Apollo's anger.

Chorus I was performed directly after the second act of the spoken drama. It begins with Melia and her father in high spirits, discussing the possibility of Melia's marriage to Apollo – the uncommon union of a god and a mortal. Their good humour is soon dampened, however, when Zephyr arrives with bad news: as he, Apollo, and Hyacinth sported in the woods, Hyacinth was fatally struck by a discus thrown deliberately by Apollo. Immediately, Oebalus falls into a rage over the murder of his son and orders that Apollo be banished from his kingdom – a command that Zephyr (confessing his guilt in an aside to the audience, lest we believe his story about Apollo) is all too eager to execute. He wastes no time, however, in making amorous advances towards Melia, advances that she is in no mood to consider. During Zephyr's rather inopportune proposals, Apollo suddenly appears, at once declaring his innocence and transforming the cowering Zephyr into a wind, which instantly dissolves into the air. Poor Melia, who still believes Apollo to be the murderer of her brother, now faces yet another series of unwelcome advances, this time from the amorous god.

Chorus II, performed before the final act of *Clementia Croesi*, begins with Hyacinth's dying breaths, which he uses to describe the truth of his murder to his father. Oebalus watches his son die, finally realizing Zephyr's guilt. There is more bad news to follow; Melia appears and informs her father that she has repelled the murderous Apollo's advances. She soon learns the terrible truth from Oebalus, however. With Hyacinth dead and their god and protector angered, the father and daughter bemoan their unlucky fate. Yet here – at the low point of their fortunes – Apollo appears once again. Love for Hyacinth has compelled him to return and he immediately causes a wondrous profusion of flowers to rise from the beautiful youth's grave. The god first reassures Oebalus that he will never forsake his lands and then asks for Melia's hand in marriage for the last time. Melia gratefully accepts his offer. Although Hyacinth is dead, the kingdom will flourish eternally under the protection of Apollo.

The singers at the first performance of *Apollo et Hyacinthus* were, of course, all boys from the grammar school, whose ages ranged from twelve to eighteen: none as young as the boy composer. It does not seem that Mozart spared them technical difficulties, although the nature of the cast – whose voices were presumably in different stages of development – probably accounts for certain peculiarities, such as the unusually low alto parts for Apollo and Zephyr. The parts of Melia and Hyacinth are given to sopranos, and Oebalus to a tenor. The two high priests of Apollo, who add to the GLUCK-like sacrificial chorus (with Oebalus's solo) that opens the piece, are basses – just about possible, at ages sixteen and eighteen.

Most of the arias aim to crystallize a particular emotional state triggered by events that take place in the recitatives; the majority are da capo arias, which repeat the text and music from an A section immediately after a contrasting B section. Occasionally, Mozart curtails or removes the repeat altogether, however – for example, in Apollo's short E major aria that concludes the prologue, which ends with the opening instrumental ritornello but no text repetition. Perhaps the most impressive numbers, from the point of view of the young Mozart's handling of the instrumental and vocal forces involved, as well as his attention to their dramatic function, feature multiple characters. The moving C major duet for the grieving Oebalus and Melia is an extraordinary through-composed movement containing some arresting orchestral effects, such as the muted first violins, under which the rest of the strings play pizzicato. The scene that opens Chorus II, in which Hyacinth dies in the presence of his father, is a strong piece of musical drama and the first example of accompanied recitative in all of Mozart's music. It shows, perhaps more than any other part of this short drama, how soon the eleven-year-old composer had absorbed the myriad techniques of eighteenth-century dramatic composition. NICHOLAS MATHEW

R. Freeman, 'The Applausus Musicus, or Singgedicht: A Neglected Genre of Eighteenth-Century Musical Theatre', in *Music in Eighteenth-Century Austria*, ed. D. W. Jones (Cambridge, 1996), 197–209

C. Gianturco, *Mozart's Early Operas* (London, 1981), 37–46

Arco family. One of SALZBURG's most illustrious noble families and keen supporters of the Mozarts. Surprisingly, there is no Mozart work known to be connected with them.

The head of the family in Mozart's time was Count Georg Anton Felix von Arco (b. Vienna, 24 Apr. 1705; d. Salzburg, 2 Sept. 1792). From 1786 he was court Obersthofmeister. On 17 April 1731 he married Maria Josepha Viktoria von Hardegg (b. 2 Mar. 1710; d. 31 Dec. 1775) and they had numerous children. He was known for his iron will and forceful expression. LEOPOLD MOZART described his heated reaction, in conversation with Count Starhemberg, to

Mozart's first resignation from Salzburg service (letter of 29 Dec. 1777; in the standard English translation by Anderson, the phrase 'Well, let's chuck it!' is better translated as 'What shit!'). The Mozarts always paid appropriate courtesies to the Arcos.

For their daughter Maria Antonia, see LODRON. Their daughter Maria Anna Felicia (b. 17 Dec. 1741; d. 6 Feb. 1764) married the Bavarian ambassador to Paris, Count Maximilian van Eyck. She died while the Mozarts were staying with her during their visit to Paris in 1763–4 (Leopold's letter of 22 Feb. 1764). Their son Joseph Adam (b. 27 Jan. 1733; d. 1802) was Bishop of Königgrätz, and helped secure Mozart's appointment as Salzburg organist in 1778. Another son, Karl Joseph Felix (b. 9 Mar. 1743; d. 1830) was Salzburg Oberstküchenmeister. He accompanied Archbishop Colloredo to Vienna in March 1781, and was involved in Mozart's second resignation from Salzburg service, which (according to Mozart's letter of 9 June 1781) was decisively concluded when Arco kicked Mozart from the antechamber. The Arcos' grandson Leopold Ferdinand (b. 19 Aug. 1764, d. 29 May 1832) became Leopold Mozart's music pupil. See also LODRON FAMILY

RUTH HALLIWELL

R. Halliwell, *The Mozart Family: Four Lives in a Social Context* (Oxford, 1998)
H. Schuler, *Mozarts Salzburger Freunde und Bekannte* (Wilhelmshaven, 1995), 64–75

aria (It.: 'air', feminine noun). Term deriving from the Latin *aer*, meaning 'air, atmosphere'. The early use of the term with a musical meaning (fourteenth–fifteenth century) has the sense of 'manner, style', as referred to a melody. During the eighteenth century, in the context of music, the term referred to a closed piece for solo voice, either independent or intended as a part of a larger work (cantata, opera, oratorio, *festa teatrale* etc.). 'Aria' (and more often its diminutive 'arietta') also describes the poetic texts written for a set-piece in the context of the above-mentioned genres. A somewhat archaic use of the term survived into the eighteenth century, as in the expression 'cantare ad aria' for 'singing by heart' as opposed to 'singing from the score'. Occasionally the term has also been used in the context of instrumental music, referring generically to the 'manner' of the vocal aria.

Depending on the stylistic context, the term might assume slightly different connotations and/or a more or less precise meaning. In its most generic usage, 'aria' describes any solo piece for voice and orchestra (rarely, versions of 'arias' for solo voice and keyboard accompaniment have also been transmitted). Some solo pieces, however, are described in the sources with other and more specific terms such as 'cavata', an abbreviaton of the expression 'aria cavata' (more often 'cavatina' during the eighteenth century), 'rondeaux' and 'rondò' (the two terms having different meanings).

A. Aria texts
B. The aria as a musical object and its theatrical implications

A. Aria texts

1. The aria as a verbal text
2. General implications of aria texts
3. Aria texts in opera buffa and characterized as 'buffo'

1. THE ARIA AS A VERBAL TEXT

Within the context of a whole *dramma* or *commedia per musica* or even of non-staged compositions, such as oratorios, the 'aria' is a section consisting of a few lines assigned to a single character (six to ten on average) normally introduced by a longer series of lines (in the form of a monologue, a dialogue, or a speech involving multiple characters). The section preceding the aria, named recitative (and characterized most conspicuously by the style of its musical setting), is distinct from the aria on account of various functional and formal traits. The 'aria' is then a self-contained text but at the same time has a more or less strong connection with the preceding recitative, as regards subject matter and expression. From the point of view of its dramatic position, an aria usually has a final and climactic function within the scena (that is, the dramatic unit defined by the constant presence on stage of the same character or group of characters). Normally, the character to which an aria is assigned exits the stage after the conclusion of the piece (hence the oft-used term 'exit aria'). The same climactic function is characteristic of the rondeaux and rondò (arias adopting particular formal features), while a cavatina, in addition to presenting specific formal and stylistic features, occurs at the beginning of the scene – in which case it might not be introduced by a recitative – or in an intermediate position. (In both cases the singing character remains on stage after the end of the piece.)

The formal features of aria texts are better understood in the contexts of their functional relationship (and contrast) with the recitative. The latter is arranged as a series of freely mixed *endecasillabi* (eleven-syllable lines) and statistically less numerous *settenari* (seven-syllable lines), without any fixed pattern concerning the alternation of the two line-types. The rhyme patterns are not as regular as in the aria and consist characteristically of *rime baciate* (rhyming couplets) occasionally emphasizing the end of individual cues and always marking the end of the recitative part, just before the beginning of the aria (see ex. 1a and b). Only exceptionally do the rhymes within the recitative form more complex structures (ex. 1c).

Ex. 1a P. Metastasio, *Il re pastore*, I, 2

	[recitative]	rhymes
	[. . .]	
Aminta:	Perdono, amici dèi: fui troppo ingiusto	
	lagnandomi di voi. Non splende in cielo	
	dell'astro che mi guida, astro più bello.	a
	Se la terra ha un felice, Aminta è quello.	a
Agenore:	(Ecco il pastor).	
Aminta:	Ma fra' contenti oblio	
	la mia povera greggia.	
	[. . .]	

Ex. 1b P. Metastasio, *Il re pastore*, II, 4

	[recitative]	
Aminta:	[. . .] Ah fate, o numi,	
	fate che Aminta in trono	a
	se stesso onori, il donatore e il dono.	a
	[aria follows]	

Ex. 1c P. Metastasio, *Il re pastore*, I,1

	[*recitative*]	
Elisa:	[. . .] Dal dì primiero	
	che ancor bambina io lo mirai, mi parve	
	amabile, gentile	a
	quel pastor, quella greggia e quell'ovile;	a
	e mi restò nel core	b
	quell'ovil, quella reggia e quel pastore	b

Recitatives are thus characterized by a certain irregularity of rhythm (defined by the accents of the individual words). This feature was meant to represent some sort of relatively 'natural' – albeit stylized – speech and contrasts with the more regular rhythmical and metrical features of the aria text. For Metastasio, who established a number of theoretical principles generally still followed in the second half of the eighteenth century, the difference between recitative and aria had to correspond to a functional differentation within the drama: the recitative carried on the action, while the arias represented more lyrical, pensive or at any rate expressive moments (close in conception to the chorus of the Greek tragedy). In practice, however, the difference is often much less clear-cut.

While the above-mentioned aspects of the aria texts apply specifically to the tradition of opera in Italian, they also influenced German texts to a remarkable extent (see for example the arias set by Mozart in BASTIEN UND BASTIENNE). In any case the use of spoken dialogue instead of recitative in the German tradition of singspiel provided a quite different frame for aria texts.

The Metastasian arias, which can be taken as representative especially of opera seria, are divided into two *strofe* (stanzas), commonly referred to as parts A and B (*prima parte* and *seconda parte* in literary contexts), the second of which aims at presenting relatively 'new' conceptual contents or images (see ex. 2a and b).

Ex. 2a P. Metastasio, *L'olimpiade* (III, 6). See Mozart's setting in K294 and K512.

Non sò d'onde viene	a
quel tenero affetto,	b
quel moto che ignoto	b/b (note the 'internal rhyme' between *moto* and *ignoto*)
mi nasce nel petto,	b
quel gel che le vene	a
scorrendo mi va.	c
Nel seno a destarmi	d
sì fieri contrasti	e
non parmi che basti	e
la sola pietà.	c

Ex. 2b P. Metastasio, LA CLEMENZA DI TITO (III, 8). See Mozart's setting in K621, No. 20.

Se all'impero, amici dèi,	a
necessario è un cor severo,	b

o togliete a me l'impero b
o a me date un altro cor. c

Se la fe' de' regni miei a
Con l'amor non assicuro, d
d'una fede non mi curo d
che sia frutto del timor. c

The line-length is determined by the count of syllables, which has to account for phenomena such as the synaloepha (fusion of two syllables). In the aria texts the position of the accents is recurrent and some rhyme pattern – not necessarily a rigid one – is always present. The 'local' regularity of the individual aria texts was counter-balanced by the variety of line types used by the librettists for the numerous arias in a single *dramma per musica* (about twenty to twenty-five pieces around the middle of the eighteenth century). In the Metastasian corpus the line types used most often are the *settenario*, the *ottonario*, the *senario*, the *quinario*, the *decasillabo* and the *quaternario*.

Usually, but not necessarily, a *strofa* ends with a truncated word (the whole line is then considered a *verso tronco*) and this determines a stronger ending, reinforcing functionally the end of the syntagm. Also, the rhymes connecting final words of two stanzas establish a sense of closure at a higher structural level (note that the introduction of *versi tronchi* implies one less syllable in the line but this does not produce irregularity, because the accent patterns within the line remain the same: in ex. 2b, typically, a sequence of *ottonari* is ended by a *settenario tronco*). Very rarely a sort of functional inversion occurs in connection with the *tronco* lines, as for instance in DA PONTE's 'Ah fuggi il traditor' from DON GIOVANNI – in this case the lines of the stanza are mostly *tronche* whereas the final lines are accented on the penultimate syllable forming the more usual *versi piani* (see ex. 3).

Ex.3 L. Da Ponte, *Don Giovanni*, I, 10 (see Mozart's setting in K527, No. 8)
Ah fuggi il traditor,
non lo lasciar più dir:
il labbro è mentitor,
fallace il ciglio.

Da' miei tormenti impara
a creder a quel cor,
e nasca il tuo timor
dal mio periglio

Such features are of great importance for the versification and the expressive character of the text as a whole, but also for the arrangement of melodic materials within the musical setting.

2. GENERAL IMPLICATIONS OF ARIA TEXTS

The prevailing structure of a mid-eighteenth-century aria was related to a set of assumptions about the general musical features of the setting: after the presentation of Part A, Part B was assumed to present 'new' musical materials. After Part B was sung, Part A was resumed and repeated, thus determining an A–B–A structure known as da capo aria. This 'closed' structure had originated in the later seventeenth century from the singers' desire to provide semi-improvised variations in the repeated Part A, as well as from the audiences' call for an ever more spectacular performance. In sum, the general formal features of the aria (as a verbal text) derived in part from pre-existing assumptions having a musical meaning related rather to the performance dimension of music than to composition proper. Such features, in turn, represented for eighteenth-century composers a formal 'standard' that could be slavishly complied with, altered, or even contradicted.

Other 'types' of texts, although used less often than A–B–A arias, were also recognized as standard. The cavatina, used to present a character and leaving the character on stage after its conclusion, is a short text (generally four or five lines), describing one single 'affection' and implying a shorter musical setting as well as a simple, mostly syllabic melody (see ex. 4).

Ex. 4 L. Da Ponte, LE NOZZE DI FIGARO, II, 1 (see Mozart's setting in K492, No. 10)

Porgi Amor, qualche ristoro
al mio duolo, a' miei sospir.
O mi rendi il mio tesoro
O mi lascia almen morir.

The rondò is a type of text that originated in the second half of the eighteenth century and is conceptually different from the classic Metastasian aria. Not only is the text of a rondò usually longer, encompassing three sections, but it often includes a change of metre (see ex. 5). The rondò calls for a long and elaborate musical setting in two movements according to a slow–fast climactic progression (and might last twice as long as an aria). In contrast to the aria proper, which is for any of the characters, a rondò is the main set-piece of the principal singers (the primo uomo and the prima donna). It is also characterized by its position towards the end of an opera, representing a climax not only of local significance but also of one principal's performance in the opera as a whole. The fortune of the rondò in the second half of the century is in any case to be understood in the context of a changing sensibility towards the dramatic meaning of musical form. While the quantitative diffusion and the formal stability of the rondò as a verbal form is inferior to that of the A–B–A Metastasian aria, its function is pivotal in the evolution of musical dramaturgy (ex. 5).

Ex. 5 C. MAZZOLÀ, 'Non più di fiori' after P. Metastasio's, *La clemenza di Tito* (see Mozart's setting in K621, No. 23)

Non più di fiori
vaghe catene
discenda Imene
ad intrecciar.
Stretta fra barbare
aspre ritorte
veggo la morte
ver me avanzar.

Infelice! Qual orrore!
Ah, di me che si dirà?
Chi vedesse il mio dolore,
pur avria di me pietà.

A limited number of pieces in Mozart's output are termed 'rondeaux' or 'aria en rondeau' (for example *Il re pastore*, K208, No. 10 or K255, 'Ombra felice – Io ti lascio'). Such terms do not correspond to any particular text form but rather apply to (or superimpose upon) a traditional 'Metastasian' aria text the musical principle of a recurring theme in the principal key according to the basic structure ABACA.

3. ARIA TEXTS IN OPERA BUFFA AND CHARACTERIZED AS 'BUFFO'

The A–B–A structure of the aria, while connected above all with opera seria (as well as oratorio), was also used in opera buffa for comic, serious and *mezzo-carattere* situations. Typically, a serious situation called for an opera seria structure like Arminda's *aria d'ira* 'Vorrei punirti indegno' in LA FINTA GIARDINIERA, K196, Act 2 (libretto ascribed to G. Petrosellini). But the lexicon and subject matter could well make a text appropriate to the genre and/or local dramatic situation independently of its formal features, as in Simone's 'Con certe persone' in LA FINTA SEMPLICE, K51, Act 2 (libretto by GOLDONI–COLTELLINI). In general, however, the texts found in *commedie per musica* tend to be longer and to accumulate images towards their climax. This approach is fundamentally different from approaches prevalent in the serious genre and is unique in fact to opera buffa. It is possible that one of the originating factors of such texts is the performing ability of specific buffo singers, based on acting and mimicry rather than on vocal display (as was the case in opera seria). While musical expansion in opera seria arias was often brought about by the introduction of extensive melismatic passages, the accumulation of text and images worked well in a buffo context.

While not all the buffo arias in opera buffa necessarily contain long texts, the term buffo has recently been used in this more restricted sense (by John Platoff) to define an aria with a comparatively high number of lines usually encompassing two different poetic metres and providing the material for a musical setting designed for the *principal* buffo singer/actor, usually a bass or baritone. The best-known example of this type in Mozart's repertory is 'Madamina, il catalogo è questo' by Lorenzo Da Ponte, sung by Leporello in *Don Giovanni* and articulated in two quatrains of *decasillabi*, one sextet and five more quatrains of *ottonari*. This type of aria buffa is in a sense analogous from the perspective of theatrical function – but not form or style – to the rondò: both constitute a 'pièce de résistance' for the principal singer/actor in the cast. Ultimately, the musical implications behind the aria buffa are connected to the theatrical and specifically 'comical' prowess of the great buffo singers of the time; the pieces recur frequently to words suitable for 'patter' singing or onomatopoeia (as in *La finta semplice*, No. 8, 'Ella vuole ed io vorrei') and are perhaps indebted to the tradition of the *tirade* in the spoken theatre.

B. The aria as a musical object and its theatrical implications

Beyond its literary dimensions, an aria can be defined as a musical and theatrical object. The compositional work can be seen as a complication and amplification of the formal and expressive potential of the text. Relationships with the literary materials and with their visual implications range from straightforward parallelism to friction or even contrast (both at the formal and expressive levels). The self-evident principle that analyses of arias should comprise an investigation of the relationship between textual, musical and visual elements has been fully exploited by scholars only fairly recently. The lasting influence of nineteenth-century idealism assigned to music a central, absolute value that transcended the relevance of textual elements and their interplay.

In Mozart's arias one finds some texts set according to the common expectations associated with the operatic lingua franca of the time, and other texts in which the musical strategies are apparently original. (One should note that the current knowledge of the lingua franca itself is far from complete.) In general, compliance and variance from operatic traditions is perhaps more easily evaluated in the realm of opera seria than opera buffa because the seria tradition appears to have been comparatively more stable and based on a limited number of formal patterns.

In contrast, arias in opera buffa were rather freely conceived (both as verbal and musical texts). The verbal texts were less strictly associated with formal expectations and suggested at best, through their formal structure, one among various possible dispositions of the musical materials.

As mentioned above, Mozart was not especially concerned with departing from prevailing traditions. Seminal nineteenth-century writers (notably Otto Jahn) underrated much of the seria production, however, on account of its conventionality. More recently scholars have focused on the uniqueness of each piece and on those expressive features that transcend conventional norms. Mozart's own concern was probably the effectiveness of his music within a set of practical as well as dramatic circumstances (the abilities and rank of a certain singer, the position of a piece within the dramatic exposition and/or its impact as a concert piece). The formal element is not negligible, but is better understood through an evaluation of specific historical circumstances rather than through an abstract morphological approach. Recent studies have also emphasized musical elements such as texture and tessitura in relation to form, as well as non-musical aspects such as narrative and visual implications.

Mozart's arias from his youth through to his late years moved from relatively 'rigid' interpretations of form towards more fluid, flexible and through-composed solutions, without, however, rejecting any of the inherited forms. Ternary da capo or da capo-like arias are found as late as *La clemenza di Tito* but acquire new meaning in late works as they are no longer the prevalent form.

The standard use of ternary forms (either da capo, dal segno or da capo-like) is evident in Mozart's first opere serie, starting with MITRIDATE RE DI PONTO. The common ternary layout of most arias of the time was subjected to one of two interpretations by Mozart: the 'great' da capo, characterized by maximum formal expansion through repetition of the first stanza (up to eight times in the piece, as in No. 1 of *Mitridate* 'Al destin che la minaccia'); and the 'small' ternary form (with half as many repetitions of the first stanza and a written-out da capo with a varied presentation of the vocal materials and instrumentation).

Such forms did not have a strictly normative value during the eighteenth century but rather provided a predictable frame that the composer could exploit for dramatic purposes. For instance, while a fairly long instrumental introduction was customary, arousing expectation of a singer's entrance (and at the same time slowing down the action), some arias began immediately with the vocal melody, stressing urgent continuity rather than repose (for example, 'Va' l'error mio palesa', No. 11 in *Mitridate*).

Mozart's early arias have typically been judged as ranging in aesthetic value from the standard or even mediocre to the relatively innovative (especially in regard to the clarity of formal articulation). The mature works in any case show a degree of compositional confidence that overshadows any sense of formal constraint. This is also apparent in the treatment of poetic texts, which in the early arias features strict parallels between literary and musical forms. As time progressed, however, Mozart increasingly altered and recombined for dramatic purposes both the order of different segments of text and the musical structure, revealing a less formalistic approach. (This might have been prompted by Jommelli's style of text setting in *Armida abbandonata*, a work that Mozart heard in Naples in 1770.) Conspicuous examples of this process are found in arias such as 'Pupille amate', No. 21 from LUCIO SILLA (where the repetition of the first line is anticipated with respect to the melodic and harmonic return) or in the scena and aria (rondeau form) K255, 'Ombra felice – Io ti lascio', where the lines and formal sections are combined in an unusually free manner.

The form of Mozart's arias has often been related by critics to instrumental genres and forms, especially to the concerto and to sonata form. The proximity to the concerto is especially apparent in the layout of the first part of the aria vis-à-vis the 'double exposition'. Also the treatment of the voice in opera seria and particularly in virtuosic pieces for the principals is close in conception to instrumental display in the concerto, as is the function of ritornellos. Some of the arias written by Mozart as concert pieces (for example 'Io non chiedo, eterni Dei', K316 and 'Ah! se in ciel, benigne stelle', K538) are extreme in their exposure of concerto-like passage-work, but are not typical. In any case the term 'concert aria' was never used by Mozart and appears to have been introduced only in the early nineteenth century.

The compositional principles associated with 'sonata form' certainly played a role in Mozart's composition of arias in his middle and late periods (and an early example is 'Biancheggia in mar lo scoglio', No. 9 of *Il sogno di Scipione*), although scholars debate how the operatic manifestation of this form should be understood. According to Webster, the first part (or exposition) of the piece usually includes two sections, called 'paragraphs' (as opposed to the first and second 'groups' of instrumental sonata form). These usually correspond to two stanzas of text and cadence in two different tonal areas (usually tonic and dominant). Such a conception is only broadly related to instrumental sonata form, however; the first paragraph of an aria, for example, might end with an authentic cadence in the tonic and a caesura. The treatment of the sections following the exposition is unpredictable compared to instrumental music, the only standard feature being the re-establishment of the tonic towards the end. The materials of the exposition may be recapitulated in their entirety, in part, or not at all. In most cases there is no trace of development proper. An analogy can thus be made between the 'first group' and the musical space occupied by the first stanza of text, and between the 'second group' and the music for the second stanza (the B section of a ternary aria). However, the B section of ternary arias has also been described as functionally akin to a 'development' despite the fact that these sections share with the instrumental forms neither motivic elaboration nor tonal mobility. The different interpretations reveal the vitality of a value system centred around sonata form but the form per se does not explain necessarily the musical and dramatic strategies that characterize individual pieces. These are often transparently related to the rhetoric of the text or to particular stage implications (which of course do not preclude the appropriation of compositional elements of the sonata-form paradigm). 'Venite, inginocchiatevi' (No. 13 in LE NOZZE DI FIGARO), is an extreme case of where the verbal text is a complement to an ongoing visual action (rather than a vehicle for affective expression in its own right); it introduces a very clear (as well as unique) two-theme exposition and a development, but it ends with a simple 'tonal return' rather than with a regular recapitulation. Sometimes, a particular connotation of 'style' rather than the thematic material per se, is the most relevant element of an aria: the reprise of the main materials might then 'sneak in unawares' (Webster) as in Elvira's 'Ah, fuggi il traditor' (*Don Giovanni*, No. 8), a piece that makes capital out of a transfigured Handelian gesture. 'Ah pietà, signori miei', No. 20 in *Don Giovanni*, contains a free recapitulation where much of the motivic material is familiar but reordered and recomposed, suggesting an elusiveness that reflects Leporello's attitude on stage. Multiple reprises, such as those in the second part of the catalogue aria or Anna's 'Or sai chi l'onore' (in *Don Giovanni*, Nos. 4 and 10) do not hint at a rondo form (in the instrumental sense) but simply represent a rhetorical peroration.

Viewed collectively, the relationships between verbal, motivic and tonal elements are quite freely interpreted by Mozart through forms that tend to be either 'rounded' (with a final abridged and/or reworked recapitulation of materials), or 'linear' (stressing the difference between the end of an aria and its beginning). In the latter case, obviously, the sense of musical closure is entrusted to the tonal and textural elements more than to the motivic ones.

'Linear' types of arias include those with a sectional and additive layout in two or more different tempos that might follow either a slow–fast plan or the opposite. While in opera buffa the alternation of slow and fast tempos is comparatively free, in opera seria such pieces tend towards a final fast climax (occasionally with a double acceleration, as in 'Parto, ma tu ben mio', No. 9 in *Tito*). In the context of opera seria, the slow–fast pattern is prevalent although it is applied to arias with different dramaturgical emphases, such as two-tempo arias and the rondò. Both two-tempo arias and rondòs begin with a tonally open-ended slow section (usually a Larghetto or Andante) cadentially linked to the ensuing Allegro. The fast C section is balanced in length with the slow movement in the case of two-tempo arias but is longer and comparatively more complex in the rondòs, including two alternating groups of thematic materials, the second of which often has a 'gavotte-like' character (hence the neologism gavotte-rondò, sometimes used in the secondary literature). The main theme of the first movement of a rondò often (but not always) returns in a varied form in the Allegro and a part of the text of the first stanza always appears in the fast section. One or the other or both recurring elements might account for the use of the term 'rondò'. The recurrence, however, is also found in some two-tempo arias (for example K369, 'Ah! non son io che parlo'). In any case, the full meaning of rondò is related to dramatic function as much as to musical form, to the pre-final position within the narrative exposition and to the rank of the singer/character.

The term 'rondeaux' or 'rondeau' has been used by Mozart (albeit with some inconsistency, as in the case of K416, 'Ah, non sai qual pena sia') to describe arias with formal organization that features the periodically recurring section of the instrumental rondo (for example ABACA). Cases in point are 'L'amerò, sarò costante', No. 10 in *Il re pastore* and 'Or che il cielo a me ti rende', K374. From an expressive standpoint, these pieces have little to do with rondos in that their characterization is less extreme and the vocalization far less virtuosic.

In his treatment of the poetic text, Mozart does not hesitate to go beyond certain formal implications when these implications are deemed musically uninteresting. Cherubino's Arietta 'Voi che sapete' (No. 12 in *Figaro*) is an example of 'realistic' music (a piece that, ideally, would be sung also in the context of spoken theatre). As such it assumes an iconic function (a lover's serenata) and is structured by Da Ponte as a strophic song that suggests the repetition of the same music for each stanza. Mozart, who had used the simple strophic structure years before in the Romance 'In Mohrenland' (*Entführung*, No. 18), now adopts a more flexible solution, setting each of the first five stanzas to different music in terms of melody and harmony but retains a constant phrase disposition (which preserves the song-like character). Once this 'variation' pattern has been established and explored, the rhythm of stanzas 6 and 7 is doubled, thus providing a pre-final intensification just before the return of the first stanza (and its music) that now functions as a recapitulation. Finally, beyond the frequent instances of 'enrichment' or 'complication' of the dramaturgy as defined merely by the verbal text, Mozart sometimes takes the liberty to contradict (or rather redirect) the meaning of the words through musical means, virtually reshaping situations and/or characters (for example 'Batti batti o bel Masetto', No. 12 in *Don Giovanni* and 'S'altro che lagrime', No. 21 in *Tito*).

SERGIO DURANTE

A. P. Brown, 'Music, Poetry, and Drama in Mozart's Arias before "Die Entführung aus dem Serail"', in *Studies in Eighteenth Century Culture*, vol. XVIII, ed. J. W. Yolton and L. Ellen (East Lansing, MI, 1988), 263–88

S. Döhring, 'Die Arienformen in Mozarts Opern', *Mozart-Jahrbuch* 1968–1970, 66–76

S. Durante, 'Analysis and Dramaturgy: Reflections towards a Theory of Opera', in *Opera buffa in Mozart's Vienna*, ed. M. Hunter and J. Webster (Cambridge, 1994), 311–39

M. Feldman, 'Mozart and His Elders: Opera-seria Arias, 1766–1775', *Mozart-Jahrbuch* 1991, 564–75

'Ritornello Procedure in Mozart: from Aria to Concerto', in *Mozart's Piano Concertos: Text, Context, Interpretation*, ed. N. Zaslaw (Ann Arbor, 1996), 149–86

M. Hunter, *The Culture of Opera Buffa in Mozart's Vienna: A Poetics of Entertainment* (Princeton, 1999)

K. Küster, 'Von *Mitridate* zu *Il Rè pastore*: Stationen auf Mozarts Weg zur Konzertform', *Mozart-Jahrbuch* 1991, 956–62

J. Platoff, 'The Buffa Aria in Mozart's Vienna', *Cambridge Opera Journal* 2 (1990), 99–120

J. Rice, 'Rondò vocali di Salieri e Mozart per Adriana Ferrarese', in *I vicini di Mozart*, ed. M. T. Muraro and D. Bryant (Florence, 1989)
M. F. Robinson, 'The Da Capo Aria as a Symbol of Rationality', in *La musica come linguaggio universale. Genesi e storia di un'idea*, ed. R. Pozzi (Florence, 1990)
J. L. H. Sibbons, 'Tonality Structure and Key Changes in Idamante's 3rd Act Aria in Mozart's Opera "Idomeneo" K366', *Mozart-Jahrbuch 1980–1983*
J. Webster, 'The Analysis of Mozart's Arias', in *Mozart Studies*, ed. C. Eisen (Oxford, 1991)

arias, concert. Writers in the eighteenth century distinguished between music written for the theatre, Church and chamber. Although Mozart and his contemporaries did not use the term 'concert aria', composers wrote arias specifically for concerts or musical academies. Thus we can usually distinguish between 'insertion arias' written to replace another in an opera, 'favourite songs' or arias taken from an opera and sung in concert, and 'concert arias'. Mozart's concert arias in particular were limited to a small group of his friends and pupils, especially ALOYSIA WEBER, Josepha DUSCHEK, VALENTIN ADAMBERGER and LUDWIG FISCHER.

Like other composers of the period, Mozart compared the composer's task to that of a tailor (see his letter of 28 Feb. 1778). And just as a tailor measured and cut cloth to fit a person's physique, so a composer sketched a melody to accommodate the range, tessitura and vocal abilities of a singer. An artful composer went beyond these minimum requisites to suit the tastes of an individual singer so that the strengths of that singer's expressive qualities were emphasized. Mozart makes this clear in describing the aria 'Se al labbro mio non credi', K295, written for the tenor ANTON RAAFF. Mozart chose this text because Raaff already had one to the same words (written by HASSE for the opera *Artaserse*), so that 'he will sing mine with greater facility and more pleasure'; Raaff was especially taken with the 'charming' middle section in 3/8, an old-fashioned form which would have been very familiar to the singer; finally, Mozart offered to alter it or even compose another aria if Raaff would prefer. (Apparently, Raaff asked him to shorten it a little, 'for I am no longer able to sustain my notes'; Mozart complied and told him that he had made it long on purpose, 'for it is always easy to cut down, but not so easy to lengthen'.) The most striking quality of the piece is its cantabile style, a method of singing that Raaff had perfected from his earliest days of study with Bernacchi, the famous castrato and singing teacher.

Throughout the eighteenth century, composers collaborated closely with singers. Indeed, composers depended on the singers to win them success, and singers depended on composers to write stylish and effective arias for them to display their talents. When getting to know a voice, Mozart first sketched a vocal melody and bass, then sought the singer's approval before completing the orchestration. Such *particelli* were learning vehicles for composer and singer alike, and it was part of the composer's task to act as a teacher or coach to help the singer interpret the work. Concert arias enabled the singers to explore subjects of interest (for example a favourite text, role or dramatic situation) outside a full-scale opera production.

While visiting London as a boy, Mozart studied singing with the castrato GIOVANNI MANZUOLI, who later sang the title role in ASCANIO IN ALBA (MILAN, 1771). One of Mozart's first arias, 'Va, dal furor portata', K21, might have been used in a pasticcio version of *Ezio*, given in LONDON during the 1764–5 season. Another early aria, K36, was performed in December 1766, shortly after the family returned home to SALZBURG. Following his European tour, Mozart wrote a series of Italian arias, many of them on texts from METASTASIO's *Demofoonte*, probably in preparation for further study in Italy beginning in 1769. These are not real concert arias but rather exercises in writing contrasting types of arias. The best-known work from Mozart's three trips to Italy is the sacred Latin solo cantata, *Exsultate, jubilate*, K165, written for VENANZIO RAUZZINI, who created the primo uomo role in *LUCIO SILLA*. Although it is not a concert aria per se, given its liturgical function, it shares many of the features of opera arias and demonstrates the virtuosity of the singer.

Mozart's first mature concert aria, K272, was written for Josepha Duschek in August 1777, the month before his departure from Salzburg to seek a position elsewhere. It is a scena from *Andromeda* by V. A. Cigna-Santi, blending accompanied recitative with an aria and cavatina in contrasting tempos and keys. The piece is virtually a solo cantata but without the strict divisions between recitative and aria; one emotional state follows close behind another. It is scored for a pair of oboes and horns in addition to the full complement of strings; in the cavatina a solo oboe weaves a graceful counter-melody to the voice (Ex. 1).

Ex. 1. Formal structure of K272

Recitativo [obbligato] (bars 1–27)	Allegro risoluto (C)
Ah, lo previdi! Povero Prence, con quel ferro istesso, Che me salvo, it lacerasti il petto. Ma tu si fiero scempio Perché non impedir? Come, o crudele, D'un misero a pietà non ti movesti? Qual tigre ti nodri? Dove nascesti?	
Aria (bars 28–176)	Allegro (¢), C minor
Ah, t'involа agl'occhi miei, Alma vile, ingrato cor! La cagione, oh Dio, tu sei Del mio barbaro dolor. Va, crudele! Ca, spietato! Va, tra le fiere ad abitar.	
Recitativo [obbligato] (bars 177–216)	
Misera! Invan m'adiro,	Allegro (C)
E nel suo sangue intanto Nuota già l'idol mio . . .	Andante
Con quell'acciaro, Ah Perseo, che facesti? Mi salvasti poc'anzi, or m'uccidesti.	Allegro
Col sangue, ahi, la bell'alma, Ecco, già usci dallo squarciato seno. Me infelice! Si oscura Il giorno algi occhi miei,	Adagio
E nel barbaro affanno il cor vien meno.	Allegro–Adagio
Ah, non partir, ombra diletta, io voglio	

	Unirmi a te. Sul grado estremo, intanto Che m'uccide il dolor, fermati alquanto!	cadence on B flat
Cavatina (bars 217–306)		Andantino (3/4), B flat major
	Deh, non varcar quell'onda, Anima del cor mio. Di Lete all'altra sponda. Ombra, compagna anch'io Voglio venir con te.	
[Coda] (bars 307–23)		allegro (¢), B flat major

As a concert piece, the action is not staged, but Mozart clearly expected the singer to portray its dramatic qualities. Indeed, he brought the aria with him on his trip to MANNHEIM and PARIS, and gave it to Aloysia Weber. In his letter to her of 30 July 1778, Mozart exhorted the young soprano to study the aria carefully and to put herself 'in all seriousness into Andromeda's situation and position! – and to imagine that you are that very person'. The texts for most concert arias came directly from opera, and singers were expected to act out the aria's dramatic content, although the venue was quite different from the theatre. This would include informal concerts, such as the ones Mozart describes at Christian CANNABICH's home in Mannheim (letters of 14 Feb. and 24 Mar. 1778), as well as the subscription concerts given in the Viennese theatres during Lent.

More often than not, singers commissioned Mozart to write arias for them, normally for a particular occasion such as a benefit concert. An aria could become a singer's signature for concert performances. For example, Raaff sang J. C. BACH's setting of 'Non sò d'onde viene' with success not only in opera houses in Italy, but also at the Concert spirituel in Paris, as well as at the Mannheim and Munich court. MICHAEL KELLY heard Raaff sing this aria in the 1780s, when the tenor was almost seventy years old. Mozart composed a setting of this text (K294) for Aloysia Weber in February 1778 and he wrote an entirely new version for the bass Ludwig Fischer in March 1787 (K512). In its original context, Metastasio's text is sung by a male character in the third act of *Olimpiade*. But as a concert aria, that is, as abstract poetic sentiment, the text is equally appropriate for a male or female singer. (Although Mozart claims his setting for Aloysia 'does not resemble [Bach's] in the very least', it is clearly modelled on the older composer's setting, while the later version for Fischer is quite different.)

Between 1778 and 1788 Mozart wrote several arias for his pupil and future sister-in-law, Aloysia Weber. These five concert arias, K294, K316, K383, K416 and K583, constitute the most arias Mozart wrote for any particular singer. This of course is no accident: during his visit to Mannheim during the autumn and winter of 1777–8, Mozart fell in love with his pupil and wanted to take her to Italy. For his budding prima donna, Mozart wrote K294 and K316, and according to Alan Tyson, K538 survives in a *particella* (vocal line and bass only) dating from this period. From his letter to his Leopold (7 Feb. 1778), we also know that Mozart gave her his concert aria K272, ANNA DE AMICIS's arias from *Lucio Silla* and four arias from IL RE PASTORE. The title role of Zaide was also probably intended for her: 'Ruhe sanft' (a cantabile aria in E flat major) and 'Tiger!' (a rage aria in G minor) make a contrasting pair (not unlike K418 and K419) for the prima donna, and they exhibit many qualities typical of the other arias written for Aloysia.

Is it possible that the bravura concert aria, 'Sperai vicino il lido', K368 – composed during the summer or autumn of 1778, when Mozart travelled back to Salzburg from Paris – was also written for Aloysia Weber? (This scenario would fit better with the paper and handwriting studies of Alan Tyson and Wolfgang Plath, who have assigned the aria to no later than the summer of 1780.) At any rate, it was certainly not intended for Elisabeth WENDLING (the first Elettra), as Alfred Einstein suggested. The bravura arias in Wendling's other roles, including Elettra, made less stringent demands on the singer's range and agility.

The scena K505 was written in December 1786 for NANCY STORACE, who was about to depart Vienna for London. The text comes from the revised version of *Idomeneo*, performed in March 1786 at Count Auersperg's palace. But here the role of Idamante is transposed to a woman, who pledges 'Non temere, amato bene, / Per te sempre il cor sarà' (Do not fear, my beloved, my heart will always be yours). Many writers have commented on the intimate interplay between the soprano and the obbligato keyboard part, which Mozart himself played at the farewell concert, suggesting that the composer had a special fondness for the first Susanna. Perhaps he did, but being a professional and experienced opera composer, Mozart could cater to the demands of the text, whoever the singer. Less than a month before leaving Mannheim in March 1778, he wrote a passionate farewell aria (K295a) for the local prima donna, Dorothea Wendling, who chose the text ('Ah, non lasciarmi, no, / Bell'idol mio') from Metastasio's *Didone abbandonata*.

Overall, German singers received far more concert arias from Mozart than did Italian singers, although most of them were settings of Italian texts. Mozart wrote concert arias for Raaff (the first Idomenco; K295), Adamberger (the first Belmonte; K420 and K431), Fischer (the first Osmin; K423 and K512), Gottfried von Jacquin (K513), and Franz Xaver Gerl (the first Sarastro; K612). Along with Aloysia Weber, Adamberger and Fischer were frequent guests on Mozart's subscription concerts in Vienna (see his letter of 29 Mar. 1783). The rondo, 'Per pietà, non ricercate', K420, was written for Adamberger as a substitute aria in Anfossi's *Il curioso indiscreto*, but because of various intrigues, the tenor did not sing it in the revival. Although we have no direct evidence, it is likely that he would have used it in concert. Mozart mentions that Adamberger sang 'a rondo of my composition', probably K420, in a letter of 24 December 1784. Fischer, who was a pupil of Raaff at Mannheim, almost certainly asked Mozart to set the text of the tenor's favourite aria as a homage to his teacher. Fischer sang the piece (K512) at his benefit concert in March 1787. Although it is not certain for whom Mozart intended the bass aria, K430, the large leaps in the vocal part are typical of Fischer's other arias.

In addition to those already mentioned, Mozart wrote concert arias for Princess Caroline Nassau-Weilburg (K23), Countess Paumgarten (K369), Francesco Ceccarelli (K374), Mme Duschek (K528) and Constanze Weber (K440, which he apparently began but did not finish before or after he married her). All of these pieces are to Italian texts; only Aloysia's 'Nehmt meinen Dank, ihr holden Gönner', K383, is to a German text. (The latter was written several months before the premiere of DIE ENTFÜHRUNG and before JOSEPH II closed the German Nationaltheater.) For his sister-in-law JOSEPHA HOFER, the first Queen of the Night, Mozart began a German aria, 'Schon lacht der holde Frühling', K580, but this was intended as an insertion aria for a German version of PAISIELLO's *Barber of Seville*. The only other finished German piece is the 'Turkish' strophic song, 'Ich möchte wohl der Kaiser sein!', K539, written for the amateur bass Friedrich Baumann.

When LE NOZZE DI FIGARO was revived in 1789 with La Ferrarese as Susanna, Mozart took advantage of the occasion to enlarge the part with an elaborate new rondò, 'Al desio, di chi t'adora', K577. This piece seems to be a preparatory study for Fiordiligi's 'Per pietà, ben mio', a role created by the same soprano (he also supplied a second, more modest aria for Susanna in Act 2, 'Un moto di gioia', K579. Also as a prelude to COSÌ FAN TUTTE, Mozart wrote three insertion arias for LOUISE VILLENEUVE, the first Dorabella. The first, K578, 'Alma grande e nobil core', dating from August 1789, was inserted in Cimarosa's *I due Baroni di Rocca Azzurra*; the other two ('Chi sa, chi sa, qual sia', K582, and 'Vado, ma dove?' K583) were interpolated in VICENTE MARTÍN Y SOLER's *Il Burbero di buon cuore* in October 1789.

If operas were his major public commissions, Mozart's concert arias are more often than not intimate vocal portraits of the singers he knew best, both personally and vocally. The best are on the same high level as his best opera arias. We should keep in mind that individual arias were given side by side with concertos and symphonies in almost every concert of the period: indeed, singers typically had a higher status than orchestral musicians. Mozart's letters are full of references to singers, and throughout his career he worked in close collaboration with them. The concert arias, together with the opera arias in their repertory, supplement the documentation we have of various singers' voices. Although we lack recordings of eighteenth-century singers, such as Aloysia Weber, Mozart's arias give us detailed vocal portraits of them.

PAUL CORNEILSON

P. Corneilson, 'An Intimate Vocal Portrait of Dorothea Wendling: Mozart's "Basta vincesti" – "Ah non lasciarmi, no" K. 295a', *Mozart-Jahrbuch 2000*, 29–45

A. Einstein, *Mozart: His Character, his Works* (New York, 1945)

D. Heartz, 'Raaff's Last Aria: A Mozartean Idyll in the Spirit of Hasse', *Musical Quarterly* 60 (1974), 517–43

S. Kunze, 'Die Vertonungen der Arie "Non so d'onde viene" von J. Chr. Bach und W. A. Mozart', *Anelecta Musicologica* 2 (1965), 85–111

Artaria & Comp. Austrian art, map and music publishers. Originally from the area around Lake Como, the Artaria family established an art dealership in MAINZ in 1765, two of them – the cousins Carlo (1747–1808) and Francesco (1744–1808) – removing to VIENNA in 1766. There they expanded their activities to include maps and music, first as dealers and later, from 1778, as publishers. Mozart probably came into contact with Artaria shortly after settling in Vienna in 1781. In July of that year he wrote to his father that Artaria was to engrave six of his accompanied sonatas (K296, 376–80), which appeared in November. Over the next ten years, the firm issued numerous editions of Mozart's works, including first editions of nearly thirty, among them the piano sonatas K330–2, the 'Haffner' symphony, K385, the six string quartets dedicated to Haydn, the string quintets K515 and K516 and the C minor Fantasy and Sonata, K475 + 457. On the whole these editions are reliable; several of them, including the six string quartets dedicated to Haydn, include additional articulation and dynamic marks that almost certainly derive from the composer himself – as such they represent valuable sources for the texts of Mozart's works. Not all of the editions were proof-read by Mozart, however, and several of them include errors or other readings that may not derive from the composer after all. The textual worth of these editions therefore needs to be evaluated on a case-by-case basis. Artaria's music-publishing business survived until 1858 (the Mainz branch existed until 1793 when it moved to MANNHEIM and amalgamated with the art bookshop and publishing business of Mathias Fontaine) although a few editions appeared as late as 1918 (notably the series *Denkmäler der Tonkunst in Österreich*); during its heyday it published numerous works, including many first editions, by HAYDN, BEETHOVEN, HUMMEL and Rossini. CLIFF EISEN

Ascanio in Alba, K111. Serenata composed 1771, text by Giuseppe Parini (1729–99); first performance: MILAN, 16 October 1771. MITRIDATE, RE DI PONTO, K87, of 1770 proved that the teenage Mozart could compose a successful *dramma per musica*. As a result, the imperial court commissioned Mozart at the end of March 1771 to compose an opera for the marriage of MARIA THERESIA's son, the Archduke Ferdinand, to the Princess Maria Beatrice d'Este. On 21 August Mozart and his father arrived in Milan and on 29 August he received the libretto by Giuseppe Parini. By the middle of September, all of the recitatives and choruses were written and finally the arias in consultation with the singers. Mozart also composed ballet music which, except for the bass part, is lost. The marriage took place on 16 October and on the next day *Ascanio* was first performed.

Ascanio in Alba is a serenata or, as stated on the printed libretto, a *festa teatrale*. The latter term had a long tradition at the imperial court extending back at least to the beginning of the eighteenth century and was reserved for special imperial occasions. Rather than depending on solo numbers, choral and ballet scenes also play an important role.

The argument centres around the son of Aeneas, Ascanio. Venus, his grandmother, reveals that she is going to provide him with Silvia from the family of Hercules as his wife. Silvia has dreamed of a handsome youth who is to be her husband. Ascanio, however, has been told by Venus to conceal his identity from Silvia so that her true feelings might be revealed. When Silvia meets the unidentified Ascanio, she is deeply disturbed by her attraction to him, not knowing that he is her chosen husband. The expected recognition scene follows and having passed tests of their political virtues (that is, duty over love), Venus advises Ascanio and Silvia of their obligation to be just and loving towards their subjects. This basic outline is embellished by a host of pastoral and mythological characters and by elaborate scenes including Venus arriving as a dea ex machina. The allegory of this plot was transparent to all. Maria Theresia was represented by Venus, Ferdinand by Ascanio and Beatrice by Silvia. In addition, Beatrice's father was Duke Hercules III of Modena making her identity unmistakable. The Graces, Genii and the like were their diverse subjects.

Most notable about *Ascanio* is how the choruses glue together a structure larger than the scene. After a single-movement overture and a ballet for the Graces, a chorus of Genii and Graces is sung (No. 2), followed by an aria for Venus (No. 3), a return of No. 2 (No. 4), after which Ascanio sings his first aria (No. 5). The refrain returns again at the end of the first part. Though the choruses of Genii and Graces provide an umbrella over the first part, beginning with Scene 3, a chorus of shepherds provides a refrain between recitatives and arias to the end of Scene 4. The second part is similarly laid out and culminates in a combined ensemble (No. 33) of these groups in praise of Venus, alias the Empress Maria Theresia. The trio for Silvia, Aceste and Ascanio (No. 31), though itself a closed form, returns (No. 32) after a recitative. Even though there is one moment in No. 31 where the singers simultaneously express different sentiments with individual melodic profiles, one should not read this as a breakthrough; Mozart still is more comfortable with his characters singing alone or in homophony.

Mozart's ARIAS are distributed hierarchically with four each to Ascanio and Silvia and two each to Venere, Aceste and the Fauno and use the expansive and flexible forms found in *Mitridate*. Here, besides the da capo and dal segno types, Mozart also uses the cavatina (that is, the first section of a da capo aria), a binary shape with alternating tempos, and a structure (Nos. 13 and 14) that adumbrates the cavatina–cabaletta sequence of the grand scena in nineteenth-century Italian opera. These two adjacent arias for the same character also coordinate with a crucial moment in the drama: Silvia has resolved her conflicting feelings.

Of the two arias for Silvia in the second part, No. 19 is a big three-part piece deriving from the da capo tradition: the A section is a closed binary structure; B changes metre, tempo and mode; and the return is like a written-out dal segno as it quickly moves from E minor to G major for the return of the last part of A. Here the text with its 'soaring and cooing heart' contrasts with her pleas for the presentation of her beloved. As in her pair of arias in the first part, this allows for a display of both lyric and coloratura styles. Silvia's final aria (No. 23) also changes tempo; however, its central Allegro maintains a declamatory style. This is preceded by an extended accompanied recitative making her final piece part of a large scena, which is marred by a less than vocally stellar, though dramatically effective, aria as she pleads to be delivered from her suffering.

Ascanio is characterized by his own big scena (I/2) consisting of an accompanied recitative followed by a binary aria featuring the *messa di voce* on the word 'cara' ('dear one'), which the castrato GIOVANNI MANZUOLI was said to deliver with particular effectiveness. In I/5 (No. 16) Mozart allows the text to shape the form with its changing tempos, metres, and moods:

Adagio	Allegro 4/4	Andante grazioso 3/8	Adagio	Allegro 4/4
D major	——→	A Minor mod.	D Major	——→
lines 1–2	lines 3–5, 1–5	lines 6–9	lines 1–2	lines 3–5, 1–5
Nobility of Soul	Virtues of Silvia	Peace, to recall her virtues	Nobility of Soul	Virtues of Silvia

His aria in II/4 also contains a series of tempo changes highlighting Ascanio's frustrations. His final aria (II/5) is less varied and more galant in style; it is notable for the colourful wind scoring with flutes, serpentini, bassoons and horns.

Venere's two arias found in the first part are rather one-dimensional Allegros (I/1, I/5) with elaborate coloraturas. One should not be surprised that she sings the opening aria; this was merely an imperial protocol. Aceste's pair of arias (I/4, II/5) are also elaborate, confirming that the tenor must have had an agile voice. Mozart writes his most demanding pieces (I/8, II/3) for the *secondo uomo*, who played the Fauno. His castrato soprano voice must have been in first-class shape to negotiate the coloraturas, particularly in his second piece (II/3) whose final flourish line culminates with a high D sharp.

Though Mozart scholarship has tended to dismiss *Ascanio in Alba* as just another ceremonial opera, it represents a significant moment. For the same celebration, METASTASIO and HASSE, the doyens of Italian opera, reluctantly undertook their last collaboration, *Il Ruggiero, ovvero L'Eroica gratitudine*, which was, in contrast to *Ascanio*, received without enthusiasm. In October 1771, the art of operatic composition had in a sense passed from the Metastasio–Hasse generation to that of Mozart. A. PETER BROWN

C. Gianturco, *Mozart's Early Operas* (London, 1981)
D. Heartz, *Haydn, Mozart and the Viennese School 1740–1780* (New York, 1995)
W. Mann, *Mozart's Operas* (London, 1977)

Attwood, Thomas (baptized London, 23 Nov. 1765; d. London, 24 Mar. 1838). English composer and organist; pupil of Mozart. Attwood was a chorister at the Chapel Royal and from 1781 to 1783 studied in Italy with Felipe Cinque and Gaetano Latilla. In VIENNA, he was a pupil of Mozart's from August 1785 to February 1787; his composition exercises, with Mozart's corrections, survive in the British Library. According to MICHAEL KELLY, Mozart said that 'Attwood is a young man for whom I have a sincere affection and esteem; he conducts himself with great propriety and I feel much pleasure in telling you, that he partakes more of my style than any scholar I ever had; and I predict, that he will prove a sound musician'. Mozart's assessment was prescient: after his return to England Attwood was appointed organist at St Paul's and composer to the Chapel Royal, professor at the Royal Academy of Music in 1823, musician-in-ordinary to George IV in 1825, and organist of the Chapel Royal in 1836. Although in later years he increasingly wrote church and organ music, during the 1790s and early years of the nineteenth century he was a prolific composer for the stage. Attwood left a short reminiscence of Mozart as well, probably written down during the 1820s: 'Mozart at the time I was with him, appeared to be of a cheerful habit, his health not very strong. In consequence of being so much over the table when composing, he was obliged to have an upright Desk & stand when he wrote . . . He was so fond of [JOHANN] SEBASTIAN BACH's Preludes & Fugues that he had a separate Pianoforte with Pedals, fixed under the Other – was very kind to all of Talent who came to Vienna & generally played at their Benefit Concerts with the Pianofortes as directed above.' CLIFF EISEN

D. Heartz, 'Thomas Attwood's Lessons in Composition with Mozart', *Proceedings of the Royal Musical Association* 100 (1973–4), 175–83
E. Hertzmann, 'Mozart and Attwood', *Journal of the American Musicological Society* 12 (1959), 178–84
C. B. Oldman, 'Thomas Attwood, 1765–1838', *Musical Times* 106 (1965), 844–5

Auernhammer, Josepha Barbara (b. Vienna, 25 Sept. 1758; d. Vienna, 30 Jan. 1820). Auernhammer was a student of Mozart's in VIENNA in the early 1780s and a fine pianist, judging by contemporary accounts. The Viennese musician Benedikt Schwarz described her as 'a great dilettante on the pianoforte' and Mozart admired her 'enchanting' playing, while also explaining that 'in cantabile playing she has not got the real delicate singing style'. ABBE MAXIMILIAN STADLER, an Austrian theologian and musicologist, was 'enchanted by the playing of master and pupil' in the violin sonatas K296, 376–80, works Mozart dedicated to Auernhammer upon publication in 1781. Mozart and Auernhammer are known to have performed together on a number of occasions, taking the solo roles in the Concerto for Two Pianos in E flat, K365 (1779) at her family residence in Vienna on 23 November 1781 and at the Augarten in Vienna on 26 May 1782. Cramer's *Magazin der Musik* for 23 April 1787 reports that Auernhammer also 'supervised and corrected the engraving of many sonatas and ariettes with variations by Mozart at [the publisher] ARTARIA'. Auernhammer fell in love with Mozart in 1781, but he did not reciprocate: 'she is not content if I spend a couple of hours with her every day. She wants me to sit there the whole day long – and, what is more, she is *sérieusement* in love with me! I thought at first it was a joke, but now I know it to be a fact. When I noticed it . . . I was obliged, not to make a fool of the girl, to tell her the truth very politely' (22 Aug. 1781). SIMON P. KEEFE

O. E. Deutsch, 'Das Fräulein von Auernhammer', *Mozart-Jahrbuch* 1958, 12–17

Augsburg. City in Bavaria, GERMANY; birthplace of LEOPOLD MOZART. A city of distinguished cultural achievement, Augsburg during Leopold Mozart's childhood was still suffering from the ravages of the Thirty Years War, and unlike most German cities of the time was split between Lutherans and Catholics, a situation that was to have consequences for Mozart. Musical activity had been revived first at the Lutheran Barfüsserkirche and the cathedral, St Anna; prominent Catholic institutions included St Ulrich and St Afra, the Augustinian monastery of the Holy Cross, the collegiate chapter of St Moritz and the Jesuit church of St Salvator. Lutheran composers, including Johann Caspar Seyfert and F. H. Graf, modelled themselves on works by north German composers, including J. S. BACH and Telemann; Catholics were oriented more towards south Germany and AUSTRIA. In addition to church music, Augsburg offered numerous other opportunities for music-making, including a collegium musicum founded in 1713, frequent theatrical productions at the schools of St Salvator and St Anna, and at the court of the prince-bishop, whose chapel included among its composers J. M. Schmid, P. P. Sales and J. G. Lang.

Leopold Mozart had studied at the Augsburg Gymnasium and the Lyceum adjoining the Jesuit school of St Salvator, where he frequently performed as an actor and singer in theatrical productions. And he maintained close contacts there after his departure for SALZBURG in 1737, with his family and with his friends, among them Johann Jakob LOTTER, later the publisher of Leopold's important *Versuch einer gründlichen Violinschule* (1756), and the keyboard builder J. A. STEIN. The collegium musicum often purchased Leopold's symphonies and incidental orchestral music, and even from Salzburg he was able to monitor their performance and distribution. Understandably, Augsburg was among Leopold's first ports of call when he began touring with Wolfgang. The family first visited in 1762, from 22 June until 6 July; Mozart and his sister gave concerts on 28 and 30 June and on 4 July. On 19 July, an article praising them appeared in the local *Extract-Schreiben oder . . . Europäische Zeitung*: '[Leopold Mozart] afforded the inhabitants of his native city the pleasure of hearing the effect of the extraordinary gifts which the great God has bestowed on these two dear little ones in such abundant measure.'

Mozart made a slightly longer stop at Augsburg in October 1777, en route to MANNHEIM and PARIS. They arrived on 10 October; on 12 October Mozart's uncle, Franz Alois Mozart, introduced him to the city governor, Jakob Langenmantel vom Wertheim and Ottmarshausen, on 12 October he visited the piano maker Stein, and on 13 October he visited the Holy Cross Monastery. He gave a public concert on 22 October; among the works performed on this occasion were the CONCERTO for three keyboards K242, a solo concerto (K175 or K238), a SYMPHONY, a SONATA and a contrapuntal fantasy; according to the *Augsburgische staats- und gelehrte Zeitung*, 'One found here mastery in the thought, mastery in the performance, mastery in the instruments, all at the same time.' While he was there, Leopold cautioned him to be sensitive to the city's Lutheran/Catholic split, writing to Wolfgang on 15 October:

> If you find that you are warmly applauded and are very highly esteemed, I should like *a special article, praising your gifts, to appear in the Augsburg papers, after you have left*, an article my brother could perhaps dictate to Herr Stein or which Herr Glatz could draft and Herr Stein could arrange to have published. You know why! It would make someone here [Archbishop COLLOREDO] very angry, but Herr Stein and some other Evangelicals would get a lot of fun out of it. You know, of course, that the Lutherans should be called *Evangelicals*, for they do not like to be called Lutherans. Thus, for instance, you should talk of an *evangelical church* and not of a *Lutheran church*; similarly the Calvinists like to be called *Protestants*, and not Calvinists. It has just occurred to me that I ought to tell you this, for no more than a single wrong word may often lead to an unpleasant experience with some irritable person, though, of course, sensible people pay no attention to such formalities.

Nevertheless, Mozart soon found himself embroiled in a row with the Evangelical patricians, a row that it required Stein's intervention to resolve.

Later visits were brief: while in MUNICH for the premiere of IDOMENEO, Mozart and his father travelled to Augsburg for four days in March 1781 and he briefly passed through the city on the return trip from LEOPOLD II's Frankfurt coronation in late 1790. Even after Mozart's move to VIENNA, however, his music was actively sought in Augsburg, with Leopold supplying copies of his church music in particular; after his death in 1787, several manuscripts were bequeathed to the Holy Cross Monastery. CLIFF EISEN

K. Dorfmüller, 'Mozart, das Augsburger Bürgerkind', *Die Sieben Schwaben* 6 (1956), 67–70
J. Mancal, 'Augsburg "Meine Vaterstadt" (L. Mozart 1756), "die vatterstadt meines Papa" (W. A. Mozart 1777), "meine eigentliche Stammstadt" (Fr. X. W. A. Mozart 1821)', *Acta Mozartiana* 46 (1999), 3–31
Mozart-Schätze in Augsburg (Augsburg, 1995 = Beiträge zur Leopold-Mozart-Forschung, 3)
E. Preussner, *Die bürgerliche Musikkultur. Ein Beitrag zur deutschen Musikgeschichte des 18. Jahrhunderts* (Hamburg, 1935)

Austria, Austrian, Austrian Monarchy. By the eighteenth century the noun 'Austria', and still more the adjective 'Austrian', had acquired a most confusing variety of meanings. 'Austria' originally referred to the archduchy of Austria, spread out along the Danube and divided into the *Länder* (provinces) or duchies of Upper and Lower Austria, the former with Linz as its capital, the latter with VIENNA. This was still the basic meaning of 'Austria' in the eighteenth century, though sometimes it was applied to Lower Austria alone. If an individual was described as an Austrian, that normally meant that he or she came from the archduchy. In this sense 'Austria' referred to an area much smaller even than that of the modern republic of Austria. The archduchy was known as a fertile, wine-growing district. It was notable too for the exceptional wealth and power of its monasteries: the tag 'Österreich Klösterreich' has the double meaning 'Austria rich in monasteries' and 'Austria under monastic rule'. Among the most important houses were Kremsmünster and Lambach in Upper Austria and Melk and Klosterneuburg in Lower Austria, all of them noted for their musical establishments and libraries and known to Mozart. Upper and Lower Austria each had an ancient constitution, a royal governor and a representative assembly or 'estates' that met regularly.

Sometimes, however, 'Austria' designated a group of duchies more nearly corresponding to present-day Austria (excluding SALZBURG, but including south Tyrol, now Italian, and Carniola, now Slovenian): Lower Austria, Upper Austria, Styria (*Steiermark*), Carinthia (*Kärnten*), Tyrol, Gorizia and Carniola (*Krain*). These lands incidentally constituted the 'Austrian circle' of the Holy Roman Empire, the area in which the Habsburgs were exempt from imperial 'interference'. Styria, Carinthia, Gorizia, Tyrol and Carniola together were known as 'Inner Austria'. 'Further Austria' (*Vorderösterreich*) referred to the scattered Habsburg lands in southern Germany.

It was also not uncommon to speak of 'the Austrian lands of the monarchy' as shorthand for the lands administered from Vienna after 1749 by the *Directorium in publicis et cameralibus* or 'Austro-Bohemian Chancellery', that is the western part of the central bloc of territories, also often called 'the hereditary lands' (*Erbländer*), i.e. the Austrian duchies and Bohemia, as opposed to the Hungarian lands.

In addition, the term 'Austria' had acquired another much wider meaning because the ruling Habsburg dynasty had since the late Middle Ages called itself 'the House of Austria'. In Grete Klingenstein's words, 'it was, so to speak, the name of the family firm' and 'the simplified and abbreviated description of a highly complicated body politic'. Hence 'Austria' became the most common designation, especially among foreigners, for the state which also came to be officially known in the eighteenth century as 'the Austrian Monarchy'. This huge collection of territories, acquired by the dynasty over many centuries, included the lands of the present-day Austrian republic (except the province of Salzburg); Bohemia (including Moravia), now the Czech Republic; greater Hungary (which then embraced, as well as modern Hungary, Slovakia, Croatia and the south-western tip of modern Ukraine); Transylvania and the banat of Temesvar (both for a time treated as part of Hungary and now mostly part of Romania); the duchy of Carniola (now Slovenian); south Tyrol, much of Lombardy and certain other lands now within Italy; small and scattered possessions in southern Germany; the 'Austrian Netherlands' (that is Luxemburg and the greater part of modern Belgium); Galicia after 1772 (now divided between Poland and Ukraine) and, after 1775, the Bukovina (now divided between Romania and Ukraine). This 'state' was not territorially unified, since its possessions in Lombardy, south Germany and the Netherlands were separated from the central bloc of the monarchy and within some of its provinces there were enclaves not ruled from Vienna, such as the bishoprics of Trent and Brixen. The sovereigns of this vast agglomeration ruled its many provinces under a wide variety of titles, of which the most important were Archduke of Austria, King of Hungary and King of Bohemia. The ruler had no title that applied to the whole monarchy.

In 1740, under the so-called Pragmatic Sanction, a declaration which had been accepted by all the lands of the monarchy and by most foreign powers, MARIA THERESIA (r. 1740–80) became sovereign of all the territories possessed by her father Charles VI, and the inheritance was declared to be indivisible. Each province had a distinct constitution, which in some cases, like Hungary and the Belgian lands, was based on a written document. On her accession Maria Theresia obtained for her husband Francis (Stephen), titular Duke of Lorraine and ruling Grand-Duke of Tuscany, the title of 'co-regent' to give him precedence in the monarchy and to enable her to delegate any of her powers to him if she so wished; and, after he died in 1765, she appointed her son JOSEPH II to succeed him in that capacity.

During her reign she greatly diminished the autonomy of the non-Hungarian provinces of the central bloc, particularly in matters of taxation. But her attempts to carry out similar measures in Hungary foundered on the opposition of the country's 'diet' or parliament, especially at its meeting in 1764, and it was not called again until 1790. As for the outlying Netherlands, she was for the most part content to enjoy the substantial revenues they supplied. Her son Joseph (r. 1780–90), however, believed fanatically that the territories he ruled, however diverse and scattered, should be made administratively homogeneous and be equally subject to his absolute sovereignty, which he claimed to exercise from above for their good. In his so-called 'pastoral letter' of late 1783, addressed to all his officials and soon published, he declared:

> Since the good can only be one, namely that which concerns the whole and the greatest number, and likewise all the provinces of the Monarchy only form a single whole, and thus can have only one purpose; . . . in all of them nationality and religion must make no difference, and as brothers in one Monarchy all should set to work equally in order to be useful to one another.

He and some of his supporters tried to excite feelings of patriotism towards it as the 'fatherland', especially during the war against the Turks from 1788 to

1791 – a campaign reflected in several of Mozart's dances and two of his songs ('Ich möchte wohl der Kaiser sein') (I wish I were the Emperor) and *Beim Auszug in das Feld* (When Troops are Leaving for the Front). But the monarchy was essentially the fortuitous creation of the dynasty, wars and treaties. If its western lands were in great majority Catholic and had developed over centuries feelings of loyalty to the Habsburgs, its huge eastern territories had been won from the Turks only since 1683 and contained large Protestant and Orthodox populations. Furthermore, even after Joseph in 1784 made German the language of administration in all his provinces except Lombardy and Belgium, the bureaucracy had to resort to at least a dozen more languages to get his orders understood. When his programme resulted late in 1789 in successful rebellion in the Netherlands and the threat of it in Hungary, he was finally brought to see on his deathbed the necessity of withdrawing his centralizing reforms. His successor LEOPOLD II (r. 1790–2), who was a believer in constitutionalism, restored the position of the ruler by a judicious mixture of concession, peace-making and procrastination.

Among the reasons for the absence of a global title for the ruler of the monarchy was the pride of each of its provinces in its distinctive relationship with the sovereign. Another was the existence of the Holy Roman Empire. (See also GERMANY.) This entity included all of modern Germany and Austria, Bohemia, modern Belgium and Luxemburg and parts of modern Poland, Slovenia and Italy. Its head was the emperor, who ranked as the senior sovereign of Europe. He was elected by the chief German princes, known as 'electors'. From 1438 to 1740 they always chose the ruler of Austria to be emperor, which meant that the imperial bureaucracy, though distinct from that of the House of Austria, was based in Vienna. But a woman could not be elected, and so the accession of Maria Theresia led to a forty-year period when the emperor and the ruler of the Austrian Monarchy were different persons. In 1742 the elector of Bavaria became emperor as Charles VII. He died in 1745, when Maria Theresia's husband was elected as Francis I, bringing the imperial administration back to Vienna. Joseph II succeeded him in 1765. When she died, the two roles of emperor and ruler of the monarchy were reunited in Joseph. He was interested in the affairs of the Empire only in so far as he could exploit them to serve the monarchy, and he had long-term plans to abolish the Empire, which he died too soon to put in hand.

Maria Theresia was usually referred to as 'Empress' (which she was by marriage), and Joseph and Leopold as 'Emperor', because this was their senior title. The existence of the Holy Roman Empire and its emperor made it virtually impossible to think and speak of the Austrian Monarchy as an empire, and the term was virtually never applied to it until in 1803, under the aegis of Napoleon, the map of Germany was redrawn and the Holy Roman Empire destroyed in all but name. In the following year Leopold II's son and heir, Francis (r. 1792–1835), assumed the title Emperor of Austria. The Holy Roman Empire was formally dissolved in 1806. 'Habsburg Monarchy' and 'Habsburg Empire' are designations invented by modern historians, especially inappropriate to the time of Joseph II, since the male Habsburg line had died out with Charles VI and the official name of the dynasty had become 'Habsburg-Lorraine'.

The relation between Austria, the Austrian Monarchy and the Holy Roman Empire mattered in Mozart's career because he was born a subject of the Archbishop of Salzburg. The archbishop was a prince of the Holy Roman Empire and not under Austrian rule, and so he had a court of his own and an important musical establishment. He and his lands belonged to the 'Bavarian circle' of the empire and not to the 'Austrian circle'. On the other hand, since his state was a buffer between Austria and Bavaria, and since his archdiocese covered much Habsburg territory, the Vienna government cared greatly who was appointed to the see. In 1772 it procured the election of COUNT HIERONYMUS COLLOREDO, who was the son of Prince Colloredo, the head of the imperial bureaucracy in Vienna directly responsible to Joseph II in his capacity as emperor. It was this important functionary whom the archbishop was visiting when he dismissed Mozart from his service in Vienna in 1781.

The best estimates of the population of the various regions within the monarchy are shown in table 1 (for the year 1787 except where otherwise stated):

Table 1.

'Austrian lands'		
Lower and Upper Austria	1,646,051	
Styria	829,229	
Carinthia	297,384	
Carniola	419,411	
Gorizia	122,081	
Tyrol	684,357	
Further Austria	355,718	
SUBTOTAL		4,354,231
Bohemia		4,383,842
Galicia and Bukovina		3,435,056
Greater Hungary		8,555,832
Austrian Netherlands (1784)		2,273,000
Lombardy (1785)		1,338,518

The grand total is more than 24 million, making the Austrian Monarchy comparable in size to France and Russia, and much more populous than the other two great powers, Britain and Prussia. Within the monarchy, the figures show how small a percentage (less than 20 percent) of the total population was to be found in the Austrian lands, and how large a proportion was located in what is now thought of as eastern Europe. If Austria and Bohemia are taken together, as often in the eighteenth century, their population still amounted to barely a third of the whole monarchy's.

Throughout this period the ruler's city of residence was Vienna, a fact that greatly helped to identify the state with Austria. See table 2 for the populations of the principal towns in the 1780s. The figures illustrate the exceptional position of Vienna, and the relatively limited importance of towns anywhere in the monarchy except Belgium and Lombardy.

Table 2.

Vienna	202,729
Milan	132,233
Brussels	74,427
Prague	72,874
Antwerp	48,665
Pozsony (Pressburg, Bratislava)	c.30,000
Graz	29,382

In foreign affairs the period is dominated by the threat from Frederick II ('the Great') of Prussia (r. 1740–86), who in 1740 seized nearly all the rich province of Silesia from Maria Theresia and made good the annexation during the following 'First Silesian War' (1740–5), in European terms 'the War of the Austrian Succession' (1740–8). But she, and later Joseph, always aimed to recover Silesia, and it was to further this objective that in 1756 she abandoned the long-standing Austro-British alliance in favour of an alliance with France in the 'Diplomatic Revolution' masterminded by her State Chancellor, Count (after 1763 Prince) KAUNITZ, who was the state's chief minister from 1753 to 1792. The 'Second Silesian War' or 'Seven Years War' (1756–63) produced a stalemate. Austria's attempt to enhance her position in Germany by exchanging Belgium for Bavaria, whose ruling dynasty died out in 1777, caused the 'Third Silesian War' or 'War of the Bavarian Succession' (1778–9), which also ended in stalemate, with only a tiny gain for Austria, the *Innviertel*, from Bavaria. In a renewed attempt to out-match Prussia, Joseph and Kaunitz succeeded in 1780–1 in tempting Empress Catherine II of Russia into an alliance with Austria, with a view to reviving the Bavarian exchange plan and also to dividing between them the supposedly moribund Turkish Empire. However, Frederick frustrated the Bavarian scheme, and the Turks proved resilient and declared war on Russia in 1787, forcing Joseph under the terms of his alliance to join in the struggle. After an inglorious first campaign in 1788, Austrian armies captured Belgrade in the following year; but the general situation of the monarchy made Joseph and Kaunitz begin to work for peace, which Leopold concluded on the basis of the convention of Reichenbach with Frederick William II of Prussia in July 1790, leading to a peace with the Turks re-establishing the pre-war boundaries.

DEREK BEALES

D. Beales, *Joseph II, I: In the Shadow of Maria Theresa, 1741–1780* (Cambridge, 1987)
Enlightenment and Reform in Eighteenth-Century Europe (London, 2005)
T. C. W. Blanning, *Joseph II* (Harlow, 1994)
P. G. M. Dickson, *Finance and Government under Maria Theresia, 1740–1780* (Oxford, 1987)
G. Klingenstein, 'The Meanings of "Austria" and "Austrian" in the Eighteenth Century', in *Royal and Republican Sovereignty in Early Modern Europe*, ed. R. Oresko, G. C. Gibbs and H. M. Scott (Cambridge, 1997), 423–78

B

Bach, Carl Philipp Emanuel (b. Weimar, 8 Mar. 1714; d. Hamburg, 14 Dec. 1788). GERMAN composer; son of J. S. BACH. Carl Philipp Emanuel Bach received his musical training from his father and from about the age of fifteen took part in performances at the Leipzig Thomaskirche and by the local collegium musicum. He studied law at the Leipzig University but in 1734 moved to Frankfurt an der Oder, where he continued his studies and was musically active, performing works by his father as well as his own. In 1738 he was appointed to the court of Frederick of Prussia: his duties chiefly included composing and teaching, which may have inspired his *Versuch über die wahre Art das Clavier zu spielen* (Berlin, 1753), the most important eighteenth-century German-language treatise on the subject. Bach was under-appreciated in Berlin (the court was also home to HASSE, Graun, Quantz and Agricola) and he sought appointments elsewhere although his applications for the post of cantor at the Leipzig Thomaskirche of 1750 and 1755 failed, as did a 1753 application for the post of organist at the Johanniskirche in Zittau. But he was successful in his application to succeed Telemann as music director of the principal churches in Hamburg in 1767, moving there the next year. His duties included teaching at the Lateinschule and organizing music at the city's five principal churches, which amounted to nearly two hundred musical performances a year. Among his original compositions of the time, the oratorios *Die Israeliten in der Wüste* and *Die Auferstehung und Himmelfahrt Jesu* were particularly successful. He was also respected for his solo keyboard music, which was widely disseminated throughout German-speaking Europe.

Although Mozart and C. P. E. Bach never met, it is fair to say that Bach's music, as well as his writings on performance, loomed large in the Mozarts' musical consciousness and that they were well acquainted with his keyboard works. A version of the variations from the *Musikalisches Allerley von verschiedenen Tonkünstler* (published Berlin, 1761) appears in NANNERL MOZART's early study book, also used by Wolfgang, and Bach's 'La Boehmer' from the *Musikalisches Mancherley* (published Berlin: G. L. Winter, 1762–3) was arranged by Wolfgang as one of movements in his pasticcio concerto K40. On 6 October 1775 LEOPOLD MOZART wrote to the Leipzig publisher Breitkopf: 'As I decided some time ago to have some of my son's compositions printed, I should like you to let me know as soon as possible whether you would like to publish some of them, that is to say, symphonies, quartets, trios, sonatas for violin and violoncello, even solo sonatas for violin or clavier sonatas. In regard to the latter perhaps you would like to print clavier sonatas in the same style as those of Carl Philipp Emanuel Bach "with varied reprises"? These were printed by Georg Ludwig Winter in Berlin and this type of sonata is very popular.' The *Versuch* is mentioned in Leopold's letter of 11 June 1778. Bach continued to figure in Mozart's musical life even after his move to VIENNA in 1781. On 10 April 1782 he wrote to his father, 'I go every Sunday at twelve o'clock to the BARON VAN SWIETEN, where nothing is played but HANDEL and Bach. I am collecting at the moment the fugues of Bach – not only of Sebastian, but also of Emanuel and Friedemann.' And in February 1788 he composed wind parts for Bach's oratorio *Die Auferstehung und Himmelfahrt Jesu*, which he conducted at Count Johann ESTERHÁZY'S. CLIFF EISEN

A. Holschneider, 'C. Ph. E. Bachs Kantate Auferstehung und Himmelfahrt Jesu und Mozarts Aufführung des Jahres 1788', *Mozart-Jahrbuch 1968/70*, 264–80

L. Silke, '"Er is der Vater, wir sind die Bub'n". Über Mozarts schöpferische Auseinandersetzung mit Carl Philipp Emanuel Bach', in *Festschrift Christoph-Hellmut Mahling zum 65. Geburtstage*, ed. K. Pfarr and W. Ruf (Mainz, 1997), 755–69

J. Stevens, 'The "Piano Climax" in the Eighteenth-Century Concerto: An Operatic Gesture?' in *C. P. E. Bach Studies*, ed. S. Clark (Oxford, 1988), 245–76

C. Wolff, 'Carl Philipp Emanuel Bach und Wien', in *Carl Philipp Emanuel Bach und die europäische Musikkultur des mittleren 18. Jahrhunderts*, ed. H. J. Marx (Göttingen, 1990), 119–31

Bach, Johann Christian (b. Leipzig, 5 Sept. 1735; d. London, 1 Jan. 1782). German pianist and composer, resident mainly in LONDON. The youngest son of JOHANN SEBASTIAN BACH, Johann Christian was the member of the family who most obviously broke away from his Protestant Church background. After studying with his brother CARL PHILIPP EMANUEL BACH in Berlin, he left for Italy in 1755 for further study with Padre GIOVANNI BATTISTA MARTINI; here he composed operas for Turin and Naples, and liturgical music for the Catholic Church (to which he had converted). In 1762 he was invited to London to write two Italian operas for the King's Theatre, and he remained there for the rest of his life. Eagerly embracing the emerging Classical style, Bach fully exploited the commercial opportunities provided by London's thriving concert life and publishing industry; and though not a virtuoso himself, he seized the expressive potential of the developing piano in sonatas and concertos, working closely with London manufacturers such as Zumpe.

His initial commitment, however, was to the Opera House. *Orione* and *Zanaida* were premiered in 1763; and after a year's absence thanks to the opposition of Giardini, he returned in 1765 with *Adriano in Siria* for the celebrated male soprano GIOVANNI MANZUOLI. But high anticipation was not fulfilled, and Bach never truly succeeded at the King's Theatre: partly through Italian opposition, but also because the succession of mellifluous arias, however beautifully scored with sensuous woodwind colours, failed to sustain a whole opera. Individual arias, however, were called for in pasticcios, of which 'Non sò d'onde' was much the most popular (and a favourite of the great tenor ANTON RAAFF, the first Idomeneo). Bach's elegant Italianate manner was also disseminated outside the King's Theatre, through songs and duets he wrote or adapted for English operas in 1765 (*The Maid of the Mill* and *The Summer's Tale*) and for Vauxhall Gardens from 1766.

Already in 1763 Bach had been appointed music master to Queen Charlotte, to whom he dedicated his first set of concertos in March, and later he was a member of the Queen's chamber band. Another of the Queen's musicians was C. F. ABEL, with whom Bach gave a benefit on 29 February 1764; and the following year they were engaged by Mrs Cornelys to direct her subscription concerts at Carlisle House, Soho Square (see LONDON). Here Bach's symphonies Op. 3 were performed, and probably the orchestrally inspired piano sonatas Op. 5, published in 1766.

When in 1764 the Mozart family arrived in London, Bach acted as a mentor to the young composer, according to anecdote playing sonatas and improvising with Wolfgang between his knees, though there is no evidence of formal lessons. A warm personal relationship ensued, and Bach became a musical father figure to the young Mozart. We know that he played Bach's trios Op. 2, and presumably he heard a great deal of Bach's music at the Opera and at concerts. But one might question Bach's initiative in furthering the Mozarts' cause: neither Bach nor Abel assisted at their benefits, and the Mozarts may not even have performed at Soho Square. The year 1765 saw the inauguration of Bach's first major concert series, an important opera and new opportunities at the English theatre: there was little for him to gain socially or professionally from public association with a nine-year-old from a distant German court, especially one whose genius he must surely have recognized.

There is no doubt, however, that Mozart was strongly influenced by Bach's melodious style, by the sharply etched orchestral contrasts and colourful woodwind writing, by the combination of Italian opera melody with German symphonic manner (the so-called 'singing Allegro'). As Wyzewa and Saint-Foix identified, J. C. Bach's idiom formed the basis of Mozart's mature musical style; and the two London symphonies K16 and K19 are largely indistinguishable from his models.

After the family left London in 1765, Mozart continued to revere Bach, and his letters contain many favourable references to Bach's music. The family library contained a wide selection, including an autograph early version of the sonata later known as Op. 17 No. 3. In 1772 Mozart turned three of the Op. 5 sonatas into concertos (K107), around the same time that he wrote cadenzas for three arias by Bach (K293e). In 1778 Mozart took up the text 'Non sò d'onde' (K294), paying tribute to Bach's beautiful setting: 'Just because I know Bach's setting so well and like it so much, and because it is always ringing in my ears, I wished to try and see whether in spite of all this I could not write an aria totally unlike his' (letter of 28 Feb. 1778). Despite the tribute, there is surely a sense of Oedipal relationship with his musical father here – and he returned to the same text in 1787, in a quite different setting for the bass LUDWIG FISCHER (K512). Later in 1778 the two composers met in Paris, where Bach was preparing for a French opera commission. Mozart's description is highly revealing, not only of his own relationship with Bach, but also of that of Leopold: 'You can easily imagine his delight and mine at meeting again; perhaps his delight may not have been quite as sincere as mine – but one must admit that he is an honourable man and willing to do justice to others. I love him (as you know) and respect him with all my heart' (letter of 27 Aug. 1778).

The Bach–Abel concerts were successful for many years: in 1768 the two entrepreneurs transferred to Almack's, and in 1775 to their new Hanover Square Rooms. Here Bach produced some of his most ambitious music, especially the symphonies published as Op. 18 (three for double orchestra) and elaborate sinfonie concertanti that revel in the shifting colours of the modern symphonic idiom. In 1778 he achieved a final success at the Opera with *La clemenza di Scipione*, in which one massive aria with obbligato flute, oboe, violin and cello strikingly anticipates Mozart's 'Martern aller Arten' in DIE ENTFÜHRUNG AUS DEM SERAIL.

Bach was also gaining European fame, not only through publications but also through operas performed at Mannheim in 1772 and 1774, and at Paris in 1779 (*Amadis des Gaules*). Yet his later years were clouded by financial burdens, with competition from younger musicians and from the more varied concerts at the Pantheon: his bank account reveals declining receipts and substantial loan repayments to the piano maker Gabriel Buntebart (foreshadowing Mozart's relationship with MICHAEL PUCHBERG). He died on New Year's Day 1782.

Mozart remembered Bach with genuine affection, if also slightly laconically, at the end of a letter to his father: 'I suppose you have heard that the English Bach is dead? What a loss to the musical world!' (10 Apr. 1782). More warmly, he honoured him in music, quoting sotto voce the Andante from the overture to *La calamità de' cuori* in his Piano Concerto in A major, K414, written later that year.

SIMON MCVEIGH

H. Gärtner, *John Christian Bach: Mozart's Friend and Mentor* (Portland, OR, 1994)
C. S. Terry, *John Christian Bach* (London, 1929; 2nd rev. edn 1967)
T. de Wyzewa and G.de Saint-Foix, *W.-A. Mozart: sa vie et son œuvre* (Paris, 1912–46)

Bach, Johann Sebastian (b. Eisenach, 21 Mar. 1685; d. Leipzig, 28 July 1750). German composer. In biographical sketches of Mozart, the name of J. S. Bach usually appears twice in the context of Mozart's dramatic encounters with Bach's works – first, the *Well-Tempered Clavier* (*WTC*) introduced to him by BARON GOTTFRIED VAN SWIETEN in 1782, and later Bach's motet *Singet dem Herrn ein neues Lied* (BWV 225), which he heard at the Thomaskirche in Leipzig in 1789. In both cases, Bach is often characterized as a forgotten master, whose works were out of fashion at that time.

Three manuscript copies of Bach works that Mozart possessed survive. Two of them contain four-part fugues from *WTC* II, which he set in open score for string quartet: K 405 consists of fugues in C minor (BWV 871/2), E flat major (BWV 876/2), E major (BWV 878/2), D sharp minor (BWV 877/2, transposed to D minor) and D major (BWV 874/2); and K *deest* contains the B flat minor fugue (BWV 891/2, transposed to C minor, written by Mozart only up to bar 39 and subsequently completed by ABBE STADLER). All of these, interestingly, are STILE ANTICO fugues. Apparently, then, Mozart selected the fugues not only according to performing forces available at Sunday matinées at van Swieten's residence but also according to their style. The remaining item is a copy of *Singet dem Herrn* acquired on his Leipzig visit, on which Mozart noted, 'NB müßte ein ganzes Orchestre dazu gesetzt werden.'

Aside from the scores that have survived, there are undoubtedly many others that did not. One of these is the set of parts that Mozart presumably wrote out from his scores, so that the fugues could be performed at van Swieten's. Mozart also possessed a copy of the *WTC* itself (or the fugue-only collection of it) as reported by Thomas Attwood: 'this volume of fugues was always lying open on his pianoforte.' In fact Mozart's estate documents do not mention any of these except for the manuscript copies of *Clavier-Übung II* – consisting of the Italian Concerto (BWV 971) and the French Overture (BWV 831) – as well as the Small Harmonic Labyrinth (BWV 591, possibly by Johann David Heinichen).

In addition to those Bach works mentioned in contemporary sources, it is also possible that Mozart got to know many more works by Bach. It is highly likely, for example, that LEOPOLD MOZART or Padre MARTINI introduced some of Bach's keyboard works to him. JOHANN CHRISTIAN BACH, Bach's youngest son and one of Mozart's early mentors, could also have done so; his death in 1782, which coincided almost exactly with Mozart's awakening to Bach's fugues, may have played a role too.

1. The dissemination of Bach's works in Vienna
2. Mozart's editorial work in K405
3. Bach's influence on Mozart

1. The dissemination of Bach's works in Vienna

It is unclear how and when Bach's music was first introduced to VIENNA. The city was predominantly Roman Catholic, and for this reason Bach's works – especially those clearly identifiable as 'Lutheran' – would not have been immediately appealing. While reports by BURNEY and Reichardt that Bach's music was relatively unknown in Vienna appear to support this, there are in fact indications that Bach's keyboard works were already in circulation before 1770: Gottlieb Muffat possessed a 1740 copy of the fugue in A minor (BWV 904/2), and GEORG CHRISTOPH WAGENSEIL taught his pupils Bach's preludes and fugues. The real turning point, however, came in 1777 when van Swieten returned from Berlin – then the most important centre for the promotion of Bach's music – with a number of Bach manuscripts, doubtless including the *WTC*. Further works were acquired from C. P. E. BACH in Hamburg, including copies of the Magnificat (BWV 243) and the St Matthew Passion (BWV 244). The informal musical gatherings van Swieten organized on Sundays at his residence were typical of Viennese amateur musical life. Mozart participated regularly from spring 1782 until at least the winter of 1783–4, making his arrangements of Bach's fugues (K405) for these events. There are also several other anonymous collections of string trio, quartet and quintet settings that feature not only Bach's fugues but also accompanying 'introductions', including K404a. Although source evidence suggests that these may well date from after Mozart's death, they certainly attest to the increasing popularity of Bach's fugues at this time in Vienna. While van Swieten's musical library was doubtless the primary resource for Mozart, he probably encountered further Bach works through others as well. Prince Karl Lichnowsky is an obvious candidate as he brought from Göttingen to Vienna manuscript copies of Bach's keyboard works that included Inventions and Sinfonias (BWV 772–801), English and French Suites (BWV 806–17), the Suite in E flat (BWV 819), the Fantasy and Fugue in C minor (BWV 906) and the Fughetta in C minor (BWV 961). By the mid-1780s, Bach's keyboard works were being recognized more publicly than ever before; on 30 April 1785, a copy of Bach's 'Variationen per il Clavicemb' (possibly the Goldberg Variations) was advertised for sale by music trader JOHANN TRAEG, who was steadily building up his list of Bach's works. There were several dedicated collectors too, including Johann Georg Anton Mederitsch (1752–1835), a Viennese copyist (known as Gallus) who established a fairly substantial collection of Bach's organ and keyboard works, and Franz Joseph von Hess (1739–1804). In spite of inconclusive evidence, then, it is reasonable to infer that Mozart came in contact with a good range of Bach's works in Vienna.

2. Mozart's editorial work in K405

Mozart's letters from April 1782 provide an illuminating account of his delight at discovering Bach's fugues. Recent research shows that Mozart used several sources when he wrote K405, borrowed not just from van Swieten but from ALBRECHTSBERGER as well. These Viennese copies of Bach's fugues contained numerous errors; even before Mozart joined the van Swieten circle, the fugues were being edited with a view to improving certain stylistic elements of Bach's fugal writing. K405 seems to have been Mozart's principal contribution to this exercise. Mozart acted responsibly to produce a playable arrangement on the strings, while occasionally making small adjustments to Bach's textures and voice-leading where the composer was seen to be breaking the rules of strict *stile antico* counterpoint. There is little doubt that the depth of thought and the range of issues Mozart considered in the process taught him matters of real import, above all the powerful logic and beauty of Bachian fugal style.

3. Bach's influence on Mozart

Although Bach's influence was certainly an important factor in Mozart's artistic development, its significance has often been overemphasized at the expense of wider forces of influence, such as the emerging trend of the 'Gothic Revival' and the *Sturm und Drang* movement that directly relate to the increasing uses of traditional fugal procedures in the works of Viennese composers. In response to such a stereotyped image, some writers assert that all we witness in Mozart's encounter with Bach is Mozart trying to please his fiancée (who loved the fugues) and to pay his respects to van Swieten, rather than a profound impact on his musical psyche. While Mozart wrote many fugues in 1782, it is sometimes noted that the great majority of them were unfinished, thus rendering them more technical experiments than works of genuine artistic expression. Recently, Robert Marshall has made great strides towards improving our understanding of the issue by observing four stages in Mozart's reception of Bach's music (transcription, imitation, assimilation/synthesis and transcendence), a gradual process of absorbing the essence of Bach's counterpoint. Elaborate counterpoint is increasingly common in Mozart's post-1786 works, most clearly in the finale of the 'Jupiter' symphony, K551.

Mozart's visit to Leipzig in 1789 brought with it a different type of influence, that of stylistic imitation. The archaic idiom of the Baroque is clearly identifiable in certain late works, for example the REQUIEM, not only in fugal passages but also in the many sections that are elaborated with strict counterpoint.

YO TOMITA

G. Croll, 'Wolfgang Amadeus Mozarts Bach- und Händel-Studien 1782', *Händel-Jahrbuch* 1992, 79–93
W. Kirkendale, *Fugue and Fugato in Rococo and Classical Chamber Music*, trans. M. Bent and Kirkendale (Durham, NC, 1979)
R. Marshall, 'Bach and Mozart's Artistic Maturity', in *Bach Perspectives 3: Creative Responses to Bach from Mozart to Hindemith*, ed. Michael Marissen (Lincoln, NE, and London, 1998), 47–79
S. Sadie, 'Mozart, Bach and Counterpoint', *Musical Times* 105 (1964), 23–4
Y. Tomita, 'Bach Reception in Pre-Classical Vienna: Baron van Swieten's Circle Edits the "Well-Tempered Clavier II"', *Music & Letters* 81 (2000), 364–91

ballets. In his memoirs, the singer MICHAEL KELLY quotes CONSTANZE MOZART as saying 'that great as his [Mozart's] genius was, he was an enthusiast in dancing, and often said that his taste lay in that art, rather than in music'. Indeed, Mozart's first public appearance, at the age of five, was as a dancer, and in later years he was an eager participant in amateur balls and composer of orchestral dances. But for a musician of his extraordinary talents, there was little glory in composing ballet (as opposed to ballroom) music, which during this period was often produced anonymously. Furthermore, though some of the most important innovations in eighteenth-century dance had occurred in VIENNA, by the time of Mozart's residence there ballet was at a low ebb.

The Mozarts witnessed pantomime ballets by Angiolini and JEAN-GEORGES NOVERRE during visits to VIENNA in 1762 and 1767, and one Noverre ballet, *Les Jalousies du sérail*, was restaged by Charles Le Picq as an entr'acte to Wolfgang's opera LUCIO SILLA (Milan, Carnival 1771/2). Sketches in Mozart's hand were long believed to prove his borrowing of JOSEPH STARZER's music for that work, but they seem rather to have been copied by ear, and represent Mozart's keen interest in the dances that accompanied his opera.

Mozart renewed his acquaintance with Noverre in 1773, and again during his extended PARIS sojourn of 1778, when he also produced the only independent pantomime ballet of his career, *Les petits riens*, for the Opéra. The piece was Noverre's reworking of an earlier Viennese ballet; its Paris premiere was on 11 June 1778, with Niccolò Piccinni's opera buffa *Le finte gemelle*. As its title suggests, the ballet was hardly ambitious or heroic; rather, it was an episodic, anacreontic piece of the sort that audiences and soloists still demanded. The action of the ballet's three scenes depicted, respectively, 'Cupid caught in a net and put in a cage', 'the game of blindman's bluff', and 'a prank of Cupid, who introduces a shepherdess disguised as a shepherd to two other shepherdesses'. According to Mozart, the music was not even completely his own: his contributions included 'the Overture, and Contredanse, and in all some 12 pieces'; the six or so non-Mozartian numbers were arrangements of 'mere old, wretched French tunes' (letter of 9 July 1778). Recourse to such pieces was common in French ballets, and not just because of laziness: the tunes carried allusive value for audiences, because of the texts associated with them. The second number in *Les petits riens*, for instance, 'Charmante Gabrielle', was appropriate for amorous situations, and the next air, 'Dans un détour', was even more apt, being about an attempt to steal the sleeping Cupid's arrows. The dances ascribed to Mozart sustain the ballet's pastoral mood, but are neither particularly suggestive of gestures or actions, nor any more ambitious than the arrangements of 'wretched French tunes'.

Judging from the papers on which he wrote them, several other of Mozart's dances date from this same Parisian sojourn, including two sketch leaves (K299c) for a pantomime ballet: one featuring dance numbers, and the other, its continuation, with various simple pantomimes ('avec le chapeau', 'avec le baton'). The contrast between these single-line, fragmentary sketches and Mozart's next ballet composition, for his opera IDOMENEO (Munich, 1781), could hardly be more striking. For this latter music Mozart usurped the role of the ballet composer (all too often a hack from the orchestra), in order that it be 'by a master', as he wrote to his father. Indeed, the magnificent Chaconne (with contrasting ensemble and solo sections) betrays Mozart's close study of similar movements in GLUCK's Parisian operas. The seeming inevitability with which the Chaconne follows the opera's final chorus, and the finality of its conclusion make problematic the placement of the other dance movements, a G major Gavotte, and a Passacaille in E flat.

Dance comes to the fore at crucial moments also in Mozart's LE NOZZE DI FIGARO and DON GIOVANNI, despite the lack of a regular ballet troupe in either of the theatres of their premieres (Vienna's Burgtheater and PRAGUE's Estates Theatre respectively). In the former work Susanna passes a *billet doux* to the Count during a fandango at her betrothal celebrations, and in his memoirs, the librettist LORENZO DA PONTE recounts his and Mozart's struggles against intrigues to excise this dramatically important ballet. Court records speak of payment to the choreographer Jean Huber de Camp only for a '3. mal gestelte[n] kleinen Ballet', and recent researches of Dexter Edge indicate that the ballet was indeed cut sometime before or during the first production. Whatever the fate of this scene, dance rhythms pervade much of the rest of the opera, notably in Figaro's aria 'Se vuol ballare', and in the slow, 'theatrical-style' minuet as Susanna emerges from a closet and confounds the Count in the second-act finale. A similarly noble-sounding minuet is the linchpin of the first-act finale in *Don Giovanni* where it combines with dances in differing metres to evoke the musical and social confusion of many real-life ballrooms.

Perhaps the most remarkable of Mozart's ballets is the *Faschingspantomime*, K446, that he created and performed with his in-laws the Langes and several friends during Carnival of 1783. In writing to his father to request that he send his Harlequin costume, Mozart proudly stated that 'the invention of both the pantomime, and the music for it, was by me' (12 Mar. 1783), though the 'old dancing master' Merk (playing Pantalone) had helped with the staging. Only incomplete drafts of the first-violin part survive, annotated with rudimentary indications for the action. Even from such meagre evidence, it is clear that Mozart captured the vivid gestural repertory of his commedia dell'arte characters, in a fluid and varied series of movements.

Not until the last months of Mozart's life was ballet (a particular interest of the new emperor, LEOPOLD II) again included among the offerings of the court's theatres. One can only speculate as to whether Mozart, had he lived, would have contributed to the revival of Viennese ballet with scores more ambitious than that of his informal carnival pantomime. BRUCE ALAN BROWN

W. J. Allanbrook, *Rhythmic Gesture in Mozart: 'Le nozze di Figaro' and 'Don Giovanni'* (Chicago, 1983)
G. Croll, 'Bemerkungen zum "Ballo primo" (KV Anh. 109/135a) in Mozarts Mailander *Lucio Silla*', *Analecta musicologica* 18 (1978), 160–5
W. Salmen, ed., *Mozart in der Tanzkultur seiner Zeit* (Innsbruck, 1990)

Barisani family. Physicians, active in SALZBURG, and friends of the Mozarts. Silvester Barisani (b. Castelfranco, 1719; d. Salzburg, 25 Jan. 1810) was personal physician to Archbishop SCHRATTENBACH from 1766; his son Sigmund (b. Salzburg, 1 Jan. 1758 or 1761; d. Vienna, 3 Sept. 1787), from 1786 active at the General Hospital in VIENNA, was a close friend of Wolfgang in Salzburg. Johann Joseph Barisani (1756–1826) was LEOPOLD MOZART's doctor in the mid-1780s. Silvester Barisani was also an active amateur musician: in 1784 a private orchestra regularly met at his house; its repertory included Mozart's 'Linz' symphony, K425. CLIFF EISEN

G. Barth-Scalmani, 'Vater und Sohn Mozart und das (Salzburger) Bürgertum oder "Sobald ich den Credit verliere, ist auch meine Ehre hin"', in *Genie und Alltag. Bürgerliche Stadtkultur zur Mozartzeit*, ed. G. Barth-Scalmani, B. Mazohl-Wallnig und E. Wangermann (Salzburg and Vienna, 1994), 173–202
F. Breitinger, 'Die Familien Barisani und Mozart', in *Mozartiana. 'Gaulimauli Malefisohu': Erhebungen von Friedrich Breitinger*, ed. Prodinger (Salzburg, 1992), 177–80

Barrington, Daines (b. London, 1727; d. London, 14 Mar. 1800). English lawyer and magistrate. The fourth son of John Shute, first Viscount Barrington, Daines Barrington, a fellow of the Royal Society, held various public offices between 1751 and 1785 but gave up his legal career in 1785 in order to pursue his other interests including archaeology, history, geography, natural history and music. Earlier, during the Mozarts' stay in LONDON in 1764–5, he examined Mozart and set the young composer several musical tests. His report was read at a meeting of 15 February 1770 and printed in the *Philosophical Transactions* for 1771; it reads, in part:

> Having been informed . . . that he was often visited with musical ideas, to which, even in the midst of the night, he would give utterance on his harpsichord; I told his father that I should be glad to hear some of his extemporary compositions. The father shook his head at this, saying, that it depended entirely upon his being as it were musically inspired, but that I might ask him whether he was in humour for such a composition. Happening to know that little Mozart was much taken notice of by Manzoli [MANZUOLI], the famous singer, who came over to England in 1764, I said to the boy, that I should be glad to hear an extemporary *Love Song*, such as his friend Manzoli might choose in an opera. The boy on this (who continued to sit at his harpsichord) looked back with much archness, and immediately began five or six lines of a jargon recitative proper to introduce a love song. He then played a symphony which might correspond with an air composed to the single word, *Affetto*. It had a first and second part, which, together with the symphonies, was of the length that opera songs generally last; if this extemporary composition was not amazingly capital, yet it was really above mediocrity, and shewed most extraordinary readiness of invention . . . After this he played a difficult lesson, which he had finished a day or two before: his execution was amazing, considering that his little

fingers could scarcely reach a fifth on the harpsichord. His astonishing readiness, however, did not arise merely from great practice; he had a thorough knowledge of the fundamental principles of composition, as, upon producing a treble, he immediately wrote a base under it, which, when tried, had very good effect. CLIFF EISEN

D. Barrington, 'Account of a Very Remarkable Musician. In a Letter from the Honourable Daines Barrington, F. R. S. to Mathew Maty, M. D. Sec. R. S.', *Philosophical Transactions of the Royal Society* 60 (1770), 54–64

'Experiments and Observations on the Singing of Birds', *Philosophical Transactions of the Royal Society* 63 (1773), 249–58

Miscellanies (London, 1781) [with accounts of W. A. Mozart, William Crotch, Samuel and Charles Wesley and the Earl of Mornington]

[Obituary], *Gentleman's Magazine* 70 (1800), 291–4

Bassi, Luigi (b. Pesaro, 4 Sept. 1766; d. ?Dresden, 1825). Italian baritone. He sang the role of Count Almaviva in the first PRAGUE production of LE NOZZE DI FIGARO in 1786 and, in 1787, also in Prague, the title role in DON GIOVANNI (1787). A student of Pietro Morandi and Pietro Laschi, Bassi had made his reputation in operas by Anfossi (*Lo sposo pereqivoco* and *I viaggiatori felici*) before joining BONDINI's company in Prague in 1784, where he sang in SOLER's *Una cosa rara* and PAISIELLO's *Il barbiere di Siviglia*. Widely considered a fine actor, opinions were divided over Bassi's singing. He left Prague in 1806 and in 1815 was engaged at Dresden as both a singer and opera producer. It was during his Dresden years that he gave a brief description of Mozart: 'Mr Mozart was an extremely eccentric and absent-minded young man, but not without a certain spirit of pride. He was very popular with the ladies, in spite of his small size; but he had a most unusual face, and he could cast a spell on any woman with his eyes.'

According to an article published in the *Allgemeine musikalische Zeitung* in 1800, 'Bassi was an excellent singer before he lost his voice, and he still knows very well how to use what remains. It lies between tenor and bass, and though it sounds somewhat hollow, it is still very flexible, full and pleasant. Herr Bassi is furthermore a very skilled actor in tragedy with no trace of burlesque, and with no vulgarity or tastelessness in comedy. In his truly artful and droll way he can parody the faults of the other singers so subtly that only the audience notices and they themselves are unaware of it. His best roles are Axur, Don Giovanni, Teodoro, the Notary in *La molinara*, the Count in *Figaro* and others.'

CLIFF EISEN

Z. Pilková, 'Prazstí mozartovstí pevci v drazdanskych pramenech [Mozart's Prague singers in sources from Dresden]', *Hudební veda* 28/4 (1991), 299–304

T. G. Waidelich, '*Don Juan von Mozart, (für mich componirt.)*: Luigi Bassi – eine Legende zu Lebzeiten, sein Nekrolog und zeitgenössische *Don Giovanni*-Interpretationen', *Mozart-Studien* 10 (2001), 181–212

Bastien und Bastienne, K50. Singspiel, composed at VIENNA in 1768. Mozart penned his first German opera, the charming one-act *Bastien und Bastienne*, during his family's year-long sojourn in Vienna in 1768. The libretto, by Friedrich Wilhelm Weiskern, was not newly written for the twelve-year-old composer, but taken from the comic repertory of Vienna's Kärntnertortheater. The young composer later altered his autograph with textual revisions provided by ANDREAS SCHACHTNER of SALZBURG.

The plot, derived from Jean-Jacques Rousseau's *Le Devin du village*, is simple and pastoral. The shepherd Bastien has left his shepherdess Bastienne for the company of a woman from the town. Bastienne visits Colas, the village soothsayer, who recommends that she feign indifference to Bastien when he returns. Colas intercepts Bastien on his homeward journey and warns him of Bastienne's new attitude. Colas recites a magic spell to make Bastienne appear. When Bastienne materializes, the two lovers argue, but they soon make up. Colas returns to wish them well and to take credit for the happy ending.

In his 1828 biography of Mozart, GEORG NIKOLAUS NISSEN stated that *Bastien und Bastienne* was first performed in 1768 in the garden theatre of F. A. Mesmer (see MESMER FAMILY), the founder of the hypnotic cure called Mesmerism, who lived in a Viennese suburb. Presumably Nissen got this information from Mozart's wife, Constanze, who had heard it while married to the composer. There are no eyewitness accounts or other evidence to confirm Nissen's claim. Some later historians have argued against the likelihood of a performance in this outdoor theatre, citing municipal records that place the construction of Mesmer's house in the same year Nissen cites as the year of the performance. But the notion of a premiere that brought together the famous hypnotist and the musical prodigy has proven too intriguing to surrender in the face of evidence that weakens, but does not disprove, the possibility of the event. The first satisfactorily documented performance of the work did not take place until 1890 in Berlin.

While *Bastien und Bastienne*'s origins can be traced back to Rousseau's *Devin du village*, there were several intervening versions between Rousseau and Mozart. Rousseau's *intermède*, after enjoying hundreds of performances at the Académie Royale de Musique, was parodied in 1753 in the nearby Comédie Italienne. The parodists completely reworked Rousseau's text, converting his recitatives and fourteen set-pieces into forty-six 'airs', poetic stanzas sung to already popular tunes. The dependence on such 'vaudevilles' rather than on newly composed songs was a tradition in French musical comedy, influenced by the commedia dell'arte.

The Comédie Italienne's parody, entitled *Les Amours de Bastien et Bastienne*, travelled from PARIS to VIENNA, where it played in French at the Laxenburg Palace and Burgtheater. In 1764, Friedrich Weiskern, a comic writer and actor at the Kärntnertortheater, translated the work into German. In doing so, Weiskern converted the parody into a Viennese musical comedy, translating most of the airs into spoken German prose, and adapting only fourteen of them into German poetry to be sung as airs to the original French tunes. In essence, Weiskern's conversion reversed what the *comique* writers had done in parodying Rousseau's text, but the Austrian's work was still very different from Rousseau's, preserving as it did the sometimes unusual poetic structure of the fourteen airs from the parody, with humorous touches caught in slang and dialect.

It was Weiskern's version that Mozart first set to music, and this would have been the text allegedly performed at Mesmer's. But the text would undergo yet another revision, most likely after the Mozarts returned to Salzburg in 1769.

The poet Andreas Schachtner, court trumpeter in Salzburg and a friend of the Mozart family, made this last revision. Schachtner's major change was to versify the spoken dialogue so that the young Mozart could set it as recitative. (The music survives for only four of the recitatives.) Schachtner made only small revisions to words and phrases in the set-pieces, because the music was already finished. He softened harsh rhymes, eliminated Viennese idioms, and brought his own poetic polish to the aria and ensemble texts.

Mozart's music for *Bastien und Bastienne* defies simple classification, and scholars have offered an array of suggestions as to the operatic tradition Mozart followed in it. As Hermann Abert notes, Mozart 'returned to Rousseau's conception' but depended as well on conventions of *opéra comique*, opera buffa, and south German folksong.

Almost all of the music in the opera is characterized by relatively simple melodies, rhythms, harmonies and textures, similar to the styles of *opéra comique* and German song. Most of the melodic phrases are short and symmetrical, the melodic movement is conjunct or triadic, and the rhythmic patterns correspond rather strictly to the poetic metre. Mozart avoids melismatic embellishment, long-held notes, extreme high or low pitches and elaborate accompaniment. Here and there he indulges in quick patter, a trademark of opera buffa, for comic effect. There is little variety in the orchestration or in the roles the instruments play – the violins dominate the texture, either doubling the voice or playing a simple counter-melody. Most of the orchestral introductions consist of a brief statement of one of the forthcoming melodies.

Colas's incantation aria and Bastien and Bastienne's reconciliation duet give an inkling of Mozart's later operatic powers. In Colas's aria, Mozart draws on Italian opera seria mannerisms for a mock-heroic effect. Dramatically swirling semiquaver notes in the violins set the scene in the minor-key introduction. Colas intones the incantation with a slow, nearly monotonic melody. Rhythmic variety and playfulness gradually increase as it becomes clear that this is an amiable spoof of arias about supernatural forces. The progression of the piece from seria to buffa and the rhythmic vitality offer pleasurable glimpses into the young composer's operatic instincts.

In Bastien and Bastienne's duet, Mozart moves the dramatic action along through a series of short connected sections. As each lover brings a new point into the argument – the possibility of other lovers, remembrance of past happiness, suicidal remorse – Mozart shifts rhythmic and melodic patterns. While the young composer almost never allows the voices to sing at the same time, and his text settings lack the breadth and distinction of later operas, his differentiation of characters, moods and stages in the conversation shows his interest and early facility in musical drama. LINDA L. TYLER

L. Tyler, '*Bastien und Bastienne*: The Libretto, its Derivation, and Mozart's Text-Setting', *Journal of Musicology* 8 (1990), 520–52

Beaumarchais, Pierre-Augustin Caron de (b. 24 Jan. 1732; d. 18 May 1799), French playwright, watchmaker, music teacher, judge, spy and arms dealer. After penning two Diderot-influenced *drames* and numerous scurrilous *parades*, Beaumarchais wrote three 'Figaro' comedies, two of which gained fame both as spoken plays and as operas. *Le Barbier de Séville*, conceived as an *opéra comique*, retained several musical numbers even when revised (1775) as a play, including Almaviva's serenade 'Je suis Lindor', on which Mozart wrote a set of piano variations, K354. The popularity of *Le Barbier* in VIENNA, first as a German play and then as an opera buffa (in PAISIELLO's setting), paved the way for DA PONTE and Mozart's transformation of its sequel, *La Folle Journée, ou Le Mariage de Figaro* (1784), as LE NOZZE DI FIGARO. EMPEROR JOSEPH II had banned performances of a German translation of Beaumarchais's *Figaro*, on account of its political and sexual audacity, but permitted its publication, with necessary retrenchments. The playwright was already known in Vienna, from a dubious pamphlet-suppressing mission in 1774 that included both an audience with the Empress and a stay in jail.

Da Ponte's preface to the libretto of *Figaro* gives some notion of the difficulty of adapting Beaumarchais's long, complex drama. The play included various songs, dances and even the enactment of writing a vaudeville, which Da Ponte cleverly elaborated in operatic terms (the latter in a 'canzonetta sull'aria . . .' – 'song to the tune of . . .'). While eliminating several characters, and compressing five acts into four, he translated much of Beaumarchais's text quite directly, in recitative, or in action arias and ensembles (for example, measuring for a bed, dressing Cherubino), which Mozart set in brilliant fashion; Da Ponte termed the result 'almost a new genre of spectacle'. To their credit, both librettist and composer managed to preserve Beaumarchais's unprecedented combination of theatrical artifice and sentiment, while adding new layers of meaning.

BRUCE ALAN BROWN

D. Heartz, 'From Beaumarchais to Da Ponte: The metamorphosis of *Figaro*', in Heartz, *Mozart's Operas*, ed., with contributing essays, T. Bauman (Berkeley and Los Angeles, 1990)

S. Castelvecchi, 'Sentimental and Anti-Sentimental in *Le nozze di Figaro*', *Journal of the American Musicological Society* 53 (2000), 1–24

Beecke, (Notger) Ignaz (Franz) von (b. Wimpfenam Neckar, 28 Oct. 1733; d. Wallerstein, 2 Jan. 1803). Keyboard player and composer. Beecke was personal adjutant to Count Kraft Ernst Oettingen-Wallerstein who in 1774 became Prince of Oettingen-Wallerstein, appointing him as his director of court music. Mozart met Beecke in PARIS in 1766 and again in MUNICH during the winter of 1774–5, where they played a piano duel. In October 1777, when Mozart was at Hohen-Altheim, he wrote to his father: 'Well, would Papa like to know how Beecke received me? Why, very favourably and most politely . . . We fell to talking of various things, among them VIENNA, and how the Emperor was no great lover of music. "That is true", he said; "he knows something about counterpoint but that is all. I can still remember (here he rubbed his forehead) that when I had to play to him, I had not the least idea what to play. So I started to play fugues and such-like foolery, and all the time I played I was laughing up my sleeve." When I heard this, I was scarcely able to contain myself and felt that I should love to say to him: "Sir, I well believe that you laughed, but surely not as heartily as I should have done, had I been listening to you"' (letter of 13 Nov. 1777). Mozart and Beecke met once more, in Frankfurt or Mainz in October 1790, where they performed together in public.

CLIFF EISEN

Ernst Fritz Schmid, 'Ignaz von Beecke', in *Lebensbilder aus dem bayerischen Schwaben*, vol. I, ed. G. F. von Pölnitz (Munich, 1952), 343–64

Beethoven, Ludwig van (b. Bonn, ?16 Dec. 1770; d. Vienna, 26 Mar. 1827). German composer. Beethoven, who admired Mozart profoundly, was fully conscious of the composer's nascent canonic status in the musical world: recognizing the importance of studying the music of his predecessor, Beethoven repeatedly asked publishers to send him copies of Mozart's vocal and instrumental works. Mozart was, in Beethoven's words, one of music's 'great men'.

In all likelihood Beethoven and Mozart met once – in VIENNA in April 1787 – with the sixteen-year-old from Bonn performing for the established master. But Beethoven's trip to Vienna in 1787, cut short by the death of his mother, is poorly documented and details of the meeting are non-existent. Further, it is not known whether Beethoven heard Mozart perform; two of his closest associates, Ferdinand Ries and Carl Czerny, disagree on this point. In any case, Mozart's supposed statement after hearing Beethoven play that he was 'the man to watch' and 'someday . . . will give the world something to talk about' was almost certainly fabricated for publicity purposes by early nineteenth-century promoters of Beethoven's music.

From an early age Beethoven's prodigious talent was compared to that of Mozart, as if the youngster was groomed from the outset to succeed his illustrious predecessor. Beethoven's teacher, Christian Gottlieb Neefe, stated in 1783 that 'He would surely become a second Wolfgang Amadeus Mozart were he to continue as he has begun'. Similarly, the Bonn intellectual Johann Heinrich Crevelt, writing in an album presented to Beethoven prior to his move to Vienna in November 1792, explained that 'Mozart's genius hovers over you and, smiling at you, lends its approbation'. Most famously, Count Waldstein, aware that Beethoven would study with HAYDN, wrote in the same album:

> Dear Beethoven. You are going to Vienna in fulfilment of your long-frustrated wishes. The Genius of Mozart is still mourning and weeping the death of her pupil. She found a refuge but no occupation with the inexhaustible Haydn; through him she wishes to form a union with another. With the help of assiduous labor you shall receive the spirit of Mozart from Haydn's hands. Your true friend, Waldstein.

Thus, expectation was high that the young Beethoven would match Mozart's remarkable artistic success in the cosmopolitan musical centre of Vienna.

There is no doubt that Mozart's music exerted a particularly strong influence on Beethoven in his early Viennese and his pre-Viennese years. As many critics have noted, however, the issue of influence is complicated in Beethoven's case by the fact that it needs to account for conventional expressive and stylistic techniques and practices from the Classical period as well as Beethoven's motivations towards the purportedly influential works in question. In the Symphony No. 1 in C, Op. 21, for example, it is likely that he chose models such as the first movement of the 'Jupiter' symphony in C, K551 and Haydn's Symphony No. 97 in C with, in Elaine Sisman's words, 'the purpose of homage, of placing himself within a tradition, laced with one-upmanship, and casting the result in the most brilliantly conventional and instantly recognizable of eighteenth-century symphonic modes: the "C major symphony" tradition with its trumpets and drums and "ceremonial flourishes"'. Equally, Beethoven will presumably have hoped to learn from Mozart's compositional expertise by basing the voice-leading and harmonic structure of the first movement's development section on the corresponding section of the 'Jupiter' symphony.

When Beethoven modelled individual movements or entire compositions on those of Mozart, he never did so slavishly, even in early works such as the C major and E flat major piano quartets, WoO 36 (1785), based on Mozart's violin sonatas K296 and K379 respectively. Moreover, in his variations for violin and piano on Figaro's aria 'Se vuol ballare', WoO 40 (1792), and Variations for Two Oboes and Cor anglais on Don Giovanni and Zerlina's duet 'La ci darem la mano', WoO 28 (1795), Beethoven exploits the popularity of these numbers as much as revealing his stylistic debt to their composer. In any case, by the late 1790s we are certainly witnessing 'deliberate "appropriation" by a truly major artist' as opposed to 'imitation by a gifted beginner' as Lewis Lockwood puts it. For example, the reappearance of the slow introduction to the first movement of the Piano Sonata in C Minor, 'Pathétique', Op. 13 (1799) at the end of the movement is indebted to the corresponding procedure in Mozart's String Quintet in D Major, K593 (1790), but is also part of a uniquely Beethovenian process in that the material reappears at the beginning of the development section as well. Similarly, the String Quartet in A Major, Op. 18 No. 5 (1800), although inspired by Mozart's String Quartet in A, K464 (1785), reinterprets and reshapes musical procedures from Mozart's composition as much as it uses them as a straightforward model.

Even though Mozart's impact on Beethoven was strongest in his early-period works, Beethoven continued to work with the music of his predecessor in his middle and late periods. He wrote stylistically bold cadenzas for the first and last movements of Mozart's Piano Concerto in D minor, K466 (probably in 1809), was inspired by the Piano Concerto in G major, K453, when composing his own Piano Concerto No. 4 in G, Op. 58 (1805–7), and analysed the Kyrie fugue from the Requiem, K626, while sketching parts of the *Missa solemnis*, Op. 123, in 1819–20. Shortly before his death, Beethoven clarified in categorical fashion that his admiration for Mozart was unwavering: 'I have always counted myself amongst the greatest admirers of Mozart and shall remain so until my last breath', he wrote in a letter of 6 February 1826.

After attending a 1799 performance of Mozart's Piano Concerto in C minor, K491, with the pianist Johann Baptist Cramer Jr, Beethoven allegedly proclaimed: 'Cramer, Cramer! We shall never be able to do anything like that!' It is true that K491 had a considerable impact on Beethoven, not least in his Piano Concerto No. 3 in C minor, Op. 37 (published 1804); it is equally true, however, that in many respects Beethoven fashioned compositional and performance styles quite unlike those of Mozart. The cadenza to the first movement of K466 in which, as Richard Kramer says, the 'tunes are Mozart's, but the touch, the rhetoric, is emphatically Beethoven's' is a case in point. Equally, Beethoven cultivated a style of piano performance very different from Mozart's. Antoine Reicha probably exaggerated about the number of strings that Beethoven broke in a performance of a Mozart concerto for which Reicha acted as page turner, but his account of the roughness and harshness of Beethoven's playing is consistent with early nineteenth-century criticism and identifies a style that is the complete antithesis of Mozart's delicacy: 'I was mostly occupied in wrenching out the strings of the piano, which snapped, while the hammers stuck among the broken strings. Beethoven insisted upon finishing the concerto, so back and forth I leaped, jerking out a string, disentangling a hammer, turning a page.'

Even though he forged a unique stylistic path that had a profound impact on the subsequent course of western music, Beethoven always remained aware of Mozart's place in the shaping and reshaping of his compositional style. Neither blindly in awe of Mozart nor dismissive of Mozart's compositional prowess at any stage of his creative development, Beethoven knew that had to get to grips with and continue to re-evaluate this element of his compositional inheritance. In so doing his own extraordinary position in music history would begin to take shape. SIMON P. KEEFE

E. Anderson, ed., *The Letters of Beethoven* (London, 1961)

T. DeNora, *Beethoven and the Construction of Genius: Musical Politics in Vienna, 1792–1803* (Berkeley, 1995)

R. Kramer, 'Cadenza Contra Text: Mozart in Beethoven's Hands', *19th Century Music* 15 (1991), 116–31

L. Lockwood, 'Beethoven Before 1800: The Mozart Legacy', *Beethoven Forum* 3 (London, 1994), 39–52

E. Sisman, '"The Spirit of Mozart from Haydn's Hands": Beethoven's Musical Inheritance', in *The Cambridge Companion to Beethoven*, ed. G. Stanley (Cambridge, 2000), 45–63

Benucci, Francesco (b. c.1745; d. Florence, 5 Apr. 1824). Italian singer. Benucci had enjoyed a successful career in Italy before joining the Italian opera company in VIENNA in 1783; he made his debut there as Blasio in SALIERI's *La scuola de' gelosi*. His other roles included Titta in SARTI's *Fra i due litiganti il terzo gode*, Taddeo in PAISIELLO's *Il re Teodoro in Venezia*, Trofino in Salieri's *La grotta di Trofino*, Tita in MARTÍN Y SOLER's *Una cosa rara*, and the title role in Salieri's *Axur, re d'Ormus*. An outstanding singer and actor, Benucci was described by Mozart as 'particularly good' (letter of 7 May 1783); he sang Figaro at the premiere of LE NOZZE DI FIGARO (1786), Leporello in the first Vienna performance of DON GIOVANNI (1788), when Mozart composed an extra duet for him ('Per queste tue manine', with Zerlina), and Guglielmo in the premiere of COSÌ FAN TUTTE (1790). In his memoirs, MICHAEL KELLY wrote that during rehearsals for *Le nozze di Figaro*, Mozart '*sotto voce*, was repeating, Bravo! Bravo! Bennuci' and that the passage 'Cherubino, alla victoria, alla gloria militar' was 'electricity itself'. In 1789 Benucci sang with Nancy STORACE at the King's Theatre, LONDON, in GAZZANIGA's *La vendemmia*, interpolating in the performance the duet of Almaviva and Susanna, 'Crudel! perchè finora farmi languir così' from *Le nozze di Figaro*. Benucci last performed in 1795 at La Scala, MILAN, in operas by Sarti ad Angelo Tarchi. CLIFF EISEN

D. Heartz, 'When Mozart Revises: The Case of Guglielmo in *Così fan tutte*', in *Wolfgang Amadè Mozart: Essays on his Life and his Music*, ed. S. Sadie (Oxford, 1996), 355–61

D. Link, *The National Court Theatre in Mozart's Vienna: Sources and Documents 1783–1792* (Oxford, 1998)

Arias for Francesco Benucci, Mozart's First Figaro and Guglielmo (Recent Researches in the Music of the Classical Era, 72, Middleton, WI, 2004)

J. Rushton, 'Buffo Roles in Mozart's Vienna: Tessitura and Tonality as Signs of Characterization', in *Opera buffa in Mozart's Vienna*, ed. M. Hunter and J. Webster (Cambridge, 1997), 406–25

Berchtold von Sonnenburg, Johann Baptist Franz (b. Salzburg, 22 Oct. 1736; d. St Gilgen, 26 Feb. 1801 during the French occupation). Third of eight children of Franz Anton Virgil Berchtold von Sonnenburg and Maria Anna Elisabeth Gschwendtner von Freyenegg; husband of NANNERL MOZART. Franz Anton Virgil was *Pfleger* (administrator) of Hüttenstein and St Gilgen. Johann Baptist studied philosophy and law at SALZBURG University, and returned to St Gilgen as his father's assistant. He became *Pfleger* when his father died on 7 November 1769. On 8 July 1792 he was ennobled. Johann Baptist was married three times: to Maria Margarethe Polis von Moulin (d. 10 Nov. 1779), with whom he had four children; to Jeanette Maria Mayrhofer von Grünbichl (d. 15 Apr. 1783), with whom he had a son; and to Nannerl Mozart on 23 August 1784, with whom he had three children. RUTH HALLIWELL

R. Halliwell, *The Mozart Family: Four Lives in a Social Context* (Oxford, 1998)

Bertati, Giovanni (b. Martellago, 10 July 1735; d. Venice, c.1815). Italian librettist. The author of mostly comic texts, Bertati was closely associated with Baldassare Galuppi, who took him to VIENNA in 1770. Bertati wrote more than seventy librettos, mostly concerning domestic intrigue, chiefly for the Teatro S. Moisè in Venice where he was the principal comic librettist from 1771 to 1791; his texts rely heavily on disguises, mistaken identities, class and generational conflicts, and other devices of the Italian commedia dell'arte. In 1791 he succeeded LORENZO DA PONTE as chief poet to the imperial theatre; his *Il matrimonio segreto*, with music by Cimarosa, was an outstanding success. He returned to Venice in 1794 and from then on mostly gave up writing librettos and worked as a civil servant in Venice. Bertati's one-act libretto *Don Giovanni, o sia Il convitato di pietra*, set by GAZZANIGA in 1787, was the model for Da Ponte's DON GIOVANNI for Mozart; Da Ponte took over the outlines of Bertati's work, adding to it the Act 1 finale and most of the second act. Other Bertati texts set by Mozart include the quartet 'Dite almeno in che mancai' (K479) and the terzetto 'Mandina amabile' (K480), both composed for a production of BIANCHI's *La villanella rapita* at the Burgtheater on 25 November 1785. CLIFF EISEN

D. Heartz, *Haydn, Mozart, and the Viennese School, 1740–1780* (New York, 1995)
S. Kunze, *Don Giovanni vor Mozart: die Tradition der Don-Giovanni-Opern im italienischen Buffa-Theater des 18. Jahrhunderts* (Munich, 1972)

Betulia liberata, La. Mozart's oratorio K118 (1771). See ORATORIOS

Bianchi, (Giuseppe) Francesco (b. Cremona, c.1752; d. Hammersmith, London, 27 Nov. 1810). Italian composer. Bianchi's first operatic success was *Giulio Sabino* (Cremona, 1772); thereafter he worked at PARIS as a harpsichordist and composer of comic operas for the Théâtre-Italien. He served as deputy maestro at the Metropolitana, MILAN, from 1782 to 1793, and as second organist at San Marco, Venice, from 1785. Bianchi worked with the progressive librettists DE GAMERRA and Sertor from the late 1770s, including action-ensemble finales, programmatic storms and ballets, large ensembles and other innovative elements in his works. Although chiefly known as a composer of serious opera, he wrote numerous comic ones as well, including *La villanella rapita* which was performed in VIENNA in 1785 with Mozart's quartet 'Dite almeno in che mancai' (K479) and the terzetto 'Mandina amabile' (K480). CLIFF EISEN

M. G. Accorsi, 'Teoria e practica della variatio nel dramma giocoso: a proposito della "Villanella rapita" di Giovanni Bertati', in *I vicini di Mozart* (Venice, 1987), 139–63
M. McClymonds, 'The Venetian Role in the Transformation of Italian Opera Seria during the 1790s', in *I vicini di Mozart* (Venice, 1987), 221–40

Böhm, Johannes Heinrich (b. c.1740; buried Aachen 7 Aug. 1792). Perhaps the son of the puppeteer Johann Böhm from Lorraine, Böhm first came to notice in 1770, when he took over Kajetan Schaumberger's travelling troupe in Brünn (Brno). The company specialized in a repertory of Italian and French singspiels, ballets and German comedies and farces, though *Hamlet* and other Shakespeare plays were also given. He sang in, and adapted and translated, several operas. In early summer 1776, in collaboration with NOVERRE, he directed a season of fourteen singspiels at the Kärntnertortheatre, VIENNA, mainly works translated from the French. In summer 1778 he and his wife (and some of their children) were members of the Burgtheater company. They then played in SALZBURG (where Böhm became acquainted with the Mozarts; he remet Mozart at Frankfurt in September 1790), and in AUGSBURG. After 1788 the company played mainly in Koblenz and Cologne. Böhm revived Mozart's LA FINTA GIARDINIERA in German in 1779, and performed it frequently in southern Germany. He chose DIE ENTFÜHRUNG to open the new theatre at Koblenz in 1787, and used some of the THAMOS, KÖNIG IN ÄGYPTEN score for incidental music to Plümicke's play *Lanassa*; he also gave early performances of DON GIOVANNI and FIGARO in the Rhineland. In a letter of 24 April 1780 Mozart mentioned to his cousin that he was composing an 'aria for Böhm'. PETER BRANSCOMBE

H. G. Fellmann, *Die Böhmische Theatertruppe und ihre Zeit* (Leipzig, 1928)
E. Pies, *Prinzipale. Zur Genealogie des deutschsprachigen Berufstheaters vom 17. bis 19. Jahrhundert* (Ratingen, 1973), 57–8

Bondini, Caterina (fl. 1780s). Soprano; wife of PASQUALE BONDINI. Caterina Bondini, who had sung Susanna in the December 1786 PRAGUE production of LE NOZZE DI FIGARO, created the role of Zerlina in DON GIOVANNI; according to the *Prager Oberpostamtszeitung* for 12 December 1786, she particularly distinguished herself in the former, which a few days later, on 14 December, was given for her benefit. NISSEN recounts that Mozart, during rehearsals for DON GIOVANNI, taught Bondini how to scream convincingly by suddenly pinching her. Possibly she was the sister of TERESA SAPORITI, the first Donna Anna. CLIFF EISEN

Zdenka Pilková, 'Prazstí mozartovstí pevci v drazdanskych pramenech' [Mozart's Prague singers in sources from Dresden], *Hudební veda* 28/4 (1991), 299–304

Bondini, Pasquale (b. ?Bonn, ?1737; d. Bruneck, 30/1 Oct. 1789). Italian singer and impresario, husband of CATERINA BONDINI. Bondini was chiefly active in PRAGUE and Dresden during the 1760s and 1770s; in 1784 he leased the Prague National Theatre built by Count Franz Anton Nostitz-Rieneck. The production that he mounted there in late 1786 of LE NOZZE DI FIGARO was so successful that Mozart was invited to Prague in January 1787; while there he was commissioned by Bondini to write a new opera, DON GIOVANNI, which was first given on 29 October 1787. Bondini proselytized for Mozart elsewhere too: he mounted performances of DIE ENTFÜHRUNG AUS DEM SERAIL in Leipzig in September 1783 and at Dresden in 1785. CLIFF EISEN

R. Prochazka, *Mozart in Prag* (Prague, 1892; 4th edn, 1938, ed. Paul Nettl as *Mozart in Böhmen*)
A. Campana, 'La compagnia di Pasquale Bondini: Praga 1787' (Ph.D. diss., University of Rome, 1987–8)

Bonno, Giuseppe (b. Vienna, 29 Jan. 1711; d. Vienna, 15 Apr. 1788). Viennese composer, mostly of opera and sacred music, and music director; Hofkapellmeister 1744–88 and president of the Tonkünstler-Sozietät. Trained in Italy, Bonno brought to his music, especially his settings of METASTASIO's librettos and oratorio texts, all the mellifluousness of the Neapolitan school.

When the Mozarts visited VIENNA in 1768, Bonno witnessed a demonstration of young Wolfgang's compositional facility at his house; Leopold announced that the twelve-year-old would set to music on the spot any aria text that Bonno and his guests might choose from the complete works of Metastasio. The Mozarts renewed their acquaintance with Bonno in 1773 on a later visit to Vienna; and in 1781, when Mozart came to Vienna in the retinue of Archbishop Colloredo, he wrote to his father that one of his symphonies had recently been performed at Bonno's house. JOHN A. RICE

D. Heartz, *Haydn, Mozart, and the Viennese School 1740–1780* (New York, 1995)

Born, Ignaz von (b. Carlsburg or Kapnik, Transylvania, 26 Dec. 1742; d. Vienna, 24 July 1791), mineralogist and Freemason, son of Ludwig Born, an army officer, and his wife Maria Katharina. He was educated by the Jesuits in VIENNA and became a novice in the Order in 1760, though he left after a few months and associated with a group of young intellectuals (whose somewhat older leader was JOSEPH VON SONNENFELS) before commencing legal studies at Prague University. However, he was more drawn to geology and was soon devoting himself exclusively to the sciences; in 1767 he completed mineralogical and mining studies at the Mountain Academy at Schemnitz. By then he had married into the wealthy Montag family of PRAGUE. He returned to Vienna in 1777 to classify the royal and imperial collection of minerals. In 1781 he was appointed court councillor and in 1785 was ennobled in recognition of his new method for smelting metals; it was in celebration of this honour that Mozart wrote the cantata *Die Maurerfreude* (Masonic Joy, K471).

Born had swiftly risen to prominence in Viennese FREEMASONRY, becoming Master of the newly founded lodge 'Zur wahren Eintracht' (True Concord) in 1782. It attracted men of distinction from various walks of life, and published short-lived but important journals: *Physikalische Arbeiten der einträchtigen Freunde in Wien* (Works in Physics of the Friends of Concord in Vienna) and – of particular significance in a Mozartian context – *Journal für Freymaurer* (Journal for Freemasons). Another of Born's writings is the anonymous, strongly anticlerical satire *Monachologia*, first published in Latin (1783), then in German, and translated into various foreign languages.

Following the decree of JOSEPH II in December 1785 limiting the number and membership of the Viennese lodges, Born became Master of the newly formed

'Zur Wahrheit' (Truth), but soon resigned from Freemasonry. For this reason it must be doubted whether, despite his lengthy contribution to the *Journal* 'On the Mysteries of the Egyptians', he should be seen as the model for Sarastro in DIE ZAUBERFLÖTE. He died after a lengthy and painful illness.

PETER BRANSCOMBE

D. Lindner, *Ignaz von Born. Meister der Wahren Eintracht. Wiener Freimaurerei im 18. Jh.* (Vienna, 1986)
P. Branscombe, *W. A. Mozart. Die Zauberflöte* (Cambridge, 1991)

Bossler, Heinrich Philipp Carl (b. Darmstadt, 22 June 1744; d. Gohlis, near Leipzig, 9 Dec. 1812). German music printer and publisher. Bossler founded his publishing firm in Speyer in 1781, opening a branch in Darmstadt in 1785. Later, in 1799, he settled in the Leipzig area. Bossler's publications chiefly included works by south German composers as well as the periodical *Musicalische Realzeitung* (1788–90). Although there is no evidence that Mozart and Bossler were acquainted during the 1780s, he nevertheless published the first edition of the Flute Quartet, K285b, in 1788 as well as early editions of the sonata for keyboard and violin K481 (1788) and selections from DIE ENTFÜHRUNG AUS DEM SERAIL (1790). It is likely, however, that they met in VIENNA in 1790 when Bossler accompanied the harmonica virtuosa MARIANNE KIRCHGÄSSNER to Vienna; it was for KIRCHGÄSSNER that Mozart composed the Adagio and Rondo, K617, and possibly the Adagio, K365. Bossler's *Musikalische Korrespondenz der teutschen Filarmonischen Gesellschaft*, the successor to the *Musicalische Realzeitung*, published the first lengthy obituary of the composer, on 4 January 1792.

CLIFF EISEN

A. Rosenthal, 'Der früheste längere Nachruf auf Mozart', in *Collectanea Mozartiana*, ed. C. Roleff (Tutzing, 1988), 134–6
H. Schneider, *Der Musikverleger Heinrich Philipp Bossler (1744–1812)* (Tutzing, 1985)

Bretzner, Christoph Friedrich (b. Leipzig, 10 Dec. 1748; d. Leipzig, 31 Aug. 1807). German playwright and librettist. Bretzner, a businessman in Leipzig, began writing plays in 1771 and a set of four comic opera texts printed in 1779 quickly established him as a fashionable librettist in Germany. More colourful than the librettos of C. F. Weisse, they were soon taken up not only by composers in north Germany but in VIENNA as well. Bretzner is best remembered as the author of *Belmont und Constanze*, written for the Berlin composer Johann André in 1780 and adapted by Stephanie the younger for Mozart as DIE ENTFÜHRUNG AUS DEM SERAIL. The success of Mozart's opera notwithstanding, the text of *Belmont und Constanze* was considered substandard; J. F. Schink's *Dramaturgische Fragmente* of 1782 described it as 'one of the most inept of his lyric pieces'. Bretzner's disavowal of Mozart's 1782 setting is a fabrication, although in 1783 Bretzner did publicly ridicule Stephanie's textual additions. In addition to writing original opera texts and one melodrama, Bretzner also translated several Italian texts for the German stage, including Mozart's COSÌ FAN TUTTE (as *Weibertreu, oder Die Mädchen sind von Flandern*, 1794) and SALIERI's *La scuola de' gelosi* (*Die Schule der Eifersüchtigen*, 1794).

CLIFF EISEN

Bullinger, Franz Joseph Johann Nepomuk (b. Unterkochen, Württemberg, 29 Jan. 1744; d. Diepoldshofen, Württemberg, 9 Mar. 1810). Taught for the Jesuits until the dissolution of the order in 1773. Arriving in SALZBURG between 1774 and 1776 to tutor Count Leopold Ferdinand von Arco (see ARCO FAMILY), he was soon an intimate friend of the Mozarts. He played the viola. When Mozart resigned court service in 1777 and travelled to PARIS with his mother, Bullinger lent LEOPOLD MOZART a substantial sum of money and was the only person other than NANNERL MOZART to whom Leopold unburdened his worries. Mozart too asked Bullinger for help when he had to tell Leopold of MARIA ANNA MOZART's death in Paris. In his letter of 3 July 1778, Mozart asked Bullinger to prepare Leopold for the possibility that his wife was dead, but in fact Bullinger gently broke the news himself. Writing again to Bullinger on 7 August 1778, Mozart sarcastically listed his grievances with Salzburg: the musicians were not respected; the musical personnel was wholly inadequate for the performance of first-rate music; and there was no opera or theatre to be seen in the town. Bullinger left Salzburg around 1784 and was parish priest in Diepoldshofen when he died. RUTH HALLIWELL

E. F. Schmid, 'Der Mozartfreund Joseph Bullinger', *Mozart Jahrbuch* 1952, 17–23

Burney, Charles (b. Shrewsbury, 7 Apr. 1726; d. London, 12 Apr. 1814). English composer and music historian. Burney's lasting contributions to musical scholarship are his two books, *The Present State of Music in France and Italy* (LONDON, 1771) and *The Present State of Music in Germany, the Netherlands, and United Provinces* (London, 1773). The first describes his meeting with Mozart at the church of S. Giovanni in Monte, Bologna, on 30 August 1770: 'I met with M. [LEOPOLD] MOZART and his son, the little German, whose premature and almost supernatural talents so much astonished us in London a few years ago'; and the second reports a negative opinion expressed to him by Louis de Visme, the British minister in MUNICH, who visited the Mozarts in SALZBURG: 'If I may judge of the music which I heard of his composition in the orchestra, he is one further instance of early fruit being more extraordinary than excellent.' Although Burney was familiar with Mozart's music, in his article for *Rees Encyclopedia* (London, 1819) he under-represented its dissemination and importance in London at the end of the eighteenth century. Nevertheless, the impression of Mozart's early visit to London remained vivid in his memory; when Mozart's pupil HUMMEL visited London in 1790, Burney wrote: 'It is odd that 30 years after his Master Mozart had been recommended to me, and played on my knee, on subjects I gave him, that this little Man should also claim and merit my kindness.' CLIFF EISEN

K. S. Grant, *Dr. Burney as Critic and Historian of Music* (Ann Arbor, 1983)
S. Klima, G. Brown and K. S. Grant, eds., *Memoirs of Charles Burney*, vol. I: 1726–1769 (Lincoln, NE, 1988)
A. Ribeiro, ed., *The Letters of Dr. Charles Burney*, vol. I: 1751–1784 (Oxford, 1991)
W. Weber, 'The Intellectual Origins of Musical Canon in Eighteenth-Century England', *Journal of the American Musicological Society* 47 (1994), 513–16

Bussani, Dorothea (b. Vienna, 1763; d. after 1810). Austrian mezzo-soprano who played an important role in the Viennese opera buffa troupe of the 1780s and early 1790s, creating the roles of Cherubino in LE NOZZE DI FIGARO and Despina in COSÌ FAN TUTTE. Her maiden name, Sardi, suggests the possibility that she was related to the Viennese keyboard player and composer Joseph

Sardi. She married the comic bass FRANCESCO BUSSANI in 1786. The *Grundsätze zur Theaterkritik*, an essay on Viennese theatre published in 1790, praised Bussani's 'beautiful and graceful chest voice'; three years later, after she won much applause for her portrayal of Fidalma in Domenico Cimarosa's *Il matrimonio segreto*, a reporter for the *Berlinische musikalische Zeitung* wrote: 'I found her lovely low voice especially striking . . . Her attractive figure and her unforced, natural acting prove very useful to her on the stage.' Bruce Alan Brown notes that, 'Paradoxically, the only unattached characters in *Così* were played by the married couple of Dorothea and Francesco Bussani [as Alfonso]. Da Ponte, no friend to either of them, turned the twenty-year difference between their ages into a joke, when Despina tells Alfonso that "an old man like you cannot do anything to a girl".' JOHN A. RICE

B. A. Brown, *W. A Mozart. Così fan tutte* (Cambridge, 1995)

Bussani, Francesco (b. Rome, c.1740; d. after 1796). Comic singer of remarkable versatility and longevity for whom Mozart wrote the role of Don Alfonso in COSÌ FAN TUTTE. He began his career in Rome in the early 1760s, one of several buffi of the period who sang both bass and tenor (or high baritone) roles. Already a veteran of the comic stage when he came to VIENNA in 1783, he frequently portrayed fathers and other old men ('Ho i crini già grigi' are Alfonso's first words). Bussani also played an administrative role within the troupe, a position from which he was removed by EMPEROR LEOPOLD II as part of this theatrical reorganization of 1791. On his retirement from the stage he returned to his native city, Rome, where he served, from 1796, as impresario of the Teatro Alibert. JOHN A. RICE

C

Calvesi, Teresa (fl. 1776–1801). Italian soprano. Her first known appearance was in Genoa in 1776. At Easter 1785 she and her husband Vincenzo were engaged for the court theatre in VIENNA. Although ZINZENDORF judged her as 'not bad' at her debut on 18 April 1785, her career in Vienna did not blossom. In 1788 she accompanied her husband to Naples on a year's leave of absence, but she did not sing there. She did not return with him to Vienna but pursued her own, apparently successful, career in Palermo, Vicenza, London and elsewhere in Italy until at least 1801. DOROTHEA LINK

Calzabigi, Ranieri (de') (b. Livorno, 23 Dec. 1714, d. Naples, ?12 or 13 July 1795), Italian librettist. The Mozart family were in VIENNA for performances of his and GLUCK's 'reform' operas *Orfeo ed Euridice* (1762) and *Alceste* (father and son only, 1767–8), but seem not to have encountered Calzabigi directly. The libretto of Mozart's LA FINTA GIARDINIERA, written for MUNICH, was long thought to be by Calzabigi, with revisions by Marco COLTELLINI, but this attribution is mistaken, based on confusion with concurrent performances in Munich of Antonio Tozzi's resetting of *Orfeo* (as revised by Coltellini). Neither the Munich libretto of *La finta giardiniera*, nor the original one for Rome (1774, set by Pasquale Anfossi) is signed, but Giuseppe Petrosellini has been suggested as the actual librettist based on mention (by the 'Interessati') in the Rome libretto of another opera by that author. However, this attribution remains conjectural.

BRUCE ALAN BROWN

R. Calzabigi, *Scritti teatrali e letterari*, ed. A. L. Bellina (Rome, 1994)
F. Marri, ed., *La figura e l'opera di Ranieri de' Calzabigi* (Florence, 1989)

Cannabich family. German musicians. (Johann) Christian (Innocenz Bonaventura) Cannabich (baptized Mannheim, 28 Dec. 1731; d. Frankfurt, 20 Jan. 1798) was a violinist, conductor and composer; he was a pupil of Johann Stamitz. Cannabich was promoted to Konzertmeister of the MANNHEIM orchestra by 1758 and in 1774 was made director of instrumental music. He followed the Mannheim court to MUNICH in 1778 when Karl Theodor became Elector of Bavaria and in 1788, following the death of Carl Toeschi, he became sole director of the Munich court orchestra.

Mozart first met Cannabich in 1763 at Schwetzingen and came to know him well during his visit to Mannheim in 1777–8, when he was a frequent guest in the Cannabich household. He had a high regard for Cannabich's conducting, describing him as 'the best conductor I have ever seen' (letter of 9 July 1778). But he was less impressed with Cannabich's compositions; on 20 November 1777 he wrote to his father: 'Cannabich is now a much better composer than he was when we knew him in PARIS. But what Mamma and I noticed at once about the symphonies here is that they all begin in the same manner, always with an introduction in slow time and in unison.' Apparently Cannabich took an active part in the preparations for IDOMENEO and may have conducted the premiere. It was about this time that Mozart wrote to his father: 'I cannot describe to you what a good friend Cannabich is to me' (24 Nov. 1780).

Cannabich's daughter Rosina ('Rosa') Theresia Petronella (baptized Mannheim, 18 Mar. 1764; d. ?Breslau, after 1805) was for a while Mozart's pupil; it was for her that he wrote the piano sonata K309, the Andante of which Mozart intended as her musical portrait. In a letter of 6 December 1777 he described Rosa as 'serious-minded, does not say much, but when she speaks, she does so in a charming and friendly manner'. She played the piano concerto K238 at a concert at the Cannabichs' on 12 February 1778 and at a later concert, on 12 March, she took part in the Concerto for Three Pianos, K242.

CLIFF EISEN

R. Münster, 'Mozart bearbeitet Cannabich', in *Festchrift Walter Senn*, ed. E. Egg and E. Fässler (Munich, 1975), 142–57

D. Patier, 'Vers une meilleure compréhension de l'expression de Léopold Mozart: le "vermanierierte Mannheimer Goût" ', in *Off-Mozart: Musical Culture and the "Kleinmeister" of Central Europe 1750–1820*, ed. V. Katalinic (Zagreb, 1995), 153–66

E. K. Wolf, 'Mannheimer Symphonik um 1777/1778 und ihr Einfluss auf Mozarts symphonischen Stil', in *Mozart und Mannheim Kongressbericht Mannheim 1991*, ed. L. Finscher, B. Pelker and J. Reutter (Frankfurt, 1994), 309–30

canons. By the mid-eighteenth century, *stile osservato* counterpoint, of which canon was an integral part, had become a largely academic discipline, as exemplified by JOHANN JOSEPH FUX's treatise of 1725, *Gradus ad Parnassum*. Nevertheless, canonic writing persisted in Mozart's day, both as a pedagogical discipline and in the form of vocal canons intended for light entertainment at social gatherings. Mozart's initial impetus for composing canons appears to have been the contrapuntal studies he undertook with Padre MARTINI in Bologna during his first visit to Italy (1769–71). Mozart also wrote out solutions to several 'puzzle canons' from Padre Martini's *Storia della musica* (Bologna, 3 vols., 1757–70) (K73x) and composed four similar examples himself (K89aII), closely modelled on those of Martini.

A notebook belonging to THOMAS ATTWOOD, who studied with Mozart in 1785–7, includes several canonic studies and copies of some canons by Mozart. In addition to a group of two-voice canons (K508a, 3 June–August 1786) at various intervals, from a unison to a seventh, there are a number of three- and four-voice examples (such as K507) and a double canon for four voices (K228) which Mozart entered in the album of his friend Josef Franz von JACQUIN on 24 April 1787.

The only canons to be found in Mozart's thematic catalogue (*Verzeichnüss*), which he began in February 1784, are K553–62, a group of ten with diverse texts, entered on 2 September 1788. Two have sacred texts: 'Alleluia, amen' (K553) and 'Ave Maria' (K554). The former opens with a melody that closely resembles the plainchant Alleluia for Easter Saturday. K556 ('Grechtelt's enk, wir gehn im Prater') and K558 ('Gehn wir im Prater, gehn wir in d'Hetz'), both in Viennese dialect, make reference to the Prater, a public park and fairground in Vienna. Mozart probably wrote the texts for these two canons and also for those of K559 and K560a, which satirize the accent of the Bavarian tenor Johann Nepomuk Peyerl. The nonsensical Latin of 'Difficile lectu mihi mars et jonicu' when sung with Peyerl's pronunciation presumably resembled 'O leck mich doch geschwind im Arsch', a phrase that occurs in K560a. Mozart clearly relished the incongruity resulting from ribald verse set as a canon, traditionally regarded as the most learned of all compositional techniques. 'Leck mich in Arsch', K231, if it is by Mozart, provides a good example of this juxtaposition, with successive lines of the round employing different species of strict counterpoint. In early editions, such as those published by Breitkopf & Härtel, the coarse or obscene texts of several rounds were supplanted by innocuous verses. As a result, only the incipits of the original texts are known in many cases. The alternately comic and pedantic associations of canonic procedures did not preclude their achieving genuinely expressive ends, as Mozart demonstrated in his setting of 'Caro bell'idol mio' (K562), a text taken from a canon by Antonio Caldara, as well as in the Act 2 finale of *Così fan tutte*. MICHAEL QUINN

M. Ochs, '"L.m.i.a": Mozart's Suppressed Canon Texts', *Mozart-Jahrbuch*, 1991), 254–61

cantata. In January 1785 Mozart received a commission from the Viennese Tonkünstler-Sozietät (a benevolent organization dedicated to helping musicians) to write a new work for two charity concerts, to be held the following Lent. Having accepted this project, Mozart intended to compose a new cantata for the Sozietät, but, either because he thought the fee was too low, or because of time limitations and prior commitments (including several performances, an academy at the Burgtheater among them), he offered instead to perform a psalm setting that had not yet been heard in VIENNA. This offer, recorded in the Sozietät's archives, was evidently not accepted, and Mozart, by February, had decided to rework his unfinished Mass in C minor, K427, as a cantata. He adapted eight movements from the Kyrie and Gloria to an Italian libretto and added two new arias. The authorship of the libretto, based on paraphrases from the Book of Psalms, is not known, but it has been attributed to LORENZO DA PONTE, whom Mozart had got to know two years earlier, and who later collaborated with him on LE NOZZE DI FIGARO, DON GIOVANNI and COSÌ FAN TUTTE. Vincent and Mary NOVELLO, on their visit to Vienna in 1829 (K469) were told by Abbé STADLER that Da Ponte was in fact the author.

The title by which this cantata is commonly known, *Davidde penitente* (along with the variant spelling *Davide*), was not assigned to it by the composer. Mozart entered incipits of the two newly composed arias into his thematic catalogue (*Verzeichnüss*) with the brief heading 'Zur Societäts Musique'. The concert notice announced it as 'a completely new cantata, adapted to this occasion by Sig Amadeo Mozart', thereby avoiding the potentially awkward issue of the work's originality. The theme of the cantata was a popular one. A letter of LEOPOLD MOZART, dated 29 December 1755, refers to an oratorio to be produced in SALZBURG on the 'penitent David', and in December 1785 the Tonkünstler-Sozietät produced *Davidde il penitente* set by Ferdinando Bertoni, in Vienna.

No autograph score of the cantata is extant, and it is likely that none was produced; the autograph of the C minor mass contains several annotations by Mozart that reflect its reworking as *Davidde penitente*. Autographs of the two new arias (Nos. 6 and 8) plus the short cadenza for the soloists interpolated towards the end of the final chorus (No. 10, bars 186–232) are extant in separate manuscripts. Mozart entered these two arias into his thematic catalogue on 6 and 11 March 1785 respectively, suggesting that he was working to a tight deadline; the general rehearsal was 12 March, with the two concerts taking place on 13 and 15 March. On this occasion, Mozart probably used the orchestral material from the Salzburg performance of the C minor mass (26 Oct. 1783), with the final movement amended and parts for the two new arias newly copied.

Mozart's adaptation of his C minor mass for the purpose of fulfilling this commission not only allowed him to produce a suitable cantata in a relatively short period of time, but also gave him the opportunity to perform the music from one of his large-scale (but unfinished) choral works – one, moreover, that was unlikely to be heard in a liturgical context after the strictures imposed by JOSEPH II. As with his operatic arias, he composed the two new arias with the voices of his soloists in mind. For the tenor JOHANN VALENTIN ADAMBERGER, Mozart wrote 'A te, fra tanti affanni' (No. 6), while 'Fra l'oscure ombre funeste' (No. 8) was added for the distinguished soprano CATERINA CAVALIERI; both singers were already well known to the composer, having appeared in the first performances of DIE ENTFÜHRUNG AUS DEM SERAIL in 1782.

The premiere of *Davidde penitente*, conducted by Mozart, took place at the Nationaltheater in Vienna, as part of a programme that also included the first performance of JOSEPH HAYDN's Symphony in D minor (Hob. I/80). An audience of over 650 was present on 13 March, but the second concert attracted only a third as many.

Davidde penitente has often been a neglected work in Mozart's oeuvre, perhaps because critics are unwilling to acknowledge that exigencies of time required him, in this case, to reuse existing music intended for a different text. Despite this fact, the text setting is, on the whole, convincing, and the two newly composed arias merit further critical attention. MICHAEL QUINN

cassation. See SERENADE

Cavalieri, Caterina (Catharina Magdalena Josepha Cavalier) (b. Vienna, 18 Mar. 1755; d. Vienna, 30 June 1801). Soprano. A pupil of SALIERI, Cavalieri made her debut as Sandrina in Anfossi's *La finta giardinera* at the Kärntnertortheater in 1775; she later appeared in IGNAZ UMLAUF's *Die Bergknappen* at the German National Theatre and in Salieri's *La scuola de' gelosi* at the Burgtheater when Italian opera was re-established in 1783. Allegedly she was also Salieri's mistress. Highly praised for her beautiful voice, Mozart described her as having a 'supple throat' (letter of 26 Sept. 1781) and a singer of whom 'Germany could be proud' (21 May 1785). She created the roles of Konstanze in DIE ENTFÜHRUNG AUS DEM SERAIL and Mademoiselle Silberklang in DER SCHAUSPIELDIREKTOR; in 1788 she appeared as Donna Elvira in the first Viennese production of DON GIOVANNI and in 1789 as Countess Almaviva in the revival of LE NOZZE DI FIGARO. In addition, Mozart composed for her the soprano part in the cantata *Davidde penitente* and the role of Bettina in *Lo sposo deluso*. She retired from the stage in 1793. CLIFF EISEN

P. L. Gidwitz, ' "Ich bin die erste Sängerin": Vocal Profiles of Two Mozart Sopranos', *Early Music* 19 (1991), 565–74
D. Link, *The National Court Theatre in Mozart's Vienna: Sources and Documents 1783–1792* (Oxford, 1998)

Ceccarelli, Francesco (b. Foligno, c.1752; d. Dresden, 21 Sept. 1814). Castrato in SALZBURG service 1777–88 (initially paid 100 florins per month, ten times the amount paid to the female court singers). LEOPOLD MOZART's lukewarm opinion of Ceccarelli's soprano voice (letter of 27 Oct. 1777) later developed into admiration. Ceccarelli took beginning violin lessons from Leopold, joined the family's shooting circle (sometimes being depicted humorously on the target), and made music frequently with Leopold and Nannerl. These occasions are important as evidence for the Mozarts' domestic practice of playing vastly scaled-down versions of orchestral works (see Leopold's letter of 12 Apr. 1778).

In 1781, Mozart wrote the recitative and aria *A questo seno deh vieni – Or, che il cielo a me ti rende*, K374, for Ceccarelli to sing at a concert given on 8 April by their employer Archbishop COLLOREDO in VIENNA. They collaborated again when Ceccarelli sang in Mozart's concert in Frankfurt on 15 October 1790. RUTH HALLIWELL

H. Schuler, *Mozarts Salzburger Freunde und Bekannte* (Wilhelmshaven, 1995), 105–6

chamber music

A. String duos and trios
B. String quartets
C. String quintets
D. Piano trios
E. Piano quartets
F. Mixed ensembles

A. String duos and trios

Mozart wrote just six extant works for string duo or trio. The duos for violin and bass K46d in C and K46e in F, written in VIENNA (dated 1 Sept. 1768 on the autograph), consist of an Allegro and two minuets; and the trio for two violins and bass K266 in B flat, composed in SALZBURG (early 1777), comprises an Adagio and a minuet. Their more celebrated successors, the violin and viola duos, K423 in G and K424 in B flat (see also SONATAS), and the String Trio in E flat, K563, labelled 'Divertimento di sei Pezzi' in the *Verzeichnüss*, come from Mozart's final decade: K423 and K424 were probably composed in Salzburg during Mozart's and Constanze Mozart's three-month stay in the city in 1783, or at least written in Vienna and then taken to Salzburg, as Mozart subsequently asked LEOPOLD MOZART to send them on to Vienna (letters of 6 Dec. and 24 Dec. 1783); and K563, perhaps intended for Mozart's friend and fellow Mason MICHAEL PUCHBERG, was completed on 27 September 1788, just six weeks after the 'Jupiter' symphony, K551 (10 August).

K423, K424 and K563 are stylistically noteworthy in several important respects. In the duets, for example, Mozart introduces considerable textural variety in spite of being limited to two instruments, K423/i featuring protracted imitation and frequent participatory parity, melody and accompaniment writing, and double-stopping that creates the impression of an ensemble of more than two players (see the beginning of the development section). K424/i includes both an adagio slow introduction that opens with a note-for-note transposition (B flat–D–G–E natural–F) of the fugal theme from the G major string quartet, K387/iv, and an eighteen-bar coda. And K424/iv, like its close contemporary, the D minor string quartet, K421 (June 1783), consists of a theme and variations followed by a concluding allegro section. The six-movement K563, widely regarded as one of Mozart's greatest chamber works, is altogether more imposing than K423 and K424, with two minuet and trios and a long, rich central Andante movement. The opening of the first-movement development section is perhaps the most remarkable passage in the work, moving between B flat and C#^{7} in a mere five bars, only to return to B flat a few bars later. This procedure invokes comparably rapid and distant modulations in approximately contemporary late works such as the piano concertos K537/iii and K595/i (completed in 1791 but probably begun in 1788) and the G minor symphony K550/i. SIMON P. KEEFE

B. String quartets

In Mozart's day the string quartet – often thought to represent the epitome of Classical chamber music – was still an emerging genre. By the time Mozart wrote his first quartet, K80 in G, completed at Lodi on 15 March 1770, flourishing Italian and Austrian traditions of string chamber music with and without keyboard continuo had been established, and JOSEPH HAYDN had issued his Opp. 1, 2, 9 and 17, in so doing almost single-handedly developing the quartet into a reputable art-form. In AUSTRIA, chamber works for strings without continuo were composed by Franz Asplmayr (1728–86) among others; there was also a tradition of performing symphonies 'a quattro' – one player to each of the (usually four) principal polyphonic lines. But these various precursors to the string quartet were still relatively new and un-coordinated; there was, as yet, no long-established 'tradition' of Classical string quartets comparable to, say, the sonata or the symphony into which Mozart's fell, making his achievement in the field over less than twenty years all the more remarkable.

1. The early quartets
2. The 'Haydn' quartets: K387, 421, 428, 458, 464, 465
3. K499 and the 'Prussian' quartets

1. THE EARLY QUARTETS

The G major quartet, K80, is stylistically indebted to Sammartini, whom Mozart had met at Count FIRMIAN's the previous month. LEOPOLD MOZART reports this meeting with pride in a letter of 10 February 1770: 'It would take too long to describe in detail the evidence of his knowledge which Wolfgang has given in the presence of Maestro Sammartini and a number of the most brilliant people, and of how he has amazed them.' Unusually for such an Italianate piece, K80 has four movements, beginning with a binary-form Adagio that cries out at times for continuo filling, as does the ensuing Allegro (the tempo marking is in Leopold's hand, as is often the case in the early quartets). Inner-part textures such as that at bar 9 of the Allegro, and the fugato at bar 16 seem to call for greater weight than a string quartet could muster, and are strongly reminiscent of contemporary orchestral divertimenti (such as K136–8). In short, K80 is something of a hybrid, showing that as yet there remained a degree of uncertainty, or at least ambivalence, in Mozart's mind about the precise identity of the quartet genre.

The six quartets K155–60 were composed in MILAN in late 1772–early 1773. On 28 October 1772 Leopold casually remarked that Mozart was writing a quartet (possibly K155) 'to pass the time'; references to other quartets, possibly K157 or K158, appear in another letter a few months later (6 Feb. 1773). K155–60 are arranged in a deliberate key sequence of falling fifths: D, G, C, F, B flat, E flat. Each is in three movements, typical of contemporary Italian practice. Several (K156, 157, 158 and 159) have notably expressive minor-key middle movements, of which the most forceful is that of K159, featuring passages of strongly contrasting texture, register and mood more usual in an orchestral than a chamber piece, including furtive chromatic lines (*piano*) and wild syncopations (*forte*) in an idiom not far removed from the G minor symphony K183 (October 1773). Mozart's early quartets betray their Italian influence, particularly in their tendency towards simple textures in which the two outer parts, treble and bass, set out the melodic and harmonic framework, while the inner parts provide an often subsidiary 'filling'. Tonally too, the idiom is uncomplicated; the opening paragraph of K158 in F, for example, utilizes a simple unison statement of the opening triplet idea to implant the secondary key area, C, without ceremony. At times the marked polarity of treble and bass is reflected in the appearance of the extant autographs (formerly Preussischer Staatsbibliothek, Berlin, now at Tübingen) – in the opening Allegro of K155 in D, the alignment of the first-violin part against the supporting chords at the beginning of the first movement strongly suggests that Mozart conceived (or at least, wrote down) the melody of this passage first, before returning to add the accompaniment, once the essential strands, theme and bass, had been determined. Other 'fingerprints' of the Italianate idiom include: the repeated-note quaver bass-line (K80/i, K157/i, K160/i), establishing a generally slow and uniform rate of harmonic change, against which the primary melody stands out all the more clearly; modulation to the dominant (or 'secondary' dominant) by means of a prominent chromatic rising step in the bass just before the cadence (K80/i, bars 7–8, K155/i, bars 19–20, K157/i, bars 29–30), a procedure associated with the repeated-note quaver bass patterns; cantabile melodies played in thirds (K155/i, bars 64–7, K157/i, opening, K159/i, bars 4–6), and occasionally octaves (K155/iii, opening); an engaging rhythmic verve, with pronounced variety of articulation (K155/iii, opening, K157/i, bars 31–8, K160/i, bars 16–23 and 24–9); 'predictable' phrase extension by means of sequence, sometimes in a pattern akin to the falling suspension chain so familiar in the works of Corelli, Vivaldi and, indeed, Sammartini (K157/i, bars 109–16); and an almost unrelieved symmetry of phrasing in four- and eight-bar groups with relatively little concern for variation upon reprise.

While the early quartets are predominantly light in idiom, it would be a mistake to consider them lightweight works. In particular, the slow movements contain some impressively affective melodic writing, as in the Adagio of K156, or the Andante of K157 (which perhaps overplays its chromaticism). Elsewhere, Mozart turns to counterpoint as a means of offsetting otherwise routine inner parts (especially the viola's). Fugatos occur in a variety of locations, usually timed to coincide with the arrival of a new section or key (K80/i, bars 16 and 36; K155/i, bar 54; K156/i, bar 72; K158/ii, opening). Possibly, the composition of these quartets taught Mozart some valuable lessons about musical proportion and structure. He substantially revised his original Adagio for the G major quartet K156, retaining the same key, tempo and time signature, and theme, but significantly reducing the prominence of the diminished-seventh harmonies that had saturated the original. All in all, the autographs of these early string quartet attempts reveal a great deal about the emerging genius.

Mozart's next six quartets, K168–73, were composed only a few months after K155–60, in VIENNA in autumn 1773. Unfortunately no specific mention of their origins is made in Mozart's surviving letters from this time. Wolfgang Plath, in the introduction to the NEUE MOZART-AUSGABE volume of the quartets, proposed that the idea of a new set of quartets was Leopold's and that Wolfgang completed these pieces in order to satisfy his father's ambitions to have works in this genre ready to supply to eager publishers. Whatever their true intention, these quartets were not issued until 1785, in manuscript copies by the publisher CHRISTOPH TORRICELLA. Clearly, a group of quartets would have been a useful and potentially marketable addition to the young composer's portfolio while in the Austrian capital, and it is quite plausible that Mozart senior was seeking preferment to a court chamber music appointment for his talented son by way of some novel quartets demonstrating a mastery of the medium, and more especially of the traditional skills of counterpoint.

There is a good deal more fugal writing in these pieces than in K155–60. Imitative counterpoint is quite common in the first-movement development sections (K168, K169) and also in the slow movement of K171, the minuet of K172 and the finales of K168 and K173. In the muted Andante of K168 Mozart shows off his canonic skill in a highly concentrated treatment of the same theme used by Haydn in his Op. 20 No. 5 (and in the same key, F minor). The finales of K168 and K173 are, in fact, fully developed fugues. At times, Mozart's fugal writing assumes the status of a technical demonstration. In K173, the manifold stretto entries of the chromatic D minor theme during the course of the finale, occurring in a variety of temporal and intervallic positions, would have appealed to those Viennese musicians who esteemed a composer for being able to handle traditional contrapuntal formulas. (A simpler, presumably original, version of K173 survives, so we know that Mozart took great pains over the details of this culminating movement of the set.) There is an altogether more 'serious' attitude at work here than in K155–60, perhaps implying an external, rather than internal stylistic motivation on Mozart's part, as if he intended these works to stand less as unified artistic statements than as a kind of 'sales brochure' to be perused by a likely secular or ecclesiastical Viennese employer.

Many commentators have remarked on the 'influence' of Haydn's quartets Opp. 17 and 20 on Mozart's K168–73. It is true that in some respects, such as the positioning of the minuet in second place, and the 'borrowing' of the theme from Haydn's Op. 20 No. 5, mentioned previously, Mozart's quartets appear indebted to Haydn's. But the link, if any, remains elusive: Haydn's Op. 20 quartets (or 'Divertimentos' as they were entitled) were not published until 1774 (the year after Mozart composed K168–73), and then not in Vienna, where Mozart might have known about them, but in PARIS, by La Chevardière. So, if Mozart had encountered Haydn's quartets by mid-1773, he must have done so via unauthorized, manuscript copies – unlikely, perhaps, though not altogether impossible. (A recent attempt to sort out this problem was made by A. Peter Brown.) In 1962, Walter Senn made a case for Mozart having bought a set of playing parts of Haydn's Op. 17 quartets in Vienna in 1773, to which he made some handwritten additions; again, this has been taken as proof positive of Haydn's influence on the young Mozart. According to Wolfgang Plath, however, Mozart's additions appear not to have been made until the late 1770s. The case for influence thus remains to be convincingly established.

2. THE 'HAYDN' QUARTETS: K387, 421, 428, 458, 464, 465

The 'Haydn' quartets embrace some of Mozart's most memorable melodic writing, and some of his most refined compositional thinking, often animated by counterpoint. It is true that counterpoint had been an important factor in his earlier quartets (K155–60 and K168–73), but it is arguably a weakness in these works, rather than a strength, since no attempt is made to integrate the strictly fugal writing into the prevailing 'galant' environment of elegant melodies, supported by simple harmonies, within a symmetrical, even predictable periodic framework. The result is a rather uncomfortable mix of different expressive types, representative of a genuine stylistic crisis during the early 1770s. This crisis required for its resolution a new way of integrating the melodic and harmonic elements of the emerging Classical style in such a way that neither element was merely passive support for the other.

The 'Haydn' quartets run a remarkably wide range of emotions, including the 'Sturm und Drang' idiom of K421's first movement, the tonal mystery of K428's hushed opening unison phrase (luxuriously reharmonized upon restatement), the serenity of the 6/8 Andante of the same quartet, and that of the 'Dissonance', K465, and the opera buffa high jinks of the finales of K458 ('Hunt'), K428 and K465, the last two of which notably introduce new counter-themes in their concluding sections, as if to hint that the action could so easily continue beyond the confines of the form.

The earliest mention of these quartets comes in a letter Mozart wrote to the Parisian music publisher JEAN-GEORGES SIEBER on 26 April 1783: 'I have been composing six quartets for two violins, viola and cello. If you would like to engrave these . . . I will gladly let you have them. But I cannot allow these to go . . . cheaply; I mean, I cannot let you have these six quartets under fifty Louis d'or.' In fact, by 26 April 1783 he had completed only one of the six quartets, K387; the sixth, K465, was not completed until 14 January 1785. The full set of six was subsequently published by ARTARIA in September 1785.

It has traditionally been assumed that these quartets were written in two relatively short bursts of creative activity: K387, 421 and 428 between late December 1782 and July 1783, and K458, K464 and K465 between November 1784 and

January 1785. The manuscript of K387 is dated 31 December 1782; K458 was entered in Mozart's own handwritten thematic catalogue on 9 November 1784, while K464 and 465 were entered on 10 and 14 January 1785, respectively. We have no first-hand documentary evidence giving specific composition dates for K421 and K428 besides an anecdote, reported by CONSTANZE MOZART to Vincent and Mary NOVELLO in 1829, that her husband had been working on the D minor quartet, K421 while she was in labour with their first child, Raimund, and therefore around 17 June 1783. Manuscript evidence suggests that K428 also dates from about this time.

It is not known for certain at what stage Mozart decided to dedicate these works to Haydn. The older composer's approval of K387, K421 and K428 at private performances on 15 January and 12 February 1785 evidently provided encouragement. In the published dedication to Haydn (1 Sept. 1785) Mozart wrote: 'Your good opinion encourages me to offer them to you and leads me to hope that you will not consider them wholly unworthy of your favour.' An alternative stimulus may have been the success of the Op. 2 string quartets by IGNAZ PLEYEL (1757–1831) that had appeared in 1784, with a dedication to his teacher, Haydn. Mozart knew Pleyel's quartets and recommended the Op. 1 set to his father in a letter of 24 April 1784. Perhaps he felt that there was something to be gained in the marketability of his own quartets by following suit. At any rate, Haydn was clearly impressed by Mozart's quartets, since at the second of the two private performances (12 Feb. 1785) he declared to Leopold: 'Before God, and as an honest man I tell you that your son is the greatest composer known to me either in person or by name. He has taste, and, what is more, the most profound knowledge of composition.'

Fortunately, the autograph score of the 'Haydn' quartets survives (and is housed at the British Library in London). Careful examination of it affords a valuable insight into Mozart's compositional process, and in particular bears out a comment he made in the dedication to Haydn that they were 'the fruits of a long and laborious toil' ('il frutto di una lungha, e laboriosa fatica'). There are a significant number of revisions in points of detail (individual notes, scorings of chords), as well as large-scale alterations to sections and even entire movements. The autograph was Mozart's composing score and among the more interesting revisions are: a false start for the 2/4 finale of the 'Hunt' quartet, K458, featuring a more contrapuntal opening than in the final version in double the eventual notated values (an entirely separate sheet, containing a sketch for a polonaise-style finale that must pre-date both the duple-time versions, exists in a private collection in Paris); a reordering of the variations in the Andante of K464; and, most dramatically of all, no fewer than three discarded attempts at a section of the finale of K387. This is the passage following the exposition that Mozart began in the main body of the manuscript, then drafted again on a blank folio further on in the gathering, then revised still further at the bottom of the same folio, before returning to the main text with a version that was still not entirely satisfactory (though he subsequently carried on to the end of the work, dating it 31 December 1782). K387 remained in this state for about six months before Mozart revised the passage yet again on a separate sheet that he tipped in to the main gathering on which the finale of K387 was written.

The reason we can be so sure about the final delay of six months is thanks to the pioneering work done in recent decades on Mozart's manuscript paper by Alan Tyson. In this case, Tyson has shown through a careful examination of watermarks that the additional sheet of paper bearing the final revision to this passage of K387 is the other half of a sheet on which the concluding bars of K421 were written (June 1783). All told, Mozart used no fewer than ten different types of paper in the autograph of these quartets and there are several other 'overlaps' where the same paper type occurs in different quartets. Folio 38 of the autograph, for example, containing the last part of K428's slow movement, consists of a single leaf, which was once, according to Alan Tyson's painstaking study of the watermarks, part of the same sheet as fols. 14–15, containing the first movement of K421 (June–July 1783). Perhaps, then, Mozart was working on these two quartets simultaneously. Tyson's examinations reveal much more that is of interest regarding the genesis of this set of quartets, including the fact that the first 106 bars of K458 were evidently left as an incomplete torso for over a year (between about May–June 1783 and November 1784, when he entered it in his catalogue) before Mozart proceeded with the rest of the movement. Possibly Mozart got 'stuck' with K458, or, alternatively, became distracted by the need to compose other works in the intervening period.

The 'authentic' text of these six quartets presents a number of difficulties. The first edition (in separate playing parts) differs in a number of vital respects from Mozart's autograph. For instance, the 'Hunt' quartet, K458 in B flat, is placed fourth, whereas in the print it comes third (the manuscript evidence showing that it was probably begun before K428, but was only finished after K428 had been complete for well over a year); there are also some discrepancies in the movement headings and tempo markings. The minuet and trio of both K428 in E flat and K465 in C are 'Allegro' in Mozart's autograph, but 'Allegretto' in the print; the finale of K464 in A is given as 'Allegro' in the autograph, but as 'Allegro non troppo' in the first edition. Mozart probably intended these emendations, along with a large number of minor changes in matters of articulation and dynamics, to supersede the text of the autograph.

In these six quartets Mozart achieves that sureness of touch in the integration of counterpoint and Classical periodicity that had characterized Haydn's Op. 33, published in Vienna in 1782, and written, according to the composer, 'in an entirely new and special manner'. To some degree, this 'new and special manner' can be read as a metaphor for contemporary ENLIGHTENMENT ideals, a 'society' in which the capacity for individual freedom of action is tempered by the regulation of the corporate body. In the string quartet it is achieved by relating the four instruments in a shifting flux of texture in which individual lines alternately come to the fore as melody and then recede into the background as accompaniment, rather like a conversation.

There are hints even on the first page of K387 that Mozart had begun to engage with Haydn's 'new and special manner'. His approach to composition was always more overtly melodic than Haydn's typically pithy motivic idiom. Nevertheless, the opening theme of K387, first stated as a tune with accompaniment, is soon recast in a contrapuntal setting (bars 10ff.) in which each instrument has an active and essential role, leading up to the secondary theme in D at bar 24. Further evidence of the influence of Haydn's motivic working on Mozart is provided by the almost imperceptible genesis of an upbeat figure through the transition (bars 10–24). Beginning in bar 13 a three-quaver dialogue evolves between the two violins (heightened by the addition of a trill); though shifting in intervallic shape, the three-quaver upbeat is subtly maintained through the next several bars by exact placement of dynamics, even surviving a transition to semiquavers in the first violin from bar 21, now accompanied by a 'factured' presentation, shared out in contrasting rhythmic patterns between the three lower strings in bars 20–3 (reinforced by *f* and *fp* dynamics). There is a new purposefulness about this kind of continuation that recurs throughout the six quartets. It is witnessed to even greater effect in the corresponding exposition transition of the D minor quartet, K421, a section Arnold Schoenberg memorably described as 'musical prose' in his essay 'Brahms the Progressive' (1947) published in the collection of his writings *Style and Idea*. Similar claims could be made for the exposition and large chunks of the development section of the 'Dissonance' quartet, K465.

Another way of integrating counterpoint and periodicity is revealed in the finale of K387. Here Mozart designs a sonata form whose main thematic materials are introduced as fugatos, interspersed by overtly dance-like 'episodes'. In the central development section the main fugue theme is worked out in novel contrapuntal settings (as a counter-theme to a repeated staccato crotchet pattern, for example) while moving around the circle of fifths and adapted to the regular phrase and cadence schemes so symbolic of Classical periodicity. The sonata reprise omits further reference to the main theme at the beginning, launching immediately into a subdominant restatement of the first 'episode' (bar 175). Both fugue themes are subsequently combined from bar 209 – an exemplary piece of 'timing' that lends the reprise a sense of culmination, not just to this movement, but to the quartet as a whole. The sense of a higher unity among the four movements of K387 is supported to some extent by the prominence of chromaticism in each one (note the alternate *piano/forte* dynamics in the minuet), though it is dangerous to read too much into 'cyclic' claims.

Playing a part in the definition of a movement's form is only one way in which Mozart exploits counterpoint in this set. Frequently, counterpoint is one factor among several in determining the local continuity of a passage. The opening theme of K458's finale is put to contrapuntal service in the development section (particularly from bar 140), where its role is to create textural contrast with the strongly periodic character of the surrounding sections. In the development section of K465 imitative dialogue between the first violin and viola at the outset takes place within the context of a series of pedal points falling gradually from B flat, the flattened seventh degree of the scale, to F, at which point there is a radical change of texture (to fractured broken chord patterns) before the main theme reappears again in the bass (against a new three-part chordal counter-theme above it), giving way eventually to an energetic exchange between treble and bass tethered by strong syncopations from the inner parts. Though counterpoint is the surface effect we notice most in this development it unfolds within a carefully planned tonal frame and the transitions from one contrapuntal setting to another are always timed to coincide with these important moments of key change, approaching ever closer to the tonic, C, for the reprise. In K464,

Mozart treats us to a minuet that combines three themes (stated in the opening phrase) in a virtuoso succession of imitations, featuring stretto and inversion; but the idiom of the dance is never forfeited. The finale of K464 in A is likewise contrapuntal in character, though without losing its lightness of touch; its opening thematic snippets soon reveal their propensity for combination in imitation (as at bars 25ff., derived from bars 3 and 4, and bars 39ff., building up stretto patterns over a dominant pedal). Imitation persists to the very end of the piece, reformulating the combinations of themes once more in its coda before dissolving in a delightful 'throwaway' ending.

For the first time in Mozart's quartets the slow movements become the 'emotional centre' of each work. They are particularly notable for their rich cantabile melodic writing; here Mozart departs entirely from the Haydnesque mode, luxuriating in thematic multiplicity and rich embellishment. In K387, 458 and 465 the form is abridged sonata (with no 'development'); in K428, there is a full-scale sonata form, complete with extended development of the main theme; in K421, extended ternary (ABA–aba–ABA); and in K464 a set of variations.

Examples of thematic multiplicity abound. The first subject and transition of K458 contain at least a dozen discrete themes, most of them merely stated in passing, as if Mozart's imagination was overflowing with more ideas than he could make use of. Arguably, the sheer thematic saturation of this movement is a weakness rather than a strength, focusing attention on the level of the beat rather than the bar, and resulting in a uniformity of accent that is perhaps a little cloying. More successful in this respect is the Andante of K421, which, for all its *embarras de richesses*, never loses sight of the proportion of upbeat to downbeat.

Melodic embellishment is a constant delight in these works. The Andante of K465 affords an especially beautiful example at the beginning of its reprise (bar 45), where the first-violin line illustrates how to vary an already elegant line by means of triads, syncopation and chromaticism, without ever destroying its essential grace. Rather more exuberant decoration is demonstrated at times in the variations of K464, especially variation 1.

Frequently in the sonata-type slow movements Mozart enhances the restatement of the tonic key in the reprise by highlighting related keys on the flat side of the tonic, possibly as a way of compensating for the lack of any true 'development'. In K387, bars 58–69, for example, Mozart expands upon the transitional phrase originally heard at bar 7, introducing the new element of antiphony and then diverting the cello theme into darker harmonic territory (lingering in D flat at bars 63–5) and continuing by chromatic descent in the cello (supporting some diminished seventh and augmented sixth chords) towards the extended dominant pedal at bar 70. Further 'quasi-development' is seen at bars 74–7 in which the first violin's demisemiquavers are accompanied by a sequentially founded quaver pattern in the second violin, derived from the material of bar 58.

The minuets, while never a parallel for Haydn's scherzos of Op. 33, are richly varied in character. The most straightforward, retaining the courtly dance feature of a minuet, are those of K428, 458 and 465, although their phraseology is unpredictable. In K387 and 421 the dimensions approach those of a sonata-form movement; indeed, elements of developmental writing and dramatized tonal reprise are readily apparent. Trios are normally opportunities for contrast. Sometimes this involves a shift to the opposite mode of the minuet (K387, 421, 465 all revert to the tonic minor and K428 to the relative minor). That of K421, featuring delicate pizzicato and octave passages, is a perfect foil for the tersely argued counterpoint of its minuet partner. In K387 the trio is the more 'aggressive' partner; its uncompromising unison and octave writing, and its asymmetrical phrasing may have been among those elements that caused Leopold Mozart to describe K387 as one of the more 'difficult' of his son's quartets (letter of 15 Feb. 1785; K458, 464 and 465 were, he believed, 'somewhat easier').

Perhaps the most 'difficult' movement among the six 'Haydn' quartets is the Adagio introduction to the 'Dissonance' quartet, K465. (It is from this section that the work acquired its nickname.) It features prominently in the early reception history of the quartets. Detailed discussions of Mozart's Adagio (and some hypothetical 'improvements') were published in the late 1820s and early 1830s in music periodicals such as the *Allgemeine musikalische Zeitung* and *La Revue musicale* by, among others, GIUSEPPE SARTI and Fétis. Selections from this debate were reprinted in translation in the London periodical, *Harmonicon* (vol. 10 (1832) 243–6) including extracts from Sarti's venomous attack (in which he described this passage of Mozart's quartet as 'barbarous'). Sarti's main objection to the opening of K465 concerned false relations, for example of A flat and A natural in bar 2 ('a most execrable commencement') and such chromatic extremes as the A sharp/F juxtaposition in bars 20–1 ('most miserable in an adagio').

Actually, the Adagio contains only mild dissonances, such as the brief whole-tone clusters at the beginning of bars 3 and 7; otherwise the chords in themselves (founded on a chromatically descending bass-line that is not at all unusual in the Classical period) are quite easy to describe in the context of eighteenth-century notions of tonality. What is so unusual here is the shifting succession of chords in bars 1–9, which confuse, rather than clarify, our tonal perspective and do not establish C at all clearly from the outset. In bar 1 the repeated cello C weakly implies a tonic, though as soon as the other strands of polyphony begin to enter in bars 1–4 we recognize instead a first inversion chord of A flat, preparing a chromatically inflected G chord in bars 3–4. This much – a hint of C followed by several beats' worth of G – is perhaps enough to suggest that C is indeed the tonic – at least until bar 5, which starts a sequential repetition of the preceding phrase one whole tone lower, seriously undermining the tonal stability. A sense of anxiety throughout this section is successfully achieved by the withholding of clear tonal (and for a while, accentual) reference points; it resembles a blurred image eventually adjusted into sharper focus. Functionally, it is a perfect harbinger of the sunny Allegro that follows.

3. K499 AND THE 'PRUSSIAN' QUARTETS

Mozart's next quartet after the 'Haydn' set, K499 in D (the so-called 'HOFFMEISTER' – named after its Viennese publisher), was completed on 19 August 1786.

The reason for its composition – an isolated quartet, composed during an intense period of concerto production – is unclear. No commission for such a work is known; the legend stemming from NIEMETSCHEK that this quartet was one of a number of pieces promised to COUNT WALSEGG-STUPPACH (in advance of the REQUIEM) is now discredited. It has been suggested by Ludwig Finscher that it was offered by Mozart to Hoffmeister in 1786 as a partial substitute for a projected series of piano quartets that failed commercially before it could be realized. At any rate the 'Hoffmeister' quartet was praised in a 1791 review of Mozart's chamber music by the publisher Heinrich Bossler who described it as 'composed with the fire of imagination and craftsmanship through which Mozart has long enjoyed the reputation of being one of the best composers in Germany . . . It is industriously written, woven through with [a quality of] canonic imitation, which is wanting in compositions by even the famous masters.' This contrapuntal manner is apparent even on the first page, with duets for the two violins being imitated by the lower strings, and during the course of the exposition (extended to a far greater length than is normal in the 'Haydn' quartets). Mozart positions his long-limbed opening theme in a variety of different imitative settings, at one stage in the exposition re-citing the original antecedent as a cadential suffix within an easygoing harmonic pace and then transforming this material to turbulent effect in the development, exploiting extremes of register conflict and inversion of the main theme. Perhaps the minuet and trio were even more to Bossler's taste: 'woven through with canonic imitation' is an apt description for the second half of the energetic trio.

'Craftsmanship' is another quality identified by Bossler, and it combines strikingly with contrapuntal expertise in the Adagio of K499. In addition to finely tuned melodic embellishment, Mozart inverts the opening texture at bar 11, transferring the tune – in paired thirds – to the viola and cello beneath a new counter-theme in the violins. From this point on the basic textural principle of this sonata design is one of florid episodic writing alternating with restatements of the main theme, which is itself sounded in canon at the fifth between lower and upper pairs of instruments at bar 40. 'Craftsmanship' may also allude to the handling of tonal and rhythmic contrast, a vital ingredient in the quicksilver finale that includes a digression into the flat mediant key, F, at bar 237 (followed yet again by a stretch of deft counterpoint).

The three 'Prussian' quartets, K575 in D, K589 in B flat and K590 in F, owe their origins to Mozart's visit to Berlin and Potsdam in early 1789. He began work on the first, K575, once he had returned to Vienna in June of that year and in his thematic catalogue described the piece as 'a quartet . . . for his Majesty, the King of Prussia'. Mozart originally intended this as the first of a set of six quartets (along with a group of six 'easy' piano sonatas for the King's daughter, of which only K576, in D was ever written). He probably believed – or at least hoped – that the dedication to Friedrich Wilhelm II of a set of quartets (like Haydn's Op. 50 set) would result in a position at court. Mozart soon decided on allocating prominent parts for the cello (the King's own instrument, on which he was a competent player). There are several brief solos for his Majesty within the first movement and some more extended appearances in the Andante exploiting the cello's high register. A sketch of an early version of the finale was abandoned after eight bars; Mozart's second attempt (the one with which we are familiar) begins with the stately 'royal' theme, this time for the cello rather than the first violin (as in the original). Close analysis of the completed autograph reveals some interesting insights into Mozart's compositional process. At first sight, the appearance of the very opening of this quartet in Mozart's manuscript tends to support the commonly held view that melodic inspiration came easiest to him and that the harmonic and accompanimental details were filled out as a secondary stage of work. In K575's first subject, the ink colour, the alignment of the four parts and the separate bar-lines for the first-violin part show that the treble tune was written down in the score independently of the lower parts, which were filled in once each melodic phrase had been determined. Possibly, though, the true state of affairs was not so straightforward. While there are numerous examples in Mozart's autographs of pages in which the melodic line is drafted for many bars without any chordal support, or even a bass-line, the fact that the underlying harmony in such cases was left to a later stage of writing out can only mean that this was already fairly obvious to him, and could safely be written into the score at a later stage, once the melodic 'descant' had been safely notated. Perhaps, then, it was *melody* that Mozart found more difficult to retain in his mind since this was what he was most anxious to write down on paper – why else would he apparently sketch forwards feverishly for bars, even pages, at a time in his autographs unless he feared forgetting (and thus losing) a specific melodic formulation? The evidence of the opening of the autograph of K575 points tentatively to the conclusion that its harmonic basis – admittedly rather slow-moving and uniform – was to some degree formulaic (that is, a basic chordal pattern that might subsequently be elaborated in any one of several satisfying ways), while its treble theme, containing specific intervallic and rhythmic patterns, required the composer's most urgent attention and needed to be captured on paper as soon as possible. The true picture may be impossible to paint in detail, and was perhaps a combination of both melodic and harmonic elements in various proportions, depending on the nature of the particular phrase. While it is conceivable that Mozart refined the melodic shape on sketch staves now lost (or unknown), the very fact that the alignment of the parts is not vertically exact – it is far from exact, in fact – strongly suggests that the autograph was indeed a composing score (otherwise, all four parts would surely have been copied into the autograph neatly, and in perfect alignment, a bar at a time from a pre-existing sketch leaf).

Attention has understandably focused on the prominent role of the cello in these quartets. One illustration among many is the glorious opening theme of K589's Larghetto. The sure handling of texture required for such a passage was perhaps attained in part by the experience of the duet sonatas for violin and viola, K423 and 424 (1783), in which, in order to accommodate a viola theme, Mozart had to provide convincing accompaniments in a suitable register of the violin – a valuable stimulus to his imagination. At the opening of K589's slow movement the accompaniment to the 'royal' theme is no less inventive – the viola holds a pedal E flat while the second violin spins out an Alberti-type pattern, filling out the harmony beneath the cello line. Other remarkably transparent textures in this movement include bars 32ff., in which the first violin's delicate tracery, in a higher register than the solo cello, is shaped in such a way as to suggest chords. (A similar technique, though entirely different in character, is found at bars 63ff. of the first movement of K590.)

In addition to prominent cello solos (sometimes attaining a considerable degree of virtuosity, in the trio of K589, for example) Mozart has the royal instrument participating in dialogue textures, as in its first entry in K589 (following an irregular, five-bar phrase) where it anticipates the viola in a brief canon. Later in the first movement (bars 45ff.) the cello rises once again to soloistic prominence, although this time it serves a broader plan, providing the leading portion of a section answered by the first violin. Structurally, too, the King's part stands out, marking the important digression into D flat at bar 81 of the development section. Appearances of the cello do not always need to be prolonged or particularly demanding to be of significant effect, of course. This is especially true of the F major quartet, K590, perhaps the most gratifying of the three in terms of instrumentation. Within its first movement the cello takes on a number of roles: sounding the main theme in unison at the very beginning; announcing the second main theme in the dominant key, as well as the first appearance of the exposition's closing theme (bar 63); providing a 'ticking' motivic bass, derived from bar 76, at the start of the development and then swapping lines with the first violin in a passage of invertible counterpoint (the same texture reappearing in the coda). Throughout this quartet, Mozart demonstrates how a judicious blend of individual presence and social deference may be expressed in music, most particularly, perhaps, in the finale, whose opening melody weaves in and out of the texture like a silver thread through all 309 bars.

Achieving a satisfying balance between concertante writing featuring the cello and the demands of the integrated quartet ensemble may have been one of the reasons that Mozart described his compositional task as 'troublesome' in a letter to MICHAEL PUCHBERG of 12 June 1790, about the same time as he was completing the third quartet, K590. There were evidently other difficulties too. So far as K589 (May 1790) is concerned, there is a cancelled attempt at a B flat minuet (KAnh 75) and another for a 2/4 finale (KAnh 71), in addition to a first draft of a 6/8 finale preceding the eventual (different) version in the autograph. Sketches for K590's minuet and for a 6/8 finale (KAnh 73) also survive.

In the event, Mozart completed only three quartets and by June 1790 had evidently given up all hope of dedicating them to the Prussian monarch. The three that were completed were published at the end of 1791, after Mozart's death. On New Year's Eve, 1791, Artaria placed an advert in the *Wiener Zeitung* for 'Three completely new concertante quartets . . . by Herr Kapellmeister Mozart, Op. 18. These quartets, which flowed from the pen of this great musical genius shortly before his death, are among the most estimable works of the composer Mozart, ([who has] too soon departed this world), [that] have evoked pleasure and admiration among all those with an interest in the realms of musical art, beauty and taste, not just in amateurs, but also in the keenest connoisseurs.'

JOHN IRVING

W. J. Allanbrook, ' "To Serve the Private Pleasure": Expression and Form in the String Quartets', in *Wolfgang Amadè Mozart: Essays on His Life and His Music*, ed. S. Sadie (Oxford, 1996), 132–60

A. P. Brown, 'Haydn and Mozart's 1773 Stay in Vienna: Weeding a Musicological Garden', *Journal of Musicology* 10 (1992), 192–230

L. Finscher, 'Aspects of Mozart's Compositional Process in the Quartet Autographs: I. The Early Quartets, II. The Genesis of K.387', in *The String Quartets of Haydn, Mozart, and Beethoven: Studies of the Autograph Manuscripts*, ed. C. Wolff (Cambridge, MA, 1980), 121–53

Marius Flothuis, 'A Close Reading of the Autographs of Mozart's Last Ten Quartets', in *The String Quartets of Haydn, Mozart, and Beethoven: Studies of the Autograph Scores*, ed. C. Wolff (Cambridge, MA, 1980), 154–73

J. Irving, *Mozart: The Six 'Haydn' String Quartets* (Cambridge, 1998)

S. P. Keefe, 'An Integrated "Dissonance": Mozart's "Haydn" Quartets and the Slow Introduction of K. 465', *Mozart-Jahrbuch* 2002, 87–103

W.-D. Seiffert, 'Mozart's "Haydn" Quartets: An Evaluation of the Autograph and First Edition, with Particular Attention to mm. 125–42 of the Finale of K. 387', in *Mozart Studies* 2, ed. C. Eisen (Oxford, 1997), 175–200

J. A. Vertrees, 'Mozart's String Quartet K. 465: The History of a Controversy', *Current Musicology* 17 (1974), 94–114

J. Webster, 'Towards a History of Viennese Chamber Music in the Early Classical Period', *Journal of the American Musicological Society* 27 (1974), 212–47

C. String quintets

The origin of the string quintet is frequently traced to the Italian sinfonia and concerto or to other soloistic ensemble music but it is also close in spirit to the south GERMAN and AUSTRIAN symphony, including works in five parts whose style is often indistinguishable from one-to-a-part chamber music; it was first cultivated in Austria during the 1750s and early 1760s, chiefly at monastic institutions.

Mozart's first string quintet, K174, completed in December 1773, is a relatively isolated work, not only within his early output but among SALZBURG chamber music generally, which well into the 1760s usually counted on two melody instruments and basso continuo. Some isolated examples of more exotic scorings can be found among LEOPOLD MOZART's works (including trios for violin, violoncello and double bass) but on the whole, chamber music in Salzburg was a traditional affair. MICHAEL HAYDN seems to have been largely immune from this tradition and his two quintets (titled *Notturni*) of 1773 – also isolated in the Salzburg repertory – appear to have been the immediate stimulus for Mozart's. Not only are there structural and thematic similarities between them, but the contrapuntal finale of K174 was apparently revised after Mozart became acquainted with Haydn's example. It is clear, in any case, that Mozart admired Haydn's quintets, which he took on tour to MANNHEIM and PARIS in 1777–8.

Mozart's quintet is a work of unusual proportions: except for the small-scale Adagio, the other movements exceed in dimensions all other comparable movements in his early instrumental music to that time. But even though it is a quintet, it still smacks of the old trio-sonata tradition: some of the writing pits either the two violins or the two violas against the cello, resulting in a succession of trio sonata textures, rather than a work in five genuine parts; it also relies heavily on thematic repetition between first violin and first viola. A. H. King described it as 'experimental', a 'mixture of styles'. Nevertheless, Mozart thought well enough of the work to take it with him on tour to Mannheim and Paris; he also had a copy made for his patron and later Viennese lodge brother Freiherr OTTO VON GEMMINGEN-HORNBERG (letter of 24 Mar. 1778).

It was nearly fourteen years before Mozart returned to writing quintets: K515, in C major, was completed on 19 April 1787 and K516, in G minor, on 16 May the same year. On the whole, they are generally considered to be the finest works of their kind; and more than that, Mozart is often credited with more or less 'inventing' the genre. It is more likely, however, that Mozart saw in the quintet an opportunity not only to compose for five voices but also a genre that since the early 1780s had been all the rage in VIENNA; by the time of K515 more than fifty quintets had been composed or printed in Vienna, including works by PLEYEL, HOFFMEISTER, ALBRECHTSBERGER, Boccherini and Anton Zimmermann, among others. Nevertheless, Mozart's surpass these other examples by far and remain the only string quintets in the repertory before BEETHOVEN's Op. 29.

The quintet K515 is among Mozart's most substantial works: the first movement alone is 365 bars; in this respect it is not dissimilar to the expansive first movement of K174. But whereas the earlier quintet harks back to older generic styles, the first movement of K515 is thoroughly modern, with dialogue effects, sudden and unexpected changes of mode, interrupted cadences, tonal digressions and a wealth of textural devices and variety. There is no reason to suppose, however, that the medium itself led to this internal expansion even if frequent exchanges between the first violin and first viola are characteristic of the repertory as a whole. In this respect K515 is anomalous: except for its first movement, the first movements of the later quintets are comparable in length, if not shorter, to the first movements of the six quartets dedicated to JOSEPH HAYDN and the 'Hoffmeister' quartet, K499. Rather, it is Mozart's deliberate choice to treat the material at length that accounts for K515's substantial dimensions, not, as is frequently claimed, the genre's uncertainty about its identity as either 'pure' chamber music or something approaching orchestral music. Each movement has its own special character: while the first movement is expansive, the Adagio is full of concealed echo effects and the minuet and trio exploit the possible combinations to which the thematic material gives rise. The finale is no less remarkable. Its opening paragraph, cast in ABA form, suggests a rondo: a balanced sixteen-bar phrase, with a strong tonic close, is followed by an extended dominant that eventually rises chromatically to the return of the main theme in the home key. And the expectations aroused by the first fifty-seven bars of the Allegro (coincidentally, the opening paragraph of the first movement is also fifty-seven bars) are seemingly confirmed by what follows – an episode with a new idea in the tonic followed by an aggressive arrival at the dominant of the dominant. But it is not clear where the new idea actually begins: in retrospect, the conclusion of this transition must represent the first bar of a 'new theme'. In effect, then, Mozart conflates rondo and sonata procedures, a device that he exploits to even greater effect in the late quintets.

The G minor quintet (K516), unlike the C major, is a study in concision and motivic integration, telescoping statement and development in general and development and recapitulation in particular. The first movement struggles mightily to escape G minor but barely manages to do so; even when it does reach the dominant, the new key is often inflected with its subdominant minor. And the chromaticism is pervasive: the development touches on A flat major, D flat major, E flat minor, F minor and G minor before approaching the dominant and the recapitulation. A particularly striking motivic gesture throughout the Allegro is the leaps in the violin (and occasionally other voices as well), rising through successively larger intervals to a climax on a minor ninth. The idea of rising intervals lies behind the minuet and trio as well, including frequent leaps of a major seventh (on the way to a minor twelfth) and, in the G major trio, a sixth rising to an octave. By contrast, the Adagio ma non troppo appears to be a study in the fracturing and reassembling of sonorities: at the very start, a homophonic, five-voice texture gives way to solo first-violin and cello parts separated by as much as three octaves before the inner voices reconstitute the full ensemble. But even then, motivic leaps are not far away: a characteristic gesture of the first-violin and first-viola parts is a rise through a major twelfth, literally lifting the music into a sweeter major key, a tonal region that is the topic of the finale (following a pathetic Adagio introduction: the juxtaposition at the start of the last movement of minor and major seems to recapitulate the first movement's attempt to break free of G minor, here successfully, there not).

The two late quintets, K593 and K614, composed in December 1790 and April 1791, respectively, are frequently dismissed as second-rate works reflecting the composer's straitened circumstances towards the end of his life. Hans Keller described K614 as 'a bad arrangement of a wind piece in mock-Haydn style' and, adding insult to injury: 'Mozart entered it in his diary on 12 April [1791], and the writing looks somewhat shaky to me; perhaps he was ill.' This may be facetious but in fact Keller appeals to a long tradition of excusing Mozart's late works on grounds of failing health, depression, financial anxiety or the necessity to compose on demand. The real reason for their dismissal, however, may be that they do not correspond to the 'Classical' ideal formulated primarily on the basis of the six quartets dedicated to Haydn and the quintets of 1787. Instead, they represent a new path for Mozart, one that sometimes eschews surface variety for the sake of a single motivating idea that frequently governs both the surfaces and structures of his works.

The quintet K593, for example, has a first movement in a style more spare in texture than that of the preceding quintets but polyphonically richer, especially in the recapitulation where the exposition material is extended and elaborated. The same can be said of K614, the minuet of which is canonic while in the finale the development section includes a double fugue. At the same time, both quintets self-consciously exploit similar topics – each first-movement Allegro begins with a passage imitating horns (in K593 immediately following the introductory gesture) – while making use of textures in novel ways. The Adagio of the D major quintet, unlike the earlier quintet slow movements, is a study in sonorities: each of its five large paragraphs is similarly structured around a recurring pattern, beginning with the full ensemble, reducing to three parts (the violins and first viola alternating with the violas and cello) and then returning to five. K614 is novel in a different way. Here the first movement can be read as a contest between the first violin and the rest of the ensemble, each vying with the other not only to assert superiority but also to control and direct the musical discourse, achieving rapprochement only in the final bars.

The notion of a contest in the first movement of K614 suggests that generic play, consisting in this case of tension between the 'brilliant' and 'Classical' styles identified by early writers on string chamber music, is self-consciously present in Mozart's works of the late 1780s. Generic play is hardly foreign to Mozart's earlier style: the Quintet for Piano and Winds, K452, takes over the ethos of the concerto, the slow movement of the Horn Quintet, K407, of 1782 is also based on the model of the concerto, and the piano sonata K333 includes a cadenza. But in the case of K614 there is a twist: Mozart manipulates not merely markers of genre but markers of form and procedure as well. The slow movement, ostensibly a theme and variations (and among the most popular of Mozart's late variation sets as several contemporaneous arrangements for keyboard show) not only takes over characteristic gestures of the rondo, including tonic restatements of the main theme, but of sonata as well. The passages linking the variations are typically transitional, while the climax of the movement, which includes some of the sharpest dissonances in all of Mozart, corresponds to the increase in harmonic tension characteristic of a sonata development. A clear return to both tonic and main theme characterizes the final variation, which is followed by a sonata-like coda, drawing together the main procedural gestures of the movement. (The same pervasive exploitation of underlying topics characterizes the 'Prussian' quartets as well – and the slow movement of K590 in particular is reminiscent of K614: here an almost obsessive set of variations masks a sonata structure that eventually gives rise to a coda of stunning beauty.)

The essence of the 'late' style, characteristic in particular of the two last quintets, is a return to an earlier aesthetic, one of unity of affect. It is not a return to an earlier style, one marked by uniformity of surface: for Mozart, the surface often remains as varied as ever, sometimes more varied, more disjunctive. But underneath, there is a uniformity of idea or topic that motivates and is expressed by the music. In this respect, the later quintets are strikingly different from the quintets of 1787, where variation, change, disruption and disjunction, even at the level of the whole, is paramount. Nor is this newly conceived and executed unity of affect a feature of the chamber music alone: it also informs the REQUIEM, DIE ZAUBERFLÖTE, LA CLEMENZA DI TITO and the last concertos.

CLIFF EISEN

C. Eisen and W.-D. Seiffert, *Mozarts Streichquintette. Beiträge zum musikalischen Satz, zum Gattunskontext und zu Quellenfragen* (Stuttgart, 1994)

I. Emerson, 'A Question of Order: Andante, Minuet, Or Minuet, Andante – Mozart's String Quintet in C major, K. 515', *Mozart-Jahrbuch 1989/90*, 89–98

H. Keller, 'The Chamber Music', in *The Mozart Companion*, ed. H. C. Robbins Landon and D. Mitchell (London, 1956), 132–4

H. King, *Mozart Chamber Music* (London, 1968)

S. Newmann, 'Mozart's G-minor Quintet (KV. 516) and its Relationship to the G-minor Symphony (KV. 550)', *Music Review* 17 (1956), 287–98

C. Rosen, *The Classical Style* (New York, 1971)

D. Piano trios

Mozart was eight years old when he first wrote for keyboard and two other string instruments, composing six sonatas (K10–15) for piano, violin (or flute) and cello in 1764. Twelve years later he wrote his 'Divertimento à 3' for piano, violin and cello and in 1786 and 1788 composed his six mature piano trios. These three stages in Mozart's life can be traced in the heterogeneity of the thirteen works; and diversity is present even within the final group. The first and last of the final six, K496 and K564, both in G major, are less weighty than the central four; K564, in fact, is surprisingly slight. The second trio of the six, the 'Kegelstatt' trio, K498, is scored for piano, clarinet and viola.

The primary differentiating feature among the works is the shifting parity in instrumental roles, and this reflects the evolution of the piano trio genre beyond the work of Mozart. Basil Smallman considers Mozart's 1786 trios to be milestones in their genre since the potential of the medium was realized here for the very first time: the piano trio was the last of the Viennese chamber media to reach maturity. Contemporary composers writing for the trio (CLEMENTI, JOSEPH HAYDN, HOFFMEISTER, KOZELUCH, PLEYEL, Sterkel and VANHAL) seem to have striven for participatory equality only fairly haphazardly: although instrumental parts were gradually becoming more equal, some composers were still writing continuo-like cello parts towards the end of the 1780s. The trio medium was an emerging genre and Mozart's six late trios are exceptional in their sophisticated handling of the ensemble.

Mozart's sensitivity to the trio's capabilities was no doubt aroused by his experiences with string quartet, violin and piano duo, piano quartet and piano concerto; his early sonatas K10–15 and even the divertimento K254 need not be regarded as precursors to the mature trios. K10–15, in B flat, G, A, F, C and B flat major, were written in LONDON and published as Op. 3 with 'optional' cello parts. Characteristically for their time (and in line with works by ECKARD, SCHOBERT, HONAUER and J. C. BACH), the sonatas could even function without the violin or flute, contributing to a growing repertory of keyboard sonatas with other instruments that were added for 'colouristic' purposes.

J. C. Bach's harpsichord sonatas with accompanying violin and cello (heard by Mozart in London in 1764) may have inspired his Divertimento à 3 in B flat major, K254; he had also enjoyed Schobert's trios in PARIS in 1763–4. 'Divertimenti' (chamber works or pieces for larger ensembles), were often written for family celebrations such as name days, although the only record we have of K254's performance is a letter in which Mozart mentions giving it at a concert in MUNICH in 1777. The piece is in three movements (anticipating later violin sonatas and trios), with an outer Allegro assai and final Rondeau (Tempo di Menuetto) of the light and sparkling nature that befits a divertimento and a central Adagio in E flat that provides complementary lyrical writing. The violin offers significant melodic and textural interest throughout the work but the cello barely diverges from the piano's left-hand part.

Although the early and late works are very different types of chamber music, they share the envisaged platform of a domestic scene. Mozart's early trios were ideally suited to the amateur *Hausmusik* market: harmony and phrasing are straightforward; no serious technical demands are made; instrumentation is flexible; and the pieces overall will probably interest players more than their audiences. Mozart's mature trios were written in a city enjoying a trio 'boom': between 1781 and 1790, seventy original keyboard trios (of which fifty-one were first editions) and eleven trio arrangements of other works were published in VIENNA, surpassing figures for most other genres, and reflecting the emerging Viennese bourgeoisie's search in the 1780s for chamber music that they could play at home. Two references to trios in Mozart's letters suggest that they were written for informal gatherings with or for friends. Mozart almost certainly played all the piano parts himself, however, and made no concessions for dilettantes: the pieces demand a high level of technical and musical ability. For this reason too, the trios stand out among contemporary works for the same genre.

1. Piano Trios in G major, K496 and K564
2. Piano Trios in B flat major, K502, in E major, K542, and in C major K548
3. Trio in E flat major ('Kegelstatt' trio), for Piano, Clarinet and Viola, K498

1. PIANO TRIOS IN G MAJOR, K496 AND K564

K496's flamboyant opening bars, consisting of an elaborated ascending G major scale in the piano, provide a simple, energetic impulse that continues throughout the Allegro movement. The same octave figure is grasped by the three players in unison at the beginning of the development section and then passed between one another in imitative ascents of C major and C minor (and their dominants). In contrast, K564 opens with a piano theme masked by unison sustained strings. The mid-bar entry of this theme establishes a gently offset rhythmic character that pervades the movement: the second thematic area elaborates the same rhythmic idea and the cello's accompaniment figure is given *tenuto* marks on the second and fourth beats. The extreme brevity of the movement (117 bars) is also striking: it has been suggested that the trio was written for 'beginners', like the piano sonata K545.

Overall, K496 is certainly the more sturdy of the two G major works, especially from the second movement onwards, when Mozart's cello writing becomes particularly resourceful. K564's C major central movement is disappointingly facile in both its Andante theme and six variations, whereas K496's central Andante (also in C major), takes an initially innocuous theme through an inventive sonata development and into C minor, as well as conjuring up a brief episode of five-part counterpoint in the coda.

The codas of several Mozart trios contain exquisite chamber-music writing and the finales of both G major works are well served in this respect. In K564, the Allegretto rondo breaks into imitative counterpoint in a movement otherwise limited to simple allocation of melody or accompaniment to the various parts. The final coda of K496 plays a synthesizing role in relation to its preceding theme and variations. Variation 4 departs considerably from the light, bouncy 'home' atmosphere through a departure to the tonic minor and creates a sinewy four-part texture of interweaving lines; variation 5, back in the major, provides further contrast with its Adagio tempo and delays resolution into the *Primo tempo* of variation 6 through a recitative-like link and fermata. The nineteen-bar coda, touching on the minor mode but also 'correcting' the minor material into the major, represents an ideal counterweight.

2. PIANO TRIOS IN B FLAT MAJOR, K502, IN E MAJOR, K542, AND IN C MAJOR, K548

Among the opening Allegro movements of these three trios, the one with the most obvious 'chamber' atmosphere is that of K542; the mellifluous nature of its opening piano theme and the unusually detailed and intricate shades of dynamics marked in the score, including the marking of 'dolce' to the second theme, both provide chamber-like intimacy. K502, on the other hand, opens with a piano solo suggestive of an intrepid piano concerto soloist; such commanding piano writing (contrasted with 'tutti' strings in dialogue with it) shapes the entire movement. K548's unison opening of bold ascending arpeggios in dotted rhythms initially evokes the more cohesive world of the string quartet, before shifting in similar fashion into more concerto-like textures.

Much of the restrained K542 is shaped by gentle interruptions from the cello part. When the strings enter after the piano's twelve-bar theme, they repeat it, but the cello interpolates an imitation of the piano's 'sigh' motif after ten bars, through which the unit is extended; and this 'sigh' to which the cello has drawn attention will be the first material presented in the development section. Also in the exposition, the cello pre-empts the close of theme 2 with a stretto entry of this theme – in a surprise turn towards G major (bar 74).

The central Andante grazioso of K542 employs the cello in a manner that is fundamentally linked to the movement's harmonic structure, and recalls Mozart's autograph scores (for the keyboard quartets and piano concertos) in which the cello is notated on a stave beneath that of the piano. The first presentation of the movement's stately theme is in the piano alone; in the second presentation the cello and the violin surround the piano. The cello's provision of the bass-line in bar 13 in particular is a potent registral and harmonic feature of the altered theme.

There is one moment in this movement that the cello is given an authentic melody, in a repetition of a section in which the piano left hand takes a similarly infrequent melodic turn (bars 64–7). More commonly in the trios as a whole, link passages and accompaniment figures provide the cello with its most interesting contributions. Accompaniment figures are particularly effective in K502's central Larghetto, in which a sustained e♭′ in the alto range contributes to the special atmosphere of the middle section, one that seems to occupy a different realm from the rest of the movement (bars 57–62). In contrast the cello breaks into one of the most beautiful 'tenor' melodies in all of Mozart's trios in the central Adagio cantabile of the C major K548 (bars 16–20).

This middle movement of K548 provides a weighty core to the trio as a whole: melodic, harmonic and textural invention is woven together in a particularly rich and intricate fashion. The outer Allegro movements contrast significantly with the Adagio and with each other as well. The rondo is in a lilting 6/8 metre, is playful in spite of a central minor episode, and features regular phrase structure and understated chromatic inflections. While these qualities are essentially small-scale ones, the opening Allegro polarizes two dramatic characters in its first theme and seems to want to burst out of the trio medium. Aside from the common tonality, the most striking point of comparison between the movements is their lack of the sort of intense thematic development that characterizes K502 and K542.

Thematic development in K502 and K542 can even be observed between movements. In K542, for example, there are several motivic 'types' that appear in the themes of the outer movement: descending parallel thirds in both crotchets and quavers; descending quaver runs (often phrased in pairs); a group of three quavers used as an upbeat; and a 'mordent plus turn' figure. The prominence of the 'sigh' motif of the first movement finds a relation in a slow three-note figure in the third movement that is used in the context of a plethora of different affects. Such inventiveness in characterization and subtle motivic linking highlights Mozart's remarkable ability to create unity with variety and vice versa.

A close examination of motivic development also illuminates similarities between works: K542's 'turn plus mordent' figure plays a prominent role in both outer movements of K502. The final Allegretto rondo of this trio provides such a profusion of thematic evolution and overlap that tracing 'origins' of note groups to particular themes yields a dazzlingly complicated picture. The listener is also dazzled, initially by the discontinuities of the movement (strikingly open-ended phrases, abrupt shifts in register and disruption to bar structure) and then by the plethora of thematic references in the magnificent synthesis of the collage-like coda.

3. TRIO IN E FLAT MAJOR ('KEGELSTATT' TRIO), FOR PIANO, CLARINET AND VIOLA, K498

K502, 542 and 548 were written shortly after Mozart had composed what is arguably the most beautiful of all his trios; indeed, it is tempting to think of the 'Kegelstatt' ('Skittle-Alley') of August 1786 as a catalyst for Mozart's further trio explorations. It may indeed have been so, but Konrad Küster points out that the ensemble has a different heritage from that of the traditional violin and cello combination. Neither viola nor clarinet functions in the bass register: clarinet and viola are associated less with accompaniment than with melody, although neither instrument at this stage had a tradition of duo sonatas with keyboard. A trio of two melody instruments plus keyboard finds its nearest relative in the 'enriched' trio sonata of the Baroque.

Mozart's two melody instruments were probably selected for a circle of people meeting at the weekly musical gatherings of his friend Professor Nikolaus von JACQUIN. Anton STADLER, a friend of both Mozart and Jacquin, very likely played clarinet and Mozart may well have played the viola on this occasion, with Jacquin's daughter Franziska, a favourite piano pupil of Mozart, on the piano. The unusual instrumental combination was played down in Artaria's 1788 publication of the work for keyboard, viola and violin (*or* clarinet), pointing perhaps towards a conservative attitude on the part of the trio-buying public.

There is no evidence that Mozart actually wrote the piece *while* playing skittles (as he himself claimed for the horn duos K487), in spite of its nickname. The precise origin of the name remains obscure, but it reminds us that Mozart was advised by his doctor to take some exercise in the summer of 1786; and, as we know, he was fond of both billiards and skittles.

The opening Andante, with its notably fluid, conversational style, appears to evoke the informality of Jacquin's soirées and the cordial relationships between Stadler, Franziska and Mozart. The first theme, for example, comprises short rhetorical 'question–answer' phrases between viola and piano, separated by rests, followed by a more extended melodic passage on clarinet, which is then echoed by the piano. The second theme, introduced on the clarinet, draws on the opening figure of the first theme in its third phrase: boundaries between the two are thus broken down. When the first theme returns in the tonic in the recapitulation, the opening 'question' phrase is passed between the piano's two hands and then to viola and clarinet in stretto. The rests before the 'answer' are thus filled in by the harmoniously concurring voices, to the extent that the 'question–answer' construct has now been dissolved.

K498/i is the only first movement among Mozart's trios that is an Andante. The middle movement is equally unusual: it is a minuet and trio. Rather than consisting of simple binary units, moreover, both minuet and trio are expansive sections. The minuet's repeated units are of 12 bars and 29 bars; the trio falls into 23-bar and 32-bar repeated sections, followed by an eight-bar link passage; the recapitulated minuet is slightly compressed, but followed by a 15-bar coda. In terms of texture, too, the movement breaks out of conventional moulds. The piano uses octaves in the left hand in areas of both accompaniment and melody, creating a sturdy, solid minuet that would be less conspicuous if a cello had done the equivalent doubling. This potentially lumbering effect is avoided when a contemporary fortepiano is used for performance; it also stands in stark contrast to areas of more obviously dance-like music and to the trio.

The clarinet's warmly melodious theme sweeps gentle conflicts away in the ensuing Allegretto. The two principal players in the first section of this rondo are the clarinet and piano; the viola tends only to fill out the alto range with accompaniment figures. In the first reprise, however, the viola introduces the main theme, a prominent role for which the first episode gives ample preparation. This episode is in C minor and is dominated by vigorous viola statements and later, viola triplet figuration. This writing highlights the difference between Mozart's viola and cello material: he wrote no such dramatic material for the cello. In the A flat major second episode the clarinet is back in its prominent role and many of the melodic lines resemble the main theme, but when it finally returns properly, it is elaborate and florid. The surfeit of creative ideas in the closing pages brings about a joyous conclusion to the work.

RACHEL BECKLES WILLSON

K. Küster, *Mozart: A Musical Biography*, trans. M. Whittall (Oxford, 1996)
B. Smallman, *The Piano Trio* (Oxford, 1990)

E. Piano quartets

According to Mozart's early biographer GEORG NIKOLAUS NISSEN the publisher FRANZ ANTON HOFFMEISTER commissioned three piano quartets from Mozart, but cancelled the agreement (with the composer's consent) after poor sales of K478 in G minor (16 Oct. 1785); K493 in E flat (3 June

1786) subsequently appeared with ARTARIA as Op. 13 in 1787. Initial lack of success in VIENNA, however, did not preclude a mini craze for one of the piano quartets (probably K493) elsewhere in GERMANY. Reporting the popularity of the work soon after its publication, a correspondent for the Weimar-based *Journal des Luxus und der Moden* (1788) also explained that it was a work for the musical professional rather than the fashionable amateur:

> The cry soon made itself heard: 'Mozart has written a very special Quartet and such a such a Princess or Countess possesses and plays it!' and this excited curiosity and led to the rash resolve to produce this original composition at grand and noisy concerts and to make a parade with it . . . Many another piece keeps some countenance even when indifferently performed; but this product of Mozart's can in truth hardly bear listening to when it falls into mediocre amateurish hands and is negligently played. – Now this is what happened innumerable times last winter . . . What a difference when this much-advertised work of art is performed with the highest degree of accuracy by four skilled musicians who have studied it carefully, in a quiet room when the suspension of every note cannot escape the listening ear, and in the presence of only two or three attentive people!

The critic hereby hits on one of the most important aesthetic features of Mozart's piano quartets that has influenced their reception ever since, namely that they intersect with the musical spheres of public and private. While the work in question featured at the kind of 'grand and noisy [public] concerts' at which orchestral works such as symphonies and concertos were regularly performed, it was much better served (according to this critic at least) by being played in a private, chamber-music setting of 'a quiet room' with 'only two or three' people in attendance.

Stylistically, too, K478 and K493 can be regarded as hybrids of the public and private realms of Mozart's piano concertos and string chamber music; Mozart treats K478, Alfred Einstein explains, 'as the purest and most characteristic chamber music, making just as exacting demands on the virtuosity of the pianist, however, as many a concerto of the period'. It is revealing to probe stylistic matters further. In the development section of K493/i, for example, Mozart retains the technique of piano–orchestra confrontation from corresponding sections of piano concertos such as K449/i, K466/i and K493/i, but transforms it in such a way as not to run completely counter to the cooperative spirit of late eighteenth-century chamber music. Two-bar units of transition material heard in unison in the viola and cello contrast forcefully with two-bar units of flamboyant semiquavers in the piano (bars 106–17), but confrontation is tempered by the first violin playing the transition material simultaneously with the piano semiquavers. As a result, the piano is pitted against only one segment of the string group, not the group in its entirety as in the strongest confrontations in the piano concertos. The hybrid stylistic status of K493 is equally evident elsewhere in the movement as well. On the one hand, the transition has an affinity with the corresponding sections of both the piano concertos – showcasing piano passage-work that is ever present in this section of Mozart's 1784–6 concertos – and the string quartets (featuring dialogue among participants, but not *all* the participants, as is the case in Mozart's 'Haydn' quartet first movements, as the cello is not involved); on the other hand, Mozart avoids pronounced soloistic virtuosity between the end of the secondary theme and the close of the exposition (bars 79–95), in similar fashion to the quartets but in contrast to the piano concertos.

On 30 November 1791, just a few days before Mozart's death, one critic remarked that K493, like the 'Hoffmeister' String Quartet, K499, was 'written with that fire of the imagination and that correctness, which long since won for Herr M. the reputation of one of the best composers in Germany'. Over two hundred years later few would surely deny that K478 and K493 both represent masterpieces of creative and cerebral compositional activity. SIMON P. KEEFE

A. Einstein, *Mozart: His Character, his Works* (New York, 1945)
K. Küster, *Mozart: A Musical Biography*, trans. M. Whittall (Oxford, 1996)
B. Smallman, *The Piano Quartet and Quintet: Style, Structure and Scoring* (Oxford, 1996)

F. Mixed ensembles

Mozart's mixed chamber ensembles involving winds include seven works for one wind instrument with strings (the flute quartets K285, K285a and K285b – if they are by Mozart – and K298; the Oboe Quartet, K370; the Horn Quintet, K407 and the Clarinet Quintet, K581) and two works with keyboard (the quintet K452 for piano, oboe, clarinet, horn, and bassoon as well as the trio K498 for piano, clarinet, and viola). He composed each of these for particular performers or special occasions and with the exception of the flautist, the players were accomplished professionals. Mozart was also responding to a local trend. In the context of late eighteenth-century VIENNA mixed quartets and quintets were popular and fashionable (over 400 are listed in the publisher JOHANN TRAEG's 1799 catalogue alone) as were accompanied keyboard genres. Both types of ensembles, as well as other chamber-music genres, were in demand for the private musical gatherings and salons so important to Viennese musical life. At the same time, the proliferation of mixed wind/string quartets and quintets paralleled the establishment during the 1770s and 1780s of the string quartet as the predominant chamber-music genre and the most widely published composers of the mixed quartet/quintet repertory were those who actively composed string quartets and quintets: PLEYEL, HOFFMEISTER, WRANITZKY, Krommer and GYROWETZ. The majority of mixed works were for flute, an instrument popular with the dilettantes (the hundreds of operas and ballets arranged for flute quartet further attest to this ensemble's vogue). But unlike Mozart's works, those of his contemporaries catered principally to amateur consumers of music; they were galant in style, easy in both execution and comprehension. Piano trios were the most widely cultivated accompanied keyboard genre in the late eighteenth century; the repertory of quartets and quintets was considerably smaller. While the majority of the ensembles were for piano and strings, publishers' catalogues also included a selection of various scorings involving winds. The only mixed piano/wind/string ensemble to appear with regularity was the piano trio with flute as an alternative to the customary violin. As far as we know, the scorings of Mozart's K452 and K498 were unprecedented and unique.

The quality of being 'mixed' affected the reception of the mixed instrumentation chamber works. The pre-eminence of the string quartet and the valuation of its ideal attributes, including equality of partnership among the four instruments, pureness of sound, and homogeneity of timbre, had a powerful effect on closely related genres. Thus mixed quartets and quintets were often seen as weak alternatives to string quartets and the mixed instrumentation understood to create an undesirable timbral imbalance at odds with string quartet values. According to one nineteenth-century critic from the *Allgemeine musikalische Zeitung* (16 May 1810): 'The effect of quartet music is based in part on the beautiful unison of four instruments . . . On account of the diversity of timbres, a combination of wind instruments never gives as beautiful and pure a result as four string instruments, with which sustained notes flow together in a single harmonious sound.' Chamber music with keyboard was also held to a different standard since in the late eighteenth century it was composed primarily for amateurs (Liebhaber), whereas string quartets were intended increasingly for connoisseurs (Kenner).

Mozart's mixed works, as well as those of the Viennese repertory generally, exhibit a range of styles, textures and approaches to instrumental balance. They are also 'mixed' with respect to genre, incorporating a blend of features from other types of works; an evaluation of Mozart's wind/string works, for example, invites comparison with his STRING QUARTETS and STRING QUINTETS and with the wind CONCERTOS. Compared to his string works, the mixed works have shorter cyclic structures of three or two movements (except for K581), and are simpler in texture and style. While solo versus tutti textures and other concerto-style gestures, as well as an occasional highlighting of the wind instruments, demonstrate concerto influence, the overall hierarchical arrangement of instruments resembles the string chamber works more than the concertos. Structurally, the piano/wind works are similar to the piano quartets and trios; stylistically they are influenced to differing degrees by public-style piano concertos and private-style chamber pieces.

The flute quartets K285 and K285a probably stem from a commission for 'three little, easy, and short concerti and a pair of quartets for the flute' Mozart received while in MANNHEIM (1777–8) from the amateur flautist FERDINAND DEJEAN. Current opinion is that K285b may be inauthentic and date from 1781 while Mozart most likely composed K298 in 1786–7 privately for the JACQUIN FAMILY. All four flute quartets are galant in style. The flute part dominates K285 in a way that the first violin does not in Mozart's string quartets, an indication that he already viewed the two quartet types differently. Though written to an amateur's specifications the parts are not especially easy. Concerto style influences the other movements, a pizzicato-accompanied aria for flute, and an ebullient rondo. The remaining three quartets are short, easy and appropriate for amateurs of modest ability. K285a and K285b are each in two movements. The light style and use of popular contemporary tunes in each movement of K298 has prompted some scholars to suggest that Mozart intended it as a light-hearted parody of the Parisian *quatuors d'airs variés* cultivated by his contemporaries. The movement types are also simple in style: a moderate-tempo variations movement, a short minuet and trio, and a monothematic rondo with the jocular heading *Rondieaoux.*

Allegretto grazioso, mà non troppo presto, non troppo adagio. Così-così-con molto garbo ed esspressione.

Mozart wrote the Oboe Quartet, K370, in 1781, while in MUNICH, for FRIEDRICH RAMM, principal oboist in the orchestra of the Elector of Bavaria. Mozart provided Ramm with ample opportunity to display his talent in this quartet while at the same time integrating the parts: the result is equality-minded chamber music rather than miniature concerto. While not as texturally dense as many string quartet movements, the principles of thematic distribution are similar. For example, in the opening of the first movement the oboe is the leader rather than the soloist and while it carries the tune, the violin and viola contribute material with rhythmic and contrapuntal interest. The final two movements draw generically upon the concerto. The Adagio treats the oboe throughout like a vocal soloist: the string opening evokes an aria ritornello while the oboe's *messa di voce* entrance, virtuosic flourishes, wide leaps and cadenza recall soloistic gestures of the sorts found in opera arias. The light-hearted rondo almost exclusively treats the oboe as soloist and includes an impressive polymetric section with the virtuosic oboe part in 4/4 and the strings in 6/8 time.

Of the mixed works with one wind, K407 has the greatest kinship with the concerto. Mozart's friend IGNAZ LEUTGEB, principal horn in the Archbishop of Salzburg's court orchestra, was the likely recipient of the quintet as well as the four concertos K412, K417, K447 and K495, all of them composed during the 1780s. Thus it is not surprising that the quintet shares a stylistic language with the concertos and that the horn plays a soloistic role, especially in the first movement. In contrast to the equality-minded texture at the outset of K370, K407 heightens the effect of the horn's lyrical entrance by preceding it with tutti fanfares in the strings, a gesture evocative of a concerto's preparation for the soloist's entrance. However, the horn does not act exclusively as soloist but also acts as concertante partner with the violin in the first movement, sharing responsibility for conducting the musical argument. While the slow movements of K285, K370 and K581 feature the wind as concerto-type soloist, the intimate chamber writing and frequently changing instrumental groupings of K407's middle movement promote balance within the ensemble and downplay soloistic display.

Mozart wrote the Clarinet Quintet, K581, for ANTON STADLER, who premiered the work on 22 December 1789. The original version (now lost) was for Stadler's special 'Bassettklarinette', an instrument with a downward extension of four semitones. Among Mozart's mixed works K581 is the only one in four movements; it is also the only one to replace the usual rondo finale with a theme and variations movement. A significant departure from other works is its synthesis of concertante and equality-minded chamber styles. As with his string quintets, there is antiphonal writing between various groupings of instruments and with the exception of the concerto-like slow second movement (written in the same vein as the slow movement of the Clarinet Concerto, K622), the clarinet does not predominate; each instrument receives concertante treatment. An interesting and subtle feature is the way in which the opposition of wind to strings is a topic of the work. For example, the opening foregrounds the inclusion of a heterogeneous element into the homogeneous string quartet ensemble: the idiomatic four-part textured string passage accentuates the timbral homogeneity of that group while the clarinet's soloistic and ornamental flourishes following the complete phrases of the tune accentuate its outsider status. The clarinet continues its distance from the strings; the full ensemble does not play together until bar 36. In the course of the movement the ensemble integrates the clarinet into the texture and the group so that in the recapitulation all five parts play the opening theme.

Mozart entered the Quintet for Piano and Winds, K452, in his thematic catalogue on 30 March 1784; it was first performed, with the composer at the piano, on 1 April 1784 at a benefit concert in the Burgtheater, together with the piano concertos K450 and K451. In a letter of 10 April Mozart reported to his father: 'I composed two grand concertos and then a quintet, which received enthusiastic applause. I myself consider it to be the best work I have ever written.' The four dissimilar wind timbres pitted against the piano in this extraordinary work must have posed Mozart with a compositional challenge. He contended with the instrumental balance by constructing themes easily divisible into small motifs and by changing textural groupings every few bars for a kaleidoscopic array of tone colours. The quintet shares with the contemporaneous piano concertos the integral feature of dialogue and close interplay between the winds and piano. Yet, while it was written in the spirit of the piano concertos and the piano part is occasionally virtuosic, the piano does not predominate; each of the wind instruments receives concertante and idiomatic treatment. An explicit reference to concerto style is the final movement's 'cadenza in tempo' for all five parts that yet remains within the bounds of chamber style.

While the other late piano trios exhibit the influence of concerto style, the Trio for Piano, Clarinet and Viola, K498, completed in August 1786 (and discussed in detail in CHAMBER MUSIC: PIANO TRIOS), remains within the sphere of chamber music. Its relaxed pace, close interplay between parts, and the absence of virtuosic display reflect the intimate domestic setting for which it was probably written: the Jacquin family musical circle. According to Karoline von Pichler, Mozart composed the piano part for his pupil, Franziska von Jacquin; the first performance may have included Mozart on viola and Anton Stadler on clarinet. Its unique instrumentation may have determined its unique scoring and form. It is the only work to modify the fast–slow–fast cyclic structure with two outer movements of moderate tempo and an interior minuet, the only minuet in Mozart's trios. With one member each of the strings, winds and keyboard families – three contrasting timbres – none stands out as potential soloist; each instrument is treated as a melody instrument, leading to complete independence of the three parts. The distribution of thematic material is most equitable in the rondo finale, which devotes each return of the theme after the first and each episode to a different instrument. SARAH ADAMS

S. Adams, 'Quartets and Quintets for Mixed Groups of Winds and Strings: Mozart and his Contemporaries in Vienna, c.1780–c.1800' (Ph.D. thesis, Cornell University, 1994)

E. Hüppe, *W. A. Mozart: Innovation und Praxis zum Quintett es-dur KV 452* (Edition Text und Kritik, 1998)

W.-D. Seiffert, 'Schrieb Mozart drei Flötenquartette für Dejean?', *Mozart-Jahrbuch 1987/88*, 267–76

church sonatas. The church sonatas, also known as 'epistle sonatas' or 'organ sonatas' were written for the liturgy of SALZBURG Cathedral, where Mozart was appointed Konzertmeister on 9 August 1772. The autograph copies are entitled 'sonatas', and the term *Sonata all'Epistola* is found in a letter written by LEOPOLD MOZART (in Wolfgang's name) to Padre MARTINI (dated 4 Sept. 1776). They were intended for performance during Solemn Mass while the celebrant, after reading the Epistle, moved from the south side of the choir to the north, in order to read the Gospel. Formally, they comprise sonata allegro movements, all in major keys, with an abbreviated development section.

The majority of the seventeen church sonatas are scored for two violins and bass (marked 'Organo e Basso' in the original sources). The size of forces intended is not specified, but a complement of one player per part, in the manner of an Italian sonata da chiesa is a possibility; archival sources from Salzburg Cathedral suggest that two-to-a-part performance was the norm for string players. Three sonatas are scored for larger ensembles, which include oboes, horns, trumpets and timpani. The designation 'basso' for the bass part also occurs elsewhere in Mozart's oeuvre; here it probably implies violone (with cello and bassoon ad libitum). The organ usually functions as a continuo instrument, with its part either notated as a figured bass or fully written out. The later sonatas feature obbligato organ solos, which, in the case of K336, result in a concerto-like movement. Contrary to the editorial suggestion of the NEUE MOZART-AUSGABE, the source for this sonata implies a performance with one organ (rather than two), which alternates between soloistic and continuo roles.

The continuo function of the organ, together with the chamber-like scoring of many of these sonatas, indicates that they were intended for performance on one of the smaller cathedral organs. This is corroborated by Leopold Mozart's account of church music in Salzburg for Marpurg's *Historisch-critische Beyträge zur Aufnahme der Musik* of 1757, which details the size and disposition of instrumental forces in the cathedral. In addition to the main organ, used exclusively for solo preludes, there were smaller organs in each of four galleries at the cathedral crossing, together with one at ground level, which accompanied the choir.

The only indication for registration given in the sources of these sonatas is the marking 'Copel allein' in the autograph of K244 and 245; this refers to a stopped flute register of 8-foot pitch, fuller-toned than its modern equivalent. The pedals are used sparingly, in order to sustain bass notes, and only required in K245, 274, 328 and 329.

Mozart's church sonatas, composed between 1772 and 1780, were the only such works written in Salzburg after about 1760 and suggest that he had a keener interest in instrumental music than in the vocal music expected of a musician employed as Konzertmeister to the Archbishop of Salzburg.

MICHAEL QUINN

T. Harmon, 'The Performance of Mozart's Church Sonatas', *Music & Letters* 51 (1970), 51–60
R. S. Tangeman, 'Mozart's Seventeen Epistle Sonatas', *Musical Quarterly* 32 (1946), 588–601

Clementi, Muzio (b. Rome, 23 Jan. 1752; d. Evesham, Worcestershire, 10 Mar. 1832). Keyboard player and composer. Although Italian born, Clementi was chiefly based in England from 1766, when he was brought there by Peter Beckford. He had a highly successful career as a pianist and composer, as a teacher (his most important pupils were J. B. Cramer and John Field) and as a publisher. Clementi undertook several continental tours, including one to VIENNA in 1781, where on 24 December he played a piano duel with Mozart that was arranged by JOSEPH II; the contest included improvisation, sight-reading and performances of their own works. Clementi later wrote of Mozart: 'I had never before heard anyone play with such spirit and grace.' Mozart, however, was less generous, writing to his father: 'He is an excellent keyboard player, but that is all. He has great facility with his right hand. His star passages are thirds. Apart from this, he has not a kreutzer's worth of taste or feeling; he is a mere *mechanicus*' (12 Jan. 1782). The next year he wrote of Clementi's sonatas: 'anyone playing or hearing them will realize that they are worthless compositions' (7 June 1783). It seems likely, given Mozart's continuing need to justify himself and to demean Clementi, that the Italian pianist was a more challenging opponent than he had anticipated and that the contest may have been a draw. CLIFF EISEN

K. Komlós, 'Mozart and Clementi: A Piano Competition and its Interpretation', *Historical Performance* 2 (1989), 3–9
L. Plantinga, *Clementi: His Life and Music* (London, 1977)
A. Tyson, 'Clementi as an Imitator of Haydn and Mozart', *Haydn Yearbook* 2 (1963/4), 90–2

clemenza di Tito, La, K621 (The Clemency of Titus). Serious opera in two acts on a libretto by PIETRO METASTASIO adapted by CATERINO MAZZOLÀ; first performed PRAGUE, 6 September 1791.

1. Genesis
2. Text and music
3. Reception

1. Genesis

On 8 July 1791, less than two months before the premiere, DOMENICO GUARDASONI, impresario of the Italian opera in Prague, signed a contract with representatives of the Estates of Bohemia (essentially the nobility and clergy) in which he agreed to present a new opera seria to celebrate the forthcoming coronation of LEOPOLD II as King of Bohemia. He promised to engage, in addition to a *musico* and a prima donna of the highest quality, 'a distinguished composer' who was to set to music one of three librettos. The only one of these librettos identified in the contract was the one chosen: *La clemenza di Tito*.

Guardasoni's contract refers repeatedly to his intention of going to Italy to engage singers. If he did so, he probably stopped on his way in VIENNA, where he asked ANTONIO SALIERI, imperial-royal court music director, to compose the coronation opera. When Salieri, occupied with the responsibilities of running the court opera and perhaps also lacking confidence in his ability to satisfy the Italianate tastes of the imperial couple, turned down the commission, Guardasoni went to Mozart, who accepted it.

In 1959 the Czech musicologist Tomislav Volek suggested that Mozart began composing *Tito* before he received the commission, and that the opera was consequently not the product of haste that earlier scholars and critics had found easy to dismiss. Although Volek's thesis contributed to a remarkable revival of interest in the opera on the part of both scholars and performers, the preponderance of evidence now supports the view (argued persuasively by Sergio Durante) that Mozart did not begin composition until after accepting the commission, probably around the middle of July 1791. Caterino Mazzolà, house poet to the court theatre in Dresden, served briefly in the same capacity in Vienna during 1791. Guardasoni or Mozart turned to him for the task of bringing Metastasio's fifty-seven-year-old libretto up to date.

Mazzolà's revision was extensive. He reshaped Metastasio's three-act libretto into two acts. He cut much dialogue, replacing some of it with orchestrally accompanied ensembles. He omitted several arias, replacing some of them with new aria texts. His most remarkable innovation, the finale with offstage chorus that ends Act 1, was crafted out of fragments of Metastasio's dialogue and arias. Mozart must have approved of Mazzolà's work. When he entered *Tito* into the catalogue of his works he noted that the libretto had been 'reworked into a true opera'.

For most of the cast Guardasoni called on members of his own troupe in Prague. In addition to the tenor Antonio Baglioni (Tito) he engaged Carolina Perini (Annio), Gaetano Campi (Publio), and Antonia Miklaszewicz (better known under her married name Campi; Servilia). For the prima donna role of Vitellia he engaged Maria Marchetti Fantozzi, a singer of leading roles in some of Italy's biggest theatres, and for the role of Sesto, Domenico Bedini, a distinguished and experienced *musico*.

Pressed for time, Mozart probably departed from his normal practice of waiting until he knew the vocal qualities or even the identity of some of these singers before beginning to compose their music. Some sketches of Sesto's music show that Mozart, at this early stage in the compositional process, believed that Sesto would be portrayed by a tenor. Perhaps he thought that Baglioni, whom he knew from having written the role of Don Ottavio for him in DON GIOVANNI, would sing Sesto, and that the *musico* required by Guardasoni's contract would take the role of Tito. Mozart may also have written some of Vitellia's music before he knew Marchetti Fantozzi's voice. The trio 'Vengo . . . aspettate . . . Sesto' and the fast section of the rondò 'Non più di fiori' do not match the vocal profile of Marchetti Fantozzi that emerges from music written for her by other composers in the 1780s.

Mozart and his wife arrived in Prague on 28 August, accompanied by FRANZ XAVER SÜSSMAYR, the student and assistant who came to Prague probably to help with copying, proof-reading and rehearsals. The next few days must have been full of last-minute composing for Mozart, and probably also for Süssmayr. With the exception of a few bars, Mozart's autograph score contains no simple recitative. A report published shortly after the premiere in a Berlin journal claimed that 'only the arias and choruses were by his [Mozart's] hand; the recitatives were by another'. It is likely that Süssmayr was the unnamed composer of the simple recitative. Mozart's compositional labours continued to the day before the premiere: he entered the opera in his thematic catalogue under the date 5 September.

2. Text and music

Mozart's coronation opera takes place in Rome in AD 79, ten years after the famous 'year of the four emperors', when Vespasian had become emperor by defeating the upstart Vitellius, brutally killed by a mob of victorious soldiers. Now Vespasian's son Titus (Tito in the opera) is emperor. Vitellius' daughter Vitellia – goaded by a confused mixture of desire for revenge for the death of her father, political ambition and love (she says that Tito's greatest crime is that he has seduced her 'almost into loving him') – hopes to become empress as Tito's wife. But Berenice, the Judean princess whom Tito loves, blocks her way to the throne and inflames her jealousy.

The brief but brilliant overture establishes C major as the opera's framing key. Its pomp bespeaks both the grand occasion for which the opera was composed and the imperial subject matter. The drama begins with a heated conversation between Vitellia and Sesto, a young nobleman who loves her. She has exploited his passion by persuading him to lead a rebellion against Tito and to assassinate him. But now Sesto has second thoughts, and reminds Vitellia of Tito's virtue. Enraged, she absolves him of his promise and is about to leave when Sesto relents. He begins the duet 'Come ti piace, imponi' by telling Vitellia that he will do whatever she commands; she responds that he must kill Tito before sunset. In their contrasting musical statements – Sesto's sweet and lyrical, Vitellia's angular and emphatic – we hear a musical depiction of their contrasting characters that complements the verbal depiction provided by Metastasio in the preceding dialogue.

Sesto's friend Annio enters with news that Tito, yielding to his subjects' unwillingness to have a foreign princess on the throne, has broken off his relations with Berenice; she has left Rome. Vitellia sees an opportunity for herself in this news and tells Sesto to postpone the rebellion. When he protests at her manipulation of his feelings, she teases him with her charming aria 'Deh, se piacer mi vuoi', in which she expresses the combination of imperiousness and the flirtatiousness so characteristic of her powerful personality. The aria begins with two bars borrowed from an aria in Salieri's *Il talismano* (1788), 'Guida l'industre amante'.

Annio loves Sesto's sister Servilia. After Vitellia has left the stage, Annio asks Sesto to help him obtain Tito's approval of his marriage to Servilia. Sesto promises to do so, and the two men celebrate their friendship in a gently amiable duet, 'Deh prendi un dolce amplesso'. This is the first of many short numbers in *La clemenza di Tito* (mostly for characters of secondary importance), a feature that keeps the action moving forward at a satisfying pace and the audience's attention focused on the principal characters.

The imperial ambience alluded to in the overture returns with a march that begins with a fanfare for trumpets and drums. This music accompanies a change of scene (the Forum) and announces the arrival of Tito, Publio (commander of the praetorian guards), other officers of state and a great throng of people, who sing a joyful chorus, 'Serbate, o Dei custodi'. Tito expresses his virtue by refusing to allow a temple to be built in his honour; let the money be used instead, he orders, for the relief of those affected by the eruption of Vesuvius that recently destroyed Pompeii. The people and officers disperse, leaving Tito alone with Sesto and Annio. The Emperor tells Sesto that since his subjects wish him to marry a Roman, he has decided to marry Sesto's sister. Annio, stunned and heartbroken, can think of nothing to do except to praise the Emperor's choice of Servilia. When Sesto warns Tito that too much generosity will make his subjects ungrateful, he responds, in the aria 'Del più sublime soglio', that benevolence is his only source of happiness. Sesto and the audience know, however, that in blessing Sesto's family the Emperor will make Annio and Servilia miserable.

Annio, alone, is soon joined by Servilia, whom he tells of Tito's intentions. Momentarily forgetting that she is Tito's bride-to-be, he calls her his beloved. He begins the lovely duet 'Ah, perdona al primo affetto' by asking Servilia to forgive this lapse in decorum. As a woman, Servilia is less afflicted than Annio by the contradictory claims of romantic love and loyalty to the Emperor. Her love for Annio comes first. She goes immediately to Tito and tells him the truth. The Emperor welcomes her honesty and blesses the union. He declares, in the aria 'Ah se fosse intorno al trono', that he would be happy to rule if only all his subjects were as honest as Servilia.

Vitellia comes upon the overjoyed Servilia, and congratulates her sarcastically for having been chosen as Tito's bride. When Servilia, leaving, tells Vitellia that she has reason to hope that Tito will marry her, Vitellia thinks that Servilia is mocking her; her anger rises to a new level of intensity. Sesto arrives, and to him she directs all her fury. In a long harangue she breaks down his resistance. He promises again to lead a rebellion against Tito, but on the point of leaving he asks for but a loving glance from her. His exit-aria 'Parto, ma tu, ben mio', with the gorgeous clarinet solo that Mozart wrote for his friend ANTON STADLER, builds in energy and excitement as it accelerates in tempo from Adagio to Allegro to Allegro assai.

Immediately after Sesto leaves to start the uprising, Publio and Annio arrive to tell Vitellia that Tito has chosen her to be his wife and to ask her to go to him. The news puts her in a state of confusion and horror, which she expresses in 'Vengo! aspettate! Sesto!' – a trio, or, perhaps better, an aria for Vitellia in which Annio and Publio are *pertichini* or bit players. Many leaps in Vitellia's vocal line, its fragmentation into small phrases separated by rests, together with frequent, abrupt shifts in dynamics in the orchestra, all contribute to this depiction of emotional turmoil, which is enhanced by irony as Annio and Sesto express their belief that Vitellia's excitement arises from joy at her impending marriage to the Emperor.

A change of scene takes us from Vitellia's indecision to that of Sesto, whom we find standing before the Capitol. (Although this scene is sometimes depicted on stage as taking place at night, there is nothing in the opera's stage directions or dialogue to suggest this.) In an emotionally tense monologue, Sesto struggles with his conflicting desires to win Vitellia and to remain loyal to Tito. He finally decides in favour of loyalty to the Emperor; but just at that moment he sees a fire breaking out on the Capitol and hears the sound of crashing arms. He realizes, with a cry of agony, that his change of heart has come too late. Throughout this scene Sesto's plight is intensified for the audience by its knowledge that Vitellia is desperately trying to find him in order to tell him to call off the rebellion.

In the great finale of Act 1, Mazzolà presented on stage events only described in Metastasio's libretto, giving wonderful opportunities for theatrical display not only to Mozart but to the scenic designer Pietro Travaglia (whose design for this scene was recently identified by Durante) and to the technical crew of the National Theatre in Prague. The fire that consumes the Capitol may have reminded the audience in Prague of another fire first staged in the same theatre: the one into which the hero fell at the end of *Don Giovanni*. (Leopold and his court had attended a revival of *Don Giovanni* just four days before the premiere of *Tito*.)

The finale begins with Sesto praying to the gods to save Tito. Annio enters, followed by Servilia; at about the same time Sesto disappears into the fray. Excitement increases as the music moves from E flat major to C minor, whose arrival is accompanied by string tremolos and the sound of trumpets and drums. The people of Rome, in the form of an offstage chorus, express their horror by crying out 'Ah!' on a diminished seventh chord. Tonal instability, syncopations and abrupt shifts of dynamics all help to convey an atmosphere of menace and violence.

Sesto returns, announcing that Tito has been killed. Servilia, Annio and Publio ask who committed this crime; Sesto is about to confess his responsibility when Vitellia interrupts him and tells him to keep quiet. The finale ends with a mournful ensemble – almost a funeral march – for soloists and chorus, 'Oh nero tradimento'. To end an act with a slow movement was rare in eighteenth-century opera; in doing so Mozart earned the disapproval of Salieri, whose student Anselm Hüttenbrenner remembered his teacher arguing 'that Mozart completely mishandled the final scene of the first act of Titus. Rome is burning; the whole populace is in tumult; the music should also storm and rage. But Mozart chose a slow, solemn tempo and expressed more horror and shock. I did not allow myself to be led into error by Salieri, and agree even today with Mozart's view.'

At the beginning of Act 2 Annio tells Sesto that the rebellion has been suppressed and that Tito has survived unharmed. Sesto, happy and relieved at the news, admits his guilt and tells of his intention to flee Rome. Annio urges him to stay, to confess everything to Tito and to trust in his clemency. His aria 'Torna di Tito al lato' expresses the tenderness of his feelings for both Sesto and the Emperor.

After Annio leaves, Vitellia enters; she tells him to take just the opposite course, to flee. She still hopes for the crown, and she is afraid that Sesto, if he stays in Rome, will ruin her chances by confessing everything to the Emperor, including her part in the plot. They are interrupted by Publio, who takes away Sesto's need to make a decision by arresting him and informing him that the man whom Sesto stabbed was not Tito but the conspirator Lentulo dressed as Tito. Having survived the wound, Lentulo has implicated Sesto in the rebellion.

The trio 'Se al volto mai ti senti' conveys beautifully the evolving feelings of Sesto, Vitellia and Publio. Like so many of his melodies, the tune with which Sesto bids Vitellia farewell is gentle and sweet. (It is preceded by an instrumental introduction for solo winds, depicting the breeze to which Sesto refers in his opening words.) Vitellia, in contrast, is accompanied by more active rhythms and tonal instability – a violent turn to the minor – and several sudden drops into her low register. Publio repeats the command 'Vieni' with stony indifference to Sesto's plaintiveness and Vitellia's confusion. The tempo shifts from Andantino to Allegretto and Sesto addresses Vitellia with a sentimental tune, 'Rammenta chi t'adora' that causes even Publio to feel pity for his prisoner.

In an audience chamber in the imperial palace, patricians, praetorian guards and citizens of Rome thank the gods for Tito's survival in the chorus 'Ah grazie si rendano'. Awaiting the Senate's investigation of Sesto's role in the rebellion, the Emperor expresses confidence that his friend will be found innocent. Publio warns him that Lentulo's testimony is damning. In his only aria, 'Tardi s'avvede', the commander of the praetorian guards reflects on the inability of the virtuous to see treachery in others; but Tito's faith in Sesto is unshaken.

Annio enters, followed by Publio, who hands Tito a document. In response to Sesto's confession the Senate has sentenced him, along with the other conspirators, to be thrown to the wild beasts in the arena. Annio pleads for mercy for his friend in the aria 'Tu fosti tradito', and he and Publio leave Tito alone to express his horror and disappointment. His orchestrally accompanied recitative begins with an instrumental cry of pain: a repeated, syncopated diminished seventh chord in the orchestra's highest register. Tito is about to sign the death sentence when he changes his mind, deciding he must give Sesto a chance to explain his actions. As he waits for Sesto to appear, his anger dissipated, he meditates on the unhappy fate of rulers, without the peace of mind that even a simple peasant, in his rustic cottage, enjoys.

Publio returns, followed shortly by Sesto. Tito and Sesto look into each other's faces – Tito's is angry, Sesto's shameful – and begin the trio 'Quello di Tito è il volto' by expressing surprise at how recent events have transformed them. Publio perceives not only anger in Tito's face but also the emotional conflict stemming from the fact that he still loves Sesto, an idea that Mozart conveys with a strikingly beautiful cadence (at 'lo seguita ad amar'). The change of tempo from Larghetto to Allegro accompanies a change of focus from Tito to Sesto, who sings a melody ('Non può chi more') whose frequent rests suggest that he is gasping for breath. Publio and Tito, linked together in a canon, comment on the prisoner's distracted state.

Left alone with Sesto, Tito asks his friend if he has really betrayed him. Sesto, kneeling, admits his guilt once again and begs for death as the only suitable punishment for his crime and the only thing that will end his suffering. Moved by Sesto's anguish, Tito pleads for some explanation of Sesto's actions; if he understood Sesto's motivation, he might be able to help find a way to justify a pardon. Sesto cannot tell Tito the truth without betraying Vitellia. He becomes increasingly desperate, and Tito finally reaches the end of his patience. Sesto will die, if that is what he wants. He calls the guards to take away Sesto, who begs to be allowed to kiss Tito's hand for the last time and launches into the touching strains of his rondò 'Deh per questo istante solo'.

Tito, alone, returns to the death sentence that awaits his signature. His anger brings him almost to the point of signing it; but again he hesitates, struggling between the claims of friendship, which urge him to pardon Sesto, and responsible government, which encourage him to follow the recommendation of the

Senate in approving the execution of a man clearly guilty of trying to overthrow the government. He signs; but then he tears up the death sentence. Clemency has triumphed. But this is a secret that Tito shares with the audience only. When Publio enters, asking the Emperor if Sesto's fate has been decided, Tito says yes, leading Publio to conclude that the Emperor has approved Sesto's execution. For the next several scenes all the characters in the drama except Tito act in the belief that Sesto is about to die.

Tito celebrates his decision to pardon his friend in 'Se all'impero, amici dei', his last and greatest aria. Like all of Tito's aria texts, this one is by Metastasio; and the music too partakes of venerable traditions. The opening melody has the shape – three phrases, the first phrase a setting of the first line of text, the second and third phrases settings of the second line of text – that composers of opera seria had exploited since the 1730s. The large-scale form also looks to the past: it has the symmetrical shape characteristic of the da capo aria, but a tonal plan characteristic of sonata form. The opening A section, an exposition, modulates to the dominant; the 'second theme' is a brilliant display of coloratura. The B section, a development, evokes the darker and more serious side of Tito's personality with a slow tempo and a turn to the minor mode. The A′ section, a recapitulation, differs from the first A section in staying in the tonic.

Tito goes off to the arena. Publio follows, but not before telling Vitellia of Sesto's fate. She believes Sesto has given away her role in the conspiracy. But when Annio and Servilia tell her that Tito still plans to marry her, she realizes that Sesto has remained silent. Moved by his love and fidelity, she decides immediately to follow Annio and Servilia to the amphitheatre. But when, overcome by tears, she hesitates, Servilia tells her that tears alone will not help Sesto. 'S'altro che lacrime', Servilia's only aria, is a beautifully crafted little piece whose repeated crescendos in the orchestra convey the same sweetly prayerful tone as the *Ave verum corpus* (in the same key of D major) that Mozart wrote a few months earlier.

After Tito and Sesto have faced so many moral dilemmas and expressed so much indecision, it is only fair that Vitellia, finally, is forced to face herself and to open her heart. The orchestral motif that introduces her monologue reminds us of the motif that dominates Sesto's monologue near the end of Act 1: both are three bars in length, with the harmonic plan tonic–dominant–tonic. Both begin with a *forte* unison and continue with a rest, a sudden shift to *piano*, a trill, and a bar of staccato notes, and a tonic chord on the following downbeat. The musical parallel seems to suggest that Vitellia is finally going through the kind of torment she imposed on Sesto and, through him, on Tito.

Looking inward, Vitellia realizes that she must confess her part in the plot and, in so doing, give up her chance to become empress. In her rondò 'Non più di fiori' she continues to remind us of Sesto's earlier experiences. As a rondò, of course, it represents a response to Sesto's rondò. If 'Deh per questo istante solo' depicted Sesto at his most tragic and pitiful impasse, 'Non più di fiori' shows that Vitellia could fall even lower. Her melodies are even more moving; the modulations through which Mozart leads her are even more dramatic. The clarinet solo in Sesto's 'Parto, ma tu ben mio', finds an echo here in the basset horn solo. In 'Parto' Sesto bids farewell to Vitellia; in 'Deh per questo istante solo' he bids farewell to Tito. Here Vitellia says 'addio' not only to her dreams of power and marriage, but to life itself.

The orchestral drive to the final cadence is interrupted by a transition whose dotted rhythms and trumpets and drums – unheard since the finale of Act I – announce a change of scene. The arena has been referred to several times in previous scenes. Shortly after the chorus 'Ah grazie si rendano', much earlier in the act, Publio says to Tito: 'The hour of the public games has arrived . . . All the people have assembled in the festive arena, and they wait for nothing but your presence. Everyone longs, after the danger known to all, to see you safe. Do not delay your Rome's enjoyment of such happiness.' The very considerable delay that follows (including arias sung by all six characters) intensifies the dramatic effect of the audience's first glimpse of the amphitheatre and its unnaturally patient crowd.

The people praise Tito and celebrate his escape from danger in the chorus 'Che del ciel, che degli dei', whose old-fashioned sequences and suspensions give it something of an ecclesiastical quality. The majestic dotted notes in the orchestra and the off-beat entry of the chorus remind us in particular of 'Rex tremendae majestatis' in the REQUIEM (in G minor, the parallel minor of this chorus's G major). Since the people sing of Tito's resemblance to the gods, it makes sense that the music should call to mind music written in praise of the king of heaven.

To Annio and Servilia, who ask for mercy, Tito says, a little teasingly: 'If you come to ask it for Sesto, it is too late. His fate has already been decided.' He addresses Sesto, listing his crimes, and is about to pardon him when Vitellia rushes in. To the astonishment of all she confesses her guilt. Tito expresses indignation and frustration in his third and final monologue, but his anger quickly yields to generosity and forgiveness. He orders the conspirators to be freed. Although he does not mention Vitellia, we have to assume that he forgives her too. Mazzolà left out an amusing exchange between Tito and Vitellia in Metastasio's original libretto:

Tito: Vitellia, I promised you my hand in marriage, but . . .
Vit: I understand, Caesar: it is no longer mine. After such an error, the match would be unthinkable.
Tito: I want you to be at least partly happy. You will not see a rival on the throne: that I promise you. I want no other wife than Rome.

With the final ensemble and chorus, 'Tu, è ver, m'assolvi, Augusto', Mozart returned to C major, the key of the overture. The ensemble gradually builds in strength. Solos for Sesto and Tito are followed by a trio for Vitellia, Servilia and Annio, and finally the chorus, accompanied by trumpets and drums, enters to pray to the gods to protect Tito.

3. Reception

COUNT JOHANN KARL ZINZENDORF, a Viennese bureaucrat and tireless theatregoer, left us in his diary a reference to the first performance of *La clemenza di Tito*: 'At 5 o'clock to the theatre in the Old Town, the spectacle that the Estates are presenting. I was put in a box in the first tier . . . The court did not arrive until half past seven. We were presented with the most boring spectacle, *La clemenza di Tito* . . . Marchetti sings very well; the emperor is enthusiastic about her. It was extremely difficult to get out of the theatre.'

That Zinzendorf found *Tito* boring does not mean that the entire audience did. He seems have been uninterested in opera seria in general and equally unresponsive to the serious operas that Leopold II presented a few months later in Vienna. But it is true that Zinzendorf was not the only member of the coronation-day audience disappointed by *Tito*. Empress Maria Luisa also found Mozart's opera tedious. 'Porcheria tedesca' – German rubbish: this judgement of Tito has long been attributed to the Empress, but the words have been traced back no further than 1871. Confirmation of her opinion, however, survives in the form of a letter that she wrote the day after the premiere to her daughter-in-law Maria Theresa. Writing in French, the normal language of correspondance among many of the rulers of Germany, Austria, and Italy, she made her opinion of *Tito* quite clear: 'In the evening to the theatre, the grand opera is not so grand, and the music very bad, so that almost all of us went to sleep. The coronation went marvelously.'

If *Tito* failed to please part of its first audience, later audiences began to appreciate it quickly. Performances continued through September, and the opera seems to have won increasing applause. Mozart wrote to his wife on 7 October that the final performance was a great success. He reported news he had received from his friend Stadler, for whom Mozart wrote the opera's clarinet and basset horn solos:

> And the strangest thing of all is that on the very evening when my new opera [DIE ZAUBERFLÖTE] was performed for the first time with such success [30 Sept. 1791] *Tito* was given in Prague for the last time with tremendous applause. Bedini sang better than ever. The little duet in A major ['Ah perdona al primo affetto'], which the two girls [Carolina Perini as Annio and Antonia Miklaszewicz as Servilia] sing was repeated; and had not the audience wished to spare Marchetti, a repetition of the rondo ['Non più di fiori'] would have been very welcome. Cries of 'Bravo' were shouted at Stodla [Stadler] from the parterre and even from the orchestra. 'What a miracle for Bohemia,' he writes, 'but indeed I did my very best.'

Mozart's statement that 'a repetition of the [Marchetti's] rondo would have been very welcome' is of special interest in view of the lack of any kind of musical closure after 'Non più di fiori', and consequently the lack of an occasion for the audience to applaud and to cry out for an encore. One wonders if Mozart allowed the aria to come to a full stop so that Marchetti could reap the applause that her performance deserved. That would help to explain marks on the last page of the autograph score of 'Non più di fiori' that might indicate that at some point Mozart called for the aria to end before the beginning of the transition to the chorus that follows.

During the first two decades of the nineteenth century *La clemenza di Tito* was one of the most frequently and widely performed operas by Mozart, although many of these performances, in common with those of other opere serie of the time, involved the omission of numbers and the insertion of music by such composers as WEIGL and Portogallo. Audiences throughout the German-speaking part of Europe heard *Tito* often until 1820. It was the first of

Mozart's operas to be performed in London, in 1806, as a vehicle for Elizabeth Billington. W. T. Parke wrote: 'I was highly gratified with the refined science, elegant taste, and natural simplicity displayed in this fine production.' The following year a highly bowdlerized version was presented in Naples; Paris heard *Tito* in 1816; Milan and St Petersburg in 1817. Thereafter it began gradually to fall from favour, and during the second half of the nineteenth century and the first half of the twentieth it was rarely performed.

A new appreciation for *La clemenza di Tito* in the last third of the twentieth century coincided with a reappraisal of opera seria in general, which scholars, performers and opera lovers discovered to be not quite as moribund as they had read in books. Several skilful and successful productions of *Tito* (especially those of Jean-Pierre Ponnelle in the late 1960s and early 1970s and the one at Covent Garden in 1974) inspired fruitful research by musicologists, revisionist thinking by critics and many subsequent productions. In the 1980s alone *Tito* was performed over twenty times in many parts of the world. Although it will probably never be as popular as LE NOZZE DI FIGARO, *Don Giovanni* and *Die Zauberflöte*, few will now share Edward Dent's opinion, expressed half a century ago, that 'for the stage of today it can only be considered as a museum piece'. JOHN A. RICE

S. Durante, 'The Chronology of Mozart's *La clemenza di Tito* Reconsidered', *Music & Letters* 80 (1999), 560–94
J. A. Rice, *W. A. Mozart. La clemenza di Tito* (Cambridge, 1991)
'Mozart and His Singers: The Case of Maria Marchetti Fantozzi, the First Vitellia', *Opera Quarterly* 11 (1995), 31–52
E. Senici, *La clemenza di Tito di Mozart: I primi trent'anni (1791–1821)* (Turnhout, 1997)

Closset, Thomas Franz (1754–1813). Physician. A well-regarded doctor who set up his own practice in 1787, Closset included among his patients PRINCE WENZEL ANTON KAUNTIZ, Count Johann Philipp Cobenzl and Mozart; he attended on the composer during his final illness, in consultation with MATHIAS VON SALLABA. According to Mozart's sister-in-law, SOPHIE HAIBEL, Closset, on the night Mozart died, would not immediately leave the theatre to attend on his patient and when he did arrive, 'he ordered cold compresses to be put on his burning head. These affected him so greatly that he lost consciousness, and he remained unconscious until he died' (letter of 7 Apr. 1825). CLIFF EISEN

A. J. Werner, 'Seine Ärzte, seine Krankheiten, sein Tod', in *Wolfgang Amadeus: Summa summarum*, ed. P. Csobádi (Vienna, 1990), 101–18

Colloredo, Hieronymus Joseph Franz de Paula von (b. Vienna, 31 May 1732; d. Vienna, 20 May 1812). Prince-Archbishop of SALZBURG from 1772 to 1803. Son of the Reichsvizekanzler in VIENNA, Colloredo was educated in Vienna and Rome, became a Salzburg canon in 1747, and Prince-Archbishop of Salzburg on 14 March 1772. This election was bitterly controversial – Salzburg's political position was sensitive, and both AUSTRIA and Bavaria had favourite candidates. Colloredo was Austria's choice; Bavaria's was Ferdinand Christoph von Waldburg-Zeil, the popular Dean of Salzburg.

Colloredo inherited huge debts from his predecessor SCHRATTENBACH, and immediately tried to reduce them. He also began to implement his ENLIGHTENMENT reforms, a task of bewildering enormity, since

Schrattenbach had been ultra-conservative. Colloredo had to establish like-minded people in each institution – ecclesiastical, educational, legal, medical, fiscal, administrative and publicistic – and persuade the reluctant populace to change its entire mentality. Colloredo ruled Salzburg for thirty years and was ultimately successful in his main aims, but the struggle was a perpetual one. He was hampered by shortage of funds and his inability to be popular, as he was both sarcastic and misanthropic – a typical view was represented by the slogan 'Enlightenment and love of mankind on paper'.

Colloredo was no puppet of Vienna's. He drew on Enlightenment models from Protestant Germany, Rhineland-Franconia, Italy, the Austrian Netherlands, Swabia, and Bavaria as well as Austria. Recognizing and defending Salzburg's historical position as a Catholic state, he pursued his reforms within the broad structures of the Church, attracting European-wide admiration for his efforts.

Colloredo's pastoral letter of 1782 shunned outward pomp, espousing simplicity and tolerance of other creeds. Pilgrimages and superstitious practices were banned, processions were restricted, church decoration was limited, musical settings of the Mass were shortened, and sacred German hymns introduced. Purely instrumental music was discouraged in church. These changes led to deep resentment, and Colloredo and the architect of the pastoral letter, Johann Michael Bönike, were called 'secret Lutherans'.

In 1775 Colloredo opened a public theatre, and in 1778 the university theatre was closed, depriving Salzburg musicians of an important outlet for musical performance. The church music reforms represented another restriction, and Colloredo's strict financial policies also limited musical opportunities at court.

Mozart was given his first Salzburg salary under Colloredo. Nevertheless, the Mozarts strongly disliked him. Travel leave was difficult to obtain, and they complained that extra presents of money for compositions were stingy, and that Colloredo was scathing about Mozart's abilities. After Mozart's second resignation in 1781, Leopold continued to bemoan the failure to replace musicians who had left or died, and the consequent shambles in the court music. Colloredo was himself a music lover as well as an intellectual, and sometimes played the violin in the court orchestra, but he had larger concerns.

In 1800 Colloredo had to flee Salzburg, because of the turbulent political situation in Europe. He resigned as head of state in 1803 and Salzburg was secularized.

RUTH HALLIWELL

H. Dopsch and H. Spatzenegger, eds., *Geschichte Salzburgs: Stadt und Land* (Salzburg, 1988)

C. Eisen, 'Salzburg under Church Rule', in *The Classical Era. From the 1740s to the End of the 18th Century*, ed. N. Zaslaw (London, 1989), 166–87

'Mozart and Salzburg', in *The Cambridge Companion to Mozart*, ed. S. P. Keefe (Cambridge, 2003), 7–21

F. Martin, *Salzburgs Fürsten in der Barockzeit* (Salzburg, 1982)

Coltellini family (1) Marco (b. Livorno, 13 Oct. 1719; d. St Petersburg, Nov. 1777), Italian librettist, whose text Mozart used for LA FINTA SEMPLICE. He began writing librettos in Livorno in 1761, moved to VIENNA (where he produced his most significant work) in about 1763, and was appointed to the Russian court in

1772. Like RANIERI DE' CALZABIGI, Coltellini contributed to the revitalization of Italian serious opera by incorporating French elements – ballet, chorus, scene complexes and multiple ensembles – into the dramatic framework of opera seria. His most celebrated collaborators were Tommaso Traetta (*Ifigenia in Tauride*, 1763), CHRISTOPH WILLIBALD GLUCK (*Telemaco*, 1765), FLORIAN LEOPOLD GASSMANN (*Amore e Psiche*, 1767), and ANTONIO SALIERI (*Armida*, 1771). JOSEPH HAYDN made a setting of his text *L'infedeltá delusa* in 1773. (2) Celeste (b. Livorno, 26 Nov. 1760; d. Capodimonte, Naples, 24 July 1829), soprano, daughter of Marco, active mainly in Naples. Her career intersected with Mozart's the first time she was engaged in Vienna, for the 1785–6 season. She was the soprano in FRANCESCO BIANCHI's *La villanella rapita* who sang in the trio and quartet supplied by Mozart (K479–80). As Tonina in Antonio Salieri's *Prima la musica, poi le parole*, she competed for the title of first soprano not only with the Italian company's NANCY STORACE but also with the German company's CATERINA CAVALIERI and ALOYSIA LANGE in GOTTLIEB STEPHANIE's and Mozart's companion work DER SCHAUSPIELDIREKTOR. A return engagement in Vienna in spring 1788 was prematurely terminated after only three months, owing to differences between her and the management. Back in Naples she created one of the most famous roles of the period, Nina, in PAISIELLO's opera of that name (1789). (3) Anna (fl. 1780–93), sister of Celeste, almost invariably sang in the same productions as her sister at the Teatro dei Fiorentini in Naples. DOROTHEA LINK

C. Baldi, 'Marco Coltellini, librettista Toscana a Vienna', *Il teatro musicale italiano nel sacro romanao impero nei secoli 17. e 18.: Loveno di Menggio 1997 nei secoli XVII e XVIII* (Como, 1999), 205–12

compositional method. Even a mere overview of Mozart's compositional processes requires a basic clarification of certain assumptions. What do we mean when we talk about compositional creativity, the process of musical creation or compositional method? What is its object? If it is tangible, where does it reside? Does it lend itself to historical research or to depiction by scholarly treatment? The questions are elementary, but the answers are complicated.

The general usage of the word 'creative' in connection with the production of musical works of art betrays in itself a tendency to mythologize. Practically no one would talk about the creative process of a tailor, even when referring to highly crafted work, for example the completion of a well-fitting lady's coat. The portrayal of composers as creators or musical artists in a categorical sense is really a feature of the modern era, to be seen in close conjunction with the new definition of the genius in the course of the eighteenth century. Mozart does not anywhere indicate that he regards himself as a creator or a genius in this sense. He simply says of himself that he *has* genius (not that he *is* one), meaning that he has a superior talent for making music. This 'making of music' was only mythologized as a creative act in the nineteenth century. Subsequently, anyone engaging with the creative process was also dealing with a myth; and, whether consciously or unconsciously, the enquiries and the language used to formulate them were guided by this myth. In Mozart's case, doubtless because of his history of early compositional activity and the consequent stylization of his person and work, the myth of impulsive and improvisatorial composition as an almost vegetative act of creation has become closely and lastingly linked with him.

The tangible result of a compositional procedure is the written score, a material product. However, the significance of Mozart's 'Jupiter' symphony for our musical understanding does not consist only in the forty-seven sheets of music written by the composer, but is formed in our consciousness as a fleeting sound event at its performance. As readers of music and as historians we can describe the special features of the material product by reference to the manner of what is written, and the way in which it was written down. In this way we create for ourselves a point of departure for conclusions about the 'inner' procedures of the composer, which led to the tangible results. These conclusions about 'inner' or intellectual procedures form the core of the pronouncements that musicologists can make about the compositional process of a composer. The process is not, however, actually rendered accessible: it cannot be ascertained by a scholar working with historical methods. For this reason, it is not reasonable to speak here primarily of the creative *process*, but of the creative or compositional *method*.

Questions about Mozart's compositional method are, first of all, matter-of-fact: they concern habits, routines and rituals in the composer's workshop. It is recognized that Mozart himself saw composition as conscious work, work that had to be actively pursued and that could be accomplished according to necessity. Waiting for inspiration, or the self-assurance that he was a medium through which an external force composed, plays no recognizable role in this. Obviously Mozart's general psychological predisposition (for example his mood, his pleasure in the work or his inner aversion to a commission) is not denied by the expression of this kind of conscious work, and neither are thought processes and the activities of his fantasy, which elude conscious regulation.

Mozart's contemporaries had no experience of the composer's working procedures. They presumably only observed that Mozart (like other musicians) wrote a lot, and published a series of works in quick succession, something which merely corresponded to general expectations. Only as a child prodigy, occasionally urged to give spontaneous proof of his creative abilities, did he cause a stir (see, for example, a representative report in LEOPOLD MOZART's letter to Lorenz HAGENAUER of 10 Nov. 1766). Mozart's outstanding gift for improvisation was well known and could give the impression that he composed extemporaneously, as indeed he himself reported (see his letter of 24 Oct. 1777). But individual reports of this kind did not grow into a realistic conception of Mozart at his compositional work.

The first 'idealistic' portrait of Mozart was drawn during the first quarter of the nineteenth century, partly through the publication of anecdotes whose essentially factual kernels are overgrown with groundless decorations. And the man chiefly responsible for this process was the Leipzig author and music publisher FRIEDRICH ROCHLITZ. As editor of the *Allgemeine musikalische Zeitung*, he disseminated the most influential document about Mozart's creative processes: the 'letter from Mozart to Baron . . .' (AMZ 17 (1815), 561–6). This 'authenticated' letter – in fact based on no authentic source whatsoever and proving by its style in the published version that it cannot possibly have been written by Mozart – developed a veritably overpowering effect far into the twentieth century. Three key statements took hold in the public consciousness and still have some effect today. First, Mozart simply composed in his head, without any compositional aids (for example, an instrument, or written notes); second, the work in question rapidly reached its completed form in this way in the composer's imagination and was recorded as such in his memory, never to be forgotten; third, 'fixing' the composition on manuscript paper was then merely a mechanical act, which proceeded very quickly, uninfluenced by external circumstances. Modern scholarship has a markedly different view of Mozart at work although one point remains uncontroversial: Mozart was in fact capable of extraordinary feats of intellect and memory. As his statement concerning the Prelude from K394 shows, he could compose one work in his head while writing down another which was already finished (see his letter to his sister of 20 Apr. 1782). On the other hand, there are equally uncontroversial reports indicating very carefully considered procedures, planning and laborious progress. Mozart's high level of intellectual consciousness when dealing with musical form in the broadest sense is clearly expressed in his own words: 'you know that I immerse myself in music, so to speak – that I think about it all day long – that I like experimenting – studying – reflecting . . .' (letter to Leopold, 31 July 1778).

Based on an assessment of all the authentic sources, Mozart's compositional processes can be broken down into four 'ideal/typical' phases. The first phase begins before any writing takes place, with the composer's concentration on a concrete idea for the work and the engagement of his fantasy, aimed at realizing this idea. As well as purely mental processes, trying things over at the keyboard was important to Mozart. We can infer this from repeated reports of occasions when Mozart had no instrument available, and for this reason could not compose – or, if he could, only with difficulty. Apart from later statements to this effect by third parties such as CONSTANZE MOZART or FRANZ XAVER NIEMETSCHEK, Mozart himself twice explicitly mentions the significance of the keyboard for his work. In 1778, he reports regularly leaving his own Parisian lodgings in order to compose at the house of the concert impresario JOSEPH LEGROS, 'because there's a keyboard there' (letter from MARIA ANNA MOZART to Leopold of 5 Apr. 1778). Three years later Mozart mentions new lodgings in VIENNA in connection with his current work on DIE ENTFÜHRUNG AUS DEM SERAIL, K384: 'My room that I'm moving to is being prepared; – I'm just off now to hire a keyboard, because I can't live there until that's been delivered, especially as I've got to write just now, and there isn't a minute to be lost' (letter to Leopold, 1 Aug. 1781). A further strand to his 'experimenting – studying – reflecting' was his engagement with the compositions of other musicians, with works that were taken as models for his own plans. Analytical research in this area is not yet far advanced, but there are several striking examples of this type of model, including the double chorus 'The people shall hear' from Handel's oratorio *Israel in Egypt* for the 'Qui tollis' of the C minor mass, K427, and the slow movement of Joseph Haydn's symphony Hob. I:75 for the Andante variations movement of the Piano Concerto in B flat, K450.

The second phase is undoubtedly the first notated 'fixing' of the musical content in a shorthand and fragmented form, its full sense only comprehensible to the composer. Mozart always maintained these jottings in an unmistakably private script and partly cryptic form, thereby denying their communication to others – his sketches therefore belong wholly to the sphere of his private workshop. A clear appraisal of the significance of Mozart's sketches is hindered by the highly differentiated quantity of the notations to be observed in the manuscripts. From barely decipherable individual notes embracing mere splinters of thought, through melodic or polyphonic parts extending to several bars, to completely fixed passages of one or more voices amounting to regular sketched-out scores, all conceivable manner of forms make their appearance. There is a large gap between a musical event that is merely hinted at, and whose larger context was known to the composer but remains completely hidden from the outside observer, and a sketch that can be reconstructed unambiguously in its intended significance. Those who would orient themselves in this field seek a description and categorization of the sketches that satisfies at least pragmatic considerations. Such a description resides in the simple demarcation between 'running sketches' and 'sketches-in-extract'.

The main purpose of a 'running' sketch is to fix the overall disposition of a work, part of a work or one of the constitutive formative lines (for example, the voice part of an aria). It can be for one part only – this predominates with Mozart – or for several parts (in which case, as a rule, the number of parts is smaller than it is for a performance of the composition). The purpose of the 'sketch-in-extract' is to master a particular musically striking factor in an excerpt which is short in relation to the whole work (perhaps concerning the harmony, the counterpoint, the form or some other element), concentrating on the requirements of each individual compositional task. It is usually encountered in several voice parts. In any system of categorization, it needs to be considered if both the 'running sketch' and the 'sketch-in-extract' should be given further reference to whether they are for vocal or instrumental works, and within these groups whether they are for one or more voices.

With the third phase, public or at least potentially public manuscripts start to be produced. Mozart notates the musical passage emerging from its constituent parts as a 'draft score'. This forerunner of the complete score is characterized (like the finished manuscript) both by 'public' handwriting and by every possible external feature of the structure. This consists of both the part carrying the melody and substantial sporadic additional details germane to the motivic and harmonic progression as well as the bass part over whose harmonic foundation the upper part unfolds. When the draft score is finished, the work counts in Mozart's parlance as composed, something which comes across clearly in his letters; not infrequently an entry was then made in the *Verzeichnüss aller meiner Werke* (Catalogue of all my Works) that he kept from 1784 onwards.

The concluding fourth phase transforms the draft score into the completed score. The most important task here is the amplification of the main instrumental part by means of the inner voices. This includes all the parts which are not designated as melody parts (in the narrower sense), above all the parts through which the harmony unfolds and which determine the sonority. Mozart called the process in this fourth phase 'the writing'. Among relevant references to the relationship between composing and writing down, a remark by Mozart concerning IDOMENEO is particularly significant: 'I must finish now, because

I've got to write at breakneck speed – everything's composed – but not written yet –' (letter to Leopold, 30 Dec. 1780). Mozart emphatically does not mean (something which is often misunderstood) that he had composed everything 'in his head' but not yet committed a single note to paper; as his consistent use of the words 'compose' and 'write' in this context shows, he distinguishes between music written in the draft score and the filling out of the complete score. In general, Mozart's practice was not a matter of individual custom, but followed a procedure observable in the work of other composers as well. And the differentiation of the two written procedures in Mozart's work is in many cases made clear by the different shades of the ink he used.

Mozart's compositional process cannot be demonstrated in the ideal/typical form described here by the example of any single work. The reason for this is obvious: all of the procedures belonging to the first, 'pre-written', phase are invisible. The length and intensity of this phase can at best be estimated by assumptions. For example, the absence of sketches for solo keyboard works may be explained by the composer's close relationship to the instrument; improvisation or the actual trying out of particularly challenging imaginative possibilities could compensate in these cases for the lack of sketches. Moreover, the possibility must be entertained that the purely mental processes and the sketched and then final written ones did not happen in vector-like sequence, but in a sort of jerky movement back and forth. Several facts support this assumption: Mozart composes in clearly defined units of musical meaning, perhaps according to the end point of a modulating section, or perhaps according to the formal function of an extract; sketches do not begin or break off at any old place, but demarcate these units of meaning (for example, the initial and final context of a theme, the bridge section between the first and second themes in a sonata movement, or a section from the development); sketches-in-extract refer to material already composed, and are therefore linked to something preceding them, and develop as a continuation from that point. It is very difficult to establish which passages Mozart composed in his head in advance, and any attempt at this can be based only on a precise analysis of the longer running sketches or sketches-in-extract. (The development of the first movement of the 'Prague' symphony, K504, may perhaps show how the final form of this passage, and the path by which it was reached, was only reached via a number of sketched stages: the writing down of the sketch breaks off just at the point where a passage already composed for the exposition can be linked up as the concluding block of the development.)

In the compositional endeavour of any composer, unfinished works offer significant insights. In this respect, Mozart takes a special place: no composer of the same rank left so many fragments as he did. What is the significance of this fact? Any attempt to answer this question depends on looking first at the stage of the work where a fragment breaks off.

Mozart's pieces which can be described as fragments are products of the third phase of the creative process. Expressed quite simply, they are characterized by something lacking, by the fact that they did not complete the transition to the fourth phase. But although this is fundamentally true, the situation in the majority of cases is somewhat more complicated. For the draft score does not necessarily indicate the complete course of the composition in the main part, but rather it often indicates merely one or more of the musical elements. And in the majority of cases, it even breaks off long before the end. Equally typical are the features shared by the fragments with completed compositions, for example the external construction and the form of writing. Precisely these external features lead us towards the profound insight that Mozart's music recorded in the fragments is 'finished', that the notated version is final. They count as independent works, and are to be understood not as early or alternative forms of compositions that will eventually be completed, but as pieces potentially 'finishable' by Mozart. This characteristic feature is the reason why the composer, as far as we can see, never used the unfinished pieces as raw material for other works. Rather, it can be shown that many completed works (for example, the keyboard concertos K449, 488, 503 and 595, or the Clarinet Concerto, K622) remained fragments for a long time before Mozart completed them.

Mozart's surviving fragments are spread over practically all genres and the kernel of the collection consists of about 150 manuscripts. The available stock may once have been more comprehensive: Constanze spoke of having destroyed 'unusable' ones; what is more, numbers written on the autographs by GEORG NIKOLAUS NISSEN suggest substantial gaps in places when compared with the collection known today. Nevertheless, it was Constanze who first articulated the suggestion 'to append such fragments to the end of each genre', that is to say, to publish the fragments in each genre together with the corresponding completed compositions: 'They will surely always be educational, and their ideas can even be used and followed through by others' (letter to Breitkopf & Härtel, 15 June 1799). Mozart's legacy of ideas was thus envisaged as a kind of quarry for posterity.

The question of why so many compositional beginnings were not seen through to the end has provoked much general speculation about Mozart's creative processes. Until very recently, the fragments seemed to bear witness to the composer's creative abundance. Erich Hertzmann expressed this view of the situation in 1957: 'The existence of these numerous fragments proves once again the overflow of his musical inventiveness. His wealth of melodic ideas, a manifestation of his creative exuberance, never seemed to diminish throughout his lifetime.' Nevertheless, there yawns a great gap, in terms of explanation, between the factual establishment of a permanently active musical fantasy, and the sheer presumption that this must have given vent to the same driving force even in mere beginnings. For that which is evaluated in positive terms by Herzmann and others could easily be turned to negative ones: was then Mozart not capable of controlling his creative forces, to see through his inventive gift confidently to the end? What is the use of musical ideas if they do not progress beyond the beginning? Moreover, according to the view that Mozart had always completed his works in his head before he wrote them down, should not the fragments stand for at least 150 imagined completed compositions?

Similar scepticism is appropriate in the face of Alfred Einstein's older 'springboard theory'. According to this, Mozart often began by writing the opening of a work, then noticed the inadequacy of his attempt, and next, through this insight, succeeded in writing a different, final, form. The opening of the work created the point where the 'filo' or thread was established, the thread with which the urgent musical train of thought was spun (the image comes from Leopold Mozart, in his letter to Mozart of 13 Aug. 1778). According to Einstein, Mozart followed this thread, which was 'critically dependent on the right opening: the opening had to be "on the highest level" '. But precisely here lies the weakness of the theory. Einstein, perhaps subconsciously, assigns a low value to the pieces that remained fragments – they were not on the highest level, and qualitatively it was not worth Mozart's while to finish them. Yet against this speaks the fact that there are completed compositions which existed for a long time as fragments. All this is quite apart from the insoluble claim of recognizing criteria for the definition of artistic heights.

For the fragments as for the sketches, Mozart displayed austere judgement in every case, oriented towards concrete compositional commissions. In the first place, it must be borne in mind that composition plans remained unfulfilled if the opportunity for performance lapsed: for example, Mozart began to notate an ambitiously scored concerto for himself and the violinist Ignaz Fränzl in Mannheim in November 1778. This double concerto for violin and keyboard, KAnh 56, failed to thrive beyond the opening ritornello and the soloists' exposition: presumably it became clear to Mozart that in view of his urgently expected return to Salzburg, there was no realistic chance of completing the piece for performance at a concert yet to be organized. A similar observation applies to the stage works ZAIDE, K344, L'OCA DEL CAIRO, K422, and *Lo sposo deluso*, K430, all begun without a commission.

A completely different point of view is provoked by a striking observation arising from the allocation of the fragments to particular types of movement. Many of the uncompleted manuscripts contain beginnings to middle and final movements rather than to first movements. Considering Mozart's usual practice of composing cyclical works forward from the beginning, these fragments must be seen in connection with something preceding them: they do not stand alone. (This observation does not necessarily apply to operas.) Mozart did not arbitrarily place together three or four movements in concerto or sonata form. He had a very precise sense of the way movements suited each other as musical characters. To be sure, it seems that this sense only served him reliably when retrospectively judging the relationships between movements – he did not always succeed with the placements the first time, and therefore a further attempt had to be made. If this assumption is right, the frequent occurrence of second and third movements in the fragments would find a plausible explanation. Furthermore, it could be established that a misjudgement in the sense described would only have to be applied to the element of cyclical form, but not to the musical success of the individual fragment. An attempt at a movement can therefore be seen as 'wrong' in a certain larger context, but artistically successful in itself.

To take a closer look at what this means, let us consider the string quartet fragment in B flat, KAnh 68. For a long time it was considered to be the opening of the final movement of the second 'Prussian' quartet, K589, and was dated to 1790. But paper and handwriting permit no doubt that the fragment should actually be assigned to 1783 and seen in conjunction with the string quartet K458, the 'Hunt'. Are there any conclusions that can be drawn from a comparison of the fragment and the completed last movement that would explain Mozart's decision to give up the first beginning? Even the external state of the fragment makes clear the chief feature of his musical creation: after notating the eight-bar theme in score, Mozart continued only with the leading melody part of the first violin as far as bar 57. This dominance, and the consequent complete subordination of the other parts, sits badly with the style of the other movements of the quartet. The strongly Polonaise-like theme, and its related construction in the fragment at a fairly moderate tempo, poses a strong contrast with the turbulent 6/8 first movement. Did Mozart see this contrast as a danger both to the balance within the larger form, and to the harmony of the movements' characters? At any rate, the accepted finale is clearly related in mood and musical gesture to the first movement, and rounds off the whole work satisfactorily. At all events, when listening to the fragment and the finale of the 'Hunt' quartet one after the other, it is possible to feel how far the ramifications of Mozart's creative thought processes could stretch.

The fragments may hold a yet further significance to Mozart's creative process. A survey of the genres covered by the transmitted manuscripts shows informal groupings, concentrating on the one hand on chamber music, keyboard concertos and masses, but on the other also showing time-specific 'nests': these groupings suggest a strong interest by Mozart in particular genres during certain periods. Perhaps Mozart created for himself something akin to a stock of musical material by turning his musical attention purposefully to the mastery of genres which had a claim on him, or which particularly attracted him – as, for example, with the string quartet during his Viennese years, or with forms of sacred music towards the end of his life. In that case, the fragments could be understood as a 'fixing' of departure points, as a delineation of intellectual places to which Mozart could return as necessary, and from which he could strike out on the road to the final works. This would speak above all for a productive economy, which emphatically did not result in an overflow of ideas aimlessly fizzling out, but consciously secured for itself the cultivation of areas of thought.

The description of the features of Mozart's creative processes, above all of the relationship of the purely mental to the written constituents of his composing, must be based on an adequate infrastructure of sources. Obviously it has to be conceded that even given this, scholars and historians cannot answer or explain all the questions, or even all the observable pieces of evidence in individual works. But it has not yet been shown whether other disciplines, such as psychology or the physiology of the brain, might advance further with respect to these points. Psychological examinations in particular suffer in Mozart's case from an uncritical evaluation of questionable transmissions, or from overvaluing secondary reports from contemporary witnesses. Recent progress in understanding has therefore only been achieved where scepticism with respect to the myths has been married to strict methodical procedures for the interpretation of the primary documents.

ULRICH KONRAD (Trans. RUTH HALLIWELL)

J. Arthur, 'Some Chronological Problems in Mozart: The Contribution of Ink-Studies', in *Wolfgang Amadè Mozart: Essays on His Life and His Music*, ed. S. Sadie (Oxford, 1996), 35–52

A. Einstein, *Mozart: His Character, his Works* (New York, 1945)

U. Konrad, *Mozarts Schaffensweise* (Göttingen, 1992)

L. Somfai, 'Sketches During the Process of Composition: Studies of K504 and K414', in *Wolfgang Amadè Mozart: Essays on His Life and His Music*, ed. S. Sadie (Oxford, 1996), 53–65

A. Tyson, *Mozart: Studies of the Autograph Scores* (Cambridge, MA, 1987)

I. Woodfield, 'Mozart's Compositional Methods: Writing for His Singers', in *The Cambridge Companion to Mozart*, ed. S. P. Keefe (Cambridge, 2003), 35–47

concert arias. See ARIAS, CONCERT

concertos. Mozart's prolific contribution to the concerto genre includes twenty-seven works for piano, five for violin, four for horn, two for flute, and one each for bassoon, oboe, clarinet and flute and harp. Admired from the late eighteenth century onwards for their musical intricacies, expressive subtleties and dramatic force, Mozart's concertos remain among his most popular works and landmarks in the history of the genre.

1. Violin Concertos and the Sinfonia concertante
2. Concertos for wind instruments
3. Piano concertos

1. Violin concertos and the Sinfonia concertante

The five violin concertos, K207 in B flat, K211 in D, K216 in G, K218 in D and K219 in A, were all written during Mozart's years in SALZBURG, following his third and final trip to Italy. Although traditionally assigned a date of April 1775, K207 is now thought to have been completed two years earlier (April 1773), making it in all likelihood Mozart's first original concerto; the remaining four date from June, September, October and December 1775 respectively. The majority of late eighteenth-century concertos were written for composers themselves to perform and Mozart, a violinist of considerable talent, certainly used these works as a showcase for his compositional and performance skills. After playing one of them in AUGSBURG in October 1777, he wrote to his father (23 Oct. 1777) that it 'went down a treat. Everyone praised my beautiful, pure tone.' But it is equally likely that Mozart wrote the violin concertos for initial performance by one of the virtuoso violinists of the Salzburg court orchestra, Antonio Brunetti. In any case, the Adagio in E major for violin and orchestra, K261, was written for Brunetti as a substitute for the original middle movement of K219: LEOPOLD MOZART reports on 9 October 1777 that the latter 'was too studied for [Brunetti's] liking'. The Rondo in B flat for violin and orchestra was probably also intended for Brunetti to replace the original finale of K207. The association between composer and performer continued for several years – Brunetti premiered the Rondo in C major for violin and orchestra, K373, for example, at a concert at Prince Rudolf Colloredo's residence in VIENNA on 8 April 1781, shortly after Mozart moved to the city.

Viewed collectively, Mozart's violin concertos are characterized by formal and affective ingenuity and by strong links to his contemporary operas. There are surprises in abundance in the rondo finales of the final four concertos:

a G minor Andante is brusquely interjected into K216; two musette themes feature in K218; and, most famously, an 'alla turca' section – itself incorporating Hungarian folk material – appears in K219. There is a deft touch in the first movement of K219 too, when Mozart introduces his soloist. Instead of bringing back the orchestra's first theme at this juncture Mozart gives the violinist new material in a six-bar Adagio and concludes it with the opportunity for a cadenza, thus drawing attention temporally, thematically and affectively to this crucial juncture of the work.

Stylistic correspondences between Mozart's violin concertos and LUCIO SILLA (1772), LA FINTA GIARDINIERA (1775) and IL RE PASTORE (1775) are not surprising given the chronological proximity of these works. Aminta's 'Aer tranquillo' from *Il re pastore* has gestures and expressive features similar to those in K207 and K216; and Giunia's 'Ah, se il crudel periglio' from *Lucio Silla* demonstrates close formal and procedural parallels with the first movement of K219. The cross-fertilization of musical materials and procedures between these two genres was, in any case, a compositional reality for Mozart throughout his career.

Mozart's final complete concerto-related work for strings, the Sinfonia concertante in E flat for violin and viola, K364, dates from 1779–80. It was not Mozart's first orchestral work for two or more string soloists – the Concertone in C for two violins, K190, pre-dates K364 by five years and a 134-bar fragment of a Sinfonia concertante in A for violin, viola and cello, K320e is contemporary with it – but is certainly his best known. A concerto in all but name, K364 prefigures Mozart's piano concertos of the 1780s in several important stylistic respects: the soloists engage in subtle interaction with the orchestra; the orchestral and solo expositions of the first movements diverge considerably in thematic terms (like several later works); and the expressive minor-key slow movement sets the stage for similarly expressive minor-key middle movements in K456, 482 and 488.

2. Concertos for wind instruments

Mozart wrote concertos for all of the principal wind representatives of the late eighteenth-century orchestra – flute, oboe, clarinet, bassoon and horn. The Bassoon Concerto in B flat, K191, was completed on 4 June 1774, just five days after the Concertone, K190, and the Flute Concerto in G, K313, if it is by Mozart, four years later in MANNHEIM to fulfil a commission from the Dutch amateur musician FERDINAND DEJEAN, 'a great friend and admirer', according to Mozart. The Oboe Concerto in C, K314 (1777), written for the virtuoso GIUSEPPE FERLENDIS and subsequently performed on several occasions in 1778 by the equally renowned German oboist FRIEDRICH RAMM, was transcribed, presumably early in 1778 at Dejean's request, as the Flute Concerto in D (as with K313, it is not certain that the transcription derives from Mozart). The Concerto in C for Flute and Harp, K299, dating from Mozart's six-month stay in PARIS in 1778, derives from his association with the flautist Adrien-Louis Bonnières de Souastre, Comte de Guines and his harpist daughter (who also took composition lessons with Mozart). All of these concertos feature carefully crafted writing for the soloists, demonstrating Mozart's striking ability, even relatively early in his career, for writing highly idiomatically for instruments with which he was unacquainted as a performer. Late eighteenth-century theorists and aestheticians often counselled concerto composers to consult specialist performers when writing technically challenging passages for instruments with which they were unfamiliar as players, and it seems likely that Mozart followed this advice.

Mozart's fruitful musical relationship with Anton STADLER provided the stimulus for his last wind concerto – indeed his last completed instrumental work – the Clarinet Concerto in A, K622 (1791). A clarinet technician as well as virtuoso performer praised by the playwright Johann Friedrich Schink for performing on an instrument that 'has so soft and lovely a tone that no one with a heart can resist it', Stadler pioneered the development of the basset clarinet, which extended the standard range of the instrument down by four semitones; it was for this particular instrument that Mozart wrote K622. The work was recognized as a 'masterpiece' in the 1804 issue of the *Allgemeine musikalische Zeitung*, which carried a lengthy review of the Breitkopf & Härtel edition. The reviewer remarks that it is a genuine challenge for the soloist, but certainly worth the effort, as 'good execution ... will bestow honour and admiration upon every able clarinettist as it will bestow pleasure upon every listener, whatever his sensibilities and whichever type of music he may love most'. He goes on to praise the 'splendidly crafted' first movement, drawing attention to canonic alterations and imitations in double counterpoint, the 'incomparably beautiful adagio, which transports one to a tender melancholy' and the witty and humorous rondo finale, lamenting the fact that space constraints require him to reproduce musical examples in short score rather than in full orchestral score: 'What extraordinary effects Mozart could achieve through the most precise knowledge of all the customary instruments and their most advantageous employment; that especially in this respect Mozart has been equalled by nobody: this everyone knows.'

The qualities of the Clarinet Concerto identified in 1804 are still central to our appreciation of the work 200 years later. Although implicit and explicit twentieth-century links between the work's perceived melancholy, transcendence and resignation and Mozart's impending death are ultimately unsustainable biographical tropes, the beautifully serene and seemingly effortless effects in the work are hard to ignore, combining masterful writing for the soloist with inspired deployment of orchestral instruments. In the development section of the first movement, Mozart moves with magical smoothness from the dominant of F sharp minor to D major in the space of just six bars, in the process bringing together simple clarinet–orchestra imitation of a three-crotchet figure, sustained notes in the winds and strings and modestly flamboyant solo arpeggios; in the coda of the famous Adagio the flutes, bassoons and horns are omitted and brought back right at the end to offer up a pristinely rounded final chord; and in the second episode of the finale, a six-bar sequence alternates calmly between the upper and lower ranges of the clarinet, with delicate support from tied notes in the flutes and bassoons and repeated quavers in the upper strings.

Mozart's association with another prominent Austrian instrumentalist, JOSEPH LEUTGEB (1732–1811), produced four horn concertos, K417 in E flat (1783), K495 in E flat (1786), K447 in E flat (1787) and K412 + 514 in D

(1791), all written in Vienna. Leutgeb was admired across Europe after acclaimed performances in the 1760s and 1770s in Vienna, Paris, Frankfurt am Main and MILAN and became particularly friendly with Mozart in the early 1780s. Their friendship is witnessed, unusually, in jovial remarks Mozart writes in the autograph scores of the concertos. 'Wolfgang Amadé Mozart has taken pity on Leutgeb, ass, ox and fool at Vienna, 27 March 1783' appears on the first page of K417; elsewhere, comments such as 'Now over to you, Sir Donkey', 'And don't you ever finish? Oh, you infamous swine!' 'take a break!' and 'You beast – oh, what a dreadful noise – Oh dear!' litter the scores. Mozart played a more conventional practical joke on Leutgeb in June 1791, announcing himself as a 'good friend from Rome' and roaring with laughter when Leutgeb arrived in perfect formal attire. 'I always need to make a fool of someone', he explained to CONSTANZE MOZART.

Musically, Mozart's horn concertos are characterized by considerable attention to the technical demands of the solo instrument and by gestural and stylistic similarities to his other Viennese concertos. Mozart skilfully accounts for the limitations of the natural horn (which did not have valves and relied on techniques of over-blowing and hand-stopping in the bell of the instrument to achieve a wide range of notes) and incorporates frequent rests in order to allow the soloist adequate recovery time. K412 + 514, a two-movement work whose second movement was completed by FRANZ XAVER SÜSSMAYR in April 1792, is particularly interesting in reference to the latter point. The soloist plays for only ten bars in the development section. The contraction of the horn's role in this section is complemented by the expansion of the orchestra's role, including a leisurely six-bar statement of the main theme at the beginning and a twelve-bar tutti immediately preceding the recapitulation. In contrasting the terse and expanded thematic statements, Mozart aligns this section procedurally with the development sections of the first movements of his late Piano Concerto in B flat, K595, and his Clarinet Concerto, K622, both of which also incorporate prominent stylistic contrasts (textural and harmonic disjunction followed by smooth, mellifluous interaction in K595 and harmonic leisureliness followed by the aforementioned compressed modulation in K622). Elsewhere in the horn concertos, echoes of the Viennese piano concertos abound: the first movements of K447 and K495 contain similar ritornello material to the corresponding movement of K482 in E flat (1785); the secondary theme of the first movement of K447 is similar to the same theme in the first movement of K467 (1785); and the run-up to the recapitulation of the opening movement of K495 is procedurally and thematically close to the corresponding passage in K450 in B flat (1784).

3. Piano concertos

Mozart's piano concertos span almost his entire compositional career, from 1767 to 1791, collectively providing a rich account of his stylistic development. As a leading pianist of his day and a master of orchestral writing, Mozart's prodigious talents were naturally suited to the genre. The resulting works, in particular the seventeen written in Vienna, are a landmark in musical history.

Mozart's earliest works in the genre are transcriptions of solo keyboard sonatas and accompanied violin sonatas by prominent mid- and late eighteenth-century composers. K37, 39, 40 and 41 (1767) draw on movements from sonatas by HERMANN FRIEDRICH RAUPACH (1728–78), LEONTZI HONAUER (1737–90), JOHANN SCHOBERT (c.1740–1767), JOHANN GOTTFRIED ECKARD (1735–1809) and CARL PHILIPP EMANUEL BACH (1714–88), while K107/1–3 (1772) are based on three solo keyboard sonatas by JOHANN CHRISTIAN BACH (1735–82), his Op. 5 Nos. 2–4. All of the works produce the requisite formal contrast between soloist and orchestra by adding tuttis (usually four for the sonata-form first movements) to the transcribed sonata material, thus providing fascinating evidence of the birth of Mozart's piano concerto style from the sonata genre. Leopold's handwriting is present in the autograph scores of the concertos; as his markings include notational and harmonic corrections of Mozart's work, it would appear that these works partially detail Leopold's tutelage of his son as well.

K175 in D, Mozart's first original piano concerto, dates from December 1773. Mozart held it in high regard, performing it in Mannheim in February 1778 and on at least four occasions in Vienna between March 1782 and March 1783, where he reported it was a real 'favourite'. The Viennese performances substituted a new finale, the Rondo in D, K382 (actually a theme and variations) for the original sonata-form finale, and Mozart remarked to Leopold on 23 March 1782 that the new movement made 'such a furore' in the city. He continues: 'I beg you to guard it like a jewel and not to give it to a soul to play . . . I composed it specially for myself and no one else but my dear sister must play it.'

Late eighteenth-century composers were justifiably concerned about pirated editions of their works appearing without their consent – hence Mozart's strongly articulated request not to circulate K382 – but this did not usually discourage them from writing concertos for performers other than themselves. Three of Mozart's next four piano concertos in fact, K242 in F for three pianos (1776), K246 in C (1776) and K271 in E flat (1777) were written in the first instance for other distinguished pianists – Countess Antonia LODRON and her daughters Aloisia and Josephina, COUNTESS ANTONIA LÜTZOW, and Mademoiselle JENAMY (formerly thought to be 'Jeunhomme') respectively. Mozart knew the Lodron family and Lützow, a pupil of Leopold, as fellow Salzburg residents, but only became familiar with the French virtuoso Jenamy and her reputedly splendid playing when she performed in Salzburg in December 1776. Mozart subsequently performed all three works – as well as K238 in B flat (1776), a work probably intended from the outset as a solo vehicle for the composer – in October 1777 in Augsburg and MUNICH. A review of the K242 performance in Augsburg, featuring JOHANN MICHAEL DEMMLER (an organist) and JOHANN ANDREAS STEIN (a renowned piano maker) in the solo roles in addition to Mozart, was published in the *Augsburgische staats- und gelehrten Zeitung* on 28 October 1777 and was effusive in its praise of work and performers alike. The composition as a whole was 'thorough, fiery, manifold and simple; the harmony so full, so strong, so unexpected, so elevating; the melody so agreeable, so playful, and everything so new; the rendering on the fortepiano so neat, so clean, so full of expression and yet at the same time extraordinarily rapid, so that one hardly knew what to give attention to first, and all the hearers were enraptured. One found here mastery in the thought, mastery in the performance, mastery in the instruments, all at the same time.'

K271, the last of the four 1776–7 piano concertos, is a landmark in Mozart's piano concerto oeuvre. Its stylistic boldness is signalled right at the outset, with the orchestra presenting the antecedent phrase of the main theme, but handing over to the piano for the consequent phrase; the process is repeated and the piano then sits out the remainder of the section. Thus, the soloist enters unexpectedly at the beginning of the work, rather than waiting for its appointed place at the onset of the solo exposition. Its re-entry fifty bars later is as subtle as its initial entry is strident, with a quietly evocative three-bar trill that accompanies tonic–dominant articulation of E flat leading to a poignantly expressive four-bar solo phrase that directs us back to the reappearance of the main theme. Overall, K271 is characterized by a conciseness of thematic development, a depth of expression (in the Andantino in particular) and a level of exuberant virtuosity (especially in the finale) that surpasses anything witnessed in his preceding piano concertos.

Mozart's next piano concerto, and his last in Salzburg, is K365 in E flat for two pianos (1779), probably written for him to perform with his sister NANNERL MOZART. While the accompanying orchestra is large – two clarinets, two trumpets and timpani in addition to two oboes, two bassoons, two horns and strings – it has not yet been proven beyond doubt that the clarinet, trumpet and timpani parts are Mozart's work. Neither the autograph nor early German editions of the work from ANDRE in 1800 and Breitkopf in 1804 contain these parts, but it is entirely possible that Mozart added them for concerts in the early 1780s. It is known from Mozart's correspondence that he played the work with his student JOSEPHA AUERNHAMMER (1758–1820) at her family residence in Vienna on 23 November 1781 and again at the Augarten, a prominent Viennese concert venue, on 26 May 1782. Irritated by Auernhammer's amorous intentions in 1781, Mozart nevertheless admired her 'enchanting' playing (albeit with the qualification that 'in cantabile playing she has not got the real delicate singing style') and dedicated to her his set of six violin sonatas (K296, 376–80, published in 1781). ABBE MAXIMILIAN STADLER, an Austrian theologian and musicologist who knew Mozart and Constanze, was 'enchanted by the playing of master and pupil' in these sonatas. Such charm would surely also have characterized their performances of K365, a work that contains numerous instances of dialogue and other delicate interaction between the two soloists.

About a year and a half after his move to Vienna in March 1781, and with a successful production of the opera DIE ENTFÜHRUNG AUS DEM SERAIL behind him, Mozart returned to the piano concerto genre with a set of three works composed in the autumn and winter of 1782–3, K414 in A (completed first), K413 in F and K415 in C. Still a new resident of the city who needed to generate a substantial income from his freelance musical activities, Mozart offered manuscript copies to the general public on subscription, placing an advertisement to this effect in the *Wiener Zeitung* on 15 January 1783. They are 'three new, recently finished piano concertos' that 'will not appear until the beginning of April this year, and will be issued (finely copied and supervised by [Mozart]) only to those who have subscribed thereto'. Mozart was keen to explain that these concertos could be performed in two different ways, 'either with a large orchestra with wind instruments or merely *a quattro*, *viz.* with 2 violins, 1 viola and violoncello [i.e. one to each part]', thus maximizing the number of potential purchasers of the scores. A famous letter to Leopold on 28 December 1782 also clarifies that these works were written with broad appeal in mind: 'These concertos are a happy medium between what is too easy and too difficult; they are very brilliant, pleasing to the ear, and natural, without being vapid. There are passages here and there from which the connoisseurs alone can derive satisfaction; but these passages are written in such a way that the less learned cannot fail to be pleased, though without knowing why.' It would appear, however, that Mozart's subscription scheme was not particularly successful, certainly not at the price at which he initially advertised them in the *Wiener Zeitung* (four ducats for the set): he failed to attract the requisite number of subscribers by April, subsequently negotiating sales of the works through the publishers SIEBER, TRAEG and ARTARIA, and on each occasion lowering his price.

Mozart almost certainly began another piano concerto alongside the so-called 'subscription' set in 1782–3, K449 in E flat, but completed only the first half of the first movement. He returned to it about a year later, finished it off and made it the first entry in the catalogue of his works, the *Verzeichnüss aller meiner Werke*, on 9 February 1784, completing the piano concertos K450 in B flat, K451 in D and K453 in G on 15 March, 22 March and 12 April 1784, respectively. K449 is, in fact, a fascinating stylistic hybrid of K413–15 and K450/451/453. In letters to his father Mozart explained the difference between K449 and the later concertos: it was, like K413–15, 'composed rather for a small orchestra than for a large one' and 'can be performed *a quattro* without wind instruments'. In a similar fashion to K450/451/453, however, the orchestra assumes a newly prominent position, witnessed (in K449 at least) in powerful confrontations between the piano and the orchestra in the development and recapitulation sections of the first movement. The confrontations are themselves intensifications of mildly disjunctive musical procedures from K413–15 and are subsequently reshaped in K450/451/453. Mozart's description of K449 as 'a concerto of an entirely special manner' should be taken literally – it is indeed a unique work and one of considerable significance to his future development as a concerto composer.

Alongside K450 and 451, K449 initiated a new venture for Mozart the composer-performer in spring 1784, a series of subscription concerts, held in a private hall of the Trattnerhof in Vienna, the residence of JOHANN THOMAS VON TRATTNER (1717–98). Instead of selling manuscript copies of his new concertos to raise revenue, Mozart put on a series of three orchestral concerts on 17, 24 and 31 March 1784, showcasing his piano concertos above all, and invited Viennese residents to subscribe. It was clearly a very successful venture, in both financial and artistic terms. On 20 March he sent a complete list of subscribers to Leopold containing 176 names, boasting that the number represented 'thirty more than [Ludwig] Fischer and [Georg Friedrich] Richter combined'. The first concert, he explained, 'won extraordinary applause' and had the hall 'full to overflowing'. Spring 1784 was, in any case, one of the high points of Mozart's career in Vienna. He had an extraordinary twenty-two engagements between 26 February and 3 April alone, including a 'most successful' concert at the high-profile Burgtheater (the National Theatre) that included performances of K450 and 451 as well as the Quintet for Piano and Winds, K452.

Just as K449 established an elevated, forceful role for the orchestra (as a single entity) in Mozart's piano concertos, so K450 initiated a special, inimitable role for the winds. Mozart described K450, 451 and 453 as 'grand concertos' with 'wind-instrument accompaniment' and, symbolically, signalled the obligatory nature of their participation at the very opening of K450. Here the oboes and bassoons present the first part of the main theme without the support of the strings, thus establishing the winds as independent interlocutors in their own right. These three works are characterized throughout by prominent writing for the winds, especially dialogue with the piano (for example split phrases and themes, full themes passed from one part to another, imitations and echoes and segues from one phrase to the next).

K453 and Mozart's next piano concerto, K456 in B flat (dated 30 Sept. 1784) were written for two distinguished female pianists, BARBARA VON PLOYER (1765–c.1811) and MARIA THERESIA VON PARADIES (1759–1824), respectively. Ployer (to whom K449 was also dedicated) was Mozart's student in 1784. She is known to have performed K453 on 13 June 1784 at the home of Gottfried Ignaz von Ployer (her father's cousin) in Döbling on the outskirts of Vienna. Paradies, blind from infancy, toured Europe twice between 1783 and 1786, perhaps performing K456 in Paris, LONDON, Brussels or Berlin in October 1784. Mozart also played K453 and 456 himself, of course, the latter in a concert on 13 February 1785 given by the Italian soprano and original Countess Almaviva in LE NOZZE DI FIGARO, LUISA LASCHI (c.1760–c.1790). Leopold, who visited Mozart in Vienna between 11 February and 25 April, attended this concert and reflected poignantly on the experience in a letter to Nannerl. K456 is 'a glorious concerto . . . I was sitting only two boxes away from the very beautiful Princess of Württemberg and had the great pleasure of hearing so clearly all the interplay of the instruments that for sheer delight tears came into my eyes. When your brother left the platform the Emperor waved his hat and called out "Bravo Mozart!"' One can well imagine Leopold's delight at witnessing such a successful performance by his son, compounding the joy he must have felt only one day earlier (12 February) when JOSEPH HAYDN told him, after playing through the three string quartets K458 in B flat, K464 in A and K465 in C ('Dissonance'): 'Before God and as an honest man, I tell you that your son is the greatest composer known to me either in person or by name. He has taste and, what is more, the most profound knowledge of composition.'

Leopold had plenty more opportunities to witness Mozart's 'profound knowledge of composition' during his visit to Vienna, not least at the six subscription concerts at the Mehlgrube Casino from 11 February 1785 onwards and at the Burgtheater academy event on 10 March. Mozart's next three piano concertos, K459 in F (11 Dec. 1784), K466 in D minor (10 Feb. 1785) and K467 in C (9 Mar.

1785) were all performed at these concerts, with K466 premiered at the first of them. Leopold reported proudly that 'a great many members of the aristocracy were present' at this concert, that it was 'magnificent' and that 'the orchestra played splendidly'. The demands on the orchestra – especially the wind instruments – are such that 'splendid' playing is, indeed a *sine qua non* for a successful rendition of these works. The first and second movements of K459 contain particularly rich dialogue between the piano and winds, quickly establishing and maintaining an atmosphere of intimate collaboration in the solo exposition, through sensitive and delicate exchanges of material, and rendering the atmosphere more intimate still in the recapitulation through the inclusion of additional dialogue and even more subtle exchange. K466 and K467 are scarcely less significant in terms of interaction between the soloist and the orchestra, the famous slow movement of K467 in particular containing a seamless flow of melodic and triplet-quaver accompaniment figuration between the piano, winds and strings, starting with as sensitive an introduction of a soloist as one finds even in a Mozart concerto – sonorous full-wind triplets are passed to the left hand of the piano and an F major pizzicato string arpeggio foreshadows in outline the singing theme in the right hand.

Although poles apart in affect and mood, K466 and K467 are similar to each other – and to all of the piano concertos from K450 onwards in fact – in carefully balancing ostensibly contrasting aesthetic and stylistic features of grandeur (represented primarily by orchestral tutti sections and tutti interjections), brilliance (solo virtuosity) and intimacy (dialogue and other subtle solo/orchestra interaction). Both the ominous, dark and strident tutti material in the first movement of K466 and the bright, bold and upbeat tutti material in the corresponding movement of K467, for example, are offset by interaction of great delicacy and poignancy, and solo passage-work of great brilliance.

Mozart's next three piano concertos date from the winter and spring of 1785–6 and bring to an end his most productive period in the genre. K482 in E flat (entered into the *Verzeichnüss* on 16 Dec. 1785) was probably premiered at the Burgtheater on 23 December and K488 in A (dated 2 Mar. 1786) at a subscription concert in the spring. While K482 is broad in scope (especially in the first movement) and K488 more intimate, both are beautifully orchestrated and, for the first time in a Mozart concerto, scored for clarinets in preference to oboes. Both also contain minor-mode middle movements (K488's is in the extremely unusual key of F sharp minor) that demonstrate soloistic fragility and elegance in equal measure.

In many respects the awe-inspiring K491 in C minor (completed on 24 Mar. 1786 and first performed in all likelihood on 7 April) is a climactic work in Mozart's piano concerto cycle. It contains the longest and most formally complex first movement (including an extended solo exposition section punctuated by a piano cadential trill at the mid-point) and the largest accompanying orchestra (flute, two oboes, two clarinets, two bassoons, two horns, two trumpets and timpani in addition to strings). The scale of the orchestra enables Mozart, in the first movement of the work at least, to write music that is both grander and more intimate than hitherto – the gravitas and noble magnificence of the sequentially spiralling confrontation between piano and orchestra in the development section and the volume and sophistication of organization of piano–orchestra dialogue in the recapitulation are simply unmatched. With the exquisite wind writing from the middle movement and the unremittingly intense theme and variations finale factored in as well, it is difficult to avoid the conclusion that, even by Mozart's extraordinary standards, K491 is one of his greatest instrumental works.

K503 in C, completed on 4 December 1786, is hardly less impressive than K491. The first movement, for example, is certainly as bold, broad, majestic and technically demanding as that of its predecessor. After the apotheosis of dialogic sophistication and confrontation in K491 it is perhaps not surprising that there are signs of stylistic change. The combination of intimacy, brilliance and grandeur at the piano's entry in the first movement and in the immediately ensuing passages is unprecedented – the piano creeps in innocuously in alternation with cadence-making in the strings, progresses through sweeping, brilliant semiquavers to the return of the orchestra's archetypically grand main theme, decorates the continuation of the main theme with magical, exquisite semiquavers and – in dialogue with the winds – transforms the theme to convey poignant intimacy. Unusually for Mozart, too, the first half of the development section is a tour de force of collaborative dialogue among the strings, winds and piano.

Mozart's last two piano concertos, K537 in D (nicknamed the 'Coronation' on account of Mozart's performance of it at the festivities for LEOPOLD II in Frankfurt in October 1790) and K595 in B flat, completed on 24 February 1788 and 5 January 1791, respectively, continue the theme of stylistic experimentation initiated in K503. They remain fundamentally misunderstood works, K537 gratuitously dismissed by generations of critics as uneven, empty and generally second-rate (Arthur Hutchings, in a famous book on Mozart's piano concertos from 1948, wished he 'had the end seats' regretting 'that Mozart stooped so low') and K595 regularly described as nostalgic, resigned, reticent and introspective, implicitly assuming that Mozart was somehow aware that this would be his last piano concerto and decided to sign off with an exquisite swansong. In fact, the first movements of K537 and 595 together represent a systematic attempt at stylistic reinvention. Passages such as the contrapuntal rumination of the solo piano after the secondary theme in the solo exposition and recapitulation of K537 and the stuttering, harmonically disjunctive dialogue followed by mellifluously flowing dialogue in the development section of K595 move away from Mozart's standard modus operandi in a search for new stylistic paradigms.

It is still not known exactly why Mozart wrote only three piano concertos in the last five years of his life (K503, 537 and 595), after having written fourteen in the previous four years, although the increasing demand of opera on his compositional time surely offers at least a partial explanation. (LE NOZZE DI FIGARO, DON GIOVANNI, COSÌ FAN TUTTE, DIE ZAUBERFLÖTE and LA CLEMENZA DI TITO were all completed after K491.) In any case, K537 and 595 do not bear witness to a loss of interest in the piano concerto, as many critics have suggested, but rather to an active reappraisal of its stylistic features. Had Mozart lived beyond 1791, it is highly likely that he would have continued to write works in the genre that served him so well. SIMON P. KEEFE

J. Irving, *Mozart's Piano Concertos* (Aldershot, 2003)
S. P. Keefe, *Mozart's Piano Concertos: Dramatic Dialogue in the Age of Enlightenment* (Woodbridge and Rochester, NY, 2001)
'"An Entirely Special Manner": Mozart's Piano Concerto No. 14 in E flat K449 and the Stylistic Implications of Confrontation', *Music & Letters* 82 (2001), 559–81
'A Complementary Pair: Stylistic Experimentation in Mozart's Final Piano Concertos, K. 537 in D and K. 595 in B flat', *Journal of Musicology* 18 (2001), 658–84
C. Lawson, *Mozart: Clarinet Concerto* (Cambridge, 1995)
N. Zaslaw, ed., *Mozart's Piano Concertos: Text, Context, Interpretation* (Ann Arbor, 1996)

Consoli, Tommaso (b. c.1753; d. after 1808). Italian castrato. Consoli was active at the MUNICH opera from 1773 to 1778; he probably took the part of Ramiro at the first performance of Mozart's LA FINTA GIARDINIERA (Munich, 13 Jan. 1775). That April he sang in SALZBURG as Adone in DOMENICO FISCHIETTI's *Gli orti esperidi* and, on 23 April, as Aminta in the premiere of Mozart's IL RE PASTORE; both works were composed to celebrate the visit there of ARCHDUKE MAXIMILIAN. Mozart met Consoli again in Munich in 1777 but the next year his contract was cancelled by the new Elector, Karl Thomas, and he returned to Italy, where he was active in Turin and Rome. CLIFF EISEN

'Coronation' concerto. Mozart's Piano Concerto in D, K537 (completed 24 Feb. 1788). See CONCERTOS

'Coronation' mass. Mozart's Mass in C, K317. See MASS

Così fan tutte, ossia La scuola degli amanti, K588 (Women are all the Same, or The School for Lovers), *dramma giocoso per musica* in two acts, libretto by LORENZO DA PONTE; first performed VIENNA, Burgtheater, 26 January 1790.

1. Genesis
2. Music and text
3. Reception

1. Genesis

We know little about the genesis of the last of three operas that Mozart produced in collaboration with Da Ponte, who called *Così fan tutte* 'the drama that holds third place among the sisters born of that most celebrated father of harmony'. Da Ponte always referred to the libretto by its subtitle; he probably conceived it originally for SALIERI, for whom it could have represented a kind of sequel to his *La scuola de' gelosi*. But Salieri, having composed one trio and written the vocal lines for another, gave up the opera. Much later CONSTANZE MOZART was to remember, as paraphrased by VINCENT NOVELLO, that 'Salieri first tried to set this opera but failed, and the great success of Mozart in accomplishing what he could make nothing of is supposed to have excited his envy and hatred, and have been the first origin of his enmity and malice towards Mozart'.

By the end of December 1789 rehearsals were already in progress. Mozart wrote to his friend PUCHBERG, asking for a loan and promising to pay it back when he received payment for the opera. After cancelling an engagement, he wrote (December 1789): 'But I invite you (and you alone) to my apartment at 10 in the morning on Thursday for a little opera rehearsal – I'm inviting only you and [Joseph] HAYDN.' The 200 ducats that he told Puchberg he was expecting from the theatrical management may have been an over-optimistic prediction. Payment records show that Mozart received only 100 ducats, the normal fee, for *Così fan tutte.*

As several critics have pointed out, *Così fan tutte* is an opera about opera: a tightly knit, gorgeously variegated web of allusions to operatic traditions, to individual works, and even to individual operatic numbers of the past. The symmetrical layout of the plot recalls METASTASIO's *drammi per musica*, as does Da Ponte's use of six characters, common in Metastasio and his followers. In the trio 'È la fede delle femmine', Da Ponte had Don Alfonso parody an aria by Metastasio; and the decorous vocabulary and diction of opera seria is maintained through much of the opera. Yet Da Ponte chose for his characters names that clearly suggest opera buffa. Dorabella, Fiordiligi and Despina may have sounded to some early audiences like a scrambling of Doralba and Fiordispina, two characters in Cimarosa's *L'impresario in angustie*, a comedy first performed in Rome in 1787 and very frequently and widely thereafter (though not in Vienna until 1793).

In superimposing the title *Così fan tutte* over the one that Da Ponte preferred, Mozart alluded to a tradition of derogatory generalizations about the opposite sex that goes back to the librettos of GOLDONI, whose works are full of arias and dialogues in which men criticize all women and women criticize all men. Such generalizations sometimes found expression in phrases that anticipate the title of Mozart's opera. In Francesco Puttini's libretto *La vera costanza*, set by Anfossi in 1776 and Joseph Haydn in 1778, Rosina complains to Lisetta, a servant, of Count Errico's attentions: 'I fled every encounter, but he followed me to the mountains, the seaside, the forest.' Lisetta responds: 'All men act like that' ('Fan così tutti gli uomini'). In Mozart's own FIGARO, Count Almaviva's discovery of Cherubino hiding in Susanna's room causes Basilio to comment: 'Così fan tutte le belle, / Non c'è alcuna novità.'

Opera buffa frequently explored themes of seduction and jealousy, faithfulness and sexual betrayal. Several librettists before Da Ponte used a plot device involving a man who hopes to demonstrate or to test the virtue of his fiancée by disguising himself and trying to seduce her, or by arranging for someone else to try to seduce her. In Antonio Sacchini's comic opera *La contadina in corte* (performed in Rome during Carnival 1766 and then, over the next twenty years, all over Europe, including Vienna), Baron Ruggiero decides to test the faithfulness of the peasant girl Sandrina, his wife-to-be. He persuades another peasant girl to disguise herself as a nobleman and to try to seduce Sandrina. The attempt, which involves a beautiful duet for the two sopranos, fails. Satisfied with his bride's virtue, Ruggiero looks forward to wedded bliss. Closer to *Così* is an episode in Goldoni's libretto *Le pescatrici* in which the fishermen Burlotto and Frisellino test the fidelity of their girlfriends by disguising themselves as noblemen. The women quickly succumb to their advances.

Mozart wrote his opera for a cast that, to the extent that we know their special skills and experience, must have inspired him and helped shape the individual roles. Alfonso, an old man whose 'philosophical' outlook on life comes from many years of experience, was created by the baritone FRANCESCO BUSSANI, a comic singer near the end of a thirty-year career that had demonstrated extraordinary dramatic and vocal versatility. The comic bass FRANCESCO BENUCCI sang Guilelmo (as his name is spelled in Mozart's autograph score and in the libretto printed for the first production). Having earlier created the role of Mozart's Figaro, he impressed Viennese audiences not only with his big voice and comic talents but also with a subtlety of characterization rarely found in those Italian male singers known as *buffi caricati* – caricature comics. 'He never exaggerates', marvelled a critic in 1793. The tenor Vincenzo Calvesi, who took the role of Ferrando, was a so-called *buffo di mezzo carattere*, a male singer in comic opera who specialized in the portrayal of young, often noble, lovers. 'Calvesi has a silvery tenor voice, and he enunciates with astonishing clarity', wrote COUNT ZINZENDORF in 1780; one of his Viennese admirers found that he combined 'a voice that is naturally sweet, pleasant, and sonorous with a technique that, without being too refined or studied, cannot but please our audience'.

The role of Fiordiligi was created by the prima donna of the Viennese troupe, ADRIANA FERRARESE DEL BENE, a young singer who brought with her to Vienna when she arrived in 1788 experience in both serious and comic opera. She excelled in bravura singing, but could also act. Singing in comic opera in London in 1786, she had won praise not only for 'the inexpressible feeling and pathetic manner' in which she sang a serious aria, but for giving her whole part 'the most lively colouring by her action'. Of LOUISE VILLENEUVE, who sang the role of Dorabella, we know little except that she had enjoyed a short career in comic opera in Italy before joining the Viennese troupe in 1789. Although she had sung in a couple of opere serie (in the minor theatre of Pavia in 1787) she clearly was no match for Ferrarese in the heroic style. Despina, finally, was created by Bussani's wife DOROTHEA SARDI BUSSANI. The only Viennese native in the cast, this mezzo-soprano had sung, among other roles, Cherubino in *Figaro*. She must have been a lively and charming actress. The *Gazzetta universale* of Florence praised her portrayal of Lisotta in Salieri's *La cifra*, another role that required excellent acting. She 'showed herself in this opera, as in many others, worthy of universal applause'.

2. Music and text

The overture presents twice, in the slow introduction and near the end of the scurrying Presto, the distinctive cadence to which Don Alfonso will pronounce the opera's motto near the end of the opera. The Presto alludes to Basilio's 'Così fan tutte le belle' by an almost literal quotation of the music to which he sang these words.

In a Neapolitan coffee-house two young military officers, Ferrando and Guilelmo, and an older civilian, Don Alfonso, are involved in a heated discussion. 'La mia Dorabella' is the first in a series of three trios that together represent the opera's *introduzione*, the ensemble (which often includes finale-like changes of tempo and metre) with which opere buffe of the second half of the eighteenth century frequently begin. The officers boast that their fiancées, the sisters Dorabella and Fiordiligi, are as faithful as they are beautiful. Alfonso, speaking from long experience, tells them that any woman is capable of infidelity. The young men insist that he prove his statement. He prefers not to do so, but they threaten to challenge him to a duel. He reacts philosophically, reflecting on the absurdity of man's desire to discover things that are sure to make him unhappy.

Alfonso tries to soothe his young friends' feelings; he has no intention to fight duels, but asks only that they keep in mind that their fiancées are not only human beings, with all the frailities of the species, but also women. In the second trio, 'È la fede delle femmine', a parody by Da Ponte of an aria text from Metastasio's *Demetrio*, Alfonso tells Ferrando and Guilelmo that constancy in a woman is like the legendary Phoenix: something that one talks of frequently without finding it. Each claims that his fiancée is the Phoenix, and in the following recitative they reject Alfonso's Metastasian paraphrase as 'nonsense written by poets' and 'the foolish talk of old men'.

When Alfonso asks them what proof they can offer of their beloveds' eternal constancy, they respond with a list of empty clichés they probably read in books: 'long experience', 'noble education', 'lofty thoughts', 'analogous temperaments' and so on. The old man laughs at their naivety. He offers to bet that Dorabella and Fiordiligi are just like other women. Ferrando and Guilelmo accept. The amount wagered, 100 zecchini, perhaps involved an inside joke between Da Ponte and Mozart, since this was exactly the fee that Mozart was later to receive for composing *Così fan tutte*. (Italians frequently referred to ducats as zecchini.)

In the third and final trio, 'Una bella serenata', Ferrando and Guilelmo are more clearly differentiated than earlier, both in words and music. Ferrando emerges as tender, romantic and artistically inclined. With a lyrical and noble melody, he says that with his share of the winnings he will organize a serenade for Dorabella. Guilelmo is more down-to-earth; he will give a dinner party in honour of Fiordiligi, he sings to a melody dominated by the two-bar phrases and disjunct contours typical of music written for *buffi caricati*. All three men join together in anticipation of toasts to the goddess of love, which they sing to music similar to that which Mozart would later use in another piece expressing masculine joy: 'Laut verkünde unsre Freude' in the *Freimaurerkantate*, K623. Mozart returned in 'Una bella serenata' to the key and to much the same orchestration (with trumpets and drums) as the overture. The cadential material at the end of this number resembles that at the end of the overture (note the characteristic drum-roll that continues while the rest of the orchestra is silent), encouraging one to hear 'Una bella serenata' as the end of a musical unit that began with the overture.

The shift to a key a third below C, A major, accompanies a change of scene to a garden by the sea and a move from the masculine to the feminine sphere. In its length and change of tempo the duet 'Ah guarda sorella' resembles an introduzione. If the three trios that preceded it can be thought of as an introduzione for the men, this duet can be thought of as a separate, parallel one for Dorabella and Fiordiligi. The sisters look at portraits of their husbands-to-be and praise their handsomeness with music that conveys the sensuousness and sweetness of erotic desire. In the Allegro that follows they unknowingly allude to future events when they pray to the god of love to make them suffer if they ever fall in love with someone else. The high-pitched horns in A playing in octaves in the orchestral postlude, by alluding to cuckoldry, undercut the women's protestations of constancy.

Talk of the forthcoming weddings is interrupted by Alfonso, who announces, in 'Vorrei dir, e cor non ho', a very short aria in F minor (Allegro agitato) that he has bad news. Ferrando and Guilelmo have been called to active duty. The young men enter. In the quintet 'Sento, o Dio', they address the women in the formal, tragic language of opera seria. The women respond in the same high tragic style, demanding that their lovers run them through with their swords. The young men express, in the short duettino 'Al fato dan legge', their hope that they will soon return to the beloveds' arms. In an aside, Alfonso declares his approval of their performance, referring to the deception that he has set in motion as a 'delightful comedy'.

Suddenly the sound of a military drum in the distance calls the men to arms. The chorus 'Bella vita militar' begins with a long orchestral introduction that serves as a march accompanying the arrival of troops. Civilian men and women assemble to watch, and a ship pulls up to shore. Clearly Alfonso has organized this charade on a grand scale, and at great expense. Even if he wins the bet, he will make no money; but it was to teach his young friends a lesson rather than to make money that he made the bet in the first place.

In the quintet 'Di scrivermi ogni giorno' the women ask their lovers to write to them every day, the men promise to do so, and they bid one another a final farewell. It is tempting to laugh at Dorabella's request that Ferrando write to her two times a day; but Da Ponte may not have intended this as comic exaggeration. Only a few years after the composition of *Così fan tutte* Emperor Francis of Austria and his wife Marie Therese sometimes corresponded twice a day; she once wrote, in the midst of a campaign against Napoleon that was going disastrously for the Austrians: 'Dearest, best husband. Still no news from you. Today is the fourth letter-less day. Have you entirely forgotten me?' Out of the simplest harmonic material the quintet gradually blossoms into music of exquisite beauty, whose pathos, parodoxically, is intensified rather than undercut by Alfonso's aside: 'I'll burst if I don't laugh.'

The quintet's contemplativeness is swept aside by a repetition of the chorus (this time without the orchestral introduction) as the boat departs with Guilelmo and Ferrando on board. Don Alfonso joins the women in the terzettino 'Soave sia il vento', a prayer for calm winds and a safe voyage. The muted violins depict the sea's gentle surface with a rippling stream of semiquavers. Instead of simultaneously expressing his point of view in an aside, as he did in the previous quintet, Alfonso waits until after the women have left before congratulating himself ('I'm not a bad actor') and looking forward to a quick and favourable conclusion to his plot. Perhaps prompted by the view of the sea and the maritime imagery of the previous trio, he quotes the Renaissance poet Sannazaro to the effect that trusting a woman's heart is as futile as ploughing the sea (the strings here serve as musical quotations marks).

A change of scene reveals a room inside the sisters' house. Their servant Despina complains, like many operatic servants before her, of all the work she has to do. She is astonished when her mistresses enter, removing all their jewellery and other adornments. Fiordiligi asks for a sword, and Dorabella begins a violent orchestrally accompanied recitative, ordering Despina to close the windows and then to leave her alone. The aria that follows, 'Smanie implacabili', is reminiscent of Alfonso's 'Vorrei dir, e cor non ho' not only in tempo (Allegro agitato) but in its almost constant use of a single rhythmic motif in the violins that features a rest on the beat. Despite this aria's heroic trappings, Dorabella's agitation sounds like something imitated rather than sincerely felt.

Despina, on hearing that the young men have gone off to battle, consoles the sisters. Their lovers are likely to return home safe and sound; but should they die, there are plenty of equally good men to take their place. In the meantime, since they cannot trust the men to be faithful, why should the women not amuse themselves while the men are gone? In her light, cheerful aria 'In uomini, in soldati' Despina mocks her mistress's naive trust in men's capacity for fidelity and urges them to dispense their amorous affections as freely as their absent lovers surely will.

Alfonso, alone, expresses fear that Despina might recognize the men in the disguises that he has had them put on. He offers her a gold coin, with a promise of more to come, if she introduces to her mistresses two handsome young acquaintances of his. She accepts his proposition. At the beginning of the sextet 'Alla bella Despinetta' the march-like melody sung by Alfonso sounds like a duple-metre version of the tune to which Don Giovanni and Zerlina sing the words 'Andiam, andiam mio bene' – as if Alfonso is confidently looking forward to the successful seduction of Fiordiligi and Dorabella. He presents to Despina Guilelmo and Ferrando, who are disguised as Albanians in exotic clothes and moustaches. They immediately begin acting the part of debonair ladies' men, their first words a series of sweet endearments. In an aside, Despina laughs at their appearance; meanwhile, all three men express to one another relief that she has not penetrated the disguises.

At the approach of the sisters, Alfonso hides. A change of metre from duple to triple accompanies the entrance of the women, who berate the maid for allowing men to enter their house and order her to ask them to leave immediately. Kneeling, Despina and the young men ask for mercy in a passage in A minor whose descending chromatic lines offer a musical counterpart to the word 'languir'. The Neapolitan-sixth harmony (at 'spasimanti') might sound sincerely tragic if it were not extended and repeated to the point of parody. Despina and the men plead for calm, but the women explode with anger as the tempo suddenly accelerates to Molto allegro. Ferrando and Guilelmo, meanwhile, are delighted to witness this evidence of the women's constancy, while Despina and Alfonso (in his hiding place) think the ladies do protest too much.

Alfonso appears, asking the reason for the commotion. Fiordiligi and Dorabella point to the two strange men, whom Alfonso greets as old friends whose presence is as surprising as it is delightful. Guilelmo and Ferrando respond in similar fashion, and then, turning to the sisters, declare their love in the most florid language of serious opera, set by Mozart as orchestrally accompanied recitative. The personalities of the two sisters begin to differentiate, with Dorabella asking her sister what they should do, and Fiordiligi taking charge. As the recitative continues, she orders the men to leave in language just as florid as theirs. Her aria, 'Come scoglio', is a splendid bravura showpiece conceived to give Ferrarese ample opportunity to show off her *cantar di sbalzo* (the technique of leaping between the top and bottom of one's tessitura) and coloratura. 'Come scoglio' refers, in its opening melody, its huge leaps and its triplet coloratura, to an earlier aria, Angelo Tarchi's 'Se il nome mio non basta', that Ferrarese had sung in Martín y Soler's *L'arbore di Diana*.

About to leave the stage, as we would expect a character to do after such an imposing aria, Fiordiligi is called back by Ferrando, while Guilelmo begs Dorabella to stay. Alfonso pleads on their behalf, reminding the sisters that they are gentlemen, and his friends. Guilelmo launches into a short comic aria, 'Non siate ritrosi', in which he speaks for both himself and Ferrando, boasting of their physical charms and inviting the sisters to inspect their skin, their noses, and their moustaches. (Mozart wrote this aria late in the preparation of the opera to replace a much longer, more traditional comic aria for Guilelmo, 'Rivolgete a lui lo sguardo'.) Near the end of 'Non siate ritrosi' the women leave. Guilelmo and Ferrando laugh, as they continue to do in the trio that follows. 'E voi ridete' closely resembles a trio for three men in Salieri's *La grotta di Trofonio* (1785), 'Ma perchè in ordine', a very fast comic number that may have inspired this one. While the young men laugh because they think they have won the bet, Alfonso warns them that the laughing will end in tears.

Guilelmo wonders when he and Ferrando will have a chance to eat; a concern with eating is typical of characters portrayed by *buffi caricati* like Benucci. Ferrando, displaying the more noble and romantic character associated with *buffi di mezzo carattere* like Calvesi, assures his friend that they will partake of a more delightful meal when the current business is concluded. In his aria 'Un' aura amorosa', a tender and passionate Andante cantabile in A major, he sings of the refreshment that their hearts will find in the amorous sighs of their beloveds.

Alfonso considers for the first time the possibility that the sisters are examples of that rare thing, the faithful woman; but he quickly rejects this idea and turns to Despina for help in breaking down the women's resistance.

The finale of Act I takes place in a garden, where we find Fiordiligi and Dorabella peacefully expressing their melancholy. They are interrupted by the sound of the Albanians, offstage. Accompanied by tremolos in the strings and violent contrasts of dynamics, the men cry out that their death alone will satisfy the ungrateful objects of their passion. Alfonso pleads with them not to kill themselves. They enter, drink from glasses that they throw away, and soon begin to show the effects of poison. Now that they are near death, Alfonso tells the sisters, the woman can at least show them some compassion. He and Despina go off to find a doctor. While Dorabella and Fiordiligi express horror at being left alone with two dying strangers, Ferrando and Guilelmo comment, in an aside, on the charming play that they are taking part in. Their sighs begin to have an effect on the women, who take pity on them. They move closer, and Dorabella's feelings evolve from pity to a kind of admiration: 'Che figure interessanti!' The men notice the change, and accept, for the first time, the possibility that their fiancées might give in.

Don Alfonso returns with Despina disguised as a doctor who greets the sisters in mangled Latin. Having ascertained the type of poison used, she pulls out a magnet and cures the young men with its Mesmeric powers. As they gradually regain consciousness, Alfonso, Dorabella and Fiordiligi praise the doctor for the seeming miracle that he has achieved.

A shift of a third from G major to B flat major, a new tempo, and a new metre together lend credence to the play-acting of Ferrando and Guilelmo, who pretend, as they stand up, that they think they are dreaming and that the women they see are Minerva and Venus. They take the women's hands and kiss them. Despina tells the sisters not to be alarmed; it is only an effect of the poison. The women protest, but only weakly. They know that their ability to resist has limits.

Another third-relation takes us to D major, the key with which the finale began, and to the sound of a cheerful tune the men try to take advantage of their gains by asking for a kiss. The request stuns the women and restores to them suddenly their sense of honour and virtue. In this Allegro and the Presto that follows, they express their outrage with a unanimity suggested by their frequent singing in unison. Against their anger further appeals for kisses from the young strangers and further attempts at mediation by Despina and Alfonso are useless. The act ends with a tumult of conflicting emotions.

The dust has settled by the time Act 2 begins, with Despina trying to persuade Fiordiligi and Dorabella to accept the advances of the two young strangers and to enjoy their attention. In her aria 'Una donna a quindici anni' she gives a lesson in flirting. The pure, transparent cheeriness of this music has an effect on the sisters, who, left alone, persuade one another to accept Despina's arguments. But at first only Dorabella is prepared to act on their new understanding that as long as their fiancés are unaware of their dalliance with the Albanians, there is no harm in it. Dorabella announces that she has already decided which of the men she will flirt with. When she begins the duet 'Prenderò quel brunettino' by saying she will take the nice dark-haired one, Fiordiligi, following her lead, says she will laugh and joke with the blond. The sisters' concern with the men's physical attributes reminds us of their very first duet, when they praised their fiancés' appearance rather than their character.

Alfonso appears; he tells the women to hasten outside, where a delightful treat awaits them in the form of instrumental and vocal music. The scene changes to the seaside garden, to which has arrived a wind octet (pairs of flutes – held in reserve until the chorus enters – clarinets, bassoons and horns) on a boat decorated with flowers. The players accompany Ferrando and Guilelmo in the performance of a serenade in which the young men, like several of Metastasio's heroes and heroines, ask the breeze to carry their sighs to their beloveds. The appeal to the wind to further their desires ironically recalls the women's much earlier prayer, shortly after the departure of their lovers, that the wind be soft, the waves gentle, and 'every element respond propitiously to our desires'.

The combination of visual and sonic stimuli puts the women in a receptive mood, which leaves the men tongue-tied. The quartet that follows corresponds the closest of any single number to the opera's subtitle. This is the school for lovers, team-taught by Alfonso (who begins by taking Dorabella's hand) and Despina (who takes Fiordiligi's). Alfonso tells the men what to say, and they, the good pupils that they are, repeat his words and music exactly. Satisfied that the women will soon capitulate, the teachers leave their students on their own.

The new couples make small talk with amusing awkwardness. Fiordiligi and Ferrando walk off, leaving Dorabella alone with Guilelmo, who asks her to accept a heart-shaped pendant as a token of his love for her. She hesitates only a little before accepting it. In their duet 'Il core vi dono' she delays her complete surrender to Guilelmo by saying that although she has accepted his heart, she cannot give hers to him because she has already given it to another. He gently turns her head away so she does not observe his removing Ferrando's portrait from her locket and replacing it with his heart, while she, fully aware of what he is doing, says in an aside that she feels Vesuvius in her breast. The parallel tenths with which they celebrate their union represent a kind of relationship that we have not seen in this opera. The sisters have sung frequently in parallel thirds and sixths with one another; so have the young men. But the passionate love that was supposed to have existed between Fiordiligi and Guilelmo and between Dorabella and Ferrando was never represented with erotically charged parallel intervals. That is why the audience may agree, and probably was intended to agree, with Dorabella and Guilelmo when they celebrate the 'cambio felice' that has resulted in this electrifying new relationship. They leave the stage arm in arm, the most explicit way that eighteenth-century dramatists could tell an audience that a couple is about to consummate their union.

Ferrando and Fiordiligi return, filled with the stormy passions characteristic of these more noble characters. He begs her to look at him, and when she does, he expresses his delight in the aria 'Ah lo veggio quell'anima bella'. But when she moves away from him in silence, the tempo accelerates from Allegretto to Allegro to depict Ferrando's renewed desperation. Telling Fiordiligi that she has condemned him to death, he leaves as if about to kill himself. To threaten suicide is the most common and most effective technique of operatic seduction, and it works here, just as it worked in the finale of Act I. Fiordiligi, alone, admits in an anguished recitative that she desires Ferrando, but her passion is hopelessly mixed with remorse. In her great rondò, 'Per pietà, ben mio, perdona', she begs the absent Guilelmo's pardon for the illicit passion that she feels for the noble stranger who courts her so ardently.

Ferrando and Guilelmo, in the opera's only scene in which just the two of them converse, report to each other on their success, or lack of it, in seducing each other's fiancées. Guilelmo is delighted to hear of Fiordiligi's stubborn resistance to Ferrando's advances; but Ferrando, expecting to hear the same about Dorabella, is horrified and outraged on learning that she has capitulated. Restrained by Guilelmo from going to confront the unfaithful woman, he asks his friend for advice. Guilelmo has none to give, except to expand upon the opera's motto (in his light-weight aria 'Donne mie, la fate a tanti') by characterizing women as prone to infidelity.

Left alone, Ferrando gives expression to his shame and anger in an orchestrally accompanied recitative. He resolves to forget Dorabella, but quickly realizes that he still loves her. His aria 'Tradito, schernito', in its rapid shifts from minor to major, reflects his conflicting emotions. By ending in C major, with a cadence in the vocal part very close to one that he sang in praise of Dorabella near the beginning of the opera ('Una bella serenata', also in C), Ferrando reaffirms his passion for his fiancée, though it is a love now largely fuelled by jealousy.

Guilelmo and Alfonso have been listening in on the latter part of Ferrando's aria; they now enter. Guilelmo, whose previous aria showed that he had begun to learn Alfonso's lesson, either does not notice the inconsistency between that lesson and Fiordiligi's apparent constancy, or if he does notice, he attributes her virtue to himself: 'Do you really think that a fiancée could be unfaithful to a Guilelmo?' When he asks Alfonso for the 50 zecchini he has won, the old man reminds him that he and Ferrando have promised to do as he says for the whole day, and the day is not over yet.

From the garden by the seaside a change of scene takes us back inside the house of Fiordiligi and Dorabella. When Fiordiligi admits that she loves her blond suitor, her sister and Despina try to persuade her to give in to her feelings. Dorabella, adopting Despina's compound metre and cheerful manner of expression, portrays Cupid as a little thief, a little serpent, who finds ways to penetrate even the most heavily armoured soul. She and Despina leave Fiordiligi alone to struggle with her nascent passion for the mysterious stranger. She suddenly decides that she and Dorabella will put on extra uniforms left by Ferrando and Guilelmo and will join their fiancés on the battlefield. Watched from the doorway by Guilelmo and Alfonso, she tears off her headdress.

As the duet 'Fra gli amplessi' begins, with Fiordiligi looking forward to embracing her faithful lover, we have no way of knowing that it is not a heroic aria for Fiordiligi. But a sudden shift from the dominant, E major, to its parallel minor, E minor, dramatizes the entrance of Ferrando, who tells her he will die of grief. Fiordiligi steers the tonality from E minor to C major and Ferrando follows her lead. The melody he sings is full of irony for the audience. He had sung it near the beginning of the opera, in the same key, to the words 'Una bella serenata / Far io voglio alla mia dea'; he had alluded to it at the end of his aria 'Tradito, schernito', again in reference to Dorabella; now he serenades another goddess, very likely with more passion than he had ever mustered for Dorabella. Still controlling the direction of the conversation, Fiordiligi nudges the tonality towards A minor (at 'Sorgi, sorgi') in order to prepare for a return to the tonic A major that will coincide with her surrender. She encourages Ferrando with questions to which she already knows the answer: 'Per pietà da me che chiedi?' She realizes now, repeating Zerlina's 'Non son più forte' in *Don Giovanni*, that she is about to succumb. She can only give the dominant of A one final reiteration, asking the gods for advice. But it is of course Ferrando, sensing now that she is ready to give in, who answers her plea, in the gorgeous A major Larghetto, 'Volgi a me pietoso il ciglio'. To the horror of Guilelmo, who is still eavesdropping, she tells Ferrando to do with her what he will. Their singing in parallel sixths and tenths represents their embrace, as do the canonic passages that follow. They leave the stage, but not, like Dorabella and Guilelmo at the analogous place earlier in the act, arm in arm. Ferrando, aware that Guilelmo and Alfonso are watching, cannot take Fiordiligi immediately to bed.

Ferrando reappears less than a minute after his exit, delighted that he can now give Guilelmo a taste of his own medicine. When Guilelmo looks for a way to punish the women, Alfonso says the best way to do so would be to marry them. The men reject this idea at first, but then admit that they still love

Fiordiligi and Dorabella. In a brief Andante accompanied by strings, Alfonso calls women's tendency to be unfaithful 'necessità del core', something that lovers cannot condemn since they should expect it. He asks the men to repeat the final lesson in this school for lovers: 'Già che giovani, vecchie, e belle, e brutte, / Ripetete con me: Così fan tutte.' The list of physical types here, in reminding us of Don Giovanni's 'non picciol libro', reminds us also that a corollary to Alfonso's dictum is that men should satisfy woman's inclination by widely distributing their favours.

Despina enters to announce that the women have agreed to marry their new suitors and to leave with them in three days. A change of scene reveals a magnificently appointed room with a table set for four and an orchestra in the background; and the finale of Act 2 begins with Despina and Alfonso making sure all the preparations for the wedding are done. Orchestra and chorus accompany the entry of the two young couples with solemn, march-like music in E flat major.

Ferrando, Guilelmo, Dorabella and Fiordiligi raise their glasses in a toast that takes the form of a ravishingly beautiful canon, 'E nel tuo, nel mio bicchiero'. Only Guilelmo, for reasons not at all clear, refuses to join in, muttering instead in an aside that he wishes the women would take poison.

An extraordinary tonal shift, from A flat major to E major, abruptly pulls us away from the canon's timeless spell. Alfonso informs the young people that the marriage contract is ready. The notary – Despina in her second disguise – reads the contract in a comic monotone, mentioning for the first time the men's assumed names, Tizio and Sempronio. The women sign the contract, but before the men have a chance to do so, the chorus from Act 1 that accompanied the departure of the men, 'Bella vita militar', is heard in the distance.

The ceremony is suddenly put on hold as Alfonso looks out of the window. Another very abrupt tonal shift, from D major to E flat major, conveys Alfonso's pretended shock; he announces in horror that the sisters' original fiancés have returned. The women hide the Albanians in another room; the men have just enough time to shed their disguises and put on their military hats and coats before returning as Guilelmo and Ferrando. But their play-acting is not over. Now they must pretend to be happy to see Dorabella and Fiordiligi, who are speechless. Guilelmo finds Despina, still disguised as a notary, hiding in a neighbouring room; she quickly reveals her identity, adding to the sister's confusion. Alfonso drops the wedding contract on the floor to be noticed by the young men, who express astonishment when they see that their fiancées have signed it. The fast scales in the strings accompanying their expression of rage were frequently used in the late eighteenth century for depicting storms.

The sisters tell their former fiancés that their crime deserves punishment by death, but Fiordiligi points accusingly at Alfonso and Despina as the ones who should tell what happened. By way of explanation, Alfonso directs the young men back into the room in which they earlier hid. They return with their Albanian clothes, but without the rest of their disguises, and mock the women (including Despina) by quoting music from memorable moments earlier in the opera.

Shocked yet again, the sisters realize now that Alfonso was behind the whole charade. He admits it, but quickly deflects any further criticism from them by claiming that his deception had the benefit of undeceiving their lovers. He joins the young people together in pairs.

Mozart and Da Ponte did not say explicitly in the libretto or score whether the women are united with their new lovers or their old ones. In favour of a return to the state of affairs at the beginning of the opera, one could argue that the resolution of a great many, probably most Italian comic operas of the eighteenth century represented a reaffirmation of the social ties presented at the beginning: Susanna begins and ends with Figaro, the Countess begins and ends with the Count. In favour of bringing together the new pairs, one could argue that *Così* began with emotional and social mismatches: the earthy and jocular Guilelmo, sung by a *buffo caricato*, had no business getting married to the passionate and noble-hearted Fiordiligi; nor should the romantic, tender Ferrando, sung by a *buffo di mezzo carattere*, have been involved with cheerful, superficial Dorabella. The two women, in any case, go back immediately to their old habit of singing in parallel thirds with one another, leading us to believe that the whole experience has not taught them much.

In the opera's final Allegro molto all the soloists recite a moral that takes Alfonso's views on relations between the sexes to a higher, more general plain, and suddenly puts his philosophy in the context of famous ancient Greek philosophical traditions. To laugh in the face of life's hardships was the central teaching of the ancient cynics, led by Diogenes, 'the laughing philosopher'; the 'lovely calm' that one can find amidst the world's whirlwinds is the *ataraxia* – the freedom from passion – that Epicurus urged his followers to seek.

3. Reception

The first performance of *Così fan tutte* was the most heavily attended operatic performance in the Burgtheater during the 1789–90 operatic year. The performances that followed were also well attended, suggesting that Mozart had a hit on his hands. Count Zinzendorf, who was at the premiere, wrote that 'Mozart's music is charming, and the subject rather amusing'. One of the earliest published reports of the opera, in the Weimar *Journal des Luxus und der Moden*, was also favourable: 'I announce to you another excellent work of Mozart that our theatres has received . . . Concerning the music: that it is by Mozart says all, I believe.' EMPEROR JOSEPH II's death on 20 February, less that a month after the premiere, was followed by a period of mourning during which the Burgtheater was closed; but when it reopened, *Così* returned for several more performances. That it left the stage after early 1791 had more to do with a theatrical reorganization by the new emperor, LEOPOLD II, than with the merits of Mozart's opera. Leopold's reorganization, which involved the reintroduction of opera seria and ballet, left practically no place in the repertory for comic operas first brought to the stage during Joseph's reign, whether composed by Salieri, Martín or Mozart.

During the nineteenth century *Così fan tutte* was subject to many and various adaptations by those who found its plot frivolous or offensive. But these did nothing to find a place in the repertory for a work that Eduard Hanslick dismissed, despite its 'lovely music', as 'no longer stageworthy'. A revival of interest in *Così* began in 1897 with an influential production in Munich conducted by Richard Strauss; Edward Dent, in the first edition of *Mozart's Operas* (1913), urged a critical reappraisal of what he called 'the best of all Da Ponte's librettos and the most exquisite work of art among Mozart's operas'. Performances at Glyndebourne from 1934, and a recording of the Glyndebourne cast made in 1935, helped to establish the opera's honoured place in the Mozart canon. JOHN A. RICE

B. A. Brown, *W. A. Mozart: Così fan tutte* (Cambridge, 1995)
M. Hunter, *The Culture of Opera Buffa in Mozart's Vienna* (Princeton, 1999)
Edmund Goehring, *Three Modes of Perception in Mozart: The Philosophical Pastoral, and Comic in Così fan tutte* (Cambridge, 2004)

'Credo' mass. Mozart's Mass in C, K257. See MASS

Czernin family. Noble Bohemian family linked to the Mozarts in SALZBURG. Count Prokop Adalbert Czernin (b. 23 Mar. 1726; d. 30 Jan. 1777) married Maria Antonia von Colloredo (b. 21 Apr. 1728; d. 2 Oct. 1757, eldest sister of Archbishop COLLOREDO). Two of the couple's children lived in Salzburg: Antonie (b. 26 Mar. 1750; d. 25 Apr. 1801), who moved there after her marriage to Johann Nepomuk Gottfried von LÜTZOW, commander of the fortress in Salzburg, and Johann Rudolph (b. 9 June 1757; d. 23 Apr. 1845), who went to university there. Both were musical. Antonie was a keyboard player who occasionally performed at court; and Johann Rudolph was a violinist.

On 13 December 1776, soon after Johann Rudolph's arrival in Salzburg, an arrangement was made whereby Count Prokop offered to pay Mozart 20 ducats annually for compositions. However, the plan foundered because of Prokop's death. Though the contredanses K269b have been linked to the Czernins, it is not certain that they are authentic Mozart works.

Johann Rudolph Czernin was an indefatigable amateur musician. He was sometimes scorned by the Mozarts for his poor violin-playing and his general ineptness (see Leopold's letter of 29 June 1778, entertainingly describing his ham-fisted attempt to serenade Countess LODRON on her name day). Nevertheless, he was a supporter of Mozart and his name appears on the list of subscribers to Mozart's Viennese concerts in 1784. Antonie, Countess Lützow, was the dedicatee of Mozart's keyboard concerto K246, written in 1776. It does not make great technical demands of the soloist, and was used by the Mozarts as part of their teaching repertory – in 1777 Mozart took it with him on his journey to PARIS and taught it to his pupil Therese Pierron in MANNHEIM. Of particular interest is the surviving source material for the concerto, especially its three sets of cadenzas, differentiated as to technical demands, and its autograph continuo part throughout: this material offers valuable information about performance practice in Mozart's concertos. RUTH HALLIWELL

C. Eisen, 'The Mozarts' Salzburg Copyists: Aspects of Attribution, Chronology, Text, Style, and Performance Practice', in *Mozart Studies*, ed. C. Eisen (Oxford, 1991), 253–307
F. Ferguson, 'Mozart's Keyboard Concertos: Tutti Notations and Performance Models', *Mozart Jahrbuch* 1984/85, 32–9
H. Schuler, *Mozarts Salzburger Freunde und Bekannte* (Wilhelmshaven, 1995), 47–52

D

Da Ponte, Lorenzo (b. Ceneda, 10 Mar. 1749; d. New York, 17 Aug. 1838), Italian librettist; Mozart's collaborator on LE NOZZE DI FIGARO (1786), DON GIOVANNI (1787) and COSÌ FAN TUTTE (1790). His picaresque lifestyle took him from his birthplace, Ceneda (now Vittorio Veneto), through Venice, VIENNA and LONDON to New York.

Da Ponte was born Emmanuele Conegliano, adopting the name of the Bishop of Ceneda on his family's conversion from Judaism to Christianity. Like his friend Casanova, he was a raffish figure plagued by scandal at every turn. After being exiled from Venice, he worked with the poet CATERINO MAZZOLÀ in Dresden before moving to Vienna in late 1781 (Mazzolà recommended him to ANTONIO SALIERI), where he attracted the favour of EMPEROR JOSEPH II. When the Emperor abandoned his pursuit of German opera and revived the Italian company at the Burgtheater, in 1783, Da Ponte was appointed the main poet to the theatre. His subsequent involvement in the remarkable flowering of opera buffa in Vienna in 1783–90 and his collaborations with MARTÍN Y SOLER (*Il burbero di buon cuore*, *Una cosa rara*), Salieri (*Il ricco d'un giorno*, *Axur, re d'Ormus*), Mozart and others made him the most significant librettist of his generation.

Da Ponte was an ideal theatre poet, with a facility for versifying, a ready wit and a sound knowledge of languages; the much admired CARLO GOLDONI was his model. His work included translating texts from French to Italian, reworking old librettos for revivals and providing new texts (themselves often adaptations) for Viennese composers. As poet, he would also have been in charge of production. Mozart was somewhat suspicious of his arrogance and his penchant for intrigue (so he wrote to his father on 7 May 1783), and Da Ponte in turn was ambivalent about Mozart in his memoirs, recognizing his genius but (as was common in the early nineteenth century) doubting his stage skills. He regarded his *L'arbore di Diana* for Martín y Soler as his best libretto. But Da Ponte and Mozart's working relationship appears to have been amicable, and probably more so than the composer's previous dealings with other librettists. Mozart also knew that he had to keep Da Ponte on his side if he was to achieve his desired success in the Viennese theatre.

Da Ponte may not have been the librettist of Mozart's early attempt to capitalize on the new fashion for Italian opera in Vienna, *Lo sposo deluso* (1783). But he pulled off the difficult task of turning Beaumarchais's controversial play *La Folle Journée, ou Le Mariage de Figaro* into an opera, despite LEOPOLD MOZART's dire predictions (see his letter of 11 Nov. 1785) and potential political scandal. *Don Giovanni*, drawing on a long tradition of plays and librettos dealing with the character, provided just the right mixture of the serious and the comic to enable Mozart to appeal to his PRAGUE audience. Only in *Così fan tutte*, a masterpiece by any poetic standard, do librettist and composer appear to have been on different wavelengths: Mozart seems to have missed Da Ponte's rich vein of literary references, allusions and parody – referring both to the Renaissance masters and to METASTASIO – and took things more, perhaps too, seriously.

Da Ponte had only half a tongue in his cheek when he made Ferrando dismiss Don Alfonso's 'sciocccherie di poeti' ('poets' nonsense'): he knew that libretto writing was more a craft than an art. His texts do what was expected, using seven- and eleven-syllable *versi sciolti* (blank verse) for the recitatives and more structured verse in other line-lengths (five-, six-, eight- or ten-syllable lines) for the arias and ensembles. For the most part, Mozart responds accordingly, with only the occasional mismatch between text and music: for example, the Act 3 sextet of *Figaro* (No. 18) was probably intended by Da Ponte to be in two musical sections (it shifts from eight- to six-syllable lines), while the Act 1 'letter' quintet in *Così*, 'Di scrivermi ogni giorno' (No. 9), was designed as recitative.

What is most attractive in Da Ponte is his compressed syntax and witty rhymes. Take, for example, Despina's hilarious comment on the strange appearance of the 'Albanians' in the Act 1 sextet of *Così* ('Alla bella Despinetta', No. 13):

Despina	Che sembianze! che vestiti! che figure! che mustacchi! Io non so se son Vallacchi o se Turchi son costor.
Don Alfonso	Che ti par di quell'aspetto?
Despina	Per parlarvi schietto, schietto, hanno un muso fuor dell'uso, vero antidoto d'amor.

(Des. What looks! What clothes! What appearances! What moustaches! I don't know whether they are Poles or Turks.
D.A. What do you think of their appearance?
Des. To speak quite frankly, they have a very unusual face, a true antidote to love.)

Few poets would have dared to match 'mustacchi' with 'Vallachi', or repeat the 'schietto', while the internal 'muso'–'uso' rhyme is carefully pointed up by Mozart.

This kind of patter worked well within opera bulfa, with the music left just to carry the words. But sometimes the verse has more specifically musical implications. In the Act 3 sextet of *Figaro*, Susanna enters to pay off her fiancé's debt to Marcellina:

Alto, alto, signor Conte,
mille doppie son quì pronte,
a pagar vengo per Figaro
ed a porlo in libertà.

(Stop, stop, my lord Count, I have a thousand doubloons here, I come to pay for Figaro and to free him.)

Here the third-line *verso sdrucciolo* (with the accent on the antepenultimate syllable, 'Fí-ga-ro') prompted Mozart to produce an achingly beautiful phrase, while the final *verso tronco* (the accent on the last syllable, the line thus ending weak-strong rather than the more common strong-weak) provides both a poetic and a musical cadence. Only very rarely did Mozart need to play around with this wonderful verse, or to add words of his own accord (for example, the 'sua madre'/'suo padre' repetitions in the same sextet).

Da Ponte was dismissed from Vienna in 1791 as a result of court intrigue after the death of Joseph II. He resumed his wanderings around Europe, ending up in London, where he spent some ten years at the King's Theatre, Haymarket. In 1805 he was forced to flee his creditors, taking passage to America. He became a grocer and general merchant in New York, then Philadelphia, while supplementing his income with private teaching. He returned to New York in 1819, became involved in various abortive theatrical ventures, and occupied the (largely honorary) post of Professor of Italian at Columbia College. His memoirs suggest a degree of disillusionment – a projected final volume was never completed – but on his death his remarkable achievements received significant recognition. TIM CARTER

S. Hodges, *Lorenzo Da Ponte: The Life and Times of Mozart's Librettist* (London, 1985)
C. Pagnini, ed., *Memorie di Lorenzo Da Ponte da Ceneda scritte da esso* (1823–7) (Milan, 1971); trans. E. Abbott (Philadelphia, 1929, repr. 1967)

Dalberg, Wolfgang Heribert, Rechsfreiherr von (b. 18 Nov. 1750; d. 27 Sept. 1806). Diplomat, Intendant of the Mannheim National Theatre 1778–1803 and amateur author; Schiller's *Die Räuber* and *Fiesko* were first performed under his direction. During his stay in MANNHEIM, Mozart wrote to Dalberg (24 Nov. 1778), indicating his difficulty in securing an audition with him and asking whether he should consider prolonging his stay by two months to write and direct a monodrama. Mozart also politely stated his reservations about setting a libretto by Dalberg. At least ten Dalbergs are referred to in the Mozart correspondence and Leopold remarked blasphemously (in a letter of 3 Aug. 1763) on the antiquity of the Dalberg family (the original name was Cämmerer von Worms), members of which were helpful to them in the Rhineland; it was probably Baron Wolfgang's brother Johann Friedrich Hugo (b. 17 May 1752; d. 26 July 1812) who appears in the list of subscribers to Mozart's VIENNA concerts and some of whose songs were erroneously included in Rellstab's edition of Mozart's songs (Berlin, 1798). PETER BRANSCOMBE

E. L. Stahl, *Shakespeare und das deutsche Theater* (Stuttgart, 1947)

dances. Dancing played a central role in the social life of Mozart's time. On the one hand, it was traditionally considered a valuable component of education among the upper classes, promoting bodily well-being and elegant deportment. On the other, it was the highlight and centre of an evening's social intercourse, where class barriers were temporarily lifted. The resulting exuberance often went so far that dancing regulations had repeatedly to be instituted to keep the unbridled passion for dancing in check.

These different roles are mirrored in the different dance types of the age. The central dance form of the Baroque, the minuet, was still very popular as a dance for couples: it begins and ends with a bow and typically describes a Z pattern, with each basic step drawn out over two bars of music. With its dignified, triple metre and its graceful, stylized bearing, it was considered the touchstone of the art of dancing.

At the other end of the spectrum from the minuet is the *Deutsche* or German Dance, which stemmed from the lower social classes and thrust its way into the dance repertory during Mozart's time. As an immediate precursor of the waltz, it is also in triple time (albeit at a much faster tempo), and is also a dance for couples, but with a completely different character. The *Deutsche* is distinguished by the elaborate intertwining of the arms and close embraces of the dancers, leading to unusually close bodily contact. Combined with a constant twirling motion, it gradually leads to dizziness, and was consequently attacked from the beginning as immoral. Nevertheless its triumphal entry, even into the highest social circles, could not be halted.

Between these two extreme forms, the contredanse – which has its origins in the seventeenth-century English country dance – stands as a third central type. Danced *en compagnie* to duple metre, catchy music, rich in figures, and with a great variety of forms, its execution could be learned quickly, and it afforded great social pleasure. Of all the dance forms, it was the contredanse that most united all the social classes.

Opportunities to practise these various dance forms were manifold. Dancing was common at semi-private family celebrations, especially weddings and domestic balls, at taverns and at institutionally organized balls. During *Fasching* or Carnival, which was celebrated with particular exuberance, the so-called *Redouten*, or routs, were especially popular. These were masked balls which often took place in designated rooms: the town hall ballroom in SALZBURG, or the *Redouten* rooms in VIENNA, which still form part of the imperial palace today. At bigger *Redouten*, several ensembles played in different rooms; the crush was sometimes so great that dancing was in fact impossible. Towards the end of the eighteenth century, the *Redouten* were thrown open to all classes of society. Because of the wearing of masks, class distinctions were significantly neutralized.

In the 1780s, Vienna was gripped by a regular addiction to dancing, something hinted at by LEOPOLD MOZART in a letter of 30 January 1768: 'As long as Fasching lasts, people here think about nothing but dancing. In every corner there's a ball.' Mozart himself must have felt something of this unbridled passion for dancing: his biographer GEORG NIKOLAUS VON NISSEN, CONSTANZE MOZART's second husband, affirmed that 'apart from playing billiards, he also passionately loved dancing, and missed neither the public masked balls in the theatre, nor his friends' domestic balls. And he danced very well indeed, particularly the minuet.' One of Mozart's comic verses makes it clear how naturally dancing permeated his everyday life: 'Come on here quickly, my friends, we'll soon get up a little dance.' As young as five he was named as part of a dance ensemble in a Salzburg *Finalkomödie*, a dramatic production performed at the end of the academic year in Salzburg and as a fourteen-year-old he wrote to his sister Nannerl from Bologna: 'my sole amusement at the moment consists of English [contredanse] steps, and Capriol and spaccat' (letter of 4 Aug. 1770). Copious reports in the letters about local customs testify to the family's general interest in the dance culture of the time, and to their lively participation in it. Mozart in turn continually asked about the course of

Salzburg's dancing engagements, and several times in his Italian correspondence exchanged his own and other people's dance compositions with his sister. In 1773, after returning from Italy, the Mozart family moved into the *Wohnhaus* (now a Mozart museum), that had previously belonged to the dancing master Karl Gottlieb Speckner. On the first floor is the 'Dancing Master's Hall', which was used by the Mozarts for domestic concerts and small-scale dances.

Mozart must also have derived considerable pleasure from dressing up for masked balls. According to contemporary reports of the Salzburg *Redoute* of 1776, Leopold Mozart appeared as a porter and Mozart as a 'barber's boy'. And Mozart expressly asked his father, in a letter from Vienna dated 22 January 1783, for a Harlequin costume – 'but so that no one knows about it'. He probably appeared in this same costume in the pantomime described a little later, which he staged with some friends as a 'masked company' at the *Redoute*. The music (K446, of which only the violin part survives) and the theatrical arrangement of the half-hour pantomime were by Mozart himself, an actor wrote the text, and a dancing master helped rehearse it.

Mozart's output includes more than 200 orchestral dances; this represents the complete spectrum of the dance forms practised at the time and span the whole of his creative life. They can properly be divided into Salzburg and Viennese groups, because the circumstances and conditions of their composition were very different.

The dances of the Salzburg period – mainly minuets – were very probably occasional works, whose origins are no longer known. We only have indirect information about such occasions, for example when Mozart complains from MANNHEIM on 7 February 1778 at not having been informed about the impending marriage of the family friend Schiedenhofen: 'I would have composed him new minuets for it.' The early dances in particular also served the function of composition and orchestration exercises: the participation of Mozart's father is clearly recognizable in the autographs. And it was Leopold who in 1768 collated all Mozart's contributions to the genre in the first catalogue of Mozart's works with the phrase 'many minuets for all types of instrument'.

The Viennese works are dominated by the more 'modern' dance types, the contredanse and the German Dance and in the overwhelming majority of cases their origins are known exactly. On 7 December 1787 Mozart was named k. k. Kammerkompositeur (imperial and royal chamber composer): it was among his duties to compose dance music for the *Redouten* balls. These 'Viennese dances' display a simpler phrase structure compared to the early orchestral dances, and show richer and sometimes also more original instrumentation. Names given individual dances, such as 'The Battle' (K535), 'The Canary' (K600), or 'The Sleigh-Ride' (K605), indicate a programmatic character, which is realized through the use of side-drum, tambourine, posthorn, piccolo, triangle, jingle bells and cymbals. In one German Dance (K602) there is even a hurdy-gurdy. These dances are described in detail in Mozart's own catalogue of his works.

The situation regarding source material is completely different for the dances of the Salzburg and Viennese periods. Whereas the early orchestral dances are known almost without exception from their autographs, the later dances have been transmitted above all through contemporary copies, early editions and keyboard arrangements. As a rule, Mozart's Viennese dance music immediately found a publisher, was printed in manifold arrangements and thus achieved wide dissemination even during his lifetime, the composer probably enjoying a proportion of the income.

A set of orchestral dances was obviously more quickly and easily composed than a symphony – Georg Nikolaus Nissen even told an anecdote of Mozart composing four contredanses for full orchestra in less than half an hour. Nevertheless, the dance music was long undervalued, for although it was composed primarily for the ballroom, or for semi-public occasions, it also found its way indirectly into the keyboard and instrumental music. And Mozart's awareness of its effectiveness on the stage is shown by the famous ballroom scene in DON GIOVANNI. In the finale to the first act, the representatives of the nobility – Donna Anna, Donna Elvira and Don Ottavio, with Don Giovanni – begin a minuet; then Don Giovanni invites Zerlina to dance a contredanse; and finally the servant Leporello dances a German Dance with the peasant Masetto. The special feature of this scene is that each set of dancers is accompanied by its own orchestra, so that three different dance melodies sound simultaneously. Through the characteristic association of dancers and dance types, Mozart holds fast to traditions that were already no longer valid. Conversely, popular melodies from the stage repertory were reworked as dance music. Mozart himself experienced this when he attended a ball during his visit to PRAGUE in 1787, writing to his friend JACQUIN on 15 January: 'I didn't dance or flirt . . . but I watched with great pleasure as all these people danced around so contentedly to the music of my FIGARO, arranged purely as contredanses and German Dances; – because nothing is talked about here except – *Figaro.*'

Without doubt, many of Mozart's dances are lost, while the authenticity of others is still not established. However, those that are accessible today, brought to life in the concert hall or in recordings, represent a precious treasure, the immediate expression of the joy of life. ANDREA LINDMAYR-BRANDL

(Trans. RUTH HALLIWELL)

W. J. Allanbrook, *Rhythmic Gesture in Mozart: 'Le nozze di Figaro' and 'Don Giovanni'* (Chicago, 1983)

S. Dahms, 'Tanz und Ballett in Wien zur Zeit Mozarts', in *Europa im Zeitalter Mozarts*, ed. M. Csáky and W. Pass (Vienna, Cologne, Weimar, 1995), 365–71

M. Mittendorfer, 'Salzburger Quellen zur Tanzkultur der Mozart-Zeit' (Ph.D. diss., University of Salzburg, 1991)

S. B. Reichart, 'The Influence of Eighteenth-Century Social Dance on the Viennese Classical Style' (Ph.D. thesis, City University of New York, 1984)

W. Salmen, ed., *Mozart in der Tanzkultur seiner Zeit* (Innsbruck, 1990)

Davidde penitente. See CANTATA

Dejean, Ferdinand (baptized Bonn, 9 Oct. 1731; d. Vienna, 23 Feb. 1797). Physician and amateur musician. Dejean was a surgeon with the Dutch East India Company from 1758 to 1767; after his return to Europe he spent much of his time travelling. Mozart met Dejean in MANNHEIM in 1777; he described him to his father as 'a man of independent means, a lover of all the sciences, and a great friend and admirer of myself' (10 Dec. 1777). Although the Mozart family letters are contradictory with respect to details, Dejean apparently commissioned three flute concertos and several flute quartets from Mozart. By early 1778, however, he had completed only two quartets, K285 and K285a, and – possibly – only one concerto, K313 (which lacks authentic sources and cannot be securely dated; the concerto K314 is not an original flute concerto by Mozart but an arrangement, probably not by the composer, of his Oboe Concerto). Consequently Mozart was paid only 96 gulden, not the 200 he might have had for completing the commission. Dejean settled in VIENNA around 1780 but there is no evidence of any further contact between him and Mozart. CLIFF EISEN

F. Lequin, 'Mozarts "... rarer Mann" ', *Mitteilungen der Internationalen Stiftung Mozarteum* 29/1–2 (1981), 3–19
J. H. Moolenijzer and S. Sas Bunge, *Mozart en de Hollanders: een winter in Mannheim* (Haarlem, 1969)

Demmler, Johann Michael (baptized Hiltenfingen, Swabia, 28 Sept. 1748; buried Augsburg, 6 June 1785). German composer and keyboard player. Mozart met Demmler, who from 1774 was organist at AUGSBURG Cathedral, during his visit there in October 1777; on 22 October, Demmler, J. A. STEIN and Mozart gave a performance of the Concerto for Three Pianos, K242. Mozart described him as 'a very strange fellow: when something pleases him greatly, he just howls with laughter. In my case, he even started to curse' (letter of 24 Oct. 1777). But he also thought highly of Demmler as a musician and in 1778 recommended him to his father for the post of cathedral organist in SALZBURG, a post that Mozart himself took over on 25 February 1779. CLIFF EISEN

A. Layer, 'Johann Michael Demmler', in *Landkreis Schwabmünchen* (Augsburg, 1974), 496
E. F. Schmid, 'Mozart und das geistliche Augsburg', in *Augsburger Mozartbuch*, ed. H. F. Deininger (Augsburg, 1942–3), 40–202, esp. 120ff.

Deym von Stržitéž, Joseph Nepomuk Franz de Paula, Count (b. Vojnice, Bohemia, 2 Apr. 1752; d. Prague, 27 Jan. 1804). Formerly an officer in the Austrian army, Deym fled the country following a duel, returning to VIENNA about 1780, where he opened an art gallery under the name Müller; chiefly he exhibited wax effigies and mechanical music instruments and toys. In March 1791 Deym also opened a mausoleum dedicated to Fieldmarshal Baron Gideon Laudon, hero of the Turkish war, who had died on 14 July 1790. Among its attractions was a piece of mechanical funeral music by Mozart that sounded hourly. Traditionally this work is thought to be K594, composed in December 1790, although the fantasia K608 and the Andante K616 are also likely candidates. Deym is said to have taken a death mask of Mozart but neither the original nor a copy made for CONSTANZE MOZART survives. CLIFF EISEN

W. Krieg, 'Um Mozarts Totenmaske: Ein Beitrag zur Mozart-Ikonograhie', *Neues Mozart-Jahrbuch* 3 (1943), 118–43

'Dissonance' quartet. Mozart's String Quartet in C, K465 (14 Jan. 1785), sometimes referred to as the 'Dissonant'. See CHAMBER MUSIC. B. STRING QUARTETS

Dittersdorf, Carl Ditters von (b. Vienna, 2 Nov. 1739; d. Neuhof, near Sobeslav, Bohemia, 24 Oct. 1799). German composer and violinist. Ditters held a variety of posts, with Prince Joseph Friedrich von Sachsen-Hildburghausen, Count Giacomo Durazzo (at the Burgtheater), Adam Patachich, Bishop of Grosswardein (now Oradea, Romania), and Count Philipp Gotthard von Schaffgotsch, Prince-Bishop of Breslau (now Wrocław); on 5 June 1773, Empress MARIA THERESIA granted him a patent of nobility, by which he acquired the additional 'von Dittersdorf' and in 1785 JOSEPH II took over administrative control of the archbishopric. Dittersdorf undertook an extended trip to Vienna where he enjoyed success with performances of his oratorio *Giob* (given for the benefit of the Tonkünstler-Sozietät) and his German comic opera *Der Apotheker und der Doktor*. There is no unequivocal evidence that Mozart and Dittersdorf were acquainted although it is very likely they met. And despite his local fame, as well as the high regard in which *Der Apotheker* was held as a potential rival to the hegemony of Italian opera in Vienna, it is likely that he felt overshadowed by Mozart. Certainly he was not beyond insulting his better-known colleague, even if obliquely; in 1788, shortly after the composition of six quartets, he wrote to the publisher ARTARIA: 'I offer you the original manuscript or, more accurately, my own score of them for the same price you paid for Mozart's . . . and I am certain that you will do better with mine than you did with Mozart's (which, indeed, I and still greater theorists consider to deserve the highest praise, but which because of their overwhelming and unrelenting artfulness are not to everyone's taste).' CLIFF EISEN

E. Badura-Skoda, 'Dittersdorf über Haydns und Mozarts Quartette', in *Collectanea mozartiana*, ed. C. Roleff (Tutzing, 1988), 41–50
Karl von Dittersdorfs Lebensbeschreibung (Leipzig, 1801; English trans., 1896)
D. Heartz, *Haydn, Mozart, and the Viennese School, 1740–1780* (New York, 1995)

divertimento. See SERENADE

Doles, Johann Friedrich (b. Steinbach-Hallenberg, Thuringia, 23 Apr. 1715; d. Leipzig, 8 Feb. 1797). German composer and choral director. Doles was a pupil of J. S. BACH and cantor at the Leipzig Thomaskirche 1756–89. Mozart met him during his stay at Leipzig in April 1789; according to a later anecdote, it was for Doles that Mozart improvised the six-part canon K572a and it may have been from him that Mozart acquired a manuscript copy of J. S. Bach's motet *Singet dem Herrn ein neues Lied*, BWV225. In 1790, Doles dedicated his cantata *Ich komme vor dein Angesicht* jointly to Mozart and the Dresden Kapellmeister Johann Gottlieb Naumann. CLIFF EISEN

'Dominicus' mass. Mozart's Mass in C, K66, performed in Salzburg on 15 October 1769. See MASS

Don Giovanni, K527, *dramma giocoso* in two acts on a libretto by LORENZO DA PONTE, first performed at the Nostitzsches Nationaltheater, PRAGUE, 29 October 1787; revived with changes at the Burgtheater, VIENNA, 7 May 1788

1. Genesis and sources
2. Da Ponte's contribution
3. Baroque elements
4. Buffo and serio
5. A web of contradictions

1. Genesis and sources

We have only sparse information about the commissioning of *Don Giovanni*, and much of it is ambiguous. The most suggestive item is the recurrence of the same singer's name in two librettos printed within nine months of each other: the tenor ANTONIO BAGLIONI, who performed in GIUSEPPE GAZZANIGA's *Don Giovanni, o sia Il convitato di pietra*, first staged at the San Moisè Theatre in Venice on 5 February 1787, was also the first Don Ottavio of Mozart's *Don Giovanni*. Even if the exact nature of the connection between the San Moisè and Nostitz Theatres remains unclear, we may plausibly surmise that it was Baglioni who brought GIOVANNI BERTATI's opera libretto from Venice to Prague. And if we are to believe the *Extract from the Life of Lorenzo Da Ponte* (New York, 1819), the director of the Prague theatre at first requested Mozart to set the Bertati libretto – it was only at the composer's insistence that he instructed Da Ponte to write a new text based on the Don Juan fable.

To this brief outline of the work's prehistory we may add three further observations. In the first place, it is no coincidence that Bertati's libretto attracted the notice of the Prague impresario: two operas on the Don Juan theme had already been staged there, *La pravità castigata* in 1730 and, in 1776, Vincenzo Righini's *Il convitato di pietra, ossia Il dissoluto*, whose subtitle lies behind the main title of Da Ponte's libretto, *Il dissoluto punito, ossia Il Don Giovanni*. The subject matter of the new opera commissioned in 1787 was thus already familiar to its intended audience, a factor all the more important in view of CHARLES BURNEY's observation that few musicians in Bohemia spoke any other language than Czech. Second, the commission came to Mozart from a city which had shown exceptional enthusiasm for his music, and – as with the 'Prague' symphony (K504) – Mozart took advantage of this favourable microclimate to create an especially complex work, confident that he need not fear the reproach, so often levelled at him, that he was a 'difficult' composer. Finally, the direct link between Venice and Prague in the person of Baglioni, confirmed by Da Ponte's mention of Bertati's name, shows that 'Mozart's *Don Giovanni*', as it was henceforth to be known, would not have been composed without the prior existence of Bertati's text. Paradoxically, for a work which rapidly came to be considered as daringly original, *Don Giovanni* was a 'remake'.

When Da Ponte says in his memoirs that he stimulated his imagination by reading Dante's *Inferno*, he gives us a valuable indication of what was, for him, the distinctive character of *Don Giovanni* in comparison with the two other librettos he was also writing at the time, *L'arbore di Diana* (for MARTÍN Y SOLER) and *Axur, re d'Ormus* (for SALIERI). In invoking the greatest name in Italian literature, however, Da Ponte was also laying a false trail designed to mask his plagiarism. This implies no value judgement: the creation of new operas had always relied on the rewriting of pre-existing topoi, and also on inserting quotations from literary works, references which cultured readers or spectators could take pleasure in recognizing. Our first task, therefore, is to ascertain the degree of novelty in Da Ponte's libretto as compared to Bertati's, and then to look beyond this direct antecedent to the older theatrical tradition within which the Don Juan fable was tirelessly reworked. This accomplished, we shall finally be in a position to discuss Mozart's *Don Giovanni* without attributing to the composer what rightly belongs to the librettist or crediting Da Ponte with the invention of material which derives from his predecessors (see table 1).

In direct contrast to Da Ponte's efforts at concealment, Bertati deliberately tells the spectator what his sources are through the mouth of a character in his *Capriccio drammatico*, the miniature opera that serves as a prologue to his *Don Giovanni*. Here is what the impresario Policastro announces in scene 11: 'la nostra commedia, ridotta com'ell'è fra la spagnuola di Tirso de Molina, tra quella di Molière, e quella delli nostri commedianti' ('Our comedy, distilled as it is from comedies by the Spaniard Tirso de Molina, by Molière and by our comedians'). The explicit reference to Tirso de Molina's *El burlador de Sevilla* (Barcelona, 1630, first performed c.1620) prompts us to include it in the left-hand column of the table. We should also refer here to its Italian adaptation by Giacinto Andrea Cicognini, *Il convitato di pietra*, which served as a model for many later plays based on the Don Juan theme. The most important of these was Molière's *Dom Juan*, whose chief contribution, from the viewpoint of Bertati and Da Ponte, was the creation of the new character Elvira.

The original *Convitato* by Tirso–Cicognini required considerable compression and selection before it could be transformed into an opera, a task that Bertati carried out with considerable skill, although the key idea of this adaptation did not originate with him: the notion of placing a tragic scene at the beginning of the drama, in which Donna Anna's father is killed by Don Juan, is first encountered in GLUCK's *Don Juan*, a pantomime-ballet based on a scenario by the choreographer Gasparo Angiolini and staged in Vienna in 1761. After this momentous opening, Bertati introduces three other women, also victims of Don Juan's false promises: Donna Elvira, the abandoned wife; Maturina, a peasant girl on the point of marrying; and Donna Ximena. Finally, we see Don Giovanni coming across the statue of Anna's father, the Commendatore, and the meal during which the Commendatore returns to drag the libertine down with him to the kingdom of the dead.

2. Da Ponte's contribution

Bertati's principal aim was to reduce into one act a Baroque play rich in speeches and fantastic or picturesque episodes, with the attendant risk of forfeiting its poetic flavour and theological implications. Da Ponte's approach was precisely the opposite: he needed to expand Bertati, since the new version no longer had to share the evening with the *Capriccio drammatico*. One of the principal innovations of Da Ponte's libretto nevertheless consists of a further shortening: he eliminated the Ximena character from his plot. For Mozart this offered the advantage of leaving him with three women whose profile matched the usual typology of opera buffa to perfection: the *parte seria* Donna Anna, the *parte buffa* Zerlina, and Donna Elvira, the *mezzo carattere*. This serves at the same time to establish the three levels of language that are symbolized in the music of the three dances played simultaneously in the Act 1 finale: while Don Giovanni, by the wide reach of his conquests, perverts society as a whole, the expressive means of opera buffa make it possible to distinguish the different classes by allotting to each an appropriate musical style.

If we now consider Da Ponte's additions – in all probability carried out with Mozart's active collaboration – one of the most striking features is the new prominence given to Anna, who plays an essential function – from both a dramatic and an expressive viewpoint – in the economy of the opera. Anna's new-found centrality is commensurate with her responsibility in triggering the initial unfolding of the action. After all, even before the rise of the curtain, she had let into her bedroom a man to whom she was not yet married (she took him to be her fiancé Don Ottavio), and it is this breach of decorum which sets in motion the tragic mechanism that leads to the death first of her father and then of Don Giovanni. It is strange that we are made to wait until the middle of Act I for Anna to give Ottavio a detailed account of what happened, but this is probably not for reasons of psychological development alone: on the one hand, the already long opening sequence had to be kept to manageable proportions; and on the other, Anna's return after the episodes devoted to Elvira and Zerlina allows for a timely restoration of opera seria's elevated tone. All of Anna's subsequent appearances are dominated by the expression of her mourning: the initial tragedy is thus regularly recalled through the grave and serious style of her music. Anna is more than a character, she is the embodiment of a dramatic genre.

As devised by Da Ponte, the action ties together the whole group of characters only at scene 11, at which point, in Bertati's version, Don Giovanni's succession of encounters with various female victims is brought to an end. But where Bertati concludes the section with a dispute between Maturina and Elvira, Da Ponte's women unite in a coalition against Don Giovanni. As a result of this they contrive to be invited to the feast at Don Giovanni's house, intending to lure him into seducing Zerlina so that they may catch the libertine *in flagrante*. Although this is the subject of the first-act finale, it would be simplistic to see in it a purely dramatic function: the celebration at Don Giovanni's is equally justified by the opportunity it provides for the staging of a ball and thus for drawing attention to the music itself. At first, in the distance, we hear a contredanse (scene 18), then, emerging through an open window, the first rendering of a minuet (scene 19). Once the listener has identified them, these two dances are then heard in full, this time superimposed on each other in scene 20, with the addition of a German dance ('Teitsch'). Each dance corresponds to a participating couple and to a well-defined social class: aristocratic in the case of the minuet, mixed for the contredanse, popular for the German dance. The close attunement between the music and the social rank of the characters was decided upon by Mozart himself, who rearranged the libretto so as to allow Anna to dance with Ottavio, Don Giovanni with Zerlina, and Masetto (Zerlina's fiancé) with Leporello (Don Giovanni's servant). But the trap set for Don Giovanni eventually proves ineffectual: he defeats it by assaulting Zerlina offstage (her cries convey that he has had enough time to attempt rape), and his adversaries, though they thwart his attack, nevertheless remain powerless. The finale ends with a static tableau in which each character is rooted to the spot. Such a state of affairs is typical of middle-act finales in opera buffa, and it would be rash

Table 1.

Tirso de Molina, *El burlador de Sevilla y convidado de piedra* (no scene numbers in the original)	Molière, *Dom Juan, ou le Festin de pierre* (only the relevant scenes have been included)	Bertati, *Don Giovanni, o sia Il convitato di pietra*	Da Ponte, *Il dissoluto punito, o sia il Don Giovanni*
Naples. Duchess Isabela, betrothed to Duke Octavio, is seduced by Don Juan, disguised as Octavio			
A beach in Tarragona. DJ seduces Tisbea, a fisherwoman			
Seville. Octavio is now betrothed to Doña Ana, who is in love with marquess Mota. She asks Mota to join her in her apartments but DJ intercepts her note and takes Mota's place. Ana recognizes him and leaves. DJ kills her father D. Gonzalo		scenes 1–2 as in Tirso, but Mota is excluded from the plot. Don Giovanni's servant, Pasquariello, witnesses the scene	I: 1 (Pasquariello is renamed Leporello, literally, 'little hare')
		scenes 3–4 D. Anna, Duke Ottavio	I: 3 (Anna's narration is delayed until scene 13)
		scene 5 DG, Pasquariello	I: 4
	I: 3 Elvire's entrance	scenes 6–8 D. Elvira	I: 5–6
		scenes 9–10 Donna Ximena	
Dos Hermanas, in the country. DJ seduces Aminta, who is about to marry Batricio	Act II Charlotte (betrothed to Pierrot) and Mathurine vie for Dom Juan's favours. This act also takes elements from Tirso's scenes with Tisbea	scenes 11–15 Maturina and Biagio, then Donna Ximena	I: 7–9 Zerlina and Masetto (without D. Ximena)

Isabela meets Tisbea in Tarragona	II: 4 quarrel between Charlotte and Mathurine	scenes 16–18 the same, then D. Elvira, who quarrels with D. Maturina	I: 10–12 Elvira meets Zerlina, then Anna and Ottavio
			I: 13 (Bertati scene 3)
			I: 14–20: preparations for the feast and ball scene. II: 1–10: DG and Leporello swap their clothes and have separate adventures
DJ sees Gonzalo's statue in a church and invites him to supper	III: 5 DJ bids Sganarelle to invite the Commandeur	scene 20	II: 11
			II: 12 Anna, Ottavio
	IV: 6 Elvire attempts to save DJ's soul	scene 22 Elvira (Da Ponte II: 14)	
DJ, while supping in his tavern, is visited by Gonzalo's statue, who invites him to supper in his church	IV: 7–8	scenes 23–24	II: 13–15 (scene 14 with Elvira, scene 15 with Commendatore)
DJ visits Gonzalo and dies in his sepulchre, which engulfs both of them	V: 6		
Epilogue in the king's palace		scene 25 final ensemble without DG	II: 16

to draw interpretative conclusions from that; it nonetheless remains the case that the absence of stage directions at the close of this finale makes for an equivocal situation in which those who argue for a diabolical and superhuman Don Giovanni find ready support.

The finale as a whole was Da Ponte's invention, even if, as John Rice has demonstrated, the ball scene has its roots in a topos from Goldonian opera buffa. The first half of the second act also evinces this mixture of originality with a reliance on dramatic themes from the tradition of comedy and opera buffa. Nothing in Bertati could have prompted Da Ponte to base this new development on the use of disguises, though he may have taken the idea from Molière's *Dom Juan* (Act 2, scene 5). This gives Don Giovanni an opportunity to sing the same serenade twice – at least as far as the beginning of the melody is concerned: first to Elvira in the central section of the trio 'Ah taci ingiusto core', and then to her maid, with a mandolin accompaniment. But events do not proceed as planned: Don Giovanni soon finds himself face to face with a group of vengeful peasants, and he owes his escape only to his disguise as a servant. For his part, Leporello, after wandering aimlessly in the darkness with Elvira, is caught by the enemies of Don Giovanni and saves his skin only by revealing his true identity.

Over and above their entertainment value, these episodes offer excellent opportunities to two aspects of Mozart's talent: the art of clothing membership of a social class in appropriate music, and that of extracting pathos from apparently farcical situations. On the level of musical disguise, Da Ponte and Mozart deny Leporello the ability to mimic aristocracy in formal song, so that he can only address Elvira in recitative – in contrast to Figaro, who in the last finale of LE NOZZE DI FIGARO raises himself to the noble style when he woos the (false) Countess. Don Giovanni, on the other hand, brilliantly deploys the popular idiom, first with a serenade in hendecasyllables whose text follows the same poetic conventions as Susanna's 'Deh vieni non tardar, o gioia bella'; and next with an action aria, 'Metà di voi qua vadano', where Mozart gives him the key associated elsewhere with Leporello (F major) and a musical tag already enunciated at the very beginning of the opera to the words 'Ma mi par che venga gente' ('But I think someone is coming'). It involves an alternation between strings and wind instruments that Mozart was to use again in *Die Zauberflöte*, in the scene where Papageno tries to commit suicide; this play on timbre is there combined with the stage direction 'looking around' which, transferred to Leporello, would suggest turning his eyes first in one direction and then in another.

Just as rich, musically, is the part played by Elvira in this first half of the second act. From a psychological point of view, the determination that she displays in seeking to reconquer Don Giovanni, followed by her failure to recognize Leporello in the clothes of his master, ought to make her into a profoundly ridiculous figure. But Mozart provides her with music of great depth, as much in the first stanza of the trio 'Ah taci ingiusto core' as in that of the sextet 'Sola sola in buio loco'. In the trio the clarinets give voice to her sensuality through languorous chromatic thirds and with a melodic line that obviously contradicts the words 'È colpa aver pietà' ('To pity him is a sin'). Elvira's role in the sextet is once again coloured by the clarinets and by the chromatic lines of the orchestra, this time displaying a more anguished nuance; the way in which she shields Leporello ('È mio marito', 'He is my husband'), which might appear ludicrous, is rendered musically in such a heart-rending manner that the spectator is moved closer to tears than to laughter. Later, in the Act 2 finale, Mozart again masterfully exploits Elvira's emotional potential by disregarding what might seem exaggerated in her words, 'Restati, barbaro, nel lezzo immondo' ('Remain, barbarous one, in the vile stench'): not only does he powerfully restate a phrase previously heard in the Act 1 quartet ('Te può tradir ancor', 'He can betray you too'), but he also provides Elvira with octave leaps that endow her fury with the superhuman dimension of a magical incantation. Even though Da Ponte may have been surprised by the depth of passion that Elvira's intrusion would unleash in his collaborator, we must give the librettist credit for the skill with which he placed it just before the arrival of the Commendatore, creating a crescendo of tension not sought by Bertati.

3. Baroque elements

These modifications and additions of Da Ponte's do not stem from Tirso de Molina's original outline. What does remain from the Baroque play, however, is a cluster of dramatic characteristics that set *Don Giovanni* in a class of its own: it may be compared only with other works on the same subject. It departs from the common practice of opera buffa in many respects, first and foremost by the Christian supernatural element, which drew from Mozart the most violent music that he would ever compose. If we except the overture, of which the first section (Andante) introduces material that will recur with the arrival of the statue during the penultimate scene of Act 2, it is with the cemetery scene (Act 2, scene 11) that the supernatural makes a spectacular entrance. Don Giovanni and Leporello have just found each other again and are recounting the events of their night of madness in a simple recitative that is at once tense and witty, where Leporello, despite his social inferiority, throws his master's arguments back at him with an acerbic irony. The spectator comes to forget that Don Giovanni is amusing himself in a sacred place, so that the voice of the Commendatore, emerging from a tomb, strikes in with tenfold solemnity. Mozart has characterized the Commendatore's two ghostly interventions with music in the style of the 'Voce' of Neptune in IDOMENEO, which itself harked back to the oracle of Apollo in the first act of the *Alceste* of Calzabigi and Gluck. The spare melodic line conveys the impassive utterance thought appropriate to the dead; and the voice is supported by archaic harmonies, coloured by the sepulchral sonority of the trombones and other wind instruments. This style of music returns overwhelmingly in the final confrontation between Don Giovanni and the Commendatore's statue, where Mozart remains in the minor mode for more than five minutes, creating a nightmarish atmosphere that Leporello's comic terror cannot hope to lighten. The scene ends with an apocalyptic 'coro di spiriti', who promise Don Giovanni unimaginable sufferings in hell; the bass-line covers the interval of a descending and then an ascending fourth and, at the moment when the ground is about to open beneath the feet of the sinner, two successive cadences ring out which also bear the stamp of the church style: first the chord progression i–VI–iv–V–i, then a plagal cadence with a *tierce de picardie*. Never had divine power been unleashed in music with such violence, even if, taken individually, the various supernatural topoi of this scene may each be found in other operas of the period, such as Righini's *Armida* (Vienna, 1782) and Salieri's *Les Danaïdes* (Paris, 1784).

The ecclesiastical or archaic musical language suffuses the whole opera in varying degrees right from the opening confrontation between Don Giovanni and the Commendatore. In order firmly to reinforce the symmetry between the two death scenes, Mozart conceived of the opera's opening as a musical unit of vast dimensions: not only does he join the first scene (*Introduzione*) without interruption to the overture but, extending beyond the recitative of scene 2, he even connects it with Anna and Ottavio's duo of scene 3, which displays a close kinship with the overture and the *Introduzione* through a variety of harmonic and melodic techniques. The formal coherence of this first unit allows Mozart to multiply the number of musical signs that may, by the end of the opera, be construed retrospectively as anticipations of the statue scene. This is clearly the case with the overture, which prefigures it almost literally: the terrible explosion of the first two chords, the descending octave leaps and the chromatically falling bass immediately impress the hearer as a kind of *memento mori*, whose victim is clearly designated by the title of the libretto, *Il dissoluto punito*. Again, in the Andante of the overture, a fearsome E flat chord rings out in which we later recognize the Commendatore's order 'repent!', Don Giovanni's refusal of which leads inexorably to the D minor cadence. In the *Introduzione*, this key is brought back significantly for the cadence that accompanies the words 'Se vuoi morir' ('If you want to die'), a phrase with which Don Giovanni unknowingly seals his own fate. The rocketing scales of the violins and basses during the duel reappear in the bass in the verbal duel of Act 2 between Don Giovanni and the Commendatore's statue. In the sword fight, the Commendatore is mortally wounded to the sound of a terrifying diminished seventh (a harmony heard in Elettra's first aria in *Idomeneo*, where she portrays a character invoking the Furies of Hades). It is this very chord that recurs, amplified by the trombones, at the precise instant in the finale when Don Giovanni opens the door to the statue.

The two death scenes are far from being the only moments of terror and violence in *Don Giovanni*. The anguished screams of Zerlina during the ball find an echo more frightening still when Elvira, also in the wings, encounters the Commendatore's statue as she leaves Don Giovanni's villa (Act 2, scene 14). At the mid-point of Act 1, Anna's narration shares similar connotations of panic, signalled by the return of the trumpets to reinforce the powerful chords evoking her cries in the night. Less brutal but just as solemn are the successive appearances of the key of D minor, a once 'dorian' key identified with the other world in church music and made memorable by Gluck's ballets *Don Juan* and *Semiramis* and his overture to *Alceste*. Certain resumptions of D minor are even embodied in a common melodic motif that thematically signals the return of the fateful key. We hear it twice from the mouth of Anna (in the duo 'Fuggi crudele fuggi' and during the Act 2 sextet, on the words 'Lascia lascia alla mia pena'), and once from Elvira, then Ottavio, in the first finale ('Bisogna aver coraggio'); in the latter case this motif affords the extra advantage of inviting the audience to associate the notion of death and vengeance with persons whose faces are hidden. It is perhaps no coincidence that part of this motif surges out at the beginning of Richard Strauss's *Elektra*, also in D minor, and the same notes are repeated later in that opera, associated with the name of Agamemnon, a murdered father whose death the daughter wishes to avenge, blood for blood.

Still in the realm of the archaic style, *Don Giovanni* includes incursions of the Baroque idiom in places where one would not expect to find it. Elvira's second aria, 'Ah fuggi il traditor', is a veritable pastiche of an opera or oratorio of HANDEL's era, with its relentless dotted rhythm, its contrapuntal orchestral accompaniment and its rhythmic effects displacing the accents within a 3/4 bar. Elsewhere it is the pure contrapuntal writing that comes as a surprise, exemplified in the sextet at the words 'che impensata novità' ('what unthought-of novelty'), as if to underline what it is about the technique, already used by Mozart in the quartet of *Idomeneo*, that was 'new' in the context of an opera bulfa. In the same fashion, the conclusion of the opera begins with species counterpoint, switches to a homophonic style, but soon reverts to strict counterpoint for the word 'sempre', illustrated by a seemingly interminable descending scale that extends from high A to low D, giddy with the vertigo of an endless fall. The evident exaggeration here steers us towards another aspect of *Don Giovanni* that we must not forget: it belongs to the category of the *dramma giocoso*, that is to say to the comic genre.

4. Buffo and serio

The horizon of expectation of audiences in Prague and Vienna, to judge by Righini's *Il convitato di pietra* (performed in those two cities in 1776 and 1777), had in its purview a genre whose heterogeneity was twofold: first through the presence of the Christian supernatural, which is diametrically opposed to farce, and second because in the 1780s most comic operas made room for serious roles. If we except the harrowing Andante of the overture, the opera proper begins in the comic mode with Leporello's abortive aria, which, in some respects, is reminiscent of the opening aria of Uberto in *La serva padrona*, with its verses abruptly cut short by a masculine rhyme. Similarly, *Don Giovanni* does not end – in the Prague libretto at least – with the demise of Don Giovanni, but with the semi-parodic 'antichissima canzon' of the final sextet.

In addition to the formal freedom of the arias and multiplicity of ensembles, the comic genre as a musical style normally employs poetic material drawn from everyday reality, whether in descriptive details or in the representation of the body's gestural language. From this point of view, Da Ponte's libretto furnished Mozart with exceptionally congenial words and situations, starting with Leporello's introductory aria as he paces back and forth outside the Commendatore's house, stamping his feet like a sentinel on his beat. As for expressions of tenderness, the roles of Don Giovanni and Zerlina abound in melodic lines that envelop the listener like caresses. The second verse of Zerlina's aria 'Vedrai carino', for example, is prefaced by a three-bar passage where we hear the bass throbbing, over which the violins trace a descending arabesque, resembling a tender and consoling gesture: Zerlina lays Masetto's hand on her heart, as the manuscript score indicates – but not the printed libretto, since the imperial censor would scarcely have allowed such liberties. Less subtle are the allusions to the sexual act itself: in Masetto's aria, the words 'Faccia il nostro cavaliere cavaliera ancora te' ('Let our lord make a lady of you') inspired Mozart to an imitation of a frenetic 'cavalcade'. We meet with a similar emphasis on a repetitive and rudimentary melodic motif, suggesting a relentless pumping, in the coda of 'Fin ch'han dal vino', with untiring repetitions and telling *forte–piano* alternations at the beginning of each bar.

In such a context, it is hardly astonishing that the serious characters, Anna and Ottavio, do not always appear in a light that matches the nobility of their language. This is particularly true of Ottavio, whose bellicose rhetoric is doomed to failure, given the premises of the fable, according to which only 'heaven' is capable of halting Don Giovanni's career as a libertine. Anna's case is more complex still, in so far as the grief that she feels for her father, mingled with respect for social conventions, is stronger than her avowed love for Ottavio. Certainly there remains no trace in Da Ponte's libretto of the moral ambiguity with which Anna's character is presented in Tirso's original – where she is engaged to Ottavio against her will and has another lover – or in Goldoni's play *Don Giovanni Tenorio, o sia Il dissoluto* (from which Da Ponte also took ideas) where Anna allows herself fleeting moments of tenderness for Don Giovanni. If we confine ourselves to what Mozart's music portrays, the final impression that Anna leaves is of a sincere love for Ottavio: the duo 'Al desio di chi t'adora' in the Act 2 finale substantially expands a mere two lines of text, and allows the two lovers to sing in sixths for as long as possible. But other passages from Anna's role show that what preoccupies her above all is the loss of her father. The clearest example is the end of the accompanied recitative that precedes her second-act aria: the words 'abbastanza per te mi parla amore' ('love already pleads your cause') are set to music in an unmistakable D minor, as if to denote that the shadow of the Commendatore had extinguished in her the possibility of any other bond of affection.

5. A web of contradictions

The problematic positioning of the serious characters is only one aspect of the fundamental heterogeneity that reigns in Mozart's *Don Giovanni* and in all the plays and operas upon the same subject. The most enlightened men of letters of the eighteenth century, Voltaire, GOLDONI and GOETHE among them, clearly expressed their disdain for these works, where all manner of implausibilities and dramatic irregularities were permitted as long as the public's principal curiosity was to see the seducer destroyed by a statue of stone. Such irregularities throw up an evident contradiction between the uninterrupted hurly-burly of events and the tight time-frame within which the action takes place. Between the Commendatore's death (in the course of a first night) and that of Don Giovanni (during a second night), there elapse a mere twenty-four hours, or scarcely more.

This profusion of episodes crowded into so short a time affects the construction and balance of the musical drama. It explains the relative brevity of the recitatives, which give us far less information than we might normally expect about the motives of the characters: if we examine the original version of *Don Giovanni* as set out in the Prague libretto of 1787, we find that the simple recitatives comprise only 37 per cent of the total text, compared to 44 per cent in *Le nozze di Figaro* and *Così fan tutte*. As if to compensate for this, the arias are tightly bound to the immediate action, as we may see (again in the 1787 libretto) from the astonishing fact that arias in the form of monologues are almost totally absent. The only moment when a character in *Don Giovanni* is presented in isolation for an aria is the beginning of the *Introduzione*, 'Notte e giorno faticar', which does not even reach its natural close, since Leporello is interrupted by the sudden arrival of Don Giovanni and Anna; the remainder of the opera is nothing but a series of continual exchanges where no single character – not least Don Giovanni himself – is permitted to devote any time to solitary effusions of sentiment. A particularly striking example of this embedding of arias in the action is Elvira's first aria, 'Ah chi mi dice mai', which Mozart interrupts on six occasions with comments from Don Giovanni and Leporello, thus transforming a serious protest into a piece half-serious, half-comical, and eliding its end with the ensuing musical material. By way of compensation, Elvira received, for the 1788 Vienna performances, a supplementary aria, 'Mi tradì quell'alma ingrata', entirely characteristic of the tradition of introspective arias; but her character thereby loses some of its coherence, because all hint of parody has disappeared from her words and music. It is also customary to perform a second monologue aria added for the Vienna performance, Ottavio's 'Dalla sua pace', while still retaining his second-act aria, even though the 1788 Vienna libretto leads us to suppose that the insertion of a new aria in the first act entailed the elimination of the other.

The restricted scope allowed for the expression of intimate sentiments leaves a clear field for pure theatricality through the twin techniques of the play within the play and music within music. Theatricality is the essence of Don Giovanni's character: he not only tries to pass for that which he is not – his servant Leporello, or a lover besotted with Elvira – but also stage-manages the characters who gravitate around him. It is Don Giovanni who organizes the ball of the first act and it is he who 'directs' Leporello when he leaves him in Elvira's hands. We have already seen the musical consequences of this play upon identities in connection with the aria 'Metà di voi qua vadano', where Don Giovanni describes himself in words that Leporello might employ; at that point we have music which, as W. J. Allanbrook puts it, depicts 'Giovanni playing Leporello playing Giovanni'. These mirror effects extend to the staging of the music itself, in no less than five instances. First there is the chorus with dancing before the wedding of Zerlina and Masetto, marked out by Bertati as a 'tarantella' and realized as such by Mozart. Next come the three dances of the ball, Don Giovanni's serenade, the extracts from then well-known operas during the dinner scene, and finally the 'antichissima canzon' with which the work ends. All in all, the result is a strong insistence on music as music. This overflowing is especially noticeable in the sextet and at two points in the first-act finale: Don Giovanni's cry 'Viva la libertà', repeated at length by all his guests, and the masked trio sung by Anna, Ottavio and Elvira. Some commentators have seen in the first a profession of libertarian faith and in the second the expression of an elevated spirituality; but we can also understand these passages as powerful moments of sheer musical expression, where Mozart gives free rein to his compositional virtuosity, with extreme brilliance in the one and extreme inwardness in the other.

It is one of the many paradoxes associated with *Don Giovanni* that these and other such episodes, long developments driven by a purely musical logic, do not detract from its success as a piece of theatre; nor do the repeated affirmations of its theatricality. If anything, the musical citations from other operas inserted into the supper scene evoke an impression, even today, of an immediate context of reality: we still recognize the melody of Figaro's 'Non più andrai farfallone amoroso' (though this was not the case in the New York production of 1826 where Leporello at this point remarks, 'Questa è un'aria di Figaro'). It is one thing, however, to acknowledge the spectator's willingness to suspend disbelief, whatever the extravagances of the story, but quite another to try to frame a rationale, a coherent explanation that accounts for all the manifold aspects of *Don Giovanni*; for, wherever we look, contradictions abound. How can we possibly accept the ostensibly moralizing pretensions of a drama entitled *Il dissoluto punito* in which the supposed villain is so often presented in a sympathetic light, while at the same time we are led to perceive Anna as cold-hearted, Ottavio as apathetic, Elvira as hysterical, Zerlina as immoral and Masetto as cowardly? How are we to accept as the *lieto fine* (happy ending) of a *dramma giocoso* this denouement where Anna and Ottavio do not marry and Elvira remains desperately alone?

Bertati's *Capriccio drammatico* offered a simple response to such questions: a Don Juan play must be accepted on its own terms, exactly as transmitted by tradition – it would be pointless to try and judge it through the lens of ENLIGHTENMENT rationality: 'the action is not believable, the libretto defies all the rules' and the play 'is even older than the invention of the roasting-jack'. With Da Ponte and Mozart the answer is not quite so simple, because their work lacks the framing device provided by the sarcastic remarks of Bertati's *Capriccio*. Yet the presence of the older traditional comedy remains strong, even if ruptures in stylistic continuity are much more consciously introduced, not only between one section and another, but often within the confines of a single musical number, as in the duo where Don Giovanni orders Leporello to invite the Commendatore to supper. Altogether, it seems as if Da Ponte and Mozart were deliberately pushing the Baroque conception to its very limits, confident that the mimetic power of the music would bestow the necessary credibility on the dramatic representation. This aesthetic of the disparate, here elevated into a structural principle, allowed them from the first to take for granted the coexistence of the comical, the serious and the supernatural, even if there have always been people mean-spirited enough to find this coherence problematic.

It remains to be decided whether the kaleidoscopic richness of *Don Giovanni* sufficiently justifies the importance that Mozart himself – according to several witnesses – attached to the opera, and in particular to its serious elements. Was it, on a more personal level, because his Catholic upbringing was profoundly attuned to a moralizing subject? Or was it, conversely, because the enlightened circles that he frequented in Vienna prompted him to sympathize with a figure who wished to break with the established order? Or yet again, was it because his father had died during the composition of *Don Giovanni* and that Mozart's mind became possessed with the idea of death? There is no evidence that enables us to answer these questions. What is beyond doubt, however, is that the Don

Juan tale provided Mozart with an unrivalled opportunity to demonstrate the full range and variety of his creative talent. The ultimate paradox is that in order to do this he needed a subject a century and a half old, and that the music of *Don Giovanni*, which more than any other was to make him famous in the nineteenth and twentieth centuries, should have afforded so large a place to musical idioms from an earlier age than his own. MICHEL NOIRAY (Trans. RAPHAËL TAYLOR)

W. J. Allanbrook, *Rhythmic Gesture in Mozart: 'Le nozze di Figaro' and 'Don Giovanni'* (Chicago, 1983)
L. Da Ponte, *Il Don Giovanni*, ed. G. Gronda (Turin, 1995 (critical edition of the libretto, based on the 1787 Prague libretto))
D. Heartz, *Mozart's Operas*, ed. T. Bauman (Berkeley, 1990)
S. Kunze, *Don Giovanni vor Mozart: die Tradition der Don-Giovanni-Opern im italienischen Buffa-Theater des 18. Jahrhunderts* (Munich, 1972)
N. Pirrotta, *Don Giovanni's Progress: A Rake Goes to the Opera*, trans. Harris S. Sanders, Jr (New York, 1994)
J. Rushton, *W. A. Mozart: Don Giovanni* (Cambridge, 1981)
D. Buch, 'The Otherworld as Past: Operatic Conventions for the Supernatural in the Eighteenth Century and Mozart's *Don Giovanni*', in *The Past as Present. Papers Read at the Intercongressional Symposium, Budapest and Visegrád, August 2000* (Budapest, 2003), 193–206

Duschek (Dussek) family. Czech musicians. Franz Xaver Duschek (František Xaver Dušek) (b. Chotěborky, near Jaroměř, Bohemia, baptized 8 Dec. 1731; d. Prague, 12 Feb. 1799), who settled in PRAGUE about 1770, was influential there as a music teacher and pianist; the most outstanding of his pupils was LEOPOLD KOZELUCH. As a composer, he was particularly successful in instrumental music. His wife, Josepha (née Hambacher, baptized Prague, 6 Mar. 1754; d. Prague, 8 Jan. 1824), had been his pupil before they married in 1776. Her family had connections to SALZBURG: Josepha's maternal grandfather was the merchant Ignaz Anton Weiser, mayor of Salzburg 1772–5 and author of the text of *Die Schuldigkeit*, K35. The Duscheks first met the Mozarts in Salzburg in August 1777; at the time, Mozart wrote the scena *Ah, lo previdi – Ah, t'invola agl'occhi miei*, K272 for Josepha. Later, in 1787, he stayed at their summer home, the Villa Betramka, when he was in Prague for the premiere of DON GIOVANNI; on this occasion he composed the scena *Bella mia fiamma – Resta, o cara*, K528. Mozart and Josepha collaborated on other occasions as well: in March 1786 he accompanied her at the Viennese court and in 1789 she sang at concerts he gave in Dresden and Leipzig. Although Josepha's singing was generally praised (JOHANN BAPTIST SCHIEDENHOFEN described her voice as 'uncommonly clear and agreeable, she had taste and sang very nicely'), LEOPOLD MOZART was critical of her, writing to NANNERL MOZART on 21 April 1786: 'How did Madame Duschek sing? I have to say it! She shrieked an aria by Naumann, quite astonishingly, with exaggerated expression as before but even more annoyingly.' But the Duscheks remained good friends of the Mozarts and were apparently in fairly regular contact with both Wolfgang and his father; on 28 April 1786, Leopold wrote to Nannerl: 'Herr & Mme Duschek told me recently that it is on account of the very great reputation which your brother's exceptional talent and ability have won for him that so many people are plotting against him.'

CLIFF EISEN

E

Eberl, Anton (Franz Josef) (b. Vienna, 13 June 1765; d. Vienna, 11 Mar. 1807). Austrian pianist and composer. A child prodigy, Eberl gave private piano recitals at the age of eight; his first public recital in VIENNA took place on 9 March 1784 and his first stage work, *Die Marchande des Modes* (1787), is said to have been praised by GLUCK. It is sometimes claimed that Eberl was Mozart's pupil although there is no evidence to support this assertion. Beginning in 1788, some of Eberl's piano pieces began to appear under Mozart's name, including variations on IGNAZ UMLAUF's *Zu Steffen sprach im Traume* and a piano sonata in C minor. In the winter of 1795–6 he toured with CONSTANZE MOZART and her sister ALOYSIA LANGE, performing piano concertos and piano quartets, possibly by Mozart. He returned to Vienna in the early 1800s where for a while he was considered Beethoven's equal, especially as a composer of concertos and symphonies.

CLIFF EISEN

F. J. Ewens, *Anton Eberl: ein Beitrag zur Musikgeschichte in Wien um 1800* (Dresden, 1927)
R. Haas, 'Anton Eberl', *Mozart-Jahrbuch* 1951, 123–30

Eberlin, Johann Ernst (b. Jettingen, Bavaria, 27 Mar. 1702; d. Salzburg, 19/21 June 1762). Composer and music director. Eberlin, director of the SALZBURG court music during LEOPOLD MOZART's early tenure as a court violinist, had a life and career that is in some ways strikingly reminiscent of his younger compatriot's. He was educated at the AUGSBURG Gymnasium and in 1721 enrolled in the law faculty of the Salzburg Benedictine University; like Leopold, however, he gave up his studies in order to join the court. He was made fourth organist in 1725 and succeeded to the post of cathedral organist in 1729; following the death of Karl Heinrich von Bibern in 1749 he was appointed court and cathedral Kapellmeister. Eberlin was a prolific composer of church music, much of which Mozart would have heard in his youth, and highly regarded as a contrapuntist; according to a notice from 1757, presumably written by Leopold Mozart, 'if anyone deserves to be called a thorough and accomplished master of composition, it is indeed this man'. Mozart, in 1782, asked his father to send him some of Eberlin's fugues for performance at the house of BARON GOTTFRIED VAN SWIETEN; but he later cancelled his request, noting that 'they are far too trivial to deserve a place beside HANDEL and [J. S.] BACH' (letter of 20 Apr. 1782). Eberlin's family was apparently close to the Mozarts in Salzburg, especially his daughter Maria Cäcilia Barbara (1728–1806), who is frequently mentioned in the family letters. CLIFF EISEN

A. Layer, 'Johann Ernst Eberlin', in *Lebensbilder aus dem bayerischen Schwaben*, ed. G. F. von Pölnitz (Munich, 1958), VI, 388–405
M. H. Schmid, *Mozart und die Salzburger Tradition* (Tutzing, 1976)

Eckard (Eckardt, Eckart), Johann Gottfried (b. Augsburg, 21 Jan. 1735; d. Paris, 24 July 1809). German pianist and composer, active in France. In his youth he became a professional copper engraver and taught himself music, chiefly from C. P. E. BACH's *Versuch*. In 1758 the piano and organ manufacturer JOHANN ANDREAS STEIN took him to PARIS, where he lived for the rest of his life. LEOPOLD MOZART became acquainted with Eckard during his visit there in 1763–4, and expressed high regard for him. BARON VON GRIMM, in his *Correspondance littéraire*, described Eckard as 'the strongest' of all Parisian composers, J.-B. de La Borde wrote that his execution was 'the most brilliant and pleasing', and BURNEY noted that 'there are many great German musicians dispersed throughout Europe, whose merit is little known in England, or even in their native land; among these is Eckard, who has been fifty years at Paris. This musician has published but little; yet by what has appeared, it is manifest that he is a man of genius and a great master of his instrument.' Only three of his works were published, six keyboard sonatas Op. 1 (1763), two sonatas Op. 2 (1764) and variations on the 'Menuet d'Exaudet' (1764). Both the variations and sonatas were known to Mozart who in 1767 transcribed Op. 1 No. 4 as the slow movement of his keyboard concerto K40. CLIFF EISEN

E. Reeser, *Ein Augsburger Musiker in Paris: Johann Gottfried Eckard (1735–1809)* (Augsburg, 1984)
T. de Wyzewa and G. de Saint-Foix, *W.-A. Mozart: sa vie musicale et son œuvre* (Paris, 1912–46)

Ein musikalischer Spass. Mozart's 'Musical Joke', K522, a divertimento scored for two horns and solo strings. See SERENADE

Eine kleine Nachtmusik. Mozart's G major serenade for strings, K525 (10 Aug. 1787). See SERENADE

Enlightenment. At the time of Mozart's birth, the Enlightenment held Europe very much in its grip, with little intellectual thought and artistic activity remaining untouched by its pervasive influence. This, of course, does not imply that the Enlightenment took the same form throughout Europe or that its thrust was necessarily welcomed by those in power. In the great centres of intellectual ferment, including Britain, northern Germany, and PARIS, enlightened thought ranged from the foundation of political stability to subversion punishable by imprisonment or public flogging. We may be tempted to assume that the young Mozart, well travelled throughout the continent and England, grew up with an awareness of the breadth and scope of the international Enlightenment, somehow absorbing its essence at each port of call. But while travel may have played a disproportionate role for Mozart, he spent his formative years in SALZBURG, where the Enlightenment, while not unnoticed, took a form unlike that of most other parts of Europe. The Enlightenment of Mozart's early experience was the distinctive one of Salzburg and his father, and its inseparability from authority figures made it fairly unappealing to a boy with one of the most fertile minds of his generation.

Unlike northern Germany with its secularization in matters of state and higher education, the Habsburg Empire under the rule of MARIA

THERESIA remained solidly Roman Catholic and immune to many of the forces of tolerance or equality characteristic of the Enlightenment. After the death of her husband, Maria Theresia relinquished much of her power to her son EMPEROR JOSEPH II and other ministers of state, allowing for more liberal policies. The most notable of these ministers, including JOSEPH VON SONNENFELS, GOTTFRIED VAN SWIETEN and PRINCE WENZEL KAUNITZ, reformed education, the distribution of land and the justice system. Joseph himself issued the *Toleranzpatent* of 1777, ending the persecution of non-Catholics (although still not giving them the full rights of Catholic citizens), and during his reign from 1780 to 1790 effected numerous other reforms, particularly before the conservative backlash accompanying the FRENCH REVOLUTION.

Reform came to Salzburg as well, under Mozart's patron Archbishop HIERONYMUS COLLOREDO, much maligned in musical circles because of his treatment of the Mozarts, but nevertheless an important force in restructuring the Church and secular society. As head of both Church and State in Salzburg, his situation was somewhat different from that of VIENNA, but he proceeded on a path of reform with Joseph II as his model, making education more accessible, restructuring the system of privileges, the agrarian economy, the military and the financial system, and patronizing the arts – especially music and the theatre. His church reforms were even more far-reaching, culminating in his *Hirtenbrief* (pastoral letter) of 29 May 1782, in which worship and devotional practice were restructured to become simpler and less ostentatious. He even went so far as to improve the lot of Protestants hidden in his realm, by leaving them undisturbed provided their dissent remained unobtrusive.

While one would expect the enlightened reforms of Joseph and Colloredo to be welcomed by a tyrannized population, this was not the case. Unlike the enlightened movements in other countries which originated from the intellectuals in response at least in some part to repression, in Salzburg and the Habsburg Empire it came from the heads of state themselves, in many respects forced on an unwilling population which regarded the changes as nothing more than new forms of despotism.

Eighteenth-century visitors to VIENNA from northern Germany, such as Friedrich Nicolai or Gotthold Ephraim Lessing, doubted the existence of an AUSTRIAN Enlightenment, finding the tenets of the Enlightenment and the Catholic Church incompatible. If that could be questioned about Vienna, it would apply doubly to Salzburg with its fusion of church and secular rule and its relative lack of any intellectual life. The Enlightenment came late to Austria where it was much more a matter of response to existing thought than an original impetus, and it should come as no surprise that Austrians looked to writers of the earlier part of the century for direction, writers whose moral outlook did not clash with that of established religion. A German observer such as Nicolai, in coming to Vienna in 1781, discovered outdated attitudes typical of those in Germany from the 1740s. For the Austrians, previously mired in feudalism, intolerance and religious dogma, these were the first important steps, and few exemplified this new sense of the old Enlightenment as well as Mozart's father.

As a reform Catholic, LEOPOLD MOZART remained a devout Christian, antagonistic to a freethinker like Voltaire whom he regarded as an atheist. Unlike the authorities of Salzburg who expelled Protestants in 1731, Leopold embraced Protestants as fellow Christians, and for him the popular German Protestant writer CHRISTIAN FÜRCHTEGOTT GELLERT exemplified enlightened thought and expression. Aside from Gellert, he admired the works of Johann Christoph Gottsched, CHRISTOPH MARTIN WIELAND and his acquaintance Solomon Gessner; his friend BARON MELCHIOR GRIMM, the founder and editor-in-chief of the *Correspondance littéraire*, also exerted a strong influence.

Mozart's encounters with notable persons of the Enlightenment happened during three fairly distinct phases of his life. The first encompasses his years spent primarily in Salzburg, with his father as mentor and the Archbishop as employer. The second phase, while the shortest, appears to have had the greatest impact: this was the journey to MUNICH, AUGSBURG, MANNHEIM and Paris, from September 1777 to January 1779, a time of freedom from his father except for their extensive correspondence. In Paris, particularly after the death of his mother, Mozart was in close contact with two of the notable figures of the century, Baron Grimm and Grimm's mistress Mme Louise d'Epinay; each exercised a distinctly different influence on him. During the third and final phase, living in Vienna, he came into contact with all the best minds of the Habsburg capital, and here too he found two approaches to the Enlightenment, one of which was no more appealing than the authoritarian approach he had so deeply resented in Salzburg.

Leopold attempted to transmit to his son the spirit of the Enlightenment that he personally admired, and the most outstanding example of this spirit was Leopold's sometime correspondent Gellert. Possibly the most popular German writer of the mid-eighteenth century, and well known in France and England through translation, Gellert brought a style of moral writing that appeared to satisfy the emerging middle-class readership. Himself a pupil of Gottsched and admirer of the Third Earl of Shaftesbury, Gellert wrote plays, odes, fables, moral lectures, criticism, treatises on letter-writing, letters and a novel. Not only did he attempt to inculcate in his readers a sense of morality, but he also strove to raise the level of taste, cultivating, like Gottsched, a higher level of German and instructing his readers how to improve their own epistolary writing. The young Mozart was well aware of the works of Gellert, not only from his father but on at least one occasion through a gift of Gellert's *Geistliche Oden und Lieder* from a relative stranger.

For the sojourn of late 1777 and 1778, Leopold had arranged for Wolfgang to meet various persons who might assist in his career quest; the most notable of these was Baron Grimm in Paris. Leopold had met Grimm as early as 1764, regarding him as a friend, a man of learning and a strong advocate of humanity, and also as someone able to facilitate virtually anything in the literary or musical world. While Grimm's work with the *Correspondance littéraire* may have brought him into contact with some of the more radical elements of the Paris intelligentsia, his own German virtue and good sense would shield him – or so Leopold thought – from being corrupted and would make him the ideal guide to shepherd Wolfgang through the perils of Paris. Leopold's plan was fundamentally sound, although he miscalculated the nature of the relationship between his son and Grimm and the gravitation of Wolfgang to Mme d'Epinay, about whom Leopold knew considerably less.

When Mozart made his permanent move to Vienna in 1781, he met virtually every leading figure of the Austrian Enlightenment. These included the poets Aloys Blumauer, Johann Baptist von Alxinger, Michel Denis and Lorenz Leopold Haschka; the mineralogist and Masonic leader IGNAZ VON BORN; the President of the Court Commission on Education GOTTFRIED VAN SWIETEN; Court War Secretary Franz Sales von Greiner; the government official TOBIAS GEBLER; and, perhaps the most influential of all, the political and cultural leader JOSEPH VON SONNENFELS. Sonnenfels's obsession with elevating the German language and raising the level of entertainment in the theatre made him – Joseph II's dislike notwithstanding – a suitable adversary in the assault on ignorance, superstition and crude entertainments. The front line of attack became Sonnenfels's attempt to eradicate HANSWURST from the Austrian stage. This foul-mouthed, pot-bellied theatrical ancestor of the Italian Harlequin held a place in the affection of the population, representing the distinctive spirit of the commedia dell'arte in Austria with all its delights and idiosyncratic invective. Sonnenfels argued that Hanswurst's crudity affronted authority and deterred enlightened refinement and morality, and in fact he was remarkably successful in his cause, forcing the comedians to try their hand at serious drama.

Mozart's own reactions to these various enlightened forces can be seen in his letters and works. If he had any admiration for Archbishop Colloredo's reforms, that has been lost in a sea of invective which both son and father could indulge in towards the autocratic and mean-spirited prelate. Based on Colloredo's manner in dealing with the Mozarts, one should not be surprised that his reforms failed to win the hearts of the Salzburg citizenry. This surely represented the Enlightenment at its worst, an official, high culture forced on people from above – a cold, ordered, repressive culture impossible to disentangle from its authoritarian source. Mozart had no more interest in this type of Enlightenment than he had in remaining in the service of the Archbishop.

Mozart's reaction in his letters to Sonnenfels's reforms in Vienna may be somewhat vague, but certain approaches taken by him in his operas place the issues in perspective. Sonnenfels, who disliked not only Hanswurst and the commedia dell'arte tradition but any comedy, measured all opera against the standard of GLUCK's serious works. Hanswurst or commedia dell'arte-like characters appear regularly in Mozart's operas, including Osmin, Antonio (from LE NOZZE DI FIGARO), Leporello, Despina and Papageno. According to Sonnenfels, any opposition to morality in a dramatic work should be conquered; no issues should be left unresolved at the end. The mission of the theatre was 'to defend the good, to fight evil, to uphold authority, to obviate subversion'. One would almost think that Mozart had read these words, completely contradicting them in his DON GIOVANNI. Leporello, like Harlequin, makes light of serious matters, while Don Giovanni in his demise can taunt God himself. The ultimate snub to Sonnenfels's serious, moral dictum comes in the moral at the end of the work: here Mozart uses music in a liturgical style but full of solecisms, with misplaced accents and absurd emphases, adding the final subversive touch.

While Mozart had no sympathy for the official, high Enlightenment of the Habsburg territories, there were other forms of it that he found more attractive, both in Vienna and Paris. Vienna had its share – if somewhat smaller than other major centres – of intellectuals, people who, while supporting Joseph's paternalistic reforms, preferred something more independent of Joseph's reach for themselves. They found this in the Masonic lodge 'Zur wahren Eintracht' (True Concord), which emerged more as an academy of arts and sciences than a typical Masonic lodge, including among its members leading representatives of all fields of endeavour.

Mozart was never an official member of 'Zur wahren Eintracht', but he was a frequent guest, and unlike many, continued as an active Mason after Joseph's restructuring in 1785. While his involvement with FREEMASONRY appears to have been genuine, one sees even here an element of irony in his public representation of Masonry, perhaps related to hypocrisy within the order itself concerning religious intolerance, racial prejudice and gender inequality. The most public of these manifestations, the opera DIE ZAUBERFLÖTE, treats Masonry and the Enlightenment in a very peculiar manner. In direct defiance of Sonnenfels's theatrical legislation, this work revives Hanswurst on the Austrian stage: SCHIKANEDER's Papageno stands as a true descendant of this unenlightened figure, the anathema of all that Joseph had attempted to achieve. Not only must the trials and the ascent to the stuffy and formal order be seen in the context of the much more appealing Papageno, but the leading representative of the Enlightenment, Sarastro, appears anything but enlightened when he stoops to meting out torturous punishments to disobedient servants. The male hegemony of the Enlightenment takes a battering in this opera as well, as women are seen to be able to achieve the same status as men, and the representation of the place of the Moors confirms the status quo of racial attitudes in Masonic circles.

If Mozart did embrace the Enlightenment in any of its various guises, this was most likely the direction he encountered in Paris in 1778. While his relationship with Grimm may have gone badly, that was not true of the other prominent figure of this household, Louise d'Epinay, with whom Mozart remained on good terms. Considering the credentials and free-spirited nature of Mme d'Epinay, it is little wonder that Mozart found her appealing. A colleague of Rousseau, Diderot, d'Holbach, Galiani and Voltaire, her achievements as a writer included a 2,000-page novel, her three-volume *Mémoires et correspondance*, and active participation in Grimm's *Correspondance littéraire*.

In all likelihood Mozart discovered at the table of Mme d'Epinay much about the *philosophes*, especially Voltaire and her close colleague and friend Diderot. In fact, the shift in Mozart's approach to his letters to his father at this time, to something more subtly dissimulating and evasive, may very well have been cultivated in response to this new knowledge. But the element of revolt in Mozart did not make him sympathetic to revolution abroad or Jacobins at home; his own actions were not designed to overthrow but simply to subvert, and the subversion often goes unnoticed because of its subtlety. Unlike his literary compatriot, Johann Pezzl, who in his novel *Faustin* starts with the scepticism of Voltaire's *Candide* but ends by finding, instead of irony, the ideal society in Joseph's Habsburg Empire, Mozart did not reveal the best of all possible worlds in his works, and leaves it to his listeners to come to their own conclusions.

DAVID SCHROEDER

R. Darnton, *Mesmerism and the End of the Enlightenment in France* (Cambridge, MA, 1968)
R. A. Kann, *A Study in Austrian Intellectual History* (New York, 1960)
N. Till, *Mozart and the Enlightenment: Truth, Virtue and Beauty in Mozart's Operas* (New York and London, 1992)
E. Wangermann, 'Reform Catholicism and Political Radicalism in the Austrian Enlightenment', in *The Enlightenment in National Context*, ed. R. Porter and M. Teich (Cambridge, 1981), 127–40
R. Weinreb, *Eagle in a Gauze Cage: Louise d'Epinay Femme de Lettres* (New York, 1993)

Entführung aus dem Serail, Die, K384 (The Abduction from the Seraglio), singspiel in two acts, text by GOTTLIEB STEPHANIE after CHRISTOPH FRIEDRICH BRETZNER; first performed at the Burgtheater, VIENNA, 16 July 1782. *Die Entführung* marks a decisive turning point in Mozart's career as an opera composer. Amazingly mature and impressive as are the early Italian operas, highly promising his first attempts at singspiel, the culmination of opera seria his IDOMENEO – his own, and German opera's, future path is marked out by this, his first work commissioned for the court theatre in Vienna. The subject matter is merely a variant on the by then well-established topos of the initially fearsome, ultimately generous oriental autocrat; what raises this work far above all other treatments of the theme is the genius of Mozart's score. To be sure, some of the numbers are overlong; there are weak touches in the motivation of characters and the placing of events and musical numbers; Pasha Selim is a difficult, ungrateful role in that it alone (apart from the tiny character-role of Klaas, a sailor, in the opening scene of Act 3) is solely a spoken part; further, Mozart in later years would not have been content for the climax of the singspiel, the attempted elopement itself, to be carried out in dialogue rather than as a musical ensemble. Yet the brilliance of every aspect of the music – its originality, boldness and melodic, instrumental and harmonic richness – is quite new in opera.

1. The topos of the generous Turk
2. Bretzner's libretto
3. The composition
4. Mozart's score
5. Synopsis and music
6. Premiere and performance history

1. The topos of the generous Turk

The subject already had a lengthy history by the time of Mozart, with examples occurring in dramas, operas and the literatures of Britain, Italy and France as well as of German lands. Stephanie's most interesting departure from previous versions is that Belmonte, his young Spanish hero, finds himself confronted at the climax of the action not, as he had imagined, by a Turk, but by a fellow countryman who had been forced into exile by the cruelty of the hero's father.

In an act of the greatest generosity, the Pasha not only pardons the intruder, who had sought to abduct his beloved, the Pasha's would-be favourite, but allows all four of his prisoners to return to their homeland. Though Pasha Selim is by name, appearance and apparent character a stereotypical eastern potentate, he is finally revealed as a renegade Spaniard, thus forfeiting his place among generous Turks; but of course, the circumstances of the story up until the denouement lead us to regard him, as do his prisoners, as a Turk.

There is no agreement as to the priority and relative importance of numerous possible sources that have been proposed for Bretzner's libretto. The twin elements of an elopement and a Turkish setting were so widespread in European culture by the second half of the eighteenth century that many of the seeming parallels between *Die Entführung* and its forerunners may be attributable to conventions and the constant recurrence of stock situations in an age in which originality was less important than the ability to adapt common property to one's own purpose and advantage. Nevertheless, it is appropriate to mention some of the most important texts from which Bretzner may have derived inspiration.

Of possible British sources, Dryden's *Don Sebastian* (1689), Isaac Bickerstaffe's *The Captive* (1769), his *The Sultan, or A Peep into the Seraglio* (1775) and Dibdin's *The Seraglio* (1776), as well as Miss Marsh's *The Female Captive. A Narrative of Facts, which happened in Barbary in the Year 1756* (London, 1769), have all been put forward as having possibly exerted some influence on Bretzner, perhaps (in the case of *The Sultan*, via the Marmontel/Favart *Soliman II* of 1761) at second hand. Several French works have been plausibly proposed as relevant in this context: Marmontel's *Soliman II, anecdote turque* (1756) arranged by Favart for P. C. Gibert's opera *Soliman second, ou Les Trois Sultanes* (1761); and GLUCK's *La Rencontre imprévue* (1764), which is a reworking by L. H. Dancourt of *Les Pélerins de la Mecque* (1726) by A. R. Lesage and D'Orneval. (Grétry's *La Caravane du Caire*, 1783, postdates Mozart's singspiel.) Of Italian works, Jommelli's setting of G. Martinelli's *La schiava liberata* (Ludwigsburg, 1768) has points of contact with Bretzner; the libretto was translated into German by J. C. Kaffka. JOSEPH HAYDN's opera *L'incontro improvviso* (Eszterháza, 1775) is in its story very close to Gluck's. Of German-language versions, ABBE VOGLER's *Der Kaufmann von Smyrna* (1771), to a libretto by C. F. Schwan, based on a French text by S. Chamfort, has little direct relevance to the Bretzner/Mozart work, whereas G. F. W. Grossmann's libretto *Adelheit von Veltheim* (1780) has perhaps the strongest claim of all to be the most significant antecedent to *Die Entführung*, not least because it is written in Bretzner's language; it was set to music by C. G. Neefe (1781).

2. Bretzner's libretto

Bretzner's libretto, published at Leipzig (by Carl Friedrich Schneider) in 1781, bears on its title page *Belmont und Constanze, / oder: / Die Entführung aus dem / Serail. / Eine Operette / in drey Akten / von / C. F. Bretzner. / Componirt vom Herrn Kapellmeister Andre / in Berlin*. In Johann Andre's setting it was first performed at the Döbbelin Theater, Berlin, on 25 May 1781, and by the time of the Mozart premiere had also been given in Munich, Leipzig and Hamburg; thereafter it seems to have been staged only in Karlsruhe and Schwedt. Bretzner's supposed reaction to learning that his text had been altered and reset by a Viennese composer is well known: 'A certain individual, Mozart by name, in Vienna has had the audacity to misuse my drama *Belmonte und Constanze* for an opera text. I herewith protest most solemnly against this infringement of my rights, and reserve the right to take the matter further'; this statement is probably inauthentic, in that it was not published until 1868, by C. von Wurzbach in his *Biographisches Lexikon des Kaiserthums Oesterreich*. However, Bretzner's heavy-handed and detailed protest directed against the (unnamed) librettist appeared in the Berlin *Litteratur- und Theater-Zeitung* on 21 June 1783. The principal alterations introduced by Stephanie and Mozart are outlined below. In short, they amount to development of the role of Osmin, the inclusion of more sung numbers, and improvements to the dramaturgy.

3. The composition

We are more fully informed about the progress of work on the composition of *Die Entführung* than is the case with any Mozart opera other than *Idomeneo*, for which the composer in Munich, and his father and the librettist, VARESCO, in Salzburg, had to rely on correspondence for contact during the vital weeks leading up to the completion and performance of the work. In the case of the German singspiel, Mozart (and his librettist) were in Vienna, his father in Salzburg. The correspondence about the new opera was instigated by Mozart (LEOPOLD MOZART's letters to his son from this period do not survive), who was anxious to assuage his father's fears that his removal to Vienna was a foolish and retrograde step (indeed, a libretto by Stephanie was under discussion as early as 18 April 1781, before the ultimate break with the Salzburg archiepiscopal court). Accordingly, Mozart took every opportunity to emphasize his successes as he sought to establish himself in Vienna; in this respect, the commission to compose a brand-new work for the royal and imperial court theatre was a trump card that he played for all it was worth, even if it soon became clear that the Emperor and his advisers were not after all going to mount the new singspiel, as had at first been mooted, as part of the celebrations for the forthcoming visit of the Grand Duke Paul of Russia and his German wife; the court decided to play safe, and restage two of Gluck's operas.

The librettist, Gottlieb Stephanie (known as Stephanie 'the Younger', to distinguish him from his older brother, also an actor, Gottlob), was known to the Mozarts at least as early as 1773. He had been taken prisoner by the Austrians during the Seven Years War, then became an actor, playwright, librettist and eventually stage manager of the National Singspiel in Vienna. He had 'the worst Renomèe in all Vienna', Mozart mentions to his father on 16 June, 'as a coarse, deceitful, slanderous man', but already on 26 May Mozart had been pleased to refer to him as 'my good friend'. On 1 August Mozart reports: 'the day before yesterday the younger Stephani gave me a libretto to set . . . the book is pretty good. The subject is Turkish and it's called; Bellmont and konstanze, or die verführung aus dem Serail. – the Sinfonia, the chorus in the first act, and the closing chorus I shall do with turkish music. Mad:^{selle} CAVALIERI, Mad^{selle} TEYBER, M:^{r} FISCHER, M:^{r} ADAMBERGER, M:^{r} Dauer and M:^{r} Walter, are to sing in it.' And Mozart adds that he has already composed the first arias for

Cavalieri and Adamberger, and the terzetto that concludes the first act. 'Time's short', he continues, 'for it's to be performed in mid September.' On 8 August he writes that he has just finished the Janissary chorus, and that Countess THUN (a good judge) seconded the three principal singers' statement that they were 'uncommonly pleased with their arias'. By 29 August Mozart has heard that the Russian visit has been postponed until November; but he seems not to have divined that the revival of Gluck's *Iphigenie in Tauris* (in German) and *Alceste* (in Italian) was to be at the expense of *Die Entführung*. On a date between 20 and 26 September he sends his father the cast-list 'as a little Praegusto of the opera', from which it is already clear that Jautz is to play the Pasha ('Bassa Selim – Herr Jautz an acteur has nothing to sing'; Walter had not been re-engaged for the new season). Exactly what Mozart sent is not known, but as he starts his next letter on 26 September with an apology for causing his father to pay 'extra heavy postage' last time, he must have sent a copy of some of the completed music from the singspiel. This is the often-quoted letter in which he discusses the changes he has had made to the libretto, and also the music of Osmin's 'Solche hergelauf'ne Laffen', with his explanation of how he has depicted Osmin's rage; then he goes on to discuss Belmonte's 'O wie ängstlich', the Janissary chorus, Konstanze's 'Ach, ich liebte', the terzetto that concludes Act 1; and he mentions that he has sent his father the first fourteen bars of the overture. Then comes the indication that, although the first act was completed more than three weeks ago, also an aria and the drinking duet from Act 2, he has been brought to a standstill because, at his own insistence, the plot is being altered, and Stephanie is too busy to make the necessary changes at once – the most important of which, the placing as finale to Act 2 of 'a charming quintet, or rather, finale' that Bretzner had in Act 3, brought with it the need for a sizeable revision, even for 'a new intrigue'. Again Mozart refers to Stephanie's bad reputation, adding 'but after all, he's arranging the book for me, what's more, just the way I want it, and Heavens, I can't ask more of him than that'.

By 6 October it is clear that Mozart was going to have to wait to get his opera performed, and he was growing impatient for the librettist's revisions. 'Of course I'm composing other things meanwhile – but the passionate enthusiasm [for my opera] is there, and what would normally take me a fortnight would take four days now. I composed Adamberger's aria in A, Cavallieri's in B♭, and the terzett, in one day, and wrote them out in a day and a half. – but it wouldn't help if the whole opera were completed, for it would have to lie there until Gluck has got his two operas ready, and they've still got an awful lot of work to do on them.' A week later (on 13 October) Mozart replies to his father's evident criticism of Stephanie's libretto, saying he is well aware of the limitations of the verse, but that it accords so well with his musical thoughts that it couldn't but please him, and that – in the well-known phrase – 'in an opera the poetry absolutely must be the music's obedient daughter'. Italian comic operas delight because the music dominates; 'how much more must an opera succeed where the plan of the libretto is well worked out; and the words are written solely for the music, not here and there for the sake of a wretched rhyme. . . . Verses are surely absolutely vital for music – but rhymes for the sake of rhyme are the most detrimental . . . It's best when a good composer who understands the theatre and is capable of contributing something himself, and a clever poet, that true

Phoenix, get together. – then there's no need to worry about the applause even of the ignorant person.' It was 17 November before Mozart next had anything to report, however laconically: 'Now I have at last received something to work on for my opera.' On 30 January 1782 he writes: 'The opera hasn't fallen asleep, but has been postponed owing to the big Gluck operas and to many very necessary alterations in the text; but it is to be given just after Easter.' On 8 May he reports: 'I was at Countess THUN's yesterday and put my second act through its paces for her, with which she is no less pleased than with the first.' As the ultimate date for the premiere approached, so, tantalizingly, there are large gaps in the surviving correspondence. The letter of 29 May mentions that Mozart and Constanze are to dine at Countess Thun's the next day, when he will play Act 3 through to her; he also says that the first rehearsal is scheduled for the following Monday, 3 June.

The next letter we have is dated 20 July; Mozart hopes his father received the letter in which he told him of the opera's favourable reception at the premiere. It was given again yesterday, he writes – and had to overcome a strong cabal, which hissed during the first act; however, there were bravos for the arias. Mozart had set his hopes on the concluding terzetto:

> But misfortune caused Fischer to go wrong, which caused Dauer (Pedrillo) to go wrong – and Adamberger alone couldn't make up for the others – so the whole effect was lost, and this time it was – not encored. – I was so angry that I didn't know myself, Adamberger too – and I said at once that I wouldn't let the opera be performed again without holding a small rehearsal (for the singers) beforehand. – In the 2nd act the two duets, as on the first night, and in addition Belmont's Rondeau wenn der freude thränen fliessen were encored. – the theatre was almost fuller than the first time. – the day before you couldn't get a reserved seat in the Noble parterre or the 3rd circle; and there wasn't a box to be had. the Opera has brought in 1200 gulden in the 2 days. – I send you the original [score], and 2 librettos. – You will find much crossed out in it; that is because I knew the Score would be copied here at once – consequently I let my thoughts run riot – and before I handed it over for copying I first made my changes and cuts here and there. – and as you have it, so was it performed. – the trumpets and timpani are missing here and there, flutes, clarinet, turkish music – because I could get no paper with sufficient lines. – they are written on additional sheets – the copyist has probably lost them, for he couldn't find them. – the First Act (when I was having it carried somewhere, I forget where) unfortunately fell in the dirt; that's why it's so soiled. – Now I've got no small task. – by Sunday week my opera must be arranged for wind instruments – otherwise someone will beat me to it – and get the profit of it, instead of me.

(In the event, Mozart failed to complete the arrangement.) It is clear from Mozart's next mention of the opera (in the letter of 31 July) that his father was cross – surely more about Mozart's continuing insistence on marrying Constanze than truly expressing disappointment about reports of his son's having boasted of the success of the opera. For his part, Leopold speaks coolly of the opera's success in the surviving fragment of his letter of 4 October to the publisher Breitkopf. On 5 October Mozart urges his father to have the score copied swiftly, as he has promised it to Baron Riedesel (the Prussian ambassador in Vienna). Hereafter the opera is occasionally mentioned in the family correspondence, usually in the context of Mozart's failure to gain profit by completing the vocal score, or with mention of performances in other operatic centres.

4. Mozart's score

Mozart never again achieved quite the superabundance of his score to *Die Entführung*; indeed, it is a sign of his ever-increasing maturity and experience that he would not have wanted to do so. He himself became aware that in his exuberance he was letting his imagination run away with him, as is suggested by the comparative austerity of means in his later operas, as well as by the numerous cuts that he made in many of the individual numbers of the *Entführung* manuscript. Never again in his operas did he demand so rich and varied an orchestra; he employs basset horns and piccolo as well as standard timpani, double woodwind and brass (only trombones are missing from the orchestra he used for *Idomeneo*, DON GIOVANNI and DIE ZAUBERFLÖTE); further, he requires the 'Turkish' instruments in several numbers: triangle, cymbals, 'Turkish' and German drums. Despite this orchestral richness, many of the numbers are austerely scored, and the sheer range of his instrumental palette allows him to vary the orchestration between numbers to telling effect. With so full an instrumentarium, no wonder Mozart sent his father on 5 October, for the copying of the score, '5 books of 12-staff-lined Paper', a size that was not available in Salzburg.

5. Synopsis and music

The overture, as Mozart mentions to his father on 26 September 1781, 'is quite short, constantly changes between forte and piano [and, he might have added, between Presto and Andante, C major and C minor]; in the fortes turkish Music comes in each time.' After a second reprise of the Presto, the Andante returns, now in the tonic major, to lead directly into the opening scene.

Act 1: Courtyard in front of the Pasha Selim's palace at the seaside. Belmonte enters, singing of his hope of finding here his beloved Konstanze ('Hier soll ich dich denn sehen'; Andante, C major). Osmin, the Pasha's supervisor, enters with a ladder and begins picking figs, singing of the joy of finding a true and honest girl ('Wer ein Liebchen hat gefunden'; Andante – Allegro, B flat). Belmonte tries to interrupt Osmin by asking whether this is the Pasha's house, but Osmin ignores him and continues his song. The tempo increases to Allegro as Osmin becomes aware of Belmonte's presence; the latter, in what has become a duet, grows angry at Osmin's ignoring of him, and for his part Osmin gives as good as he gets, grudgingly agreeing that Belmonte has found the house he is looking for. Their mutual antipathy, and the tempo, increase and the duetto ends (Presto, D major) with Osmin pushing Belmonte out.

Pedrillo, Belmonte's servant, now in charge of the Pasha's gardens, enters and finds Osmin in angry mood. The latter's F major aria, 'Solche hergelauf'ne

Laffen', exploits Fischer's exceptional bass voice as well as proclaiming Mozart's masterly control of the depiction of musical rage. Osmin then enters the house, leaving Pedrillo to be joined – and of course recognized – by Belmonte, who learns of Konstanze's continued opposition to the Pasha's desire to make her a full member of his harem. Pedrillo will introduce Belmonte to Selim as an architect, building and gardens being his hobbies. Pedrillo exits, leaving Belmonte to sing the aria 'O wie ängstlich, o wie feurig' (Andante, A major), which is preceded by a brief accompanied recitative. Pedrillo then returns, urging Belmonte to conceal himself until Selim, about to return from a boat trip, has been told of his arrival.

A short C major Marcia (discovered only recently and probably authentic, but seldom played) accompanies the entry of Selim's boat party; it is scored for woodwind, brass and both German and Turkish drums. The Janissaries (who have been accompanying Selim in a second boat) sing the praises of their master in a brilliant four-part chorus (C major) that includes solo voices. They leave the stage to Selim and Konstanze, who continues her opposition to his desire to make her first among his wives, in the aria 'Ach ich liebte, war so glücklich!' (Adagio – Allegro, B flat); she sings of her unshakeable fidelity to her beloved. He grants her one further day's respite, and she leaves. Pedrillo then enters and introduces Belmonte as a young architect who wishes to enter Selim's service; the latter tells Pedrillo to see to Belmonte's needs, he will interview him properly the next day. Pedrillo warns the excitable Belmonte to be constantly on his guard. As they are about to enter the palace, Osmin blocks their way. In the terzetto 'Marsch, marsch, marsch! trollt euch fort!' (Allegro – Allegro assai, C minor – C major) that ends Act 1, Pedrillo and Belmonte eventually manage to push past Osmin.

Act 2: A palace garden; Osmin's dwelling to one side. Blonde, Konstanze's maid, vigorously opposes Osmin's command to love him. In the aria 'Durch Zärtlichkeit und Schmeicheln' (Andante grazioso, A major, accompanied by strings alone) she tells him that good women can be won, if at all, only by tenderness and flattery. In the dialogue that follows, she lets him know that she is an Englishwoman, not a slave; if he values his eyes, he shouldn't get too near her fingernails. Her trump card is that she need only tell Konstanze of his intended treatment of her, and she will see to it that the Pasha has him whipped. In a duetto ('Ich gehe, doch rate ich dir'; Allegro – Andante – Allegro assai, E flat) he is mocked by her, and sent packing; his protestations make no impression. Konstanze enters, and in a brief, poignant accompanied recitative she laments her separation from Belmonte, then moves into the aria 'Traurigkeit ward mir zum Lose' (Andante con moto, G minor, accompanied by flutes, oboes, basset horns, bassoons, horns and strings), in which she laments her grief. Blonde attempts to cheer her, confident that they will manage to escape to their homeland. When she spies the Pasha approaching, Blonde exits. Konstanze tells him that she cannot love him, even though he threatens her with torture. There follows the aria 'Martern aller Arten', in which she takes up this threat and swears constancy to her absent lover. This number (Allegro – Allegro assai, C major, accompanied by pairs of clarinets, bassoons, horns, trumpets, timpani and strings, with demanding obbligato solos for flute, oboe, violin and cello) is easily the longest, most exacting, and from the producer's viewpoint most taxing, in the opera: not only must the Pasha stand and listen, or pace to and fro while Konstanze sings (almost immediately after her previous aria), the number also dangerously retards the action. Mozart marked the deletion of twenty-seven bars with two cuts, yet that scarcely affects an aria of 319 bars. It is a wonderful tour de force; but it does help us to understand the general criticism attributed to EMPEROR JOSEPH: 'Very many notes, my dear Mozart!' She storms off, followed by the Pasha after he has wondered what gives her the courage to oppose his desires – he will now use cunning, where threats and entreaties have failed. Blonde re-enters, surprised to find neither the Pasha nor Konstanze in the garden. Pedrillo enters and imparts the news of Belmonte's arrival, and of the nearby ship in which all four of them will escape that very night. In the merry aria 'Welche Wonne, welche Lust' (Allegro, G major) Blonde sings of the joy this news will bring to her mistress; she hurries off, leaving Pedrillo to summon up courage for the task that lies before them. In his D major aria 'Frisch zum Kampfe! Frisch zum Streite!' (Allegro con spirito, D major, accompanied by oboes, horns, trumpets and timpani as well as strings), he manages to overcome his fears. Osmin enters, wondering at Pedrillo's unexpected cheerfulness, and despite Mohammed's ban on alcohol he is unable to resist Pedrillo's invitation to drink with him: he is given the larger of two wine-flasks (which has been doctored with a sleeping-draught), and in the duetto 'Vivat Bacchus!' (Allegro, C major, with 'Turkish' instruments added to the texture, which includes piccolo and pairs of flutes, oboes, clarinets, horns and trumpets) they drink together, once Osmin has overcome his doubts. The latter already displays signs of the effect of the wine and the sleeping-draught in the dialogue scene that follows, during which Pedrillo manages to lead him off into his house, before returning almost at once. He is joined first by Belmonte, then by Konstanze and Blonde. Belmonte sings to Konstanze the aria 'Wenn der Freude Tränen fliessen' (Adagio – Allegretto, B flat) in which he welcomes the tears of joy that he kisses from her cheek. Only after the aria do they get down to practicalities: Belmonte has a boat at the ready; at midnight the men will be beneath the women's windows with a ladder; Pedrillo will give the signal with a song. The act ends with the quartetto 'Ach Belmonte! ach mein Leben' (D major). Its frequent changes of tempo mirror the mood of the participants, as love, joy, practical concerns, and the men's fears that their loved ones have been unable to remain faithful to them, lead to apologies and then forgiveness; finally, with jealousy overcome, the four unite in praise of love.

Act 3: Courtyard in front of the Pasha's palace; the palace on one side, Osmin's dwelling on the other, a view of the sea beyond. It is midnight. Pedrillo enters with Klaas, a sailor (spoken part), who brings a ladder. Pedrillo, relieved when Belmonte enters, leaves to see if the coast is clear, advising Belmonte to sing (as he himself is in the habit of doing) so that the Janissary guards will not be suspicious if they find him in the courtyard. Needing no second bidding, Belmonte sings the most leisurely and elegant of his four arias, 'Ich baue ganz auf deine Stärke' (Andante, E flat; flutes, clarinets, bassoons, horns and strings). Pedrillo enters with a mandoline, and while Belmonte keeps watch, he sings his strophic Romance (basically in D major) 'In Mohrenland gefangen war / Ein Mädel hübsch und fein', the four verses being separated by rapid dialogue with Belmonte, and with Pedrillo speaking in melodrama during his pre- and postluding. At last Konstanze appears at her window, Belmonte climbs up the ladder and into the room, a few moments later appearing with her in the doorway; Pedrillo hustles them towards the shore, then climbs and enters Blonde's room. Before they emerge, a black mute slave appears, and signals to the inebriated Osmin that he has heard suspicious noises. Osmin's lantern then reveals the ladder, on which he sits; when Pedrillo begins to climb down the ladder, Blonde sees Osmin and gives warning; Osmin attempts to climb up after Pedrillo, but has to resort to shouting for the guards – who fail to recognize Osmin, but then set out in pursuit of the escapers. First the servant pair, then Belmonte and Konstanze are led back in as prisoners; Belmonte's attempt to bribe Osmin fails, and the latter rejoices in the thought of his revenge, as the prisoners are led away to face Pasha Selim. In his aria 'O, wie will ich triumphieren' (Allegro vivace, D major), Osmin celebrates his forthcoming triumph when the prisoners are led to the place of execution and strung up, their treachery rewarded.

The Pasha's room: Selim orders an officer to investigate the disturbance that has awoken him. Osmin, still under the influence of drink and the sleeping-draught, enters to report the attempted elopement. Then Belmonte and Konstanze are led in, she admitting her guilt, and prepared to die if Belmonte is spared; he bends his knee before Selim and says his Spanish family will pay whatever ransom Selim demands. 'My name is Lostados', he concludes. – 'Is the Commandant of Oran known to you?' the Pasha asks. – 'He is my father', replies Belmonte. Selim rejoices to learn that the son of his greatest enemy is in his hands. 'Know, wretched man! Your father, that barbarian, is the cause of my having to leave my native land. His inflexible avarice tore from me a woman whom I esteemed higher than my life. He robbed me of position, of honour, fortune, everything. In short, he destroyed my entire happiness. And now I have this man's only son in my power! Tell me, were he in my position, what would he do?' – 'My fate would be pitiable.' – 'So it shall be', he concludes, bidding Osmin follow him to plan their torture, and the guard to watch them carefully. In the accompanied recitativo e duetto 'Welch ein Geschick! . . . Meinetwegen sollst du sterben!' (Adagio – Andante – Allegro, B flat) Belmonte and Konstanze each express grief at causing the death of the other, but together, they will die happily. Then Pedrillo and Blonde are led in. Selim enters, and demands of Belmonte whether he is prepared to hear his sentence. 'Yes,' he replies, 'slake your vengeance on me, extirpate the wrong my father did you. I am prepared for everything, and do not blame you.' – 'I have despised your father far too much to be able to follow in his footsteps. Take your freedom, take Konstanze, sail to your homeland, tell your father that you were in my power, that I let you go so that you might say to him that it is a far greater pleasure to repay with beneficence an injustice suffered, than to extirpate one vicious crime with another.' Anticlimax is avoided only by the bitter tone with which Selim bids farewell to Belmonte and Konstanze, then grants permission for Pedrillo and Blonde too to leave, Osmin's jealous fury being temporarily assuaged only by Selim's comment that at least he will no longer live in danger of having his eyes scratched out. 'Calm yourself', he tells his overseer, 'one must rid oneself of persons whose good will one cannot obtain through beneficence.' The closing Vaudeville and Janissaries' Chorus (Andante – Allegro vivace, F major – C major) has each of the soloists sing in turn of the Pasha's goodness and generosity, the others joining in praise of him, until Blonde's mocking remark about the bestiality of Osmin leads the latter into a further explosion of fury, and he takes up again the Allegro assai section of his Act I aria. He storms off, and there follow a few bars of sotto voce moralizing from the four freed prisoners before musical peace is restored. The brief, brilliant chorus of the Janissaries in praise of their master brings the singspiel to its close.

6. Premiere and performance history

As usual, Mozart conceived the roles with specific singers in mind. If this is not wholly true of *Die Entführung*, the reason lies in the abnormally long gestation period. His principals were both excellent singers: the Konstanze was the Vienna-born Caterina Cavalieri, a SALIERI pupil who sang in opera buffa; Johann Valentin Adamberger, a renowned opera seria tenor, who had sung with success in LONDON as well as in Italy, was the Belmonte. Mozart's need to win their approval and write to their strengths undoubtedly had an adverse effect on the economy of the score; Mozart indeed confessed to his father (letter of 26 Sept. 1781) that he had found it necessary to make sacrifices in favour of Cavalieri's 'flexible throat'; and the placement of two arias for Konstanze back to back in Act 2 was only marginally preferable to Bretzner's placing Konstanze's third aria at the end of the work, after the denouement. In the case of Belmonte, his four arias are one too many; it is arguable that they reveal too little musical variety; and to give him an aria that fatally delays the Act 3 elopement is a serious miscalculation (such as Smetana was also to commit in *Dalibor*). Adamberger seems not to have been a very talented actor. In that vital respect Mozart was more fortunate with the remainder of his cast. Therese Teyber, the Blonde, had studied with Vittoria Tesi and was by 1782 an excellent soubrette. The Pedrillo, Johann Ernst Dauer, had gained considerable experience in theatres in central and northern Germany, as well as in Vienna, where he had success as actor and as singer. The star performer in terms of imposing stage presence, as well as resplendent voice, was the Osmin, Ludwig Fischer, a basso profondo who clearly also had a good top register, and who, the Prince-Archbishop of Salzburg opined, 'sang too low for a bass' (see Mozart's letter of 26 Sept. 1781). The one role that then as now presents problems is Bassa Selim, a spoken part. The tenor Joseph Walter, who was to have sung it (see the letter of 1 Aug. 1781), was among those dismissed from the company before the opening of the 1781–2 season. It was the actor Dominik Jautz who ultimately played Selim. Though a cast combining spoken and singing roles was by no means uncommon in Mozart's day, it is unfortunate that this key character alone (apart from the sailor, Klaas) does not sing.

Die Entführung was the most frequently performed opera of Mozart in his lifetime, being staged all over German lands, and very soon in foreign countries as well (PRAGUE autumn 1782, Warsaw May 1783, Riga March 1785, Amsterdam and Budapest 1791), quite often in translation. In Vienna it proved to be the most popular and successful work written for the National Singspiel company that Joseph II inaugurated in 1778, with a total of forty-two performances, including the very last night of this enterprise, 4 February 1788 (the two works that rang up more performances were both French originals, taken into the repertory in German translation, Gluck's *La Rencontre imprévue* under the title *Die Pilgrime von Mekka*, and Grétry's version of the tale of Beauty and the Beast, *Zémire et Azor*). Mozart attended a performance of his singspiel in Berlin on 19 May 1789, as an amusing memoir of Ludwig Tieck relates, who got into conversation before the performance with a stranger in the pit, who turned out to be Mozart himself. Despite periods when its German singspiel form rendered it less popular, it has retained a place in the repertories of most German and Austrian houses, and it continues to be frequently performed throughout the world. Though it is best suited to small or medium-sized theatres, it has also been performed with success in large houses. PETER BRANSCOMBE

T. Bauman, *W. A. Mozart: 'Die Entführung aus dem Serail'* (Cambridge, 1987)
M. Head, *Orientalism, Masquerade and Mozart's Turkish Music* (London, 2001)
Edward W. Said, *Orientalism. Western Conceptions of the Orient* (London, 1978, repr. 1995)
W. Daniel Wilson, *Humanität und Kreuzzugsideologie um 1780* (New York, 1984)

Esterházy von Galántha. Two members of the extensive Esterházy family have connections with Mozart. A double memorial celebration, for Georg August, Duke of Mecklenburg-Strelitz and for the imperial and royal chamberlain Franz Esterházy von Galántha (b. ?19 Sept. 1715; d. Vienna, 7 Nov. 1785), held at the lodge 'Zur gekrönten Hoffnung' on 17 November 1785, featured a performance of Mozart's *Maurerische Trauermusik* (MASONIC FUNERAL MUSIC), K477; Esterházy was a subscriber to Mozart's March 1784 Trattnerhof concerts. His cousin, Johann Baptist Esterházy von Galántha (b. Vienna 6 June 1748; d. Vienna, 25 Feb. 1800), imperial and royal chamberlain and court councillor, was a prominent patron of music. Mozart played at his palace ten times during March 1783 and Johann Baptist, like Franz, was a subscriber to the Trattnerhof concerts. In February and March 1788, Mozart conducted performances of C. P. E. BACH's *Die Auferstehung und Himmelfahrt Christi* at Esterházy's; performances were also given there of Mozart's arrangements of HANDEL's *Acis and Glatea* (30 Dec. 1788) and *Messiah* (6 Mar. and 7 Apr. 1789). Esterházy was a member of the lodge 'Zur neugekrönten Hoffnung'. CLIFF EISEN

Ettore, Guglielmo d' (b. c. 1740; d. Stuttgart, 1771). Italian tenor and the first Mitridate in Mozart's opera of the same name. The Mozarts first met d'Ettore in MILAN in early 1770 and during rehearsals for MITRIDATE, in November, he proved a thorn in Mozart's side, demanding at least four rewrites of the aria 'Se di lauri il crine adorno', two of 'Vado incontro al fato estremo' and two of the recitative 'Respira alfin'; in the performance itself, d'Ettore substituted GASPARINI's aria on 'Vado incontro' for Mozart's. In a letter of 6/11 May 1778, Leopold alluded to d'Ettore's bad behaviour: 'you must not let yourself be discouraged or unnerved by those who envy you; for it is the same everywhere. Remember Italy and your first opera, and your third opera too, and d'Ettore and so forth; likewise the intrigues of DE AMICIS and all the rest.' CLIFF EISEN

H. J. Wignall, 'Mozart's first Mitridate', *Opera Quarterly* 10 (1994), 93–112.
'The Genesis of "Se di lauri": Mozart's Drafts and Final Version of Guglielmo d'Ettore's Entrance Aria from "Mitridate" ', *Mozart Studien* 5 (1995), 45–99.

Exsultate, jubilate. Mozart's motet K165 written for VENANZIO RAUZZINI and first performed in Milan on 17 January 1773. See MOTET

Eybler, Joseph Leopold von (b. Schwechat, 8 Feb. 1765; d. Vienna, 24 July 1846). Austrian composer, Viennese court Vizekapellmeister from 1814 and court Kapellmeister, succeeding SALIERI, from 1824. An acquaintance of JOSEPH HAYDN and a student from 1777 to 1779 of ALBRECHTSBERGER (who in 1793 described him as 'the greatest musical genius VIENNA possessed after Mozart'), Eybler reportedly helped at rehearsals for COSÌ FAN TUTTE; in May 1790 Mozart wrote a testimonial for the young composer, describing him as 'a well-grounded composer, equally skilled in chamber music and the church style, fully experienced in the art of song, also an accomplished organ and keyboard player'. Shortly after Mozart's death, Eybler was asked to complete the REQUIEM but he soon abandoned the task, which was left to SÜSSMAYR; ironically Eybler suffered a stroke while conducting the Requiem at a performance in February 1833. CLIFF EISEN

Robert Haas, 'Josef Leopold Edler von Eybler', *Mozart-Jahrbuch* 1952, 61–4

Johanna Senigl, 'Neues zu Joseph Eybler', in *De Editione Musices. Festschrift Gerhard Croll zum 65. Geburtstag*, ed. Wolfgang Gratzer and Andrea Lindmayr (Laaber, 1992), 329–37

F

Ferlendis, Giuseppe (b. Bergamo, 1755; d. Lisbon, 1810). Italian oboist and composer. Ferlendis joined the SALZBURG court music establishment on 1 April 1777; that summer Mozart composed the Oboe Concerto, K314, for him, according to LEOPOLD MOZART. But he did not remain in Salzburg for long, resigning from the orchestra in June 1778. At the time, Leopold wrote to Wolfgang: 'Now for a piece of news! Ferlendis . . . left the service at the end of June. This has been the more unexpected and upsetting as during the last two months whenever Ferlendis played a concerto, the Archbishop had been in the habit of giving him one or two ducats. Moreover he was the favourite in the orchestra and since Besozzi's [Carlo Besozzi, the Italian oboe virtuoso who played in Salzburg in May 1778] arrival in Salzburg had learnt a good deal from him' (letter of 3 Aug. 1778). After his departure from Salzburg, Ferlendis was active in Turin, Venice, LONDON (from 1795) and Lisbon. He was a specialist on the cor anglais and possibly responsible for improvements to the instrument. CLIFF EISEN

A. Bernardini, 'The Oboe in the Venetian Republic, 1692–1797', *Early Music* 16 (1988), 372–87

Ferrarese del Bene, Adriana [baptized Andriana Augusta] (b. 19 Sept. 1759; d. 1804 or after). Prima donna of the Viennese opera buffa troupe 1788–91; she sang Susanna in the 1789 revival of LE NOZZE DI FIGARO and created Fiordiligi in COSÌ FAN TUTTE. After training and performances of oratorio at the Ospedale de' Mendicanti in Venice (1778–82) she eloped with the son of the papal representative to the Venetian government, Luigi del Bene. Shortly thereafter she embarked on an operatic career that took her to many of Italy's leading theatres as well as those of LONDON, VIENNA and Warsaw. Although her early operatic work in Italy was in serious opera, in London she also sang opera buffa. In Vienna she specialized in roles (such as that of Diana in MARTÍN Y SOLER'S *L'arbore di Diana*, to which she added two serious arias by Angelo Tarchi) that allowed her to make good use of her experience and abilities in both genres. The music that Mozart wrote for her, including two new arias for *Figaro* ('Al desio di chi t'adora' and 'Un moto di gioia mi sento') gave her plenty of opportunity to sing brilliant coloratura and leap dramatically between her lowest and highest notes, but also required her, in numerous ensembles and extensive dialogue, to display her comic and dramatic skills. JOHN A. RICE

P. L. Gidwitz, 'Mozart's Fiordiligi: Adriana Ferrarese del Bene', *Cambridge Opera Journal* 8 (1996), 199–214
L. Nassimbeni, *Paganini, Rossini e La Ferrarese* (Udine, 1999)
J. A. Rice, *Antonio Salieri and Viennese Opera* (Chicago, 1998)

Fiala, Joseph (b. Lochovitz (now Lochovice), western Bohemia, 2 Mar. 1748; d. Donaueschingen, 31 July 1816). Bohemian composer, oboist, cellist and viol player. From 1774, Fiala served in the chapel of Kraft Ernst von Oettingen-Wallerstein, in Swabia, and in 1777 he was appointed oboist in the MUNICH Hofkapelle of Elector MAXIMILIAN III JOSEPH. Fiala met Mozart in Munich that year and in 1778 he visited LEOPOLD MOZART in SALZBURG; shortly afterwards he joined the court music establishment there. He was dismissed from Salzburg service in 1785 and then travelled to St Petersburg, returning to Germany in 1792. The Mozarts and Fiala were close, and the oboist took Mozart's side in his disputes with Archbishop COLLOREDO; on 23 November 1778 Leopold wrote to his son: 'Yesterday Herr Fiala was with the Archbishop, who questioned him about the MANNHEIM musicians and especially about their compositions. Fiala told him that the best music in Mannheim was Mozart's, that at the very first concert, there being one every Monday in the Kaisersaal, apart from CANNABICH's symphony everything else was Mozart's, and that immediately after the symphony Mlle WEBER had sung an aria by Mozart, the like of which he had never heard in his life.' CLIFF EISEN

E. Hintermaier, 'Die Salzburger Hofkapelle von 1700 bis 1806' (Ph.D. thesis, University of Salzburg, 1972), 112–16
S. E. Murray, 'Introduction', in *Seven Symphonies from the Court of Oettingen-Wallerstein, 1773–1795*, ed. Murray (New York, 1981)

Finalmusik. See SERENADE

finta giardiniera, La, K196 (The Feigned Gardener's Girl). *Dramma giocoso* in three acts, composed 1774–5. First performance: MUNICH, 13 January 1775. Sometime in 1774 Mozart received a contract from the Munich court theatre to compose the *dramma giocoso La finta giardiniera* for Carnival. By September, Mozart was already at work composing the recitatives and on 6 December, he, with his father, left SALZBURG for Munich in order to become acquainted with the capabilities of the singers so that he could compose the set numbers. *La finta* received its premiere on 13 January and was performed three times in total.

K196 has been plagued by source problems. First, since there is no extant libretto from the Munich performances, its authorship remains uncertain. It has been attributed to RANIERI CALZABIGI and MARCO COLTELLINI. Most recently, the libretto has been attributed to the Abbate Giuseppe Petrosellini, but this attribution has also been called into question. Second, for many years there was no complete musical text for the Italian version; one had to conflate Mozart's autograph for Acts 2 and 3 in its authentic German version of 1779/80, and the recitatives by Anfossi. In 1978 a copy from c.1800 of the complete Italian version was recovered. In contrast to the old Mozart edition, which printed the singspiel version of Act 1 and Italian/German texts for Acts 2 and 3, the NEUE MOZART-AUSGABE presents a uniform Italian version.

The action centres around seven characters who have or have had various relationships with each other. Arminda of noble birth at one time was in love with Ramiro, who still loves her, but Arminda is now the betrothed of the Contino Belfiore. The Contino was formerly in love with the Countess Violante, alias Sandrina, the pretended gardener's maid, who still has feelings for him. Don Anchise, the Podestà (Mayor of Lagonero), finds himself taken with Sandrina.

Roberto, alias Nardo, is Violante's servant and the pretended gardener of the Podestà, who is in love with the Serpetta, who in turn is in love with the Podestà.

In a jealous quarrel, the Contino has stabbed the Countess Violante (Sandrina) thinking her to have died. When the Contino arrives on the scene Sandrina has fainted and he is totally mystified to discover that this is the still breathing Violante. The Podestà is also confused. Everyone seems unhappy with their situations. In the end, all the complications are resolved: Sandrina (Violante) and Belfiore are reconciled; Arminda rekindles her love for Ramiro; and the Serpetta settles for Nardo. The Podestà declares that he will continue to be happily unattached.

The characters are divided into seria and buffa roles with Arminda and Ramiro belonging to the serious realm. Ramiro is a male soprano, which further underlines his station. The Countess Violante, the Contino Belfiore, and the Podestà could also by their position be serious roles, but neither their texts nor their music consistently portray them in this way. As such, some have claimed *La finta* to be the first buffa libretto to introduce *parti serie*; hence, its designation as a *dramma giocoso*. Nevertheless, in the end all the couples are matched by their class; the Serpetta does not gain the Podestà, but rather Violante's servant Roberto (Nardo). Additionally, besides the two pretended roles (Violante and Roberto), several other characters derive from the commedia dell'arte: the Podestà is a reincarnation of Pantalone, Roberto (Nardo) a Pulcinella, and the Serpetta a Columbine.

In *La finta giardiniera* the set numbers play a vital role in character development. Mozart's most fully developed character is the Contino Belfiore who sings four solo numbers (Nos. 6, 8, 15 and 19) and two duets (Nos. 24 and 27). No. 6 introduces us to the Contino with music that reeks of his and Arminda's station: dotted rhythms and scales, a demisemiquaver figure (a bowing motif? or kiss of the hand?), and a certain elaborateness of melody. As the Serpetta observes: 'What a beautiful caricature!' The caricature of the Contino is further built in No. 8; he traces his lineage with a catalogue of ancient Romans; Mozart again fills the music with noble codes. In No. 15, the Contino sings to Sandrina and takes the Podestà's hand in slapstick fashion. His underlying confusion comes to a head in his mad scene (No. 19), whose accompanied recitative carefully enhances the text. His loss of sanity is expanded in his duet with Sandrina (No. 24) and fully resolved in their final duet (No. 27), as they both gradually return to sanity.

The Podestà's first aria (No. 3) is a response to the love triangle with the Serpetta and Sandrina in which instruments of the orchestra underline his changing moods: the sweetness of flutes and oboes, the sombreness of the violas, and the noise of trumpets, drums, bassoons and basses drive him to the brink. Here, the sections of text are also defined by mode (verse 2) and by tempo (verse 3) as well as orchestration. In Nos. 17 and 25, the Podestà acts in an official capacity though he, too, is finally afflicted by insanity.

Violante, alias Sandrina, is allotted five solo numbers. All except for one, No. 21, portray her in her feigned state as a gardener, which is underlined by their simple structures. No. 21 turns to the high seria style; it includes a number of STURM UND DRANG characteristics: minor mode, agitated rhythms and an urgent declamation.

Arminda and Ramiro consistently reveal their elevated status. The text of Ramiro's first aria (No. 2) defines a serious character with the metaphor of 'a lover as a bird in a cage', which is ornamented by a series of different musical figures and shaped in a sonata form. His second aria (No. 18) is a seria gesture marked by elaborate melismas at the two principal cadences, while his final piece (No. 26) is saturated by a C minor *Sturm und Drang* style. Of Arminda's two arias, only No. 13 carries a serious affect similar to Violante's No. 21 and Ramiro's No. 18, while No. 7 has a rather neutral cast. In neither of these seria arias does Arminda display any coloratura.

In contrast, the Serpetta and Roberto, alias Nardo, have less elaborate pieces. Together they share a simple strophic song (Nos. 9a and 9b). The Serpetta's first aria (No. 10) includes two contredanses in 6/8 and 3/8 time, and her second (No. 20) begins as a bourrée and concludes with another 6/8 Allegro. Nardo's No. 5 identifies iron and marble as more malleable than women. Mozart uses riding music and hammer-blows to conjure up the image of a blacksmith and stonemason. In the opera's best-known piece (No. 14), Nardo temporarily becomes a *galant homme*. He unsuccessfully tries to charm the Serpetta in French, English and Italian; Mozart responds with dances that underline each national style.

The finales to Acts 1 and 2 show how far the eighteen-year-old composer had come since LA FINTA SEMPLICE; in K196 everything is assured and polished with a variety of styles and a convincing tonal plan that at times underlines the dramatic situation. The finale to Act 1 (No. 12) moves nowhere dramatically; it recapitulates the situations and leaves the characters confused and deceived. The Act 2 finale proper (No. 23) has an ambiguous beginning since the music is continuous, starting with No. 20. However, it fails to resolve all the dramatic strands and by its end only Sandrina (Violante) and the Contino are satisfied, even though they are both still delirious. The Act 3 finale is merely a chorus in praise of love.

La finta giardiniera is the first indication we have of Mozart's mastery of an idiom that would serve him well in the Italian buffo and *giocoso* idioms during the last decade of his life in Vienna. Though *La finta*'s libretto has its dramatic problems, Mozart makes it work through a series of set numbers – arias, duets and the two big finales – that are effective both in treating the text and in developing the characters. Nearly every number has its own delights.

A. PETER BROWN

C. Gianturco, *Mozart's Early Operas* (London, 1981)
D. Heartz, *Haydn, Mozart and the Viennese School 1740–1780* (New York, 1995)
W. Mann, *Mozart's Operas* (London, 1977)

finta semplice, La, K51 (The Feigned Simpleton). Opera buffa in three acts, libretto by MARCO COLTELLINI after CARLO GOLDONI. First performance: SALZBURG, ?Archbishop's Palace, ?1 May 1769. Everything we know about the circumstances surrounding Mozart's first opera, *La finta semplice*, comes from LEOPOLD MOZART, who during the family's 1768 residence in VIENNA wrote letters to Lorenz HAGENAUER in Salzburg and on 21 September petitioned in writing the EMPEROR JOSEPH II. Apparently Joseph II asked Wolfgang if he would like to compose and conduct an opera, which Leopold took to be an imperial command; accordingly, he made arrangements to acquire a libretto for Wolfgang. After K51 was completed, all sorts of intrigues were mounted against the work by people in the court theatre, who were fearful of Wolfgang's prodigious talent. In the end, *La finta semplice* was never heard in the imperial city; its premiere may have been at the Salzburg Archbishop's residence on 1 May 1769. Though the date is not certain, Mozart's sister and the existence of a printed libretto with a Salzburg cast confirm its performance.

The libretto by Carlo Goldoni was reworked by the imperial court poet Marco Coltellini. In Acts 1 and 2, his alterations were few: Cassandro's aria of Act I/6 was redone, in Act II/8 Cassandro's aria was reconceived as a duet with Fracasso, and a duet for Rosina and Fracasso was eliminated. However, for Act 3 Coltellini made alterations to every scene and added a fully-fledged finale.

The plot involves Rosina, the pretend simpleton, Hungarian baroness, and sister of Fracasso, who attracts the love interests of Cassandro and Polidoro. Cassandro is a foolish and avaricious gentleman, prone to outbursts of anger and misogyny, who drinks too much; Polidoro is his foolish brother. Donna Giacinta, the sister of Cassandro and Polidoro, wants to get married and is subject to fits of temper. Ninetta is the chambermaid to Donna Giacinta; Fracasso, a brother of Rosina and a Hungarian captain, controls Cassandro's estate; and Simone acts as Fracasso's officer and servant. After much manoeuvring and foolery, Ninetta and Donna Giacinta agree to marry Simone and Fracasso, and Rosina declares her love for Don Cassandro, even though up to the last minute she plays on the rivalry between the two brothers, leaving Don Polidoro out in the cold. Virtually every one of these characters is derived from the commedia dell'arte : the brothers Cassandro and Polidoro are reincarnations of Pantalone, Fracasso is the captain, Ninetta the servette, Simone is Harlequin as well as the captain's servant, and, of course, the three couples take on characteristics of the lovers.

The numbers are almost entirely for solo voices. There is but one duet (Act II/8), the duelling scene for Fracasso and Cassandro. Here Mozart plays on the action with the first and second violins exchanging figures. Though the challenger Cassandro withdraws, the situation is never resolved. Act 1 begins with an ensemble for Giacinta, Fracasso, Ninetta and Simone presenting their individual situations and coming together for the opening and closing refrains, which praise love, springtime and freedom. As to the act finales, they do not begin to approach the sophistication found in the DA PONTE operas nor do they compare even with those in LA FINTA GIARDINIERA. Granted, they are sectional with changing tempos and keys coordinating with the addition of characters, but the dramatic situations are less powerful, a defect that Mozart seems to compound through his tutti scoring rather than through gradually increasing the instrumentation, and by his less than strategic use of accelerating tempos (at the end of the Act 1 finale, for example, the tempo moderates). The Act 2 finale leaves the listener dramatically suspended but hardly surprised by the situation. Mozart again displays a lack of control over the larger structure, which is revealed by his sequence of metres: rather than moving from large to small, he inverts the process, which tends to impede surface acceleration: 3/8–2/4–3/8 –2/4–3/4. The Act 3 finale has many of the same deficiencies, although the wonderfully controlled melody of the un poco Adagio foreshadows Mozart's mature lyric gifts.

The arias are rather evenly spread with two each for Polidoro and Fracasso, three for Cassandro, Giacinta, Ninetta and Simone, and four for Rosina. Though Rosina is of the highest social rank, Ninetta has as many numbers as her mistress Giacinta, and Simone has more than his captain Fracasso. The class hierarchy that aria distribution represents in the *dramma per musica* is inoperative for this *dramma giocoso*/opera buffa.

Rosina not only has the most arias, but two of them are the opera's most elaborate and memorable. Her second number (Act I/7) belongs to the echo tradition. Also belonging to the seria genre is the simile structure of the verses, which demand contrasting sections. Its orchestration is unusually rich with an oboe solo, pairs of cors anglais and French horns, and strings. Rosina's 'Amoretti' (Act II/5) is probably the opera's best-known and most rococo-type piece. It too is richly scored with pairs of bassoons, violins and violas, which share the *circulatio* figure that paints the flying cupids.

Of Cassandro's arias, his last (Act II/6), where he proclaims that he is not drunk, deserves notice. Here is one of Mozart's simplest and shortest numbers with but one statement of the text and a few short motifs shaped into a binary structure. Most revealing of Polidoro is his Act II/6 piece where he comforts Rosina and threatens Cassandro. Each thought has its own metre and tempo as the text is stated twice. With their bland lyricism, Fracasso's arias in Acts I/3 and II/11 are hardly pieces one would expect of a Hungarian captain. However, Mozart's original Act I/3 piece with its Adagio maestoso opening with rushing hemidemisemiquavers and dotted rhythms seems more appropriate to a captain, who melts into a softened *galant homme* when he comes under a lady's spell. Fracasso's third aria (Act III/2) is a bolder piece more indicative of his profession. His servant, Simone, proves in his three arias to be a more consistent character than his captain as he is introduced twice by elevated dotted rhythms (Act I/1 and Act III/1).

Two of Ninetta's arias (Acts I/8 and III/1) are Tempo di Menuettos, which is hardly the way one would expect a servette to be portrayed. Her Act II/1 piece is a bourrée with a contredanse, a decidedly neutral portrayal. Indeed, Mozart's treatment of this servant is surprisingly aristocratic. One could even argue that Donna Giacinta's arias in I/2 and III/3 are less aristocratic than those given to her servant. However, Giacinta does have a fully-fledged rage aria (Act III/2) in the minor mode with a telling modulation, driving surface rhythms and breathless declamation. Mozart deepens its impact by breaking its cadence as Fracasso interrupts with a recitative, which produces the opera's most potent stream of emotion. It anticipates pieces for such characters as Lucio Silla, Elettra, Donna Anna and Donna Elvira. However, the overall impression is that Mozart has not yet discovered how to portray his characters appropriately.

La finta semplice's main interest is historical. It tells us something about Mozart's capabilities at the age of twelve in a genre with which he had limited experience. It is therefore not surprising that the most successful numbers use styles from the serious operatic genres; Mozart had already composed a series of arias in the seria idiom. A. PETER BROWN

C. Gianturco, *Mozart's Early Operas* (London, 1981)
D. Heartz, *Haydn, Mozart and the Viennese School 1740–1780* (New York, 1995)
W. Mann, *Mozart's Operas* (London, 1977)

Firmian family. One of SALZBURG's leading noble families; several members had impressive art collections. They were well disposed to the Mozarts, but no Mozart work is known to be connected with them.

Leopold Anton Eleutherius (b. 27 May 1679; d. 22 Oct. 1744) was Prince-Archbishop of Salzburg from 1727. Under his rule the Protestants were expelled from Salzburg in 1731–2. He was LEOPOLD MOZART's first court employer, though Leopold's position was unpaid. Franz Alphons Georg (b. 8 June 1686; d. 1 Mar. 1756) was the Archbishop's brother. With his wife Barbara Elisabeth von Thun-Hohenstein he had four sons, three of whom were often mentioned by the Mozarts.

Leopold Ernst (b. 22 Sept. 1708; d. 13 Mar. 1783) was Bishop of Passau and later a cardinal; Leopold and Wolfgang Mozart celebrated this translation in MILAN in 1772. Franz Lactanz (b. 28 Jan. 1712; d. 6 Mar. 1786) was Salzburg Obersthofmeister from 1736. He represented the archbishop in secular matters and had jurisdiction over the court musicians. He was a gifted amateur artist and his picture collection was famous throughout Europe (for Leopold's entertaining description of his real-life Figaro-type role of Count Almaviva, see GILOWSKY). Karl Joseph (b. Deutschmetz, Trentino, 6 Aug. 1716; d. Milan, 20 July 1782) became Governor-General of Lombardy – CHARLES BURNEY called him 'a sort of King of Milan'. He was a powerful patron of the arts and read several languages; his library contained 40,000 books. Through his support for Leopold and Wolfgang Mozart from 1770, when they first visited Milan, he was directly and indirectly responsible for many of Mozart's successes in Italy, including the commissions of the operas *MITRIDATE*, *RE DI PONTO*, *ASCANIO IN ALBA* and *LUCIO SILLA*.

RUTH HALLIWELL

R. Halliwell, *The Mozart Family: Four Lives in a Social Context* (Oxford, 1998)
H. Schuler, *Mozarts Salzburger Freunde und Bekannte* (Wilhelmshaven, 1995), 75–83

Fischer, (Johann Ignaz) Ludwig (b. Mainz, 18/19 Aug. 1745; d. Berlin, 10 July 1825). German bass singer and the first Osmin in *DIE ENTFÜHRUNG AUS DEM SERAIL*. Fischer began his career singing at Mainz with later appointments at MANNHEIM, MUNICH and, from 1780, VIENNA; he was considered the finest bass singer in Germany. Renowned for his two-and-a-half octave range, his voice was described by Friedrich Reichardt as having 'the depth of a cello and the natural height of a tenor'. Fischer spent three years in Vienna and it was for him that Mozart specifically added the aria 'Solche hergelauf'ne Laffen' to *Die Entführung*, writing to his father on 26 September 1781: 'one must make good use of such a man, especially as he is such a great favourite with the audiences here'. After 1783, Fischer sang throughout Italy and German-speaking Europe, including return engagements in Vienna where he performed Mozart's *Non so donde viene*, K512, at a concert on 21 March 1787. It is possible that the scena *Così dunque tradisci – Aspri rimorsi atroci*, K432, was also composed for Fischer although there is no unequivocal evidence to support this assertion.

CLIFF EISEN

P. Corneilson: 'Vogler's Method of Singing', *Journal of Musicology* 16 (1998), 91–109, esp. 108–9
A. Gottron, 'Klein Beiträge zur Mainzer Musikgeschichte, I. Die Selbstbiographie des Bassisten Ludwig Fischer aus Mainz', *Mainzer Almanach* (1959), 113–25

Fischietti, Domenico (b. Naples, c.1725; d. ?Salzburg, after c.1810). Italian composer. Fischietti's greatest successes came during the 1750s when he worked in Venice with the librettist GOLDONI on the comic operas *Il mercato di Malmantile* and *Il signor dottore*. From about 1762 he was active in PRAGUE as part of the Molinari opera company and in 1765 he became court Kapellmeister in Dresden. Apparently he was ineffective in the post and dismissed in 1772, only to be hired in SALZBURG, where he was similarly unsatisfactory and superseded first by Giacomo Rust and later by LUIGI GATTI. He taught the choirboys at the Chapel House from 1779 and 1783 but his whereabouts thereafter are uncertain. His one moment of relative success in Salzburg came in 1775 when he composed a serenade to celebrate the visit there of ARCHDUKE MAXIMILIAN; it was for the same occasion that Mozart composed IL RE PASTORE K208. CLIFF EISEN

Freemasonry. The history of Freemasonry can be traced back to the groups or guilds of craftsmen, mainly stonemasons, who in medieval Scotland, and probably elsewhere, sought to preserve the secrets of their craft and to help each other in adversity. Various theories have been advanced about the origins of modern Freemasonry, but it is generally agreed that the beginnings of the craft in the modern sense of the term lie in the institution of the Grand Lodge of England in 1717, which itself grew out of smaller, less formalized lodges.

On the continent, particularly in France and Germany, lodges after the British pattern were quickly established and gained considerable popularity, especially among the aristocracy, the professional classes, military officers, intellectuals and even members of the established Churches. The rise of Freemasonry may be seen as a reaction against political absolutism and religious intolerance; the emphasis was on brotherly love and charity, and normal social barriers were largely absent. Symbolic rituals, loosely connected with those of earlier ages, were important; and the secrecy of beliefs and practices, to which members bound themselves, inevitably provoked suspicion, and at times downright enmity, from representatives of interests who felt themselves threatened – Pope Clement XII condemned the Order as early as 1738, but it continued to thrive and grow.

1. Freemasonry in Austria
2. Mozart as Mason
3. Masonic music

1. Freemasonry in Austria

The first Viennese lodge was constituted in 1742 ('Aux trois Canons') and MARIA THERESIA's consort, Franz Stephan von Lothringen, had been admitted a Freemason as early as 1731. However, there is no evidence that he took an active part in Masonry after his accession as Emperor Francis I in 1745, though he may, despite the often-attested antagonism of the Empress towards the craft, have had a hand in the prevention of the publication in Habsburg lands of the papal bull condemning Freemasonry that was promulgated in 1751. The first of the major Viennese lodges were founded in 1770: 'Zur Hoffnung' ('Hope'), which numbered many leading aristocrats, civil servants and men from the world of the arts among its members; and 'Zu den drei Adlern' ('The Three Eagles'), reformed in 1776 as 'Zum Palmbaum' ('The Palm-Tree'); these two lodges united in 1781. Two Viennese lodges under foreign patronage also began their activities in the 1770s, 'Zum heiligen Joseph' ('St Joseph'), which was constituted in 1771 under the Grand Lodge of Berlin; and 'Zur Beständigkeit' ('Constancy'), which was formed in 1779 under the aegis of the Regensburg lodge 'Zu den drei Schlüsseln' ('The Three Keys'), to which EMANUEL SCHIKANEDER briefly belonged before his move to VIENNA. The most famous of the lodges in Vienna, 'Zur wahren Eintracht' ('True Concord') was formed in 1781; in 1783 the last two of the Vienna mainstream lodges were founded: 'Zu den drei Feuern' ('The Three Fires'), and 'Zur Wohltätigkeit' ('Beneficence').

'True Concord' was founded by leading members of 'Hope' and, following the election on 9 March 1782 of IGNAZ VON BORN as its Master, it swiftly gained eminence. Among its members were the African prince, Angelo Soliman, JOSEPH HAYDN (who seems to have attended only one meeting – his normal place of residence, far from Vienna, may be more to blame than any lack of interest on his part), the eminent lawyers Franz von Zeiler and JOSEPH VON SONNENFELS (the latter was the most prominent representative of the Austrian ENLIGHTENMENT), men of letters (including Blumauer, Ratschky and Alxinger), also noblemen and politicians, doctors, explorers and artists. Meetings were often held twice a week, and the average attendance at lodges was around eighty. Learned papers were presented and debated, and in 1783 publication began of the *Physikalische Arbeiten der Einträchtigen Freunde in Wien* (Works in Physics of the Friends of Concord in Vienna); by 1788 eight numbers had appeared, ranging in subject matter from botany and ornithology to astronomy and geography. More important was the *Journal für Freymaurer*, the first number of which appeared in a print run of 1,000 copies in 1784. In all, twelve numbers were published, edited by Blumauer; the contents covered intellectual and natural historical themes, and news of Masonic activity in royal and imperial lands and abroad. Born's essay 'Ueber die Mysterien der Aegyptier', which was to influence the background to DIE ZAUBERFLÖTE, opened the series.

These lodges followed the English ritual of St John ('symbolic' or 'blue' Masonry, named for the colour of the heavens and of the Order of the Garter). Of Viennese lodges observing other rites, the most important were the Rosicrucians' 'Zu den drei Schwertern' ('The Three Swords', 1772–8) and 'Zur Liebe und Wahrheit' ('Love and Truth', 1790); and the Asiatic Brethren's 'Zu den sieben Himmeln' ('The Seven Heavens', founded in 1784). Also from 1784 dates the foundation of the National Grand Lodge of AUSTRIA, one of the aims of which was to regularize Masonic activity. The most fruitful years of Freemasonry were then almost at an end. Though JOSEPH II was not himself opposed to the Masons, and some of his senior advisers were dedicated members of the Craft, restrictions were introduced in 1785, largely to counteract what was seen by some as the threat posed by powerful, semi-autonomous secret societies. That summer, Leopold, Count Kolowrat, Deputy Master of 'True Concord', warned that the Emperor was intending to make lodges register with the police and supply lists of their members. The imperial edict, promulgated on 11 December 1785, effectively ended the brief period of the Order's intellectual and artistic splendour. This 'Masonic Patent' ordained that there should henceforth be only one lodge in the capital of each province and just two (or at most three) lodges in Vienna, but none in smaller towns and country estates, and explained that each lodge should supply quarterly lists of its members to the provincial governor. Finally, the Emperor's edict permitted 'this Brotherhood, which consists of so many honest men who are known to me, truly to show itself useful to its fellow men and to learning'. The decree was published in the official *Wiener Zeitung* on 17 December 1785, and took effect from 1 January 1786.

Prince Dietrichstein, the Provincial Grand Master, assisted by Ignaz von Born, the Grand Secretary, supervised the reorganization. 'St Joseph' and 'Constancy' closed immediately. 'True Concord', 'The Three Eagles' and 'The Palm-Tree' were reconstituted under Born's leadership as the united lodge 'Zur Wahrheit' ('Truth'), which opened on 6 January. The other three lodges, 'Crowned Hope', 'Beneficence' and 'The Three Fires' formed the united lodge 'Zur neugekrönten Hoffnung' ('New-Crowned Hope') under BARON TOBIAS GEBLER. As neither of the new lodges was to number more than 180 members, perhaps as many as 600 former Masons were excluded, or would have to wait for vacancies to occur. Neither Dietrichstein nor Born remained Masons for much longer, and under Francis II the Order was finally driven to suspend all its activities in December 1793.

Though some important records of Austrian Masonic activity have survived and been published, the comparative rarity of such information has encouraged much speculation among scholars, including attempts to link Mozart with the Rosicrucians and with other forms of Masonry.

2. Mozart as Mason

On 5 December 1784 the secretary of the small lodge 'Beneficence' circulated to the sister lodges the name of 'Kapellmeister Mozart' as a candidate for initiation. Nine days later Mozart was duly admitted by the Master, his old Mannheim acquaintance from 1779, OTTO, BARON VON GEMMINGEN-HORNBERG (author of the drama *Semiramis*, which Mozart had intended to set as a melodrama). Mozart appears in the attendance records of 'True Concord' on Christmas Eve as a 'visiting brother', and it was at this lodge on 7 January 1785 that he advanced to the Fellow Craft (Journeyman) degree. Records do not note when he was raised to the degree of Master, but it must have been before 22 April, when he attended a Master Lodge at 'True Concord' (on this occasion the signature of his father, then only a Fellow Craft, was erased as being not yet eligible). Mozart's name appears frequently in lodge records, and he wrote a number of works for Masonic occasions. Indeed, some commentators maintain that the song *O heiliges Band* ('O sacred bond', K148), which probably dates from 1773, should be numbered among these; Alfred Einstein argued persuasively that the Adagios for wind instruments, K410 and 411, are Masonic in mood, and perhaps also in purpose.

We can only speculate as to the features of Freemasonry that attracted Mozart, and indeed, why he joined 'Beneficence', rather than the leading lodge 'True Concord', the meetings of which he most often attended. Several of his friends and colleagues were Masons; and the Craft's emphasis on virtue, discretion, the search for wisdom, charitable acts and brotherly love (all exemplified in DIE ZAUBERFLÖTE) must have drawn him as they did so many of his prominent contemporaries. If hope for personal advantage was among his motives, he remained true to his vows long after the majority of Vienna's Masons had resigned. Further, we have to assume that the speed with which LEOPOLD MOZART, on his visit to his son and daughter-in-law in 1785, was admitted a Mason and advanced to the third degree, was at least in part due to filial persuasion and protection; in the only surviving letter (4 Apr. 1787) to his father from the last two years of the latter's life, Mozart refers obliquely to the consolation in the face of death that is present for the Christian and Mason.

The earliest undisputed Masonic composition by Mozart is *Gesellenreise*, K468, written on 26 March 1785 and presumably intended for his father's passing to the degree of Fellow Craft, which took place during the latter's extended visit to his son and daughter-in-law that spring. This short, piano-accompanied song depicts the movement of the initiate on his path towards wisdom and light; the words are by Mozart's fellow Mason J. F. von Ratschky. On 20 April of the same year Mozart completed a cantata, *Die Maurerfreude* ('Masonic Joy', K471) for the celebration of Born's ennoblement, which took place at 'Crowned Hope' on 24 April. The full score was published in August 'for the benefit of the poor' in an elegant edition, in the production of which all involved were Masons. The work, to words by Franz Petran, consists of two fast-moving tenor arias separated by a brief recitative and arioso; a three-part chorus joins the soloist in the closing bars in praise of 'Joseph the Wise', who has 'twined laurels round the brow of the wisest of the Masons'. At its first performance the tenor solo was taken by VALENTIN ADAMBERGER, the first Belmonte in DIE ENTFÜHRUNG AUS DEM SERAIL. The best-known of Mozart's Masonic compositions followed in July, *Maurerische Trauermusik* ('Masonic Music of Mourning', see 'MASONIC FUNERAL MUSIC', K477). Its first known performance was probably at a lodge of sorrows in November for two prominent Masons, but it has been proposed that it was first heard in a choral version ('Master Music') in the summer. In its final form it is a brief, solemn movement in C minor, scored for clarinet, three basset horns, two oboes, two horns, double bassoon and strings. The mood of austere grief is lightened in the final bar by a *tierce de Picardie* (major third). From this year probably also date other Masonic compositions, the songs *Zerfliesset heut, geliebte Brüder* ('Flow this day, beloved brothers', K483) and *Ihr, unsre neuen Leiter* ('You, our new leaders', K484) for tenor, organ accompaniment and closing chorus, and two further, lost, songs written for the opening and closure of lodge meetings.

Although Mozart continued his membership of the Order after its reorganization in January 1786, he does not seem to have composed further works for the lodge until summer 1791. The German cantata *Die ihr des unermesslichen Weltalls Schöpfer ehret* ('You who honour the creator of the infinite universe', K619), written in July, is not strictly a Masonic work, though Franz Ziegenhagen, who commissioned it and wrote the text, was a Mason in Regensburg. It is scored for solo voice and keyboard accompaniment and consists of an opening flourish followed by a recitative and five brief aria-like sections, some of them separated by a phrase of recitative. The text is pacifist in tone, and – as is appropriate for a work written for Ziegenhagen's 'Colony of the Friends of Nature' – pantheistic. More strictly Masonic is the last of these works, *Eine kleine Freymaurer-Kantate*, K623, which was the last work Mozart completed, and the last he conducted – at the inaugural meeting of the new temple of 'New-Crowned Hope' on 17 November 1791. He died eighteen days later, and this cantata (easily the longest of Mozart's Masonic works in spite of its title) was published by subscription a year later 'in order to assist his distressed widow and orphans'. It opens with a three-part chorus (with solo voices) leading into a recitative in which the tenor praises the completion of the new temple of the lodge. There follow a tenor aria, another recitative, a duet in which the second soloist, a bass, takes part, and the opening chorus is then repeated. The most likely author of the words is C. L. Gieseke, long but erroneously held to have written the libretto of *Die Zauberflöte*.

3. Masonic music

Music played an important part in the activities of most Masonic lodges in the eighteenth century. In the lodges in smaller towns there was probably seldom more in the way of accompaniment for singing than a keyboard instrument; in Vienna, where many of the leading musicians of the city were Masons, quite elaborate instrumentation was frequently employed. Records survive of performances of instrumental concertos as well as of vocal works. Choral songs (often in three parts) were sung for the opening and closure of lodge meetings; for special occasions ambitious compositions were sometimes written, and visiting musicians were given the opportunity to display their skills. Various collections of Masonic songs were published.

Attempts to characterize Masonic music tend to founder on the paucity and the disparate nature of surviving material. Much of the music heard in the lodges was imported from everyday experience: hymns, popular and patriotic songs, mostly simple in style and within the compass of untrained voices. Choral repetition of the last lines of solo songs was frequent; examples occur in Mozart's *Die Maurerfreude* and Sarastro's first aria in *Die Zauberflöte*. Symbolism is common, as Philippe Autexier in particular has demonstrated: the use of seconds (the smallest of intervals, betokening close fraternity) and thirds; tied notes; and the frequency of key signatures employing three flats (though it may be pointed out that Sarastro only sings in this key at the very end of *Die Zauberflöte*). The rhythmic knocking characteristic of Masonic practice is present in several of Mozart's compositions (not only the strictly Masonic ones): the cretic (– ⏑ –) for the Entered Apprentice, the bacchius (⏑ – –) for the Fellow Craft, and the anapaest (⏑ ⏑ –) for the Master Mason.

PETER BRANSCOMBE

P. Autexier, 'Freemasonry', in *The Mozart Compendium*, ed. H. C. Robbins Landon (London, 1990), 132–4
P. Branscombe, *W. A. Mozart: 'Die Zauberflöte'* (Cambridge, 1991)
A. Einstein, *Mozart: His Character, his Works* (New York, 1945)
H.-J. Irmen, *Mozart: Mitglied geheimer Gesellschaften* (Mechernich, 1988)
H. C. Robbins Landon, *Mozart and the Masons: New Light on the Lodge 'Crowned Hope'* (London, 1982)
E. Lennhoff and O. Posner, *Internationales Freimaurerlexikon* (Vienna and Munich, 1932, repr. 1980)
P. Nettl, *Mozart and Masonry* (New York, 1957, repr. 1970)
K. Thomson, *The Masonic Thread in Mozart* (London, 1977)

French Revolution. Early in the twenty-first century we can look back at the French Revolution as one of the great defining points of modern history, but over two centuries ago reaction from abroad proved much less enthusiastic. The English, who had already made many of the reforms that the Revolution brought about, roundly condemned the events in France as a display of the worst form of human barbarism. VIENNA as well regarded the French with great alarm, not because of the reforms, many of which JOSEPH II had previously instituted in Habsburg lands, but because of the mob mentality driving change in France. As a reformer, Joseph could envisage change happening only in one way, from above, and he abhorred any interference from the masses. With his sister, Marie Antoinette, as Queen of France, Joseph had a personal reason to be very interested in political developments in France, although during the last year of his life (he died on 20 Feb. 1790), revolution in distant parts of his own realm occasioned much greater concern and reaction from him. He commented bitterly on French attempts to create a better constitution, which resulted in destruction: 'The same stupidity reigns partially in Brabant. The only difference is that the French intoxication is due to champagne, which is swift but passes quickly; while that of Brabant comes from beer, which is slow and obstinate.'

After two centuries the French Revolution may appear as a force of inevitable progression, with great acts of courage and daring, but during the decade that it took place beginning in 1789 chaos no doubt was its most characteristic feature, especially during the reign of terror. The fiscal ineptitude of the Bourbon kings provided the trigger, with the meeting of the Estates-General at Versailles on 5 May 1789 – the first gathering of this body since 1614 – for the purpose of levying taxes. The Third Estate broke away because of the unfairness of these taxes to the lower classes and created a National Assembly. The storming of the Bastille two months later, another event regarded as a defining moment, looms much larger in mythology than reality since the Bastille held few prisoners at the time. Nevertheless, the Paris mobs continued to play a major role and attracted the attention of the world during the next decade.

For Joseph and his brother who succeeded him as LEOPOLD II, France necessarily took second place to more immediate revolutionary activity within the Habsburg realm. Joseph started his reign in 1780 with great enthusiasm as a reformer, moving with surprising speed towards a more egalitarian society, with, of course, a strong monarchy in place. Not everyone welcomed his reforms, and this was particularly true of the aristocrats who saw their traditional powers eroded and treasuries drained, especially those in the more far-flung reaches of the Empire. Trouble brewed most noticeably in the Netherlands (Belgium) and Hungary, where discontent led to open rebellion as early as 1786, and forced Joseph to reconsider the direction of reform over the next few years. Enlightened advisers such as GOTTFRIED VAN SWIETEN and JOSEPH VON SONNENFELS fell into disfavour during the late 1780s as he deferred to the likes of Count Johann Anton Pergen, who gained unprecedented power as Minister of Police. At Pergen's instigation reforms ground to a halt, freedom of the press ended, political discussion disappeared as activities of the secret police expanded rapidly, and censorship reached a new level of oppressiveness. Intellectuals and artists encouraged by the heady days of the early 1780s now had to be careful to avoid criminal activities. While Joseph had previously tolerated criticism, by December 1787 he wrote that 'scribblers and publishers who indulge in libels must be severely punished. Those who oppose us with ridicule or threats must be arrested, whipped and kept in jail.'

Mozart had been one of the beneficiaries of Joseph's reforms, his own arrival in Vienna more or less coinciding with Joseph becoming the sole ruler. Mozart had thrived under these conditions, writing an opera for Joseph's German theatre in 1782 (DIE ENTFÜHRUNG AUS DEM SERAIL), and later being able to use a text Napoleon claimed as groundwork for the revolution – LE NOZZE DI FIGARO. *Figaro*, of course, would not have flown in German in a popular theatre, just as the censors banned the works of Voltaire in German translation, not wishing subversive material to fall into the hands of lower-class agitators in a language they would understand. By the time of DON GIOVANNI'S performance in PRAGUE in 1787 and Vienna in 1788, the new censorship of Pergen was in place, and while this work pushes subversion in one way, it may have served Joseph's goals in presenting members of the aristocracy as degenerates deserving of punishment.

Mozart's last three operas appeared with the French Revolution in full swing, although the extent to which they may be political relates more to Habsburg issues than anything outside the realm. With strict censorship in place one would not expect Mozart to dabble in political issues, although it appears that he does, disguising them with great subtlety. Drama of such finesse and irony would not be seen for another generation in AUSTRIA after Mozart, until Nestroy used it during the repressive Metternich era. The foundation of the *ancien régime* lay in a rigorously maintained symmetry between monarch and subjects, Church and parishioners, and all other forms of authority and the people. Breaking that symmetry down could be seen as an act of democratization, but if the dismantling occurred in music rather than text, censors would probably not notice it. In COSÌ FAN TUTTE, Mozart goes out of his way to generate symmetry in the first act and part of the second, but after Fiordiligi's revelations in 'Per pietà' it comes unstuck, as Mozart abandons balanced ensembles and replaces them with a string of arias that probe the wilful loss of enlightened morality which a pat ending cannot resolve. Here Mozart reveals his own revolutionary tendencies, not anything connected with the mob spirit of the French Revolution, but nevertheless a plea for the return to freedoms that Joseph had initiated.

DAVID SCHROEDER

R. Darnton, *The Kiss of Lamourette* (New York, 1990)
N. Till, *Mozart and the Enlightenment* (New York, 1993)
E. Wangermann, *The Austrian Achievement 1700–1800* (London, 1973)

Freysinger family. Friends of the Mozarts, resident in MUNICH. Franziskus Erasmus Freysinger (dates unknown), a court councillor in Munich, had known LEOPOLD MOZART from their days together at the St Salvator school in AUGSBURG; Wolfgang met them during his stay in Munich in 1777. According to a letter of 3 December 1777, he had promised Freysinger's daughter, Josepha, a keyboard sonata that is sometimes claimed to be K311. There is no evidence, however, that Mozart finished the work or its exact identity. CLIFF EISEN

Freystädtler, Franz Jacob (b. Salzburg, 13 Sept. 1761; d. Vienna, 1 Dec. 1841). Composer and keyboard player. Freystädtler was organist at St Peter's, SALZBURG, from 1778 to 1784 before travelling to MUNICH and, in 1786, VIENNA, where he had composition lessons from Mozart. Apparently he had close relations with the composer: Freystädtler's hand appears in the autograph of the String Quintet in G minor, K516, and, about the same time, he made a copy of the Piano Concerto in B flat, K456. It was for Freystädtler that Mozart invented the nickname 'Gaulimauli', a sobriquet that reappears in the canon *Lieber Freistädtler, lieber Gaulimauli*, K232. CLIFF EISEN

M. Lorenz, 'Franz Jakob Freystädtler (1761–1841). Neue Forschungsergebnisse zu seiner Biographie und seinen Spuren im Werk Mozarts', *Acta Mozartiana* 44/3–4 (1997), 85–108

Friedrich Wilhelm II (b. Berlin, 25 Sept. 1744; d. Potsdam, 16 Nov. 1797). King of Prussia and an accomplished cellist. Mozart played before Friedrich Wilhelm II on 26 May 1789 at the royal palace in Berlin. According to a letter of 12 July 1789 to MICHAEL PUCHBERG, Mozart was 'composing six easy keyboard sonatas for Princess Friederike [Frederika, 1767–1820, daughter of Friedrich Wilhelm II] and six quartets for the King . . . the two dedications will bring me in something'. Whether these were commissions or just speculations on Mozart's part remains unclear; in the end he composed only three quartets (K575, 589, 590, the so-called 'Prussian' quartets) and one sonata (K576), writing to Puchberg around 12 June 1790: 'I have now been obliged to give away my quartets (those very difficult works) for a mere song, simply in order to have cash in hand to meet my present difficulties.' The quartets, published by ARTARIA in 1791, lack a dedication. CLIFF EISEN

C. Sachs, *Musikgeschichte der Stadt Berlin bis zum Jahre 1800* (Berlin, 1908)

fugue. Fugue is generally considered to be a texture rather than a form; it was only in the mid-eighteenth century that structure and form became associated with fugal writing when the influential theorist Friedrich Wilhelm Marpurg, in his *Abhandlung von der Fuge* (1753–4), described fugues in this way. In a structural/formal sense, a fugue may be considered as a composition that is made up of several formal parts, the defining feature of which is the opening section, the exposition. It begins with an introduction of the principal theme, the 'subject', which may be accompanied or unaccompanied. The subject is always followed by an 'answer', usually in the dominant, and accompanied by a 'counter-subject' which is normally an extension of the subject theme. Answers may be real or tonal depending on whether they are exact replications of the subject or whether they are adapted in order to remain in the overall tonic key. When all voices have entered as either subject or answer, the exposition is complete. However, an extra entry of the first voice – a 'redundant entry' – may occur at this point. The exposition is then followed by an episode, which, in a strict fugue, would comprise looser contrapuntal treatment of the subject material; in freer fugues, new material may be introduced. From there the development of a fugue can take many different turns, using common techniques such as stretto (closer subject–answer entries than in the exposition), augmentation (note values of the subject lengthened), diminution (note values shortened), abbreviation (subject truncated), and inversion (subject presented upside down). In eighteenth-century Viennese fugues, the exposition may even lead into homophonic, galant-style sections.

Mozart uses fugal technique in both his vocal and instrumental works. In common with the practice of the time, his vocal fugues are generally stricter than the instrumental varieties. Fugues feature in many of his masses, most commonly in the Gloria and Credo sections. However, Mozart also used fugue technique in, for example, the Agnus Dei of the Mass in C, K167, the Benedictus of the Mass in C, K337 and the Kyrie of the REQUIEM, K626. In these sections, the style of writing varies considerably according to the choice of subject type and degree of strictness in fugal procedures. The subjects used in the Gloria and Credo are invariably longer because of the textual setting and are based mainly on traditional models, all employing alla breve metre. The fugues found in other movements of the mass are more 'modern' in outlook, using short subjects founded on 'classical' melodic styles. The 'dona nobis pacem' setting in the Agnus Dei of K167 mixes fugal procedures with galant-style accompaniments. In the Sanctus of the *Missa brevis*, K194, the fugal exposition leads into homophonic sections. Rarely occupying a whole movement, fugue appears most often in the closing sections (for example, the 'cum sancto spiritu, in gloria dei patris' of the Gloria or the 'et vitam venturi saeculi. Amen' of the Credo), as it was most commonly understood rhetorically as a closing gesture in eighteenth-century Classical music.

The use of strict fugal procedures in Mozart's instrumental writing is less common. Its appearance is related to compositional ideas that appealed to Mozart at distinct phases of his creative life. The two finales in his early string quartets (K168 and K173, 1772) were in part a response to the three fugal finales in Haydn's Op. 20 set of quartets (1772). The finale in the first quartet of Mozart's set of six 'Haydn' quartets (K387, 1782) and the finale of the 'Jupiter' symphony (K551, 1788) are certainly no direct imitations of Haydn's fugal procedures but were undoubtedly a reaction to an attitude towards mixing fugue and sonata styles that emanated most prominently from Haydn. Strict fugal expositions using traditional alla breve subjects are presented at (or near) the beginning of both movements, features that should define them as fugues. Because of the extensive use of homophony and formal divisions by double barlines, however, they are usually understood by theorists nowadays as sonata-form movements with fugal episodes; nineteenth-century theorists such as

Simon Sechter, however, described the finale of the 'Jupiter' as 'a model for an instrumental fugue in free style'.

Another strong influence on Mozart's attitude towards fugue was J. S. BACH. Under the direction of BARON VAN SWIETEN, Mozart was introduced to works by north German composers, most notably Bach and HANDEL. Mozart arranged some of Bach's fugues from the *Well-Tempered Clavier* for string quartet (K405, 1782) composing the piano fugues (K426 for two pianos, 1782) – which he later scored for string quartet as Adagio and Fugue (K546, 1788) – and the Prelude and Fugue in C major (K394, 1782) around the same time. His last instrumental fugue, the Fantasia and Fugue in F minor (K608, 1791) was written for the mechanical organ. Other than these complete fugues, Mozart also wrote many fugal fragments that show his diligent experiments with different fugal techniques and styles.

Evidence of Mozart's approach to fugal writing can also be observed in his teaching. The most extensive document that reveals Mozart's teaching style is found in the ATTWOOD studies (1785–6). Here Mozart follows Haydn's didactic principles of basing his teaching mainly on the study of FUX's *Gradus ad Parnassum*. In addition, Mozart's elaborations and comments on Fux's methods are similar to those found in Haydn's heavily annotated copy of the treatise. This suggests that the main ingredients that shaped Mozart's idiosyncratic approach to fugal writing were fashioned from a combination of the strict technique instituted by Fux, Haydn's Classical procedures, and Bach's north German Baroque style. SHARON CHOA

S. A. Choa, 'Sonata–Fugue Synthesis in Joseph Haydn's String Quartets' (Ph.D. thesis, King's College London, 1998)
S. P. Keefe, 'The "Jupiter" Symphony in C, K551: New Perspectives on the Dramatic Finale and its Stylistic Significance in Mozart's Orchestral Oeuvre', *Acta musicologica* 75 (2003), 17–43
W. Kirkendale, *Fugue and Fugato in Rococo and Classical Chamber Music* (Durham, NC, 1979)
A. Mann, *The Study of Fugue* (New York, 1965)
E. Sisman, *Mozart: The 'Jupiter' Symphony* (Cambridge, 1993)

Fux, Johann Joseph (b. 1660; d. 13 Feb. 1741). AUSTRIAN composer and theorist. Fux was first and foremost a composer of concerted liturgical music in late Baroque style, which he wrote in his capacity as Kapellmeister to the court of the Holy Roman Emperor in VIENNA. His extant compositions – catalogued by Köchel, like Mozart's – include about ninety concerted mass settings, eighty large-scale liturgical works and ten oratorios. He also wrote extensively for the court opera.

Fux's important theoretical work, the *Gradus ad Parnassum* (1725), published in Vienna at imperial expense, is a Latin treatise on composition cast in the form of a dialogue between master ('Aloysius', that is, Palestrina) and pupil ('Josephus', namely Fux himself). It represents a profoundly conservative attempt to rationalize contemporary styles of composition in terms of modal polyphony, seeking out the basis of compositional technique in a radical systematization of late Renaissance textures. The concept of 'species counterpoint' (taken from seventeenth-century Italian theorists such as Angelo Berardi and Giovanni Maria Bononcini) is lucidly established as the foundation of compositional thought and ensured the treatise its long reception history and significant influence in European art music.

JOSEPH HAYDN appears to have been responsible for Mozart's knowledge of and recourse to the *Gradus* as a composition manual; the older composer's heavily annotated copy of the Latin original was in Mozart's possession at some point during the early 1780s. Mozart made his earliest references to Fux's text in a notebook dated 1784 that was devoted to the instruction of BARBARA VON PLOYER and one year later used the *Gradus* extensively as the basis for exercises in two-, three- and four-part counterpoint given to THOMAS ATTWOOD. The Attwood studies demonstrate that as with Haydn before him, Mozart frequently deviated from or modified Fux's modal procedures in light of current tonal practice. Haydn's annotations to the *Gradus* are undoubtedly more thoroughgoing than Mozart's, but the absorption of Fux's procedures by both men testifies to the enduring influence of the treatise as a source of technical instruction during the Classical period. HARRY WHITE

A. Mann, 'Zur Kontrpunktlehre Haydns und Mozarts', *Mozart-Jahrbuch 1978/79*, 195–9
'Joseph Fux's Theoretical Writings: A Classical Legacy', in *Johann Joseph Fux and the Music of the Austro-Italian Baroque*, ed. H. White (Aldershot, 1992), 57–71
H. White, 'The Afterlife of a Tradition: Fux, Vienna and the Classical Style', in *Musical Cultures in the Adriatic Region during the Age of Classicism*, ed. Vjera Katalinić and Stanislav Tuksar (Zagreb, 2004), 23–32

G

Gamerra, Giovanni de (b. Livorno, 1743; d. Vicenza, 20 Aug. 1803). Italian poet, dramatist and librettist. Gamerra, who as a young man studied law and subsequently served in the AUSTRIAN army, was poet at the Teatro Regio Ducale, MILAN, from 1770 to 1774 and the librettist for Mozart's LUCIO SILLA (Milan, 26 Dec. 1772). In 1781 Mozart set an aria from Gamerra's text for PAISIELLO's *Sismano nel Mogol* ('A questo seno deh vieni – Or che il cielo a me ti rende', K374). Gamerra was court poet in VIENNA 1774–6 and again 1793–1802; in 1794 his Italian translation of DIE ZAUBERFLÖTE was performed in PRAGUE. CLIFF EISEN

Gasparini, Quirino (b. Gandino, near Bergamo, 1721; d. Turin, 30 Sept. 1778). Italian composer. A student of G. A. Fioroni, *maestro di cappella* of MILAN Cathedral, and G. B. Martini, Gasparini was appointed *maestro di cappella* of Turin Cathedral in 1760. In 1767 he set *Mitridate*, a libretto set by Mozart for Milan three years later. According to LEOPOLD MOZART's letter of 2 January 1771, the singers had wanted to substitute some of Gasparini's numbers for Mozart's; in the event, the tenor GUGLIELMO D'ETTORE performed the older composer's 'Vado incontro' (Act 3), as a result of which the aria was later incorrectly attributed to Mozart. Nevertheless, relations between the Mozarts and Gasparini, whom they met later in January 1771, were good. Possibly as late as 1783, Leopold Mozart copied out Gasparini's *Adoramus te*. CLIFF EISEN

L. F. Tagliavini, 'Quirino Gasparini and Mozart', in *New Looks at Italian Opera: Essays in Honor of Donald J. Grout*, ed. W. W. Austin (Ithaca, NY, 1968), 151–71

Gassmann, Florian Leopold (b. Brüx (now Most), 3 May 1729; d. Vienna, 20 Jan. 1774). Bohemian composer. Gassmann's earliest documented musical activity is the production of his *Merope* at the Teatro S. Moisè, Venice, in 1757; in 1763 he moved to VIENNA as GLUCK's successor and later took on SALIERI as his pupil. In 1770 he wrote his most popular opera, *La contessina* and in March 1772 succeeded Georg von Reutter as Hofkapellmeister. It may have been Gassmann's ill health in 1773 that prompted the Mozarts to travel to Vienna in search of employment – as LEOPOLD MOZART noted in a letter of 4 September 1773, however, 'Herr Gassmann has been ill but is now better. I do not know how this will affect our stay in Vienna.' And Mozart did not hold his German operas in high regard. Writing to his father concerning Johann Mederitsch's *Rose, oder Pflicht und Liebe im Streit* he remarked that 'Still, it is better stuff than its predecessor, an old opera by Gassmann, *La notte critica*, in German *Die unruhige Nacht*, which with difficulty survived three performances. This in turn had been preceded by that execrable opera of UMLAUF [*Welche ist die beste Nation?*] . . . which never got so far as a third performance. It really seems as if they wished to kill off before its time the German opera' (letter of 5 Feb. 1783). CLIFF EISEN

D. Heartz, *Haydn, Mozart and the Viennese School, 1740–1780* (New York, 1995)

Gatti, Luigi (Maria Baldassare) (b. near Mantua, 11 June 1740; d. Salzburg, 1 Mar. 1817). Italian composer. The Mozarts first met Gatti, then serving in Mantua at the church of S. Barbara, in 1770; at the time, he copied out one of Mozart's early masses. And LEOPOLD MOZART was acquainted with him in the 1780s: on 1 February 1783 he became the last Kapellmeister at the SALZBURG court, where he also directed the chapel boys' choir, taught composition and wrote a significant amount of church music. Leopold, who already thought little of Gatti, had sought the post; Mozart described him as an 'ass' (letter of 12 Oct. 1782). Nevertheless, Gatti helped NANNERL MOZART secure copies of Mozart's works from the cathedral archives for sale to the Leipzig publisher Breitkopf in the late 1790s although it is likely that he also recognized this as an opportunity for his personal profit and began to deal with Breitkopf directly. CLIFF EISEN

M. Schimek, *Musikpolitik in der Salzburger Aufklärung: Musik, Musikpolitik und deren Rezeption am Hof des Salzburger Fürsterzbischofs Hieronymus Graf Colloredo* (Frankfurt, 1995)
C. Schneider, *Geschichte der Musik in Salzburg* (Salzburg, 1935)

Gazzaniga, Giuseppe (b. 5 Oct. 1743; d. 1 Feb. 1818). Italian composer of operas whose treatment of the Don Juan story influenced that of DA PONTE and Mozart. After training in Naples under Porpora and Piccinni, he emerged in the early 1770s as a leading composer of comic and serious opera. His *dramma giocoso L'isola d'Alcina* (Venice, 1772) was one of the most widely performed operas of the decade. *Don Giovanni, ossia Il convitato di pietra* was originally performed as the second act of a two-act comedy about the production of an opera (*Il capriccio drammatico*, with a libretto by GIOVANNI BERTATI; Venice, Carnival 1787). Several parts in Da Ponte's *DON GIOVANNI* – the *introduzione* in Act 1, Leporello's catalogue aria, the supper scene in Act 2 – show that he knew Bertati's libretto well and that he made effective use of Bertati's dramatic ideas and verse. Although we have no reason to believe that Gazzaniga's music was performed in VIENNA or PRAGUE during 1787, occasional musical parallels between his opera and Mozart's – the most remarkable is the entrance of Don Giovanni and Donna Anna in the *introduzione* – suggest that Mozart was familiar with at least some parts of the Venetian's score. JOHN A. RICE

Gebler, Tobias Philipp, Baron (b. Zeulenroda, 2 Nov. 1726; d. Vienna, 9 Oct. 1786). AUSTRIAN civil servant, with a special interest in the theatre; dramatist and translator. In 1752 he transferred from Netherlandish to Austrian service, becoming a privy councillor and vice-chancellor in the Bohemian/Austrian chancellery. He was a prominent supporter of the Austrian ENLIGHTENMENT and a leading FREEMASON, becoming Master of the 'New-Crowned Hope' lodge in 1786. Mozart's first contact with him came with the commission in 1774 to write music for Gebler's drama *THAMOS, KÖNIG IN ÄGYPTEN*, Gebler evidently being dissatisfied with the score composed for it in the previous year by J. T. Sattler. After writing choruses for *Thamos* in 1774, Mozart revised his instrumental numbers for a new production in 1776–7, adding a final chorus in 1779–80. Johann Böhm later used some of Mozart's *Thamos* music for a production of Plümicke's tragedy *Lanassa*.

PETER BRANSCOMBE

R. M. Werner, ed., *Aus dem josephinischen Wien. Geblers und Nicolais Briefwechsel aus den Jahren 1771–1786* (Berlin, 1888)

Gellert, Christian Fürchtegott (b. 4 July 1715; d. Leipzig, 13 Dec. 1769). German poet and prose writer. After studying at Leipzig University he became a private tutor, then, from 1751, professor of poetry, rhetoric and ethics. His first volume of poems, *Lieder* (1743), was followed by two volumes of comedies (1747) and by the dull but influential novel *Leben der schwedischen Gräfin von G . . .* (1747–8). He is remembered for his *Fabeln und Ezählungen* (1746, 1748), which extol morality, and contentment with one's lot; and above all for his *Geistliche Oden und Lieder* (1757). His contemporaries, including LEOPOLD MOZART, valued highly his volume of model letters, *Briefe, nebst einer praktischen Abhandlung von dem guten Geschmacke in Briefen* (1751, 'Letters, with a practical treatise on good taste in letters'). Among composers drawn to his verses are C. P. E. BACH, JOSEPH HAYDN and BEETHOVEN. The fifteen Gellert settings included in recent editions of the Köchel catalogue as Anhang C8.32–46 were published by Löschenkohl in VIENNA in 1800 and 1801–5 as 'Odes and Songs of Gellert set to music by Mozart', allegedly youthful compositions intended for 'first instruction of the young'; almost certainly the works are not by Mozart.

PETER BRANSCOMBE

H. and M. Garland, 'Gellert', in *The Oxford Companion to German Literature* (Oxford, 1976)
D. Schroeder, *Mozart in Revolt: Strategies of Resistance, Mischief and Deception* (New Haven, 1999)

Gemmingen-Hornberg, Otto Heinrich, Baron (b. Heilbronn, ?5 Nov. 1755; d. Heidelberg, 15 Mar. 1836). Councillor, diplomat, FREEMASON and playwright. He befriended Mozart during the latter's residence at MANNHEIM in 1777–8 and gave him a letter of introduction to Count Sickingen in PARIS. In November 1778 he invited Mozart to set his melodrama *Semiramis*. Although Mozart mentioned this as a work in progress, and for several years it was listed among his works in the Gotha *Theater-Kalender*, he probably never began the composition; certainly no trace of it survives. Gemmingen was in VIENNA between 1782 and 1786, and founded short-lived periodicals. In 1782 he joined the 'Crowned Hope' lodge, in the following year becoming Master of the 'Beneficence' lodge, to which Mozart was admitted on 14 December 1784. In 1786 they both transferred to the 'New-Crowned Hope'. His best-known drama is *Der deutsche Hausvater*, an adaptation of Diderot's *Le Père de famille*. PETER BRANSCOMBE

L. Abafi, *Geschichte der Freimaurerei in Österreich-Ungarn* (Budapest, 1893)

genius. The *word* 'genius' (and its German equivalent 'Genie') has had several meanings. In its broadest sense it may signify the peculiar character of a person, nation or place: in this sense of the word everyone has a genius. Or it may refer to an aptitude or talent for a particular activity – poetry, gardening or organizing:

in this sense many people have a genius. Or it may refer to an outstanding and rare ability for creative work, and to those who have such ability: in this sense very few are geniuses. It is to this last concept that we shall turn.

Its roots lie in Greek thought, for example in Plato (c.428–347 BC) and 'Longinus' (first century AD). The Greeks launched ideas such as that poetic invention is mysterious and inexplicable, that it cannot be reduced to rules and taught and learnt, that it is a gift of the Gods and may stem from inspiration, that it is associated with a kind of frenzy akin to madness and that poets are typically given to dark melancholy. Greek philosophy was ambivalent about artists; for example Aristotle (384–322 BC) thought that those who were dominated by imagination were on a decidedly lower level than those governed by reason. All of these ideas were recuperated by modern thought, after the close of the Middle Ages (during which interest in individuality and originality in art reached a low ebb). The first stage of recuperation occurred during the Renaissance, when artists and theorists of art sought to win high status by insisting that artists were special and extraordinary. They promoted the notion of the artist as a *creator*, whose activity was akin to that of God himself.

But the critical period for the emergence of the fully-fledged concept of 'the genius' was the eighteenth century. The context was the high prestige, in the late seventeenth and early eighteenth centuries, of French Classicism, with its emphasis upon imitation and upon the rules of art. This presented a problem for aesthetic theory in England on account of the adoration of Shakespeare, whose dramas manifestly failed to conform to the rules. Hence the steady rise of the notion of untutored genius – in Homer and Shakespeare, for example – as something that was more important than teachable rules or techniques – genius as a gift of God or Nature as distinguished from mere *talent*. The exaltation of natural genius finds expression in Edward Young's *Conjectures on Original Composition* (1759). This book had a particularly large impact in Germany, where young artists yearned to throw off the yoke of French cultural dominance. The rebels of the STURM UND DRANG movement of the 1770s such as Hamann, Herder and GOETHE promoted the concept of genius in extreme form. And although some of them, for example Goethe, later drew back from the excesses of the 'Geniezeit' and returned to an enriched Classicism, German Romanticism of the nineteenth century placed the idea of genius centre stage, to such an extent that the other meanings of 'Genie' dropped out of most dictionaries, leaving the field clear for defining genius as outstanding creative ability.

This concept of genius has had a very considerable, and largely malign influence on the way that Mozart was understood from his death until the end of the twentieth century. To speak of a *single* concept is to an extent misleading – different thinkers presented different combinations of ideas – but we may identify a number of pervasive themes that contributed to the construction, in the biographical tradition, of Mozart the genius. Nineteenth- and early twentieth-century German biographers were strongly motivated to construct him in this way. For the Romantics, the paradigmatic musical genius was BEETHOVEN. The danger was that Mozart would be contrasted with Beethoven and depicted merely as a Classical composer, skilled in the techniques of his art, and composing according to rules. And since German critics associated Classicism with France and Italy, and thought that Romantic genius expressed the German soul, such a contrast would call into question Mozart's place in the national pantheon. He *had* to be constructed as a genius.

Genius, and the artistic creativity stemming from it, is thought of as inexplicable, and incapable of being reduced to a set of learnable rules or techniques. Kant's *Kritik der Urteilskraft* (1790) gives this idea its classic philosophical expression. Aristotle divorced poetic imagination from reason; it was commonplace for the *Sturm und Drang* movement, and later Romantic thinkers to regard artistic creativity as stemming from the sub-rational and even the subconscious – from passion, emotion and instinct. Diderot (1713–84) influentially proposed that the artist, remarkable in the field of his natural gift, might be mediocre or even below par in all other respects. From this it may follow that learning and general culture are not necessary to the genius, who outside his art may be passionate, sensual, irrational, disorderly – quite the reverse of an admirable specimen of humanity. This construction contributed to the biographical tradition – in SCHLICHTEGROLL, Suard, Arnold, Stendhal, Schurig and Einstein among others – of depicting Mozart as a strange mixture of angel and beast, Tamino and Papageno: sublime where his music was concerned, but pathetically inadequate in worldly matters.

The Greek idea of the artist as divinely or demonically inspired, developed in the *Sturm und Drang* 'Geniezeit' by Hamann (1730–88), continued to be highly influential in German Romanticism. This inspiration could be thought of in religious terms as coming from without; or, drawing on Romantic philosophies of nature such as that of Schopenhauer (1788–1860), could be conceived as a welling up of an underlying, sub-rational, perhaps dark and destructive life force. French Catholic biographers – Boschot, Curzon, Ghéon and Wyzewa and Saint-Foix – tended to think of Mozart's inspiration as divine and angelic. German Romanticism, darker and inclined to believe that only the tragic could be profound, emphasized the demonic in Mozart. Alfred Heuss's article 'Das dämonische Element in Mozarts Werken' (*Zeitschrift der Internationalen Musikgesellschaft* 5 (1906–7), 175–86) is a classic expression of a theme also found in the biographies of Schurig and Abert. From this perspective Mozart's minor-key works are greater than those in the major, and *Don Giovanni* a greater opera than LE NOZZE DI FIGARO or COSÌ FAN TUTTE. Such inspiration may be thought of as something that speaks through the artist, spontaneously and as it were independently of his will. When the idea of inspiration is combined with the notion of genius as a natural gift, not learnt or acquired by effort, we are led to the construction of Mozart's genius whereby he composes rapidly and effortlessly – NIEMETSCHEK and ROCHLITZ launched this interpretation, and it became a standard trope after NISSEN's biography.

The genius, according to Romantic conceptions, is thought of as utterly unlike ordinary men and women. On account of his or her exceptionality, those of mere talent may react with envy and dislike. The genius is characterized by originality; never a mere imitator or follower of norms. Obsessed with his art, driven by his mission to create, he is unwilling to conform and adapt himself to social requirements, largely indifferent to his audience. Hence he tends to be an outsider, a misfit, perhaps a social rebel. The young rebels of the *Sturm und Drang* set themselves the task of shocking the conventionally minded. In the period of Romanticism proper the alien, semi-autism of the genius, lost in his ideal world and cut off from everyday reality, was a theme of the influential writings of E. T. A. HOFFMANN (1776–1822) (who wrote a little 'demonic' story about Mozart's *Don Giovanni*). Hoffmann also picked up the Classical and Renaissance notion of an affinity between genius and madness. The theme of a connection between genius and mental abnormality or lack of mental health continued through the nineteenth and twentieth centuries: for example Lombroso in his *Genio e Follia* wrote of genius as a degenerative psychosis, and Freud thought that artistic creation was rooted in escapism and a reluctance to come to terms with reality. Recently there has been interest in those suffering from autism who in a limited area are capable of genius-like performance, for example incredibly rapid calculations or amazing feats of memory. Some biographies of Mozart have accordingly constructed him as an alienated outsider or as abnormal because of his genius, for example the Massins' account of him as a social rebel, or Hildesheimer's depiction of him as tragically cut off from human understanding and contact. The idea that he composed to satisfy an inner need and was indifferent or cavalier towards his audience was propagated by Niemetschek, Rochlitz and Nissen.

But how did Mozart think of himself? Our best hope of finding an answer lies in the substantial body of letters by Mozart and his father: what do they reveal? They give little evidence that Mozart and his father were touched by the *Sturm und Drang*-inspired theory of genius. Leopold thought of his remarkable son in religious terms; the boy was a prodigy, an astonishing wonder, his accomplishments miraculous, his talents (Leopold uses 'Talente' more than 'Genie') a gift from God. Mozart rarely uses the word 'Genie' in his own letters, and when he does, he uses it in the broad sense to mean simply his particular character or disposition, not his outstanding gifts. Nowhere does he describe his own artistic productivity in Romantic terms, as a spontaneous outpouring or inspired rapture, coming to him as in a dream from he knows not where; significantly, the alleged letter by him to the 'Baron von P–.' providing this kind of description is a forgery that first appeared in 1815, an account of his creativity that a Romantic critic (probably Rochlitz) thought that he *ought* to have written. The Romantic conception even still contaminates editions and translations of the correspondence. Take for example the following letters about his pupil (I have italicized the crucial terms):

> She has a great deal of talent and *even genius* . . . She is, however, extremely doubtful as to whether she has any *talent* for composition, especially as regards invention or ideas. . . . If she gets no *inspirations or ideas* . . . then it is to no purpose, for – God knows – I can't give her any . . . It is too soon, even if there really were genius there, but unfortunately there is none. Everything has to be done by rule. (Mozart to Leopold, from Paris, 14 May 1778, in Emily Anderson's translation)

> You say that you have given the Duke's daughter her fourth lesson and you seem to expect her to be able to invent melodies. Do you think that everyone has got your genius? (Leopold to Mozart, from Salzburg, 28 May 1778, in Emily Anderson's translation)

On a quick, casual reading, these passages do not challenge the Romantic notion of genius. But as we read more carefully, and especially as we consult the original German, doubts arise. Anderson's translation says 'she has a great deal of talent, and even genius'. That word 'even' does a lot of work here, making sense of the passage in accordance with Romantic preconceptions. From this point of view, it is odd that Mozart should refer to his pupil as a genius; but that word 'even' reduces the oddity. It suggests that *maybe* she has *just a little bit* of genius – it qualifies the attribution of genius to her. But the word 'even' is not in the original German; Mozart baldly writes 'sie hat viell Talent, und genie' – she has much talent, and genius.

Further down, Anderson has Mozart writing 'if she gets no inspirations' – inspiration, that idea so closely connected to the Romantic conception of genius. But Mozart does not use that word; he writes 'wenn sie keine idéen oder gedancken bekömmt' – 'if she gets no ideas or thoughts'. Anderson's translation subtly adjusts the text to make sense to a twentieth-century reader. Hence she substitutes 'talent' for 'genius' in the passage where Mozart actually writes 'sie zweifelt aber starck ob sie auch genie zur Composition hat' – 'she is, however, extremely doubtful as to whether she has any genius for composition'. From the point of view of Romantic usage, 'genius' is out of place here. But if we remove our twentieth-century spectacles, Mozart does *not* mean talent rather than genius, because he does not make that distinction and does not have the Romantic conception.

It is significant that the standard modern German edition of the Mozart letters indexes the one use of 'Genie' in the letter from Leopold to his son, but fails to index the three uses of 'Genie' in Mozart's letter to his father. Perhaps the German editors have fallen into the same trap as Anderson. They index Leopold's use of the word, because 'Do you think that everyone has got your genius' can be read in accordance with modern understandings of genius. They opt not to index Mozart's use of the word because, from their point of view, he is not using it properly. The *word* in his letter does not refer to the *concept* that they wish to index, so they ignore it.

Mozart himself writes about the effort he put into his works (for example, the quartets dedicated to JOSEPH HAYDN) or about his technical mastery that will be understood and appreciated by 'Kenner' (experts). His creativity did not stem from some mysterious other world, or express itself heedless of social requirements: in his youthful travels he had imbibed the practice of all the great music centres of Europe, and he prided himself in his skill that enabled him to produce what the occasion demanded. He was not alienated from, but thoroughly connected to, his musical environment.

Arguably 'genius' has outlived its (always dubious) usefulness as a concept. More recent work by psychologists and sociologists (represented in the Steptoe collection cited below) has begun the task of demystifying it, searching for genetic, social and cultural explanations of the components of 'genius'. Such work has tended to explode many of the myths, showing that great artists and scientists may be slightly more likely to suffer from depressive illness but for the most part enjoy fine mental health. They tend to show ability on a broad front, not the narrow excellence of some autistics. And their achievement requires not isolation but rather a social environment that provides them with at least a minimum of training, support and recognition. WILLIAM STAFFORD

P. Murray, ed., *Genius: The History of an Idea* (Oxford, 1989)
J. Schmidt, *Die Geschichte des Genie-Gedankens, 1750–1945* (2 vols., Darmstadt, 1985)
W. Stafford, *Mozart's Death: A Corrective Survey of the Legends*, (London, 1991; also published by Stanford University Press as *Mozart Myths and Legends*)
A. Steptoe, ed., *Genius and the Mind: Studies of Creativity and Temperament* (Oxford, 1998)

Gerl, Franz Xaver (b. Andorf, Upper Austria, 30 Nov. 1764; d. Mannheim, 9 Mar. 1827). Bass singer, composer and actor. In 1777 he was a chorister at SALZBURG, and between 1782 and 1784 he studied at Salzburg University. In 1785 he joined a theatre troupe at Erlangen, transferring to the Grossmann company and, in 1787, to SCHIKANEDER's, who was then playing in Regensburg. In 1789 he and his future wife, Barbara Reisinger, moved with Schikaneder to VIENNA to join the latter's new venture at the Freihaus-Theater auf der Wieden; he sang numerous bass roles and composed much music for the company. He is best remembered for creating Sarastro in DIE ZAUBERFLÖTE, and is one of the singers who reportedly sang through the REQUIEM with Mozart on the latter's deathbed. The Gerls left Vienna for Brünn c.1793 and moved to the MANNHEIM court theatre in 1802. PETER BRANSCOMBE

German language and literature. By comparison with other major European languages, German was slow to reach its definitive form as a literary vehicle. There are two main reasons for this: until well into the nineteenth century, Germany was divided into a very large number of mainly quite small states, each having its own administration and its own linguistic peculiarities; and almost the entire area of modern Germany was harshly affected by, and slow to recover from, the ravages of the Thirty Years War. The one form of German that was more generally used, and comprehensible to the educated classes, was the official language of administration, used in the chancelleries; this so-called *Kanzleistil* had local variants, but the advent of printing had helped in the gradual process of linguistic standardization. Although the chancellery language was characterized by cumbrous constructions and frequent use of loan-words, mainly from Latin and French, and was archaic in nature, its influence continued to be felt well into the eighteenth century, as – even in Roman Catholic regions – did the language of Luther's Bible. Stages in the process leading to standardization of the language include the publication in 1578 by Johannes Clajus (or Klaj) of the first German grammar, the work of Martin Opitz in the seventeenth century on behalf of German as an appropriate language for literature, and the various locally based societies that sought to purify the language.

The most influential of these societies (*Sprachgesellschaften*), all of them instituted between 1617 and 1660, were the Fruchtbringende Gesellschaft in Anhalt-Köthen, the Tannengesellschaft based in Strasburg, the Teutschgesinnte Genossenschaft in Hamburg, the Hirten- und Blumenorden an der Pegnitz in Nuremberg, and the short-lived Elbschwanenorden, also based in Hamburg. In terms of literary achievement, few of these societies have lasting importance; all of them, however, by encouraging writings in and discussion of the German language, deserve honourable mention. Among their members a few achieved more than temporary fame – Opitz, Harsdörffer and Logau of the Fruchtbringende, Weckherlin of the Tannengesellschaft, Zesen of the Teutschgesinnte, Harsdörffer, Klaj, Birken, Rist and Staden of the Blumenorden, and Rist of the Elbschwanenorden. Independent German authors of the seventeenth century include Johann Jakob Christoffel von Grimmelshausen, whose series of six picaresque novels depicting the life of Simplicissimus from his youthful exploits in the Thirty Years War on to his old age and death on a desert island, has continued until the age of Brecht and Grass to entertain and delight.

During the first half of the eighteenth century, German at last began to be recognized as a literary language. Credit for this development must be shared among a number of men, in particular Gottsched and GELLERT. Johann Christoph Gottsched (1700–66) worked for the wider acceptance of a single educated German language, based on Saxon usage, though for literary purposes borrowing liberally from French. Gottsched's principal theoretical publications (and he was far more important as a theorist than as a creative writer) were *Versuch einer critischen Dichtkunst vor die Deutschen* (1730, 'Attempt at a Critical Theory of Literature for the Germans'), and *Grundlegung einer deutschen Sprachkunst* (1748, 'Foundation of a German Linguistic Art'). Christian Fürchtegott Gellert (1715–69), though admired by his contemporaries for his moral verse fables and hymns, is in the present context more important for his presentation of model letters, which exerted a strong influence: *Briefe, nebst einer praktischen Abhandlung von dem guten Geschmacke in Briefen* (1751, 'Letters, with a Practical Treatise on Good Taste in Letters'); LEOPOLD MOZART exchanged letters with Gellert, whose epistolary style he sought to emulate.

The Ciceronian principle was a major element in Gottsched's theory and practice. *Subtile in probando, modicum in delectando, vehemens in flectendo* summarizes Cicero's three stylistic levels: the plain style is for instruction, the middle style is to give pleasure, the grand style is passionate and eloquent in moving its audience; in Gottsched's formulation in his *Ausführliche Redekunst* (1736, 'Thorough Rhetoric'), the equivalents are *natürlich* (natural), *sinnreich* (witty, ingenious), and *bewegend/beweglich* (moving, appealing to the emotions). The middle road is the one he recommends, often citing examples from France: 'For this is the rule in good writing, that one must fully understand one's subject, but then formulate one's thoughts about it as they occur to one; without pondering whether one is achieving one's aim with simple or with complex periods.' Here he comes close to the principles of Seneca's looser prose style.

What was the state of German literature in Mozart's formative years? 'Poor, but improving (in two senses)', the answer has to be, with few native products of high quality and with even the most popular translations of foreign works being dutiful and leaden rather than idiomatic or inspired. From the early years of the eighteenth century onwards, a new and growing German literate public was weaned on a series of mainly short-lived periodical publications along the lines of the *Spectator* and the *Tatler*; for longer literary works, the reader had to rely on translations and adaptations of what the Germans called *Robinsonaden*, or variants on the theme of the shipwrecked mariner in the manner of Defoe's *Robinson Crusoe* (1719) – and of the 'Continuatio', the sixth and last book of

Grimmelshausen's *Simplicissimus* cycle. J. G. Schnabel's *Die Insel Felsenburg* (1735–43, originally entitled *Wunderliche Fata einiger See-Fahrer*, 'Strange Fortunes of some Mariners') was one of the most popular of these imitations; older books continued to be reprinted, and thus to find readers, such as Ziegler's oriental novel *Die asiatische Banise* (1689), a heroic-galant tale of love and vengeance. From the 1740s, the novels of Richardson and Fielding began to reach the German public in translation. And important younger German writers began to emerge: Klopstock, with his sub-Miltonic epic *Der Messias* (1748–73), the art-historian Winckelmann, Lessing, WIELAND, Gessner, Herder, then the young GOETHE (whose poem 'Das Veilchen' Mozart lived long enough to set to music).

If one examines the German-language texts that Mozart set, very few of them are of high literary quality – but then, as he himself pointed out more than once, notably in the correspondence at the time of DIE ENTFÜHRUNG AUS DEM SERAIL, high literary quality was not a major desideratum in a text intended for musical setting. Indeed, many of the minor changes that Mozart introduced in texts during the composition process were aimed at reducing the 'literary' quality in favour of greater clarity and directness ('wie bald' replacing BRETZNER's 'im Hui' in Konstanze's first aria, for instance – Bretzner's complaints about changes made to his book bounce back against himself).

The great majority of Mozart's German settings can be divided into four categories: works for the theatre, works for the Freemasons, lieder and canons mainly intended for his own immediate circle, and some quasi-religious works, such as the early oratorio *Die Schuldigkeit des ersten Gebotes* and the *Grabmusik*. It is not unfair to remark that scarcely any of these texts has much literary merit – yet for their purpose they served admirably, giving the eleven-year-old Mozart the opportunity in the oratorio to depict in music of remarkable maturity the rivers bursting their banks, or the angry lion (with growling horns). Later, in the Masonic music, Mozart responded to often undistinguished texts with music that, in its use of conventional symbols (knocking rhythms, the prominence of seconds and thirds, the three flats of E flat major and C minor) underlined its purpose – which was to encourage informed participation in the activities of the Craft.

What did Mozart know of German literature? With the necessary reservations that possession of a book does not necessarily betoken knowledge of the contents of that book, and that acquaintance with the contents of a book is not dependent on actual ownership of it, one can nevertheless point to titles that Mozart either refers to knowledgeably in his letters or, from reported comments of others, seems to have known. As examples one may cite the letter to Leopold Mozart of 16 June 1781 in which he praises two 'certainly very good' comedies by STEPHANIE, and the letter to his sister of 15 December 1781 in which he discusses plays by Stephanie and Schröder. The comparatively frequent mention of Stephanie in the family correspondence is largely to be explained by Mozart's working relationship with him on *Die Entführung* and DER SCHAUSPIELDIREKTOR. Most of the references to specific plays and authors occur in the context of theatre in SALZBURG, Leopold Mozart informing his daughter at St Gilgen of plays performed in Salzburg when she could no longer keep up her own diary records after her marriage. The paucity of definite information about Mozart's knowledge of literature is exemplified by his sole reference to a play of Shakespeare: writing from MUNICH on 29 November 1780 about his problems with the oracular voice in IDOMENEO, he comments: 'If the Ghost's speech in *Hamlet* wasn't so long, it would have even greater effect' (Mozart had probably attended the performance of *Hamlet* given in Salzburg a few weeks earlier by Schikaneder's company and in Schröder's adaptation).

Examination of the list of volumes in Mozart's possession at the time of his death reveals thirty-three titles in German, mainly works by contemporaries, out of a total of thirty-nine items, for few of which is there any indication in his works and letters that he was familiar with their contents. He was an inveterate theatregoer ('My sole entertainment is the theatre', he wrote to CONSTANZE MOZART on 3 October 1790 and variants on this phrase occur elsewhere in the letters), but usually we have to rely on circumstantial evidence to back up a claim that he was influenced by, or even pondered, this or that work that he saw, or read. In his letter of 7 May 1783 he claims to have perused 'easily a hundred – indeed more' librettos in the search for one that he would feel drawn to set to music; he is not looking for literary quality, but for a text that would provide the foundation for a successful opera. It is extremely doubtful if he had much say in the choice of the books he set to music, though the facts that he owned a copy of a German translation of BEAUMARCHAIS's *Le Mariage de Figaro*, and that DA PONTE stated that the subject of LE NOZZE DI FIGARO was Mozart's suggestion, provide evidence that at least sometimes the choice may have been his.

Whereas Leopold Mozart had enjoyed the standard education of a reasonably fortunate lower-middle-class boy – he was the son of a bookbinder – with secondary schooling at the AUGSBURG Gymnasium and the Jesuit Lyceum, and went on to make a successful start to a course in philosophy and law at Salzburg University, neither his son nor his daughter had a normal education, both being instructed in the basics as well as in music theory and practice by their father. Further, they spent so much of their time in travels that a conventional education would in any case have been impracticable. We know from the reminiscences of his sister that young Wolfgang had a talent for drawing and arithmetic. He also had a gift for languages, mastering Italian and French as well as writing a lively, often idiosyncratic German, heavily marked by dialect; and in the mid-1780s he began to study English seriously, with a view to undertaking a second visit to Great Britain. By comparison with our knowledge of many of his contemporaries we have to admit to possessing very little knowledge about his literary interests.

Mozart's father enjoyed a close working relationship with JOHANN JAKOB LOTTER, the Augsburg publisher of his *Violinschule*; and he was also in contact with Breitkopf & Härtel. Wolfgang Mozart knew well the VIENNA publisher and bookseller JOHANN THOMAS EDLER VON TRATTNER – indeed Mozart and his wife lived in Trattner's house on the Graben from January 1784; Trattner's wife, Maria Theresia, was one of Mozart's most talented keyboard pupils and the recipient of the dedication of the C minor keyboard Sonata and Fantasia (K457 + 475). Mozart had close connections with several of the Viennese music dealers, including TRAEG, ARTARIA and

HOFFMEISTER; some of them were also more general booksellers. We know, however, of few personal links between Mozart and leading members of the Vienna literary scene. Indeed, one could go so far as to say that, during Mozart's years there, Vienna almost entirely lacked authors worthy of more than passing attention from posterity. EMANUEL SCHIKANEDER was the most important German-language author with whom Mozart had a close friendship and working relationship; and his reputation is largely dependent on the fact that Mozart set (and in so doing textually improved) his libretto of DIE ZAUBERFLÖTE.

An area of which little is known is Mozart's relations with publishers and censors. True, he seems not to have taken further the project mentioned in his letter of 28 December 1782 to write a monograph on music theory. But one looks in vain for evidence that he had any contact with publishers or censors; he certainly knew SONNENFELS (who, however, did not become censor until 1810, long after Mozart's death), who is mentioned in Mozart's letters of 6 May and 22 December 1781, and whose name appears early on Mozart's concert subscription list of March 1784. Given the paucity of evidence that Mozart took much interest in current affairs, it may even be that he was unaware how fortunate he was that he lived and worked in Vienna during a period when JOSEPH II had considerably restricted the powers of the censors, and when book production had begun to be recognized as an economically significant factor in the nation's life. PETER BRANSCOMBE

E. A. Blackall, *The Emergence of German as a Literary Language 1700–1775* (Cambridge, 1959)
D. Breuer, *Geschichte der literarischen Zensur in Deutschland* (Heidelberg, 1982), esp. 98–113
H. and M. Garland, *The Oxford Companion to German Literature* (Oxford, 1976)
D. Schroeder, *Mozart in Revolt: Strategies of Resistance, Mischief and Deception* (New Haven and London, 1999)

Germany, German. ' "Germany" did not exist' in this period, declares Professor James Sheehan – there was certainly no state or administrative unit officially so called. However, 'Germany' figured on maps, designating an area of which the German Republic occupies the greater part today. Foreigners did not doubt that Germans and the German language, despite its many dialects, were identifiable. The Holy Roman Empire (*Reich*) was nominally 'of the German Nation' and its business was mostly conducted in German. It cannot be called a state in the proper sense since its head, the emperor, and his bureaucracy had less power over the inhabitants of the more than 300 political entities that composed it than was possessed by the technically subordinate rulers. But it had precise, if in some cases disputed, frontiers embracing modern Germany and AUSTRIA; its laws, courts and officials facilitated commerce and travel throughout the overlapping and jostling jurisdictions of the Empire; and in extreme cases the emperor and his court for imperial business (the *Reichshofrat* or 'Aulic Council', which sat in VIENNA) could still bring a major ruler to book: in 1770 they forced Karl Eugen, Duke of Württemberg, to abandon the unconstitutional practices that had enabled him to spend far beyond his legitimate income on his army and his opera.

If the prime loyalty of Germans as of most Europeans was to smaller units, cities and *Länder* (often translated 'provinces'), many of them, like the Mozart family, thought of themselves as German and regarded the French, the English and the Italians as different and foreign. The Reformation, by insisting on the use of the vernacular, and Luther, by translating the Bible into German, had made his followers conscious of their linguistic identity. In Catholic western and southern Germany the emperor and the Empire were seen as the guarantors of the gains of the Counter-Reformation and of the continued existence of the numerous states ruled by prince-bishops and prince-abbots. One of the emperor's titles was 'King in Germany', and he and the Empire were foci of German patriotism. Even in Hamburg, Protestant and remote from his court, prayers were regularly said for him and his birthday was celebrated. GOETHE famously described in *Dichtung und Wahrheit* the pride he felt as a citizen of Protestant Frankfurt during the coronation there in 1764 of JOSEPH II as King of the Romans, that is, as the next emperor. There was something of a revival of imperial feeling when Joseph, young and a reformer, became emperor in 1765. In that year, one of the Protestant members of the *Reichshofrat*, Friedrich Carl von Moser, published *Of the German National Spirit*, followed in the next year by *What is Good in an Emperor, and What is not Good?* and in 1767 by *Patriotic Letters*, all maintaining that the emperor's rights were the best protection for the Empire as a whole. In 1768, however, Justus Möser produced an alternative justification of the Empire in his *History of Osnabrück*, namely, that it preserved the division of Germany into small units, like the prince-bishopric of Osnabrück where he had been born and was a minister, units that he claimed served their inhabitants well and commanded their affection and loyalty. Joseph soon tired of his probably hopeless attempt to make significant reforms of imperial institutions. But his conversion of the Vienna court theatre into a National Theatre in 1776 and his encouragement of vernacular plays and librettos (like Mozart's *DIE ENTFÜHRUNG AUS DEM SERAIL*) appealed to pan-German if not to imperial sentiment. A later wave of imperial patriotism accompanied the formation in 1785 of the League of Princes (*Fürstenbund*) under the aegis of Frederick the Great of Prussia, this time directed against the ambition of Joseph II as ruler of the Austrian monarchy to annex Bavaria.

Sheehan's negative judgement, however, has much to be said for it. The major states within the Empire, including Austria, pursued their own interests with little or no regard to those of the *Reich*. Several of them – Austria, Prussia, Hanover and until 1763 Saxony – had rulers who also possessed substantial territories outside its borders. Although religious toleration was growing, Catholics and Protestants generally regarded each other with deep suspicion. If the great majority of German speakers lived within the Empire, the Swiss and the colonists who dominated the towns of eastern Europe were excluded. On the other hand, among the inhabitants of the Empire were the French- and Flemish-speaking Belgians, the Czech speakers of Bohemia and some northern Italians. Latin was still so much used by the churches, in administration, in the universities and by learned authors that travellers could get around the country using that language alone. German rulers and aristocrats aped French manners and wrote in French. Frederick II of Prussia always used French except for internal administration and publicly maintained that German-language literature was a contradiction in terms. Very few foreigners troubled to learn German and it was only from the late 1760s that literature in the vernacular began to rival French, Spanish, Italian and English. DEREK BEALES

J. G. Gagliardo, *Reich and Nation: The Holy Roman Empire as Idea and Reality, 1763–1806* (London, 1980)
J. J. Sheehan, *German History, 1770–1866* (Oxford, 1989)
P. H. Wilson, *The Holy Roman Expire, 1495–1806* (London, 1999)

Gilowsky von Urazowa family. Salzburg barber surgeons. Two brothers, Franz Anton (b. 27 May 1708; d. 12 Jan. 1770) and Johann Wenzel Andreas (b. 30 Nov. 1716; d. 21 Aug. 1799) produced children mentioned by the Mozarts. From Franz Anton's first marriage came Johann Joseph Anton Ernst (b. 12 Jan. 1739; committed suicide 10 June 1789) who followed an administrative career, was a court councillor, FREEMASON and represented Mozart in the settlement of LEOPOLD MOZART's estate. From Franz Anton's second marriage came Maria Anna Katharina (b. 1753; d. 11 June 1809), the 'Figaro story' chambermaid: according to Leopold Mozart's letter of 29 June 1778, Salzburg's Obersthofmeister Franz Lactanz von FIRMIAN arranged for her to marry his servant Simon Ankner in order to have her sexual services close by. Johann Wenzel Andreas's daughter Maria Anna Katharina ('Katherl', b. 19 Apr. 1750; d. 1802) was NANNERL MOZART's boisterous friend and the butt of the Mozarts' humour, often appearing on their shooting targets desperate to catch a man and in other unflattering situations. Her brother, Franz Xaver Wenzel (b. 16 Dec. 1757; d. 22 Mar. 1816), was a witness at Mozart's wedding. RUTH HALLIWELL

H. Schuler, *Mozarts Salzburger Freunde und Bekannte* (Wilhelmshaven, 1995), 107–15

Gluck, Christoph Willibald (b. Erasbach, Upper Palatinate, 2 July 1714; d. Vienna, 15 Nov. 1787), composer and leading exponent of opera and ballet reform. Despite their difference in age, Mozart learnt important musical and dramatic lessons from Gluck, who like him was both a papal Knight of the Golden Spur and a Habsburg court composer. (It was the elder composer's death that opened a position for Mozart as *Kammermusikus*, though with much lower compensation.)

In October 1762, while in VIENNA to exhibit his children's talents, LEOPOLD MOZART heard Gluck's opera *Orfeo ed Euridice* – though he was silent on the work in letters home to his non-musical neighbour Lorenz HAGENAUER. During a more extended visit in 1767–8 Leopold (and his son, presumably) heard the composer's *Alceste*, Leopold commenting that this tragic work was performed by 'mere opera buffa singers'. Though initially supportive of Leopold's idea to have Wolfgang compose an opera buffa (LA FINTA SEMPLICE) for the court theatre, Gluck later opposed the project. Towards the start of Mozart's decade of residence in the capital, Gluck again (though inadvertently) obstructed Mozart's theatrical ambitions, in that the production of DIE ENTFÜHRUNG AUS DEM SERAIL was delayed by performances of various Gluck operas – particularly *La Rencontre imprévue* (performed in German as *Die Pilger von Mekka*), which used many of the same singers as *Entführung*. But the delay also gave Mozart time to make some 'very necessary alterations' in his opera, and to profit from close acquaintance with Gluck's 'Turkish' opera, on a tune from which he later composed a set of piano variations, K455. Some spectators perceived *Die Entführung* to be overly derivative of

La Rencontre, but Gluck himself helped silence such talk by requesting a performance of Mozart's opera, and complimenting the composer publicly on the work.

Gluck's influence is also evident in Mozart's IDOMENEO of 1781, as Wolfgang had taken his father's advice to accompany the oracle's pronouncement with swelling and diminishing wind chords, as in *Alceste*. In a wider sense, *Idomeneo* shows Mozart profiting from Gluck's various sacrifice dramas (including the two *Iphigénie* operas), in the integration of music and spectacle, careful balancing of personal and ceremonial aspects, and many specific musical details. More rigorously even than in his later operas, in *Idomeneo* Mozart was concerned (as was Gluck) to maintain continuity, so as to further the audience's complete immersion in the spectacle. Yet Mozart fundamentally reversed Gluck's prioritization of words over music, by finding dramatically appropriate ways to use vocal virtuosity, and later stating that 'in an opera the poetry must be altogether the obedient daughter of the music'.

Gluck's first major 'reform' ballet, *Don Juan, ou Le Festin de pierre* (1761) left its mark on two of Mozart's DA PONTE operas, inspiring the fandango in the third-act finale of LE NOZZE DI FIGARO, and providing the model for the cemetery scene of DON GIOVANNI.

BRUCE ALAN BROWN

G. Croll, 'Gluck und Mozart', *Österreichische Musikzeitschrift* 28 (1973), 300–7
D. Heartz, 'Sacrifice Drama', in *Mozart's Operas*, ed., with contributing essays, T. Bauman (Berkeley and Los Angeles, 1990)
Haydn, Mozart, and the Viennese School, 1740–1780 (New York, 1995)

Goethe, Johann Wolfgang (b. 28 Aug. 1749; d. 22 Mar. 1832). German writer, one of the outstanding figures of the European literary tradition. Goethe heard the seven-year-old Mozart play in Frankfurt in 1763; clearly impressed by the prodigy, he remembered the occasion in old age. To Goethe, Mozart's talent was both marvellous and inexplicable. He admired the composer's works, in particular DON GIOVANNI, and lamented the fact that his own *Faust* was not set to music by Mozart. Goethe produced four singspiel texts between 1775 and 1782, among them *Erwin und Elmire* (1775), which includes the song *Das Veilchen*, set to music by Mozart in 1785 (K476). Goethe considered DIE ENTFÜHRUNG AUS DEM SERAIL to be a turning point in the history of singspiel – it also marked the end of his own work in that area. From 1791 to 1817, Goethe was director of the court theatre at Weimar, during which time *Die Entführung*, LE NOZZE DI FIGARO, *Don Giovanni* and DIE ZAUBERFLÖTE were produced regularly. After a production of *Die Zauberflöte* in 1794, Goethe decided to write a sequel to the opera. A fragment of *Der Zauberflöte zweiter Teil* remains, but the work was never finished.

ÁINE SHEIL

J. W. von Goethe, *Conversations of Goethe with Johann Peter Eckermann*, trans. J. Oxenford, ed. J. K. Moorhead (New York, 1998)
R. Spaethling, *Music and Mozart in the Life of Goethe* (Columbia, SC, 1987)
F. W. Sternfeld, *Goethe and Music* (New York, 1979)

Goldoni, Carlo (b. Venice, 25 Feb. 1707; d. Paris, 6/7 Feb. 1793). Italian playwright and librettist. Goldoni was among Italy's finest dramatic authors; his texts are mostly comic but also include serious operas, cantatas and oratorios. At first he was chiefly active in Venice, where he worked with the composers

Galuppi, Cocchi, Giuseppe Scarlatti, Bertoni and FISCHIETTI; in 1762 he settled permanently in PARIS. Mozart set several Goldoni texts, including LA FINTA SEMPLICE, K51 (with a text revised by M. COLTELLINI) and the soprano aria 'Voi avete un cor fedele', K217 (from *Le nozze di Dorina*). In early 1783 he considered setting a German adaptation of *Il servitore di due padroni*, K416a, but nothing came of the project. CLIFF EISEN

T. Emery, *Goldoni as Librettist: Theatrical Reform and the drammi giocosi per musica* (New York, 1991)
D. Pietropaolo, ed., *Goldoni and the Musical Theatre* (New York, 1995)

Gottlieb, (Maria) Anna (b. Vienna, 29 Apr. 1774; d. Vienna, 4 Feb. 1856). Soprano. Gottlieb was barely twelve when she created the role of Barbarina in LE NOZZE DI FIGARO; she joined SCHIKANEDER's Freihaus-Theater in 1789 and in 1791 was the original Pamina in DIE ZAUBERFLÖTE. Thereafter she specialized in singspiels and comedies, retiring from the stage in 1828. CLIFF EISEN

E. Komorzynski, 'Sänger und Orchester des Freihaustheaters', *Mozart-Jahrbuch* 1951, 138–50
H. Schuler, 'Das Zauberflöten-Ensemble des Jahres 1791: Biographische Miszellen', *Mitteilungen der Internationalen Stiftung Mozarteum* 39 (1991), 92–124

Grimm, Friedrich Melchior, Baron (b. Regensburg, 26 Dec. 1723; d. Gotha, 19 Dec. 1807). Author and diplomat. In 1753, Grimm, who had settled in PARIS in 1749, founded the *Correspondance littéraire*, a journal of cultural affairs that circulated throughout Europe in handwritten copies. He was the Mozarts' chief patron during their first visit there, arranging an appearance at court as well as two public concerts in March and April 1764; Grimm also wrote the dedications to Madame Victoire de France and to the Comtesse de Tessé of Mozart's sonatas K6–7 and K8–9, respectively. His first article on Mozart appeared in the *Correspondance littéraire* on 1 December 1763, where he wrote: 'I cannot be sure that this child will not turn my head if I go on hearing him often; he makes me realize that it is difficult to guard against madness on seeing prodigies.' A further article appeared in July 1766, after the Mozarts' return visit to the French capital. Relations with Grimm were strained, however, during Mozart's stay in Paris in 1778. Although he was helpful – Mozart's mother had earlier written to LEOPOLD MOZART 'we can assuredly rely on him, as he is a sincere and true friend to us' (letter of 7 Mar. 1778) – Wolfgang felt that he was treated inappropriately: 'M. Grimm may be able to help *children*, but not grown-up people – and – but no, I had better not write anything – and yet I must. Do not imagine that he – is the same as he was. Were it not for Madame d'Epinay, I should not be in this house. And he need not be so proud of his hospitality – for there are four houses where I could have had both board and lodging. The good fellow doesn't know that, *if I had remained in Paris*, I should have cleared out of his house next month and gone to a less boorish and stupid household, where people can do you a kindness without constantly throwing it in your face' (letter of 11 Sept. 1778). CLIFF EISEN

Guardasoni, Domenico (b. ?Modena, c.1731; d. Vienna, 13/14 June 1806). Tenor and impresario. Guardasoni was engaged at VIENNA from 1772 and subsequently sang in Dresden, Leipzig and PRAGUE where, from 1785, he was affiliated with PASQUALE BONDINI's company at the National Theatre, later succeeding him as director of the company. Guardasoni was in charge of the premiere of DON GIOVANNI (Prague, 29 Oct. 1787) and in 1791 the opera festivities connected with the second coronation of LEOPOLD II. He first approached SALIERI, who turned down the commission for a festival opera, and then Mozart, who was engaged to compose LA CLEMENZA DI TITO; the opera was produced at Prague on 6 September. Guardasoni's company included in its repertory operas by Salieri and Stephen STORACE, among others, in addition to LE NOZZE DI FIGARO and COSÌ FAN TUTTE. CLIFF EISEN

Gyrowetz, Adalbert (b. 19 or 20 Feb. 1763; d. 19 Mar. 1850). Composer of symphonies, chamber music, opera and ballets; music director and resident composer at the Viennese court theatres from 1804 to 1831. Born and raised in Bohemia, Gyrowetz came to VIENNA in the mid-1780s. In his autobiography he recalled visiting Mozart, who praised the young man's symphonies and arranged to have one performed in one of his subscription concerts in the Mehlgrube: 'Mozart, out of the goodness of his heart, took the young artist by the hand and introduced him to the public as the symphony's author.' Shortly thereafter Gyrowetz travelled to Italy, on the first leg of a tour that would, over several years, take him to PARIS, LONDON and Berlin. When Mozart heard of his impending departure, he said: '"You lucky man! If only I could go with you, how happy I would be! But now I must give another lesson, to earn something for myself". These were the last words that Mozart spoke to Gyrowetz. With tears in their eyes and a handshake they parted.' JOHN A. RICE

A. Gyrowetz, *Biographie* (1848), ed. A. Einstein (Leipzig, 1913)

H

Habsburg monarchy. See AUSTRIA, AUSTRIAN, AUSTRIAN MONARCHY

Haffner family. SALZBURG family of factors, whose business encompassed banking, haulage and the import and export of goods for merchants. Under Siegmund Haffner the elder (b. 1699; d. 12 Jan. 1772) the firm reached its zenith, and was known throughout GERMANY, AUSTRIA and Italy. Siegmund was mayor from 1768 to 1772 and left enormous wealth. He was married twice – from 3 February 1733 to Anna Elisabeth Kaltenhauser (b. 1712; d. 25 Dec. 1744), and from 3 August 1745 to Eleonore Mezger (b. 1716; d. 2 June 1764). From these marriages five daughters and a son reached adulthood, the daughters marrying into mercantile families. Mozart wrote music for two of the children: Maria Elisabeth (b. 24 Oct. 1753; d. 1 Nov. 1781) and Siegmund the younger (b. 30 Sept. 1756; d. 24 June 1787).

When Maria Elisabeth married Franz Xaver Späth on 22 July 1776, Mozart wrote the 'Haffner' serenade, K250 (plus the march K249), in celebration. It was performed on the eve of the wedding at the Haffners' summer residence by Salzburg's Loreto convent. On 9 July 1782 Siegmund the younger was ennobled, and Mozart wrote what became the 'Haffner' symphony, K385, to mark the event. By now living in VIENNA, he completed it in two weeks. It had a march (possibly K408, No. 2), and may originally have had two minuets, though only one survives. Later Mozart added flutes and clarinets, and dropped the march, leaving the four movements that now comprise the 'Haffner' symphony.

Siegmund the younger had little active interest in the family business, and his brother-in-law Anton Triendl managed it instead. Siegmund never married, despite an attempt, coarsely derided by Mozart's parents, to do so in 1778 (letters of 29 Apr.–11 May), and became melancholy and reclusive before his early death. He was nevertheless a great Salzburg benefactor, dispensing wealth lavishly to charitable causes. RUTH HALLIWELL

H. Schuler, *Mozarts Salzburger Freunde und Bekannte* (Wilhelmshaven, 1995), 196–8
N. Zaslaw, *Mozart's Symphonies: Context, Performance Practice, Reception* (Oxford, 1989), 376–82.

'Haffner' serenade. Mozart's D major serenade, K250 (1776). See HAFFNER FAMILY and SERENADE

'Haffner' symphony. Mozart's Symphony No. 35 in D, K385 (1782). See HAFFNER FAMILY and SYMPHONIES

Hagenauer family. Landlords, bankers and close friends of the Mozarts. From 1673, when Georg III Hagenauer acquired a *Spezerei* (combined delicatessen and medicaments) business, they played a prominent role in SALZBURG life; the geographical scope of the business eventually reached the Adriatic, the Mediterranean, the Atlantic and the North Sea. Georg Hagenauer's grandson Johann Lorenz (b. 10 Aug. 1712; d. 9 Apr. 1792) inherited the business in Salzburg's Getreidegasse, and married Maria Theresia Schuster (d. 2 Feb. 1800). Their eleven children grew up with Mozart and NANNERL MOZART, because the Mozarts rented an apartment from the Hagenauers in the Getreidegasse house from 1747 until 1773. When the Mozarts started to travel, the Hagenauers provided loans, put their mercantile credit network at Leopold's disposal, and performed numerous extra favours.

The two families corresponded from 1762 to 1768. The Hagenauers' letters have not survived, but LEOPOLD MOZART's to them (some pamphlet-length) give rich information about Mozart's astonishing development, and fascinating details of travel and society in eighteenth-century Europe. Although the families were intimate in many ways (socializing daily, swapping gossip, giving mutual support and offering Masses for each other in times of trouble), the Hagenauers' situation as the Mozarts' bankers made the relationship unequal. This observation has implications for the interpretation of Leopold's letters: he may sometimes have given a view of his finances that was more optimistic than accurate; and he may sometimes have written to flatter the Hagenauers' conservative religious and moral views.

There is one Mozart work known to have a Hagenauer connection. Their fifth child was Kajetan Rupert (b. 23 Oct. 1746; d. 4 June 1811). He entered St Peter's Benedictine Abbey in Salzburg as novice in 1764, taking the name Dominicus, and in 1769 Mozart wrote the Dominicusmesse, K66, to mark the celebration of his first Mass on 15 October. The following day, Mozart and Nannerl played the music for a grand dinner given by the Hagenauers at their garden house in the Nonntal district. RUTH HALLIWELL

G. Barth, 'Die Hagenauers: Ein Salzburger Bürgergeschlecht aus Ainring', in *Ainring: Ein Heimatbuch* (Ainring, 1990)
R. Halliwell, *The Mozart Family: Four Lives in a Social Context* (Oxford, 1998)

Haibel, Sophie (née Weber, b. Oct. 1763; d. Salzburg, 26 Oct. 1846). Younger sister of CONSTANZE MOZART. She married Jacob Haibel on 7 January 1807 and moved from VIENNA to Diakovar when he became cathedral choirmaster there; on Haibel's death in 1826, Sophie moved to SALZBURG to live with Constanze, whose second husband NISSEN had also just died. Sophie is remembered for her reminiscences of Mozart, especially those of his final illness. When Nissen was compiling material for his biography of Mozart, Sophie wrote with information on 7 April 1825. Nissen copied and annotated her letter in an apparent attempt to clarify details. Most of her material found its way into the posthumously compiled biography, together with more information purportedly (but unverifiably) from her. Later, in 1829, Sophie gave Vincent and Mary NOVELLO oral accounts of Mozart. The sum of Sophie's information, Nissen's annotations and the use of her material in Nissen's biography raises issues about Mozart's death that have aroused interest ever since, but shows inconsistencies and inaccuracies.

With respect to Mozart's illness, both in her letter to Nissen and in a passage in Nissen's biography purporting to derive from Sophie (but *not* in her letter), criticisms are voiced about Mozart's treatment. Carl Bär believes that these criticisms (together with others deriving from Constanze and articulated in NIEMETSCHEK's biography) underlie the subsequent controversy about the diagnosis of Mozart's final illness. Then, as concerns Mozart's preparation for death, Sophie stated in her letter to Nissen that she had great difficulty persuading a priest to attend Mozart. Though the statement seems to imply that a priest did eventually come, Nissen's annotation of this part of the letter claims that no priest attended, because Mozart had not himself made the request. A later annotation states that although Mozart did not receive the last rites (presumably absolution and Holy Communion), he was given extreme unction. Yet Nissen's biography claims that he was refused extreme unction. Thus there is confusion about which, if any, of the sacraments for the sick and dying Mozart received. And, finally, Sophie's report to the Novellos that Mozart was writing part of the REQUIEM on the day he died is at odds with her statement that he had swollen, inflamed limbs. Her letter to Nissen, although indicating that Mozart was actively concerned with its completion, did not make this claim. As Bär points out, Sophie's letter to Nissen contains one verifiable inaccuracy, concerning the chronology of Mozart's illness; since it was written thirty-three years after the death, there may be other inaccuracies as well.

RUTH HALLIWELL

C. Bär, *Mozart: Krankheit, Tod, Begräbnis* (Salzburg, 1972)

R. Lewicki, 'Aus Nissens Kollektaneen', *Mitteilungen der Internationalen Stiftung Mozarteum* 2 (1919), 28–30

G. N. von Nissen, *Biographie W. A. Mozarts* (Leipzig, 1828), 573–5

V. and M. Novello, *A Mozart Pilgrimage: Being the Travel Diaries of Vincent and Mary Novello in the Year 1829*, ed. N. Medici di Marignano and R. Hughes (London, 1975).

Handel, George Frideric (Georg Friedrich, Händel) (b. Halle, 23 Feb. 1685; d. London, 14 Apr. 1759). German, later English composer. Mozart's first contact with Handel's music was probably at his audiences with King George III in LONDON in the spring of 1764: the King placed before him music by WAGENSEIL, J. C. BACH, ABEL and Handel, which he played fluently at sight; he also extemporized a melody to a bass part by Handel 'in a manner that astonished all who were present'. Mozart undoubtedly heard music by Handel when he was in London, for example at a concert in June 1764 at which music from *Acis and Galatea* and *Alexander's Feast* was performed.

Mozart had no further contact with Handel's music for several years; there was a performance of part of *Messiah* in MANNHEIM when he was there in 1777 but he was not present. His interest in music of an earlier era was, however, stimulated when in his first Viennese years he performed at the salon of BARON GOTTFRIED VAN SWIETEN. Van Swieten, who had served as a diplomat in Berlin and London, where music of the late Baroque era had in some degree been kept alive, notably at Princess Anna Amalia's Berlin establishment, was keenly interested in J. S. BACH and Handel. In April 1782 Mozart wrote to his father asking him to send 'Handel's six fugues [pub. 1735, HWV605–10] and EBERLIN's toccatas and fugues'. He continued: 'I go every Sunday at 12 o'clock to the Baron van Swieten's – there nothing is played other than Handel and Bach. I am making a collection of Bach fugues, including Sebastian's as well as Emanuel and Friedemann's – and also of Handel's.' A few days later he remarked in a letter to his sister on CONSTANZE MOZART's enthusiasm for fugues by Bach and Handel, and he also countermanded the request for Eberlin's, which he now realized were much inferior. It was at about this time that Mozart made his string transcriptions of fugues by Bach, mainly from the '48'. But it is not generally known that he also at least began work on one by Handel, the fourth movement of Suite No. 2 in F, HWV427 (1720), and completed one side of a folio; either he broke off at that point, or he continued on a further sheet that is now lost. New articulation markings are included, for string quartet performance.

Whether or not the fugal music of Handel and Bach had any influence on Mozart's own music is a question that has been much debated. Some critics have been eager to claim Mozart's recognition of the greatness of these earlier composers and to see their influence as seminal in the formation of his mature style. Others, perhaps more realistically, have seen the contrapuntal elements in such work as the string quartet K387 and the symphony K551 as more directly derived from the usage of MICHAEL HAYDN and other early Classical composers.

Mozart's most decisive encounter with Handel came towards the end of his life, when he arranged a number of major Handel works for performance in Baron van Swieten's programmes and elsewhere. These are *Acis and Galatea*, K566, performed in November 1788; *Messiah*, K572, March 1789; and *Alexander's Feast*, K591 and the *Ode for St Cecilia's Day*, K592, arranged in July 1790 (no performances are documented, but the works were probably given late in 1790). It was believed for a time, in the early nineteenth century, that Mozart also made a setting of *Judas Maccabaeus*, but the version once ascribed to him has been shown to be the work of JOSEPH STARZER; a different version purporting to be his was discovered recently but in the absence of firm evidence concerning its authenticity, must be regarded as at best doubtful.

These versions, which Handelians have heavily criticized (even as early, at least in England, as the beginning of the nineteenth century), need to be understood in the context of performing practices and the favoured orchestral textures of the time. The works were to be performed in German, which involved some revision of the vocal lines to accommodate the text. Second, the techniques of trumpet playing called upon in Handel's scores (three of the four make use of trumpets) were no longer practised in the late eighteenth century and the parts had to be revised and any essential music reassigned. Third, much of the original articulation was adjusted, softened and made more uniform, and in conformity with bowing styles of the late eighteenth century.

Fourth, and most significant, the scoring was substantially supplemented. The spare textures and the dependence on continuo-supplied harmony of late Baroque music were not acceptable to audiences in late eighteenth-century VIENNA and will certainly have seemed primitive and excessively austere to Mozart and his colleagues. To all four scores he added one or two flutes, two clarinets, independent bassoon parts and music for two horns. He not only filled out the textures, providing a warmer and fuller tutti sonority and extra rhythmic activity but occasionally – the most famous, or infamous, example is 'The people that walk'd in darkness' from *Messiah* – supplied new, sinuous, chromatic lines for the woodwind. Sometimes picturesque colour was supplied, as in the bleating woodwind of 'All we like sheep'. Simple top-and-bottom textures were anathema to Mozart and his times; where Handel wrote two-part string textures, a filling-in viola part is sometimes added, often much more. But Mozart could leave well alone where the music was eloquent and purposeful as it stood, for example in 'Behold a ghastly band' in *Alexander's Feast*, with its dark bassoons and violas. Sometimes Mozart's wider knowledge of Handel's music is evident: in the overture to the *Ode for St Cecilia's Day* he uses the longer version of the minuet that appeared in the concerto grosso Op. 6, No. 5 but not originally in the ode. It is clear, however, from his versions of these works that Mozart had great respect for Handel's music and particularly for his mastery of grand choral effect. STANLEY SADIE

R. Cowgill, 'An Unknown Handel Arrangement by Mozart? The Halifax *Judas*', *Musical Times* 143 (Spring 2002), 19–36

Hanswurst. Stock character of German-language literature and theatre. Hanswurst is best known as the clown of eighteenth-century Viennese popular folk theatre but the name can be traced back as far as a 1519 version of Sebastian Brandt's satirical poem *Das Narrenschiff* (The Ship of Fools) where it appears in the form Hans Worst, as it does in two tracts by Luther from 1530 and 1541.

Hanswurst the stage character contains elements of Pickelhering, a clown brought to Germany by wandering English theatre troupes, and of Arlecchino, one of the Italian commedia dell'arte figures. The Viennese version was created in the early eighteenth century by Joseph Anton Stranitzky (1676–1726), director of a company resident at the Kärntnertortheater. His Hanswurst was of SALZBURG peasant stock but the character spoke in Viennese dialect, thus bringing the action of the play – generally a translation of an Italian libretto – closer to Viennese theatregoers. Stranitzky himself would take the role of Hanswurst, extemporizing and communicating directly with the audience. His character was cowardly but shrewd, greedy for physical pleasure and money, and shamelessly vulgar. His attitudes and manner of speaking formed a comic counterpoint to the concerns and language of the characters surrounding him and he became a wildly popular stage figure. In the 1730s, the German writer J. C. Gottsched complained about the vulgarity of Hanswurst comedy and called for the character to be driven from the stage. In 1770 the Viennese censor JOSEPH VON SONNENFELS banished Hanswurst from the city of Vienna, but the character lived on in suburban theatres where he became known as Kasperl, Thaddädl or Staberl.

By the time Mozart wrote his operas, Hanswurst had evolved into a more diffuse character than the original Stranitzky conception. A number of his characters display what could, however, be described as Hanswurst tendencies: in DON GIOVANNI, Leporello makes many witty asides, he displays both cunning and fear, he is easily won over with money and he is greedy for food and female company. In some respects, Don Giovanni is similar: he has a voracious appetite for women, food and wine, and could be regarded as an overblown Hanswurst were it not for his imperious and fearless manner. In DIE ZAUBERFLÖTE, Papageno displays Hanswurst characteristics as well: he has a strong interest in women, a preoccupation with his own well-being and safety, a disregard for the higher things in life and an ability to communicate directly with the audience. ÁINE SHEIL

H. G. Asper, *Hanswurst* (Emsdetten, 1980)
M. Dietrich, ed., *Hanswurst lebt noch* (Salzburg, 1965)
H. Würtz, ed., *Hanswurst und das Zaubertheater, von Stranitzky zu Raimund* (Vienna, 1990) (exhibition catalogue)

Harmonie. See WIND MUSIC and WENT, JOHANN (NEPOMUK)

Hasse, Johann Adolph (baptized Bergedorf, 25 Mar. 1699; d. Venice, 16 Dec. 1783). German composer. Hasse, one of the most successful and highly respected opera composers of the eighteenth century, served as Kapellmeister at the court of Frederick August of Saxony from 1731 and lived in VIENNA for much of the time between 1760 and 1772, when he retired to Venice. He was music tutor to MARIA THERESIA, a favourite of King Philip V of Spain, and described by LEOPOLD MOZART as 'the father of music' (letter of 30 July 1768). Hasse was apparently one of the few musicians in Vienna to take Leopold Mozart's side in his dispute with the court over the suppressed performance of *LA FINTA SEMPLICE* and wrote letters of recommendation for Mozart in anticipation of his first trip to Italy; one, to G. M. Ortes, describes Mozart as 'already a composer and a master of music.... The boy is moreover handsome, vivacious, graceful and full of good manners; and knowing him, it is difficult to avoid loving him.' Mozart and Hasse met again in MILAN in 1771: both were commissioned to write theatrical works for the wedding of Archduke Ferdinand and Maria Beatrice Riciarda d'Este. But while Mozart's serenata *ASCANIO IN ALBA* was a success, Hasse's opera *Il Ruggiero* was a failure; a local newspaper reported that 'The opera has not met with success... The serenata, however, has met with general applause, both for the text and for the music', confirming Leopold Mozart's assertion in a letter of 19 October 1771 that 'Wolfgang's serenata has killed Hasse's opera'. CLIFF EISEN

Hässler, Johann Wilhelm (b. Frankfurt, 29 Mar. 1747; d. Moscow, 29 Mar. 1822). German composer, music director and keyboard player. Mozart met Hässler in Dresden on 15 April 1789, when they played in an informal keyboard duel on the organ of the court church and on the piano at the house of Prince Alexander Mikhailovich Beloselsky, Russian ambassador to Saxony. In a letter of 16 April Mozart wrote to CONSTANZE MOZART from Dresden: 'you must know that a certain Hässler, who is organist at Erfurt, is in Dresden . . . He is a pupil of a pupil of [J. S.] BACH's. His forte is the organ and the clavichord. Now people here think that because I come from VIENNA, I am quite unacquainted with this style and mode of playing. Well, I sat down at the organ and played. PRINCE LICHNOWSKY, who knows Hässler very well, after some difficulty persuaded him to play also. This Hässler's chief excellence on the organ consists in his foot-work, which, since the pedals are graded here, is not so very wonderful. What is more, he has done no more than commit to memory the harmony and modulations of old Sebastian Bach and is not capable of executing a fugue properly.' CLIFF EISEN

Hatzfeld, August Clemens Ludwig Maria, Count (baptized Bonn, 10 Nov. 1754; d. Düsseldorf, 30 Jan. 1787). Member of the cathedral chapter at Eichstätt.

Hatzfeld met Mozart in January 1786 while on a pilgrimage to the Mariahilfekirche in VIENNA. An accomplished violinist, he and Mozart became fast friends; in March, for the performance of IDOMENEO at Prince Auersperg's, Mozart wrote an obbligato violin part for the aria 'Non temer, amato bene' specifically for him. Hatzfeld, who returned to Eichstätt shortly afterward, died prematurely in April 1787; at the time Mozart wrote to his father of the 'sad death of my best and dearest friend' (letter of 4 Apr. 1787). CLIFF EISEN

G. Hedler, 'Mozarts bester Freund, August Clemens Graf Hatzfeld', *Acta Mozartiana* 10 (1963), 10–14
E. F. Schmid, 'August Clemens Graf Hatzfeld', *Mozart-Jahrbuch* 1954, 14–33

Haydn, (Franz) Joseph (b. Rohrau, Lower Austria, 31 Mar. 1732; d. Vienna, 31 May 1809). AUSTRIAN composer who achieved international pre-eminence in his lifetime and whose relationship with Mozart was characterized by mutual affection and admiration. Although later scholarship described them as the primary exponents of a 'Classical school', their careers were substantially different and personal contact was restricted to the last period of Mozart's life.

Haydn was born in Rohrau, near the boundary of Lower Austria and Hungary, the eldest son of a wheelwright. In this rural, artisan background Haydn learned the violin and keyboard instruments and showed an above average talent as a treble. In 1737 or 1738 he moved to the nearby town of Hainburg, singing in the church and boarding with a relative, Johann Mathias Franck, the headmaster of the local school. A couple of years later, Georg Reutter, the Kapellmeister of St Stephen's in VIENNA, was travelling in the district looking for new recruits for the choir. Haydn was auditioned and subsequently moved to Vienna where he spent the next ten years as a daily participant in the rich musical offerings that accompanied the church services at the cathedral and at court. In comparison with that of Mozart, Haydn's musical upbringing was much more restricted, focused almost exclusively on church music, and, although Haydn was clearly talented he was not a *Wunderkind*; in this regard he enjoyed the same respect as his younger brother, MICHAEL HAYDN, who joined him at St Stephen's in 1745.

Both Haydn brothers were to comment in later life that Reutter neglected his duties as a teacher. But it is probably a mistake to over-personalize the issue since formal education in Austria in the 1740s was altogether haphazard. At the age of seventeen Haydn's voice broke and he was dismissed from the choir school. For the next eight years he led a freelance life in Vienna, singing and playing the violin and the organ in church services, accompanying singing lessons given by Porpora, giving his own keyboard and theory lessons, and providing music for a GERMAN theatre company. Although his musical background and much of his freelance activity would, most naturally, have led to a career as a church composer, Haydn's growing reputation as a composer of instrumental music was encouraged by his appointment as Kapellmeister to the Morzin family, probably in 1757. It was for this court that Haydn composed his first symphonies. At about the same time his first quartets were composed for another patron, Baron Fürnberg.

Because of financial difficulties Morzin had to disband his musical retinue and Haydn moved in 1761 to the ESTERHÁZY family, in whose employment he remained for the rest of his life, first as Vice-Kapellmeister and then, from 1766 as Kapellmeister. The Esterházy family was one of the richest aristocratic families in the Austrian territories, extensive landowners in Hungary with palaces in Eisenstadt, Vienna, Pressburg (Bratislava) and Kittsee. Haydn served four successive princes: Prince Paul Anton up to his unexpected death in 1762; the most lavish of them, Prince Nicolaus, from 1762 until 1790; Prince Anton and, finally, Prince Nicolaus II. In a way that Mozart would probably have found uncongenial, Haydn relished life as a courtier, including the occasional tensions, viewing his circumstances as an aid rather than a hindrance to musical creativity.

Apart from ensuring the smooth running of the musical establishment, Haydn's duties at first included providing music for the court orchestra, some seventy symphonies by the early 1780s. Prince Nicolaus was especially interested in opera and at a new summer palace named after the family, Eszterháza, built two opera houses, one for Italian opera, the other for marionette operas performed in German. As Kapellmeister, Haydn was responsible for directing these performances and composed himself. Today, Haydn's reputation as an opera composer is insignificant in comparison with that of Mozart but for nearly a quarter of a century his daily schedule involved opera in some way and he acquired a knowledge of Italian opera that was comprehensive if slightly more dated than the one Mozart's acquired more intermittently on his various travels.

One consequence of Haydn's employment at the Esterházy court up to 1790 was that he was based most of the time in the new summer palace at Eszterháza or in Eisenstadt; visits to Vienna were occasional events, typically in the 1780s for a few weeks in December and January. It is easy to exaggerate Haydn's isolation and it would be a mistake to maintain that he was unaware of musical life beyond the court, for its repertory, whether sacred, operatic or instrumental, featured a range of works by many of his contemporaries. Although there is no direct evidence, Haydn would have been aware of the reputation of the young Mozart in the 1760s and 1770s, if only through Joseph Haydn's brother, Michael, now working in Salzburg. Mozart, for his part, would have become increasingly aware of Haydn's music, from the works that reached Salzburg or were available in Vienna and, in PARIS in 1778, the many printed editions (some completely spurious) that were sold in that city. Probably the nearest the two composers came to a meeting was in March 1768: Mozart spent virtually the whole of that year in Vienna and he could have attended a performance of Haydn's Stabat mater that was directed by the composer in the church of the Barmherzige Brüder in the Leopoldstadt on the afternoon of Friday 25 March.

After Mozart moved to Vienna in 1781 there were greater opportunities for the two composers to meet. A plausible first meeting has been suggested for 22 and 23 December 1783, the dates of an important pair of charity concerts in the Burgtheater organized by the Tonkünstler-Sozietät. The programmes that year included works by both Haydn and Mozart; although there is no actual evidence that Haydn was in Vienna at the time, he quite often spent Christmas and New Year in the capital and had he done so in that particular year would certainly have attended this leading musical-cum-social event. The first documented evidence of a meeting between the two composers relates to the following year. In a celebrated account, the Irish tenor MICHAEL KELLY describes how he attended a musical party in which quartets were played by Haydn (first violin), DITTERSDORF (second violin), Mozart (viola) and VANHAL (cello). Kelly's memoirs were written several decades later and his account is not entirely convincing since Dittersdorf (a very capable violinist) is much more likely to have played first violin and Vanhal is not otherwise known to have played the cello; perhaps he conflated more than one social event in his account.

Mozart, by this time, was already working with great resolve on six quartets, stimulated by the appearance of Haydn's Op. 33 in 1782. By 1785 they were complete and were performed privately in Mozart's apartment in the Domgasse in the presence of LEOPOLD MOZART and Haydn. In a letter to NANNERL MOZART, Leopold proudly reported Haydn's comments about his son's music, its aesthetic quality and its craftsmanship: 'Before God and as an honest man, I tell you that your son is the greatest composer known to me either in person or by name. He has taste and, what is more, the most profound knowledge of composition.' The following autumn Mozart reciprocated the compliment when he dedicated his six quartets to Haydn, 'celebrated man and my dearest friend'.

Haydn and Mozart's mutual acquaintances in Vienna were numerous, including VAN SWIETEN, the Auernbrugger sisters, BARBARA VON PLOYER, PLEYEL, WEIGL, JOSEPH LEUTGEB and many FREEMASONS, Mozart having joined in December 1784 and Haydn in February 1785. Towards the end of the decade Haydn occasionally vented his frustration at life at the Esterházy court, wishing he could spend more time in Vienna. For his part, Mozart might well have envied the international esteem that Haydn acquired during the decade, whether in terms of commissions for new works, offers of publication, or invitations to travel.

For Haydn 1790 turned out to be a decisive year. It began, ordinarily enough, with performances of operas by Cimarosa, PAISIELLO, and SALIERI; they were to be joined later in the season, probably in late August or September, by the first production of a Mozart opera at the court, LE NOZZE DI FIGARO. In the summer Prince Nicolaus became ill and was taken to Vienna where he died in September. Musical life, including the planned performances of *Le nozze di Figaro*, was abruptly halted. The new reigning prince, Anton, immediately put in place his plans to reduce the musical personnel at the court and Haydn moved to Vienna in the autumn. On 10 November Mozart returned from his journey to southern Germany and for the next four or five weeks the two composers seem to have been in almost daily contact. MAXIMILIAN STADLER recalled that the two played the viola parts in performances of the string quintets in C (K515), D (K593) and G minor (K516).

In December, the London violinist and impresario JOHANN PETER SALOMON arrived in Vienna with the express intention of persuading Haydn to travel to LONDON to be the resident composer in a forthcoming season of concerts. Mozart, who was a much more experienced traveller, allegedly remarked, 'Papa, you have had no training for the great world, and you speak too few languages.' Haydn's reply reflected the international popularity that his music enjoyed: 'Oh, my language is understood all over the world.' Vague arrangements were made that Mozart should join Haydn in London, but these never materialized.

Haydn subsequently made two visits to London, from January 1791 to June 1792, and from February 1794 to July 1795, where he not only capitalized on but extended his existing popularity, principally through the composition of the twelve London symphonies (Nos. 93–104). It was while he was in London that he heard of Mozart's premature death. He wrote to their mutual friend, JOHANN MICHAEL PUCHBERG: 'For some time I was beside myself about his death, and I could not believe that Providence would so soon claim the life of such an indispensable man. I only regret that before his death he could not convince the English, who walk in darkness in this respect, of his greatness.' He went on to suggest that he try to organize a memorial concert in London and on his return to Vienna would give composition lessons free of charge to FRANZ XAVER WOLFGANG MOZART 'so that he can, to some extent, fill his father's position'; neither plan came to fruition.

For the remainder of his life Haydn continued to lament the early death of Mozart but was also able to witness the beginnings of his posthumous popularity as both composers were increasingly linked together as the leading figures in Viennese musical life. NIEMETSCHEK's biography of Mozart, which appeared in 1798, was dedicated to Haydn and contains many anecdotes, presumably related by CONSTANZE MOZART, about the warm relationship between the two composers. In April 1805, the thirteen-year-old Franz Xaver Mozart made his debut in Vienna in a concert in the Theater an der Wien; the main item in the concert was a cantata, unfortunately lost, written to celebrate Haydn's recent seventy-third birthday. In a symbolic gesture Haydn was to have led the young boy on to the stage but the ageing composer had become a frail man and he was unable to attend.

Haydn's last major work, the 'Harmoniemesse', had been written in 1802, part of a remarkable period of composition that included five other masses and two oratorios, *The Creation* and *The Seasons*. His life was a comfortable one, supported still by the Esterházy family and enhanced, both materially and psychologically, by international fame.

Although many authors have written about the influence of Haydn on Mozart, and vice versa, there is no systematic or comprehensive account. Casual comments are sometimes simplistic, such as attributing all uneven phrase lengths in Mozart to the influence of Haydn or descending chromatic passages in Haydn to the influence of Mozart. The fundamental truth is that scholarship still has only the most superficial experience of the lingua franca of the day, necessary to distinguish between the common, the special and the unique. For instance Mozart's quartets K168–73 have often been said to show the influence of Haydn's Op. 20 but they seem to owe much more to broader traditions of quartet-writing at the time, traditions that are reflected too in Haydn's Op. 20.

The composition of quartets, however, is one area where there is testimony that Mozart sought to learn from Haydn (as, indeed, BEETHOVEN was later to do). On manuscript copies of Haydn's Op. 17 quartets in F, C and D Mozart added copious additional dynamic markings, in a very conscious attempt to internalize the music. A short fragment of a quartet in E major, from c.1780–2 is clearly modelled on Haydn's quartet in E major, Op. 17. Mozart's dedicatory letter in the 'Haydn' quartets remarks that they were 'the fruit of a long and laborious study' and there are a number of striking correspondences between them and earlier quartets by Haydn: the finales of Op. 33 No 5 and K421, the minuets of Op. 33 No. 2 and K428, and the slow movements of Op. 33 No. 1 and K465. Stadler's story of the two composers playing quintets together in the autumn of 1790 also invites comparison between the following pairs of movements: the opening fast movements of Op. 64 No. 5 ('Lark') and K593 and the final movements of Op. 64 No. 6 and K614. Mozart's last three symphonies had been completed in the summer of 1788 and it is perhaps significant that their keys, E flat major, G minor and C major, are exactly the ones found in the ARTARIA print of three of Haydn's 'Paris' symphonies, Nos. 84, 83 and 82, published the previous December; there are some musical allusions here too. More generally, Mozart's increasing interest in monothematic sonata form towards the end of his life, as in the two late piano sonatas and the overture to DIE ZAUBERFLÖTE, almost certainly owes something to Haydn.

As regards the influence of Mozart on Haydn, it is difficult to find similar correspondences but his broadening harmonic language in the 1780s and 1790s, especially the increasingly resourceful use of secondary dominant and diminished harmonies, are significant. Some commentators have heard echoes of *Die Zauberflöte* in certain passages in *The Creation*, such as the trio 'On thee each living soul awaits', with its windband scoring, but this may be part of musical development in general in the 1790s. Undeniable in its intent, however, is the quotation from the slow movement of the G minor symphony, K550, in the penultimate number of *The Seasons*, when the onset of winter is compared to the end of human life. DAVID WYN JONES

M. E. Bonds, 'The Sincerest Form of Flattery? Mozart's "Haydn" Quartets and the Question of Influence', *Studi musicali* 22 (1993), 365–409
A. P. Brown, 'Haydn and Mozart's 1773 Stay in Vienna: Weeding a Musicological Garden', *Journal of Musicology* 10 (1992), 192–230
M. S. Cole, 'The Rondo Finale: Evidence for the Mozart–Haydn Exchange?', *Mozart-Jahrbuch* 1968/70, 242–56
D. W. Jones, 'Why did Mozart Compose his Last Three Symphonies? Some New Hypotheses', *Music Review* 51 (1990), 280–9
H. C. Robbins Landon, *Mozart. The Golden Years. 1781–1791* (London, 1989)

Haydn, (Johann) Michael (baptized Rohrau, 14 Sept. 1737; d. Salzburg, 10 Aug. 1806). Composer, younger brother of JOSEPH HAYDN. As a youth, Michael Haydn was a chorister at St Stephen's, VIENNA; his first significant appointment was in Grosswardein, where he was Kapellmeister to the bishop there. He joined the SALZBURG court music establishment, as concert master, in 1763. After the death of A. C. ADLGASSER in 1777, Haydn served as organist at the Dreifaltigkeitskirche; in 1782 he was appointed court and cathedral organist, succeeding Mozart.

Haydn was a prolific and successful composer of sacred and secular music (his sacred music in particular was performed well into the nineteenth century); in 1767 he collaborated with Mozart and Adlgasser on the composition of *Die Schuldigkeit des ersten Gebots*. At least some of his music was admired by both Mozart and his father (on 24 Sept. 1778 LEOPOLD MOZART wrote to Wolfgang, 'You would surely not deny Haydn certain achievements in music?') and in addition to apparent citations in Wolfgang's works, there are cases where compositions by Haydn were mistakenly attributed to the younger composer: these include the minuets K61b, 104 and 105, the terzetto 'Liebes Mädchen, hör mir zu' (KAnh. C 9.04), and the canons K562a and K562b. Presumably for study purposes, Mozart copied out several of Haydn's church works, among them two Pignus futurae gloriae (KAnh. A11 and A12), a Tres sunt (KAnh. A13) and an Ave Maria (KAnh. A14); in 1783 he asked his father to send some of Haydn's music to him in Vienna, for performance at VAN SWIETEN's.

The Mozarts' admiration for Haydn's music notwithstanding, they were frequently critical of his personal behaviour and in particular his excessive drinking. On 29 December 1777 Leopold wrote to Wolfgang, 'Who do you think has been appointed organist at the Dreifaltigkeitskirche? Herr Haydn. Everyone is laughing. He will be an expensive organist; after each LITANY he swills a quart of wine.' A few months later he reported to Wolfgang that 'in the afternoon, Haydn played the organ during the litany and Te Deum, the Archbishop being present, and he played so abominably that we were all terrified and thought he was going the way of Adlgasser of pious memory. But it was only a slight tipsiness, which made his head and his hands refuse to agree.' Nevertheless, Mozart, his father and Haydn seem to have maintained good relations, even if Leopold sometimes felt he had to lord Wolfgang's success over him; on 23 March 1786 he wrote to NANNERL MOZART, 'We had our concert yesterday. MARCHAND played the concerto in D minor, which I sent to you the other day. As you have the keyboard part, he played it from the score and Haydn turned over the pages for him and at the same time had the pleasure of seeing with what art it is composed, how delightfully the parts are interwoven and what a difficult concerto it is.' Mozart seems to have been fairer: as late as 1787–8 he not only wanted to borrow masses by Haydn but also invited him to visit him in Vienna.

CLIFF EISEN

R. Angermüller and J. Senigl, 'Biographie des Salzburgischen Concertmeisters Michael Haydn von seinen Freunden verfasset', *Mitteilungen der Internationalen Stiftung Mozarteum* 37 (1989), 199–231

G. Croll and K. Vössing, *Johann Michael Haydn, sein Leben, sein Schaffen, seine Zeit: eine Bildbiographie* (Vienna, 1987)

M. H. Schmid, *Mozart und die Salzburger Tradition* (Tutzing, 1976)

Heina, François-Joseph (b. Mieschitz, near Prague, 20 Nov. 1729; d. Paris, Feb. 1790). Music publisher. The Mozarts first met Heina in PARIS in 1763 when he was a horn player in the service of the Prince de Conti; later, in 1778, Heina and his wife befriended Mozart and his mother, visiting them often and securing for Mozart's mother, when she fell ill, the services of a German doctor and a German priest. Heina was present when she died on 3 July and the next day attended her funeral at St Eustache. Heina's publishing business, founded in

1773, concentrated chiefly on chamber music; among other works he published the first editions of Mozart keyboard variations K179, 180 and 354 (on the French song from BEAUMARCHAIS's *Le Barbier de Séville*, 'Je suis Lindor' set by Antoine-Laurent Baudron), the divertimento K254, and the keyboard sonatas K309, 310 and 311. CLIFF EISEN

Hofdemel, Franz (b. ? c.1755; d. Vienna, 6 Dec. 1791). Clerk at the court of justice, Vienna. Although it is not known when Mozart and Hofdemel met, they were on good terms at least by 1789 when Mozart wrote to him, requesting a loan (late March 1789); it was about the same time that Hofdemel was admitted to Mozart's lodge, 'Zur neugekrönten Hoffnung'. On 6 December 1791, however, Hofdemel attempted to murder his wife and then committed suicide; it was alleged that his wife, a keyboard student of Mozart's, was having an affair with the composer. This, in turn, led to the suggestion that Hofdemel poisoned Mozart although it was not taken seriously at the time. The episode did give rise to at least two later works of fiction, Leopold Schefer's *Mozart und seine Freundin* (1841) and Wolfgang Goetz's *Franz Hofdemel: Eine Mozart-Novelle* (1932). Hofdemel's wife, Maria Magdalena, left VIENNA in 1792, returning to her family home in Brünn, where she gave birth to a son on 10 May. CLIFF EISEN

G. Gugitz, 'Von W. A. Mozarts kuriosen Schülerinnen', *Österreichische Musikzeitschrift* 11 (1956), 261–9

Hoffmann, Ernst Theodor Amadeus (b. 24 Jan. 1776; d. 25 June 1822), German writer, critic and composer; he assumed the name Amadeus as a tribute to Mozart. After law studies at Königsberg University, Hoffmann worked in law from 1796 to 1806. During this time he devoted much attention to music (composition in particular) and in 1808 was appointed music director at the theatre in Bamberg. Hoffmann was a regular contributor to the *Allgemeine musikalische Zeitung* between 1809 and 1815; in his writings he championed the works of BEETHOVEN and frequently professed his admiration for Mozart, whom he saw as a Romantic composer – an artist of genius whose works were transcendent and profound. He reserved special praise for DON GIOVANNI; in a review of a performance from 1815, Hoffmann described it as the 'opera of all operas' and called for the performance of all recitative passages, a practice not common at the time. In 1813 and 1814 he was conductor of Joseph Seconda's company; performances took place in Dresden and Leipzig and included *Don Giovanni*, DIE ZAUBERFLÖTE and DIE ENTFÜHRUNG AUS DEM SERAIL.

It is for his literary output – in particular his stories, many of which display a fascination with the bizarre – that Hoffmann is chiefly remembered. *Don Juan* (1813) tells the tale of a traveller who attends a performance of *Don Giovanni*; it contains an element of the supernatural and an original, if characteristically Romantic, interpretation of the opera. ÁINE SHEIL

E. T. A. Hoffmann, *Selected Letters*, ed. and trans. J. C. Sahlin (Chicago, 1977)
E. T. A. Hoffmann's Musical Writings: Kreisleriana, The Poet and the Composer, Music Criticism, trans. M. Clarke, ed. D. Charlton (Cambridge, 1989)
H. von Kleist, L. Tieck and E. T. A. Hoffmann, *Six German Romantic Tales*, trans. R. Taylor (London, 1985) (includes Hoffmann's *Don Giovanni*)

Hoffmeister, Franz Anton (b. Rothenburg am Neckar, 12 May 1754; d. Vienna, 9 Feb. 1812). Music publisher and composer. Hoffmeister arrived in VIENNA in 1768 where he pursued a career in music, founding a publishing house in January 1784; among other works, he published the first editions of the piano quartet K478, the piano trio K496, the so-called 'Hoffmeister' quartet K499, and the sonatas for keyboard with violin accompaniment K481 and K526. For his part, Mozart wrote variations on Hoffmeister's song *An die Natur* as the first movement of his flute quartet K298. Apparently the two were well acquainted: Mozart owned a number of other publications by Hoffmeister and in the autumn of 1790 the publisher apparently loaned him money. Hoffmeister retired from music publishing in 1806 and the branch office that he had established in Leipzig with Ambrosius Kühnel was eventually purchased by C. F. Peters, Leipzig, one of the foremost music publishers of the nineteenth and twentieth centuries.

CLIFF EISEN

A. Weinmann, *Die Wiener Verlagswerke von Franz Anton Hoffmeister* (Vienna, 1964)

Hofmann, Leopold (b. Vienna, 14 Aug. 1738; d. Vienna, 17 Mar. 1793). AUSTRIAN composer. Hofmann, a pupil of WAGENSEIL, was active at the Michaelerkirche in VIENNA by 1758 and Kapellmeister at the Peterskirche from 1766. In 1769 he succeeded Wagenseil as court keyboard master and in 1772 he was appointed Essential- und Gnadenbildkapellmeister at St Stephen's Cathedral. Apparently he virtually withdrew from professional life after 1783 and Mozart, who had been appointed his unsalaried deputy in 1791, may have directed performances of church music in his absence. Hofmann enjoyed considerable fame in his lifetime, not only for his compositions but for his violin-playing as well.

CLIFF EISEN

D. Heartz, *Haydn, Mozart and the Viennese School 1740–1780* (New York and London, 1995), 464–72

B. MacIntyre, *The Viennese Concerted Mass of the Early Classic Period* (Ann Arbor, 1986)

Honauer, Leontzi (b. Strasburg, 2 June 1737; d. ?Strasburg, ?1790). Alsatian keyboard teacher and composer. Honauer, the son of a musician at Strasburg Cathedral, arrived in PARIS by 1761 at the latest, where he was probably in the retinue of Prince Louis de Rohan, the coadjutor of the diocese of Strasburg. In a letter of 1 February 1764, LEOPOLD MOZART described him as one of a group of German composers 'taking the lead [in Paris] in publishing their sonatas' and Wolfgang used movements from Honauer's sonatas Op. 1 No. 1, Op. 2 No. 1 and Op. 3 as the basis for movements in his pasticcio concertos K41, 37 and 40, respectively. Honauer's other works include two suites for keyboard and winds (1770) and four quartets for keyboard and strings with ad libitum horns, Op. 4 (1771).

CLIFF EISEN

E. Reeser, *De Klaviersonate met vioolbegeleiding in het Parijsche muziekleven ten tijde van Mozart* (Rotterdam, 1939)

Hübner, Beda (b. Temesvar, 18 Dec. 1740; d. Salzburg, 2 Apr. 1811). Priest and librarian. Hübner was the nephew of Beda Seeauer, abbot of St Peter's, SALZBURG, from 1753; he was consecrated in 1763 and thereafter served as Seeauer's librarian and secretary. Hübner's diary, which he kept from 1764 to 1767, provides a valuable documentary record of some of Mozart's activities in Salzburg and his growing reputation; in an entry dated 29 November 1766 he wrote: 'There is a strong rumour that the Mozart family will again not long remain here, but will soon visit the whole of Scandinvia and the whole of Russia, and perhaps even travel to China . . . I believe it to be certain that nobody is more celebrated in Europe than Herr Mozart with his two children.' CLIFF EISEN

H. Klein, 'Unbekannte Mozartiana von 1766/67', *Mozart-Jahrbuch* 1957, 168–85

Hummel, Johann Nepomuk (b. Pressburg/Bratislava, 14 Nov. 1778; d. Weimar, 17 Oct. 1837). Pianist and composer, and Mozart's most successful student. Hummel, who lived with the Mozarts in 1786 and 1787, may have been introduced to the composer by FRANZ JAKOB FREYSTÄDTLER. A child prodigy, Hummel undertook his first extended European tour in 1789; Mozart heard him play in Berlin on 23 May of that year. Later, after studies with CLEMENTI, SALIERI, ALBRECHTSBERGER and JOSEPH HAYDN, Hummel served as concert master to Prince Nikolaus ESTERHÁZY at Eisenstadt and, from 1817, as Kapellmeister at Weimar. CONSTANZE MOZART was insulted that Hummel left her no money in his will, writing to his sons that 'he had so often promised, in speaking to me, that once he was successful he would not fail to recompense me richly for all the trouble I took, for the love and care he received, the cost of his board and lodging, and for the lessons my late husband Mozart gave him'. She threatened legal action but gave up her claim the following year. In the 1820s, Hummel arranged several of Mozart's symphonies and piano concertos for piano, flute, violin and violoncello. CLIFF EISEN

D. Zimmerschmied, 'Mozartiana aus dem Nachlass von J. N. Hummel', *Mozart-Jahrbuch* 1964, 142–50
H. Schmid, ed., *Johann Nepomuk Hummel, ein Komponist zur Zeit der Wiener Klassik* (Eisenstadt, 1989)

'Hunt' quartet. Mozart's String Quartet in B flat, K458 (9 Nov. 1784). See CHAMBER MUSIC. B. STRING QUARTETS

I

Idomeneo, re di Creta, K366 (Idomeneus, King of Crete). *Dramma per musica* in three acts, K366, libretto by GIAMBATTISTA VARESCO. First performance: MUNICH, court theatre, 29 January 1781. *Idomeneo* bridges Mozart's final period of employment in SALZBURG and his years in VIENNA. It was the principal production of the Munich Carnival season in 1781 at the court theatre of Karl Theodor, former Elector Palatinate in MANNHEIM and since 1778 Elector of Bavaria. *Idomeneo* was well received, and the Elector was warm in his praise (Mozart reports him saying at rehearsal, 'Who could believe that such great things could be hidden in so small a head?'). Nevertheless it seems to have been performed only three times, on 29 January and 5 and 12 February 1781. There is no record of a revival in Munich, where a performing score (not the autograph) and performing materials survive. Nor, as Mozart already hoped on his extended visit to Mannheim in 1777–8, did Karl Theodor offer him a job. Despite a single revival in Vienna in 1786, what is without question Mozart's finest serious opera was to him as much a source of frustration as of satisfaction.

1. Origin and composition
2. The subject
3. Synopsis
4. Genre, music and characterization
5. Revision and reception

1. Origin and composition

The commission for *Idomeneo* may have been obtained by the veteran tenor ANTON RAAFF, who had known Mozart since his 1777 Mannheim visit, and who took the title role. The theatre intendant Count Seeau, who knew Mozart from 1775 when LA FINTA GIARDINIERA was performed in Munich, or Karl Theodor himself, may have been responsible for selecting the subject of the opera; there is no reason to suppose that it was Mozart's own choice, and it may be no coincidence that the Carnival opera of 1780 was Grua's *Telemaco*, for the story of *Idomeneo* derives from Fénelon's *Télémaque.* Mozart is unlikely to have had any previous acquaintance with the French libretto that was the immediate literary source.

The libretto was entrusted to Abbate Giambattista Varesco, chaplain to the Archbishop of Salzburg, and work began in Mozart's home city. The composer left for Munich on 5 November 1780 to finish composing the opera and supervise rehearsals. His father and sister joined him in late January. In the meantime LEOPOLD MOZART acted as mediator between librettist and composer, and the resulting correspondence provides the fullest documentation of the creative process of any Mozart opera. Much of it concerns the performers, but questions of large-scale planning and versification were also discussed, with Leopold sometimes taking the librettist's side against his son who was, however, by far the most experienced dramatist of the three.

Among the performers were the WENDLING FAMILY, known to the Mozarts from their travels in the 1760s. Johann Baptist Wendling had also been Mozart's particular companion when he was not haunting the WEBER household in 1777. His wife Dorothea took the role of Ilia and his brother's wife Elisabeth that of Elettra. Mozart had already written a Sinfonia concertante for the Mannheim wind players' visit to PARIS in 1778 (unperformed and lost: but see K297b). He now composed a multiple obbligato in Ilia's second aria for Wendling (flute), FRIEDRICH RAMM (for whom Mozart also wrote the Oboe Quartet and Concerto), Ritter (bassoon) and a horn of uncertain identity. The contribution of the Wendling singers can hardly be overestimated; they fell in with Mozart's plans ('Madame Dorothea Wendling', he reported in his first letter home, 'is arcicontentissima' with the opening of Act 1), and the music he wrote for them is superb.

The principal male singers caused real stress. Raaff was friendly but, at sixty-six, set in his ways; he could no longer sustain long phrases and he had never been much of an actor. Mozart treated him with affectionate care in the arias, the second of which is of considerable brilliance. But he firmly disallowed an aria at the climax of Act 2: 'the thunderstorm is not likely to subside during Herr Raaff's aria, is it?' he remarked (forgetting that it has to die away for the recitative). He rebuffed Raaff's complaint about his modest role in the quartet: 'there is nothing in this opera with which I am more pleased.' Raaff's last aria gave endless trouble, initially because the singer could not stand the poetry; Mozart supported him against Leopold and Varesco. The ineffectuality of the Idamante (VINCENZO DAL PRATO, alluded to ironically as 'mio molto amato Castrato dal Prato'), was a serious drawback; his previous experience seems not to have prepared him for a truly dramatic role and Mozart, whose views on singers tended to extremes, criticized his musicianship: 'I have to teach him every note, like a child.' He was another weak actor, and Mozart cut ruthlessly into the high-minded dialogues between Idomeneo and his son supplied by Varesco. Fortunately the Arbace (Domenico de Panzacchi) and High Priest (GIOVANNI VALESI) were competent. There is no doubt that the strengths and weaknesses of the singers affected the style and quality of Mozart's music, and consequently the dramatic meaning of the work in performance even today.

When Mozart proceeded directly to Vienna after *Idomeneo*, presumably taking the autograph with him (it is now divided between libraries in Berlin and Kraków), performance at the court theatre was very much on his mind. He made notes on casting, planning to adapt Idamante's role for tenor and Idomeneo's for bass, using VALENTIN ADAMBERGER and JOHANN LUDWIG FISCHER, who later created the principal male roles in DIE ENTFÜHRUNG AUS DEM SERAIL. A German version was mooted, perhaps by J. B. Alxinger, who in 1781 translated GLUCK's *Iphigénie en Tauride*. However, the occasion propitious for such an enterprise, a royal visit from Russia, was given over to revivals of Gluck; and Mozart turned his attention to *Die Entführung*. Isolated numbers from *Idomeneo* appeared in concerts, and a rendering of the quartet in Salzburg in 1783 caused Mozart to run off in tears. *Idomeneo* was revived once, on 13 March 1786, by noble amateurs, at the private theatre in the Auersperg Palace. Idamante became a tenor, but the adaptation of Idomeneo for bass was never undertaken, and it is possible that Mozart never attained his ideal vision for this opera.

2. The subject

Idomeneo belongs to the plot archetype in which a father has to sacrifice a child to propitiate a deity. Except with Abraham and Isaac, where the sacrifice was never meant to be consummated, the proper end of these stories is the death of the child. *Idomeneo* also belongs to a plot-type in which a successful hero overcomes danger, only to find worse trials at home: Agamemnon is murdered by his wife and Theseus discovers his wife's incestuous passion for Hippolytus. This tradition is explicitly alluded to in Idomeneo's Act 2 aria 'Fuor del mar' ('Free of the sea, I have a sea in my breast more deadly than the first'). The biblical story of Jephthah combines both elements. The warrior vows to sacrifice the first living thing he meets if he is victorious; to his eternal grief, and as punishment for *hubris*, it is his own child. This is essentially the story of *Idomeneo.*

The story is told in Fénelon's famous didactic novel *Télémaque* (1696), which the young Mozart is known to have read. Idomeneus, King of Crete, returns from the ten-year Trojan war laden with prisoners and spoils, but the hostile sea-god Neptune (Poseidon), defender of Troy, threatens him with shipwreck on his return. In sight of Crete, Idomeneus saves his life and that of his crew by promising to sacrifice the first living person he meets on shore. When the victim proves to be his own son, Idomeneus refuses to fulfil his vow. Neptune takes vengeance upon the island people, the attack from the sea symbolically embodied in a huge monster. In Fénelon, the son is duly sacrificed, and the King is driven into exile.

In 1712, following a dramatization in 1706 by P. J. de Crébillon, an opera *Idomenée* appeared in PARIS, composed by André Campra to a libretto by Antoine Danchet. In this the son, Idamante, kills the monster, making Neptune still more angry; Idomenée still refuses the sacrifice, but is driven mad by Nemesis and kills his son. Danchet introduced a complex love-interest: a Trojan princess, Ilione, has been sent back to Crete as a prisoner, and she and Idamante fall in love. Agamemnon's daughter Electre is exiled on the island, following the murder of her father; she too is in love with Idamante, and the match is supported by the King, who wishes to marry Ilione himself.

Varesco based his drama on Danchet, but simplified the love-rectangle. He preserved Ilia [Ilione] from the attentions of the King, while retaining her prolonged internal struggle, in which loyalty to her dead father prevents her from admitting her love for Idamante. In the French opera Electre, once she realizes she cannot win Idamante's love, intrigues to bring about his downfall. There was no room for this in the new opera, so her role is dramatically reduced, but even as an impotent avenging fury, Elettra is one of Mozart's most vivid characterizations. More radically, Varesco brings about the happy ending by adopting the convention of an oracle from operas such as Gluck's *Alceste* and

Iphigénie en Aulide, the latter a child-sacrifice opera whose happy ending was anticipated in dramas by Euripides and Racine.

3. Synopsis

The D major overture introduces several thematic shapes that play a role in the opera. A single dynamic form, rather than the three-movement design of opera seria, it dies away with utmost pathos, merging with the opening scene. In the palace of Sidon, the Cretan capital, Ilia, alone, meditates on her conflicting feelings: Greece is the cause of her country's woes, but she loves a Greek, and assumes that Idamante must be in love with Elettra, his compatriot (recitative and aria: 'Padre, germani, addio!'). Idamante enters with words of comfort, even affection, but she rejects him; he blames the gods for his suffering (aria, 'Non ho colpa'). He frees the Trojan prisoners (chorus, 'Godiam la pace'), which displeases Elettra. Arbace brings news of Idomeneo's shipwreck and presumed death. Idamante runs off to see for himself; Ilia follows and Elettra, alone, foresees that if Idamante is king he will marry Ilia (aria, 'Tutte nel cor vi sento').

Without a cadence, the music sweeps through the change of scene, to the seashore. We witness the agony of the sailors, about to drown, and the prayers of those on shore; Neptune appears and calms the waves. Idomeneo lands, and dismisses his followers to meditate on the implication of his vow (aria, 'Vedrommi intorno'); he fears that the victim will return to haunt him. Idamante duly appears. Their awkward dialogue is broken off at the moment of recognition, when Idomeneo, giving no reason, forbids his son to come near him. Idamante is left alone in fear and perplexity (aria, 'Il padre adorato'). In an entr'acte, the Cretan soldiers and populace join in rejoicing at the safe delivery of the King, and ironically praising Neptune (ballet and choral chaconne, 'Nettuno s'onori').

Act 2 begins with Idomeneo confessing the truth to Arbace. After the latter's aria ('Se il tuo duol'), Ilia sings of her happiness in finding a father (aria, 'Se il padre perdei', with four obbligato wind instruments). Idomeneo realizes with horror that she is in love with Idamante; the sacrifice will bring not one death, but three, for he and Ilia will not survive it; he must defy the gods and find a means of escape (aria, 'Fuor del mar'). He decides to send Idamante away, as escort for Elettra; she believes their proximity will bring love (aria, 'Idol mio').

The scene changes to the port of Sidon (March). Elettra and the chorus welcome a propitious calm ('Placido è il mar, andiamo'). Idamante and Idomeneo join her in a trio ('Pria di partir, oh Dio!'), in which their mutual misunderstanding is exposed. As they are about to embark, a tempest breaks out and a sea-monster terrorizes the chorus ('Qual nuovo terrore'). Idomeneo challenges the god; why should he sacrifice an innocent victim when he himself is guilty? That their king has brought this on them terrifies the people still more, and they flee ('Corriamo, fuggiamo'). Varesco wrote in the libretto that this sufficed for an entr'acte.

Act 3 begins peacefully. Believing Idamante to be at sea, Ilia prays for his safety and asks the breezes to convey her still suppressed feelings to him (aria, 'Zeffiretti lusinghieri'). But he appears; taken off guard, she admits her love and they embrace (duet, 'S'io non moro'). They are surprised by Idomeneo and Elettra; Idamante, banished by his father and feeling himself at fault, prepares to depart, determined to kill the monster or die in the attempt. This critical point in the drama is conveyed by its highest musical achievement, the wonderful quartet ('Andrò, ramingo e solo'). Arbace surveys the suffering of Crete and begs for the King and Prince to be spared (recitative, 'Sventurata Sidon'; aria, 'Se colà ne' fati è scritto').

The scene changes to a public square. The high priest confronts the King (recitative, 'Volgi intorno lo sguardo'): he must name the victim. Idomeneo, broken, admits that it is his son; the awed Cretans are deeply moved (chorus, 'O voto tremendo'). To a ritual march, the scene changes to the temple of Neptune. Idomeneo leads the prayer ('Accogli, o re del mar'). A jubilant cry is heard offstage; Idamante has killed the monster. But when he enters ('Padre, mio caro padre'), he is robed for sacrifice, and begs his father to fulfil the terrible vow for the sake of the people. His only regret is in leaving Ilia (aria, 'Nò, la morte io non pavento'). At the moment of sacrifice, Ilia intervenes, offering her own life instead. The confusion is ended by the oracle announcing the remission of the sacrifice. Idomeneo must abdicate; Idamante will reign in his place, with Ilia as his consort. Only Elettra is left out of the happy ending, and she lets us know it (recitative and aria, 'D'Oreste, d'Aiace'). Idomeneo addresses his people for the last time (recitative, 'Popoli! a voi l'ultima legge') and welcomes retirement (aria, 'Torna la pace al core'). There is a brisk final chorus ('Scenda amor') followed by a ballet.

4. Genre, music and characterization

Idomeneo is not a traditional opera seria, consisting almost entirely of arias, like Mozart's MITRIDATE and LUCIO SILLA; nor does it just add ensembles and chorus to an opera seria framework to make 'a real opera', as was to occur with LA CLEMENZA DI TITO. Its origin and generic background derive from two different and related elements: French *tragédie lyrique* and Italian reform opera. Both genres were devoted, as opera seria was not, to subjects taken from classical mythology and consequently requiring elaborate decoration and machinery to bring about a visual analogue to the supernatural elements in the plot, which the French called the 'marvellous'. Deeply influenced by the French model, and imitating some of its forms and greater orchestral elaboration, Italian reform opera nevertheless retained the simple and orchestral recitative styles, the advanced musical language, and the cantabile singing style of opera seria, while reducing the number of arias, varying their forms, and incorporating song, chorus and dance into a simpler dramatic framework.

The first stirrings of reform are found in works mostly written outside Italy by Jommelli, Traetta and GLUCK, although Traetta's reform operas began at Parma, whose court had intimate connections with France. In Stuttgart and Mannheim (Jommelli), and Vienna (Traetta and Gluck), the reform flourished in courtly opera houses where the principal patrons, including Karl Theodor, were interested in high rather than popular art; but only Gluck's *Orfeo ed Euridice* had much international success and that usually with alterations to suit local taste. When Gluck grafted his ideas back onto the French stem with his series of operas written for Paris from 1774, however, the reform became commercially successful.

Mozart had been aware of this operatic tendency since he saw Gluck's *Alceste* as a boy in Vienna. The choral scene with solo (Giunia), exceptional within *Lucio Silla* (Act I) is a typical product of reform. Mozart later witnessed Gluck's French reforms at first hand in Paris in 1778, and their adaptation to Italian taste by Piccinni; he knew Holzbauer's attempt to develop this tradition in German (*Günther von Schwarzburg*). *Idomeneo* follows operas by Traetta and Gluck in being based on an old French libretto (such revivals became common in France itself from the 1750s) and *Idomeneo* benefited from Mozart's earlier experience with serious opera (including IL RE PASTORE) and from his experiments with orchestral expression underlying spoken text (melodrama) in ZAIDE, the unfinished opera which preceded *Idomeneo*. But perhaps the greatest stimulus to the extraordinary richness of the music was frustration: at not having had an opera performed since 1775, and at not having been asked to write one for Mannheim or Paris.

In Munich, *Idomeneo* ended with a magnificent ballet, for which Mozart composed the music; it was usual for this task to be confided to someone else, and he was pleased to be able to control the whole evening's entertainment and afford it a unity. This he did, in part, by emphasizing the key of D major in the superb Chaconne (the ballet music is catalogued separately as K367; it is uncertain how much of it was actually performed).

An unusual feature of *Idomeneo* is that every act ends with the same keynote. D major was the key most brilliant for strings while equally suited to trumpets and timpani. Other significant sections employ this key, notably Idomeneo's central aria 'Fuor del mar' and his recitative in defiance of the gods. However, Act I proper ends with Idamante's second aria, in F major, and D is restored only in the entr'acte; Act 2 ends in D minor. Another instance of D minor is Elettra's first aria, 'Tutte nel cor vi sento'. In a striking musical, as well as theatrical, coup, Mozart reaches the recapitulation in C minor before modulating back to the home key; then he modulates without changing speed into the music of the tempest, also in C minor and making use of a similar motif to the aria. Elettra is thereby identified with the storm which breaks out with renewed fury, in C minor, in her final aria, 'D'Oreste, d'Aiace', as she compares herself to the Greek heroes most noted for being driven mad by the furies.

Idomeneo's first aria, nominally in C major, is deeply coloured by C minor. The relative key of C minor, E flat, is used for Ilia's central statement, 'Se il padre perdei', which is musically linked to the recitative preceding 'Fuor del mar', for the great quartet, and for Idomeneo's speech of abdication. Thus a large part of the opera relates to these two key-complexes that are brought into close relationship at critical points. It is also noteworthy that Idamante tends to sing in B flat at each entrance, and this is the key of his first aria. But his third aria, when he heroically wills his own sacrificial death, is in D major, whereas Idomeneo's last aria is in B flat, the exchange of keys reflecting their exchange of roles. Among other tonalities employed, E major stands out for its use as a sign of serenity, in the chorus 'Placido è il mar' and in Ilia's third aria; while Ilia's first aria is part of a great series for suffering women in which Mozart used the key of G minor.

A tonal design has been identified in Act 1, and in Act 2 a progression by fifths has been detected, interrupted by the E major of 'Placido è il mar' and destroyed by the tempest: where the progression would imply a descent from F to B flat, it founders in F minor and the stupendous passage representing the people in panic, which is almost atonal, emerges arbitrarily into D for Idomeneo's confession. The last act, in which no such systems have been identified, is equally effective dramatically; the case for the significance, rather than the existence, of tonal organization in Mozart operas will no doubt continue to be the subject of debate.

Another feature of *Idomeneo* often remarked upon is the permeation of the musical texture by a few short motifs, one of which in particular has been identified with Idamante and the sacrifice. A handful of occurrences might have been fortuitous, but the total is nearer thirty; the motif often appears at the mention of Idamante, as in Ilia's first aria, and in the third-act duet when she says 'You will be my husband.' It is prominent at the end of the overture and versions of it appear as Idomeneo gains land, in Elettra's second-act aria in which she apostrophizes Idamante, when Idomeneo names Idamante as the victim, and in Idomeneo's final recitative in which he abdicates in favour of his son. The vigorous ascending arpeggio that opens the overture also recurs at crucial moments in the drama, such as the recognition and the introduction to the High Priest's speech. A sensitive turning motif seems to relate to the restoration of peace, and the reconciliation of the human and divine orders whose discord brought about the entire plot; it too figures in Idomeneo's abdication speech.

The latter is an example of orchestrally accompanied recitative (*recitativo obbligato*), which in *Idomeneo* reaches an extreme stage in Mozart's work. Indeed, in cutting the Act 3 arias (see below), Mozart ended with an extended sequence of ensemble, chorus, a march and recitative, of which a strikingly high proportion is orchestrated. Gluck himself hardly suppressed the solo voice as much; however, he had already orchestrated all the recitatives in *Orfeo*. What singles out *Idomeneo* is the unrivalled richness of motivic allusion in the recitative accompaniments (which even affects some of the *recitativo semplice*, accompanied by continuo alone), and the harmony. Disturbing chromatic harmonies are a feature from the first recitative, Ilia's solo, moving quickly when she thinks of Elettra. In the second scene, in *recitativo semplice*, Idamante's bitterness at his chilly reception by Ilia brings a tonal shock (following E minor, the substitution of C minor for C major). Tonal deliquescence affects the *recitativo semplice* when Arbace announces the death of Idomeneo and the orchestral recitative before Elettra's aria, reaching a climax when Ilia interrupts the sacrifice and declares that the gods want her as a victim instead of Idamante.

This thrilling passage leads directly to the pronouncement of the oracle, for which Mozart specified trombones, or meant to. He composed four versions of this speech; probably the one performed was the only one without trombones, as Count Seeau considered it an expense too far to hire these instruments for a couple of minutes. The trombones are a sign of the sacred, the numinous, and echo another opera dependent on an oracle, Gluck's *Alceste*. The richness of woodwind writing extends far beyond the obbligatos in Ilia's aria, where soloists, more eloquent than virtuosic, dialogue with the voice (quite differently from the instrumental solos in 'Marten aller Arten' in *Die Entführung* or the aria added for Idamante in 1786). Searching for special sonorities, Mozart had trumpet mutes sent over from Salzburg for the Act 2 march; and for the first time he was able to deploy clarinets, to particularly lovely effect in the E major pieces 'Placido è il mar' and 'Zeffiretti lusinghieri'. The string writing, too, is richly inventive, from the filigree-work that adds depth to Idomeneo's abdication speech, to the brilliance of the closing chaconne.

This richness would avail nothing, however, without strength of plot and characterization. Although Varesco's libretto is too long and conventional in language and versification, it is a solid structure, adapting the Baroque French original to the requirements of the Metastasian moral drama favoured by the ENLIGHTENMENT. The characters are as vivid as possible within a mythical framework, particularly, as so often in Mozart, the women. Ilia and Elettra represent opposite effects of love: Ilia willing to sacrifice herself, Elettra so jealous she would prefer Idamante to die rather than love her rival: 'O qual contrasto', as she mutters on seeing Ilia fling herself between Idamante and the sacrificial knife. The music brings out every nuance of tenderness in Ilia, and balances the STURM UND DRANG vehemence of Elettra's minor-key arias with the chilly possessiveness of her second-act 'Idol mio' (in G major, scored for strings only). Yet these mettlesome princesses are equally proud of their ancestry, something perhaps hinted in the chromatic ascent towards the cadence in Ilia's first aria and at the same point, with more vehemence than pathos, in Elettra's 'D'Oreste, d'Aiace'. (Vastly augmented, this chromatic slide introduces the frighteningly desolate C minor chorus, 'Già regna la morte'.)

Idamante's arias are sometimes considered weak, but they entirely suit the characterization of the young prince. He matures more than any other character, as is seen in his merging with the musical languages of Ilia and Idomeneo in the third-act duet and quartet, which he leads and concludes. Mozart had to keep his arias relatively simple, and may not have been sorry to maintain momentum in the sacrifice scene by omitting 'No, la morte'. Idomeneo's arias reveal the tact with which Mozart accommodated the elderly Raaff. The first, 'Vedrommi intorno', is a movingly expressive vision of the sacrificial victim returning to haunt him; the second, 'Fuor del mar', is an essay in Baroque heroism, updated in style, with brilliant contrapuntal virtuosity in the orchestra, and providing opportunities for vocal display that enhance the expression of defiance. The final aria crowns the work with mellowness; Daniel Heartz has demonstrated how in tailoring it to Raaff, Mozart also paid tribute to the tenor's favourite composer, HASSE.

The most powerful being in *Idomeneo* scarcely appears. Neptune is seen in a short 'Pantomime', during the chorus of despairing sailors, receiving Idomeneo's vow. He is heard in the speech of the oracle, which Mozart wanted to be kept as short as possible, claiming (from recent experience with SCHIKANEDER's troupe in Salzburg) that the ghost's speech in *Hamlet* would be more effective if it were shorter. Yet Neptune is ubiquitous; everything stems from his wrath and his willingness to accept propitiation by the sacrifice of Idamante, or, finally, by the proffered self-sacrifice of Ilia: the oracle proclaims that 'Love has conquered'. The supernatural gives rise to the most extraordinary music in all three acts, appropriately as the underlying theme of the opera is the necessary balance between earthly and divine.

5. Revision and reception

Whatever his grand design, Mozart yielded to the demands of theatricality even before the first performance. Since the ballet could not be omitted, the opera was far too long, particularly its final act. He therefore cut the last three arias, for Idamante, Elettra and Idomeneo himself. He had expanded the recitative ('Sventurata Sidon') before Arbace's second aria because Panzacchi was a good actor. But the leisurely progress Varesco made through the crucial scenes of recognition, in Act 1, and sacrifice, in Act 3, given that neither of the original singers could act well, led to further cuts in the recitative. Idamante's aria may have been restored, but not Idomeneo's, despite the trouble Mozart had taken to fit both text and music to Raaff's requirements. Mozart prepared a shorter recitative for Elettra so that she could still leave sensationally after the oracle.

Mozart's first thoughts about a revision, soon after his arrival in Vienna, were never implemented; he left no notation making Idomeneo into a baritone or bass. In 1786, however, Idamante was sung by a tenor, Baron Pulini, and while much of the role need not be affected by the change of octave, Mozart carefully recomposed the trio and quartet, and substituted a new third-act duet with Ilia ('Spiegarti non poss'io', K489; this retains the 'Idamante motif'). Mozart composed a new recitative and aria for Pulini ('Non temer, amato bene', K490), including a violin obbligato for COUNT HATZFELD. Countess Hatzfeld (the violinist's sister-in-law and a star among Viennese amateurs) sang Elettra, and Anna von Pufendorf was Ilia. A shortened version of 'Fuor del mar' omitting the most challenging coloratura was once thought to have been made to assist Raaff; in fact it was for Giuseppe Antonio Bridi, later known as the finest amateur tenor in Vienna, but only twenty-two in 1786.

Otherwise the 1786 performance confirmed the Munich cuts, while also removing Arbace's recitative and arias. The only change in dramatic pace results from the new aria, placed at the start of Act 2, in which Idamante makes his feelings plain to Ilia; this if anything undercuts her subsequent aria, 'Se il padre perdei'. The new aria is in the rondò form Mozart exploited in all his operas from 1786, with an elaborate violin obbligato; both form and idiom make it stand out ineffectively from its surroundings. Another drawback is that this, Idamante's third aria, follows his second, which ends Act 1, too closely. The words, of unknown authorship, were used again for a finer setting, K505, with piano obbligato, composed for Nancy STORACE and known as 'Ch'io mi scordi di te' from the first words Idamante sings in recitative.

Modern performances usually reject the tenor version, and must balance the advantage of having Idomeneo and his son sing in different registers against the drawback of having a female take the heroic role (not an uncommon choice in the eighteenth century). What is unforgivable is to have a tenor sing the original version an octave lower, disregarding Mozart's careful recomposition of the trio and quartet.

While it remains hard to determine exactly what music was performed in Munich (the three performances may have differed in detail), the original version as planned possesses an integrity that the Vienna version lacks. It is not surprising that none of it was published in the composer's lifetime; it is more remarkable that three vocal scores were marketed before 1800. The next revival, in German, was at Kassel in 1802, followed by Vienna and Berlin in 1806. *Idomeneo* was known on many German stages during the nineteenth century, usually performed in German and severely cut. The first French and British productions had to wait until the twentieth century.

Idomeneo was widely mistaken for an opera seria, and certain adaptations, paradoxically, aimed to enhance precisely those elements that it already possessed and that differentiate it from that once-despised genre. To modernize *Idomeneo* in the light of Wagnerian symphonic opera seems to have been the objective of Ernst Lewicki, whose version was performed in 1917 and 1925, and two experienced opera composers, Richard Strauss and Ermanno Wolf-Ferrari, whose versions (among other productions) marked the opera's 150th anniversary in 1931. Even after 1950, some productions used greatly altered texts. It is only recently that *Idomeneo* has been felt not to require any apology, so that today both the Italian language and, increasingly, the Munich score have been restored, particularly in recordings, often running to a greater length than in any performance supervised by Mozart. While never likely to become a repertory piece, *Idomeneo* can now be properly valued as one of Mozart's most remarkable achievements. JULIAN RUSHTON

Bayerische Staatsbibliothek, *Wolfgang Amadeus Mozart: Idomeneo 1781–1981* (Munich, 1981)
P. Gallarati, *La forza delle parole: Mozart drammaturgo* (Turin, 1993)
D. Heartz, *Mozart's Operas*, ed. T. Bauman (Berkeley, 1990)
R. Münster, 'Neues zum Münchener *Idomeneo* 1781', *Acta Mozartiana* 25 (1982), 10–20
J. Platoff, 'Writing about Influences: *Idomeneo*, a Case Study', in *Explorations in Music, the Arts, and Ideas: Essays in Honor of Leonard B. Meyer*, ed. E. Narmour and R. Solie (New York, 1980)
J. Rushton, *W. A. Mozart: Idomeneo* (with contributions from S. Sadie, M. Everist, C. Walton, D. Neville, C. Ayrey) (Cambridge, 1993)

Internationale Stiftung Mozarteum. The Internationale Stiftung Mozarteum (ISM) was founded thanks to the efforts of SALZBURG's inhabitants, who in 1841 participated in the creation of the Dom-Musik-Verein und Mozarteum under the auspices of Mozart's widow CONSTANZE MOZART, and her two sons CARL THOMAS MOZART and FRANZ XAVER WOLFGANG MOZART. The first aim of the society was to create a school of music to organize concerts in Salzburg, using the best students and their teachers. In 1844 Franz Xaver Wolfgang Mozart stipulated in his will that 'the manuscripts and fragments of music written by his illustrious father, which form part of his legacy, together with sundry family documents, the family portrait and other portraits, and also the keyboard on which the great Mozart composed the celebrated works of his last years, together with his complete library, should be given to the Mozarteum to erect a lasting monument to the memory of his father'. The manuscripts and music fragments form the basis of the ISM's Bibliotheca Mozartiana (Mozart Library), while the musical instruments and portraits are some of the jewels of the two Mozart museums in Salzburg.

In 1858, scores and the voice and piano arrangements of the operas and singspiels were added: these were part of Carl Mozart's legacy, and became known as 'Mozarts Nachlass' (Mozart's estate). After the separation of the Mozarteum and the Dom-Musik-Verein in 1880, the ISM saw a rapid development, immediately opening a conservatory over which it presided until 1922 and for which it had a building called the Mozarteum constructed. This building, erected between 1910 and 1914 by the MUNICH architect Richard Berndl (1875–1955) in Salzburg's *Jugendstil*, comprises lecture rooms, two concert halls, administrative offices and a library.

A concert-organizing body was responsible for the first 'musical festival' in Salzburg in 1877. These musical festivals can be seen as precursors of the SALZBURG FESTIVAL; in 1906, the Vienna Philharmonic Orchestra and the Vienna Opera were engaged for the first time. The concerts committee now puts on a substantial programme all the year round, and the Mozart Week, which has formed the climax of each musical season since 1956, takes place at the end of January and the beginning of February, to coincide with the composer's birthday.

The seat of the ISM was established in Salzburg and has always had as its aim the cultivation and promulgation of Mozart's music (as well as music more generally). Its main endeavour is to collect as completely as possible artefacts connected with Mozart, to establish the Mozart Archive, to keep up to date the constantly expanding Bibliotheca Mozartiana, to encourage research into Mozart, and to preserve buildings connected with him, in particular his birthplace at Getreidegasse 9, his second home (the Wohnhaus, restored and partly reconstructed in 1996, at Makartplatz 8), the *Magic Flute* hut in the garden of the Mozarteum, and the commemorative museum in St Gilgen, not forgetting the building of the Mozarteum itself. The ISM is chiefly responsible for the most complete edition of Mozart's works (the NEUE MOZART-AUSGABE or NMA), for other publications and activities designed to deepen our knowledge of Mozart's life and work, and for maintaining the collaboration with the Hochschule für Musik und darstellende Kunst (College of Music and Representational Art, an institution which has borne the name Mozarteum since 1970), in periodically organizing, among other events, an international Mozart competition.

In addition to organizing concerts throughout the year and within the framework of the Mozart Week, enriching the Bibliotheca Mozartiana, seeking out all the current publications, and buying Mozart autographs (when market conditions permit), the work of the ISM focuses more particularly on the Mozart museums (Mozart's Birthplace and the Mozart Wohnhaus) and on the Mozart Ton- und Film-Sammlung (Mozart Collection of Film and Sound, recently opened in the Wohnhaus). By 2005 this new museum had about 19,000 sound and video recordings; it offers eight listening posts and eight video booths, each for two people, and a film projection room capable of accommodating forty people. The ISM possesses a huge collection of theatrical and iconographical documentation and regularly organizes exhibitions on Mozartian themes.

The Akademie für Mozart-Forschung (Academy for Mozart Research), comprising musicologists of international renown, is the research arm of the ISM, organizing workshops and international conferences. The ISM is currently overseeing the completion of the NMA and the production of a series of digital recordings of Mozart works on original instruments owned by the composer, using soloists of international renown. Since 1993 a bibliography can be consulted at www.mozarteum.at, under 'Wissenschaft', 'Bibliotheca Mozartiana'.

The ISM maintains privileged links with c.eighty Mozart associations operating under its auspices in twenty-six countries worldwide, and has about 1,000 regular members and patrons. It publishes an annual musicological journal, the *Mozart-Jahrbuch*. Since 1975 the ISM has published, in conjunction with the *Mozart-Jahrbuch*, a Mozart bibliography, which is updated every five years. The ISM is also preparing the *Digital Mozart Edition* (DME), which is housed at the NMA website, www.nma.at.

The Bibliotheca Mozartiana, at the centre of Mozartian research, has collected practically all the international Mozart literature (c.27,000 titles); it also collects original and early editions of Mozart, and possesses a vast holding of autographs: around 700 Mozart family letters (c.190 by Mozart, 370 by Leopold, and the rest by Mozart's mother, by NANNERL MOZART, by Constanze Mozart and GEORG NIKOLAUS NISSEN, and by Mozart's sons); it also preserves about a hundred musical autographs, of which about sixty are sketches of great interest for musicological research.

GENEVIEVE GEFFRAY (Trans. RUTH HALLIWELL)

R. Angermüller and G. Rech, eds., *Hundert Jahre Internationale Stiftung Mozarteum Salzburg. 1880–1980* (Kassel, 1980)

Karl Wagner, *Das Mozarteum. Geschichte und Entwicklung einer kulturellen Institution* (Innsbruck, 1993)

Ippold, Franz Armand d' (b. Doxan, near Leitmeritz, c.1730; d. Salzburg, 25 Feb. 1790). SALZBURG neighbour of the Mozarts and unsuccessful suitor of NANNERL MOZART; captain in the imperial and royal army, then director of the Virgilianum (the school for noble boys) in Salzburg from 1775, and in 1777 (additionally) court war councillor. D'Ippold and Nannerl wanted to marry, but there was a hindrance of unknown nature. Mozart wrote to Nannerl from VIENNA on 19 September 1781 urging her to persuade d'Ippold to move to Vienna to work – LEOPOLD MOZART could then retire and move with them. Nothing came of this suggestion, probably because Leopold refused to allow anything so financially risky. After Nannerl's marriage in 1784, her first child ('Leopoldl') lived with Leopold in Salzburg from his birth in 1785. D'Ippold continued to visit Leopold, becoming very attached to the baby. When Leopold died in 1787, it was d'Ippold who wrote to tell Mozart the news. Mozart then asked him to represent his interests in the settlement of Leopold's estate, but in the event Johann Joseph Anton Ernst GILOWSKY von Urazowa did this. It is usually assumed that d'Ippold declined to act in a way that set him legally against Nannerl.

RUTH HALLIWELL

R. Halliwell, *The Mozart Family: Four Lives in a Social Context* (Oxford, 1998)

J

Jacquin family. (Emilian) Gottfried von Jacquin (b. 1767; d. Vienna, 24 Jan. 1792) worked at the court chancellery in VIENNA; his friendship with Mozart probably dates from before 1783. It seems likely that Mozart helped Jacquin, an amateur composer and singer, with several compositions, or at least that he composed some works jointly with him; these include the six *notturni* K346 and K436–9. And in 1791 Gottfried published under his name six songs, two of which were composed by Mozart: *Als Luise die Briefe ihres ungetreuen Liebhabers verbrannte*, K520, and *Das Traumbild*, K530. Mozart composed the aria *Mentre ti lascio, o figlia*, K513 for Gottfried; and according to CONSTANZE MOZART's letter of 25 May 1799, Gottfried wrote the aria *Io ti lascio, o cara, addio*, K621a – only the violin parts are by Mozart. Gottfried's sister, Franziska (1769–1850) was a keyboard student of Mozart's; it was for her that he wrote the so-called 'Kegelstatt' trio for clarinet, viola and piano, K498, and the piano duet sonata K521. CLIFF EISEN

H. Kraus, 'W. A. Mozart und die Familie Jacquin', *Zeitschrift für Musikwissenschaft* 15 (1932–3), 155–68

Jenamy, Victoire (b. 1749; d. 1812). French pianist, daughter of J. G. NOVERRE. A first-rate pianist, Jenamy, the daughter of Mozart's friend, the ballet master J. G. Noverre, commissioned from him the piano concerto K271 (January 1777). In their letters, Mozart and his father variously refer to her as 'jenomy' and 'Madame genomai'; until recently she was supposed to be an unidentified French virtuosa, dubbed by the French scholars Théodore de Wyzewa and Georges de Saint-Foix 'Jeunehomme'. CLIFF EISEN

Jeunehomme, 'Jeunehomme' Concerto. See JENAMY and CONCERTOS

Joseph II, Joseph(in)ism. Joseph II (b. Vienna, 13 Mar. 1741, d. Vienna, 20 Feb. 1790), the eldest son of MARIA THERESIA and her husband, Francis Stephen of Lorraine (grand-duke of Tuscany from 1737, Holy Roman Emperor as Francis I, 1745–65), became emperor when his father died on 18 August 1765 and a month later was made (as his father had been) co-regent of the AUSTRIAN monarchy. On his mother's death on 29 November 1780 Joseph became the sole ruler of the monarchy. He was married twice: first, happily, to Isabella (Elisabeth) of Parma from 1760 to 1763, and then, miserably, to Josepha of Bavaria from 1765 to 1767. He thereafter refused to marry again; his only child, a daughter, died in 1770, so his brother LEOPOLD II succeeded him.

He has been generally regarded as one of the three chief exemplars of 'Enlightened despotism' or 'Enlightened absolutism', the other two being Frederick the

Great of Prussia (r. 1740–86) and Catherine the Great of Russia (r. 1762–96). Few people have called Joseph 'the Great', but in compensation he has had a programme or movement named after him, 'Joseph(in)ism'.

1. Joseph's activity before 1781
2. Joseph's sole reign
3. Joseph(in)ism
4. Joseph II and Mozart

1. Joseph's activity before 1781

As heir to the lands of the Austrian Habsburg dynasty – its first male heir to survive infancy in the eighteenth century – Archduke Joseph was given an excessively elaborate education in the duties of rulers to God and to their subjects, in the highly complex constitution of the monarchy, in the languages he would need for its administration (German, French, Italian, Latin and 'Slav') and in soldiering. It was understood that, like his mother and her predecessors, he would himself govern his lands as an 'absolute' ruler with the power to make laws – except, according to the Hungarians and Belgians, in their provinces, whose ancient constitutions insisted on the right of the Diet (in Hungary) or Estates (in the Netherlands) to approve or reject royal legislation). It was also presumed that, following his father's example, and in hopes of emulating the victories of Austria's great enemy, Frederick the Great, Joseph would personally command his armies in the event of war.

He was first given the opportunity to influence the monarchy's policy when he was called to sit in on the meetings of the newly created Council of State (*Staatsrat*) in 1761. This was a unique body, with strictly limited and defined membership, in principle excluding executive ministers and concerned solely with considering and advising on policy questions. It was the brain-child of the powerful chief minister, count (after 1763 prince) WENZEL ANTON VON KAUNITZ(-RIETBERG) (1711–94, state chancellor or *Staatskanzler* 1753–92), who saw it as a mechanism for planning the domestic reform of the monarchy as a whole in order to modernize it and enable it to succeed in war and diplomacy. The Council had been founded at a critical time, when it was becoming clear that the Austrian attempt to destroy Prussia in the war begun in 1756 was doomed to failure, leaving the monarchy bankrupt. As had evidently been expected by those who knew him, the young Archduke at once showed himself a headstrong proponent of radical reform. His extremism was best shown in a document so shocking that it was kept strictly secret for more than a century, his *Rêveries* (reflections) of 1763. In it he declared his aim of procuring 'the absolute power to be in a position to do all possible good to the state'. For the sake of establishing a big enough army, he demanded an end to the exemptions from taxation enjoyed by the nobility and by some provinces, proposing to 'humble and impoverish the grandees' and to persuade the provinces that they should accept 'despotism' for ten years. In this and other early manifestos he expressed his conviction that the state's servants were too numerous, lazy and overpaid, and signalled his almost pathological revulsion from pomp, ceremony and display. Although he later dissembled some of these views, he never abandoned them.

His father's death increased his influence, but only in certain areas. As emperor he had no standing in the monarchy, and the terms of the co-regency left Maria Theresia's sovereignty intact. She felt it necessary to put Joseph in charge of the army, where he forced through changes that greatly increased its size and somewhat improved its efficiency. Throughout his life he made a point of attending at least one military camp a year, and in the War of the Bavarian Succession in 1778, as in the war against the Turks in 1788, he commanded his armies in the field – though with little success. Under Maria Theresia he played a considerable role too in foreign policy and was partly responsible for the Austrian annexation of Galicia in the first partition of Poland in 1772, and of the Bukovina from Turkey in 1775. But his attempt to exchange Belgium for Bavaria in 1778–9 led to an inconclusive war and only a very small territorial gain, the *Innviertel* on the Austro-Bavarian border.

Internally, the Empress refused to make the fundamental changes Joseph proposed, but she made many concessions to his vehement and bitter demands, backed up as they were by the unrivalled knowledge he acquired on his extensive travels within the monarchy and to Italy, France and (in 1780) Russia. His main domestic achievements during her lifetime were to cut down drastically the cost and elaboration of the court, to establish in VIENNA a so-called 'national theatre' in 1776 and, in collaboration with Prince Kaunitz, to obtain her consent to important reforms affecting religion and the Church.

The significance of these changes can be understood only if it is realized how pervasive the influence of religion and the Roman Catholic Church was within the monarchy, especially before the 1750s. The consolidation of the Habsburgs' power in Austria and Bohemia had been carried through in the seventeenth century in ardent collaboration with the resurgent Catholic Church of the Counter-Reformation, and particularly with the Jesuits. When, after the raising of the Turkish siege of Vienna in 1683, the monarchy conquered Hungary and Transylvania, the war was represented as a Christian crusade against Islam. Vienna formally agreed to measures of toleration towards Protestant and Greek Orthodox in these new lands, but both Charles VI (1711–40) and Maria Theresia regarded the conversion of Protestants and other heretics to Catholicism as a necessary goal of the state, and were not too scrupulous in their methods of promoting it. The Church, chiefly in the persons of Jesuits, was in control of the universities and of a strict censorship. Nearly all education at lower levels was in the hands of the clergy. Great monasteries dominated the Estates of the Austrian and Belgian lands. Most of Austria belonged to dioceses whose bishops had their cathedrals outside the Habsburgs' territories and were therefore difficult for the government in Vienna to control.

As throughout Catholic Europe, from around 1750 the rulers of Austria came to regard the Church as the major obstacle to the state's carrying through essential modernizing reforms. They also found the Church an easier target than the nobility. It is difficult to apportion responsibility for the programme of reform between Maria Theresia, Kaunitz and Joseph. The devout Empress certainly wanted to restrict the power of the Jesuits, whose casuistical theology and vow of obedience to the Pope she deplored, and in 1759 she took away their monopoly of professorships and the censorship. More generally, her hope was that, by reforming the Church, it could be made more effective in proselytization. In the late 1760s Kaunitz began to offer her more radical advice, arguing both for a reduction of the number of monks and nuns, partly on economic grounds, and for the explicit subordination of the Church to the state. Joseph supported these proposals but, unlike Kaunitz, was a pious Catholic who cared deeply that the pastoral provision of the Church should be improved. Kaunitz and the Emperor both favoured a degree of religious toleration that Maria Theresia was unable to reconcile with her conscience. During the period of the co-regency a small number of monasteries were suppressed in Lombardy and Galicia; the age at which binding monastic vows could be taken was raised to twenty-four; and, after the Pope had suppressed the Jesuits at the instance of other Catholic powers in 1773, the state set about promoting a new and more effective educational system less dominated by the Church. It even laid down what was to be taught in the theology courses of the universities.

2. Joseph's sole reign

Maria Theresia's legislative activity surpassed that of her predecessors, but in the nine years of his reign Joseph averaged nearly seven times as many enactments per annum as his mother. Revealing his hostility to the nobility, he accorded the serfs certain personal rights and at the time of his death was trying to push through a fundamental reform of the whole seigneurial system. This involved a redistribution of the tax burden so that nobles paid rather more and peasants rather less. Whereas she had treated Hungary and Belgium circumspectly and kept him from meddling in their affairs, after his accession he at once set about making their administration as similar to that of the other provinces as possible. He treated their constitutions as absurd antiquarian survivals, refused to be crowned King of Hungary and gave gratuitous offence by removing the crown to Vienna. In 1784, in the interests of homogeneity and modernization, he replaced Latin by German as the language of Hungarian administration.

Over the whole monarchy he imposed a much more radical church policy than his mother's. He suppressed all monasteries of purely contemplative Orders, and all other houses that could not show themselves to be 'useful', which normally meant in providing parish priests. Altogether he dissolved more than a third of the 2,000 houses in the monarchy. He abolished all brotherhoods and applied their property, like that of the dissolved monasteries, to other charitable purposes. He created several bishoprics and hundreds of new parishes. Church services were simplified. Marriage was made a civil contract. It was decreed that all those wishing to become priests must be trained in a small number of general seminaries organized by the state, with a standard curriculum. In 1781–2 a measure of toleration was conceded to the main Protestant denominations, the Greek Orthodox and the Jews. He transformed the censorship rules, making it possible for many works hitherto condemned by Church and State to be published and releasing a 'flood of pamphlets', many of them strongly anticlerical. The pope and his cardinals thought Joseph's legislation constituted the greatest threat to the Church since the Reformation and in 1782 Pius VI made the first papal journey out of Italy since the sixteenth century in order to reason with the Emperor – but to very little effect.

In foreign policy he was equally restless. He tried a second time to exchange Bavaria for Belgium, achieving nothing except to provoke strong hostility from other powers and within Germany. The alliance he made in 1781 with Catherine of Russia led to him being drawn into a war against the Turks in 1787. In the following year he led his troops against them in an inglorious campaign that shattered his health.

All his reforming was done too quickly and with no or little consultation. While Joseph was paying his second visit to Russia in 1787, Brabant, the most important of the Belgian provinces, staged its first rebellion. Concessions seemed to calm the situation but, despite the costs and demands of the Turkish war, the Emperor soon revived his policy of centralization. When the Estates and courts of Brabant and other Belgian provinces refused to accept his administrative reforms, he declared 'I do not need your consent to do good' and abolished the old constitutions. But the bankruptcy of the French government and the Revolution of 1789 rendered his other ally, Louis XVI, unable to assist him and permitted a Belgian rebellion, masterminded by its abbots, to drive out his troops at the end of that year – just after his forces in the east had taken the great prize of Belgrade from the Turks. Desperately ill with tuberculosis and threatened with revolt in Hungary backed by Prussia, he was at last persuaded by Kaunitz and others of the hopelessness of his 'grand project' and revoked nearly all his Hungarian and Belgian measures.

News of his death a few weeks later was greeted with relief by foreign governments, his ministers and many of his subjects. But he retained the gratitude and admiration of Protestants, Jews, Orthodox and serfs – and of those numerous petitioners of all classes whom he had received without ceremony day after day in the Hofburg or on his travels. The young BEETHOVEN's first significant large-scale piece, written in Bonn, was a setting of an ode on the death of Joseph II, part of which ran: 'A monster, whose name was Fanaticism, rose from the caverns of Hell . . . and it was night. Then came Joseph . . . dragged the frenzied monster down . . . and crushed it. Then mankind rose up into light.' The memory of Joseph's reign remained an inspiration to liberals and radicals during the period of severe repression that followed it.

3. Joseph(in)ism

(In German the term is Josephinismus or Josefinismus, in English traditionally Josephism, but nowadays commonly Josephinism.) The natural meaning of Josephism is 'the policies of Joseph and the principles they embody'. But modern historians using the term give it a different sense or range of senses, wider in some respects, narrower in others. The main writers on the subject agree more or less in defining it as a movement for change within the Austrian monarchy affecting many aspects of life, but especially associated with claims made and measures taken by the state to control and reform the Roman Catholic Church within its borders, involving not only obviously ecclesiastical matters like the exclusion of papal bulls, the dissolution of monasteries and the introduction of religious toleration but also wider issues such as the reform of education in all its aspects, the liberalization of censorship, the secularization of marriage and the reorganization of poor relief.

This is to carry the story of Josephism back at least to the early years of Maria Theresia, before Joseph had the slightest influence on policy, and forward at least to the 1840s, because much of the Emperor's legislation in these fields survived him. His successors, though they made important changes such as to strengthen policing and censorship, maintained the strict control of the Church by the state more or less as he had left it. It was in the 1830s that the term was coined, precisely in order to categorize the many surviving measures of Maria Theresia, Joseph and their successors that Metternich and other sympathizers with Catholic Reaction wished to see repealed. Their particular objection was to Joseph's establishment of civil marriage.

The principal historians of the subject have been Ferdinand Maass, who between 1951 and 1961 published *Der Josephinismus*, five substantial volumes of documents with commentary, ranging from 1760 to 1850 and focusing on Church–State relations; Eduard Winter, the second edition of whose book *Der Josefinismus*, published in 1962, had as its subtitle 'The History of Austrian Reform Catholicism' and who was chiefly interested in the changes observable in Catholic attitudes in Austria and Bohemia between 1740 and 1848; and Fritz Valjavec, the earliest of the three and the one to depart furthest from the original usage of the word, whose book of 1945, *Der Josephinismus*, treated it as a wider intellectual movement difficult to distinguish from the Austrian ENLIGHTENMENT. But if modern usage extends the chronological application of the term 'Josephism' and treats Joseph as part of a broader movement rather than confining the term to his personal contribution, it restricts the sense of the word in other ways. It limits Josephism to domestic policy, with principal reference to matters that in a broad sense concern the Church and religion. It is not usual to include discussion of his mitigation of serfdom under the heading 'Josephism' or his administrative and military reforms, still less his foreign policy and wars.

That Maria Theresia herself, her husband and her ministers, especially Kaunitz, took steps in some of the directions that Joseph later moved is indisputable; and it is important that much educated opinion across Catholic Europe and in the Austrian lands supported these tendencies in varying degrees. It is also plain that even Joseph, with all his energy and his absolute power, could not have been personally responsible for everything that was done during his sole reign; that Kaunitz's role was always significant, sometimes encouraging his master to press forward, at other times trying to hold him back; and that the Emperor could not have carried through his programme of ecclesiastical reform if he had not had a considerable body of supporters willing and ready to implement it. His successor, Leopold, while abandoning much of Joseph's legislation on serfdom, proved remarkably skilful at preserving the great mass of his brother's legislation in the ecclesiastical field. The bulk of the measures classed as Josephist were originally enacted during Joseph's sole reign, and no one who worked with him or observed him at close quarters during that period had any doubt that he was the prime mover. He informed the Pope that he had an inner voice telling him what it was right for him to do and not do as legislator and protector of religion. Secure in this conviction, he selected a particular group of measures from among those that were being suggested, and was strong-willed enough to impose the great majority of them on his subjects.

Josephism is sometimes seen as the Austrian monarchy's version of the Enlightenment, or of Enlightened despotism or absolutism. It is true that measures such as the enactment of religious toleration, the suppression of monasteries and the liberalization of the censorship unquestionably rank as Enlightened. In these respects Joseph went further than any other Catholic ruler of the day. He himself spoke of having encouraged Enlightenment, and a number of well-disposed civil servants and writers hailed him, down to the mid-1780s, as a philosopher-king. The imposition of reform from above runs counter to the usual perception of the Enlightenment in the United States, Britain and France, where it is identified with the growth of effective public opinion and representative government. But east of the Rhine, though there was a marked growth of public discussion, the only prospect of serious change, short of revolution, lay in the legislative power of absolute or despotic rulers. While despotism was generally regarded as a dirty word, some thinkers, like Joseph himself in his *Rêveries*, were prepared on occasion to give it a favourable sense. They often contrasted the beneficent power of the Enlightened ruler with the malign influence of others who, they said, could more properly be called despots, such as oppressive local lords and subordinate officials, and the Pope.

It is difficult too for modern writers to accept that a ruler could be beneficent who was as concerned as Joseph was (like Frederick and Catherine) to enhance the size of his army and increase the area of his state. Voltaire's reply to that objection was that, the more subjects an Enlightened ruler gained, the more people in the world would be happy. A more convincing reply might be that in the conditions of the eighteenth century a major state was expected, and perhaps needed to be, expansionist. Prominent among the motives of Joseph's (and Maria Theresia's) reforms was the desire to create an effective army with a view to security and perhaps aggrandizement. But many of the changes had no obvious relevance to those aims and cannot be explained without taking more benevolent motives into account.

4. Joseph II and Mozart

Joseph's musical knowledge and attainment were considerable. He played the piano, organ, violin and cello, and sang. When in Vienna, he set aside time each day to hear and play music. Since (subject to financial constraints) he controlled the court opera and since he enacted laws to simplify church services, his liking for German opera, opera buffa, *Harmoniemusik* and short and simple church music, together with his dislike of court entertainments, opera seria and ballets, set the pattern of Viennese music of the 1780s. His attitude to Mozart and his work has provoked much controversy. On the one hand it is asked how a discerning ruler-musician could have allowed such a genius, who had chosen to come to his court, to suffer financial hardship and die in penury. Joseph has been condemned for his remarks that DIE ENTFÜHRUNG AUS DEM SERAIL had too many notes and that Mozart's music was too difficult for the singers. On the other hand, he had shown the composer favour as long ago as 1768, encouraging him to write LA FINTA SEMPLICE and trying to get it staged in Vienna. After Mozart settled there, Joseph clearly advanced his career by the favour he showed him. We may regret that his policies ensured that Mozart wrote no opere serie between IDOMENEO and LA CLEMENZA DI TITO, that *Idomeneo* received only a private performance in Vienna, and that he wrote no large-scale church music during the reign except the Mass in C minor, K427, composed for a special occasion in Salzburg. But the Emperor personally engaged DA PONTE as librettist and encouraged the writing and production of Mozart's LE NOZZE DI FIGARO, DON GIOVANNI and COSÌ FAN TUTTE. In the case of *Figaro* he stretched one point to allow the text to be sung at all, and another to permit the inclusion of the ballet as an integral part of the action. He actually commissioned DER SCHAUSPIELDIREKTOR. At the end of 1787 he created a post for the composer, with limited duties, at a salary that most musicians would have considered generous, 'solely out of consideration that so rare a genius in the world of music should not be obliged to seek abroad for recognition and his daily bread'. The Emperor's quoted remarks were not in fact criticizing Mozart's music but scoffing at the failure of others to appreciate it.

In four texts set by Mozart the Emperor is praised by name, two of them attempts to enlist the Emperor as a patron of FREEMASONRY, and the other two patriotic songs written at the time of the Turkish war. Some of his dances celebrate victories against the Turks. Mozart liked Joseph's affable, unstuffy ways and Da Ponte called him 'this adorable prince'. Since the Emperor was careful with his money and had strong musical preferences, he was not an absolutely perfect patron for Mozart. But the composer was very fortunate to find in so powerful a ruler, presiding over the most musical city in Europe, a discriminating admirer. DEREK BEALES

D. Beales, *Joseph II, I: In the Shadow of Maria Theresa, 1741–1780* (Cambridge, 1987)
Enlightenment and Reform in Eighteenth-Century Europe (London, 2005)
T. C. W. Blanning, *Joseph II* (Harlow, 1994)
V. Braunbehrens, *Mozart in Vienna* (Oxford, 1991)
P. von Mitrofanov, *Joseph II: Seine politische und kulturelle Tätigkeit* (2 vols., Vienna, 1910)
H. M. Scott, ed., *Enlightened Absolutism* (London, 1990)
F. A. J. Szabo, *Kaunitz and Enlightened Absolutism, 1753–1780* (Cambridge, 1994)

K

Karl Theodor, Elector Palatine and Elector of Bavaria (b. Dorgenbos Castle, near Brussels, 11 Dec. 1724; d. Munich, 16 Feb. 1799). Karl Theodor became Elector Palatine in 1742 and Elector of Bavaria on 30 December 1777, succeeding his cousin MAXIMILIAN III JOSEPH. A flautist and cellist, Karl Theodor lavished attention on the MANNHEIM court music; under his leadership it was one of the outstanding centres for music in the eighteenth century. The court was particularly renowned for its orchestra, which LEOPOLD MOZART described as 'unquestionably the best in Germany' (letter of 19 July 1763). The Mozart children first played for Karl Theodor at his country home, Schwetzingen, in July 1763, and Mozart visited Mannheim twice in 1777 and 1778, first on the way to PARIS and then on the way home to SALZBURG. Although he hoped to gain an appointment at court, he was not successful; he was also unsuccessful in MUNICH in December 1778 after the Mannheim court's move there. Nevertheless, Karl Theodor must have been well disposed towards Mozart, whose IDOMENEO was first given at Munich in January 1781; Mozart wrote to his father that after hearing a rehearsal of Act 2, Karl Theodor said to him, 'Who would have believed that such great things could lodge in so small a head!' (27 Dec. 1780). Mozart met Karl Theodor once more, in Munich in early November 1790 when the composer was returning from LEOPOLD II's coronation festivities in Frankfurt; on this occasion he was invited to play at court on 4 or 5 November.

CLIFF EISEN

'Kegelstatt' trio. Mozart's Trio for Clarinet, Viola and Piano, K498 (5 Aug. 1786). See CHAMBER MUSIC: D. PIANO TRIOS

Kelly, Michael (William) (b. Dublin, 25 Dec. 1762; d. Margate, 9 Oct. 1826). Irish tenor, composer, theatre manager and music publisher. Kelly made his singing debut as the Count in Piccinni's *La buona figliuola* in 1777; from May 1781 to 1783 he was active in Italy. While in Venice, Kelly was recruited by Count Giacomo Durazzo for the newly created Italian opera company in VIENNA; he spent four years there, singing in operas by MARTÌN Y SOLER, PAISIELLO and Mozart. The roles of Don Basilio and Don Curzio in LE NOZZE DI FIGARO were written for him. Kelly's memoirs (ghosted by Theodore Hook in the early 1820s) are a valuable source of information about Mozart. Kelly, together with the STORACES and THOMAS ATTWOOD, left Vienna in early 1787, travelling by way of SALZBURG (where they visited LEOPOLD MOZART) to LONDON. There he established himself as the principal tenor at Drury Lane; from 1793 he was also stage manager at the King's Theatre, Haymarket. Numerous compositions by him also survive, including songs for various theatrical productions and the popular 'grand dramatic romance' *Blue Beard*. CLIFF EISEN

S. M. Ellis, *The Life of Michael Kelly, Musician, Actor and Bon Viveur* (London, 1930)
M. Kelly, *Reminiscences* (London, 1826)

Kirchgässner (Kirchgessner), Marianne (Mariane, Maria Anna) (Antonia) (b. Bruchsal, 5 June 1769; d. Schaffhausen, 9 Dec. 1808). German glass harmonica player. Blind from the age of four, Kirchgässner made several successful concerto tours as a glass harmonica virtuosa beginning in 1791 when she visited MUNICH, SALZBURG, Linz and VIENNA, where she gave a concert on 10 June. It was for her second concert, on 19 August, that Mozart composed the Adagio and Rondo, K617; the Adagio, K356, for solo glass harmonica, was also probably composed for her. Her death in 1808 was attributed to nerve damage caused by the vibrations of her instrument. CLIFF EISEN

K. M. Pisarowitz, 'Zum Bizentenar einer Blinden', *Acta mozartiana* 16 (1969), 72–5
H. Ullrich, *Die blinde Glasharmonikavirtuosin Mariane Kirchgessner und Wien: eine Künstlerin der empfindsamen Zeit* (Tutzing, 1971)

kitsch. Kitsch is a buzz word, coined in the 1870s, that is hard to define and even harder to set limits for: it implies the taking over of current means, forms and contents, and enriching them with exaggerated feelings. A. Moles believes that kitsch most affects the 'middle classes of a replete society', but according to Umberto Eco its meaning has changed because market forces are now moving in the direction of an art *industry*. Shops in museums, at exhibitions and at birthplaces offer related goods to a wide market, a practice rendering the boundary between art and kitsch so fluid that the definition is increasingly left to the judgement of the individual.

Thanks to his worldwide popularity, Mozart is a perfect example of limitless marketability, and this marketability applies not only to commerce, advertising and tourism, but to theatre, the film industry and politics as well. Today Mozart's name transcends all subject and national boundaries to which any specific attributes and definitions can be linked. Neither Mozart as a historical figure, nor his work, have anything to do with it. Mozart's music, the cause of his popularity, has to accommodate manipulations as gross as those endured by its creator: anything goes that promises success. And because the manufactured products are sought by so many special interest groups, and have to be tailored to the needs of these groups, the limits of good taste can no longer be established. The rococo dolls and china figures à la Mozart offered for sale in AUSTRIA and elsewhere, Austrian TV's 1985 advertisement 'Mozart with the ice-cream cornet', Leherb's poster to promote Austrian tourism in the 1980s (showing the *Wunderkind* roaring through the ether on a motorbike, woollen shawl flapping behind), and the widespread use of his name in the confectionery, cheese, spirits, clothing and tobacco industries – all these exemplify the point. Moreover, the broad spectrum of Mozart offers – postcards, stickers, placards, watches, commemorative coins, perfumes, calendars, cookery books and so on – are by no means offered only by enterprises far removed from art and music and driven purely by turnover: in addition to shops in museums and at exhibitions, there exists in SALZBURG the 'Mozart-Haus Handels- und Versandgesellschaft' (Mozart museums trade and export company). Behind it stands the august INTERNATIONALE STIFTUNG MOZARTEUM as a limited company, its name appearing in Salzburg's business register since 1990. It draws its profit from the sale of souvenirs in all tastes and sizes, and its annual turnover long ago surpassed 2 million shillings (c.£110,000/$200,000).

It is clear that behind the trade name of Mozart is the attempt to create a stereotypical image of the composer that will immediately spring to mind. And thanks to the worldwide dissemination of these products, a young man in knee breeches, white silk stockings, gala costume and plaited wig will always be identified as 'Mozart' rather than as EMPEROR JOSEPH II, JOSEPH HAYDN or the young Lord Nelson. Similarly, depictions of Mozart on stage and film have disseminated to a wide audience a few well-known episodes from Mozart's life, through constantly repeated anecdotes, thereby creating a clichéd fate for the composer: the *Wunderkind* playing the keyboard to MARIA THERESIA (in Gaellmo's *Wolfgangerl*, 1990); the young man's love affairs (in Shaffer's/Foreman's *Amadeus*, 1979); and the premonition of his own death through the secret-laden commissioning of the REQUIEM (in Wilder's *Mozart and the Gray Stranger*, 1928).

The broad field of kitsch relegates Mozart's music to second place. Among the great number of his works, only a small number of melodies is marketed, albeit with great persistence, since wide recognition secures success. At a symposium at Salzburg University in 1990, the German musicologist Inka Stampfl produced the following order of popularity: first movement of the Symphony No. 40, K550; second movement of the Piano Concerto No. 21, K467; the 'Rondo alla turca' from the piano sonata K331; the first movement of the Serenade in G, *Eine kleine Nachtmusik*, K525; excerpts from *DON GIOVANNI* and *DIE ZAUBERFLÖTE*.

Music used in this way serves not only to intensify the commercial image of Mozart as a composer, but is even more important as an acoustic signal for products alien to music and art such as yoghurt and beer. Similarly, classic rock music by groups such as Vanilla Fudge, Ekseption, and the Beatles uses the popularity of Mozart's melodies for purposes of self-promotion, rather than as any kind of retrospective link to the composer.

Perhaps the most sensitive area concerning the use and abuse of Mozart is the world of politics: a good example is the pseudo-cultural ambitions of the Nazis, who completely took over Mozart. In 1938 'Mozart as Apollo' was used as the official slogan for the Salzburg Festival of the now Greater German Empire; in 1939 Mozart stood as the symbol of Hitler's pact with Mussolini; and in 1941 Mozart's name fronted VIENNA's Imperial Music Festival. According to the Nazi party organ *Völkischer Beobachter* (29 Nov. 1941), the invocation of Mozart's spirit would be a balm to the minds of the fighting soldiers. A few days later, at the premiere of the film *Whom the Gods Love* (written and directed by Karl Hartl), the propaganda minister, Joseph Goebbels, asserted that Mozart's music was part of that 'which defends our soldiers against the onslaught of eastern barbarians'. After 1945 the Republic of Austria again made use of Mozart. He was the 'ambassador of Austria' (*Die Furche*, 12 Apr. 1947), his 'genius hovered over the country' (*Arbeiter Zeitung*, 11 Apr. 1946), and the Masonic song, *Brüder, reicht die Hand zum Bunde* (K623a and of uncertain authorship, although at the time believed to be by Mozart) became the Austrian national hymn, albeit with new words.

The many-faceted uses of Mozart shows no sign of abating after 200 years: there is too much to be made from his name. As Rosendorfer and Eder put it in the opera *Mozart in New York* (1991), whether on MOZARTKUGELN or the Austrian 5,000-shilling banknote, 'Mozart is money!'

FRIEDL JARY (Trans. RUTH HALLIWELL)

U. Eco, 'Kitsch' in *Brockhaus-Lexikon* (Wiesbaden, 1990), vol. XII, 35–6
C. Grag, *Rockmusik-Lexikon* (Hamburg, 1986)
A. Moles, *Psychologie des Kitsches* (Stuttgart, 1972)

Köchel, Ludwig (Alois Ferdinand), Ritter von (b. Stein, near Krems, 14 Jan. 1800; d. Vienna, 3 June 1877). Austrian music historian. After graduating in law from the University of Vienna in 1827, Köchel and his friend Franz Freiherr Scharschmid von Adlertreu took over the education of the four sons of Archduke Karl; he was appointed k.k. Schulrat in Salzburg and Gymnasialinspektor for Upper Austria in 1850, but gave up this post after only two years, returning to Vienna, where he remained until his death in 1877.

As an independent scholar of private means, Köchel published numerous articles on botany and mineralogy, as well as translations of Virgil, Ovid and Horace. His chief claim to fame, however, is his work on Mozart. In 1851, Köchel's friend Franz Lorenz published an anonymous pamphlet, *Im Sachen Mozarts*, drawing attention to the very unsatisfactory state of knowledge about Mozart's music and its sources, and this prompted Köchel to compile a chronological catalogue of Mozart's works, first published in 1862 as *Chronologisch-thematisches Verzeichnis sämtlicher Tonwerke Wolfgang Amadé Mozarts*. It gave the first few bars of each work, including all movements or vocal numbers, and identified it by a number; it also listed the autograph and other manuscript sources, if extant, the first edition, and references to the recent biography by Otto Jahn, to whom it was dedicated. In compiling his catalogue, Köchel was helped by material from the collections of Josef Hauer, a doctor in Öd (Lower Austria), Aloys Fuchs and Leopold von Sonnleithner, in addition to his own large collection of first and early editions. He also made, or had made, manuscript copies of many of Mozart's works, some of which served as printers' copy for Breitkopf & Härtel's complete works. Subsequent editions of the catalogue (2nd edn Leipzig, 1905, by Paul Graf von Waldersee; 3rd edn 1937, by Alfred Einstein; 6th edn 1964 by Franz Giegling, Alexander Weinmann and Gerd Sievers) added enormously to the amount of information, often radically altering the presumed datings, but these have become unworkable: more recent work by Wolfgang Plath and Alan Tyson, among others, has rendered many of these datings, both traditional and revised, obsolete (see SOURCES). A new edition of Köchel (*Studienköchel*, by Ulrich Konrad and Cliff Eisen) will be published in 2006.

After the completion of his catalogue, Köchel turned to other matters: in 1869 he published the still useful *Die kaiserliche Hof-Musikkapelle in Wien von 1543 bis 1867* and in 1872 a thematic catalogue of the works of FUX; eighty-three of BEETHOVEN's letters to Archduke Rudolph appeared in 1865 and *Die Pflege der Musik am österreichischen Hofe vom Schlusse des XV. bis zur Mitte des XVII. Jahrhunderts* in 1866. But Köchel's interest in Mozart remained, and he was instrumental in bringing about the first complete edition of the composer's works, published by Breitkopf & Härtel beginning in 1877; to this end he left the publishers a significant subvention. Mozart's REQUIEM was performed at his funeral.

CLIFF EISEN

O. Biba, 'Ludwig Ritter von Köchels Verdienste um die Mozart-Gesamtausgabe', in *Bürgerliche Musikkultur im 19. Jahrhundert Salzburg* (Salzburg, 1980), 93–104

O. E. Deutsch, 'Aus Köchels Jugendtagen', in *Festschrift Hans Engel zum siebzigsten Geburtstag*, ed. H. Heussner (Kassel, 1964), 70–5

A. H. King, 'Köchel, Breitkopf, and the Complete Edition: Studies in Criticism and Bibliography', in *Mozart in Retrospect* (London, 1955, 3rd rev. edn 1970), 55–65

L. Ritter von Köchel, *Studienköchel*, ed. Ulrich Konrad and Cliff Eisen (Wiesbaden, 2006)

T. E. Konrad, *Ludwig Ritter von Köchel* (Vienna, 1998)

Kozeluch, Leopold (Jan Antonin Koželuh) (b. Velvary (Bohemia) 26 June 1747; d. Vienna, 7 May 1818). Composer, keyboard player and music publisher, resident in VIENNA from 1778. Having refused (in 1781) an offer to succeed Mozart as court organist to the Archbishop of SALZBURG, he achieved considerable success in many of the genres in which Mozart worked, including piano SONATAS, piano CONCERTOS and SYMPHONIES. Ludwig Gerber, in his *Historisch-Biographisches Lexikon der Tonkünstler* (1790–2), called him 'without question, and for young and old alike, the most beloved of living composers; and with good reason. His works are distinguished by a combination of liveliness and grace, the most elegant melody and the purest harmony, and the most pleasing arrangement of rhythm and modulation.' Kozeluch's publication of a set of three symphonies (including one in G minor) in Vienna in 1787 may have helped to inspire Mozart to compose the three symphonies of 1788, perhaps with publication in mind. The success of Kozeluch's cantata in praise of EMPEROR LEOPOLD II, performed in PRAGUE a few days after the first performance of LA CLEMENZA DI TITO, exceeded the initial reception of Mozart's opera. The following year Emperor Franz II named him Kammer Kapellmeister and Hofmusik Compositor, a position similar to the one Mozart had occupied from 1788 to his death.

JOHN A. RICE

O. E. Deutsch, 'Kozeluch ritrovato', *Music & Letters* 26 (1945), 47–50

A. Weinmann, *Verzeichnis der Verlagswerke des Musikalischen Magazins in Wien* (Vienna, 1950)

L

Lange (née Weber), (Maria) Aloysia (b. Zell or Mannheim, c.1761; d. Salzburg, 8 June 1839). German soprano, Mozart's sister-in-law and daughter of Fridolin Weber (b. ?Zell im Wiesental, 1733; d. Vienna, 23 Oct. 1779). Mozart first met Lange during his stay in MANNHEIM in 1777–8, when he gave her musical instruction and composed for her the concert arias K294, K316 and probably the early version of K538; he also fell in love with her, mooting to LEOPOLD MOZART his plans to take her to Italy (an idea to which his father objected strenuously). In 1778 she moved to MUNICH where she made her debut in Schweitzer's *Alceste*; shortly afterwards she was engaged at the Nationaltheater in VIENNA. From 1782, when German opera was removed to the Kärntnertortheater and Italian comic opera reinstated at the Burgtheater, she was a leading singer of the Italian troupe; Mozart composed the arias 'Vorrei spiegarvi, oh Dio!', K418 and 'No, che non sei capace', K419 for her debut as Clorinda in Anfossi's *Il curioso indiscreto*. Apparently Lange fell out of favour and in 1785 was transferred to the less prestigious Kärntnertortheater, where among other roles she sang Konstanze in Mozart's *DIE ENTFÜHRUNG AUS DEM SERAIL*; occasionally she was engaged for the Italian opera, most notably in 1788 when she sang the role of Donna Anna at the Viennese premiere of *DON GIOVANNI*. From 1790 she was engaged by LEOPOLD II as a *seconda donna* for opera seria. Leopold Mozart described her voice in a letter of 25 March 1785: 'It can scarcely be denied that she sings with the greatest expression: only now I understand why some persons I frequently asked would say that she has a very weak voice, while others said she has a very loud voice. Both are true. The held notes and all expressive notes are astonishingly loud; the tender moments, the passage work and embellishments, and high notes are very delicate, so that for my taste the one contrasts too strongly with the other. In an ordinary room the loud notes assault the ear, while in the theatre the delicate passages demand a great attentiveness and stillness on the part of the audience.' CLIFF EISEN

P. Lewy Gidwitz, 'Vocal Profiles of Four Mozart Sopranos' (Ph.D. thesis, University of California, Berkeley, 1991)
R. P. von Thurn, *Joseph II als Theaterdirektor* (Vienna and Leipzig, 1920)

Lange, (Johann) Joseph (b. Würzburg, 1 Apr. 1751; d. Vienna, 17 Sept. 1831). Actor, husband of ALOYSIA LANGE and Mozart's brother-in-law. As an actor, Lange was best known for his serious roles, including Hamlet and Romeo. He was also a talented painter and his unfinished portrait of Mozart from 1789 or 1790 (now in the Mozart Geburtshaus, Salzburg) is perhaps the most famous likeness of the composer; according to CONSTANZE MOZART, it exactly resembled him. Lange married Aloysia Weber, Constanze Mozart's sister, on 31 October 1780; relations between the two couples were friendly.

CLIFF EISEN

V. and M. Novello, *A Mozart Pilgrimage: Being the Travel Diaries of Vincent & Mary Novello in the Year 1829*, ed. R. Hughes (London, 1955)
H. Schuler, 'Zur Familiengeschichte des Johann Joseph Lange', *Mitteilungen der Internationalen Stiftung Mozarteum* 22 (1974), 29–37

Laschi-Mombelli, Luisa (b. Florence, 1760s; d. c.1790). Italian soprano. Laschi-Mombelli was engaged at VIENNA from August 1784 to February 1785 and from April 1786 to 1790; she made her debut there as Giannina in Domenico Cimarosa's *Giannina e Bernardone* in September 1784. Her roles for Mozart included the Countess in LE NOZZE DI FIGARO and Zerlina in the first Viennese production of DON GIOVANNI (when she was seven months pregnant). A review of her 1787 performance in MARTÌN Y SOLER's *L'arbore di Diana* praised both her acting and singing: 'what painter has ever depicted a mischievous smile more perfectly, what sculptor has portrayed more graceful gestures, what other singer is capable of producing such melting, marvellously smooth singing with such simplicity and genuine emotion?'

CLIFF EISEN

D. Link, *The National Court Theatre in Mozart's Vienna: Sources and Documents 1783–1792* (Oxford, 1998)

Lausch, Lorenz (b. ?1737/8; d. Vienna, 23 Nov. 1794). AUSTRIAN music copyist and publisher. Lausch's music-copying business, established in the early 1780s, concentrated chiefly on vocal music; in 1786 he advertised manuscripts of LE NOZZE DI FIGARO and in 1788 similar parts for DON GIOVANNI; he was also the first to advertise the German song 'Ich möchte wohl der Kaiser sein', K539. Whether these manuscripts were authorized by Mozart, however, remains an open question; according to JOSEPH HAYDN, at least, Lausch was not above buying stolen manuscripts from other publishers.

CLIFF EISEN

D. Edge, 'Recent Discoveries in Viennese Copies of Mozart's Concertos', in *Mozart's Piano Concertos: Text, Context, Interpretation*, ed. N. Zaslaw (Ann Arbor, 1996), 51–65
A. Weinmann, *Wiener Musikverlag 'am Rande'* (Vienna, 1970)

Legros, Joseph (b. Monampteuil, 7/8 Sept. 1739; d. La Rochelle, 20 Dec. 1792), French singer and impresario. Legros, a leading *haute-contre*, sang at the PARIS opera from 1764 to 1783; among his numerous roles were Sandomir in Philidor's *Ernelinde* and principal tenor parts in GLUCK's *Iphigénie en Aulide*, *Alceste*, *Armide*, *Iphigénie en Tauride* and *Echo et Narcisse*. From 1777 to 1790 he was director of the Concert spirituel. Mozart became acquainted with him during his visit to Paris in 1778, when he visited Legros frequently and used his piano for composing. It was for Legros and the Concert spirituel that Mozart composed the 'Paris' symphony, K297, and movements for a 'Miserere' by Holzbauer; presumably it was for the Concert spirituel that he also composed the lost Sinfonia concertante K297B for flute, oboe, horn and bassoon. According to Mozart, Legros treated him badly, suppressing performances of the Sinfonia concertante and claiming that the slow movement of the 'Paris' symphony had 'too many modulations and that it is too long' (letter of 9 July 1778), as a result of which Mozart composed a replacement movement. But he also thought

Cambini may have been behind Legros's mistreatment. In 1782, Mozart wrote to the impresario concerning a possible contract for 1783; it is not known if Legros replied. CLIFF EISEN

Leopold II, Emperor (b. Vienna, 5 May 1747; d. Vienna, 1 Mar. 1792). Brother of JOSEPH II; crowned Holy Roman Emperor at Frankfurt on 9 October 1790 and King of Bohemia at PRAGUE on 6 September 1791. Although they may have met as early as 1762, Mozart's first documented acquaintance with Leopold II was at Florence on 1 April 1770, when he was received at the Pitti Palace; the next day Wolfgang performed for him at the Villa Poggio Imperiale. Leopold succeeded Joseph II in 1790 and Mozart travelled at his own expense to the coronation in Frankfurt, where he gave a concert on 20 October 1790; additionally, DIE ENTFÜHRUNG AUS DEM SERAIL was given on 12 October. Later that year, in Prague, DON GIOVANNI was given as part of the coronation ceremonies, for which Mozart also composed LA CLEMENZA DI TITO. After Mozart's death, CONSTANZE MOZART applied to Leopold for a pension but this was not granted until 31 March 1792, by Leopold's successor Francis II. During his short reign, Leopold undertook a radical transformation of the court opera, dismissing LORENZO DA PONTE and reintroducing opera seria and ballet to the repertory of both the Burgtheater and Kärntnertortheater. CLIFF EISEN

Leutgeb, Joseph (b. Vienna, 8 Oct. 1732; d. Vienna, 27 Feb. 1811). Horn player and friend of the Mozarts. Leutgeb, who joined the SALZBURG court orchestra in 1762 or 1763, had frequent contacts with the Mozarts both at home and on their travels: they met up in MILAN in February 1773, where Leopold tried to arrange a concert for him. Leutgeb later left Salzburg, settling in VIENNA where he became a cheesemonger and, after Mozart's move there in 1781, one of the composer's close friends. He also continued to perform: it was for Leutgeb that Mozart wrote the Horn Quintet, K407, and the Horn CONCERTOS K417, 447 and 495; the autograph of K417 includes the jocular comment 'Wolfgang Amadè Mozart has taken pity on Leutgeb, ass, ox and fool, at Vienna, 27 March 1783.' CLIFF EISEN

D. Heartz, 'Leutgeb and the 1762 Horn Concertos of Joseph and Johann Michael Haydn', *Mozart-Jahrbuch* 1987/88, 59–68

K. Küster, *Mozart: A Musical Biography* (Oxford, 1996), 227–33

K. Pisarowitz, 'Mozarts Schnorrer Leutgeb: Dessen Primärbiographie', *Mitteilungen der Internationalen Stiftung Mozarteum* 18/3–4 (1970), 21–6

Lichnowsky, Karl (Alois Johann Nepomuk Vinzenz Leonhard), Prince (b. Vienna, 21 June 1761; d. Vienna, 15 Apr. 1841). Court councillor and chamberlain, patron of the arts and possibly a student of Mozart. Lichnowsky and Mozart may have met at their Masonic lodge, 'Zur Wohltätigkeit', which Lichnowsky had joined in 1783 (he later belonged to the lodges 'Zur wahren Eintracht' and 'Zur Wahrheit'). In 1789 they travelled together to PRAGUE, Dresden and Leizpig; on 10 April 1789 Mozart wrote to CONSTANZE MOZART, 'I am now taking the Prince to see DUSCHEK, who is expecting us, and at nine o'clock we are starting off for Dresden.' There may have been a falling out between them, however: in May 1789 Lichnowsky apparently abandoned Mozart in Berlin and, as Mozart reported to Constanze, 'I had to lend him a hundred gulden, as his purse was getting empty. I could not well refuse him: you will know why' (23 May 1789). Later, in November 1791, Lichnowsky successfully sued Mozart for 1,435 gulden, a substantial sum. The cause of Lichnowsky's action, the legal proceedings surrounding it, and details of any settlement, however, are unknown; Mozart died less than a month afterwards. Lichnowsky became a staunch supporter of BEETHOVEN, who dedicated his Piano Trios Op. 1, 'Pathétique' sonata, Symphony No. 2 and other works to him. But Beethoven also had problems with the Prince, later filing a suit against him for shirking his financial obligations. According to Countess Lulu Thürheim Lichnowsky was a 'cynical degenerate and a shameless coward'. CLIFF EISEN

W. Brauneis: '"... wegen schuldigen 1435 f 32 xr": neuer Archivfund zur Finanzmisere Mozarts im November 1791', *Mitteilungen der Internationalen Stiftung Mozarteum* 39 (1991), 159–63

T. DeNora, *Beethoven and the Construction of Genius. Musical Politics in Vienna, 1792–1803* (Berkeley, 1995)

Ligniville, (Pierre) Eugène (François), Marquis of, Prince of Conca (b. near Nancy, 1730; d. Florence, 10 Dec. 1788). Italian composer. A French nobleman by birth, Ligniville nevertheless spent most of his adult life in Italy, as a member of the Bolognese Accademia Filarmonica from 1758 and, from 1761, in Florence at the court of Grand Duke Pietro Leopoldo. Mozart met Ligniville on 2 April 1770; LEOPOLD MOZART described him as 'the best contrapuntist in all Italy' and noted 'he presented Wolfgang with the most difficult fugues and themes, which Wolfgang played and worked out as easily as one eats a piece of bread' (3 April). The Kyrie K89 was apparently influenced by Ligniville's 1768 Stabat mater, nine movements of which Mozart copied out in the early 1770s (Anh A17). CLIFF EISEN

Linley, Thomas (b. Bath, 5 May 1756; d. Grimsthorpe, 5 Aug. 1778). English violinist and composer. Linley, a child prodigy and pupil of William Boyce, studied violin in Florence with Pietro Nardini from 1768 to 1771; it was there that he met Mozart, in Apr. 1770. Wolfgang and Linley became fast friends, frequently playing together; LEOPOLD MOZART wrote to his wife: 'In Florence we came across a young Englishman, who is a pupil of the famous violinist Nardini. This boy, who *plays most beautifully* and who is the same age and the same size as Wolfgang, came to the house of the learned poetess, Signora Corilla, where we happened to be ... The two boys performed one after the other throughout the whole evening, constantly embracing each other. On the following day, the little Englishman, a most charming boy, had his violin brought to our rooms and played the whole afternoon, Wolfgang accompanying him on his own. On the next day we lunched with M. Gavard, the administrator of the grand ducal finances, and these two boys played in turn the whole afternoon, not like boys, but like men! Little Tommaso accompanied us home and wept bitter tears, because we were leaving on the following day' (21 Apr. 1770). Mozart and Linley subsequently corresponded although only one of their letters survives, from Wolfgang to Thomas (10 Sept. 1772). After his return to England, Linley played concerts in Bath and became leader of the Drury Lane orchestra; he died prematurely in a boating accident in 1778. CLIFF EISEN

G. Beechey, 'Thomas Linley, Junior, 1756–1778', *Musical Quarterly* 54 (1968), 74–82
'Thomas Linley, 1756–78, and His Vocal Music', *Musical Times* 119 (1978), 669–71

'Linz' symphony. Mozart's Symphony in C, K425 (1783). See SYMPHONIES

Lipp family. Bavarian musicians active in SALZBURG. The composer and organist Franz Ignaz Lipp (b. Eggenfelden, Lower Bavaria, 1 Feb. 1718; d. Salzburg, 15 Aug. 1798) arrived in Salzburg as a fourteen-year-old choirboy and was appointed court and cathedral organist in 1754. At first his duties were restricted largely to performance at the cathedral; it was only after the death of ADLGASSER in 1777 that he was active as an accompanist at court. LEOPOLD MOZART initially thought well of Lipp, writing in 1757 that in addition to his keyboard playing, he 'also plays the violin, sings with a beautiful tenor voice, and composes not badly'. Less than a year after succeeding Adlgasser, however, Leopold Mozart wrote to his son: 'You can easily imagine how abysmal things are now that . . . Lipp accompanies at court. Whenever CECCARELLI sings, he complains loudly and publicly.' Mozart also had a low opinion of him, ironically describing one of his own performances as including fugues played 'with all the skill of a Lipp' (18 July 1778). It is probably no coincidence that Mozart succeeded Lipp on his return to Salzburg in 1779. Lipp's daughter, Maria Magdalena (b. Eggenfeld, Bavaria, 1745; d. Salzburg, 10 June 1827), who in 1778 married MICHAEL HAYDN, was an accomplished soprano who studied in Venice from 1761 to 1764; she sang the role Göttliche Barmherzigkeit at the premiere of *Die Schuldigkeit des ersten Gebots* (Salzburg, 1767) and, according to the libretto of LA FINTA SEMPLICE, was the first Rosina. CLIFF EISEN

T. Aigner, 'Wenn Mozart mit aller Kunst des Lipp fugierte', *Wiener Figaro* 45 (1978), 3–10
H. Schuler, *Mozarts Salzburger Freunde und Bekannte: Biographien und Kommentar* (Wilhelmshaven, 1996), 144–6

litany. Between 1771 and 1776 Mozart completed four litanies for chorus, soloists, and orchestra: two Loreto litanies for the Blessed Virgin Mary (K109 and 195) and two sacramental litanies venerating the Holy Sacrament upon the altar (K125 and 243). Seldom performed today, the litanies include some of the composer's finest and most operatic music for the church.

As the name suggests, a litany consists of a series of prayers ('Litaniae') punctuated by a repeated, formulaic response from the congregation, often in connection with a procession. In Mozart's litanies the recurring petitions are 'miserere nobis' and, in the Loreto litanies, 'ora pro nobis'. The litanies open and close with acclamations similar to those that open and close the Mass Ordinary: Kyrie and Agnus Dei.

Liturgical calendars and personal diaries mention litany performances in SALZBURG during late afternoons or early evenings for the forty-hour 'Gebet' (prayer vigil) starting on Palm Sunday in the cathedral, for the feast of St John Nepomuk (16 May) and its octave in the chapel of Mirabel Palace and at the Franciscan church, as well as for the feasts of St Roch of Montpellier (16 August), its octave, and St Michael the Archangel (29 September) at other local churches. Litanies were also part of the Marian devotions from 15 May onwards at Mirabel.

Written for solemn occasions, Mozart's litanies are extended compositions with total lengths ranging from 272 bars (K109, five movements) to 791 bars (K 243, nine movements). The litanies use the mixed, concerted style of the polyphonic litany that had come from Italy in the late seventeenth century. They offer an engaging juxtaposition of homophonic choral movements, bravura solo arias, operatic ensembles, and, occasionally, old-fashioned choral fugues. Mozart's direct models were the multi-movement litanies of comparable length by Salzburg composers such as J. E. EBERLIN, A. C. ADLGASSER, LEOPOLD MOZART and MICHAEL HAYDN.

K109 has the basic scoring shared by all Mozart's litanies: chorus, soloists, two violins, basses (cello and double bass), organ continuo, and the standard three *colla parte* trombones (ATB) of Salzburg practice. In addition to this traditional 'church trio' accompaniment, the other three litanies require two oboes, two horns and viola, plus the following: in K125, two flutes (only in 'Panis') and two clarini; in K243, two flutes (in 'Dulcissimum'; one in 'Agnus'), a second viola, and obbligato violoncello (solo in 'Agnus').

1. Litany of Loreto
2. Sacramental litanies

1. Litany of Loreto

The Litany of Loreto (*Litaniae Lauretanae*) is the best known of the litanies dedicated to the Blessed Virgin Mary. Assigning Mary her special place in the heavenly hierarchy, the litany was often sung in a procession or devotional service on a Marian feast. Loreto, near Ancona, Italy, is one of the oldest Marian pilgrimage sites, and since 1601 this litany had been the only sanctioned Litany of Our Lady. Emperor Ferdinand II (r. 1619–37) was influential, according to J. I. Armstrong, in 'establishing the importance and popularity of the Litany of Loreto throughout Habsburg lands'.

The autograph score of *Litaniae Lauretanae [de] B[eata] M[aria] V[irgine]*, K109 (B flat major), is dated 'Salzburg, May 1771'. Mozart's first, shortest and simplest litany, K109 has the five-movement structure typical for the Loreto litany. As concert master to the archbishop, Mozart probably wrote it for that May's Marian feasts at the cathedral and modelled the work on his father's Loreto Litany in F major.

The Kyrie is a concise chorus (Allegro; B flat major) in ABA′ form. The 'Sancta Maria' (Andante; F major) begins softly, as the soloists take turns with graceful, minuet-like phrases that close with 'ora pro nobis'. The chorus enters with the appropriately *forte* petition 'Virgo potens' (Virgin most powerful). 'Salus infirmorum' is for chorus only. After a short majestic introduction (Adagio; D minor), a faster, equally brief 'Auxilium Christianorum' (Allegro; G major) closes the movement. In 'Regina Angelorum' (Vivace, E flat major, 2/4) the soloists separately announce the Virgin's eight regal titles with a light, jaunty melody reminiscent of Pergolesi and opera buffa. (Mozart had completed his first Italian trip only two months earlier.) The 'ora pro nobis' after each appellation is emphasized by longer note values. Tonic B flat major and the chorus return for the concluding Agnus Dei (Andante), a solemn movement haunted by the sadness of the soft, chromatic 'miserere nobis' sung by the soloists.

The second *Litaniae Lauretanae de B.M.V.*, K195 (D major), has the solemnity, ample proportions and operatic qualities typical of Mozart's remaining litanies. Completed at Salzburg in 1774 and more than twice as long as his first litany, it has a greater variety of accompanying instruments and more frequent orchestral ritornellos. Sonata-form principles influence most of its five movements. Perhaps to reduce redundancy but enhance drama, Mozart omits some of the 'ora pro nobis' pleas from this setting. Scholars are not sure of the occasion for its first performance. Einstein believes K195 was written 'for one of the smaller Salzburg churches', while Federhofer-Königs suggests that it was for the Marian feasts of May.

The Kyrie opens with a majestic adagio introduction in which the subdued solo quartet is dramatically interrupted at 'Christe' by forte choral entrances. In the following allegro Kyrie the chorus juxtaposes contrasting textures, twice relieved by a melismatic soprano–alto duet. In a hasty, ascending closing theme, sopranos are answered by the rest of the chorus. In the graceful solo quartet 'Sancta Maria' (Andante; G major), the soprano sings extended melismas on 'inviolata' and 'nobis'. Twice the chorus compellingly highlights 'ora pro nobis' (subito *forte*) as well as 'Virga potens'.

'Salus infirmorum' (Adagio; B minor–G major) sounds Handelian with its pervasive dotted rhythms. The solo quartet highlights each 'ora pro nobis' as well as 'Consolatrix' and 'Auxilium'. 'Salus' ends with the strings alone playing a two-bar modulation to the key of the next movement. With virtuosic coloratura for the tenor soloist, 'Regina Angelorum' (Allegro con spirito; D major) reminds us of opera seria. The chorus emphasizes the recurrent 'ora pro nobis' and provides a structural framework. Solemnity returns with the sublime Agnus Dei (Adagio; D major). Accompanied by muted strings, the soprano sings the repeated calls to Christ with impressive coloratura, leaps and a cadenza. Typically, descending chromaticism for 'qui tollis peccata mundi' alludes to the Crucifixion. Chorus and full orchestra dramatically interrupt with the believer's imploration 'parce nobis' (spare us). Sumptuous demisemiquaver runs above a dominant pedal lead to a quiet, penitential conclusion that includes one of Mozart's rare decrescendo markings.

2. Sacramental litanies

Sacramental litanies venerate the Holy Sacrament or Eucharist upon the altar. They were used in the forty-hour prayer vigil starting on Palm Sunday, on Corpus Christi, at sacramental devotions, and for pilgrimages and processions in cloisters and brotherhoods.

Mozart's two sacramental litanies each consist of nine movements, with different starting points, however, for their sixth movements. Both show strong influences from the symphony and concerto as well as opera. Movements often connect directly from one to the next, with slow movements (3, 5, 7) often functioning as introductions to the faster movements that follow.

Litaniae de venerabili altaris sacramento (Litany in Honour of the Blessed Sacrament), K125 (B flat major), is dated 'Salzburg, March 1772'. The original occasion for the work is unknown, but the initials that Mozart wrote at the score's end – 'I [n]: O[mnibus]: G[lorificetur]: D[eus]:' – suggest that completion of the work had a special meaning for him.

K125 seems closely modelled on a C major sacramental litany by Mozart's father, as K. A. Rosenthal has explained. Indeed, no other litany shows such involvement by Leopold in the preparation of his son's manuscript. Leopold's notation in the Agnus Dei indicates that the soprano part was to be rewritten for baritone JOSEPH NIKOLAUS MEISSNER.

The joyous Kyrie of K125 (Molto allegro; B flat major) uses the double-exposition sonata form of a concerto. After an orchestral exposition, an *adagio* Kyrie introduces the chorus, which then sings its own exposition. The presence of regal-sounding clarini trumpets in the choral movements suggests that timpani should also play, ad libitum. 'Panis vivus' (Andante; F major), which describes the spiritually nourishing sacrament, is a charming soprano aria that also uses the double-exposition sonata form. Two flutes in place of the oboes add a pastoral touch.

In the short 'Verbum caro factum' (Adagio; D minor) chorus and full orchestra proclaim the mystery of the 'Word made flesh, dwelling among us'. At the litany's mid-point, 'Hostia sancta' (Molto Allegro; B flat major) addresses the sacrament with thirteen appellations, most punctuated by 'miserere nobis'. Each soloist takes a turn, and the chorus dramatically enters to emphasize 'Praecelsum' (most exalted) and 'Stupendum supra omnia' (wonderful above all). With a single modulatory chord the movement leads directly into the fifth movement, 'Tremendum' for chorus (Adagio–Allegro; G minor–B flat major). To evoke the sacrament's 'awesome' aspect, agitated triplets accompany tortured-sounding suspensions above a chromatically descending bass. Like a revived soul, the tonic key and a fast tempo return for the joyful 'ac vivificum sacramentum' (life-giving sacrament). 'Panis omnipotentia' is an elegant opera seria-like aria for tenor (Andante; E flat major) with extended melismas, sustained *messe di voce* and three cadenza opportunities.

In the choral 'Viaticum' (Adagio; B flat minor) sudden dynamic changes, dramatic pauses and chromatic part-writing evoke the 'journey of those who die in the Lord'. A half cadence connects 'Viaticum' to the eighth movement, 'Pignus futurae gloriae' (pledge of future glory). This choral fugue is based on a monumental nine-bar subject of repeated notes, octave leaps and jubilant melismas. Mozart is using the old convention of imitative polyphony referring to the eternity of God. The fugue's impressive climax is augmented by the basses' rising sequence upon the subject and by harmonic instability.

The serene Agnus Dei (Un poco adagio; F major–B flat major) is another operatic aria for the soprano who must negotiate *messe di voce*, coloratura and large leaps. After a cadenza the tonic B flat major returns, and the chorus and full orchestra present the final Agnus Dei. Striking modal shifts and dynamic juxtapositions underscore 'miserere nobis' at the end of the litany.

Using one of his most expressive keys (E flat major) and imaginative scoring, Mozart's *Litaniae de venerabili altaris sacramento*, K243, is his grandest litany, indeed one of his most sublime contributions to sacred music. It was completed in March 1776 for use on Palm Sunday (31 March) at Salzburg Cathedral with the Dicasteries (civil servants from the archbishop's central administration).

Triplicate violin and basso ripieno parts in Salzburg and AUGSBURG suggest that a large ensemble originally performed the work.

The solemn Kyrie (Andante moderato; E flat major) has an ABA′ form and alternates between solo quartet and chorus. The 'Panis vivus' (Allegro aperto; B flat major) is a heroic tenor aria with extended ritornellos, impressive coloratura and a sonata-like design. In the short chorus 'Verbum caro factum' (Largo; G minor) the mysterious eucharistic transformation in St John's words are evoked by unexpected melodic and harmonic twists. The chorus emphasizes 'miserere' with a series of *fp* dynamics. As in K125, the 'Hostia sancta' (Allegro comodo; C major) resolves the half cadence at the end of the previous movement and sets the thirteen sacramental appellations with alternations between the soloists and chorus.

This movement leads via a three-bar transition into the sombre, intense choral 'Tremendum' (Adagio; C minor) which poignantly uses three obbligato trombones, chromaticism, dynamic contrasts and an agitated violin accompaniment. Mozart unifies this awe-inspiring movement by having the chorus later repeat as a kind of refrain the words and music of the beginning. Ending upon a half cadence, the movement leads into the graceful soprano aria, 'Dulcissimum convivium' (Andantino; F major). Two flutes replace the oboes, while upper strings play *con sordino*. In the final four bars the strings remove their mutes and start the opening ritornello, which suddenly goes astray harmonically and leads into the next movement. 'Viaticum'(Andante; C minor–G minor) recalls the dead, and Mozart uses eerie-sounding pizzicato violins and sustained winds (three trombones, two horns, and two oboes) to accompany the sopranos' long notes intoning what sounds like an adaptation of the medieval chant 'Pange lingua' (Sing, O tongue, the mystery of the glorious body), a hymn associated with the Divine Offices on Corpus Christi. Mozart's cantus firmus technique resembles the chorale treatment in J. S. BACH's cantatas, while the supernatural scoring recalls GLUCK and looks forward to the nineteenth century. 'Pignus futurae' (E flat major) exploits old-fashioned imitative counterpoint, this time in a double fugue which pits a leaping, disjunct subject against a 'miserere' counter-subject. For contrasting episodes Mozart uses a softer, undulating semitone motif ('miserere nobis') that suddenly explodes *forte* with syncopated descending arpeggios. The magnificence of this contrapuntal tour de force is augmented by Mozart's introducing yet another subject when the dominant key is reached (bars 41ff.) as well as by his use of stretto techniques and a sonata-like recapitulation (bars 93ff.).

In the majestic Agnus Dei (Andantino; B flat major) obbligato oboe, flute and cello accompany a soprano aria that requires delicate coloratura and improvised 'Eingänge' (lead-ins) at two fermatas. As in K125, Mozart provides a simple one-bar transition to connect directly with the next movement, 'Miserere'. The four soloists and then chorus sing this quiet, closing movement (Andante moderato; E flat major) in which music from the Kyrie returns. Such a thematic recall occurs in none of the other litanies, yet, with such a captivating hymn-like melody as this one, the composer found a suitably pious and serene way to set the final repetitions of 'Have mercy on us.'

Mozart wrote no more litanies after K 243, perhaps because of JOSEPH II's 1783 *Gottesdienstverordnung*, an imperial decree limiting devotional services and prohibiting the use of instruments in Vespers. Nonetheless, extant manuscript copies show that Mozart's litanies had some popularity and were used outside Salzburg even during his lifetime. Early in the nineteenth century K109 and parts of K125 were published as *contrafacta* cantatas with German texts. In 1856 ANDRE of Offenbach first published K243 in its original form.

BRUCE C. MACINTYRE

J. I. Armstrong, *The Litany of Mary and Devotional Worship at the Eighteenth-Century Viennese Imperial Court* (Munich and Salzburg, 2000)
A. Einstein, *Mozart: His Character, his Works* (New York, 1945)
R. Federhofer-Königs, 'Lauretanische Litaneien KV 109 (74e) und 195 (186d)', *Mozart-Jahrbuch* 1967, 111–20
K. G. Fellerer, *Mozarts Kirchenmusik* (Salzburg-Freilassing, 1955)
K. A. Rosenthal, 'Mozart's Sacramental Litanies and Their Forerunners', *Musical Quarterly* 27 (1941), 433–55
C. H. Sherman and T. D. Thomas, *Johann Michael Haydn (1737–1806): A Chronological Thematic Catalogue of His Works* (Stuyvesant, NY, 1993)

Lodron family. One of SALZBURG's leading noble families, linked by marriage with the FIRMIAN and ARCO families. Mozart wrote three pieces of music known to have a connection with them. Ernst Maria Joseph Nepomuk von Lodron (b. 30 May 1716; d. 18 Feb. 1779 and nicknamed 'Count Potbelly' by the Mozarts) married Maria Antonia von Arco (b. Salzburg 13 Oct. 1738; d. Salzburg, 14 Dec. 1780) on 4 Apr. 1758; she was the fourth child of Georg Anton Felix von Arco. She and her husband must have been friends with HIERONYMUS COLLOREDO before he became Archbishop of Salzburg, because their fifth child, Hieronymus Maria ('Momolo', b. 21 May 1766) was Colloredo's godson. After Colloredo was elected Salzburg's prince-archbishop in 1772, Maria Antonia became the most influential woman at court. She shared her love of music with Colloredo and was a fine keyboard player. For her name day (Antony of Padua, 13 June) it became customary to serenade her with specially written music: in 1776 Mozart wrote the divertimento K247 (with its march K248), and in 1777 the divertimento K287. In 1778, when Mozart was in PARIS, LEOPOLD MOZART gave an amusing description, full of *Schadenfreude*, of Count Johann Rudolph CZERNIN's bungled attempt to serenade the Countess with his own and Hafeneder's music instead (letters of 11 and 29 June).

Maria Antonia was well disposed to the Mozarts, and in 1778 played a key part in easing Mozart's return to Salzburg as organist, after ADLGASSER's death. After this event, too, Leopold Mozart began to give keyboard lessons to her two elder daughters, Aloisia and Giuseppina, while NANNERL MOZART taught two of the younger three. It was for the Countess, Aloisia and Giuseppina that Mozart had written the Concerto for Three Keyboards, K242, in 1776. Despite the Countess's protection, the Mozarts found her cold and false. After her early, lingering death, the family was broken up, because her husband had already died.

RUTH HALLIWELL

R. Halliwell, *The Mozart Family: Four Lives in a Social Context* (Oxford, 1998)

London. London in 1764 was a city of opportunity, of vitality and optimism, the centre of a thriving trading empire, flushed with military success around the globe. Affluence and stability meant time and leisure for an expanding urban society, whether nobility and gentry in London for the season or wealthy bourgeoisie:

merchants, bankers and professionals, men of letters and the arts. For the leisured classes – and especially their wives and daughters – the season was a frantic round of pleasure, of public performances and private assemblies, balls, card-parties, operas, plays and concerts. For LEOPOLD MOZART, coming from the quiet courts of central Europe, it was a maelstrom ('the number of entertainments which really weary one here'). During the hedonistic 1760s music was indeed viewed primarily as entertainment, and though there was a serious side to operatic criticism and to oratorio after HANDEL, it was the energy and charm of the new symphonies and comic operas that really caught the imagination of the London public.

Cosmopolitan and ever welcoming towards foreign musicians, London was a magnet to adventurous Europeans seeking to try their fortune in an unregulated commercial environment, which offered lucrative opportunities for concerts and publishing unrivalled on the continent. Yet competition also entailed risks, and though Leopold Mozart marvelled at taking 100 guineas in one evening, he was ultimately less successful than he had anticipated. The cost of living in London was high: lodgings in fashionable Westminster near aristocratic patrons, clothing, transport, even the cost of music-copying (Leopold himself copied the parts for his son's symphonies). And the season was short, for most concerts took place between February and May; during the summer months the only regular employment for musicians, unless invited to the country seats of their patrons, was at the pleasure gardens (such as Ranelagh, where Mozart affected 'the English patriot' at a charity benefit on 29 June 1764).

Furthermore marketing two prodigies required a delicate balance. London was, of course, used to concerts by young musicians, their age usually lopped by a year or two. But such concerts were occasional or at best annual events, fitted into the normal run of benefits rewarding good service from patrons known to the concert-giver. This was not a privilege that could be over-extended: the market for high-priced West End concerts was limited (essentially a few hundred habitués of opera and concerts), and the *beau monde* would have resented any appearance of commercial exploitation. There was simply no structure for mass market repetition that retained prestige, and advertising the two prodigies as an exhibition or sideshow was a capitulation only to be taken later in the visit. Where Mozart's talents could have been more advantageously exploited was as a scientific phenomenon, something worthy of learned investigation in the spirit of the ENLIGHTENMENT (compare their advertisement as 'prodigies of nature'). But DAINES BARRINGTON's thorough investigation of Mozart's musical skills and improvisation took place only in June 1765, and his report was not presented to the Royal Society until 1770.

London already numbered some 700,000 inhabitants, and Leopold Mozart's letters revel in amazement at the size of the sprawling metropolis, the number of churches and squares, the learned societies and libraries, the shops and taverns, the victuals it consumed. He was clearly shocked by the contrast between the violence of a rioting mob, protesting against French silk imports, and the gentility and ease of cultured society, the broad avenues and fine squares of the West End, the brilliant lighting, the fine horses and carriages. Yet he was also intrigued by the mix of society milling together around the open-air bandstand at Vauxhall Gardens, whose magical setting he found so enchanting.

His primary object was to gain favour with the higher echelons of society, for London's commercial musical life was underpinned by layers of traditional patronage. For Leopold Mozart, an inevitable first step was an appearance at court, achieved on 27 April 1764 only five days after their arrival; and at a second appearance on 19 May Mozart flattered the King's taste for the music of Handel. But the royal court had little direct influence on London's musical life, not even the young Queen, whose musicians included J. C. BACH and C. F. ABEL. The Mozarts made a third court appearance on 25 October, and received 50 guineas from the Queen for the dedication of the Op. 3 sonatas. But it was more important to cultivate other contacts. As Leopold Mozart wrote in the fallow autumn of 1764, 'During the coming months I shall have to use every effort to win over the aristocracy and this will take a lot of galloping round and hard work.' Public concerts, though much the most visible part of London's music-making, formed only a small part of a professional career, and indeed they often acted as an entrée to more lucrative private engagements. Leopold Mozart's notebook reveals his success in forging aristocratic contacts, and the Mozarts must have appeared at numerous private concerts, including one at the Clive family's London residence on 13 March 1765, only recently discovered.

The strata of London's musical life closely reflected its topology. The West End (the areas around St James and Soho) was the centre of elite culture, embodied in the first place in the Italian Opera at the King's Theatre. Though management of the Opera was always financially hazardous, opera on two evenings a week was central to upper-class life, both socially and culturally. The return of comic operas in 1760, especially those of Galuppi, occasioned lively debate about artistic status and operatic finances; and even Italian dominance was questioned with an invitation to J. C. Bach for the 1762–3 season. The new manager Felice Giardini restored Italian hegemony, but without success; and the 1764–5 season was more interesting, with new operas by J. C. Bach and Thomas Arne, as well as an international star in GIOVANNI MANZUOLI, whose £1,500 advance made Leopold Mozart's eyes water. Manzuoli's musicianship made a strong impact on the young Mozart, who even took some singing lessons from the great castrato.

Directed at much the same clientele – and indeed sharing many of the same performers – were concerts at West End halls, such as Hickford's in Brewer Street or the Spring Gardens room. Not that concerts were as profuse as ten years earlier when the Opera was closed; and with Hickford's already in decline, London had no well-established concert hall until the opening of the Hanover Square Rooms in 1775. But the early 1760s initiated a rising tide of concert activity that culminated in the concerts of SALOMON and JOSEPH HAYDN three decades later. This coincided with an influx of German musicians such as Abel and Bach, who both took up residence in London, as well as visitors such as Richter from MANNHEIM. The publishers Robert Bremner and Peter Welcker seized the initiative in the market not only for the latest songs and keyboard music, but also for galant chamber music and symphonies. Bremner's Periodical Overtures of 1763–4 were dominated by Stamitz and other Mannheimers, leading the English composer Charles Avison to rail against 'the inumerable foreign Overtures, now pouring in upon us every Season, which are all involved in the same Confusion of Stile'. The Seven Years War (1756–63) also brought to

London innovative German keyboard manufacturers such as Zumpe, following in the steps of Shudi, whose most elaborate two-manual harpsichord was exhibited at the Mozart concert on 13 May 1765.

In the development of concert life the crucial catalyst was Mrs Theresa Cornelys, a singer and self-created society hostess, who fitted up Carlisle House, Soho Square, in superb style, and succeeded in attracting high society for assemblies and masquerades through a deliberately exclusive admission policy. Concerts were part of the entertainment: only in 1764 was a more formal series entrusted to Gioacchino Cocchi, who was supplanted in 1765 by Bach and Abel for ten concerts featuring their latest symphonies. Presumably the Mozart family attended: one reference suggests that Leopold Mozart might have attempted to give concerts here himself, although this may refer to the main series. Certainly the Bach–Abel concerts provided the foundation for London's later concert structure, fixing the subscription series at the centre of the social and artistic calendar of the *beau monde*.

Surrounding subscription concerts were single benefits for principal performers and other entrepreneurs, mostly similarly high-priced concerts in the West End. A benefit was a high-risk undertaking requiring energetic promotion; in the 1764 season there were twenty-two, but a year later just ten. The Mozarts' late arrival in 1764 allowed little time for the delivery of tickets to patrons: by 5 June many had already left for their country seats, although with the King's birthday the day before the audience numbered over 200, including ambassadors and 'the principal families in England' (the Earl of March sold as many as thirty-six tickets). The following season Leopold Mozart put on two concerts, but difficulties arose from clashes of dates, and the concert on 21 February (at which Mozart's new symphonies were performed) had to start at six to enable patrons to attend Mrs Cornelys', while ticket prices for 13 May were reduced to five shillings, suggesting that novelty interest was already waning. Nevertheless even a moderately attended concert could raise over £100 (especially if some of the performers waived their fees), a sum that exceeded Leopold Mozart's annual salary in SALZBURG.

Midway between the West End and the City, with graduated prices ensuring variegated company, were the two main English theatres, Covent Garden and Drury Lane. In 1764–5 the fare ranged from serious spoken drama to the English operas of Arne and revivals of *The Beggar's Opera*. Covent Garden was also the venue for oratorios on Wednesdays and Fridays during Lent, the pattern established by Handel and carried on by his successors Smith and Stanley. Handel oratorios – or pasticcios derived from them – continued to draw crowds, with *Messiah* as the invariable closing work, a continuity of repertory unprecedented for the time. Whether the Mozarts attended is unknown: they would certainly have heard Handel choruses at the Ranelagh concert in 1764, and there were obsequious references to Handel in their concert advertisements and the dedication of Mozart's Op. 3 sonatas.

The musical culture of the City, the commercial heart of London, differed markedly from that of the West End. Although the bourgeoisie to some extent emulated upper-class culture, the City itself maintained a distance from its perceived excesses and degeneracy, preferring amateur musical societies such as the Castle Concerts for the enjoyment of concerti grossi and the occasional oratorio. The Academy of Ancient Music, formed in 1726 for the cultivation of Renaissance and early Baroque music, was organized on similar lines, although it still retained a commitment to older vocal music.

In the early 1760s a different kind of concert came to prominence: the daily exhibition, on the lines of those scientific or zoological demonstrations that periodically caught the public's imagination. The venue was typically a minor hall or even a private house, and the concert inexpensive and informal, responding to the wishes of the passing visitor. Often there was some particular curiosity in the form of a new instrument (the musical glasses were in vogue) or a notorious personage. Clearly on the same lines were the Mozarts' daytime performances at their lodgings in March 1765, repetitive commercial exhibitions that can only have weakened their artistic and social standing. The final venue in July (the Swan and Hoop, a minor City tavern) and the shameless circus tricks – the young Mozarts playing with a handkerchief covering their hands – was an admission that prestige had been sacrificed for money for their return journey.

One of the family's last visits was to the British Museum, an honour that Leopold returned with donations of Mozart's music, including his only setting of English words, the short chorus 'God is our refuge and our strength' (K20). Leopold seems to have left London with mixed feelings. Although forever complaining about the expenses he endured, he clearly exulted in London's opulence and the 'good catch of guineas' to be made there. Only after the most anxious soul-searching did he turn down an opportunity to remain in London, and this apparently for a different reason: 'I will not bring up my children in such a dangerous place (where the majority of the inhabitants have no religion and where one only has evil examples before one).' Mozart himself hankered after a return to London for the rest of his life, imagining England as a haven offering escape from daily travails. His father was strongly against such a move, as we learn from his impassioned pleas in 1778, and again eight years later when the care of Mozart's own children was an obstacle.

Mozart lived on in London's memory as a prodigy to be recalled alongside his friend THOMAS LINLEY. Only gradually did his reputation as a mature composer reach England; and though appreciated by professionals, his music seems to have encountered resistance from London audiences. Throughout the late 1780s, however, there were serious plans to entice Mozart to London. In 1786 his English friends in VIENNA – Nancy and Stephen STORACE, MICHAEL KELLY, his pupil THOMAS ATTWOOD – seem to have persuaded him to plan the journey, with a vague idea of opera and concert engagements. Back in London in 1787, the Storaces remained in contact, Stephen publishing a number of keyboard works (including the first edition of the piano trio K564) and Nancy inserting arias into pasticcio operas, such as the unpublished 'Batti, batti' in 1790. Later the same year she was behind an invitation from the manager of the new Pantheon Opera, Robert O'Reilly, inviting him to write two operas and hinting at an engagement from the Professional Concert (successor to the Bach–Abel concerts). Other possibilities soon followed: a proposal from Salomon in December 1790 that he succeed Haydn as composer at his Hanover Square series; and another the following year from DA PONTE. It has been suggested that the three last symphonies and even COSÌ FAN TUTTE may have been intended for London; but we can only fantasize with Mozart about the wealth and acclaim he surely would have received there. SIMON MCVEIGH

J. Jenkins, *Mozart and the English Connection* (London, 1998)
S. McVeigh, *Concert Life in London from Mozart to Haydn* (Cambridge, 1993)
I. Woodfield, 'New Light on the Mozarts' London Visit: A Private Concert with Manzuoli', *Music & Letters* 76 (1995), 187–207

Lotter family. GERMAN music publishers and printers. Founded by Johann Jakob Lotter (b. AUGSBURG, c.1683; d. Augsburg, 1738), the firm was among the most important south German music publishers, primarily of works by south German Catholic composers; Lotter's son, also Johann Jakob (b. Augsburg, 1726; d. Augsburg, 1804), later expanded the firm's list to include composers from north Germany, Italy and France as well as pedagogical music literature. The firm's most important customers included court orchestras, monasteries and schools. LEOPOLD MOZART may have been acquainted with Johann Jakob Lotter the younger during his early years in Augsburg; in 1756 Johann Jakob published Leopold's *Gründliche Violinschule*. For his part, Leopold was Lotter's agent in SALZBURG, offering for sale the publisher's many works at Salzburg book fairs. Their correspondence shows that they were friends as well: Johann Jakob was among the first to be informed of Wolfgang's birth on 27 January 1756. The firm, later managed by Esaias Daniel Lotter (b. Augsburg, 1759; d. Augsburg, 1820), survived well into the nineteenth century. CLIFF EISEN

A. Layer, 'Johann Jakob Lotter der Jüngere, Leopold Mozarts Augsburger Verleger', in *Leopold Mozart 1719–1787: Bild einer Persönlichkeit*, ed. L. Wegele (Augsburg, 1969), 117–28
H. Rheinfurth, *Der Musikverlag Lotter in Augsburg (ca. 1719–1845)* (Tutzing, 1977)

Lucio Silla, K135. *Dramma per musica* in three acts (MILAN, Teatro Regio Ducale, 26 Dec. 1772), libretto by GIOVANNI DE GAMERRA. The success of MITRIDATE, RE DI PONTO (1770) encouraged the ducal theatre in Milan to commission a second opera from Mozart to open the 1772–3 carnival season. The contract (4 Mar. 1771) offered Mozart 130 gold gigliati for the work (a 30 per cent increase on the fee for *Mitridate*) and stated that he should send the recitatives by October 1772 and be in Milan by November to write the arias and rehearse the whole; it was normal to compose the overture and recitatives first, and then the arias only in the presence of the singers so that their abilities could be gauged and exploited. Mozart and his father in fact were in Milan in August–December 1771, when Mozart wrote the serenata ASCANIO IN ALBA for the marriage of Archduke Ferdinand. After ten months in SALZBURG, they returned to Italy for a third time, leaving on 24 October (and arriving back on 13 March 1773).

As with *Mitridate*, the main evidence for the work's preparations and performance come from the Mozart letters, which are somewhat muted compared with Leopold's excitement over the earlier work. Perhaps this was because of difficulties over the preparations and rehearsals, or perhaps because Leopold was suffering from rheumatism. Gamerra, the theatre poet in Milan, fretted over the libretto in the light of criticisms from the great METASTASIO; singers arrived late (the primo uomo and prima donna appeared in only late November and early December), fell ill and were replaced at the last minute; and the first performance was delayed by some three hours by the Archduke having to write his New Year letters. The performance was also overlong thanks to the presence of three (unrelated) ballets. But towards the end of the run (twenty-six performances), LEOPOLD MOZART was happier to report on the success gradually being gained by *Lucio Silla*, and rightly so: it is Mozart's first operatic masterpiece.

The subject is typically drawn from Roman history (after Plutarch) turned into fiction and then cast into an opera seria mould, with a heroic pair of lovers (Giunia, Cecilio) opposed by an authority figure (Lucio Silla), a second pair of lovers (Celia, Lucio Cinna) and a minor confidant (Aufidio). The plot as usual revolves around the conflict of love and duty, the virtues of constancy, fidelity and self-sacrifice, and the ultimate reform of a tyrant for the sake of the common good. The whole is presented in a rich variety of scenes (as with *Mitridate*, designed by the Galliari brothers and perhaps repeating some of the same sets). These are stock themes and the countless works elaborating them were conventionally structured – such that audiences could then enjoy the nuances of playing upon convention – but nonetheless offered powerful lessons in appropriate modes of human behaviour in an age when autocratic absolutism was increasingly a matter of debate. This is not to say that *Lucio Silla* is a 'revolutionary' opera – the genre would not permit such political or social critique – but for all the historical distance, it offers an intriguing mirror on its times.

The scene is set in Rome in 79 BC. In Act 1, Cecilio (Cecilius), an exiled Roman senator in love with Giunia (Junia), has secretly returned to Rome and asks for news of his beloved from his friend Lucio (Lucius) Cinna. Lucio Silla (Lucius Sulla) enlists the aid of his sister Celia in gaining Giunia's hand for himself, but Giunia hates him as the enemy of her father, the murdered Gaius Marius: Silla is torn but decides for anger and revenge. Cecilio, on Cinna's advice, has gone to wait for Giunia by Marius' tomb, where she goes every day to weep; they meet and embrace in joyous reconciliation.

In Act 2, Aufidio (Aufidius) tells Silla that he should declare Giunia his wife in public, and Silla and Celia decide that drastic action is needed: he will give Celia to her beloved Cinna if she aids his suit. Cecilio decides to kill Silla but is restrained by Cinna, who urges instead a conspiracy whereby Giunia should marry the tyrant but kill him on her wedding night. She refuses so violent an act but asks Cinna to protect Cecilio in fear for his safety. Silla once again woos Giunia; she again scorns him and is left in despair with Cecilio, who decides that he himself must murder Silla. Celia urges Giunia to accept Silla's hand but she again refuses: she would rather die. On the Capitol, Silla is fêted by the Roman people and proclaims Giunia his wife; she would kill herself but is prevented by Cecilio, who draws his sword on Silla and is put in chains. The two lovers are consoled by thoughts of a shared death, while Silla is enraged by their constancy.

In Act 3, Cinna promises to marry Celia if she can change Silla's mind, and reassures Cecilio. Giunia takes a sad farewell of her beloved, promising to join him in death. Cecilio is brought before the Senate and, to everyone's surprise, Silla pardons both him and Cinna, offering them their respective brides. He renounces public life and is praised for his magnanimity, while the lovers rejoice in their freedom.

Mozart had come a long way since *Mitridate, re di Ponto*; he had also developed his technique by way of an important group of SYMPHONIES and string quartets. Although *Lucio Silla* is in the grand opera seria mould (and of a similar size to *Mitridate*), there is a new formal fluidity that is matched on the smaller scale by a more flexible melodic and harmonic style. Mozart may have been frustrated by the problems over the singers: the first Silla, Bassano Morgano, was a last-minute replacement and so did not receive music to do the character justice. But Mozart had the famous soprano castrato VENANZIO RAUZZINI as Cecilio (he also wrote *Exsultate, jubilate*, K165, for him at the same time) and as Giunia the soprano prima donna ANNA DE AMICIS. Leopold Mozart noted (28 Nov. 1772) that Rauzzini sang his first aria 'Il tenero momento' (Act 1, scene 2; No. 2) 'like an angel'; the initial long note showed his *messa di voce* at its best. He said nothing about the first Cinna, the female soprano Felicità Suardi, although she must have had a fine voice to take on this difficult role. But he was particularly pleased at Anna de Amicis's favourable response to her arias, especially the phenomenally virtuosic 'Ah se il crudel periglio' (Act 2, scene 5; No. 11) with its 'passages which are unusual, quite unique and extremely difficult and which she sings amazingly well' (12 Dec. 1772).

These and other arias in the opera are typical showpiece numbers in the expanded da capo format also found in *Mitridate*: Cinna's first aria, 'Vieni ov'amor t'invita' (Act 1, scene 1; No. 1) has a long opening ritornello, four full statements of the first stanza of the text, one of the second, and a full da capo (minus the opening ritornello), with the result that the first stanza is heard eight times in all. However, there are alternatives. As in *Mitridate*, two-tempo arias provide emotional contrast, but Mozart also starts to use more compressed structures. Cecilio's delightful 'Pupille amate' (Act 3, scene 4; No. 21) sets a two-stanza text in a simple ternary form with a hint of rondo. Silla's 'D'ogni pietà mi scoglio' (Act 2, scene 8; No. 13) is a typical 'indecision' aria, where Silla veers between fury at Giunia's intransigence and the love he feels for her. Unusually, the text is not stanzaic and it changes metre: Mozart responds with a through-composed setting (and with no opening ritornello), including a brief passage of recitative as Silla questions his motives.

Such deviations from the norm may be because the librettist De Gamerra was becoming interested in more fluid structures on the model of the 'reform' operas of Traetta and Jommelli. That, in turn, may explain the increasing emphasis on accompanied (rather than just simple) recitatives: there are eight in *Lucio Silla* (not counting the scene-complex at the end of Act 1 discussed below) compared with six in *Mitridate*, and five are in the intense Act 2. Both Cecilio and Giunia in particular are given ample chance to exploit the expressive possibilities of the medium. In Act 2, scene 10, Giunia is left alone on stage fearing for her future. Her powerful soliloquy is set as an accompanied recitative that ranges widely in terms of gesture and tonality, leading to an aria, 'Parto, m'affretto' (No. 16) – again irregularly structured in mixed metres – combining resolve with emotional confusion that is once more, in effect, through-composed.

These strategies soften the boundaries between recitative and aria, and also loosen the formal constraints of aria, to produce a more 'natural' and continuous dramatic flow, in so far as that is possible within the constraints of opera seria: IDOMENEO is not far around the corner. Mozart also explores the possibilities of ensemble writing: the trio for Silla, Cecilio and Giunia at the end of Act 2, 'Quell'orgoglioso sdegno' (No. 18), pits the tyrant against the lovers by way of contrasted melodic ideas in a single musical framework in ways that were to become typical of Mozart's later ensembles. And thanks to his librettist, he was also able to combine accompanied recitative, aria and ensemble to powerful effect. In Act 1, scene 7, Cecilio meets Giunia in the mausoleum containing her father's remains: such tomb (so-called 'ombra') scenes were conventional in opera seria of the period, and there may be a hint of GLUCK here. Silla's aria ending scene 6 is followed by a nine-bar instrumental interlude (presumably covering the set change) with almost DON GIOVANNI-like chromaticism introducing an accompanied recitative in A minor (Cecilio's 'Morte, morte fatal, della tua mano'). Giunia enters with her companions, and the chorus (in E flat major; shades of DIE ZAUBERFLÖTE) frames an intense arioso passage for Giunia ('O del padre ombra diletta' in G minor; Pamina's key) as she laments the death of her father. The scene continues in accompanied recitative, with appropriate musical gestures for Cecilio's sudden appearance to Giunia's great surprise, leading meltingly into the duet 'D'Elisio in sen m'attendi' (No. 7 in A major) moving from Andante to Molto Allegro as the lovers are united in harmonious parallel thirds. *Mitridate* also included a love duet in A major (always the most seductive of keys) at the end of Act 2, but the one in *Lucio Silla* is far more intense, confirming what was to become a topos in the later operas, whether as parody (Don Giovanni and Zerlina's 'Là ci darem la mano') or in deadly earnest (Fiordiligi and Ferrando's 'Fra gli amplessi in pochi istanti' in COSÌ FAN TUTTE).

It is not entirely idle to suggest that *Lucio Silla* somehow stayed in Mozart's memory. As with *Mitridate*, he dropped the opera once it had served its purpose: it was not revived until 1929 (in PRAGUE). But he remained fond of its music, particularly the arias for Giunia: ALOYSIA LANGE (then Weber) with whom Mozart was in love, sang 'Ah se il crudel periglio' (No. 11) 'most excellently' and 'Parto, m'affretto' (No. 16) in MANNHEIM in early 1778 (see the letters of 17 Jan., 7, 14 and 19 Feb. 1778); Leopold sent three other arias from the opera to Mannheim at the same time; and 'Parto, m'affretto' was performed in a concert in Vienna in March 1783. Mozart was also very curious to see J. C. BACH's setting of the revised libretto (Mannheim, 1775). He must have known that his own *Lucio Silla* was the best work of his yet to reach the stage, bearing all the hallmarks of an operatic composer in full maturity. TIM CARTER

M. Feldman, 'Staging the Virtuoso: Ritornello Procedure in Mozart, from Aria to Concerto', in *Mozart's Piano Concertos: Text, Context, Interpretation*, ed. N. Zaslaw (Ann Arbor, 1996), 149–86
C. Gianturco, *Mozart's Early Operas* (London, 1981)
D. Heartz, *Haydn, Mozart and the Viennese School 1740–1780* (New York, 1995)
W. Mann, *Mozart's Operas* (London, 1977)

'Lützow' concerto. Mozart's Piano Concerto in C, K246 (1776). See LÜTZOW, COUNTESS ANTONIE VON and CONCERTOS

Lützow, Countess Antonie von (b. 26 Mar. 1750; d. 25 Apr. 1801). Dedicatee of Mozart's keyboard concerto K246. Countess Lützow was the niece of Archbishop HIERONYMUS VON COLLOREDO; on 4 May 1772 she married Johann Nepomuk Gottfried von Lützow (b. 4 Aug. 1742; d. 6 Feb. 1822), who was then offered a post as Commander of the fortress in SALZBURG. Countess Lützow was a keyboard player, occasionally playing informally at court after her move to Salzburg. K246 was written in April 1776. It does not make great technical demands of the soloist, and was used by the Mozarts as part of their teaching repertory; in 1777 Mozart took it with him on his journey to PARIS, and taught it to his pupil Therese Pierron in MANNHEIM. Of particular interest is the surviving source material for the concerto, because of the information it offers about performance practice in Mozart's concertos. RUTH HALLIWELL

M

Magic Flute, The. See ZAUBERFLÖTE, DIE

Mandini, Stefano (1750–c.1810). A leading Italian baritone in VIENNA in the 1780s, praised for the beautiful, unforced quality of his voice, Mandini probably made his debut in the city in Domenico Cimarosa's *L'italiana in Londra* (5 May 1783). He played a number of prominent operatic roles in Vienna in the 1780s, to considerable critical acclaim, including Mingone in Giuseppe SARTI's *Fra i due litiganti il terzo gode* (28 May 1783), Count Almaviva in Giovanni PAISIELLO's *Il barbiere di Siviglia* (13 Aug. 1783) and Giorgio in *La contadina di spirito* (6 Apr. 1785), where he performed alongside FRANCESCO BENUCCI. On 1 May 1786, he sang Count Almaviva in the premiere of LE NOZZE DI FIGARO at the Burgtheater (again with Benucci, who sang Figaro). A few months earlier (on 28 Nov. 1785), he was a soloist at the same venue in two Mozart ensembles performed at the premiere of *La villanella rapita* by FRANCESCO BIANCHI – the quartet for soprano, tenor, two basses and orchestra 'Dite almeno, in che mancai', K479, and the trio for soprano, tenor, bass and orchestra 'Mandina amabile', K480. Mandini left Vienna for Naples in 1788, after a grand farewell concert on 15 February 1788. He subsequently moved on to PARIS in 1789 – where he reprised the role of Almaviva in Paisiello's *Il barbiere di Siviglia* – then to Venice in 1794–5. SIMON P. KEEFE

D. Link, *The National Court Theatre in Mozart's Vienna: Sources and Documents 1783–1792* (Oxford, 1998)

Mannheim. City in GERMANY at the confluence of the Neckar and Rhine rivers. During Mozart's lifetime, Mannheim was ruled by Karl Theodor, a patron of both the arts and the sciences. 'Gala' days, celebrating the name days of Karl Theodor or his wife, Elisabeth Auguste, were particularly elaborate, including the performance of grand masses, operas, ballets, French comedies or opere buffe and concerts. So too was Carnival, which additionally included masked balls. The splendour of the court, and Karl Theodor's support, attracted numerous prominent musicians to Mannheim, including a contingent of Bohemian horn players, the Kapellmeister Ignaz Holzbauer, Anton Fils, Johann Baptist WENDLING and Innocenz Danzi; among local musicians, Johann Stamitz and Christian CANNABICH were perhaps the most important. Performances took place not only at court but also at Schwetzingen, the Elector's summer residence, which boasted a theatre built in 1752.

Above all, Mannheim was famous for its orchestra; in 1772 CHARLES BURNEY wrote, 'There are more solo players and good composers in this, than perhaps in any other orchestra in Europe; it is an army of generals, equally fit to plan a battle, as to fight it.' Discipline was all-important, including precise attacks, attention to dynamic nuance and uniform bowing; and much of the credit for this went to Stamitz and Cannabich. C. F. D. Schubart wrote of Cannabich that 'He has invented a totally new bowing technique and possesses the gift of holding the largest orchestra together by nothing more than the nod of his head and the flick of his elbow. He is really the creator of the co-ordinated execution characteristic of the Palatine orchestra. He is the inventor of all those magical devices that are now admired by the whole of Europe.' LEOPOLD MOZART described the Mannheim ensemble as 'unquestionably the best in Europe'.

Chamber music was frequently performed as well, with Karl Theodor sometimes taking the flute or cello part, while opera was under the direction of Holzbauer, Kapellmeister 1753–78. The repertory included opere serie by Galuppi, Traetta, Jommelli, HASSE and SALIERI as well as J. C. BACH, whose *Temistocle* (1772) and *Lucio Silla* (1775) were both written for Mannheim. Italian comic opera figured at Schwetzingen in particular: works by Piccinni, Sacchini, Anfossi and PAISIELLO were performed in the 1770s as were French *opéras comiques*, including Grétry's *Zémire et Azor*. Some French operas, in German adaptations, were given during the summers, by the Theobald MARCHAND troupe which performed in a temporary theatre on the Fruchtmarkt and these no doubt led to the encouragement of native German opera during the 1770s: among the most notable of these was Anton Schweitzer's *Alceste* and Holzbauer's *Günther von Schwarzburg*. In general, the close connection to PARIS contributed significantly to the court's musical life and provided an additional outlet for Mannheim's prominent instrumentalists, many of whom travelled at one time or another to perform at the Concert spirituel. Understandably, then, Mannheim was an important destination for Mozart, who visited the city four times.

The first visit was brief: on 18 July 1763, en route to Paris, the Mozarts played for the court at Schwetzingen. Considerably more extended was Mozart's stay in 1777 and 1778. Wolfgang and his mother arrived at Mannheim on 30 October 1778; the purpose of their visit was to secure for Mozart a position at court. But despite numerous attempts to secure the patronage of Karl Theodor, including a performance at court on 6 November and the support he received from Cannabich, the court music Intendant Count Louis Aurel Savioli, the Kapellmeister Ignaz Holzbauer and the flautist J. B. WENDLING, among others, nothing came of it. Instead Mozart busied himself with private teaching, commissions for compositions and with private music-making. He composed the keyboard sonata K309 for Cannabich's daughter Rosa and frequently performed at their house, including a concert on 13 February 1778 where Aloysia Weber (later LANGE) sang arias from LUCIO SILLA, Rosa played the concerto K238 and Mozart himself performed K175. At a semi-public concert on 23 February, another pupil of Mozart's, Therese Pierron, played the concerto K246. His other compositions from the time include the sonata K311 and five accompanied sonatas (K296, K301–3 and K305) inspired by similar works by J. Schuster. He was also asked by FERDINAND DEJEAN, an employee of the Dutch East India Company who had worked in eastern Asia for many years as a physician, to compose three flute concertos and two flute quartets, but in the event he failed to deliver and may have written only a single quartet.

Mozart dawdled in Mannheim, in no small part because he had fallen in love with Aloysia Weber, a daughter of the court music copyist Fridolin Weber (and the older sister of his future wife, CONSTANZE MOZART); it was for her that he composed the aria *Alcandro lo confesso – Non sò donde viene*, K294. Mozart even put to his father the idea of taking Aloysia to Italy, where she would become a famous prima donna and he her composer, but the proposal infuriated Leopold. Nevertheless, Mozart continued to spend time with the family, travelling with them in January 1778 to Kirchheim-Bolanden, where they visited the court of Princess Caroline of Nassau-Weilburg and Aloysia performed two arias from *Lucio Silla*.

When Mozart finally left Mannheim, on 14 March 1778, he had nothing to show for his visit there and there is no doubt that for the most part he had only himself to blame, even if the political situation was complicated by the death on 30 December 1777 of MAXIMILIAN III JOSEPH, Elector of Bavaria, and Karl Theodor's move to Munich in January 1778 as Elector of the Pfalz and Bavaria. By the time he returned to Mannheim in the autumn of 1778, following his unsuccessful stay in Paris and against his father's wishes (who felt that since the removal of the Elector's court there was little opportunity for advancement in Mannheim), Aloysia had moved to Munich; when he saw her in Munich at the end of December, she received him coolly. But he did become acquainted with Benda's melodrama *Medea* and resolved to write one himself (the work, *Semiramis*, if started, was never performed and is now lost).

Mozart's final visit to Mannheim was in 1790, during the return trip to Vienna from LEOPOLD II's Frankfurt coronation, when he attended a performance there of LE NOZZE DI FIGARO on 24 October. A review of the performance, published in the Berlin *Annalen des Theaters*, described the music as 'full of expression and truth'.

CLIFF EISEN

L. Finscher, ed., *Die Mannheimer Hofkapelle im Zeitalter Carl Theodors* (Mannheim, 1992)
B. Pelker and J. Reutter, eds., *Mozart und Mannheim. Kongressbericht Mannheim 1991* (Frankfurt, 1992)
S. Mörz, *Haupt-und Residenzstadt. Carl Theodor, sein Hof und Mannheim* (Mannheim, 1998)
E. K. Wolf, 'The Mannheim Court', in *The Classical Era: From the 1740s to the End of the 18th Century*, ed. N. Zaslaw (London, 1989), 213–39
R. Würtz, ed., *Mannheimer Mozart-Buch* (Wilhelmshaven, 1996)

Manzuoli, Giovanni (b. Florence, c.1720; d. Florence, 1782). A leading European castrato in the second half of the eighteenth century, Manzuoli sang to great acclaim in Madrid, Lisbon, VIENNA and Bologna before heading to LONDON's King's Theatre for the 1764–5 season. LEOPOLD MOZART's letter from London to his friend Lorenz HAGENAUER (8 Feb. 1765) gives a good indication of Manzuoli's esteemed reputation at this time (and the rich rewards he received): 'This winter, nobody is making much money except Manzuoli and a few others in the opera. Manzuoli is getting 1500 pounds sterling for this season and the money has had to be guaranteed in Italy . . . otherwise Manzuoli would not have come to London. In addition he is giving a benefit, that is, an evening recital for himself, so that this winter he will be drawing more than 20,000 German gulden. He is the only person whom they have had to pay decently in order to set the opera on its feet again.' Manzuoli elicited lavish praise from CHARLES BURNEY: 'Manzuoli's voice was the most powerful and voluminous soprano that had been heard on our stage since the time of Farinelli; and his manner of singing was grand and full of taste and dignity.' BARON FRIEDRICH MELCHIOR GRIMM also remarked in the *Correspondance littéraire* of 15 July 1766 that he 'sings with as much taste as soul'.

Manzuoli befriended the Mozart family in London in 1764–5, and probably gave Mozart singing lessons. He also performed a private concert with the Mozarts at the home of Lord and Lady (Robert and Margaret) Clive in Berkeley Square. They met in Florence in 1770, first by chance on 2 April, and again in MILAN in late 1771, when Manzuoli sang Ascanio in the first production of Mozart's ASCANIO IN ALBA (17 Oct. 1771), written for the wedding of Archduke Ferdinand of Austria and Maria Beatrice Ricciarda of Modena. But a disagreement over Manzuoli's fee ensued, as reported by an irritated Mozart to his sister on 24 November 1771: 'Manzuoli, who up to the present has been generally looked upon as the most sensible of the castrati, has in his old age given the world a sample of his stupidity and conceit. He was engaged for the opera at a salary of five hundred cigliati, but, as the contract did not mention the serenata, he demanded another five hundred for that, that is one thousand cigliati in all. The court only gave him seven hundred and a fine gold snuff-box (quite enough, I think). But he like a true castrato returned both the seven hundred cigliati and the snuff-box and went off without anything. I do not know how it will all end – badly, I expect.' SIMON P. KEEFE

I. Woodfield, 'New Light on the Mozarts' London Visit: A Private Concert with Manzuoli', *Music & Letters* 76 (1995), 187–207

Marchand family. Theatrical and musical family. Theobald Marchand (b. 21 Nov. 1746; d. 25 Nov. 1800) directed Elector Karl Theodor's German court theatre in MUNICH from 1777 to 1793. He married Magdalena Brochard (b. c.1749; d. 25 Aug. 1794), an actress and dancer. Two of their children and their niece were Mozart family resident pupils after Mozart had left SALZBURG, until NANNERL MOZART's marriage: their son Heinrich (b. 4 May 1769; d. after 1812) from 1781 to 1784, their daughter Margarethe ('Gretl'; b. c.1768; d. 1798 or 1800) from 1782 to 1784, and their niece Johanna Brochard ('Hanchen'; b. 31 Jan. 1775; d. after 1807) from 1783 to 1784. Gretl was a keyboard player, composer and professional singer. Her abilities and character were admired by LEOPOLD MOZART above Heinrich's. Heinrich was a violinist, keyboard player and composer. In 1786 he returned to Salzburg as court violinist, lived with Leopold again, and gave the first Salzburg performance of Mozart's D minor keyboard concerto, K466, on 22 March 1786.

The Mozart correspondence and Nannerl's diary give an engaging idea of the educational experience of these pupils. They lived as part of the family, helping with household tasks and joining in all social activities, including the musical jamborees planned by Leopold whenever the children's parents visited. It is striking that Leopold encouraged Gretl, as well as Heinrich, to publish compositions, and Hanchen also became a composer, as well as an actor, singer and keyboard player. RUTH HALLIWELL

R. Halliwell, *The Mozart Family: Four Lives in a Social Context* (Oxford, 1998)
H. Schuler, *Mozarts Salzburger Freunde und Bekannte* (Wilhelmshaven, 1995), 98–100 and 191–2

Maria Theresia, Empress (b. Vienna, 13 May 1717; d. Vienna 28 Nov. 1780). Daughter of Emperor Charles VI (1685–1740) and wife of Emperor Francis I (1737–65), Maria Theresia became Dowager Empress in 1765 when her son, Joseph, assumed the position of Emperor JOSEPH II after the death of his father. She first encountered Mozart when the six-year-old prodigy performed for her and her husband at Schönbrunn in VIENNA on 13 October 1762. LEOPOLD MOZART proudly recalled the event, and the impetuous behaviour of his son, in a letter to his friend Lorenz HAGENAUER (16 Oct. 1762): 'Their Majesties received us with such extraordinary graciousness that, when I shall tell of it, people will declare that I have made it up. Suffice it to say that Woferl [Mozart] jumped up on the Empress's lap, put his arms around her neck and kissed her heartily.' Maria Theresia continued to see the Mozarts in 1762 and then again on their trip to Vienna in 1768: 'you cannot possibly conceive with what familiarity her Majesty the Empress conversed with my wife, talking to her partly of my children's smallpox and partly of the events of our grand tour; nor can you imagine how she stroked my wife's cheeks and pressed her hands', Leopold reported to Hagenauer on 23 January 1768. But Leopold struck a sourer note only a week or so later: the Empress's 'amazing graciousness and . . . indescribable friendliness' was overshadowed by the Emperor's frugality – they were presented with only a 'worthless' medal. Three years later, Maria Theresia wrote nastily to her son Archduke Ferdinand about the possibility of giving Mozart a position at court in MILAN: 'You ask me to take the young Salzburger into your service. I do not know why, not believing that you have need of a composer or of useless people. If however it would give you pleasure, I have no wish to hinder you. What I say is intended only to prevent your burdening yourself with useless people and giving titles to people of that sort. In addition, if they are in your service it degrades that service when these people go about the world like beggars.'

SIMON P. KEEFE

Marriage of Figaro, The. See NOZZE DI FIGARO, LE

Martin, Philipp Jakob (b. ?Regensburg, n.d.; d. ?Vienna, n.d.). An impresario based in VIENNA, Martin arranged a series of Friday concerts for amateurs at the Mehlgrube (winter 1781–2) and then a comparable series of Sunday concerts at the Augarten in which Mozart participated (summer 1782). Martin advertised the 'very cheap prices' of these concerts in the *Wiener Zeitung* (1 June 1782). Mozart reported to his father, predicting a profit of 300 hundred gulden from the events (8 May 1782): 'The subscription for the whole summer is two ducats. So you can imagine that we shall have plenty of subscribers, the more so as I am taking an interest in it and am associated with it.' After the first concert, attended by luminaries such as ARCHDUKE MAXIMILIAN, COUNTESS THUN and BARON VAN SWIETEN, Mozart described Martin as 'a very worthy young man, who is trying to make his way by his music, by his elegant writing and generally by his ability, intelligence and sound judgment'. Mozart had dinner with Martin on 29 September 1782, poking fun at him as a 'little angel' in a letter to BARONESS VON WALDSTÄTTEN (28 Sept. 1782). Martin also stood in for BARON WETZLAR VON PLANKENSTERN, godfather to Mozart and CONSTANZE MOZART's first child, Raimund Leopold, at Raimund's christening in June 1783. He advertised another series of outdoor concerts in Vienna in 1791 (*Wiener Zeitung*, 14 May 1791), but was forced to delay the start of the series for more than a week on account of 'insufficient ticket sales' (4 June 1791). SIMON P. KEEFE

M. S. Morrow, *Concert Life in Haydn's Vienna: Aspects of a Developing Musical and Social Institution* (Stuyvesant, NY, 1989), esp. 53–8

Martín y Soler, Vicente (Martini) (b. Valencia, 2 May 1754; d. St Petersburg, 30 Jan./10 Feb. 1806), Spanish composer of Italian opera. Born and raised in Valencia, he composed operas in Italy from 1777 to 1785, spent the next three years in VIENNA, and in 1788 moved to St Petersburg, where, except for an engagement in LONDON in 1795, he spent the remainder of his life. His Viennese period represents the peak of his career. With LORENZO DA PONTE, who in his memoirs writes more warmly about him than Mozart, he produced *Il burbero di buon cuore* (4 Jan. 1786), *Una cosa rara* (17 Nov. 1786) and *L'arbore di Diana* (1 Oct. 1787).

The enormous popularity of the latter two had a strong and lasting impact on opera in Vienna. Mozart acknowledged the success of *Una cosa rara* by quoting from it the tune 'O quanto un sì bel giubilo' in the supper music of DON GIOVANNI. In 1789 LOUISE VILLENEUVE made a successful debut in Vienna as Amore in *L'arbore di Diana*. When Mozart came to compose Dorabella for her in COSÌ FAN TUTTE, he alluded to her role of Amore in the aria 'È Amore un ladroncello', a joke that would have been appreciated by the audience. Meanwhile he had already provided Villeneuve with two new arias (K582, K583) for the revival of *Il burbero di buon cuore* in 1789. The canon in *Così fan tutte* 'E nel tuo, nel mio bicchiero' also owes its existence to Martín. It was composed in friendly competition with SALIERI, who had written a canon in his opera *La cifra* (1789) evidently in response to the inferior canons introduced by Martín into *Una cosa rara* and *L'arbore di Diana*. This episode launched a local tradition, which survived to BEETHOVEN's *Fidelio*. Mozart's other response to Martín's canons was to change the title of his vocal canon 'O du eselhafter Peierl' to 'O du eselhafter Martin' (K560).

Martín's popularity lies in his tuneful style, which contemporaries described as 'sweet' and 'graceful'. Characterized by the use of thirds, dance rhythms and unexpected melodic turns, it comes most strongly into its own in lyrical numbers, which often assume the pastoral topos. DOROTHEA LINK

D. Link, '*L'arbore di Diana*: A Model for *Così fan tutte*', in *Wolfgang Amadè Mozart: Essays on his Life and Music*, ed. S. Sadie (Oxford, 1996), 362–73

C. Martin, *Vicente Martín y Solers Oper 'Una Cosa Rara': Geschichte eines Opernerfolgs im 18. Jahrhundert* (Hildesheim, 2001)

J. Platoff, 'Review-Essay: A New History for Martín's *Una cosa rara*', *Journal of Musicology* 12 (1994), 85–115

Martini, Giovanni Battista (Padre) (b. Bologna, 24 Apr. 1706; d. Bologna, 3 Aug. 1784). A Franciscan monk, and a composer and scholar of considerable repute, Martini met Mozart and LEOPOLD MOZART while they were in Bologna in March 1770 on the first of Mozart's Italian tours. Writing to his wife (27 Mar. 1770), Leopold called Martini the 'idol of the Italians' and described the 'tests' Martini had set Mozart to investigate his prodigious talent: 'We have visited him twice and each time Wolfgang has worked out a fugue, for which the

Padre had only written down with a few notes the *ducem* or *la guida*.' These tests 'increased [Mozart's] reputation all over Italy'. Later in 1770, when Leopold and Mozart were back in Bologna, they met frequently; Martini furnished Mozart with a written testimonial on 12 October 1770 detailing his performing and compositional skills, 'above all . . . playing on the Harpsichord various subjects given him to improvise, which with great mastery he carried out according to all the conditions demanded by Art'.

Mozart and Leopold clearly liked and admired Martini. In a letter signed by Mozart, but in Leopold's hand (4 Sept. 1776), they expressed their affection: 'how often have I longed to be near you, most Reverend Father, so that I might be able to talk to and have discussion with you. . . . Alas we are so far apart.' In summer 1777, Leopold commissioned a painting of Mozart wearing his Order of the Golden Spur and sent it to Martini, as Martini had requested. The painting can now be seen at Bologna's Civico Museo Bibliografico Musicale.

SIMON P. KEEFE

C. Burney, *The Present State of Music in France and Italy* (London, 1773; repr. New York, 1969)

Masonic Funeral Music. Mozart wrote most of his music for Viennese Masonic lodges, including the *Gesellenreise*, K468, the songs for male chorus K483 and K484, the cantata *Die Maurerfreude*, K471 and the orchestral *Maurerische Trauermusik* (Masonic Funeral Music), K477 between 14 December 1784 – the date of his initiation into the 'Beneficence' lodge – and mid-January 1786. (By the end of this period his lodge had merged with two others to become 'New-Crowned Hope'.) Each work was written for a specific occasion: K468 probably in recognition of LEOPOLD MOZART acquiring the status of 'journeyman' at the 'True Concord' lodge (26 Mar. 1785); K483 and 484 for an initial gathering of the newly formed 'New-Crowned Hope' (14 Jan. 1786); and K471 for a ceremony honouring IGNAZ BORN, a prominent Viennese Freemason who was Master of 'True Concord' (24 Apr. 1785). The Masonic Funeral Music, performed on 17 November 1785 in memory of Duke Georg August zu Mecklenburg-Strelitz, a senior figure in the Austrian army, and Count (Franz) ESTERHÁZY von Galántha, an official at the Hungarian-Transylvanian Chancery, was no exception, although it was not conceived initially at least as a memorial for these two men. Both the Duke and Count died in November 1785, but Mozart entered the work into his thematic catalogue, the *Verzeichnüss*, in July 1785, listing a single basset horn and no bassoon when the final version in fact has three basset horns and a double bassoon. It is possible that the work was performed in its original instrumentation on an earlier occasion.

K477 is short – sixty-nine bars and about four and a half minutes in length – but exhibits a wide range of affects and packs a strong punch. Mozart begins, for example, with eight bars of doleful, but rounded and harmonious *piano* wind writing on a simple motif – first the two oboes alone, then the three basset horns, bassoon and horns, then the wind ensemble in its entirety – followed by a passage for winds and strings featuring raw *forte* surges that interrupt the prevailing *piano* dynamic. In the middle section Mozart introduces a Gregorian chant (Lamentations of Jeremiah) in the oboes and clarinet, creating pronounced textural contrast between string and wind sections. It has been suggested that the use of this particular chant, associated with the destruction of the Temple of Solomon (a topic referenced in Masonic ritual) indicates that K477 was initially intended for performance at another Viennese lodge event in August 1785. SIMON P. KEEFE

P. A. Autexier, 'Wann wurde die Mauererische Trauermusik uraufgeführt?' *Mozart-Jahrbuch* 1984–5, 56–8
Mozart & Liszt sub rosa (Poitiers, 1984), 23–6
K. Küster, *Mozart: A Musical Biography*, trans. M. Whittall (Oxford, 1996), 200–4

mass. Mozart composed fifteen complete settings of the Mass Ordinary for chorus, soloists and orchestra over a thirteen-year period from 1768 to 1780. In addition, there are five individual mass movements, eight incomplete mass movements and the incomplete C minor mass (K427). According to a source at Lambach, the debated *Missa brevis* in G, K140, is probably by Joseph Mathias Kracher (1752–1827/30) and should no longer be considered authentic Mozart. The unfinished REQUIEM mass is treated elsewhere in this volume.

The masses are of two basic types: the *missa longa* and the *missa brevis*. The first was usually associated with more solemn and festive church occasions when the archbishop or other high church authorities presided. Mozart composed six masses of this type: K139, 66, 167, 262, 257 and 317. In addition to their length and solemnity, these masses usually require pairs of oboes, trumpets, timpani and, in K66, 262, 317, and 427, French horns. Orchestral introductions start movements, intonation texts at the opening of the Gloria and Credo are set, and traditional, fully-fledged choral fugues occur at 'Cum Sancto Spiritu' and 'Et vitam venturi'. In three masses there is a double fugue for one of these texts or the 'Hosanna'.

Mozart's nine completed *breves* are for regular Sundays and smaller feasts; they include K49, 65, 192, 194, 220, 258, 259, 275 and 337. The longest is 569 bars and they usually have the following traits: accompaniment by a small orchestra (the so-called 'church trio' of two violins and organ/bass), along with three trombones doubling the alto, tenor and bass choral parts; each part of the Mass Ordinary is treated as a single, continuous movement (with tempo changes usually at 'Et incarnatus', 'Et resurrexit', 'Pleni sunt coeli', 'Osanna in excelsis' and 'Dona nobis pacem'); minimal repetition of the text which, in the Gloria and Credo, tends to be set syllabically; and fugato writing rather than strict fugue for the 'Cum Sancto Spiritu', 'Et vitam venturi' and 'Osanna in excelsis'.

That most of the masses are of the *brevis* type is largely due to time restrictions for masses at SALZBURG Cathedral under Archbishop COLLOREDO. In a letter of 4 September 1776 to Padre GIOVANNI BATTISTA MARTINI, Mozart wrote: 'Our church music is very different from that of Italy, since a mass with the whole Kyrie, the Gloria, the Credo, the Epistle sonata, the Offertory or Motet, the Sanctus and the Agnus Dei must not last longer than three quarters of an hour. This applies even to the most Solemn Mass said by the Archbishop himself. So you see that a special study is required for this kind of composition. At the same time, the mass must have all the instruments – trumpets, drums and so forth.' The final sentence corroborates the existence in Salzburg of the hybrid *missa brevis et solemnis*; examples among Mozart's works include K220,

258, 259 and 337. (Mozart also later added two trumpets to the *missa brevis* K192 to make it suitable for a Solemn Mass.)

Nine of Mozart's fifteen masses have as their central key C major, the commonest key for this genre at the time and a suitable one for the clarini trumpets. All such C major masses are either a solemn *missa longa* or a *missa brevis et solemnis*. The two C minor masses (K139, 427) are also long and solemn in nature. The regular *missae breves*, however, are based on several other keys (one to two sharps or flats).

When Mozart's masses are compared to those of his predecessors in Salzburg and VIENNA, one sees that, early on, he assimilated and used effortlessly the traditional musical rhetoric of the genre. For example, there are the rising, high fanfare motifs at 'Gloria in excelsis' and 'Et resurrexit'; the descent to lower pitches for 'Et in terra pax'; colourful chromaticism and contrasts at 'Qui tollis', 'miserere', 'Crucifixus', 'passus', 'et mortuos' and 'mortuorum'; falling melodies for 'descendit', 'Crucifixus', 'mortuorum' and 'miserere'; mournful minor tonalities for 'Qui tollis', 'Crucifixus' and 'Agnus Dei'; choral unison at 'Et unam sanctam catholicam'; and softer dynamics and slower rhythms for 'miserere,' 'et sepultus est' and 'mortuorum'.

1. Salzburg
2. Vienna
3. Mass movements, fragments, misattributed works

1. Salzburg

The *Missa brevis* in G, K49, is the earliest surviving mass by Mozart; it was probably composed in Vienna in 1768. Although the teenage Mozart had not yet fully learned the typical attributes of a *missa brevis*, the composer's promising talents are readily apparent. The long, multi-movement Credo resembles that of a longer, number mass: three movements with ten changes of tempo, ending with an 'Et vitam' fugue. K49 is Mozart's only *missa brevis* to have a viola part in addition to the usual church string trio. The 'Et incarnatus' is beautifully ethereal, as angelic strings with slowly moving harmonies in repeated quavers accompany the chorus, and dramatic rests and descending chromatic lines heighten the magic of 'passus et sepultus'.

The Mass in C minor, K139, is Mozart's first and longest complete *missa longa*, a multi-movement 'cantata' or number mass with solo arias and ensembles. This was probably the mass that Mozart wrote for the consecration service of Jesuit Father Ignaz Parhammer's 'Waisenhaus' (orphanage) chapel in Vienna on 7 December 1768. It is scored for a pair each of high and low trumpets (two clarini, two trombe) – a scoring commonly used at the imperial court of Vienna. In addition, there are two oboes, three trombones, timpani, divisi violas and the usual strings. At more than 1,100 bars, K139 is matched in size only by K66, K427 and the Kyrie K341. The work shares many stylistic traits with contemporary Viennese *missae longae* by HASSE, Reutter, Monn, Sonnleithner, DITTERSDORF and others.

While its eclectic collection of church, chamber and operatic styles was surely meant to impress everyone with the *Wunderkind*'s talents, the daring chromaticism ('Qui tollis', 'Et vitam'), harmonic surprises ('Gratias') and unorthodox text repetition ('Christe eleison' appears in three separate movements) set the work apart from its contemporaries. Daniel Heartz notes a C–F♯–G unifying figure in several movements. The Gloria has six separate movements with seven changes of tempo. The 'Quoniam' aria and the start of the 'Et resurrexit' have dazzling coloratura for the soprano soloist. The Credo uses nine tempos for its five movements. A striking contrast occurs between the 'Et incarnatus' duet in a pastoral siciliano style and the following dirge-like 'Crucifixus' with its muted trumpets. The 'Hosanna' interruptions by the chorus in the midst of the soprano's Benedictus were unusual for the time but fit the acclamatory text. The mournful trombone trio that opens the Agnus Dei is particularly poignant.

The next year Mozart again completed two masses, K65 and 66. K65 is dated 14 January 1769, shortly after the composer's return to Salzburg from Vienna. Some scholars believe this mass was the 'solennem missam' performed 5 February 1769, in Salzburg's University Church to open a forty-hour vigil. With only 356 bars, K65 is Mozart's shortest mass and his only *missa brevis* in a minor key. Occasionally in the sacred music of Salzburg from this time, one hears melodies that resemble a chanted plainsong, Psalm tone or LITANY. The Gloria opens with sopranos singing repeated tones reminiscent of a Psalm tone. For the start of the triple-metre 'Hosanna' Mozart curiously writes duple-metre rhythms. The Benedictus is a Baroque-like duet with a lament-like, continually descending chromatic melody. The closing 'Dona nobis' with its 3/8 metre and double counterpoint (using another chant-like theme) offers dance-like finality.

The Mass in C, K66, is dated October 1769 and bears the nickname 'Dominicus' because it was written for the first Mass celebrated by Mozart's friend Cajetan HAGENAUER, now Pater Dominicus, at the abbey church of St Peter's, Salzburg, on 15 October 1769. The orchestral accompaniment, like that of K139, includes two high (clarini) and two low (trombe) trumpets, timpani, two horns, two oboes, and violas along with the usual strings and trombones. This is the first of Mozart's four masses with horn parts. Aside from the incomplete K427 and Kyrie K341, it is the only complete mass requiring flutes in lieu of oboes for one movement ('Et in Spiritum Sanctum'). Dynamic contrasts play a significant role in K66. The tenor's 'Domine Deus' aria resembles a *tempo di menuetto*, with Scotch snaps and a mannered, rococo mix of beat subdivisions. The slow 'Qui tollis' has shades of STURM UND DRANG with its nervous string accompaniment and chromaticism while the 'Quoniam' coloratura soprano aria even includes an opportunity for a cadenza. The 'Cum Sancto Spiritu' fugue has a commanding eight-bar subject. The 'Et incarnatus' is a quiet solo quartet accompanied only by strings. The 'Crucifixus' follows with the re-entry of the winds and a powerful choral unison suggesting the mob. The closing 'Dona nobis' in 3/8 resembles a dance-like operatic finale with quick alternations between soloists and chorus.

Almost four years later, in June 1773, Mozart completed the *Missa in honorem SSme Trinitatis*, K167. The work's title, festive key of C major and scoring (including two high and two low trumpets) suggest that it was composed for the feast of Trinity at the Church of the Holy Trinity in Salzburg. Mozart's only mass not requiring vocal soloists, this *missa solemnis* has a *brevis*-like Kyrie and Gloria. The extended Credo, however, corresponds to the solemn type, with five movements and seven changes of tempo that culminate in a joyful 'Et vitam' fugue. Starting with this mass, all of Mozart's remaining complete masses lack a viola part. In addition, sonata form, which had started influencing Viennese mass settings in the 1760s, begins to appear regularly in Mozart's settings. The 'Et incarnatus' has a beautiful unaccompanied chorus at the moment of incarnation ('ex Maria Virgine') and 'tortured' chromaticism at 'Crucifixus'. Throughout K167 there is effective dynamic contrast and variety, including a rare crescendo in the Agnus Dei. Mozart seldom relies on immediate melodic repetition as a way of composing out a section of text, as he had in earlier masses.

There then began a three-year period in which Mozart produced at least two new masses each year. On 14 June 1774 he finished the *Missa brevis* in F, K192. The longest and perhaps best of his *missae breves*, this popular work is called 'kleine Credo Messe' (Little Credo Mass) because of its unifying four-note 'Credo' refrain, a melody better known from the finale of the composer's 'Jupiter' symphony, K551. The Kyrie is a fine example of sonata-form use in this genre, with the 'Christe' serving as a 'development' section. The Credo is compelling not only because of the seven returns of its opening subject but also because the theme is used for the contrasting 'Crucifixus', 'Confiteor', 'Et vitam' and 'Amen'.

Two months later, on 8 August 1774, Mozart completed another mass with the same scoring, also probably for Salzburg's Cathedral, K194. This was the first of Mozart's masses to appear in print, albeit posthumously (in 1793). The Kyrie is unified by a fanfare-like theme, and the Gloria has expressive chromaticism ('Agnus Dei, Filius Patris') and dynamic contrasts ('Qui tollis'). The Agnus Dei has solo voices over a chilling, Baroque-like descending chromatic bass of repeated quavers, before the full chorus enters *forte* with the imploring 'miserere nobis'. The attractive 'Dona nobis' is a clear example of sonata form. The tender, simple melody and the playful give-and-take between soloists and chorus recall the finale qualities of an operatic vaudeville of the period.

Mozart next wrote a series of five C major masses over the next two or possibly three years. The *Missa [brevis et solemnis]* K220 was probably composed during 1775 or at the start of 1776. It is called the 'Spatzenmesse' ('Sparrow' mass) because of the chirping violin figure in the Sanctus. Despite its brevity the work includes two clarini and timpani. The mass (or possibly K257, 258 or 259) may have been performed on 7 April 1776, when the Archbishop celebrated Easter Mass. A letter the next year suggests that Mozart loaned a copy of the mass to Heiligenkreuz Monastery. K220 offers a strong sense of musical unity, thanks both to its brevity, resemblance of later themes to the first theme of the 'sonata-form' Kyrie, and the return of the Kyrie's music (in reverse order) for the closing 'Dona nobis pacem'. In its fast alternation between soloists and chorus the Gloria is a good example of how the soloists' textual assignments in a *missa brevis* clearly mimicked those commonly found in a *missa longa* (that is, solos for 'Laudamus', 'Domine Deus' and 'Quoniam'). The syllabic, homophonic Credo is Mozart's shortest. The Sanctus, with its waltz-like triple metre, simple harmonies and drinking-song-like 'Hosanna' has a secular tone; the Benedictus is a touching solo quartet. The minuet-like Agnus Dei concludes with a particularly Mozartian dramatic touch when C major's return is delayed by a dark, mysterious passage of diminished-seventh chords above a chromatically descending bass.

Paper studies show that the *Missa longa* K262 comes before K257 and was probably written in June or July 1775. The inclusion of two horns (along with two oboes, two trumpets, timpani, three trombones and strings) and the extended length suggest that K262 was written for St Peter's, but there is evidence that the work (along with other masses having two horns) was performed in the cathedral as well. Thus this well-crafted, highly unified work, and not K258, is probably the 'Spaur-Messe' mentioned by LEOPOLD MOZART in his letter of 28 May 1778. (Ignaz Josef, Count von SPAUR, a family friend, was installed as titular Bishop of Chrysopel on 17 November 1776, in Salzburg Cathedral.) In sonata form, the Kyrie opens with a double fugue and has Mozart's traditional softer dynamics and vocal-solo homophony for the second theme at 'Christe'. Abert considered the Gloria's 'Qui tollis', with its pointed dynamic contrasts, tortured harmonic course, and dotted-rhythm ostinato in the accompaniment, 'one of the most touching moments of this Mass'. The Credo is Mozart's longest and consists of five sections, each with a different tempo. A chromatic, choral 'Crucifixus' dramatically interrupts the tender solo quartet of the 'Et incarnatus'. Near the Credo's end, the sopranos hauntingly sing 'mortuorum' on the first four notes of Mozart's G minor symphony, K183, written less than two years earlier; this motif anticipates the melodic outline of the 'Et vitam' fugue subject that follows. The Benedictus is unusual for the refrain-like, choral exclamations of 'Hosanna in excelsis' that interrupt the solo quartet while the Agnus Dei makes further use, at 'miserere,' of the 'mortuorum' motif. As in K194, the cheerful character and the solo-chorus repartee in the 'Dona nobis' recall the vaudeville operatic finale. The main theme's insistent repeated notes evoke a Psalm tone.

The final three masses of the C major series, K257–9, consist of one *missa longa* and two *missae breves et solemnes* originally assigned to the year 1776 through a misreading of tampered dates on the autograph scores. The publisher ANDRE guessed that K257 was from November and that K258 and 259 were from December of that year. Paper studies suggest, however, that K257 dates from November 1776 and K258 from a year earlier, December 1775. The year of K259 remains uncertain and could be either 1775 or 1776.

The earliest of the three, K258, was given the unwarranted title 'Piccolomini-Messe' by Schneider and Algatzy; it also used to be considered the 'Spaur-Messe'. Despite its solemn scoring of two oboes, two clarini, timpani, three trombones and strings, K258 is a true *missa brevis* in its economy and concision. Melodic mundaneness and textural simplicity suggest that Mozart completed the work in extreme haste. At the centre of the Credo, the Adagio 'Et incarnatus' solo ends with an expressive 'Crucifixus' solo quartet over a chromatically ascending bass. The Benedictus is highly unusual on account of its fast tempo and antiphonal, echo-like effects between the chorus and the solo quartet. Few composers, however, have suggested so successfully the joyful, acclamatory, Palm-Sunday nature of the Benedictus text. This is the only Mozart mass where the 'Dona nobis' is not a movement separate from that of the Agnus Dei.

Completed almost a year later, in November 1776, K257 is known as the 'grosse Credo-Messe' (Great Credo Mass) because – as in K192 – the Credo is unified by a recurrent refrain. This was the most widely disseminated of Mozart's masses during the eighteenth and early nineteenth centuries. Daniel

Heartz notes that 'for sheer inspiration and cogency K257 is Mozart's greatest Mass if not, indeed, his greatest composition in any genre up to this date'. Scored for two oboes, two clarini, timpani, three trombones and strings, the work shows Mozart abandoning the old conventions of the *missa longa*. The short Kyrie opens with a slow introduction that sounds recitative-like and *in medias res*. The triple-metred Credo's recurring theme seems inspired by one of the most commonly chanted Credo intonations (the theme's four pitches are the same as the opening of the English hymn 'O God, Our Help in Ages Past'). In the slower, siciliano-style 'Et incarnatus', the suffering of the 'Crucifixus' is suggested by the choral *forte–piano* accents and the sopranos' chromatically descending fourth. Unusual non-harmonic tones add to the anguish of the scene, which ends with a powerful textural crescendo and more destabilizing chromaticism. Like most of the mass, the Credo is homophonic, without a formal fugue at the end. We hear only a brief fugato at 'Et vitam'. In the Sanctus the sopranos' first four pitches correspond with the Credo motif from the other Credo mass, K192. In the sonata-form Benedictus two magical a cappella moments for the solo quartet occur during the retransition back to the tonic while the Agnus Dei is one of Mozart's most regal sounding. In another example of Mozart's growing concern for cyclical connections between movements, the lyrical, contrasting theme of the solo quartet 'miserere' inspires the main theme of the faster 'Dona nobis pacem' that follows in finale fashion. Here a rare Mozart crescendo appears twice in the chorus parts.

The 'Orgel messe' (Organ Solo Mass), K259, is one of Mozart's two masses with obbligato organ, a relatively common genre in eighteenth-century Austria. The last of the series of five C major masses, this *missa brevis et solemnis* was completed in 1775 or 1776 and possibly premiered with the Epistle Sonata in C, K 263, which is similarly scored. Early on, the Benedictus was shortened; oboe parts were probably added later. The Kyrie uses sonata form and is Mozart's shortest Kyrie, while the Gloria resembles his first mass, K49, in brevity and general deployment of soloists. Heartz notes the audible motivic connections between the energetic 'Pleni sunt caeli' of the Sanctus (with its chromatically descending 'Hosanna') and other sections of the mass. The Benedictus opens with the eight-bar organ obbligato that gives the work its nickname, although such a short organ introduction could not by itself have provided enough music for the elevation of the Host at this point in the Mass. The Benedictus ends with an elegant written-out 'cadenza' for the solo quartet, before the 'Hosanna' music returns, now cleverly reworked in triple metre. With a lyrical first-violin/soprano melody (reminiscent of the Kyrie) above pizzicato lower strings, the intimate texture of the Agnus Dei resembles a slow aria from Mozart's operas or a cantabile slow movement from his chamber music.

Mozart probably completed the *Missa [brevis]* K275 in the summer of 1777, just before leaving Salzburg in September for his tour to MUNICH, MANNHEIM and PARIS. Like its immediate predecessor, K275 is an efficient, straightforward and functional setting of the Mass Ordinary. Bassoon and trombone parts formerly in the possession of the Mozart family suggest that these instruments played in addition to the strings of the traditional church trio. The through-composed Gloria opens with a haunting *piano* descent using parallel diminished twelfths between the outer voices of the chorus while the anguish of the Agnus Dei is heightened by angular melodies above diminished-seventh chords, as well as by the chromaticism of each *forte* 'miserere'. As in K194 and 220, a witty and folksong-like 'Dona nobis' recalls the rondo-like form of an operatic vaudeville.

After his return to Salzburg from Paris in January 1779, Mozart was appointed court and cathedral organist to the Archbishop. He immediately began the Mass in C, K317. Dated 23 March 1779, and perhaps intended for Easter Sunday or Monday, the work is known today as the 'Krönungsmesse' ('Coronation' mass) because of its use at the coronation ceremonies for either Emperor LEOPOLD II in PRAGUE in 1791 or, more likely, his son, Francis II, as King of Bohemia in 1792. The connection of this mass with Mozart's memorial vow to the Virgin Mary at the pilgrimage church Maria Plain in Salzburg is considered apocryphal. K317 is Mozart's best-known and most often performed mass, probably because of its attractive melodies and its full, solemn scoring including two horns along with the oboes, clarini, timpani, trombones and strings. Curiously, melodies of two movements of the mass resemble those in later Mozart operas: the Kyrie is like 'Come scoglio' from COSÌ FAN TUTTE and Agnus Dei like 'Dove sono' from LE NOZZE DI FIGARO. The Epistle Sonata in C, K329, which was written at the same time with the same orchestration (plus obbligato organ), was probably premiered with the mass.

K317 is Mozart's shortest *missa longa*. Indeed some sources describe it as a *missa brevis* despite the sizeable orchestration and word repetitions. The short Kyrie opens and closes with a regal Andante maestoso that encloses a faster, more lyrical central section briefly highlighting the vocal soloists. In this mass, sonata form clearly influences the structure of the Gloria rather than the Kyrie. Heartz notes how the Gloria has the characteristics of a *ciaccona* that is also found in the next mass, K337, and in the *Ciaccona* that ends the first act of IDOMENEO. During the Credo's expressive 'Et incarnatus' muted violins play an ethereal demisemiquaver commentary above the chorus, and at 'Crucifixus' the mode turns minor and a chromatically rising bass leads to the climactic moment of death ('passus'), suggested by a crescendo, sudden *pianissimo* (*senza organo*), and fragmented words. The Agnus Dei soprano solo, with its three varied presentations of the theme against muted (later pizzicato) strings, wonderfully demonstrates Mozart's melodic art. This solo segues operatically, quasi-cadenza fashion, into the faster 'Dona nobis' where the Kyrie theme returns. The full ensemble enters for a tumultuous, stretto-like coda using this theme and a motif derived from its opening notes.

The next year Mozart finished his last complete mass, K337, a *missa brevis et solemnis* dated Salzburg, March 1780. The Epistle Sonata K336 dates from the same month and was probably written for the same occasion, possibly Easter. The scoring is the same as K317, except that K337 lacks horns, and the organ and bassoons play obbligato in the Agnus Dei and Credo respectively. Evidence shows that by the start of the 1790s, K337 was performed by the Imperial Hof-Musikkapelle in Vienna. Hence in some sources the work is entitled 'Hof-Messe'. It was probably also used in connection with the imperial coronations of 1791 and 1792.

The Kyrie is a subdued, legato choral setting of remarkable continuity, while the energetic, syllabic Gloria has a sonata-like form. The Gloria's only melismatic writing is in the 'Amen' passage where the soprano soloist has two extended flights of coloratura. The rondo-like Credo is indebted to the operatic *ciaccona* with its rhythmic ambiguities and a chaconne-like refrain over a recurring descending bass. A magical moment occurs at the end of the slower 'Et incarnatus' when the unison chorus, accompanied by undulating woodwind motifs, softly moves downward on the word 'Crucifixus'. In the Sanctus the chorus enters with monolithic unison octave leaps and dramatic dynamic contrasts while the *stile antico* fugue of the choral Benedictus sounds old-fashioned. Empress MARIA THERESIA died the same year as this mass was composed, so perhaps Mozart hoped soon to impress her son, Emperor JOSEPH II, who was quite fond of fugues. (This apparently was, after all, the first Mozart mass to be added to the imperial music collection.) The Agnus Dei starts in a fresh-sounding E flat major, one of Mozart's most affective keys, and an organ obbligato dialogues with the colourful oboe and bassoon texture that accompanies a scintillating soprano 'aria' reminiscent of the Countess's 'Porgi amor' in *Figaro*. Muted strings heighten the other-worldly effect of the movement. The flavour of the Credo's *ciaccona* returns for the joyful, rondo-like 'Dona nobis pacem'. Contrary to convention, the vocal soloists sing the final, quiet notes of the mass. This peaceful passage takes on added poignancy when we realize that Mozart would never complete another mass.

2. Vienna

Although incomplete, the Mass in C minor, K427, is one of Mozart's grandest church works. In size, layout and overall musical weight, this operatic *missa solemnis* harks back to the earlier Neapolitan 'cantata' masses, works that were also models for J. S. BACH's B minor Mass and JOSEPH HAYDN's first *Missa Cellensis*. Only Mozart's early 'Waisenhaus' mass (K139), his last two litanies (K195, 243), the D minor Kyrie (K341), and the unfinished Requiem approach the scope of this mass. Despite its incomplete state, K427 is longer than any other mass by Mozart. The Gloria consists of seven separate movements that, together, are longer than an entire *missa brevis*. With a full string section (including two violas), timpani, and twelve obbligato wind parts (two each of trumpets, oboes, bassoons, and horns, one flute for 'Et incarnatus' and three trombones), the orchestra is the largest for any Mozart mass except the isolated Kyrie K341.

Mozart composed K427 in Vienna and Salzburg in 1782–3 as part of a promise to his new bride, Constanze. MARIA ANNA MOZART's diary indicates that the mass was performed on 26 October 1783, the feast of St Armand, at St Peter's, Salzburg. Although Mozart completed only the Kyrie, Gloria, Sanctus and Benedictus, extant first drafts of the Credo through the 'Et incarnatus' have been the basis for full versions published later. The 'Et resurrexit' and Agnus Dei were not composed, although a brief 'Dona nobis pacem' double-fugue sketch survives. Completions of the mass include those published by Joseph Drechsler (1847), Alois Schmitt (1901, using other mass movements by Mozart), H. C. Robbins Landon (1956) and, more recently, Franz Beyer, Helmut Eder, Richard Maunder and Robert Levin. In March 1785 Mozart reused the music of this mass for his oratorio *Davidde penitente*, K469.

Mozart tailored the large range and challenging coloratura of the soprano solos (namely, 'Christe,' 'Laudamus te' and 'Et incarnatus') to Constanze's voice, so she could suitably display her vocal gifts during their visit to Salzburg in 1783. Both 'Christe' and 'Et incarnatus' have written-out cadenzas, the latter unusually accompanied by a flute, oboe and bassoon. Other arresting elements of K427 include its powerful Handelian double choruses and the engaging interplay of woodwind obbligatos and solo voices. Mozart seems to have purposely imitated many Baroque features: extended ritornellos that frame movements, two- and three-part aria forms, basso ostinato ('Qui tollis'), French-overture double-dotting ('Gratias'; 'Qui tollis'), double fugues ('Cum Sancto Spiritu', 'Hosanna') and extended vocal melismas. Mozart also showed concern for the mass as a unified cycle. Several movements are linked by an ascending triadic motif, and the number of soloists increases as the work proceeds, from aria ('Laudamus'), duet ('Domine Deus') and trio ('Quoniam') to quartet (Benedictus).

3. Mass movements, fragments, misattributed works

Of the five individual mass movements, Kyrie in D minor, K341, stands out for requiring the largest orchestra in any of Mozart's sacred music. In addition to the chorus and strings (with two viola parts), there are four horns and pairs of flutes, oboes, clarinets, bassoons, trumpets and timpani. It is Mozart's only church composition requiring clarinets. The sonata-form Kyrie was to be part of a grand *missa longa* perhaps destined for Munich during Mozart's stay there from November 1780 to March 1781 although recent studies suggest that the work may have been written during his later Viennese years, about 1788, when Mozart resumed the study and composition of sacred music and was perhaps hoping to secure a Kapellmeister position.

Three of the other isolated mass movements were apparently part of Mozart's contrapuntal studies in mid-1772: the Kyries in G major and D minor (K89 and 90) and the Hosanna in G (K223). The Kyrie in F, K33, is for chorus, strings and organ and was completed in Paris on 12 June 1766. ABBE MAXIMILIAN STADLER completed two Kyrie fragments: K322 in E flat and K323 in C. A few masses listed in earlier editions of the Köchel catalogue are spurious, now attributed to other composers. The *Missa brevis* in C, K115, and the Kyrie, K116, for example, are by Leopold Mozart, and the Kyrie in C, K221, is by J. E. EBERLIN. Because the young Mozart learned the church style partly through copying works by his Salzburg contemporaries, some pieces surviving in his autograph were incorrectly attributed to him; many other, similar works are also wrongly credited to Mozart.

The masses were chiefly disseminated in manuscript copies starting in the 1770s and the most popular ones soon acquired various nicknames. On 13 November 1780, Mozart asked that the scores for K275, 317 and 337 be sent to him in Munich at the time of the premiere of *Idomeneo*. Similar requests came after his move to Vienna and in 1791 choir director ANTON STOLL in Baden borrowed the autograph scores and performed all three works. The Viennese copy shop of JOHANN TRAEG disseminated numerous copies of these and other masses during the 1790s.

Among the trademarks of Mozart's concerted masses are: harmonic boldness of a dramatic nature, operatic solo arias and ensembles, effective a cappella interludes for the choir, suspenseful pauses, metric ambiguities, striking contrasts in melodies and dynamics, unorthodox divisions of the text, cogent blending of sonata and contrapuntal procedures, use of sonata-form structures (from K167 onwards), masterful fugues or fugatos, and cyclic unity derived from the use of similar motifs and themes in different movements of the same mass. Mozart's final work, the incomplete Requiem, exhibits most of these qualities, making it all the more frustrating to ponder what his future masses would have been like. BRUCE C. MACINTYRE

K. G. Fellerer, *Mozarts Kirchenmusik* (Salzburg-Freilassing, 1955; rev. as *Die Kirchenmusik Mozarts*, Laaber, 1985)
D. Heartz, *Haydn, Mozart and the Viennese School, 1740–1780* (New York, 1995)
B. C. MacIntyre, *The Viennese Concerted Mass of the Early Classic Period* (Ann Arbor, 1986)
M. H. Schmid, *Mozart und die Salzburger Tradition* (Tutzing, 1976)

Maximilian Franz, Archduke (b. Vienna, 8 Dec. 1756; d. Hetzendorf, near Vienna, c.26 July 1801). The youngest son of Emperor Francis I and EMPRESS MARIA THERESIA, Archduke Maximilian was a keen musician, who played violin in the court orchestra and in private chamber-music groups with his brother, JOSEPH II. He first encountered Mozart on 16 October 1762 during Mozart's initial visit to VIENNA as a child prodigy, and apparently held him in high esteem. Writing to LEOPOLD MOZART on 23 January 1782, Mozart reported: 'he thinks the world of me. He shoves me forward on every occasion and I might almost say with certainty that if at this moment he were Elector of Cologne [a position he attained in 1784], I should be his Kapellmeister.' After one occasion when Maximilian had tried to do a favour for Mozart – introducing him to Duke Friedrich Eugen of Württemberg and daughter, Princess Wilhelmine Louise, on 16 November 1781 and recommending that he be assigned the Princess for private piano tuition – Mozart recorded his personal antipathy to Maximilian: 'Stupidity oozes out of his eyes. He talks and holds forth incessantly and always in falsetto.' Maximilian is known to have attended a number of Mozart's performances – in SALZBURG on 23 April 1775, again the following day when 'the famous young Mozart was heard on the clavier and played various things by heart with as much art as pleasantness' according to his travel journal, and on 26 May 1782 at the Augarten in Vienna, where he performed the Concerto for Two Pianos in E flat, K365, with JOSEPHA AUERNHAMMER as well as his Symphony in C major, K338. A few weeks after Mozart's death, Maximilian donated 24 ducats to CONSTANZE MOZART. SIMON P. KEEFE

M. Braubach, *Maria Theresias jüngster Sohn: Max Franz. letzter Kurfürst von Köln und Fürstbischof von Münster* (Vienna, 1961)

Maximilian III, Joseph (b. Munich, 28 Mar. 1727; d. Munich, 30 Dec. 1777). Elector of Bavaria, 1745–77, and oldest son of Elector Karl Albrecht (1697–1745), the German Emperor Karl VII from 1742. He received musical instruction from Francesco Peli, Joachim Setzkorn (valet of his uncle, Duke Ferdinand Maria) and Andrea Bernasconi. Although his main instrument was the gamba he also played the violin, viola, violoncello and keyboard. LEOPOLD MOZART first met him around 1744 and Wolfgang played for him during visits to MANNHEIM in 1762, 1763 and 1766. On 13 January 1775 the premiere of Wolfgang's LA FINTA GIARDINIERA, K196, took place in his presence in the Salvator Theatre; he later commissioned the Offertorium 'Misercordias Domini', K222. On 30 September 1777, in the small Knights' Hall in his palace in MUNICH, Mozart tried in vain to gain an engagement with him.

Maximilian III was a passionate lover of music: J. Michl, J. MYSLIVEČEK, P. P. Sales, T. Traetta and A. Tozzi, as well as A. Bernasconi, were given commissions for the annual carnival opera. Among the Elector's compositions, four *Concerti a piu istromenti* and his best work, a Stabat mater in C minor, were printed at J. C. dall'Abaco's instigation in Verona in 1765–6. A Sinfonia a 2 chori with a partial oboe part, a Sinfonia for strings and two horns, twelve Sinfonie for strings and basso continuo and twelve trios for two violins and bass survive in manuscript. A *Missa pastoralis*, two litanies, a Salve regina and three Sonate per il gallichona are lost. ROBERT MÜNSTER (Trans. RUTH HALLIWELL)

F. J. Lipowsky, *Baierisches Musiklexikon* (Munich, 1811)
R. Münster, *'Ich bin hier sehr beliebt': Mozart und das kurfürstliche Bayern* (Tutzing, 1993)

Mazzolà, Caterino (b. Longarone, near Belluno, c.1745; d. ?Venice, 1806). An Italian librettist who served as poet to the Italian theatre at Elector Frederick Augustus III's Dresden court between 1780 and 1798, Mazzolà adapted and shortened PIETRO METASTASIO's libretto of LA CLEMENZA DI TITO (first set in 1734 by Antonio Caldara) for Mozart's opera seria premiered in PRAGUE on 6 September 1791. Mozart recorded Mazzolà's contribution to *Tito* in his entry for the work in the *Verzeichnüss* (thematic catalogue). The Prague impresario DOMENICO GUARDASONI, who commissioned *Tito*, knew Mazzolà's work well from having already staged operas that set his librettos. Mazzolà's version features eleven arias, three duets, three trios, one quintet, one sextet and five choruses, in contrast to Metastasio's twenty-five arias and four choruses. A number of operas featuring Mazzolà's librettos were staged at the Burgtheater in VIENNA during Mozart's period of residence in the city, by eminent composers such as ANTONIO SALIERI, Giacomo Rust, JOSEPH WEIGL and Pierre Dutillieu. Mazzolà's testimonial for LORENZO DA PONTE – whom he first met in Dresden around 1780 – led to Da Ponte's appointment as poet to Vienna's Italian company (1783). SIMON P. KEEFE

K. Küster, 'An Opera Seria for the 1790s: *La clemenza di Tito*, K. 621', in *Mozart: A Musical Biography*, trans. M. Whittall (Oxford, 1996), 346–55

mechanical instruments, music for. From at least the third century BC, Greek and Roman writers described organs powered by water or the heat of the sun and 'programmed' to play by themselves. Similar instruments were known to Byzantine and Arabic writers in the Middle Ages, and from the thirteenth century to as late as the first half of the eighteenth century large-scale examples were constructed in Italy and elsewhere. With the introduction of mechanisms powered by springs or pendula in the fifteenth century, however, the building of musical automata gradually came under the aegis of clock builders rather than hydraulic engineers. Municipal or church towers were often equipped with bells or chimes that rang the hours and played melodies by means of clockwork mechanisms. Mozart grew up within earshot of three such automata: the 'Salzburger Hornwerk' in the Hohensalzburg Fortress, built in 1502 but completely refurbished in 1753 by the local organ builder Johann Rochus Egedacher, which apparently sounded twice a day (rebuilt again in 1893, this organ now plays every day at noon); the so-called 'Dutch carillon' dating from 1704, which played three times a day in the archbishop's residence; and a 'water organ' at Hellbrunn Castle (actually a pneumatic organ driven by hydraulically operated bellows) also constructed by Egedacher. The Mozarts must also have heard other mechanical musical instruments during their European tours, although they made no mention of it in their correspondence.

In the eighteenth century, elegant table-top clocks incorporating small organs of flute pipes – the so-called 'Flötenuhr' – were popular among the nobility. These usually had two clockwork mechanisms, one for the timepiece, the other to work the bellows and rotate the barrel from which protruded 'pins', carefully placed to activate the various pipes at precisely the right moment and in precisely the right sequence. The barrels were usually pinned with popular airs, dances, or sets of variations, though original compositions were sometimes commissioned. C. P. E. BACH, JOSEPH HAYDN and BEETHOVEN were among those who wrote such pieces. None of the clocks for which Mozart composed is known to have survived. Instruments that play music of unknown provenance attributed to Mozart or variations on tunes from DIE ZAUBERFLÖTE and his other 'hits', as well as an instrument in Leipzig that plays a drastically shortened version of K616, were built in the early nineteenth century; none has been convincingly shown to have been copied from one associated with Mozart.

The earliest documented connection between Mozart and mechanical instruments is found in a letter of 3 October 1790, which he sent to his wife from Frankfurt:

> I have most firmly resolved to undertake at once the Adagio for the clockmaker and then to slip a few ducats into my dear little wife's hand. I would have done it sooner, but it is such hateful work that unfortunately I have not been able to finish. I write some of it every day – but I must always knock off because it bores me. And indeed, I would surely abandon the whole thing if there weren't such a strong reason to go on with it. Thus I still hope to manage to complete it little by little. Of course, if it were for a large clock and the thing would sound like an organ, then it might give me some enjoyment. But as it is, the works [of the instrument] consist solely of shrill little pipes, which sound too high-pitched and too childish for my taste.

The 'clockmaker' to whom Mozart referred was Father Primitivus (Joseph Niemecz), librarian at Esterháza Palace and pupil of Joseph Haydn. Some of Haydn's mechanical clock music survives in staff notation, some survives pinned on the barrels of Father Primitivus's clockwork organs, and some in both forms. The piece Mozart claimed he was working on in Frankfurt may possibly be represented by a nine-bar fragment, the Adagio in D minor for mechanical organ K593a, which is notated on three treble staves and calls for an instrument with a three-octave range d–d‴.

After returning to VIENNA Mozart entered three mechanical compositions into his catalogue of his own works: 'A piece for an organ in a clock' (K594) in December 1790, 'An organ piece for a clock' (K606) on 3 March 1791, and the 'Andante for a cylinder in a small organ' (K616) on 4 May. The first two pieces are dramatic outpourings in F minor, lasting about ten minutes, notated on three treble staves and a bass staff for an instrument with two ranks of pipes (flute and bassoon) with a range of three octaves and a tone, c–d'''. The commissioner of these works was one Joseph Nepomuk Franz de Paula, Baron Deym von Stržitéž (see DEYM), who operated under the alias Müller after having had to flee from his post as an officer in the AUSTRIAN army following an illegal duel. Deym's art gallery and museum, operated by him at various locations in Vienna between c.1780 and 1804 and then by his widow until 1819, contained curious works of art, plaster-cast copies of ancient sculptures and handsomely clad wax statues of famous personages. Among Deym's wax heroes was the Austrian Field Marshal Ernst Gideon, Baron von Laudon (or Loudon), to whom Haydn had dedicated his Symphony No. 69. After Laudon died on 14 July 1790, Deym decided to construct a monument in which the Field Marshal's effigy could be viewed in a glass coffin. As described in the *Wiener Zeitung* (26 Mar. 1791) the scene must have been striking:

> On March 23rd Herr Müller . . . opened the Mausoleum erected by him, which he has at great expense created in memory of the unforgettable and world-famous Field Marshal Baron von Laudon . . . Here on the ground floor this remarkable monument may be seen in a setting especially designed for it, splendidly illuminated from 8 o'clock in the morning till 10 o'clock at night . . . [T]he sight of it will not fail to surprise everyone who visits this Mausoleum and thereby renews the memory of this great and meritorious man . . . The seats are arranged in the best possible way, and each person pays 1 fl. for a first place and 39 kr. for a second; upon the stroke of each hour a Funeral Musique will be heard, and will be different every week. This week the composition is by Herr Kapellmeister Mozart.

The function of the two F minor compositions thus becomes clear. No other composers are mentioned in subsequent accounts of the Mausoleum – only Mozart. And after a while K608 was preferred to K594, and only the former employed. K608 was soon published in an arrangement for piano four-hands whereas K594 was more or less forgotten.

Years later Ignaz von Seyfried, said to have studied with Mozart, described the effect K608 had had on him:

> I still recall from my youth the lively sensation that repeated – oft repeated – hearings of this ingenious production ineradicably impressed upon my memory. A thousand varying emotions were aroused by that (I might almost call it) terrifying Allegro, with its artful fugue subject in the strict style. The listener is startled at the violent modulation to F sharp minor, and imagines the ground shaking beneath him. The lovely, so tenderly expressed Adagio [recte Andante] in A flat major is music of the spheres; it elicits tears – salutary tears of longing for heaven. The repeat of the opening Allegro catapults us back into troubled human existence. The two mutually belligerent fugue subjects impart a striking, serious, powerful image of the

battle of the passions. Only at the end is there calm. Power is exhausted, human nature has died, and the soul escapes the body. The end signifies the life to come.

Mozart's third and final contribution to mechanical music, the Andante in F major 'for a cylinder in a small organ', falls at the other end of the affective and aesthetic spectrum from the first two. A highly ornamented lyrical effusion lasting six or seven minutes, the rondo tinkles away in tones that Mozart had described as 'too high-pitched and too childish'. The scene it is thought to have accompanied was 'The Bedroom of the Graces', in which stood 'a resilient bed which is dimly lit in the evenings by alabaster lamps, with a beautiful sleeping figure, and behind these the most enchanting music, which was composed especially for the place and presentation. In an eighteen foot niche stands [a replica of] the beautiful Kalliygos Venus, admirably coloured, and with the aid of the artfully placed mirror the three graces from which the bedroom takes its name.'

In the half year that had elapsed since Mozart complained to Constanze about the small pipes and narrow range, he perhaps had come to see artistic possibilities in the 'too high-pitched and too childish' sounds, for K616 is a miniature of lapidary beauty. NEAL ZASLAW

O. E. Deutsch, 'Count Deym and his Mechanical Organs', *Music & Letters* 29 (1948), 140–5

A. H. King, 'Mozart's Compositions for Mechanical Instruments: The Background and Significance', *Musical Times* 88 (1947), 11–14; repr. in King, *Mozart in Retrospect* (London, 1956), 198–215

A. Richards, 'Automatic Genius: Mozart and the Mechanical Sublime', *Music & Letters* 80 (1999), 366–89

N. Zaslaw, 'Wolfgang Amadè Mozart's Allegro and Andante ('Fantasy') in F minor for Mechanical Organ, K. 608', in *The Rosaleen Moldenhauer Memorial. Music History from Primary Sources: A Guide to the Moldenhauer Archives*, ed. J. Newsom and A. Mann (Washington, DC, 2000), 327–40

Meissner, Joseph (Dominikus) Nikolaus (b. Salzburg, c.1725; d. Salzburg, 12 Mar. 1795). A court singer in SALZBURG, famed for his broad vocal range, Meissner was internationally admired. He sang the role of the Hungarian captain Fracasso in the production of LA FINTA SEMPLICE at Archbishop SCHRATTENBACH's palace in Salzburg in 1769 and performed with Mozart on 2 May 1770 at the Collegio Germanico in Rome. Mozart had mixed feelings about Meissner, however, as his comparison between Meissner's and ANTON RAAFF's voices makes clear (letter to LEOPOLD MOZART, 12 June 1778). Meissner, unlike Raaff, 'has the bad habit of making his voice tremble at times, turning a note that should be sustained into distinct crotchets, or even quavers – and this I could never endure in him'. In contrast, 'so far as real cantabile is concerned, I prefer Meissner to Raaff'.

Appointed to his Salzburg position in 1747, Meissner was earning a yearly salary of 378 florins (plus dining rights and a teaching stipend) by 1758, while his father, Nikolaus (a violinist and horn player) received only 282 florins. According to Leopold, Meissner was a 'great favourite', but occasionally he courted controversy. On 18 March 1768 he received an official warning (as did Leopold) that his pay would be suspended the following month if he did not return to Salzburg. And on 6 October 1777 Leopold reported to his wife and son that the Chief Steward had threatened Meissner with dismissal if he did not 'sing and perform regularly in the church services', even though he had been absent through illness. SIMON P. KEEFE

R. Halliwell, *The Mozart Family: Four Lives in a Social Context* (Oxford, 1998)
H. Klein, 'Unbekannte Mozartiana von 1766/67', *Mozart-Jahrbuch* 1957, 168–85

Mesmer family. The Mozarts were friendly with two Viennese-based members of the Mesmer family in particular, Franz Anton Mesmer (b. Iznang, near Lake Constance, 23 May 1734; d. Meersburg, 5 Mar. 1815) and his cousin Joseph Conrad Mesmer (1735–1804). Franz Anton was a physician who used magnets on hypnotized patients. 'Mesmerism', as his practice became known, remained popular into the nineteenth century but was highly controversial; Franz Anton had to leave VIENNA in 1778, accused of medical deceitfulness, taking up residence first in PARIS, then in Versailles, Switzerland and GERMANY. His large house in the Landstrasse suburb of Vienna was the venue for the premiere of Mozart's first singspiel, BASTIEN UND BASTIENNE (September or October 1768). Mozart and LEOPOLD MOZART visited Mesmer and his wife on several occasions during their two-and-a-half-month visit to Vienna in July–September 1773; it is quite likely that Mozart's string quartets K168–73, which date from this trip, were also played at their residence. Mozart wrote his first letter to Leopold following his move to Vienna in 1781 (dated 17 March) 'in the Mesmers' garden', but reported to NANNERL MOZART just a few months later (13 Dec. 1781) that the family house 'is no longer what it was'.

Joseph Conrad Mesmer, director of the St Stephen's Cathedral School in Vienna, obviously held Mozart in high esteem. Just a few days before Franz Anton left for Paris, he wrote to Leopold with a generous offer (c.23 Jan. 1778): 'Why did you not send your son to Vienna? Or why do you not send him even now? I assure you herewith most faithfully that he will have board, lodging and everything with me as long as he likes, and that I and all our other friends would endeavour to obtain a good appointment for him quickly . . . After all, there is always a good opening here for a great talent.' Joseph (junior), Joseph Conrad's son, also possessed considerable musical skills, according to Mozart (28 Mar. 1781), although his level of application left a lot to be desired: 'His son plays magnifique, but, as he imagines that he knows quite enough already, he is lazy. He has also considerable talent for composition, but is too indolent to devote himself to it, which vexes his father.' SIMON P. KEEFE

O. E. Deutsch, 'Die Mesmers und die Mozarts', *Mozart-Jahrbuch* 1954, 54–64
A. Steptoe, 'Mozart, Mesmer and *Così fan tutte*', *Music & Letters* 67 (1986), 248–55

Metastasio (Trapassi), Pietro (Antonio Domenico Bonaventura) (b. Rome, 3 Jan. 1698; d. Vienna, 12 Apr. 1782). Italian poet, librettist and moralist. Although a commentator on the dramatic practices of antiquity and a lyric poet in his own right, Metastasio is best known for his twenty-seven opera seria librettos. Other works intended for musical setting include some forty stage and concert pieces for court and aristocratic occasions, oratorios, cantatas, canzonettas and a set of *strofe per musica*. During the period c.1720 to c.1835, these works caught the attention of over 400 composers.

Metastasio's early education in Rome was guided by Cardinal Pietro Ottoboni, a generous patron of music and the theatre. Gianvincenzo Gravina, a founding member of the first Arcadian Academy established in Rome in 1690, took over this task when he adopted the boy in 1708, subsequently changing his surname from Trapassi to Metastasio. Under Gravina, young Pietro received a classical education and became well versed in the literary aspects of the Arcadian movement, in Cartesian moral philosophy and in Christian doctrine. In 1719, Metastasio moved to Naples where his early career blossomed through works written for well-connected members of the aristocracy and through opera seria texts set by the leading Italian composers, Vinci, Porpora and Sarro, and performed in the principal opera centres: Naples, Rome and Venice. By imperial invitation, he moved to VIENNA in 1730 where he soon gained, for life, the title of Imperial Court Poet.

The decade 1730–40 proved to be the most intensely prolific for Metastasio. During these years he wrote eleven of his twenty-seven opera librettos, eleven occasional pieces, and seven of his eight oratorios, as well as cantatas, canzonettas, sonnets and other lyrical poetry for which the dates are uncertain. With the death of his first patron, Charles VI, began a period of decline – the result of essential changes under MARIA THERESIA that brought economic restrictions, the passing of court theatre to private enterprise and a shift in taste from Italian opera to French and subsequently to German theatre. After 1740, a number of Metastasio's best works were premiered outside Vienna where, in some centres, settings of his texts remained in vogue well into the nineteenth century, accounting for the several references to such operas in the Mozart correspondence. In Vienna, however, Metastasian opera left the stage around 1765 and did not return until the 1790s when a short-lived Metastasian revival brought with it the first performance in Vienna of Mozart's LA CLEMENZA DI TITO.

Mozart became aware of Metastasian opera and its texts from an early age and remained so throughout his life. Indeed, an entire history of opera seria and its aria forms can be sketched from this association. Such a history begins with the composer's first extant vocal piece, the independent aria 'Va, dal furor portata' (K21), and ends with the full setting of *La clemenza di Tito* (K621), premiered in PRAGUE just three months before his death. Poet and composer met during the visit of the Mozarts to Vienna in 1767–8, when Metastasio, among others, championed the cause of LA FINTA SEMPLICE, and was one in whose house the young Mozart proved his ability as an opera composer by setting any randomly chosen Metastasian aria text in a short space of time. The first extant Metastasian arias, however, K21 and 'Conservati fedele' (K23) were composed during the British–European tour of 1764–5, and both are essentially in full da capo form.

In MILAN, in 1770, Mozart received the 1757 Turin edition of Metastasio's works as a gift, and from this source, another group of texts were chosen, now set in either a broad binary form or in a modified da capo format. In addition to the dubious 'Non curo l'affetto' (K74b), extant and complete among these works is the aria *Per pietà, bell'idol mio* (K78), the two *scene ed arie*, 'Misero me . . . Misero pargoletto' (K77) and 'Oh, temerario Arbace . . . Per quel paterno' (K79), and the arias 'Se adire, e speranza' (K82), 'Se tutti i mali miei' (K83) and 'Fra cento affani' (K88). Modified da capo forms permeate MITRIDATE,

RE DI PONTO, the Milan opera of the same year and two Metastasian works performed in SALZBURG in 1771 and 1772 respectively: the oratorio, *La Betulia liberata*, and the *azione teatrale*, *Il sogno di Scipione*. In the oratorio, Amital's 'Con troppo rea' is binary, while his 'Non hai cor' provides one of many examples of the modified da capo form. Both forms are still present in the two Milan works of the same two years: the *festa teatrale*, ASCANIO IN ALBA and the opera, LUCIO SILLA, for which text Metastasio made additions and alterations. In the *festa*, however, sonata forms, such as that found in Ascanio's 'Caro lontana ancora', begin to dominate. As would be expected, the texts of both Metastasio pieces were curtailed, but neither to the extent to which the libretto for the next Metastasian work was adapted: the opera seria, IL RE PASTORE, which Mozart set as a serenata. The original work, reluctantly written and staged by the poet for a gentleman and four ladies of the imperial court in Vienna, was already limited in its dramatic content; the abridged version simply drained dramatic aspects further.

Mozart's command of the sonata principle as a means of aria structure, however, becomes particularly prominent in *Il re pastore*, just as it will in IDOMENEO. Further, Aminta's aria 'L'amerò, sarò costante' provides an example par excellence of the rondeau structure with recurring refrain which Mozart had previously used in LA FINTA GIARDINIERA, and would exploit in the future, most immediately in the *scena ed aria* 'Ombra felice . . . Io ti lascio' (K255) of which only the aria's first couplet is Metastasian. In four subsequent independent scenas, two written in MANNHEIM prior to *Idomeneo* and two in MUNICH after it, the texts are drawn entirely from Metastasio and the arias are all built on the sonata principle: *Alcandro, lo confesso . . . Non sò donde viene* (K294), 'Ma, che vi fece . . . Sperai vicino il lido' (K368) and 'Misera, dove son . . . Ah! non son' io' (K369) and 'Basta vincesti . . . Ah non lasciarmi' (K486a).

Mozart turned to Metastasio for five subsequent arias written in Vienna, a group that includes 'Schon lacht der holde Frühling' (KV 580). This aria, left incomplete, was intended for a performance, in 1789, of a German version of PAISIELLO's opera, *Il barbiere di Siviglia*. The original Italian text, which begins 'Già riede primavera', is drawn from Metastasio's canzonetta, *La primavera*, and the aria appropriately occurs in the opera's singing-lesson scene. Also left incomplete is the aria, 'In te spero' (K440). Of the remaining three arias, the earliest, that of the *scena ed aria* 'Così dunque tradisci . . . Aspri rimorsi atroci' (K432) of 1783 exemplifies the sonata form without development, a form that occurs in L'OCA DEL CAIRO and *Lo sposo deluso* of the same year and which continues, with tremendous dramatic advantage, into the last operas. The resources of a full sonata-form return for the display piece, 'Ah se in ciel' (K538) of 1788, and the two-tempo structure, vital to the psychological action of the rondò arias in the late operas, finds representation in the aria of the scena, *Alcandro lo confesso . . . Non sò donde viene* (K512) of 1787.

Not to be missed is Mozart's use of Metastasian texts for three of his 1783 *Notturni* (K436, 437 and 438), the trio fragment (K532) from 1787 and the Canzonetta (K549) of 1788. Also significant is Mozart's mention of possibly setting an adaptation of Metastasio's *Demofoonte* in Paris in 1778 and the prospect, as suggested by a sketch sheet dated c.1786–7, that had he visited London in the late 1780s, he may have offered a setting of the court poet's *Olimpiade*.

Mere possibilities aside, however, Mozart's most outstanding association with a Metastasian text is his rendition, in music, of the full moral and psychological implications of what Metastasio had expressed in words in *La clemenza di Tito.* Reflecting principles laid down by Descartes, Metastasio demonstrates in this opera how morality rests in reason's ability to control the actions incited by emotion. The morally weak who lack this control will fall prey to emotional dictates, and certain states of suffering will inevitably follow. Such is the case with Vitellia and Sesto until redirected and morally strengthened, towards the opera's conclusion, by the model of the morally strong Tito. The musical forms range from a simple, one-part duet of twenty-four bars through binary, ternary and strophic forms, sonata and two-tempo structures, to act-ending finales where, for the first time, Mozart combines the voices of solo ensemble and chorus, against which, for the opera's second finale, he features a solo voice – that of the title role, as moral hero, championing Cartesian devotion, one of two states of mind Descartes considered best suited to promote moral strength. Already presented in the opera with the tonal solidity of two ternary arias and one in sonata form, Tito is heard to stand firm against the tonal digressions and shifting tempos that characterize the music of his temporary opponents. Although Metastasio might have disapproved of Mozart's and CATERINO MAZZOLÀ's reshaping of his libretto, no other setting rendered his fundamental ideals more faithfully.

DON NEVILLE

R. Angermüller, 'Mozart and Metastasio', *Mitteilungen der Internationalen Stiftung Mozarteum* 26 (Feb. 1978), 12–36

D. Neville, 'Cartesian Principles in Mozart's *La clemenza di Tito*', in *Studies in the History of Music* (New York, 1988), vol. II: *Music and Drama*, 97–123

J. A. Rice, *W. A. Mozart: 'La clemenza di Tito'* (Cambridge, 1991)

Milan. City in northern Italy, capital of Lombardy. Milan, earlier under Spanish rule, entered a new age of peace and prosperity in 1706 with the advent of AUSTRIAN rule. Culture flourished: the splendid Teatro Regio Ducale, with five tiers of boxes, was opened in 1717 and for more than fifty years represented the centrepiece in the city's cultural life; its programme included intermezzos and ballets, as well as operas by G. B. Lampugnani and G. B. Sammartini (Kapellmeister at several of the city's churches), sung by the most prominent artists in Italy – the castratos TENDUCCI and Farinelli and the prima donnas Bordoni and Aguiari. When the opera house burned down in 1776, Archduke Ferdinand, from 1771 Governor of Lombardy, built two new theatres: the smaller Teatro della Cannobiana and the larger Teatro alla Scala, which was inaugurated on 3 August 1778 with SALIERI's *L'Europa riconosciuta*. During Lent, when the theatres were closed, private concerts featuring symphonies were given, as well as sacred cantatas. Open-air instrumental music concerts, featuring symphonies, a Milanese speciality, were also given on the ramparts of the Castello Sforzesco – in part these led to the founding of the Accademia Filarmonica in 1758; members were obliged to compose a sonata or sinfonia annually.

As a centre for both opera and orchestral music, as well as a traditional destination for musical travellers and at the same time under Austrian rule, Milan was in many ways an ideal destination for the Mozarts: Wolfgang and his father visited several times between 1770 and 1773. They first visited in early 1770, lodging at the Augustinian monastery of San Marco and attending a performance of Jommelli's *Didone abbandonata* on 26 January. On 7 February they dined with the Governor-General of Lombardy, Count Karl Joseph FIRMIAN, who presented Wolfgang with an edition of METASTASIO's works; Mozart played for the guests and on 23 February gave his own public concert. He played at Firmian's again on 18 February and 12 March. Firmian was a firm supporter of the young composer: he was instrumental in arranging a contract for MITRIDATE and wrote several letters of recommendation for Wolfgang, to Count Gian Luca PALLAVICINI at Bologna, to Guglielmo du Tillot, Marchese di Felino, at Parma and to Franz Xaver Wolf, Count Rosenberg-Orsini, the Tuscan minister of state, at Florence.

The composition of *Mitridate*, first given on 26 December at the Teatro Regio Ducale, was probably started that summer and at least from mid-November Mozart and his father, after visiting several other Italian cities, were lodging near Milan with Leopold Troger, Firmian's secretary. The opera was a notable success; according to the *Gazzetta di Milano*, 'The young *maestro di capella*, who has not yet reached the age of fifteen, studies the beauty of nature and exhibits it adorned with the rarest of musical graces.' Firmian held a farewell lunch for them on 2 February – on 4 February they headed for Venice. A month later Mozart was sent a contract for a second Milanese opera (for Carnival 1773), LUCIO SILLA. Wolfgang and his father returned to SALZBURG but in the meantime Wolfgang was also asked to write a serenata for the wedding of Archduke Ferdinand of Austria and Maria Beatrice Ricciarda of Modena, so father and son spent only four months at home, setting out again on 13 August. They arrived at Milan on 21 August and on 29 August he received the libretto to ASCANIO IN ALBA, which went into rehearsal at the end of September. The opera was produced on 17 October and overshadowed by far the principal opera for the occasion, HASSE's *Ruggiero*; according to the *Notizie del Mondo* for 26 October, 'The opera has not met with success, and was not performed except for a single ballet. The serenata, on the other hand, has met with great applause, both for the text and for the music.' In the days after, Mozart lunched at Count Firmian's and gave a concert at the house of Johann Adam Mayr, and was received by Archduke Ferdinand.

Ferdinand had wanted to give Mozart a post at court but this was squelched by his mother, MARIA THERESIA, who wrote to him on 12 December: 'you ask me to take the young Salzburger into your service[.] I do not know why, not believing that you have need of a composer or of useless people . . . if they are in your service it degrades that service when these people go about the world like beggars.' The origin of Maria Theresia's enmity is unclear, and her characterization of the Mozarts unfair; nevertheless, no post was offered.

Leopold and Wolfgang arrived back at Salzburg on 15 December, where they celebrated the election of the new archbishop, HIERONYMUS COLLOREDO, in April. But in October they set out again, arriving at Milan on 4 December. The first rehearsals for *Lucio Silla* were held on 12 December and on 18 December they were at Firmian's. The opera premiered on 26 December and was given twenty-six times during the 1772–3 carnival season. The next month Mozart composed the motet *Exsultate, jubilate* for VENANZIO RAUZZINI, which he sang at the Theatine Church on 17 January, and on 30 January they heard the second opera commissioned for the season, PAISIELLO's *Sismano nel Mogol*. They left Milan on 4 March, arriving in Salzburg on 13 March. The third Italian journey was Mozart's last south of the Alps. The success of his operas notwithstanding, and the good contacts and impression they made there, they had no lasting result. Whether Maria Theresia poisoned their Italian chances altogether remains unclear; but after a promising start, the Mozarts seem to have abandoned any hope for further advancement in Italy. CLIFF EISEN

Milano e la Lombardia al tempo dei soggiorni milanesi di Mozart (Milan, 1991)
A. Pryer, 'Mozart's Operatic Audition. The Milan Concert, 12 March 1770: A Reappraisal and Revision', *Eighteenth-Century Music* 1 (2004), 265–88
H. Wignall, 'Mozart in Milan: Between Triumph and Disappointment', in *Wolfgang Amadeus Mozart: Mitridate. Mozartwoche und Salzburger Festspiele 1997* (Salzburg, 1997), 25–31

Mitridate, re di Ponto K 87 (Mithridates, King of Pontus), *dramma per musica* in three acts (MILAN, Teatro Regio Ducale, 26 Dec. 1770), libretto by Vittorio Amedeo Cigna-Santi after Racine. LEOPOLD MOZART knew that if his son was to gain success in the musical world, it would be by way of opera. He also knew that real operatic experience could only be gained in Italy; if Mozart himself was not Italian, he needed at least to learn and demonstrate a skill in Italian styles. Leopold and Wolfgang's first tour through the peninsula (December 1769–March 1771) involved a leisurely trip passing through Verona, Mantua, Milan, Bologna, Florence, Rome, Naples, back to Milan and ending in Venice.

On their first stay in Milan (January–March 1770), the Mozarts met Count Carl Joseph FIRMIAN, Governor-General of Lombardy, who offered the commission of an opera to open the forthcoming carnival season (which traditionally began on St Stephen's day). Mozart received the libretto of *Mitridate, re di Ponto* in Bologna on 27 July; the contract made the standard requirement of him to send the recitatives by October and arrive in Milan by 1 November to compose the arias to suit the singers. The fee was 100 gold gigliati plus accommodation.

The Mozarts arrived in Milan on 18 October 1770, whereupon Mozart began serious work on the opera. Events are described in a series of excited letters home by Leopold and occasionally Wolfgang. There were some six weeks before the rehearsals started, and work was hampered by the late arrival of the primo uomo, forcing Mozart to delay writing his arias 'so as to fit the costume to his figure' (letter of 24 Nov. 1770). As usual, the libretto was not new – it was first set by QUIRINO GASPARINI in 1767 – and Leopold feared that the prima donna might be persuaded to drop Mozart's music in favour of Gasparini's. Mozart also had to work hard – the number of drafts and discarded versions that survive is surprising for a composer who was normally so fluent – and the singers required extensive revisions: in the end, too, the lead tenor did indeed sing an aria by Gasparini, causing some rancour. But on the whole, the singers were pleased with the music, so Leopold said, and he considered that 'Wolfgang has written the opera well and with great intelligence' (8 Dec. 1770). *Mitridate* received twenty-two performances, the first three directed by the composer at the harpsichord. No doubt the spectacular scenery by the Galliari brothers aided the opera's success.

The subject concerns the ancient enemy of Rome, Mithridates (c.164–135 BC), despotic King of Pontus. It was popular – there are *Mitridate* operas by

Alessandro Scarlatti, Caldara, Porpora and Graun, amongst many others – in part because of the critical favour received by Racine's play *Mithridate* (1673). As usual, too, there are significant deviations from history to conform to the requirements of the opera seria genre in terms of casting and subject matter, both of which are served by conventional love triangles and clashes of honour and ambition.

The scene is set in Nymphaeum in 63 BC. In Act 1, Mitridate (Mithridates), betrothed to Aspasia (Monime in Racine), is thought dead in battle against the Romans. His two sons, Sifare (Xiphares) and Farnace (Pharnaces), are in love with Aspasia, who in turn loves Sifare. Mitridate returns unexpectedly with the Parthian princess Ismene, whom he has destined for Farnace. He fears conspiracy from his sons, although the Governor of Nymphaeum, Arbate (Arbates), assures him of Sifare's loyalty. Farnace, however, is in league with the Romans. In Act 2, Farnace scorns Ismene, while Mitridate suspects Aspasia. Sifare resolves to leave Pontus, taking a fond farewell of Aspasia. Farnace is accused of treachery by Mitridate, who also discovers Sifare's illicit love; both sons are imprisoned. Act 3 begins with the preparations for the final battle with the Romans. Mitridate attempts to poison Aspasia but she is saved by Sifare, who resolves to die nobly in the fight. Farnace is freed from prison by his friend Marzio (Marcius) and shifts his allegiance from Rome to his father. The Romans are defeated but Mitridate has engineered his own death: he unites Sifare and Aspasia, and forgives Farnace, who marries Ismene.

The premiere was given by a star-studded cast headed by GUGLIELMO D'ETTORE (tenor; Mitridate), Antonia Bernasconi (soprano; Aspasia), Pietro Benedetti (soprano castrato; Sifare) and Giuseppe Cicognani (alto castrato; Farnace); several were already known to the Mozarts (as Leopold explains in a letter of 28 July 1770). The musical sources are complicated by the drafts, revisions, excisions and additions (the last including in Act 1, scene 10 the march K62, written in SALZBURG in summer 1769 for the Serenade in D, K100), and some of the recitatives survive only incomplete. Clearly there were also problems of length: the first performance, which included three (unrelated) ballets by Francesco Caselli, lasted some six hours. It is not surprising (and entirely typical) that the opera runs out of steam towards the end, making almost nothing of the final reconciliation which is played just in recitative for all its more musical potential. One problem is the lengthy virtuoso arias which, as usual in the genre, dominate the score; there is just one duet (Sifare and Aspasia's touching scene at the end of Act 2, which the singer Benedetti much admired) and a conventional final quintet.

Almost every aria is in the usual two-stanza format to be set as a da capo aria (an A section for the first stanza, a B section for the second, and a repeat of the A section). In earlier da capo arias (say, by HANDEL) the first stanza is generally stated twice in the A section between three statements of an orchestral ritornello in tonic, dominant (or relative major in a minor key) and tonic. By the second half of the eighteenth century, however, the form had expanded to include four or more statements of the first stanza (two before the middle ritornello and two after), which could thus be heard eight or more times in the aria as a whole. Mozart often adopts the expanded form here – hence the length – although he generally makes some attempt to cut the da capo down from four statements to two or even one by beginning the reprise of the A section somewhere in its middle, leading to some rather abrupt tonal transitions.

All of this is conventional enough: the composer's art (perhaps better, craft) lies instead in responding to the librettist's contrasts of style and mood in successive arias while retaining opportunities for virtuoso display. Mozart manages to produce some striking music: Sifare's moving farewell to Aspasia in Act 2, scene 7 ('Lungi da te, mio bene'; there are three extant versions, one with an obbligato horn part) and Farnace's change of heart in Act 3, scene 9 ('Già dagli occhi il velo è tolto') are worthy of the best Italian masters. One can also see Mozart flexing his muscles and exercising his right to vary the scheme. 'Già dagli occhi il velo è tolto' is in a rich E flat major with oboes, horns and (at times) divisi violas – the last is always significant for Mozart – and contrasts an Andante for the A section with an Allegretto for the B section. Similarly, Mozart elsewhere uses two-tempo arias to highlight emotional issues, and he may have had some influence over the unusual number (six) of accompanied (rather than just simple) recitatives that enhance the dramatic expression; not surprisingly, three are in the intense Act 2. Few can have expected his handling of Aspasia's poison scene in Act 3, scene 4, with its curious mixture of recitative and arioso. And the A major love duet at the end of Act 2 consolidates a model that was to bear significant fruit in Mozart's next Milan opera, LUCIO SILLA, and beyond.

It is tempting to see in *Mitridate* hints of IDOMENEO and even LA CLEMENZA DI TITO but this probably misses the point. Mozart was just discovering the trade of the opera house, and once the lessons were learnt he dropped the work: there is no mention of it in the letters after March 1771, and it was revived only in 1971 in Salzburg. The only difference from countless other would-be opera composers was that Mozart was not quite fifteen years old. TIM CARTER

C. Gianturco, *Mozart's Early Operas* (London, 1981)

monodrama (melodrama, duodrama, melologo). A form of composition in which the spoken word is accompanied, or interrupted, by passages of instrumental music; the effect can be very powerful, as Mozart perceived. In some situations melodrama takes on the function of operatic recitative, in others of arioso; its greatest advantage is that words are clearly comprehensible. Although the genre may be of ancient vintage, the form as it is normally understood dates from the middle of the eighteenth century. It is generally accepted that it was invented by Jean-Jacques Rousseau, whose *Pygmalion* was first performed at Lyons in 1770, though it had probably been written eight years earlier. Some of the musical numbers were probably by Rousseau himself, the rest by Horace Coignet. Other composers were swift to seize on the potential of the form, and Rousseau's text was set by FRANZ ASPLMAYR in VIENNA in 1772, by Anton Schweitzer in the same year, and in 1779 by GEORG BENDA. The last-named is the master of monodrama, as he showed with his earliest experiments in it, *Ariadne auf Naxos* and *Medea*, both dating from 1775. His normal pattern is to separate the characters' speeches by usually brief musical phrases, which may either intensify the mood already created, or prepare the listener for what is to come; at moments of heightened passion, the verbal phrase is spoken against the (then briefly continuous) musical line.

Mozart's enthusiasm for monodrama is evident from his letters of 12 and 24 November and 3 and 18 December 1778; there are fine examples in ZAIDE and THAMOS, KÖNIG IN ÄGYPTEN; though the point is almost universally overlooked, it is clear from the libretto that the long ritornello to Papageno's first aria in DIE ZAUBERFLÖTE should accompany the last words of Tamino's speech.

Despite the enthusiasm with which monodrama was taken up, it enjoyed a comparatively short vogue as an independent musical genre (apart from in Czechoslovakia, where Fibich in particular kept it alive; see his trilogy *Hippodamia*, 1889–91). However, the use of spoken phrases in an otherwise wholly sung opera can make an effect out of all proportion to the import of the words themselves; familiar examples are the letter scenes in Verdi's *Macbeth* and *La traviata*. The term melodrama is also used for a dramatic entertainment with sensational content that may, though does not always, use music as an intensifier of the drama; in Italian, *melodramma* denotes an opera's libretto.

PETER BRANSCOMBE

K. G. Holmström, *Monodrama, Attitudes, Tableaux vivants: Studies on Some Trends of Theatrical Fashion 1770–1815* (Upsala, 1967)

U. Küster: *Das Melodrama. Zum ästhetikgeschichtlichen Zusammenhang von Dichtung und Musik im 18. Jahrhundert* (Frankfurt, 1994)

motet. In the eighteenth century, the term 'motet' referred to both a genre and a style. There was no consistency in regard to when a choral work was designated a motet. In a famous letter describing SALZBURG church music to Padre MARTINI, Mozart almost equates the motet with OFFERTORY, as he says the parts of an entire mass include 'the Offertory or Motet' (4 September 1776).

Johann Mattheson (1739) defines *motetti* as 'multi-voiced vocal pieces, filled with nothing but fugues and imitations, and laboriously worked out over a short Biblical saying'. Mattheson pleads, however, for interspersing 'concerto style' with this strict motet style (in chapter 13 of his treatise *Der vollkommene Kapellmeister*, trans E. C. Harriss). By then motet style also included choral sacred works with *colla parte* instruments, as Mattheson notes: 'Yet the instrumentalists here play not a note more, different, or less than the singers, which is an essential trait of motets.' J. J. Quantz (1752) notes that a cappella motets 'have now been almost completely abandoned in the Roman Catholic Church' and that 'the French call all their church pieces indiscriminately *des motets*'. Quantz also describes the contemporary motet in Italy as 'a sacred Latin solo cantata that consists of two arias and two recitatives and closes with an Alleluia, and is ordinarily sung by one of the best singers during the Mass after the Credo'. This definition of motet fits well with most of the works described here. (See the article SMALLER CHURCH WORKS below for other choruses – including liturgical hymns, antiphons, psalms, Te Deum – that may, in some sources, also be considered motets. For example, K47, 108, 127 and 276 each end with an Alleluia that could make them motets according to Quantz's definition above.)

Mozart's two solo and two choral motets were composed over twenty-six years and include two of his most popular vocal works, the *Exsultate, jubilate*, K165, and the *Ave verum corpus*, K618. Unless their text indicated another liturgical function, his motets were performed during Mass, usually in lieu of the

Gradual/Alleluia sung between the Epistle and Gospel readings; hence they were part of the 'Gradualmusik'. Sometimes this 'Figuralmusik' (that is, polyphonic vocal or instrumental music) was heard in place of the Communion chant that followed the Agnus Dei. Mozart's letter to Martini also suggests that a 'motet' would not be sung for 'Gradualmusik' if the choir were singing a choral offertory. As more analysis of the sources and performance dates for these works is completed, we shall know more about the specific occasions of their use.

'God is our refuge and strength', K20, is Mozart's earliest known sacred composition. The brief setting of the opening verse of Psalm 46 (King James version) was probably written in late June 1765 during the family's extended stay in London. Manuscript emendations by Mozart and his father show that the nine-year-old was still learning his compositional craft. The influence of HANDEL and English church anthems in the style of sacred madrigals is apparent. K. Pfannhauser indicates that K20 was intended to be a short opening anthem for the Anglican Communion liturgy.

'Ergo interest, an quis male vivat – Quaere superna', K143, was probably one of the Latin 'Motetti' for two young castrati to which LEOPOLD MOZART and Wolfgang refer in letters from MILAN in 1770. It was presumably written in early February 1770, although some doubt still remains about the work's authenticity because of its style and its extremely clean autograph score. The seven-minute work for soprano, strings (2 vn, va, vc/db), and continuo opens with a brief secco recitative about a solitary soul deciding whether to follow a good or evil course in life. The following aria, 'Quaere superna' (Andante, G major), gives the soul's decision to forget earthly things and delight in the eternal joy and comfort of seeking 'things above'. The extended aria sets two quatrains in a concerto-like sonata form with double exposition. The impressive solo part includes elaborate melismas, a tender *Eingang* leading into the recapitulation, extended trills and a cadenza.

Exsultate, jubilate, K165, is Mozart's most often performed solo motet. The virtuosic work was composed in January 1773 in Milan for the castrato VENANZIO RAUZZINI, who had sung Cecilio at the premiere of *LUCIO SILLA* the previous month. The motet premiered 17 January 1773, at the city's Theatine Church. As with K143, the author of the text remains unknown.

With its three arias, recitative and closing 'Alleluia', the fifteen-minute motet K165 closely fits Quantz's definition of the genre. The orchestra is the basic church trio (two violins, cellos/basses) and continuo, supplemented by pairs of oboes, horns and violas. Upon returning to Salzburg and as late as 1779, Mozart prepared a version of the motet with two flutes instead of oboes. The opening fast aria 'Exsultate, jubilate' (F major) sets a psalm-like text (cf. Psalms 47, 66, 81 and 95) encouraging believers to praise the Lord. It blends the Baroque ritornello form of an opera seria aria with sonata form. The presentation of the main themes during an introductory ritornello prior to the soloist's exposition recalls, as in K143, the 'double exposition' of contemporary instrumental concertos; the first theme, however, does not return in the tonic. The extended coloratura passages, both here and in the final movement, demonstrate the agility of Rauzzini's voice. A twelve-bar recitative calms the believers' fears and invites them to rise up and give 'handfuls of lilies' to the new dawn. The slow, cantabile aria 'Tu virginum corona' (A major; without oboes and horns) is a prayer to the Blessed Virgin Mary as the giver of peace and comfort. A concerto-like sonata form is again used. A three-bar modulatory bridge leads directly into the well-known, exuberant 'Alleluia' (F major). Based upon a symmetrical eight-bar melody in a quasi-rondo layout, this finale becomes a showcase of extended, jubilant melismas (bars 99–116 being the longest). Near the close we twice hear a descending sequence (bars 135–8, 143–6) which Haydn seems to have quoted in his Emperor's Hymn twenty-four years later. The penultimate high c‴ often sung in performances does not appear in the autograph score. Several melodic ties to the first movement can also be heard.

Ave verum corpus, K618, is Mozart's last and most beloved choral motet. According to the autograph score, the four-minute work was composed 17 June 1791, in Baden, a spa town near VIENNA where his wife Constanze was staying. The motet was probably written for use by Baden church musician and schoolmaster ANTON STOLL on Corpus Christi (Thursday 23 June 1791). Also used as a benediction, offertory, and private devotion, this Eucharistic hymn is primarily a sequence associated with the votive Mass of the Most Holy Sacrament and the feast of Corpus Christi.

The solemn, subdued work (Adagio; D major) is scored for four-part chorus, strings (two violins, viola, cellos/basses) and continuo. All parts are marked sotto voce; and all voices except the bass are restricted to a range of less than an octave. The solemnity reminds us of Mozart's Masonic music from this period. Subtle control of musical rhetoric is evident in the affective chromaticism and twisting harmonic modulations. In the emphatic repeat of 'in mortis' the sopranos leap expressively to their highest pitch, d″. The only lapse in the overall homophonic texture comes, appropriately, with the paired imitative entries at 'Esto nobis praegustatum' (be for us a foretaste).

Mozart's unfinished 'Hostias' for the REQUIEM has much of the same spirit as *Ave verum*. During the nineteenth century the work was often performed at Vienna's imperial Hofmusikkapelle where the autograph score was originally kept. The innate calm, spirituality and beauty of K618 has made it one of the best-known sacred works of all time. BRUCE C. MACINTYRE

G. Krombach, *Die Vertonungen liturgischer Sonntagsoffertorien am Wiener Hof: Ein Beitrag zur Geschichte der katholischen Kirchenmusik im 18. und 19. Jahrhundert* (Munich, 1986)
J. Mattheson, *'Der vollkommene Capellmeister': A Revised Translation with Critical Commentary*, trans. E. C. Harriss (Ann Arbor, 1981)
K. Pfannhauser, 'Mozarts kirchenmusikalische Studien im Spiegel seiner Zeit und Nachwelt', *Kirchenmusikalisches Jahrbuch* 43 (1959), 155–98
K. A. Rosenthal, 'The Salzburg Church Music of Mozart and His Predecessors', *Musical Quarterly* 18 (1932), 559–77
M. H. Schmid, *Mozart und die Salzburger Tradition* (Tutzing, 1976)

Mozart, (Maria) Constanze (Caecilia Josepha Johanna Aloisia) (née Weber, later Nissen) (b. Zell im Wiesental, 5 Jan. 1762; d. Salzburg, 6 Mar. 1842). Wife of W. A. Mozart. Mozart first met Constanze during his visit to MANNHEIM in 1777–8, at which time he was infatuated with Constanze's elder sister, ALOYSIA LANGE (née Weber). Their relationship blossomed only in 1781, by which time both Mozart and the Webers were living in VIENNA. For a short spell in the spring and early summer, Mozart was the Webers' lodger; in order to scotch rumours linking him with Constanze, however, he moved to rooms on the

Graben in the late summer. Even then, Mozart still harboured feelings for Aloysia, by then married, writing to his father on 16 May: 'I admit I was a fool about Aloysia Lange, but what does not a man do when he is in love? Indeed I loved her truly and even now I feel that she is not a matter of indifference to me.' By December, however, he was fully committed to Constanze, describing her to his father as 'the martyr of the family and probably for that very reason, is the kindest-hearted, the cleverest and, in short, the best of them all . . . I must make you better acquainted with the character of my dear Constanze. She is not ugly, but at the same time far from beautiful. Her whole beauty consists in two little black eyes and a pretty figure. She has no wit, but she has enough common sense to enable her to fulfil her duties as a wife and mother . . . She understands house-keeping and has the kindest heart in the world. I love her and she loves me with all her heart. Tell me whether I could wish myself a better wife? One more thing I must tell you, is that when I resigned the Archbishop's service, our love had not yet begun. It was born of her tender care and attentions when I was living in their house' (15 Dec. 1781). By January 1782 Mozart was committed to Constanze although it also appears he was forced by her guardian, Johann Thorwart, to give a written understanding that he would either marry her within three years or pay her compensation. They married on 4 August 1782 and the apparent messiness of their courtship and Mozart's seemingly lukewarm praise notwithstanding, Constanze seems to have been a good wife to Wolfgang. It is clear that their marriage was, on the whole, both a happy one and one that kept Mozart satisfied, as his letters to her from 1791 document. The couple visited SALZBURG in 1783, to meet Mozart's father and sister, and relations among them appear to have been cordial if slightly distant. While there, Constanze may have sung in a performance of Mozart's C minor Mass, K427, at St Peter's in October.

Following Mozart's death, Constanze was granted a pension by Francis II for an annual sum of 266 gulden and over the next few years she arranged performances of his works and toured GERMANY with her sister Aloysia; on several occasions she took part in performances of LA CLEMENZA DI TITO. Towards the end of the decade she arranged for the sale of Mozart's manuscripts to the Offenbach publisher J. A. ANDRE; many of her business affairs were handled by GEORG NIKOLAUS NISSEN, a Danish diplomat whom she married in 1809. The couple lived in Copenhagen from 1810 to 1821; after his retirement they settled in Salzburg. Nissen died in 1826 while collecting materials for a biography of Mozart, which Constanze then had finished and published in 1828.

CLIFF EISEN

Mozart, Franz Xaver Wolfgang (b. Vienna, 26 July 1791; d. Carlsbad, 29 July 1844). The younger of Mozart's two surviving sons, Franz Xaver followed in his father's footsteps becoming a pianist, composer and Kapellmeister. Like Mozart, he started his musical career as a young child, performing (aged six) at a memorial concert for his father in PRAGUE on 15 November 1797. He published his Op. 1 piano quartet in 1802, and performed the Piano Concerto in C, K467, at VIENNA's Theater an der Wien on 8 April 1805. A series of eminent teachers included ALBRECHTSBERGER, HUMMEL and SALIERI; the latter predicted a great future for him in a testimonial dated 30 March 1807. Johann Baptist

Gänsbacher (1778–1844), a composer and cathedral organist, also reported in the *Allgemeine Wiener Musik-Zeitung* (1844) that by the early 1800s Wolfgang 'was already an excellent pianist, who could among other things transpose Bach fugues into another key at sight'. Before moving to Copenhagen with GEORG NIKOLAUS NISSEN, her second husband, in 1810 CONSTANZE MOZART left Franz Xaver one of Mozart's keyboards.

Franz Xaver performed widely in eastern and central Europe (he lived in Lemberg, Poland for much of his life), carrying out a concert tour between 1819 and 1821 that he documented in a travel diary. Other important performances included conducting Mozart's REQUIEM in SALZBURG in August 1826 at a memorial service for Nissen and playing at celebrations surrounding the unveiling of the Salzburg Mozart statue in 1842. (The Requiem was performed at Franz Xaver's own memorial services in Carlsbad, Salzburg, Vienna and Lemberg in 1844.) Among his compositions, the Piano Concerto No. 2 in E flat was especially popular in the early nineteenth century. SIMON P. KEEFE

R. Halliwell, *The Mozart Family: Four Lives in a Social Context* (Oxford, 1998)
W. Hummel, *W. A. Mozarts Söhne* (Kassel, 1956)
F. X. W. Mozart, *Reisetagebuch 1819–1821*, ed. R. Angermüller (Bad Honnef, 1994)

Mozart, Karl Thomas (b. Vienna, 21 Sept. 1784; d. Milan, 31 Oct. 1858). The elder of Mozart's two surviving sons, Karl Thomas studied in VIENNA and PRAGUE and moved to Livorno in 1797 before settling in MILAN in 1805. He intended at first to be a musician, studying with Bonifazio Asioli, the Milanese court Kapellmeister – after JOSEPH HAYDN had written to Asioli on Karl's behalf on 23 April 1806 – but later turned away from the profession (warned against it by CONSTANZE MOZART who feared that unfavourable comparisons would inevitably have been drawn between him and his father). In 1810 he took a civil service position with the Viceroy of Naples in Milan. He continued to perform privately, however, and remained closely involved with perpetuating his father's legacy, attending the Salzburg celebrations in 1842 (the unveiling of the Mozart statue) and 1856 (the centenary of Mozart's birth). L. A. Zellner reported in the *Blätter für Musik, Theater und Kunst* (1856) that Karl Thomas was 'a small, thin man with black eyes and slightly greying hair, simple and extremely modest in his manner . . . [H]e assured me when I asked him that he remembered his father very clearly, and that he recalled two circumstances in particular. Firstly, that his father often had to take him out for walks, because his mother Constanze had at that time long been ailing and had to keep to the house. Thus he was often taken to the theatre by his father.' Mozart partially corroborated the latter point, explaining in a letter to Constanze on 14 October 1791 that he took seven-year-old Karl to a performance of DIE ZAUBERFLÖTE the previous day: 'Karl was absolutely delighted at being taken to the opera.' SIMON P. KEEFE

R. Halliwell, *The Mozart Family: Four Lives in a Social Context* (Oxford, 1998)
W. Hummel, *W. A. Mozarts Söhne* (Kassel, 1956)

Mozart, (Johann Georg) Leopold (b. Augsburg, 14 Nov. 1719; d. Salzburg, 28 May 1787). Composer, violinist and theorist; father of W. A. Mozart.

Leopold Mozart, the son of an AUGSBURG bookbinder, Johann Georg Mozart (1679–1736), attended the Augsburg Gymnasium (1727–35) and the Lyceum adjoining the Jesuit school of St Salvator (1735–36); a frequent performer in local theatrical productions, he was also an accomplished organist and violinist. In 1737, Leopold broke with his family and matriculated at the SALZBURG Benedictine University, where he studied philosophy and jurisprudence. He took the bachelor of philosophy degree in 1738, with public commendation, but in September 1739 he was expelled for poor attendance and a failure to show proper deference to his professors and the university establishment. It is unclear why Leopold became disenchanted with his studies and why he deliberately provoked the university officials; possibly he felt that a career in the Church, chosen for him by his parents, did not suit his nature or interests. As his later correspondence shows, Leopold was a gregarious youth and a willing performer. No doubt he had always been attracted to a career in music and shortly after leaving the university he became a valet and musician to Johann Baptist, Count of Thurn-Valsassina and Taxis, Salzburg canon and president of the consistory; it was to Thurn-Valsassina that he dedicated his *Sonate sei da chiesa e da camera*, Op.1 (1740), which he engraved in copper himself.

It may have been the composition around this time of several German passion cantatas that led to his appointment in 1743 as fourth violinist in the court orchestra of Archbishop Leopold Anton Freiherr von FIRMIAN; in addition to his court duties he taught violin to the choirboys of the cathedral oratory and, later, keyboard. By 1758 he had advanced to the post of second violinist and in 1763 to deputy Kapellmeister. During these years he composed prolifically; according to the 'Nachricht von dem gegenwärtigen Zustande der Musik Sr. Hochfürstl. Gnaden des Erzbischoffs zu Salzburg', published by F. W Marpurg in 1757, Leopold had by that time composed

> many contrapuntal and other church items; further a great number of symphonies, some only à4 but others with all the customary instruments; likewise more than 30 large serenades in which solos for various instruments appear. In addition he has brought forth many concertos, in particular for the transverse flute, oboe, bassoon, Waldhorn, trumpet etc.: countless trios and divertimentos for various instruments; 12 oratorios and a number of theatrical items, even pantomimes, and especially certain occasional pieces such as martial music . . . Turkish music, music with 'steel keyboard' and lastly a musical sleigh ride; not to speak of marches, so-called 'Nachtstücke' and many hundreds of minuets, opera dances and similar items.

Only a fraction of these works survive, chiefly symphonies and other occasional orchestral works (including *Die musikalische Schlittenfahrt* and *Die Bauernhochzeit*), divertimenti for strings, keyboard sonatas, sacred and secular songs, and numerous masses, litanies and offertories. Tentative dates can be established for most of this repertory but they do not answer the most intractable and significant chronological question: whether Leopold continued to compose after Wolfgang began his own career. The latest substantiated dates of composition are April 1762 for the Trumpet Concerto and August 1762 for a litany in D major. It is almost certain, however, that the fragmentary mass K116, previously attributed to Wolfgang, was composed in Vienna in 1768 and the so-called 'Lambach' symphony, also claimed for Mozart, a year earlier, in 1767.

References in the family letters show that Leopold Mozart considered himself a 'modern' composer and his extant works, both early and late, bear this out. The church music, including the sacramental litany in D major, the litany in E flat major and the *Missa solemnis* in C minor, is surprisingly dramatic, juxtaposing traditional *stile antico* counterpoint with arias based on models from Italian opera. The symphonies, too, are generally finely wrought and the most mature of them stylistically approximate German symphonies by composers a generation younger than Leopold. It speaks for itself that several of his works were at one time thought to be compositions by Wolfgang. The 'popular' bias frequently cited as characteristic of his style affects only a small part of his output and is of little significance; in general it is more a reflection on the demands of his patrons and the particular occasions for which the works were written. Curiously, Leopold seems to have written little for his own instrument; no violin concertos by him are known. The *Violinschule* of 1756, however, was highly regarded. It was revised by Leopold for second and third editions published in 1769–70 and 1787 respectively. A Dutch translation appeared in 1766, and a French edition, by Valentin Roeser, apparently not authorized, in 1770; elsewhere, revisions of Mozart's text continued to be published as late as 1817. Based chiefly on the Italian method, and Tartini in particular, the *Violinschule* nevertheless shows Mozart's acquaintance with a broad range of music theory from Glarean on. While not universally applicable as a guide to pan-European eighteenth-century performing practices, the work nevertheless represents the source closest to Mozart and is the most valuable guide to the musical and aesthetic education of the younger composer.

Mozart married MARIA ANNA MOZART (née Pertl) on 21 November 1747; of their seven children only two, Maria Anna ('NANNERL' MOZART, b. 1751) and Wolfgang Amadeus (b. 1756), survived to adulthood. And while Leopold continued to compose and teach throughout the late 1750s, there is no doubt that the 'miracle which God let be born in Salzburg', as he later described Wolfgang, changed his life. It is not true, as Nannerl later reported, that he 'entirely gave up both violin instruction and composition in order to direct that time not claimed in service to the prince to the education of his two children'; even after Wolfgang's musical talents became apparent, Leopold continued to perform his works, to direct the court music, to teach violin, to arrange for the purchase of music and musical instruments, and to attend to numerous other details as part of his court duties. Nevertheless, the recognition of this 'miracle' struck Leopold with the force of a divine revelation and he felt his responsibility to be not merely a father's and teacher's but a missionary's as well; at least in part this was the motivation for the journeys that he undertook, at first with his entire family but after 1769 chiefly with Wolfgang alone.

Leopold's collaboration in Wolfgang's early works up to about 1770 was probably considerable; in addition to editing the manuscripts, he frequently made compositional suggestions; at least one of his works, the trio of the serenade in D major, appears as Menuet II in Wolfgang's sonata K6, and scarcely a single autograph of Wolfgang's is without additions or alterations in his father's hand. Even later, the attributions and dates on Mozart's autographs are frequently by Leopold, who apparently preserved his son's manuscripts with painstaking orderliness. Thus the elder Mozart fulfilled a universal function as teacher, educator and private secretary to his son, and when necessary also served as valet, impresario, propagandist and travel organizer.

During the 1770s, when the Mozarts travelled less and Wolfgang began to assert his independence, Leopold felt increasingly distant from Salzburg's musical life; a letter of 4 September 1776 to Padre MARTINI, written by Wolfgang but composed by Leopold makes this clear: 'My father . . . has already served this court for thirty-six years and as he knows that the present Archbishop cannot and will not have anything to do with people who are getting on in years, he no longer puts his whole heart into his work, but has taken up literature, which was always a favourite study of his.' And his final decade was one of rebuffs, setbacks at court and personal tragedy. His wife died in PARIS in 1778 while accompanying Wolfgang on tour and Leopold was subsequently compelled to mediate in the ever worsening relations between his son and Archbishop COLLOREDO. Although he managed to secure a temporarily satisfactory resolution of this conflict – in 1779 Wolfgang was appointed court and cathedral organist – his efforts finally came to nothing when in 1781 Mozart left the Archbishop's service and took up permanent residence in VIENNA. Wolfgang's marriage to CONSTANZE MOZART (née Weber) was seen by Leopold as a misalliance and he became increasingly alienated from his son, although in the spring of 1785, while visiting Vienna, he experienced at first hand Mozart's triumphs and heard with pride and satisfaction Haydn's famous words in praise of Wolfgang: 'Before God and as an honest man, I tell you that your son is the greatest composer known to me either in person or by name. He has taste and, what is more, the most profound knowledge of composition' (letter of 16 Feb. 1785). But after this visit especially, Salzburg must have seemed remote and isolated to him. Earlier, in August 1784, Nannerl had married JOHANN BAPTIST VON BERCHTOLD ZU SONNENBERG and moved to St Gilgen, the birthplace of Mozart's mother; one consolation was the birth in July 1785 of his grandson, Leopold (Nannerl and Berchtold's first child), who was brought to Salzburg to live with the elder Mozart, then sixty-six years old.

Leopold Mozart died in May 1787 and was buried in the cemetery of St Sebastian. On the same day, Dominicus HAGENAUER, Abbot of St Peter's in Salzburg and a long-time family friend, noted in his diary:

> Leopold Mozart, who died today, was a man of much wit and wisdom, and would have been capable of good services to the state beyond those of music . . . He was born in Augsburg, spent most of his days in court service here, and yet had the misfortune always to be persecuted and was far less beloved here than in other great places of Europe.

Mozart's personality could not be more accurately summarized, nor his misrepresentation at the hands of later biographers more strikingly contradicted. A man of broad cultural achievement, a passionate reader of literature and natural science, an admirer of Gottsched, a correspondent of GELLERT's and a friend of WIELAND, Leopold Mozart may have been haughty, difficult to please and at times intractable, but even his contemporaries gave him full credit for Wolfgang's development; HASSE, who once described him as 'equally discontented everywhere' also wrote to Ortes, 'you will not be displeased to know a father who has the merit of having known how to form and give so good an education to a son'. There is no compelling evidence that Leopold was excessively manipulative, intolerant, autocratic or jealous of his son's talent. On the contrary, a careful reading in context of the family letters reveals a father who cared deeply for his son but who was frequently frustrated in his greatest ambition: to secure for Wolfgang a worldly position appropriate to his genius.

CLIFF EISEN

W. Baer, ed., *Leopold Mozart zum 200. Todestag, Stadtarchivs Augsburg, 23 May–16 Aug 1987* (Augsburg, 1987) (Exhibition catalogue)

C. Eisen, 'The Symphonies of Leopold Mozart: Their Chronology, Style, and Importance for the Study of Mozart's Earliest Symphonies', *Mozart-Jahrbuch 1987/88*, 181–3

R. Halliwell, *The Mozart Family: Four Lives in a Social Context* (Oxford, 1998)

L. Mozart, *Versuch einer gründlichen Violinschule* (Augsburg, repr. 1756, 2nd edn 1769–70, enlarged rev. 3rd edn 1787, 4th edn 1800; Dutch trans., repr. 1766; French trans., 1770; numerous other unauthorized reprintings and edns; Eng. trans., 1948, 2nd edn 1951)

[L. Mozart, presumed author], 'Nachricht von dem gegenwärtigen Zustande der Musik Sr. Hochfürstl. Gnaden des Erzbischoffs zu Salzburg im Jahre 1757', in F. W. Marpurg, *Historisch-kritische Beyträge zur Aufnahme der Musik*, 3 (Berlin, 1757/R), 185–98; Eng. trans. in N. Zaslaw, *Mozart's Symphonies: Context, Performance Practice, Reception* (Oxford, 1989), 50–7

Various letters and notebooks in *Mozart, Briefe und Aufzeichnungen*, ed. W. Bauer, O. E. Deutsch and J. Eibl (Kassel, 1962–75; some trans. in E. Anderson, ed., *The Letters of Mozart and his Family* (3rd edn London, 1985))

W. Plath, 'Zur Echtheitsfrage bei Mozart: 2. Leopold Mozart', *Mozart-Jahrbuch 1971/72*, 19–36; repr. in W. Plath, *Mozart Schriften*, ed. M. Danckwardt (Kassel, 1991), 179–201

F. Posch, 'Leopold Mozart als Mensch, Vater und Erzieher der Aufklärung', *Neues Mozart-Jahrbuch 1941*, 49–78

M. H. Schmid, *Mozart und die Salzburger Tradition* (Tutzing, 1976)

Mozart, Maria Anna (née Pertl, b. St Gilgen, 25 Dec. 1720; d. Paris, 3 July 1778). Mozart's mother. Her father (Wolfgang Nikolaus Pertl, *Pfleger* or administrator of St Gilgen) died when she was three, and her childhood was penurious. On 21 November 1747 she married LEOPOLD MOZART, and they lived in SALZBURG's Getreidegasse as tenants of the HAGENAUER family. Of their seven children, five died in infancy.

Information about Maria Anna is limited to snippets of news in Leopold's letters to the Hagenauers when the family was away (Maria Anna did not write herself); Leopold's and Mozart's letters to her when they were travelling on their own (her replies have been lost); and her letters to Leopold from September 1777 to June 1778 (when she and Mozart were travelling to PARIS on Mozart's quest for an appointment), together with Leopold's answers. Her writing style and orthography show that she was not as well educated as her daughter NANNERL MOZART, but she was a capable housekeeper, a role then encompassing highly developed skills like needlecraft, food preservation and the preparation of medicaments.

The correspondence of 1777–8 illuminates the stresses of the last year of Maria Anna's life. The journey was physically challenging; Mozart sometimes made her feel an encumbrance; and money was short, causing her difficulties in accounting to Leopold for their expenditure. Her lonely death (for which Leopold blamed Mozart) after a short febrile illness appears to cap the pathos of this period, causing biographers to depict her with sympathetic piety, but in a somewhat restricted way, as a woman possessing far-reaching devotion to her family, robust humour and a love of friendship and gossip.

It may be possible to deepen the understanding of Maria Anna by studying her life in particular local contexts. For example, the documentation exposes riddles, one concerning her relationship with Leopold. Many passages in the letters reveal Leopold's love and respect for her, but he could also be impatient, sarcastic and insistently determined to be right. Yet Maria Anna, despite her economic dependence and educational inferiority, evidently had little fear of him, confidently showing comfort and tenderness. A contextual study of male/female relationships in Salzburg might illuminate the social mechanics that apparently made it possible for couples to feel affectionately at ease in spite of such profound inequalities.

Other intriguing questions concern religion: her trust in prayer to improve the family's position sometimes replaced action to bring about the desired result. Mozart too betrayed this kind of passivity during the journey of 1777–8, while Leopold had a more complex vision of how man's choices and deeds would interact with God's will. To what extent was such passivity a characteristic of women and the inexperienced young, unused to taking responsibility for their actions? Again, a contextual study of religious thinking in Salzburg – the minutiae showing how a religion was actually lived both by women and by men – might shed light on this question. RUTH HALLIWELL

R. Halliwell, *The Mozart Family: Four Lives in a Social Context* (Oxford, 1998)
E. Valentin, *'Madame Mutter': Anna Maria Walburga Mozart (1720–1778)* (Augsburg, 1991)

Mozart, Maria Anna ('Nannerl') (b. Salzburg, 30/1 July 1751; d. Salzburg, 29 Oct. 1829). Mozart's older sister. On her eighth name day LEOPOLD MOZART gave her a music book he had prepared, the so-called 'Nannerl Notenbuch', which soon began to record how quickly Mozart learnt its pieces. This example of precociousness became a pattern: Mozart overshadowed Nannerl.

Though she was involved in the concert tours of 1762–9, Nannerl did not publicly demonstrate the same musical abilities as Mozart. She won high praise for taste and execution in keyboard performance, but Mozart also played the violin and organ, and developed compositional arts intensively. Nevertheless, Nannerl was certainly taught some of these skills: surviving exercises and references in the correspondence indicate that she practised varying a melody, composing a bass to a melody, accompanying at sight, and improvising. She also learnt to sing and teach, and Leopold wanted her to be capable of earning a musical living. From 1769 to 1775 Leopold made several journeys with Mozart alone, so Nannerl experienced some neglect. From this period, her lack of autonomy was problematic – wanting opportunities for performance in SALZBURG, she was dependent on a man to provide a livelier place of residence.

Until Mozart moved to VIENNA, he and Nannerl were very close: his letters from Italy in 1769–71 encouraged her compositions (which do not survive), and teased her about her 'unbearable' voice, her 'wonderful horse-face', and her unsuccessful suitors. The highlights of their public appearances were duet performances, and the concerto for two keyboards K365 was probably written for them. Mozart usually arranged to serenade Nannerl on her name day, and it is likely that the 'Nannerl Septet', K251 was written for her in 1776. Nannerl depended on Mozart for keyboard music (though apart from several short, improvisatory preludes such as the capriccio K395, there is no keyboard music known to have been written explicitly for her), and they shared a passion for the theatre and for making music. Many facets of their Salzburg life, from her piety to the family's tireless socializing, are illustrated by her diary.

Nannerl's hopes that Mozart would enable her to leave Salzburg dwindled after his move to Vienna without a salary in 1781, and his marriage in 1782. From this date she appears to have shared with Leopold a degree of disenchantment with Mozart. Disappointed in her apparent wish to marry FRANZ ARMAND D'IPPOLD, on 23 August 1784 she married the twice-widowed JOHANN BAPTIST BERCHTOLD VON SONNENBURG, and moved to St Gilgen to direct his household of five children. She and Berchtold had three further children: Leopold Alois Pantaleon (b. 27 July 1785; d. 15 May 1840); Johanna ('Jeanette', b. 22/3 Mar. 1789; d. 1 Sept. 1805); and Maria Babette (b. 27 Nov. 1790; d. 24 Apr. 1791). Because of difficulties in her situation, Leopold kept her baby 'Leopoldl' ('little Leopold') with him in Salzburg until Leopold's death in 1787. Leopold's letters to Nannerl for the period between her marriage and his death not only illuminate the situation of her marriage and his Salzburg service, but also provide news about Mozart. Despite difficulties in keeping her fortepiano working in St Gilgen, Nannerl regularly demanded new pieces, and Leopold sent her Mozart's latest keyboard music. It is because of Nannerl's requests for music that Mozart's own cadenzas survive for several of the keyboard concertos – Mozart sent these to her, and she kept them. These and the preludes mentioned above (together with the letters about them) are valuable for what they show about Nannerl's skills, Mozart's ideas on improvisation, and PERFORMANCE PRACTICE.

Nannerl had become involved with Mozart biography soon after Wolfgang's death in 1791. In 1792 she wrote an essay for SCHLICHTEGROLL'S *Nekrolog*; unknown to her, this essay acquired a postscript critical of Mozart and CONSTANZE MOZART, written by Albert von Mölk. In 1799 she supplied Breitkopf & Härtel with anecdotes about Mozart, and in the 1820s she cooperated with Constanze Mozart's second husband GEORG NIKOLAUS NISSEN by giving him letters for use in his Mozart biography. She and Constanze played a great role in handing down biographical and musical source material.

RUTH HALLIWELL

R. Halliwell, *The Mozart Family: Four Lives in a Social Context* (Oxford, 1998)

W. Plath, 'Leopold Mozart und Nannerl: Lehrer und Schülerin', in Plath, *Mozart-Schriften: Ausgewählte Aufsätze*, ed. M. Danckwardt (Kassel, 1991), 375–8

E. Rieger, *Nannerl Mozart: Leben einer Künstlerin im 18. Jahrhundert* (Frankfurt am Main, 2nd edn 1991)

Mozart, Maria Anna Thekla (b. 25 Sept. 1758; d. 25 Jan. 1841). Mozart's Bäsle ('little cousin'), daughter of LEOPOLD MOZART's brother Franz Alois. She did not conform to Leopold's pattern of female modesty, and bore an illegitimate daughter in 1784. Mozart befriended her on his way through AUGSBURG to PARIS in 1777. The two corresponded, and nine of his 'Bäsle letters' survive, unfortunately without her answers. In contrast to the letter Mozart wrote on 30 July 1778 to his new love Aloysia Weber (later LANGE) which is formal, even pompous, those to his cousin show riotous irreverence. When Mozart was returning to SALZBURG from Paris, Aloysia rejected him, and Maria Anna Thekla softened his homecoming by visiting him in SALZBURG.

The Bäsle letters are about play – almost devoid of news, they are rumbustious verbal fantasias demonstrating Mozart's subversive sense of humour. Exploiting current comic conventions (especially those of the Hanswurst popular comedy tradition), they parody literary and musical genres, using rhymes, puns, echoes, and other techniques. Their scatological and erotic allusions put them at great risk of destruction: they survived by a hair's breadth, were not printed complete until 1938 (in Emily Anderson's edition), and awoke bewildered disgust that the 'divine' Mozart could have written so coarsely. Some commentators see the erotic allusions as proof that Mozart and his cousin had sexual relations; others suggest that they may simply show Mozart behind the mask of HANSWURST; others again proclaim the validity of deeper psychological analysis, however playful Mozart intended the letters to be. RUTH HALLIWELL

J. H. Eibl, 'Zur Überlieferungsgeschichte der Bäsle-Briefe', *Mitteilungen der Internationalen Stiftung Mozarteum* 27 (1979), 9–17

W. Hildesheimer, *Mozart*, trans. M. Faber (London, 1985)

A. Kühn, 'Komik, Humor und Musikalität in Mozarts Bäslebriefen', in *Neues Augsburger Mozartbuch* (= Zeitschrift des historischen Vereins für Schwaben, Augsburg, 1962), 107–89

D. Schroeder, *Mozart in Revolt: Strategies of Resistance, Mischief and Deception* (New Haven and London, 1999)

Mozart, (Johann Chrysostom) Wolfgang Amadeus (b. Salzburg, 27 Jan. 1756; d. Vienna, 5 Dec. 1791). Composer and keyboard player.

A. Biography
B. Personality
C. Education
D. Religious beliefs
E. Medical history and death
F. Mozart as author
G. Mozart as letter writer
H. Biographies
I. Mozart: literature and the theatre

A. Biography

1. Childhood and early travels
2. Salzburg, Mannheim and Paris, 1772–1780
3. Vienna, 1781–1788
4. The final years, 1788–1791

1. CHILDHOOD AND EARLY TRAVELS

Mozart was the seventh and last child of LEOPOLD MOZART and MARIA ANNA MOZART (née Pertl). His first two names record that 27 January was the feast day of St John Chrysostom; Wolfgangus was the name of his maternal grandfather and Theophilus the name of his godfather, the merchant Joannes Theophilus Pergmayr. He sometimes preferred the Latin form, Amadeus, but more frequently Amadè, Amadé or the German form Gottlieb.

As far as is known, Leopold was entirely responsible for Wolfgang's early education, which included mathematics, reading, writing, literature, languages, dancing and moral and religious training. But it was his musical talent that manifested itself early and won him lasting fame. By the age of four he had learned to play simple keyboard pieces. And his earliest compositions, the Andante and Allegro, K1a and 1b, were written in 1761, when he was five.

Mozart's first known public appearance was at the SALZBURG University in September 1761, when he took a dancing part in a performance of *Sigismundus Hungariae rex*, an end-of-term play by Marian Wimmer with music by the Salzburg Kapellmeister J. E. EBERLIN. Leopold took him to MUNICH in 1762, where he played the harpsichord for MAXIMILIAN III JOSEPH, Elector of Bavaria, and to VIENNA, where he twice appeared before MARIA THERESIA and her consort, Francis I; COUNT KARL VON ZINZENDORF, later a high state official, wrote in his diary that 'the poor little fellow plays marvellously, he is a child of spirit, lively, charming'.

In February 1763, Leopold was promoted to deputy Kapellmeister in Salzburg but less than four months later the family set out on a three-and-a-half-year journey through Germany, France, the Low Countries, England and Switzerland. Travelling by way of MUNICH, AUGSBURG, Frankfurt, Coblenz, Aachen and Brussels, the family arrived in PARIS by the end of the year. Mozart and his sister played before Louis XV on 1 January 1764 and gave public concerts in March and April at the private theatre of M. Félix. Before they left the French capital, Mme Vendôme published the sonatas K6–9, the first of his music to appear in print.

The family arrived in England on 23 April 1764: they played twice for George III, on 27 April and 17 May, and were scheduled to appear at a benefit for the composer and cellist Carlo Graziani but Wolfgang was taken ill and unable to perform. A concert for their benefit was mounted on 5 June at the Great Room in Spring Garden and later that month Mozart performed several of his own works on the harpsichord and organ at Ranelagh Gardens, during breaks in a performance of HANDEL's *Acis and Galatea*. At some time during their fifteen-month visit, Mozart was tested by the philosopher DAINES BARRINGTON, who in 1769 furnished the Royal Society with a report on him. Barrington's tests were typical of others that Mozart was set on the Grand Tour and, later, in Italy:

> I said to the boy, that I should be glad to hear an extemporary *Love Song*, such as his friend Manzoli might choose in an opera. The boy . . . looked back with much archness, and immediately began five or six lines of a jargon recitative proper to introduce a love song. He then played a symphony which might correspond with an air composed to the single word, *Affetto*. It had a first and second part, which, together with the symphonies, was of the length that opera songs generally last: if the extemporary composition was not amazingly capital, yet it was really above mediocrity, and shewed most extraordinary readiness of invention . . . After this he played a difficult lesson, which he had finished a day or two before: his execution was amazing, considering that his little fingers could scarcely reach a fifth on the harpsichord. His astonishing readiness, however did not arise merely from great practice; he had a thorough knowledge of the fundamental principles of composition, as, upon producing a treble, he immediately wrote a base under it, which, when tried, had very good effect. He was also a

> great master of modulation, and his transitions from one key to another were excessively natural and judicious; he practised in this manner for a considerable time with a handkerchief over the keys of the harpsichord.

The Mozarts remained in LONDON until late July 1765: they played at court again in October 1764 and gave public concerts on 21 February and 13 May 1765; in December 1764 Mozart published six sonatas for keyboard and violin (K10–15), dedicated to Queen Charlotte, and it was probably during this time that he composed his first symphony (K16). They also became acquainted with the composer C. F. ABEL, with the singer GIOVANNI MANZUOLI and with J. C. BACH, with whom the family became intimate and whose influence on Mozart was lifelong.

From London the Mozarts travelled via Canterbury to Lille, Ghent and Antwerp, arriving at The Hague in September 1765. There the children gave two public concerts and played before the Princess of Nassau-Weilburg, to whom Mozart later dedicated the keyboard and violin sonatas K26–31. In Amsterdam Mozart composed the *Gallimathias musicum*, K32, for the installation of Wilhelm V on 11 March and in April they set out again for Paris, arriving in early May. Then they travelled home by way of Dijon, Lyons, Lausanne, Zurich, Donaueschingen, Augsburg and Munich, arriving in Salzburg on 29 November. On the day of their arrival, Beda Hübner, librarian at St Peter's, wrote in his diary:

> I cannot forbear to remark here also that today the world-famous Herr Leopold Mozart, deputy Kapellmeister here, with his wife and two children, a boy aged ten and his little daughter of 13, have arrived to the solace and joy of the whole town . . . The two children, the boy as well as the girl, both play the harpsichord, or the clavier, the girl it is true, with more art and fluency than her little brother, but the boy with far more refinement and with more original ideas, and with the most beautiful harmonic inspirations . . . There is a strong rumour that the Mozart family will again not long remain here but will soon visit the whole of Scandinavia and the whole of Russia, and perhaps even travel to China, which would be a far greater journey and bigger undertaking still: de facto, I believe it to be certain that nobody is more celebrated in Europe than Herr Mozart with his two children.

Contrary to what is usually assumed, much of the Grand Tour was not planned in advance. When he left Salzburg, Leopold was undecided whether to travel to England and he had no intention to visit the Low Countries. There were miscalculations too, especially in London, where the family probably outstayed its welcome: by June 1765 Mozart was reduced to giving public displays at the down-market Swan and Hoop Tavern in Cornhill. Also, travel was not easy at the time: routes were often unsafe and usually uncomfortable, expenses were substantial and the family was frequently mistreated, ignored or prevented by potential patrons from performing. In a letter of 4 November 1763, Leopold wrote from Brussels: 'We have now been kept [here] for nearly three weeks. Prince Karl . . . spends his time hunting, eating and drinking . . . Meanwhile, in decency I have neither been able to leave nor to give a concert since, as the prince himself has said, I must await his decision.' Unexpected detours and delays added nearly two years to the tour. But detours and delays also gave the Mozarts an opportunity to become acquainted with some of Europe's most significant composers and performers: in addition to Abel, Manzuoli and J. C. Bach, they heard the violinist Pietro Nardini at Ludwigsburg and met SCHOBERT, ECKARD and HONAUER in Paris.

The Mozarts remained in Salzburg for nine months, during which time Wolfgang wrote the Latin comedy APOLLO ET HYACINTHUS, the first part of the oratorio DIE SCHULDIGKEIT DES ERSTEN UND FÜRNEHMSTEN GEBOTS (a joint work with MICHAEL HAYDN and ANTON CAJETAN ADLGASSER) and the *Grabmusik*, K42. But on 15 September they set out again, for Vienna. It is presumed that Leopold had timed this visit to coincide with the festivities planned for the marriage of the sixteen-year-old Archduchess Josepha to Ferdinand IV of Naples. Josepha, however, contracted smallpox and died on the day after the wedding was to have taken place, throwing the court into mourning. Leopold removed his family from the city, first to Brünn (Brno) and then to Olmütz (Olomouc), where both Mozart and his sister had mild attacks. Shortly after their return to Vienna, Leopold conceived the idea of securing for Mozart an opera commission. This was LA FINTA SEMPLICE but intrigues at court conspired to defeat his plans. Leopold wrote an indignant petition to the Emperor in September and presumably as compensation, in December Mozart directed performances before the imperial court of a festal mass (K139), an offertory (K47b, lost) and a trumpet concerto (K47c, also lost). That same month he completed the symphony K48.

The Mozarts arrived home on 5 January 1769 and remained there for nearly a year. *La finta semplice* was performed at court on or about 1 May and Mozart wrote the mass K66 in October (for the first Mass celebrated by his friend Cajetan HAGENAUER, son of the family's Salzburg landlord); other important works from this time include three orchestral serenades (K63, 99 and 100), some shorter sacred works (K117 and 141) and several sets of dancing minuets. On 27 October he was appointed, on an honorary basis, Konzertmeister.

Less than two months later, on 13 December, Leopold and Wolfgang set out for Italy. The journey followed the now usual pattern with concerts at towns along the way or at the homes of influential noblemen. Mozart gave a concert at the Accademia Filarmonica in Verona and had his portrait painted, probably by Saverio dalla Rosa. And on 16 January he gave a public concert at Mantua; a report in the *Gazzetta di Mantova* described him as 'incomparable'. From Mantua the Mozarts travelled to MILAN, where Wolfgang performed several times at the home of Count Karl FIRMIAN, the Austrian minister plenipotentiary; shortly afterwards he was commissioned to write MITRIDATE, RE DI PONTO for the carnival season in December. Father and son left Milan on 15 March, stopping at Lodi (where Mozart composed his first string quartet, K80), Bologna (where they met Padre MARTINI) and Florence (where Wolfgang became friendly with the young English composer THOMAS LINLEY). They arrived at Rome on 10 April, where Mozart may have composed two or three symphonies, visited Naples, and returned to Rome where, on 5 July, Pope Clemens XIV made Mozart a Knight of the Golden Spur. From Rome they returned to Bologna, where Mozart was admitted to membership of the Accademia Filarmonica, and then to Milan, for work on the opera. Although the composition itself went quickly, there were various intrigues among the singers who demanded numerous revisions of Mozart's arias; in one case,

'Vado incontro al fato estremo', the primo uomo GUGLIELMO D'ETTORE substituted an aria by GASPARINI for Mozart's. The opera premiered on 26 December at the Teatro Regio Ducale. Leopold had not been confident that the opera would be a success but it was, running to twenty-two performances.

The Mozarts left Milan on 14 January 1771, stopping at Turin, Venice, Padua and Verona before arriving at Salzburg on 28 March. The fifteen-month trip had been an extraordinary success, widely reported in the international press. And even before their return home, Leopold had laid plans for two further trips to Italy: when the Mozarts were in Verona, Wolfgang was commissioned to write the serenata ASCANIO IN ALBA for the wedding in Milan the following October of Archduke Ferdinand and Princess Maria Beatrice Ricciarda of Modena; and the same month he was issued a contract by the Teatro Regio Ducale at Milan for the first carnival opera of 1773, LUCIO SILLA. As a result, Mozart spent barely five months at home in 1771, during which time he wrote the Regina coeli K108, the litany K109 and the symphony K110. Father and son set out again on 13 August, arriving at Milan on 21 August. They received the libretto for *Ascanio in Alba* on 29 August and the opera went into rehearsal on 27 September; the premiere was on 17 October. HASSE's Metastasian opera *Ruggiero*, also composed for the wedding festivities, had its first performance the day before; according to Leopold, *Ascanio* 'struck down Hasse's opera' (letter of 19 Oct. 1771), a judgement confirmed by reports in local newspapers. The Mozarts remained in Milan until 5 December, during which time Wolfgang wrote the divertimento K113 and the symphony K112. He may also have sought employment at court but his application was effectively scotched by Ferdinand's mother, MARIA THERESIA, who in a letter of 12 December advised the Archduke against burdening himself with 'useless people' who go 'about the world like beggars'.

The third and last Italian journey began on 24 October 1772; probably Mozart had been sent the libretto and cast list for *Lucio Silla* during the summer, when he also began to set the recitatives. On his arrival at Milan he wrote the choruses and composed the arias, having first heard each of the singers so that he could suit the music to their voices. The premiere, on 26 December, was a mixed success, chiefly because of a patchy cast. Nevertheless, the opera ran for twenty-six performances. Before leaving for home (they arrived in Salzburg on 13 March 1773), Mozart wrote the solo motet *Exsultate, jubilate* for the primo uomo in the opera, VENANZIO RAUZZINI.

2. SALZBURG, MANNHEIM AND PARIS, 1772–1780

ARCHBISHOP SCHRATTENBACH, who had generously supported the careers and travels of both Leopold and Wolfgang, died on 16 December 1771, the day after the Mozarts' return from the second Italian tour. He was succeeded by HIERONYMUS COLLOREDO, an unpopular choice whose election was bitterly contested. Colloredo sought to modernize the archdiocese along Viennese models but his reforms met with local resistance. The court music in particular suffered and many traditional opportunities for music-making were eliminated, including the university theatre (which was closed in 1778). The mass was generally shortened, restrictions were placed on the performance of purely instrumental music at the cathedral and other churches, and local traditions, among them the famous pilgrimage to Pinzgau, were abolished. Concerts at court were curtailed.

While these changes profoundly affected traditional composition and performance in Salzburg, they also encouraged other kinds of musical activity. In 1775 Colloredo ordered that the Ballhaus in the Hannibalgarten be rebuilt at the city's expense as a theatre for both spoken drama and opera. The first troupe to play there, directed by Carl Wahr, included in its repertory GEBLER's tragedy THAMOS, KÖNIG IN ÄGYPTEN, possibly with incidental music by Mozart; and in 1780 SCHIKANEDER put on Gozzi's *Die zwei schlaflosen Nächte*, for which Mozart composed the aria 'Warum, o Liebe . . . Zittre, töricht Herz', K365a. Private orchestras were also established, the first of them by Colloredo's nephew, Count Johann Rudolf CZERNIN.

Mozart composed prolifically during the early years of Colloredo's rule: between 1772 and 1774 he wrote the masses K167, 192 and 194, the litanies K125 and 195, the Regina coeli K127, more than a dozen symphonies (K124–202), the keyboard concerto K175, the Concertone, K190, the serenade K204, the divertimenti K131, 166 and 205 and the string quintet K174. The family prospered financially: in late 1773 they moved from their apartment in the Getreidegasse to a larger one, the so-called Tanzmeisterhaus, in the Hannibalplatz; no doubt this move reflected Leopold's awareness of their status in Salzburg society. Nevertheless, encouraged by rumours of a possible opening at the imperial court, Leopold took Wolfgang to Vienna in July 1773. While there, Mozart composed the serenade K185 and the string quartets K168–73, although nothing came of Leopold's grander plans.

They returned from Vienna in late September and with the exception of three months spent in Munich between December 1774 and March 1775 (where Mozart composed LA FINTA GIARDINIERA), he remained in his native city until September 1777. In the absence of any sustained family correspondence, his activities there can only be surmised. They included performing at court and at the cathedral, frequent musical gatherings at home, a rich social life and composition. Among the few documented events of these years are the composition of IL RE PASTORE for the visit to Salzburg of Archduke Maximilian Franz in April 1774 and Mozart's participation in celebrations marking the 100th anniversary of the pilgrimage church at Maria Plain, also in 1774.

It was about this time that Mozart began to withdraw from the Salzburg court music, although the root cause of his dissatisfaction remains unclear. Family letters document Leopold's frustrating inability to find suitable positions for both of them and his annoyance with Colloredo's preference for Italian musicians. (DOMENICO FISCHIETTI was appointed Kapellmeister in 1772 and Giacomo Rust in 1777: Leopold, who had been deputy Kapellmeister since 1763, had reasonable but unrealized expectations of promotion.) Yet there is no compelling evidence of Colloredo's mistreatment of the Mozarts early in his rule. IL SOGNO DI SCIPIONE, originally composed for the fiftieth anniversary of Schrattenbach's ordination, was reworked early in 1772 and performed as part of the festivities surrounding Colloredo's installation; on 21 August 1772 Mozart was formally taken into the paid employment of the court, as Konzertmeister, with an annual salary of 150 gulden; Leopold continued to run the court music on a periodic basis and was entrusted with securing musicians, music and instruments; and the Mozarts travelled to Italy, Vienna and Munich. Their discontent with Salzburg must therefore have had grounds beyond the conditions of their employment, Colloredo's difficult personality, or his attempts to reform music-making and cultural life in Salzburg. No doubt Colloredo was displeased by Leopold's excessive pride, his superior manner (in November 1766 Leopold had written to Lorenz Hagenauer, 'after great honours, insolence is absolutely not to be tolerated') and by his continuing attempts to find jobs for the family elsewhere. Mozart may have contributed to their problems as well: his rejection of court musical life was transparent. He continued to compose church music, the primary duty of Salzburg composers, but with little enthusiasm; his output from 1775 to 1777, including masses and shorter church works, is meagre compared with Michael Haydn's. Instead, he established himself as the chief composer in Salzburg of instrumental and secular vocal music, including four violin concertos and four keyboard concertos, the serenades K204 and K250, numerous divertimenti (among them K188, 240, 247 and 252) and several arias. Many of these works were intended for friends and private patrons rather than the court.

Matters came to a head in the summer of 1777. In August Mozart wrote a petition asking the Archbishop for release from his employment and Colloredo responded by dismissing both father and son. Leopold, however, felt he could not afford to leave Salzburg and so Mozart, accompanied by his mother, set out from his native city. The purpose of the journey was clear: to secure well-paid employment so that the family could move. Mozart first called at Munich, where he offered his services to the Elector but met with a polite refusal, and then travelled to Augsburg, where he gave a concert, became acquainted with the keyboard instrument maker J. A. STEIN, and embarked on a relationship with his cousin, MARIA ANNA THEKLA MOZART (the 'Bäsle' with whom he later had a scatalogical correspondence). From there Mozart travelled to Mannheim, where he and his mother remained until the end of March. Wolfgang became friendly with the Konzertmeister Christian CANNABICH, the Kapellmeister Ignaz Holzbauer and the flautist J. B. WENDLING; he recommended himself to the Elector but with no success. While in Mannheim, Mozart composed five accompanied sonatas (K296, K301–3 and K305), two arias (K294 and 295) and was commissioned by FERDINAND DEJEAN, an employee of the Dutch East India Company, to write three flute concertos and two flute quartets; in the end, Mozart failed at the commission and may have written only a single quartet. The aria *Alcandro lo confesso*, K294 was written for ALOYSIA WEBER, the daughter of a Mannheim copyist and the sister of his later wife, CONSTANZE MOZART. Mozart, who was in love with Aloysia, put to Leopold the idea of taking her to Italy to become a prima donna, a proposal that infuriated his father, who accused him of dilatoriness, irresponsibility over money and family disloyalty.

Leopold ordered Wolfgang to Paris and it was decided that his mother should accompany him there rather than return to Salzburg. They arrived in the French capital on 23 March and Mozart immediately re-established his acquaintance with BARON VON GRIMM. He composed additional music, mainly choruses, for a performance of a *Miserere* by Holzbauer and, according to his letters, a sinfonia concertante for flute, oboe, bassoon and horn, now lost. A symphony

(K297) was performed at the Concert spirituel on 18 June while a group of ballet pieces, *Les petits riens*, was given with Piccinni's opera *Le finte gemelle*.

Mozart was unhappy in Paris: he claimed to have been offered but to have declined the post of organist at Versailles, and his letters make it clear that he despised French music and suspected malicious intrigue. He was not paid for a flute and harp concerto (K299) that he composed in April for the Comte de Guines, and his mother fell ill in mid-June. Although Grimm's doctor was called in to treat her, nothing could be done and she died on 3 July. Mozart wrote to his father to say she was critically ill and by the same post to his close Salzburg friend ABBE BULLINGER, telling him what had happened. Leopold was thus prepared when Bullinger broke the news to him.

These events triggered another round of recriminatory letters: Leopold accused Mozart of indolence, lying and improper attention to his mother; Wolfgang defended himself as best he could. Although this correspondence is usually taken to represent the first and most compelling evidence of an irreparable fissure in the relationship between Mozart and his father, it reflects more on their attempts to come to grips with a family tragedy. And Leopold's uncompromising devotion to Mozart was never in question: in his first letter to Wolfgang after learning of Maria Anna Mozart's death, Leopold does not lay blame but is concerned chiefly with his son's well-being.

Mozart stayed with Grimm for the rest of the summer. He gave another symphony at the Concert spirituel on 8 September, renewed his acquaintance with J. C. Bach (over from London to hear the Paris singers before composing his opera *Amadis de Gaule*), and wrote a now lost scena for the castrato TENDUCCI. But his friendship with Grimm deteriorated and on 31 August Leopold wrote to him that, following the death of Adlgasser, a post was open in Salzburg for court organist; the Archbishop had offered an increase in salary and generous leave. Mozart set out for home on 26 September, via Nancy, Strasburg, Mannheim and Munich, where he was coolly received by Aloysia Weber, now singing at the court opera. He arrived back in Salzburg in the third week of January 1779.

Mozart's new duties at court included playing in the cathedral, at court and in the chapel, and instructing the choirboys. At first he seems to have carried out his duties with determination: in 1779 and 1780 he composed the 'Coronation' Mass, K317, and the mass K337, the vespers K321 and 339 and the Regina coeli, K276. But Colloredo was not satisfied. In an ambiguously worded document appointing Michael Haydn court and cathedral organist in 1782 he wrote that 'we accordingly appoint [Haydn] as our court and cathedral organist, in the same fashion as young Mozart was obligated, with the additional stipulation that he show more diligence . . . and compose more often for our cathedral and chamber music'. It may be that Colloredo was disappointed that Mozart turned his energies to works such as the Concerto for Two Pianos, K365, the Sonata for Keyboard and Violin, K378, the symphonies K318, 319 and 338, the 'Posthorn' serenade, K320, the Sinfonia concertante, K364 and incidental music for *Thamos*, few of which would have been heard at court – and this notwithstanding his contract, which stated only that 'he shall as far as possible serve the court and the church with new compositions made by him'. During his final years in Salzburg, then, Mozart reverted to the pattern of 1774–7: his appearances at court as both performer and composer were half-hearted and his music-making was intended chiefly for a small circle of friends and the local nobility.

3. VIENNA, 1781–1788

In the summer of 1780, Mozart received a commission to compose a serious opera for Munich and the Salzburg cleric GIOVANNI BATTISTA VARESCO was engaged to prepare a libretto based on Danchet's *Idoménée*. Mozart began to set the text in Salzburg, completed it in Munich in January, and the opera was first given on 29 January 1781; both Leopold and Nannerl were at the premiere. During his stay in Munich, Mozart also composed the recitative and aria *Misera! dove son – Ah! Non son' io che parlo*, K369, the Oboe Quartet, K370, and possibly the three piano sonatas K330–2. On 12 March he was summoned to Vienna where Archbishop Colloredo was temporarily in residence for the accession of EMPEROR JOSEPH II; Wolfgang arrived there on 16 March.

Fresh from his triumphs in Munich, Mozart was offended at being treated like a servant and his letters home over the next three months reflect his increasing resentment: on 8 April Colloredo refused to allow him to perform for the Emperor at COUNTESS THUN's. But his letters also show a growing enthusiasm for freelancing in Vienna and matters came to a head on 9 May. At a stormy interview with the Archbishop, Mozart asked for his discharge. This was refused but later, at a meeting on 8 June with the chief steward, Count Arco, he was finally and decisively released from Salzburg service, 'with a kick on my arse . . . by order of our worthy Prince Archbishop' as he wrote to his father (letter of 9 June).

Mozart moved to the house of the Webers, his former Mannheim friends who had relocated after Aloysia's marriage to the court actor JOSEPH LANGE, although in order to scotch rumours linking him with the third daughter, Constanze, he moved in late August to a room in the Graben. He made a modest living at first, teaching three or four pupils (among them JOSEPHA VON AUERNHAMMER and MARIE KAROLINE, COUNTESS THIENNES DE RUMBEKE). He also participated in, or had works performed at, various concerts: the Tonkünstler-Sozietät gave one of his symphonies on 3 April, and on 23 November he played at a concert sponsored by Johann Michael von Auernhammer; later, in May 1782, he participated in a series of Augarten concerts promoted by PHILIPP JAKOB MARTIN. His own first public concert took place on 3 March 1782, possibly at the Burgtheater: the programme included the concertos K175 (with the newly composed finale K382) and K415, numbers from *Lucio Silla* and IDOMENEO, and a free fantasy. He also played regularly at the home of BARON GOTTFRIED VAN SWIETEN, where HANDEL and J. S. BACH were staples of the repertory.

By this time, Mozart had established himself as the finest keyboard player in Vienna and although he was not without competitors, few could match his pianistic feats. The most serious challenge, perhaps, came from MUZIO CLEMENTI, with whom he played an informal duel at court on 24 December 1781. Clearly he was perturbed by the event although he was judged to have won, and Clementi later spoke generously of his playing, while Mozart in his letters repeatedly disparaged the Italian; Joseph II must have been impressed too, for he continued to speak of the contest for more than a year. The same month saw the publication of the sonatas for keyboard and violin K296 and K376–80. They were well received: a review in C. F. Cramer's *Magazin der Musik* described them as 'unique of their kind. Rich in new ideas and traces of their author's great musical genius.' The most important composition of this period, however, was DIE ENTFÜHRUNG AUS DEM SERAIL, the libretto of which was given to Mozart at the end of July 1781. Originally planned for September of that year, the premiere was postponed until 16 July 1782; productions were soon mounted in cities throughout German-speaking Europe and the earliest lengthy obituary of Mozart, published in the *Musikalische Korrespondenz der Teutschen Filarmonischen Gesellschaft* for 4 January 1792, described the opera as 'the pedestal upon which his fame was erected'.

Shortly after the premiere of *Die Entführung*, on 16 July, Mozart decided to go forward with his marriage to Constanze Weber. Possibly events gave him little choice: his future mother-in-law's scheming may have placed him in a position where, because of his alleged intimacy with Constanze, he had to agree either to marry her or to compensate her. Mozart wrote to his father on 31 July, asking for his approval, the couple took communion together on 2 August, the contract was signed on 3 August and the next day they were married at the Stephansdom. Forced or not, the marriage appears to have been a happy one. Although Mozart described Constanze as lacking wit, he credited her with 'plenty of common sense and the kindest heart in the world'; his letters to her, when he was on tour or she was taking the cure at Baden, are full of affection. There is little reason to think that she was solely or even primarily to blame for their later financial troubles; according to Nannerl Mozart's statement in 1792, Wolfgang was largely incapable of managing his own affairs and Constanze was unable to help him. She nevertheless showed herself a sharp businesswoman after Mozart's death and a manipulator of truth for her own benefit: she was an unreliable and sometimes dishonest witness concerning the history, completion and sale of the REQUIEM, and was probably responsible for many of the myths surrounding Mozart's death.

Mozart's wedding to Constanze set off another acrimonious exchange with Leopold, whose letters from this period are lost (although their contents can be inferred, at least in part, from Mozart's). Leopold accused Wolfgang of concealing his affair with Constanze and, worse, of being a dupe, while Wolfgang became increasingly anxious to defend his honour against reproaches of improper behaviour; he chastised his father for withholding consent to his marriage and for his lukewarm reaction to *Die Entführung*. Mozart had reason to be upset: Leopold had repeatedly pressed him to return home and in his dealings with Colloredo, Wolfgang had been told by Count Arco that he could not leave his post without his father's permission. Despite his numerous successes in Vienna, he felt thwarted in his attempt to achieve a well-earned independence.

Presumably in order to heal the rift with his family, Mozart determined to take Constanze to Salzburg to meet his father and sister, but the visit was postponed several times: the opera had catapulted him to success (it was performed on 9 October in the presence of the visiting Russian Grand Duke Paul Petrovich) and between November 1782 and March 1783 he played at concerts sponsored by Auernhammer, the Russian Prince Dmitry Golitsyn, Countess Maria Thun, Philipp Jakob Martin, his sister-in-law Aloysia Lange, Count ESTERHÁZY and the singer THERESE TEYBER. On 23 March he gave his own academy at the Burgtheater, in the presence of the Emperor. Mozart composed several new works for these occasions, including the piano concertos K413–15 and three arias (K418–20) intended for a production of Pasquale Anfossi's *Il curioso indiscreto*. He also began work on the so-called 'Haydn' quartets, the first of which, K387, was completed in December 1782; the second was finished in June 1783, about the time Constanze was giving birth to their first child, Raimund Leopold, on 17 June.

Mozart and Constanze finally set out in July; they remained in Salzburg for about three months. (Raimund Leopold, who was left behind, died on 9 August.) Later evidence suggests the visit was not entirely happy but details are lacking. While in Salzburg, he composed two duos for violin and viola (K423 and 424) and parts of the mass K427 (which he never completed) may have had their first hearing at St Peter's on 26 October. On the return journey to Vienna, Mozart stopped off at Linz, where he composed a symphony (K425) and probably a piano sonata (K333).

With his return to Vienna in late November, Mozart entered on what were to be the busiest and most successful years of his life. On 22 December he performed a concerto in a concert given by the Tonkünstler-Sozietät and on 25 January 1784 he conducted *Die Entführung* for the benefit of Aloysia Lange. He gave three subscription concerts in the private hall of the Trattnerhof in March and a grand musical academy at the Burgtheater on 1 April; the programme included a 'quite new' symphony (possibly the 'Linz', K425), a new concerto (K450 or K451), the quintet for piano and winds (K452) and an improvisation. The 1785 season was just as busy: there were six subscription concerts at the Mehlgrube beginning on 11 February and another grand academy at the Burgtheater on 10 March; it was chiefly for these and other similar concerts that he composed a dozen piano concertos (from K449 to K503) between February 1784 and December 1786. In addition to his public performances, Mozart was also in demand for private concerts: in March 1784 alone he played thirteen times, mostly at the houses of Count Johann Esterházy and the Russian ambassador, Prince Golitsyn. And newly commissioned works by him were frequently given by visiting and local virtuosos and concert organizations: on 23 March 1784 the clarinettist Anton STADLER mounted a performance of the wind serenade K361 and on 29 April Mozart and the violinist REGINA STRINASACCHI played the sonata for keyboard and violin K454. The Tonkünstler-Sozietät gave the cantata *Davidde penitente*, arranged from the unfinished C minor mass, in March 1785 and Mozart played a concerto for the same group in December. These works brought Mozart considerable acclaim: a review in the *Wiener Zeitung* of the December Tonkünstler-Sozietät concert noted 'the deserving fame of this master, as well known as he is universally valued' and earlier that year, when Wolfgang's father visited him in Vienna, Leopold wrote to Nannerl describing a quartet party at Mozart's home at which JOSEPH HAYDN told him: 'Before God and as an honest man, I tell you that your son is the greatest composer known to me either in person or by name. He has taste and, what is more, the most profound knowledge of composition.'

Mozart's publications were numerous. In July 1784 TORRICELLA brought out the three sonatas K333, K284 and K454 and LAUSCH advertised manuscript copies of six piano concertos; in February 1785 TRAEG offered copies of three symphonies. In March of that year Artaria published the concertos K413–15 and in September the six quartets dedicated to Haydn. The success of these works may have brought about a fundamental shift in Mozart's attitude to composition. After mid-1786, several works were conceived primarily with a view to publication rather than public performance; these included the piano quartets K478 and K493, the three piano trios K496, K542 and K548, the string quintets in C major and G minor, K515 and K516, the 'Hoffmeister' quartet K499 and the sonata for keyboard and violin K526.

Although opera remained central to Mozart's ambitions, there were few opportunities to build on the success of *Die Entführung*: by late 1782 Joseph II had decided to close down the Nationaltheater and to re-establish Italian opera. Mozart was eager to capitalize on this change but had little luck finding a text; on 7 May 1783 he wrote to his father: 'I have looked through at least a hundred librettos and more, but I have scarcely found a single one with which I am satisfied.' He began, but abandoned, L'OCA DEL CAIRO and in 1785 he worked on *Lo sposo deluso*, after a text used by Cimarosa, but this too was left unfinished. A one-act comedy, DER SCHAUSPIELDIREKTOR, was given early in 1786 at Schloss Schönbrunn, together with SALIERI's *Prima la musica e poi le parole* (both were commissioned for a visit to Vienna by the Governor-General of the Austrian Netherlands) and in March a private performance of a revised version of *Idomeneo* was given at Prince Auersperg's.

The libretto of Mozart's first documented collaboration with LORENZO DA PONTE, LE NOZZE DI FIGARO, was carefully chosen. BEAUMARCHAIS's play, *La Folle Journée, ou Le Mariage de Figaro*, had been printed in German translation in Vienna in 1785 and the opera was a sequel to the same author's *Le Barbier de Séville, ou La Précaution inutile*, which had been successfully performed in PAISIELLO's operatic version in Vienna in May 1784. Work on *Figaro* was started by October or November 1785 and the opera premiered at the Burgtheater on 1 May 1786. The initial run was a success: several items were encored at the first three performances, prompting Joseph II to restrict encores at later ones to the arias. Letters from Leopold to Nannerl Mozart make it clear that there was intrigue against the opera, allegedly by Salieri and Vincenzo Righini; and a review in the *Wiener Zeitung* obliquely points the finger at cabals by lesser lights: 'Herr Mozart's music was generally admired by connoisseurs already at the first performance, if I except only those whose self-love and conceit will not allow them to find merit in anything not written by themselves.'

The presumed political implications of *Figaro*, as well as Mozart's Masonic activities, may be overstated. On 11 December 1784 he had joined the lodge 'Zur Wohltätigkeit' ('Beneficence'), which in 1786, at Joseph II's orders, was amalgamated with the lodges 'Zur gekrönten Hoffnung' ('Crowned hope') and 'Drei Feuern' ('Three Fires') into 'Zur neugrekrönten Hoffnung' ('New-Crowned Hope') under the leadership of the well-known scientist IGNAZ VON BORN. The society was essentially one of liberal intellectuals, less concerned with political ideas than with the philosophical ones of the ENLIGHTENMENT, including nature, reason and the brotherhood of man. The organization was not anti-religious and membership was compatible with Mozart's faith. Wolfgang frequently composed for Masonic meetings: the cantata *Die*

Maurerfreude, K471, was written to honour Born and the *Maurerische Trauermusik* (MASONIC FUNERAL MUSIC), K477 was given in November 1786 in memory of Duke Georg August von Mecklenburg and Count Franz Esterházy; several songs and other occasional works were also composed for lodge meetings.

Even with the successes of the mid-1780s, Mozart continued to teach: the most important of his pupils was JOHANN NEPOMUK HUMMEL, who lodged with the composer between 1786 and 1788. Mozart also taught the English composer THOMAS ATTWOOD, whose surviving exercises testify to his careful, systematic teaching methods. Mozart's English connections were strong at this time: the first Don Curzio in *Figaro* was MICHAEL KELLY (in fact an Irishman) and the first Susanna was the soprano Nancy STORACE. It is likely that Nancy's brother Stephen also consulted Mozart (even if informally) on matters of composition and after his return to London, Storace prepared a series of publications that in 1789 included the first edition of Mozart's keyboard trio K564.

It was the departure from Vienna in 1787 of the English contingent that led Mozart to consider a journey to London, although the plan foundered when Leopold took a strong stand against it and refused to look after Mozart's children. Wolfgang did, however, accept an invitation to PRAGUE, where *Figaro* had been a great success. He spent approximately four weeks there, beginning 11 January 1787: he directed a performance of *Figaro*, gave a concert including a new symphony (the 'Prague', K504) and received from the impresario PASQUALE BONDINI an opera commission for the following autumn. On his return to Vienna, Mozart asked Da Ponte for a libretto. The new opera, DON GIOVANNI, was originally scheduled for 14 October 1787 but its premiere was postponed to 29 October because of inadequate production. In the meantime, Mozart, who had arrived in Prague on 1 October, directed three or four performances of *Figaro*. He also visited his friends the DUSCHEK FAMILY and wrote the difficult aria *Bella mia fiamma*, K528 for Josepha.

The two Da Ponte operas, together with the increased success of his publications, initiated a new phase in Mozart's career: he now gave fewer public concerts – a grand academy at the Burgtheater on 7 April 1786 was his last in that venue – and other genres came to the fore in his output, including the symphony. The final trilogy, K543, K550 and K551 ('Jupiter'), composed between June and August 1788, was apparently intended for a concert series that autumn; it is striking that Mozart chose these works, rather than concertos, for what may have been his first public concert appearance in two years. (There is no evidence the concerts took place.) Possibly these changes related to Mozart's appointment the previous December as court chamber musician although he was apparently required to do little more than write dances for court balls. Nevertheless, he welcomed the appointment, which gave him a dependable income and advanced his standing in Viennese musical circles. There is little reason to think that the salary (800 gulden, considerably less than the 2,000 gulden paid GLUCK, the previous incumbent) was an insult to Mozart, for the post was superfluous to begin with; Joseph II later remarked that he had created the position solely to keep Mozart in Vienna.

More significant, perhaps, was the death in May 1787 of Leopold Mozart, which may have triggered a fallow period for the composer. Mozart wrote relatively few works immediately following the Prague premiere of *Don Giovanni*; a similar fallow period had followed the death of his mother in Paris in July 1778. What is more, Leopold's death marked the final breakdown of the Salzburg Mozart family. Only Nannerl, who in 1784 had married the magistrate Johann Baptist Franz von Berchtold zu Sonnenburg and moved to St Gilgen, remained and except for settling their father's estate, Mozart apparently failed to keep in touch with her. Nannerl was probably hurt by Mozart's lack of attention: in 1792, when she was asked about her brother's life in Vienna, she pleaded ignorance despite the fact that she had become personally acquainted with Constanze in 1783 and still had in her possession numerous letters from her father detailing Mozart's activities at the time.

4. THE FINAL YEARS, 1788–1791

Mozart's financial well-being in Vienna can be measured in part by the size and location of his rented lodgings there. In September 1785 he moved to a flat, now Domgasse 5, in the heart of the town, close to the Stephansdom. By mid-1788, however, he had removed to the distant suburb of Alsergrund where rents were cheaper. It is from this time, too, that a series of begging letters to his fellow Freemason MICHAEL PUCHBERG survives; they continued well into 1790. Nevertheless, Mozart's finances at this time must be counted a mystery. He was never forced to do without a maid or other luxuries although his income was unstable; estimates of his earnings are incomplete and unreliable. His main sources of income included profits from his public concerts and gifts from private patrons, teaching, honoraria for publications and, from 1788, his salary as court chamber musician. During his early years in Vienna, performances were a good source of income: his subscription series of 1784 attracted over 100 patrons; but this largely disappeared after 1786. Teaching brought in less although Mozart enterprisingly formulated a scheme to ensure some regularity of payment: 'I no longer charge for 12 lessons' he wrote to his father, 'but monthly. I learned to my cost that my pupils often dropped out for weeks at a time; so now, whether they learn or not, each of them must pay me 6 ducats' (letter of 23 Jan. 1782). And publication may have brought in substantial sums as well although the 450 gulden he received from ARTARIA for the six quartets dedicated to Haydn was exceptional; he received less for symphonies, sonatas and other chamber music. On occasion he acted as his own publisher, sometimes with sorry results: a 1788 subscription for his string quintets apparently failed. In 1791, however, he may have sold copies of DIE ZAUBERFLÖTE for 100 gulden each; for the composition of an opera he generally received 450 gulden from the court theatre. But he also had expenses, which have been little explored. In addition to rent and food, his income had to cover substantial medical bills, many of them resulting from Constanze's frequent cures, child-rearing expenses, a costly wardrobe, books, music and manuscript paper. By all accounts he was also generous to his friends, sometimes lending them money.

Perhaps in an effort to alleviate his presumed financial woes, Mozart undertook a concert tour of Leipzig, Dresden and Berlin in the late spring of 1789. Details of the journey are scarce: he played at court in Dresden and at Leipzig he reportedly improvised on the Thomaskirche organ in the presence of J. F. DOLES, the local cantor and a former pupil of J. S. Bach. He may also have sold some of his compositions. But the trip was not a financial success, even if it had its rewards: in Leipzig Mozart renewed his acquaintance with Bach's music; and he conceived the idea to write six string quartets for King Friedrich Wilhelm II, an avid amateur cellist, in addition to keyboard sonatas for Princess Friederike (in the event, only three more quartets were finished, K575, K589 and K590, and when they were published by Artaria in 1791 they lacked a dedication; Mozart wrote to Puchberg on 12 June of that year, 'I have now been obliged to give away my quartets . . . for a pittance, simply in order to have cash in hand').

Mozart's circumstances began to improve in late 1789. In addition to the first of the 'Prussian' quartets, he wrote two replacement arias, 'Al desio di chi t'adora', K577, and 'Un moto di gioia mi sento', K579, for a new production of *Figaro* on 29 August and substitute arias for productions of Cimarosa's *I due baroni* and MARTÍN Y SOLER's *Il burbero di buon cuore*. His work attracted international interest: the poet Friedrich Wilhelm Gotter wanted to offer Mozart his opera libretto *Die Geisterinsel* and in 1791 he was apparently offered a pension by two groups of patrons, one in Amsterdam, the other in Hungary. But his main energies were directed to the composition of COSÌ FAN TUTTE, which premiered on 26 January 1790. There were four further performances, then a break because of the death of Joseph II in February, and five more in the summer.

Joseph II was succeeded by Leopold II and in September 1790 Mozart travelled to the coronation festivities in Frankfurt although he had no official role. He gave a public concert there on 15 October that was poorly attended and on the way home a concert at Mainz; he heard *Figaro* at Mannheim, played before the King of Naples, then in Munich, and reached home about 10 November. A trip to England again became a possibility: Mozart was offered a commission for an opera and the promise of an engagement like Haydn's but apparently declined. But he was busy in Vienna: during the winter months he composed the concerto K595 (possibly performed by his pupil BARBARA PLOYER at court in January 1791) and two string quintets, K593 and K614. He played a concerto at a concert organized by the clarinettist Josef Bähr and an aria and symphony by him were given at the Tonkünstler-Sozietät concerts in April. That same month Mozart secured from the Vienna city council the reversion to the important and remunerative post of Kapellmeister at the Stephansdom, where the incumbent LEOPOLD HOFMANN was old and in poor health. He was appointed deputy without pay; in the end, Hofmann outlived him.

During the summer, Mozart composed LA CLEMENZA DI TITO, commissioned for the Prague coronation of Leopold II in September. Reports published soon after Mozart's death suggested that it was written in only eighteen days but it is more likely to have been composed over a period of six weeks. The impresario DOMENICO GUARDASONI signed a contract with the Bohemian Estates on 8 July; his first choice to compose the coronation opera was Salieri. But Salieri refused the commission and it fell to Mozart, probably in mid-July. The text, based on METASTASIO, was arranged by CATERINO MAZZOLÀ and the premiere took place on 6 September.

Mozart was well along with the composition of DIE ZAUBERFLÖTE, composed for Emanuel Schikandeder's suburban Theater auf der Wieden, even before he received the commission for *La clemenza di Tito*, as a reference in a letter to Constanze of 11 June makes clear; and except for a few vocal items, the priests' march and the overture, it may have been finished in July. Premiered on 30 September, contemporary opinion on the music was universally favourable. The text, however, was roundly criticized; according to a report published in Hamburg, 'the piece would have won universal approval if only the text . . . had met minimum expectations'. And it was probably about the time that he finished most of *Die Zauberflöte*, in July, that he was also commissioned by COUNT WALSEGG-STUPPACH, under conditions of secrecy, to compose a Requiem for his wife, who had died on 14 February 1791. It is likely that Mozart was aware of Walsegg's identity: his friend Puchberg lived in Walsegg's Vienna villa and the inclusion of basset horns in the score suggests that Mozart could count on the participation of specific players who would have been booked far in advance for a date and place already known to him. It is likely that actual composition did not begin until the autumn, after the premieres of his two operas, and while later sources describe him as working feverishly on it, filled with premonitions of his own death, these accounts are hard to reconcile with the high spirits of his letters from much of November. Constanze's earliest account, published in NIEMETSCHEK's biography of 1798, states that Mozart 'told her of his remarkable request, and at the same time expressed a wish to try his hand at this type of composition, the more so as the higher forms of church music had always appealed to his genius'. There is no hint that the work was a burden to him as was widely reported in German newspapers from January 1792 on.

Mozart was confined to bed at the end of November, attended by two leading doctors, CLOSSET and SALLABA, and nursed by Constanze and her youngest sister, Sophie. His condition seemed to improve on 3 December and the next day his friends SCHACK, Hofer and GERL gathered to sing over parts of the unfinished Requiem; he may also have been visited by Salieri. That evening, however, his condition worsened and Closset (who had refused to leave the theatre until the end of the production) applied cold compresses, sending Mozart into shock. He died just before 1 a.m. on 5 December 1791. The cause of his death was registered as 'severe miliary fever' (where 'miliary' refers to a rash resembling millet-seeds) and later described as rheumatic inflammatory fever on evidence from Closset and Sallaba, a diagnosis consistent with his medical history. There is no credible evidence to suppose that he was poisoned, by Salieri or by anyone else.

In accordance with contemporaneous Viennese custom, Mozart was buried in a communal grave at the St Marx cemetery outside the city on 7 December. Later reports claimed that no mourners attended but according to Jahn, Salieri, SÜSSMAYR, van Swieten and two other musicians were present. The day was calm and mild.

At the time of his death, Mozart was flourishing in Vienna and widely recognized, along with Haydn, as the leading composer in Europe. His last year already gave testimony to this. Not only were his works widely disseminated (Viennese dealers produced nearly a dozen editions of his works in that year alone) but he was commissioned to write for audiences that ranged far beyond court and noble circles: in addition to the keyboard concerto, string quintets, two operas and unfinished Requiem, he also composed the Clarinet Concerto,

K622 for Anton Stadler, the Masonic cantata *Laut verkünde unsre Freude*, K623, the aria *Per questa bella mano*, K612 and the motet *Ave verum corpus*, K618. There was, in addition, the likelihood of both Dutch and Hungarian patronage as well as a steady stream of publications (most of them pirated) outside Vienna. Obituary notices appeared across the continent, including London; and according to the *Staats- und gelehrte Zeitung des hamburgischen unpartheyischen Correspondenten* for 16 December, Mozart was 'a rare musical talent [who] rose to the rank of a great master through the felicitous development of his exceptional natural gifts and assiduous industriousness; this is shown by his universally loved and admired works and it gives the measure of the irreplaceable loss which music has suffered because of his death'. CLIFF EISEN

B. Personality

Views of Mozart's personality display extreme oppositions, even his letters being interpreted in contradictory ways. For example, those Mozart wrote to his father LEOPOLD MOZART after his mother's death have been seen by some as showing mature consideration for Leopold's feelings, by others heartless self-preoccupation. Such contradictions have provoked increasingly sophisticated debates about the complexities of his character. Furthermore, as contextual studies of Mozart proliferate, a broader spectrum of insights into historical mentalities becomes available. Finally, the development of more careful analyses of the personalities of highly creative people challenges the stereotype of the genius as someone excepted from 'normal' human development.

Some of Mozart's generally accepted adult character traits can be progressively traced from earliest childhood; others appear to have developed as later responses to unique aspects of his environment. From infancy Mozart was the centre of his family's attention, because of his musical abilities, charm, gaiety and wit. The need to be loved was strong – initially he depended particularly on Leopold's love, later on that of his wife CONSTANZE MOZART. The family letters, the reminiscences of the SALZBURG friend SCHACHTNER, and the reports of observers of the childhood European tours, offer abundant evidence for these childhood characteristics. Schachtner also commented that Mozart was 'full of fire', so impressionable that he might have become a dastardly villain had it not been for Leopold's teaching (letter of 24 Apr. 1792). This impetuousness can be seen in the adult Mozart, especially during his involvement with ALOYSIA Weber (later LANGER). And Leopold, in his letter of 23 August 1782 to Baroness von WALDSTÄTTEN, mentioned Mozart's burning impatience, contrasting it with his indolence when exertion was unnecessary.

Because Mozart's talents determined all the family's activities during his childhood, he was used to having his developmental needs generously met. While other musical boys were in the choir school, Mozart's rich education was tailor-made for him by Leopold, and he never had to be one of many. He was petted by nobles and encouraged to believe that a magnificent future awaited him – on 15 July 1766, when Mozart was ten, BARON VON GRIMM predicted that monarchs would vie to attract the Mozarts. When this did not happen, Mozart's frustration showed itself in a number of character traits not evident in the surviving documentation about his childhood.

First, he could not abide tedium, and began to display arrogance and tactlessness. To Leopold he wrote from MANNHEIM on 7 February 1778 about teaching: 'I leave that to people who can't do anything else except play the keyboard. I am a composer and was born to be a Kapellmeister.' (Leopold himself was then teaching heavily, to supply Mozart with travel money.) Second, the childhood triumphs probably made Mozart complacent about his adult prospects, hindering his recognition of the value of Leopold's contribution (ceaseless toil on the organizational front). Complacency and a lack of flair for practicalities made a bad combination, and Grimm wrote to Leopold from PARIS on 27 July 1778: 'To make his fortune I wish he had half as much talent and twice as much savoir-faire' (Leopold's letter of 13 Aug. 1778). Third, he became extremely sensitive about his social worth, complaining that his class barred him from the company of people who, though higher-ranking, were not intellectually or morally superior. This exclusion contrasted starkly with the friendliness shown to him as a child by members of upper classes. The longing to be accepted for his merits was surely a key reason for his espousal of FREEMASONRY, which gave him the opportunity to converse on equal terms with a wide range of people.

Mozart had also been spoilt within the family, and as an adult often displayed selfishness and thoughtlessness. One example is his letter from Mannheim on 4 February 1778, announcing his love for Aloysia Weber, and upturning Leopold's plans for helping his own family financially. When the horrified Leopold replied, mentioning NANNERL MOZART's misery at the news, Mozart threatened, on 19 February 1778, never to return unless she stopped crying over 'every piddling little thing'. Nannerl was twenty-six, unmarried and dependent on the financial support of her father and brother. Countless passages in the correspondence, as well as the evidence of kind deeds to friends, suggest that Mozart had a charitable and loving disposition. But his generosity was sometimes unrealistic, and the promises from 1781 to Leopold and Nannerl that his move to Vienna would be beneficial for them as well as him proved empty.

Mozart had been so dependent on Leopold during childhood that his transition to adult life was problematic. He was sometimes able to use persuasion against Leopold's insistently expressed opinions (as when he resigned for the first time from Salzburg service), but his attempts at a degree of autonomy also sometimes involved concealment. This happened strikingly in Mozart's letter from Paris to the family friend BULLINGER on 7 August 1778, in which Mozart simultaneously told Bullinger that he had no secrets from Leopold, and asked Bullinger to keep one.

Mozart was tirelessly sociable, and loved laughter, dancing, cards, shooting and billiards. As a young man his humour displayed riotous frivolity, and (like Leopold) he always had a keen eye for the ridiculous in human behaviour. Perhaps the most engaging character traits in adult life were his almost indefatigable optimism, his courage in persevering through the personal difficulties besetting him and Constanze and his determination to preserve his artistic integrity. Though he occasionally gave expression to despair, his letters to Constanze display to a remarkable degree the ability to comfort and encourage her even when his own spirits were so low that composition was a struggle.

RUTH HALLIWELL

D. Schroeder, *Mozart in Revolt: Strategies of Mischief, Resistance and Deception* (New Haven and London, 1999)
M. Solomon, *Mozart: A Life* (London, 1995)
W. Stafford, *Mozart's Death: A Corrective Survey of the Legends* (London, 1991)
A. Steptoe, 'Mozart's Personality and Creativity', in *Wolfgang Amadè Mozart: Essays on his Life and his Music*, ed. S. Sadie (Oxford, 1996), 21–34

C. Education

Mozart received such thorough musical instruction from his father, LEOPOLD MOZART, that it is easy to forget how comprehensive his education was. Its foundation was in fact not music, but religion. In the Mozarts' Roman Catholic society, the goal of each life was the soul's salvation: development of God-given talents like musicianship was merely one aspect of a properly lived life. And because SALZBURG recognized only Catholicism, this ethos permeated every social network. It was against this background that all Leopold's moralizing remarks were made, his name-day greeting to Mozart of 23 October 1777 being typical: 'you should take heed for your soul, that you do not cause your father any anxiety at the hour of his death . . .'. Nevertheless, family life was saturated with music. From their earliest days, listening to the music-making of their father and friends, through the later rigour of practice and study, and in Mozart's case his youthful court work and compositions for Salzburg acquaintances, Leopold's children were absorbing phenomenal amounts of varied musical experiences. Had Leopold not taught Mozart himself, the alternatives would have been a choir school education, like that received by the HAYDN brothers; an apprentice-style education, like that received by Leopold's resident pupils the MARCHANDS; or education at an Italian conservatory. The factors favouring home tuition were that Leopold was a first-class teacher, and not only of music; Mozart was too precocious for school; being away would have been expensive; and the Mozarts valued their family life.

Mozart's musical education was characterized by remarkable breadth and depth. Leopold was methodical and dedicated, as his *Violinschule* suggests, and as evidence about his pupils (whom he involved in the family's daily informal music-making sessions) corroborates. At four, Mozart began to play the keyboard. At six he added the violin and organ, while from five he was composing. Several primary sources illuminate Leopold's teaching and Mozart's learning (and, later, teaching): the so-called 'Nannerl-Notenbuch' (prepared by Leopold for NANNERL MOZART, but used by Mozart too); the 'London Sketchbook' (given to Mozart for private compositional experiments by Leopold in 1764); and the PLOYER, ATTWOOD and FREYSTÄDTLER studies (Mozart's tuition courses for his pupils Barbara Ployer, Thomas Attwood and Franz Jakob Freystädtler). The book formerly known as the 'Wolfgang Notenbuch' is not authentic.

The 'Nannerl-Notenbuch' contains keyboard music for beginners, technical exercises, a table of intervals, simple modulating figured basses, and Mozart's earliest compositions. It shows that from an early stage Leopold taught music theory, and that his compositional tuition methods involved a starting point – a given bass, a melody to be continued or varied, or a structural model. Because

Leopold's help was needed for years in writing down Mozart's ideas, it is difficult to untangle the contributions of father and son in the childhood manuscripts. The 'Nannerl-Notenbuch' also shows Leopold's sensitivity to the need for encouragement – initially he notated Mozart's pieces precisely, only later suggesting amendments. A similar sensitivity is shown by the 'London Sketchbook' – its pieces are entirely in Mozart's hand, with no corrections, and were never reworked for publication, suggesting that Leopold understood Mozart's need for privacy and freedom.

Mozart himself later became a careful teacher, and the Ployer, Attwood and Freystädtler studies show teaching methods like Leopold's. Mozart required Ployer to set a bass to a minuet melody, and to add inner parts to a melody and figured bass set by Mozart. He also used FUX's counterpoint manual *Gradus ad Parnassum* with her. Attwood was systematically taught theory and free composition. These studies challenge the view of Mozart as an uninterested, superficial teacher – his suggested improvements to the pupils' exercises, and the occasional alteration even of a Fuxian motif, show an almost inexhaustible capacity for devising alternative possibilities, hinting at Mozart the lifelong learner.

Leopold designed the European tours partly to expose his children to musical influences absent from Salzburg, so enriching their skills and taste. While abroad, Leopold cultivated musicians who could develop some aspect of Mozart's education (arranging singing lessons in London in 1764 with MANZUOLI, and counterpoint lessons in Bologna in 1770 with Padre MARTINI), and also collected music by composers whose works seldom reached Salzburg. On each return, therefore, Mozart was able to absorb further the new influences to which he had been exposed. The tours were also important for his wider education: the family assiduously engaged with the culture of the places visited, and critically observed human nature from the wealth of characters they encountered.

Mozart's education in subjects other than music is not well documented, but arithmetic, French, Italian and Latin were apparently all taught systematically. Leopold, a respected man of letters, had been educated by Jesuits, and probably drew on his own education. He strongly believed that young minds were broadened and sharpened by good literature in different languages. The Mozarts were also passionate theatregoers, and Wolfgang was certainly exposed to enormous quantities of European drama.

Though Mozart studied intensively, the family was also indefatigably sociable. Friends of several classes, all ages and both sexes called almost every afternoon to go walking, shoot with airguns, play cards, go to the theatre, make music and dance. It is a myth that Mozart was a solitary child, cooped up with nothing but music: recreation, exercise and fresh air were crucial to the family's health regimen; and beyond this, the Mozarts belonged to a community whose common values formed an integrated whole, accommodating musical expertise within the social and religious framework. Perhaps the main drawbacks of Mozart's education were over-protection from drudgery, making him reluctant to be an ordinary court musician and possibly hindering his independence; and excessive closeness to Leopold, causing emotional problems between them. But there can be little doubt that it was ideal for his development as a composer, dramatist, teacher and active member of society's different strata.

RUTH HALLIWELL

Neue Mozart-Ausgabe IX: 27/1 (Notebooks), X: 30/2 (Ployer and Freystädtler Studies) and X: 30/1 (Attwood Studies)

D. Religious beliefs

(See also RELIGION AND LITURGY.) Detailed, direct evidence for the adult Mozart's religious beliefs is virtually non-existent, a frustrating situation because of its contrast with the much better documented picture of his all-pervasive Catholic upbringing.

Mozart's father LEOPOLD MOZART (himself educated by Jesuits) believed that the purpose of life was to live as a Catholic Christian, preparing the soul for judgement at death. Daily family routines were dominated by devotional requirements, decisions were scrutinized for their accordance with God's will, and name-day greetings contained hopes for eternal well-being. The optimum development of God-given talents was one Christian responsibility, so Mozart's musical development was extremely important, but nevertheless a means to the larger end.

During Mozart's childhood SALZBURG was religiously conservative, and Leopold's Catholicism appeared at its most devout, probably encouraged by the attitudes of Archbishop SCHRATTENBACH. Leopold wrote of his duty to show to the world 'a miracle . . . which God has caused to be born in Salzburg' (letter of 30 July 1768); had prayers said at the altars of carefully chosen saints while the family was away; and searched the Bible for clues to the outcome of his daughter NANNERL MOZART's dangerous illness in The Hague in 1765 (letter of 5 Nov. 1765). However, he also criticized aspects of the Catholic Church, and enjoyed conversation with non-Catholics. Questions therefore arise concerning the interpretation of his letters. Were some of his remarks about Catholicism made to flatter the views of others? Did some of his opinions change as he encountered ENLIGHTENMENT ideas? And did he simultaneously hold contradictory beliefs?

Though such family practices as the veneration of saints probably developed more at Mozart's mother's (MARIA ANNA MOZART's) instigation than at Leopold's, Leopold certainly held lifelong to his fundamental beliefs about man's responsibilities to God, and he checked that the young adult Mozart went to Mass and confession regularly. Mozart's letter to his father of 13 June 1781, however, suggests that Mozart had a more relaxed attitude to some church stipulations – he explained that while he acknowledged the principle of fast day requirements, he did not interpret them strictly.

The correspondence of 1777–9, when Mozart was travelling with Maria Anna in search of a job, exposes the contrasting attitudes of Leopold and Mozart to the interaction of divine predetermination and human choices. The twenty-one-year-old Mozart had been taught that all events were willed by God. When Leopold disapproved of Mozart's actions, Mozart's sanguine replies expressed his faith that everything would turn out as God intended. Leopold found this attitude too passive, and urged on Mozart the duty to plan ahead. The debate resurfaced after Maria Anna's death in PARIS: Mozart took a fatalistic stance, arguing that nothing could have saved her because God had determined the hour of her death, while Leopold considered this attitude reprehensible. (See MEDICAL HISTORY AND DEATH.)

One boon to posterity of Mozart's correspondence with Leopold is that it was in disagreements with his father that Mozart's views were most rigorously tested. It is therefore regrettable that this source of evidence, through loss of letters and then Leopold's death, peters out from 1781. Mozart's adult letters to his other correspondents reveal almost nothing about his religious beliefs, and he died too young to write educative letters to his sons.

Interpreting the small amount of direct evidence for Mozart's adult beliefs is also problematic. Sometimes Mozart may have wanted to flatter the views of his correspondent, for example when he told Leopold on 3 July 1778 that 'the godless' Voltaire had 'rotted away like a dog, like a beast'. And sometimes he used religious arguments to support actions for which he had ulterior motives, for example when he withdrew from a plan to accompany the flautist JOHANN BAPTIST WENDLING to Paris in 1778. To Leopold (on 4 February) he cited Wendling's lack of religion, but the stronger reason was his desire to stay in MANNHEIM with Aloysia Weber (later LANGE).

Mozart's decade in VIENNA (1781–91) was one of increasing religious tolerance, but it is easier to say what influences he was exposed to than to find evidence for his beliefs about them. His library contained works by Enlightenment authors, but the listing is not complete, and it is also impossible to say what Mozart thought about his books. He became a FREEMASON in 1784, but his membership was not incompatible with Catholicism, and he composed both Christian and Masonic texts. His most devout allusion to his church music, the statement (in a letter to Leopold of 4 January 1783) that the C minor Mass, K427, had been written to fulfil a vow, may have been made to impress Leopold. During 1791 he became unpaid assistant to the organist of St Stephen's, and was trying to get his son KARL MOZART accepted by the Piarists' school, so clearly he observed some Catholic duties. Though a priest was asked to attend Mozart's deathbed, it seems that Mozart did not himself request one. But it is not clear why, nor is it clear which sacraments he received (see HAIBEL). He did, however, have a funeral service in St Stephen's Cathedral, and a Requiem Mass in St Michael's Church.

On 4 April 1787, shortly before Leopold's death, Mozart wrote him a consolatory letter, speaking of death as 'the key to our true bliss'. An entry in his album also expressing belief in an afterlife suggests (through the private nature of the source) that his words to Leopold were sincere. The entry was made on 3 September 1787, on the death of Mozart's doctor, Sigmund BARISANI – Mozart wrote of seeing Barisani again 'in a better world – and *never to part*'. An educated guess at the totality of Mozart's beliefs based on reconciling the motley evidence would probably posit a broad belief in Christianity, but impatience with many of the requirements of the Catholic Church: however, the salient word in this sentence is 'guess'.

RUTH HALLIWELL

D. Beales, 'Court, Government and Society in Mozart's Vienna', in *Wolfgang Amadè Mozart: Essays on his Life and his Music*, ed. S. Sadie (Oxford, 1996), 3–20
N. Till, *Mozart and the Enlightenment* (London, 1992)

E. Medical history and death

Although the diagnoses of Mozart's illnesses have been exhaustively debated, there is another type of investigation concerning Mozart and medicine whose importance has scarcely been noted: that of eighteenth-century south German society and mentality, based on wide-ranging medical material from the family correspondence.

Underpinning the discipline of the social history of medicine is the observation that medicine was once knit far more densely into the fabric of society than it is in the modern developed world, and that to engage with its ramifications for a particular society is to understand better the dynamics of that society, and the mentality of its people. For the Mozarts, no less than for other historical figures, this has profound implications for the interpretation of the correspondence, and the evaluation of characters and relationships.

Yet the medical biography of Mozart, for reasons unique to Mozartian mythology, belongs in a category not easily assimilated into the frameworks developed by social historians of medicine: many Mozart-lovers remain interested solely in the cause of his death. It is true that in pursuit of this quest (which is defeated by a dearth of good evidence) historians have engaged with eighteenth-century medical literature, but this has never been integrated into a more holistic study of medicine in Mozart's society.

1. The medical world of the Mozarts
2. Mozart's medical history and death

1. THE MEDICAL WORLD OF THE MOZARTS

The Mozarts' medical culture was based on ideas evolving from Hippocratic humoralism, and a hierarchy of causes of disease, the first being supernatural or divine. Humoralism explained sickness and health in terms stressing individual responsibility for the maintenance of health. According to this model, four bodily 'humours' (blood, phlegm, yellow bile and black bile) needed to be kept balanced. Further, each body had its individual constitution, so that although a disease could follow a recognized course up to a point, illness was basically understood as the *expression* of disease in a particular body. External influences on the body needed to be perpetually controlled, to avoid the humoral imbalance that was constantly threatening: prophylaxis and therapy were equally important.

The external influences were the 'six things non-natural': air and environment; food and drink; sleep and wakefulness; motion and rest; evacuation and repletion; and passions of the mind. Neutral in themselves, they could change the body's humoral balance for better or worse, according to its already-existing state. Hence everyone followed a lifelong daily regimen: a ceaseless, almost instinctive, watchfulness over the state of the body and the influence of the non-naturals; and a corresponding set of bodily habits embracing such elements as diet, exercise, purging and bloodletting. Among copious examples from the Mozart correspondence of this earnest attention to regimen are LEOPOLD MOZART's exhortations to MARIA ANNA MOZART of 11 May 1778, when she was in PARIS ('My dear wife, don't forget *to be bled*, remember that you're not at home'), and to Mozart of 28 September 1777, when he was in MUNICH ('I'm just asking you, my dear Wolfgang not to go in for any excess . . . you know that you soon become heated . . . so strong wines and a lot of wine-drinking are bad for you').

Despite its age by the eighteenth century, humoralism had not been superseded by medical developments. Apart from smallpox inoculation, the century was not one of startling innovations so much as of the formation of certain medical infrastructures, paving the way for nineteenth-century breakthroughs. Maternal and infant mortality were high: obstetric forceps were not yet commonly used, puerperal fever not understood, and breastfeeding feared. Surgery lacked effective anaesthesia, and the importance of antisepsis was not appreciated. Instrumental diagnosis was not used, and autopsies were performed too sporadically to permit significant improvements in understanding disease progressions inside a sick body. The role of disease vectors like lice was not understood.

In this climate, the patient's own views on his or her illness were paramount, because the symptoms were the main means of assessment. Lacking the diagnostic resources with which to refine these views, the physician's role was to attend painstakingly to the patient's words and constitution. Institutional developments during the eighteenth century changed this type of doctor/patient relationship, spelling the death of humoralism and laying the foundations of modern scientific medicine, but the changes did not become visible until the nineteenth century. The developments were the increasing use of hospitals to treat the sick poor (collecting together a body of less assertive patients for observation), the professional split between surgeons and barbers (increasing the surgeons' status until they could collaborate with the higher-class physicians), and a host of medical record-keeping projects (paving the way for keeping individual patient records, which in turn enabled therapies to be assessed more systematically). Whereas the humoral model of disease had posited a state of sickness for the whole body, in which the *site* of the malady was relatively immaterial, these developments gradually produced an alternative model based on lesions: through autopsies it was realized that the lesions inside a dead body were like those treated by surgeons outside a sick body, and should be amenable to similar treatment if only they could be identified and reached. The principle of a living anatomization being established, medical endeavours then focused on increasing use of physical diagnosis with specially developed instruments, and on improvements in surgery. As doctors became able to challenge patients' accounts of their illnesses, they became more independent and the patients more passive.

None of these changes are present in the Mozarts' descriptions of sickness and health: these are decisively humoral in character. The consultative encounters are based primarily on the patient's presentation of the symptoms to the doctor: an example is Leopold's description, on 5 Nov. 1765, of Professor Schwenke's meticulous attention to the desperately ill NANNERL MOZART in The Hague. The Mozarts did not use hospitals, though these existed both in

SALZBURG and VIENNA. The sites of their ailments were not crucial to the medical explanation: Nannerl's first (incompetent) doctor had 'stopped up' her cough and expectoration by a 'milk cure', but this had merely driven the phlegm down into her lower abdomen, where it continued to endanger her life.

The most rewarding aspect of the Mozarts' medical writings concerns the interaction of supernatural and natural causes of disease, for here can be glimpsed clues to a moral code, a complete philosophy of life and death, for eighteenth-century Roman Catholic south German society. The Mozarts' regimens, cures, and medical explanations cannot be dismissed as quaint irrelevances while their social interactions are judged on the same terms as those of modern societies: rather, they are indicative of a profoundly different mental outlook, and one important purpose of studying them is to identify this difference, so developing historical sensitivity in questions of interpretation.

In the complete correspondence (still unavailable in English) there are more than twenty-five letters giving detailed descriptions of illness, shorter passages and allusions almost without number, and eighteen Latin pharmaceutical recipes. The subjects covered embrace every aspect of life and death as a 'good Catholic Christian'. The interaction of natural and supernatural causes of illness meant that it was seldom described simply in terms of symptoms and treatment: what we find, rather, are illness *narratives*, one of whose purposes is to try to explain the central, paradoxical, belief that God had already determined the outcome of each ailment, but that in principle each was curable. The key to the correct behaviour was humility: in a letter of 22 February 1764, Leopold repudiated as theologically presumptuous the idea of inoculating Mozart against smallpox; and when Nannerl's two-month-old baby Leopoldl was close to death, Leopold (who was looking after him) wrote on 22 September 1785: 'I pray each day that God might preserve him, *only for his salvation*; and *that not my will, but God's, will be done*.' Nevertheless, humility did not imply passivity for Leopold, and he strenuously rejected Mozart's plea (in his letter of 31 July 1778) for him to believe that Maria Anna '*had* to die – no doctor in the world could have brought her through it this time – because it was evidently the will of god to be thus; her time was up at that point – and god wanted to have her'. Leopold's counter-assertion was that she would not have died if he had been with her, even though he accepted the hour of her death as fixed: the reasons he offered for her death, therefore, included her own and Mozart's neglect of their duty to care for the body, and (using a tortuous argument) her separation from him through Mozart's inability to manage his life without parental help (letters of 13 July and 3 and 27 Aug. 1778).

Because sick people and their families were allegedly striving to achieve the outcome intended by God, they looked for supernatural signs. These signs then too became absorbed into the narratives of sickness: Leopold and Maria Anna searched the Bible for clues to the outcome of Nannerl's illness in The Hague (letter of 5 Nov. 1765); Leopold listed the signs portending the death of the Empress's daughter Josepha (letter of 17 Oct. 1767); his account of the death of the Mozarts' pregnant acquaintance Eleonore von Weyrother included premonitory features (letter of 23 Oct. 1777); and Mozart's sister-in-law SOPHIE HAIBEL reported the inexplicable extinction of her candle as she was thinking about the dying Mozart (letter of 7 Apr. 1825). Other illness narratives focused on incompetent doctors (whose deficiencies were also sometimes worked into the divine scheme), punishment for personal failings, and 'proper' deathbed scenes, providing illumination of the significance of life, death, humanity and spirituality for the Mozarts' society.

A more elusive, imaginative, endeavour is needed to understand the dynamics of the Mozarts' society through medical matters. Because death loomed so large, there was a certain universal, underlying, 'silent' state of mind, fundamentally different from that of affluent modern societies. It is possible to recapture some sense of this by considering incidents of illness and death within individual families in a chronologically cumulative way (adding up, in effect, the experiences of disaster which formed new strata of dark possibilities in people's minds over time). By keeping fresh this imagined state of mind, the characters and social interactions of historical people may bear different interpretations from those that may otherwise be given.

The number of deaths reported by the Mozarts is enormous. Babies died so frequently of commonplace ailments such as catarrhs and stomach upsets that their infancy was gruelling. Even in families whose children (unusually) all survived, the ordeal was only partly mitigated: parents were spared the grief of bereavement, but not the dread. Married women routinely died in childbirth, leaving motherless children: this happened to the first two wives of Nannerl's husband. Married men died leaving their families in penury and their children without guidance: this happened to the Niderl and ADLGASSER families, both within the Mozarts' circle. By adulthood, most people had a sad fund of experience of domestic turbulence, loss and sometimes family break-up: to live then was to endure a chronic background fear of death, which gnawed more insistently at each dangerous illness or death among acquaintances, and threatened panic when a loved one became ill. Although common experiences created social solidarity, the ways in which people came to terms with bereavement had more to do with the painful development of a particular kind of courage than with any form of emotional insusceptibility. The greatest source of strength was religion, whose teachings and routines helped people to continue leading a dignified Christian family life.

These facts of life cannot but have implications for the interpretation of the Mozart correspondence. Humoralism meant believing that merely being away from home carried a significant health risk through the difficulties of controlling the non-natural elements of air, climate and food; and doctors were not credited with understanding the constitutions of foreigners. Hence passages that can seem crudely xenophobic may be viewed more charitably, as manifestations of genuine fears for health. One example is Leopold's letter of 13 September 1764 (written just after his near-death in London) about English medicine and diet: 'The esteemed doctors here treat their patients in their own way, it doesn't matter if they've got Germans in front of them, who have different constitutions and temperaments . . . the whole way of life of the English is as different from ours as night is from day . . . they guzzle down congealed fat with gusto.' Passages that can seem morbidly obsessive take on a different hue if respect is given to the belief that once the humoral balance was disturbed, anything taken into the body would interact with the 'matter' of the disease, and could become literally corrupted, causing wholesale bodily putrefaction. Such a case is offered by Leopold's minutely detailed letters of 25 and 30 November and 4 December 1780 to the twenty-four-year-old Mozart on how to treat his catarrh, complete with the assurance that Leopold himself would willingly travel from Salzburg to Munich to nurse Mozart if necessary. 'If I'd been with your mother, I could hope that she'd still be alive', he wrote. Beyond questions of interpretation raised specifically by humoralism is the issue of the more general underlying state of mind, whereby death and its consequences loomed so large. Thus in the letters from September 1777 to January 1779, which chronicle difficulties between Leopold and Mozart, Leopold's stance may be viewed more sympathetically if we engage with his fears: his salary was the family's only security; Nannerl was still unmarried; and his colleague Adlgasser (ten years his junior) died suddenly, leaving his family to splinter into impoverished fragments. These few examples of the significance of medical assumptions for questions of interpretation could be multiplied many times over from the Mozarts' family correspondence, but a systematic, interdisciplinary, study of their medical world (embracing elements from disease ecology to folklore, and pharmacology to etymology) is a necessary prerequisite for more detailed scholarly enquiry.

2. MOZART'S MEDICAL HISTORY AND DEATH

Just as illness narratives played a fundamental role in articulating the meaning of life, sickness and death in the Mozarts' society in general, so too they have proved central to the vexed question of the diagnosis of Mozart's final illness in particular: most of the sources for this are in fact stories. These legends – of Italian enmity, poisoning and the supernatural commissioning of the REQUIEM – have urged scholars to discover all of the circumstances of Mozart's death and to study his previous illnesses (see table 1) for clues to the state of his body in 1791. At the same time, the unsatisfactory nature of the stories, whose accuracy cannot adequately be tested, severely limits the usefulness of the diagnostic enterprise, and many specialists now see the main worth of the evidence as historiographical, using it to explore how Mozart and his medical history have been treated by biographers.

Mozart died on 5 December 1791, and by January 1792 several newspaper reports of unknown origin had alluded to dramatic elements such as his debts and helpless dependants, his enemies and the possibility of poisoning, and his conviction that the Requiem would be his own. The only official record of the final illness is the death register, which named it 'hitziges Frieselfieber' (heated miliary fever, where 'miliary' denotes a rash resembling millet seeds), and there are no physical remains securely attributable to Mozart. The first surviving accounts were not given until 1798, and further sporadic details followed until 1856. This material includes stories associated with CONSTANZE MOZART's circle, stories concerning SALIERI, and miscellaneous claims.

The 'Constanze' stories are found chiefly in NIEMETSCHEK's biography of 1798, NISSEN's biography of 1828 and the NOVELLOS' journals of 1829. The Nissen and Novello sources include the reminiscences of Constanze's sister SOPHIE HAIBEL, who had helped nurse Mozart. As well as relating the symptoms, treatment and length of the illness, the women's stories encompass features familiar from the illness narratives sketched above: the preoccupation with making a 'good death' is suggested, among other things, by the efforts

Table 1. *Mozart's illnesses*

No	Date	Age	Duration	Place	Symptoms (Sources)
1	1762	6	2 weeks	Vienna	Fever, pain, scarlet rash of raised kreutzer-sized marks on buttocks, shins, elbows, and possibly feet (letters of 16 and 30 Oct., and 6 Nov. 1762)
2	1763	7/8	?	Salzburg	Fever, agonizing pain in knees and toes (letter of 15 Nov. 1766)
3	1764	8	4 days	Paris	Fever, catarrh, virulently sore throat, with danger of choking (letter of 22 Feb. 1764)
4	1765	9	4 weeks	The Hague	Fever (with crisis nearly leading to death), stupor, emaciation (letter of 12 Dec. 1765)
5	1766	10	at least 10 days	Munich	As illness 2 above (letters of 15 and 22 Nov. 1766)
6	1767	11	2 weeks	Vienna, Olmütz	Those of smallpox, and illness designated such by Leopold Mozart (letters of 7, 14, and 17 Oct., 10 and 29 Nov. 1767, and 6 Aug. 1768)
7	1772	16	?	Salzburg	Unknown, but left Mozart sickly and yellow (letter of Nannerl of 2 July 1819 explaining Mozart's appearance in a portrait)
8	1783	27	?	Vienna	Virulently sore throat, headache, tight chest (letters of 30 May and 7 June 1783)
9	1784	28	?	Vienna	Fever and raging colic with vomiting, designated 'rheumatic fever' by physician BARISANI (letter of 14 Sept. 1784)
10	?	?	?	Vienna	All details unknown (Barisani's entry in Mozart's album, 14 Apr. 1787)
11	1790	34	?	Vienna	Ailments allegedly involving 'rheumatic' head pains, toothache, chills, and fever (Mozart's begging letters to PUCHBERG of 8 Apr., beginning of May, and 14 Aug. 1790)

made to persuade a priest to visit Mozart; and supernatural elements are present in Sophie's story of the extinguished candle, but above all in accounts of the Requiem.

The 'Salieri' stories began with entries in BEETHOVEN's conversation book about the deranged composer Salieri, who claimed in 1824 to have poisoned Mozart. The same year Salieri's friends engaged Dr Eduard Guldener von Lobes, who had known Mozart's doctors and said he had seen the body, to disprove Salieri's claim. Guldener von Lobes stated that Mozart had died naturally of a 'rheumatic inflammatory fever' with 'a deposit on the brain'.

The miscellaneous stories include reminiscences (sometimes at one remove) of sundry acquaintances of Mozart, and anecdotes in the *Allgemeine musikalische Zeitung*. As well as mentioning details of the illness, some of these accounts repeat and add claims about Mozart's rivals and the attempted completion and supernatural significance of the Requiem.

There are insuperable problems in evaluating all these stories: the long time-span throws into doubt the accuracy of memories, and means that some statements could have been influenced by already-printed material; Constanze and Sophie were not objective witnesses, because Constanze's continuing quest for charity gave her reasons to disseminate sentimental and sensationalist views; and the integrity of ROCHLITZ, the editor of the AMZ, has been utterly discredited. Inconsistencies in and between the accounts of Constanze, Sophie and others make it impossible to judge which, if any, details are accurate. This has enabled later authors to accept or reject evidence from a range of incompatible statements, in numerous permutations, providing fertile ground for murder theories. These have been encouraged further by Mozart's third-class burial in a shared, unmarked and later reused grave, enabling some authors to speculate on the concealment of evidence and others to claim knowledge of the whereabouts of parts of the body. Not only did Salieri's claim (despite its rebuttal) acquire accretions until the mid-twentieth century, but more sinister conspiracy theories positing Mozart's murder by Jesuits, Jews and Freemasons have been aired from the mid-nineteenth century.

To clarify the debate, Carl Bär published a comprehensive review of the evidence in 1972. Studying eighteenth-century Viennese medical procedures, government regulations and record-keeping, and burial practice, Bär concluded that there was nothing suspicious or unusual about Mozart's death. Cautiously accepting Constanze's and Sophie's accounts of the main symptoms (especially the fever and the inflamed hands and feet), and considering these in conjunction with Mozart's previous medical history, he suggested that the most likely cause was rheumatic fever with complications from the treatment, which probably included excessive blood-letting. He warned, however, that a confident diagnosis was unrealistic, that some of the reported symptoms (for example, vomiting) could have been part of the treatment, and that modern disease progressions cannot be uncritically assumed for historical diseases. Since Bär's work there has been a general consensus that Mozart died naturally, though many diagnostic suggestions other than rheumatic fever have been made, kidney disease being the chief contender.

Although the allegations of murder have subsided, there is still enormous interest in why Mozart died, rather than recovered. Here too narratives have been hard at work from the beginning, as successive biographers have linked aspects of Mozart's life with his death. One group of stories suggests that Mozart wrecked his body through a dissipated lifestyle entirely opposed to his 'divine' creative force. Another argues that he was debilitated through overwork and financial and family worries, either because he was too much of a lonely genius to handle life's practicalities, or because he lost patronage by rebelling against certain social strictures, or simply through an unfortunate accumulation of external and personal difficulties. The most exotic suggestion is that Mozart died through outright divine decree, with the Requiem commission as a sign; the plainest is that his death was as banal as the early deaths of many others. All these competing suggestions, which have been analysed by William Stafford, contribute to a historiographical portfolio: we will never know for sure what killed Mozart, but by studying the accounts of his death we can learn a good deal about the nature of biography. RUTH HALLIWELL

Carl Bär, *Mozart: Krankheit, Tod, Begräbnis* (Salzburg, 1972)
W. F. Bynum and R. Porter, eds., *Routledge Companion Encyclopedia of the History of Medicine* (London, 1993)
R. Halliwell, *The Mozart Family: Four Lives in a Social Context* (Oxford, 1998)
R. Ludewig, 'Zum derzeitigen Stand der Forschung über die Ursachen des Todes von Mozart', *Mozart-Jahrbuch* 1991, vol. 1, 132–44
William Stafford, *Mozart's Death: A Corrective Survey of the Legends* (London, 1991)

F. Mozart as author

A minor but significant aspect of Mozart's oeuvre is his writings that do not fall within the bounds of his letter-writing. If the verses that occasionally figure in his letters are marginal in this context, the two sketched spoken comedies that he wrote deserve more attention than they have received; his other literary products include the well-known Italian-language dedication to JOSEPH HAYDN for the set of six string quartets, and various alterations in, and additions to, the librettos of his operas and singspiels. Much of this output can only hypothetically be attributed to Mozart, since the material no longer exists in his hand. Only fragments survive of Mozart's commonplace book, into which he entered trifles such as the purchase of and obituary for his pet starling; and he made entries in the albums of a number of his friends. Above all, of course, he is the author of a correspondence that for quality and quantity, exuberance and depth of feeling, is fully the equal of the achievements in this field of even the most distinguished of his contemporaries.

Apart from doggerel in letters, and entries in albums, an eighty-two-line-long poem survives, called 'Der kunstreiche Hund. Ein Gedicht' (undated, 'The artistically gifted dog. A poem', published in *Mozart: Briefe und Aufzeichnungen, Gesamtausgabe*, ed. W. A. Bauer, O. E. Deutsch and J. H. Eibl (Kassel, 1962–75), vol. IV, 164–7). Mainly in *Knittelvers* (here four-lined stanzas of irregular length, rhyming aa, bb), and with a preponderance of dactyls, Mozart sings the praises of 'Gross-Buzigannerl . . . the god of all dogs'. He invites his listeners to gather round him on the grass, and then tells his story – or rather, begins to tell it, for he gets no further than the love-making and impregnation. Buzigannerl, we learn, was born in VIENNA to a much-travelled, but sexually ignorant, bitch called Zemir; the identity of the father was uncertain, though he was certainly an

Austrian aristocrat, even if he behaved towards her in an initially unchivalrous manner, and excuses his ravishing of her by praising her irresistible sexual charms. Some scholars detect the influence of Alois Blumauer in this undated (and undatable) effusion, while pointing out that Mozart was familiar with Blumauer's verse (for example, 'Lied der Freiheit', K506) by 1785 at the latest.

The two dramatic fragments, though again undatable, may have been written around the time of the masquerade (K446) Mozart devised for Carnival Monday 1783 and about which he informed his father on 12 March. Recent editions of Köchel, as well as the *Briefe und Aufzeichnungen*, incline to date them to the period of the canon 'Lieber Freistädtler, lieber Gaulimauli' (K232, probably early 1787). The first of the fragments consists of a prose sketch for the first four scenes of a play that would have had at least two acts. It is headed *Der Salzburger Lump in Wien* ('The SALZBURG dolt in Vienna', published in *Briefe und Aufzeichnungen*, vol. IV, 167–8), and tells how Herr Stachelschwein ('Mr Porcupine'; names of this kind were a long-established tradition of the popular stage) learns of his father's death in Salzburg, is saddened, but also delighted at his inheritance. His friend, 'the Intriguer', with whom he had been in prison, is not permitted to delay him, as he is on his way to Frau von Scultetti and her daughter, the latter being his unwilling intended.

The other fragment, *Die Liebes-Probe. Ein LustSpiel in Drey Aufzügen* ('The Love-Test. A comedy in three acts', published in *Briefe und Aufzeichnungen*, vol. IV, 168–73), contains three more or less fully worked-out scenes in dialogue, with stage directions. The characters named are in the tradition of the talented mid-eighteenth-century Viennese comic dramatist Philipp Hafner, including the young lover, Leander, his servant Wurstl (that is, HANSWURST), and Kasperl; Leander's rival for Rosaura, daughter of Herr von Dumkopf ('Fool'), is Herr von Knödl ('Dumpling'); there are also Rosaura's maid, Trautel, the witch Slinzikicotinzki, a female dwarf and a giantess. The ridiculous names recall Mozart's letter of 15 January 1787 to GOTTFRIED VON JACQUIN from PRAGUE, in which he imparts the names by which their circle are to be called. The surviving scenes show Wurstl pushing his master in on a wheelbarrow, then dumping him outside his beloved Rosaura's house (only, which of two identical houses is it?). Wurstl's inventive wit lets him be cheeky, but seemingly unintentionally so, to Leander. Despite his confidence that he has smelt out the house in which his beloved Trautel lives, he seems to have chosen wrong: his knock is answered by a giantess who, however, maintains that she is indeed Trautel – and that the female dwarf who approaches is Leander's Rosaura. The fragment ends there, without explanation for the transformation of the girls (the witch has yet to appear), whether owing to the loss of further sheets or, more likely, Mozart's loss of interest in the project, and more pressing concerns.

Mozart's poetic effusions are mostly ephemera that entertain but hardly edify. One of the earliest is the farcical doggerel postscript of 15 September 1773 to Herr [Franz Friedrich] von Hefner, a friend; being wise after the event we can see a truth hidden in the final brief couplet, 'I am at all times / from now unto Eternity.' His cousin MARIA ANNA THEKLA MOZART (the 'Bäsle') was the recipient of various coarse verses in his letters, as was his sister and the young family friend Rosalie Joly (in a letter of 20 Dec. 1777). His mother was recipient of an unusually extended verse letter written from Worms on 31 January 1778.

The additions and alterations Mozart made to the librettos he set to music represent a significant if quantitively small part of his literary output. A well-known example occurs in the letter to his father of 26 September 1781, where, referring to Osmin's famous Act 1 aria in DIE ENTFÜHRUNG AUS DEM SERAIL, he mentions having 'outlined to Herr STEPHANIE the whole aria; – and the main part of the music to it was already complete before Stephanie knew a word about it'. Numerous instances occur in DIE ZAUBERFLÖTE – most of them are minor details, but include significant alterations to text and rhythmic pattern in the Queen's Act 2 aria, and several changes in the Act 2 finale. For instance, in the scene of Papageno's attempted suicide, Mozart in his autograph inverts the epithets from the libretto's 'Papagena! Herzenstäubchen! / Papagena! liebes Weibchen' ('. . . dove of my heart! . . . dear little wife!') to 'Herzensweibchen . . . liebes Täubchen' – surely as an encoded tribute to his wife, whom in letters over the previous couple of years he had several times addressed as his 'Herzensweibchen'.

Finally, it should be pointed out that in his letter to his father of 28 December 1782, Mozart mentioned his desire 'to write a book, a short critique of music ["eine kleine Musicalische kritick"], with examples – but NB: not under my own name'. Whether or not the idea owed anything to Johann Mattheson's *Critica musica* of 1722–5, Mozart does not seem to have taken it any further.

PETER BRANSCOMBE

P. Branscombe, 'Die Zauberflöte: some Textual and Interpretative Problems', *Proceedings of the Royal Musical Association* 92 (1966), 45–63

G. Mozart as letter writer

The correspondence of Mozart and his family has long been regarded as one of the most vital sources of information not only about the man himself and his circle, but also about contemporary society, and the position of the artist within society – as well, of course, as about Mozart's musical activities. English-language readers are likely to have at best limited and partial knowledge of other contemporary correspondence in German, or of the expectations of letter writer or reader at that time; even for the specialist, Mozart's letters stand out for their vividness and apparent spontaneity.

The art of letter-writing in the German language in the eighteenth century was influenced, broadly speaking, by either the Ciceronian style or the Senecan, the former characterized by periodic sentence structure and participial phrases, the latter more loosely knit, less formal. Both forms existed side by side and were to some extent interchangeable (depending on the linguistic level desired by a writer – complex and formal in a literary context, lighter and less formal in personal communication); both still contained elements drawn from the *Kanzleistil*, or cumbrous, extremely formal and archaic chancellery language of legal documents, with highly complex constructions and frequent borrowings from French and Latin.

The influence of LEOPOLD MOZART on his son is strongly marked in epistolary style, as in most other matters. For Leopold, the models tended to be contemporary writers more highly regarded for their style than the artistic content of their writings: Salomon Gessner, Johann Christoph Gottsched, and CHRISTIAN FÜRCHTEGOTT GELLERT. The last-named was valued by his contemporaries especially for his *Briefe, nebst einer praktischen Abhandlung von dem guten Geschmacke in Briefen*, published in 1751. Leopold Mozart, who corresponded with, and greatly admired, Gellert, was happy to take one of the latter's letters to him as a model of epistolary style; further, Gellert recommended his *Leben der schwedischen Gräfin von G . . .* to Leopold – a novel modelled on those written in letter form by Samuel Richardson. The reader of Leopold Mozart's letters to his friend, and publisher of his *Violinschule*, JOHANN JAKOB LOTTER in AUGSBURG, will be struck by their blend of formality and slightly forced humour, especially where the writer's financial interests seem to be at stake.

Strange as it may seem to a non-specialist modern reader, Mozart was probably more correct in his control of Italian, which he learnt on his travels as a boy, than in his use of his native language. High German in the late eighteenth century was by no means the settled language that it was to become in the nineteenth, and regional variations and dialects were then even more idiosyncratic. Mozart's epistolary styles owe far more to the mood of the moment than to strict schooling, which he never enjoyed. Tutored by his father, often of course during bumpy coach journeys or overnight stops in strange inns, and with the emphasis usually on musical instruction rather than German grammar, style and literature, he developed a mode of spelling, and idiosyncratic use of capitalization and punctuation, that not surprisingly strike the modern reader as highly personal and unusual. But even the finest writers of the German language among his contemporaries – Kant, Lessing, Herder, GOETHE – were guilty of what the modern specialist would consider to be errors in grammar and spelling.

By comparison with the 'learned' style of many of his father's letters, Mozart's own reveal right from the beginning a quirkiness, quick-wittedness and only partially successful effort to rein in the flow of his thoughts. The juxtaposing of the serious and the frivolous elements is there from a very early stage, the instantaneous hopping from one subject to another, at times from one language to another, the exaggeration, the scattiness (as well as the scatological); and it is not inappropriate that in one of his earliest postscripts, that to his father's letter of 10 February 1770, he identifies himself to his sister as 'the same old HANSWURST'. The lavatorial humour of many letters in the collected correspondence has often been commented on as if it were something exceptional – which, in an age before the development of modern methods of hygiene, it certainly was not. Especially in his early letters, Mozart's orthography tends to be aural, with spelling that even in those unregulated days is highly erratic (though seldom incomprehensible); dialect forms play a significant role, though Mozart probably failed to recognize them as such. That the impression of spontaneity in his letter-writing can be misleading is shown by the existence of a sketch for the postscript to his sister that he added to his father's letter from Rome of 21 April 1770. And the reader must be warned that one should not automatically accept statements in Mozart's letters as representing the truth, even the truth as he himself saw it.

Especially from the years of Mozart's maturity date letters that the modern reader at his peril takes at face value. The often-cited comment of 14 February 1778 on his dislike of the flute makes no sense in the context of the fine, idiomatic music he wrote for the instrument; and in the letters to his father he claimed to have completed the composition of works that he had hardly begun to write, or gave the impression of being financially much better off than was the case. Yet in the most touching instance in the correspondence, he has the tact, love and sense of duty to warn his father on 3 July 1778 of the gravity of his mother's illness – when, as reported to the family's friend, ABBE BULLINGER, on the same date, she had already died; Mozart requests Bullinger gently to prepare his father and sister for the sad news. All of life, and indeed of death, is contained in the Mozart correspondence. We read it not only because it is the vital link between the man and the music, but also because the blend of immediacy and perspective, banality and brilliance, hold out the promise that we might by reading be brought a little nearer to understanding the nature of his genius.

PETER BRANSCOMBE

E. A. Blackall, *The Emergence of German as a Literary Language 1700–1775* (Cambridge, 1959)
R. Halliwell, *The Mozart Family. Four Lives in a Social Context* (Oxford, 1998)
D. Schroeder, *Mozart in Revolt: Strategies of Resistance, Mischief and Deception* (New Haven and London, 1999)

H. Biographies

Biographical writings on Mozart, now a veritable scholarly industry, began in modest fashion in 1793 with a 6,000-word obituary by FRIEDRICH SCHLICHTEGROLL, published in his *Nekrolog auf das Jahr 1791*. Although he did not meet Mozart, Schlichtegroll corresponded at length with those who did, especially Albert von Mölk in SALZBURG, who in turn drew much of his information from NANNERL MOZART. The biography is slanted strongly towards Mozart's childhood and adolescence – Schlichtegroll apparently gleaned little or no information from his Viennese correspondent, Joseph Friedrich Retzer – with a resulting emphasis on Mozart's childlike qualities and perceived lack of maturity. FRANZ XAVER NIEMETSCHEK, whose *Life of Mozart* first came out five years later in PRAGUE (1798), drew heavily on Schlichtegroll for its account of Mozart's career before 1781, but redressed the balance somewhat by giving substantially more attention to Mozart's career from 1781 onwards. In its way no less biased than Schlichtegroll – as a patriotic Czech, Niemetschek all too eagerly stressed Mozart's successes in Prague – Niemetschek's biography nevertheless contains genuine insights, especially on aesthetic matters relating to instrumentation and orchestration. The trilogy of important biographical accounts of Mozart published in the decade after his death is completed by FRIEDRICH ROCHLITZ, who published anecdotes about Mozart in early issues of the *Allgemeine musikalische Zeitung* (1798–1801) based (he claimed) on his own personal recollections and other observations of Mozart. Many of the anecdotes are now known to have been falsified, but may well have had the desired effect for Breitkopf & Härtel (publishers of both the AMZ and of editions of Mozart's works) – namely to increase public interest in Mozart in order to sell copies of his scores.

Vested interests continue to feature prominently in the next landmark biography of Mozart (1828), by GEORG NIKOLAUS NISSEN, CONSTANZE MOZART's second husband. Nissen began collecting materials for his volume around 1820, but died in 1826 before completing it. Constanze drafted in Johann Heinrich Feuerstein to help finish it off, but the end result was a long (920 pages), chaotic and poorly edited volume, containing demonstrable falsities and misrepresentations. On the positive side, it published for the first time voluminous extracts from the family correspondence, now (in twentieth-century editions) an absolutely essential biographical resource.

Representing a significant scholarly advance over the likes of Schlichtegroll, Niemetschek and Nissen, Otto Jahn's seminal, four-volume biography appeared in 1856 to coincide with the hundredth anniversary of Mozart's birth. Well versed in the rigours of academic and philological work, Jahn approached his task more methodically, soberly and cautiously than any of his predecessors more intimately connected to Mozart could ever realistically have done. He believed firmly in the standard biographical idea that his protagonist's life and works were fundamentally linked, working to uncover such connections in spite of his relative lack of knowledge of musico-historical issues. Subsequent revisions to Jahn, especially by Hermann Abert (Leipzig, 1919–21), expand considerably on Mozart's position in music history and include more protracted discussion of his music.

Biographies of Mozart proliferated in the twentieth century, especially in the scholarly boom of the post-war era. Alfred Einstein set the ball rolling with a lucid, rational account, *Mozart: His Character, his Work* (London, 1945), that served as a standard biographical text for several decades. (Einstein himself was strongly influenced by the five-volume *W.-A. Mozart: sa vie musicale et son œuvre* by T. de Wyzewa and G. de Saint-Foix (Paris, 1912–46), a combination biography–stylistic study.) It demonstrated considerable advances in knowledge over its predecessors, especially in matters of compositional chronology, and contained protracted, insightful commentaries on Mozart's music still relatively rare in mid-twentieth-century biographies. Unafraid to probe Mozart's psyche, and to criticize his protagonist's purportedly complex personality in the process, Einstein also set the stage for the more overtly psychological portrayals by Wolfgang Hildesheimer (*Mozart*, Frankfurt am Main, 1977, trans. 1979) and Maynard Solomon (*Mozart: A Life*, London, 1995). For Hildesheimer, Mozart was an other-worldly figure incapable of relating in a normal fashion to the world around him. Thus, Hildesheimer believes, Mozart was not deeply affected by the deaths of either of his parents, or with the earlier 'estrangement' (if it can be so described) from his father; nor was he able to hold down friendships in Vienna or feel guilt in the way that most of us do. In fact, Hildesheimer's book (with its provocative stance and unusual organization, eschewing a systematic chronological approach) owes as much to styles of popular biographical writing that blur distinctions between fact and fiction as it does to scholarly traditions, even though it is written in a considerably more erudite fashion than, say, Marcia Davenport's rip-roaring *Mozart* of 1932 ('When the Duscheks did not have a big party on [in Prague], Wolfgang . . . with whatever other men were about, would put on their hats and sway off to town to spend the evening in a royal bout of music, wit and noise, in some tavern where they were treated like kings') and Francis Carr's patently preposterous account of FRANZ HOFDEMEL'S poisoning of Mozart in *Mozart and Constanze* (New York, 1983). Firmly back in the scholarly camp, Solomon uses Freudian analytical techniques to probe the relationship between Mozart and his father, LEOPOLD MOZART, in almost every case to the detriment of Leopold, who comes across (unjustly in the opinion of many) as a quasi-daemonic, obsessively controlling figure. A much more measured and sensitive account of the relationship between Leopold and Mozart can be found in Ruth Halliwell's *The Mozart Family* (Oxford, 1998), a model of even-handed biography richly elaborated through discussion of social contexts. Other carefully researched, well-argued and occasionally controversial biographies of recent years include Volkmar Braunbehrens, *Mozart in Vienna, 1781–1791* (trans. New York, 1989), Georg Knepler, *Wolfgang Amadé Mozart* (trans., 1994), Robert Gutman, *Mozart: A Cultural Biography* (New York, 1999) and Cliff Eisen and Stanley Sadie's article on Mozart for *The New Grove Dictionary of Music and Musicians*, 2nd edn (London, 2001). Konrad Küster's *Mozart: A Musical Biography* (trans. Oxford, 1996) is also a welcome addition to the literature, promoting musical discussions over biographical facts.

Irrespective of their methodological orientations, twentieth-century scholarly biographers – alongside those carrying out archival, interpretative, contextual, analytical and source-related work – have collectively worked hard to counteract deep-seated stereotypes and myths about Mozart and his creative processes – about, say, his blissful ignorance aligned with genius and his perpetual facility for composition. But narrative themes and patterns are so deeply entrenched in biographical writings about Mozart that they are difficult to escape completely; fascination with issues such as his death, his apparent fall from favour with Viennese concert audiences in the late 1780s, and his purported financial difficulties reveal priorities on the part of biographers – however fastidiously these issues are researched – that tell us as much (or nearly as much) about the author writing the book as they do about Mozart. Future biographies will have to engage self-consciously both with the Mozartian biographical tradition and with the very act of writing biography, part of which may involve not necessarily viewing Mozart's life exclusively from Mozart's perspective.

SIMON P. KEEFE

W. Stafford, 'The Evolution of Mozartian Biography', in *The Cambridge Companion to Mozart*, ed. S. P. Keefe (Cambridge, 2003), 200–11

I. Mozart: literature and the theatre

Mozart's interest in the theatre is attested almost throughout his life by references in the family correspondence as well as, indirectly, by the evidence provided by his compositions and other writings. The matter of his interest in, and knowledge of, literature is more elusive, giving rise to speculation in the absence of firm documentary evidence. We are faced with the conundrum that Mozart, for all his evident cultured state, seldom indicated in his letters (or in his comments to contemporaries that have survived) his knowledge of literary or dramatic works. At least in the case of theatre, an abundance of information is available about the buildings and the theatrical activity in most of the cities and towns with which Mozart had contact.

In SALZBURG, his birthplace, Mozart early gained first-hand experience of the forms of theatre then favoured there: school drama, usually performed at the end of the academic year for the benefit of pupils, their families and alumni of the institution; ecclesiatical drama; and the operatic and spoken theatre productions that were given by visiting or semi-resident companies (an example are the well-documented seasons given by EMANUEL SCHIKANEDER and his troupe, for which Mozart wrote an aria in 1780, KAnh 11a (365a)). During the Mozart family's travels, their first concern on arriving in a city was usually to attend whatever theatrical performances were available. And in capital cities – VIENNA and PARIS – their thought was to attempt (usually unsuccessfully, at least in Wolfgang's early years, though he was invited to write the ballet *Les petits riens* for Paris in 1778) to secure a commission for the composition of an opera; at all events, under LEOPOLD MOZART's guidance, care was taken to assess the kinds of work that were staged with success, local taste being an important factor in plans for what Mozart should compose.

If we look more precisely at the stage works that Mozart wrote, we at once notice the number and variety of the kinds of theatres that at one period or another offered him opportunities, as well as the number of cities that were involved: at Salzburg he composed the Latin intermezzo APOLLO ET HYACINTHUS for the university in 1767, the opera buffa LA FINTA SEMPLICE (at first intended for Vienna) was given at the Archbishop's palace in 1769 (he later wrote the serenata *Il sogno di Scipione* for the same venue in 1772, and the *dramma per musica* IL RE PASTORE in 1775); during the Italian journeys he wrote three serious operas for the Teatro Regio Ducale, MILAN: in 1770, MITRIDATE, RE DI PONTO, the *festa teatrale* ASCANIO IN ALBA in 1771, and LUCIO SILLA in 1772; MUNICH commissions were LA FINTA GIARDINIERA (Assembly Rooms, 1775) and IDOMENEO (Hoftheater, 1781); he was invited to set OTTO VON GEMMINGEN's duodrama *Semiramis* by HERIBERT VON DALBERG, intendant of the influential MANNHEIM Theatre, in 1778. His first work for Vienna was the singspiel BASTIEN UND BASTIENNE, traditionally said to have been written for DR ANTON MESMER's garden theatre; for travelling companies he wrote incidental music for THAMOS, KÖNIG IN ÄGYPTEN (Salzburg, late 1770s) and the unfinished singspiel ZAIDE (1779–80). After he had settled in Vienna, Mozart composed DIE ENTFÜHRUNG AUS DEM SERAIL for the German National Singspiel (premiered at the Burgtheater), DER SCHAUSPIELDIREKTOR for a court entertainment at Schönbrunn Palace, LE NOZZE DI FIGARO and COSÌ FAN TUTTE for the court opera buffa company; DON GIOVANNI was commissioned by a PRAGUE theatre director who had enjoyed great success with *Figaro*, and it was later taken into the repertory of the Vienna court theatre; and LA CLEMENZA DI TITO was written for the Prague festivities on the occasion of the coronation of LEOPOLD II as King of Bohemia; finally – and, had Mozart lived, this was a direction in which he might have travelled far – for Schikaneder's suburban Theater auf der Wieden he wrote part of the score for *Der Stein der Weisen* (1790), as well as DIE ZAUBERFLÖTE (1791).

Some guidance about Mozart's knowledge of literature is provided by the 'List and valuation of the books of the late Herr W. A. Mozart, Imperial Kapellmeister' that is appended to the inventory and valuation of his personal estate. With the cautious reservations that possession of a book does not necessarily betoken knowledge of the contents of that book, and that acquaintance with the contents of a book is not dependent on actual ownership of it, one can nevertheless point to books that Mozart either refers to in his letters or, from reported comments of others, seems to have known. At the time of his death, he owned thirty-three titles in German, mainly works by contemporaries, out of a total of forty-one items, for few of which is there any indication in his music and letters that he was familiar with their contents; the most important German-language writers whose works appear in the List include Gessner, Ewald von Kleist, Moses Mendelssohn, SONNENFELS, C. F. Weisse and WIELAND.

Among the volumes in his estate are Johann Nikolaus Forkel's *Musikalischer Almanach für Deutschland* (Leipzig, 1782–4), which includes three reviews of works by Mozart, and Karl Friedrich Cramer's *Magazin der Musik* (Hamburg, 1783–9), which contains no fewer than eight critiques of his compositions. Closer to home, *Philosophische Fragmente über die praktische Musik*, by Amand Wilhelm Smith, published anonymously (Vienna, 1787), also mentions Mozart. It is safe to assume that Mozart at least skimmed through, and decided to acquire, and keep, these volumes. There is no discernible pattern to the list of the books in his possession at the time of his death, which suggests that they were chance purchases, or gifts (we know that various books and sets of books were presented to him at different times, for example, METASTASIO's works in nine volumes; 10 Feb. 1770), rather than representing systematic choice; and of course we do not know whether Mozart lost books or other possessions during his numerous changes of address.

Of the works of his two great literary contemporaries, Mozart seems to have known little. JOHANN WOLFGANG VON GOETHE (1749–1832) first came to the attention of the wider public with his letter-novel *Die Leiden des jungen Werther* (1774), though by that time he had already published, and had had produced, some early plays. We can be thankful that Mozart at least set Goethe's *Das Veilchen* (1785); given the poet's dislike of any tampering with his texts, he may well have taken exception to Mozart's closing *a piacere* repetition of 'Das arme Veilchen! es war ein herzigs Veilchen'. Be that as it may, he paid Mozart the long-posthumous compliment of saying that Mozart would have been the ideal composer to set *Faust* to music.

Friedrich Schiller (1759–1806) gained notoriety and celebrity through the production by DALBERG in Mannheim of his plays *Die Räuber* (1782) and *Fiesko* (1784). Neither author had reached the indisputable status of a literary giant by the time of Mozart's death, though Goethe (who at the end of his life recalled seeing 'the little fellow with his wig and sword', aged seven, in Frankfurt), was by then well on the way towards eminence. Austrian literary and theatrical censorship meant that comparatively little of their output could have been familiar to the wider public in the royal and imperial capital. Further, Mozart's daily existence was so filled with the tasks of composition, performance and teaching, family concerns and business matters, not to mention his well-attested love of social intercourse, that he can have had little time left for reading, even if he were to have been a keen reader.

Through his membership of and attendance at Masonic lodges, Mozart was certainly in contact with a number of Vienna's leading men of letters. Few of these, however, rank highly in the eyes of posterity. K. J. Michaeler, custodian of the Vienna University Library and a member of 'True Concord', the lodge that Mozart often attended, edited a version of Hartmann von Aue's medieval epic, *Iwain*, which seems to have influenced the opening scenes of *Die Zauberflöte*. Among the talented Freemasons whose acquaintance Mozart is almost bound to have made are the poet and satirist Alois Blumauer, whose *Gedichte*, in the second edition of 1784, was among the books that Mozart owned; the setting of his 'Lied der Freiheit' (K506) is not, however, among Mozart's most memorable songs. Other then-prominent literary and Masonic figures, who have to an extent escaped posthumous oblivion, include JOSEPH VON SONNENFELS, the leading figure of the ENLIGHTENMENT in Vienna, and the men of letters Johann Baptist Alxinger and Joseph Franz von Ratschky. The prolific Leopoldstadt Theatre dramatist Carl Friedrich Hensler, who gave the Masonic oration for Mozart at the 'Crowned Hope' lodge, clearly knew him. And it is likely that Mozart was also acquainted with J. M. C. Denis, whose long 'bardic song', *O Calpe!* ('Gibraltar', KAnh 25), Mozart began to set in 1782, following the naval action that relieved the British base, and gave rise to Mozart's comment to his father that he was a thoroughgoing Englishman in his sympathies (letter of 19 Oct. 1782).

Among the poets whom Mozart set in his lieder, few cause any surprise: anacreontic lyricists like Hagedorn, Hölty, Jacobi, J. M. Miller, Uz and C. F. Weisse (Mozart set four of his poems, more than of any other poet). The three lyrics of J. T. Hermes that Mozart set (K340a–c) are taken from his novel *Sophiens Reise von Memel nach Sachsen*; it should not be assumed that Mozart had actually read the novel, or indeed more generally, that he selected the texts he set from individual volumes of the poets concerned – lyrics were widely published in anthologies and periodicals, and doubtless also circulated in manuscript copies, so Mozart may have come across them in any one of a number of ways.

How good was Mozart's literary discernment? The fact that he set just one lyric of Goethe's, and even there could not resist revising Goethe's ending, is redolent of the somewhat puerile lack of respect characteristic of other aspects of his personality. His judgement of *O Calpe!* (see his letter of 28 Dec. 1782), is certainly not free of irony; 'the ode is exalted, beautiful, everything you like – only – it's too exaggeratedly bombastic for my fine ears – . . . the golden mean – truth in all things is no longer known or valued – to earn applause one must write things that are so easily understood, that a coachman could sing them, or so impenetrable – that, because no sane man can understand them, they find favour for that very reason'. This comment could also be applied to many of Mozart's own writings: the dramatic sketches on the one hand, the nonsense doggerel verse on the other. Most of the poems that form the texts of Mozart's lieder are for modern taste of very limited literary value; however, he endowed them all with at least a touch of distinction, and in the case of the finest, *Das Lied der Trennung* (K519, 'The song of parting'), *Als Luise die Briefe ihres ungetreuen*

Liebhabers verbrannte (K520, 'When Luise burnt her unfaithful lover's letters') and *Abendempfindung* (K523, 'Impressions of evening'), he turned trifles into major works of art. PETER BRANSCOMBE

P. Branscombe, *W. A. Mozart: 'Die Zauberflöte'* (Cambridge, 1991)
D. J. Buch, 'Mozart and the Theater auf der Wieden: New Attributions and Perspectives', *Cambridge Opera Journal* 9 (1997), 195–232
H.-J. Irmen, *Mozart. Mitglied geheimer Gesellschaften* (Mechernich: Prisca-Verlag, 1988)
Theatergeschichte Oesterreichs (Vienna: Österreichische Akademie der Wissenschaften, 1964–), esp. vols. III/1, III/2, VI/1

Mozart in Literature. It is not surprising that a composer of extraordinary gifts, who died young, should be the subject of works of literature either through direct portrayal of him, or through reference to his music, in particular the operas. Mozart's older contemporary, GOETHE, was among the inaugurators of this trend, and it continues into our own day, with poets, novelists and dramatists attempting, with greater or less success, to bring Mozart and his family, friends and colleagues back to credible life. Few professions and callings have been able to resist the temptation – philosophers and scholars, as well as lyric poets, novelists and dramatists, are to be numbered among those who have succumbed. A scholar and Mozart biographer like Egon von Komorzynski should have known better than to write a novel, *Pamina: Mozarts letzte Liebe* (Pamina: Mozart's Last Love; Berlin, 1941), in which Mozart falls for Anna Gottlieb, the first Barbarina and, five years later, the first Pamina. A more recent novel, Francis Carr's *Mozart and Constanze* (New York, 1984), makes play with marital infidelities, the poisoning of Mozart and the mysterious episode involving the HOFDEMELS. John Heath-Stubbs has celebrated Mozartian themes in several poems (most memorably in 'Leporello') while DIE ZAUBERFLÖTE has attracted numerous authors, including Thomas Bernhard in his play *Der Ignorant und der Wahnsinnige* (The Ignoramus and the Madman; 1972), in which we meet a prima donna who has already sung the Queen of Night innumerable times, and Marion Zimmer Bradley in her 'shimmering fantasy of music and magic', *Night's Daughter* (1985). Also centred on this opera is a fascinating, generally forgotten work of 1920, G. Lowes Dickinson's *The Magic Flute. A Fantasia*. This is an evocation and reinterpretation of the story, almost a parable of the state of civilization in Europe after the First World War. Jill Paton Walsh updates the story of COSÌ FAN TUTTE to a contemporary Oxford setting in her novel *A School for Lovers* (1989) and Elaine Feinstein in the long poem 'Gold', which gives her most recent book of verse (2000) its title, concentrates on the life and changing fortunes of LORENZO DA PONTE, told from his viewpoint as an old shopkeeper in early nineteenth-century America, looking back on his years of scandal and success as a librettist in VIENNA and elsewhere in Europe. Two other recent novels deserve mention: Giorgio Taboga's *L'assassinio di Mozart* (1997) has Franz Hofdemel, jealous husband of Mozart's pupil and – it is claimed – mistress, Magdalena, attack and mortally wound Mozart; the Emperor commands Mozart's family and friends to conceal the scandal, and Hofdemel to commit suicide. Most recently the American musician and musicologist Harrison James Wignall in *NightMusic* (2002) writes of a young musicologist who discovers what he believes to be an authentic Mozart diary. He is invited to an arts foundation located in a French palace, but soon realizes that he is involved in a world of intrigue, money-laundering and murder.

In a short article one can hope at best to comment on a selection of writings that stand more or less in the debt of Mozart. The outstanding fictionalization of Mozart was achieved by Eduard Mörike (1856) in the short prose tale that he wrote as a tribute to his favourite composer at the time of the first centenary of his birth, *Mozart auf der Reise nach Prag* (Mozart on his Journey to Prague). With a poet's insight and subtlety he portrays Mozart and his wife making an unscheduled break on the journey from Vienna that will end with the premiere of DON GIOVANNI: lost in thought as he sits in a castle garden, Mozart abstractedly plucks, and cuts in half, an orange that was being tended for the forthcoming betrothal ceremony of the daughter of the castle; Mozart is 'arrested' for his crime but is soon forgiven when he is recognized by the ladies of the house. He and Constanze entertain the family and their guests, she with anecdotes from his past, he especially by his playing and singing of excerpts from the still uncompleted new opera. The story ends with the count's gift to the Mozarts of a handsome coach; his daughter, more deeply moved than the others, foresees in the 'Bohemian folksong' she finds lying on the keyboard, 'Denk es, o Seele!' (later to be set memorably by Hugo Wolf), the composer's premature death. If later scholarship has shown a few details of Mörike's tale to be historically incorrect, his insight into Mozart's character, and into the mysteries of creation, is an extraordinary achievement.

Before Mörike, there are numerous instances of works by Mozart moving writers to include incidents or characters from them in their works. Goethe in his verse epic *Hermann und Dorothea* (1797) makes play with the naivety of someone ignorant of the identity of Tamino and Pamina; and in his novel *Die Wahlverwandtschaften* (Elective affinities; 1809) he has been held (somewhat unconvincingly) to have incorporated elements of the story of *Così fan tutte*. E. T. A. Hoffmann in the prose tale *Don Juan* (1814) has his narrator experience an outstanding performance of the opera in a small-town theatre, the Donna Anna appearing to him as an inspired *Doppelgängerin* before her sudden death.

Pushkin twice tackled Mozartian themes in what he subtitled 'little tragedies': *The Stone Guest* (1830), which Dargomyzhsky set to music in 1872, though he left it unfinished at his death; and *Mozart and Salieri* (also 1830), which Rimsky-Korsakov turned into an opera in 1897. Kierkegaard's *Either/Or* (1843) is a celebrated attempt to come to philosophical terms with *Don Giovanni*, and specifically with its principal character. Later in the nineteenth century, Shaw takes up the same Don Juan theme. In the story *Don Giovanni Explains* (1887), a woman returning by train from a performance of the opera is accosted by the shade of Giovanni; and the play *Man and Superman* (1903) concerns the nature of sexual attraction and marriage in what is in part a modern adaptation of the Don Juan theme.

An Austro-Hungarian dramatist who returned several times to Mozartian subject matter is Ödön von Horváth (1901–38), most notably in *Figaro lässt sich scheiden* (Figaro gets a divorce; 1937) and *Don Juan kommt aus dem Krieg* (Don Juan's return from the war; completed 1936, performed 1952 and revised in various guises). A further German-language variant to this latter theme is Max

Frisch's play, *Don Juan, oder Die Liebe zur Geometrie* (1953), in which Juan's passion is mathematics, not amorous conquests. More recent is Anthony Rudel's *Imagining Don Giovanni* (2001), a novel that embroiders the known fact that Casanova was in PRAGUE at the time of the completion and performance of the opera, and had a small hand in it.

Without doubt the best-known, most often discussed and witnessed modern depiction of the figure of Mozart is to be found in Peter Shaffer's play *Amadeus* (London, 1980), later revised by its author, and most familiar from the filmed version by Milos Forman. This product, in whichever medium, draws forth the most profound differences of opinion, dependent largely on the extent of the knowledge of the facts of Mozart's life and character of the individual commentator, in contrast to the often supercilious superiority of the Mozart 'expert'. That said, play and film present a vivid and fascinating study of the relationship of two composers, centring on the envy felt towards Mozart by his rather older, talented but limited contemporary, ANTONIO SALIERI, and the scatty, scatological insouciance of the young genius, Mozart. Rolf Hochhuth has also written a drama, *Nachtmusik* (2000), analysing the relationship between Mozart (who does not appear in the play – it is set on the day of his funeral), his pupil Magdalena Hofdemel, her jealous husband, Franz, accused of poisoning the composer before attempting to kill his own wife, and the Emperor LEOPOLD II, who plays a game of bargaining with Magdalena.

There is every reason to expect that the topic of Mozart and literature will continue to inspire dramatists, composers, poets and novelists for the next two centuries and beyond. PETER BRANSCOMBE

Mozarteum. See INTERNATIONALE STIFTUNG MOZARTEUM

Mozartkugeln. The core ingredients of the sweet confection known as the Mozartkugel are marzipan, nougat and chocolate. The quality of individual Kugeln depends on the ingredients used and on differences in the recipes, which each manufacturer keeps secret. There are 'Original SALZBURG Mozartkugeln', 'Genuine Mozartkugeln', 'Genuine Salzburg Mozartkugeln', 'Salzburg Mozartkugeln', and simply 'Mozartkugeln'. What is the reason for this variety?

The origin of the confusion lies in the failure of the master baker Paul Fürst to protect his recipe by patent. In 1884, Fürst came from Steiermark to Salzburg where he opened a small Café-Konditorei that is still there today. An internationally trained master of his craft, his hand-made chocolate creations won a staggering market and justifiably earned him the gold medal at the world exhibition in PARIS in 1905. In 1914 the Berlin jam factory Fassbender marketed its machine-made Mozartkugeln and soon several other German firms followed. Fürst took them to court but with little success: each manufacturer made slight variations to the ingredients and the product description. Hence the plethora of names to this day.

After the Second World War, there was a veritable boom in Mozartkugeln in AUSTRIA. The small Konditorei Fürst, although it still has a turnover for its 'Original Salzburg Mozartkugeln', wrapped in silver paper, plays no part in the profits of the big firms, which are worth millions. The global success of the product is mirrored in the advertising costs put up by the manufacturers: for

Austria alone they are about 5 million shillings, more than $500,000. The slogan of the Mirabell firm in Salzburg is that their 'enjoyment is entrancing', and the advertisement suggests that anyone eating them will visibly be transformed into 'Amadeus'. Small wonder, then, that Mozartkugeln are found everywhere, from Austrian hotels to aeroplanes. FRIEDL JARY (Trans. RUTH HALLIWELL)

U. Müller and P. Csobadi, eds., *Das Phänomen Mozart im 20. Jahrhundert* (Salzburg, 1991)

Munich. City in Bavaria, southern GERMANY. At the time of the Mozarts' visit to Munich, in January 1762, the city had about 30,000 inhabitants; Elector MAXIMILIAN III JOSEPH heard them play at the Residenz. They also stayed in Munich from 12 to 22 June 1763 (at the inn 'Zum Goldenen Hirschen', today Theatinerstr. 18), on their way to PARIS and LONDON; Mozart played at Schloss Nymphenburg on 13 June and the two following days, with his sister, for Duke Clemens Franz (Maximilian III Joseph's cousin). On the return trip to SALZBURG they stayed at the 'Zum Goldenen Hirschen' again, from 8 to ?28 November 1766; Mozart composed a now-lost work, possibly for keyboard, based on a theme given to him by the Elector.

A third visit took place in 1775, for the premiere of LA FINTA GIARDINIERA, K196; Mozart and his father lodged with Johann Nepomuk von Pernat, canon at the Frauenkirche. Presumably the commission, intended to take advantage of the success of Pasquale Anfossi's setting of the same libretto for Rome in 1773, had been arranged by the Hofmusikintendant Joseph Anton Graf von Seeau, who presented it at his court-subsidized theatre. The first performance, at the Salvatortheater, took place on 13 January; an abbreviated version was repeated on 2 February, in the presence of Elector Karl Theodor of the Pfalz, and a repeat performance of the original the next day, also at the Salvatortheater. LITANIES by Leopold and Wolfgang were given at the Stiftskirche zu Unserer Lieben Frau at the beginning of March and on 12 and 19 March Leopold directed MASSES by Wolfgang in the court chapel; the OFFERTORY K222 had its first performance during High Mass on 5 March. IGNAZ VON BEECKE, Musikintendant to Prince Karl Kraft von Oettingen-Wallerstein, was also in Munich at this time and the vintner Franz Joseph Albert arranged a piano duel between Mozart and Beecke at his inn 'Zum Schwarzen Adler'. It was about this time that a Bavarian officer, Thaddädus Wolfgang von Dürnitz, commissioned keyboard sonatas from Mozart; the result of this commission was the Sonata in D major, K284.

Mozart and his mother stayed at the 'Zum Schwarzen Adler' again in late September and early October 1777. Mozart met with his Munich friends, including the court flautist Johann Baptist Becke and the court castrato TOMMASO CONSOLI, visited the noble La Rosée family, and performed on three successive days at the home of Count Joseph Ferdinand Maria von Salern. He was looking for a position at court and after several meetings with Count Seeau (who was well disposed to Mozart) and the Archbishop of Chiemsee, Ferdinand Christoph Count Waldburg-Zeil, Mozart thought he was making progress. The court cellist Franz Xaver Woschitka arranged a meeting for 30 September with the Elector at the Residenz, but nothing came of it. The vintner Albert wanted to bring together ten friends to support Mozart financially and keep him in Munich but Leopold energetically opposed this plan. As a result, Mozart and his mother continued on their way to MANNHEIM and PARIS. Wolfgang did stop in Munich during the return trip, from 25 December 1778 until early January 1779, by which time his first love, ALOYSIA LANGE (née Weber), was singing at the court opera; he gave her the aria *Popoli di Tessaglia*, K316 but she brusquely rejected him. On 7 January he presented the Elector's wife, Elisabeth Auguste, with a copy of his six accompanied sonatas K301–6 (recently published in Paris) and on 11 January he heard Aloysia sing the title role in Anton Schweitzer's *Alceste*; he was also visited by his cousin MARIA ANNA THEKLA MOZART, the 'Bäsle'.

In 1780 Mozart was commissioned to write the carnival opera, IDOMENEO, for the next season by the Elector KARL THEODOR; probably this was arranged by his friend Christian CANNABICH and the music-loving Countess Joseph von Paumgarten, the mistress of the Elector. Mozart arrived in Munich on 6 November, lodging with a 'Mr. Fiat' in the Burggasse (today Burgstrasse 7). He completed the score, undertook revisions, worked with the singer and consulted with Seeau, the scenic designer Lorenzo Quaglio, and the ballet master Claudius Legrand. The opera was given on 29 January and 12 and 19 February 1781; although it was successful with the Elector, some of the nobility and with other connoisseurs, it was not well received by the general public. The probable author of the only short notice about the opera in the *Münchner Staats-, gelehrte und vermischte Nachrichter* was their editor Lorenz Hübner. While he was in Munich Mozart also composed the arias *Misera, dove son*, K369, for Countess Paumgarten and *Ma, che vi fece*, K368, presumably for Elisabeth Augusta WENDLING. He is also presumed to have composed the Oboe Quartet, K370, for the court oboist FRIEDRICH RAMM and the songs *Die Zufriedenheit*, K349, and *Komm, liebe Zither*, K351, for the horn player Martin LANG. From Munich, Mozart went straight to VIENNA, in March 1781.

Mozart's last visit to Munich took place from 29 October to 7 or 8 November 1790, on his return from LEOPOLD II's Frankfurt coronation. On 4 November he played at a concert arranged in honour of the visiting King Ferdinand IV of Naples. As a mark of the esteem in which Mozart was held at Munich, the composer Carl Cannabich in 1797 wrote a mourning cantata, *Mozarts Gedächtnisfeyer*, partly based on tunes from the operas.

ROBERT MÜNSTER (Trans. CLIFF EISEN)

R. Angermüller and R. Münster, eds., *Wolfgang Amadeus Mozart. Idomeneo 1781–1981* (Munich, 1981)

R. Münster, *La finta giardiniera. Mozarts Münchener Aufenthalt 1774–75* (Munich, 1975)

'Ich bin hier sehr beliebt': Mozart und das kurfürstliche Bayern (Tutzing, 1993)

'ich würde München gewiss Ehre machen'. Mozart und der Kurfürstliche Hof zu München (Weissenhorn, 2002)

'Musical Joke'. Mozart's serenade K522 (*Ein musikalischer spass*). See SERENADE

Mysliveček, Joseph (b. Horní Sarka, near Prague, 9 Mar. 1737; d. Rome, 4 Apr. 1781). A Czech composer, well known in the late eighteenth century for his operas, oratorios and instrumental music, Mysliveček befriended Mozart and LEOPOLD MOZART in Bologna in 1770. (Mysliveček was in the city for a production of his opera, *La Nitteti*.) Their paths crossed twice in MILAN – in autumn 1771, when Mozart's ASCANIO IN ALBA coincided with preparations for Mysliveček's *Il gran Tamerlano* (premiered on 26 Dec. 1771) and in late 1772. Mozart met Mysliveček again in MUNICH in 1777, by which time his face had become badly disfigured after treatment for venereal disease. Leopold suggested rather bluntly that Mozart avoid Mysliveček, condemning his purportedly promiscuous behaviour in the process (30 Sept. 1777): 'your excuse, if you do not wish to visit him [in Munich], will have to be that your Mamma forbids you to do so and that other people have persuaded you, and so forth . . . What a disgrace he is before the whole world! Everybody must fly from him and loathe him. It is indeed a real calamity, which he has brought on himself.' But Mozart was much more sensitive in his attitude to his friend, visiting him in hospital, professing to be moved by what he saw and imploring Leopold 'to reply to Mysliveček. Write to him as often as you have time. You can give him no greater pleasure.' They chatted warmly, Mysliveček encouraging Mozart to return to Italy and subsequently attempting (albeit unsuccessfully) to secure him an operatic commission at the Teatro San Carlo in Naples. The esteem in which Mozart held Mysliveček's piano sonatas is also evident at this time (13 Nov. 1777): 'They are quite easy and pleasing to the ear. I should advise my sister . . . to play them with plenty of expression, taste and fire, and to learn them by heart. For they are sonatas which are bound to please everyone, which are easy to memorize and very effective when played with the proper precision.' SIMON P. KEEFE

N

Neue Mozart-Ausgabe (New Mozart Edition). Shortly after the publication of the third edition of Ludwig Ritter von Köchel's Mozart catalogue (edited by Alfred Einstein and published in Leipzig in 1937), and more than fifty after the completion of the main part of the so-called *Alte Mozart-Ausgabe* – the first 'complete' edition of Mozart's works, issued between 1877 and 1883 (with additional stray volumes appearing until 1910) – calls arose for a new Mozart edition, initially planned in connection with the Mozart year 1941 and with a 'directive' from the highest ranks of the Nazi regime. For obvious reasons, the project was never launched, and it was only following the Second World War that there was renewed discussion of the project within the newly reinstituted INTERNATIONALE STIFTUNG MOZARTEUM, SALZBURG. As a result, a plan for a new, complete edition was announced in the *Mozart-Jahrbuch* for 1953.

Within a remarkably brief period, the JOSEPH HAYDN and Mozart scholar Ernst Fritz Schmid established philological foundations for scholarly work on the *Neue Mozart-Ausgabe* (NMA) and the inaugural volume, with works for two pianos (edited by Schmid himself), was published in 1955. While at first it was planned to publish Mozart's oeuvre over a period of approximately fifteen years, drawing upon older philological precepts and recruiting a string of editors known for their expertise in eighteenth-century music research, it quickly became evident that the older scholarly approach, still prevalent in the early 1960s, was in need of serious revision, not only with respect to the selection of volume editors but also – and perhaps above all – as a result of a new philological orientation prescribed by Wolfgang Plath at the International Mozart Congress of 1964 in Salzburg in a paper with the unassuming title 'Der gegenwärtige Stand der Mozart-Forschung' ('The Present State of Mozart Research'). Plath expanded on his ideas further in a two-part publication for the *Mozart-Jahrbuch* for 1960/1 and 1976/7: 'Mozart-Autographie'. Plath's groundbreaking conclusions, together with the paper and watermark studies of Alan Tyson, were the twin pillars for the continuation of the NMA along the lines of the originally conceived plan of a critical edition aimed at both scholars and musicians.

Ernst Fritz Schmid published the first set of editorial guidelines for the NMA in 1954 and revised them substantially in 1955. Wolfgang Plath and Wolfgang Rehm thoroughly revised them again in 1962; this third edition was the last to be undertaken. This is not to say that from then on editorial techniques were not further developed. On the contrary, the basic concepts of the edition were intentionally so flexibly conceived that the ongoing editorial work could be moulded to the present state of research, could recognize new problems and attempt to solve them. In the same manner, Plath's revolutionary 'course correction' of 1964 was a product of daily work on the NMA and took as its point of departure the problems arising in relation to this work.

Externally, the musical text of the NMA resembles that of the slightly older *Neue Bach-Ausgabe* but, of course, with minor variations and additions that eventually found their way into later editions such as the *Neue Schubert-Ausgabe*. The scholarly, critical commentary, which provides information concerning editorial decisions, is published separately from the musical volume and in a somewhat smaller format. The forewords to the editions treat in concise, or occasionally even extended, fashion the origins of the works, the sources, and their relation to musical practice, without sacrificing the intended uniformity of the musical volumes and critical commentary as first defined in 1955.

The NMA is divided into ten series: Series I to IX, the main corpus with 105 volumes that include the indisputably authentic works of Mozart (as far as present-day knowledge allows) was completed in 1991 with the edition of COSÌ FAN TUTTE. At that time, the supplemental series (X) included thirteen volumes, together with the seven-volume edition of the correspondence of the Mozart family (not actually a part of the NMA but produced in close association with it. Today the supplemental series has grown to over twenty volumes, including volumes 2 and 3 of the doubtful works which, together with the first volume (including the violin concerto K271i and the so-called 'Wind Concertante' K297b/AnhC 14.01), attempt to treat and offer a final word about the sometimes confused problems of attribution in Mozart through the use of well-chosen examples; an annotated facsimile edition of Mozart's handwritten catalogue of his own works, a two-part watermark catalogue, editions of Mozart's sketches and fragments (facsimile editions with commentary, the sketches, however, with transcriptions in multicolour print as well) and, finally, an addenda volume with piano music (including cadenzas to the piano concertos and a revised edition of the Rondo in A, K386). By the time of its completion in 2006, the edition will include approximately thirty volumes, among them Wolfgang Plath's projected handwriting chronology, drafts, studies and miscellaneous works, addenda (including corrigenda), a licensed edition of the newly edited Köchel catalogue and finally, an intricate, keyed index to the NMA.

Since 1991 and the completion of the main corpus of the NMA's 'daily work', the edition has focused on completing the outstanding critical commentaries. While nearly 100 commentaries have appeared to date, a substantial number (among them some of the longer operas) nevertheless remains to be published by 2006. This state of affairs arose chiefly for financial reasons: those responsible for the edition were forced early on to concentrate their energies on the musical volumes in order not to endanger the edition as a whole. Ultimately, the decision proved to be musicologically advantageous since sources for many of the outstanding critical commentaries, removed from Berlin and deposited in the east during the course of the Second World War and since 1945 considered lost, resurfaced in 1979/80 in the Biblioteka Jagiellonska, Kraków.

WOLFGANG REHM (Trans. FAYE FERGUSON)

Neukomm, Sigismund Ritter von (b. Salzburg 10 July 1778, d. Paris 3 Apr. 1858). Born opposite Mozart's birthplace (now Hagenauerplatz 1/Getreidegasse 10) Neukomm's SALZBURG teachers, comprising members of the court Kapelle, university personnel and other Salzburg citizens, introduced him to Mozart's music, encouraging Neukomm to hear, play and study Mozart's works during his time in the city (1778–97). In January 1797 he produced DON GIOVANNI in Salzburg's court theatre, and on 12 August 1803 he gave a public performance of Mozart's Piano Concerto in D minor, K. 466, in the Town Hall. He attacked Ludwig Wenzel Lachnith's bowdlerized version of DIE ZAUBERFLÖTE in PARIS in 1801 in the strongest terms. On 24 January 1821 Neukomm finished a 'Libera me Domine, for large orchestra' for Mozart's REQUIEM in Rio de Janeiro.

Neukomm's name is closely associated with the celebrations surrounding the unveiling of the Mozart monument in Salzburg (4–6 September 1842); he gave the address, conducted Mozart's 'Coronation' mass, K317, and his Requiem, and composed the national hymn 'Oestreich'. He also made arrangements of a large number of Mozart's works (although these are not listed in Appendix C of the sixth edition of the Köchel catalogue), including the symphonies K385 ('Haffner'), K425 ('Linz'), K504 ('Prague'), K543, K550, K551 ('Jupiter'), the piano chamber works K452, 478, 493, 498 and the string quintets K515, 516, 593, 614. RUDOLF ANGEMÜLLER (Trans. RUTH HALLIWELL)

New Mozart Edition. See NEUE MOZART-AUSGABE

Niemetschek, Franz Xaver (František Xaver Němeček) (b. Sadska, Bohemia, 24 July 1766; d. Vienna, 19 Mar. 1849). Niemetschek, a native Czech and professor of philosophy at PRAGUE University from 1802, got to know Mozart in all likelihood during Mozart's final trip to Prague in August–September 1791. Following Mozart's death he took KARL THOMAS MOZART (1784–1858), the composer's older son, under his wing, housing him in Prague between 1794 and 1797; he also looked after the younger son FRANZ XAVER WOLFGANG MOZART (1791–1844) for six months in 1795–6, while CONSTANZE MOZART was on a concert tour in GERMANY.

Alongside FRIEDRICH SCHLICHTEGROLL's *Nekrolog auf das Jahr 1791* (Necrology for the Year 1791) Niemetschek's *Leben des k. k. Kapellmeister Wolfgang Gottlieb Mozart* (given as *Life of Mozart* in the 1956 translation) is the most important early biographical account of the composer. It was first published anonymously in Prague in 1797, again in 1798 (now attributed to 'Niemtschek') and then in an expanded second edition in 1808. Niemetschek draws almost exclusively on Schlichtegroll for his account of Mozart's life in SALZBURG and on his travels up to 1781, but devotes the lion's share of his biography to Mozart's period in VIENNA from 1781 onwards, giving special attention to Mozart's associations with Prague. Constanze was one of Niemetschek's primary sources and she is known to have falsified some information, for example on the topic of the REQUIEM. Thus, Niemetschek unwittingly became an early perpetuator of myths about the work, such as its commissioning by a mysterious messenger, whose identity remained a mystery to Constanze and from whom she heard nothing after Mozart's death. In spite of demonstrable biographical falsities and an unabashedly hagiographical tone, Niemetschek's book contains a number of trenchant, aesthetically significant observations. On Mozart's orchestration, for example, he comments: '[Mozart] judged with extreme accuracy the nature and range of all instruments, plotted new paths for them and from each of them obtained the utmost effect, so that the greatest melodic potentiality was realised . . . Never is an instrument wasted or misused, and, therefore, redundant. But he alone knew how to achieve his most magical effects with true economy, entailing the least effort, often through a single note on an instrument, by means of a chord or a trumpet blast.' SIMON P. KEEFE

G. Gruber, *Mozart and Posterity*, trans. R. S. Furness (London, 1991)
F. X. Niemetschek, *Life of Mozart* (1798), trans. Helen Mautner (London, 1956)
W. Stafford, 'The Evolution of Mozartian Biography', in *The Cambridge Companion to Mozart*, ed. S. P. Keefe (Cambridge, 2003), 200–11

Nissen, Georg Nikolaus (b. Haderslav, 22 Jan. 1761; d. Salzburg, 24 Mar. 1826). A Danish diplomat, who held a series of positions in Regensburg, VIENNA and Copenhagen before moving to SALZBURG for his retirement in 1820, Nissen met CONSTANZE MOZART around 1797, marrying her in Bratislava on 26 June 1809. Nissen started to assemble materials for a biography of Mozart in the early 1820s; his *Biographie W. A. Mozarts* was eventually published posthumously by Breitkopf & Härtel in 1828. At 920 pages, it is an unwieldy, disorganized volume containing demonstrable errors, contradictions and misrepresentations – it suffers too from the multiple authorship of Nissen, Constanze and Johann Heinrich Feuerstein (a medical doctor), whom Constanze drafted in to complete the volume after her husband's death. (It is quite possible, in fact, that Nissen wrote very little of the final text.) Nevertheless, the volume represents an important contribution to the Mozartian biographical tradition, containing numerous extracts from the family correspondence. It also exerted a strong influence on the next generation of Mozart biographers, including Alexander Ulybyshev (*Nouvelle Biographie de Mozart* (1843)) and Edward Holmes (*Life of Mozart* (1845)). A second edition of Nissen's biography was published in 1849.

SIMON P. KEEFE

R. Halliwell, *The Mozart Family: Four Lives in a Social Context* (Oxford, 1998)
R. Münster, 'Nissens *Biographie W. A. Mozarts*: Zu ihrer Enstehungsgeschichte', *Acta Mozartiana* 9 (1962), 2–14
G. N. Nissen, *Biographie W. A. Mozarts* (Leipzig, 1828)
W. Stafford, 'The Evolution of Mozart Biography', in *The Cambridge Companion to Mozart*, ed. S. P. Keefe (Cambridge, 2003), 200–11

notturno. See SERENADE

Novello, Vincent and Mary. Mozart enthusiasts who visited SALZBURG and VIENNA from LONDON in 1829, seeing Mozart's sister NANNERL MOZART and his widow CONSTANZE MOZART, and writing a diary about their experiences. Vincent Novello (b. 6 Sept. 1781; d. 9 Aug. 1861) married Mary Sabilla Hehl (b. c.1789; d. 25 July 1854) in 1808. Vincent was organist at the Portuguese Embassy in London, and a composer, teacher, editor and publisher, whose publishing mission was the dissemination of 'sterling' music at affordable prices. They passed a total of five days in Salzburg and nine in Vienna. Nannerl could hardly speak because of her enfeebled state, but they saw plenty of Constanze, her sister SOPHIE HAIBEL, and Mozart's younger son FRANZ

XAVER WOLFGANG MOZART. In Vienna they met several people who had known Mozart well, including ABBE MAXIMILIAN STADLER and JOSEPH EYBLER, both of whom had been involved in the tangled story of the REQUIEM. But though the Novellos wanted to discover the fate of Mozart's autograph scores, and to glean information for Vincent's intended biographical sketch of Mozart, they were hampered by shortage of time and lack of access to primary documents. However, their reports add further strands to the web of secondary accounts of Mozart, and give many interesting details about music in nineteenth-century Europe, and the attitudes to and state of knowledge about Mozart. RUTH HALLIWELL

V. and M. Novello, *A Mozart Pilgrimage: The Travel Diaries of Vincent and Mary Novello in the Year 1829*, ed. N. Medici di Marignano and R. Hughes (London, 1975)

Noverre, Jean-Georges (b. Paris, 29 Apr. 1727; d. St Germain-en-Laye, 19 Oct. 1810). A dancer and choreographer of international repute, Noverre played a pivotal role in the evolution of the dramatic ballet. He travelled widely across Europe, working for lengthy periods in Stuttgart (coinciding with the first publication of his important book, *Lettres sur la danse et sur les ballets* in 1760), VIENNA, LONDON and, as the Opéra's ballet master between 1776 and 1781, PARIS. He probably got to know the Mozarts in MILAN in October 1771, when a staging of his ballet *Roger et Bradamante* coincided with a production of ASCANIO IN ALBA, and certainly met them in Vienna in 1773.

Acquaintances were renewed in PARIS in 1778 when Mozart contributed to a revised version of Noverre's ballet, *Les petits riens*. First staged at the Vienna Burgtheater on 5 January 1768, it was revived at the Paris Opéra on 11 June 1778. Mozart wrote thirteen out of twenty numbers, plus the overture (KAnh.10/299*b*), describing his involvement in the project as 'an act of friendship to Noverre' (9 July 1778). Noverre also tried (albeit unsuccessfully) to secure an operatic commission for Mozart in Paris. Issuing fatherly advice about operatic composition, LEOPOLD MOZART encouraged his son to consult Noverre on textual issues (6 May 1778) and on 'how the emotions are to be expressed' (28 May 1778). SIMON P. KEEFE

E. Fairfax, *The Styles of Eighteenth-Century Ballet* (Lanham, MD, and London, 2003)
D. Lynham, *The Chevalier Noverre, Father of Modern Ballet: A Biography* (London, 1950)

nozze di Figaro, Le, K492 (The Marriage of Figaro). Mozart's first collaboration with LORENZO DA PONTE was first performed at VIENNA's Burgtheater on 1 May 1786. It received nine performances during the seven months of its first run, and was revived in August 1789 for a further twenty-nine performances over the course of eighteen months (the last performance of this production occurring on 9 February 1791). The second run of the opera overlapped with the premiere of COSÌ FAN TUTTE, such that at the beginning of 1790, these two operas were the primary fare at the Burgtheater, with the dramatic soprano ADRIANA FERRARESE DEL BENE appearing alternately as Fiordiligi and Susanna. Although thirty-eight performances in two runs over the course of five years was no better (and no worse) than average for Burgtheater operas during this period, *The Marriage of Figaro* had distinctly better than average success in PRAGUE during Mozart's lifetime; and over the last two centuries, it has become a staple for regional and touring companies as well as for major opera houses. It alternates with DON GIOVANNI as the most popular Mozart opera.

1. The plot
2. The prehistory and origins of *The Marriage of Figaro*
3. *The Marriage of Figaro* in the context of the Burgtheater repertory
4. Understanding *The Marriage of Figaro*

1. The plot

The plot of *Figaro*, which is based on BEAUMARCHAIS's *Le Mariage de Figaro* (written by 1781, first performed 1784), is simple in outline but complicated in detail, involving a number of secondary characters who revolve around two central couples: the Count and Countess Almaviva, and the servants Figaro and Susanna. The opera takes place in the Almaviva estate, 'Aguas Frescas', near Seville. The trigger for the plot is that the Count has designs upon the Countess's maidservant Susanna, hoping to revive and exercise his long-abolished *droit de seigneur* (the manorial lord's right to deflower a woman on his estate) before she is handed over to her true love, Figaro, who is the Count's valet. The first act begins with Susanna revealing the Count's intentions to Figaro, who immediately begins to plot ways to thwart the Count by hastening the wedding (which the Count has to bless). Figaro's own situation is, however, complicated by his relation to Doctor Bartolo and his old servant Marcellina. Marcellina is in love with Figaro and plans to hold an old debt over his head as blackmail to make him marry her, and Bartolo is still smarting from Figaro's part in *The Barber of Seville* (Beaumarchais's 'prequel' to *The Marriage of Figaro*), in which Figaro helped Rosina (now the Countess Almaviva, then Bartolo's ward) escape Bartolo's lustful clutches. Bartolo does not want Figaro to be happy, and Marcellina does not want the young and charming Susanna to enjoy the advantages of her youth. The plot is further complicated by the Count's jealous but incorrect suspicion that the adolescent page Cherubino is having an affair with the Countess, and his (correctly directed) irritation that Cherubino and the gardener's daughter Barbarina are romantically involved. The Count's sense that the youth is everywhere he isn't supposed to be is reinforced in the wonderfully funny quartet, 'Cosa sento', during which, in re-enacting for Susanna and the music master Basilio how he found Cherubino under a table pretending he had not been with Barbarina, the Count finds him again, hiding in a chair under a dress. The first act ends with the Count trying to get rid of Cherubino (who is not only a romantic nuisance but also knows too much about the Count's philandering) by sending him off to the military: Figaro pretends to give him a rousing send-off, but has actually told him to stay so that he can participate in the plots to ensnare the Count.

The Countess does not appear until the second act, which opens with a tender aria ('Porgi, amor') in which she laments her husband's lack of interest in her. From this point on she becomes increasingly involved in the imbroglio, realizing the need to act in order to bring her husband back into the fold. She agrees to Figaro's idea that Susanna should accept an assignation with the

Count in the garden, but sends Cherubino, dressed as a woman, in Susanna's stead. This plot leads to a scene in which Cherubino, overcome with adolescent desire for the Countess, is dressed up in female clothing by the two women, much to everyone's delight. The Count interrupts this occasion, however, and the famous second-act finale begins as he tries to prise open the closet in which the Countess has confessed to hiding Cherubino, half-dressed and in deep trouble for being on the estate at all. Unbeknownst to the Count and Countess, Susanna has managed to persuade Cherubino out of a window and hide herself in the closet while the Count and Countess were out of the room. Her astonishing emergence from the closet is one of the great moments of the opera. Complication follows upon complication in the finale, as the Count discovers Cherubino's non-departure and Figaro's implication in this; the gardener Antonio arrives and describes having seen Cherubino leaping from a window into his carnations; and finally Marcellina, Bartolo and Basilio arrive to urge the Count to make Figaro honour his promise to marry Marcellina if he cannot repay the money he owes her.

The chief events of the third act are the discovery that Marcellina and Bartolo are Figaro's long-lost parents, which effectively nullifies Marcellina's interest in Figaro as a husband, and produces matrimonial plans between the old couple, and the solidification of the plan to ensnare the Count. The Countess swallows her pride sufficiently to suggest that Susanna accept the Count's invitation to a garden rendezvous, but that instead of Susanna, the Countess herself will make this date, dressed in her servant's clothes. The act ends with a ceremony supposedly preparatory to the double wedding of Bartolo with Marcellina and Figaro with Susanna. Local country girls (among them Cherubino, who is once more revealed to have postponed his departure) present the Countess with flowers, Barbarina reveals that the Count has dallied with her as well, and the Count promises a great feast later that evening to celebrate the weddings. Susanna, however, passes the Count a note setting a time and place for her meeting and telling him to return the pin that seals it. Figaro sees this exchange but does not comprehend.

The fourth and last act begins as Barbarina has dropped the pin which the Count commissioned her to return to Susanna. Figaro offers to help, and in the process learns that the Count's assignation is with Susanna. He confides in his mother, who defends women in general from the usual accusations of deceit and infidelity. Figaro is not mollified, and decides to watch the proceedings, ready to intervene if necessary. Susanna, who knows he is lurking in the wings, is annoyed that he does not trust her, and sings a ravishing amorous serenade, 'Deh vieni, non tardar', ostensibly to the Count, but actually to Figaro. The central events of the last finale involve the private reconciliation of Susanna and Figaro – she has disguised herself as the Countess and approaches Figaro pretending to want revenge on the Count, but Figaro recognizes her voice and they make up – and the public revelation of the Count's philandering and the Countess's moving forgiveness of him. The 'crazy day' (the first part of Beaumarchais's title is *La Folle Journée*) ends with one couple newly united (Figaro and Susanna), one reunited (Bartolo and Marcellina), one reconciled (the Count and Countess) and forgiveness all round.

2. The prehistory and origins of *The Marriage of Figaro*

The Marriage of Figaro was Mozart's first complete Italian-language opera since IDOMENEO (Munich, 1781), and his first complete opera buffa since LA FINTA GIARDINIERA of 1775. Opera buffa had been banned from the Burgtheater in 1776, when JOSEPH II re-created the venue as an entirely German national theatre, but in 1783 Joseph thought better of this decision and replaced the singspiel again with the Italian genre. Thus Mozart's 1782 success with DIE ENTFÜHRUNG AUS DEM SERAIL could be neither repeated nor built upon, and in order to make the desired splash on the imperial stage he had to write an opera buffa. He was, however, famously exacting about the choice of a libretto. His letter to his father of 7 May 1783 describes how he 'looked through at least a hundred libretti and more, but I have hardly found a single one with which I am satisfied'. This extraordinary reading spree was reported a mere two weeks after opera buffa had returned to the Burgtheater stage, which suggests genuine eagerness on Mozart's part. During this year he seems to have started two opere buffe: L'OCA DEL CAIRO (text by VARESCO) and *Lo sposo deluso* (text originally by Petrosellini), but neither work got very far. Mozart had had his eye on the imperial poet Da Ponte as a librettist since the latter's arrival in Vienna in 1783, and had tested the waters with him in some substitution and insertion numbers in Anfossi's *Il curioso indiscreto* (performed in Vienna in 1783) and BIANCHI's *La villanella rapita* (performed in Vienna in 1785). Evidently each man found the other a satisfactory prospect for a longer-term project, even in the absence of a firm commission.

Both Da Ponte and tenor MICHAEL KELLY (the first Don Curzio) claim that it was Mozart's idea to turn Beaumarchais's play into an opera, but there is no indication in Mozart's correspondence one way or the other. It is, however, clear both that there was no commission from the Burgtheater establishment and (in an apparent contradiction) that the Emperor did not oppose it in the way that Da Ponte describes in his memoirs. Joseph did indeed forbid a performance of the play in January 1785, though he also permitted its publication in an unabridged German translation by Johann Rautenstrauch later the same year. He also attended the dress rehearsal of the opera on 29 April 1786, according to Daniel Heartz, and (according to Da Ponte's memoirs) squashed the attempts of the 'Italian faction' to make nonsense of the end of Act 3 by removing the music for the march and fandango. (Separate ballets had been banned in operas at the Burgtheater, and ROSENBERG-ORSINI and others evidently used this rule to forbid the music that accompanies the mime in which Susanna passes the Count the note about their assignation in the garden – and that also accompanies dancing by the assembled subjects of the Almaviva estate. The Emperor, Da Ponte explains in his memoirs, ordered the music restored and authorized the hiring of dancers.) One can read the politics of this opera in many ways (see below), but one perfectly plausible reading is that Joseph saw the opera as a useful corrective to aristocratic abuses of privilege – abuses that he himself, from a position above the aristocracy, was also trying to curb. It is also possible that Joseph felt some sympathy for Mozart as a German composer, particularly in light of his own attempts to make the Burgtheater into a German-nationalist temple. For example, the 1786 Viennese libretto for

Figaro announces the composer as 'Signor Volfgango Mozart, Maestro di Cappella, Tedesco' (Mr Wolfgang Mozart, Composer, German), which is, on the one hand, evidence of Mozart's lack of a position with an aristocratic household, but also an unusual way of describing a composer. VICENTE MARTÌN Y SOLER, a Spanish composer who had three operas premiered in Vienna during Mozart's time there, for example, was never described as 'Spagnuolo', though his appointment as composer to the Prince of the Asturias was noted on at least one libretto.

Mozart evidently began the composition of *Figaro* in mid-1785, and by the autumn it was well under way, even sending ripples of its gestation to Paris. Mozart seems to have composed the four acts in order, but within each act working in general on the ensemble numbers before the solo pieces. The overture was, as was his habit, among the last items to be written. Like any opera in this repertory, however, revisions were made until the last moments and even beyond – the libretto, for example, includes an arietta for Cherubino in Act 3 that was either never composed or that left no trace in the score. It also includes a reiteration of his 'Voi che sapete' right before the Act 4 finale, which was also evidently not performed (it is crossed out in the libretto and does not appear in the score). In part because of various sorts of evidence of last-minute tinkering, and in part because of some dramatic awkwardness in this very complex plot, various reorderings of material in the third and fourth acts have been proposed, the most famous of these in 1965 (before the whole autograph was available to scholars) by Robert Moberly and Christopher Raeburn, in which scenes 7 and 8 of Act 3 (a little recitative between Barbarina and Cherubino, and the Countess's great scena including the aria 'Dove sono i bei momenti', in which she decides to save her marriage) were said to belong (as if they were scenes 3 and 4) immediately after the Count's rage aria, 'Vedrò mentr'io sospiro', and before the events leading up to the sextet in which Figaro and Susanna recognize and embrace Bartolo and Marcellina as parents. The autograph score, which may or may not have been used in performance, neither supports nor refutes this ordering. The autograph does suggest, however, that the order of the last act – especially the relation between Susanna's serenade, 'Deh vieni non tardar', and Figaro's anti-female tirade, 'Aprite un po' quegl'occhi' – was the result of decisions made very late in the process of composition. This has given at least one conductor (John Eliot Gardiner) licence to place Figaro's aria as a response to Susanna's. Mozart's difficulty with this spot in the action is evidenced by the fact that he wrote a recitative and the first thirty-six bars of a completely different aria for Susanna (a rondò (like 'Dove sono') entitled 'Non tardar, amato bene'), in E flat, the same key as Figaro's 'Aprite un po' ', before coming up with 'Deh vieni, non tardar', in F. Naturally today we think of the traditional order and Susanna's wonderfully understated and deliciously ambiguous song as Mozart's 'last, best' thoughts on the subject – and on this topic we may be right. On the other hand, as Alan Tyson has shown, many of Mozart's latest thoughts on the details of the opera are recorded in copies used for the performance rather than in the autograph, and may not be what we might deem 'best': these include a recitative version of the tiny (but very fast) duet for Susanna and Cherubino, 'Aprite, presto aprite', which Tyson suggests may have been written as an emergency back-up in case the performers couldn't manage the ensemble. For the revival in 1789, and its new cast, especially Adriana Ferrarese del Bene, the new Susanna, Mozart wrote two new arias, 'Un moto di gioia', to replace 'Venite inginocchiatevi', in Act 2, and 'Al desio di chi t'adora', to replace 'Deh vieni, non tardar', in Act 4. Tyson also suggests that Mozart revised the Countess's 'Dove sono' for this revival.

One might draw a number of plausible conclusions from the compositional history of this text. One is that Mozart worked exceptionally hard at the musical dramaturgy of his operas; we know this in any case from the mountain of correspondence surrounding *Idomeneo*, and the evidence of last-minute tinkering in the sources for *Figaro* certainly bears it out. Another plausible conclusion is that Mozart paid close attention to an opera's actual effect on stage, and was willing to make literally endless adjustments to ensure that the performance was effective. Again, this is borne out by other documentation about Mozart's compositional practices with respect to opera. Another conclusion one finds in the literature discovers the 'tyranny' of singers in operatic composition: the fact that Mozart wrote two new arias especially for La Ferrarese – arias, moreover, that modern critics find less dramatically effective than what they replace – is said to show the 'imbalance' of power in the Viennese operatic establishment at the time. The judgements suggested here do not reflect the values of eighteenth-century operatic composition (excepting, perhaps, Gluckian 'reform' opera), which included, (a) that 'the work' in the sense of a single, finished, and integral text, was always the result of some degree of collaboration with its singers, and (hence) that (b) as the singers changed, the work did too: there was (and was intended to be) no single text which represented 'the work' in its perfect form. Thus our sense that there is a single *Figaro* to which all performances should be faithful is, while defensible in some respects (many elements of Mozart's and Da Ponte's text are fixed and clear and apparently final), still conceptually at odds with eighteenth-century Viennese and Italian notions of what an opera was.

The premiere of the work on 1 May 1786 was evidently a mixed success. Beforehand, LEOPOLD MOZART reported intrigues and cabals against the opera by the 'Italian faction' – court composer ANTONIO SALIERI, Joseph II's theatrical administrator Count Rosenberg-Orsini, and Giambattista Casti, who had been displaced as imperial poet by Da Ponte. The *Wiener Realzeitung* reported that 'some bravos were heard from unbiased music lovers', but also that some 'uncouth louts' in the highest balcony tried to deafen singers and audiences with their hissing, and thus that opinion at the end of the evening was divided. However, as the performers became used to playing this unusually difficult work, and as the audience had a chance to get to know the music, opinion swung in favour of the work. Indeed, by the third performance, the same newspaper reported, so many numbers were encored that a new rule was put into effect, that no number with more than one voice could be encored. The nine-performance run in 1786 did not make *Figaro* a horrible failure by the standards of the time, but neither did it count among the great successes of the period. PAISIELLO's *Il barbiere di Siviglia*, for example, had had thirty-eight performances by the time *Figaro* appeared, and continued in the repertory for a total of over fifty, a popularity that must have been galling given the thematic closeness of the two works. However, *Figaro* was produced in Prague in December 1786, where it had a stunning success. As Mozart gleefully noted in a letter to his friend the Baron Gottfried von Jacquin, 'here they talk about nothing but "Figaro". Nothing is played, sung or whistled but "Figaro". No opera is drawing like "Figaro". Nothing, nothing but "Figaro" '. Even allowing for exaggeration born of excitement, it is hard not to hear a tone of vindication in these comments.

3. *The Marriage of Figaro* in the context of the Burgtheater repertory

Whoever was the source of the idea for the opera, and whatever the reasons for Joseph's evident lack of opposition to the project, adapting the Beaumarchais play was a marvellous idea, given the nature of the repertory and Mozart's position in Vienna at the time. Several things about the project ensured that it would make a splash as a novelty, while other aspects balanced the novelty out by projecting the 'tried and true' elements of the project. As we have seen, Beaumarchais's play was politically and perhaps sexually too bold for Vienna: if it had been staged more or less complete it would certainly have stood out from its 'colleagues' in terms of its direct treatment of questions of power. Even with the more rebellious material excised, however, the libretto would still have seemed quite novel. Da Ponte's preface to the libretto announces it as a 'quasi nuovo genere di spettacolo' (a newish kind of entertainment); its cast of eleven characters (reduced from the sixteen of the original) was significantly larger than the norm of seven or eight characters per opera, and thus even a glance at the front matter of the libretto (which was available for purchase beyond the Burgtheater) would have suggested something more theatrically complex than usual. Mozart as a composer of Italian opera was a novelty, and the theatrical politics surrounding the premiere would also have given the opera an aura of excitement. At the same time, many things about the opera would have seemed quite familiar to its first audiences: indeed it is not inappropriate to think of *The Marriage of Figaro* (as of any other opera in the Burgtheater repertory) as part of a complex and multi-layered 'conversation' with the genre of opera buffa itself, with specific other works, with other performances and with the experiences of the audience.

One familiar aspect of this opera was its roots in a French play: Da Ponte had very recently adapted another such in *Il burbero di buon core* (an adaptation of GOLDONI'S *Le Bourru bienfaisant*, first performed in January 1786) for Martín y Soler; GAZZANIGA'S *Il finto cieco* (performed in February 1786) was Da Ponte's adaptation of Marc-Antoine Legrand's *L'Aveugle clairvoyant*; and most relevant of all, of course, the ever-popular *Il barbiere di Siviglia* was a remarkably literal adaptation of Beaumarchais's *Le Barbier de Séville*. Although the length and complexity of *The Marriage of Figaro* were unprecedented, and the play itself was perceived as scandalous, many of its themes – even its central ones – would have been entirely familiar to Mozart's first audiences. The importuning of an appealing servant or peasant by an untoward nobleman, for example, was a standard element in this genre. Perhaps the most striking example of this theme in the repertory immediately surrounding *The Marriage of Figaro* was BERTATI'S and Bianchi's *La villanella rapita* (first performed in Vienna in 1785), in which a country girl is abducted by the local Count, rescued by her father and bumpkin lover, and then chased down again by the Count and his armed men. The peasants have quickly married by the time the Count catches up with them, so he is left grumbling in the background. Mozart wrote two ensembles for the Viennese production of this opera. The foundling theme in *The Marriage of Figaro* is also common in opere buffe performed in Vienna: it is more usual for the person of unknown birth to be female, but the relation of birth to merit was of enormous importance in the years before 1789 (and after, of course) and the foundling theme was a theatrically convenient and politically non-confrontational way of addressing that issue. The overturning or humiliation of a patriarch figure by the wit and wile of his inferiors is a dramatic element as old as comedy itself, and it was certainly familiar to the audiences of late eighteenth-century opera buffa. Here, however, *The Marriage of Figaro* reconfigures the convention rather than adopting it more or less whole. The most usual version of this theme was that exemplified in *The Barber of Seville*: namely, the duping of an inappropriately lustful or greedy (old) guardian or father to allow the *ingénue* and her lover to marry. In operas on this theme, the guardian is typically widowed or single, and never actually apologizes: he either simply blesses the young lovers or grumbles away in the background. In either case, the triumph of young love effectively pushes the guardian aside, obliterating him both as a focus of dramatic interest and as a locus of power. This is not the case in *Figaro*, where the overthrow is moral rather than generational and the Count stays in charge of his household at the same time as he is unambiguously corrected.

In addition to recognizing certain familiar themes (however reconfigured), the first audiences for *The Marriage of Figaro* would also have heard connections to particular previous works, and *Figaro* in turn would have served as part of the web of references for works that came after. GIUSEPPE SARTI's setting of *Fra i due litiganti il terzo gode* ('The third of two contenders wins') an anonymous adaptation of Goldoni's *Le nozze*, for example, features a philandering Count, his unhappy wife and a much-importuned servant, Dorina, who is eventually allowed to marry the servant Masotto. The connections here are essentially verbal and narrative: Mozart does not refer to Sarti's music. He does, however, refer quite strikingly and pervasively to Paisiello's setting of *Il barbiere di Siviglia*. Figaro's aria of defiance, 'Se vuol ballare', for example, essentially quotes a passage in 'Scorsi già molti paesi', Figaro's description of his past life for the Count in *Il barbiere*. Curiously enough, music from 'Se vuol ballare' then reappears in an aria specially written for the Viennese production of Sarti's *I finti eredi* (August 1786) in which a bumpkin lover shouts defiance at an over-amorous marquis. The narrative and musical connections among these works were no doubt further reinforced by continuities in the performers, who were often typecast. The singing actress Nancy STORACE, for example, played not only Susanna, but also Dorina in *Fra i due litiganti*, the importuned peasant girl Giannina in *I finti eredi* and the lively *ingénue* Rosina in *Il barbiere di Siviglia* (soon to grow up as the Countess Almaviva). The much-prized comic bass FRANCESCO BENUCCI, Mozart's first Figaro, played an unsuccessful bumpkin lover in *Fra I due litiganti*, the successful bumpkin lover in *I finti eredi* (thus quoting himself singing 'Se vuol ballare') and the blustering Dr Bartolo in *Il barbiere di Siviglia*. Later in the same year, Da Ponte and Martín y Soler's *Una cosa rara* took Vienna by storm: also set in Spain, it featured another too-much-loved heroine, played by Storace, and a queen, played by Luisa Laschi-Mombelli, who was Mozart's first Countess. These connections – which are in any case not particularly subtle – would not have been missed by contemporary listeners, many of whom (and especially the aristocrats with season subscriptions) attended each opera multiple times. It is important to remember nowadays that although for us *The Marriage of Figaro* dwells on the isolating pedestal of transcendent art, and despite the fact that even in its own time it stood apart from its 'colleagues' in the Burgtheater repertory in terms of ambition, scale and difficulty, its contemporary audiences could not have avoided understanding it as a contribution to a multi-layered and immediate operatic dialogue.

4. Understanding *The Marriage of Figaro*

One common view of *The Marriage of Figaro* is that Da Ponte de-politicized Beaumarchais's play, turning it into a work more universal in its concerns about human relations, if also as witty and funny as its model. This reading of the relation of the two works is based in part on Da Ponte's most striking omissions, and in part on the extraordinary variety and beauty of Mozart's music, which is generally understood to give depth and 'humanity' to the characters in ways that make the drama more psychological than political. Da Ponte's most notable omissions include most of Beaumarchais's Act 3, especially the trial scene, in which the magistrate Don Gusman Brid'oison (a cruel portrait of a contemporary Parisian judge) hears Marceline's case against Figaro, and some parts of Beaumarchais's Act 5, especially Figaro's tirade against the (absent) Count, which includes the famous outcry, 'What did you do to deserve such riches? You took the trouble to get born, nothing more. Otherwise, you are quite an ordinary man; while I, for goodness' sake! lost in the crowd, I have had to use more science and calculation simply to survive than it has taken to govern Spain for the last hundred years!' In Da Ponte's adaptation, this three-page disquisition is reduced to Figaro's 'Aprite un po' quegl'occhi', the complaint against womankind that takes only the first three or four sentences of Beaumarchais's speech. In the sense of removing the most obviously rebellious or locally satirical elements, then, Da Ponte's adaptation does soften the political edge of the play. If 'political' is interpreted more broadly, to mean having to do with the nature and distribution of power, then *Figaro*, in its words, but more particularly in its music, is profoundly so. Even without the trial and the tirade, the Almaviva household is quite transparently a miniaturization of feudal society, and the main questions of the plot quite obviously have to do with the rights and obligations of people in variously unequal stations. The main *agon* of the Beaumarchais play is between the servant Figaro and his master the Count – each standing in for a broader social status. Beaumarchais also uses the women in the plot essentially as currency in the play's economy of power. The opera, however, suggests a much more complicated relation between social class and gender; the characters exercise power within and between social layers in a much more fluid way than in the play, and the political message of the opera is communicated more in the ways Da Ponte and (especially) Mozart manipulate our sympathies than in disquisitions on equality and difference.

Late eighteenth-century music had various ways of embodying and communicating social content, among the most powerful of which were musical-rhetorical topoi, or topics: rhythmic, melodic and textural motifs or gestures that derived from or were associated with distinct social occasions. Thus the clearly audible march-like rhythms and the triadic tune of Figaro's 'Non più andrai', the aria at the end of Act 1 where he describes Cherubino's victorious military future, make audible and real the content of the text. The use of trumpets and drums in this aria also heightens the aria's connection to ceremony and military magnificence. More politically, Figaro's use of minuet rhythm (a steady, more or less equally accented triple metre) in 'Se vuol ballare' accentuates the vitriol of the text, since the minuet was characteristically a dance of the aristocracy, and we hear Figaro turning the language of his betters against them. The second part of this aria (to the text 'L'arte schermendo', etc.) uses a sort of country-dance rhythm, which suggests Figaro's capacity to engage in the sort of scheming and imbroglio typical of comic servants. Topoi might also derive from opera itself: thus, accompanied recitative and coloratura signify the 'high' style of opera seria, while patter and a more syllabic manner of declamation signify the 'lower' associations of opera buffa. Figaro's and Susanna's adoption of accompanied recitative before their arias in the fourth act ('Aprite un po'', and 'Deh vieni, non tardar', respectively) thus suggests that they are capable of a level of emotional seriousness not uniformly or necessarily typical of servant-class characters. The story told by Mozart's brilliant and subtle deployment of these topoi is not only politically charged, but also psychologically complex.

The Countess, for example, can be read as both the emotional and the political centre of the opera. Mozart's music for her is exceptionally rich, both in its multi-layered deployment of topoi and in its purely compositional strategies. For example, the unusually prominent use of wind instruments – especially clarinet and oboe – in her two arias, 'Porgi, amor, qualche ristoro', at the beginning of the second act, and 'Dove sono i bei momenti', in Act 3, draw on the 'outdoor' and 'serenading' associations of those instruments to suggest that she has associations with the green and classless world of the pastoral. Those same wind instruments, and especially the solo oboe in 'Dove sono', also connect to the more immediate opera buffa tradition of representing a serious (usually female) character's 'inner voice' with a solo wind instrument. To have an 'inner voice' usually means that a character is emotionally serious and has an inner life in which we might be supposed to be interested. On an even more specific level, the use of clarinets, the E flat tonality and the opening upward leap of 'Porgi, amor' refer to the Countess's earlier existence as the young Rosina in the *Barber of Seville*, as they echo these aspects of Paisiello's aria of despair for Rosina, 'Giusto ciel, che conoscete', sung when she thinks her schemes to elope with the Count will never work. The interaction of these different sorts of associations – ideal, generic and specific – lends the Countess a multifaceted penumbra of potential significance, and thus assists the illusion that she is real. Within the *Marriage of Figaro* itself, some critics have heard the high A in the faster part of 'Dove sono', sung to the word 'cangiar' ('to change [this heart]') as she decides to act to reclaim her husband, as a sort of completion and fulfilment of the notably unfulfilled high A♭ halfway through 'Porgi, amor', sung in the depths of self-pity, to the word 'morir' ('die'). This connection, which is quite audible, suggests that Mozart wanted to highlight the Countess's *process* of psychological movement from her initial self-absorbed misery to her later capacity to involve herself in the action and thus (paradoxically) position herself to forgive her husband. Although all the main characters in the opera learn something in the course of the day, the Countess is the only one whose emotional progress matters to the audience as much as, if not more than, her involvement in the imbroglio.

The richness and immediacy of the Countess's emotional life has meaning beyond the fact that generations of critics have found her a marvel of humanity and a demonstration of Mozart's uncanny ability to express a woman's psychology. As the character who demands the lion's share of the audience's empathy, and eventually as the vindicated centre of the opera's moral economy, she occupies a position exactly analogous to the emerging notion of the wife and mother as emotional, spiritual and moral hub of the bourgeois home. The triumph of her values over the Count's is a triumph of a bourgeois notion of exclusive companionate marriage over the Count's aristocratic notion of marriage as the dynastically necessary point of departure for more casual liaisons. In the context of a Vienna whose emperor assumed bourgeois values and demeanour in conspicuous and self-conscious opposition to the traditional protocol of aristocratic display, Mozart's (and it is mostly Mozart's) representation of bourgeois morality in the compelling guise of the Countess assumes a quite explicitly political significance. Mozart's and Da Ponte's Countess also lends weight to the appeal of the social middle through her intimacy with Susanna – whom, after all, she has to pretend to be in order to recapture her husband's affections. As many critics have pointed out, Susanna and the Countess develop an unusually intimate friendship, in which their difference in status takes second place to their need and evident affection for one another. Not only does Susanna sing higher than the Countess in several ensembles (a fact which, despite its likely origins in the relative ranges of the two singers, is still not without political significance), but in the 'letter duet' in Act 3, where the two women construct a letter to the Count inviting him to meet 'Susanna' in the garden, their music is essentially indistinguishable. When Susanna sings her fourth-act serenade, 'Deh vieni, non tardar', to the Count (but 'really' to Figaro), the elaborate use of winds and the pastoral topoi in both the text and the music link her with the Countess. This both elevates her love for Figaro into something more than the usual cosy affection demonstrated by servant-class characters in opera buffa, and, conversely, reminds us that the Countess's language is not exclusive.

One persuasive reading of the two women's friendship is that it is the central item in an opera which is, at its most profound level, a pastoral. The world that this extraordinary friendship occupies is 'hors de combat', an idealized literary and imaginative location where relationships and attitudes can be explored without being constrained by the divisions of the real world. But it is also the case that together, the Countess and Susanna define a place *in* the real world that stands between the cold rigidities of the aristocrats and the antics of the serving classes. It is an idealized – and thus potentially prescriptive – vision of a middle class that unites the 'true nobility' of the Countess's generosity towards her husband with the social adaptability of the 'lower orders'. This adaptability is demonstrated by Susanna's participation in duets with all the main characters of the opera, from the Count to Cherubino, as well as by Figaro's capacity to speak, as the occasion demands, at all the rhetorical levels of the opera from the grandest to the most ridiculous, and from the most pompous to the most sentimental. It is interesting that the appeal of a middle social space is expressed in aesthetic and emotional terms: this attraction is allowed for by Da Ponte's text, but only realized by Mozart's music. In that sense, the contemporary critic who commented that 'what cannot be said may now be sung' was wrong: what is sung in *Figaro* is in fact rather different from – and arguably more political – than what was left to be said. Mozart did not replace the animus that Da Ponte perforce left out of the Beaumarchais, but he did imagine and communicate a social order that values merit as much as birth, and rewards community over division.

It would, however, be wrong to construe *The Marriage of Figaro* as first and foremost, or only, a political tract. It is also a comedy whose verbal and theatrical wit (much of it taken from Beaumarchais) still makes audiences laugh: it is an opera buffa that calls on the resources of its genre at the same time as it spills over its generic boundaries; and it is a masterpiece of musical dramaturgy, in which 'purely musical' processes of tension and release, expectation and fulfilment, departure and return, match and animate the dramatic processes of the text. The combination of social relevance, humour, generic virtuosity and musical richness allow the opera to communicate a remarkably immediate sense of 'real time' action and psychological plausibility, at the same time as it opens a window onto the issues and circumstances of the 1780s in Europe.

MARY HUNTER

W. J. Allanbrook, *Rhythmic Gesture in Mozart: 'Le nozze di Figaro' and 'Don Giovanni'* (Chicago, 1983)

R. Angermuller, *Mozart's Operas*, trans. Stewart Spencer (New York, 1988)

T. Carter, *W. A. Mozart, 'Le nozze di Figaro'* (Cambridge, 1987)

D. Heartz, 'Constructing *Le nozze di Figaro*', and 'Setting the Stage for *Figaro*', both in his *Mozart's Operas*, ed., with contributing essays, Thomas Bauman (Berkeley and Los Angeles, 1990), 133–56 and 123–32

A. Steptoe, *The Mozart–Da Ponte Operas* (Oxford, 1988)

A. Tyson, *Mozart: Studies of the Autograph Scores* (Cambridge, MA, 1987)

O

oca del Cairo, L', K422 (The Goose of Cairo) (1783–4). Early in 1783, Mozart was on the lookout for a new opera libretto; JOSEPH II had just established an opera buffa troupe in VIENNA and Mozart was eager to show himself equal to the challenge of Italian comic opera after the success of DIE ENTFÜHRUNG AUS DEM SERAIL (1782). Searching for a suitable subject, he worked his way through more than a hundred texts sent to him from Italy. Finding nothing that inspired him, however, Mozart eventually resolved to request a brand-new libretto from GIOVANNI VARESCO, the chaplain to the Archbishop of SALZBURG; the result was the ill-fated project *L'oca del Cairo*, an unfinished opera buffa that survives only as a fragmentary first act.

Varesco had collaborated with Mozart before, on the opera seria IDOMENEO, commissioned in 1780 by the MUNICH court. That Varesco had been resident in Salzburg had given Mozart ample opportunity to intervene in the design of the libretto during the early stages of its composition; with the constant help and mediation of his father, Mozart likewise became closely involved in the creation of the text of *L'oca del Cairo*. Indeed, Mozart's constant tinkering with the libretto for *Idomeneo* had caused considerable friction between the composer and the poet, and one can surmise that the composer's rather demanding attitude, coupled with Varesco's own shortcomings and relative inexperience as a librettist, were contributing factors in the premature demise of *L'oca del Cairo*. It certainly does not seem that the difficult experience of collaborating on *Idomeneo* with Varesco had diminished Mozart's self-assurance: on 21 June 1783, he wrote to his father that Varesco 'must alter and recast the libretto as much and as often as I wish'.

An important letter of 7 May 1783 makes Mozart's specifications for his new libretto quite clear. He wanted the text itself to be absolutely new and by no means an adaptation of an older libretto – above all, something 'really comic'. He further stipulated that there be two substantial female roles of more or less equal importance, one of which should be serious, the other light-serious or 'mezzo carattere', as it was sometimes called; any other female parts and all of the male roles could be 'entirely buffa' if the plot required it. The following June, in response to the composer's commission, Varesco sent Mozart a synopsis of *L'oca del Cairo*.

Although Mozart was moderately pleased with the opera to begin with – unlike Varesco himself, who began to express doubts about the quality of his work almost as soon as it was on paper – it rapidly became clear that certain elements of the plot needed to be curtailed or altered, while others needed to be removed altogether. Indeed, most modern critics agree that Varesco's rather inexpert handling of the story was foremost among the reasons for the failure of the entire project. Without a doubt, the storyline that survives is a rather scrambled concoction, although recent research by J. Everson has helped to clarify some of its more outlandish details, not least the eponymous goose. Indeed, because the opera remained unfinished, there is no single 'plot' to speak of, especially since the original synopsis that Varesco sent to Mozart and the scraps of surviving libretto appear to diverge a great deal. Suffice it to say that the story concerns an old nobleman, Don Pippo, whose wife has fled into exile and spread rumours of her death owing to her husband's persistent ill-treatment, and lives in disguise on the other side of the city. Don Pippo, thinking himself a widower, resolves to remarry a young friend of his daughter's, at the same time compelling his daughter to marry an old count. Since the two unfortunate young women already have lovers, the tyrannous nobleman imprisons them in a high-walled garden, although he loses no time in challenging his daughter's young suitor Biondello to enter the garden and woo her (helpfully setting the time limit of a year). Surprising as it may seem, this complicated set-up is merely the backdrop for the story. The action within the opera itself concerns Biondello's plan to breach the walls of the garden with the help of Don Pippo's wife – a ridiculous scheme to approach Don Pippo's palace concealed within a giant mechanical goose. The action of the fragmentary first act as Mozart set it is, however, thoroughly confused by a lack of any reference to the back-story and much superfluous detail relating to servants and other minor buffo characters. J. Everson has argued that the peculiar element of the goose from Cairo (about which Mozart perhaps understandably had his reservations) derived from a distant model for Varesco's libretto – a *novella* from the romance *Il mambriano* by Francesco Cieco da Ferrara, parts of which continued to circulate as cheap pamphlets in Italy and AUSTRIA even into the nineteenth century.

As it stands, almost all of Mozart's music survives only in a skeletal form – as melody and bass-lines, with important instrumental parts also added. Aside from a few unfinished scraps, there survives an opening A major duet and a pair of arias with a light, buffo character. Mozart also completed the barest outline of a D major aria for Don Pippo, an E flat quartet for the two imprisoned women and their young lovers, and a large-scale finale that begins and ends in B flat. The fullest part of the surviving score did not come to light until the middle of the twentieth century, however – a more or less completely orchestrated setting of Don Pippo's aria 'Siano pronte alle gran nozze', which unexpectedly becomes a trio (including the two servants Chichibio and Auretta) at roughly the point at which the other sketch of the piece breaks off. The trio had been in the collection of the Bavarian-born composer Johannes Simon Mayr (1763–1845); it seems to have come into his possession through CONSTANZE MOZART at some time in the early years of the nineteenth century.

In a letter dated 10 February 1783, Mozart informed his father that he was putting aside his opera in order to work on more profitable projects; there is no indication that he considered the opera a lost cause at this stage; indeed, it seems clear that he believed that he would eventually return to it. Of course, this might have been wishful thinking, or perhaps the reluctance of a son to disappoint his father, who had been closely involved in the project from the very beginning. As it is, *L'oca del Cairo* survives only as a record of Mozart's abortive first attempts in the world of Italian comic opera. NICHOLAS MATHEW

J. Everson, 'Of Beaks and Geese: Mozart, Varesco, and Francesco Cieco', *Music & Letters* (1995), 369–83
W. Mann, *The Operas of Mozart* (London, 1977), 322–30
H. Redlich, '*L'oca del Cairo*', *Music Review* 2 (1940), 122–31

offertory. Liturgically, offertories are antiphon texts from the *Proprium de Tempore* of the Mass and are performed at the start of the Liturgy of the Eucharist (Mass of the Faithful). Mostly derived from the Gospels of Luke and Matthew, the Psalms, or other Old Testament books, their texts usually refer to the Gospel reading of the day.

By the second half of the eighteenth century in German-speaking lands, however, there was inordinate flexibility in applying the designation 'offertory' to a particular text setting. Depending upon local parish customs, there was extraordinary leeway in the use of non-liturgical, 'free' texts for offertories (except during Advent and Lent). Thus, works which were not offertories in strict liturgical terms were designated so nonetheless. The practice of using new Latin poetry for an 'Offertoriumseinlage' (substitute offertory) apparently came from Italy. According to some sources, the term 'motet' rather than 'offertorium' was used when the polyphonic offertory was not liturgically proper but 'free', and by the second half of the eighteenth century the terms *Offertorium*, *Motette* and *Graduale* were being used quite loosely, often interchangeably.

Mozart's offertories reflect this loosening practice. Of his seven extant 'offertories' – all written for SALZBURG – only 'Benedictus sit Deus' is truly an offertory; the remainder use 'free' texts. A similar freedom in offertory texts is found in MICHAEL HAYDN, only sixteen of whose fifty-six Latin offertories are found in the Roman rite. As will be seen below, some of Mozart's offertories have texts that are also used outside the mass. 'Sancta Maria, mater Dei' (1777), K273, which is considered a Marian offertory by some sources is actually a Gradual and is therefore treated in the separate article SMALLER CHURCH WORKS.

Mozart's seven offertories are short, motet-like works of one to three movements, for chorus and/or soloists, accompanied by a small orchestra. Following local practices and examples by his Salzburg predecessors, the works are part of the final flowering of the polyphonic offertory, a genre that first appeared in the fifteenth century.

'Scande coeli limina', K34, is a C major offertory for the Feast of St Benedict (21 March). Allegedly, Mozart wrote it while staying at Seeon Monastery, Bavaria, in the autumn of 1766. The text is probably by a local monastic poet. It consists of two movements, Andante–Allegro: soprano aria 'Scande coeli' (ABA′ form; with strings only) and chorus 'Cara o pignora' (adding two clarini trumpets and timpani), and is accompanied by the conventional church trio (two violins, continuo bass and organ). For the profound question of the aria's middle section and coda ('What will happen to one's children left on earth?'), the music turns restless, approaches accompanied recitative and goes astray harmonically. In the following chorus of St Benedict's words, we hear God's assurance of protection. Trumpets and timpani announce God's arrival, and the basses declaim God's message. Mozart depicts the 'Coeli ut patria societ nos' ('so that the heavenly homeland may bring us together') with a texture that evolves from imitative to chordal for the repeated 'societ nos' ('bring us together'). Indeed, the precocious composer already understood the conventions of musical-textual rhetoric in church music.

'Benedictus sit Deus', K117, is Mozart's only liturgical offertory, albeit with a pastiche text wherein only its first movement sets an actual offertory. This is probably the 'grosses Offertorium' that, according to LEOPOLD MOZART's catalogue, was performed on 7 December 1768, for the dedication of the Waisenhaus-Kirche in VIENNA (cf. K47). The autograph score dates from October to November 1768. A. Einstein considered this the offertory used at the premiere of the 'Dominicus' mass', K66 (see MASS). There are three movements, fast–slow–fast: 'Benedictus sit Deus' (chorus), 'Introibo domum tuam' (soprano aria), and 'Jubilate Deo omnis terra' (chorus). The texts are, respectively, the offertory for Mass on Trinity Sunday, Psalm 66, and the Introit for the third Sunday after Easter. The instrumentation for the nine-minute work is the church string trio plus two trumpets, timpani, viola, and, in the second movement, two flutes, two horns, and an additional viola part.

'Benedictus sit Deus' (C major) is a joyful chorus with alternating homophonic and polyphonic phrases punctuated by trumpets and timpani. 'Introibo' (F major) is a two-part aria written for a soprano (castrato?) able to negotiate the movement's impressive coloratura and one cadenza. The flutes and horns here are merely decorative doublings. Early on, 'Introibo' was also disseminated as a separate work. After a cheerful homophonic opening, the sublime 'Jubilate' (C major) presents the eighth Psalm tone sung successively by each section of the chorus on 'Psalmum dicite' ('sing a Psalm').

'Inter natos mulierum', K72, is a single-movement chorus (Allegro moderato; G major) that was probably completed in May or June 1771. The autograph score is lost, however, and the earliest copies date from the late 1770s. The 'free' text, an encomium to St John the Baptist, who 'prepared the way for the Lord', and an invocation of Jesus as 'Lamb of God', is drawn from Matthew 11: 11 and John 1: 29. The first part of the text also serves as the fourth antiphon for second Vespers on the feast of St John the Baptist (24 June). Allegedly, the tender, recurring theme of 'Joanne, Joanne Baptista' and the 'Alleluja' at the end were part of Mozart's homage to a Pater Johannes of the Benedictine monastery at Seeon where the work may have premiered. The church string trio plus optional *colla parte* trombones (ATB) accompany the eight-minute chorus. The quieter second part of the movement, 'Ecce agnus Dei' (Behold the Lamb of God), offers an inspiring, prayerful contrast and seems to foreshadow Mozart's later *Ave verum corpus*, K618.

'Sub tuum praesidium', K 198, is a jewel of a soprano duet (Andante; F major) whose authenticity had been doubted until R. Münster discovered a late eighteenth-century copy in 1962. The date of the six-minute work remains uncertain. Comparison of internal characteristics with those of other works have led scholars to assign the work to Salzburg, and to 1774 or later. The church string trio accompaniment is augmented with an independent viola part. A nineteenth-century version of the offertory is arranged for soprano and tenor.

A Marian antiphon upon one of the oldest prayers for protection from the Blessed Virgin Mary, 'Sub tuum praesidium' was said after every Low Mass. In the Roman rite, it was also the antiphon before the Magnificat in Vespers of the Little Office of the Virgin. At Göttweig Abbey the antiphon was known as 'Offertorium de B.M.V.', while elsewhere it was used as a Gradual. At the Viennese court it was regularly included in settings of the Loreto Litany (cf. LITANY above). There is no evidence, however, that this 'Sub tuum' was used in that function.

Following an eighteen-bar ritornello, each soprano makes a similar but separate entry. Then, in a Mozartian dramatic stroke that foreshadows later operatic duets, like 'La ci darem la mano' from DON GIOVANNI, the two voices begin to interact more actively, as the second soprano 'interrupts' the first with pleas to the Virgin. A sonata-like form supports the drama, especially when the thematic/harmonic recapitulation occurs precisely at the point where the prayer asks the Virgin to 'reconcile us' with her Son ('Nos reconcilia'). The sense of reconciliation is confirmed by the two soloists harmonizing simultaneously for the first time. This coordination of sonata design with textual meaning supports the mid- to late 1770s as a date for the work.

'Misericordias Domini', K222, is a single-movement chorus (Allegro; D minor) of about eight minutes' duration. Mozart wrote the work during January or February 1775, while in MUNICH for a performance of LA FINTA GIARDINIERA. The offertory was first performed there on 5 March. In sending a copy to Padre MARTINI on 4 September 1776, Mozart explained that the Bavarian Elector had wanted 'to hear some of my contrapuntal music'. In his response of 18 December Martini was 'delighted' with the 'motet' and noted that it has 'all that is required by Modern Music: good harmony, mature modulation, a moderate pace in the violins, a natural connection of the parts and good taste'. In a letter of 20 November 1777, Mozart calls the work his 'contrapuntal Offertory in D minor'.

Based on a single line of text, the work alternates between the soft, solemn refrain of 'Misericordias Domini' and the loud, more agitated and melismatic STILE ANTICO polyphony of 'cantabo in aeternum' ('I shall sing for ever'). One of the two 'cantabo' subjects is based upon the motet 'Benedixisti Domine' by Mozart's Salzburg predecessor EBERLIN. Striking to modern ears is how each time the chorus chants 'Misericordia' in unison (bars 23ff., 49ff., etc.) there is an uncanny resemblance between the violins' legato counter-melody and Beethoven's 'Ode to Joy'. The accompaniment is the basic church trio; a doubling viola part is of questionable authenticity. The text slightly rearranges the opening five words of Psalm 89, a Psalm for the third Nocturn of Matins of the Nativity. Mozart's setting became one of the more popular offertories used at Vienna's Hofmusikkapelle.

'Venite populi,' K260, an *Offertorium de venerabili sacramento*, is dated Salzburg, 1776 (probably June), and is Mozart's only work for double chorus other than parts of the C minor Mass, K427. Accompanied by the church trio and optional *colla parte* trombones (ATB), this joyful six-minute work consists of three connected movements, fast–slow–fast: 'Venite populi' (D major), 'O sors cunctis beatior' (modulating), and 'Eja ergo epulemur' (G–D major). The origin of the text is unknown, but its poetry clearly celebrates the arrival of the Holy Sacrament at this part of the Mass. In 'Venite populi' various combinations of the two choruses reinforce the idea of inviting multitudes from far and wide to partake of the Eucharist. The choral writing recalls the Venetian polychoral style that spread to Salzburg in the seventeenth century. A prolonged dominant pedal surrounded by overlapping vocal entries increases the excitement and tension. For the description of the solemn Eucharist at 'O sors cunctis beatior' the tempo slows down, the mode changes, the harmonies become unsettled, and the choruses alternate dramatically between *forte* and *piano* phrases. The a cappella rendition of 'communio' is especially touching. The opening music returns in varied form for the closing, seemingly intoxicated celebration of the Communion feast. Brahms, who admired the offertory, both conducted and published the work.

The *Offertorium de B.M.V.* 'Alma Dei creatoris', K277, was composed in Salzburg, probably in the summer or autumn of 1777. The Marian offertory appeals for assistance from the Blessed Virgin Mary. Einstein suggests that the work was for the same occasion as the *Missa brevis*, K275. Using responsorial alternation between solo and choral renditions of the words, the six-minute, single-movement work (Allegro; F major) is in sonata form. The soprano soloist begins both the primary and secondary themes. The song-full melodies and the sudden *piano* for each 'mater clementissima' ('most merciful mother') are especially poignant. BRUCE C. MACINTYRE

J. I. Armstrong, Jr., *The Litany of Mary and Devotional Worship at the Eighteenth-Century Viennese Imperial Court* (Munich and Salzburg, 2000)
A. Einstein, *Mozart: His Character, his Works* (New York, 1945)
G. Krombach, *Die Vertonungen liturgischer Sonntagsoffertorien am Wiener Hof: Ein Beitrag zur Geschichte der katholischen Kirchenmusik im 18. und 19. Jahrhundert* (Munich, 1986)
The Liber Usualis (Tournai, 1956)
K. A. Rosenthal, 'The Salzburg Church Music of Mozart and His Predecessors', *Musical Quarterly* 18 (1932), 559–77
M. H. Schmid, *Mozart und die Salzburger Tradition*, 2 vols. (Tutzing, 1976)
C. H. Sherman and T. D. Thomas, *Johann Michael Haydn (1737–1806): A Chronological Thematic Catalogue of His Works* (Stuyvesant, NY, 1993)

opera. Opera (literally 'work') is an Italian feminine noun of international use, deriving from the expression 'opera in musica' or 'opera per musica'. It indicates a type of theatre in which the action is mainly carried out through music and a sung text. As late as the 1740s the term, in use since the seventeenth century, is not found in its musical meaning in the *Vocabolario degli Accademici della Crusca*; it achieved a sort of 'official' recognition through Francesco Algarotti's *Saggio sopra l'opera in musica* (1755). It was then synonymous with *melodramma* although this term became increasingly widespread from the nineteenth century on. Many other compound expressions have been used to designate various sub-genres or forms which became popular in particular times or places including opera seria (or opera regia) and opera buffa. Opera seria is in turn synonymous with *dramma per musica*, the latter being used more often by literati and/or in the context of literary discussion. 'Singspiel' is the term generally used for an opera with German text in which spoken dialogue is used instead of sung recitative.

The precise meaning of the term 'opera' must be established within specific historical contexts. As far as the Mozart literature is concerned, 'singspiel' generally refers to his works on German texts even though contemporary sources (including Mozart himself) chiefly use 'Oper' or 'opera'. Mozart, by his own account, considered opera one of his finest genres. Although a historical outline of opera is useful for a full understanding of Mozart's achievements, it should be clear that his own approach to musical theatre largely left out a historical sensibility in the modern sense, concentrating instead on the multifarious practical aspects of composing a successful work. Like other composers of the time, Mozart had no interest in studying the work of his remote predecessors; the only models relevant to him belonged to the immediately preceding generation (among them J. C. BACH and C. W. GLUCK). He also listened with interest to the works of selected contemporaries, such as G. PAISIELLO.

Although western examples of musical theatre or spoken theatre interspersed with music date back to the Middle Ages (or further, to classical Greek theatre, the music of which is, however, entirely lost), the birth of opera proper can be dated to around the end of the sixteenth century. An aristocratic endeavour promoted by intellectuals who convened at the house of Count Giovanni Bardi in Florence, opera in its initial phase was characterized by a desire to revive the intense effects of classical theatre by devising a type of vocal monody, exploiting the expressive as well as implicitly ethical potential of a literary text. In this sense, early opera represented a statement against the primacy of the predominantly polyphonic music of the time. A particular musical language was developed for such purpose, 'recitar cantando', the successful effect of which was mainly based on a high standard of vocal as well as rhetorical presentation.

Although a significant number of operas, based mainly on mythological subjects rewritten in Italian verse, were produced during the first decades of the seventeenth century (among the best known are *Euridice* on a text by O. Rinuccini, set by J. Peri for the Florence court in 1600, and *Orfeo*, on a text by A. Striggio set by Monteverdi for the Mantua court in 1607), the genre itself would deserve only a limited place in music history had it not met with favour among broader and more diverse audiences. This process started in 1637 with the opening of the first public opera house in Venice (Teatro S. Cassiano). While this did not imply an immediate popularization of opera, it paved the way for a progressive and comparatively fast increase in the number of opera houses in Italy and in other parts of Europe. About the middle of the seventeenth century, itinerant troupes performing mostly in makeshift theatres played an important role in opera's dissemination. But as specially built public houses became the main opera venue, the substance of the spectacle expanded beyond restrained aristocratic representations to include more elaborate and surprising plots, complicated and allusive scenography (at least by the standards of the time), farcical characters, vocal virtuosity based on melismatic melodies and ornaments, and a frequent indulgence in sexual allusion. Moreover, opera texts often nested more or less transparent political and/or ethical statements. This phase peaked towards the end of the seventeenth century in a type of show based on extremely convoluted plots, intended to increase opportunities for solo pieces (mostly arias), a relatively high number of characters, and a mix of tragedy and comedy (the latter usually confined in scenes relatively detached from the main plots, a sort of opera within an opera). The later part of the seventeenth century was also characterized by increased stability of the two general styles of operatic writing, recitative and aria.

As a rule, operas of this time were not produced for more than one run in the same city; the increase in opera houses, on the other hand, provided opportunities for the circulation of titles (and casts) in different cities. In Italy, the prevailing pattern of production was based on the central responsibility of a manager (impresario), frequently subsidized by the local public authorities, who was responsible for contracting the librettist, the musician, the scenographer and the singers. This was different from north of the Alps, where opera personnel were generally attached to one particular theatre or belonged to a stable opera company. Towards the end of the seventeenth and especially in the first decades of the eighteenth centuries, opera production assumed the character of a modern 'market' within which the balance of power mainly favoured the principal singers who came to represent the chief attractions of a composite type of entertainment. The ever-increasing production of operas, however, was not accompanied by stability of repertory; the stage life of each title (text and music) encompassed no more than ten to fifteen years (with rare exceptions). At the same time, the use of old librettos set to new music was established as a frequent (albeit not prevailing) pattern. This lasted until the end of the eighteenth century, affecting Mozart's and most other contemporary composers' output.

The multifarious spectacle of opera was strongly opposed in Italy by the literary movement known as *Accademia dell'Arcadia*, which first flourished in Rome in the last decade of the seventeenth century and soon assumed a pan-Italian character, eventually affecting the style of opera librettos all over Europe. This process is often referred to as the 'first reform' of opera. Reactions against the irrational traits of late-Baroque opera had a number of complex and interrelated consequences: from the beginning of the eighteenth century, a number of authors (*poeti* or, somewhat derogatively, *librettisti*) simplified their plots, reducing the number of characters to six or seven, and consequently the number of set-pieces (mostly arias with rare ensembles); at the same time, the literary worth of librettos improved (A. Zeno, who worked for the commercial theatre as well as for the Habsburg court in VIENNA, offered the best examples of this trend). All farcical elements were excluded from reformed opera seria and relegated to small comedies for two or three characters to be performed as entr'actes (*intermezzi*) by specialized actor-singers (Pergolesi's *La serva padrona* is the best-known example). Around the 1740s, longer and more complex comedies for music were developed and soon gained popularity in Italy and elsewhere. This type, named opera buffa or *commedia per musica*, became an alternative to opera seria, both on account of its characters (a mix of bourgeois, aristocratic and peasant) representing class and gender relationships in daily life (the best-known author in the genre was C. GOLDONI) and its subjects. With few exceptions, buffa and seria singers were specialists in their respective genres; castrati (male sopranos or altos) were especially valued and acted exclusively in seria productions. Also, the scenographies of buffa were often 'generic' and belonged to the theatre's stock, while seria productions boasted new sets as a special and almost regular attraction.

Opera buffa did not replace seria; the two genres had parallel developments throughout the century. In fact, opera seria peaked in the work of PIETRO

METASTASIO, whose *drammi per musica* became a model for most theatrical poets, writing either in Italian or in other languages. Metastasio was the successor of Zeno in Vienna and his position, no less than the elegance, dramatic effectiveness and musical functionality of his poetry, was important for the projection of his work on the broader European scene. Most of his librettos, according to theatrical practice, were slightly or substantially adapted by theatrical poets to local conditions.

A distinctive trait of opera buffa with respect to seria was the approach to musical forms and dramatic action. The action conveyed in buffa works was increasingly entrusted to set-pieces: *introduzioni*, ensembles and *finali*, consisting of long stretches of music sectionally articulated (chain-finales), with the participation of most or all characters, leading to a climax. By contrast, the paradigm of seria was to entrust almost all the dramatic-narrative progress of the action to the recitatives, while the set-pieces were reserved for lyrical or reflective moments in which characters expressed their feelings. This pattern of alternation was explicitly theorized by Metastasio and resulted in a limited formal flexibility compared to buffa. Towards the end of the century, a reaction to the rigidity of Metastasian seria resulted in the inclusion in opere serie of chain-finales (G. de Gamerra's *Pirro*, set by Paisiello in 1787, was the first self-conscious example), *introduzioni* and a greater number of ensembles. This trend also affected the modified versions of Metastasian librettos circulating at the time.

Rather distinct from but related to the evolution of 'Metastasian' seria was the so-called 'second' or 'Viennese' reform of opera seria, a product of the combined efforts of the poet RANIERI DE' CALZABIGI and of C. W. Gluck. Aiming at a more effective and powerful interpretation of the classical sensibility, this eminently intellectual project is best represented by works such as *Orfeo ed Euridice* first produced in Vienna in 1762 (a subject looking back to the beginnings of opera) and *Alceste* (Vienna, 1767). These works, while not entirely free of Metastasian features, avoid complications in the plot and largely reject simile arias and standard da capo form. They are based on a dramaturgical taste deriving in part from Calzabigi's experience of French *tragédie lyrique* (including large-scale tableaux and ballets). The aim of dramatic continuity and expressive intensity was fully achieved by Gluck's accompanied recitatives and multifarious musical forms.

Mozart experienced virtually every operatic sub-genre during his career. IDOMENEO was the mature work in which Mozart most clearly approached the Gluckian experience, but his finest achievements are generally considered to be his late opere buffe on texts by L. DA PONTE, written for Vienna (LE NOZZE DI FIGARO and COSÌ FAN TUTTE) and for PRAGUE (DON GIOVANNI). DIE ZAUBERFLÖTE, composed in his last year, soon came to be regarded as a sort of national German masterpiece and exerted a strong influence on subsequent generations. LA CLEMENZA DI TITO, his last opera, also circulated widely in German translations during the first decades of the nineteenth century but soon fell into oblivion until its revival during the late twentieth century.

At a more general level, Mozart managed throughout his career to manipulate the musical medium at such a high level of artistry that he made it the guiding dramaturgical element, taking at the same time full advantage of verbal and acting resources. This meant no less than a reversal of the centrality of the verbal text, which had in principle characterized opera from its beginnings. Mozart did not theorize this approach, although his self-consciousness in regard to this issue is clear in his letters. His operas provoked a deep fascination for many later composers, eventually affecting perceptions of the genre in its entirety.

SERGIO DURANTE

L. Bianconi and G. Pestelli, eds., *Storia dell'opera italiana* (Turin, 1988), esp. vols. IV–VI
D. Heartz, *Mozart's Operas*, ed. (with contributing essays) T. Bauman (Berkeley, 1990)
M. Hunter, *The Culture of Opera Buffa in Mozart's Vienna: A Poetics of Entertainment* (Princeton, 1999)
N. Till, *Mozart and the Enlightenment: Truth, Virtue and Beauty in Mozart's Operas* (London, 1992)

oratorio. Mozart's only complete oratorio, or *azione sacra*, is *La Betulia liberata* (K118), composed in 1771 to a libretto by PIETRO METASTASIO. Mozart received the commission on his first visit to Italy, accompanied by his father LEOPOLD MOZART. It was intended for performance in Padua, as Leopold relates in a letter to his wife from Vicenza, dated 14 March 1771. Leopold mentions the work again a few months later (19 July) in a letter written from SALZBURG to Count Gian Luca PALLAVICINI (of Bologna), and notes that it had been commissioned by Don Giuseppe Ximenes, Prince of Aragon, presumably for performance at his private residence. Ximenes was a well-known musical patron in Padua, and apparently preferred earlier music to that of his contemporaries. He was well informed on musical matters, and corresponded with the theorist and pedagogue Padre MARTINI. Mozart's oratorio was completed in Salzburg during the summer of 1771, but not performed in Padua, as planned; perhaps the music proved too modern for Ximenes's rather conservative tastes. The lack of documentary evidence on this point leaves the question unsettled. It is unlikely that the oratorio had been intended for performance in Lent 1771, as some writers have suggested, since this would have left Mozart only two weeks to complete it – a difficult task while simultaneously travelling around Italy. Moreover, Leopold's second letter indicates that he expected to attend a rehearsal in Padua on his second visit to Italy, which lasted from August to December of that year. A setting of the same libretto by the local composer Giuseppe Calegari took place in Padua in 1771, presumably in place of Mozart's version. Mozart later intended to rework some of his oratorio to satisfy a commission from the Viennese Tonkünstler-Sozietät, as he asked NANNERL MOZART to send him a copy of it (letter of 21 July 1784); this plan was not fulfilled, however, and *La Betulia liberata* remained unperformed.

In southern GERMANY and AUSTRIA, Italian oratorio was cultivated at courts that favoured Italian opera, such as VIENNA and Dresden. Oratorios were usually performed at times of year when opera was not permitted, namely Advent and Lent. Holy Week in particular was marked by an oratorio, often on the theme of the Passion, termed a *sepolcro*, since the setting usually included a depiction of Christ's tomb; after about 1705 *sepolcri* were often supplanted by performances of oratorios on other subjects. Salzburg was a noted centre of oratorio performance, with JOHANN ERNST EBERLIN, Leopold Mozart and MICHAEL HAYDN all contributing settings. Wolfgang's earliest foray into this genre was composing the first part of a three-part work in German, *Die Schuldigkeit des ersten Gebots* (K35), in 1767; parts 2 and 3, by Michael Haydn and ADLGASSER, have not survived.

Mozart's setting employs a libretto by Metastasio dating back to 1734, which was originally commissioned by the Emperor Charles VI to be set by Georg Reutter. Since Ximenes disliked most contemporary music, which he believed did not respect the 'true principles of counterpoint' (as he observed in a letter dated 15 Jan. 1781), his choice of an early libretto by a well-respected author, Metastasio, is hardly surprising. It had been set by several other composers before Mozart, including Jommelli (1743), and Holzbauer (1752); later versions were composed by KOZELUCH (c.1780), Schuster (1787) and SALIERI (1821). Metastasio was one of the leading librettists for both oratorios and opere serie in Vienna in the period 1730–40. Although usually set in the original Italian, some of his librettos were set in translation; Eberlin's *Das Leiden unsers Heilanders Iesu Christi* is based on a German version of Metastasio's *La Passione*.

The subject of *La Betulia liberata* is drawn from the Old Testament (Apocrypha) Book of Judith. Metastasio begins his libretto at the point where the Israelites, besieged in the city of Bethulia by the Assyrians, under the command of their general Holofernes, beg their governor Ozìa to surrender. He agrees to do so if the siege is not lifted within five days. Giuditta (Judith), a pious young widow, gains entry to the enemy's camp on the pretext of betraying her city; she feasts with Holofernes, pretends to seduce him and, when he has fallen asleep, kills him and bears his head back to Bethulia. A sudden attack by the Israelites then defeats the Assyrians, who are caught unawares, and without their general. Achior, a former ally of Holofernes, is initially horrified by the sight of Holofernes' head, but acknowledges the power of the Israelites' god, and converts to Judaism. Metastasio situates the events inside the city of Bethulia, so that most of the action occurs offstage, a common dramatic technique in the *azione sacra*. His libretto serves to emphasize Judith's unswerving courage in the face of adversity, and the victory achieved though her perseverance, thereby drawing a moral from this tale of violence and conflict. Achior's conversion is upheld as a demonstration of the power of true faith.

Mozart's accomplished setting of *La Betulia liberata*, cast in an appropriately heroic mould, demonstrates his familiarity with the conventions of the opera seria tradition. It draws on the experience he had gained the previous year by writing the opera MITRIDATE, RE DI PONTO for the Teatro Regio Ducale in MILAN. There are six soloists in this oratorio (of whom three are soprano/castrato roles), a chorus and orchestra, which includes horns and trumpets. In addition to independent choral movements, the chorus participates in the drama through its dialogue with both Ozìa ('Pietà se irato sei') and Giuditta ('Lodi al gran Dio'), and is even heard briefly during a recitative. The integration of the chorus in this manner recalls the operatic developments of GLUCK. Two accompanied recitatives for Giuditta display Mozart's command of dramatic techniques. Although aged only fifteen, he had also clearly mastered the established aria types common to both oratorio and opera seria. Achior's 'Terribile d'aspetto' (No. 7) with its trumpet scoring and vigorous bass-line is a typical 'rage aria'. A contrasting mood is illustrated by 'Con troppa rea viltà', a heartfelt plea for mercy, sung by Amital (a noble Israelite woman). Scored for strings alone, it consists of two contrasting thematic ideas, in different tempi, which alternate with each other. Amital's second aria, 'Quel nocchier che in gran procella' makes extreme demands on the soloist, encompassing long sustained notes in high register, large leaps and virtuosic coloratura passages. Most of the full-length arias employ modified versions of da capo form, usually with the opening ritornello abridged on its return.

The work concludes with 'Lodi al gran Dio', a large-scale chorus in two parts. It begins in E minor with a choral setting of the well-known 'tonus peregrinus' chant, alternating with solo verses sung by Giuditta; this leads directly into a victorious D major chorus. The oratorio is preceded by a stirring overture in D minor, featuring two trumpets and four horns. It is tripartite in form, with the three sections (Allegro–Andante–Presto) connected by incomplete cadences. Despite its smaller scale, the overture is also noteworthy for pre-dating Mozart's Symphony in G minor, K183 – his first in a minor key – by two years.

La Betulia liberata marks an important stage in Mozart's development as a dramatic composer. Within the conventions of the oratorio, he created an effective musical setting that anticipates, in certain modest respects, his later achievements in the operatic realm. MICHAEL QUINN

D. Neville, 'Opera or Oratorio? Metastasio's Sacred "Opere serie" ', *Early Music* 26 (1998), 596–607

S. Sadie, 'Mozart's "Betulia liberata" ', *Musical Times* 109 (1968), 1015–17

H. E. Smither, *A History of the Oratorio*, vol. III: *The Oratorio in the Classical Era* (Chapel Hill, NC, 1977), 34–42, 76–83, 340–7

N. Zaslaw, *Mozart's Symphonies: Context, Performance Practice, Reception* (Oxford, 1989), 184–5

orchestra. Mozart composed over 300 works that involve the participation of an orchestra. These include symphonies, operas, concertos, masses and other liturgical music, sets of dances and other works. Almost all of these pieces were written with a particular orchestra in mind. DIE ENTFÜHRUNG AUS DEM SERAIL, LE NOZZE DI FIGARO and COSÌ FAN TUTTE, for example, were written for the orchestra at the Burgtheater in VIENNA, MITRIDATE and LUCIO SILLA for the orchestra of the Teatro Regio Ducale in MILAN, DON GIOVANNI for the orchestra of the National Theatre in PRAGUE. Mozart composed symphonies for the orchestra of the Archbishop's court in Salzburg (K114, K124, K128, K130 etc.), for the orchestra of the Concert spirituel in PARIS (K297), for the private Kapelle of the Thun family (K425), and for the theatre orchestra in Prague (K504). Mozart often participated in performances of his orchestral works: as the soloist in piano and in violin concertos; as the keyboard player in operas and other vocal works; and as a violinist in symphonies and serenades.

Notwithstanding the immediacy of this connection between orchestra and work, Mozart did not tailor his music to the orchestra for which he wrote it to anywhere near the extent that he tailored an aria for a particular singer. By the last half of the eighteenth century the orchestra had become considerably standardized as an institution in the larger cities and courts of Europe. The orchestra of a London concert hall contained more or less the same instruments in more or less the same proportions as the orchestra of a German court or an Italian opera house. Mozart conceived most of his orchestral works for the 'same' orchestra, an ensemble of first and second violins, violas, cellos and double basses, plus pairs of oboes, horns and bassoons. Flutes were available in most orchestras, but they were often played by the oboists; trumpets and timpani were available as needed. Most orchestras also included a keyboard instrument – organ in church, harpsichord for opera, organ, harpsichord or piano in concert settings. In a few instances (usually in operas) Mozart called for special instruments, not available in most orchestras: piccolo (*Entführung*, *Zauberflöte*), mandolin (*Don Giovanni*), trombones (*Don Giovanni*, *Zauberflöte*), basset horn (*Così fan tutte*, *La clemenza di Tito*). Clarinets constitute a special case, because they were just coming into fashion during Mozart's lifetime and were available in some orchestras but not in others. Mozart had an opportunity to write for them first in MUNICH (IDOMENEO) and in Paris (Symphony K297), and they were available for many of his Viennese orchestral works.

Because he composed his orchestral music for a more or less standard ensemble, Mozart could perform the same works with several different orchestras. On their grand tour through Holland, France and Germany in 1765–6 and on their visits to Italy (1769–73), the Mozarts carried young Wolfgang's symphonies with them, both in score and as sets of parts, to be performed by the orchestras of the courts and towns where the young prodigy showed off his talents. In his Viennese concerts of the 1780s, Mozart often programmed music that he had written earlier in his career for other orchestras. For example at the concert of 23 March 1783 at the Burgtheater the orchestra played an aria from *Lucio Silla*, originally written for the orchestra of the Teatro Regio Ducale in Milan, an aria from *Idomeneo*, written for the MUNICH court Kapelle, the 'Haffner' symphony (K385), written for the Archbishop's Kapelle in Salzburg, and the Piano Concerto in D major, K175, written for Salzburg and performed also at Munich (1774) and at Mannheim (1778). When the resources of the orchestra at hand differed from those of the original orchestra, Mozart sometimes adjusted the scoring. For the Burgtheater concert he added flutes and clarinets to the first and last movements of the 'Haffner' symphony; he rewrote the oboe and horn parts of the concerto K175, and he composed an entirely new rondo (K382) for the last movement.

Some of the orchestras for which Mozart composed were much larger than others. Mozart's largest orchestras were probably the eighty and more instrumentalists who performed his symphonies, concertos and a cantata at the Tonkünstler-Sozietät concerts in Vienna. It is impossible to know which were the smallest, perhaps the orchestras at some of the churches around Salzburg, which consisted of only a few violins, a double bass and an organ, with trumpets or horns added for festive occasions. Not all church orchestras were small, however. In a letter from Mannheim in 1777 Mozart describes an orchestra of over forty instruments that played High Mass on All Saints' Day. The unfinished mass that Mozart began at Mannheim (K322) seems to have been intended for this large orchestra. The orchestras that played Mozart's operas also varied greatly in size. *Mitridate* at the Teatro Regio Ducale in Milan in 1770 was played by an orchestra of over fifty, with fourteen first and fourteen second violins, according to LEOPOLD MOZART's count. *Don Giovanni* was premiered by an ensemble about half as big, the orchestra of the National Theatre in Prague, with only four violins in each section. Mozart's symphonies were performed by orchestras ranging in size from the orchestra of fifty-six at the Concert Spirituel, which introduced the 'Paris' symphony, to an orchestra at the City Theatre in Frankfurt which had only five or six violins, with whom Mozart performed symphonies and piano concertos at a benefit concert during his tour in 1790.

The two places in which Mozart worked for the longest periods and where he composed the most orchestral music were Salzburg and Vienna. The orchestras and the orchestral milieux in the two cities were very different. Salzburg was a small ecclesiastical principality with a limited number of instrumentalists, most of them members of the Prince-Archbishop's Kapelle. Vienna was a world of musical freelancers, where a large number of instrumentalists made their livings playing in several orchestras. Table 1 shows some Salzburg orchestras that played Mozart's music or with which he was connected in some way. Table 2 shows some of Mozart's Viennese orchestras.

Mozart's Salzburg orchestras have been described in detail by Cliff Eisen. The instrumentalists of the Archbishop's Kapelle functioned as an orchestra in several different contexts. They played concerted masses, vespers, other liturgical music and even symphonies in the cathedral. They played at concerts, musical academies and other entertainments that the Archbishop gave at court. The Kapelle also accompanied sung Latin school dramas at the Benedictine University, and each year in August it played a serenade (*Finalmusik*) at the university's graduation exercises. During the second half of the eighteenth century the Salzburg Kapelle contained between twenty and thirty players, exclusive of trumpeters and organists (table 1). In the cathedral, however, it often performed at less than full strength, as shown by an 'Ordnung' dated 1746 and also by sets of parts in the cathedral archives (see table 1). On the other hand, when necessary the Kapelle could muster more than thirty instrumentalists, because many of the trumpeters doubled on stringed instruments. At court concerts the Kapelle's numbers were swelled by noble dilettantes, like the Archbishop himself and his nephew Count CZERNIN, both of whom often joined the orchestra on violin. Besides the court Kapelle Salzburg had two other groups of professional instrumentalists: the town waits, who sounded the watch on brass instruments and provided music for civic events, and the Archbishop's military music, which included a parade band, a wind ensemble (*Harmonie*) and Turkish music. Members of these ensembles could be called upon to reinforce the Kapelle as needed. Mozart often took the opportunity in his letters to express his poor opinion of the Archbishop's Kapelle: the court musicians were 'coarse', 'slovenly' and 'dissolute' and the orchestra was required to play 'far too many performances'. These utterances may reflect Mozart's exasperation with Salzburg in general and with the Archbishop in particular rather than a considered judgement of the quality of the Kapelle.

Besides the court, the cathedral and the university, there were other less official contexts for orchestral music in Salzburg. Minor nobility and prominent burghers often commissioned music and hired orchestras to celebrate special occasions. For example Mozart composed his serenade K185 for the graduation of Judas Thaddäus von ANTRETTER, a family friend, and the serenade K250 for the marriage of Elisabeth HAFFNER and Franz Xaver Späth. It is hard to tell how large or small the orchestras were for these and similar occasions, because no lists of players have survived. Mozart's Salzburg serenades and

Table 1. *Mozart's Salzburg Orchestras*

Date, venue	Keyboard	Bowed strings	Woodwinds	Brass and percussion	Mozart works performed
1746 – Salzburg Cathedral	1 organ	8 violins and violas 1 cello 1 double bass	3 bassoons	3 trombones	
1757 – Court Kapelle	3 organs	10 violins 2 violas 3 cellos 2 violoni	3 oboes 4 bassoons	2 horns 1 trombone 10 trumpets 2 timpani	
1760s?, Benedictine University	[1 harpsichord]	12 violins 2 violas 1 cello 2 double basses	2 oboes 1 bassoon	2 horns	*Apollo et Hyacinthus*, K38
1768, Court Kapelle	2 organs	11 violins and violas 2 cellos 2 double basses	2 oboes 2 bassoons	3 horns 10 trumpets 2 timpani	Serenade K62a, 74g?
1775?, Cathedral	2 organs	8 violins 2 double basses	2 bassoons	2 trumpets 2 trombones 1 timpani	Mass K220 (196b)
1778, Czernin's amateur orchestra	1 harpsichord	8 1st violins 6 2nd violins 2 violas 5 cellos 3 double basses	2 oboes	2 horns	
1780, Court Kapelle	3 organs	13 violins 2 violas 2 cellos 4 double basses	5 oboes (flutes) 3 bassoons	2 horns 9 trumpets 2 timpani	Symphonies K318, 319, 320, 338, 385, 425

Sources: Eisen 1992; Marpurg; Eisen 1992; Hintermaier; Eisen 1992; *Mozart Briefe* (12 April 1778); Hintermaier

cassations were clearly intended to be performed with several string players on a part, while pieces entitled 'divertimento' were more likely to be one-to-a-part music. Most likely some of the performers were drawn from the Archbishop's Kapelle, while others were amateurs. Some orchestras were composed almost entirely of dilettantes, like the orchestra of twenty-eight members that Count

Table 2. *Mozart's Viennese Orchestras*

Date, work, venue	Keyboard	Bowed strings	Woodwinds	Brass and percussion	Work
April 1774, Kärntnertor-theater		13 violins 2 violas 3 cellos 4 double basses	2 oboes ? bassoons	2 horns 1 trumpet 1 timpani	*Thamos König in Ägypten*, K345
3 April 1781, Tonkünstler-Sozietät, Kärntnertor-theater		40 violins 8 violas 9 cellos 11 double basses	2 flutes 7 oboes 2 cors anglais 6 bassoons	4 horns 2 trumpets 1 timpani	Symphony K338?
July 1782, Burgtheater	[1 harpsichord]	6 1st violins 6 2nd violins 4 violas 3 cellos 3 double basses	3 flutes 2 oboes 2 clarinets 2 bassoons	4 horns	*Die Entführung aus dem Serail*, K384
Feb.–Mar. 1785, Mehlgrube Concert		12 violins 4 violas 3 cellos 4 double basses	2 flutes 2 oboes 2 clarinets 2 bassoons	4 horns 2 trumpets 1 timpani	
23 Dec. 1785, Tonkünstler-Sozietät	?	19 1st violins 19 2nd violins 6 violas 7 cellos 7 double basses	2 flutes 6 oboes 4 bassoons	4 horns 2 trumpets 1 timpani 2 trombones	Piano concerto, K482?
May–Dec. 1786, Burgtheater	[1 harpsichord]	6 1st violins 6 2nd violins 3 violas 3 cellos 3 double basses	2 flutes 2 oboes 2 clarinets 2 bassoons	2 horns 2 trumpets [timpani]	*Le nozze di Figaro*, K492
16–17 April 1791, Tonkünstler-Sozietät		18 1st violins 19 2nd violins 8 violas 8 cellos 6 double basses	2 flutes 7 oboes 2 clarinets 4 bassoons	4 horns 2 trumpets 1 timpani	soprano aria symphony
Sept. 1791 Theater auf der Wieden		3 1st violins 3 2nd violins 2 violas 1 cello 2 double basses	2 flutes 2 oboes 2 clarinets [and basset horns] 2 bassoons	2 horns 2 trumpets [3 trombones] 1 timpani	*Die Zauberflöte*, K620

Sources: Edge 1992; *Mozart Briefe* (11 April 1781); Edge 1992; Edge 1992; Edge 1992; Edge 1992; Edge 1992; Schönfeld

Czernin organized to meet every Sunday at the LODRON palace to play symphonies, arias and concertos.

When Mozart moved to Vienna in 1781 he entered an orchestral milieu of a very different sort. The imperial court Kapelle played only a minor role in Viennese musical life. The most important standing orchestras were those at the Burgtheater, where several of Mozart's operas were introduced, and the Kärntnertortheater, where his operas were repeated and where he performed in many concerts. Dexter Edge has described these orchestras in detail. Both numbered about thirty players, with twelve or thirteen violins and pairs of winds, including clarinets (see table 2). The Burgtheater and Kärntnertortheater orchestras included most of the best instrumentalists in Vienna, and there was considerable demand for their services. On evenings when there was no opera or spoken drama in the theatres, the musicians were free to play in other orchestras, at public concerts or in the homes of wealthy patrons. Members of the theatre orchestras also turn up on the rosters of Viennese churches, as participants in dance orchestras, and as members of the imperial Kapelle. Theatres in the Vienna suburbs also maintained standing orchestras, but somewhat smaller than those of the theatres in town. The theatre in Leopoldstadt had an orchestra of twenty-five in 1796; the orchestra at Schikaneder's Theater auf der Wieden, where *Zauberflöte* premiered, numbered twenty-four.

Concert orchestras in Vienna were seldom standing ensembles; instrumentalists were usually engaged for the occasion, either for a single concert or for a series. No personnel records have been preserved from Mozart's subscription concerts, but his orchestras on those occasions can probably be assumed to have been similar to those of the two major theatres. Indeed, according to GYROWETZ, Mozart engaged the entire Burgtheater orchestra for his subscription concerts at the casino in the Mehlgrube in 1785. The semi-annual benefit concerts of the Tonkünstler-Sozietät, which sponsored a pension fund for the families of musicians, featured orchestras with seventy-five and more instrumentalists; Viennese musicians were obliged to volunteer their services or to pay a fine. Mozart remarked enthusiastically in a letter about the large size of the orchestra that had performed one of his symphonies at a Tonkünstler concert in April 1781. The cantata (*Davidde penitente*), concert arias and piano concertos that he contributed to other concerts were probably played by large orchestras as well. Mozart was also associated for a time with the entrepreneur PHILIPP JAKOB MARTIN, who organized concerts in the Mehlgrube and the Augarten. 'The orchestra' Mozart informed his father, 'consists principally of dilettantes, with the exception only of the bassoons, the trumpets and the drums.' Music-loving Viennese aristocrats held concerts in their homes, often on a weekly basis, and often with fairly large orchestras, again consisting mainly of amateurs.

The orchestras for which Mozart composed and with which he performed elsewhere in Europe resembled his Salzburg and Vienna orchestras to a considerable extent in make-up and in social role (table 3). The orchestra that performed his *Galimathias musicum* in The Hague 1766 was the court Kapelle of William V of Orange, similar in size and shape to the Archbishop's Kapelle in Salzburg. *Mitridate* in Milan in 1770 was accompanied by the orchestra of the Teatro Regio Ducale, similar to the orchestras in the Viennese theatres, but with

Table 3. *Mozart's European Orchestras*

Place, date, venue	Keyboard	Bowed strings	Woodwinds	Brass and percussion	Work
The Hague, 1766, Installation of William V		15 violins and violas 3 cellos 2 double basses	4 oboes and flutes 2 bassoons	4 horns 6 trumpets 1 timpani	K32
Mantua, Jan. 1770, Teatrino del Accademia Filarmonica		6 violins 2 violas 1 cello 2 double basses	2 oboes 1 bassoon	2 horns	3 symphonies
Milan, Dec. 1770, Teatro Regio Ducale	2 harpsichords	14 1st violins 14 2nd violins 6 violas 2 cellos 6 double basses	4 flutes and oboes 2 bassoons	4 horns 2 trumpets 1 timpani	*Mitridate, re di Ponto*, K87
Mannheim, Nov. 1777, High Mass at Court	[1 organ]	10–11 1st violins 10–11 2nd violins 4 violas 4 cellos 4 double basses	2 flutes 2 oboes 2 clarinets 4 bassoons	2 horns trumpets timpani	
Paris, 18 June 1778, Concert spirituel		22 violins 5 violas 8 cellos 5 double basses	2 flutes 2 oboes 2 clarinets 4 bassoons	3 horns 2 trumpets 1 timpani	'Paris' symphony, K297
Munich, Jan. 1781, Residenz-theater	[2] harpsichords	12 violins 2 violas 2 cellos 2 double basses	1 piccolo 2 flutes 2 oboes 2 clarinets 2 bassoons	4 horns 2 trumpets 1 timpani	*Idomeneo*, K366
Prague, 1787, Nationaltheater	[1 harpsichord]	8 violins 2 violas 1 cello 2 double basses	2 flutes 2 oboes 2 clarinets 2 bassoons	2 horns 2 trumpets 1 timpani [3 trombones]	'Prague' symphony, K504, *Don Giovanni*, K527
Dresden, 14 April 1789, Concert at Elector's palace		20 violins 6 violas 4 cellos 5 double basses	2 flutes 4 oboes 4 bassoons	4 horns [2] trumpets [1] timpani	'Coronation' piano concerto, K537?
Leipzig, 12 May 1789, Gewandhaus Conzert		12 violins 3 violas 2 cellos 2 double basses	2 flutes 2 oboes 2 bassoons	2 horns 2 trumpets	K528 (concert aria), 'Jupiter' symphony, K.551?

Sources: De Smet; Deutsch; *Mozart Briefe* (15 Dec. 1770); *Mozart Briefe* (4 Nov. 1777); *Almanach* 1779; Zaslaw 1991; Schönfeld; Mahling; Schering

more violins. The orchestra at the Concert spirituel, for which Mozart wrote his 'Paris' symphony in 1778, was a professional concert orchestra, something as yet unknown in Vienna or Salzburg. Its membership overlapped to a considerable extent, however, with the orchestra of the Paris Opéra. Compared to Viennese orchestras it had more cellos and fewer double basses, but otherwise its proportions were similar. *Idomeneo* in 1781 was accompanied by the Munich court Kapelle, many of whose members Mozart knew already as members of the Mannheim Kapelle, which LEOPOLD MOZART called 'indisputably the best orchestra in Germany', and whose concert master, Christian CANNABICH, Wolfgang called 'the best orchestra leader I have even seen'. The Munich Kapelle had to be reduced somewhat to fit in front of the stage at the Residenztheater, but there was also an offstage band. The orchestra of the National Theatre in Prague, which premiered both *Don Giovanni* and the 'Prague' symphony (K504) was small compared to those of the Burgtheater and Kärntnertortheater. On the other hand, the orchestra at the Leipzig Gewandhaus, an amateur concert society that had turned into a professional orchestra and with which Mozart performed on his tour of 1789, closely resembled the theatre orchestras in Vienna.

The calibre of the orchestras that Mozart encountered on his travels through Europe varied widely. In 1766 Leopold listed in his travel diary the names of the members of an orchestra that performed his son's works in Dijon, along with judgements of their abilities. The violinists were 'asses, all of them' (*asini tutti*); the violist was 'a scraper' (*un racleur*), and the oboists were characterized (in English) as 'rotten'. On the other hand the orchestra they encountered in Mantua was 'not bad', according to Wolfgang, and the orchestra in Cremona was actually 'good'. The orchestra of the Concert spirituel in 1778 sounded so bad in the rehearsal that Mozart contemplated snatching the concert master's violin and leading the 'Paris' symphony himself; but in concert they played well enough that the audience applauded a passage midway through the first movement and another in the last.

Mozart's scoring practices in his orchestral works depended on the genre of the music and on the available orchestra. The so-called 'high classical' scoring, with strings in four parts and pairs of flutes, oboes, clarinets, bassoons, horns and trumpets plus timpani, is found almost exclusively in operas. Only theatre orchestras, by and large, included clarinets and had separate players for flutes and oboes. The 'Paris' symphony (K297) has this scoring because it was written for the Concert spirituel; so does the revision of the 'Haffner' symphony for the Burgtheater. In the symphonies, serenades and concertos written for Salzburg and for his tours, Mozart usually scored for strings plus pairs of oboes and horns, with trumpets and drums added for festive occasions. Flutes replace oboes either for individual movements (K110, K133, K185) or for entire pieces (K130, K134, K209), standard practice in eighteenth-century orchestral music, since the instruments were played by the same persons. In symphonies and concertos written after his move to Vienna in 1781, Mozart often added a single flute alongside the two oboes, a scoring that few other composers used. Some of Mozart's earlier works with trumpets lack drum parts (K125, K181, K184, K250 etc.), but it is quite possible that timpani were added ad lib in performance. In operas written for large orchestras Mozart occasionally scored for four rather than two horns (*Mitridate*, *Idomeneo*), and likewise in a few symphonies he wrote for Salzburg (K130, K132, K318), where court trumpeters could be enlisted to play horn.

In church music – masses, vespers, church sonatas – Mozart often scored for two violins and bass without viola, even in rather large-scale works (K167, K257, K262, K337). Other sacred works do have viola parts (K127, K165, K195, K273), and it is not clear whether the difference has to do with the size of the orchestra, the intended venue, or other factors. In dance music Mozart almost always omitted violas; the only exceptions are ballets written for theatre orchestras. The omission of violas in dance music seems to have been a matter of convention rather than necessity, since personnel rosters for dance orchestras list many violinists, most of whom could play viola if needed. On the other hand Mozart not infrequently scored for violas on two separate parts, sometimes as a temporary divisi (K74b, K139) and sometimes for entire movements (K84).

Throughout his career Mozart maintained the notion of the basso, a single bass-line that could be played by several sorts of instruments simultaneously, and he almost always wrote 'basso' on the lowest part of his orchestral scores. The basso might be played by double basses, cellos, bassoons and/or keyboard (harpsichord, piano, organ). Over the course of his career Mozart increasingly tended to give each of the bass instruments its own part. Before about 1775 an obbligato part for one or two bassoons was a special effect that Mozart used in an occasional opera aria (K51, K126, K135). And a few Salzburg serenades and symphonies have obbligato parts (K183, K203, K250). After his trip to Mannheim and Paris in 1778, Mozart began to give the bassoons their own part in most of his orchestral music. Mozart never gave cellos and double basses separate staves in his scores, and his copyists usually wrote out the same part for both instruments, but he made increasing use of cues, usually to let the basses drop out in soft or difficult passages, but sometimes to take advantage of the tone colour of one or the other instrument.

The presence or absence of a keyboard instrument on the basso part in Mozart's works is a contentious issue. When the orchestra accompanied a singer or singers, Mozart would almost certainly have expected a keyboard to realize the basso line – organ in church music, harpsichord in the theatre. The keyboard set the tempos, kept the singers on pitch, and filled in when they missed their entrances. In Italian theatres there were two harpsichords in the orchestra. For the first three performances of *Mitridate* in Milan, Mozart played harpsichord himself as was customary for the composer to do, while Lampugnani, the resident *maestro*, played second harpsichord. In piano concertos, the soloist played along with the orchestral bass in the tutti sections; for this purpose the basso line was written into the soloist's part, with occasional cues or figures. In purely orchestral works, like serenades, symphonies and concertos for other instruments leadership of the orchestra was clearly the responsibility of the first violinist, as Mozart's comment about Cannabich above emphasizes. However, a keyboardist may have played along on the basso nonetheless. A letter from Leopold states that in the concert at the Lodron Palace (see Table 1) NANNERL MOZART 'accompanied all the symphonies' on a harpsichord, though Czernin, a violinist was manifestly the leader. ABBE VOGLER reported from Mannheim at about the time Mozart visited that symphonies were 'accompanied' by a keyboard instrument; this was musically unnecessary, he said, since all the harmonies were written into the instrumental parts. At the Concert spirituel in Paris, on the other hand, the keyboard did not play in orchestral music: in his fantasy of taking over the leadership of the 'Paris' symphony, Mozart chose the violin rather than the harpsichord as his instrument. JOHN SPITZER

Almanach des spectacles de Paris . . . (Paris, 1752–91)

M. De Smet, *La Musique à la cour de Guillaume V, prince d'Orange* (Utrecht, 1973)

O. E. Deutsch, ed., *Mozart und seine Welt in zeitgenössischen Bildern* (Kassel, 1961)

D. Edge, 'Mozart's Viennese Orchestras', *Early Music* 20 (1992), 64–88

'Manuscript Parts as Evidence of Orchestral Size in the Eighteenth-Century Viennese Concerto', in *Mozart's Piano Concertos: Text, Context, Interpretation*, ed. N. Zaslaw (Ann Arbor, 1996), 427–60

C. Eisen, 'Mozart's Salzburg Orchestras', *Early Music* 20 (1992), 89–103

'The Scoring of the Orchestral Bass Part in Mozart's Salzburg Keyboard Concertos: The Evidence of the Authentic Copies', in *Mozart's Piano Concertos: Text, Context, Interpretation*, ed. N. Zaslaw (Ann Arbor, 1996), 411–26

E. Hintermaier, 'Die salzburger Hofkapelle von 1700 bis 1806, Organisation und Personal' (Diss., Salzburg, 1972)

C.-H. Mahling, 'Orchester und Orchestermusiker in Deutschland von 1700 bis 1850' (Diss., Saarbrücken, 1971)

F. W. Marpurg, ed., *Historich-kritische Beyträge zur Aufnahme der Musik, vol. III (Berlin, 1757)*

Mozart Briefe und Aufzeichnungen, ed. W. A. Bauer and O. E. Deutsch (Kassel, 1962–75)

A. Schering, *Musikgeschichte Leipzigs*, vol. III (Leipzig, 1941)

J. von Schönfeld, *Jahrbuch der Tonkunst von Wien und Prag* (Vienna, 1996)

J. Spitzer and N. Zaslaw, *The Birth of the Orchestra: History of an Institution, 1650–1815* (Oxford and New York, 2004)

E. K. Wolf, 'On the Composition of the Mannheim Orchestra, ca. 1740–1778', *Basler Jahrbuch für historisches Musikpraxis* 17 (1993), 113–38

N. Zaslaw, *Mozart's Symphonies: Context, Performance Practice, Reception* (Oxford, 1989)

'Mozart's Orchestral Flutes and Oboes', in *Mozart Studies*, ed. C. Eisen (Oxford, 1991), 201–11

'Mozart's European Orchestras', *Musicology Australia* 17 (1994), 13–18

Organ Solo Mass, 'Orgelmesse'. Mozart's *Missa brevis* in C, K259. See MASS

P

Paisiello, Giovanni (b. Roccaforzata, near Taranto, 9 May 1740; d. Naples, 5 June 1816). Famed above all for his opere buffe, Paisiello worked for most of his life in Naples, aside from eight years in St Petersburg (1776–84) and two in VIENNA (1802–4). He met Mozart in Naples in mid-1770, in Turin in early 1771 and in Vienna in 1784 on his way back to Naples from Russia. On the latter occasion, he attended a private concert given by Mozart and his pupil BARBARA VON PLOYER (13 June 1784); Mozart duly reciprocated by going to the premiere of Paisiello's *Il re Teodoro in Venezia* (23 August) at the Burgtheater. (The opera was performed another thirteen times before the end of the year.) In his 'Reminiscences' (1826) MICHAEL KELLY, the original Don Basilio and Don Curzio in LE NOZZE DI FIGARO and a popular singer in Vienna in the 1780s, recalled one of the meetings between Paisiello and Mozart in 1784: 'it was gratifying to witness the satisfaction which they appeared to feel by becoming acquainted; the esteem which they had for each other was well known'.

Paisiello was easily the most popular operatic composer at the Viennese court theatres during Mozart's decade in the city (1781–91) – he had over a hundred more performances in this period than SALIERI, his nearest rival. Mozart exploited Paisiello's widespread popularity by composing new settings of a number of arias from his operas, including 'A questo seno deh vieni', K374 (1781) from *Sismano nel Mogol* and 'Mentre ti lascio', K513 (1787), from *La disfatta di Dario*, for FRANCESCO CECCARELLI and Gottfried von JACQUIN respectively. Writing to ALOYSIA LANGE (née Weber) from PARIS (30 July 1778) Mozart encouraged her to sing his setting of 'Ah lo previdi' (K272) from Paisiello's *Andromeda*, originally written for Josepha DUSCHEK (1777), 'for I assure you that it will suit you admirably – and that you will do yourself great credit with it'. A few years later in a letter to LEOPOLD MOZART (29 Mar. 1783) Mozart reported playing his newly composed piano variations on 'Salve tu, Domine' from Paisiello's *I filosofi immaginari* (K398) to great acclaim at a Viennese concert.

SIMON P. KEEFE

M. Hunter, *The Culture of Opera Buffa in Mozart's Vienna: A Poetics of Entertainment* (Princeton, 1999)

Pallavicini family. Count Giovanni Luca Pallavicini and his distant relative Cardinal Count Lazzaro Opizio Pallavicini, enthusiastic patrons of the arts based in Bologna and Rome respectively, acted generously towards Mozart and LEOPOLD MOZART on their first Italian sojourn in 1770. Before Mozart and Leopold arrived in Bologna, the Milanese Count Karl Joseph FIRMIAN wrote a letter to Gian Luca (14 Mar. 1770) recommending Mozart as 'one of those musical talents but rarely produced by nature, in as much that at his tender age he not only equals the Masters of the art, but even exceeds them, I believe, in readiness of invention'. Gian Luca duly received the Mozarts, had them perform at a concert attended by 150 noblemen (26 March) and agreed in his reply to Firmian (28 March) that Mozart was 'a boy of such singular talent'; on the same day he also wrote to Lazzaro of the 'prodigy' of 'truly extraordinary merit', asking for him to be received in Rome. After arranging a performance for Mozart, Lazzaro remarked to Gian Luca on Mozart's 'truly amazing' talents; a few months later (5 July) he presented Mozart with his papal order insignia, three days before Mozart's formal audience with the Pope. Heading back north after visits to Rome and Naples, Mozart and Leopold (sporting a fairly serious shin injury as a result of a coaching accident) stayed at Gian Luca's country residence near Bologna (10 Aug.–1 Oct. 1770). Mozart reported 'often' performing MICHAEL HAYDN minuets to Gian Luca's wife, Countess Maria Caterina, at this time (letter to NANNERL MOZART, 22 September). SIMON P. KEEFE

Paradies, Maria Theresia von (b. Vienna, 1759; d. Vienna 1 Feb. 1824). Blind from the age of three, Paradies became one of VIENNA's leading pianists in the 1780s. She completed successful European concert tours between 1783 and 1786, calling on Mozart and LEOPOLD MOZART in SALZBURG in the autumn of 1783. (Mozart and Constanze visited Leopold between late July and late October.) Mozart is presumed to have written his Piano Concerto in B flat, K456, for her; she may have performed it on tour in PARIS, LONDON, Brussels or Berlin in October 1784. Her travels certainly took her to London in 1785 – her presence in the city is recorded in the *Public Advertiser* on 9 March 1785. From the late 1780s onwards her musical activities were primarily confined to teaching and composition. SIMON P. KEEFE

E. Komorzynski, 'Mozart and Marie Therese Paradis', *Mozart-Jahrbuch* 1952, 110–16

Paris. Capital of France. During the 'Grand Tour' of 1763–6, the Mozarts were in Paris from 18 November to 24 December 1763, from 8 January to 9 April 1764 and from 10 to 17 May and 2 June to 8 July 1766. At first they lodged with the Bavarian envoy, Maximilian Emanuel Franz Graf von Eyck (1711–77) in the rue St Antoine at the Hôtel Beauvais (today 68 rue François Miron, Paris X). One of their sponsors was the Regensburg-born BARON FRIEDRICH MELCHIOR GRIMM, who on 1 December 1763 praised the Mozart children in his periodical *Correspondance littéraire*: 'True prodigies are sufficiently rare to be worth speaking of, when you have had occasion to see one. A Kapellmeister from SALZBURG, Mozart by name, has just arrived here with two children who cut the prettiest figure in the world. His daughter, eleven years of age, plays the harpsichord in the most brilliant manner . . . Her brother, who will be seven years old next February, is such an extraordinary phenomenon that one is hard put to believe what one sees with one's eyes and hears with one's ears. It means little for this child to perform with the greatest precision the most difficult pieces.'

On Christmas Eve 1764, the Mozarts travelled to Versailles, lodging at the hotel 'Au Cormier' in the rue des Bons-Enfants (today rue du Peintre-Lebrun), near the palace. On New Year's day they attended Louis XV's gala evening assembly; Madame de Pompadour, whom LEOPOLD MOZART described as a woman 'of great arrogance', was present. Wolfgang played on the organ in the royal chapel; NANNERL MOZART also performed. For these appearances, Leopold received the above-average sum of 1,200 livres.

Although the weak-willed Louis XV's policies were wasteful and extravagant, he sought to bring the state's finances into better order; nevertheless craftsmen, workers and peasants sank deeper into misery. As far as Louis was concerned, his chief enemies were England and Prussia.

On 8 January 1764, the Mozarts returned to Paris where they met with several expatriate German musicians including JOHANN SCHOBERT, Christian Hochbrucker and GOTFRIED ECKARD, all of whom composed accompanied sonatas and, according to Leopold's letter of 1 February, adored his children. Wolfgang's first printed works, the accompanied SONATAS K6–7, dedicated to Madame Victoire de France (Louise-Marie-Thérèse de Bourbon), were published on 1 Feburary 1764. On 10 March and 9 April, Wolfgang and Nannerl gave concerts at the theatre of M. Félix in the rue et porte Saint-Honoré. In April, the accompanied sonatas K8–9, dedicated to Comtesse Adrienne-Catherine Tessé, were published. And before their departure for LONDON, Leopold had Christian von Mechel produce an engraving of the family based on a painting by Louis Carrogis *dit* Carmontelle.

It is striking that in their correspondence the Mozarts say nothing about performances at the Académie Royale de Musique – it seems that operatic life in the capital was of little interest to them. At the time of their first visit to Paris, only older works by Rameau and Mondonville were performed. It was only in 1766 that the family could hear a real novelty, Monsigny's *Aline, Reine de Golconde* (first performed on 15 April 1766). So Parisian opera had little influence on Mozart's works – what was important were the singers, dancers and scenic designs.

More than ten years later, after Mozart had left court service, he and his mother arrived at Paris on 23 March 1778, where they stayed in the rue Bourg l'Abbé with a Herr Mayer, an agent of the AUGSBURG merchant Joseph Felix Arbauer. At this time, a battle raged between supporters of GLUCK and supporters of Piccinni; if Mozart wanted to get ahead he would have to take sides. But he remained neutral. Above all, he wanted to write for the orchestra of the Concert spirituel and on 7 March 1778 he wrote to his father, 'I've now got all my hopes pinned on Paris.' These hopes were not fulfilled. The Parisian public, the court and influential nobles gave him little notice. In 1763 he had been a *Wunderkind*; in 1778 he was just another artist among artists, another musician among musicians. Both Wolfgang and his father were mistaken if they thought the name Mozart would travel from mouth to mouth and that everyone would remember the child of 1763. So Mozart had to appeal to influential patrons. Grimm, who had sponsored the Mozarts before, was not a great help and Wolfgang required entirely more substantial and broad-ranging backing to succeed, backing that he did not have – in fact he altogether rejected the idea of appealing and paying respect to those who were influential. He seems to have had no contact with Grétry, director of the Comédie Italienne, and neither Philidor or Francœur, music master of the Chambre du Roi, gave him any help.

The most distinguished philosophers of the time, including Voltaire and Diderot, were both concerned with the relationship between music and the

French and Italian languages. Voltaire saw arias as moments of reflection, which demanded carefully calculated situations. Diderot, on the other hand, looked for 'real' tragedy, calling for a mixture of genres, even generic confusion, which – like real life – mixed tragedy and comedy. Other important thinkers at the time included d'Alembert, who wanted to see opera renewed but was little interested in instrumental music, and Rousseau, who was particularly concerned with French as an operatic language and played the French and Italians against each other. Under any circumstances, music theatre was the chief interest in Paris and instrumental music, a flourishing private concert life notwithstanding, was of secondary importance.

It is no surprise that Mozart did not compose an opera for the Académie Royale de Musique: new French operas were not in demand, and because Mozart had not yet composed a well-known and frequently played Italian opera, a new one by him would have been a risky venture. (Coincidentally, during his lifetime, not one of his operas was performed in Paris.) As a result, Mozart's lack of success resulted in part from the policies of the opera director, Devismes, who favoured Italian operas that were inexpensive to produce and already known. Primarily, however, it was Mozart's own fault: he over-valued himself, did not understand the intrigues of the Parisian music world, and was oriented chiefly to Italian music; Leopold Mozart thought that Wolfgang was unsuccessful in adapting himself to the French style.

In May 1778 the director of the Concert spirituel, JOSEPH LEGROS, commissioned a symphony from Mozart. Legros had fundamentally revamped the concerts: he contracted internationally known soloists, programmed contemporary works (included works by German composers such as J. C. BACH, CANNABICH and JOSEPH HAYDN and Italians such as Anfossi, Cambini, Jommelli and Sacchini), and reduced the size of the chorus and orchestra.

Mozart probably composed his 'Paris' symphony, K297, at the end of May and into the beginning of June; the successful first performance was on 18 June. Legros was exceptionally happy with the work and told Mozart it was the best symphony he had – except for the Andante which Mozart replaced with a new one for a performance on 15 August. The final version exceeded by far the dimensions of Mozart's earlier symphonies and, according to the *Spectacles de Paris*, the orchestra that performed it included twelve first and ten second violins, six violas, eight cellos, six double basses, two flutes, two oboes, two clarinets, two or possibly four bassoons, two horns, two trumpets and timpani; among the distinguished performers were the concert master Pierre La Houssaye, the second concert master Marie-Alexandre Guénin, the violist Anton Stamitz, the cellist Jean-Louis Duport and the double bassist Jean-Baptiste Rochefort. It is surprising, therefore, that Mozart had a low opinion of the ensemble; he even wrote to his father that at one point he considered jumping on the stage, taking the concert master's violin and directing himself (letter of 3 July).

In order to support himself, Mozart arranged to give well-paid lessons, even if these frequently bored him. We have his acquaintance with Adrien-Louis de Bonnières, Comte de Guines, a highly decorated military man and one-time envoy in Berlin and LONDON, to thank for the Concerto for Flute and Harp, K299. According to Wolfgang, the Count, a music lover and patron par excellence, was an incomparable flautist and his daughter 'magnificent' on the harp. Mozart gave the Countess composition lessons in May and although the commission for the concerto came early in Mozart's stay, by 31 July he had still not been paid; the work itself, composed for virtuoso dilettantes, represents a type that was all the vogue in Paris.

Mozart's acquaintance with the dancer and choreographer J.-G. NOVERRE, from 1776 ballet master at the Académie Royal de Musique, resulted in his music for *Les petits riens*, which was performed on 11 June together with Piccinni's opera buffa *Le finte gemelle*. The ballet, only part of which was composed by Mozart, was performed six times. About this time, Mozart also composed a Sinfonia concertante (K297B) for the Concert spirituel, for Johann Baptist WENDLING (flute), FRIEDRICH RAMM (oboe), GIOVANNI PUNTO (horn) and Georg Wenzel Ritter (bassoon). The autograph is lost, as are all contemporaneous copies. But the work may be preserved, at least in part, by a nineteenth-century manuscript, now in Paris, of a sinfonia concertante for flute, clarinet, horn and bassoon (KAnh C14.01).

In the end, though, whatever his successes or failures, the 1778 visit to Paris was overshadowed by a single event: the death of his mother on 3 July.

RUDOLF ANGEMÜLLER (TRANS. CLIFF EISEN)

'Paris' symphony. Mozart's Symphony No. 31 in D, K297 (1778). See PARIS and SYMPHONIES

patronage. For musicians of Mozart's father's generation and earlier, there were limited possibilities for employment, chiefly as a servant in a household or court or attached to a religious institution. Exceptions to this feudal pattern of employment were rare. After an early period where, accompanied by his father, Mozart exhibited his talent through extensive concertizing in the cities of Europe, his career was secured in the traditional manner when he was appointed paid Konzertmeister by the newly elected Archbishop of SALZBURG, HIERONYMUS COLLOREDO in 1772. (Mozart had first been appointed to the Salzburg court music in 1769, during the reign of SIGISMUND SCHRATTENBACH, but without pay.) Petitioning the Archbishop for leave in 1777, Mozart left court service, albeit temporarily, and embarked on further concert tours to MUNICH, AUGSBURG, MANNHEIM and PARIS. He was reappointed in 1779 as court and cathedral organist. Mozart held these posts until an altercation with the Archbishop during a visit to VIENNA in 1781, when his contract was terminated. He remained in the capital thereafter and embarked on a quasi-freelance career.

Through the efforts of the imperial court and its aristocrats, Vienna was recognized after 1750 as a major European music capital and a centre of musical prestige. During the final quarter of the century, from roughly 1775 onwards, the traditional aristocratic *Hauskapellen* (resident house ensembles) were disbanding. Their decline was recorded by the ennobled publisher Johann Schönfeld who noted in his 1795 publication, *Jahrbuch der Tonkunst von Wien und Prag*, that 'this worthy custom has been lost – one house orchestra lost after another, so that, apart from Prince Schwarzenberg, perhaps no more exist'. In place of the *Hauskapellen* came a growing cadre of quasi-freelance musicians and the earliest forms of public concerts, and it is into this context that Mozart was thrust when he made Vienna his new home in the early 1780s.

The enterprise of music patronage was socially significant and those who took part did so for a variety of reasons – love of music was often intertwined with the pursuit of social status. As the *Hauskapellen* continued to decline, Vienna's aristocrats continued their involvement in musical affairs by supporting musicians through salon performances, after-dinner concerts and balls as well as larger-scale events. The Gesellschaft der Associierten Cavaliere, for example, albeit founded by BARON GOTTFRIED VAN SWIETEN who was not himself a member of 'first society', was otherwise composed of Vienna's most highly ranked aristocrats. The group organized private concerts, usually held at Prince Joseph Schwarzenberg's palace. It was active well into the 1800s, growing gradually more powerful as it absorbed three of Vienna's most important public concert venues later on.

On the surface, these new patronage practices appeared compatible with older formats because events were controlled by Vienna's 'old' aristocrats (that is, not by members of the newly ennobled or 'second society' and not directly by members of the middle class). But the newer organization was conducive to the rise of independent musicians, most of whom, however, enjoyed at best a modicum of autonomy in Mozart's day. Dependent upon teaching as a primary income source, musicians had to rely for the most part on ad hoc modes of making a living. The emergence of quasi-freelance forms of income was not initially accompanied by improved economic status; if anything, the general economic position of musicians declined. During these transition years, musicians relied upon the patronage of aristocrats and yet, at the same time, they were far less likely to benefit from *Naturgeld*, the non-cash presents of food and other necessary goods and clothing. Other options available at the time were emigration, in order to work as the house musician or Kapellemeister in a foreign court, or an itinerant virtuoso career, managed by a handful of Mozart's contemporaries (Johann Samuel Schroeter, MUZIO CLEMENTI and the blind female pianist, MARIA THERESIA PARADIES).

The benefit and subscription concert – one of the most 'public' forms of presentation in Mozart's day – was still a rarity. Mozart profited from a subscription series in 1784 and was pleased to report that he had managed to attract 174 subscribers, thirty more than his two rivals (Georg Friedrich Richter and LUDWIG FISCHER) together. But in 1789 when he attempted to mount a second series, the response was disastrous with only one subscriber, his patron and key backer at that stage, van Swieten. The failure of Mozart's proposed subscription series in 1789 should not be read as a clear indication of his growing unpopularity during the late 1780s, but rather as an indication of a more general decline of aristocratic interest in the public concert forum.

Late eighteenth-century Viennese society was rigidly hierarchical and often perceived as 'haughty' by foreign observers. Historians of the AUSTRIAN aristocracy have observed that the old and established aristocrats were actively concerned with distancing themselves from their newly ennobled counterparts. Yet the mechanics of the newly emerging basis of music patronage during the final quarter of the eighteenth century made it possible for members of the second society and middle class to lead more or less the same sort of musical life as an aristocrat: they could patronize the same musicians and hear music by the same composers (albeit at different times and in different places). By the late eighteenth century, Vienna's older aristocrats thus risked being dispossessed of the primary means for maintaining their identities as cultural leaders. Whether or not they were conscious of the fact, they thus had an interest in impeding large-scale public and commercial developments in musical life, which they could and did accomplish by continuing their musical affairs in private, through the sponsorship of exclusive music in socially sequestered venues. It would appear that the tendency in favour of public musical life was curtailed during the late 1780s and into the 1790s and the feudal mould was modified rather than broken at the time of Beethoven's arrival in Vienna in 1792. Key among Mozart's patrons and subscribers were PRINCE KARL LICHNOWSKY, who escorted Mozart on a foreign concert tour in the 1780s, Baron van Swieten, who encouraged Mozart's interest in older musical forms and counterpoint, and Count Johann Joseph Anton Thun-Hohenstein (see THUN), whose guest Mozart was in Linz and PRAGUE.

Because musical life remained dependent on the activities of individuals rather than institutions, employment opportunities for musicians were far less regular and made for especial hardship. For a composer like BEETHOVEN in the 1790s, it was advantageous to comply with the aristocrats since the institutional mechanisms for commercial musical life that were available during this time in places such as LONDON were not present in Vienna. For Mozart, who during the 1780s had begun to make the tenuous journey towards occupational independence, the shift away from public sponsorship later in that decade frequently placed his livelihood in peril. TIA DENORA

T. DeNora, *Beethoven and the Construction of Genius* (Berkeley and London, 1995)
H. C. Robbins Landon, *Mozart: The Golden Years* (London, 1988)
J. Moore, 'Mozart in the Market Place', *Journal of the Royal Musical Association* 114 (1989), 18–42
M. S. Morrow, *Concert Life in Haydn's Vienna: Aspects of a Developing Musical and Social Institution* (New York, 1989)

performance practice. Generally understood as the study of how Mozart's music was performed in his own day, and in particular how he himself might have performed his works, performance practice is nevertheless a complicated issue, encompassing not only questions of ensemble, tempo, dynamics, articulation and ornamentation, but also the extent to which modern-day performers ought to be bound by performance practice studies.

The make-up of Mozart's ensembles is in some ways the least problematic practice to reconstruct: numerous documents survive detailing the size and seating plans of the orchestras that performed his music. These range from small ensembles with few or no winds and only a handful of violins to the enormous orchestra of the Tonkünstler-Sozietät, at which Mozart gave several of his own works. The size, nature and direction of these ensembles is dealt with separately (see ORCHESTRA). CONCERTOS, however, may represent an exception to the standard orchestral ensemble, at least during the years before 1780. Evidence from the family letters and surviving parts used by Mozart suggests that for the concertos to K365, Mozart's orchestra included double basses but not violoncellos. This would ally the genre with that of the orchestral SERENADE, which according to current thinking also dispensed with cellos. There are historical grounds for associating the two genres in SALZBURG:

orchestral music in Salzburg prior to about 1750 consisted chiefly of serenades that included two or three soloistic concerto movements; the composition of these sorts of concertos pre-dates the writing of independent solo concertos and therefore, in a sense, represents its origin. It would not be surprising, then, to discover that they shared a common scoring. For concertos written after Mozart's move to Vienna, the evidence shows that Mozart regularly wrote parts for cellos. This, too, is in line with contemporary practice: the splitting of the orchestral bass-line into its chief components – cello, double bass and bassoon – was more or less accomplished and standardized by this time.

The scoring of Mozart's chamber music, especially during the Salzburg years, is also not clear. Salzburg traditions included some exotic scorings with or without cello on the bass-line; early trios can use a variety of instruments for the lower part. Although it is likely that this was frequently the cello, it cannot be assumed that this was always the case. The string quintet K174, for example, may have been intended for a double bass; not only is Mozart's terminology equivocal (the part is labelled 'basso', a generic term) but similar, exactly contemporaneous examples by MICHAEL HAYDN are unequivocally scored for that instrument. As with orchestral music, the situation is less fraught after 1780 when almost without exception Mozart's chamber music is scored for ensembles that by then had become more or less standardized in VIENNA: string quartets with two violins, viola and violoncello, and quintets with two violins, two violas and violoncello. The watershed represented by 1780, which not only mirrors general European practice but also the biographical fact of Mozart's leaving Salzburg, is less applicable to his keyboards. Although his earliest keyboard music was conceived with the harpsichord in mind, it is clear by the mid-1770s his works were intended for the piano, as a letter to LEOPOLD MOZART of 17 October 1777 describing the pianos of J. A. STEIN shows:

> Before I had seen any of his make, Späth's . . . had always been my favourites. But now I much prefer Stein's for they damp ever so much better than the Regensburg instruments. When I strike hard, I can keep my finger on the note or raise it, but the sound ceases the moment I have produced it. In whatever way I touch the keys, the tone is always even. It never jars, it is never stronger or weaker or entirely absent; in a word, it is always even. It is true that he does not sell a pianoforte of this kind for less than three hundred gulden, but the trouble and the labour which Stein puts into the making of it cannot be paid for. His instruments have this special advantage over others that they are made with escape action. Only one maker in a hundred bothers about this. But without an escapement it is impossible to avoid jangling and vibrations after the note is struck. When you touch the keys, the hammers fall back again the moment after they have struck the strings, whether you hold down the keys or release them. He himself told me that when he has finished making one of these instruments, he sits down to it and tries all kinds of passages, runs and jumps, and he shaves and works away until it can do anything.

Metronomes are an invention of the nineteenth century; although there were various late eighteenth-century attempts to fix tempos (usually based on the normal heart rate of a mature male), tempo words give only a general idea. And tempo is almost always related to character: both C. P. E. BACH and

Leopold Mozart, for example, state that tempo derives from 'mood' and from a consideration of the fastest notes in a movement or characteristic passage, which 'shows' the correct tempo. Tempo also depended on genre and performing venue: an allegro in church music is almost always slower than an allegro in chamber music; the large physical space and reverberance of a church necessitated slower tempos that allow the music to 'speak' clearly. Charles Avison, in his *Essay on Musical Expression* of 1752, makes exactly this point: 'The words Andante, Presto, Allegro, etc., are differently apply'd in . . . different kinds of music . . . For the same terms which denote lively and gay in the opera or concert style, may be understood in the practice of church-music as . . . serene; wherefore, the Allegro etc. in this kind of composition should always be performed somewhat slower than is usual in concertos or operas.' Other conventions governing the choice of tempo relate to the concept of fixed tactus, a relationship among all tempos generally in which, other things being equal, time signatures with smaller denominators move more quickly than those with larger ones, and to dance types which inform specific passages or even whole movements: Mozart himself, for example, noted that Italian minuets are slower than GERMAN ones and include more notes.

Numerous eighteenth- and early nineteenth-century treatises give charts relating tempos to each other; more or less they agree on which tempos are slower and which are faster. One problematic case, however, is Andantino: for some this is considered slower than Andante, for others faster. Evidence deriving from Mozart, scanty though it is, suggests that for him Andantino was a slower tempo, sometimes approaching Larghetto. One peculiarity of Mozart's notation deserves special mention: whereas treatises often give a vast array of possible tempos, both Leopold, in his violin method, and Mozart, in his autographs, use a relatively restricted range of tempo indications. It is tempting to see in this a tacit recognition of the necessity to divine the correct tempo according to character, venue and genre. As a general rule, though, it is probably safe to say that tempos were generally faster in the eighteenth century: this applies not only to allegros and minuets, but in particular to andantes, which were generally considered movements to be taken at a 'walking' tempo; the idea of a genuine 'slow' movement, common to the nineteenth and twentieth centuries, is on the whole foreign to Mozart. Tempo modification – at least the agogic type of rubato where stretches of a movement are taken either faster or slower – was also probably foreign to the composer except possibly in soloistic movements (and even there changes in tempo would have been slight). But a rubato that allowed the right hand to linger behind the left was common; writing to his father in 1777, Mozart noted that 'they all marvel that I always stay in strict time. They don't realize that tempo rubato in an adagio does not apply to the left hand.'

Articulation is central to Mozart's musical style, a fact borne out by the details of his slurs and staccato markings. There is still controversy about whether Mozart used two signs, the dot and the stroke, for his staccatos, as well as the intended meaning of the two. Although several treatises of the time distinguish between them, or at least admit the possibility that some composers see them differently, Leopold Mozart's violin treatise mentions only the stroke. And a careful study of Mozart's autographs and the copies used by him to perform his music shows that, except for dots under slurs, Mozart wrote only strokes, even if through haste these sometimes approximate dots. But the stroke did not have the specific meaning then that it does now, a short, light articulation. It could also denote a more weighty articulation akin to the later accent sign (which does not appear in Mozart's autographs), mark phrase endings or serve to countermand a previous articulation, usually a slur. It is up to the performer to decide, given the musical context, which type of articulation a stroke represents. Slurs, according to Leopold Mozart and other contemporaneous treatises, represent not only legato – it is assumed that the absence of a slur means some degree of separation between notes – but also diminuendos, with the last note under a slur normally lighter and shorter; in keyboard music, slurred Alberti basses are understood to indicate a finger pedal, the holding down of the bottom note throughout the group.

Mozart sometimes uses dynamics in imaginative ways, differentiating various musical strands through their dynamic levels. There is, however, no clear evidence of what the eighteenth century considered to be loud or soft in absolute terms. Nevertheless, Mozart is generally clear about indicating the dynamic shape of a movement and this serves to articulate not only a broad structure but also specific affective gestures. It is unlikely, for example, that changes in dynamic level represent a sudden change from loud to soft or soft to loud; more often than not these markings should be understood as nuanced movement towards a new dynamic level. Part of the misunderstanding concerning Mozart's dynamics derives from modern, normalized publishing conventions which always reproduce his *forte* and *piano* as *f* and *p*. Quite often, however, Mozart's spelling is *for*: or *pia*:, spread across several notes. Significantly, perhaps, these expanded spellings often occur where phrases are elided, inviting the speculation that such markings do not indicate sudden dynamic change but dynamic gradation, crescendo and diminuendo. Numerous examples can be found throughout Mozart's works.

Improvised ornamentation is, by its nature, the least fixed and most difficult, perhaps, of eighteenth-century performance practices. It is commonly understood that such ornamentation was expected in slow movements, on long-held notes and in repeats. But it could also be applied elsewhere although in moderation, as examples from Mozart show: ornamentation by him survives for piano sonatas, arias and, in one instance, for the piano concerto K450; these are reproduced in most modern editions of his works and can serve as a guide to improvising ornamentation where none survives. The prosodic appoggiatura represents one thorny issue: where the last two notes of a vocal phrase drop a third, it is sometimes common to fill in the leap; but it is unclear whether this was universally applied in the eighteenth century or not. In any case, virtually all eighteenth-century treatises warn against excessive ornamentation: as with other aspects of performance practice, proper execution depends chiefly on the innate good 'taste' of the performer. Fixed or notated ornamentation, including trills, turns, mordents and appoggiaturas, was widely described at the time, although practice varied from place to place and author to author. Perhaps the best guide to notated ornamentation in Mozart is his father's

Gründliche Violinschule of 1756, which gives numerous examples of realized ornamentation.

A final question remains: having discovered (as far as possible) how Mozart is likely to have performed his works, are present-day performers obligated to play his works the way we think he performed them? By and large this question revolves around the issues of 'the work' and compositional authority. One school of thought holds that 'works' exist, that a text represents only a pale reflection of the substance of a composition, at best a road map to its performance and meaning, something that can be divined only by an insightful performer – who in turn speaks 'for' the composer. Another view, however, suggests that the surviving evidence – chiefly Mozart's autographs and performing parts – documents successive stages in the performance of a piece and that, as performances, these texts may give us an idea how Mozart performed but, more importantly, obligate us to think for ourselves rather than slavishly follow convention (old or new) or try to speak for the composer. It was, after all, Mozart's practice to reinterpret his music at each successive performance; it seems likely, therefore, that he expected others to interpret as well.

CLIFF EISEN

H. M. Brown and S. Sadie, eds., *Performance Practice. Music after 1600* (New York and London, 1989)

C. Eisen, 'Notation and Performance', in *A Performer's Guide to Classical Music*, ed. A. Burton (London, 2002), 15–38

C. Lawson and R. Stowell, *The Historical Performance of Music: An Introduction* (Cambridge, 1999)

R. Levin, 'Performance Practice in the Music of Mozart', in *The Cambridge Companion to Mozart*, ed. S. P. Keefe (Cambridge, 2003), 227–45

L. Mozart, *Versuch einer gründlichen Violinschule* (Augsburg, 1756; English trans. E. Knocker as *A Treatise on the Fundamental Principles of Violin Playing*, Oxford, 1948)

S. Rosenblum, *Performance Practices in Classic Piano Music* (Bloomington, IN, 1988)

R. Stowell, *Violin Technique and Performance Practice in the Late Eighteenth and Early Nineteenth Centuries* (Cambridge, 1985)

R. Taruskin, *Text and Act* (Oxford, 1995)

petits riens, Les. Mozart's ballet music, K299b, performed in PARIS on 11 June 1778. See BALLETS and NOVERRE, JEAN-GEORGES

piano concertos. See CONCERTOS

piano quartets. See CHAMBER MUSIC: E. PIANO QUARTETS

piano quintet. Mozart Quintet for Piano and Winds, K452. See CHAMBER MUSIC: F. MIXED ENSEMBLES

piano trios. See CHAMBER MUSIC: D: PIANO TRIOS

Pleyel, Ignaz Josef (Ignace Joseph) (b. Ruppersthal, 18 June 1757; d. Paris, 14 Nov. 1831). One of Europe's most famous musicians in the last two decades of the eighteenth century, Pleyel studied with JOSEPH HAYDN in his youth (c.1772–7), travelled to Italy in the early 1780s and worked in Strasburg (c.1784–95) and LONDON (1791–2) – where his works competed with those of Haydn given at the SALOMON concerts in the same season – before moving to PARIS in 1795. Here he set up a prestigious publishing house, later adding piano making to his firm's business activities. He enjoyed extraordinary popularity early in his career, CHARLES BURNEY remarking (1789) that 'lately . . . a rage for the music of Pleyel . . . has diminished the attention of amateurs and the public to all other violin music', and a critic for the London-based *Morning Herald* (1791) pointing out that he 'is becoming even more popular than his master [Haydn], as his works are characterized less by the intricacies of science than the charm of simplicity and feeling'.

Mozart encountered Pleyel's first set of string quartets, Op. 1 (1782–3), in VIENNA, writing to LEOPOLD MOZART (24 Apr. 1784): 'I must tell you that some quartets have just appeared, composed by a certain Pleyel, a pupil of Joseph Haydn. If you do not know them, do try to get hold of them; you will find them well worth the trouble. You will see at once who was his master. Well, it will be a lucky day for music if later on Pleyel should be able to replace Haydn.' It is possible that Pleyel's dedication of his next set of quartets, Op. 2 (1784), to Haydn inspired Mozart to do the same with his own six quartets K387, K421, K428, K458, K464 and K465, published in Vienna in 1785. SIMON P. KEEFE

R. Benton, *Ignaz Pleyel: A Thematic Catalogue of his Compositions* (New York, 1977)
J. Kim, 'Ignaz Pleyel and His Early String Quartets in Vienna' (Ph.D. thesis, University of North Carolina, Chapel Hill, 1996)
I. Pleyel, *Six String Quartets, Op. 1*, ed. S. P. Keefe (Ann Arbor, 2005)

Ployer, Maria Anna Barbara von (b. Sarmingstein, Upper Austria, 2 Sept. 1765; d. c.1811). Barbara Ployer was Mozart's student in 1784. He wrote two piano concertos for her, K449 in E flat (begun in 1782–3 and completed on 9 Feb. 1784) and K453 in G (12 Apr. 1784). She certainly performed K453 on 13 June 1784 at the home of Gottfried Ignaz von Ployer (her father's cousin) in Döbling on the outskirts of VIENNA, playing the Sonata for Two Pianos in D, K448, with Mozart at the same concert. Nine months later on 23 March 1785, COUNT KARL ZINZENDORF recorded a 'marvellous' performance by Ployer in his diary. Ployer's father, Franz Kajetan von Ployer (1734–1803) readily recognized the impact Mozart's association with his daughter had had on her career, describing Mozart in 1787 as '[surpassing] all in divine Apollo's art'. SIMON P. KEEFE

W. Senn, 'Barbara Ployer, Mozarts Klavierschülerin', *Österreichische Musikzeitschrift* 33 (1978), 18–28

'Posthorn' serenade. Mozart's D major Serenade, K320 (3 Aug. 1779). See SERENADE

Prague. At the time of Mozart's visits to Prague, between 1787 and 1791, it was the capital of Bohemia and the Czech crown lands, and second largest city in the AUSTRIAN Empire. A solid tradition of musical education established after Austrian domination of the Czechs in the seventeenth century, and to a large extent propagated by a network of Jesuit schools and seminaries, meant that Prague provided considerable opportunities for visiting musicians. Paradoxically, many native musicians did not choose to remain in Prague; while generally approving of the high standards of Czech musicians, BURNEY was quick to observe of their situation: 'a man of genius among them, becomes an admirable musician . . . ; but, when that happens, he generally runs away, and settles in some other country, where he can enjoy the fruit of his talents'.

Although Prague developed a well-founded municipal musical scene in the mid-nineteenth century, in the eighteenth the material circumstances of Czech musicians were largely dependent on the aristocracy. While many of the most significant Czech-Austrian nobility had palaces in Prague, they were predominantly resident near the imperial court in VIENNA. In fact, a considerable number of them, including members of the Waldstein and Sternberg families, and the Princes Joseph LOBKOWITZ and Alois Joseph Liechtenstein, appear in the list of subscribers to Mozart's series of concerts in Vienna in Lent 1784 (as given in Mozart's letter to Leopold on 20 Mar. 1784). Thus, Czech musicians were to be found seeking employment all over Europe and Mozart's professional life was rich in encounters with these expatriates, among them JOSEF MYSLIVEČEK in Italy, in PARIS František Hejna, who offered sympathetic assistance during the final illness and after the death of Mozart's mother, and in Vienna LEOPOLD KOZELUCH, Jan Stich-PUNTO, and JOHANN BAPTIST VANHAL, with whom, according to MICHAEL KELLY, he played string quartets. In addition, Mozart was much attracted by the musical advances of Czech composers, notably the symphonic legacy of the Stamitzes in MANNHEIM and the melodramas of Georg (Jiří) Benda, of whom he wrote to his father (12 Nov. 1778): 'of all the Lutheran Kapellmeisters Benda has always been my favourite'.

Despite this diaspora of many of the finest Czech musicians, the picture of musical life in Prague, aided by the reforms of MARIA THERESIA and JOSEPH II as well as a doubling of the population, was one of increasing dynamism during the eighteenth century; in some ways, Mozart's relationship with the Bohemian capital can be seen as the climax of its pattern of developing creativity. Austrian linguistic, religious, and, to a large extent, cultural domination had begun in the years after the Battle of the White Mountain (1620) and intensified with the activities of the Jesuits. By Mozart's time Prague had been primarily a German-speaking town for decades, and legislation by Maria Theresia and Joseph II attempted to extend this linguistic hegemony to the countryside; nevertheless, Czech, as Burney noted, was spoken widely among musicians, many of whom had their origins in country towns and villages. In addition to the predominantly provincial background of many musicians, there was also a marked tendency for musical careers to run in families: the Stamitzes and Bendas are but the best-known examples of a large number of such dynasties.

Much of what Mozart would have seen of Prague is still visible today. The city's three main divisions, the Lesser Town on the west bank of the Vltava (Moldau), connected by the Charles Bridge to the Old and New Towns on the east bank, were present from the middle of the fourteenth century. As tastes changed in the mid-eighteenth century the Gothic outlines of Prague – in particular the castle height, which was badly damaged by the Prussian bombardment of 1757 – gave way to Baroque and neo-Classical styles of architecture. Although the Jesuit order was suppressed by Pope Clement XIV and expelled from the Austrian Empire by Joseph II in 1773, its influence was to be observed everywhere in Prague, not just in a legacy of well-educated Czech musicians, but architecturally in many seminaries and churches, one of the most striking of which was St Nicholas in the Lesser Town, designed by Christoph Dientzenhofer and completed by his son Kilian in 1753.

Owing to the seasonal nature of the richest noble families' sojourns in Prague and the lack of an imperial court orchestra, much of the general encouragement of music and the arts fell to aristocrats of slightly lesser rank. The most significant of these for Prague's musical development and Mozart's relationship with the city was Franz Anton Nostitz (also Nostitz-Rienek, 1725–94). Italian opera performances in Prague, though by no means unknown, only became a regular feature of musical life with the conversion of Count Franz Anton Sporck's comedy theatre in 1724. These productions ran, with increasing financial difficulty, until 1735. Performances continued at the Kotzentheater by itinerant, mainly Italian, impresarios and singspiels were eventually introduced, including Mozart's DIE ENTFÜHRUNG AUS DEM SERAIL in 1782. Prompted by a desire to preserve Prague from falling too far behind Vienna in the cultural stakes (hence its original name, the Nostitzsches Nationaltheater, and the inscription above its entrance: *Patriae et Musis*) Nostitz commissioned a thousand-seat theatre designed by Haffenecker on the site of the Fruit Market in the Old Town which opened on 21 April 1783.

The rising fortunes of Prague as a musical centre are reflected in the Mozart family's view of the city as a potential source of employment. Mention of Prague was made by LEOPOLD MOZART as early as 13 November 1777 in the context of Franz Xaver DUSCHEK having prompted Mozart to petition for release from the Archbishop of SALZBURG's service. Still more significantly, in a letter to Leopold dated 16 May 1781 about his discontent with the Archbishop, Mozart mentioned that 'The road to Prague is now less closed to me than if I were at Salzburg'. Long before his renowned visits to Prague, Mozart would have been aware of the benefits of the patronage of the more cultivated branches of the Bohemian nobility. In 1775 he became acquainted with Count Johann Rudolph CZERNIN and his sister COUNTESS ANTONIE LÜTZOW, nephew and niece of the Archbishop of Salzburg and the children of Count Prokop Adalbert Czernin, head of a well-known Prague noble family. He composed the C major keyboard concerto (K246) the following year for Antonie and may well have written more for the family since Count Prokop resolved by the end of 1776 to pay Mozart an annuity for regular compositions. Mozart also had dealings from at least 1777 with the THUN family, who along with their home in Linz kept an extensive establishment in Prague, dedicating the 'Linz' symphony (K425) to Count Johann Josef Anton. NIEMETSCHEK states that Count Thun invited Mozart to Prague in January 1787 and is known to have entertained him handsomely.

Apart from contacts with influential aristocrats, Mozart counted a number of Czech musicians among his friends, notably the oboist, cellist and composer JOSEPH FIALA whom he had met in MUNICH in 1777. Later that year Fiala came to play in the Archbishop's orchestra in Salzburg and often played chamber music at the home of the Mozarts. Closer still was Mozart's friendship with Franz Xaver and Josepha (née Hambacher) Duschek. Josepha had relatives in Salzburg and took a friendly interest in the Mozarts; according to Leopold (28 Sept. 1777), she sympathized with Mozart's difficulties over Salzburg and the Archbishop and with prophetic perceptiveness wrote that Mozart 'should come directly or indirectly to Prague, where he will always be given a very warm welcome'.

For all the good intentions of the Duscheks, it was Mozart's music that first commended him to the citizens of Prague. Writing about the Prague premiere of *Die Entführung aus dem Serail* Niemetschek delivered a panegyric: 'I was witness to the enthusiasm which it aroused in Prague among knowledgeable and ignorant people alike. It is as if what had hitherto been taken for music was nothing of the kind. Everyone was transported – amazed at the novel harmonies and at the original passages for wind instruments. Now the Bohemians proceeded to seek out his works, and in the same year, Mozart's symphonies and piano music were to be heard at all the best concerts. From now onwards preference for his works was shown by the Bohemians. All the connoisseurs and artists of our capital were Mozart's staunch admirers, the most ardent ambassadors of his fame.' The event that transformed enthusiasm into sensation was the first Prague performance of LE NOZZE DI FIGARO given by the impresario PASQUALE BONDINI's company late in 1786. The *Prager Oberpostamtszeitung*'s account captures the flavour of the event: 'No piece . . . has ever caused such a sensation as the Italian opera *Die Hochzeit des Figaro*, which has already been given several times here with unlimited applause by Bondini's resident company of opera virtuosi . . . The music is by our celebrated Herr Mozart. Connoisseurs who have seen this opera in Vienna are anxious to declare that it was done much better here; and this is very likely, since the wind instruments, on which the Bohemians are well known to be decided masters, have a great deal to do in the whole piece.' (The comment on the wind instruments is interesting: though past its heyday, wind playing in Bohemia, as Burney affirmed, was superior to that in Vienna.) The same review also set running the rumour that Mozart was expected in Prague to hear the opera for himself. When Mozart and CONSTANZE MOZART arrived in Prague on 11 January 1787 the city was in the grip of *Figaro* mania much advanced, as the composer observed, by arrangements of its most popular melodies as: 'contredanses and German dances. . . . Nothing is played, sung or whistled but *Figaro*' (15 Jan. 1787). Mozart himself conducted the opera on 22 January and had, on 19 January, played the fortepiano at a concert in the Nostitz Theatre, including an improvisation on 'Non più andrai' from *Figaro*, and with the theatre orchestra the Symphony in D major (K504), named by popular acclaim after the city, but not composed for it. Both the reception and the fee of 1,000 gulden netted from Prague surpassed his experiences of the fate of *Figaro* in Vienna. Moreover, Bondini had contracted Mozart, for the usual sum of 100 gulden, for another opera buffa for the autumn season.

Mozart worked on DON GIOVANNI during the summer of 1787 with a view to a premiere in Prague on 14 October, but, as he rather caustically observed: 'the stage personnel here are not as smart as those in Vienna, when it comes to mastering an opera of this kind in a very short time' (15 Oct. 1787). *Figaro* was given instead on 14 October, though even this performance was in doubt. On a brief stop in Prague during her honeymoon, Maria Theresia, the niece of Joseph II, was due to attend the opera. According to Mozart a mischievous claque of ladies persuaded the local government that an opera with the soubriquet 'The Crazy Day' was unsuitable for the Princess, but she eventually allowed that:

'if the new opera could not be given, *Figaro* was to be performed!' (15 Oct. 1787). The premiere of *Don Giovanni*, delayed yet again owing to the illness of one of the singers, eventually arrived on 29 October and was, in Mozart's own words: 'received with the greatest applause' (4 Nov. 1787); once again Prague gave a Mozart opera the kind of reception it failed to achieve at its Viennese premiere. A veritable mythology has arisen regarding how much of the opera was composed in Prague; the arguments for and against the overture being composed the night before the premiere and other parts of the work being written in Prague are summarized by Julian Rushton in his book *Don Giovanni*.

Mozart's third and (very brief) fourth trips to Prague were stopovers to and from his April and May trip to Germany in 1789. The chief fruit of his visit was a contract with the impresario DOMENICO GUARDASONI – whose company had premiered *Don Giovanni* – which seems to have prompted an interest in METASTASIO's LA CLEMENZA DI TITO. There is also reasonable evidence (reported by T. Volek) that a version of 'Non più di fiori' – a rondo with basset horn used in *La clemenza* – was performed by Josepha Duschek in Prague on 26 April 1791, four months before the premiere. Guardasoni signed his contract from the Bohemian Estates for an opera seria to celebrate the coronation of LEOPOLD II as King of Bohemia, a traditional honorific for the Holy Roman Emperor, on 8 July 1791. Then, it seems, he first approached SALIERI before Mozart, who, busy with DIE ZAUBERFLÖTE, composed most of the opera to a revised text by CATERINO MAZZOLÀ from July till shortly before its premiere in Prague on 6 September 1791. Old-fashioned in tone at a time when opera buffa was the rage and by a composer who was far from a favourite at court, it is perhaps unsurprising that in *La clemenza* the imperial party found little to entertain them. Once again, Prague audiences delivered a more positive verdict, the climax of which was a hearteningly successful final night on 30 September.

Prague's reaction to Mozart's death hardly more than two months after this event was heartfelt and found eloquent expression in a lavish commemoration with a Requiem setting by Rössler-Rosetti, given in St Nicholas on 14 December 1791 and performed by 120 musicians – including Josepha Duschek as solo soprano – to a congregation of four thousand. When *Die Zauberflöte* reached Prague on 25 October 1792, the first time it was performed outside Vienna, it proved as great a success as *Figaro*, as reported by Niemetschek. Nevertheless, the Mozartian legacy was for Prague something of a double-edged sword. His music was performed and his memory cherished; notable sentiment appears in the biography of Niemetschek, who seems to have reflected the feelings of his fellow Czechs in statements such as: 'The Bohemians are proud that he recognised and honoured their good taste with so noble a work [*Don Giovanni*], coming from the depths of his genius.' Memories of Mozart were long in Prague and the Czech sense of loyalty towards him decades later prompted commemorations of his birthday (1869 and 1882) and death-day (1864, 1874 and 1882) in the Prague Provisional Theatre. This affection extended to care over text: the theatre's conductor, Jan Maýr, was among the first to reintroduce the secco recitatives (though accompanied by strings) into *Don Giovanni* (15 Nov. 1864) and quite possibly the first in the later nineteenth century to bring back the second act finale's concluding sextet (18 Dec. 1865). Smetana protested that Mozart had provided the model for *The Bartered Bride* and Dvořák admitted Mozart's influence on his early chamber music. There is also, however, an air of self-congratulation in Niemetschek's comment that has often shadowed the way in which the Czechs construe their understanding of Mozart's music: namely, as superior to the Austrians. A more serious downside to their pervasive admiration of Mozart's music was that many Czech composers became locked into an imitation of his style well into the nineteenth century. JAN SMACZNY

P. Demetz, *Prague in Black and Gold* (London, 1997)
J. A. Rice, *W. A. Mozart: 'La Clemenza di Tito'* (Cambridge, 1991)
J. Rushton, *W. A. Mozart: 'Don Giovanni'* (Cambridge, 1981)
J. Smaczny and C. Hogwood, 'The Bohemian Lands', in *The Classical Era: From the 1740s to the End of the 18th Century*, ed. N. Zaslaw (London, 1989), 188–212
T. Volek, 'Über den Ursprung von Mozarts Oper *La Clemenza di Tito*', *Mozart-Jahrbuch* 1959, 274–86.

'Prague' symphony. Mozart's Symphony No. 38 in D, K504 (6 Dec. 1786). See PRAGUE and SYMPHONIES

Prato, Vincenzo dal (b. Imola, 1756; d. Munich, c.1828). An Italian castrato, based for much of his career in MUNICH (1780–1805), dal Prato was the original Idamente in Mozart's IDOMENEO premiered on 29 January 1781. Mozart was decidedly unimpressed, complaining about him on several occasions during the rehearsal period. On 20 November Mozart heard him sing 'most disgracefully', predicting that he would 'never get through the rehearsals [for *Idomeneo*], still less the opera'. He also lacked experience: 'I have to sing with him, for I have to teach him his whole part as if he were a child.' Just over a month later (27 Dec. 1780), Mozart described dal Prato and ANTON RAAFF, who sang the role of Idomeneo, as 'the most wretched actors that ever walked on a stage', and considered dal Prato the 'stumbling block' in a rehearsal of the Act 3 quartet, 'Andrò ramingo e solo': 'the fellow is utterly useless. His voice would not be so bad if he did not produce it in his throat and larynx. But he has no intonation, no method, no feeling.' SIMON P. KEEFE

'Prussian' quartets. Mozart's string quartets K575 in D (June 1789), K589 in B flat (May 1790) and K590 in F (June 1790). See CHAMBER MUSIC: B. STRING QUARTETS

Puchberg, Johann Michael von (b. Zwettl, Lower Austria, 21 Sept. 1741; d. Vienna, 21 Jan. 1822). A Viennese textile merchant for whom Mozart wrote either the Piano Trio in E, K542 (1788) or the String Trio in E flat, K563 (1788), Puchberg lent Mozart about 1,400 gulden in the final years of the composer's life, individual payments ranging from 30 to 300 gulden. Nineteen begging letters survive (June 1788–June 1791) in which Mozart invariably relates his desperate financial position ('I would not wish my worst enemy to be in my present position' (12 July 1789)) and his fear of losing dignity, but appeals in rhetorically eloquent fashion to Puchberg's friendship and compassion, his status as a fellow Mason and his knowledge of Mozart's financial position and prospects. Mozart repaid small amounts (as indicated by Puchberg's annotations on letters he received from Mozart), but CONSTANZE MOZART repaid the bulk several years after her husband's death, according to GEORG NIKOLAUS NISSEN'S biography (1828). Constanze included the begging letters among material sent to Breitkopf & Härtel to assist in their publication of anecdotes about Mozart's life (designed in turn to arouse interest in their edition of his works).

SIMON P. KEEFE

J. H. Eibl, 'Ein "ächter Bruder": Mozart und Michael Puchberg', *Acta Mozartiana* 26 (1979), 41–6
R. Halliwell, *The Mozart Family: Four Lives in a Social Context* (Oxford, 1998)

Punto, Giovanni (b. Žehušice, near Čáslav, Bohemia, 28 Sept. 1746; d. Prague, 16 Feb. 1803). Born Jan Václav (Johann Wenzel) Stich and changing his name in the mid-1760s, Punto was an eminent horn player and member of orchestras in PRAGUE (1763–6) and Mainz (1769–74), who subsequently performed around Europe. Mozart wrote the horn part of his Sinfonia concertante K297b (now lost, but partially transmitted by KAnhC 14.01) for Punto in 1778 in PARIS, reporting to LEOPOLD MOZART (5 Apr. 1778) that 'Punto plays magnifique'. (The other soloists for the work were flautist JOHANN BAPTIST WENDLING, oboist FRIEDRICH RAMM and bassoonist Georg Wenzel Ritter.)

SIMON P. KEEFE

R

Raaff, Anton (b. Gelsdorf, near Bonn, 6 May 1714; d. Munich, 28 May 1797). A highly acclaimed GERMAN tenor, whose international career took him to such cities as Bonn, VIENNA, Lisbon, Madrid, Naples, Florence, MANNHEIM, PARIS and MUNICH, Raaff became a good friend of Mozart in Mannheim and Paris (1777–8). He is mentioned copiously (and affectionately) in the family correspondence, especially between 1777 and 1781, although Mozart and his mother offered mixed reports on his singing and acting. Both thought his voice was past its best in Mannheim in 1777 (14 Nov. 1777); Mozart was forced 'to pull out a handkerchief and hide a smile'. Mozart also thought him a poor operatic actor: 'he had to die [on stage], and while dying sing a very very very long aria in slow time; well, he died with a grin on his face, and towards the end of the aria his voice gave out so badly that one really couldn't stand it any longer'. But they both changed their tune somewhat in Paris a few months later. Mozart remembered writing unfavourably about Raaff's voice from Mannheim, but admitted liking it much more in Paris, in spite of the fact that Raaff was clearly past his prime (12 June 1778). MARIA ANNA MOZART particularly liked Raaff's voice (12 June 1778): 'One day he came especially to sing to me and sang three arias, which gave me great pleasure. And now whenever he comes to see us he always sings something to me, for I am quite in love with his singing.' In 1781 Raaff sang the title role at the IDOMENEO premiere in Munich (29 January). Mozart complained again about his acting: 'Raaff is like a statue' (8 Nov. 1780); and he and VINCENZO DAL PRATO, the original Idamente, were 'the most wretched actors that ever walked on a stage' (27 Dec. 1780). But Raaff at least was enamoured with his Act 2 aria, 'Fuor del mar': 'The fellow is as infatuated with it as a young and ardent lover might be with his fair one . . . Enfin, he is as happy as a king.'

In 1778, Mozart wrote the aria 'Se al labbro mio non credi', K295, for Raaff. Mozart's account of giving the aria to Raaff (28 Feb. 1778) clarifies that he was eager to consult his eminent singers in order to achieve the best results: 'I was at Raaff's yesterday and brought him an aria which I had composed for him the other day . . . I asked him to tell me candidly if he did not like it or if it did not suit his voice, adding that I would alter it if he wished or even compose another. "God forbid", he said, "the aria must remain just as it is, for nothing could be finer. But please shorten it a little, for I am no longer able to sustain my notes". "Most gladly", I replied, "as much as you like. I made it a little long on purpose, for it is always easy to cut down, but not so easy to lengthen".'

SIMON P. KEEFE

H. Freiberger, *Anton Raaff (1714–1797): Sein Leben und Wirken, als Beitrag zur Musikgeschichte des 18. Jahrhunderts* (Cologne, 1929)

I. Woodfield, 'Mozart's Compositional Methods: Writing for his Singers', in *The Cambridge Companion to Mozart*, ed. S. P. Keefe (Cambridge, 2003), 35–47

Ramm, Friedrich (1744–c.1811). A German oboist, Ramm met Mozart in late 1777 in MANNHEIM while playing in the court orchestra in the city (and before moving with a number of the court musicians to MUNICH in 1778). Mozart admired his playing, reporting to LEOPOLD MOZART (4 Nov. 1777) that he 'plays very well and has a delightful pure tone'. Likewise, Ramm admired Mozart's Oboe Concerto, K271k (a work either lost or, in fact, synonymous with K314), performing it five times in early 1778. Ramm was also the oboe soloist in the sinfonia concertante that Mozart composed in PARIS in 1778, K297b (lost, but partially transmitted by KAnhC 14.01), alongside JOHANN BAPTIST WENDLING (flute), Georg Wenzel Ritter (bassoon) and GIOVANNI PUNTO (horn). Mozart quoted Ramm's extremely warm praise for *IDOMENEO* in a letter to his father (1 Dec. 1780): ' "I must honestly confess that no music has ever made such an impression on me, and I can assure you that I thought fifty times of your father and of what his delight will be when he hears this opera." '

SIMON P. KEEFE

Raupach, Hermann Friedrich (b. Stralsund, 21 Dec. 1728; d. St Petersburg, Dec. 1778). Based for much of his life in St Petersburg in various professional capacities – as harpsichordist, Kapellmeister and court composer – Raupach wrote several operas, about fifteen ballets and three sets of sonatas (Op. 1, 2 and 3). The latter were published in the 1760s in PARIS – Raupach travelled there after losing the position of Kapellmeister in St Petersburg to Vincenzo Manfredini (1762). He met Wolfgang and LEOPOLD MOZART in Paris at this time; their encounter led to Mozart adapting three of his Op. 1 sonata movements (from Nos. 1 and 5) as concerto movements (K37/i, K39/i, K41/ii). Marvelling at Mozart's prodigious musical talents in the *Correspondance Littéraire* (15 July 1766), BARON FRIEDRICH MELCHIOR GRIMM explained that Mozart had extemporized for two hours with J. C. BACH in LONDON for the King and Queen: 'Here [in Paris] he went through the same trial with M. Raupach, an able musician . . . who improvises in a very superior manner.'

SIMON P. KEEFE

Rauzzini, Venanzio (b. Camerino, near Rome, 19 Dec. 1746; d. Bath, 8 Apr. 1810). An Italian male soprano based in MUNICH (1766–72), VIENNA (1767), Italy (1772–4) and England (from 1774), Rauzzini sang Cecilio at the premiere of *LUCIO SILLA* at the Teatro Ducal, MILAN (26 Dec. 1772). LEOPOLD MOZART was not especially impressed with Rauzzini's singing in September 1767 in Vienna (he was 'nothing exceptional'), but was far more complimentary on hearing him rehearse for *Lucio Silla*: 'he sings [his first aria] like an angel' (28 Nov. 1772). Feigning stage-fright at the premiere in order to elicit special encouragement and applause from the Archduchess, Rauzzini also made ANNA LUCIA DE AMICIS, who sang Giunia, jealous, as reported by Leopold (2 Jan. 1773). A few weeks after the premiere of his opera (which had been performed seventeen times by mid-January), Mozart exploited Rauzzini's talents again in the MOTET *Exsultate, jubilate*, K165, first performed at the Theatine Church, Milan on 17 January 1773. SIMON P. KEEFE

***re pastore*, IL**, K208 (The King as Shepherd). To modern ears, the title 'serenade in two acts' might suggest lighter fare. *Il re pastore*, however, like MITRIDATE, RE DI PONTO, LUCIO SILLA, IDOMENEO and LA CLEMENZA DI TITO, is a *dramma per musica*, one of the Mozart's contributions to the most prestigious operatic form of his time, the serious musical drama sung in Italian. Opera seria, the label often attached to *drammi per musica*, has a slightly pejorative whiff about it, suggestive of elaborate, hardly credible plots and mechanical sequences of lengthy recitatives and virtuosic set-piece arias. Mozart's efforts in this genre – with the possible exception of the somewhat reformist *Idomeneo* – have long suffered some neglect for this reason. Yet an account of his career as a composer without them would be one-dimensional, for Mozart's *drammi per musica* are like a golden thread spun through his musical life, culminating in his final opera, *Tito*. Indeed, Mozart himself was impatient throughout the 1770s and 1780s to continue writing serious operas, a task for which he had been so carefully trained by his father on their trips to Italy in his youth. In early 1778 he wrote to Leopold that his real interests in opera remained '*seria*, and not *buffa*'.

Just three years before, in the spring of 1775, a felicitous confluence of circumstances had led to the writing of *Il re pastore*. The Habsburg ARCHDUKE MAXIMILIAN FRANZ, the youngest son of Empress MARIA THERESIA, planned an official stop in SALZBURG on a journey to Italy; Mozart's employer, Prince-Archbishop HIERONYMUS COLLOREDO, deemed the occasion important enough to merit the commission of two works of musical theatre to celebrate it. One commission, unsurprisingly, went to the Naples-born Salzburg court composer DOMENICO FISCHIETTI; the other went to the nineteen-year-old Mozart, who had just returned from MUNICH with father and sister from the first performances of his LA FINTA GIARDINIERA, an opera buffa. Despite the one-off nature of this *scrittura* or commission, *Il re pastore* is no 'occasional work'. We can be sure that the young Mozart jumped at the chance to write it, sensing – beyond the prestige of the occasion – all of the ingredients of a lucky break for his career: a book by the most important librettist of the era, PIETRO METASTASIO and, perhaps more importantly, the assurance that Colloredo would spare no expense to please and flatter a prince from the Holy Roman Empire's ruling dynasty. The latter would allow for the importation from outside Salzburg of at least one star-quality singer and one top-flight instrumentalist.

By the middle decades of the eighteenth century composers like JOHANN ADOLF HASSE, CHRISTOPH WILLIBALD GLUCK, GIUSEPPE SARTI, Giovanni Battista Lampugnani, Baldassare Galuppi and Niccolò Piccinni had all set Metastasio's *Il re pastore*. It belongs to the pastoral subspecies of *dramma per musica*, and as such has earlier roots in the Italian seventeenth century. In its original form it was a *festa teatrale*. That means that it was not necessarily meant for production in a 'real' theatre, but rather for a court celebration, although some of the later composers set it as a full-blown opera seria. Metastasio wrote it in 1751 for an amateur production, to music by GIUSEPPE BONNO, at Maria Theresia's court; its five figures were portrayed by four ladies-in-waiting and a cavalier. Accordingly, its plot lacks the twisting intrigues of Metastasio's larger dramas. Not that this plot is all that simple; the bucolic setting, however, serves to focus the classic question opera seria asks (how will the noble hero solve a moral problem without compromising his rational ideals?) on to the relation between four or five main figures. The pastoral quality, then, is much more than a cliché. It bestows intimacy on the *dramma per musica* by moving it out of the politically laden sphere of elaborate public representation, where the connection between the warrior-king on the opera stage and the one in the audience is far more transparent. The imposing soundtrack of absolutism to which so many opere serie contributed is refined here to a kind of courtly chamber piece, without sacrificing the ultimate message that the ruler, chosen by the gods, always does what is right, even if he sometimes begins by getting some details wrong.

As the opera opens, Alessandro of Macedonia (that is, Alexander 'the Great') has recently freed Sidon from the clutches of the tyrant Stratone, and named the noble shepherd Armita (the pastoral king of the title) as his successor. He plans a match between Armita and Stratone's daughter Tamiri, who has fled in the disguise of a shepherdess. But she loves Agenore, a friend of Alexander's; Armita's heart, in turn, belongs to the Phoenician patrician Elisa. Armita is prepared to do his duty and sacrifice his private feelings, although in truth he would much prefer to remain a shepherd; Agenore, likewise, is ready to sacrifice his relationship with Tamiri for the greater political good. The female figures feel betrayed by their respective lovers, but just as confusion and recrimination appear to gain the upper hand, Alexander – who was unaware of Armita's and Elisa's relationship – intervenes, having seen the damage one decision has caused. Almita is commanded to take Elisa as his queen, and Agenore and Tamiri are promised the next kingdom Alexander conquers.

Mozart had been working with Metastasio's texts since he was twelve, when his father had him improvise arias to them before potential patrons in Vienna. Although little is known about the details of *Il re pastore*'s adaptation in Salzburg, twentieth-century research has shown that this version is based on three sources. The first is the Neapolitan composer Pietro Alessandro Guglielmi's setting of the work, originally written for the Teatro San Benedetto in Venice in 1767. This was revived in Munich in 1774 in a two-act version. Mozart's setting follows the Munich rendering in this redaction and in many other respects too; indeed, the many parallels between the two versions suggest that Mozart was familiar with the Munich production. The second source is an edition of Metastasio's texts, published in 1770 in Turin, known to be in the possession of the Mozart family. Mozart appears to have revised the Guglielmi version by returning some passages to their 'original' form. The third contributor seems to have been GIAMBATTISTA VARESCO, a functionary at the Prince-Archbishop's court who would later pen the libretto for *Idomeneo*. Varesco may well have written several recitative passages that appear in neither the Munich version nor Metastasio's original. These are written with a native sensitivity to Italian prosody not likely to have been within Mozart's capabilities.

Concrete information about the actual performance or performances in Salzburg is scarce. It seems unlikely that they could have been elaborate productions, as they must have been given at the Prince-Archbishop's palace. The diary entries of the Court Councillor JOHANN BAPTIST JOSEPH JOACHIM FERDINAND VON SCHIEDENHOFEN report that although the two 'serenades' were performed mostly by local forces, two star performers from outside were involved in both. These were the castrato TOMMASO CONSOLI and the flautist Johann Baptist Becke. Both were engaged at the court in Munich; in fact, Consoli had sung the role of the shepherd king Aminta in Guglielmi's *Re pastore* the previous year. Mozart's creation of the main role in the drama around the voice of a specific singer – perhaps he even suggested using the libretto after having been impressed by what he had heard in Munich – was his normal practice. Indeed, he claimed more than once in the family correspondence that he could compose an aria to a specific voice as a tailor would sew a 'fitted suit'. The appearance of a prominent flute part in Alessandro's aria 'Se vincendo vi rendo felici' (If through my victory I bring you joy) (No. 9) suggests he had the same ambitions for the virtuoso Becke.

The opera is evidence of Mozart's growing maturity and control over the contrasting tools of a mature composer of *drammi per musica*. It is marked as well by the freshness of his voice: Reinhard Strohm has written that in *Il re pastore* 'opera seria, one last time, sounds young'. The young composer seems to have written himself into the music: Armita's memorable rondeaux 'L'amerò, sarò constante' sets the composer, in his other role as Salzburg's court concert master and solo violinist, and the star singer in the scene together, much as he was to do in the concert aria with obbligato clavier K505 'Ch'io mi scordi di te' for himself and Nancy STORACE more than a decade later. THOMAS IRVINE

R. Strohm, *Die italienische Oper im 18. Jahrhundert* (Wilhelmshaven, 1979), esp. 355–77

reception. Prior to 1781, Mozart's reputation rested primarily on his accomplishments as a child prodigy and the early SONATAS and variations published between 1763 and 1766, and he was regularly mentioned in contemporary biographical works, among them Martin Gerbert's *De Cantu et Musica Sacra* (1774) and Johann Georg Meusel's *Teutsches Künstlerlexikon* (Lemgo, 1778). Otherwise, however, few of his compositions were known although some of them did enter general circulation as a result of his visits to VIENNA in 1773, MUNICH in 1775 and MANNHEIM and PARIS in 1777–9. The song *An die Freude*, K53, was published in Vienna in 1768 and the accompanied sonatas K301–6 in Paris in 1778.

In Vienna, Mozart established contacts with local publishers almost immediately after his arrival in 1781. ARTARIA published the accompanied sonatas K296 and K376–80 in December of that year and the sonatas for keyboard four-hands, K381 and K358, in 1783. The work that made Mozart's reputation, however, was DIE ENTFÜHRUNG AUS DEM SERAIL, which by 1786 had been performed in more than twenty cities across German-speaking Europe. A 1788 review from Leipzig stated that 'It is a veritable feast for the ear to hear . . . such glorious music, made for the ear and the heart. Not a single sentiment remains unsatisfied when Herr Mozart is seen to paint and present passion after passion and immediately afterwards the most droll humour.' GOETHE, in his *Italienische Reise* of 1787 wrote that 'All our endeavours . . . to confine ourselves to what is simple and limited were lost when Mozart appeared. *Die Entführung aus dem Serail* conquered all.'

Most of the other mature operas were similarly successful. LE NOZZE DI FIGARO and DON GIOVANNI were widely performed, especially in German, and COSÌ FAN TUTTE had numerous performances before 1793; DIE ZAUBERFLÖTE was an instant smash hit. Only the serious operas, IDOMENEO and LA CLEMENZA DI TITO, were slower to gain public acceptance, although CONSTANZE MOZART had taken *Tito* on tour in the mid-1790s and performed the work, usually in concert versions, in PRAGUE, Vienna, Graz, Leipzig, Berlin, Linz and probably Dresden.

The instrumental music, in particular the keyboard and chamber music, was a cornerstone in the wider dissemination of Mozart's works. In Vienna, many of these were offered first in manuscript copies; by the late 1780s almost all of them were available in printed editions as well. And often they were shipped directly to other parts of German-speaking Europe; TORRICELLA sold his edition of K333, 284 and 454 in Hamburg, and ARTARIA offered SYMPHONIES, CONCERTOS, quartets and sonatas in Dessau. A further stimulus to the dissemination of Mozart's works during the 1780s was his tours of Leipzig, Dresden, Berlin and Frankfurt. Almost certainly Mozart sold some of his compositions in Berlin; from there they circulated throughout northern Germany and Denmark.

In France Mozart's reputation as a child prodigy lingered on well into the 1770s and it was only with his visit in 1778 that he became known as a mature composer: aside from performances of the 'Paris' symphony, K297, and the BALLET *Les petits riens*, he published several works there, including the variations K179 and 354 and the accompanied sonatas K301–6. Still others may have been left behind or sold to publishers, including the divertimento K254 and the sonatas K309–11, all of which were published in Paris about 1781 at a time when Mozart is not known to have had active contacts there. Regular if infrequent performances of Mozart's works in Paris are documented throughout the early 1780s; symphonies by him were given every year between 1779 and 1783 and according to *Les Spectacles de Paris ou Calendrier Historique & Chronologique*, Mozart held an official appointment, at least titularly, as *compositeur* to the Concert spirituel. Beginning in 1784, however, most of Mozart's published works became available in Paris, either through imported editions or editions produced locally. Artaria's September 1785 edition of the six quartets dedicated to JOSEPH HAYDN, for example, was available in Paris before the end of the year; and the Trio for Piano, Clarinet and Viola, K498, published in Vienna in September 1788, was reprinted in a Parisian edition, by Le Duc, in December.

As elsewhere outside German-speaking Europe, the dissemination in Paris of the vocal music was slower than the instrumental works. Apparently the first work to be performed there was the trio 'Mandina amabile', K480, which was included in a performance of the pasticcio *La villanella rapita* at the Théâtre de Monsieur in June 1789; a review published in the *Mercure de France* described it as 'charming'. Other vocal works followed later, including a pasticcio based on

Figaro given at the Académie de Musique in 1793 and a version of *Die Zauberflöte* performed in 1801 under the title *Les Mystères d'Isis*. The first Mozart operas to be given in Paris in their original forms were *Così* in 1809 and *Don Giovanni* in 1811.

England is generally thought to have been more immune to Mozart, at least before the nineteenth century. About 1803, when Mozart's juvenile works, including K6–9 and K10–15, were still on sale in LONDON, CHARLES BURNEY wrote in Abraham Rees's *Cyclopedia*, 'we know nothing of [his] studies or productions but from his harpsichord lessons, which frequently came over from Vienna; and in these he seems to have been trying experiments. They were full of new passages and new effects; but were wild, capricious and not always pleasing.' Credit for the appearance of some works during the later 1780s is usually give to Mozart's English friends, Stephen and Nancy STORACE, THOMAS ATTWOOD and MICHAEL KELLY, who in 1787 returned to London from Vienna, almost certainly bringing some of Mozart's music with them; Storace's *Collection of Original Harpsichord Music* included the first English edition of the piano quartet K493 and he published the first edition anywhere of the piano trio K564. Stephen Storace included an arrangement of part of the *alla turca* from Mozart's sonata K331 in his *The Siege of Belgrade* (1791) and in 1789 Nancy Storace and FRANCESCO BENUCCI interpolated the duet 'Crudel! perchè finora' from *Figaro* in a performance of GIUSEPPE GAZZANIGA's *La vendemmia* in 1789. In any case, it is not true that Mozart's works were widely disseminated in London only during the last years of the 1780s; ample documentation survives for performances of his music as early as 1784 when subscription concerts sponsored by Lord Abingdon included three Mozart symphonies. Printed editions of the concertos K413–15, first published in 1785, were available at least from January 1786 when the pianist Johann Baptist Cramer performed K414 in public. Other works circulating in London about this time included the accompanied sonatas K296 and K376–80, the solo sonatas K309–11, the C minor fantasy and sonata K475+457 and several sets of variations. As in France, though, the operas made a later appearance. The first complete Mozart opera performance was *La clemenza di* Tito, given in 1806; *Così* and *Die Zauberflöte* followed in 1811, *Figaro* in 1812, and *Don Giovanni* in 1817. Selections from these operas had already appeared in various printed anthologies of the 1790s, usually with different English texts.

In other parts of Europe, Mozart's works generally achieved little distribution before about 1790. In Italy his music was considered difficult. According to an anecdote in Gotifredo Ferrari's *Aneddoti piacevoli e interesanti*, 'various *dilettanti* and teachers tried [the six quartets dedicated to Haydn] but we could not play anything but the slow movements, and even these only with difficulty'; and NIEMETSCHEK wrote that a performance of *Don Giovanni* in Florence in 1798 was abandoned because the music was considered too hard. Nevertheless, at least some of Mozart's mature works were known in the south during his lifetime: *Figaro* was given in Monza (1787) and in Florence (1788) while copies of the symphonies K338, 425 and 504 circulated there during the 1790s. *Don Giovanni* may have been performed in Florence as early as 1792 although the first securely documented performances were at Bergamo and Rome in 1811;

Così was given at MILAN in 1807, *La clemenza di Tito* at Naples in 1809 and *Die Zauberflöte* at Milan in 1816 (in Italian). *Die Entführung aus dem Serail*, Mozart's first great operatic success, was not given in Italy until 1935.

Unlike the works of Haydn and other Viennese composers, Mozart's did not circulate widely in Spain and Portugal during the 1780s. A 1787 inventory of a music collection in Madrid includes not a single work by Mozart, even if his contemporaries are well represented; the only documented early opera performances are *Così* in Barcelona in 1798 and *Figaro* in Madrid in 1802. Scandinavia is similarly poorly documented although the discovery of a copy of the spurious symphony K16a shows that perhaps some of his works were known in Denmark during the 1780s and 1790s; and by 1796 a music club in Odense owned manuscript copies or editions of at least six symphonies as well as the overtures to *Figaro*, *Don Giovanni*, *La clemenza di Tito* and *Die Zauberflöte*. *Die Entführung* was given in Copenhagen in 1813 and Stockholm in 1814; *Figaro* was mounted in both cities in 1821. Evidence for early performances in eastern Europe is rare although there are some notable exceptions: *Die Entführung* was given in Warsaw in Polish in 1783 and *Don Giovanni*, in Italian, in 1789. In St Petersburg, a certain Frau Schulz performed a piano concerto, advertising herself as a student of Mozart's; and advertisements by Russian music dealers from 1788 list some of the solo keyboard sonatas and the sonatas for four hands. Travelling troupes performed *Don Giovanni* and *Die Zauberflöte* in the 1790s, *Die Entführung* was given complete, in Russian, in 1810, and *La clemenza di Tito* was staged in St Petersburg in 1817. CLIFF EISEN

G. Gruber, *Mozart and Posterity*, trans. R. S. Furness (London, 1991)

religion and liturgy. When the eighteenth century began, the State and the Church were the two pillars of community life in the Austrian Empire. By the century's end, however, the Church's role had diminished because of growing anticlerical attitudes, emerging religious toleration and new policies of reform-minded rulers. Growing up in SALZBURG, Mozart witnessed first hand an environment where the State and Church, although not separate entities, were responding to the secularizing effects of the ENLIGHTENMENT.

1. Religion in the eighteenth century
2. Salzburg as a church state
3. Other trends: toleration and anticlericalism
4. Religion in the Mozart family
5. Mozart's relations with clergy
6. Liturgy
7. Church year and musical practices at Salzburg Cathedral
8. Salzburg church music and Josephine reforms

1. Religion in the eighteenth century

In the eighteenth century Roman Catholicism faced new challenges. There was a new, Enlightenment-driven *Weltanschauung*, with emphasis on rational thought, scientific method, individual will and the natural world. There was also a growing materialism and utilitarianism in matters of state, economics and education. Irreligious, atheistic thinking was becoming more common. With its purview increasingly restricted only to religious matters, the Church experienced an ever-decreasing role in daily life.

Church authorities responded to new philosophical currents, particularly those fostered by Protestant thinkers as well as the *philosophes* (Voltaire, Rousseau et al.), the Encyclopedists (Diderot, d'Alembert), and, later, Kant. The Pope's absolute power was now balanced by a regional episcopalism, and there was movement towards a more locally oriented, national Church (for example, Gallicanism, Febronianism, JOSEPHINISM).

Natural religion promoted a rise of autonomous reason and a decline of Revelation (i.e. God's revealed truth; cf. David Hume's *Dialogues Concerning Natural Religion*, 1779). Many philosophers even doubted whether God was still around to save souls. Thus arose *Deism*, according to which God created the perfect universe but was no longer intervening directly. Revelation was unnecessary for future happiness and incompatible with 'truth'; God's Providence, without direct, divine mediation, governs the world.

An emphasis on individual free choice, rational enquiry and moral will was characteristic of religious thought as an 'enlightened Christianity' made its appearance. Faith was a personal matter between an individual and God. In *Emile* (1762) Rousseau described religious training for his student in this way:

> So long as we yield nothing to human authority, nor to the prejudices of our native land, the light of reason alone, in a state of nature, can lead us no further than to natural religion; and this is as far as I should go with Emile. If he must have any other religion, I have no right to be his guide; he must choose for himself.

2. Salzburg as a church state

Salzburg was an ecclesiastical principality, a church state ruled by a prince-archbishop. A prince of the Holy Roman Empire, the archbishop had absolute power and even appointed the city's Bürgermeister. In the seventeenth century Salzburg was designated 'Primus Germaniae', that is the highest-ranking bishopric in German-speaking lands, and the city became known as 'the Rome of the north'. The archbishop was the city's chief arts patron with his support for new drama, music, art and architecture. Politically, Salzburg was caught between MUNICH and VIENNA, whose rulers vied to have one of their loyalists be the prince-archbishop, who was elected by the canon priests of Salzburg. During the eighteenth century the sympathies of these canons shifted from Munich to Vienna. Mozart encountered two very different prince-archbishops: Siegmund Christoph, Count of SCHRATTENBACH (r. 1753–71), the last Baroque-minded prince, and Hieronymus, Count of COLLOREDO (r. 1772–1803), a man of the Enlightenment who did much to advance the secularization and blossoming of the city.

In examining Mozart's faith and his church music, one should be aware of the close proximity of three principal churches in Salzburg: the Dom,

St Peter's and the Stadtpfarrkirche. Their services and music were a fundamental part of the community in which Mozart grew, practised and matured as a musician. At the seventeenth-century Dom (cathedral), seat for the archbishop, LEOPOLD MOZART served as violinist from 1743 onwards (from 1763 as Deputy Hofkapellmeister). He worked under Hofkapellmeister Karl Heinrich von Biber (1743–9), JOHNAN ERNST EBERLIN (1749–62), Giuseppe Francesco Lolli (1763–72), DOMENICO FISCHIETTI (1772–83), Jakob Rust (1777–8) and LUIGI GATTI (1783–1817). Mozart served here as concert master (1769–77) and as court organist (1779–81).

Nearby is the Benedictine Abbey of St Peter's which, with nearly 600 services using music annually, had its own musicians, mostly students. Also close to the cathedral is the thirteenth-century Stadtpfarrkirche (City Parish Church, today's Franziskaner-Kirche). Mozart could also have frequented services at the Kollegien-Kirche (Collegiate Church; founded as the Benedictine University church in 1694) and the Dreifaltigskeit-Kirche (Holy Trinity Church).

3. Other trends: toleration and anticlericalism

One significant change in Mozart's day was the improved treatment of religious minorities in Salzburg, Vienna and elsewhere. Salzburg, for example, had a history of driving out Protestants and Jews. In 1731–2 Archbishop FIRMIAN forced some 20,000 Protestants to emigrate. Empress MARIA THERESIA mistreated both Protestants and Jews. Reducing non-Catholic infiltration was a means by which rulers believed they could protect their territories from liberal, Enlightenment ideas. The Mozarts say little about this, although in 1777 Leopold urged his travelling son not to stay long in the Protestant towns (letter of 4 December).

Emperor JOSEPH II (r. 1780–90) had more liberal, enlightened views than his mother Maria Theresia. His *Toleranzpatent* of 13 October 1781 abolished most religious discrimination but *not* against the Jews. The edict permitted private religious services for recognized denominations. Jews were allowed to settle, however, in communities previously out of bounds for them, and they could take on certain previously forbidden trades and be admitted to the university. This curious mix of despotism and humanitarianism, absolutism and egalitarianism, was typical of Josephine rule.

In the seventeenth century Jansenism, with its strict belief in predestination and emphatic reliance on the Roman Church for one's relationship with God, unsettled many lay persons' respect for ecclesiastical authority and caused breaches within the Church. New historical and philosophical writings added fuel to the flames of growing anticlericalism even after the demise of Jansenism at the start of the eighteenth century. Excommunicated and censored for his devastating 1723 attack upon the Church's power, historian Pietro Giannone left Italy for Vienna where for several years he was under the protection of the Emperor, a natural sympathizer with such anticlericalism. A veritable 'battle of books' ensued, as philosophers criticized and clerics defended the Church. Some countries like Spain, Portugal and France maintained close ties with the Catholic Church, while others like the Austrian Empire or the

Archbishopric of Salzburg sought greater, albeit amicable independence from the Holy See.

A special form of anticlericalism was the virtual elimination of the Jesuits, an order whose exemplary missionary and educational work had gained them enormous power since the Counter-Reformation. Jesuits were distrusted as a threat to the state as well as to the Roman Church. Pope Clement XI declared them heretics in 1713, and half a century later they were driven out of several countries, including Portugal (1759), France (1764) and Spain (1767). Finally, political and intellectual pressures led Pope Clement XIV to suppress the order on 21 July 1773. The far-reaching effects of this action were witnessed first hand by a dismayed Mozart family and reported in letters from 1770 and 1773.

In the 1780s, under Joseph II, anticlericalism reached a new high that directly affected church music. In what some call the 'Josephinisches Staats-Kirchentum', the Emperor named himself 'Obervormund der Kirche und Verwalter ihrer Güter' (Chief Guardian of the Church and Manager of its Properties). The Emperor's approval was required for the promulgation of papal encyclicals or diocesan exhortatory pronouncements relating to non-religious matters. In 1782 a spiritual court commission was charged with all ecclesiastical matters that were not purely religious. The guiding principles for all innovations, such as simplifying the liturgy, were reason and practicality. In 1783 the Emperor closed cloisters of purely contemplative character, abolished church sodalities (lay fellowships or *Brüderschaften*), and eliminated many church holidays. Some 738 out of 2,163 monasteries and convents were shut down, and the number of church holidays was reduced from forty-two to twenty-seven. Only cloisters dedicated to teaching or ministering to the medical and spiritual health of a parish remained. The closed cloisters' wealth went to a *Religionsfond* which was used for church purposes. Some 36,000 out of the total 63,000 monks and nuns were released from their orders and flooded the labour market. The number of public processions and pilgrimages was sharply reduced by the elimination of holidays, an act that theoretically increased the country's productivity.

A noticeable effect of Josephine reforms on church music was the cutback in sumptuous, instrumentally accompanied vocal music. For example, from 1783 onwards instrumentally accompanied masses in Vienna were restricted to only the Hofkapelle and St Stephen's Cathedral when the archbishop officiated. Such a restriction explains Mozart's smaller output of sacred music in the decade that followed. At the same time numerous church musicians lost their jobs. In 1782 Mozart expressed concern when he learned that the cutbacks observed in Viennese churches had already occurred in Salzburg (letter of 25 Sept. 1782). After Joseph II's death (1790), his successor, LEOPOLD II, retracted many of the reforms and permitted instrumentally accompanied masses only when an institution could cover the expense.

4. Religion in the Mozart family

(See also MOZART, (JOHANN CHRYSOSTOM) WOLFGANG AMADEUS: D. RELIGIOUS BELIEFS)

Although the Catholic faith did not play as central a role in Wolfgang's life as it had for his pious father, the family raised him as a good Catholic. Family letters have frequent references to Mass attendance, receiving Communion, making confession, saying the Rosary, celebrating Holy Days, etc. – all so as not to 'fall into perdition' (15 Dec. 1777). Later, in Vienna, FREEMASONRY with its humanitarian ideals and social connections attracted Mozart's interest and participation more than the Church. He shared the personal, pure, and heartfelt religion then typical of Vienna's upper classes. In a letter of 1 September 1784, Georg Forster described Mozart's religion as 'free from all superstition, the religion of gentle and innocent hearts familiar with the secrets of nature and creation'. Mozart, then, seems to have been a freethinking Catholic with a private relationship with God. Mozart's religion was utilitarian, not dogmatic; that is, he seemed to observe his faith for practical, outward appearances rather than for strong belief in doctrine.

By contrast, Leopold was a devout Catholic who believed in Divine Providence – the will of God – for his recoveries from illness or even for the premature death of his wife MARIA ANNA MOZART. Wolfgang's talent, moreover, was 'bestowed by God' (22 Dec. 1777). Never hesitating to face difficulties or death, Wolfgang also exhibited an optimistic trust in God's will and power. When Leopold was mortally ill, Mozart confidently described death as 'the true goal of our existence' (4 Apr. 1787). From remarks in his letters and the appealing poise with which he musically depicted undaunted characters in his operas, one perceives Mozart's sincere *Gottvertrauen* (trust in God).

5. Mozart's relations with clergy

Despite an outward respect for the ecclesiastical leadership of Salzburg, Mozart inherited from Leopold a generally negative view of the Archbishop. For them Archbishop Colloredo was stingy, untrusting and untrustworthy, frustrating, and even, at times, idiotic. It is no surprise that the fear of 'being caught' or of 'losing favour' prompted the Mozarts to use secret codes when referring to the Archbishop in their letters, or to wait for him to be out of town so that they could 'escape' to Munich to hear Wolfgang's new opera (18 Dec. 1780). Because of the Archbishop and the unsatisfactory musical conditions at court Mozart sorely wanted to leave Salzburg.

Wolfgang showed other anticlerical sentiments with statements like: 'a priest is capable of anything' (21 May 1783). In late 1777 Mozart criticized ABBE VOGLER several times as an incompetent composer-theorist and as an arrogant, conniving prelate who used women to help him accomplish things.

The Mozarts nonetheless had many friends among the clergy, several of whom helped and documented Wolfgang's career. In nearly every letter he enthusiastically greets the kind Abbé BULLINGER. To Padre MARTINI in Bologna Mozart openly complained about the conditions of sacred music in Salzburg (4 Sept. 1776); and it was Martini who taught Mozart strict counterpoint and gave him supportive testimonials. Many details about Mozart's life come from the diaries of clerics (for example, Beda Hübner and Cajetan

Hagenauer (Pater Dominicus)). Without the letters and diaries of these church contacts we would know much less about the composer.

The Mozarts always visited churches wherever they travelled. In 1777 Mozart's mother admitted, somewhat guiltily, that she and Wolfgang could not attend Mass on weekdays in MANNHEIM, but that 'Wolfgang goes every Sunday to High Mass at the Hofkirche in order to hear the music' (20 Dec. 1777). In spite of their dislike of the Archbishop, the Mozarts never lost their respect for the Church. Clerics, after all, had the ability and means to hire musicians, loan money and write testimonials. Indeed one of Mozart's highest honours occurred when Pope Clement XIV made him a Knight of the Golden Spur in July 1770. Orlando di Lasso was the only previous musician to have received the papal honour.

6. Liturgy

As the entire practice of corporate worship, *liturgy* includes the elements of rite, ceremony and use for the church year. Since its first systematic codification, liturgy has had a long and complicated evolution. Mozart encountered the *Tridentine Rite* formulated after the Council of Trent (1545–63). Specific ceremonies (local use) of this authorized liturgy, however, can vary from place to place. For example, there are significant differences between Roman use and monastic use such as the Rule of St Benedict.

The two official services of the Roman Catholic liturgy then, as now, were Mass and Divine Office (liturgical hours). For service *texts* on a particular Sunday or feast, one consults a *missale* or missal (for Mass) and a *breviarium* or breviary (for Offices), while *chants* are found in the *graduale* (for Mass) and the *antiphonale* or antiphoner (for Offices).

The church year consists of four intersecting cycles: the daily cycle of Office and Mass, the weekly cycle (including Monday–Saturday as *Feriae II–VII*), the annual cycle of liturgical seasons (*Temporale*), and the annual cycle of feast days (*Sanctorale*). The major feasts of the church year (for example, Christmas, Easter, Pentecost) affected the weekly cycle by extending special celebrations for an eight-day week (the Octave).

The *Temporale* (the *Proper of the Time*) corresponds to events in the life of Christ. Some of these feasts are fixed to a particular date (such as Christmas), while others are 'movable', occurring on a Sunday according to phases of the moon (such as Easter). The 'penitential' seasons are Advent and Lent, when there were special ceremonial and musical requirements (such as no orchestrally accompanied Masses). The *Sanctorale* consisted of the various saints' feast days, that is the 'lesser', fixed feasts whose observance varied according to local use. Complicated rules determined feast prioritization on occasions when the fixed dates of the *Sanctorale* coincided with a Sunday or with one of the major feasts of the *Temporale*.

There were two basic ranks of feasts: simple (*simplex*) and double (*duplex*). Double feasts, the higher in rank, could be divided into as many as four separate ranks depending on local use (principal double, semi-double etc.). Texts appropriate for a particular day were *Proper* (for example, Gradual, Offertory), while unchanging, fixed texts were *Ordinary* (for example, Kyrie, Gloria, etc. of the Mass). Use of *Ordinary* texts could vary (for example, the Gloria was omitted during penitential seasons). Throughout the year there were, of course, many other changes in ceremonial observance (such as the participants, the use of distinctive dress, seasonal liturgical colours, particular decorations and special processions).

The Divine Office was the daily cycle of liturgical prayer consisting of eight services from early morning to evening (Matins, Lauds, Prime, Terce, Sext, None, Vespers, Compline). Each service was built around the recitation of Psalms, ending with the Magnificat. A liturgical 'day' usually began with the Vespers in the late afternoon *before* a given Sunday or feast day. Vespers had the most ornate figural music of all the Offices for a major feast. Sometimes composers wrote an orchestrally accompanied setting of only the opening and closing texts ('Dixit Dominus' and 'Magnificat') rather than the entire Vespers (see K193).

In addition to the Mass and Office, there were also supplementary liturgical observances and devotionals, some occurring on a daily basis and all determined by local use (for example, Gradual Psalms, Penitential Psalms, Office of the Dead, Little Office of the Virgin, Votive Masses, Litanies). In Salzburg Litanies were performed in the late afternoon or early evening, sometimes at Mirabel Palace (see LITANY).

All services in Mozart's day, the pre-Vatican II era, were still spoken and sung principally in Latin. The attending clergy, choir and other musicians were the active participants in the services. The celebrant recited quietly *all* texts of a service, even though certain sung items might be eliminated or replaced by other music (such as a Litany in place of an Offertory). The role for lay persons observing a service was quite passive and distantly devotional. In the 1780s, however, as part of an effort to make services more meaningful for the general populace and increase congregational participation, Emperor Joseph II and Archbishop Colloredo, among others, encouraged the singing of German *Kirchen-Lieder* and *Deutsche Messen* (German Masses). In response to the Archbishop's wishes, MICHAEL HAYDN wrote several German sacred compositions.

7. Church year and musical practices at Salzburg Cathedral

Karl Gustav Fellerer (1955) was among the first to emphasize the importance of knowing both the eighteenth century's spirituality and its liturgy when assessing Mozart's sacred music. The *Chor-Ordnungen* for Salzburg's Cathedral delineate which feasts were to have a *missa solemnis* or a *missa brevis* and which instruments were used. Walter Senn's studies have corrected earlier misconceptions about Salzburg's church music practices. For example, a short, Solemn Mass with sizeable orchestral accompaniment was really not new at this time, particularly north of the Alps. This *Missa brevis et solemnis* was sometimes designated 'kurzes Hochamt'. Several *missae longae* by Michael Haydn prove that Solemn Masses longer than forty-five minutes were also heard in Salzburg, despite Mozart's famous complaint to Padre Martini in September 1776 about service time limits.

In Mozart's day the annually printed *Hof-Kalender oder Schematismus* listed the official feasts and their liturgical classification at Salzburg Cathedral. High feasts involving the archbishop were termed *Festa Palli*, that is feasts with the pallium or archbishop's vestment. In the *Ordo Festivitatum et Functionum*, an undated list prepared by LUIGI GATTI, there were, in order of diminishing importance, five categories of services determined by who officiated: *Festa Pallii primae classis*, *Festa Pallii secundae classis* (these first two types with the archbishop or appropriate designee as celebrant), *Festa Praepositi* (with the cathedral *Propst* or provost), *Festa Decani* (with the cathedral dean), *Festa Canonici* (recte Canonicorum; that is with the canon priests).

The 1746 guidelines prepared by K. H. von Biber – *Ordnung deren hochfürstlichen Kürchen-Diensten im Domb* – describe Salzburg Cathedral's *Chor-Ordnung*, according to which five explicit categories of orchestration for Masses (and solemn Vespers on the day preceding) corresponded to the character of a feast and the celebrant officiating. Together with a report allegedly by Leopold Mozart for Marpurg's *Historisch-Kritische Beyträge zur Aufnahme der Musik* (Berlin, 1757), Biber's guidelines offer a detailed view of the elaborate musical forces at the cathedral on high feasts (for example, five ensembles in five separate locations).

For *Festa Pallii* the musicians performed a *Missa solemnis* or a *Missa brevis et solemnis* (or a solemn Vespers on the day preceding), although the cathedral's *Catalogus Musicalis* from the 1780s reports the latter type also being used for *Festa Praepositi*. If the archbishop was present, two choirs of trumpets and timpani in separate balconies would play splendid *intradas* for his entrance and exit. When the provost or dean was celebrant, there were usually no wind instruments in the accompanying orchestra. A *Missa brevis* was performed when the canons were officiating. For those lesser occasions the orchestra consisted of a smaller number of strings, bassoon, the usual two organs, and three trombones (ATB).

Church music in Salzburg was mostly a local affair avoiding influences from elsewhere. The *Catalogus Musicalis* shows that more than 90 per cent of its repertory was by local composers. The archbishop's large musical establishment consisted of four groups of musicians: *Hofmusik* (musicians for use at the court and cathedral), *Hof- und Feldtrompeter* (court and field trumpeters, with timpanists, for the cathedral and court events), *Dom-Musik* (Domchorvikarien (choral deacons) and Domchoralisten (choristers) for cathedral music), and the *Kapellknaben* (choirboys) from the Kapellhaus. Leopold's 1757 report suggested that French horns were never used in the cathedral, but music later performed there includes a pair of horns as well as trumpets (for example, litanies K125 and mass K317).

8. Salzburg church music and Josephine reforms

In Mozart's era the main function of church music was to maintain an appropriately solemn, pious and penitent atmosphere. In *Etwas von und über Musik* (1778) Joseph Martin Kraus asked that church music arouse 'inspiration and total devotion' ('Begeisterung und volle Andacht'). With the increasing variety of venues for public performance, however, music was no longer restricted to just the former 'triumvirate' of church, chamber and theatre, with their 'separate' styles. More and more their styles were 'contaminating' each other. As a result, more modern, even dramatic styles were now heard in the church. Contemporaries like Kraus and Colloredo complained publicly about the overly secular nature of church music that sometimes sounded like opera. Indeed, some offertories were actually operatic *contrafacta*, that is, opera arias with new, Latin texts.

In the 1780s, in an attempt to 'modernize' rationally the diocese along Enlightenment principles in line with those of Joseph II, Archbishop Colloredo instituted reforms affecting church music. One goal was to make the liturgy simpler, shorter and more comprehensible. In a pastoral letter of 29 June 1782, the Archbishop announced his wish to remove excessive ornateness and ostentation from the liturgy of parish churches. Numerous local traditions were eliminated (such as cannon-firing, carrying pictures during processions, taking certain pilgrimages). Liturgical texts, however, were not affected by the reforms, but theoretically all instrumental music in church was abolished. For example, choral music based on liturgical texts was now to be sung as the Gradual instead of instrumental music (cf. 'Epistle Sonatas'). Michael Haydn was contracted to compose new choral Graduals (1783–90) for this purpose. The Archbishop also requested the inclusion of *deutsche Kirchengesänge* or *Kirchenlieder* (German hymns) in all church services except at the cathedral and the monasteries. More important now than the mystery of the liturgical experience was the awakening of individual religious feelings through the German hymn – an approach more in tune with the natural theology of the age. As Fellerer observes, the ornate Baroque service and its high art echoing the *majestas Domini* disappeared. Apparently, however, the Archbishop was not interested in shortening the non-Mass items of the liturgy (such as Litanies, Vespers), so that they could remain extended concerted works.

Colloredo's church music reforms may have been another annoyance that led Mozart to leave the Archbishop in 1781. In actualizing Enlightenment ideals the Archbishop sought to suppress the tradition of the liturgy and church music. Curiously, in Vienna it was the opposite, as the conservative Archbishop there, Cardinal Count Christoph Bartholomäus Anton Migazzi (r. 1757–1803), attempted to maintain the traditions against the reforms of Joseph II.

By the time Mozart died, the power of the Church was being limited by state oversight, worshippers were gaining individual spiritual freedom, and a decline in opulent church music had begun. There was no longer one definite 'church style' but, rather, a mixed, cosmopolitan style which BEETHOVEN, HUMMEL, Cherubini and others would soon use to great effect. During the nineteenth century, thanks to the purist, conservative Cecilian movement ('Caecilianism'), such instrumentally accompanied church music as Mozart's was further discouraged, and it fell into disuse in many parishes. Fortunately sound technologies of the twentieth century encouraged the performance and recording of Mozart's entire sacred output and promoted its renaissance as the viable music it remains today. BRUCE C. MACINTYRE

J. M. Creed and J. S. Boyssmith, *Religious Thought in the Eighteenth Century: Illustrated from Writers of the Period* (Cambridge, 1934)
C. Eisen, 'Salzburg under Church Rule', in *Man and Music: The Classical Era: From the 1740s to the End of the 18th Century*, ed. N. Zaslaw (Englewood Cliffs, NJ, 1989), 166–87
K. G. Fellerer, 'Liturgische Grundlagen der Kirchenmusik Mozarts', in *Festschrift Walter Senn zum 70. Geburtstag*, ed. Ewald Fässler (Munich and Salzburg, 1975), 64–74
Mozarts Kirchenmusik (Salzburg-Freilassing, 1955)
Karl Hammer, *W. A. Mozart: eine theologische Deutung. Ein Beitrag zur theologischen Anthropologie* (Zurich, 1970)
J. Harper, *The Forms and Orders of Western Liturgy from the Tenth to the Eighteenth Century: A Historical Introduction and Guide for Students and Musicians* (Oxford, 1991)
D. Heartz, *Haydn, Mozart and the Viennese School: 1740–1780* (New York, 1995)
E. Hintermaier, 'Die Salzburger Hofkapelle von 1700 bis 1806: Organisation und Personal' (Ph.D. thesis, University of Salzburg, 1972)
B. C. MacIntyre, *The Viennese Concerted Mass of the Early Classic Period* (Ann Arbor, 1986)
W. Senn, 'Der Catalogus Musicalis des Salzburger Doms (1788)', *Mozart Jahrbuch 1971/72*, 182–96
'Mozarts Kirchenmusik und die Literatur', *Mozart Jahrbuch 1978/79*, 14–18

Requiem. The Requiem in D minor, K626, was unfinished at his death on 5 December 1791. Completed chiefly by his student FRANZ XAVER SÜSSMAYR (1766–1803), it is one of Mozart's most celebrated works, shrouded in myth and controversy, even to the present day.

1. Genesis and completion
2. The work and its reception

1. Genesis and completion

In the spring or summer of 1791, Mozart received an anonymous commission to write a requiem mass. The commission came from an agent acting on behalf of COUNT FRANZ WALSEGG-STUPPACH (1763–1827), a rich estate-owner, who wanted to perform the work in memory of his wife, Anna, who had died on 14 February 1791. On 7 January 1792, one month after Mozart's death, the *Salzburger Intelligenzblatt* reported that Mozart 'received an unsigned letter, asking him to write a Requiem'; he demanded no less than 60 ducats, received 30 in advance and was told that he would be paid the remaining amount upon completion of the work. So, the reporter continued, Mozart wrote it 'often with tears in his eyes, constantly saying: I fear that I am writing a Requiem for myself; he completed it a few days before his death'.

But the Requiem, of course, was not finished by 5 December 1791 – far from it in fact. From the surviving autograph, it has been determined that Mozart completed only one movement in full, the Introit, 'Requiem aeternam', and another, the Kyrie, in all but details of instrumentation. In addition, Mozart wrote the vocal parts and a figured basso continuo for the six sections of the sequence ('Dies irae', 'Tuba mirum', 'Rex tremendae', 'Recordare', 'Confutatis' and 'Lacrymosa', although the latter for only eight bars) and both sections of the offertory ('Domine Jesu Christe' and 'Hostias et preces'), as well as leaving some indications of instrumentation. No autograph material remains for the concluding sections of the work, the Sanctus, Benedictus and Agnus Dei. An

1827 obituary notice for BENEDIKT SCHACK (1758–1826), the first Tamino in DIE ZAUBERFLÖTE, recalled Schack's account of a rehearsal of the Requiem with Mozart on 4 December 1791: 'Even on the afternoon before [Mozart] died he had the score of the Requiem brought to his bed and himself sang the alto part (it was about two o'clock in the afternoon); Schack, the friend of the family, as he had always done before, sang the soprano part, [Franz de Paula] HOFER, Mozart's brother-in-law, the tenor, and [FRANZ XAVER] GERL, later of the MANNHEIM theatre, the bass. When they got to the first bars of the Lacrimosa, Mozart began to weep violently, and laid the score aside. Eleven hours later, at one in the morning, he passed on.'

Shortly after her husband's death, CONSTANZE MOZART turned to one of his students, JOSEPH LEOPOLD VON EYBLER (1765–1846), to ask him to complete the work. Although Eybler accepted in writing on 21 December 1791 and partly orchestrated several movements, he soon withdrew from the project for reasons that are not altogether clear; neither Eybler nor the other two musicians who orchestrated parts of the work – FRANZ JACOB FREYSTÄDLER (1761–1841), a composition student of Mozart, and ABBE MAXIMILIAN STADLER (1748–1833), a friend of Mozart and Constanze – are credited in the autograph score or elsewhere in the sources. The task of completing the work finally passed to Franz Xaver Süssmayr and the exact nature of his involvement in carrying out his responsibilities remains controversial to this day. In a letter to the Leipzig-based publishers Breitkopf & Härtel on 8 February 1800 he claimed sole compositional responsibility for the Sanctus, Benedictus and Agnus Dei and for finishing the 'Lacrymosa'. Constanze argued conversely that Süssmayr's contributions to the completed work were routine and mechanical; her statement in 1826 that he obtained 'small scraps of paper' from Mozart's desk soon after his death has encouraged speculation that Mozart left material for the later movements. One such item was discovered in 1963 by the scholar Wolfgang Plath – a sketch for an 'Amen' fugue at the end of the 'Lacrymosa', where Süssmayr's completion gives only a grand plagal cadence.

Süssmayr has found himself, undeservedly, in a no-win position: where the musical quality of the Sanctus, Benedictus and Agnus Dei is deemed high, it is hypothesized that Mozart left material; where the quality is deemed low, fingers are pointed accusingly at Süssmayr. The *Allgemeine musikalische Zeitung* set the ball rolling in a review of the Requiem in 1801, claiming that Süssmayr could not have had a major involvement in the completion of the work on account of the qualitative discrepancy between his earlier works and the finished piece. Vincent NOVELLO continued along similar lines in 1829, explaining that the Sanctus, Benedictus and Agnus Dei 'bear such internal proofs of their having been written by Mozart that I never for a moment believed they could have been produced by another composer, especially such an obscure writer as Süssmayr of whom nothing whatever can be shown as having the least resemblance to the style of Mozart's Requiem'. Implicit and explicit criticisms of Süssmayr have gained a head of steam in recent times too. Christoph Wolff speculates that he did not complete the 'Amen' fugue at the end of the 'Lacrymosa' 'because he lacked confidence in his own ability to write strict polyphony to the necessary standard' and that he was left Mozart's sketches for the Sanctus,

Osanna, Benedictus and Agnus Dei 'especially in view of the quality of the vocal writing'; and Duncan Druce describes his orchestration as 'occasionally inept [and] rarely imaginative', identifying 'greater defects' such as 'the perfunctory quality of the Osanna fugues and the harmonic stagnation in the central part of the Benedictus' in the later sections of the work. Richard Maunder, in particular, leaves no stones unturned in undermining Süssmayr's involvement: Mozart must have left him a 'fairly complete draft' of the Agnus Dei, as it 'really does, for once, seem too good to be Süssmayr's, not merely in its general impression, but also in its highly ingenious yet simple construction'; he and Mozart are unlikely to have had protracted discussions about the completion of the work, and Mozart would not have chosen him for the task of completing it in any case; Mozart, Maunder claims, did not even hold Süssmayr in high esteem.

In truth, few people directly connected to the Requiem at the end of the eighteenth and beginning of the nineteenth centuries (Süssmayr included), and few scholars writing about it in the twentieth, have approached the work dispassionately, and Süssmayr has suffered more than most from highly charged agendas. Constanze, entirely understandably, needed to make money out of the work to support herself and her two young sons and was eager therefore to claim that it was almost entirely Mozart's own work, thus cashing in as much as possible on Mozart's growing posthumous reputation. Equally, scholars such as Maunder and Druce prepared their own completions of the Requiem (1988 and 1993) and would be expected, therefore, to marginalize or find faults with Süssmayr's contribution to the project. New completions, in fact, have become fairly commonplace of late – Franz Beyer (1971), H. C. Robbins Landon (1989) and Robert Levin (1994), as well as Maunder and Druce, have all tried their hand, altering Süssmayr's purported contributions to lesser and greater extents. (Both Maunder and Levin composed intelligent fugues for the 'Amen' of the 'Lacrymosa', in light of the discovery of Mozart's sketch.) All told, however, it is far from certain that any of these recent completions represent technical, aesthetic and stylistic 'improvements' over Süssmayr. And the thorny question of whether they correspond more closely to Mozart's intentions than Süssmayr's version remains unanswerable.

2. The work and its reception

There are only a few recorded performances of Mozart's Requiem in the 1790s, before the work grew remarkably in popularity in the early years of the nineteenth century. It is not impossible that parts of the Requiem were performed in VIENNA on 10 December 1791, just five days after Mozart's death; in any case, it is likely that the benefit concert on 2 January 1793 for Constanze and her children organized by BARON VAN SWIETEN (1733–1803), a friend and ardent supporter of Mozart, included a performance of it. Count Walsegg-Stuppach conducted his first performance on 14 December 1793 in Wiener-Neustadt using a score that bore the provocative inscription 'Requiem composto dal Conte Walsegg'. (It is far from certain, however, that he intended this inscription to be taken seriously.) Performances later in the 1790s took place at a concert organized by Constanze in 1796 and, in all probability (although documentation for it no longer survives), at a Leipzig concert given by Johann Adam Hiller, who called it 'the last but also the greatest of Mozart's works'. It would appear that few copies of the work were made at this early stage – in addition to Süssmayr (who seems to have had two copies) and Constanze, perhaps only the Elector of Saxony, the King of Prussia and Breitkopf & Härtel owned copies.

Publication of the Requiem, initially by the Offenbach-based JOHANN ANTON ANDRE, led to extraordinary popularity in the nineteenth century. It appeared at funerals and memorial services for musical giants such as JOSEPH HAYDN, BEETHOVEN, Weber and Chopin – the service for Haydn in Vienna on 15 June 1809 was conducted by Eybler – and non-musical figures such as Friedrich Gottlieb Klopstock and Heinrich von Collin. It is well known that the Requiem also featured at the funeral ceremony for Napoleon at Les Invalides in PARIS on 15 December 1840; it is less well known that it was included at an exhibition of pictures relating to Napoleon's funeral at St James's Bazaar in St James's Street in LONDON in 1841. As a reporter for *The Times* explained on 5 April 1841: 'The general effect of these pictures is very much assisted by military and sacred music, which is executed during the time of the exhibition by concealed musicians; it is very cleverly managed. The requiem of Mozart is more particularly well introduced.'

Alongside prominent performances came critical acclaim. As early as 1800, Breitkopf & Härtel called the Requiem 'Mozart's last and most perfect work'. Soon thereafter, the writer and critic E. T. A. HOFFMANN described it as 'the sublimest achievement that the modern period has contributed to the church' and FRIEDRICH ROCHLITZ identified the 'richness of harmony of great, profound ideas' associated with the sublime. Writers were fascinated above all by the work's biographical dimension: one of western music's greatest composers (a status well established by the early nineteenth century) was working on a requiem mass as he himself lay dying. The programme booklet for an early performance of the work, at Covent Garden in London in 1801, and an edition of it published by the Paris Conservatoire in 1804, even took the then unusual step of including biographies of Mozart, as if to emphasize to audience members that an appreciation of Mozart's desperate situation in late 1791 was an essential prerequisite to understanding the work. A reviewer of a performance at the Norwich Musical Festival in *The Times* (20 Sept. 1845) made a similar link in regard to the 'Tuba mirum': 'The whole character of this piece is plaintive and pathetic, bearing evident testimony to the state of the musician's mind at the period, when by the most solemn and unaccountable conviction he at once anticipated his death and sealed his doom by his unceasing labour to perfect the work commenced under such peculiar circumstances.'

In describing the 'Tuba mirum' as 'plaintive and pathetic', as well as identifying the 'gentle tinge of melancholy' in the 'Rex tremendae', the 'suppliant wailings of the praying penitents' in the 'Recordare' and 'the most pleasing impressions of peace and religious repose' in the choral segment of the 'Lux aeterna', this *Times* reviewer also reveals a predilection for the work's consoling qualities. Such qualities have been regularly associated with Mozart's Requiem in nineteenth- and twentieth-century criticism and can be equated, as Cliff Eisen explains, with the peaceful, quiet and Arcadian images of death that took root in the nineteenth century. But, Eisen continues, Mozart's work may in fact embody a very different conception of death as barbarous and terror-laden, a conception more in line with eighteenth-century writings. The Introit 'manifests the horror and uncertainty of death' on account of dramatic instrumental and vocal writing; the Kyrie fugue 'is an unstoppable floodtide of sound with few if any points of repose' where 'dominant tonalities are overshadowed by the darker world of the subdominant'; and in the Confutatis 'no-one takes heed of the prayers of the women to be spared the fires of Hell: like "Salva me" in the Rex tremendae, they are weak and pathetic'.

Irrespective of whether we privilege the consolatory or the terror-laden qualities of the work, it seems that Mozart wanted to situate his Requiem in the context of eighteenth-century music on the subject of death. The Introit, for example, derives much of its material from the first chorus of GEORGE FRIDERIC HANDEL's 'The Ways of Zion do mourn', HWV 264, a funeral anthem for Queen Caroline written in 1737. Mozart developed a close affinity for Handel's music in the last years of his life, making arrangements of a number of his works, including the *Messiah* and *Alexander's Feast*, so it is not especially surprising that his Requiem should reveal a general debt to his great choral predecessor. Like Handel's oratorios, too, Mozart's Requiem soon became popular with choral societies across Europe, with the result that massive choral forces were involved rather than the far more modest forces of the first performances. On 3 September 1818, *The Times* published a letter from a resident of Hamburg, describing one such occasion: 'In our great church of St. Michaelis, musical oratories the Messiah of Handel and the Requiem of Mozart will be performed by 500 persons in the evenings of the 7th and 9th of September.' According to Maunder's calculations, the earliest performances of the Requiem would probably have contained a choir of only twelve men and boys.

It is quite likely that Mozart would have added considerably to his portfolio of sacred music had he lived into the 1790s. In spring 1791 he was appointed deputy Kapellmeister to LEOPOLD HOFMANN at St Stephen's Cathedral in Vienna. While the position was unpaid, Mozart would have been firm favourite to succeed the ill, ageing Hofmann upon his death, and thus to secure a lucrative and prestigious position that reportedly paid a yearly salary of 2,000 gulden. But fate would take a hand, as Mozart died at the end of the year and Hofmann lived on until 1793. The Requiem could so easily have come to represent a new beginning for its composer rather than an extraordinary, compellingly mysterious end. SIMON P. KEEFE

F. Blume, 'Requiem but no Peace', *Musical Quarterly* 47 (1961), 147–69

C. Eisen, *New Mozart Documents: A Supplement to O. E. Deutsch's Documentary Biography* (London and Stanford, CA, 1991)

'Mozart's Leap into the Dark', in *Mozart Studies*, ed. S. P. Keefe (Cambridge, 2006), forthcoming

G. Gruber, *Mozart and Posterity*, trans. R. S. Furness (London, 1991)
D. N. Leeson, 'Franz Xaver Süssmayr and the Mozart Requiem: A Computer Analysis of Authorship based on Melodic Affinity', *Mozart-Jahrbuch* 1995, 111–53
R. Maunder, *Mozart's Requiem: On Preparing a New Edition* (Oxford, 1988)
W. A. Mozart, *Requiem for soprano, alto, tenor and bass soli, SATB and orchestra: K. 626*, edited and with a new completion by Duncan Druce (London, 1993)
C. Wolff, *Mozart's Requiem: Historical and Analytical Studies, Documents, Score*, trans. M. Whittall (Berkeley and Los Angeles, 1994)

rhetoric. Rhetoric is perhaps best understood as the art of persuasion in oratory. In the ancient world rhetoric was a fundamental discipline in the education of men of letters and especially among those who practised law. Textbooks on rhetoric were written by Aristotle, Cicero and Quintilian among others, and these writings once more became central to educational thinking from the Renaissance until the nineteenth century.

Music was considered analogous to rhetoric in some respects, and at least from the publication of Burmeister's *Musica Poetica* (1606) close connections were inferred between particular rhetorical figures and musical figures, especially in Germanic Baroque music which laid great stress on *Affektenlehre*. In the Classical era, in which the relatively 'static' concept of *Affekt* was gradually replaced by the more dynamic concept of topicality (itself stretching back at least to the time of Aristotle), the importance of rhetoric shifted somewhat, from a narrow obsession with 'figures' (almost always surface embellishments of some sort) to a more panoramic outlook dealing with the interrelationships between building blocks of Classical musical language and the form-schemes through which Classical music communicated with its audience.

The idea of communication here is vital. Rhetoric, as taught by Cicero and especially Quintilian in the ancient world and re-presented by, for example, Johann Christoph Gottsched, the eighteenth-century German lexicographer in works such as *Ausführliche Redekunst* (1736), was a series of conventions for the presentation of facts (whether verbal or, by analogy, musical), understood by both speaker and listener, according to which an argument was presented in a coherent way. These conventions included not only the *figurae* well known to Baroque orators and musicians, but structural matters – the relation of parts to the whole – the careful organization of which required skill on the part of the speaker, whose relative success or failure in persuading his audience of his case rested upon his command not only of the material but also of the conventions for presenting it. The hierarchy of this rhetorical system can be represented as follows:

SPECIES
Forensic Deliberative Epideictic
PARTES
Invention (*inventio*) Arrangement (*dispositio*) Style (*elocutio*) Memory (*memoria*) Delivery (*pronuntiatio*)

The three *Species* refer, respectively, to prosecution or defence of a legal case; a debate, in which the outcome is decided on the strength of the arguments for and against; and an oration in praise of the life and works of a notable person or benefactor. Of these, only the third (Epideictic) really applies, by analogy, to music, since its outcome is not in question: the purpose of the oration in such a case is to present what is already known. The existence of the oeuvre of a poet, praised in an Epideictic oration, is a finite concept, not in doubt (though its value may be open to interpretation); likewise, in a piece of Classical-period music the final destination (confirmation of the tonic key at the end) is not in doubt. Aristotle (*Rhetoric*) described this kind as 'especially suited to written compositions [he means words, not specifically music, of course], for its function is reading'.

While there were three separate *Species*, each with its own characteristics, the techniques for presenting an argument (for example, the development of a single idea by amplification, or repetition of a clause for effect, imperceptibly lodging a central thesis in the listener's mind) were developed primarily for use in Forensic oratory, and were transferred freely between all the *Species*. Eighteenth-century musical writers frequently make an analogy between the various techniques of oratory and those of musical composition. (For example, 'amplification', a rhetorical means of stressing an idea by piling up a number of related illustrations of the same idea in succession, has a clear musical analogy in the technique of sequence, including sequential melodic, harmonic and phrase formations often found in sonata-form development sections.)

The *Partes* of rhetoric were well known to eighteenth-century musicians. Johann Mattheson, writing in his *Kern melodischer Wissenschaft* (1737) likened music to rhetoric, as follows: '[In music] *dispositio* differs from the arrangement of ideas in a speech only in terms of its particular subject matter [notes rather than words] . . . it should observe the same six divisions normally required of the orator, that is to say . . . *exordium*, *narratio*, *propositio*, *confirmatio*, *confutatio* and *peroratio*.'

The terms *exordium* (Introduction), *narratio* (Statement of Facts), *propositio* (Proposition, or main idea, also known in German as *Hauptsatz*), *confirmatio* (Proof), *confutatio* (Refutation) and *peroratio* (Conclusion), to which Mattheson refers, belonged to the *Partes* listed above as Arrangement (*dispositio*), and were likewise central to Johann Nikolaus Forkel's important rhetorical-musical analogies in *Musikalischer Almanach für Deutschland auf das Jahr 1784* and *Allgemeine Geschichte der Musik* (1788), according to which musical composition was a kind of 'oration in sound' consisting of three stages (conforming to the first three of the above *Partes*, *inventio*, *dispositio* and *elocutio*): *Erfindung*, the creation of basic ideas (themes, for instance); *Ausführung*, the planning of a movement (for example its subdivision into sections of a recognized form, such as sonata form); and finally *Ausarbeitung*, the working-out of surface detail (including the embellishments, or *figurae*, so beloved of Baroque composers). Such was the rhetorical system of conventions in which composers of Mozart's time worked (or, at least, according to which their music was understood by some of the more prominent theorists).

The important question in relation to Mozart is whether he knew or cared about such theoretical constructs, given the practical and pragmatic concerns associated with making a living from composition. All that can be adduced with certainty is that he was educated in a household in which the intellectual traits of emerging ENLIGHTENMENT philosophy were highly prized. His father, LEOPOLD MOZART, himself the author of a textbook on violin playing that includes a 'Short History of Music' culled from his evidently wide knowledge of written musical theory traversing several centuries, was a passionate advocate of learning. He repeatedly sought out textbooks by the rhetorician Gottsched in the years before Wolfgang's birth (a number of letters survive between Leopold and the AUGSBURG publisher of Gottsched's works, Lotter), was a subscriber to GRIMM's *Correspondance littéraire* and owned a number of music theory books (including one by Mattheson).

Judging by the organization of Leopold's violin treatise, completed in the year of Wolfgang's birth, his approach to musical instruction was quite rigorous, proceeding from a solid theoretical platform. One can assume that, in the absence of a formal education, Wolfgang would have informally absorbed from his father's instruction a certain amount of the intellectual background of musical composition within which rhetoric played an important contemporary role. The impossibility of 'proving' whether or not Wolfgang composed 'rhetorically' does not remove his output from those contemporary, rhetorically inspired theoretical constructs formulated by Forkel, Türk and Koch among others; a recent attempt to situate Mozart's music in a rhetorical-theoretical framework can be found in John Irving's book on the piano sonatas. JOHN IRVING

M. E. Bonds, *Wordless Rhetoric: Musical Form and the Metaphor of the Oration* (Cambridge, MA, 1991)
J. Irving, *Mozart's Piano Sonatas: Contexts, Sources, Style* (Cambridge, 1997)

Robinig von Rottenfeld family. Salzburg friends of the Mozarts, with wealth from the iron and arsenic industries; members of the minor nobility. Georg Joseph Robinig von Rottenfeld (b. 14 Nov. 1710; d. 15 Jan. 1760) married Maria Viktoria Aniser (b. 16 Aug. 1716; d. 24 Apr. 1783) in 1743. They had three daughters and a son, Georg Siegmund (b. 20 Apr. 1760; d. 4 Oct. 1823). After her husband's death, Maria Viktoria ran the business, employing the Mozarts' landlord Johann Lorenz HAGENAUER as manager. The Robinigs owned a summer residence, the 'Robinighof' in Schallmoos, just outside SALZBURG. Siegmund was a violinist, and the two families often made music together.

Mozart's divertimento K334, with its march K445, was possibly written for Siegmund on completion of his legal studies at Salzburg University in July 1780. And although its identity is not definitely established, Mozart also wrote a piece called the 'Musique vom Robinig' (a designation indicating a masculine member of the family), mentioned in letters of 4 July 1781, and 8 and 29 May 1782. RUTH HALLIWELL

Richard M. Allesch, 'Die Robinig und ihre Nachfolger als Hüttrauchgewerken in Rothgülden', *Mitteilungen der Gesellschaft für Salzburger Landeskunde* 95 (1955), 93–119

Rochlitz, (Johann) Friedrich (b. Leipzig, 12 Feb. 1769; d. Leipzig, 16 Dec. 1842). A prominent writer and critic in the first half of the nineteenth century who met Mozart in Leipzig in 1789 and was well acquainted with such luminaries as GOETHE and BEETHOVEN, Rochlitz was the founding editor (1798) of the influential journal *Allgemeine musikalische Zeitung* published by Breitkopf & Härtel. He was general editor until 1818, but even after giving up the position continued to contribute articles and reviews. He was a great admirer of Mozart – as well as of J. S. BACH, HANDEL and JOSEPH HAYDN in particular – and wrote insightfully about his music in early issues of the AMZ, thus acting as an important promoter of the composer in the decades immediately after his death. But Rochlitz's forty-odd 'authentic anecdotes' about Mozart published in the AMZ (October 1798–May 1801) are misleading documents as many are known to have been fabricated. In addition to his writing and editorial work, Rochlitz composed a number of works early in his career, carried out an influential translation of DON GIOVANNI (1801) and wrote oratorio and cantata texts set by, among others, Carl Maria von Weber and Louis Spohr.

SIMON P. KEEFE

G. Gruber, *Mozart and Posterity*, trans. R. S. Furness (London, 1991)
R. Halliwell, *The Mozart Family: Four Lives in a Social Context* (Oxford, 1998)
M. Solomon, 'The Rochlitz Anecdotes: Issues of Authenticity in Early Mozart Biography', in *Mozart Studies*, ed. C. Eisen (Oxford, 1991), 1–59
W. Stafford, *The Mozart Myths: A Critical Reassessment* (Stanford, CA, and London, 1991)

Rosenberg-Orsini, Franz Xaver Wolf (b. Vienna, 6 Apr. 1723; d. Vienna, 14 Nov. 1796). AUSTRIAN count (from 1790 prince), diplomat, chamberlain to Emperors JOSEPH II, LEOPOLD II and Francis II, and manager of the court theatres from 1776 to 1791 and from 1792 to 1794. As chief steward to Grand Duke Leopold (later Emperor Leopold II) in Florence in 1770, Rosenberg helped Mozart and his father gain entry to the grand-ducal court, where they gave a concert. When Mozart moved to VIENNA in 1781 he reported that Rosenberg, now theatre director, received him 'politely' and heard a private performance of IDOMENEO. Rosenberg began looking for a singspiel libretto for Mozart, and shortly thereafter came the commission for DIE ENTFÜHRUNG AUS DEM SERAIL. With the success of this opera and Joseph's decision to install an opera buffa troupe in the Burgtheater, the manager urged Mozart to write an Italian opera. But relations between them had cooled considerably by the time Mozart brought LE NOZZE DI FIGARO to the stage more than three years later. DA PONTE records in some detail the controversy that arose when Rosenberg ordered, during rehearsals, that dancers be omitted from the wedding scene at the end of Act 3. Only through the Emperor's intervention were the dancers restored.

JOHN A. RICE

J. A. Rice, *Antonio Salieri and Viennese Opera* (Chicago, 1998)
C. Wurzbach, *Biographisches Lexikon des Kaiserthums Oesterreich* (Vienna, 1856–91)

Rumbeke, Marie Karoline, Countess, née Cobenzl (1755–1812). Wife of Count (Chrétien) Charles Rumbeke – they married on 12 July 1778 – Countess Rumbeke studied the piano with Mozart in VIENNA, beginning lessons only days after he arrived on 16 March 1781. (Mozart reported to his father that she was under his tutelage on 28 March and that as of 16 June she was his only pupil.) By 22 December 1781 she was having a lesson every day and paying six ducats for twelve. It is possible that Mozart wrote the piano and violin variations on the French song 'La bergère Célimène', K359 (1781) for her. On their Viennese publication in 1784 Mozart also dedicated his piano sonatas K284 in D and K333 in B flat and his violin and piano sonata K454 in B flat to Countess Rumbeke's sister-in-law, Theresia Johanna Cobenzl. SIMON P. KEEFE

S

Salieri, Antonio (b. Legnago, 18 Aug. 1750; d. Vienna, 7 May 1825). An Italian musician resident in VIENNA, he played a crucial role in the evolution of Viennese opera during thirty-five years as composer and conductor. FLORIAN GASSMANN, music director of the Viennese court theatres, brought Salieri from Venice to Vienna in 1766. The sixteen-year-old orphan's charm and musicality won the patronage of JOSEPH II, under whose protection his education and career flourished. From 1770 to 1804 he wrote many operas for the court theatres and fulfilled commissions in Italy, MUNICH and PARIS. In 1788 Joseph appointed him Hofkapellmeister, a position he occupied for the rest of his career.

Salieri probably came into contact with Mozart for the first time in 1768, when LEOPOLD MOZART and Wolfgang stayed in Vienna for several months and Wolfgang composed *LA FINTA SEMPLICE* in the vain hope of having it performed in the court theatres. On his next trip to Vienna, in 1773, Mozart must have heard Salieri's comic opera *La locandiera*, which was performed frequently during Mozart's residence in the capital. Another opera by Salieri Mozart knew was *La fiera di Venezia*, from which he borrowed, as a theme for keyboard variations, a minuet that accompanies the dancing and conversation ('Mio caro Adone') from the finale of Act 2. This ballroom scene probably served later as inspiration for the finale of Act 1 of *DON GIOVANNI*, an opera in which Mozart seems to have incorporated many aspects of Salieri's art.

It was not until Mozart settled in Vienna in 1781 that he came into close and frequent contact with Salieri, who quickly came to personify the obstacles that he perceived to be blocking the advancement of his career. Shortly after arriving in Vienna he wrote to his father that the Emperor 'cares for no one but Salieri'. Although he earned the patronage of many of Vienna's leading music lovers, commissions from the court for several operas, and a paid position in Emperor Joseph's *Kammermusik*, Mozart remained below Salieri in the court hierarchy, where the principle of seniority was rarely violated. Clearly aware of the extent to which his talent surpassed Salieri's, he resented the older composer, and rarely mentioned his name in his letters except in a tone of disappointment or animosity.

In the little world of the Viennese court theatres, jealousy, backbiting and intrigue were facts of life. Mozart and Salieri were probably both victims at different times of secret machinations – 'cabals' – that every librettist, composer and singer feared. Mozart expressed in his letters anti-Italian prejudice common among Austrians of his time, which may have encouraged him to think of the Italian troupe – with Salieri at its head – as a cabal organized against him. But there is no evidence to support the view that Salieri conspired against Mozart in any kind of long-term, systematic campaign. CONSTANZE MOZART told the NOVELLOS in 1829 that 'Salieri's enmity arose from Mozart setting the COSÌ FAN TUTTE which he had originally commenced and given up as unworthy [of] musical invention'. Constanze's statement, which has become easier to believe since the recent discovery of Salieri's settings of 'La mia Dorabella' and 'È la fede degli amanti', casts doubt on Mozart's claims that Salieri had worked against him as early as 1783.

Salieri rarely expressed his opinion of Mozart or of his works. According to his student Anselm Hüttenbrenner, 'of Mozart he always spoke with the most extraordinary respect'. At the same time, 'where he could detect a weakness in Mozart he pointed it out to his students'. Thus, for example, he criticized the finale of the first act of LA CLEMENZA DI TITO for its slow, quiet ending. JOHN A. RICE

V. Della Croce and F. Blanchetti, *Il caso Salieri* (Turin, 1994)
I. Mosel, *Über das Leben und die Werke des Anton Salieri* (Vienna, 1827; repr. 1999)
J. A. Rice, *Antonio Salieri and Viennese Opera* (Chicago, 1998)

Sallaba, Dr Matthias von (b. Prague, c.1764; d. Vienna, 8 Mar. 1797). A Viennese physician, who trained under Dr Maximilian Stoll and established his own practice in the late 1780s, Sallaba advised DR THOMAS FRANZ CLOSSET during Mozart's fatal illness in late 1791. They perhaps met on 28 November, after which (according to Dr Eduard Guldener von Lobes, a medical official in VIENNA in the 1790s) Sallaba reported Closset as saying, 'Mozart is lost, it is no longer possible to restrain the deposit [on his brain].' It is conceivable that Sallaba also visited Mozart on 4 December, the day before he died. SIMON P. KEEFE

C. Bär, *Mozart: Krankheit – Tod – Begräbnis* (Salzburg, 1967)
W. Stafford, *The Mozart Myths: A Critical Reassessment* (Stanford, CA, 1991)

Salomon, Johann Peter (b. Bonn, 20 Feb. 1745; d. London, 28 Nov. 1815). A violinist, conductor, composer and impresario, Salomon moved to LONDON in 1781, performing and promoting concerts in the city for the remainder of his life. He set up JOSEPH HAYDN's two visits to London (1790–1 and 1794–5), arranging the concerts at which Haydn's 'London' symphonies were premiered and GIOVANNI BATTISTA VIOTTI's violin concertos were showcased, and reputedly offered Mozart a contract for winter 1791–2 similar to Haydn's for 1790–1. According to Mozart's son FRANZ XAVER WOLFGANG MOZART, reporting to Vincent NOVELLO in 1829, Salomon was the originator of the nickname 'Jupiter' for Mozart's Symphony No. 41 in C, K551 (1788).

SIMON P. KEEFE

H. C. Robbins London, *Haydn: Chronicle and Works*, vol. III: *Haydn in England, 1791–1795* (London, 1976)

Salzburg. Austrian city on the Salzach river, capital of Salzburg province and birthplace of Mozart.

The city of Salzburg owes its post-Roman origin to the founding of the Abbey of St Peter by St Rupert of Worms in 696 and of the cathedral by St Virgil in 774. In 1278 Rudolph of Habsburg made the archbishops of Salzburg imperial princes and during centuries of relative peace (except for the Peasants' War of

1525–6), the power and prestige of the court increased until it was the most important and influential archdiocese and sacred state in German-speaking Europe. By 1700, half a century before Mozart's birth, its boundaries stretched north and west into what is today Bavaria and east and south as far as Wiener Neustadt and Graz.

While for visitors Salzburg could be a paradise, boasting natural beauties and a rich history, for the local citizenry, life could be less than ideal: the state was old-fashioned, education was out-of-date, censorship was frequent and society highly stratified. For local musicians, work at the court was full of vexations. This was less the case, perhaps, during the reign of Archbishop Siegmund Christoph, Graf SCHRATTENBACH (r. 1753–71), Mozart's first employer. Schrattenbach was often lavish in his support of the court music, exhibited a keen interest in instrumental works, sent his composers and performers to Italy to study, and rewarded composition with generous presents. And he was a strong supporter of the Mozarts: LEOPOLD MOZART advanced rapidly in the court music establishment during Schrattenbach's reign and during the 1760s and 1770s, when Wolfgang and his father travelled to VIENNA, PARIS, LONDON and Italy, the Archbishop subsidized their travels, at least in part. Still, Schrattenbach and the archbishops before him were not always attuned to the political currents of court musical life, as an incident from 1743 shows:

> At the archbishop's order, EBERLIN's promotion to deputy Kapellmeister had already been drawn up and was considered by everyone to be a closed matter. Then his rival, Herr Lolli (Eberlin's inferior by far in music experience), grasped a last means, threw himself at the prince's feet, and promised that, should he take over the office, he would serve without [additional] pay. And so the archbishop, who was determined to economize in every possible way, appointed him to the post, to [Eberlin's] detriment and much grumbling of almost the entire court and others.

Situations like these were exacerbated during the reign of Archbishop Hieronymus, Graf COLLOREDO (r. 1772–1803), who not only pinched pennies but also tended blindly to hire and promote Italian musicians at the expense of local talent. What is more, Colloredo was far less interested in the court music than many of his predecessors.

To judge by traditional Mozart biographies, Colloredo was a narrow-minded tyrant. And to judge by the Mozart family letters (one of the richest sources of information concerning music in the archdiocese) music-making was more or less restricted to the court and cathedral. Seen in this way, it was Colloredo's mean-spiritedness that was largely responsible for Mozart's mistreatment and sorry life in his native city. But the situation was not so simple. Colloredo had an agenda: to modernize Salzburg, to overhaul the education system, to rescue a financially failing court, and to promote both the sciences and the arts. Although he was hampered in these attempts by an unattractive personality, by his aloofness and by his general unpopularity, his reforms nevertheless favoured some aspects of local cultural life: a new sense of toleration and freedom of the press in particular attracted prominent writers, scientists and teachers to the court. At the same time, however, many of his reforms did away with traditional music-making opportunities in the archdiocese: instrumental music at local churches was restricted during some services, German hymns were made obligatory in place of more traditional liturgical compositions, and the important university theatre, home to the school drama, was permanently closed in 1778. For the court music establishment, these reforms represented a dilution of musical life and a source of dissatisfaction. Yet music in Salzburg was not entirely dominated by the court and any musician willing to negotiate the city's numerous musical opportunities was capable of carving out for himself a decent life. A musician who thought only in terms of the court, who failed to understand its implicit and explicit expectations and deliberately flouted the Archbishop – whether out of excessive ego, political miscalculation or both as seems to have been the case with the Mozarts – was bound to be disappointed. It was not Colloredo who was primarily responsible for their misery, but the Mozarts themselves.

The Salzburg court music was a sprawling institution, founded in 1591 and little changed, even in Mozart's day. In general, it was divided into four distinct and independent groups: the court music proper, which performed in the cathedral, at the Benedictine University and at court; the court- and field-trumpeters, together with the timpanists (normally ten trumpeters and two timpanists), who played in the cathedral, at court and provided special fanfares before meals and at important civic functions; the cathedral music (*Dommusik*), which consisted of the choral deacons (*Domchorvikaren*) and choristers (*Choralisten*) and performed in the cathedral; and the choirboys of the Chapel House (*Kapellhaus*), who also performed at the cathedral and who were instructed by the court musicians.

The chief duty of the court music proper, together with the *Dommusik* and choirboys, was to perform at the cathedral. For elaborate performances, the musicians numbered about forty, sometimes more; on less important occasions the performing forces were reduced. Sometimes musicians did double duty: because the woodwind players, trumpeters and timpanists played less frequently than the strings and vocalists, they were often expected to perform on the violin; when needed, they filled out the ranks of the orchestra both at the cathedral and at court, where concerts and table music were a regular if occasional part of their duties. The trumpeters and timpanists were also required to perform festive music at Christmas and New Year.

The boys of the Chapel House (founded 1677 by Archbishop Max Gandolph) usually consisted of ten sopranos and four altos. In addition to their duties at the cathedral, where they sang on Sundays and feast days, they performed at the university, at local churches and occasionally as players of instrumental music at court as well as receiving musical training from the court musicians: the theorist Johann Baptist Samber, Eberlin, ADLGASSER, Leopold Mozart and MICHAEL HAYDN all taught the choirboys. (Leopold began giving violin instruction at the Chapel House as early as 1744 and it may be that his *Violinschule* of 1756 was based at least in part on his lessons there; it is possible that other didactic music and music theory originating in Salzburg was similarly intended for the choir boys.) Teaching the choirboys meant extra income for the court musicians and it provided compositional opportunities as well. The *Unschuldigen Kindleintag* (Feast of the Holy Innocents) on 28 December was traditionally marked by music composed especially for the choirboys: Michael Haydn's *Missa Sancti Aloysii* (for two sopranos and alto, two violins and organ) of

1777 is only one example (other works composed by Haydn for the chapel boys include the cantata *Lauft ihr Hirten allzugleich*, a *Laudate pueri*, an *Anima nostra*, a litany and several other masses, among them his last completed work, the *St Leopolds-Messe*, dated 22 December 1805).

In addition to their service at court and at the cathedral, the court musicians also performed at the Benedictine University, where school dramas were regularly given. These belonged to a long tradition of spoken pedagogical Benedictine plays that during the seventeenth century developed into an opera-like art-form. Salzburg University, the most important educational institution in south Germany at the time, played a leading role in this development. At first, music in the dramas was restricted to choruses that marked the beginnings and ends of acts. By the 1760s, however, the works consisted of a succession of recitatives and arias, based at least in part on the model of Italian opera. A description from 1670 of the anonymous *Corona laboriosae heroum virtutis* shows the extent to which Salzburg school dramas represented a fusion of dramatic genres:

> The poem was Latin but the stage machinery was Italian . . . The work could be described as an opera. The production costs must have been exceptionally great. It drew a huge crowd. Part of the action was declaimed, part was sung. Gentlemen of the court performed the dances, which in part were inserted in the action as entr'actes. It was a delightful muddle and a wonderful pastime for the audience.

Mozart's sole contribution to the genre was APOLLO ET HYACINTHUS, performed in 1767 between the acts of Rufinus Widl's Latin tragedy *Clementia Croesi*.

It was the university that also gave rise to an orchestral genre unique to Salzburg: the orchestral serenade. Every year in August, in connection with the university's graduation ceremonies, the students had a substantial orchestral work performed for their professors. Typically these serenades consisted of an opening and closing march and eight or nine other movements, among them two or three concerto-like movements for various instruments. Although the origin of this tradition is not known, it was certainly established as a regular fixture of the academic year by the mid-1740s. Leopold Mozart, who composed more than thirty such works by 1757, was the most important early exponent of the genre. Wolfgang followed in his steps: K203, 204 and the so-called 'Posthorn' serenade, K320, were all apparently written for the university. Other serenades, similar in style and substance to those for the university, were composed for name days or, as in the case of the so-called 'Haffner' serenade, K250, for local weddings.

Aside from the court, Salzburg was home to several important religious institutions closely tied to, but still independent from, the state church establishment. Foremost among them was the Archabbey of St Peter's where the music chapel consisted largely of students; only a few musicians at the abbey were professionals, among them the *chori figuralis inspector*, who was responsible for the music archive. Nevertheless, St Peter's offered the court musicians numerous opportunities for both performance and composition. In 1753, Leopold Mozart composed an *Applausus* to celebrate the anniversary of the ordination of three fathers and some years later, in 1769, Wolfgang wrote the mass K66 for Cajetan Hagenauer, son of the Mozarts' landlord Johann Lorenz HAGENAUER.

Cajetan, who took the name Dominicus, was also the dedicatee of two of Michael Haydn's works, the *Missa S. Dominici* and a Te Deum, both composed to celebrate his election as abbot of St Peter's in 1786. Haydn had established close ties with St Peter's almost immediately after his arrival in Salzburg in 1763 and it was the source of his most important students and closest friends, for whom he composed his innovatory lieder for men's chorus.

In addition to St Peter's, Salzburg also boasted the important *Frauenstift* Nonnberg, founded by St Rupert c.712–14. Although strict cloistering was in effect from the late 1500s – access to the church and other external areas was walled off – some court musicians were excepted: Franz Ignaz LIPP, a contemporary of Leopold Mozart, served as music teacher there and the court music copyist Maximilian Raab as cantor. The court music frequently appeared for special occasions, such as the election of a new Abbess: when M. Scholastika, Gräfin von Wicka, was elected in 1766, the Archbishop celebrated her installation with a grand feast at which the court music played instrumental works and performed a cantata by Michael Haydn (*Rebekka als Braut*). For the most part, however, the nuns performed themselves, not only at Mass, but also the fanfares traditionally given on festive occasions or to welcome guests. A description from 1704 of a mass celebrated by the Bishop of Chiemsee and performed by the court music is telling: 'On 10 September at 10 am the Archbishop celebrated Holy Mass in the cloister church with the women performing the music. In the Johannes Chapel, where Baron FIRMIAN also celebrated mass, a song was sung, written specially for the occasion and set to music by Frau Anna Ernestina, who also accompanied.' The uncommon festivity of the ceremonies described here notwithstanding, this account includes a reference to what was perhaps the chief musical distinction of Nonnberg and other local churches: the performance of German sacred songs. Such works were composed and printed in Salzburg as early as the first decade of the eighteenth century, including the anonymous *Dreyssig Geistliche Lieder* (Hallein, 1710) and Gotthard Wagner's *Cygnus Marianus, Das ist: Marianischer Schwane* (Hallein, 1710). These songs, frequently performed instead of an offertory, continued to be written throughout the century, some of them by Salzburg's most important composers, including Eberlin and Leopold Mozart. More importantly, the cultivation at Nonnberg of German sacred songs provided opportunities for women composers; aside from singing at court, women in Salzburg had little opportunity to shine musically, no matter how exceptional they may have been (as the case of NANNERL MOZART shows).

Beyond the court and other religious institutions in Salzburg, civic music-making was important as well. Watchmen blew fanfares from the tower of the town hall and were sometimes leased out to play for weddings, while military bands provided marches for the city garrisons. And often there was a close connection with the court: it was the watchmen, not the court music, who played trombone in the cathedral during service. By the same token, private citizens – or court musicians off duty – also played. Concerts to celebrate name days and serenades to celebrate weddings were common, as was domestic music-making generally. In a letter of 12 April 1778, Leopold Mozart wrote: 'on evenings when there is no grand concert [at court], he [soprano FRANCESCO CECCARELLI] comes over with an aria and a motet, I play the violin and Nannerl accompanies, playing the solos for viola or for wind instruments. Then we play keyboard concertos or a violin trio, with Ceccarelli taking the second violin.' Nannerl Mozart's diary for 1779–80 documents other, similar occasions.

Possibly as a result of Colloredo's relative lack of interest in the court music, the local nobility started up a private orchestra, the first meeting of which was described by Leopold Mozart in a letter of 12 April 1778:

> Count Czernin is not content with fiddling at Court and as he would like to do some conducting, he has collected an amateur orchestra who are to meet in Count Lodron's hall every Sunday after three o'clock . . . A week ago today, on the 5th, we had our first music meeting . . . Nannerl accompanied all the symphonies and she also accompanied Ceccarelli who sang an aria *per l'appertura della accademia di dilettanti*. After the symphony Count Czernin played a beautifully written concerto by Sirmen alla BRUNETTI, and *doppo una altra sinfonia* Count Altham played a frightful trio, no one being able to say whether it was scraped or fiddled, whether it was in 3/4 or common time, or perhaps even in some newly invented and hitherto unknown tempo. Nannerl was to have played a concerto, but as the Countess wouldn't let them have her good harpsichord (which is *casus reservatus pro summo Pontifice*), and as only the Egedacher one with gilt legs was there, she didn't perform. In the end the two LODRON girls had to play. It had never been suggested beforehand that they should do so. But since I have been teaching them they are always quite well able to perform. So on this occasion too they both did me credit.

Finally, there were numerous institutions within the state, or just outside its borders, that maintained close contact with the court and other music establishments within the city. These included the Benedictine monastery at Michaelbeuern, four of whose abbots were rectors at the Salzburg University and some of whose musicians, among them Andreas Brunmayer, studied in Salzburg and remained there as part of the court music; and the Benedictine monastery at Lambach, which purchased music and musical instruments from Salzburg and maintained close ties with the Salzburg court and the Salzburg court musicians: both Michael Haydn and Leopold Mozart were welcome guests at Lambach. Other institutions allied with Salzburg stretched up the Salzach, along what is now the border with Bavaria: Landshut, Tittmoning, Frauenwörth, Wasserburg am Inn, Beuerberg and others. All of these institutions relied heavily on the city and their surviving archives are still home to important early copies of otherwise unknown works by Salzburg composers.

Contrary to received opinion, Mozart's Salzburg was hardly a musical backwater: it offered numerous opportunities for composition and performance, it maintained close ties with nearby institutions and cities, and music circulated freely there, including the most recent works of composers active throughout Europe. Leopold Mozart was in regular contact with Breitkopf in Leipzig, the most prominent German dealer in music manuscripts and instruments (several of which Leopold purchased for the court) and was himself the Salzburg sales agent for the music publisher Haffner in Nürnberg.

This cosmopolitanism notwithstanding, Salzburg, like all courts of the time, also clung firmly to its own performing tradition – and beyond that, there were local compositional expectations, even if these were not always spelled out. One of these expectations concerned church music: it was the primary obligation of Salzburg composers to write works for the cathedral. And while Mozart appears to have fulfilled this obligation – his church compositions amounted to some thirty works, including masses, litanies, offertories – he was, in fact, one of the least productive of Salzburg composers. During the same period, 1763–1780, Michael Haydn composed at least eleven masses, fifteen litanies and vespers and more than ninety other sacred works. Several aspects of Mozart's church music fall in line with Salzburg traditions: word-painting is common – including fanfare motifs at 'Gloria in excelsis' and 'et resurrexit' and falling melodies for 'descendit', 'Crucifixus' and 'miserere' – as are multi-movement Credos with changes of tempo, and fugues at 'Et vitam venturi' are common. In other respects, however, Mozart stands outside this tradition. His sacred works are more Italian in style than those of other Salzburg composers, no doubt a result of his contact in the early 1770s with Padre MARTINI in Bologna and Eugène, Marquis of LIGNIVILLE, in Florence and his composition of Italian opera, a genre not widely cultivated in Salzburg. Beyond that, the disruptive and disjunctive elements that inform his instrumental music of the Vienna period are often adumbrated in the Salzburg church music. Chromaticism is frequent and destabilizing while the Benedictus of K262 includes choral exclamations of 'Hosanna in excelsis' that interrupt the solo quartet (in the Benedictus of K258, the fast tempo and antiphonal exchanges between chorus and soloists are also atypical).

It is with respect to instrumental – and in particular orchestral – music, however, that Mozart most clearly flouted Salzburg norms. During Schrattenbach's reign, orchestral music was assiduously cultivated: during the 1750s, the court boasted three composers who were associated primarily with instrumental music, Leopold Mozart, Ferdinand Seidl and Caspar Christelli. By the 1770s, however, orchestral music was little cultivated, especially at court. A letter written by Leopold to Wolfgang in September 1778 makes it clear that he was disappointed both with the frequency of the concerts and with their length:

> Yesterday I was for the first time [this season] the director of the great concert at court. At present the music ends at around a quarter past eight. Yesterday it began around seven o'clock and, as I left, a quarter past eight struck – thus an hour and a quarter. Generally only four pieces are done: a symphony, an aria, a symphony or concerto, then an aria, and with this, Addio!

Indeed, the infrequency of the court concerts is indirectly documented by Nannerl Mozart's diary. Of the 151 entries for the period from 26 March 1779 to 30 September 1780, a mere two describe Mozart's official duties and both state only 'my brother had to play at court'. Apparently Colloredo did not allow much time for music, nor was he as concerned with the music establishment as he was with other aspects of court life. The historian Corbinian Gärtner, an observer well disposed towards the Archbishop, paints a picture of court life that leaves little room for entertainment, even if he does mention Colloredo's own occasional participation in the performances: 'Social gatherings began after 6 o'clock, during which [the Archbishop] often discussed business with his civic officials; otherwise he entertained foreign visitors, or played cards, or mingled with the court musicians and played the violin with them. Afterwards he had his evening meal, said his prayers, and went to bed at about 10 o'clock.' And Koch Sternfeld, in his early nineteenth-century account of Salzburg, noted that 'the Prince was less concerned with the court music than with court society and the pleasant life in Salzburg'.

On the other hand, Nannerl's diary includes numerous entries describing private music-making, including performances of quartets and quintets and rehearsals for a concerto. One entry describes a public concert given at the town hall while references to two presumably private academies are given in March 1780.

Another venue for orchestral music was the university. Although it is generally thought that the serenades and cassations performed by the court musicians were mostly composed for the traditional August graduation exercises, this may be only part of the story. The university diary for 1769 records a student performance of a *Platzmusik* in May and a similar event is documented – again by Nannerl Mozart's diary – for 24 September 1779 (the work performed was Mozart's 'Haffner' serenade). The university students, then, regularly performed (or had performed) orchestral works throughout the year, including works of a sort traditionally thought to have been given only at graduation. The same is true of other institutions. The estate inventory of Martin Bischofreiter, *chori figuralis inspector* at St Peter's, shows that orchestral music was a regular feature of musical life at St Peter's while the monastery at Michaelbeuern at one time had a collection of more than 120 symphonies, primarily works by Salzburg and Viennese composers. Salzburg's citizens also required music for their entertainment, and some of Mozart's best-known works of the 1770s were demonstrably written for private performance including not only the 'Haffner' serenade (for the wedding of Elisabeth HAFFNER and Franz Xaver Späth) but also the three-piano concerto K242 (for Countess Lodron and her daughters) and the divertimento K334 (for Georg Sigismund ROBINIG on the occasion of his law examination). The diary of the court councillor JOHANN BAPTIST SCHIEDENHOFEN describes a private concert made up entirely of Mozart's compositions:

> [25 July 1777:] to Gusseti's where the music by young Mozart, which he wanted to perform for his sister in the evening, was rehearsed. It consisted of a symphony, a violin concerto, played by young Mozart, a concerto for transverse flute, played by the violone [double bass] player Herr Castel, and everything was young Mozart's work.

All of this suggests that the court was probably not the principal venue in Salzburg for the performance of symphonies and other orchestral works – and it is in this context that Mozart's overwhelming interest in instrumental music seems like more than a curiosity: it seems like a provocation. Not only does the number of his symphonies alone almost exceed his entire output of masses, litanies, offertories and shorter sacred works, but by comparison with his contemporaries, Mozart clearly positioned himself as the city's dominant composer of orchestral music.

An obvious question, then, is why Mozart composed so many symphonies and other instrumental works in Salzburg. He was not obliged to. In fact, composition was not a specific obligation of the court musicians, not even the composition of church music. Mozart's appointment as court organist states only that 'he shall . . . carry out his appointed duties with diligence assiduity and irreproachably, in the Cathedral as well as at court and in the chapel, and shall *as far as possible* serve the court and the church with new compositions made by him'.

One possible answer to this question is hinted at in Leopold Mozart's letter of 28 May 1778 to his wife and son:

> The Archbishop of Olmütz was consecrated on the 17th. If you had not had so much to do for other people at MANNHEIM, you might have finished your mass and sent it to me. For at our practices Brunetti was chattering about who should compose the consecration mass and was hoping to arrange for Haydn to get the commission from the Archbishop. But the latter never replied; nor did Counts Czernin and Starhemberg who were approached by Brunetti and Frau Haydn. I therefore produced Wolfgang's mass with the organ solo, taking the Kyrie from the SPAUR mass.

Leopold's freedom of action was possible because the choice of works to be performed at court depended almost entirely on whoever was in charge that week, a practice documented by the 'Nachricht':

> The three court composers play their instruments in the church as well as in the chamber and in rotation with the Kapellmeister, each has the direction of the court music for a week at a time. All the musical arrangements depend solely upon whoever is in charge each week as he, at his pleasure, can perform his own or other persons' pieces.

This may explain why so few of Wolfgang's works seem to have been heard at court. Music-making in Salzburg was strictly ad hoc: the choice of works to be performed fell to the music director; the choice of works to be written fell to the composer. And because the Mozarts were not well liked by many of the court musicians, it is possible that Wolfgang's music was performed only when Leopold was weekly director (and even then under duress).

To Colloredo, it may have seemed that Wolfgang, given the opportunity, was slacking off. Certainly Mozart gave him plenty of ammunition, not only during the mid-1770s but also after the disastrous trip to Mannheim and Paris of 1777–8 when he was reinstated at Salzburg under favourable conditions as court and cathedral organist. For although in 1779 and 1780 he composed the 'Coronation' Mass, K317, and the *Missa solemnis*, K337, the Vespers, K321 and K339 and the Regina coeli, K276, Colloredo was not satisfied. In an ambiguously worded document appointing Michael Haydn to replace Mozart in 1782 he wrote: 'we accordingly appoint [Johann Michael Haydn] as our court and cathedral organist, in the same fashion as young Mozart was obligated, with the additional stipulation that he show more diligence . . . and compose more often for our cathedral and chamber music, and, in such cases, himself direct in the cathedral on every occasion'. Why this apparent criticism of Mozart? The answer, perhaps, is to be found in his other compositions of the time: the concerto for two pianos K365, the accompanied sonata K378, the symphonies K318, 319 and 338, the 'Posthorn' serenade, K320, the divertimento K334, the Sinfonia concertante, K364, incidental music for THAMOS, KÖNIG IN ÄGYPTEN, K345 and ZAIDE, K344, and, from the end of the 1770s, IDOMENEO. Few if any of these works would have been heard at court.

Even the few orchestral works by Mozart that came to the court's notice must have surprised the Archbishop – their complexity, colourful scoring, harmonic richness and, above all, expressive density, even among symphonies of the early 1770s, are not like other comparable works composed in Salzburg. A case in point is the symphony K133 that has been compared with Michael Haydn's symphony Sherman 81 (Perger 9). Haydn's symphony, which originally consisted of three movements composed in 1766, was augmented in 1772 by the addition of a finale; the autograph of this new movement is dated 15 June 1772. K133 was completed a month later, in July. Parallels between the works seem clear: both have quiet, lyrical main themes that are withheld at the beginning of the recapitulation and reappear only at the conclusion of the movement. And in both works, the theme returns *forte*, with augmented scoring (as early as the development in Haydn's symphony but not until the recapitulation in Mozart's). But these similarities are mostly on the surface and the two composers work out their ideas in strikingly different ways.

Like other Salzburg symphonies of the 1760s and 1770s, Haydn's work essentially consists of blocks of material that are shifted about and rearranged in a different order, occasionally with varied scoring and dynamics, but only rarely with different functions. It begins with a two-part theme contrasting *piano* and *forte* which is then repeated and extended into a transition; the dominant-area material is also given a double statement before moving on to closing material. The recapitulation, as noted, begins with dominant-area material before bringing back the main tune and its continuation as well as the closing. There is little that is dramatic about the movement. The restatement of the opening theme in the central section is developmental only by virtue of its location: the material is tonally stable. Even the return at the end of the movement is unexceptional: the material is stated once, more or less exactly as at the beginning of the work, and it leads directly to the exposition's cadential material, thus preserving a sense of closure that not even the reversed order of the recapitulation can disturb.

Mozart's symphony, on the other hand, invites critical response. For although it begins straightforwardly enough, with three *forte* chords, the character of the primary material is already different from Haydn's: where Haydn's main theme is harmonically and rhythmically stable, Mozart's – beginning in the second bar – has no downbeat root-position tonic chords and only deceptive cadences. The entire gesture, from the opening of the movement to the beginning of the transition, is ambiguous. Nor does Wolfgang anticipate the effect of his reversed recapitulation by giving out the theme in the development. In fact, its reappearance at the end of the movement is not recapitulatory at all: by any conventional description, the movement has run its course and the closing group has already signalled its end. What is more, Mozart's weak, unstable theme is immediately juxtaposed with its opposite: the full orchestra, *forte*, 'straightens out' the material, investing it with full cadences and strong root movements. It is functionally changed and, as closing material, makes palpable a meaningful reversal between the opening and closing of the movement. For where the opening juxtaposes a stable, *forte* gesture (the three chords) with an unstable, *piano* one (the main theme), the ending not only reverses this order but at the same time draws out the 'hidden meaning', so to speak, of the three chords: the final apotheosis is, in effect, a 'realization' of the three opening chords and the one gesture that finally gives the movement tonal stability and a convincing close.

It is no wonder Colloredo may have been perplexed by his young composer. And he was not the only one who found Mozart's Salzburg music unsatisfactory. When CHARLES BURNEY's correspondent Louis de Visme visited Salzburg in 1772, shortly after the composition of K133, he wrote: 'Young Mozhard, too, is of the band, you remember this prodigy in England . . . If I may judge of the music which I heard of his composition, in the orchestra, he is one further instance of early fruit being more extraordinary than excellent.' Possibly it was reactions such as these that led Mozart to write to his father: 'I confess that in Salzburg work was a burden to me and that I could hardly ever settle down to it. Why? Because I was never happy . . . there is no stimulus [there] for my talent! When I play or when any of my compositions is performed, it is just as if the audience were all tables and chairs.'

There is no question that Colloredo was a difficult employer. And his greatest failing may have been a blind trust in foreign-born musicians, Italians in particular, whom he frequently promoted over the heads of better-qualified local talent. Long-time employees such as Leopold Mozart and Michael Haydn, both of whom established their credentials during Schrattenbach's reign, had good reason to be disgruntled: not only were they repeatedly passed over for promotion but Colloredo's choices, even with respect to ordinary court musicians, inevitably turned out badly. Following the incapacitation in December 1785 of the violinist Wenzl Sadlo, Colloredo enlisted the two oldest choirboys from the *Kapellhaus* to play violin in the cathedral; this was a stop-gap action until the arrival in Salzburg of a new violinist from Italy, Giacomo Latouche. Leopold was upset. Not only had he hoped his pupil Joseph Breymann would be taken on, but Latouche made the worst possible impression:

> The new violinist arrived on Good Friday, but hasn't played a note of a solo yet, and as far as I can see, we'll hardly get to hear a concerto from him very soon either; something like a *quartet* maybe, because the Italians are saying: *the poor man – he's a good professor, you've got to give him that, and he'll be good leading the second violins*; but he *hasn't been used* to playing concertos. *At most he can play a trio or quartet cleanly, and what's more he's timid.* Now it can't be held against him that he's timid either, because after all he's only *30 years* old. So the archbishop has once again been nicely diddled and with a salary of 500 fl. to boot, plus 40 ducats travel money here and back making 700 fl. good luck to him! – on top of that the man isn't good looking. He's of medium build, has a pale rather puffed up face, and yet has certain bony bits to it too, like a horse's head, hangs his head forward, and chews tobacco like the Zillerthal farmers; that's what the Italians say. I pity the man, all the same it's a piece of Italian audacity to undertake something you're not capable of.

The upshot was that Latouche left court service in late 1786, excusing himself to Colloredo on grounds of poor health: the truth of the matter is that he left behind a pregnant girl.

At the same time, however, the Mozarts were not good employees. Leopold made no bones about his dissatisfaction. (Although he often wrote in cypher to keep his plans hidden from Colloredo and his censors, it is almost certain they were public knowledge.) And Mozart took over many of Leopold's opinions – whether musical or political – lock, stock and barrel. Most importantly, Leopold wrote from Schwetzingen on 19 July 1763: 'The orchestra is undeniably the best in Germany. It consist altogether of people who are young and of good character, not drunkards, gamblers or dissolute fellows.' And Mozart wrote, some fifteen years later: 'one of my chief reasons for detesting Salzburg [is the] coarse, slovenly, dissolute court musicians. Why, no honest man, of good breeding, could possibly live with them! Indeed, instead of wanting to associate with them, he would feel ashamed of them . . . [The Mannheim musicians] certainly behave quite differently from ours. They have good manners, are well dressed and do not go to public houses and swill.'

Men of good breeding, honest men, the Mozarts withdrew from the court music – from Colloredo who at least implicitly sanctioned ill behaviour and from their drunken, dissolute colleagues. And this withdrawal, at least in Mozart's case, manifested itself not simply as non-participation but in the seemingly deliberate cultivation of non-institutional music-making, of a type of music – instrumental and orchestral music – openly shunned by the court, and of a style foreign to local taste. Clearly the Mozarts saw themselves as moderns: Leopold says as much when in 1755 he describes one of his symphonies as 'composed in the most up-to-date fashion'. And they may have felt trapped in Salzburg, Colloredo's reforms notwithstanding. Certainly they felt unappreciated. Nevertheless, considering their strong attachment to the court and neglect of other institutions in the archdiocese, the Mozarts' reaction – haughty withdrawal – was bound to cause friction.

If blame is to be apportioned for the breakdown of Mozart's relationship with his native city, then it is clear that both sides were at fault. And yet history has adopted only one side of the story, namely Mozart's. It is worth asking how this came about.

Biographical accounts of Mozart published prior to the late 1820s make virtually no mention of his mistreatment in Salzburg. Not even Nannerl Mozart, in her reminiscences, has much to say about this. But with the publication in 1828 of GEORG NIKOLAUS NISSEN's *Biographie W. A. Mozart*, the story of Mozart's early suffering became a standard biographical trope. What gave Nissen (CONSTANZE MOZART's second husband) such authority was his publication of lengthy abstracts from the family correspondence – indeed, his is as much an epistolary biography (and as such at least indirectly related to the idea of the epistolary novel) as a scholarly one. The biographical power of these abstracts, including bitter complaints and frequent accounts of abuse, was beyond measurement: not only were they 'authentic', straight from the horse's mouth, but they reinforced the then-current 'idea' of Mozart as a quintessentially Romantic artist: discarded and neglected, passed over in favour of lesser talents, sickly and impoverished, doomed to an early grave. And the music composed between 1784 and 1788: so powerful, so moving, so 'absolute', so Viennese. Could a better foil be found for the creation of this classical (in the sense of exemplary) style than his miserable life in Salzburg, where he was subjugated by his father and the Archbishop and where, as most accounts have it, he was forced to toe the line musically? Almost inevitably, Salzburg came to occupy an important and thoroughly negative place in Mozart's history, fuelled by the composer's own words. Most important of all, perhaps, he was relieved of any personal culpability: it was not Mozart's fault that his life turned out the way it did – his true spirit, and the rewards that he deserved, are manifest in the grace and beauty and purity of his works.

It is a convenient story but not a convincing one. Salzburg, like all courts large and small, had its share of problems. And it was the Mozarts' misfortune to be just as problematic as their employer. Curiously, however, recognizing the complexities and realities of the situation does not much change the final outcome: whether he was a neglected Romantic artist or a rebellious *ancien régime* hothead, Mozart's story remains exceptional. And that, above all, is what posterity wants to believe. See also RELIGION AND LITURGY CLIFF EISEN

A more extended version of this article first appeared as 'Mozart and Salzburg' in *The Cambridge Companion to Mozart*, ed. S. P. Keefe (Cambridge, 2003), 7–21

K. Birsak and M. König, *Die grosse Salzburger Blasmusik: mit Ehrentafeln der Salzburger Blasmusikkapellen* (Vienna, 1983)
S. Dahms, 'Das musikalische Repertoire des Salzurger Fürsterzbischöflichen Hoftheaters (1775–1803)', *Österreichische Musikzeitschrift* 31 (1976), 340–55
H. Dopsch, ed., *Geschichte Salzburgs: Stadt und Land* (Salzburg, 1981–8)
C. Eisen, 'Mozart's Salzburg Orchestras', *Early Music* 20 (1992), 89–103
E. Hintermaier, 'Die Salzburger Hofkapelle von 1700 bis 1806: Organisation und Personal' (Ph.D. thesis, University of Salzburg, 1972)
A. Kearns, 'The Orchestral Serenade in Eighteenth-Century Salzburg', *Journal of Musicological Research* 16 (1997), 163–97
J. P. Schiedenhofen, 'Diary', in O. E. Deutsch, *Mozart: A Documentary Biography* (London, 1966)
M. H. Schmid, *Mozart und die Salzburger Tradition* (Tutzing, 1976)
C. Schneider, *Geschichte der Musik in Salzburg* (Salzburg, 1935)

Salzburg Festival. The most important predecessor of the present-day Salzburg Festival, an annual summer event and one of the most prestigious European music festivals, was organized in 1877 by the Mozart-Stiftung. Subsequent festivals – including those directed by Richter in 1879 and 1887 (for the centenary of DON GIOVANNI), Otto Jahn (1891, for Mozart's death centenary), Hofkapellmeister Joseph Hellmesberger (ii) (1901), Mottl (1904), Strauss and Mahler (1906, including a performance of LE NOZZE DI FIGARO by the VIENNA Hofoper personally subsidized by Emperor Franz Joseph), Artur Nikisch, Franz Schalk and Felix Weingartner (1910) – led to the idea of a regular event but although one was planned for summer 1914, it was cancelled at the outbreak of war. In 1917 Friedrich Gehmacher and Heinrich Damisch founded the Salzburger Festspielhaus-Gemeinde in Vienna, with a branch in SALZBURG, for the purpose of establishing an annual festival of drama and music with special emphasis on the works of Mozart; the first took place in 1920 with Max Reinhardt's production of Hofmannstahl's *Jedermann* in the Domplatz, since then a traditional event. Bernhard Paumgartner organized the first series of concerts at the 1921 festival and operas were first given at the 1922 festival in the small Stadttheater: *Don Giovanni* and COSÌ FAN TUTTE conducted by Strauss, and *Le nozze di Figaro* and DIE ENTFÜHRUNG AUS DEM SERAIL conducted by Schalk.

There were no music performances at the 1923 festival, when the first official International Society for Contemporary Music festival was held in Salzburg, and the entire 1924 festival was cancelled because of the general economic crisis.

The year 1925 was important, with the opening of the Festspielhaus, the first lieder recital and the first radio broadcast of a festival event (*Don Giovanni*, 24 August). The Festspielhaus was rebuilt in 1926 by Clemens Holzmeister to seat 1,200, first used for opera in 1927 (*Fidelio*) and altered in 1937 and 1939. Open-air performances have been given in the Felsenreitschule (Summer Riding School) since 1926; in the same year a contemporary opera, Strauss's *Ariadne auf Naxos*, was for the first time included among the festival events. During the 1930s Bruno Walter, Wilhelm Furtwängler, Hans Knappertsbusch and Arturo Toscanini were the leading conductors; Herbert Graf produced many of the operas. After the Anschluss in 1938, however, many artists left or refused to perform in Salzburg, including Walter, Toscanini, Fritz Busch and Otto Klemperer. Events were curtailed during the Second World War and the 1944 festival was cancelled.

The founding and early history of the Salzburg Festival has increasingly become a fashionable topic in cultural history; in one compelling view it is seen as a search for Austrian identity after the fall of the Habsburg monarchy, and as a conservative reaction against modernism. Since its resurrection in 1945, a number of premieres have been given at the festival, notably Strauss's *Die Liebe der Danae* (1952) and Henze's *The Bassarids* (1966); productions of early operas have also been mounted, including Cavalieri's *Rappresentatione di Anima, et di Corpo* (1968). The Vienna Philharmonic Orchestra has long been the musical backbone of the festival. In addition to playing for orchestral concerts, it has also served as the opera orchestra, chamber orchestra for the serenade concerts and for the sacred concerts. The first guest orchestra to perform was the Budapest Philharmonic Orchestra under Ernst von Dohnányi in 1931; the next was the Berlin Philharmonic Orchestra in 1957. Among conductors, the festival has been dominated in the post-war era by Wilhelm Furtwängler, Karl Böhm and Herbert von Karajan, who until his death in 1989 also served as musical director. Karajan was succeeded as director in 1991 by Gérard Mortier. Under his direction the festival has reintroduced the performance of classic twentieth-century operas, including Schoenberg's *Moses und Aron*, Berg's *Lulu*, Bartók's *Bluebeard's Castle* and Janáček's *From the House of the Dead*. CLIFF EISEN

S. Gallup, *A History of the Salzburg Festival* (London, 1987)
F. Hadamowsky and G. Rech, eds., *Die Salzburger Festspiele: ihre Vorgeschichte und Entwicklung, 1842–1960* (Salzburg, 1960)
M. P. Steinberg, *The Meaning of the Salzburg Festival: Austria as Theater and Ideology, 1890–1938* (Ithaca, NY, 1990)
R. Tenschert, *Salzburg und seine Festspiele* (Vienna, 1947)

Saporiti, Teresa (b. Milan, 1763; d. Milan, 17 Mar. 1869). Saporiti sang Donna Anna at the premiere of DON GIOVANNI at the National Theatre in PRAGUE on 29 October 1787 as a member of PASQUALE BONDINI's company. She stayed with Bondini's company until the late 1780s, moving to Venice for productions of Pietro Alessandro Guglielmi's operas *Arsace* and *Rinaldo* in 1788 and 1789 respectively and remaining in Italy for most of the 1790s. Saporiti was one of only two soloists from the original cast of *Don Giovanni* not to sing at the Prague production on 2 September 1791; the other absentee was CATERINA BONDINI (Zerlina), wife of Pasquale, and possibly Saporiti's sister.

SIMON P. KEEFE

Sarti, Giuseppe (baptized Faenza, 1 Dec. 1729; d. Berlin, 28 July 1802). An Italian composer famous for his opere buffe, Sarti held prominent musical positions in Copenhagen (1755–65; 1768–75), Venice (1775–9), MILAN (1779–83) and St Petersburg (1784–1801). Several of his operas were successfully staged in VIENNA during Mozart's decade in the city (1781–91), above all *Fra i due litiganti il terzo gode*, which was performed sixty-three times during this time, second only in popularity to *L'arbore di Diana* by MARTÍN Y SOLER. Mozart reworked the aria 'Come un agnello che va macello' from *I due litiganti* early in the Act 2 finale of DON GIOVANNI – in between citing Martín y Soler's *Una cosa rara* and 'Non più andrai' from LE NOZZE DI FIGARO – shortening it considerably. Mozart also composed piano variations on the same aria (K460) in 1784, around the time he met Sarti in Vienna as Sarti travelled through the city on his way to St Petersburg. He reported to LEOPOLD MOZART (12 June 1784): 'Sarti is a good honest fellow! I have played a great deal to him and have composed variations on an aria of his [K460] which pleased him exceedingly.' Writing sometime between 1785 and 1802, Sarti harshly criticized Mozart for cross relations in the slow introduction of the String Quartet in C, K465 ('Dissonance'), initiating protracted theoretical debate about this controversial passage.

SIMON P. KEEFE

M. Hunter, *The Culture of Opera Buffa in Mozart's Vienna: A Poetics of Entertainment* (Princeton, 1999)

Schachtner, Johann Andreas (b. Dingolfing, Bavaria, 9 Mar. 1731; d. Salzburg, 20 July 1795). SALZBURG court trumpeter, close Mozart family friend, poet, violinist and cellist. LEOPOLD MOZART's report on music in Salzburg in 1757 praised Schachtner's playing and taste and Mozart's divertimento K188 (1773) surely used Schachtner as trumpet player. In 1765 Schachtner published his *Poetischer Versuch in Verschiedenen Arten von Gedichten*, dedicating it to Gottsched. He wrote and translated texts for Salzburg composers: his best-known venture was the German translation of VARESCO's libretto for Mozart's opera IDOMENEO, but he also wrote the text for ZAIDE; revised and augmented the German version of BASTIEN UND BASTIENNE; and may have written one of the German versions of LA FINTA GIARDINIERA, the text of the *Grabmusik* and had a hand in the final chorus of THAMOS. Schachtner is remembered chiefly for his reminiscences of Mozart the child: he had been one of the Mozarts' almost daily visitors. On 24 April 1792, after Mozart's sister NANNERL MOZART had been approached by SCHLICHTEGROLL for information about Mozart to be published in his *Nekrolog*, Schachtner wrote to Nannerl answering her questions about his childhood. From him come several affectionate and well-known anecdotes (see MOZART, (JOHANN CHRYSOSTOM) WOLFGANG AMADEUS, B. PERSONALITY). His letter forms a crucial part of the reconstruction of the sequence of events culminating in the controversial postscript to Nannerl's essay.

RUTH HALLIWELL

B. Cooper Clarke, 'Albert von Mölk: Mozart Myth-Maker?', *Mozart-Jahrbuch* 1995, 155–91
H. Schuler, 'Der "hochfürstlich salzburgische Hof- und Feldtrompeter" Johann Andreas Schachtner: Ein Beitrag zu seiner Familiengeschichte', *Acta Mozartiana* 24 (Feb. 1977), 10–13

Schack (Cziak, Schak, Žák, Ziak), Benedikt (b. Mirotice, 7 Feb. 1758; d. Munich, 10 Dec. 1826). Tenor and composer. Following a period as chorister at PRAGUE Cathedral, Schack studied medicine and philosophy in VIENNA, before taking up music seriously. He held a post as Kapellmeister at a Silesian court from 1780, and in 1786 joined SCHIKANEDER's company as leading tenor; LEOPOLD MOZART praised him highly in a letter of 26 May 1786. With the company in Vienna from 1789, he was in demand in numerous roles, and as composer of scores and part-scores (often with GERL); he is best remembered for creating Tamino in DIE ZAUBERFLÖTE. He was on friendly terms with Mozart, who composed, or collaborated in, numbers for Schack's scores. Schack moved to Graz in 1793, and in 1796 to MUNICH. His wife, Elisabeth Weinhold, sang Third Lady in the premiere of *Die Zauberflöte*. PETER BRANSCOMBE

Schauspieldirektor, Der, K486 (The Impresario). Operas about opera were not all that rare in the eighteenth century – some notable examples include Benedetto Marcello's *Teatro alla moda* (1720), Domenico Scarlatti's *La Dirindina* (1715), Domenica Sarri's *L'impresario delle isole Canarie* (1724; with a libretto by PIETRO METASTASIO) and finally CALZABIGI's Viennese opera buffa, *La critica teatrale* (1769). So Mozart's *Der Schauspieldirektor*, a one-act farce about an incompetent impresario's faltering – and hilarious – attempt to assemble a cast of singers is part of a specific generic tradition, albeit one twenty-first-century audiences are apt never to have encountered. This 'Gelegenheitswerk', as its librettist called it (an 'occasional work', a term that sounds today like a mild put-down) was written expressly for a remarkable evening in which two acknowledged masters of musical theatre in the Habsburg capital, Mozart representing the newer genre of German opera, and ANTONIO SALIERI the high-prestige opera seria style, collaborated with some of the city's top celebrity singers and two prominent librettists to create elaborate 'behind-the-scenes' send-ups of VIENNA's theatrical elite.

Mozart's singspiel and Antonio Salieri's Italian comic one-act opera *Prima la musica, poi le parole* (First the music, then the words) were written for JOSEPH II, who ordered them to be performed at a celebration in the Orangerie of the Schönbrunn Palace on 7 February 1786 in honour of his sister Marie Christine and her husband Duke Albrecht of Sachsen-Techen, who were his co-regents in the Habsburg Netherlands; three public performances in the Kärtnertortheater followed later that month. JOHANN GOTTLIEB STEPHANIE supplied the libretto for the *Schauspieldirektor*; Salieri wrote his music for a text by LORENZO DA PONTE's rival Giambattista Casti. It seems that the Emperor wished to impress his guests with the quality of both his principal theatrical projects: at the conclusion of the formal meal, the actors and singers of the German Nationaltheater performed Mozart's comedy on a makeshift stage set up at one end of the Orangerie; they were followed – on an equally temporary stage on the other side of the room – by the members of the Italian-language court theatre with Salieri's contribution. Stephanie, who had also written the libretto for Mozart's DIE ENTFÜHRUNG AUS DEM SERAIL (1782), recalled later that the outlines of the *Schauspieldirektor*'s plot had been laid down by Joseph himself. Mozart worked on the music around the beginning of 1786; he entered the work into his thematic catalogue (something he did with operas only after he had finished the overture) on 3 February of that year.

The piece tells the story of the theatre director (the *Schauspieldirektor* of the title, played by Stephanie himself) Frank's futile attempts to assemble an appropriate cast of singers for an operatic season in provincial SALZBURG, a joke that would not likely have been lost on anyone in Vienna who knew of Mozart's well-documented distaste for his native city. Together with his colleague Herr Buff (a bass, portrayed by the comedian Josef Weidman) he begins by acquiring three actresses, who audition with excerpts from well-known contemporary plays. The entire fee for the first is offered by her long-suffering husband, the second is famous in serious roles but crushingly boring, the third is young and attractive yet somewhat precious. The real problems begin with the singers. Quality is not an issue; each is outstanding. Madame Herz (in the original production ALOYSIA LANGE, Mozart's former love interest, then sister-in-law, and one of Europe's most prominent sopranos) auditions with the arietta 'Da schlägt die Abschiedsstunde' ('The hour of our parting has come'), in which Mozart offers her both an almost melodramatic larghetto introduction and a brilliant, virtuosic allegro. Her rival, Mademoiselle Silberklang (created by CATERINA CAVALIERI, the original Konstanze in the *Entführung*, also a voice of top international quality), appears equally brilliant in her rondo 'Bester Jüngling, mit Entzücken nehme ich deine Liebe an' ('My dear young man, I accept your love with great delight'), which ends in a burst of coloratura fireworks.

Both are offered the same fee; and the seeds of theatrical disaster are sown. As the negotiations descend into squabbling, the two prima donnas are joined by the tenor Herr Vogelsang (in the libretto the husband of the third actress, in real life JOHANN VALENTIN ADAMBERGER, the first Belmonte) for a terzetto ('Ich bin die erste Sängerin'/'I am the prima donna'). It is the high point of the comedy, and a highlight in Mozart's entire operatic oeuvre, in which each of the would-be leading ladies tries to outdo the other. At the opening of the ensemble, in an energetic Allegro assai, Silberklang proclaims her superiority ('I am the prima donna!') to Herz's sarcastic replies ('I'm sure you are!') and over Vogelsang's pleas for compromise ('Each has her own special something'). A real coup comes next, as the expected slower section has no text beyond the single word 'adagio'; Herz tries to win the battle with heartfelt sensitivity and tasteful ornamentation. Silberklang retaliates, of course, with a brilliant, breakneck 'allegro, allegrissimo'. And so the conflict continues, until Vogelsang gives up his hope for mutual respect and wishes only for a final 'decrescendo pianissimo'. Frank, the impresario, then throws in the towel; with a company like this, he'll never make a profit. The comedy ends with Herr Buff joining the two divas and their friend Vogelsang for a moralistic final quartet: 'All artists must strive always to be worthy of advantage, yet to give oneself advantage and place oneself above the others makes the greatest artist small.' Weideman, who 'sang' Buff, had an awful voice: his couplet 'I am the first bass among the singers here' must have brought the house down.

With its clever manipulation of music within music (the audition arias) and music about music (the terzetto) *Der Schauspieldirektor*, which was written during the preparations for LE NOZZE DI FIGARO, is proof, if proof be needed, of Mozart's remarkable ability to write in several dramatic registers and 'voices' at once. It is also a fascinating document of one specific time and place, the musical Vienna of mid-1780s. For a composer like Mozart, who took special pride in his professional ability to write music to fit specific singers, it was a special chance to show this skill. By doing so, of course, he put the abilities of his colleagues in a flattering light while at the same time poking fun, with a light touch, at the institution (opera) upon which they all depended.

Der Schauspieldirektor was well received, even if the ubiquitous COUNT KARL ZINZENDORF found it 'very mediocre'. SALIERI's *Prima la musica*, which included both a caricature of Lorenzo da Ponte as an overbearing librettist and a show-stopping imitation by Nancy STORACE (who would soon create the first Susanna) of the castrato Marchesi, was no less successful. The Mozart work was revived in Vienna in the late 1790s; at around the same time it was taken up in Weimar in an adaptation by GOETHE. New productions followed intermittently in the nineteenth century, but Stephanie's text, laden as it is with cross-references to contemporary theatre, has not aged well. Mozart's voice, on the other hand, still rings loud and clear, even if we miss half the fun by not knowing his two leading ladies as he and his audience did. THOMAS IRVINE

L. Tyler, 'Aria as Drama: A Sketch from Mozart's *Der Schauspieldirekor*', *Cambridge Opera Journal* 2 (1990), 251–67

Schiedenhofen, Johann Baptist Joseph Joachim Ferdinand von (b. 20 Mar. 1747; d. 31 Jan. 1823). Mozart family friend belonging to the minor nobility, whose family owned estates at Stumm and Triebenbach. Their town house was in the Getreidegasse in SALZBURG, making them neighbours of the Mozarts. Schiedenhofen was a court administrator who eventually became Landschaftskanzler. Until his marriage in 1778 to Maria Anna Daubrawa von Daubrawaick he lived with his mother and sister Aloisia (Louise). Ten books of Schiedenhofen's diary have survived, covering the period 10 October 1774 to 18 April 1778; there are also occasional entries after this date. The diaries give a fair idea of leisure and culture in Salzburg, albeit with tantalizingly few details. Schiedenhofen's social circle included other members of the minor nobility, the family of the physician SILVESTER BARISANI, and the Mozarts. Activities included dancing, serenading, other forms of music-making, walking, hunting, shooting, card-parties, charade games, carriage outings and billiard and skittle games. The Mozarts were regularly invited to house parties at Triebenbach, and Schiedenhofen appears to have been particularly close to NANNERL MOZART during LEOPOLD MOZART's and Wolfgang's absence in Italy from 1769 to 1771, supervising her music practice and colluding with her in a jocularly undercover operation to 'steal' minuets from MICHAEL HAYDN. A number of performances of Mozart's compositions are chronicled by the diary, as is the plight of the Mozart family when Wolfgang applied to resign in 1777 and Leopold initially feared he had also been released from court service.

RUTH HALLIWELL

O. E. Deutsch, 'Aus Schiedenhofens Tagebuch', *Mozart-Jahrbuch* 1957, 15–24

Schikaneder, Emanuel (b. Straubing, 1 Sept. 1751; d. Vienna, 21 Sept. 1812). Dramatist, theatre director, actor, singer and composer. Educated at the Jesuit Gymnasium in Regensburg, where he also sang in the cathedral choir, he joined a travelling theatre troupe in 1773 or 1774. A singspiel, *Die Lyranten*, for which he wrote words and music, was performed at Innsbruck in 1775 or 1776, and at least one later piece, *Das Urianische Schloss* (SALZBURG, 1786) is recorded as having 'music, and book' by him. He was in AUGSBURG in 1776 and married an actress, Eleonore Arth, in the following year. In December 1777 he played Hamlet with great success in MUNICH, and soon after became director of a successful company that toured much of central and southern Germany. During their Salzburg season in autumn 1780 he became friendly with the Mozarts; in 1783 the troupe performed at the Kärntnertortheater, Vienna, and Schikaneder became its lessee for fifteen months. He was a member of the Nationaltheater (April 1785 until early 1786) and then took to touring again, returning to Vienna in spring 1789 as director of the Theater auf der Wieden.

For the next seventeen years he produced a stream of plays and librettos for this theatre, as well as acting and singing in many of them. He even continued to compose, as has become clear from the recently rediscovered Hamburg score of *Der Stein der Weisen*, which has the individual composers' names against the numbers they wrote. DIE ZAUBERFLÖTE is Schikaneder's supreme achievement, though a number of his other librettos and plays were highly successful and remained in the repertory of numerous theatres for many years. Among them are *Der dumme Gärtner aus dem Gebirge* and its six sequels about a gardener, Anton; *Der Spiegel von Arkadien*, *Babylons Pyramiden* and *Der tiroler Wastel* were popular opera books; and plays like *Das abgebrannte Haus*, *Der Fleischhauer von Ödenburg* and *Die Fiaker in Wien* strongly influenced the development of the Viennese local play. In spite of financial difficulties caused by the lavishness of his productions, Schikaneder continued to direct the Theater auf der Wieden until June 1801, whereupon his new house (he had found a generous backer), the superbly equipped Theater an der Wien, opened its doors. Schikaneder's triumphs were now behind him, and after he had sold the theatre to a consortium of nobles in 1806, he eked out an existence, mainly in the provinces, until his mind failed. He was brought back to Vienna penniless, and died there.

Schikaneder was one of the most talented theatre men of the era. Many of his plays and librettos show obvious signs of haste, but the best of them, most notably *Die Zauberflöte*, are skilfully constructed, with strong dramatic situations of which GOETHE spoke admiringly.

PETER BRANSCOMBE

O. E. Deutsch, *Das Freihaus-Theater auf der Wieden* (Vienna, 1937)

K. Honolka, *Papageno: Emanuel Schikaneder, Man of the Theater in Mozart's Time*, trans. J. M. Wilde (Portland, OR, 1990)

E. von Komorzynski, *Emanuel Schikaneder: ein Beitrag zur Geschichte des deutschen Theaters* (Berlin, 1901, rev. 2nd edn, Vienna and Wiesbaden, 1951)

Schlichtegroll, Friedrich Adolph Heinrich von (b. Waltershausen, near Gotha, 8 Dec. 1765; d. Munich, 4 Dec. 1822). A GERMAN scholar who taught in Gotha between 1787 and 1800 and was made director of the MUNICH Academy of Sciences in 1807, Schlichtegroll wrote a 6,000-word obituary of Mozart in his *Nekrolog auf das Jahr 1791* (Gotha, 1793), one of a series of thirty-four volumes of obituaries he published between 1790 and 1806. His information about Mozart derived from correspondence with Albert von Mölk in SALZBURG and Joseph Friedrich Retzer in VIENNA. (Both men had known Mozart.) Mölk conferred a great deal with NANNERL MOZART who in turn sought the assistance of a family friend, JOHANN ANDREAS SCHACHTNER. The input from these three sources, together with the lack of information gleaned from Retzer about Mozart's career in Vienna, resulted in a biographical account emphasizing Mozart's child-like qualities and his dependency on others. As Mölk reported to Schlichtegroll: 'Apart from his music he was almost always a child, and thus he remained . . . he always needed a father's, a mother's or some other guardian's care; he could not manage his financial affairs.' Franz Xaver NIEMETSCHEK's biography of Mozart (first published in 1797) drew heavily on Schlichtegroll for its description of Mozart's career prior to his move to Vienna in 1781. CONSTANZE MOZART, however, disapproved of Schlichtegroll's account, presumably because her late husband was portrayed as an irresponsible spendthrift. SIMON P. KEEFE

Bruce Cooper Clarke, 'Albert von Mölk: Mozart Myth-Maker? Study of an 18th-Century Correspondence Source', *Mozart-Jahrbuch* 1995, 155–91

G. Gruber, *Mozart and Posterity*, trans. R. S. Furness (London, 1991)

R. Halliwell, *The Mozart Family: Four Lives in a Social Context* (Oxford, 1998), esp. 581–9

W. Stafford, 'The Evolution of Mozartian Biography', in *The Cambridge Companion to Mozart*, ed. S. P. Keefe (Cambridge, 2003), 200–11

Schobert, Johann (b. ?Silesia, c.1735; d. Paris, 28 Aug. 1767). Resident in PARIS from c.1760 onwards as an employee of the Prince of Conti, Schobert was a well-known mid-eighteenth-century composer of instrumental music, above all sonatas, concertos and symphonies. He encountered Wolfgang and LEOPOLD MOZART in PARIS in 1763–4 and exerted an important influence on the young composer. In 1767, Mozart adapted the first movement of Schobert's sonata Op. 17 No. 2 as the second movement of his piano concerto K39. On his later trip to Paris in 1778 he taught Schobert sonatas to his pupils and quoted directly from Op. 17 No. 1 in his Piano Sonata in A minor, K310 (1778). Leopold, however, reported negatively on Schobert in a letter to his friend Maria Theresa HAGENAUER (1 Feb. 1764): 'My little girl [Nannerl] plays the most difficult works which we have of Schobert and ECKARDT and others . . . with incredible precision, and so excellently that *this mean Schobert* cannot conceal his envy and *jealousy* and is making himself a laughing-stock to Eckardt, who is an honest man, and to many others. . . . Schobert is not at all the man he is said to be. He flatters to one's face and is utterly false.' SIMON P. KEEFE

D. Heartz, *Music in European Capitals: The Galant Style, 1720–1780* (New York and London, 2003), esp. 689–97

J. Irving, 'Johann Schobert and Mozart's Early Sonatas', in *Proceedings of the Maynooth International Conference 1995*, ed. H. White and P. Devine (Dublin, 1996), 82–95

H. C. Turrentine, 'The Prince de Conti, a Royal Patron of Music', *Musical Quarterly* 54 (1968), 309–15

Schrattenbach, Siegmund Christoph von (b. ?Graz, 28 Feb. 1698; d. Salzburg, 16 Dec. 1771). Prince-Archbishop of SALZBURG 1753–71. In 1731 Schrattenbach became a canon of Salzburg Cathedral, in 1750 dean, and on 5 April 1753 archbishop. His birthday, name day (Siegmund, 1 May), and election day were celebratory occasions, when favours were bestowed. An example is his birthday in 1763, when LEOPOLD MOZART became Vice-Kapellmeister (albeit without salary increase), and the seven-year-old Mozart and eleven-year-old NANNERL MOZART played at the musical events.

Schrattenbach is often called Salzburg's 'pious' archbishop, quite different from his successor HIERONYMUS COLLOREDO. He is reported to have attended up to five church services daily, and he kept all the traditional church feast days. He was no intellectual, and was said to be not only bigoted, but also incapable of distinguishing true virtue from its counterfeit – Johann Pezzl reported that it had been possible to become a privy councillor simply by saying the rosary at an open window. There was a small nucleus of would-be reformers in Salzburg during his reign, but the ENLIGHTENMENT did not systematically penetrate institutions until after his death.

Schrattenbach followed not the Enlightenment model of a leader who was the first servant of the state, but rather the older patriarchal one. He attended weddings, was free with presents, and was fond of children, often standing as godfather. This may partly explain why the Mozarts seemed so high in his favour during Mozart's childhood. It is also possible that the development of Leopold's vision of Mozart as a miracle who had to be shown to the world (letter of 30 July 1768) owed something to Schrattenbach's particular brand of piety.

Schrattenbach encouraged native talent. He paid substantial sums of money for local female singers (including Maria Anna Braunhofer and Maria Magdalena LIPP, future wife of MICHAEL HAYDN) to be educated at the Pietà in Venice, and gave them court appointments on their return. Under him, too, many musicians enjoyed generous paid travel leave. Leopold was granted this for the Mozarts' first visit to VIENNA (1762–3), for their European tour (1763–6), and for part of their second visit to Vienna (1767–9). On this last occasion, however, Leopold's salary was withheld from April to December 1768 because he absented himself for longer than stipulated. Perhaps the court performance of Mozart's opera LA FINTA SEMPLICE on Schrattenbach's name day in 1769 rehabilitated the Mozarts, for Schrattenbach appointed the thirteen-year-old Mozart Konzertmeister (without a salary) in November 1769, and awarded Leopold 600 gulden (almost two years' salary) for Mozart's first visit to Italy from 1769 to 1771. Ironically, Schrattenbach's generosity sometimes caused trouble by fostering envy of his favourites – under his successor, Colloredo, there was certainly less favouritism altogether.

It was under Schrattenbach that the 'Neutor' or 'Siegmundstor', a tunnel under the Mönchsberg linking Salzburg with Riedenburg, was built, and opened on 26 June 1766. On Schrattenbach's death, Salzburg was deep in debt.

RUTH HALLIWELL

H. Dopsch and H. Spatzenegger, eds., *Geschichte Salzburgs: Stadt und Land* II:1 (Salzburg, 1988)
C. Eisen, 'Salzburg under Church Rule', in *The Classical Era: From the 1740s to the End of the 18th Century*, ed. N. Zaslaw (London, 1989), 166–87
F. Martin, *Salzburgs Fürsten in der Barockzeit* (Salzburg, 1982)

Schuldigkeit, Die. See ORATORIO

serenade. The terms 'serenade', 'cassation' and 'divertimento' were employed in the eighteenth century to refer to certain types of ensemble music. Often thought interchangeable, they began to acquire more distinct meanings in the latter part of the century, although exact definitions remain elusive. Examples of all three can be found in Mozart's oeuvre, although 'cassation' is the term least often used. Music in this period was broadly divided into three kinds, according to function – for church, theatre or chamber. 'Chamber' music, then, in contrast to its current usage, referred to any genre of instrumental music that did not fall into the other two categories, and encompassed SYMPHONIES and CONCERTOS as well as string quartets, serenades and divertimenti.

1. Serenades
2. Divertimenti
3. Cassations

1. Serenades

From about the sixteenth century onwards, the serenade was recognized as a song performed by a lover to his beloved in the evening, while standing beneath her window. The two characteristics of the location (out of doors) and the customary time of performance (in the evening) were retained, but by the mid-eighteenth century it had become a predominantly instrumental genre. (The 'dramatic serenade' (*serenata teatrale*) was a vocal work, closely related to opera – Mozart's ASCANIO IN ALBA is one such example.)

The orchestral serenade, particularly associated with Mozart's native SALZBURG, fulfilled a number of roles in that city's cultural and social life. One of these was to provide music, known as *Finalmusik*, for a ceremony to mark the end of the university's academic year each August. The earliest known reference to the performance of *Finalmusik* there dates from 1746, although the tradition may in fact go back further. The two bodies that made up the philosophy department of Salzburg's Benedictine University, the students of Logic and the students of Natural Science, each organized a *Finalmusik* performance. A serenade – a large-scale orchestral work – was performed in two places; firstly at the Schloss Mirabell, in honour of the archbishop, and then in the square in front of the university building, the Collegienplatz (now Universitätsplatz), for the professors. The performers, assembled from students, court musicians and possibly other amateur musicians, processed to and from each location, playing a march. LEOPOLD MOZART is known to have composed over thirty serenades for these occasions (although only one incomplete work is extant). Among Wolfgang's contemporaries, MICHAEL HAYDN and Josef Hafeneder likewise contributed to the Salzburg serenade repertory. The *Finalmusik* was commissioned from Mozart several times during the 1770s, resulting in the composition of the serenades K185, 203, 204 and 320. On occasion, a pastiche of different works was employed; this appears to have been the case in 1775, when the march K214 and other movements by Mozart were performed. The university archives show that serenades were also performed on other occasions during the academic year.

Serenade performances were in addition arranged to honour a particular individual, usually a member of the aristocracy. Mozart composed two serenades for the HAFFNER family, a family of wealthy merchants in Salzburg. His 'Haffner' serenade, K250, was commissioned by Sigmund Haffner for performance on 21 July 1776, the eve of his sister Elizabeth's marriage to Franz Xaver Späth. The second work, another serenade, intended to mark Sigmund's ennoblement in 1782, is known today only in a shortened version, as the 'Haffner' symphony, K385. In addition to the four movements that make up this symphony, a march (K408/2) has survived, but another minuet, mentioned in one of Mozart's letters to his father (27 July 1782) has not; other movements may also have been lost. Notwithstanding the original occasions for which serenades were composed, they could be reused for later performances, if required. Mozart noted that his first 'Haffner' serenade was performed again in Salzburg in September 1779, for a university professor, Herr Dell. The Salzburg serenade tradition appears to have come to an end in the 1780s – the last known *Finalmusik* performance took place in 1783.

Mozart's serenades are scored for similar forces to those established by his predecessors in Salzburg. The wind section usually includes a pair of oboes (doubling flutes) and two bassoons, along with two horns and two trumpets. In only one work, his 'Posthorn' serenade (K320), are flutes and oboes heard together in the same movement, and this serenade is unusual in featuring a 'post-horn' in the second trio of its second minuet. Remarkable too is the inclusion of timpani, which did not usually form part of the serenade orchestra. For practical reasons, they were omitted from the march associated with this serenade. The question of an appropriate string body for these serenades has been a focus for debate. In addition to the usual two violins and violas is a bass part, usually marked 'basso' or 'bassi' in the sources. This appears to have been intended for a violone (double bass), rather than a cello, although some scholars have suggested that both instruments were used (see also PERFORMANCE PRACTICE).

The marches associated with serenades were regarded as more or less independent of them, and could be performed with other serenades as required, provided both were in the same key. It is clear, however, that each serenade was preceded and followed by a march, which was evidently performed from memory, as a letter of Leopold's implies.

The majority of Salzburg serenades, including Mozart's, are between forty minutes and an hour in length, which accords with contemporary written accounts of their performance. One way to ensure that the serenade was of the requisite length for the occasion was to add movements, such as minuets, to an Allegro–Andante–Allegro outline. Minuets could be paired with one or two trios, and were sometimes set in remote keys; the first minuet from the 'Haffner' serenade is in G minor, rather than the tonic, D major. The opening movements, and some of the finales, are preceded by slow introductions.

In K250 and K320, the introductions prefigure the thematic ideas of their respective first movements.

A particular feature of Salzburg serenades was the integration of two or three concertante movements into the work. Highlighting a soloist or a small group of instruments added variety to the serenade, while providing an opportunity for the more virtuosic performers (probably court musicians) to display their skill. Wind and brass instruments are the most prominently featured in the concertante movements of the 1760s, while the violin is the usual solo instrument in Mozart's serenades. In addition to concertante trios to complement the minuets, serenades frequently included concerto-like movements, which could then be extracted from their original context to act as independent concertos. Leopold Mozart's trumpet concerto was composed as part of a (now-lost) serenade, and Wolfgang wrote to his father that 'the little concertante symphony from my last *Finalmusik*' (K320) formed part of a concert that he organized at Vienna's Burgtheater in March 1783. The 'Haffner' symphony, mentioned above, was also drawn from a serenade. The orchestral serenade, therefore, offered Mozart and other composers in Salzburg the opportunity for performances of symphonic and concerto repertory that was unlikely to be heard in other contexts.

The usual sequence of movements for Mozart's serenades consisted of a symphonic Allegro, usually in rounded binary or sonata form, two or three concertante movements, a minuet and trio, a slow movement followed by a second minuet (often with two trios), and a lively finale, scored for the full ensemble. The slow movement (often Andante) was generally scored for a reduced ensemble, as were the trios. The entire serenade was framed by a march, played by the orchestra while processing to and from the setting for their performance.

Aside from the issue of serenades being reused on other occasions, they could also be converted into four-movement symphonies by omitting the march and other movements such as second or third minuets. Besides the 'Haffner' symphony, Mozart adapted other serenades, such as K204, for symphonic performance in Vienna after he moved there in 1781. Vienna did not offer the same occasions for orchestral serenades as Salzburg and the serenades that Mozart composed there were probably intended for concert performance (see WIND MUSIC). Among them is the Serenade in B flat, K361, for twelve wind instruments (including two clarinets and two basset horns) and double bass. (It is also known as the 'Gran Partita', a title not assigned to it by the composer.) This work may have been commissioned by the clarinettist Anton STADLER, for whom Mozart later wrote his Clarinet Quintet (K581) and Clarinet Concerto (K622). Stadler, with an ensemble, premiered four movements from it in a concert at Vienna's Hoftheater in March 1784. Another serenade from the Vienna period is K525, composed in 1787. Entitled 'Serenade in G', it was entered in Mozart's thematic catalogue (*Verzeichnüss*) with the heading 'Eine kleine Nachtmusik' ('a short notturno'), which was probably meant as an indication of its function, rather than representing its title. Although scored for strings, with the bass part clearly marked 'violoncello e contrabasso', it is difficult to determine whether five solo strings or a larger ensemble was intended by the composer. Mozart's catalogue lists five movements for this serenade, but the first minuet and trio is no longer extant.

2. Divertimenti

A 'divertimento', in its most general sense, is music intended as light entertainment, either for a particular occasion, such as a name day, or as background music. Heinrich Christoph Koch, in 1802, defined the divertimento as a work with solo instrumentation, usually less developed than a sonata and eschewing contrapuntal techniques, intended 'to please the ear' rather than arouse the emotions. Such a definition cannot be upheld throughout the eighteenth century, however, as its usage was often imprecise. The majority of Mozart's divertimenti were composed in Salzburg, and comprise chamber works for ensembles of string and wind instruments, with some (such as K213 and 240) written for winds alone (see WIND MUSIC). They are generally scored for smaller ensembles than the serenades, with a group of two horns and four strings (two violins, viola and double bass) being one of the more common combinations. The Notturno, K286, is scored for four of these sextets. The two works that Mozart composed for Countess LODRON, in 1776 and 1777 (K247 and 287) were both intended as serenades for the Countess's name day, yet are entitled divertimenti, perhaps to reflect their smaller scoring of two horns and strings. *Ein musikalischer Spass* (K522), dating from 1787, is a later work for the same forces, albeit a more light-hearted one.

The divertimenti K136–8 are intended simply for four solo strings, but with the bass part played by a double bass rather than a cello.

3. Cassations

'Cassation' or 'cassatio', a less specific designation than 'serenade', was a term used in south Germany, Austria and Bohemia in the latter half of the eighteenth century. It probably derives from the German expression 'gassatim gehen' ('to perform in the streets'); Praetorius, in his *Syntagma musicum* (1619) mentions the term 'gassaten' in this context. JOSEPH HAYDN employed 'cassatio' and 'divertimento' interchangeably, generally for chamber works of a lighter character. 'Cassation' is a title rarely encountered in Mozart's works. In a letter of 4 August 1770, Mozart quoted the incipits of marches from the orchestral serenades K63, 99 and 100, referring to these works as 'cassations', but the autograph of K63 in fact bears the heading 'divertimento', in Leopold's hand. On account of this lack of precision we cannot ascribe a fixed scoring or number of movements to the cassation. It can be regarded instead as a generic term for ensemble music, usually applied to smaller-scale serenades. MICHAEL QUINN

Carl Bär, 'Zum Begriff des "Basso" in Mozarts Serenaden', *Mozart-Jahrbuch* 1960–61, 133–55
Andrew Kearns, 'The Orchestral Serenade in Eighteenth-Century Salzburg', *Journal of Musicological Research* 16 (1997), 163–97

serenata. See *SOGNO DI SCIPIONE, IL*

shorter piano pieces. Mozart's most significant contribution to the solo piano literature was undoubtedly in the field of the sonata. We must also remember, however, that in his lifetime he was especially well known as an improviser of fantasias, variations and sometimes fugues and that, to judge from the surviving details of his concert programmes as well as comments gleaned from his letters and the diaries of his contemporaries, Mozart's fame as a keyboard player and composer rested principally with works such as these, rather than with the sonatas. Sets of variations, often based on operatic arias, proved a popular 'concert' genre in the late eighteenth century and Mozart frequently played his in public concerts. The 'Fischer' variations, K179, based on a theme from the finale of J. C. Fischer's Oboe Concerto No.1 in G, were especially popular. Mozart often performed this set in MUNICH in late 1774 and early 1775, and again in PARIS during 1778. By contrast, the solo sonatas appear to have been intended largely for domestic use (see SONATAS). The ability to invent exciting variations on a theme provided Mozart with an instant entrée into Viennese concert life. At a public concert on 23 March 1783, for example, he improvised on 'Les hommes pieusement' from GLUCK's opera, *La Rencontre imprévue* in the composer's presence, and to great acclaim. This set subsequently became extraordinarily popular with Viennese audiences – and aspiring keyboard players – under its German title, 'Unser dummer Pöbel meint' (K455). Some eighteen months after this concert Mozart produced a fully notated version that he entered into his thematic catalogue on 25 August 1784; the set was published the following year. In the final published version there are ten variations on Gluck's theme, but there exists an earlier manuscript source containing just five, of which the last three are, respectively, variations 3, 5 and 8 of the eventual text. The extent to which either of these versions relates to Mozart's original extemporization for Gluck is impossible to determine, although together they provide evidence of his careful refining of the individual variations into a satisfying musical whole before he presented them to the printer, and consequently to the public at large.

To some extent, the popularity of Mozart's variations is borne out by publication statistics. Of the fifteen complete solo sets only one, the nine variations on a minuet by J. P. Duport (29 Apr. 1789) remained unpublished at Mozart's death (whereas just over half of his solo sonatas had appeared in print before 1791). Publishers were very keen to market Mozart's variations. On 14 September 1785, for example, the important Viennese music dealer JOHANN TRAEG (1747–1805) announced in the *Wiener Zeitung* that he had good-quality manuscript copies of Mozart's keyboard variations K455, as well as K359 and K360, on French tunes, for violin and piano, probably composed around the time of Mozart's move to VIENNA in 1781. K455 was also available at this time from a rival publisher, CHRISTOPH TORRICELLA. His 1785 'Prospectus' (whose contents we know from an advertisement in the *Wiener Zeitung* on 5 Aug. 1786) announced – in addition to K455 – the publication of two other variation sets for piano (probably K265, 'Ah, vous dirai-je, Maman' (1781–2), and K398, 'Salve tu, Domine' (1781), on a theme taken from PAISIELLO's *I filosofi immaginarii*) in the following, glowing terms: 'The eagerness with which the works of this famous master are on all sides especially awaited (these works win the attention of the connoisseur with their exceptional art and freshness, and so gently move our hearts with their melodies) persuaded me to make these very beautiful variations my own and thereby be once again of service to the most esteemed lovers of music.'

Altogether, Mozart completed fifteen sets of variations for solo piano. In addition to the complete variation sets there is a set of eight variations, K460 on 'Come un agnello' from SARTI's 1782 opera, *Fra i due litiganti*, which may be the variations referred to by Mozart in a letter of 9–12 June 1784. While the published text contains eight variations on Sarti's theme, the surviving autograph fragment preserves only the first two. The variation sets cover virtually the whole of Mozart's composing career: the earliest, on the Dutch song, 'Laat ons Juichen', KAnh 208, is dated January 1766 and was published at The Hague that year; the latest, 'Ein Weib ist das herrlichste Ding', K613, was written in Vienna in March 1791, based on a tune possibly by BENEDIKT SCHACK as incidental music to SCHIKANEDER's 1789 play, *Der dumme Gärtner*.

Stylistic features common to Mozart's mature variations include pensive, minor-key variations in the middle of a set that radically alter its *Affekt* and create the expectation of a subsequent, culminating return to a lighter idiom, and a tendency towards extreme virtuoso display. The phrase- and harmonic structure of the theme is generally preserved intact but at times the amount of figurative embellishment becomes so overwhelming that it is difficult, and sometimes impossible, to trace the original theme. While we may find that the quality of embellishment detracts from the overall structural integrity, it is important to bear in mind that it was their ephemeral, 'showy' effect (such as hand-crossing in K455) that so appealed to the taste of the Viennese public for which Mozart was writing.

Mozart's output of solo piano music, which extends over the whole of his life, contains an impressive variety of genres and styles. His earliest compositions are the minuets K1, 1f, 2, 3, and 5, and the Allegro in B flat, K4, written between late 1761 and early 1762. Other early piano pieces are the Allegro in C, K9a (summer 1763), an untitled work in F, K33B (October 1766) and two further minuets in D (K94, 1769) and C (K61gII, 1770). The extent to which LEOPOLD MOZART may have corrected the young Wolfgang's scribblings is unknown; his handwriting appears in some of the early manuscript sources. Entirely original is the later set of eight minuets, K315a, composed at SALZBURG in late 1773, following the third journey to Vienna. These were possibly intended for orchestral performance at the archiepiscopal court (or else at the university), though no text other than that for keyboard survives. Each piece except the last is a regular, binary-form 8 + 8-bar minuet and trio pair; Wolfgang Plath's handwriting research has shown that the final trio is probably independent of the rest of the set. The six German Dances, K509, composed at PRAGUE in February 1787, are of a similarly uncomplicated nature.

The only other independent piano piece pre-dating Mozart's permanent removal to Vienna is the C major Prelude (or Capriccio), K395, composed in Munich for Mozart's sister, NANNERL MOZART, at the beginning of October 1777. It arose in response to Nannerl's request for such a piece in her postscript to a letter from Leopold Mozart to Wolfgang (28–9 Sept. 1777). The work is in four contrasting sections (whose precise ordering is ambiguous, to judge from annotations to the autograph manuscript). Stylistically, it has very much the character of a free fantasia, depending for its effect on abrupt contrasts of register and figuration, especially, in what was evidently intended to be the opening section, and rapid arpeggiations of 'abstract' harmonic progressions, frequently outlining diminished sevenths.

Shortly after his arrival in the AUSTRIAN capital Mozart became acquainted with BARON GOTTFRIED VAN SWIETEN. Van Swieten was much taken with counterpoint, and especially fugue, and he soon gave Mozart free access to his extensive library of works by HANDEL and J. S. BACH. Handel's keyboard suites evidently provided Mozart with the inspiration to compose one of his own, in C, K399 (1782). The surviving movements (Ouverture, Allemande and Courante – a fragmentary Sarabande also survives) align themselves to no small degree with the Handelian – or, more generally, Baroque – idiom, including fingerprints such as the dotted rhythms of the Ouverture, and the cadential extension at bars 18–19 of the Courante (rhymed at the end of the second section of the binary form). On the other hand, there are features, such as the persistent chromaticism, that mark this music out as late, rather than early eighteenth-century style. In addition to various string quartet arrangements of fugues from Bach's '48', Mozart turned himself to the composition of fugues, an endeavour in which he was actively encouraged by his new wife, CONSTANZE MOZART, for whom he wrote the Prelude and Fugue in C, K394, in April 1782. In a letter to his sister (20 Apr. 1782), Mozart explains that he was working out the prelude while writing out the fugue – a casual-seeming boast nevertheless hinting that Mozart regarded the prelude as a relatively undemanding creative task that could be assembled 'in the back of his mind' while engaged in copying activity (whereas the fugue itself had presumably required more concentrated effort). The prelude is a multi-sectional piece whose purpose is to explore a few contrasting *Affekts* (sometimes touching on the *Empfindsamkeit* familiar from C. P. E. BACH's free fantasias, as at bar 33); the three-part fugue, by contrast, is very carefully composed (if a little stiff in its counter-subject), exploiting diminution and stretto presentations of the subject. According to Arthur Hutchings, it was modelled, perhaps, on J. S. Bach's A flat major fugue from Book II of the '48'. (K394 is possibly one of a projected series of six fugues for van Swieten that Mozart was composing at this time; the only others known are the fragmentary fugues in E flat, K153, and G minor, K154, completed after Mozart's death by Simon Sechter.)

Two other incomplete works are the fantasias in C minor, K396, and D minor, K397 (both possibly from early 1782). The former exists in autograph up to bar 27, initially for keyboard alone, but with a violin part added in the last five bars (concluding in the relative major, E flat). The fantasia was completed (for piano alone) by MAXIMILIAN VON STADLER after Mozart's death. The work was evidently intended as a sonata movement for violin and piano, but has found its way into the repertory of pianists. The D minor fantasia was also probably left incomplete. Its last section is a Haydnesque Allegretto, punctuated by a cadenza-like outburst and breaking off abruptly at bar 97 in the 1804 first edition. In the later Breitkopf & Härtel *Gesamtausgabe* a brief coda (probably by A. E. Müller) was added, still within the Allegretto tempo. Possibly though, had Mozart completed the fantasia himself, he would have engineered a more substantial return to the opening *Affekt* as in the more famous C minor Fantasia,

K475, completed on 20 May 1785 to precede the Piano Sonata in C minor, K457.

Most of the remaining solo piano works, composed during the last five years of Mozart's life, though varied in character and form, share an interest in chromaticism. This feature pervades the openings of the A minor Rondo, K511 (11 Mar. 1787), the Adagio in B minor, K540 (19 Mar. 1788), the *Kleine Gigue* in G, K574 (16 May 1789) and the strangely luminous Minuet in D, K355 (c.1789–1790?), whose reprise at bar 29 combines the main theme with a chromatic counter-subject. Of these late works, K511 and K540 are the finest. The rondo was perhaps originally intended to form a set of three, along with those in D major, K485 (10 Jan. 1786) and F major, K494 (10 June 1786, later reworked as the finale of the Piano Sonata in F major, K533), although in its motivic development, its tonal planning, its inventive use of the keyboard and its emotional intensity, it far exceeds them. The B minor Adagio (Mozart's only single movement work in that key, for which a six-bar sketch survives in a copy by Aloys Fuchs) is most notable for its expressive harmonic progressions (in which diminished-seventh chords play a significant part). Contrast of theme is also central to the unfolding of this sonata-form movement, and in the development, which moves purposefully through a wide tonal range, the second main idea is inverted and its structural purpose reformulated as a dramatic interruption of successive statements of the main theme.

Besides the sonatas for piano duet Mozart composed two 'single' duet pieces: the Variations in G, K501 (4 Nov. 1786) and the C minor Fugue, K426 (1783; arranged by him for string quartet in 1788, with an additional Adagio introduction, K546). The theme for the G major variations is possibly Mozart's own. It is arguably a finer work (at least, according to modern taste) than any of the solo variation sets, achieving, as it does, a fine balance between the generic characteristic of embellishment, the textural opportunities of the duet medium, and harmonic interest. While the structure of the theme (and most particularly, its rhythmic aspect) is preserved throughout, Mozart at one stage in the variations wanders into quite remote harmonic territory reinterpreting the theme chromatically and affording us a glimpse into an enchanting sound-world far removed from the innocent charm of the opening. As in the solo piano fugues, Mozart's stimulus for the composition of K426 was presumably his rediscovery of counterpoint in the works of J. S. Bach and Handel while under the spell of Baron van Swieten in the early 1780s. JOHN IRVING

E. Cavett-Dunsby, *Mozart's Variations Reconsidered: Analytical Approaches to Four Works* (New York, 1992)

A. Hutchings, 'The Keyboard Music', in *The Mozart Companion*, ed. H. C. Robbins Landon and D. Mitchell (London, 1956), 32–64

W. D. Sutcliffe, 'The Keyboard Music', in *The Cambridge Companion to Mozart*, ed. S. P. Keefe (Cambridge, 2003), 61–77

Sieber, Jean-Georges (b. Reiterswiesen, 2 Feb. 1738; d. Paris, 13 Jan. 1822). Moving to PARIS in 1758, Sieber began his career as a music publisher in 1770–1, continuing to trade from various locations in the city for the remainder of his life, latterly in partnership with his son, Georges-Julien (1775–1847). His output, impressive in quantity and quality, featured works by many of the leading composers of the late eighteenth century including J. C. BACH, Boccherini, Cambini,

DITTERSDORF, Gossec, JOSEPH HAYDN, PLEYEL, SCHOBERT, VANHAL and VIOTTI; his stock included first editions of Mozart's six violin and piano sonatas, K301–6 (1778) – Mozart's 'Op. 1' – and of the 'Paris' symphony, K297 (published c.1788) as well as the first full score of DIE ZAUBERFLÖTE, in its adapted version as *Les Mystères d'Isis* (1801). In 1783 he turned down the opportunity to publish Mozart's first three Viennese piano concertos, K413–15. Mozart had written to Sieber (26 Apr. 1783): 'I am not very well pleased . . . with the way in which works are engraved in VIENNA and, even if I were, I should like some of my compositions once more to find their way into the hands of my fellow countrymen in Paris . . . [I]n order to avoid delay, I shall quote my lowest terms to you. If you give me 30 louis d'or for them, the matter is settled.'

SIMON P. KEEFE

A. Devriès, 'Les Editions musicales Sieber', *Revue de musicologie* 55 (1969), 20–46

Sinfonia concertante. See CONCERTOS

smaller church works. These comprise Mozart's antiphon, Te Deum, psalm, and hymn settings.

According to Leopold's catalogue, Wolfgang composed 'Veni Sancte Spiritus', K47, during his visit to Vienna in 1768. A setting of an antiphon that begins like the second Alleluia verse for Mass on Pentecost (Whit Sunday), this work was composed either for Pentecost that year (22 May) or possibly during the following autumn. The opulent orchestration consisting of pairs of oboes, horns, clarino trumpets and timpani, in addition to the strings (with independent viola) and organ continuo, suggests a solemn occasion. This led some scholars to believe that the work was composed for the consecration of Vienna's Waisenhauskirche, for which Mozart wrote a mass, probably K139. The two triumphant movements ('Veni Sancte' and 'Alleluia') – paired soloists contrasting with the choral tutti passages in both – contain a rhythmic and melodic drive, as well as a textural variety, that evokes the monumental style of late Baroque church music.

Mozart's only Te Deum, K141, is believed to have been composed in SALZBURG at the end of 1769 and is modelled almost bar-for-bar on MICHAEL HAYDN's Te Deum for Grosswardein (1760). Its four movements contain functional, syllabic and homophonic choral writing, except for an impressively climactic duple-metred double fugue ('In te Domine speravi'). The 'Miserere nostri' (bars 118–25) also stands apart as a beautiful, prayerful passage for soft a cappella voices.

The a cappella 'Miserere mei, Deus, secundum magnam misericordiam tuam', K85, was probably composed during July–August 1770 in Bologna when the abilities of the fourteen-year-old Mozart were examined by that city's respected Accademia filarmonica; the 'autograph' score is in LEOPOLD MOZART's hand and it is believed that the work was left unfinished by Mozart and later completed by J. A. ANDRE. Composed for three voices (ATB) and organ continuo, it is a rigid exercise in the polyphonic STILE ANTICO. The affective use of dissonance in poignant polyphonic suspensions recalls Allegri's famous 'Miserere' that Mozart had heard only a few months earlier in Rome. Like Allegri, Mozart set only every other verse of Psalm 51: 1–14 as imitative polyphony, leaving out the intervening verses that would be sung to the original Psalm-tone chant. The lack of dynamic marks, tempos and other expressive indications is evidence of the purely pedagogical nature of the work.

Mozart wrote the a cappella motet 'Quaerite primum regnum Dei', K86, in the afternoon of 9 October 1770, as part of an academic exercise assigned to him by Bologna's Accademia filarmonica. The young teenager was isolated in a room where, according to Leopold, he composed the twenty-one-bar work in 'less than half an hour'. The Accademia then voted unanimously to accept the fourteen-year-old as a master composer – 'inter academiae nostrae magistros compositores'. For the strict four-part contrapuntal exercise in the first mode (dorian), Mozart wrote three un-texted voice parts (SAT) above a whole-note bass cantus firmus, which is the Vespers antiphon preceding the Magnificat on the 14th Sunday after Pentecost and on the feast of St Cajetan the Confessor, 7 August. Academy member Padre MARTINI also composed his own realization of the antiphon, probably for Mozart's instruction.

In Salzburg Mozart composed three festive settings of the Marian antiphon 'Regina coeli laetare', K108, 127 and 276, the first two of which were composed one year apart, in May 1771 and May 1772. The demanding soprano solos in both K108 and K127 were probably intended for Maria Magdalena LIPP, the wife of Michael Haydn; Leopold indicates that castrato FRANCESCO CECCARELLI later sang one of the settings. The influence of Neapolitan sacred and symphonic music is apparent in K108. In the second of the four movements impressive coloratura ranging from a high a″ to a low b is required for the delicate soprano part that is punctuated by two choral 'Alleluia' refrains. 'Ora pro nobis' (Pray for us) is a most effective cantabile aria with stunning ornaments and *messe di voce* upon sustained tones; only the strings accompany. The closing movement is an uplifting setting of the 'Alleluia' for chorus and a soprano soloist whose coloratura ascends at one point to a high b″.

K127 has the same text divisions and vocal requirements for its four movements as K108 and sets the opening movement in a similar double-exposition sonata form. In the two-part aria 'Ora pro nobis', one of the highlights of the work, the soprano exhibits her operatic bel canto skills while the accompanying strings spin a delicate web of undulating repeated notes and trills. Also, in the brisk, concluding 'Alleluia', the fireworks of the soloist's driving coloratura are repeatedly punctuated by the chorus's more sustained, homophonic statements.

Scholars consider 'Sancta Maria, mater Dei', K273, to be Mozart's musical 'votive offering' to seek protection from the Blessed Virgin Mary on the eve of his ambitious 1777 trip to MANNHEIM and PARIS; the autograph score is dated 9 September 1777, two weeks before his trip began. Consisting of a single movement, the setting is generally syllabic and homophonic with expressive use of appoggiaturas, and *piano* dynamics and a lower register set apart the more reverent lines of text. Here and there, however, immediate repetitions of phrases seem gratuitous, recalling a shortcoming in Mozart's earlier sacred works.

Mozart's third setting of Regina coeli, K276, is his shortest and best. Probably completed in Salzburg in 1779 – there is no known autograph score so the year has been estimated from the setting's similarities to the opening movement of Mozart's *Vesperae de Dominica*, K321 – the work contains an accompaniment appropriate for a solemn high feast, with pairs of oboes, clarino trumpets and timpani supplementing the basic church trio and organ continuo.

From 1773 onwards, Salzburg's new reform-minded archbishop, HIERONYMUS COLLOREDO, required that High Masses at the cathedral be restricted to a total duration of no more than forty-five minutes (as Mozart explains in a letter to Padre Martini on 4 Sept. 1776). Mozart seems to have made a virtue of this time restriction when he composed *missae breves* and a compact, energetic work like K276. There is seamless continuity throughout and an unrelenting dramatic repartee between the soloists and chorus. Aside from the opening line, the chorus sings only the recurring words 'Alleluia' and 'Resurrexit sicut dixit', with the repeated exclamations of the former at times recalling the start of HANDEL's 'Hallelujah' from *Messiah*. BRUCE C. MACINTYRE

K. A. Rosenthal, 'Der Einfluss der Salzburger Kirchenmusik auf Mozarts kirchenmusikalische Kompositionen', *Mozart-Jahrbuch 1971/72*, 173–81

K. A. Rosenthal, 'The Salzburg Church Music of Mozart and His Predecessors', *Musical Quarterly* 18 (1932), 559–77

M. H. Schmid, *Mozart und die Salzburger Tradition*, 2 vols. (Tutzing, 1976)

sogno di Scipione, Il, K126 (Scipio's Dream). It is almost certain that Mozart composed *Il sogno di Scipione* and the so-called *azione sacra Le Betulia liberata* in mid-1771 upon his return to SALZBURG from his first Italian sojourn with his father. Both compositions were based on librettos by the Habsburg court poet PIETRO METASTASIO, whose complete dramatic works had been presented to Mozart in Italy by the governor of MILAN, Karl Joseph Count FIRMIAN.

While it is hard to avoid seeing Mozart's early dramatic works in the light of his later development as an opera composer, such a perspective tends to obscure fundamental generic differences between his Salzburg dramatic compositions and his later stage works. *Il sogno di Scipione* belongs to a tradition of semi-staged, cantata-like dramas that marked important events in the calendar of court and Church – pieces whose primary function was to pay homage to illustrious audience members on the occasion of weddings, enthronements, anniversaries, and name days. Eighteenth-century musicians and writers used a loosely related family of terms to distinguish pieces of this sort, from the plainly descriptive *festa teatrale* and *azione teatrale*, which appeared on the title page of Metastasio's *Il sogno*, to the serenata, which generally referred to the most explicitly eulogistic compositions. Metastasio's *Il sogno* – a simple scenario drawn from Cicero's 'Somnium Scipionis' – was itself a remnant of an early eighteenth-century occasion: the Empress Elizabeth had commissioned it – along with music by the Bolognese composer Luca Antonio Predieri (1688–1767) – as part of the birthday celebrations for Karl VI in 1735.

It is understandable, therefore, that the fifteen-year-old Mozart, under the guidance of his father, should have turned to Metastasio's libretto when he laid plans for an occasional work of his own – a contribution to the festivities surrounding the fiftieth anniversary of the ordination of the Archbishop of Salzburg, Sigismund Count SCHRATTENBACH, due to take place in January of 1772. But, with the score completed, Mozart's project suffered a fatal setback: Mozart and his father returned from their second trip to Italy on

15 December 1771 only for Count Schrattenbach to die the very next day. There is consequently no record that *Il sogno* was ever performed in full; only a small alteration to the libretto reveals the intended purpose of Mozart's drama: in the concluding address or *Licenza* – which customarily turns to the immediate purpose of flattering a particular audience member – Mozart replaced Metastasio's fawning tribute to Karl VI with the name 'Sigismondo'.

Schrattenbach's unexpected demise left Mozart with a celebratory dramatic composition but nothing to celebrate; it seems that the teenage composer and his father subsequently sought out another festive occasion that might be worthy of *Il sogno*. The most obvious candidate was the impending enthronement ceremony of Schrattenbach's successor, and the autograph manuscript shows that Mozart seized the opportunity, once again adjusting the recitative of the *Licenza*: 'Sigismondo' now became 'Girolamo', the Italianized Christian name of HIERONYMUS COUNT COLLOREDO, whose appointment as Archbishop was announced in March of 1772. But it appears that Mozart was thwarted yet again: the enthronement of the new Archbishop turned out to be a modest affair – the Count, notorious for his parsimony, had no desire for elaborate musical entertainments.

Il sogno might have received a partial performance, however. For unknown reasons, Mozart composed a splendid second version of the final aria of praise from the *Licenza*. The Austrian musicologist Josef-Horst Lederer has hypothesized that this new aria, together with the preceding recitative (with its reference to 'Girolamo') and the following chorus, were performed as a short homage cantata at an evening concert around the time of Colloredo's enthronement.

Metastasio's plot is structured around a simple contest between two principal characters – a commonplace dramatic form for celebratory pieces of this kind. The bulk of the action takes place in a dream of Scipio, the Roman military commander and conqueror of Carthage, who lies sleeping in the palace of King Massinissa. The end of the Italianate two-part overture leads directly into the first scene, in which the two rivals appear – the goddesses Fortuna (Fortune) and Costanza (Constancy) – telling Scipio that he must choose only one of them as his lifelong companion and protector. Scipio's anxious opening F major aria expresses his confusion and doubt, confusion that is gradually dispelled as the drama progresses. Seeing his initial indecision, the goddesses pledge to help the hero make up his mind by addressing any questions or doubts he might have, although Fortuna urges Scipio to be quick lest she lose interest altogether, and launches into a rousing aria in praise of changeability. Having heeded Fortuna's warnings, Scipio finds himself spirited away to the Elysian fields; now it is Costanza's turn to address him. Having explained to Scipio the mysteries of divine harmony and the music of the spheres, Costanza uses her aria to compare mankind's feeble attempts to grasp the glory of heaven to the eye that is blinded when it tries to see the sun. Scipio is possessed with wonder; ignoring Fortuna's impatient demands for him to come to a decision, he begs the two goddesses to tell him more about the dwellers of Elysium. At once, a chorus of dead Roman heroes marches into view – their D major chorus bolstered by warlike timpani strokes – led by Scipio's father Emilio and adoptive grandfather Publio. Scipio is greatly agitated by this vision of the

Roman soldiers who gave their lives to conquer Africa, but Publio helps to calm his grandson by reminding him that the immortal soul lives for eternity and telling him that those who have lived and died selflessly receive the finest dwellings in Elysium. Publio's aria subsequently urges Scipio to lead a virtuous life if he wishes to receive his eternal reward.

By this time, Fortuna – in keeping with her changeable temperament – has had quite enough of Scipio's questions and presses him to come to a decision. Yet Costanza – likewise in keeping with her own character – admonishes Fortuna, reminding her that what Scipio learns will help him make an informed choice. Scipio first turns to the spirit of his father for guidance and Emilio teaches his son a lesson in perspective: from a heavenly viewpoint, the earth is a mere speck of dust among all the stars in the firmament. His aria expands on this theme: to the gods, the sorrows of mankind are like the petty troubles of a child to adults. Thus enlightened, Scipio begs to be allowed to stay in Elysium, but neither Fortuna nor Costanza can fulfil his desire; Publio and Emilio encourage him instead to fulfil his earthly destiny and do his duty for Rome. Publio emboldens his grandson with an aria comparing man's struggles to an oak tree in a storm, which sends its roots ever deeper even when it is battered by freezing winds.

The time has come to make a choice. Scipio, despondent in the face of the superior wisdom of his heavenly companions, asks Publio to tell him which goddess he ought to choose. Publio declines, however, saying that he would not deny Scipio the honour of deciding for himself. Meanwhile, Fortuna's patience is wearing thin; she urges Scipio to choose her, telling him that he will need luck on his side if he is ever to be happy. Her final aria contains a veiled threat: while fortune's favour makes for a life free of hardship, her frown incurs disaster. Yet Costanza is quick to point out that one power alone is equal to the terrible might of fortune – constancy. Her final aria counters Fortuna's threats with a description of steadfast rocks by the shore: even though they are submerged by the ocean in stormy weather, they will always re-emerge with the gentle waves lapping at their feet. Scipio is swayed. He decides against Fortuna and sings an aria condemning those who live their lives as slaves to fortune; the vicissitudes of fate have no power over a fearless spirit and a noble heart. Scipio is unmoved in his decision even when Fortuna becomes enraged and threatens him with thunder and lightening in a dramatic piece of accompanied recitative. And it is with this confusion of light and sound that the hero wakes and realizes that it was all a dream – an omen from the gods. Here, the *Licenza* begins, stripping away the allegorical veneer to reveal the drama's immediate political function: 'Scipio is not the subject of my verses', runs the recitative, 'my tongue exalts Scipio, my heart Girolamo.' The aria of the *Licenza* expands on the theme: there is no need to speak of past heroes when virtue is on hand in the person of the prince. A grand chorus ultimately joins with the strains of homage.

Even venerable twentieth-century critics – Edward Dent and Alfred Einstein among them – have ignored or dismissed *Il sogno di Scipione*, not only because it is the work of a teenage composer, but also because it is unequivocally an 'occasional work'. What is more, it represents a set of opera seria conventions that have since been routinely disparaged as retrospective and un-dramatic. *Il sogno* seems to be a remnant of all that the modern sensibility finds tiresome in the musical dramas of the Baroque: a crudely allegorical plot made from long stretches of recitative and a succession of dramatically inert arias, each centring on simple emotional utterances (for example, Scipio's opening aria of confusion), banal aphorisms (Publio's first aria, warning Scipio to lead a virtuous life), or similes (Costanza's final aria comparing the virtue of steadfastness to the rocks by the sea). Moreover, most of them can broadly be described as 'dal segno' arias, a formal type in which the music and text from an A section is partially reprised after a contrasting B section. Even the most sensitive opera critics have tended to imply that this repetition is problematic, because it is dramatically redundant or even tautological. Nowadays, however, critics and music lovers tend to be more sympathetic to these Metastasian musico-dramaturgical formulas. Every opera works according to formulas, after all, whether it be *Il sogno* or *Le nozze di Figaro*; formulas vary as widely as operatic genres themselves. And since one of the central aims of Metastasio's *Il sogno* is to arrange a narrative so that it triggers a succession of contrasting arias, each expressing a single mood or idea, one can say that the libretto is constructed with admirable neatness. And if Mozart's most engaging responses to Metastasio's text – particularly the framing arias of confusion and certainty from Scipio, Fortuna's arresting accompanied recitative, and the grandly proportioned arias for the *Licenza* – do not achieve the impossible and dispense with formulas altogether, then they might at least illustrate the difference between a winning formula and the merely formulaic. NICHOLAS MATHEW

C. Gianturco, *Mozart's Early Operas* (London, 1981), 120–30
S. Sadie, 'Mozart's Moralities', *Musical Times* (March, 1968), 222–4

sonata form. Sonata form became the essential structure for instrumental music during the second half of the eighteenth century. It is an expanded binary form whose first part cadences in a related key with the second part concluding in the tonic. The first part, often referred to as the exposition, displays three or four functions which include a primary section (P) that establishes the tonic key, a transition (T) that effects the modulation to a related key, and a secondary section (S) and closing (K) that solidifies the new key. Often, the exposition is repeated. The second part, usually also enclosed by repeats, consists of the development, which explores more distant keys and may also engage the exposition's materials in motivic play, and a recapitulation, which restates much of the material from the exposition in the tonic key.

A distinction is often made between two different approaches to sonata form depending on the nature of its thematic materials. In one approach, the expository functions, that is P, T, S, and K, contrast strongly, featuring a bold P theme, a T that exploits motivic play in the process of modulation, a lyrical S and a closing K that reinforces the secondary key. In the other approach, the expository themes are less differentiated: T may use motifs from P; and S and K may also be based on P. The exposition in this scenario can even be thought to be essentially developmental. In any case, such an exposition requires an intensified development section and a reformulated recapitulation. The exposition with related materials (the second type) is often considered characteristic of JOSEPH HAYDN, while that with contrasting themes (the first type) is often associated with Mozart. While this is a useful distinction, both composers wrote movements of both types.

Most striking about Mozart's sonata-form movements is the depth of thematic and procedural contrasts contained therein, such that P, T, S and K gain an identity rarely found in corresponding movements by other contemporaneous composers. Distinctively in the context of presentations of P, Mozart uses architectonic structures in such a way that the smallest element contributes to larger symmetries; in the first movement of the 'Jupiter' symphony in C, K551, for example, the contrasting two-bar units build clearly into two four-bar phrases (and an eight-bar P statement) articulating a I–V, V–I progression. Other examples of this symmetrical type include the P themes in the first movements of the Piano Concerto in E flat, K271, the Piano Sonata in C minor, K457, and the Piano Quartet in G minor, K478, as well as the last movement of the Symphony No. 40 in G minor, K550. A less symmetrical P structure is found, however, in the first Allegro of the 'Prague' symphony in D, K504, where Mozart strings out a series of unrelated motifs that can be combined contrapuntally.

T's harmonic rhythm often stabilizes to regular sequences moving in uniform motion. Before c.1780, T often consists of new material, but after Mozart's move to Vienna (1781) tends to be more developmental. Either way, T maintains a connection to P, if not thematically, then in terms of its surface activity; T's surface rhythms will frequently accelerate over that of P providing a rhythmically coherent P–T statement.

S frequently presents additional new material, except that after c.1780 Mozart may use, à la Haydn, material from P or less strongly contrasting ideas. S often possesses the symmetrical stabilization of P, but without its bold contrasts that are now regularly replaced by lyricism. S frequently begins as the most relaxed point in the exposition. However, like P–T, S together with K forms another swath of increasing rhythmic activity. But on this occasion, K frequently reaches a climactic point, which may be underscored by other non-rhythmic elements.

Prior to c.1780, Mozart's development sections often comprise new material and do not extend much beyond the level of tension found in the exposition. This is not to say that there are no fully-fledged and powerful development sections. A fine example of strong thematic and tonal working out is the finale to the Symphony in A, K201 (1774), where developmental aspects are already witnessed in the exposition. After c.1780, Mozart's development sections often combine potent tonal and thematic explorations, a good example being the finale of K550. After an introductory passage that approaches twelve-tone writing, Mozart continues to develop P with changes in orchestration, dynamics and texture. But it is the rapid tonal motion that drives the section as it moves upward and downward through fifths, reaching the most distant key from the tonic of G, C sharp.

Mozart's recapitulations generally match the events of the exposition more closely than Haydn's; Mozart tends to recapitulate all of the earlier material in the tonic key. In movements conceived in a more Haydn-like manner, Mozart sometimes excludes materials heard more than once in the exposition (for example, K504/i). The little Piano Sonata in C major, K545, departs from Mozart's practice of beginning the recapitulation in the tonic by commencing in the subdominant. This allows an eventual return to the tonic by transposing P–T–S–K down a fifth from the exposition. Among the smaller alterations found in Mozart's recapitulations is an intensification of the rhythmic tendencies noted in the exposition. This is especially true of K.

Mozart's concerto first movements combine the old ritornello, tutti/solo form with a structure close to that of his sonata-form Allegros. The first orchestral tutti, though not as firmly closed as a ritornello, remains for the most part in the tonic key and states material that is subsequently used in the first solo/exposition section (P–T–K). Mozart's ritornello is often linked to the solo/exposition by a solo lead-in that can gain structural significance (for example in K466/i where it becomes a principal feature of the development section). Otherwise, the solo/exposition allows T to modulate and adds an S in the related key. The second orchestral tutti is frequently a continuation of K. A second solo corresponds to the development section. Mozart postpones the next tutti/ritornello until the recapitulation, thus also delaying the next solo. A tutti at the end of the recapitulation is interrupted by a cadenza and a further tutti concludes the movement.

A concerto-like first-movement shape has been noted in some of Mozart's early arias. The most extensive and convincing case is Giunia's aria No. 11 from *Lucio Silla*, K135, which has been compared formally to the first movements of the Violin Concerto in G major, K216, and the Piano Concerto in B flat, K238. Among Mozart's arias from his Viennese period, Constanze's 'Martern aller Arten' (DIE ENTFÜHRUNG AUS DEM SERAIL, No. 11) is the clearest concerto-like, sonata-orientated piece. Only a few arias from the later Viennese operas employ anything that approximates to sonata structure (for example LE NOZZE DI FIGARO, No. 4 and DON GIOVANNI, Nos. 3 and 15). A. PETER BROWN

S. Davis, 'Harmonic Rhythm in Mozart's Sonata Form', *Music Review* 27 (1966), 25–43

M. Feldman, 'Staging the Virtuoso: Ritornello Procedure in Mozart, from Aria to Concerto', in *Mozart's Piano Concertos: Text, Context, Interpretation*, ed. N. Zaslaw (Ann Arbor, 1996), 149–86

C. Rosen, *Sonata Forms* (New York, 1980)

sonatas. The sonata is the most frequently encountered genre of solo instrumental music in the Classical era. Sonatas were written for solo keyboard and for single instruments (most frequently violin or cello) with keyboard accompaniment (although in the work of SCHOBERT, for example, the designation is most commonly 'pour claveçin avec accompagnement d'un violon'). Typically a sonata consisted of three (or less often four) movements, generally fast–slow–fast, but incorporating a variety of possible schemes including a minuet finale that is common in Viennese sonatas by Mozart's predecessors (such as WAGENSEIL, Steffan and earlier examples by JOSEPH HAYDN).

Mozart wrote eighteen sonatas for solo piano, six for piano duet, twenty-six for violin and piano, two for violin and bass, one for bassoon and cello, and two 'duos' for violin and viola that are sonatas in all but name. In addition there are a number of individual sonata movements, some of them fragmentary, and two piano sonatas of doubtful authenticity, K498a and 547a. The first of these, in B flat, has four movements (unheard of elsewhere in Mozart's solo sonatas), of which the second bears a strong affinity to the slow movement of the concerto

K450, while the 6/8 rondo finale contains an ineffective modulation from the tonic, B flat, to B major, in which the main theme appears. The other sonata, in F, was not originally conceived as a keyboard sonata, but was evidently concocted by an unknown hand (after Mozart's death?). It has just two movements, the first taken from the second movement of the violin sonata, K547, and the second from the finale of the C major piano sonata, K545 (transposed to F).

1. Piano sonatas
2. Duet sonatas
3. Violin sonatas
4. Miscellaneous sonatas

1. Piano sonatas

Mozart's approach to the external design of the piano sonata is remarkably stable: all eighteen are in three movements, the first always in some sort of SONATA FORM (except for K331 in A, a set of variations), the middle one slower (again, often in a sonata-like form, normally without central 'development', but sometimes in a ternary form, as in K284, a 'Polonoise en Rondeau'), the third fast, generally light in idiom and typically a sonata or rondo (or combination of the two). All but two conform to the fast–slow–fast scheme (K282 and K331 beginning with slow movements; K457 is prefaced with a separate multi-sectioned Fantasia, K475, incorporating an aria, a sarabande and a virtuoso passage in brilliant, extempore style between framing statements of the famous chromatic unisono theme built over a descending chromatic bass). The vast majority of the piano sonatas are in major keys, the only exceptions being K310 (1778) and K457 (1784). For the middle movements Mozart's clear preference is for the subdominant (K279, 280, 281, 283, 309, 311, 330, 332, 333, 533, 545 and 570); for the minor-key works he chooses the relative major.

While the piano sonatas have normally been dismissed in favour of the admittedly greater achievement of the concertos they contain some of Mozart's most engaging pieces. Within a genre intended mainly for domestic use (it is significant that, among reports of Mozart's own public performances of his piano music, sonatas are rarely found) he perhaps felt able to indulge in such experimental luxuries as the extraordinarily chromatic Andante of K533 or the somewhat 'abstract' counterpoint that pervades much of the first movement of K570. At times, he imports more 'public' elements into the domestic sonata environment, as in the finale of K570 which behaves rather like a concerto in the shape of its opening theme and incorporates a mock woodwind episode later on. (In the preceding Adagio there is a near-exact quotation from the slow movement of the Concerto in C minor, K491.)

It is important to remember the original environment for which the solo sonata was intended. This was the drawing-room of a private home, rather than the stage of a public theatre. While there are frequent references in the Mozart family correspondence to performances by Wolfgang of his own sonatas during the various tours that he undertook as a youth, these invariably turn out to have been in private, or semi-private settings. There are, for instance, several accounts of performances of items from the earliest sonata set, K279–84 in October–November 1777 (especially K283 and K284, which ends with a splendid set of variations of increasingly virtuosic character). However, not one was truly 'public', being either in princely chambers, a monastery or else a hall hired by a private music society. Sonatas were most often intended for performance before a learned company of (usually) upper-crust connoisseurs in the context of the salon, a forum that became increasingly popular among the upper classes during the second half of the eighteenth century, especially in France and AUSTRIA. Salons were normally given in the homes of counts and countesses, less frequently in the homes of court officials, such as L'Augier, the Viennese court physician, one of whose meetings was attended by CHARLES BURNEY in 1772. The most famous of Viennese salons was that of Countess Wilhelmine THUN, a staunch patron of Mozart during his early years in the capital, who loaned her fortepiano for the famous contest with CLEMENTI before EMPEROR JOSEPH II on 24 December 1781.

An awareness of the pedagogical connection is likewise fundamental to a proper understanding of the Classical sonata (in 1789 D. G. Türk's *Clavierschule* even included a list of keyboard composers graded according to the difficulty of their sonatas). Mozart's sonatas are no exception. His letters from MANNHEIM in late 1777 indicate that the sonata K309 was composed specifically for Rosa CANNABICH (daughter of the local Kapellmeister, Christian Cannabich) whom he was teaching at the time. Its slow movement requires great sensitivity to dynamic contrast, as Mozart notes in a letter to his father of 14 November:

> The Andante will give us the most trouble, for it is full of expression and must be played accurately and with the exact shades of forte and piano, precisely as they are marked. [Rosa] is smart and learns very easily. Her right hand is very good, but her left, unfortunately, is completely ruined . . . I have told her too that if I were her regular teacher, I would lock up all her music, cover the keys with a handkerchief and make her practise, first with the right hand and then with the left, nothing but passages, trills, mordents and so forth, very slowly at first, until each hand should be thoroughly trained.

For the most part, the 'domestic' and 'pedagogic' market for Classical sonatas was female (interestingly, C. P. E. BACH had issued a set of sonatas specifically 'à l'usage des dames' in 1770). Talented female keyboard players were not uncommon in Mozart's day: among aristocratic families, for instance, ability in this direction could be important in attracting an acceptable husband, and thus socially desirable. During the 1780s several of Mozart's Viennese pupils were ladies from the higher echelons of society: Countess Thun, COUNTESS RUMBEKE; somewhat lower down the the scale were Maria Theresia TRATTNER (wife of the important bookseller and publisher, and dedicatee of the Fantasia and Sonata K475 + 457, published by Artaria in 1785), BARBARA VON PLOYER and JOSEPHA AUERNHAMMER, the latter two of whom carved out successful careers as performers.

The most obvious case of a 'teaching piece' among the solo sonatas is that in C major, K545 ('für Anfänger' – 'for beginners'). Although this work is deceptively simple (as many a professional pianist will confirm) it does address a number of basic pedagogic issues, including general avoidance of the 'black' keys, frequent scale and arpeggio patterns, sequential phrases, calling for equally sequential finger-patterns in performance, Alberti bass accompaniments, cantabile melody in the Andante and repeated thirds in the finale. All these devices are part of the fundamental technical equipment of a keyboard player.

Other sonatas traverse much more difficult territory than K545 and were evidently designed for more advanced players and, as likely as not, vehicles for Mozart himself. The opening of K284 (written for Baron Thaddeus von Dürnitz) calls for command of mock-orchestral textures; the finale of K309 contains extended tremolandos for the right hand; the development of K310's first movement features an extended contrapuntal sequence demanding clear part-writing in the right hand, followed immediately by a difficult semiquaver continuation in the left hand, dissolving into the reprise; at the end of the finale of K457 there is an extended crossed-hands passage; while the whole of the sonata K576 is technically beyond all but the experienced performer, shifting rapidly back and forth between a variety of different textures (including, once more, intricate counterpoint).

The solo piano sonatas fall into several distinct groups. The earliest complete set of six pieces, K279–84, dates from late 1774–early 1775. Stylistically, the last sonata, in D, stands apart from the first five by virtue of its more advanced technical demands, its quasi-orchestral textures and its sheer length, including a set of twelve variations as its finale. The handwriting in the surviving autograph, while clearly a composing score, not a fair copy, betrays no signs of this stylistic gulf, however: the handwriting suggests that the pieces were written in one fell swoop and were probably completed at MUNICH in February or March 1775. The six sonatas cover an impressive range of expression, including the intimacy of K281's first movement, the *Empfindsamkeit* of K280's Adagio (just possibly modelled on the slow movement of Haydn's Hob. XVI:23 in the same key), and the delicacy of K283's opening Allegro, as well as the grandiose K284.

The next set of three sonatas, K309–11, originated during the journey Mozart undertook with his mother to Mannheim and PARIS (September 1777–January 1779). K311 was perhaps the first to be composed (it may be the piece promised to Mlle Josepha FREYSINGER in letters to Mozart's cousin, MARIA ANNA THEKLA MOZART on 5 Nov. and 3 Dec. 1777). Its first movement is notable for its dramatic reversal of the order of main themes during the reprise, so that the long postponed first subject actually functions as a coda, heralding the end of the movement. K309 in C is the piece written for Rosa Cannabich, and, in addition to a strikingly full-textured Allegro, features perhaps Mozart's most effective sonata Andante to date, an eloquent cross between sonata form, rondo and variations. The famous A minor sonata, K310, was composed in Paris in summer 1778. Its highly original dotted opening over a throbbing quaver accompaniment is succeeded by a second subject that may have been 'borrowed' from a sonata in the same key (Op. 3 No. 2, 1777) by Nicholas-Joseph Hüllmandel (1756–1823). It is undoubtedly a powerful piece, surpassing any of his earlier sonatas in its emotional range, effectively complemented by the graceful Andante and the hushed intensity of the finale.

The three sonatas K330–2 were long thought to date from Mozart's 1778 sojourn in Paris. However, the painstaking watermark investigations of Alan Tyson have shown that none is written on a French paper; in fact, all three are on a type of ten-stave paper that was available to Mozart during the early 1780s. (Analysis of Mozart's handwriting in the surviving autographs by Wolfgang Plath tends to confirm this date.) On similar grounds, Tyson has proposed that the Sonata in B flat, K333, dates from November 1783, composed perhaps in Linz during the return journey from SALZBURG to VIENNA following a family visit during which Mozart introduced his father to his new bride, CONSTANZE MOZART, for the first time. This places the sonata adjacent to the 'Linz' symphony, K425, rather than the Sonata in A minor, K310.

The fact that the right-hand parts of K330–2 are notated in the soprano clef (rather than Mozart's more usual treble clef) may be a hint that these sonatas – most especially, perhaps, the first in C – were didactic in function (Mozart normally used the soprano clef in his composition lessons, for instance, when teaching Barbara Ployer fundamental bass). There are some significant differences between the autograph and the first printed edition (by Artaria, Vienna, 1784): in the slow movement of K330 the print adds a brief coda (bars 60–4, mirroring bars 36–40) that is not found in Mozart's autograph; in the slow movement of K332 the reprises are greatly embellished in the print, compared to the autograph; and in all three sonatas the print (possibly revised by Mozart personally) incorporates a much wider range of dynamic and articulation marks, possibly suggesting that these pieces, as recorded in Mozart's manuscript, were at first intended for use in individual lessons (where the composer could suggest to a pupil varying levels and/or styles of articulation to be added to the deliberately 'plain' text), but that when the works found their way into the public domain it was felt (by Mozart or Artaria) that precise notation of dynamics, articulation and appropriate manners of embellishment were required.

Perhaps the most significant event in recent Mozart scholarship is the rediscovery of the autograph of the Fantasia and Sonata in C minor, K475 + 457. Lost since about the end of the nineteenth century, Mozart's manuscript was found in the Eastern Baptist Theological Seminary, Philadelphia, in 1990 (it is now in the INTERNATIONALE STIFTUNG MOZARTEUM, SALZBURG). Mozart composed the sonata first, and a so-called 'dedication copy' of the sonata alone (for Maria Theresia Trattner), dated 14 October 1784, has long been known. The first edition (Artaria, Vienna, about September 1785) contains both the fantasia and sonata. According to Mozart's own thematic catalogue the fantasia was completed on 20 May 1785, evidently as a kind of 'prelude' to the sonata (although its multi-sectional structure, covering a wide range of moods and keys, makes it capable of standing alone as a piece in its own right). The rediscovered autograph is important in many respects, especially, perhaps, in that it reveals previously unknown embellishments for reprises of the main theme in the central Adagio. The sequential chromatic opening of the fantasia is recaptured diatonically by the opening of the sonata, and chromaticism returns at various junctures throughout both pieces, along with intense counterpoint, for example at bar 118 of the first movement of K457, and again in the coda.

Counterpoint is a device that characterizes all of the later Viennese sonatas to some degree. The rondo finale of K533 (1788) is a reworking of an independent rondo, K494 (1786), incorporating an additional twenty-seven-bar episode of a fugal character, possibly in an attempt to produce at short notice a finale to match the character of the first movement, in which imitative counterpoint plays a significant role. The texture of theme and counter-theme pervades much of the opening Allegro of the Sonata in B flat, K570 (a magnificent work, better known for many years in a posthumous arrangement for violin and piano); imitative counterpoint, like that of K570 predominantly in just two parts, is found in the ebullient Sonata in D major, K576 – a feature that requires the utmost clarity of execution in performance. The arpeggiated main theme of this sonata suggests the idiom of the hunt, one of several 'topics' that are encountered in Mozart's solo sonatas (that of the stately minuet lies behind much of the first movement of K283 in G, for example). The application of different topics in these and other works by Mozart is an important element of eighteenth-century compositional practice that is still comparatively little understood. Topics – which can be very mobile, as at the beginning of K332, or else relatively static, as in K309's Andante (a sarabande) – clearly formed a backcloth against which Mozart's listeners perceived the unfolding musical discourse. Like RHETORIC, topics amounted to a channel of communication between composer and listener, possibly equivalent to the Baroque notion of *Affekt*. The character of the fragmentary sonata movement in G minor, K312 (evidently composed about 1790) is at times similar to that of K570's first movement. Mozart's autograph of K312 continues up to bar 106, and is thereafter completed by another (unknown) hand, possibly that of ABBE MAXIMILIAN VON STADLER, who was responsible for completing the B flat sonata movement K400, a work whose virtuosic keyboard textures resemble those of the roughly contemporary piano concertos K413–15.

2. Duet sonatas

In addition to his solo piano sonatas Mozart also composed a handful of examples for duet (at both one and two keyboards). The early sonata, K19a – if it is genuine – may have been composed in LONDON in summer 1765 (although recent research suggests the work is not by Mozart). It is nevertheless tempting to think that it is the work Mozart and his sister NANNERL MOZART are depicted playing in the famous family portrait of 1780–1 by della Croce: in the finale of the sonata the two players have to cross hands, as Wolfgang and Nannerl are doing in the painting. In 1800 Nannerl wrote to the Leipzig publishers Breitkopf & Härtel about her late brother's works, referring in passing to other duet pieces from his infancy (now lost). From Mozart's maturity come four other such works, K381 in D (1772), K358 in B flat (1773–4), K497 in F (1 Aug. 1786) and K521 in C (29 May 1787). The idiom of the first two is that of the sonatina (the modulation scheme in the opening Allegro of K358, for instance, is of the truncated variety, in which a tonic–dominant modulation in the exposition, preparing the dominant, F, is repeated exactly in the reprise, this time preparing the tonic, B flat). The F major sonata is tonally and idiomatically more developed, surer in its treatment of dialogue. Rather more inventive in the handling of texture, register and colour contrast is the Sonata for Two Pianos in D, K448 (November 1781).

3. Violin sonatas

Over two dozen sonatas survive for the violin–piano (or harpsichord) combination, covering virtually the whole of Mozart's career. In general a distinctive trend can be observed away from the so-called 'accompanied' sonata, in which the piano takes the lead and the violin has only a subsidiary function, towards the fully-fledged partnership exhibited in, for instance, K454 and K526.

The first two violin sonatas, K6–7 were published in Paris in 1764 as 'Op. 1', closely followed by 'Op. 2' (K8–9). Possibly K6 was begun in Salzburg at the end of 1762, and completed during the infant composer's first foreign tour. While the extent of Leopold's contribution to these works remains in doubt, they show that the eight-year-old Mozart was becoming aware of contemporary trends in the 'accompanied' sonata. He encountered music by Schobert, HONAUER, ECKARD and RAUPACH during his Parisian visit and was influenced by their style to some extent. One such 'fingerprint' was phrase extension, resulting in occasional uneven patterns of, say, six, rather than four bars. Schobert and his contemporaries achieved this by repeating the consequent phrase in an antecedent–consequent pair, sometimes with added embellishment, sometimes not, most commonly at the very opening of a movement (often involving transposition down an octave). Mozart's K6 and K8 feature this device prominently at their openings, as does the slightly later K28, part of a set of six sonatas, K26–31, composed at The Hague and published in 1766 with a dedication to the Princess of Nassau-Weilberg. In each case, Mozart's opening features the dominant note prominently in the antecedent phrase, following which the consequent fills in the space between this note and the lower tonic by (decorated) step. Possibly Mozart included consequent phrase-repetition in these cases in order to confirm more strongly the first significant arrival on the tonic degree (from which the transition to the second key area begins). If so, then his importation of the device would have been at least partly consequential upon the shape of his thematic material, suggesting an early awareness of the intimate relationship between thematic design and larger structural considerations.

Mozart's next violin sonatas (K301–6) were composed during a later tour, in Mannheim and Paris during the spring and summer of 1778. K301–6 were dedicated to Maria Elisabeth, Electress Palatine (the first, in G, was originally devised for piano with flute accompaniment). Only K306 is a 'normal' three-movement sonata: K301, 302, 304 and 305 each have just two movements, while K303 is a two-movement structure the first of which alternates between two tempos, slow and fast. Technically, these works are still 'avec accompagnement d'un violon', but the violin is here acquiring an independent voice. At the opening of K301 the violin states the theme, over Alberti-style figuration in the piano and throughout the exposition thematic material is equally distributed between the two instruments. In the Allegro of K304 the two instruments share a unisono opening which is strikingly reshaped at the reprise, the now soaring violin theme beginning completely alone before the entry in its second bar by throbbing chromatic quaver chords. The violin comes completely into its own in the variation finale of K305.

Also composed at this time was K296 in C (dated 11 Mar. 1778 in the autograph), published together with the slightly later K376–80, also 'Op. 2' by

Artaria in Vienna in 1781. The works are especially notable for the quality of their thematic development (shared between both instruments). K379 in G is possibly the work referred to in a letter from Mozart to his father (8 Apr. 1781); Wolfgang notes that he had still been composing the sonata between 11 and 12 o'clock at night (for performance the following day) and that in the concert itself he was forced to play his own (piano) part from memory, having had no time to write the part out. (The alignment of parts in the autograph bears this comment out to some degree. Indeed, the declamatory opening in the piano part retains something of an improvisatory quality.)

K454 in B flat, completed, according to Mozart's thematic catalogue, on 21 April 1784 (and written for the Italian violin virtuosa REGINA STRINASACCHI), was published along with the piano sonatas K284 and K333 in Vienna by TORRICELLA (as 'Op. 7') later that same year. It features a substantial slow introduction to the main sonata Allegro. Its first performance was in the presence of Emperor Joseph II at the Kärntnertortheater on 29 April 1784, at which Mozart again played the keyboard part from memory (the autograph, as in K379, bears this out, for the keyboard part is in a different-coloured ink and at times very cramped, as if 'fitted-in' to an already completed 'grid' of bar-lines encompassing the violin line). K454, and its successors, K481 in E flat (12 Dec. 1785), K526 in A (24 Aug. 1787), and the incomplete K547 in F (10 July 1788), are in no sense 'accompanied' sonatas – the musical argument is presented in a texture that allocates an equal share of activity to both players, as may be seen, for instance, in the exposition transition of K454's Allegro, the cantabile embellishments in its central Andante, the virtuoso exchange of material between the players in the outer movements of K526 and the sparse, eerie textures of its Beethovenian Adagio, in which every note makes a telling impact.

4. Miscellaneous sonatas

Five sonatas remain to be considered. The two apparently for violin and bass, K46d in C and K46e in F, each consist of two short movements, a binary form Allegro followed by a pair of minuets (I–II–da capo). These were written during the first Viennese journey and are dated 1 September 1768. Like the contemporary sonatas by Wagenseil and Steffan that Mozart may have encountered in the capital the second section of each binary movement opens with a dominant-key restatement of the main theme. As in many early works, the autograph contains corrections and additions in Leopold's handwriting. The scoring for violin and bass is conjectural – possibly the lower stave was intended as an un-figured continuo bass.

The Sonata for Bassoon and Bass in B flat, K292, dates from the beginning of 1775, and was evidently written, like the D major piano sonata K284, for Baron Thaddeus von Dürnitz. Mozart's autograph does not survive, and the designation for bassoon and cello is that found in the earliest (pre-1800) edition; possibly two bassoons were intended, the second acting for much of the time as a 'support' for the first, although true equality is attained at times, particularly in the rondo finale which features a brief canonic episode.

The two 'duos' for violin and viola, K423 in G and K424 in B flat, are, in effect, sonatas, despite the title 'Duetto', added by an unknown hand to the front page of each autograph. (See also CHAMBER MUSIC: B. STRING DUOS AND TRIOS.) These superb pieces, which deserve to be much more widely known, were composed at some time between July and October 1783, while Mozart was visiting Salzburg with his new bride, Constanze (and are thus roughly contemporary with the piano sonata K333). They were written as a favour to MICHAEL HAYDN who was due to present some duos to Archbishop Colloredo but fell ill before he could complete the task. Mozart composed them in the course of just a few days, passing them off as the work of Haydn (although the true authorship was revealed in subsequent newspaper advertisements placed by the Viennese music dealer TRAEG). The scoring is breathtaking in its inventiveness, exploiting register and colour contrasts to full effect. There is not an idea in either work that does not seem to spring naturally from the instruments themselves. Among many wonderful passages that could be cited are the extensive development section of K423's Allegro; the sublimely peaceful Adagio of the same work, in which the transitions between foreground decoration and background harmonic support are effortlessly managed; the powerful Adagio introduction to K424, resembling at times the 'French ouverture' idiom; the tonal digression into the flat mediant in the development section of the ensuing Allegro; and the deft touches of melodic chromaticism that colour its siciliana slow movement. These are works that perhaps reveal most to the players themselves, fleeting treasures to be savoured anew in each performance. JOHN IRVING

J. Irving, *Mozart's Piano Sonatas: Contexts, Sources, Style* (Cambridge, 1997)

songs. Mozart composed lieder throughout his life: his earliest song dates from 1768, his last from 1791. But the composition of these works was sporadic, infrequent and sometimes, it seems, geared to specific, private social occasions. K53, *An die Freude*, was composed during his visit to VIENNA in 1768 and published in Gräffer's didactic periodical, *Neue Sammlung zum Vergnügen und Unterricht*, together with 'Daphne, deine Rosenwangen', an arrangement for voice and keyboard, presumably by LEOPOLD MOZART, of the aria 'Meiner liebsten schöne Wangen' from BASTIEN UND BASTIENNE; like other contemporaneous Viennese songs, it is notated on only two staves, representing voice and basso continuo parts. The same is true of two songs composed in SALZBURG, *Wie unglücklich bin ich nit*, K147 and the Masonic *Logesang auf die feierliche Johannisloge*, K148 (both 1774–6) as well as three late songs, the two GERMAN church songs K343 (presumably early 1787) and *Die Alte*, K517 (also 1787). The last is something of an exception: whereas the other continuo songs are written in the 'accepted' style for works of their type, *Die Alte* self-consciously exploits an archaic manner to reinforce the sense of the text, even marking the voice part 'a little through the nose'.

Both *Oiseaux, si tous les ans*, K307, and *Dans un bois solitaire*, K308, date from Mozart's visit to MANNHEIM in late 1777 and early 1778 and were written for Augusta WENDLING – perhaps these represent a nod in the direction of French *opéra comique*, which was popular at the court of Karl Theodor; *Dans un bois solitaire* even includes an operatic-like declamatory treatment of the vocal line and quasi-orchestral gestures in the piano part, as well as changes in tempo and dramatic pauses. *Die Zufriedenheit*, K394, and *Komm, liebe Zithe*, K351, are presumed to have been composed in MUNICH in 1780–1, for the horn player Martin Lang, while *Ich würd auf meinem Pfad*, K390, *Sei du mein Trost*, K391, and *Verdankt sei es dem Glanz*, K392, probably date from Mozart's last year in Salzburg, 1780; all three are based on texts from J. T. Herme's popular, sentimental novel *Sophiens Reise von Memel nach Sachsen*.

It was not until 1785 that Mozart composed songs in Vienna, *Der Zauberer*, K472, *Die Zufriedenheit*, K473, and *Die betrogene Welt*, K474, all completed on 7 May of that year; the sudden and apparently unmotivated composition of three songs on a single date suggests they may have been written for an otherwise undocumented social occasion. The same may be true of *Abendempfindung an Laura*, K523, and *An Chloe*, K524, both of which are dated 24 June 1787, and *Des kleinen Friedrichs Geburtstag*, K529, and *Das Traumbild*, K530, dated PRAGUE, 6 November 1787. *Als Luise die Briefe ihres ungetreuen Liebhabers verbrannte*, K520, was apparently composed at the house of Mozart's friend JACQUIN and later published under his name, together with K530. And no doubt the two Prague songs were composed for the DUSCHEKs, with whom Mozart frequently socialized while in Bohemia for the premiere of DON GIOVANNI.

Mozart's best-known songs are the through-composed ones, including *Das Veilchen*, K476 (8 June 1785) and *Das Lied der Trennung*, K519 (23 May 1787). *Das Veilchen* includes a fraught middle section in a minor key, recitative textures at the climax, and a declaimed end: 'the poor violet'. *Das Lied der Trennung* repeats its first stanza, but varied, after a middle section that also includes declamation. *Als Luise die Briefe* and *Abendempfindung an Laura* are also through-composed; the latter in particular strikes a serious note, with a wide-ranging tonal scheme and a meditation on the inevitability of death.

The last songs – *Sehnsucht nach dem Frühlinge*, K596, *Im Frühlingsanfang*, K597, and *Das Kinderspiel*, K598 – all date from 14 January 1791. They are children's songs, ironically representative, perhaps, of Mozart's rejuvenation in the last years of his life.

CLIFF EISEN

E. A. Ballin, *Das Wort-Ton-Verhältnis in den klavierbegleiteten Liedern Mozarts* (Kassel, 1984)

J. Rushton, 'Mozart's Lieder: A Survey', in *Mozart in History, Theory, and Practice. Selected Papers from the International Symposium, Faculty of Music, The University of Western Ontario 1990–91*, ed. D. Neville (London, 1996), 105–30

P. Russell, *The Themes of the German Lied from Mozart to Strauss* (Lewiston, NY, 2002)

C. Schachter, 'The Violet: An Analysis of the Music', *Ostinato: Revue internationale d'études musicales* (1993), 163–73

Sonnenfels, Josef von (1733–1817). A writer, dramatist and leading figure of the AUSTRIAN ENLIGHTENMENT, Sonnenfels held a professorship at the University of VIENNA as well as official positions at the Bohemian-Austrian Chancellery and Education Commission. It seems that Mozart was on relatively good terms with him: he attended the performance of IDOMENEO at COUNTESS THUN's residence in 1781 and subscribed to Mozart's series of concerts at the Trattnerhof in March 1784. A few months after his move to Vienna, Mozart also advised his father to consult Sonnenfels (among other senior Viennese figures) 'if you really believe [i.e. incorrectly] that I am detested at Court and by the old and new aristocracy' (22 Dec. 1781). The books owned by Mozart at his death included Sonnenfels's *Gesamellte kleine Schriften* (Collected Shorter Writings). SIMON P. KEEFE

sources for Mozart's life and works. Almost everything we know about Mozart, his life and his works, derives in the first instance from contemporaneous written and musical sources. This complex of primary information includes the family letters, contemporaneous documents, and musical sources: autographs, manuscript copies and printed editions.

A. Letters
B. Documents
C. Musical sources

A. Letters

The Mozart family letters are the most extensive and richly detailed surviving correspondence of any composer of the eighteenth century or earlier. Almost 1,200 letters survive from the period 1755–91, by Mozart, his father, his mother and his sister. Another 400 letters, most of them by Mozart's widow and sister, date from after 1791.

Only a few letters by LEOPOLD MOZART from 1756 or earlier are known; mostly addressed to his AUGSBURG publisher and friend JOHANN JAKOB LOTTER, they primarily concern the publication of Leopold's *Gründliche Violinschule* of 1756. The chief part of the correspondence begins with the family trip to VIENNA in 1762 and continues with accounts of the grand tour of 1763–6 and the return to Vienna in 1767–8. The majority of these letters are addressed to the Mozarts' SALZBURG landlord, Lorenz HAGENAUER. Although they sometimes transact left-over local business, many of them were intended for public circulation, to inform the Mozarts' friends of their activities and to impress Archbishop COLLOREDO with their successes. It is likely that Leopold expected the letters to be saved, and that they were to form the basis of his projected biography of Wolfgang.

The letters written from Italy between 1770 and 1773, when only Mozart and his father were on tour, are chiefly by Leopold and addressed to his wife, MARIA ANNA MOZART. In addition to detailing their various social and performing activities, they occasionally report on Leopold's plans – often cryptically described – to secure a position for his son; apparently Leopold, who believed the Archbishop's agents were reading his correspondence, wished to keep at least some of his dealings secret. The letters from Italy also include the first correspondence by Mozart himself, usually humorous or nonsensical postscripts addressed to his sister.

Fewer letters are known from the period 1773–7 when the family was mostly in Salzburg; the only exceptions are those written during the short journeys to Vienna in 1773 and to MUNICH in late 1774–early 1775. Mozart's departure from Salzburg in September 1777, however, and his subsequent trip to Munich, Augsburg, MANNHEIM and PARIS, generated a substantial and intensely personal correspondence. Not only do they report on Mozart's frequent professional and personal failures – including his inability to secure an adequate post, his unrequited love for Aloysia Weber (later LANGE) and the death of his mother in July 1778 – but they are also among the chief witnesses to Mozart's at times troubled relationship with his father.

The Viennese letters from 1781 and later are a remarkable record of Mozart's activities at the time of his greatest success. But they also continue to document Mozart's estrangement from Leopold: the letters are full of self-justifications, particularly with regard to his marriage to CONSTANZE MOZART, a match opposed by Leopold. With his father's death in May 1787, however, the family correspondence comes to a virtual end. Leopold's estate was settled later that year and, as far as is known, Mozart did not write to his sister again after about August 1788. Most of the letters from the last years of Mozart's life are addressed to his wife and were written when he was on tour in Leipzig, Berlin and Dresden in 1789 and Frankfurt in 1790. Some well-known begging letters addressed to Mozart's fellow Mason MICHAEL PUCHBERG also survive. Finally, two important posthumous collections, those of Mozart's widow, Constanze, and his sister, NANNERL MOZART, mostly concern the sale of Mozart's estate to the Offenbach publisher JOHANN ANTON ANDRE in 1799 and Breitkopf & Härtel's attempts to collect Mozart's works for a projected complete edition (see below).

The surviving correspondence must be considered incomplete – numerous letters and other documents make reference to correspondence that is now lost. Similarly, there is convincing circumstantial evidence that Mozart must have corresponded with his English friends Nancy and Stephen STORACE after their return to LONDON in 1787 although no such letters are known. Nevertheless, the letters are a fundamental source of information concerning Mozart's biography and the authenticity, chronology and genesis of his works. Numerous details of his life – including details of the early tours and the composer's activities in Vienna – are known only from the letters. By the same token, Leopold's letters written when Wolfgang was on tour in 1777 and 1778 are the best surviving source of information concerning musical life in Salzburg, even if the opinions expressed in them are entirely one-sided.

The letters also give information concerning Mozart's compositional activities. Some works, including the Trumpet Concerto, K47c, the aria 'Misero tu non sei', K73A (Anh. 2), additional wind parts for a flute concerto by J. B. WENDLING, K284e and the Rondeau for keyboard, K284f, are known only from the letters. Similarly, Leopold Mozart's *Verzeichniss alles desjenigen was dieser 12jährige Knab seit seinem 7tem Jahre componiert* (List of everything that this twelve-year-old boy has composed since his seventh year) accompanied a letter to Emperor JOSEPH II requesting the court's intervention against the Viennese cabal trying to prevent the production of *LA FINTA SEMPLICE* in 1768. The list, the most comprehensive account of Mozart's earliest compositions, includes references to numerous lost works, among them the Stabat mater K33c, six divertimenti for various instruments K41a, the flute solos K33a and the march K41c. Because it is non-thematic, the list is also a source of controversy: the works described there do not always square with surviving compositions from the time, or cannot be accounted for adequately.

In addition to providing information concerning the genesis, authenticity and chronology of Mozart's works, the letters also give evidence concerning their performance. This is true not only of performing practices such as rubato and tempo (see, for example, Mozart's letters of 18–20 July and 7 Aug. 1782), but also with regard to sometimes uncertain questions of scoring. A letter of 13 April 1778, for example, documents the soloistic, as opposed to orchestral, performance of the divertimento K287 while others give specific information on the size of orchestras in Salzburg and elsewhere.

Perhaps the most widely studied aspect of the letters, and in particular those from the Mannheim–Paris tour of 1777–8, has been the light they shed on Mozart's personality and his troubled relationship with his father. They show not only that from Paris Mozart misled Leopold with respect to his compositional indolence and lack of success, but they have also been cited as evidence of Mozart's hypomania and cyclothymic depression, as well as his emotional insecurity.

B. Documents

1. Private and semi-private documents
2. Public documents

In addition to the family letters, contemporaneous documents of various sorts also provide direct information concerning Mozart's life and works. Generally these documents are of three sorts: those deriving directly from Mozart that are not letters strictly speaking; private or semi-private documents such as the correspondence of individuals, court records and catalogues of the music holdings of publishers, monasteries and other similar institutions; and public documents intended for broad circulation, chiefly reports in newspapers and journals of Mozart's public appearances, reviews of his published and performed works and advertisements by music dealers.

The number of documents deriving from Mozart himself – as opposed to letters – is small but significant. They include entries in various private albums such as those of his friend GOTTFRIED VON JACQUIN and his pupil BARBARA PLOYER. Mozart himself kept several albums. A smaller one included entries by KARL LUDWIG FISCHER, the first Osmin in DIE ENTFÜHRUNG AUS DEM SERAIL and IGNAZ BORN, a leading Viennese intellectual and master of the Masonic lodge 'Zur wahren Eintracht'. According to Constanze Mozart, another larger album was lost by Mozart on one of his journeys. More substantial are three undated literary efforts: the poem *Der Kunstreiche Hund*, an outline for a stage work titled *Der Salzburger Lump in Wien* and an incomplete draft of a libretto for a comedy in three acts, *Die Liebes-Probe*.

Perhaps the most important document to derive directly from Mozart is his *Verzeichnüss aller meiner Werke vom Monath Febrario 1784 bis Monath 1* (List of all my works from the month of February 1784 to the month 1), a chronological list of all his compositions beginning with the piano concerto K449. The last work in the catalogue, *Laut verkünde unsre Freude*, K623, was written in November 1791 – it is a poignant reflection on the blanks in the list's title, a sure indication that Mozart expected to live at least until the nineteenth century.

The chief importance of the catalogue is the evidence it provides concerning the dates and authenticity of Mozart's works. Almost every major work composed after February 1784 is listed there. The catalogue also represents the only surviving evidence for the composition of some lost works, including the Andante for violin and orchestra K470, the march K544 and the aria *Ohne Zwang, aus eignem Triebe*, K569. Additionally, it sometimes reports uniquely on the scoring of Mozart's works. The concerto K459, for example, is listed as having trumpets and drums although parts for these instruments are lacking in the autograph and do not otherwise survive. At the same time, the catalogue is also a source of chronological problems: the dates in it do not always square with those on Mozart's autographs. The concerto K467 is dated February 1785 on the autograph but 9 March in the catalogue. It may be that some of the entries in the list were made retrospectively; at least this appears to be the case with the earliest works listed there. What is more, the musical incipits in the catalogue sometimes differ from those of other sources deriving from Mozart. It is likely that these differences represent different performances (if only in Mozart's mind).

1. PRIVATE AND SEMI-PRIVATE DOCUMENTS

Numerous documents relating to Mozart derive from private or semi-private sources and were not intended for general circulation. These include references in private correspondences or diaries, thematic catalogues compiled by various religious and secular institutions, and the records of the courts where Mozart performed or where, as in Salzburg, he was employed.

Because the Mozarts corresponded less when they were not on tour, and because many of Leopold Mozart's early letters are lost, the majority of references to Mozart in Salzburg derive from the court records and other private sources; and although they fail to give a full record of his day-to-day activities, they nevertheless provide extensive information concerning his various appointments, dismissals, resignations and leaves of absence, his remuneration for court services and for writing specially commissioned works, subsidies for his travels, and occasionally accounts of his performances. A particularly important document concerns his appointment as court organist in 1779, which shows that composition was a secondary and non-specific condition of his employment. Also important are several contemporary diaries, among them those of Beda Hübner, librarian at St Peter's and Joachim Ferdinand von SCHIEDENHOFEN, a Salzburg court councillor. Schiedenhofen's diary in particular provides numerous otherwise unrecorded details concerning the performance of Mozart's works in Salzburg between 1774 and 1778.

Private documents are plentiful from the Mozarts' many tours. The earliest independent reference to Wolfgang's performances in Vienna in 1762 comes from the diaries of COUNT JOHANN KARL VON ZINZENDORF, and numerous letters, by Voltaire and JOHANN ADOLF HASSE among others, show the extent of the Mozarts' contacts and their importance in promoting Wolfgang's career. This is especially true for the first Italian journey of 1770: among the Mozarts' supporters at this time were Count Karl Joseph FIRMIAN, Governor-General of Lombardy, Count Gian Luca PALLAVICINI of Bologna and Cardinal Count Lazaro Opizio Pallavicini and Prince Andrea Doria Pamphili, both of Rome.

Institutional and other private documents also survive for the last decade of Mozart's life, when he had taken up permanent residence in Vienna. In addition to records of court payments for various works (chiefly the operas), other surviving documents include his marriage contract, the records of several

Masonic lodges, his appointment as imperial chamber musician and records relating to the inventory and disposition of his estate, as well as CONSTANZE MOZART's petition for a pension.

Mostly unknown, but of potential importance, are numerous thematic music catalogues drawn up by courts, monasteries and by late eighteenth-century publishers. These include a catalogue from the monastery at Lambach (1768), which provides strong if still inconclusive evidence that the symphony K17 is by Leopold Mozart and the so-called *Quartbuch* of c.1775, well known from HAYDN research, which shows that, contrary to the generally accepted view, Mozart's quartets K168–73 circulated in central AUSTRIA, and possibly in Vienna, during the 1770s. Also important is a catalogue of the Salzburg Cathedral holdings, drawn up in the late 1780s, which includes a number of Mozart's works but also suggests that not all of his sacred music was housed, or perhaps even performed, there.

Possibly the most important publisher's catalogue is the so-called Breitkopf & Härtel manuscript catalogue, an early nineteenth-century attempt to list titles and musical incipits of all works attributed to Mozart, organized by genre. In addition to listing a significant proportion of Mozart's authenticated works, the catalogue also includes entries for several compositions that are otherwise unknown, among them the symphonies K19b and K66c–e as well as the solo sonatas K33d–g. Their listing in the catalogue, however, is insufficient as unsupported evidence of Mozart's authorship.

2. PUBLIC DOCUMENTS

Whereas documents relating to Mozart's time in Salzburg derive mainly from private sources, many of those relating to his travels are found in widely circulated printed sources, primarily contemporary newspapers and periodicals. Between 1763 and 1766, substantial articles describing Mozart were published in newspapers in AUGSBURG, Frankfurt, Paris, Utrecht and Lausanne. While these articles generally report primarily on Mozart's precocity, they sometimes provide otherwise unknown biographical information; and in the absence of details in the family letters, much of our knowledge of Mozart's public concerts in LONDON and Holland derives from advertisements in local newspapers. Similar articles are plentiful for the first Italian journey (1769–71) but less common for subsequent trips, including the important and extended tour of 1777–9 to Mannheim and Paris (documented primarily by the family letters). Several explanations seem likely for this, among them that Mozart was no longer an exciting child prodigy and, as a careful study of others sources shows, that by and large he was indolent and made few public appearances.

With Mozart's move to Vienna and his increased compositional and performing activity, published documents once again become common. Primary among several sources – including the *Wienerblättchen*, the *Wiener Kronik* and the *Wiener Realzeitung* – is the court-sanctioned *Wiener Zeitung*, which includes announcements and reviews of Mozart's public concerts and his operas as well as advertisements for his works, significant numbers of which now became available for the first time. Some of the advertisements derive from Mozart himself, who sometimes tried first to sell his compositions on a subscription basis, usually unsuccessfully. The majority are by local dealers in manuscript and printed music, among them JOHANN TRAEG, LAURENZ LAUSCH, the court theatre copyist Wenzel Sukowaty and such prominent firms as Artaria and HOFFMEISTER. Also common are published reports of Mozart's trips during these years: his performances were regularly noted in local newspapers from PRAGUE (1787 and 1791), Dresden, Leipzig and Berlin (all 1789), and Frankfurt (1790) where he attended the first coronation of LEOPOLD II. Just as Mozart's personal appearances generated considerable local interest, so too did the appearance of his works in print and on stage. A large number of articles testifies to the widespread popularity of his operas, DIE ENTFÜHRUNG AUS DEM SERAIL in particular, and reviews of printed editions of his chamber and keyboard music appear in journals published as distant from Vienna as Hamburg and London.

C. Musical sources

1. Autographs
2. Manuscript copies
3. First and early editions

1. AUTOGRAPHS

Mozart's autographs are the primary musical documents transmitting his works. Although many compositions also survive in manuscript copies or printed editions, the majority of these are second- or later-generation sources (the exceptions are manuscripts and prints that derive directly from Mozart; concerning these, see below).

Considering that Mozart held no significant church or court appointment during the last ten years of his life, it is fortunate that a large number of his autographs, more than 400, survive. After Leopold Mozart's death in 1787, Mozart's early autographs, the majority of which apparently remained in Salzburg after 1781, were sent to him in Vienna, where they were carefully preserved, together with more recent scores. After Mozart's death, these remained with his widow, Constanze, who on several occasions attempted to sell parts of the collection but unsuccessfully. It remained with her throughout the 1790s. About 1799, however, she was approached by the Leipzig publishers Breitkopf & Härtel, who were collecting Mozart's works for a projected complete edition of his works; Constanze suggested that they purchase the entire collection but Breitkopf took only about forty autographs. In the same year, however, Constanze also had an offer from the publisher Johann Anton André, located in Offenbach am Main, not far from Frankfurt, and she sold what was left of the collection to him – just under 300 autographs as well as some copies. With few exceptions (mainly the last ten string quartets and some other chamber and keyboard works, now part of the collection at the British Library), the autographs remained in André's possession until his death in 1843. They then passed to his heirs and, eventually, to the Royal Library at Berlin. But they did not remain there. Attacks on Berlin during the Second World War made it necessary to move the autographs, together with other treasures, to secure hiding places, many of them in eastern Europe. Among the collections squirrelled away to safety was a significant holding of more than one hundred autographs deposited at the convent of Grüssau in

Silesia, later part of Poland. For many years these autographs were presumed lost. However, three of them surfaced in 1977 and shortly afterwards the recovery of almost the entire collection was publicly announced. Since 1980, this significant holding has been on deposit at the Biblioteka Jagiellonska in Kraków. Other Mozart autographs are owned by numerous major and minor libraries, among them the INTERNATIONALE STIFTUNG MOZARTEUM (Salzburg), the Library of Congress (Washington), the British Library (London), the Staatsbibliothek zu Berlin and the Bibliothèque nationale (Paris).

The evaluation of Mozart's autographs is not always straightforward. While a significant proportion of them are either signed, or dated, or both, in some cases the dates have been tampered with or do not square with other evidence; in many other cases they are not dated at all. In order to determine when they were written down – and to establish an accurate chronology of Mozart's works – two techniques have recently proven particularly valuable: the study of the chronological development of Mozart's handwriting (*Schriftchronologie*) and the analysis of the types of paper on which the autographs are written.

Schriftchronologie documents changes in handwriting. When these changes can be shown on the basis of securely dated manuscripts to occur at particular times, they can serve as criteria for the dating of other undated autographs. In Mozart's case, *Schriftchronologie* is uncertain for the period up to about 1770, prior to the first Italian tour: too few dated autographs survive to construct a working chronological model and for the most part Mozart's handwriting was fairly stable during the 1760s. By the same token, Mozart's handwriting was also stable during the 1780s (except, possibly to distinguish between works written before and after LE NOZZE DI FIGARO, about 1786). For the period 1770–80, however, *Schriftchronologie* has achieved striking results: many dated autographs survive from this time and the changes in Mozart's hand are readily identifiable. According to Wolfgang Plath, three main periods can be distinguished: 1770/1–2, 1772–4 and 1775–80. The notational signs most subject to change during these periods are Mozart's treble clef, crotchet, quaver and his abbreviations for *forte* and *piano* (*for:* and *pia:*). Beyond suggesting a chronology for Mozart's handwriting, Plath was also able to establish criteria for distinguishing Mozart's hand from that of his father. As a result, numerous autographs previously thought to be by Wolfgang, including the masses K115 and K116 as well as the songs K149–51, can now be shown to be by Leopold.

As for the types of paper on which Mozart's autographs are written, it is necessary first to understand how paper was manufactured during the eighteenth century. All of the papers available to Mozart were handmade. Two men, a vatman and a coucher, each worked with a sieve or mould, a rectangular frame with several wooden ribs. Across the bottom of the mould was a mesh made of two kinds of wires: many thin, closely spaced wires running parallel to the long axis of the mould (laid lines) and fewer thicker wires, spaced farther apart, running at right angles to them (chain wires). Several additional ornamental wires attached to the laid and chain wires, forming a design, letters, or some combination of these, identified the maker and sometimes the size and quality of the paper. When raw, liquid paper 'stuff' was deposited on the moulds, formed into sheets and then dried, the result of the ornamental design was a local thinning in the finished paper, a watermark. And it is on the basis of the watermarks, together with details of Mozart's staff-ruling (rastrology), that a chronology of his use of paper types, and consequently of his works, can be constructed. In this respect, the principle underlying paper studies is similar to that of *Schriftchronologie*: where a sufficiently large sample of securely dated autographs on a particular paper type survives, the occurrence of the same paper type in an undated autograph is strong evidence for its dating. Details of staff-ruling add a further refinement: it is the case, for example, that Mozart could generally obtain only ten-staff paper in Salzburg whereas in Vienna he wrote on twelve-staff paper. In cases where paper with similar or identical watermarks was available in both Salzburg and Vienna, staff-ruling often represents decisive evidence for dating.

The study of paper types is most important for the period 1781–91. Undated Viennese autographs, generally on twelve-staff Italian-made paper, can often be assigned to very exact periods on the basis of their watermarks and rastrology; this is true even for quite similar types of paper used throughout the decade. What is more, the study of watermarks and rastrology often shows that autographs were written out at one sitting. Several works, among them the six quartets dedicated to Haydn, were apparently written down over a considerable period of time.

The most immediate result of studies of *Schriftchronologie* and paper types is a revised chronology for many of Mozart's works. Often these new datings differ by as many as five or more years from those given in the standard literature. The first movement of the horn concerto K412, for example, usually thought to date from 1782, was probably started about 1786 and not finished until 1791; and the piano sonata K333 is usually assigned to Paris in 1778 but was probably composed in Linz about November 1783. By the same token, *Schriftchronologie* and paper studies have implications for Mozart's biography and his working methods. The commonly held notion that he virtually abandoned church composition in Vienna is probably incorrect: a number of Kyrie and Gloria fragments, as well as two settings of psalm text by Georg Reutter copied by Mozart (K93 and 93a), are on paper used by the composer only after about December 1787. This observation apparently confirms the report of a Danish visitor to Vienna in 1788, who wrote that '[Mozart] is now working on church music'. Similarly, paper studies show that several fragmentary works are not drafts rejected by Mozart as unsatisfactory, but merely unfinished compositions – apparently the composer often began works but put them aside for completion later (the piano concertos K449, K488 and K503 are examples). At least some of the fragments, then, should probably be understood as 'works in progress', left unfinished at the time of Mozart's death.

2. MANUSCRIPT COPIES

In addition to the evidence they offer concerning the authenticity and chronology of Mozart's works, the autographs often represent the primary texts for his composition. But they do not always represent his last thoughts or all aspects of his performances. In some cases, these are transmitted by handwritten copies of his works (and by editions, see below) as are sanctioned texts, especially in those cases where no autograph survives. Unlike autographs, however, copies have a wide range of provenances: some derive from Mozart himself, others from places and times distant from the composer. It is therefore necessary to distinguish among the various manuscript copies in order to establish their exact worth.

For the period up to 1780, the most important manuscript sources derive from Salzburg. By and large, Salzburg copies transmit accurate attributions and reliable texts. Not all of them, however, derive directly from Mozart and among generic Salzburg copies, misattributions are sometimes found: Leopold Mozart's Mass Seiffert 4/1, for example, survives in three contemporary Salzburg copies, two of them attributed to Leopold Mozart and one, dated 1753, to JOHANN ERNST EBERLIN. In order to be considered reliable witnesses to authenticity, then, Salzburg copies of Mozart's works must have title pages or autograph corrections in the parts (by Wolfgang or Leopold), be attested to by independent, unequivocal documentary evidence or be by copyists whose direct connection to the Mozarts and reliability can be demonstrated.

In Salzburg, three copyists worked for Mozart on a regular basis: Maximilian Raab, Joseph Richard Estlinger and Felix Hofstätter. All three were court musicians and Raab and Estlinger in particular were close to the Mozarts. Hofstätter's copies are reliable, too, but he may also have made additional copies for sale without Mozart's knowledge. On 15 May 1784, Mozart wrote to his father from Vienna:

> Today I sent with the post coach the symphony that I composed in Linz for Graf Thun [K425] together with four concertos [K449, 450, 451, 453]. I am not particular about the symphony, only I ask you to have the four concertos copied at home, for the copyists in Salzburg are as little to be trusted as those in Vienna – I am absolutely certain that Hofstetter copied [Michael] Haydn's music twice.

Although the majority of authentic Salzburg copies of Mozart's works date from before c.1780, some important copies were also made after Wolfgang's permanent move to Vienna in 1781. At least until 1785, Mozart continued to send new works to his father, who had them copied and performed. A number of these copies survive including important manuscripts of the 'Linz' symphony, K425, and the D minor concerto, K466. With Leopold's death in 1787, however, the flow of sanctioned Salzburg manuscripts comes to an end.

When CHARLES BURNEY visited Vienna in 1772 he wrote: 'as there are no music shops in Vienna, the best method of procuring new compositions is to apply to copyists . . . I was plagued with copyists . . . they began to regard me as a greedy and indiscriminate purchaser of whatever trash they should offer.' A decade later, the situation was different: music publishing had taken a firm hold in the imperial capital. Nevertheless, large genres such as concertos, symphonies, operas and church music continued to be disseminated chiefly in handwritten copies. During Mozart's time there, the most important copy shops were those of Laurenz Lausch, Johann Traeg and Wenzel Sukowaty, the court theatre copyist. All three handled Mozart's music although it is difficult to establish with certainty that Mozart himself provided the exemplars from which the copies were prepared. Accordingly, Viennese copies can be identified as deriving from the composer only when his autograph corrections appear in the parts or other unequivocal documentary evidence testifies to the authenticity of a manuscript.

In addition to commercial copy shops, Mozart also had dealings with individual copyists who probably worked for him on an ad hoc basis. For reasons of cost and accuracy, he relied at first on copyists in Salzburg, especially for earlier composed works; in a letter of 4 July 1781 he wrote to his father: 'copying here [in Vienna] costs far too much; and they write atrociously'. Before long, however, he had engaged local copyists of his own and if a reminiscence of Nannerl Mozart is to be believed, copyists had a free hand at Mozart's home, taking and making copies as needed. The large body of surviving manuscripts notwithstanding, however, only one of Mozart's regular Viennese copyists can be identified by name, Joseph Arthofer; among the most important copies in his hand are manuscripts of the piano concertos K413–15 (now at St Peter's, Salzburg). At least one other copyist also worked for Mozart on a regular basis throughout the 1780s although his identity remains unknown. But he was certainly close to the composer: several copies wholly or partly in his hand include Mozart's autograph corrections, including manuscripts of the G minor symphony K550, the keyboard concerto K456, the dedication copy of the C minor sonata K457 and a copy of the symphony K391 sold by Mozart to the Donaueschingen court in 1786. No doubt Mozart had dealings with other music copyists as well, although it is difficult, if not impossible, to document the exact nature of their relationship.

In addition to manuscripts from Salzburg and Vienna, copies of Mozart's works were made throughout Europe, especially during the 1780s and later. Some of these copies derive from printed editions, others from earlier manuscript copies. In a few instances they also represent the earliest or only surviving source. Lacking any demonstrable connection to the composer, however, these manuscripts are insufficient as evidence for attribution nor do they guarantee the texts they transmit. This is the case, for example, with the A minor symphony listed in the Köchel catalogue as Anh. 220 (16a). Although it represents the only surviving source for the work, its provenance cannot be tied to the composer and the style of the work suggests it was not composed by him. The situation is hardly unique in the eighteenth century: it is likely that as many as 20 per cent of symphony manuscripts from the time are misattributed.

Finally, a group of copies from the nineteenth century deserves special notice: manuscripts prepared by or for the first generation of Mozart scholars, Otto Jahn, Aloys Fuchs and LUDWIG RITTER VON KÖCHEL. For the most part these copies were based on Mozart's autographs, many of which were subsequently lost. As a result, they sometimes represent the only surviving *potentially* reliable sources for Mozart's works, even if recent research shows that they often misrepresent Mozart's texts. Nevertheless, although many previously lost autographs have now been recovered, several of these nineteenth-century copies transmit otherwise unknown works, sketches or drafts.

In general, the importance and authority of manuscripts by Mozart's regular copyists – whether in Salzburg or Vienna – does not rest solely on evidence that they were proof-read or owned by the composer, as if they were second-hand autographs, isolated from and inferior to other, similar sources. In fact, their authority stems from being part of a *complex* of sources of equal if not always identical importance. As such, their texts do not necessarily (or even exclusively) document the corruption of an Urtext but, rather, a succession of moments in the compositional and performance history of a work.

3. FIRST AND EARLY EDITIONS

During Mozart's lifetime, slightly more than 130 of his works appeared in printed editions published in Vienna, Prague, Speyer, Mainz, Paris, Amsterdam, The Hague and London. More than half of these are of works with keyboard, including solo and accompanied sonatas, piano trios, piano quartets and arrangements of dances. Others are of chamber music, including string quartets and quintets and songs. Works for larger forces are not so well represented. Before 1791, only two complete operas were published in vocal scores, *Die Entführung aus dem Serail* and DON GIOVANNI, three symphonies (K297, 319 and 385) and six piano concertos (K175 + 382, 413–15, 453 and 595). By 1805, however, more than half of Mozart's compositions had appeared in print, including almost all of the major works in each genre.

The majority of editions published before 1780 appeared under the composer's direct supervision or with his consent, often as a result of his early travels. The sonatas and variations K6–15, K24–5 and K26–31 were published during the grand tour of 1763–6, the songs K52–3 in Vienna in 1768 and the variations and sonatas K179–80, K301–6 and K354 in Paris in 1778. Often these editions carry dedications to royalty for whom Mozart composed or performed the works. More compositions were published between 1781 and 1791, the majority of them in Vienna. Indeed, Mozart seems to have established connections with Viennese publishers shortly after his arrival in the imperial capital. He was in touch with Artaria as early as August 1781; in December they published the sonatas K296 and K376–80.

In some cases, first and early editions represent the best surviving sources for Mozart's works. This is the case, for example, with the juvenile sonatas K9–15 and K24–31, the autographs of which do not survive. It is also true of some late works, including the piano quartet K493 and the songs K552 and K596–8. But it is by no means sure that these editions were carefully supervised or proof-read. A copy of the sonatas K6–7, now in the library of the Internationale Stiftung Mozarteum, includes later corrections by Leopold Mozart. And when Wolfgang published the sonatas K301–6 in Paris in 1778, he left the city before the edition actually appeared. In Vienna, some of his sonatas and variations were seen through the press by his pupil JOSEPHA AUERNHAMMER. In fact, there is little evidence that Mozart always supplied originals to publishers and it may be that they sometimes worked from second-generation sources. As a result, it is uncertain whether some textual details in the first editions, details that differ from the autographs, always derive from Mozart. Those in the first edition of the six quartets dedicated to Haydn (K387, 421, 428, 458, 464, 465) – including dynamics, phrasing and tempo indications – probably do derive from Mozart. The situation may be different, however, with other editions.

Mozart's satisfaction with Viennese editions of his works remains an open question. In a letter of 26 April 1783 he wrote, hyperbolically perhaps, to the Paris publisher SIEBER: 'You presumably know about my pianoforte sonatas with accompaniment for violin which I have had engraved here by Artaria and Company; – but I'm not entirely satisfied with the standard of engraving here.' By the same token, there is evidence that Viennese publishers were not entirely happy with Mozart and his often difficult music. According to Constanze Mozart's second husband, GEORG NIKOLAUS NISSEN, Mozart had a contract with Hoffmeister to publish three quartets for piano and strings. However, 'Mozart's first piano quartet, in G minor, was so little thought-of at first that the publisher Hoffmeister sent [Mozart] the advance honorarium on the condition that he not compose the two other agreed-upon quartets and Hoffmeister was released from his contract.'

In part because of a lack of documentation, Mozart's exact relationships with contemporary publishers remain unclear. Few of his letters to publishers survive and they do not always concern the publication of his works. Mozart's sole extant letter to Hoffmeister, for example, is a request for a loan (20 Nov. 1785). It must also be presumed that some letters are lost. Documents show that Breitkopf in Leipzig approached Mozart in 1786 and that in 1790 the London publisher John Bland claimed to have settled a contract with Mozart, Haydn, KOZELUCH and VANHAL, among others. In any case, both Mozart and his father were ambivalent about publication. While it is clear that the Mozarts wished to have at least some of Wolfgang's works printed, the family letters also show that at times they wished to suppress the dissemination of his compositions.

The sudden availability in print after 1791 of a considerable number of Mozart's works was no doubt a result of the success of DIE ZAUBERFLÖTE as well as the composer's extraordinary popularity, fuelled in no small part by Romantic stories of his last days, stories that began to circulate in early 1792. And at least some of these editions derived from Constanze Mozart's release of works from her husband's estate. Even so, a large chunk of Mozart's music remained unavailable throughout the 1790s until Breitkopf & Härtel in Leipzig launched their 'complete' works in 1798. The scheme was ambitious, and ultimately remained far from complete. Nevertheless, by 1806 they had published seventeen volumes of works for solo keyboard, chamber music with keyboard, the solo songs, the REQUIEM, *Don Giovanni*, the masses K257 and 317, twelve quartets, twenty concertos and a number of arias. Similarly important are the editions published by Johann Anton André, who in 1799 purchased the bulk of Mozart's estate from the composer's widow. In 1800 alone, André published several important first editions, including the concertos K246, 365, 482, 488 and 491, as well as the quartets K168–73. However, progress on the series was slow and it was not long before André became more interested in studying the autographs with a view to establishing a chronology of Mozart's works, than in publishing them. All the same, André's editions from the autographs represent early important sources, especially in those cases where Mozart's originals have in whole or in part subsequently been lost. CLIFF EISEN

W. A. Bauer, O. E. Deutsch and J. H. Eibl, eds., *Mozart: Briefe und Aufzeichnungen* (Kassel, 1962–1975); partial English trans. E. Anderson, *The Letters of Mozart and his Family* (London, 1938; rev. 2nd edn 1966 A. H. King and M. Carolan; rev. 3rd edn 1985 S. Sadie and F. Smart)

O. E. Deutsch, *Mozart: die Dokumente seines Lebens* (Kassel, 1961; suppl. 1978 ed. J. H. Eibl); English trans. E. Blom, P. Branscombe and J. Noble, *Mozart: A Documentary Biography* (London, 1965; repr. 1966)

D. Edge, 'Mozart's Viennese Copyists' (Ph.D. thesis, University of Southern California, 2001)
C. Eisen, *New Mozart Documents: A Supplement to O. E. Deutsch's 'Documentary Biography'* (London and Stanford, CA, 1991); in German with additions as *Mozart: die Dokumente seines Lebens: Addenda. Neue Folge* (Kassel, 1997)
'The Mozarts' Salzburg Copyists: Aspects of Attribution, Chronology, Text, Style and Performance Practice', in *Mozart Studies*, ed. Eisen (Oxford, 1991), 253–307
G. Haberkamp, *Die Erstdrucke der Werke von Wolfgang Amadeus Mozart: Bibliographie* (Tutzing, 1986)
U. Konrad, *Mozarts Schaffensweise: Studien zu den Werkautographen, Skizzen und Entwürfen* (Göttingen, 1992); suppl. in *Mozart-Jahrbuch* 1995, 1–28
W. Plath, 'Beiträge zur Mozart-Autographie I: die Handschrift Leopold Mozarts', *Mozart-Jahrbuch* 1960/61, 72–118
'Beiträge zur Mozart-Autographie II: Schriftchronologie 1770–1780', *Mozart-Jahrbuch* 1976/77, 131–73
A. Tyson, *Mozart: Studies of the Autograph Scores* (Cambridge, MA, 1987)

'Spatzenmesse'. Mozart's *Missa brevis* in C, K220 (1775–7). See MASS

Spaur family. Noble family known to the Mozarts in SALZBURG. Franz Joseph Spaur (b. 1725; d. 1797), was father of Friedrich Franz Joseph (b. 1 Feb. 1756; d. 6 Mar. 1821), a Salzburg canon from 1777, a distinguished representative of the Catholic ENLIGHTENMENT, and a FREEMASON. His brother Ignaz Joseph (b. 8 May 1729; d. 2 Mar. 1779) was Bishop of Brixen. LEOPOLD MOZART wrote to him on 31 July 1778, suggesting that Archbishop COLLOREDO had been instrumental in MARIA ANNA MOZART's death. There is one Mozart work associated with the family, the 'Spaurmesse', mentioned in Leopold's letter of 28 May 1778. It is probably, but not certainly, the mass K262, dating from 1775.
RUTH HALLIWELL

K. O. Wagner, 'Domherr Friedrich Graf Spaur und seine Werke', *Mitteilungen der Gesellschaft für Salzburger Landeskunde* 74 (1934), 14–158

'Spaur-Messe'. See MASS

Spitzeder, Franz (de Paula) Anton (b. Traunstein, Bavaria, 2 Aug. 1735; d. Salzburg, 19 June 1796). A GERMAN tenor to whom LEOPOLD MOZART refers warmly in his correspondence, Spitzeder sang solo roles at the premieres of several of Mozart's early works – *Die Schuldigkeit des ersten und Fürnehmsten Gebots*, K35 (1767), *LA FINTA SEMPLICE*, K51 (1769) and (in all likelihood) *IL RE PASTORE*, K208 (1775). He was based at court in SALZBURG for almost his entire professional life (1760–96) and was well respected by Archbishop SCHRATTENBACH, who ruled until 1771. While ANTON CAJETAN ADLGASSER suffered a seizure during a Salzburg service on 21 December 1777, Spitzeder played the left-hand organ part as Adlgasser continued with the right hand. After Adlgasser's death the next day, Spitzeder temporarily carried out his teaching at the Kapellhaus.
SIMON P. KEEFE

R. Halliwell, *The Mozart Family: Four Lives in a Social Context* (Oxford, 1998)
W. Rainer, 'F. A. Spitzeder als Klavierlehrer am Kapellhaus', *Mozart-Jahrbuch* 1964, 138–41

Stadler family. Anton Paul Stadler (b. Bruck an der Leitha, 28 June 1753; d. Vienna, 15 June 1812) was a clarinet virtuoso, composer and inventor who became a good friend of Mozart's in VIENNA; his brother Johann Nepomuk Franz Stadler (b. Vienna, 1755; d. Vienna, May 1804), was also a highly accomplished clarinettist.

The earliest documentation of the brothers performing is a 1773 programme of the Tonkünstler-Sozietät for which they performed an unidentified double clarinet concerto. In 1779, they were employed in Emperor JOSEPH II's wind octet or *Harmonie* – in which Anton initially played second clarinet because of his interest in the instrument's low register – and in the court orchestra on a per service basis. (Johann Nepomuk Franz also played first clarinet when Anton was on tour from 1792 to 1796 and after Anton retired in 1799.) By 1781, as orchestral instrumentation came to include clarinets more regularly, the brothers were designated 'indispensable' by the Emperor and were given full-time employment in the court orchestra as well as the *Harmonie*.

It is likely that Anton Stadler first met Mozart at the home of Countess Wilhelmine THUN soon after Mozart's arrival in Vienna in 1781. Four years later he became a member of the Palm Tree lodge and frequently participated in Mozart's Masonic music, especially pieces including the basset horn, on which he was also a virtuoso. In 1786, Mozart wrote the 'Kegelstatt' trio, K498, featuring Stadler (clarinet), Mozart's accomplished student Francesca von JACQUIN (piano) and Mozart himself (viola).

As early as 1787, with the collaboration of Anton Stadler, Theodor Lotz created a 'Bass-Klarinet' later called a basset clarinet, having 'two more keys at the lower end than the normal clarinet' and receiving its premiere at Stadler's concert of 20 February 1788 in Vienna. By 1790 (perhaps earlier), the instrument had a total of four basset keys of low E flat, D, C sharp and C. In newspapers of the time, this clarinet is described as having a 'full four-octave range', which Stadler played with 'amazing ease'. Mozart composed the Quintet for Clarinet and Strings, K581 (1790) and his Concerto for Clarinet and Orchestra, K622 (1791) for Anton to perform on this instrument, the latter work premiered in all likelihood in the National Theatre in PRAGUE on 16 October 1791, the beginning of his five-year tour of Europe. Basset clarinet writing also appears in the obbligato aria, 'Parto, parto, ma tu ben mio' from LA CLEMENZA DI TITO and portions of COSÌ FAN TUTTE, K588, as well as in two quintet fragments for clarinet and strings, K516c (1790) and K581a, Anh. 88 (1790 or 1791).

No other wind player dominated the Viennese musical scene of this era in quite the way Anton Stadler did. His rich, full tone was frequently commended in contemporary criticism, as was his ability to 'imitate the human voice' and to change registers quickly and 'with remarkable ease' throughout a 'four octave range'.

PAMELA L. POULIN

Karl Maria Pisarowitz, 'Müßt ma nix in übel aufnehma . . .': Beitragversuche zu einer Gebrüder-Stadler-Biographie', *Mitteilungen der Internationalen Stiftung Mozarteum* 19/1–2 (Feb. 1971), 29–33

P. L. Poulin, 'The Basset Clarinet of Anton Stadler', *College Music Symposium*, 22/2 (Fall 1982), 67–82

'A Little-Known Letter of Anton Stadler', *Music & Letters* 69/2 (Jan. 1988), 49–56

'Noch eine Bach–Mozart Verbindung', *Bach-Jahrbuch* (Jan. 1990), trans. Christoph Wolff

'A View of Eighteenth-Century Musical Life and Training: Anton Stadler's Music Plan', *Music & Letters* 71/2 (May 1990), 215–24

'A Report on New Information Regarding Stadler's Concert Tour of Europe and Two Early Examples of the Basset Clarinet', *Mozart-Jahrbuch* 1992, 270–80

'An Updated Report on New Information Regarding Stadler's Concert Tour of Europe', *The Clarinet*, 22/2 (1995), 24–8

'Discoveries in Riga: What Stadler's Basset Clarinet Looked Like and the First Documented Performance of the Mozart Clarinet Concerto', *Journal of the American Musical Instrument Society* (1996)
The Life and Times of Anton Stadler (forthcoming)
P. Weston, *Clarinet Virtuosi of the Past* (London, 1971)
More Clarinet Virtuosi of the Past (London, 1977)

Stadler, Maximilian [Abbé] (b. Melk, Lower Austria, 1748; d. Vienna, 8 Nov. 1833). A theologian and musician, Stadler first heard Mozart perform (on the organ) at Melk Monastery on 14 December 1767. In his autobiography he reported meeting Mozart fairly regularly in the 1780s. He also commented: 'In the art of free improvisation, Mozart had no equal. His improvisations were as well-ordered as if he had them lying written out before him.' Following Mozart's death, he orchestrated parts of the REQUIEM after JOSEPH LEOPOLD VON EYBLER had reneged on his commitment to CONSTANZE MOZART to complete the work. His relations with Constanze after 1791 were good: he examined several of Mozart's extant autographs in 1798 and 1799 (assisting GEORG NIKOLAUS NISSEN), made piano arrangements of several works and catalogued sketches and fragments (published in Nissen's biography). During the so-called *Requiem-Streit* ('Requiem Controversy') of the 1820s, Stadler elicited further gratitude from Constanze for arguing staunchly for Mozart's involvement in the work in a pamphlet entitled 'Defence of the Authenticity of Mozart's Requiem' (1826).

SIMON P. KEEFE

G. Croll, 'Eine zweite, fast vergessene Selbstbiographie von Abbé Stadler', *Mozart-Jahrbuch* 1964, 172–84

Starzer, Joseph (Johann Michael) (baptized Vienna, 5 Jan. 1728; d. Vienna, 22 Apr. 1787). A prolific composer of ballet scores, Starzer lived and worked in VIENNA, aside from eight years at the Russian court (1759–67), collaborating with leading choreographers such as Franz Hilverding, JEAN-GEORGES NOVERRE and Angiolini. In 1772 he became leader of the charitable organization for musicians in Vienna, the Tonkünstler-Sozietät, that he helped to set up a year earlier. He participated frequently in the society's activities as violinist, composer and conductor and, acting on BARON VAN SWIETEN's suggestion in 1779, arranged HANDEL's *Judas Maccabaeus* for the society's concerts.

Like Mozart, Starzer participated in Baron van Swieten's regular Sunday concerts, often singing tenor. Their paths crossed elsewhere too. In March 1781 Starzer invited Mozart to play in a Tonkünstler-Sozietät concert and had to persuade Archbishop COLLOREDO (who still employed Mozart) to allow him to do so. Starzer's death in 1787 paved the way for Mozart's court appointment as composer in the *Kammermusik* (6 Dec. 1787). SIMON P. KEEFE

B. A. Brown, *Gluck and the French Theatre in Vienna* (Oxford, 1991)

Stein, Johann Andreas (b. Heidelsheim, 6 May 1728; d. Augsburg, 29 Feb. 1792). Settling in AUGSBURG in 1750, Stein became an internationally famous piano maker, providing instruments (as many as 700 in total) for musicians across Europe. LEOPOLD MOZART purchased a piano from him in 1763. Mozart was highly complimentary about Stein's pianos, writing to his father from Augsburg (17 Oct. 1777): 'In whatever way I touch the keys, the tone is always even. It is true that he does not sell a pianoforte of this kind for less than three hundred gulden, but the trouble and the labour which Stein puts into the making of it cannot be paid for. His instruments have this special advantage over others that they are made with escape action. Only one maker in a hundred bothers about this.' Five days later, Stein performed Mozart's Concerto for Three Pianos in F ('LODRON'), K242 (1776), alongside Mozart and the Augsburg cathedral organist, JOHANN MICHAEL DEMMLER, providing the pianos himself. Several Mozart performances on Stein instruments are also documented in the decade 1781–91, including his Viennese contest with CLEMENTI in front of Emperor JOSEPH II on 24 December 1781 and his concert in Frankfurt on 15 October 1790 (on an instrument 'supreme of its kind' according to Count Ludwig von Bentheim-Steinfurt in his travel diary).

Stein's daughter, Maria Anna ('Nanette') (1769–1833) continued in her father's footsteps as a piano maker, first in partnership with her brother Matthäus Andreas (1776–1842) and then with her husband, Johann Andreas Streicher (1761–1833). The firm operated until 1896, latterly in the name of Nanette's son, Johann Baptist Streicher. SIMON P. KEEFE

M. Latcham, 'Mozart and the Pianos of Johann Andreas Stein', *Galpin Society Journal* 51 (1998), 114–53

Stephanie, Johann Gottlieb (b. Breslau, 19 Feb. 1741; d. Vienna, 23 Jan. 1800). A distinguished playwright, librettist and actor who had over thirty plays performed at the Viennese court theatre in the late eighteenth and early nineteenth centuries, Stephanie was the librettist of Mozart's singspiel DIE ENTFÜHRUNG AUS DEM SERAIL (1782) and the one-act *Komödie mit Musik*, DER SCHAUSPIELDIREKTOR, K486 (1786). He also performed the speaking role of Frank in the latter at the premiere at Schönbrunn Palace, VIENNA (7 Feb. 1786). He furnished singspiel librettos for other eminent composers such as CARL DITTERS VON DITTERSDORF, Joseph Barta and IGNAZ UMLAUF, and also derived singspiels from Italian and French comic operas by GIOVANNI PAISIELLO, Antonio Sacchini and André-Modeste Grétry.

Stephanie was in control of GERMAN opera in Vienna when Mozart moved to the city in 1781 and soon promised to write a libretto for him. In all likelihood Mozart had very little say in the selection of the story, CHRISTOPH FRIEDRICH BRETZNER's *Belmonte und Constanze, oder Die Entführung aus dem Serail*, which Stephanie adapted considerably in consultation with Mozart.

SIMON P. KEEFE

T. Bauman, 'Coming of Age in Vienna: *Die Entführung aus dem Serail*', in D. Heartz, *Mozart's Operas*, ed. Bauman (Berkeley, 1990), 65–87
K. Küster, *Mozart: A Musical Biography*, trans. M. Whittall (Oxford, 1996), 141–52

stile antico. A term that originated in the seventeenth century to describe church music using the old, 'antiquated' style of strict Palestrina counterpoint. When applied to music of the eighteenth century, the connotation of an old style remains, but Palestrina may not be the specific reference point. Instead, music that exhibits traits of the a capella chorus – alla breve style, canonic formations and simplicity of harmony – is regarded as a manifestation of the *stile antico*.

Many of Mozart's vocal fugues in his church music make use of alla breve, cantus firmus-type subjects. Extended employment of the alla breve style features, most notably, in the 'Cum sancto spiritu' from the Gloria of the Mass in

C minor, K427 (1783); also, the 'Laudate pueri' from the Vespers, K321 (1779) comprises an alla breve canon. In the Magnificat, K193 (1774), the entries at the beginning of the words 'et in saecula saeculorum' are specifically marked alla capella. Works written entirely in a strict sixteenth-century contrapuntal style are almost non-existent, however, in Mozart's repertory. His mode of contrapuntal writing is more consistently akin to a freer, Classical approach.

The term *stile antico* is rarely applied to instrumental or operatic settings, but music in these genres that is generally contrapuntal and 'learned' in nature rather than homophonic and galant (the then 'modern' style) may be perceived as 'antiquated'. The appearance of canonic technique in the Act 2 finale of COSÌ FAN TUTTE (K588, Act 2, scene 16, Terzetto) is the only example in Mozart's operas of his use of an explicitly learned technique. It is said to have influenced BEETHOVEN's famous quartet canon in Act 1, No. 3 of *Fidelio*, even though the effect and expressive aims of the two settings are very different. Mozart also wrote about twenty independent, short canons with text, experimenting with different canonic formations and their effects.

For instrumental music, the use of the 'old style' is a more complex issue. Mozart wrote only a few complete instrumental fugues, but many of his works incorporate a learned, contrapuntal style mixed with homophonic writing. The best-known examples are the finales of the G major String Quartet (K387) and the 'Jupiter' symphony in C (K551). Both movements employ alla breve subjects of the cantus firmus type and set the 'learned' openings against galant, homophonic sections (see FUGUE). Other compositions exhibiting mixtures of 'old' and 'new' styles include the Overture to DIE ZAUBERFLÖTE (K620), and the rondo finales of the piano concerto K459, the two string quintets K593 and K614, and the 'Musical Joke', K522. Even though alla breve contrapuntal treatment is in itself an antiquated technique in cases such as these, its combination with galant styles in the same movement is an innovative eighteenth-century musical trend. SHARON CHOA

L. G. Ratner, *Classic Music: Expression, Form, and Style* (New York, 1980)
E. Sisman, *Mozart: The 'Jupiter' Symphony* (Cambridge, 1993)

Stoll, Anton (1747–1805). A friend of Mozart who resided in Baden, near Vienna and worked as a teacher and choirmaster, Stoll performed several of Mozart's works in 1790 and 1791, including a mass (possibly the 'Coronation', K317) in 1790 and the *Missa brevis* in B flat, K275, in July 1791. Mozart's late MOTET, *Ave verum corpus*, K618, was written for Stoll, who premiered it in Baden (23 June 1791). Also in summer 1791 at Mozart's request, Stoll found accommodation in Baden for CONSTANZE MOZART. SIMON P. KEEFE

Storace family. The musical members of the Storace family included Stephen (Stefano) Storace (c.1725–c.1781), his son Stephen (1762–96) and his daughter Ann Selina 'Nancy' (b. LONDON, 27 Oct. 1765; d. London, 24 Aug. 1817). Storace senior, a double bass player, was born and brought up in Italy, spent a decade in Dublin and moved to London in 1758. His son was a composer, whose operas often showcased his sister Nancy in leading roles – for example *Gli sposi malcontenti* (premiered at the Burgtheater on 1 June 1785), *La cameriera astuta* (his only Italian opera for London) and *No Song, No Supper*. He also wrote a substitute aria, 'Compatite miei signori', for GIUSEPPE SARTI's ever-popular *Fra i due litiganti il terzo gode*, again to exploit the talents of his sister. It was he who hosted the famous quartet party in the mid-1780s at which JOSEPH HAYDN and DITTERS VON DITTERSDORF played the violin parts, Mozart the viola and VANHAL the cello.

Nancy Storace, the first Susanna in Mozart's LE NOZZE DI FIGARO premiered at the Burgtheater on 1 May 1786, was a prominent singer in VIENNA's Italian company between 1783 and 1787. She starred in a number of productions at this time, including ANTONIO SALIERI's *La scuola de' gelosi*, Domenico Cimarosa's *L'italiana in Londra*, MARTÍN Y SOLER's *Il burbero di buon cuore* and *Una cosa rara* and GIOVANNI PAISIELLO's operas *Il barbiere di Siviglia*, *La frascantana* and *Il re Teodoro in Venezia* in addition to *Figaro*. Her last performance at the Burgtheater on 19 February 1787 was followed four days later by a farewell concert at the Kärntnertortheater at which she sang the scena for soprano and piano that Mozart had composed for them to perform together, *Ch'io mi scordi di te? . . . Non temer, amato bene*, K505. She departed soon thereafter for London where she would live for the remainder of her life singing at the King's Theatre and at Drury Lane, stopping off in SALZBURG to perform at Archbishop COLLOREDO's palace. Although widely admired, Nancy's voice was, according to some critics, slightly coarse. CHARLES BURNEY reported a performance in 1788: 'though a lively and intelligent actress, and an excellent performer in comic operas, her voice, in spite of all her care, does not favour her ambition to appear as a *serious singer*. There is a certain crack and roughness . . . [In] airs of tenderness, sorrow, or supplication, there is always reason to lament the deficiency of natural sweetness.' SIMON P. KEEFE

K. and I. Geiringer, 'Stephen und Nancy Storace in Wien', *Oesterreichische Musikzeitschrift* 34 (1979), 18–25

D. Link, ed., *Arias for Nancy Storace, Mozart's First Susanna* (Recent Researches in the Music of the Classical Era, 66; Middleton, WI, 2002)

Strack, Johann Kilian (baptized Mainz, 30 Mar. 1724; d. Vienna, 16 Jan. 1793) An employee of the Viennese court who frequently organized private chamber-music performances with Emperor JOSEPH II, Strack dealt regularly with the Emperor as his chamberlain and thus became an important point of contact for Viennese musicians. Mozart was aware of Strack's potentially influential position. He admitted to his father that the 'chief reason' for composing the serenade K375 (1781) for the name day of court painter Joseph Hickel's sister-in-law 'was in order to let Herr von Strack . . . hear something of my composition; so I wrote it rather carefully' (3 Nov. 1781). A few months later Mozart reported (10 Apr. 1782): 'I have been a few times to see Herr von Strack (who is certainly a very good friend of mine) in order to let myself be seen and because I like his company, but I have not gone often, because I do not wish to become a nuisance to him, or to let him think that I have ulterior motives.' SIMON P. KEEFE

Strinasacchi, Regina (b. Ostiglia (near Mantua), 1764; d. Dresden, 11 June 1839). An acclaimed Italian violinist trained in Venice, Strinasacchi visited VIENNA in 1784, performing the violin and piano sonata K454 in B flat at the Kärntnertortheater that Mozart had written for her (29 Apr. 1784). Wolfgang and LEOPOLD MOZART both admired her playing, Mozart reporting to his father (24 Apr. 1784): 'We now have here the famous Strinasacchi from Mantua, a very good violinist. She has a great deal of taste and feeling in her playing.' Leopold was similarly impressed with the feeling and emotion she conveyed upon hearing her in SALZBURG on 7 December 1785. Strinasacchi's brother, Antonio, played violin in the Salzburg court orchestra between 1787 and 1789; Leopold felt that he fell well short of the high standards set by his sister.

SIMON P. KEEFE

string quartet. See CHAMBER MUSIC: B. STRING QUARTETS

string quintet. See CHAMBER MUSIC: C. STRING QUINTETS

string trio. See CHAMBER MUSIC: A. STRING DUOS AND TRIOS

Sturm und Drang. *Sturm und Drang* ('Storm and Stress') derives from the title of a 1776 drama by the playwright Maximilian Klinger. It came to be associated with certain writings of GOETHE (for example, *Die Leiden des jungen Werthers*) and Schiller (*Die Räuber*) and spanned the time from 1773 to 1781. As a musical term, it was first introduced in a 1909 essay on JOSEPH HAYDN by Théodore de Wyzewa and also associated there with Mozart. The *Sturm und Drang* in music has been considered both a style period covering a somewhat earlier time-frame (c.1765–c.1774) than its literary counterpart and as a powerfully expressive style that rears its head in passages, movements, arias and cycles throughout the second half of the eighteenth century. Some have seen it as a precursor or adumbration of musical Romanticism, though by the middle-period works of BEETHOVEN, it had become such a common topic that much of its contextual distinction had been lost. Its most essential feature is the presence of the minor mode; other contributory elements are driving rhythms, syncopations, accents on weak portions of a bar, leaping intervals, polyphonic textures, detailed and sudden changes in dynamics and an overall extroverted but sombre expression.

When Wyzewa and Saint-Foix made their first substantial application of the *Sturm und Drang* to Mozart, it was in connection with a series of sonatas for violin and keyboard supposedly composed in MILAN in 1772–3, but that are now considered spurious. Attempts by H. C. Robbins Landon and others to define a *Sturm und Drang* period to which Mozart was a contributor is not persuasive. To be sure, Mozart produced in 1773 both a D minor string quartet, K173 and his 'Little' G minor Symphony, K183, but since these works as well as other movements from the early Viennese string quartets (K168–73) were part of an effort to acquire a position at the imperial court, their use of 'pathétique' and learned styles represent above all an effort to gain favour with the Emperor JOSEPH II and, in the specific case of K183, to gain further facility in the symphonic idiom.

It is more persuasive to view Mozart as a user of the *Sturm und Drang* topic throughout his career, beginning most markedly with the overture to *Betulia liberata*, K118 (1771), where all three movements remain unusually in D minor. The spread of this style in Mozart's oeuvre is best revealed by looking at his instrumental cycles in the minor mode, which are rather evenly distributed over the decades of the 1770s and 1780s and include such works as the Violin Sonata in E minor, K304 (1778), the Piano Sonata in A minor, K310 (1778), the Serenade in C minor, K388 (1782), the Piano Concerto in D minor, K466 (1785), and the Symphony in G minor, K550 (1788). If any conclusion can be reached, it is that

Mozart wrote more *Sturm und Drang*-orientated works in the 1780s than in the 1770s.

Mozart also uses the *Sturm und Drang* style as a contrasting topic within a major-mode movement. In the 'Prague' Symphony in D major, K504 (1786), we can cite the massive slow introduction and the finale's development section; in the first movement of the 'Jupiter' Symphony in C major, K551 (1788) the minor-mode episode, juxtaposed with buffo and celebratory affects, is equally striking.

The *Sturm und Drang* was also employed effectively in Mozart's operas, where arias and ensembles in the minor mode underscore the drama. In the early operas, these include passages and numbers in LUCIO SILLA as well as Sandrina's (No. 21) and Ramiro's (No. 26) arias from LA FINTA GIARDINIERA; in IDOMENEO, Elettra is most fully characterized by this style (see No. 4), as is the Queen of the Night (Nos. 4 and 14) in DIE ZAUBERFLÖTE. And in DON GIOVANNI the revenge duet (No. 2) of Donna Anna and Don Ottavio as well as the demise of the protagonist (No. 26) are saturated with *Sturm und Drang* material. A. PETER BROWN

H. C. Robbins Landon, 'La Crise romantique dans la musique autrichienne vers 1770. Quelques précurseurs inconnus de la Symphonie in sol minuer (KV183) de Mozart', in *Les Influences étrangères dans l'œuvre de W. A. Mozart*, ed. A. Verchaly (Paris, 1956)

M. Rudolf, 'Storm and Stress in Music', *Bach* 3 (1972), No. 2, 3–13; No. 3, 3–11; No. 4, 8–16

T. de Wyzewa, 'A propos du centenaire de la mort de Joseph Haydn', *Revue des deux mondes* 79 (1909), 935–46

Süssmayr, Franz Xaver (b. Schwanenstadt, Upper Austria, 1766; d. Vienna, 17 Sept. 1803). An Austrian composer who studied with Mozart in 1791 and with ANTONIO SALIERI soon after Mozart's death, Süssmayr wrote popular sacred and secular works in VIENNA in the 1790s, including the operas *Der Spiegel von Arkadien* (1794, to a libretto by EMANUEL SCHIKANEDER) and *Soliman der Zweite, oder Die drei Sultaninnen* (1799). Once JOSEPH LEOPOLD VON EYBLER, another of Mozart's students, withdrew from his agreement with CONSTANZE MOZART to complete the REQUIEM, Constanze turned to Süssmayr, who finished the task. (According to Constanze's sister, SOPHIE HAIBEL (née Weber), Mozart issued instructions to Süssmayr the night before he died on how he wanted the work completed.) Süssmayr's involvement in the Requiem quickly became (and still remains) a controversial topic (see REQUIEM). On 8 February 1800 he informed the publishers Breitkopf & Härtel that he alone had finished off the 'Lacrymosa' and composed the Sanctus, Benedictus and Agnus Dei; Constanze, in contrast, claimed his contributions were purely mechanical. At any rate, he has been harshly (and somewhat unfairly) criticized by nineteenth- and twentieth-century writers, blamed when the musical quality of the later sections of the Requiem is purportedly low and said to be reliant on sketches and other materials perhaps left by Mozart when the quality is high.

Süssmayr became a trusted friend of Mozart in 1791, staying in Baden with Constanze in June as she rested before the birth of her son FRANZ XAVER WOLFGANG MOZART (26 July), copying out music for him (including for DIE ZAUBERFLÖTE) and travelling with both of them to PRAGUE for the premiere of LA CLEMENZA DI TITO (6 September). Mozart poked fun at him relentlessly in his letters, describing him as 'that idiotic fellow' and 'that great fellow' in quick succession (2 July 1791), suggested 'whippings' for him (3 July 1791), called him 'Sauermayr' (7 July 1791) – a pun on 'süss' (sweet) and 'sauer' (sour) – and 'a full blown ass' (7 Oct. 1791), and sent him 'a few good nose-pulls and a proper hair-tug' rather than more conventional greetings (8 Oct. 1791). In scatological mood, he also signed a spoof letter to his Baden-based friend JOSEPH ANTON STOLL 'Franz Süssmayr, Muckshitter' (12 July 1791). SIMON P. KEEFE

R. Maunder, *Mozart's Requiem: On Preparing a New Edition* (Oxford, 1988)
C. Wolff, *Mozart's Requiem: Historical and Analytical Studies, Documents, Score*, trans. M. Whittall (Berkeley and Los Angeles, 1994)

Swieten, Gottfried (Bernhard), Baron van (b. Leyden, 29 Oct. 1733; d. Vienna, 29 Mar. 1803) A diplomat, civil servant, court administrator and occasional composer, van Swieten held various official positions in VIENNA from 1777 onwards (after diplomatic posts in Brussels, PARIS, Warsaw and Berlin), including the directorship of the court library and the presidency of the Education and Censorship Commission. He was an ardent supporter of Mozart and his music, subscribing to his Trattnerhof concerts (1784) and to the ill-fated series in 1789 – 'I sent around a list for subscribers two weeks ago and so far the only name on it is that of the Baron van Swieten!' (12 July 1789) – and regularly attending his concerts; after Mozart's death (5 Dec. 1791) he organized a Viennese benefit concert for CONSTANZE MOZART (2 Jan. 1793) at which the REQUIEM was performed and also helped facilitate KARL THOMAS MOZART's education in PRAGUE. Even as early as 9 December 1791 a Viennese publication in Hungarian reported that the 'magnanimous Baron Swieten has . . . come to the assistance of the orphans [Karl Thomas and FRANZ XAVER WOLFGANG MOZART]'.

Having encountered van Swieten in Vienna in 1767–8, Mozart met him regularly in the 1780s, and they shared their common passion for the music of past masters (10 Apr. 1782): 'I go every Sunday at twelve o'clock to the Baron van Swieten, where nothing is played but HANDEL and [J. S.] BACH. I am collecting at the moment the fugues of Handel and Bach – not only of [Johann] Sebastien, but also of [CARL PHILIPP] EMANUEL and [Wilhelm] Friedemann.' Mozart's contact with Handel's music in particular bore fruit in his reorchestrations, at van Swieten's suggestion, of four of Handel's works – *Acis and Galatea*, K566 (1788), *Messiah*, K572 (1789), *Alexander's Feast*, K591 (1790) and *Ode for St Cecilia's Day*, K592 (1790). It has also been suggested that the Introit of the Requiem derives material from the first chorus of Handel's funeral anthem 'The Ways of Zion do mourn', HWV 264, another work Mozart is likely to have encountered through van Swieten. SIMON P. KEEFE

O. Biba, 'Gottfried van Swieten', in *Europas Musikgeschichte: Grenzen und Öffnungen*, ed. U. Prinz (Stuttgart, 1993), 120–37
T. M. Neff, 'Baron van Swieten and Late Eighteenth-Century Viennese Musical Culture' (Ph.D. thesis, Boston University, 1998)

symphonies. Mozart wrote forty-one numbered symphonies, and several others as well, beginning with K16 in E flat (1764–5) and ending with the 'Jupiter' Symphony in C, K551 (1788). Although he was by no means the most prolific late eighteenth-century symphonic composer, he stands alongside JOSEPH HAYDN as the era's most celebrated exponent of the genre.

1. In Salzburg and on his travels, 1764–1780

Mozart's initial symphonic forays, K16 (1764–5), No. 4 in D, K19 (1765), K19a in F (1765), No. 5 in B flat, K22 (1765) and K45a in G (1766) date from Mozart's three-and-a-half-year grand tour of GERMANY, France, England, Holland, Belgium and Switzerland with his father, mother and sister. They are cast in three movements, in a fast–slow–fast arrangement that features an Allegro of some kind for the first movement, an Andante for the second and a Presto for the third, and are identically scored for two oboes, two horns and strings. The principal models are likely to have been JOHANN CHRISTIAN BACH's and CARL FRIEDRICH ABEL's symphonies; Mozart got to know works by both composers on his European tour, and became friendly with Bach in LONDON. Even at such a tender age, Mozart was clearly conscious of the need to orchestrate carefully and creatively, asking NANNERL MOZART to 'remind me to give the horn something worthwhile to do' in K16; this would continue to be a preoccupation for him throughout his symphonic career.

A trip to VIENNA in 1767–8 provided the impetus for Mozart's next symphonies, chiefly No. 6 in F, K43 (1767), No. 7 in D, K45 (16 Jan. 1768) and No. 8 in D, K48 (13 Dec. 1768), although K43, at least, may have been partially composed in SALZBURG earlier in the summer of 1767. The minuet and trio movements reflect the influence of contemporary Viennese musical practice as does the orchestral scoring, which includes two trumpets and timpani (in K45 and 48) in addition to the usual two oboes, two horns and strings. K43 and K45 also marked the beginning of the strong musical association between Mozart's early symphonies and early operas; the Andante of K43 was an arrangement of a duet from *APOLLO ET HYANCINTHUS*, K38, premiered at the Benedictine University in Salzburg on 13 May 1767, and K45 was subsequently adapted as the overture to Mozart's first opera buffa, *LA FINTA SEMPLICE*, K51 (1769). In fact, the idea that Mozart's symphonies represent a self-contained, hermetically sealed orchestral genre, could not be further from the truth. In addition to the relationship between Mozart's symphonies and operas, one of his cassations (a type of orchestral work intended for 'the evenings, outdoors, or on public streets' according to the late eighteenth-century theorist Heinrich Christoph Koch), K100 in D (1769), and three of his SERENADES, K204 in D (1775), K250 in D ('Haffner', 1776) and K320 in D ('Posthorn', 1779) all reappeared in symphonic versions.

Another of Mozart's lengthy trips away from Salzburg, on this occasion to Italy (December 1769–March 1771), provided him with his next opportunity to work in the symphonic genre. On 4 August 1770 he declared that he had 'composed four Italian symphonies'. These, it is generally assumed, are K81 in D, K84 in D, K95 in D and K97 in D, although the absence of authentic sources for these works (autograph scores and authenticated copies) continues to preclude unequivocal confirmation of Mozart's authorship. No such doubts surround No. 10 in G, K74 (Milan, 1770) and No. 13 in F, K112 (Milan, 2 Nov. 1771), from Mozart's second Italian sojourn. Curiously, the autograph of the latter, a work in four movements rather than the Italianate three, includes a Menuetto written into the score by LEOPOLD MOZART, at least raising the possibility that this was originally an independent composition that was later interpolated into Mozart's symphony. K120 in D also dates from Mozart's second trip to Italy in late 1771 and comprises material used in the opera ASCANIO IN ALBA, first performed at the Teatro Regio Ducale in MILAN on 17 October 1771, while No. 12 in G, K110 (July 1771) was composed in Salzburg between the end of the first Italian trip and the beginning of the second.

Thus far, Mozart had cultivated his symphonic career almost entirely outside Salzburg. But this changed dramatically between December 1771 and 1774, during which he composed at least seventeen works in his home town, a fact all the more extraordinary when local circumstances in Salzburg are taken into consideration. Archbishop Hieronymus, Count COLLOREDO, who ruled Salzburg between 1772 and 1803, provided relatively few opportunities for the cultivation of instrumental music (certainly in comparison to his predecessor, Archbishop Siegmund Christoph, Count SCHRATTENBACH, who ruled from 1753 to 1771) and instrumental music concerts at court were infrequent at best. Mozart's primary outlets for his symphonies, then, would have been private and public concerts unconnected to his responsibilities as court organist, which required him to 'carry out his appointed duties with diligent assiduity and irreproachably, in the Cathedral as well as at the court and in chapel, and . . . *as far as possible* serve the court and the church with new compositions'. Since Mozart would have been expected consequently to compose far more MASSES, LITANIES and other sacred works than orchestral works, his proliferation of symphonies may have irritated the Archbishop and the ruling Salzburg authorities, perhaps contributing to the deterioration of relations between the Mozarts and Colloredo during the 1770s.

Several of Mozart's Salzburg symphonies from December 1771 to August 1772 – comprising No. 14 in A, K114, No. 15 in G, K124, No. 16 in C, K128, No. 17 in G, K129, No. 18 in F, K130, No. 19 in E flat, K132, No. 20 in D, K133, and No. 21 in A, K134 – feature relatively large wind sections, notably two flutes and four horns (K130), two oboes and four horns (K132), and flute, two oboes, two horns and two trumpets (K133). The official list of instrumentalists in the court orchestra includes only two/three horns and no flutes; on the few occasions when Mozart was able to avail himself of their services for performances of his symphonies, he would have had to rely on the relatively common practice of certain instrumentalists switching to a secondary instrument (oboists playing the flute, for example). In any case, Salzburg's wind instrumentalists had a good reputation in the late eighteenth century, Christian Friedrich Daniel Schubart and Friedrich Siegmund von Böcklin identifying 'especially distinguished' performers and 'several fine wind players' respectively, and Mozart often exploited their skills during the remainder of his career in the city.

Mozart's symphonies from 1773 and 1774 – K161 + 163 in D (most of which was drawn from the overture to the opera seria IL SOGNO DI SCIPIONE, K126 from 1772), No. 26 in E flat, K184, No. 27 in G, K199, No. 22 in C, K162, No. 23 in D, K181, No. 24 in B flat, K184, No. 25 in G minor, K183, No. 29 in A, K201, No. 30 in D, K202 and No. 28 in C, K200 in their most likely chronological order – continue to boast large wind sections and prominent roles for their constituent members. K183, typically acknowledged as a milestone in Mozart's symphonic output for its concentrated intensity and its status as his first minor-mode work in the genre (and sometimes referred to as the 'Little' G minor Symphony to distinguish it from No. 40 in G minor, K550), is especially striking in these respects. Scored for four horns as well as two oboes, two bassoons and strings, it contains numerous engaging instrumental effects. The main theme at the beginning of the first movement, for example, is replete with standard STURM UND DRANG characteristics, such as syncopation, frenetic activity and dotted rhythms all at a *forte* dynamic, but is completely transformed in the restatement and continuation. Here, the oboe floats mellifluously in semibreves over accompanimental material in the strings and horns, aligning the highpoint of its melody (b♭″) both with the low point in the cellos/basses and with a moment of gentle harmonic intensification (German augmented sixth). Later, in the final two bars of the development section, the oboes and four horns play a crescendo in semibreves from *piano* to *forte* unaccompanied by strings for the only time in the movement, thus carrying by themselves the important structural responsibility of directing the music towards the recapitulation. The other famous symphony from this period, K201, is equally memorable for its handling of the orchestra. Its economy of thematic development and clarity of formal articulation as well render it one of Mozart's most important instrumental works of the 1770s.

Mozart wrote no independent symphonies between 1774 and 1778, but continued to derive works in the genre from his operas and serenades, including K121 in D (1774–5) and K102 (1775) from the overtures to LA FINTA GIARDINIERA, K196 and IL RE PASTORE, K208 (both symphonic versions contain original finales), and K204 in D and K250 in D from the serenades K204 and K250. His six-month trip to PARIS in 1778 gave rise to the 'Paris' symphony, No. 31 in D, K297, a work richly documented through letters written to his father back in Salzburg. In several important respects, these letters reveal Mozart's thoroughly pragmatic attitude towards symphonic composition and his acute sensitivity to the demands of specific audiences. In spite of an apparent lack of interest in the *premier coup d'archet*, for example – the tutti chords or unisons heard at the beginning of a work that incorporate simultaneous down-bows in the strings – Mozart includes it anyway, in an effort to please the musically uneducated: 'I still hope . . . that even asses will find something in it to admire – and, moreover, I have been careful not to neglect *le premier coup d'archet* – and that is quite sufficient. What a fuss the oxen here make of this trick! The devil take me if I can see any difference! They all begin together, just as they do in other places' (letter of 12 June 1778). He admits to writing with the Parisian audience uppermost in his mind in the finale as well, playing with their expectations to successful effect: 'having observed that all last as well as first Allegros begin here with all the instruments playing together and generally *unisono*, I began mine with two violins only, *piano* for the first eight bars – followed instantly by a *forte*; the audience, as I expected, said "Shh!" at the soft beginning, and when they heard the *forte*, began at once to clap their hands' (3 July 1778). The existence of two different versions of the middle movement can also be attributed to the reaction of one of Mozart's audience members, the most important audience member of all in fact – JOSEPH LEGROS, the director of the Concert spirituel in Paris where the symphony was premiered. Legros, Mozart reports to Leopold, found the original 'too long' with 'too many modulations', so Mozart wrote a second one, 'just the reverse of what Legros says – . . . quite simple and short' (9 July 1778). Scholarly debate still rages about which of the two Andantes (in 6/8 and 3/4) is the original, but there is no doubt that Mozart's decision to write two movements represents a victory for a flexible and practical symphonic mindset, over an idealistic and naively obstinate one.

K297 has recently been criticized by eminent writers for its stylistically unadventurous writing and for exploiting extravagant gestures that render the work unconvincing when judged by Mozart's high standards. But examination of the music does not support such criticism and illustrates instead that the work is thoughtfully and carefully conceived. Whereas the grand opening gestures in K161 and K181, similar to the one that initiates K297, simply function as calls to attention that do not appear elsewhere, the *coup d'archet* in K297 (and the ascending semiquaver scale attached to it) is assimilated completely into the musical fabric of the first movement and exploited to dramatic effect. The motto reappears before and after the presentation of the secondary theme – first emphasizing a half-close on the dominant and later reconfirming the dominant in an imitative context – initiates the development while including a harmonic twist that pivots on an intrusive B flat, and resurfaces in extended form at the onset of the recapitulation, carrying both harmonic and imitative force.

Mozart's final Salzburg symphonies comprise No. 32 in G, K318 (26 Apr. 1779), No. 33 in B flat, K319 (9 July 1779) and No. 34 in C, K338 (29 Aug. 1780), as well as (perhaps) K320 in D, which consists of movements extracted from the 'Posthorn' Serenade in D (3 Aug. 1779) that have yet to be validated in their symphonic form by authentic sources. K318 is, unusually for Mozart, a one-movement work in three sections (Allegro spirituoso, Andante and Primo Tempo) indebted to the overture style of contemporary French *opéra comique*. (It is possible too that K318 was at one stage planned as the overture to the unfinished singspiel, ZAIDE, K344.) The Andante delays the recapitulation expected after the exposition and development sections of the Allegro. When the recapitulation finally arrives at the Primo Tempo, Mozart brings back the secondary theme first and delays the return of the primary theme until the end of the work, thus skilfully rendering his strident tutti unison both instigator and summarizer of the musical action. K319 is also an unusual work in Mozart's symphonic canon. He wrote it originally in three movements, but added a minuet and trio in 1784 or 1785, in all probability for a performance in Vienna, thus demonstrating – as in K297 – considerable sensitivity to the expectations of his audience.

2. The Vienna years, 1782–1788

Mozart spent relatively little time composing symphonies in Vienna, certainly in comparison to the amount spent in Salzburg and on his travels between 1764 and 1780. The resulting number of works is significantly lower as well – six in contrast to more than thirty-four. The critical tendency to marginalize the pre-1781 repertory, evident as early as the 1799 issue of the *Allgemeine musikalische Zeitung*, which dismissed four of the 1773–4 works as 'entirely ordinary symphonies . . . without conspicuous characteristics of originality and novelty', is unjust on account of the high quality of Mozart's works in the 1760s and 1770s. At the same time, however, it is difficult *not* to regard the six Viennese symphonies, No. 35 in D, K385 ('Haffner', July 1782), No. 36 in C, K425 ('Linz', October/November 1783), No. 38 in D, K504 ('PRAGUE', 6 Dec. 1786), No. 39 in E flat, K543 (26 June 1788), No. 40 in G minor, K550 (25 July 1788) and No. 41 in C, K551 ('Jupiter', 10 Aug. 1788) as climactic works in Mozart's symphonic output, such is their profusion of musical riches.

K385 was written at Leopold's request to coincide with the ennoblement of Siegmund HAFFNER the younger (1756–87), a friend of Mozart's from Salzburg, and its genesis is amply documented in the correspondence between father and son. (It was not the first work he had written for this prominent Salzburg family – Maria Elisabeth, sister of Siegmund, was the recipient of the 'Haffner' Serenade in D, K250, on the occasion of her wedding in 1776.) Following Leopold's request for a symphony in mid-July, Mozart replied testily on 20 July: 'Well, I am up to my eyes in work. By Sunday week I have to arrange my opera [DIE ENTFÜHRUNG AUS DEM SERAIL, K384] for wind instruments, otherwise someone will beat me to it and secure the profits instead of me. And now you ask me to write a new symphony! How on earth can I do so?' He explained nevertheless: 'You may rely on having something from me by every post. I shall work as fast as possible and, as far as haste permits, I shall turn out good work.' One week later, he was in a position to send only the first movement: 'it has been quite impossible to do more for you, for I have had to compose in a great hurry a serenade [K375], but for wind instruments only (otherwise I could have used it for you too). On Wednesday the 31st I shall send the two minuets, the Andante and the last movement. If I can manage to do so, I shall send a march too. If not, you will just have to use the one from the Haffner music [the serenade, K250, preceded by the march, K249], which hardly anyone knows.' Again, though, he fell short of his target, writing on 31 July: 'You see that my intentions are good – only what one cannot do, one cannot! I am really unable to scribble off inferior stuff. So I cannot send you the whole symphony until next post-day.' The date of the first performance of the completed symphony is not known, nor whether the premiere coincided with the party for Haffner's ennoblement, but it is certain from further correspondence that Leopold had at least seen the completed score by 24 August. Once again, Mozart's letters underscore his pragmatic attitude towards symphonic composition: he is happy to work very quickly; and he would have been willing to reuse material from the K375 serenade had it been scored for orchestra rather than wind band.

Mozart had the opportunity to perform K385 in spring 1783 in Vienna and requested that Leopold return the score to him, so that he could have copies made. It was at this stage, in all likelihood, that Mozart dispensed with one of the two minuets mentioned above and also added clarinet and flute parts to the outer movements. On receipt of the score, he wrote to his father on 15 February 1783: 'My new Haffner Symphony has positively amazed me, for I had forgotten every single note of it. It must surely produce a good effect.'

It was perhaps compositional bravado on Mozart's part to claim that he 'had forgotten every single note' only a few months after composing the work. Just six weeks earlier, on 4 January, he had requested that his father send him four of his old symphonies from the mid-1770s (K204, K201, K182 and K183), quoting the main themes of each. It is clear, nevertheless, that Mozart held K385 in high esteem.

Returning from a three-month visit to Salzburg at the end of October 1783, Mozart and CONSTANZE MOZART stopped off in Linz, where Mozart wrote K425 by his own admission 'at breakneck speed' for a performance at the city's theatre on 4 November. Sending K425 back to Salzburg for copying led to a performance in September 1784 of this 'new, excellent symphony' (Leopold's words) at the residence of the BARISANI family, longstanding Salzburg friends of the Mozarts. K425 is a remarkable work for several reasons. It contains Mozart's first slow introduction to one of his symphonies – deeply intense and expressive writing compressed into nineteen bars – a *forte* outburst in E minor (the submediant of the dominant) in the secondary theme section of the first movement that is certainly atypical of the contemporary symphonic repertory, and a highly sensitive yet dramatic slow movement. Another slow introduction followed soon thereafter in late 1783 or 1784, for Michael Haydn's Symphony, Perger 16 (K444).

It would be three years before Mozart composed another symphony, K504, a three-movement work without a minuet and trio. Having finished it in December 1786, he took it with him to Prague in January 1787, on the first of two month-long trips to the city that year, performing it to great acclaim. It is quite likely that the finale was written first and originally intended as a replacement finale for the 'Paris' symphony, K297, rather than as a movement for a completely new work. The Prague orchestra that performed the work was very small – just twenty-four to twenty-seven instrumentalists in total – but widely renowned as an orchestra of the highest quality. Mozart exploited their collective talents to the full, including intricate dialogue, euphonious combinations of wind instruments and technically challenging material throughout. FRANZ XAVER NIEMETSCHEK, one of Mozart's earliest biographers and a native Czech, surely had this work among others in mind (so strong are its associations with his beloved Prague) when he explained that Mozart 'judged with extreme accuracy the nature and range of all instruments' and 'the exact time and place to make his effect' thus '[evoking] the admiration of all experts . . . Never is an instrument wasted or misused, and, therefore, redundant. But he also knew how to achieve his most magical effects with true economy, entailing the least effort, often through a single note on an instrument, by means of a chord or a trumpet blast.' The first movement is probably also Mozart's most complex in terms of its lengthy, wide-ranging slow introduction, its integration of a ritornello into a symphonic sonata-form structure and its extraordinarily diverse range of allusions to musical styles, including grand, singing and march styles in the introduction and fanfare, brilliant, singing and contrapuntal styles in the Allegro.

Mozart's final trilogy of symphonies, K543, K550 and K551 have long been shrouded in mystery; Charles Rosen's remark that the Piano Concerto in D minor, K466 (1785) is 'almost as much myth as work of art' is just as applicable to these works. Fuelled no doubt by the fact that Mozart composed them incredibly in the space of just six weeks in the summer of 1788 and that no hard evidence exists for performances during Mozart's lifetime, writers traditionally assumed that he did not hear them in concert and that, by extension, he must have written them out of an inner compulsion to do so, rather than with specific performances in mind. But this romanticized view of the works runs completely counter to Mozart's practical and pragmatic attitude towards symphonic composition, indeed composition in general, and has been widely disparaged. It is quite possible – as explained recently – that Mozart wrote the works with a view to performing them either at planned subscription concerts later in 1788 (which may or may or may not have materialized) or on a projected, but unrealized, trip to England. He might also have intended to publish the three symphonies as an opus. The existence of two versions of the G minor symphony, K550 (the first without clarinets and the second with them) is the firmest evidence that performances took place during Mozart's lifetime. Mozart would surely not have rescored the work without specific performances on the horizon.

K543 is the least celebrated of the three last symphonies, but a magnificent work. The magisterial opening slow introduction to the first movement, an equal to that of K504, combines emphatic chords, visceral tutti writing, sweeping scalar material and sonorous wind writing. The lightly scored primary theme in the ensuing Allegro contrasts markedly, representing, to some extent, a release from harmonic tension evident in the introduction. Later, in the transition, Mozart skilfully transforms the introduction's scalar writing from grand expansiveness to pulsating energy. The latter characteristic is present in abundance in the finale in particular, generated by an opening motif that dominates musical proceedings even bringing the symphony to a close in unison among the strings.

The G minor Symphony, K550, stands alongside the string quartet K421 (1783), the piano concertos K466 (1785) and K491 (1786) and the string quintet K516 (1787) as Mozart's finest minor-mode instrumental work. But unlike K421, K466 and K516, Mozart's unremittingly intense finale continues in the minor right up until the final chord. The high esteem in which the work is held by the musical public at large originated at the beginning of the nineteenth century; issues of the *Allgemeine musikalische Zeitung* praise K550 as 'a true masterpiece' (1804), 'Mozart's symphony of all symphonies' (1809) and a 'classical masterwork' (1813). Not the least of its qualities are the intricate, idiomatic writing for winds – in evidence throughout – and the passages of harmonic audacity, such as at the beginning of the development sections of the outer movements.

Where reverence for Mozart's symphonies is concerned, the 'Jupiter' symphony, K551 (whose sobriquet is usually attributed to the late eighteenth-century impresario JOHANN PETER SALOMON) stands supreme. It quickly established itself as a classic, a work shattering and exalted in equal measure, and a climactic moment in music history, revealing 'all that music has achieved up to this time, and what it will do nearly a hundred years later' according to Georges de Saint-Foix. Heinrich Eduard Jacob even claimed that it has 'the allure of a God, who idly opens his hands to release it from the world'. The finale, which integrates fugal and other richly contrapuntal writing into a sonata-form structure culminating in a famous passage of five-part invertible counterpoint in the coda, has been singled out for the most lavish praise: it is 'one of the marvels of classical music' according to Hugh Ottoway, a 'triumphant exaltation' for Wilhelm Spohr, and 'a movement of unexcelled diversity and intellectual power' for Robert Gutman. More subtly – and motivated by readings of historical sources from the Classical period – the finale has been interpreted as a representative of elevated style and the bewilderment of the sublime (Sisman) and as a climactic exemplar of dramatic dialogue in Mozart's symphonic repertory (Keefe). Mozart could not have known that this would be his final symphony, of course. Even so, he could not possibly have gone out on a higher note. SIMON P. KEEFE

C. Eisen, 'Mozart and Salzburg', in *The Cambridge Companion to Mozart*, ed. Keefe (Cambridge, 2003), 7–21

'The Salzburg Symphonies: A Biographical Interpretation', in *Wolfgang Amadè Mozart*, ed. S. Sadie (Oxford, 1996), 178–212

S. P. Keefe, 'The Orchestral Music', in *The Cambridge Companion to Mozart*, ed. Keefe (Cambridge, 2003), 92–104

'The "Jupiter" Symphony in C, K. 551: New Perspectives on the Dramatic Finale and Its Stylistic Significance in Mozart's Orchestral Oeuvre', *Acta Musicologica* 75 (2003), 17–43

K. Küster, *Mozart: A Musical Biography*, trans. M. Whittall (Oxford, 1996)

F. X. Niemetschek, *The Life of Mozart* (1798), trans. H. Mautner (London, 1956)

E. R. Sisman, *Mozart: The 'Jupiter' Symphony* (Cambridge, 1993)

'Genre, Gesture and Meaning in Mozart's "Prague" Symphony', in *Mozart Studies* 2, ed. C. Eisen (Oxford, 1997), 27–84

N. Zaslaw, *Mozart Symphonies: Context, Performance Practice, Reception* (Oxford, 1989)

T

Tenducci, Giusto Ferdinando (b. Siena, c.1735; d. Genoa, 1790). A castrato who spent most of his working life in England (including at LONDON's King's Theatre), Scotland and Ireland, Tenducci is reputed to have had a beautiful, often-imitated voice, praised by CHARLES BURNEY among others. He had particular success as Arbaces in Thomas Arne's *Artaxerxes* (London, 1762). Wolfgang and LEOPOLD MOZART met Tenducci in London (1764) during their three-and-a-half-year grand tour of northern Europe. Crossing paths again in 1778 in PARIS, Mozart wrote Tenducci an aria with concertante piano and winds, KAnh.3/315b (now lost). SIMON P. KEEFE

Teyber (Deiber, Taiber, Tauber. Täuber, Tayber, Teiber, Teuber) family. Austrian family of musicians, with all or most of whom Mozart was personally acquainted from 1773. The principal members of the family were: Matthäus Teyber (b. c.1711; d. VIENNA, 6 Sept. 1785), violinist and court musician in Vienna; his wife Therese, née Ried[e]l; and their talented musician children: the soprano Elisabeth (b. c.16 Sept. 1746; d. 9 May 1816) who after successful operatic appearances in Vienna in the 1760s made her career mainly in Italy; the organist and composer Anton (b. c.8 Sept. 1756; d. 18 Nov. 1822) who toured with Elisabeth before working in Vienna (from 1781) and at the Dresden Hofkapelle (1787–91 – in his letters of 12 Mar. 1783 and 16 Apr. 1789 Mozart mentions having made music with him); and the composer, organist, bass singer and conductor Franz (b. c.25 Aug. 1758; d. 21/2 Oct. 1810). After studying in Vienna, Franz toured central Europe before joining SCHIKANEDER's company; in 1784 an aria by him was substituted for 'Martern aller Arten' at a performance of DIE ENTFÜHRUNG AUS DEM SERAIL in the Kärntnertortheater; LEOPOLD MOZART praised him highly in a letter of 5 May 1786. From 1788 he was in GERMANY and Switzerland, returning to Vienna to write the opera for the opening of Schikaneder's Theater an der Wien, *Alexander* (13 June 1801). He later worked in the Theater in der Leopoldstadt, and became court organist in 1810. The soubrette Therese Teyber (b. c.15 Oct. 1760; d. 15 Apr. 1830) studied with BONNO and Tesi; she was the first Blonde in *Die Entführung*. Mozart and Therese performed in each other's benefit concerts in 1783 (see Mozart's letters of 29 March and 12 April). She married the tenor Ferdinand Arnold in 1785, replaced LASCHI-MOMBELLI as Zerlina in later performances of *Don Giovanni* in 1788, and retired in 1791. Two other Teyber children made lesser marks: Friedrich (1748–1829), a good amateur violinist; and Barbara (?1750–1832), who in 1775 sang Sara in the premiere of JOSEPH HAYDN's *Il ritorno di Tobia*. PETER BRANSCOMBE

C. Eisen, *New Mozart Documents* (London, 1991)
D. Link, *The National Court Theatre in Mozart's Vienna: Sources and Documents, 1783–1792* (Oxford, 1998)

Thamos, König in Ägypten, K345 (Thamos, King of Egypt). The history of Mozart's only completed incidental music for a drama begins in 1773 in VIENNA. The Viennese court functionary and dramatist TOBIAS PHILIPP VON GEBLER had composed a five-act 'heroic drama' on an ancient Egyptian theme. To judge from the author's preface to the textbook his intentions must have been polemical, and might have had something to do with finding a place for music in a spoken drama. Ancient Egypt is far away, he argued, and this distance allowed him to imagine, among other details, 'entire assemblies of sanctified virgins' in temples 'where hymns were sung'. Having justified the music in the drama, he needed a composer. His first choice was the philosopher Johann Tobias Sattler, who is not otherwise known for his work as a musician. When Gebler wrote to his friend the critic Christoph Friedrich Nicolai in Berlin in May 1773, the commission seems already to have gone awry: 'Should one wish to do me the honour of producing my Thamos', he wrote, 'then I would be pleased to offer music for the choruses, which is really not bad at all, and has been checked through by His Excellency Ritter GLUCK himself.' By the time he wrote again to Nicolai in December of that year he had let Magister Sattler go and found a new composer, 'a certain Sigr. Mozzart . . . [the music] is his originally, and the first chorus very beautiful'. Gebler's play, and most probably Mozart's choruses, were performed in April 1774 in the Kärntnertortheater in Vienna.

Mozart's music to *Thamos*, however, comes down to us in a different version thought to date from 1779. By that year Mozart appears to have reworked the choruses from 1773 and added extensive instrumental interludes; a version of *Thamos* without such interludes seems to have been performed in SALZBURG in 1776. Today's Mozart scholarship is not in unanimous agreement about its compositional history. The handwriting expert Wolfgang Plath, for instance, argued that the entr'acte music dates from just before Mozart's departure for MANNHEIM and PARIS in late 1777, while the revised choruses come from 1779 or even 1780. Alan Tyson agrees that the entr'actes must have been written before 1778, but is puzzled that the composer used an upright-format paper not found in other works of the later period for the choruses. Konrad Küster, in turn, argues that the revised choruses were written in 1774.

Laurenz Lütteken, finally, suggests that the entr'actes were written during or after the journey to Mannheim and Paris, and that these might not originally have had anything to do with *Thamos* at all. In Mannheim, Mozart came into contact with the north German techniques of melodrama, in which an actor declaims a text over an orchestral accompaniment. He was, as he reported to his father, very taken with them, and apparently began to work on one himself together with the Mannheim poet OTTO HEINRICH VON GEMMINGEN in the later part of 1778. This project never came to fruition. Lütteken suggests that the entr'actes in the *Thamos* score found today in the Staatsbibliothek in Berlin are in fact the relics of the collaboration with Gemmingen, recycled as it were for a performance, or planned performance, in Salzburg sometime in 1779 (although there is no evidence that one took place). Lütteken's argument is strengthened by the fact that the text cues in instrumental interludes – some of which even suggest performance as melodrama – are all in LEOPOLD MOZART's hand, as if he were 'editing' the works for inclusion in a production of *Thamos*.

Whatever its true history, *Thamos* saw no further performances in its 1779 form. A travelling troop of actors toured GERMANY in the 1780s with Mozart's music but another play, Karl Martin Plümicke's *Lanassa*; Mozart even heard this production when it was performed in Frankfurt in the celebrations surrounding LEOPOLD II's coronation there in 1790. Scholars have often been tempted to draw connections between *Thamos* – a story of obstacles overcome through virtuous behaviour, and featuring an evil priestess – and DIE ZAUBERFLÖTE, although no direct connections can be made between the two. Manuscript copies of some of the choruses with Latin texts were found in Mozart's estate; this suggests that he might have approved of their use in this manner, as indeed they often were, long into the nineteenth century. Mozart seems to have considered his *Thamos* music worthy in every respect of a longer life, writing in 1783 to his father:

> I thank you with all my heart for sending me the music – I am very sorry that I won't be able to find any use for the music to *Thamos*! – the play is out of favour here, because it failed to please and has been thrown aside, – it ought to performed just because of the music – but that is not likely to happen – it certainly is a shame!

THOMAS IRVINE

L. Lütteken, 'Es müsste nur blos der Musick wegen aufgeführt worden: Text und Kontext in Mozarts Thamos Melodrama', in *Mozart und Mannheim*, ed. Ludwig Finscher et al. (Berlin, 1994), 167–86

Thun-Hohenstein family. Mozart knew Count Johann Joseph Anton Thun-Hohenstein (1711–88) and his daughter-in-law Countess (Maria) Wilhelmine Thun-Hohenstein (b. VIENNA, 12 June 1744; d. Vienna, 18 May 1800) benefiting greatly from their generosity. An imperial chamberlain, Count Thun owned palaces in Linz and PRAGUE and accommodated Mozart and CONSTANZE MOZART in both places. Mozart wrote his 'Linz' symphony, K425, 'at breakneck speed' while staying at his palace in Linz in Autumn 1783 on his return journey from SALZBURG to Vienna. He wrote to his father (31 Oct. 1783): 'I really cannot tell you what kindnesses the family are showering on us.' (Leopold stayed there on his way back to Salzburg from Vienna in April 1785 and was also very impressed with the Count's hospitality.) On his trip to Prague in January 1787, Mozart again stayed with Thun and was provided with a good piano as well as regular, high-quality entertainment from Thun's musicians.

Countess Thun-Hohenstein was an important supporter of Mozart during his decade in Vienna (1781–91). He ate lunch and socialized with her frequently, especially in the early part of his Viennese career, and testified to her numerous acts of kindness. For example, she made great efforts to keep him in Vienna, lent him her STEIN piano for his competition with CLEMENTI attended by Emperor JOSEPH II on 24 December 1781 and subscribed to his three concerts at the Trattnerhof in March 1784. She also listened to him perform IDOMENEO on the piano in May 1781 and repeatedly praised his compositions. On 8 August 1781, Mozart reported to Leopold: 'I played to her what I have finished composing [of DIE ENTFÜHRUNG AUS DEM SERAIL] and she told me afterwards that she would venture her life that what I have so far written cannot fail to please.' Her response to Act 2 of *Entführung* on 7 May 1782, moreover, was no less positive.

SIMON P. KEEFE

C. Preihs, 'Mozarts Beziehungen zu den Familien Thun-Hohenstein', *Neues Mozart-Jahrbuch* 3 (1943), 63–86

Torricella, Christoph (b. Switzerland, c.1715; d. Vienna, 24 Jan. 1798). A music publisher in VIENNA who issued his own editions from 1781 and who was bought out by ARTARIA in 1786 following financial difficulties, Torricella had in his stock Mozart's piano sonatas K284 in D and K333 in B flat, violin sonata K454 in B flat and piano variations K265 in C major ('Ah vous dirai-je, Maman'), K398 in F ('Salve tu, Domine') and K455 in G ('Les hommes pieusement') as well as JOSEPH HAYDN's symphonies Nos. 73, 76, 77 and 78. His advertisement for the three sonatas in the *Wiener Zeitung* (7 July 1784) described them as emanating 'from the pen of the famous Herr Kapellmeister Mozart'. Torricella advertised the sale of Mozart's six early string quartets K168–73 on 10 September 1785, just days after Artaria's publication of the six 'Haydn' quartets (K387, 421, 428, 458, 464, 465), forcing Mozart to clarify matters one week later in the *Wiener Zeitung*: 'Herr Mozart regards it as his duty to inform the estimable public that the said 6 Quartets are by no means new, but old works written by him as long as 15 years ago [*sic*], so that amateurs who had been expecting the new ones should not be wrongly served.' SIMON P. KEEFE

A. Weinmann, *Kataloge Anton Huberty (Wien) und Christoph Torricella* (Vienna, 1962)

Traeg, Johann (b. Gochsheim, Lower Franconia, 20 Jan. 1747; d. Vienna, 5 Sept. 1805). A publisher and copyist, Traeg first advertised copies of music in 1782 including, on 21 December, Mozart's SYMPHONIES and piano CONCERTOS; a few months later (27 Sept. 1783) he offered the three piano concertos K413, 414 and 415 on sale by subscription for 10 gulden after the publisher SIEBER had turned them down. He continued to sell works – many by Mozart – until 1794, whereupon he finally established his own publishing company. It remained in operation until 1820 with Traeg's son in control after his father's death, listing among its stock works by C. P. E. BACH, BEETHOVEN, Cherubini, JOSEPH HAYDN, MICHAEL HAYDN and IGNAZ PLEYEL as well as first editions of Mozart's String Quintet in B flat, K174 (published 1798) and a four-hand piano arrangement of the mechanical organ fantasia K608 (published 1799). Traeg also issued early editions of the six 'Haydn' quartets (K387, 421, 428, 458, 464, 465); Artaria had published them first in 1785. SIMON P. KEEFE

A. Weinmann, *Verlagsverzeichnis Johann Traeg (und Sohn)* (Vienna, 1973)
Die Anzeigen des Kopiaturbetriebes Johann Traeg in der Wiener Zeitung zwischen 1782 und 1805 (Vienna, 1981)

Trattner, Johann Thomas von (b. Johrmannsdorf, Hungary, 11 Nov. 1717; d. Vienna, 31 July 1798). A wealthy owner of Viennese bookshops and printing works and godfather to Mozart's sons KARL THOMAS MOZART and FRANZ XAVER WOLFGANG MOZART, Trattner built a large residence on the Graben – the Trattnerhof – that was completed in 1777. Mozart lived there with CONSTANZE MOZART in 1784 putting on three subscription concerts in the private hall (17, 24, 31 March) that featured his newly completed piano CONCERTOS K449 in E flat, K450 in B flat and K451 in D. According to Mozart (20 Mar. 1784), these were highly successful events – the first, for example, had a hall that was 'full to overflowing', 'won extraordinary applause' and elicited repeated praise. Mozart listed 176 subscribers – many from the highest intellectual, aristocratic and cultural echelons of Viennese society – and boasted to LEOPOLD MOZART that this number represented thirty more than the combined total of Richter's and FISCHER's contemporary subscription series in the city.

Mozart also knew Trattner's second wife, Maria Theresia von Nagel (1758–93). She was one of his first Viennese pupils in 1781, was godmother to his short-lived daughter Theresia (1787–8) and was the dedicatee of the Piano Sonata in C minor, K457, and the Fantasia in C minor, K475.

SIMON P. KEEFE

H. Cloeter, *Johann Thomas Trattner: Ein Grossunternehmer im Theresianischen Wien* (Graz, 1952)

travel. Eighteenth-century travel was so different from modern experience that an awareness of its distinctive conditions is essential to an understanding of the lives of those involved. The travelling undertaken by the Mozarts during Mozart's childhood had a profound effect on LEOPOLD MOZART's later views about the adult Mozart's organization of his own journeys; and these views, together with Mozart's actions, influenced the relationship between the two men.

Travel was socially differentiated, involving the poor wandering on foot and sleeping in outhouses, merchants riding on horseback and sleeping in cheap beds, and the wealthy using the structures developed to facilitate the Grand Tour. Musicians, however, had an anomalous status: dependent on wealthy patrons, they had to cultivate a socially impressive style, meaning that they partly shared the experiences of the leisured classes; but their lack of resources brought them additional responsibilities. The slow pace of journeys (causing frequent, expensive, overnight stops) made costs for everyone consume a much larger proportion of income than in modern contexts, but musicians were affected more than their patrons. On 26 September 1763 Leopold Mozart wrote to his landlord, Lorenz HAGENAUER: 'we have to travel in a noble or courtly style for the preservation of our health and the reputation of my court'. In LONDON in 1764, this principle involved moving from lodgings costing 12*s.* weekly to lodgings costing a guinea. There are telling examples of the income/travel-costs ratio for the Mozarts. The 370-mile, fourteen-week journey from SALZBURG to Koblenz in 1763 cost 1,068 gulden, three times Leopold's annual Salzburg salary of 354 gulden. Hence, even when court musicians were being paid their salary while absent (Leopold's usual situation), travel for most of them would have been unthinkable on this money alone: they had to earn their expenses by giving concerts en route.

Dependence on patrons could be frustrating, as musicians ran up expenses waiting to be summoned: the Mozarts stayed a month in Brussels in 1763 awaiting the call from Prince Karl Alexander of Lorraine, who 'does nothing but hunt, guzzle, and swill, and in the end it turns out he's got no money' (Leopold's letter of 4 Nov. 1763). Sometimes they were paid with trinkets ('on a journey you need money', wrote Mozart on 13 Nov. 1777, 'now I have five watches'), sometimes with embraces ('neither the innkeeper nor the postmaster will accept payment in kisses', wrote Leopold on 17 Oct. 1763), and sometimes with air ('[the emperor] enters it into his Book of Forgetfulness', he wrote on 30 Jan. 1768). Musicians were also hit particularly hard by illness when travelling: medical expenses were high, they could not earn, and they often had to endure the illness in an inn, the most expensive accommodation available. In The Hague in 1765, the Mozarts were confined by the children's illnesses for three months without earnings, forcing Leopold to cash a credit letter for 600 gulden.

Travellers faced numerous permutations in the interlinked choices of vehicles, horses and coachmen. The fastest system was to travel 'post', which involved regular changes of horses on mail routes; the slowest was to employ a single driver with his own horses, which had to be rested periodically. Sometimes it was difficult to get horses at all, as the Mozarts discovered when leaving Ludwigsburg in 1763, most of them having been commandeered for an aristocratic hunting party. The standard of roads varied, but the eighteenth century was only patchily seeing the first major improvements in road-building since Roman times, and many roads were still merely tracks across the countryside. Mud-filled ruts, insufficient passing room, and precipitous stretches in hills caused many breakdowns and accidents. One of the Mozarts' fastest road journeys was achieved by Leopold and Mozart from Naples to Rome in 1770: travelling non-stop post, the journey of 120 miles, which would have taken more than four days with the slower service, took twenty-seven hours (still less than 5 mph!). However, it also involved the upturning of the carriage and serious injury to Leopold's shin. 'You know that two horses and a postilion make three beasts', he wrote on 30 June.

River travel, though sometimes preferable, was also problematic: difficulties included droughts, floods, ice, rocks and unmanageable currents. An average speed was 5/6 mph. The Mozarts' slowest-recorded river journey was from Mainz to Koblenz in 1763: the sixty-mile stretch should have taken one day, but took four because of foul weather. Every evening involved struggling on foot to the nearest inn, and this one journey cost 44 gulden, about an eighth of Leopold's annual salary.

Accommodation further taxed the resourcefulness of travellers. In towns and on well-used routes people could expect comfort. But off the beaten track, 'inns' might offer neither beds nor food: travellers were paying merely for a roof, some straw, and a seat at the fire. Even the most respectable travellers could occasionally have unpleasant experiences: at least once the Mozarts had a meal at a hovel-and-yokel inn, when their carriage wheel broke on the way to PARIS in 1763. 'The door was open all the time, so we very often had the honour of a visit from the pigs, who grunted round us', Leopold wrote to Hagenauer on 17 October, inviting him to visualize a Dutch painting. Service varied enormously, and the joint vested interests of innkeepers and postilions could lead to exasperating frustrations for travellers.

When travellers expected to stay several weeks in the same place, they usually took private lodgings, which were significantly cheaper than inns. Here musicians had an advantage over other travellers: they could trade their skills for accommodation (either in private houses or in monasteries), and opera commissions usually brought free lodgings. The Mozarts took full advantage of these opportunities.

The price of the pleasures of travelling was a range of discomforts. Inside or out, winter was bitterly cold. From Mantua Leopold complained on 11 January 1770: 'I can't write to anyone, I'm a harassed man . . . and on top of that never a warm room, freezing like a dog, everything I touch is ice.' Mozart endured six days of 'house arrest' in Munich in 1774, from toothache attributed to the freezing air on his face during the two-day journey from Salzburg (Leopold's letter of 21 December). Hot weather was equally trying, forcing travellers to begin their journeys as early as 3 o'clock each morning to avoid the heat and insects. Wet clothes, bedbugs, poor food, unsafe drinking water, arguments with innkeepers, postilions, and fellow-travellers, and perpetual forward planning – all these issues were commonplace.

Because of the discomforts, the need to socialize and the fact that journeys could last several seasons, luggage was prolific. Furs, foot-sacks, hat boxes, a medicine chest, wine, and newly made fashionable clothes for each country visited – such items were standard. Most people also bought books, engravings and souvenirs everywhere. As musicians, the Mozarts took these things and more. Violins, music and even a portable keyboard instrument were carried on their longest tour. They amassed a huge collection of trinkets as payment for performances, and Leopold bought souvenirs for themselves, and artefacts both for friends and for resale for his own profit. Despite leaving possessions for later collection in France in 1764, the Mozarts' luggage quickly grew again in London. On 18 April 1765 Leopold wrote: 'It'll take time just to get away from here and put all our baggage in order, which brings the sweat to my face just thinking about it.'

Once luggage had been securely packed, the next anxiety was negotiating customs, a haphazard business often involving enforced bribery, because customs officers expected to supplement their meagre pay by tips. The Mozarts never mentioned particularly unpleasant experiences with customs – indeed, one of the best-known anecdotes of Mozart's childhood is Leopold's account of the six-year-old child charming his way through the Viennese office in 1762 by playing a minuet on his violin (letter of 16 October) – but Leopold nevertheless always anticipated possible trouble. In general, the political fragmentation of GERMANY made travel more difficult: laws and currency changed frequently, many checkpoints had to be negotiated, and there was no integrated system of planning, support or redress for travellers.

More perturbing than these inconveniences were disruptions to health. Medical assumptions meant that merely to be away from home was considered risky. Moreover, common illnesses such as catarrhs and diarrhoea claimed lives regularly, while travel increased the risk of accidents. Within the Mozart family the illustrations of near and actual disaster are striking. Mozart and Nannerl both almost died in The Hague in 1765, and could have died of smallpox in Olmütz (Olomouc) in 1767. Leopold nearly died of a catarrhal complaint in London in 1764. He and Mozart could have been killed in the carriage accident outside Rome in 1770. MARIA ANNA MOZART died in Paris in 1778. Though Leopold grieved that her grave was so far away, he was at least spared the torment of those whose relations died somewhere with the wrong established religion: Rome, for example, had no provision for the formal burial of non-Catholics until 1738, and even after that such burials were only grudgingly tolerated.

The difficulties of travel meant that socializing was crucially important to the success and enjoyment of a trip. It was common to share transport or accommodation, and evenings involved mingling round the inn's dining table with the other guests. The pressure to socialize could involve its own stress, but most people relished these encounters with other people, deriving amusement from some, information, contacts or patronage from others, help, comfort and solidarity in times of need, and occasionally a type of enlightenment that challenged prejudices. Sometimes travellers shared journeys for weeks, becoming good friends. Leopold Mozart, a critical and lively commentator on the human condition, told many stories about the absurd, contemptible, generous and humane people they met. He also wrote travel notes: for their 'Grand Tour' (1763–6) alone, hundreds of people's names were recorded, so the types of scene he described must be imagined multiplied many times to gain an idea of the wealth of experiences to which the family was exposed.

The Mozarts' situation as musicians made 'starting' in a new place arduous. With all travellers they shared the need to present their laboriously collected letters of introduction and financial credit (Leopold arrived in Rome in 1770 with twenty), find accommodation, and seek out a suitable church and a doctor who understood their constitution and lifestyle. But beyond this they had to give prestigious concerts. Because this required the support of influential local people and fellow musicians, they had to 'gallop around' paying visits, and be prepared to be summoned at short notice to entertain at salons long into the night. A practice and educational routine had to be arranged for the children, and music copied ready for performance. Since they remained at many destinations for several weeks at least, they made friends everywhere, and after a start that required a fair degree of courage, they usually also found departures difficult in emotional as well as practical terms.

The period of Leopold's greatest zest for travel was from 1762 to 1766. Escaping the tedium of the court musician's life, he entered warmly into the spirit. The letters, travel notebooks and souvenirs bought abroad testify to his appetite for sightseeing. However, by the 1770s Leopold's responsibilities were eroding his enthusiasm. By then the family had had some terrifying experiences of illness, and certain financial and professional frustrations. These pressures, together with the sheer work of planning journeys, sapped his spirit. The letters from Italy show the teenage Mozart's blissful delight in travelling, while Leopold's utterances are often more despondent.

Reflecting on these circumstances suggests a number of cautions regarding the interpretation of travel reports. First, given the difficulties of travelling, individual character attributes assumed more importance to the enjoyment or otherwise of a journey than they usually do now: the alert, resourceful, phlegmatic and well-disposed personality as opposed to the disorganized or easily discontented one was a more necessary precondition of a positive experience. This observation both heightens the need to understand a writer's character as a prerequisite for the subtle differentiation between an experience and the writer's perception of it, and points to the travel experiences themselves as tests of character.

Second, and also arising from the greater difficulties of travel, engagement with the difference between an experienced and an inexperienced traveller is fundamentally important to the interpretation of any letters between the two. When the consequences of carelessness could be calamitous, the voice of experience is likely to speak more insistently than it might now, an observation particularly pertinent to parent–child correspondences. A further point concerning the tone of letters is that ostensibly banal factors such as the speed of the postal service could also have their effect. In 1778 a letter from Salzburg took ten days to reach Paris, making it three weeks before the writer could receive a reply. In situations where advice was being offered or sought, it was vital for each letter to omit nothing of importance: disorganized letter-writing could affect the recipient more harmfully than it would now, and hence provoke a sharper response.

Third, and again of particular relevance to family correspondences, medical assumptions (now quite unfamiliar) had a significant effect on people's attitudes to their close relations: the situation whereby attention to a humours-controlling regimen was thought crucial to health but was difficult to apply abroad, was a chronic underlying worry to travellers and could be agonizing to parents when their inexperienced children were away from them. Parental fussiness about personal habits may therefore be viewed with more understanding against this background.

The Mozarts had extensive experience of all these situations and Leopold's views on organizing journeys were forged through countless occurrences of frustration, mishap, embarrassment, worry and danger. On 22 February 1764 he had written: 'Anyone who hasn't made these journeys can't imagine what's required for them. You need your hands constantly in your purse, and your wits about you all the time, and a plan for many months ahead constantly before your eyes; but a plan that can instantly be changed when circumstances change.' When Mozart travelled for the first time without Leopold in 1777, he in turn had to learn ways of dealing with these challenges, while Leopold could only offer advice through his letters. Interpretation of these letters, which underpin discussions of the relationship between Mozart and Leopold, is not well served by modern-day assumptions about travel or family life. A truer benchmark would be the travel correspondences of other eighteenth-century parents and children, but a study of the Mozarts from this perspective is still awaited.

RUTH HALLIWELL

J. Black, *The Grand Tour in the Eighteenth Century* (London, 1999)
R. Halliwell, *The Mozart Family: Four Lives in a Social Context* (Oxford, 1998)

U

Umlauf, Ignaz (b. Vienna, 1746; d. Meidling, near Vienna, 8 June 1796). A composer and conductor active in VIENNA, Umlauf held positions as Kapellmeister of the GERMAN opera (1778–83) and deputy conductor of the Italian opera (from 1783). Several of his singspiels were staged during his tenure as Kapellmeister, most notably *Die schöne Schusterin, oder Die pücefarbenen Schuhe* (1779), setting a libretto by JOHANN GOTTLIEB STEPHANIE. On 6 March 1789 Umlauf directed the singers in a performance (under Mozart's general direction) of Mozart's reorchestrated version of HANDEL's *Messiah*, K572. Professional interaction, however, did not equate with professional respect, for Mozart was disparaging about Umlauf's compositional abilities. Reporting to LEOPOLD MOZART that Umlauf had taken a year to write one opera, Mozart explained (6 Oct. 1781): 'you must not believe that the opera is any good, just because it took him a whole year. I should have thought . . . that it was the work of fourteen or fifteen days.' He goes further still in his condemnation of Umlauf's *Welches ist die beste Nation?* as an 'execrable opera' (5 Feb. 1783): 'the music is so bad that I do not know whether the poet or the composer will carry off the prize for inanity' (21 Dec. 1782).

SIMON P. KEEFE

J. A. Rice, *Antonio Salieri and Viennese Opera* (Chicago, 1998)

V

Valesi, Giovanni (Johann Evangelist Walleshauer) (b. Unterhattenhofen, Bavaria, 28 Apr. 1735; d. Munich, 10 Jan. 1816). A GERMAN tenor who was employed for much of his professional life at the MUNICH court Kapelle and who performed regularly in Italy, Valesi sang Gran sacerdote di Nettuno at the premiere of IDOMENEO in Munich on 29 January 1781 and probably Contino del Belfiore at the premiere of LA FINTA GIARDINIERA in the same city on 13 January 1775. He was also a well-known singing teacher, counting JOHANN VALENTIN ADAMBERGER and Carl Maria von Weber among his students. When Mozart heard another of his students, Margarethe Kaiser, sing in Munich, he wrote to Leopold (2 Oct. 1777): 'She has a beautiful voice, not powerful but by no means weak, very pure and her intonation is good. Valesi has taught her; and from her singing you can tell that he knows how to sing as well as how to teach.' SIMON P. KEEFE

H. Schmid, 'Zur Biographie des bayerischen Hofsängers Giovanni Valesi (Walleshauser)', *Musik in Bayern* 10 (1975), 28–30

Vanhal (Vanhall, Wanhal), Johann Baptist (Jon Křtitel) (b. Nové Nechanice, Bohemia, 12 May 1739; d. Vienna, 1813). A Czech composer well known for his orchestral, chamber, keyboard and vocal works, Vanhal worked in VIENNA for most of his professional life, studying with CARL DITTERS VON DITTERSDORF in the early 1760s and subsequently teaching IGNAZ PLEYEL. Mozart played his violin concerto in B flat, 'which was unanimously applauded', in AUGSBURG on 19 October 1777 and then met him in Vienna. As reported famously by MICHAEL KELLY (1826), Vanhal on one occasion played cello in quartets with Mozart (viola), Haydn (first violin) and Dittersdorf (second violin) at a party hosted by the English composer Stephen STORACE. SIMON P. KEEFE

D. Heartz, *Haydn, Mozart and the Viennese School, 1740–1780* (New York and London, 1995)
D. W. Jones, 'The String Quartets of Vanhal' (Ph.D. thesis, University of Wales, 1978)
B. MacIntyre, 'Johann Baptiste Vanhal and the Pastoral Mass Tradition', in *Music in Eighteenth-Century Austria*, ed. D. W. Jones (Cambridge, 1996), 112–32

Varesco, Giovanni Battista (baptized Trento, 26 Nov. 1735; d. Salzburg, 29 Aug. 1805). A resident of SALZBURG from 1766 as court chaplain, Varesco wrote the librettos for the opera seria IDOMENEO and the unfinished *dramma giocoso* L'OCA DEL CAIRO. His collaboration with Mozart on *Idomeneo*, and the back and forth in which he, Mozart and LEOPOLD MOZART engaged on plot-, text- and music-related matters is richly documented in letters Mozart and Leopold wrote to each other in late 1780 and early 1781. (Leopold acted as intermediary between composer and librettist as Mozart was in MUNICH and

Varesco in Salzburg.) Shortly before the premiere in Munich (29 Jan. 1781) relations between the Mozarts and Varesco soured over the fee Varesco was to procure from Count Joseph Anton Seeau: 'The greedy, money-grubbing fool simply can't wait for his money', Leopold reported bitterly to his son on 22 January.

Two years later, while looking for an Italian libretto in Vienna and aware that LORENZO DA PONTE might not write him one as soon as he wished, Mozart suggested to his father (7 May 1783): 'I have been thinking that unless Varesco is still very much annoyed with us about the Munich opera [*Idomeneo*], he might write me a new libretto for seven characters . . . You will know best if this can be arranged.' The resulting text, *L'oca del Cairo*, received a lukewarm reception from Mozart (19 Feb. 1784) and he abandoned the project: 'the impression I have gained from Varesco's text is that he has hurried too much, and I hope that in time he will realize this himself'. Varesco had already raised doubts about the prospective success of the work, provoking an indignant response from Mozart (21 May 1783): 'If . . . the opera is to be a success and Varesco hopes to be rewarded, he must alter and recast the libretto as much and as often as I wish and he must not follow his own inclinations, for he has not the slightest knowledge or experience of the theatre.' SIMON P. KEEFE

J. E. Everson, 'Of Beaks and Geese: Mozart, Varesco and Francesco Cieco', *Music & Letters* 76 (1995), 369–83

D. Heartz, 'The Genesis of *Idomeneo*', in Heartz, *Mozart's Operas*, ed. T. Bauman (Berkeley, 1990), 15–35

D. Neville, 'From *tragédie lyrique* to Moral Drama', in J. Rushton, *W. A. Mozart: 'Idomeneo'* (Cambridge, 1993), 72–82

Vienna. In 1781, when Mozart made his permanent move to Vienna, the city was a bustling centre of about 200,000 inhabitants. Within its medieval walls, Baroque palaces crowded up against apartments and commercial buildings, and narrow streets opened to plazas fronted by Gothic cathedrals. Outside the walls past the Glacis, a public park that ringed the city, the suburbs stretched out into the countryside, dotted with houses and apartments, shops and churches, and the various manufacturing concerns (chief among them the porcelain and silk industries) that provided employment for the working classes. It was a city well positioned to support a musical culture, but to understand the distinctive opportunities – and challenges – it presented to a talented young composer like Mozart, we must first understand Vienna itself, for its politics and social structure shaped the institutions of music.

The political structure of Vienna was Byzantine and confusing, not the least because it was the seat of two distinct, parallel governments: the Austro-Hungarian monarchy and the Holy Roman Empire. Ruled by the hereditary heir of the house of Habsburg, the Austro-Hungarian monarchy comprised much of central and eastern Europe, including modern-day AUSTRIA, Hungary, the Czech Republic, Slovakia, parts of Poland and various Balkan countries, plus territories in Italy and in the Netherlands – lands that retained their individuality and customs, sometimes to the detriment of the whole. The Holy Roman Empire, an even looser conglomeration of states and principalities that encompassed most of north-central Europe and overlapped the territories of the monarchy, was headed by an emperor elected by the rulers of the constituent states. Since the fifteenth century, these electors had unfailingly chosen the reigning head of the house of Habsburg, so that the empire and monarchy had come to be regarded as an indivisible unit. But when MARIA THERESIA succeeded to the Habsburg throne in 1740, she upset the system, because – by law – a woman could not serve as Holy Roman Emperor. She eventually managed to get her husband, Francis of Lorraine, elected in her stead, and he ruled as emperor until his death in 1765. The real seat of power, however, was in the Austro-Hungarian monarchy, which Maria Theresia kept under tight control. When JOSEPH II followed his father as Holy Roman Emperor in 1765, he had to spend fifteen years cooling his heels, working with his mother and following her lead, a role that he did not relish. After her death in 1780, he finally gained control of both monarchy and empire and ruled with pent-up fervour for a decade. He died childless in 1790 and was succeeded by his brother LEOPOLD II, whose own promising reign was cut short by his premature death in 1792.

Thus, several different personalities governed during Mozart's lifetime, shaping the city and society in which he chose to live. If we briefly consider a few of the policies they instituted, particularly those of Maria Theresia and Joseph II, we will be in a better position to understand the various forces affecting his career. For example, Maria Theresia instituted a series of reforms that improved the school and university system and provided better educational opportunity, not only for the aristocracy, but for the merchant and working classes as well. Her purpose had been to train young men to fill new positions in government offices and thus strengthen and centralize the administrative structure of the monarchy, but the effect was to create an educated administrative class that gradually began to participate in the cultural and musical life of the city, a realm previously restricted to the aristocracy. Joseph II continued many of his mother's initiatives, but throughout the years of his co-regency he had been frustrated by her measured approach to governmental reform; after her death, he quickly initiated a series of radical reforms reflecting his fervent belief in the ideals of the ENLIGHTENMENT. He abolished many (though not all) aspects of serfdom and decreed limited religious toleration for Protestants and Jews. However, whenever his progressive steps threatened to undermine state authority, he reversed himself, reinstating censorship laws he had lifted earlier and restricting the spread of FREEMASONRY. (Mozart, an enthusiastic Freemason, remained a lodge member even after the restrictive edict.) Joseph II also ran into trouble when he sought to impose his ascetic views on the customs of his subjects. In 1784, concerned with what he considered to be excessive expenditures for funerals, he decreed that the dead should be sewn naked into linen sacks, transported in reusable coffins to cemeteries beyond the city walls, and buried without a coffin in a mass grave. After the outcry among ordinary citizens proved too great to ignore (the nobility had never been affected and continued to use their private tombs as before), he lifted the prohibition against individual coffins, but the practice of using common graves and simplified burial rituals lingered, influencing the decisions about Mozart's own funeral.

Some of Joseph II's reforms, though laudable in their intent, had a deleterious affect on music and musicians. When he moved to dissolve the religious organizations known as lay brotherhoods in order to secure their property for building schools and parish churches, he was working to improve the educational and religious opportunities of his subjects. However, some of the brotherhoods had made extensive use of music, and their dissolution threw the musicians involved out of work. Any hopes that the creation of new parish churches would take up the slack would have been dashed by the liturgical reforms of 1783. Driven partly by Joseph's mania for economizing, but also by his basic distrust of splendour and ceremony, these reforms sought to simplify the divine service and enhance congregational singing, and to this end restricted orchestrally accompanied music in the Mass and Offices. Though the restrictions were lifted after his death in 1790, and perhaps not universally observed even when in effect, they did serve to temporarily choke off sacred music composition and further limit employment opportunities for musicians. Perhaps because of these circumstances, Mozart wrote almost no sacred music during his Viennese years. Had he lived to succeed to the position of Kapellmeister at St Stephen's, as he was slated to do, he might well have led a Viennese renaissance in sacred composition.

But ultimately, Joseph II's greatest impact on the musical world may have resulted not from any decree or proclamation, but from his insistence on cutting the ceremony of his court to a bare minimum. In the early eighteenth century, rulers still demonstrated their power and significance by elaborate, expensive court festivities, which often included the lavish production of operas and other musical events. During the reign of Maria Theresia, economic necessity had forced some curtailment of patronage, but a court appearance was still the necessary prelude to musical success in the city. When the Mozart family travelled to Vienna in 1762, they gave a private performance at her favourite palace of Schönbrunn, for which they received the princely sum of 450 florins (see below for the relative value of the payment, which Leopold mentions in a letter of 19 October). By the time they returned to Vienna in 1767, Joseph II had assumed the title of emperor, and their obligatory court appearance brought them only the gift of an inexpensive medal, causing LEOPOLD MOZART to complain bitterly (in a letter of 30 Jan. 1768) about the Emperor's tightfistedness. In the absence of traditional royal interest, other institutions and levels of Viennese society began to assume a leading role in the musical world, a process well under way by the time Wolfgang made the city his permanent home (and one that would have occurred even without a parsimonious emperor, though perhaps less precipitously). Mozart did not ignore or disdain Joseph II's support, but his fortunes lay elsewhere.

Those fortunes were guided by the audience he needed to cultivate, the infrastructure that provided practical support and the institutions that would feature him and his music. The potential audience during Mozart's lifetime came from a very small segment of society, one dominated by the upper aristocracy, those holding the titles of Fürst (prince) or Graf (count) in families whose patents of nobility extended back many generations. Most had country estates farmed by serf (or near-serf) labour that brought them substantial annual incomes, which could range from 20,000 florins (the Austrian unit of currency) up to the stratospheric 700,000 a year commanded by the Prince ESTERHÁZY (Haydn's patron). In addition, many held high-level positions in the court bureaucracy, which brought them even more income and influence. Though they typically retreated to their country estates in the summer, the majority spent the winter season at palatial residences in Vienna where, in imitation of the (pre-Joseph II) court, they undertook the patronage of cultural and musical events. By the 1780s, these families were increasingly joined in this endeavour by members of the lower aristocracy (the Barons, Ritter and the Edler von), who held titles of more recent vintage, often conferred for service to the empire or occasionally for artistic distinction (like Christoph Willibald, Ritter von GLUCK). Mozart found students and patrons at both levels, from the LICHNOWSKYS, the THUNS and the Johann Esterházys to the TRATTNERS, the AUERNHAMMERS and the Arnsteins.

Nipping at the heels of the lower aristocracy were the city's wealthy business and finance class and the growing numbers of educated civil servants who filled the lower echelons of the court administration. Their income levels, which ranged from 200–300 up to several thousand florins annually, reflect the wildly inequitable (from a modern perspective) income distribution typical of the time. As we shall see, financial realities would have effectively prevented most from either attending or sponsoring performances, but as a cultured, educated, quasi-middle class, they were, by the end of Mozart's life, beginning to make their influence felt. Most of the city's professional musicians would have belonged, by virtue of their education and income, to this level of society. Though musicologists have often expressed indignation at the paltry incomes (compared to the upper aristocracy) of a church music director (200–400 florins annually) or a court Kapellmeister (about 800 florins), we would do well to remember that this educated middle class – *together* with the aristocracy – constituted less than 10 per cent of the Viennese population. The remaining 90-plus per cent (the small merchants, the factory and construction workers, the domestic servants), whose annual incomes have been estimated at between 50 and 100 florins, would simply not have had the money to purchase even an occasional ticket to a concert or an opera. Not that the city's population lived in abject poverty: food was plentiful and affordable, and most visitors to Vienna commented on the relatively high standard of living of its inhabitants. Nor should we imagine the working classes existed in a state of musical deprivation. Especially before the liturgical upheavals of the 1780s, near-operatic MASSES and vespers resounded in cathedral vaults, and elaborate festive music accompanied the processionals of the lay brotherhood through the city streets. At night, a SERENADE presented underneath the window of a princess would have wafted upwards to the rooms of her chambermaid or the garret of a starving student. But the world of opera and concerts – the world to which Mozart aspired and for which he wrote most of his music – was simply not a part of the lives of most Viennese citizens. Thus, he had to concentrate his efforts on winning over the aristocracy and the educated middle class.

His task was made easier by the attitudes and education of the Viennese aristocracy; many had at least a modicum of musical training, and some reached a level of performance that compared favourably to their professional counterparts. These amateur performers sought out Mozart as a teacher and as a composer of pieces they could play, particularly SONATAS and string quartets (genres intended for private, rather than public performance). Mozart and other musicians also benefited from the fact that attendance at musical performances was considered a *de rigueur* part of the aristocratic social calendar. Even the most profoundly unmusical count or princess would have routinely attended one or two musical events each week during the winter season. While Mozart may not have relished the idea that some of his audience were snoozing behind their fans or wishing they were at the card table (or in fact actually *were* at the card table), we must acknowledge that a society so imbued with music offered many advantages to composers and performers.

By Mozart's Viennese decade, the city's musical infrastructure had also begun to provide many essential support services. In the 1760s and 1770s, for example, most fortepianos had to be imported. But beginning around 1780, when ANTON WALTER opened his shop, keyboard players could, like Mozart, have an instrument built locally. Musical scores had always been relatively easy to acquire, either in manuscript from one of the many professional copyists or in mostly foreign prints from retailers like Trattner and Kurzböck. In the late 1770s, the local firm of ARTARIA & Co. seriously entered the music publishing business and, along with several other newly founded music publishers, eagerly snapped up new sonatas and quartets by Mozart, adding substantially to his income. But Vienna did lack one critical infrastructure component: an active daily press that reported on music and musical performances. Composers and performers could advertise new compositions or concerts in the back pages of the main local paper, the *Wiener Zeitung*, but unless they happened to appear at a court function, they had no hope of any mention in the regular columns. Occasionally smaller papers like the *Realzeitung* or the *Wiener Blättchen* would comment on an opera production, but the kind of musical reporting we expect today (or that occurred in contemporary LONDON newspapers) simply did not exist in Vienna. Without it, Mozart and his musical colleagues were deprived of a powerful means of creating a public reputation and building an audience. Instead, they had to cultivate patrons and fans personally and hope to build their reputation by word of mouth.

The primary way of doing that was to enter the world of private performances: full-scale opera productions and orchestral concerts produced in the chambers and private theatres of the city's upper crust and funded by their substantial incomes. Patrons undertook private sponsorship for a variety of reasons. For some, it stemmed from a sheer love of music, as one suspects was the case with the oratorio performances of the 1780s, co-sponsored by BARON VAN SWIETEN and the Count Johann Esterházy. For aristocratic dilettantes, private events provided an opportunity to perform public genres like operas or concertos in a socially acceptable setting. (The aristocratic code of behaviour would have prevented them from appearing on a public stage, and thus would have limited their repertory to private genres like sonatas, string quartets, or Lieder.) Others used musical productions to demonstrate their largesse and create goodwill, no doubt a major factor in the concerts sponsored by foreign ambassadors. Finally, for many the impulse stemmed from a desire to imitate the court. As Joseph II withdrew from the patronage arena, he theoretically left the field wide open for other aristocratic patrons, but also, paradoxically, removed one of their main incentives. (Leopold Mozart had observed the aristocratic reluctance to outdo the court in this regard as early as 1768, in a letter of 30 January.) Moreover, with the increasing participation of the lower aristocracy and middle class, the whole enterprise became much less exclusive, certainly a disincentive for patrons whose efforts had been mainly status-driven. Still, during Mozart's lifetime, private performances made up a substantial part of Vienna's musical world, and he took full advantage of them, particularly during his most active virtuoso years. He performed regularly at the concerts of Prince Golitsyn, Prince Kaunitz, Prince Paar, the Countess Thun and others during the early 1780s, conducted a production of IDOMENEO at Prince Auersperg's private theatre in 1786, and arranged music and conducted for the van Swieten oratorio concerts in the late 1780s.

For Mozart and other professional musicians, private performances provided a source of income (albeit an uncertain one dependent on the whims of the patron) but also an opportunity to cultivate an audience and create a public, who might then eagerly purchase tickets to a later public concert or opera performance. Though public events were theoretically open to anyone who wished to purchase a ticket, in reality the potential audience was the same as that for private ones. Most concert tickets cost between one and two florins, prohibitively expensive for a schoolteacher earning only 250 florins a year. A six-month lease on a box at the Burgtheater, the city's Italian opera venue, went for 450 florins (making them the exclusive provenance of the upper aristocracy), a seat in the *parterre noble* for about 25 florins per month. Though the cheapest balcony seats could be had for as little as a sixth of a florin per performance, bringing them within the realm of possibility for a larger percentage of the educated middle class, for the most part the audiences of public and private performances were the same.

Public concerts were a relatively new phenomenon in Europe and thus lacked the physical and administrative apparatus of older cultural institutions like the theatre. Partly because of the strong private realm, they got an especially slow start in Vienna; we have, for example, no record of any public appearances during the Mozart family's visits in the 1760s (though that could simply reflect the absence of extant sources). Even by the 1780s, however, Vienna still had no hall intended specifically for concerts and no agency or institution to organize and present them. The Tonkünstler-Sozietät (a type of musicians' union) did sponsor four fund-raising concerts each year; Mozart, and later BEETHOVEN, made their earliest documented Viennese public appearances there. For the most part, though, the initiative lay in the hands of individual performing musicians, who faced considerable logistical challenges in addition to any musical ones. For example, Viennese concerts (except for oratorios) – whether organized by a composer, an instrumental virtuoso or a singer – generally opened and closed with symphonies, which of course meant the organizer had to find, and pay, an orchestra. All included an instrumental concerto and several numbers from operas. Thus a singer wishing to concertize needed not only an orchestra, but also an instrumental virtuoso to share the stage, and vice versa. For someone as versatile as Mozart, this format, however problematic, allowed him to show off his dazzling array of abilities. The programme for his 1784 concert at the Burgtheater included three symphonies, a piano concerto and a piano fantasy – all his compositions – plus three arias by unspecified composers, but which were probably his as well.

The variety of concert spaces utilized by performers in the absence of a dedicated concert hall offered very different atmospheres for the audience and posed different challenges for the musicians. During the early 1780s the two court theatres, the Burgtheater and the Kärntnertortheater, were available during Lent, when law and custom proscribed the performance of stage plays and operas. Most performers preferred them over the city's other venues, in part because of their better acoustics and greater seating capacity (at more than 1,000), in part because they had an already assembled orchestra, but also because aristocratic society's habit of attending the theatre regularly might help to boost attendance. Mozart took full advantage of these locations, presenting a concert performance of parts of *Idomeneo* in 1782, and regular, mixed-genre concerts during Lent of 1783–6. Apparently, he did well, for the *Magazin der Musik* in Hamburg gossiped that his 1783 concert brought in 1,600 florins (though then, as now, one should not take press reports as the gospel truth), and Mozart himself was very satisfied with the 559 florins profit from his 1785 concert (according to Leopold's letter of 12 March).

Other concert locations offered a smaller, more intimate atmosphere, but correspondingly lower receipts from ticket sales and a possibly less exclusive atmosphere. The publisher Johann Thomas, Edler von Trattner, maintained a hall which he leased for concerts. Judging from the subscription lists for the series Mozart presented there in 1784 (he gave others in 1786 and possibly again in 1788), the audience included many of the upper and lower aristocracy, a possible indication of its status as a prestigious location. Other venues included the Mehlgrube, a *Gasthof* and ballroom that catered to the middle class, and, beginning in the late 1780s, a restaurant run by Ignaz Jahn. In addition to rooms where patrons could dine and gamble, both establishments had a hall (seating a few hundred listeners) intended for dancing and concerts. We have few reliable descriptions of either place, and have no way of knowing if symphonies and concertos presented there had a persistent accompaniment of rattling coffee cups and the shuffling of cards, or whether the music took precedence. Nor can we reliably ascertain the likely social status of the audience. Though one might suppose these locations would have attracted fewer of the upper aristocracy, the ticket prices were similar to those for the court theatres. Mozart did not disdain to appear at either place: he gave several concerts at the Mehlgrube in 1785, and made his last documented public appearance as a pianist at a concert given by the clarinettist Franz Joseph Bähr at Jahn's in 1791.

For the most part, the concert season in Vienna was concentrated during the winter months, but during the summer, Viennese audiences could enjoy the delightful custom of garden concerts, held in the cool early morning hours, when they could be combined with breakfast and a stroll along shady pathways. Most probably, these concerts attracted those from the lower aristocracy and educated middle class, in part because many of the upper aristocracy retreated to their country estates during the summer to escape the heat and dust of the city. In 1782, Mozart joined forces with the entrepreneur PHILPP JAKOB MARTIN to organize a dozen Sunday morning concerts in the Augarten, at a price of less than a florin for each concert. The opening performance featured one of Mozart's symphonies, his E flat concerto for two pianos, various arias, a violin concerto and a symphony by Baron van Swieten, a programme no less substantial than might have been found at a Lenten concert at one of the court theatres.

Most of Mozart's documented concert appearances, both public and private, took place during his first five years in Vienna, with a sudden decline after 1786. Some scholars have speculated that the apparent absence of concerts in the later part of the decade indicates his declining popularity with a fickle Viennese public, others have suggested his performing abilities may have been hampered by illness, while others have pointed out that the decline coincided with the death of his father in 1787, at which point his informative letters home ceased, and our main source of information dries up. Though he may well have given any number of performances for which no record remains, other events beyond his control perhaps limited his opportunities. In 1786, for example, Joseph II began to lift the restrictions on theatrical performances in Lent, which meant that the court theatres were less available for concerts. Fewer concerts in general are documented for the last years of the decade (possibly reflecting the economic uncertainties caused by the Turkish war of 1778–91), and none at all took place in the Lenten season of 1790 because of the official mourning for the death of Joseph II. Perhaps, especially since the more lucrative court theatres were no longer a realistic option, Mozart simply decided that concerts were not worth the effort.

But he may also have simply decided to concentrate his energies elsewhere, particularly in the realm of opera, where we see an upswing in his activity beginning in 1786. Even more than concerts, theatre and opera lay at the very centre of the city's cultural and social life, particularly the offerings of the Burgtheater and Kärntnertortheater. The Burgtheater had originally been the court's private theatre, but the financial difficulties of Maria Theresia's early years had forced her to lease it to a series of entrepreneurs, who opened it to the public. It retained its elite status, however, and remained a place to see and be seen; a theatre-loving aristocrat might well spend several nights there each week, watching the performances and visiting friends in adjoining boxes. In 1776, however, Joseph II had taken steps that would ensure its offerings appealed to a wider range of people: He placed the Burgtheater back under direct court control, renamed it the Nationaltheater, and installed a theatrical company that would present plays in German instead of the French drama favoured by the aristocracy. In 1778, a singspiel company was formed as an outgrowth of this push for German-language theatre. Just a year after his arrival in Vienna, Mozart secured one of the lucrative commissions to write a new work for the company, and the resulting *Die Entführung aus dem Serail* premiered in July 1782 to great popular acclaim. But the following year, the company was disbanded (and replaced by an Italian opera troupe), only to be reconstituted briefly during 1785–8, with performances held at the Kärntnertortheater. *Die Entführung* remained a popular staple of the repertory in these seasons, but aside from the one-act *Der Schauspieldirektor*, Mozart did not return to singspiel composition until about 1790. By that time he had more options, for during the 1780s, several private theatres had opened in the city's ever-expanding suburbs. Smaller, less expensive and thus accessible to greater numbers of people, these theatres specialized in popular entertainment: farces, low comedy and singspiel. In 1790 Mozart began to collaborate with the staff of the Theater auf der Wieden, possibly contributing several numbers to *Der Stein der Weisen*, a fairy-tale opera with many parallels to DIE ZAUBERFLÖTE, which premiered at the same theatre the following year. With these productions, Mozart's music began to reach a wider audience.

Nevertheless, Italian opera was still the most prestigious genre for any composer and had long been one of Mozart's greatest ambitions. Though he had conquered the singspiel establishment relatively quickly, it took him longer to gain entry to the exclusive circle that received Italian opera commissions. The Burgtheater's opera company operated on a repertory system, alternating performances of a number of different works, with each season featuring a mixture of new operas (normally between five and seven each year) and revivals of older pieces. For a newly commissioned work, the composer received 450 florins and sometimes part of the box-office receipts for a performance or two. Mozart wrote LE NOZZE DI FIGARO (1786) and COSÌ FAN TUTTE (1790) on such commissions (possibly earning a double fee for the latter) and prepared a revised version of DON GIOVANNI for the 1788 season, for which he received 225 florins. It is hard for us to realize today what a triumph these three commissions represented, for at the time, Italian opera in Vienna was almost exclusively the provenance of Italian composers. Of the seventy-seven Italian operas documented during the 1783–92 seasons, sixty-three, or 82 per cent, were by Italian-born composers like GIOVANNI PAISIELLO, Domenico Cimarosa and ANTONIO SALIERI. Only four composers from the territories of the Austro-Hungarian Empire received commissions, for a total of seven operas, or 9 per cent of those presented. Mozart leads this list with his three. Moreover, Mozart's operas proved quite popular, though they never achieved the frequency of performance found for Italian composers. Still, in the 1788–9 season, *Don Giovanni*, with sixteen performances, ranked second only to the Salieri/DA PONTE piece *Axur*, and the revival of *Figaro* the two following seasons ranked in the top five. In addition, box-office receipts from the 1789–90 and 1790–1 seasons indicate a strong demand for tickets at Mozart's operas, especially for *Così*, which took in the highest average receipts per performance of the 1789–90 season. Given these circumstances, Mozart's operatic career in Vienna must be judged a success.

In fact, the startling thing that emerges from a consideration of the opportunities that Vienna offered to composers and performers is the degree to which Mozart managed to permeate and conquer all the city's musical facets. Though others may have managed greater successes in individual areas, no one else during his lifetime (or later) could boast of such all-encompassing appeal. Those who are disposed to find Mozart ill-treated by the world will lament that the practical necessity of dealing with so many institutions robbed him of precious time and energy that he could have devoted to composition. Others, however, may suspect that the city's variety energized him and stimulated his creativity. Whichever viewpoint lies closer to the truth, there can be little doubt that Vienna's society and institutions, with all their quirks and peculiarities, influenced and guided the compositional output of Mozart's maturity.

MARY SUE MORROW

D. Beales, 'Court, Government and Society in Mozart's Vienna', in *Wolfgang Amadè Mozart: Essays on his Life and his Music*, ed. S. Sadie (Oxford, 1996), 3–20
T. C. W. Blanning, *Joseph II* (London, 1994).
M. Csáky and W. Pass, eds., *Europa im Zeitalter Mozarts* (Vienna, 1995)
D. Edge, 'Mozart's Reception in Vienna, 1787–1791', in *Wolfgang Amadè Mozart: Essays on his Life and his Music*, ed. S. Sadie (Oxford, 1996), 66–117
D. Link, *The National Court Theatre in Mozart's Vienna: Sources and Documents, 1783–1792* (Oxford, 1998)
M. S. Morrow, *Concert Life in Haydn's Vienna* (Stuyvesant, NY, 1989)

Villeneuve, Louise (fl. 1771–99), soprano, the original Dorabella in *Così fan tutte* (26 Jan. 1790). She joined the opera company in VIENNA in 1789, making her debut on 27 June as Amore in MARTÌN Y SOLER's *L'arbore di Diana*. This role, which gained her immediate success and which she continued to sing throughout the season, was alluded to by Mozart in Dorabella's second-act aria 'È Amore un ladroncello'. Mozart also supplied arias for her in Cimarosa's *I due baroni* (K578) and Martín's *Il burbero di buon cuore* (K582, K583). She left Vienna at the end of the 1790–1 season, resuming an itinerant career in Italy. There is no evidence that, as is often stated, she was the sister of ADRIANA FERRARESE, the first Fiordiligi. On the contrary, Villeneuve's career path did not follow the route usually taken by Italian singers, for she seems to have started as a dancer. Upon hearing her sing for the first time, on 11 July 1789, ZINZENDORF identified her as 'a pupil of NOVERRE', and, indeed, a Mlle Villeneuve can be found in Noverre's Viennese ballet company from 1771 to 1774. DOROTHEA LINK

D. Edge, 'Attributing Mozart I: Three Accompanied Recitatives', *Cambridge Opera Journal* 13 (2001), 197–237
D. Link, 'Così fan tutte: Dorabella and Amore', *Mozart-Jahrbuch* 1991, 888–94
'A Newly Discovered Accompanied Recitative to Mozart's "Vado, ma dove" K583', *Cambridge Opera Journal* 12 (2000), 29–50

violin sonatas. See SONATAS

Viotti, Giovanni Battista (b. Fontanello da Po, 12 May 1755; d. London 3 Mar. 1824). One of the leading virtuoso violinists of the late eighteenth century, widely considered the founding father of the nineteenth-century French method of violin-playing, Viotti made his name in PARIS following a successful debut on 17 March 1782. Amidst the revolutionary fervour of the early 1790s Viotti was forced to flee to LONDON, where he lived for the remainder of his life, aside from three years in temporary exile (1798–1801). Reviewers of his performances at public concerts in London in the 1790s – including those organized by JOHANN PETER SALOMON that featured JOSEPH HAYDN – were effusive in their praise of his playing. The *Morning Chronicle* report on 12 March 1794 is typical: 'The masterly performance of Viotti exceeded all former samples; his power over the instrument seems unlimited. The grand mistake of musicians has been a continued effort to excite amazement. Viotti, it is true, without making that his object, astonishes his hearer; but he does something infinitely better – he awakens emotion, gives a soul to sound, and leads the passions captive.' Viotti's twenty-nine violin concertos, premiered by the composer himself in Paris and in London, represent his major compositional achievements. Mozart added trumpet and timpani parts to one of them, No. 16 in E minor in 1789–90 (K470a). In spring 1786, Heinrich MARCHAND (1769–c.1812), a friend of the Mozarts and a pupil of Leopold, performed a Viotti violin concerto in SALZBURG as part of his concert series that also included Mozart's piano concertos K451 and K466. Leopold reported making Marchand practise extremely hard for his Viotti performance (letter to NANNERL MOZART, 31 Mar.–1 Apr. 1786). SIMON P. KEEFE

S. P. Keefe, 'Aesthetic and Stylistic Balance and the Role of the Orchestra in Viotti's Violin Concertos', in *Viotti Essays*, ed. Massimiliano Sala (Bologna, 2005), forthcoming
H. C. Robbins Landon, *Haydn: Chronicle and Works*, vol. III: *Haydn in England, 1791–1795* (London, 1976)
M. H. Schmid, 'Ein Violinkonzert von Viotti als Herausforderung für Mozart und Haydn', *Mozart Studien* 5 (Tutzing, 1995), 149–71
C. White, *From Vivaldi to Viotti: A History of the Early Classical Violin Concerto* (New York, 1992)

Vogler, Georg Joseph, Abbé (b. Pleichach, near Würzburg, 15 June 1749; d. Darmstadt, 6 May 1814). GERMAN composer, organist and theorist. Vogler was active at the MANNHEIM court of Karl Theodor from 1771 and deputy Kapellmeister from 1775; although he did not accompany the court to MUNICH in 1778 he was nevertheless appointed Kapellmeister there in 1784; from 1786 he was active in Stockholm and from 1807 in Darmstadt. Mozart and Vogler met in Mannheim in 1777 but neither father nor son had a good opinion of his musicianship. Mozart wrote to his father on 4 November 1777, 'He is a very conceited but quite incompetent man' and LEOPOLD MOZART described his opera *Castore e Polluce* as 'music [that] pleased me very little for it gave the impression of having been composed by Herr Vogler in a paroxysm of high fever' (letter of 13 Feb. 1787). Vogler's enduring contributions to the history of music are his periodical *Betrachtungen der Mannheim Tonschule* (Mannheim, 1778–81) and his treatise *Tonwissenschaft und Tonsetzkunst* (Mannheim, 1776), even if Mozart described the latter as teaching 'arithmetic rather than composition' (letter of 13 Nov. 1777). CLIFF EISEN

G.-H. Fischer, 'Abbé Georg Joseph Vogler: A "Baroque" Musical Genius', in *Gustav III and the Swedish Stage* (Lewiston, NY, 1993), 75–102
F. Grave and M. Grave, *In Praise of Harmony: The Teachings of Abbé Georg Joseph Vogler* (Lincoln, NE, 1987)

W

Wagenseil, Georg Christoph (b. Vienna, 29 Jan. 1715; d. Vienna, 1 Mar. 1777). A court composer in VIENNA from 1739 until his death, organist at Empress Elizabeth Christine's private chapel (1741–50) and court keyboard instructor (from 1749), Wagenseil was a renowned composer of operatic, vocal, orchestral and chamber works. His prolific instrumental output alone totalled over 100 symphonies, 100 concertos and 200 works for solo keyboard. Wagenseil's prowess on the keyboard was widely praised, C. F. D. Schubart citing his 'extraordinary expressive power'. Mozart learned a Wagenseil scherzo on 24 January 1761 (as reported by LEOPOLD MOZART in NANNERL MOZART's music book), performed a Wagenseil concerto for EMPRESS MARIA THERESIA on his first trip to Vienna in 1762, and played other keyboard works by him at court in LONDON two years later. According to FRIEDRICH SCHLICHTEGROLL's biography of Mozart in his *Nekrolog auf das Jahr 1791* (Gotha, 1793), Wagenseil was present at the Vienna performance and may have turned pages for Mozart. On a later trip to Vienna, Leopold explained to his wife (30 Jan.–3 Feb. 1768): 'I was told that all the clavier-players and composers in Vienna were opposed to our advancement, with the sole exception of Wagenseil, who, however, as he was ill at home, could not help us or contribute anything to our advantage.' SIMON P. KEEFE

D. Heartz, *Haydn, Mozart and the Viennese School, 1740–1780* (New York and London, 1995)
H. Scholz-Michelitsch, *Georg Christoph Wagenseil, Hofkomponist und Hofklaviermeister der Kaiserin Maria Theresia* (Vienna, 1980)

Waldstätten, Martha Elisabeth, Baroness (baptized Vienna, 5 Jan. 1744; d. Klosterneuberg, near Vienna, 11 Feb. 1811). Waldstätten, a noblewoman and amateur pianist who may have studied with Mozart, was generous to the composer and his wife on a number of occasions in the early 1780s. She accommodated CONSTANZE MOZART three times at her residence in VIENNA's Leopoldstadt district (1781–2) and, at Mozart's request, housed his student JOSEPHA AUERNHAMMER free of charge in late 1782. She also provided Constanze and Mozart with an extravagant, 'princely' meal on their wedding day, 4 August 1782, and corresponded with LEOPOLD MOZART in an effort to convince him of Constanze's suitability as a wife. A year later she honoured a debt incurred by Mozart, eliciting sincere gratitude in return. She also subscribed to Mozart's highly successful series of concerts at the Trattnerhof in spring 1784. Mozart's letters to Waldstätten (see 28 Sept. 1782 and 2 Oct. 1782, for example) are affectionate and jovial, revealing a comfortable, friendly relationship that transcended the difference in social class between them. SIMON P. KEEFE

Walsegg-Stuppach, Franz Count (b. 1763; d. Schloss Stuppach, near Wiener-Neustadt, 11 Nov. 1827). In the spring or summer of 1791, Walsegg-Stuppach, a rich estate-owner, commissioned a requiem mass from Mozart to be performed in memory of his wife, Anna, who died on 14 February of that year. He commissioned the work anonymously, either through his lawyer, Dr Johann Sortschan, or business manager, Franz Anton Leitgeb. After Mozart's death on 5 December 1791 and FRANZ XAVER SÜSSMAYR's subsequent completion of the REQUIEM, K626, he finally received the work from CONSTANZE MOZART, conducting a performance on 14 December 1793. According to Anton Herzog in his 1839 essay 'Wahre und Ausführliche Geschichte des Requiems von W. A. Mozart' (True and Complete History of Mozart's Requiem), the concert took place at the parish church at Wiener-Neustadt as 'it was not possible to find all the necessary performers in the neighbourhood of Stuppach'. Intriguingly the score used at this concert, in the Count's hand, bears the inscription 'Requiem composto del Conte Walsegg'; whether he seriously intended to market K626 as his own work, however, is a matter of debate. Herzog claims that this was a 'joke': 'We all knew that the Count wanted to make a mystery out of the Requiem . . . for when he claimed, in our presence, that it was a composition of his own, he always used to smile.' In any case, Walsegg-Stuppach, a passionate music lover, also commissioned quartets from contemporary composers – FRANZ ANTON HOFFMEISTER (1754–1812) prominent among them – for twice-weekly music sessions at his home and insisted on 'exclusive ownership' of the works, according to Herzog. He subsequently arranged the Requiem for string quintet, presumably for private performance at one of these gatherings. SIMON P. KEEFE

O. E. Deutsch, 'Zur Geschichte von Mozarts Requiem', *Österreichische Musikzeitschrift* 19 (1964), 49–60

Walter, (Gabriel) Anton (b. Neuhausen an der Fildern, Swabia, 5 Feb. 1752; d. Vienna, 11 Apr. 1826). A highly acclaimed piano manufacturer, Walter provided instruments for many leading late eighteenth- and early nineteenth-century Viennese musicians, including Mozart and BEETHOVEN. From the early 1800s onwards he traded as 'Walter und Sohn' with his stepson, Georg Christoph Joseph Stöffstoss. Mozart's piano was frequently transported around VIENNA for concerts, as a fatigued LEOPOLD MOZART reported to NANNERL MOZART (12 Mar. 1785) during his stay with Mozart and Constanze: 'It is impossible for me to describe the rush and bustle. Since my arrival [11 February] your brother's fortepiano has been taken at least a dozen times to the theatre or to some other house.' In addition the instrument had a large pedalboard attached, which, as Leopold explained in the same letter, 'stands under the instrument and is about two feet longer and extremely heavy'. In 1810, before moving to Copenhagen with her second husband GEORG NIKOLAUS VON NISSEN, Constanze sent Mozart's instrument to their son, KARL THOMAS MOZART, in MILAN; he subsequently donated it to the Mozarteum in SALZBURG in 1856 (the centenary of his father's birth) and it is now on display at the Mozart museum in Salzburg's Getreidegasse. SIMON P. KEEFE

U. Rück, 'Mozarts Hammerflügel erbaute Anton Walter, Wien: Technische Studien, Vergleiche und Beweise', *Mozart-Jahrbuch* 1955, 246–61

Weber family. See LANGE, ALOYSIA; MANNHEIM; MOZART, CONSTANZE; HAIBEL, SOPHIE

Weigl, Joseph (b. Eisenstadt, 28 Mar. 1766; d. Vienna, 3 Feb. 1846). A composer and Kapellmeister, Weigl staged his first opera at VIENNA's Burgtheater in 1783, *Die unnützte Vorsicht, oder die betrogene Arglist*; more than thirty were to follow, including the highly successful singspiel *Die Schweizerfamilie* (1809). His other compositions included cantatas, sacred works and ballets.

Weigl had frequent contact with Mozart in Vienna. He accompanied rehearsals of LE NOZZE DI FIGARO and DON GIOVANNI and conducted *Figaro* – after Mozart had directed the first two or three performances – in 1786 and again at the revival at the Burgtheater on 29 August 1789. Like Mozart, he participated in the regular Sunday morning concerts at BARON VAN SWIETEN's residence, reflecting fondly on the experience in his autobiography (1819): 'No one can imagine this pleasure. To hear Mozart play the most difficult scores with his own inimitable skill, & sing . . . & correct the mistakes of others, could not but excite the greatest imagination.' SIMON P. KEEFE

Wendling family. A family whose lives intersected repeatedly with the Mozarts, the musical members comprised Johann Baptist (b. Rappoltsweiler, Alsace, 17 June 1723; d. MUNICH, 27 June 1797), his wife Dorothea (b. Stuttgart, 21 Mar. 1736; d. Munich, 20 Aug. 1811), their daughter Elisabeth Augusta ('Gustl') (b. MANNHEIM, 4 Oct. 1752; d. Munich, 18 Feb. 1794) and their sister-in-law Elisabeth Augusta ('Lisl') Wendling née Sarselli (b. Mannheim, 20 Feb. 1746; d. Munich, 10 Jan. 1786). LEOPOLD MOZART first heard Johann Baptist, an acclaimed flautist, in July 1763 in Schwetzingen near Mannheim, and was complimentary about his playing. Mozart and his mother socialized regularly with the Wendling family in Mannheim in 1777–8, in spite of strongly articulated reservations about the Wendlings' lack of religious values. It was Johann Baptist who suggested that they travel on to PARIS together in spring 1778 (although Mozart and his mother left on 14 March one month after Wendling and the oboist FRIEDRICH RAMM): 'Wendling assures me that I shall never regret it . . . He maintains that it is still the only place where one can make money and a great reputation' (3 Dec. 1777). While in the French capital, Mozart wrote the solo flute part of his Sinfonia concertante KAnh 9/297b for Wendling.

Dorothea, Gustl and Lisl were all sopranos. Dorothea and Lisl sang at the premiere of IDOMENEO in Munich (29 Jan. 1781), the former as Ilia and the latter as Elettra. In Mannheim Mozart wrote the scena 'Basta, vincesti . . . Ah, non lasciarmi', K486a/295a for Dorothea (1778) and the ariettas 'Oiseaux, si tous les ans', K307 and 'Dans un bois solitaire', K308 for Gustl (1777–8).

SIMON P. KEEFE

R. Halliwell, *The Mozart Family: Four Lives in a Social Context* (Oxford, 1998)

Went (Vent), Johann (Nepomuk) (b. Divice, 27 June 1745; d. Vienna, 3 July 1801). A prominent oboist first in PRAGUE and then at both the Hofkapelle and Nationaltheater in VIENNA, Went transcribed more than fifty operas and ballets for *Harmonie* (small wind band). In control of the Emperor's *Harmonie* repertory for two decades in the late eighteenth century, Went transcribed five Mozart operas, including DIE ENTFÜHRUNG AUS DEM SERAIL. His output of original compositions included more than eighty works for *Harmonie*. SIMON P. KEEFE

R. Hellyer, 'The Transcriptions for Harmonie of "Die Entführung aus dem Serail"', *Proceedings of the Royal Musical Association* 102 (1975–6), 53–66
D. Link, *The National Court Theatre in Mozart's Vienna: Sources and Documents*, 1783–1792 (Oxford, 1998)

Wetzlar von Plankenstern, Raimund, Baron (b. 1752; d. Grünberg, 29 Sept. 1810). Between December 1782 and late February 1783, Mozart and CONSTANZE MOZART lived rent-free at Wetzlar's residence on the Hohe Brücke in VIENNA. Wetzlar was godfather to their son Raimund (17 June 1783–19 Aug. 1783), named after Wetzlar. Mozart explained to LEOPOLD MOZART how this came about (18 June 1783): 'He came to see us at once [after the birth] and offered to stand godfather. I could not refuse him and thought to myself: "After all this boy can still be called Leopold". But while I was turning this round in my mind, the Baron said very cheerfully: "Ah, now you have a little Raimund" – and kissed the child. What was I to do?' Along with his father and sister, Wetzlar subscribed to Mozart's series of three concerts at the Trattnerhof in March 1784. A year or so later, according to LORENZO DA PONTE, Wetzlar offered 'with fine generosity' to pay Da Ponte for writing a libretto for LE NOZZE DI FIGARO and to have it staged in France or England, if the Emperor continued his Viennese ban on the BEAUMARCHAIS play: 'but I refused his offer and proposed that we should write the words and the music in secret, and await a favourable opportunity to show it to the theatre directors or to the Emperor'. SIMON P. KEEFE

Wieland, Christoph Martin (b. 5 Sept. 1733; d. 20 Jan. 1813). German author and translator. He was taken up by the Swiss man of letters, Jakob Bodmer, and became his guest at Zurich in the early 1750s. After appointments in Berne and Biberach, and the professorship of philosophy at Erfurt, he was invited by the dowager Duchess Anna Amalia of Sachsen-Weimar to be tutor to her sons. He remained connected with the Weimar court for the remainder of his life. He wrote verse, novels, epics, and singspiels, and translated twenty-two plays of Shakespeare, and works of Latin literature. His verse romance *Oberon* (1780) exerted a powerful appeal, but most influential in a Viennese connection was the collection of fairy stories that he edited with J. A. Liebeskind, *Dschinnistan* (Winterthur, 1786–9), which provided the stimulus both for the Perinet/Wenzel Müller *Kaspar der Fagottist* and the SCHIKANEDER/Mozart DIE ZAUBERFLÖTE.
PETER BRANSCOMBE

H. and M. Garland, *The Oxford Companion to German Literature* (Oxford, 1976)

Willmann family. Active in several locations in GERMANY and AUSTRIA, the musical members of the Willmann family comprised (Johann) Ignaz

(1739–1815), his second wife Marianne de Tribolet (1768–1813) his daughters (Maximiliana Valentina) Walburga (1769–1835) and (Johanna) Magdalena (1771–1801), and his son Maximilian Friedrich Ludwig (1767–1813). Ignaz played the flute, violin and cello, holding positions in Bonn, Brno and Kassel; Marianne, a soprano, sang Konstanze in a production of DIE ENTFÜHRUNG AUS DEM SERAIL at VIENNA's Freihaus-Theater in March 1795. Walburga, a pianist who may have studied with Mozart, Magdalena, a court singer in VIENNA from 1795, and Max, a cellist, performed together in Viennese concerts on 16 March 1784 and 7 March 1787; on the second of these occasions, Walburga played a Mozart piano concerto, possibly K503 in C. The programme for this concert explained: 'Since these three siblings were so fortunate, two years ago, to receive the adulation of such a discriminating public, so they flatter themselves that the same will be even more the case now since from that time they have not lacked for effort and diligence.' SIMON P. KEEFE

C. Eisen, *New Mozart Documents: A Supplement to O. E. Deutsch's Documentary Biography* (London, 1991)
K. M. Pisarowitz, 'Die Willmanns', *Mitteilungen der Internationalen Stiftung Mozarteum* 15 (1967), 7–12

wind music. Music for winds, or *Harmoniemusik*, was an established feature of court music long before Mozart's time; it is possible to see its origins in the simple calls played by the pairs of horns that attended the hunt. By the late 1750s, bands had grown into groups of five or more instruments, the two horns with a pair of treble instruments above and one or more bassoons beneath, and traditionally these entertained their employers with music at the dinner table or alfresco SERENADE. With only rare exceptions, a *Harmonie* of five or six players would remain standard for some twenty years or more.

1. Italy and Salzburg
2. Vienna
3. Smaller wind pieces

1. Italy and Salzburg

It is curiously at odds with normal practice that Mozart's first pieces of *Harmoniemusik* should require bands of no fewer than ten instrumentalists, to play three pairs of treble instruments, oboes, cors anglais and clarinets, above the conventional horns and bassoons. The two Divertimenti K186 and K166 were apparently the result of a commission obtained while in MILAN in 1773, the second of them being written down after the composer's return to SALZBURG. But in spite of the wealth of resources this music is only infrequently in more than three real parts. The oboes play mostly in thirds, often doubled an octave down by the cors anglais, the bassoons are rarely divided, and the clarinets function in effect as a second pair of horns. Some of the movements derive from music composed earlier, such as Mozart's own *Le gelosie del Serraglio*, Anh. 109 and a Symphony in D major written by PAISIELLO in 1772.

Resident in Salzburg, Mozart returned to *Harmoniemusik* between 1775 and 1777 with a series of divertimenti (K213, 240, 252, 253 and 270) composed for his employer, Archbishop HIERONYMUS COLLOREDO. He scored them for the traditional sextet of oboes, bassoons and horns, though the writing was anything but conventional. While the horns continue to function as the harmonic nucleus to the ensemble, Mozart found new ways of scoring the woodwind instruments independently of each other when so often in the past they had been restricted to a diet of parallel sixths and thirds. Even the first bassoon, while still doubling the bass when its weight was required, shared in this freedom as a real tenor solo voice. These divertimenti are also formally unconventional. Not one of them had the standard five movements. The third begins with a slow movement, an aria for the first oboe, while the fourth, limited to three movements only, opens with a theme with six variations wherein Mozart delighted in exploiting the full range of tonal possibilities of his ensemble.

2. Vienna

Within months of his move to VIENNA in 1781 Mozart found himself again writing *Harmoniemusik*. As it happened, he arrived when radical changes were afoot in the music of the imperial court, and the opportunity of employment must have appeared to him a most optimistic prospect. EMPRESS MARIA THERESIA had recently died, and was succeeded by her son JOSEPH II whose interest in music was altogether more enlightened. He reconstituted the Italian opera, enlarging the orchestra and at one point insisting that the two STADLER brothers, who played clarinet, 'must be taken into the orchestra, because they are still necessary on many occasions, and perhaps they might take up appointments elsewhere, or move away'. Anton Stadler and his younger brother Johann had been irregularly employed in Vienna since 1773 and it would be hard to overstate the importance of their decision to accept the permanent positions offered as it affected the use of wind instruments in music in Vienna: for Mozart in particular it would prove critical. Not only did he write a concerto and a quintet for Anton, but it is not too hard to hypothesize further connections, including the trio K498 for clarinet, viola and piano, the way he scored for clarinet, especially in the Burgtheater operas in the certain knowledge that the Stadlers would perform the parts, his introduction to the basset horn, and (Mozart and Stadler being FREEMASONS) the Masonic association Mozart undoubtedly felt for clarinet and basset horn. The Stadler brothers could well have been two of 'the poor beggars', as Mozart wrote of them to his father on 3 November 1781, who entertained the composer himself three days earlier with his Serenade in E flat major. And the great Serenade in B flat major K361 has its Stadler connection as well.

By far the most grandiose work of its genre, of dimensions that were rarely if ever surpassed, is the Serenade in B flat major, K361. Mozart wrote it in seven movements though five was the norm, adding a romanze and a large-scale theme and variation movement between second minuet and finale. He extended its dimensions still further with a slow introduction to the first movement and second trios to both minuets. It was only a late decision for him to delete a repeat of the second half of the first movement. And he wrote for a band of no fewer than thirteen instruments when six or eight were still normal. His instrumental palette consisted of two pairs of horns, in different keys, thereby providing greater tonal support where the music modulated away from the tonic. He employed three pairs of treble instruments, oboes, clarinets and basset horns, finding especial pleasure in the similar voicing of the clarinets and basset horns even to the extent of reserving one trio for them alone. The usual pair of bassoons were supported by what may be the earliest instance of the use in *Harmoniemusik* of a 16-foot instrument, in fact a double bass. Mozart's choice may have been restricted for lack of any alternative – the contrabassoon was virtually unknown in Vienna before 1785.

Such proportions make this atypical of Mozart's work whenever it was written, and it is one of the most frustrating riddles of his entire compositional career that we have no real clue as to when or why he should have written so remarkable a piece of music. We have a *terminus ante quem* in the only known contemporary performance, at a subscription concert promoted by Anton Stadler on 23 April 1784. There is a strong body of opinion that it was for this performance that Mozart wrote the serenade, though it seems inconceivable that Mozart should have created so monumental a work for so insignificant an occasion, the more so since only four of its seven movements were played. As to the *terminus post quem*, currently the only real evidence lies in the manuscript paper on which the serenade was written. Two types, which Mozart would not have purchased before his arrival in Vienna, constitute the entire autograph. The composer started to use both in 1781, and continued to use them, on and off, for the next three years, including the first version of the Serenade in E flat, K375, written for a sextet of clarinets, bassoons and horns before mid-October 1781. Herein lies perhaps the most tantalizingly inconclusive piece of evidence of all. The final page of the first movement of this serenade was written down on a sheet of paper that Mozart had used before. As was his practice with the Serenade in B flat, he had braced together eleven of the twelve staves. On the top line he had written what are probably the bars before and after the double bar in the middle of a variation, for an unnamed instrument, perhaps an oboe. The melodic line possesses an intriguing similarity, to put it no stronger, to the variation movement of the Serenade in B flat, and though critically it does not possess the same underlying chord structure it is identical in tonality and metre. It could be interpreted as the final bars of an abandoned variation movement for the serenade before the composer began again using similar but subtly different material. One thing is certain about this discarded fragment – there is no other known work of Mozart, certainly not of his early Viennese years, to which it could remotely be connected. And if it is the serenade, it places its composition in the summer months of 1781.

For the next few months, rumour among musicians must have been rife about the Emperor's reforms at the Burgtheater. The formation of his *Harmonie* was part of this process. It is unlikely to be coincidence that at precisely the same time Mozart took greater interest in *Harmoniemusik* than at any other stage of his career, seeing perhaps the possibility of court employment. Mozart related to his father on 3 November 1781 how he wrote a *Nachtmusik* (the sextet Serenade in E flat, K375) with some care in the hope of influencing Joseph von Strack, a chamberlain who had the ear of the Emperor. If this is the case,

Mozart's intelligence had misinformed him of the Emperor's intentions, since he was not planning a conventional sextet *Harmonie* at all, but an octet of oboes, clarinets, bassoons and horns, and demonstrably other noblemen (his brother Maximilian Franz, Prince Aloys Liechtenstein) had it in mind to follow his lead. It may be such circumstances that caused the composer the following summer to revise the serenade, integrating oboe parts into the texture. The considerable reworking of the first, third and fifth movements necessitated writing them out again; in the two minuet movements he was content just to add oboe parts into the original manuscript without altering the other six.

'I have hastily had to "make" a Nacht Musique, but only for harmonie', the composer wrote to his father on 27 July 1782. Mozart had used the expression *Nachtmusik* before, on 3 November 1781 when writing of the Serenade in E flat in its sextet form. This may be a coincidence, but the haste so evident in the handwriting in the second autograph as the serenade was rescored would seem to confirm that the composer here was writing of the E flat work and not, as the traditional view would have it, the C minor Serenade, K388. There is no hint of haste here, certainly not in the composer's handwriting. Supported by this probably erroneous evidence, the serenade has always been listed as a mid-1782 composition, and this date is in fact supported by the paper of the autograph. Mozart again cocks a snook at convention, composing a curiously sombre and powerful work which often conveys a mood of dramatic intensity totally alien to the informal background music normally associated with the serenade type. The constant focus on the minor key, the symphonic structure of its four movements, the display of exceptional musical ingenuity in the canonic devices of the third movement, the dramatically cumulative effect of the marvellous set of variations that form the finale, all compel the attention of the listener in a way that is atypical of *Harmoniemusik* in particular and the serenade style in general.

But, whatever Mozart's intentions with the two octet serenades, new original compositions were not at all what the Emperor had in mind for his *Harmonie*. The theatre and its music were central to his pleasures, and what he wanted was to enjoy his dinner listening to the highlights of the opera and ballet scores that were in performance on the stage in his Burgtheater, arranged for the octet *Harmonie* formed of the oboists, clarinettists (the Stadler brothers, no less), bassoonists and horn players of the Burgtheater orchestra who were especially rewarded for this additional responsibility. We can again only conjecture that Mozart was aware of this: certainly it is a logical explanation of the letter he wrote to his father on 20 July 1782 that if he did not transcribe for *Harmonie* movements from his new opera DIE ENTFÜHRUNG AUS DEM SERAIL, someone else would, and secure profits he evidently considered should be his. We have no idea how far he got with his transcription, though it has recently been argued that an anonymous arrangement which is part of the Donaueschingen collection (now at Karlsruhe) is Mozart's completed work. But there is no evidence that his transcription was ever taken up by the Emperor, even if finished, and the work of transcribing opera and ballet scores was for the next decade to be done principally by the second oboist in the Emperor's *Harmonie*, JOHANN WENT.

3. Smaller wind pieces

All too little is known of the background to Mozart's several small pieces for various combinations of horns, clarinets and basset horns. The Adagio for two basset horns and bassoon, K410, is in fact a canon between the basset horns accompanied by the bassoon. This short piece, and the Adagio in B flat for two clarinets and three basset-horns, K411, may both have been written for processional use, possibly at Masonic functions in 1782–3. Mozart may also have composed five trios Anh. 229 for basset horns. Any clues to when and why have long since disappeared, the two most probable periods being in 1781 when Anton and Johann Stadler were known to be attempting to earn money playing basset horn trios with a colleague named Griessbacher, or in the mid-1780s when Anton David and Vincent Springer, two itinerant basset horn players, spent many months in Vienna in hope of employment, before finally moving on.

The duets for pairs of identical instruments may have been written purely for the pleasure of the participants. The Sonata in B flat major, K292, is probably such a work, perhaps composed for two bassoons in about 1775 for the MUNICH amateur bassoonist Thaddäus von Dürnitz. The traditional view that the instrumentation of Mozart's twelve duos K487 must have been for strings or woodwind is equally doubtful, and was no doubt fuelled by the cautious opinion that such high and chromatic writing could not possibly have been for brass instruments. Yet twelve pieces all written in C major positively suggests music for brass instruments, presumably horns; in fact, all the chromatic notes are available to a skilled hand horn player and the extremely high notes are within a horn player's range when approached as they are here by ascending scale passages. Mozart could have written these pieces for JOSEPH LEUTGEB, who had moved from Salzburg to Vienna ahead of him, and of course was the dedicatee of the horn concertos, though Martin Rupp and Jacob Eisen, horn players in the Emperor's *Harmonie*, are equally possible recipients.

ROGER HELLYER

B. Blomhert, *The Harmoniemusik of 'Die Entführung aus dem Serail' by Wolfgang Amadeus Mozart* (Utrecht, 1987)

R. Payer von Thurn, *Joseph II. als Theaterdirektor* (Vienna, 1920)

Winter, Sebastian (b. Donaueschingen, 1743; d. Messkirch, Baden-Württemberg, 11 Apr. 1815). Servant and hairdresser to the Mozart family on their trip from SALZBURG to PARIS in 1763, Winter went on to work for Prince Joseph Wenzel Fürstenberg in Donaueschingen and later, as valet, for Prince Joseph Maria Benedikt Fürstenberg. He acted as an intermediary between LEOPOLD MOZART and Joseph Maria in the sale of copies of Mozart's piano concertos K413, 414 and 415 in 1784. (Leopold sent the works to Winter on 4 April packed 'in waterproof cloth'.) Mozart sold Joseph Maria further copies of compositions through Winter – whom he called 'Companion of my Youth!' – but was ultimately unsuccessful in his attempt to procure an annual stipend in exchange for a regular supply of pieces.

SIMON P. KEEFE

Wranitzky family. Prominent composers of orchestral, chamber and operatic works in the late eighteenth century, the Wranitzky brothers, Paul (b. Nová Říse, Moravia,

30 Dec. 1756; d. VIENNA, 26 Sept. 1808) and Anton (b. Nová Říse, Moravia, 15 June 1761; d. Vienna, 6 Aug. 1820), moved to Vienna in the late 1770s (or perhaps the early 1780s in Anton's case). Paul wrote over twenty works for the stage, including the singspiel *Oberon* (1789) given at the coronation events for LEOPOLD II in Frankfurt (15 Oct. 1790) at which Mozart was also present. The success of this work in Vienna – at which MARIA ANNA GOTTLIEB, Mozart's first Barbarina in *LE NOZZE DI FIGARO* and first Pamina in *DIE ZAUBERFLÖTE*, sang Prinzess Amande – acted as a catalyst for SCHIKANEDER to write *Die Zauberflöte* for Mozart in 1791. *Oberon* was compared unfavourably with Mozart's works by Carl Spazier in Berlin's *Musikalisches Wochenblatt* (25 Feb. 1792): it contained an 'affected, studied fullness that contrasts curiously with the genuine, original, natural wealth of ideas of a *Mozard*'. After Mozart's death, Paul – a member of the FREEMASON lodge 'Zur gekrönten Hoffnung' (The Crowned Hope) to which Mozart also belonged – helped CONSTANZE MOZART negotiate with the publisher ANDRE over the sale of Mozart's works. He also established a reputation as a leading conductor, directing JOSEPH HAYDN's *Creation* (1799 and 1800) and the premiere of BEETHOVEN's Symphony No. 1 in C (1800) in Vienna. Anton, like Paul, was a friend of Haydn and Beethoven and well known as a violin teacher and virtuoso, whose compositional output included fifteen violin concertos and twenty-one string quartets. He studied composition with Mozart in Vienna, as well as with Haydn and J. G. ALBRECHTSBERGER.

SIMON P. KEEFE

R. Hickman, 'The Flowering of the Viennese String Quartet in the Late Eighteenth Century', *Music Review* 50 (1989), 157–80

Z

Zaide, K344. By the end of the 1790s, CONSTANZE MOZART had recovered from the emotional and financial shock of Wolfgang's death, and begun – with the help of a group of her late husband's associates – to bring order to his musical estate. Among the mass of unfinished works, sketches, and other unrealized projects she found a 'GERMAN opera without a title, for the most part complete'. She and her helpers, unable to locate a libretto for it, even resorted to placing an advertisement in a widely read music journal (the *Allgemeine musikalische Zeitung* in Leipzig) asking any reader who recognized the characters in the drama to make contact with her. No one replied.

It took more than 150 years for Mozart scholarship to shed some light on the fragment, which includes sixteen musical numbers divided into two acts but lacks an overture and a finale. The piece was eventually given the name *Zaide*, after its main female figure. Like DIE ENTFÜHRUNG AUS DEM SERAIL, to which it bears more than a few similarities, *Zaide* is a singspiel in German; spoken texts are meant to advance the action between the musical numbers. In the score Constanze found (which is preserved today in the Staatsbibliothek Berlin) these spoken texts, except for cues, are missing. The challenge, then, is to find the source of the text Mozart and his librettist, the Mozart family friend JOHANN ANDREAS SCHACHTNER, used to construct their version. After approximately fifty years of back and forth, the scholarly consensus is approximately as follows: Mozart began, upon his return from his long trip to MANNHEIM and PARIS in early 1779, and perhaps at the urging of his father, to cast about for a German singspiel with an eye towards the new German-language Nationaltheater in VIENNA. One libretto seems to have caught his and Schachtner's eye: *Das Serail / Oder: / Die unvermuthetete Zusammenkunft in der / Sclaverei zwischen Vater, Tochter / und Sohn* (The Seraglio, or the Unexpected Meeting, as Slaves, of Father, Daughter, and Son). The textbook for this singspiel, by Franz Joseph Sebastiani, set to music by the Passau composer Joseph Friebert (performances of it have never been documented), was printed in Bozen (today Bolzano) sometime in 1779. Mozart and Schachtner's texts follow the texts in *Das Serail* down to the names of the characters. But there is a problem: *other* versions of a singspiel about western slaves in a Turkish seraglio, some with texts by Sebastiani, had been in circulation throughout southern Germany and AUSTRIA for more than a decade *before* 1779. In the absence of a proven performance of any of these in Salzburg, it seems impossible to conclude which *Serail* was the inspiration for Mozart's *Zaide*. The very latest research, in a forthcoming article by Thomas Betzwieser, suggests that the Mozart/Schachtner version depends too closely on the Bolzano textbook for it to have come directly from any other source.

Since this version cannot reasonably be expected to have reached Salzburg immediately after its publication in Bolzano, it follows that Mozart worked on his *Zaide* in the closing months of 1779, or, more likely, some time in 1780. *Zaide* appears in the Mozart family correspondence only three times. In a letter dated 11 December 1780 to his son, who was in MUNICH supervising the production of IDOMENEO, LEOPOLD MOZART reassures him that it is not a problem that 'Schachtner's drama' is unfinished; on 18 January 1781, Wolfgang asks Leopold to bring the score of the 'operetta of Schachtner's' to *Idomeneo*'s premiere. Since Mozart clearly did not have these materials with him in Munich, it stands to reason that he composed the fragments before his departure from Salzburg in late October 1780. Just a few months later, having travelled to Vienna in the entourage of his patron the Prince-Archbishop of Salzburg, Mozart had already experienced *Zaide's* rejection:

> As far as Schachtner's operetta is concerned, there is nothing to be done – for the very reason I have so often mentioned. STEPHANIE junior [a powerful figure at the German Court Opera in Vienna] is going to give me a new text to work with, and he says it will be a good one . . . It was impossible for me to tell Stephanie to his face that he was wrong. I only told him that the piece is a good one, except for the long dialogues, but these would be easy to change; it is just that it is not right for Vienna, where the public would rather see comedies.

The end of the *Zaide* project was the beginning of *Die Entführung aus dem Serail*. The plots of the two are similar: Zaide, enslaved to the Sultan Soliman, falls in love with her fellow westerner Gomatz. Together with the sympathetic Allazim, a favourite of the Sultan, they plot their escape. The plan succeeds, initially; Soliman is enraged, even after he is offered a beautiful replacement for Zaide by the slave dealer Osmin. Eventually, the three escapees are apprehended. In the last surviving number of the Mozart fragment, their pleas for mercy fall on the Sultan's deaf ears. In the Sebastiani version, this scene precedes a dramatic turn towards a happy ending, in which the three slaves discover they are in fact father, son and daughter. The Sultan, moved by this twist of fate, pardons them and arranges for them to return home.

The music in *Zaide* is of very high quality, and demonstrates the progress Mozart had made as a composer during his journey to Mannheim and Paris. It is especially easy to hear the influence of the first city in the operetta's two melodramatic monologues (Gomatz's 'Unerforschliche Fügung' and Soliman's 'Zaide entflohen'). Mozart had become an enthusiast there of the north German technique of melodrama, in which a speaker declaims a text over a musical accompaniment; perhaps he would have composed more of them had *Zaide* not had to be abandoned. But the big 'What if?' remains unanswered. Had Mozart been given the opportunity to refine *Zaide* further while preparing it with a fine cast of singers for a real production, there is no doubt that the end product would have been a major contribution to his operatic oeuvre, the dramatic German opera he never got to write. THOMAS IRVINE

T. Betzwieser, 'Mozarts *Zaide*: Überlegungen zu Gensese und Werkgestalt im Licht einer neuen Libretto-Quelle', in *Report of the XIII International Congress of the Gesellschaft für Musikforschung*, ed. D. Altenburger (Kassel, forthcoming)

L. Tyler, '*Zaide* in the Development of Mozart's Operatic Language', *Music & Letters* 72 (1991), 214–35

Zauberflöte, Die, K620 (*The Magic Flute*). Although DON GIOVANNI has often been called *sui generis*, it is *Die Zauberflöte*, which premiered on 30 September 1791, more than any of Mozart's other operas that truly deserves this designation. It is his only opera written expressly for the suburban Freihaustheater auf der Wieden, his only collaboration with librettist and actor EMANUEL SCHIKANEDER, producer and director of that theatre, and his only work conceived in the tradition of the magic operas and 'machine comedies' of the Volkstheater. Although extremely unlike Mozart's other operas in terms of plot, character and magic effects, *Die Zauberflöte* is a natural successor to them in its treatment of ENLIGHTENMENT themes and its dramatization of the individual quest for emotional fulfilment. IDOMENEO, DIE ENTFÜHRUNG AUS DEM SERAIL and especially LA CLEMENZA DI TITO, which was composed almost simultaneously with *Die Zauberflöte* and premiered in PRAGUE only three weeks earlier, share with *Die Zauberflöte* an emphasis on virtue, courage and clemency. It is somehow fitting that Mozart's only fairy-tale opera complete with imaginary locations, fantastic elements and magic talismans should also be his most high-minded operatic piece for the stage. For it is only here in the suburban theatre, which was attended by all ranks of society, that Mozart's representation of the themes of his age could truly parallel the vast scope of the Enlightenment, which sought to include all of mankind in its sweeping reforms.

1. Origins and contexts
2. Synopsis
3. Understanding *Die Zauberflöte*

1. Origins and contexts

The tradition of Viennese popular theatre – to which *Die Zauberflöte* is much indebted – has roots reaching as far back as the beginning of the century when Joseph Anton Stranitzky's company (famous for its HANSWURST comedies) had been in residence at the Kärntnertor and as far afield as travelling companies carried their fare of comedies, dramas and singspiels, all given in German. (Singspiel, the generic name given to eighteenth-century German opera, alternates musical numbers with spoken dialogue and is the German equivalent of the contemporaneous ballad opera in England and the *opéra comique* in France.) Perhaps the greatest experiment in this genre was JOSEPH II's establishment of a National Singspiel in 1778. The repertory of this new troupe included newly written singspiels, the most famous of which was Mozart's DIE ENTFÜHRUNG AUS DEM SERAIL (1782), as well as French and Italian operas in translation. But the Viennese still longed for Italian opera and in 1783 the Emperor replaced the German troupe with the splendid Italian company for which Mozart was to compose LE NOZZE DI FIGARO. From this point forward, German opera flourished in the suburban theatres.

Only two years before the premiere of *Die Zauberflöte* Schikaneder and his company set up shop in the Freihaustheater, opening with a comic opera, *Der Dumme Gärtner aus dem Gebirge, oder Die zween Antons* (The Foolish Gardener from the Mountains, or The Two Antons) on 12 July 1789. With a libretto by Schikaneder and music composed by two members of his troupe, BENEDIKT SCHACK (for whom Mozart created the part of Tamino) and FRANZ XAVER GERL (the first Sarastro), it was an immediate success and eventually gave rise to six sequels. Mozart evidently thought well of these 'Anton' plays for he wrote to CONSTANZE MOZART after attending a performance of a new work by Schikaneder and Schack, *Der Fall ist noch weit seltner* (a sequel to MARTÍN Y SOLER's celebrated *Una cosa rara*) that he 'liked it, but not as much as the "Antons"' (2 June 1790); he later wrote a set of keyboard variations (K613) on a tune from the second of the 'Anton' plays. Schikaneder was a consummate man of the theatre – an accomplished actor (Mozart saw him play Hamlet), singer, comedian, librettist, composer, director and producer. His repertory at the Theater auf der Wieden included comedies and tragedies – by Schikaneder himself, as well as by luminaries such as Lessing, Schiller and GOETHE – and opera in German, mostly light singspiels and French and Italian works in translation. Many of the productions, especially the newly written singspiels and plays with magic elements, featured the fantastic scenic effects for which Schikaneder and his theatre were well known: flying machines, trapdoors, thunder, elaborate lighting and other visual effects including fires and waterfalls. His theatre, in common with other Viennese theatres of the late 1780s and 1790s, specialized in *Zauberoper* (magic opera) and *Zauberkomödie* (magic comedy with song) that are the important precursors of *Die Zauberflöte*. Many of these works centred on stories drawn from German fairy tales (which were then experiencing a renaissance) and merged magic elements with stage spectacle.

The exact date and circumstances of *Die Zauberflöte*'s inception are not known, although the idea for the collaboration was almost certainly born of the long acquaintance of Schikaneder and Mozart (they met in SALZBURG in 1780). Mozart's friendship with the tenor and composer Benedikt Schack, his occasional musical contributions to new productions, including *Der Stein der Weisen* (1790), and his arias for his sister-in-law Josepha Hofer (née WEBER) and Franz Xaver Gerl also show his connection to the Theater auf der Wieden. In an oft-cited letter many years earlier, Mozart had boasted to his father that he liked 'an aria to fit a singer as perfectly as a well-made suit of clothes' (28 Feb. 1778). In composing *Die Zauberflöte* Mozart found himself tailoring music not only for the individual singers, but for the company as a whole and the theatre itself. It is surely no accident that an opera centring on the adventures of a noble hero and his magic flute was written for this company whose tenor was both a fine singer and a flautist. Many of the special effects conceived as part of the story, including the use of machines, the trials of fire and water and the illumination of the whole stage at the end are scenic effects for which Schikaneder was well known. What was unprecedented was the music.

The Theater auf der Wieden had never before attempted a new production on the scope of *Die Zauberflöte*, which the playbill for the premiere describes as 'A Grand Opera'. Musically it far exceeds the expectations of the genre, containing Italianate arias for the noble characters, complex ensemble writing for many of the scenes and full-length finales that rival those in *Figaro*, *Don Giovanni*, and *Così* FAN TUTTE in musical scope and sophistication. Fortunately, Schikaneder's company, which frequently staged opere buffe in translation, not to mention Mozart's own *Die Entführung*, was in a position to provide Mozart with accomplished singers for the central roles as well as an experienced orchestra of thirty-five players. The most important singing roles of course were those of the hero and heroine, Tamino and Pamina. The voice of the first Tamino was captured in the following eloquent description by LEOPOLD MOZART: 'he '[Schack] sings excellently, has a beautiful voice, an effortlessly smooth throat and a beautiful method' (26 May 1786). The first Pamina, ANNA GOTTLIEB, was only seventeen at the time; Mozart already knew her, however, for she had created the role of Barbarina in *Figaro* when she was only twelve. Josepha Hofer, the Queen of the Night, was the eldest of the Weber daughters; although her voice was apparently not quite so fine as that of her sister, ALOYSIA LANGE, she had a very high tessitura (both arias for the Queen reach the F above high C). Franz Xaver Gerl, the first Sarastro, then only twenty-seven, was vital to the company as composer, singer and actor. When the prominent theatre manager Friedrich Ludwig Schröder came to VIENNA in 1791, he was especially recommended to hear Schack and Gerl and described the latter as 'very good'. Schikaneder created the role of Papageno for himself and it clearly exploits his particular comic genius. Of course the success of the opera as a whole did not depend only on the central roles, which were joined on stage by a large cast of sung and spoken roles: the Speaker and three priests (all members of Sarastro's Order), three ladies (in the service of the Queen of the Night), three boys, Papagena (intended for Papageno), Monostatos (a Moor), three slaves (in the service of Monostatos), two armoured men, as well as priests, attendants and slaves.

Many sources of contemporary interest and significance appear to have influenced *Die Zauberflöte*, although the libretto, when taken as a whole, is largely original. Mozart and Schikaneder took their title (though little else) from a fairy tale by August Jakob Liebeskind, 'Lulu, oder die Zauberflöte', which appeared in WIELAND's popular collection *Dschinnistan* (1786–9). And they were no doubt inspired by the Viennese taste for magic operas on fairy-tale subjects; Schikaneder almost certainly hoped that this new production would rival the extraordinary success the Theater in der Leopoldstadt was having with its *Kaspar der Fagottist, oder Die Zauberzither* (by Wenzel Müller and Joachim Perinet). Mozart went to see *Kaspar*, which was so much the rage that he refers to the theatre as the Kasperl: 'I went . . . to the Kasperl to see the new opera *Der Fagottist*, which has made such a stir, but there is nothing in it' (12 June 1791). Various aspects of the libretto seem inspired by the three fairy-tale operas previously produced at the Theater auf der Wieden, *Oberon* (1789), *Der Stein der Weisen* (1790) and *Der wohltätige Derwisch* (1791) and one episode, the opening scene, appears to be drawn from a medieval romance, *Yvain*, which was then experiencing a renaissance in a translation by one of Mozart's Masonic brothers.

The main inspiration for the libretto, however, appears to have been the mysteries of FREEMASONRY. Both Mozart and Schikaneder were Masons, and Mozart, who joined the Viennese lodge 'Zur Wohltätigkeit' in 1784, composed several explicitly Masonic works, including *Die Maurerfreude* (K471), written to honour Master Mason and metallurgist IGNAZ VON BORN, *Maurerische Trauermusik* (MASONIC FUNERAL MUSIC, K477), and *Eine kleine Freymaurer-Kantate* (K623). Opinions vary as to what extent Mozart and Schikaneder intended a coded representation of Freemasonry and its secrets, but there can be no question that they drew heavily, and with great seriousness, on its mysteries. (Rumours that Mozart endangered his life by revealing these secrets have persisted without foundation; Vienna's Masonic community was, in fact, quite an open one.) It is of some interest to note that this was not the first opera based loosely on Masonic lore. *Osiride* (by CATERINO MAZZOLÀ and Johann Gottlieb Naumann), which premiered in Dresden in 1781, also turns on Masonic ideals.

Die Zauberflöte draws mainly on two literary sources devoted to Masonic lore: a novel by the Abbé Jean Terrasson, *Sethos, histoire ou Vie tirée des monuments anecdotes de l'ancienne Egypte* (1731), which was popular in Germany in the translation by Matthias Claudius (1777) that Schikaneder used, and an essay by the celebrated Born, 'Ueber die Mysterien der Aegyptier', which appeared in the *Journal für Freymaurer* in 1784. Several individual scenes are somewhat indebted to *Sethos*, including Tamino's arrival at the temple, his encounter with the two armoured men and the trials of fire and water. Verbal echoes of both *Sethos* and Born's essay have been demonstrated by Peter Branscombe, particularly concerning the tests for initiation and the significance of light as knowledge. The most important musical source is also of Masonic origin: Mozart's own incidental music for TOBIAS PHILIPP FREIHERR VON GEBLER's play, THAMOS, KÖNIG IN ÄGYPTEN (1780). The points of similarity with *Die Zauberflöte* are striking: the story takes place in the Temple of the Sun, features a chorus of priests and involves the symbolic use of a threefold chord.

The practice of Freemasonry provides much of *Die Zauberflöte*'s symbolism and ritual. The number three, which holds a special place in Masonic lore, permeates the opera: three ladies, three boys, three slaves, three temples, even three chances for Papageno. Three is significant in the music as well: there are three flats in the opera's home key of E flat major (which is used so frequently in Masonic music that it is known as the Masonic key); the opera opens with the famous threefold chord, which recurs at significant moments in the rituals of Act 2 (and which is borrowed from the three knocks that signal admittance to the tests of initiation in Masonic ritual); Tamino plays his magic flute in only three scenes. Other numbers of special significance to Freemasonry also appear in the opera – the five-pointed star that appears in the libretto's frontispiece, the sevenfold sun cross (the symbol of Sarastro's power), and the number eighteen (eighteen priests and their eighteen chairs).

The extent to which *Die Zauberflöte*'s mysteries derive from Masonic sources is a question that has long fascinated audiences. The special connection with Masonry was noted almost immediately by the initiated and has produced a substantial literature. But it is a mistake to read the opera as a *roman à clef* and the particularities of the mysteries and their origins are perhaps less important to the opera than the meaning they take on in their new context. Mozart and Schikaneder were indebted to but not bound by Masonic beliefs and their opera was designed to speak its message of love and knowledge to all who attended. For this reason the many passages of spoken dialogue are crucial to the meaning of the work and should not be omitted or shortened – as they frequently are – in performance.

2. Synopsis

The opera opens onto a rocky landscape with trees; 'mountains appear on both sides and between them a round temple. Tamino enters in a splendid Japanese hunting costume . . . with a bow, but no arrows; a serpent follows him.' He cries out for help (No. 1, 'Zu Hilfe! zu Hilfe!') and falls unconscious. Three Ladies, veiled, each holding a silver javelin, emerge from the temple to kill the serpent. They quarrel over which of them should stay with him but finally agree to leave together to report this event to the Queen of the Night. Tamino awakes to the sound of a panpipe and hides. Papageno enters with his panpipe and introduces himself (No. 2, 'Der Vogelfänger bin ich ja'). Tamino imagines that Papageno slew the serpent, but as the bird-catcher begins to boast, the Three Ladies appear to chastise him for telling a lie and seal his mouth with a padlock. They identify themselves as Tamino's rescuers and present him with a portrait of the Queen's daughter, Pamina. Tamino falls in love at first sight (No. 3, 'Dies Bildnis ist bezaubernd schön').

Pamina has been abducted, Tamino is told, by Sarastro. 'With a clap of thunder', the libretto directs, 'the mountains part and the stage is transformed to reveal a magnificent chamber in which the Queen of the Night sits on a starry throne.' She sings an accompanied recitative and aria (No. 4, 'O zitt're nicht, mein lieber Sohn!') in which she commissions Tamino to save her daughter. Repeated vocalises of great difficulty in the second tempo of her aria ('Du, du, du') offer a remarkable demonstration of her power. When the Queen and the Three Ladies exit, the scene returns to what it was before. Papageno, still padlocked, begins the Act 1 quintet (No. 5, 'Hm! Hm! Hm'), in which the Three Ladies remove the lock, making Papageno promise that he won't lie again. They present Tamino with a golden magic flute and Papageno with a set of magic bells to help them on their journey.

In a magnificent Egyptian room in Sarastro's castle, Three Slaves reveal Monostatos's lustful designs on Pamina and rejoice that she has escaped. But it is soon discovered that she has been recaptured. Monostatos appears with Pamina at the start of the trio (No. 6, 'Du feines Täubchen, nur herein!'). She soon faints and Papageno appears. He and Monostatos terrify each other and run off in opposite directions. When Pamina awakes Papageno tells her of the prince who is in love with her. Papageno confides that he too is interested in love, but has no Papagena. They sing a duet in praise of love (No. 7, 'Bei Männern, welche Liebe fühlen') and escape together.

The libretto describes precisely the scene for the Act 1 finale (No. 8, 'Zum Ziele führt dich diese Bahn') – a grove with three temples: at the back the Temple of Wisdom, at the right the Temple of Reason, and at the left the Temple of Nature. The Three Boys lead in Tamino, each carrying a silver palm frond. They warn Tamino to be steadfast, patient and silent. Left alone, Tamino reflects on his new surroundings in a soliloquy that makes a complete change of musical texture. The long and complex accompanied recitative that begins here marks the turning point of the drama. Certain that his purpose is honest and pure, and exclaiming that it is his duty to rescue Pamina, he approaches the door on the right and opens it. But when he tries to enter, a voice within calls out, 'Back!' He approaches the left-hand door, but receives the same reply. He approaches the last door, the Temple of Wisdom, and knocks. An old priest comes forward to ask what he seeks. Tamino replies that he seeks love and truth, but the priest challenges that he will find neither so long as death and vengeance are in his heart. In the ensuing dialogue, the priest reveals that Sarastro rules in these temples, but avoids answering Tamino's questions directly, engaging him in a Socratic dialogue in which Tamino himself must face the questions he poses. Tamino slowly begins to realize his own confusion and finally asks in desperation: 'When will the veil [of darkness] be lifted?' The priest's reply – 'As soon as the hand of friendship leads you / Into the holy place' – is signalled as important by the fact that it is accompanied by the first coherent melody complete with an authentic cadence in over seventy bars. The priest now exits. Left alone once again, Tamino cries 'O endless night!' recalling the melody of the Queen's first words to him. The recollection is an important moment of recognition and the crux of the opera. He had thought the Queen to be good and Sarastro to be evil. He now realizes the reverse is true, and this knowledge changes everything. He asks a second question: 'When will light strike my eyes?' and receives an answer from offstage – soon or never. He asks a third question: 'Does Pamina live?' and learns that she does. Rejoicing in this news, he plays his flute, which draws birds and animals to him in a wonderful miniature Orpheus drama. Just as Tamino begins to lose hope that the flute will draw Pamina to him, Papageno's panpipe replies from off stage. Tamino exits towards the sound.

Papageno and Pamina enter, looking for Tamino. When they are discovered, Papageno plays his magic bells; an enchanted Monostatos and his slaves forget their purpose and begin to dance and sing. Pamina and Papageno sing a short paean to the bells. To the tune of a march, Sarastro enters with his procession. Pamina kneels to explain why she fled from Monostatos, but Sarastro already understands. As Tamino and Pamina see each other for the first time, each immediately recognizes the other as the partner of a future life with the words, 'It is he/she!' They meet and embrace. Sarastro rewards Monostatos with seventy-seven lashes on the soles of his feet. Tamino and Papageno are acknowledged as initiates and veiled, while the priests conclude the act with a closing chorus to virtue and justice.

Act 2 begins with a solemn scene, set in a palm grove and described in detail in the libretto. The trees are made of silver with leaves of gold. There are eighteen seats covered with leaves, on each of which sits a pyramid and a horn. Sarastro and his priests, each holding a palm frond, enter to a march for wind instruments (No. 9). They have gathered in the Temple of Wisdom to determine whether Tamino, who is waiting at the north gate, may be admitted to the trials. The entire proceeding is shrouded in ritual and mystery. The priests discuss the worthiness of the initiate, and signal their agreement on each of three occasions with their horns (this is the famous threefold chord). At the conclusion, the priests join Sarastro in his aria (No. 10, 'O Isis und Osiris').

Tamino and Papageno are led in for the first trial by the Speaker and another priest, who remove the veils from their charges and leave them alone. The two initiates are immersed in almost total darkness and have difficulty seeing each other or their surroundings until their guides return with torches. When questioned, Tamino responds that he seeks friendship and love within the temple and will undergo every trial in the hope of achieving wisdom and winning Pamina. Papageno, on the other hand, is not a fighting man and does not seek wisdom; the only thing he might like is a pretty little wife. The two priests sing a short duet warning against the wiles of women (No. 11, 'Bewahret euch vor Weibertücken') in preparation for the trial of silence. When they exit, the two initiates are left in darkness. Papageno begins to chatter and no sooner does Tamino remind him to be quiet than the Three Ladies appear to challenge their vow of silence (No. 12, 'Wie? Wie? Wie?'). The ensemble is ended by the priests who intervene from offstage with the help of thunder and lightning. As the Three Ladies disappear through a trapdoor, Papageno collapses in fear. The threefold chord resounds; the Speaker and the priest enter with torches. Tamino has passed the first trial; Papageno has not. Both initiates are veiled and led offstage.

Pamina is discovered asleep in a pleasant garden. Monostatos enters and sings a brilliant, light-footed aria (No. 13, 'Alles fühlt der Liebe Freuden') in which he resolves to kiss the sleeping princess. But before the Moor can fulfil his desire, the Queen rises from a trapdoor to prevent him. The Queen has come to get the sevenfold sun cross. Her husband gave it to Sarastro when he died, she explains, and commended both mother and daughter to his guardianship. The Queen believes the cross (and its power) should rightfully be hers and charges her daughter to murder Sarastro with a dagger she provides and retrieve it. In her aria (No. 14, 'Der Hölle Rache kocht in meinem Herzen'), the Queen declares the hateful rage in her heart with a glorious pyrotechnical display. Left with the dagger in her hand, Pamina exclaims that she cannot commit murder. Monostatos, having overheard everything, seizes the dagger and threatens Pamina, but, when Sarastro appears, resolves to try his luck with the Queen. In his aria (No. 15, 'In diesen heil'gen Hallen') Sarastro explains that revenge is not known in these sacred halls. Once Tamino has passed the trials and may be joined with Pamina, the Queen will be forced to return to her castle.

Tamino and Papageno are led into a great hall, where Papageno meets an old woman (really Papagena) who tells him that her boyfriend is named Papageno. The Three Boys descend in a flying machine (which, in the original production, was made to look like a hot-air balloon, modelled on Jean Pierre Blanchard's successful balloon flight in Vienna of July 1791) with a beautifully laid table. They explain in a little trio (No. 16, 'Seid uns zum zweitenmal willkommen') that they have been sent by Sarastro to return the magic flute and bells. While Papageno partakes of the fine food, Tamino plays his flute. Pamina appears, but Tamino, still bound by his vow of silence, cannot speak to her. Confused by what appears to be rejection, she sings a hauntingly beautiful aria of despair (No. 17, 'Ach, ich fühl's'). After she leaves, the threefold chord is heard, signalling the next stage of the trials.

The following scene takes place in the vault of pyramids. The Speaker and several priests sing a chorus celebrating Tamino's initiation (No. 18, 'O Isis und Osiris, welche Wonne!'). Tamino is brought before the assembly and Sarastro commends him on his success thus far. Pamina is brought in wearing the veil of the initiates, which Sarastro loosens for her. She joins Sarastro and Tamino in the trio (No. 19, 'Soll ich dich, Teurer, nicht mehr sehn?') and the lovers bid each other farewell. All exit. Papageno is heard calling for Tamino from offstage. In a parody of Tamino's recognition scene, Papageno enters and approaches the door through which Tamino has just passed, but a voice within calls out 'Back!' Papageno retreats to the door through which he has just entered, but the same thing happens. The Speaker enters to tell Papageno that he will never be initiated. Papageno, completely unconcerned, says that all he wants from life is a glass of wine, which appears magically from below. Papageno plays his magic bells and sings how he would like to have a wife (No. 20, 'Ein Mädchen oder Weibchen'). The old woman appears and magically turns into the young Papagena. As Papageno moves to embrace her, the Speaker appears and Papageno descends through a trapdoor that suddenly opens at his feet.

The finale opens (No. 21, 'Bald prangt, den Morgen zu verkünden') in a garden. The Three Boys have come to watch over Pamina, who is in a state of despair. Pamina enters, looking half-mad and carrying the dagger her mother gave her. Believing she has said her last farewell to Tamino, she has lost all hope and plans to kill herself. Her soliloquy is the most chromatic and darkest moment of the opera and at the end of it she raises the dagger to stab herself. The Three Boys intervene. They assure her that Tamino loves her, and in so doing they give her hope. A recognition scene in its own right, this scene is the crucial counterpart to Tamino's colloquy with the priest in the Act I finale. Both Tamino and Pamina are now ready to face the final trials.

The libretto calls for the stage to be transformed into a rocky landscape crowned by two high mountains. In one of these the rush of a waterfall may be heard; the other is a volcano. Through grills in the mountains both water and fire may be seen. Two men in black armour with fire-burning helmets read Tamino the inscription that appears on a pyramid suspended high above the two mountains: 'One who travels this path full of burdens, will be purified by Fire, Water, Air, and Earth' (this is set by Mozart as a chorale, using the melody of the Lutheran hymn 'Ach Gott, vom Himmel sieh' darein'). As Tamino prepares for the final trials, Pamina appears and they once again embrace as lovers. She takes him by the hand and tells him that the flute, which was carved by her father in a magical hour, will protect them. As they enter first the mountain of fire and then of water, Tamino plays his flute while drums sound softly. When they emerge safely for the second time a door opens through which a brilliantly lit temple may be seen. After a moment of solemn silence, the chorus (offstage) rejoices in triumph.

Back in the garden, Papageno plays a little on his panpipe and calls for Papagena. Giving in to despair, he prepares to hang himself. As they did with Pamina, the Three Boys now intervene, descending in their flying machine. They remind him to play his bells and, as he does so, help Papagena out of the flying machine. When Papageno turns around, Papagena and he recognize each other at once with their well-loved 'Pa-pa-pa' duet. Papageno may not join the initiates, but he is to live in happiness and prosperity under their protection.

In the final scene, Monostatos, the Queen and the Three Ladies enter carrying black torches. (The Queen has promised Pamina in marriage to the Moor in exchange for his help.) As they approach the temple, thunder and lightning strike. 'All at once the whole stage is transformed into a sun.' Sarastro is revealed on high with Tamino and Pamina, dressed in priestly garb and attended by the priests and the Three Boys. As the music moves triumphantly from dark C minor to a bright E flat major (complete with trumpets and drums), the Queen and her entourage sink into the ground. Sarastro moralizes: 'The rays of the sun vanquish the night,' and the chorus sings a final verse in praise of the initiates. Virtue, beauty and wisdom have triumphed.

3. Understanding *Die Zauberflöte*

The opera celebrates themes of virtue and knowledge, themes that have a special resonance in an age that named itself the 'Enlightenment'. With *Die Zauberflöte*, Schikaneder and Mozart conceived a theatre piece in which these themes would depend almost entirely for their realization on an enlightenment metaphor (in which light is knowledge). Nearly every scene, speech and stage direction turns on the symbolic opposition of dark and light. While the Queen of the Night is characterized by the darkness over which she rules, Sarastro presides in the domain of wisdom and light. The central conflict of the opera is the confrontation of universals their opposition represents. As the libretto repeatedly suggests, only the dawning of light can banish the night. When Sarastro describes Tamino's entrance to the trials as his seeking 'to tear off the veil of night to see into the sanctuary of great light', when the priests explain in their chorus (No. 18) that 'The dark night is banished by the brightness of the sun', and when the Three Boys announce at the beginning of the Act 2 finale 'Soon, to herald the morning, the sun will shine on its golden path', the dawn to which they are all referring is both literal and figurative.

The Queen's association with the night sky (her throne is studded with stars) also associates her with the darkness of human thoughts and deeds. Tamino's confusion and distress are repeatedly represented in terms of darkness: 'O endless darkness' he exclaims when he first learns that Pamina has been kidnapped; 'O endless night!' at the crux of his dialogue with the priest. In her aria (No. 17) 'Ach, ich fühl's', Pamina turns to a dark G minor – the key of her mother's plea to Tamino ('Zum Leiden' in No. 4) – as she imagines Tamino has rejected her and longs for death. Even Papageno in his suicide scene says, 'Good night, you black world.' In the trials, the priests lead their charges to dark cavernous spaces where they are left alone to contemplate their worthiness. The metaphoric darkness of the initiates is made explicit by the use of veils, which impose darkness on their wearers. Even after the veils are removed in preparation for the first trial, Tamino exclaims 'A fearful night!' When the priests return bearing torches to explain the first trial, the light they shed is both symbolic and real. Later Pamina will be veiled, before the trio (No. 19), suggesting that she too undergoes trials. She is made to withstand Monostatos's repeated advances, to suffer her mother's threats, to believe that she has lost Tamino, and finally to face her own despair in her aria (No. 17) and subsequent suicide scene. As she and Tamino prepare to enter the trials of fire and water, they describe the dangers therein as 'death's dark night'.

The opposition of light and dark is dramatized vividly in the music. While the Queen is an extraordinarily high soprano, who sings quick and elaborate vocalises with fire and passion, Sarastro is a very low bass, who sings slow-moving, hymn-like tunes that descend to emphasize important thoughts and words. His chorus of priests sing stately, simple melodies in chorale style. This priestly music is indebted to the music Mozart wrote for the chorus of priests in *Thamos* a decade earlier and embodies, as did Mozart's other Masonic music, the highest ideals of brotherhood and harmony. Suggestive of the opposed worlds over which these two rulers govern, minor keys with their attendant chromaticism tend to be associated with the Queen and the darkness she represents, while major keys tend to be associated with Sarastro, his priests and the contentment both the initiated and ordinary men like Papageno share in his enlightened realm. The Queen characterizes her own situation in minor repeatedly: with G minor in the first tempo of her Act 1 aria (No. 4), with D minor in her Act 2 aria (No. 14), and in C minor in the Act 2 finale. The despair Tamino and Pamina face as they encounter various difficulties in Sarastro's realm is represented in minor and in passages of wandering tonality, while the triumphs they experience on their way to and including the trials are celebrated exclusively in major keys. In the Act 2 finale, the juxtaposition of minor and major dramatizes the conflict between darkness and enlightenment: when the Three Boys intervene to snatch the dagger from Pamina they end her wandering in minor keys by restoring E flat major; while the two armoured men read the gates' inscription to Tamino in C minor, contemplating the dangers contained therein, the Adagio march that accompanies the trials of fire and water is in the parallel major, C major, as is the brief celebratory chorus that immediately follows; at the very end of the opera, the Queen and her companions approach the temple in C minor, but are vanquished by the dazzling E flat major that accompanies the illumination of the stage. The dramatization of the ascendance of light here is perhaps the most explicit musical realization of the enlightenment metaphor ever attempted in opera.

The central vehicle for this enlightenment – the move from darkness to light – is the recognition scene. Recognition – *anagnôrisis* in Aristotle's *Poetics* – brings about a shift from ignorance to knowledge and involves the character (and the audience) in a powerful reversal of former understanding. *Die Zauberflöte* is based on a quest plot, and centres on a recognition scene in which Tamino's rescue mission is transformed into a quest for knowledge of the highest kind. This recognition scene, Tamino's long colloquy with the priest in the Act 1 finale, challenges Tamino's understanding of everything – the Queen's distress, Pamina's plight, Sarastro's true nature. The priest shows him that his world-view is false, but instead of answering his questions, leaves him in confusion. Realizing now for the first time the truth of his situation and the new direction of his quest, Tamino cries 'O endless night! When will you end? / When will light strike my eyes?' Tamino's recognition brings about a reversal; he has discovered a new purpose in his quest for enlightenment and in so doing proves himself worthy of becoming an initiate. Tamino's scene sets the pattern for similar scenes for Pamina and Papageno, in which they too will be advised by the Three Boys, face grave doubts overcome by dialogue, and arrive at a state of new awareness. The trials of fire and water, the final stage of knowledge in Sarastro's temple and the culmination of Tamino's and Pamina's quest for enlightenment and each other, cannot come until both have individually faced the darkness and become seekers of enlightenment. Papageno, of course, chooses to remain unenlightened, a self-described 'Naturmensch'. But he, unlike the Queen, is not opposed to the enlightenment of others. He is grateful in the end to find his Papagena and happiness in Sarastro's enlightened realm.

The most powerful and astonishing dramatization of Enlightenment themes is reserved for the final scene of the opera where the powers of darkness are vanquished for the last time. This final stage of the opera's representation of knowledge brings the fulfilment the preceding recognition scenes have implied. As the Queen and her entourage descend (through a trapdoor) to endless night, the dark stage is suddenly overwhelmed with light. In the words of the original libretto, 'the entire stage is transformed into a sun'. The striking contrast of musical styles, of diatonic and chromatic lines, in conjunction with this final transformation of C minor into E flat major presents the triumph of enlightenment. Schikaneder and Mozart dramatize the experience of enlightenment for the whole stage and the world it represents. Tamino and Pamina, destined for each other, having completed the trials, finally achieve enlightenment in terms of the opera's central metaphor when we see them take their places in Sarastro's temple, dressed in priestly garb, and illuminated by a great sun.

Without doubt, the opera's representation of enlightenment was intended as an all-inclusive one. Papageno, a lowly bird-catcher, is given a chance to join the band of priests and, even though he fails, is given both Papagena and a place in this world of benevolent rule. In the dialogue in Act 2 in which Sarastro and the priests consider whether or not to admit Tamino to the trials, the Speaker warns of the dangers of the trials (in which the initiate may lose his life) and reminds Sarastro that Tamino is a prince. 'More than that', Sarastro replies, 'he is a man!' The message at the end of the Act 1 finale is meant for all: 'When virtue and justice strew the path with glory, then is earth a heavenly realm and mortals are like Gods.' Only the Queen cannot coexist within this realm, not because she is excluded by Sarastro, but because her one object is to replace enlightenment with tyranny. The status of this representation of enlightenment as all-inclusive, however, has at times been called into question, primarily for three reasons: first, the misogynist comments of the priests and their deliberate exclusion of the Queen from their temple; second, the apparent racial bias in Monostatos's role as both black man and villain; and third, and most importantly, the seemingly unenlightened actions of Sarastro, including his abduction of Pamina, his placing her even temporarily under the power of Monostatos, and the punishment he metes out of seventy-seven lashes. Although these criticisms are frequently based on partial or misinformed readings of the libretto, they raise potential objections to the opera's Enlightenment message that require consideration.

On the matter of the libretto's treatment of women, it is true that the outrageously misogynist comments of the priests are highly prejudicial, but it is also true that no greater refutation of these claims could be offered than the character of Pamina. What is more, while the Masons, known for their misogynist views, did not admit women, Sarastro and his priests invite Pamina to undergo the trials of initiation and to rule at the head of their temple with Tamino. The second matter, the charge of racial bias in the role of Monostatos, is more difficult to answer, for one has to ask why the role of villain in an opera that repeatedly contrasts light and dark imagery is given to a Moor and why Mozart and Schikaneder allow Sarastro to say to him, 'Your soul is as black as your face.' But it is important to remember that Monostatos's slaves (also dark skinned), who have suffered at his hand, sympathize with Pamina and pray for her escape. The compassion and understanding of his slaves make it clear that the opera is concerned with Monostatos's actions and not with the colour of his and their skin. Monostatos is punished not because he is a Moor, but because he attempted to rape Pamina. To the further objection that it is unenlightened for Sarastro to have any slaves in his palace at all, even though they answer to Monostatos, it may only be said that slaves were not an uncommon presence in plays and operas that attempted to represent exotic cultures, and also that eighteenth-century thinkers, however enlightened, did not view slavery in the same way we do today. The signers of the 'Declaration of Independence', many of them Freemasons, proclaimed 'all men' equal, but did not find their phrase incompatible with slavery.

In regard to Sarastro's status as an enlightened and benevolent ruler it is important to remember that eighteenth- and twenty-first-century definitions of enlightenment may not agree and that it may not always be possible to wring perfect logic out of a magical libretto. Certain of Sarastro's actions, his placing Pamina in Monostatos's care for example, are never explained. He could not have intended her any harm for, as he explicitly says in Act 2, he took Pamina because she was destined for Tamino. He may have been deceived as to Monostatos's worthiness, but it is equally likely that Monostatos's attentions were meant as a trial for Pamina. In either case, the punishment Sarastro metes out of seventy-seven lashes on the soles of the feet does not seem excessive for attempted rape. Although it is true that, with the benefit of hindsight, the diverse movements and ideologies of this period no longer share the rubric 'Enlightenment' in unproblematic fashion, it should be remembered that Vienna's ruler, Joseph II, though committed to modern ideas in science and government, ruled as an enlightened despot, making many unpopular decisions and implementing them by royal decree. Sarastro's adherence to the spirit of enlightened thinking is at least as defensible as Joseph's: he does not punish Monostatos a second time for the same crime and he does not take revenge on either Monostatos or the Queen, proving, as he claims, that 'In these hallowed halls, man does not know vengeance'.

Immediately successful in Vienna, *Die Zauberflöte* was soon performed in Prague (1792), Leipzig, Munich and Dresden (1793), Berlin (1794) and elsewhere in Germany. It reached St Petersburg in 1797, PARIS in 1801 and LONDON in 1811, and has since become part of the repertory of every major opera house. By 1800 Schikaneder had given over 200 performances of it in his theatre and produced a sequel, *Das Labyrinth* (1798), with music by Peter Winter. Goethe, too, envisioned a sequel, but never completed it. How the opera's Enlightenment allegory was received by early audiences is impossible to determine, but its political resonance was assumed by many. Masonic interpretations of the work arose as early as 1794; a pamphlet published in this year reads the opera as an allegory of the FRENCH REVOLUTION in which the Queen represents the philosophy of the Jacobins, Pamina the Republic and Tamino the best hope for France. More recent criticism offers an enormous diversity of interpretation, from the proliferation of Masonic readings that run the risk of reducing the opera to its symbolism, to the recurrent tendency in commentaries that centre on Mozart's music – almost universally agreed to be sublime – to dismiss the libretto altogether. Edward Dent famously described the libretto as 'one of the most absurd specimens of that form of literature in which absurdity is regarded as a matter of course', and Joseph Kerman refers to it as 'Schikaneder's doggerel'. But the opera's mysticism and magical happenings may not be dismissed as Schikaneder's – they were Mozart's too.

In his letters, Mozart attests to the fact that he took the opera's libretto seriously and saw something profound in it. He writes to Constanze (at the spa in Baden): 'But what always gives me most pleasure is the *silent approval!* You can see how this opera is becoming more and more esteemed' (7 Oct. 1791). He reports with pleasure that SALIERI and Madame CAVALIERI (creator of the role of Constanze in *Die Entführung*), whom he has taken to see a performance, both praised the work:

> You cannot believe how polite they both were, – how much they liked not only my music, but the libretto and everything. They both said that it was an *operone* [a grand opera], worthy to be performed for the grandest festival and before the greatest monarch, and that they would often go to see it, as they had never seen a more beautiful or delightful show. He [Salieri] listened and watched most attentively and from the overture to the last chorus there was not a single number that did not call forth from him a bravo! or bello!
>
> (14 Oct. 1791)

Aware that his audience was accustomed to seeing high drama at the court theatres and light entertainment at the Volkstheater, Mozart emphasizes that Salieri and Caterina Cavalieri liked not only the music, 'but the libretto and everything', and that they thought it good enough to be performed at the 'grandest festival and before the greatest monarch'.

Of course the chance that *Die Zauberflöte*'s Enlightenment allegory would prove entertaining but miss its mark was considerable. Mozart encountered this reaction too, at another performance:

> [the name has been crossed out] had a box this evening [and] applauded *everything* most heartily. But he, the know-all, showed himself to be such a thorough *Bavarian* that I could not remain or I should have had to call him an ass. Unfortunately I was there just when the second act began, that is, at the solemn scene. He laughed at everything. At first, I was patient enough to draw his attention to a few passages. But he laughed at everything. Well, I could stand it no longer. I called him Papageno and cleared out. But I don't think the idiot understood my remark. (8–9 Oct. 1791)

Like his opera, Mozart's narrative in the letter is didactic. What underlies his account is the assumption that audience members should not be 'know-alls', that they should have come to the theatre to learn, to be enlightened. The gentleman with the box enjoys the opera, but does not seem to understand it. Mozart, like one of the priests of Sarastro's Order, attempts to lead his charge, 'to draw his attention to a few passages', but the gentleman repeatedly misses the point of the drama. Genuinely frustrated, Mozart calls his unknowing, unwilling initiate 'Papageno'. It is difficult to imagine that a more compelling argument could be made on behalf of the libretto and its mysteries. With his own example, Mozart urges us one and all to take the libretto – complete with its ritualistic dialogue, magical effects, and fairy-tale plot – seriously and to pay attention during the solemn scene. JESSICA WALDOFF

P. Branscombe, *W. A. Mozart: 'Die Zauberflöte'* (Cambridge, 1991)
D. J. Buch, 'Mozart and the Theater auf der Wieden: New Attributions and Perspectives', *Cambridge Opera Journal* 9 (1997), 195–232
D. Heartz, *Mozart's Operas*, ed. T. Bauman (Berkeley, 1990)
N. John, ed., *The Magic Flute* (London, 1980) (English National Opera Guides)
D. Koenigsberger, 'A New Metaphor for Mozart's *The Magic Flute*', *European Studies Review* 5 (1975), 229–75
J. Waldoff, 'The Music of Recognition: Operatic Enlightenment in "The Magic Flute"', *Music & Letters* 75 (1994), 214–35

Zichy, Karl, Count (1753–1826). A Hungarian-Transylvanian Court Councillor married to Countess Anna Maria Antonia Khevenhüller-Metsch (1759–1809), one of Mozart's Viennese pupils, Zichy hosted at least two private concerts at which Mozart performed. The first (20 Mar. 1784) came in the middle of Mozart's subscription series at the Trattnerhof; the next (21 Feb. 1785) coincided with LEOPOLD MOZART's visit to VIENNA. On another occasion (20 July 1782) Zichy drove Mozart to the Viennese court's summer residence, Laxenburg Palace, so that Mozart could meet Prince Wenzel Kaunitz-Rietberg. Zichy and Kaunitz-Rietberg, along with Countess THUN and BARON VAN SWIETEN were 'very much displeased with the Emperor, because he does not value men of talent more, and allows them to leave his dominions', Mozart explained to his father (17 Aug. 1782). SIMON P. KEEFE

Zinzendorf, Count Karl Zinzendorf und Pottendorf (b. Dresden, 5 Jan. 1739, d. Vienna, 5 Jan. 1813). Diarist who for half a century chronicled aristocratic life in VIENNA and elsewhere; nephew of Count Nikolaus Ludwig von Zinzendorf (1700–60), Lutheran Pietist and founder of the Renewed Moravian Church. Karl moved to Vienna in 1761 to make his career in the financial branch of the government. From 1764 to 1770 he was posted to various cities in Europe and in 1776 he was appointed governor of Trieste. In 1781 JOSEPH II appointed him President of the Court Audit Office, a position he held until 1792 when he was made Councillor of State. Other promotions followed until his retirement in 1809.

Zinzendorf kept a diary (in seventy-six volumes) from the age of eight until his death; the volumes usually called the *Tagebücher* comprise numbers VI–LVII and begin with Zinzendorf's move to Vienna. Factual and reliable, the diary is an invaluable source of information on all manner of subjects, but is somewhat disappointing for the music historian. Although Zinzendorf was a keen and knowledgeable devotee of both spoken and sung theatre, his interest did not extend to music, particularly instrumental music. He played no instrument and was conscious of the limits of his judgement on purely musical matters – the opinions he cites are those of his friends (he also liked to note VAN SWIETEN's pronouncements). Nor did he seek out the great musical events of the day, unless they were society events. Thus it was with van Swieten's performances of HANDEL as arranged by Mozart in 1788 and 1789: it was only when Count Johann ESTERHÁZY hosted them in his palace (and only at their repeat performances) that Zinzendorf heard *Acis and Galatea* and *Messiah*. While his well-known inattentiveness at the premiere of LE NOZZE DI FIGARO – 'the opera bored me' – can be excused by the distraction of his passion for the woman in his box, it is unfortunately symptomatic. He declined to attend the nobility's production of IDOMENEO in 1786 and the one time he reports hearing Mozart perform, on 10 February 1788 at the Venetian ambassador's, he says nothing at all about the man, his playing or his music; and he makes no mention of Mozart's death, although he records other deaths that struck him as historically significant. His very lack of interest in Mozart, however, is revealing of Mozart's standing in Vienna. If at a performance of *Le nozze di Figaro* on 2 January 1799 he wrote 'beautiful music by Mozart', it meant that Mozart's genius had by then been recognized. DOROTHEA LINK

D. Link, ' "Le Soir au théâtre": From the Diary of Count Karl Zinzendorf, 1783–92', in *The National Court Theatre in Mozart's Vienna: Sources and Documents, 1783–1792* (Oxford, 1998), 191–398

'Vienna's Private Theatrical and Musical Life, 1783–92, as Reported by Count Karl Zinzendorf', *Journal of the Royal Musical Association* 122 (1997), 205–47

H. Wagner, ed. and trans., *Wien von Maria Theresia bis zur Fransozenzeit. Aus den Tabegüchern des Grafen Karl von Zinzendorf* (Vienna, 1972)

Appendix 1
Worklist

This worklist primarily reports on Mozart's completed works, with additional information on works traditionally attributed to him but lacking authentic sources, and works attributed to him that are by other composers. Works are listed by the numbers assigned them in Ludwig Ritter von Köchel's *Chronologisch-thematisches Verzeichnis sämtlicher Tonwerke Wolfgang Amadé Mozarts* (Leipzig, 1862). Although many numbers were revised in subsequent editions by Alfred Einstein (1937, 3rd edition) and Franz Giegling, Alexander Weinmann and Gerd Sievers (1964, 6th edition), Mozart's works continue to be known chiefly by Köchel's original numbers, regardless of their revised order in the chronology. We have therefore decided to retain the original numbers except where a work is not listed in the 1862 catalogue; in those cases we have generally taken the number from the sixth edition. Regardless, Köchel is well cross-referenced and any number will eventually lead a user to the full entry for a work.

The dating of Mozart's works is based on a variety of sources. In many instances, his autographs are both signed and dated or there is unequivocal evidence in the family letters or contemporaneous documents; in those cases we have given a place and date without qualification. The same is true of works listed in Mozart's own thematic catalogue, which he began in February 1784 and continued for the rest of his life (*Verzeichnüss aller meiner Werke vom Monath Febrario 1784 bis Monath 1*; facsimile edition, ed. A. Rosenthal and A. Tyson, London, 1991). Another important source is Leopold Mozart's 1768 *Verzeichniss alles desjenigen was dieser 12jähriger Knab seit seinem 7ten Jahre componiert, und in originali kann aufgezeiget werden*; although this source does not generally give precise dates, it nevertheless provides a *terminus post quem non* for many of Mozart's works and additionally documents many that are now lost. For undated works, we have relied on our own research on the manuscripts, letters and contemporaneous documents, as well as the handwriting analysis of Wolfgang Plath and the watermark studies of Alan Tyson, to form an independent conclusion; these dates are given in square brackets.

Although there are countless modern editions of Mozart, we have limited ourselves to references to the standard modern edition published by the *Neue Mozart-Ausgabe* (NMA, Kassel, 1955–). These are generally given in the form Werkgruppe/Abteilung/Band although in some instances the reference is to Werkgruppe/Band only. Nevertheless, readers may wish to consult other editions which sometimes present a different view of Mozart's texts. Finally, we have included additional commentary on publication during Mozart's lifetime, contemporaneous performances, dedications, the survival of sketches and other important matters in the Remarks column.

Problems of authenticity and chronology are never as straightforward as they look; for full details, readers should consult the Köchel catalogue, the forewords and critical reports to the NMA and the extensive specialized literature. Nevertheless, we believe this list substantially represents a faithful account of Mozart's works and their places and dates of composition. For information concerning the numerous unidentified sketches and fragmentary compositions left by Mozart, readers could do no better than to consult the editions by Ulrich Konrad published as part of the *Neue Mozart-Ausgabe* (X:30/3, 1998 for the sketches and X: 30/4, 2002, for the fragments; a volume of *Studien, Entwürfe, Varia* is scheduled for after 2006).

MASSES, MASS MOVEMENTS, REQUIEM

K	Title	Key	Scoring	Place, date	NMA	Remarks
33	Kyrie	F	SATB, str, bc	Paris, 12 June 1766	I:1/1	
139	Missa solemnis	c	S, A, T, B, SATB, 2 ob, 4 tpt, timp, str, bc	Vienna, autumn 1768	I:1/1	'Waisenhausmesse', perf. orphanage in Rennweg, Vienna, 7 Dec. 1768; possibly completed by 12 Nov.
49	Missa brevis	G	S, A, T, B, SATB, str, bc	Vienna, Oct.–Nov. 1768	I:1/1	sketch 1768a
65	Missa brevis	d	S, A, T, B, SATB, str, bc	Salzburg, 14 Jan. 1769	I:1/1	perf. Salzburg, Universitätskirche, 5 Feb. 1769; sketches survive
66	Missa	C	S, A, T, B, SATB, 2 ob/fl, 2 hn, 2 tpt, timp, str, bc	Salzburg, Oct. 1769	I:1/1	'Dominicus' mass, perf. Salzburg, St Peter, 15 Oct. 1769; hn parts c.1775–6; sketches survive
89	Kyrie	G	SSSSS	[Salzburg, 1772]	I:1/1	
90	Kyrie	d	SATB, bc	[Salzburg, 1772]	I:1/1/vi	
167	Missa	C	SATB, 2 ob, 4 tpt, 2 vn, bc	Salzburg, June 1773	I:1/1/ii	'In honorem Ssmae Trinitatis'
192	Missa brevis	F	S, A, T, B, SATB, (2 tpt), 2 vn, bc	Salzburg, 24 June 1774	I:1/1/ii	tpt parts possibly added later
194	Missa brevis	D	S, A, T, B, SATB, 2 vn, bc	Salzburg, 8 Aug. 1774	I:1/1/ii	
220	Missa brevis	C	S, A, T, B, SATB, 2 tpt, timp, 2 vn, bc	[Salzburg, 1775–7]	I:1/1/ii	'Spatzenmesse'
262	Missa [longa]	C	S, A, T, B, SATB, 2 ob, 2 hn, (2 tpt), 2 vn, bc	[Salzburg, 1775–6]	I:1/1/ii2	tpt c.1777
257	Missa	C	S, A, T, B, SATB, 2 ob, 2 tpt, timp, 2 vn, bc	Salzburg, Nov. 1776	I:1/1/iii	'Credo'; sketches survive
258	Missa brevis	C	S, A, T, B, SATB, 2 ob, 2 tpt, timp, 2 vn, bc	Salzburg, Dec. 1775–6	I:1/1/iii	'Spaur', but possibly not mass composed for consecration of Count Friedrich Franz Joseph von Spaur, Feb. 1777

(cont.)

(cont.)

K	Title	Key	Scoring	Place, date	NMA	Remarks
259	Missa brevis	C	S, A, T, B, SATB, (2 ob), 2 tpt, timp, 2 vn, bc	Salzburg, Dec. 1776	I:1/1/iii	'Organ solo'; 2 ob possibly later c.1776–81
275	Missa brevis	B♭	S, A, T, B, SATB, 2 vn, bc	Salzburg, before 23 Sept. 1777/L	I:1/1/iv	perf. Salzburg, St Peter, 21 Dec. 1777
317	Missa	C	S, A, T, B, SATB, 2 ob, 2 hn, 2 tpt, timp, 2 vn, bc	Salzburg, 23 Mar. 1779	I:1/1/iv	'Coronation' (perf. Prague, Sept. 1791 at coronation of Leopold II)
337	Missa	C	S, A, T, B, SATB, 2 ob, 2 bn, 2 tpt, timp, 2 vn, bc	Salzburg, Mar. 1780	I:1/1/iv	
341	Kyrie	d	SATB, 2 fl, 2 ob, 2 cl, 2 bn, 4 hn, 2 tpt, timp, str, bc	[Vienna, late 1780s]	I:1/1/vi	lacks authentic sources; earlier thought to date Munich, 1780–1
427	Missa	c	2S, SATB, 2 basset hn, 2 bn, 2 tpt, timp, str, bc	Vienna and Salzburg, 1782–3	I:1/1/v	Credo incomplete, Agnus not composed; perf. (at least in part) Salzburg, St Peter, 26 Oct. 1783; see also *Davidde penitente*, K469; sketches survive
626	Requiem	d	S, A, T, B, SATB, 2 basset hn, 2 bn, 2 tpt, timp, str, bc	Vienna, late 1791	I:1/2/i–ii	unfinished at time of death; completed by F. X. Süssmayr and others

Spurious (selective list): K91, by G. Reutter (ii); K140, attributed to Mozart but almost certainly not by him, author unknown, *NMA* I:1/1; K115, by L. Mozart, pub. Neuhausen-Stuttgart, 1981, ed. R. Kubik; K116 + 90a + 417B + Anh18–19, Missa brevis, L. Mozart; K221, J. E. Eberlin

LITANIES, VESPERS, VESPER PSALMS

K	Title	Key	Scoring	Place, date	NMA	Remarks
109	Litaniae lauretanae BVM	B♭	S, A, T, B, SATB, 2 vn, bc	Salzburg, May 1771	I:2/i	
125	Litaniae de venerabili altaris sacramento	B♭	S, A, T, B, SATB, 2 ob/fl, 2 hn, 2 tpt, str, bc	Salzburg, Mar. 1772	I:2/i	
195	Litaniae lauretanae BVM	D	S, A, T, B, SATB, 2 ob, 2 hn, str, bc	Salzburg, May 1774	I:2/i	
193	Dixit Dominus, Magnificat	C	S, T, B, SATB, 2 tpt, timp, 2 vn, bc	Salzburg, July 1774	I:2/ii	
243	Litaniae de venerabili altaris sacramento	E♭	S, A, T, B, SATB, 2 ob/fl, 2 bn, 2 hn, str, bc	Salzburg, Mar. 1776	I:2/i	first perf. Salzburg, 31 Mar. 1776
321	Vesperae de Dominica	C	S, A, T, B, SATB, 2 tpt, timp, 2 vn, bc	Salzburg, 1779	I:2/ii	
339	Vesperae solennes de confessore	C	S, A, T, B, SATB, 2 tpt, timp, 2 vn, bc	Salzburg, 1780	I:2/ii	

SHORT SACRED WORKS

K	Title	Key	Scoring	Composition	NMA	Remarks
20	God is our Refuge	g	SATB	London, July 1765	III:9	motet
33c	Stabat mater		SATB	by late 1768	—	lost
41f	[Fugue à 4 voci]		SATB	by late 1768	—	lost
47	Veni Sancte Spiritus	C	S, A, T, B, SATB, 2 ob, 2 hn, 2 tpt, timp, str, bc	[Vienna, 1768]	I:3	traditionally considered identical to Veni in L. Mozart's list of W. A. Mozart's works, Vienna, 1768
47b	Offertory			Vienna, late 1768	—	lost; perf. Vienna, Waisenhauskirche, 7 Dec. 1768
117	Benedictus sit Deus	C	S, SATB, 2 fl, 2 hn, 2 tpt, timp, str, bc	[Salzburg, by mid-1772]	I:3	offertory
141	Te Deum	C	SATB, 4 tpt, timp, 2 vn, bc	[Salzburg, by c.1770]	I:3	orig. timp part lost
85	Miserere	a	ATB, bc	Bologna, July–Aug. 1770	I:3	
86	Quaerite primum	d	SATB	Bologna, 9 or 10 Oct. 1770	I:3	antiphon; exercise for Accademia Filarmonica, Bologna
108	Regina coeli	C	S, SATB, 2 ob/fl, 2 hn, 2 tpt, timp, str, bc	Salzburg, May 1771	I:3	
72	Inter natos mulierum	G	SATB, 2 vn, bc	[Salzburg], 1770s	I:3	offertory for feast of St John the Baptist, 24 June
127	Regina coeli	B♭	S, SATB, 2 ob/fl, 2 hn, str, bc	Salzburg, May 1772	I:3	
143	Ergo interest	G	S, str, bc	[Salzburg, late 1773]	I:3	motet

165	Exsultate, jubilate	F	S, 2 ob, 2 hn, str, bc	Milan, Jan. 1773	I:3	motet, for V. Rauzzini; perf. Milan, 17 Jan. 1773; rev. version with 2 fl in place of 2 ob, text changes, Salzburg, about 1780
222	Misericordias Domini	d	SATB, 2 vn, [va,] bc	Munich, early 1775	I:3	offertory
260	Venite populi	D	SSAATTBB, 2 vn ad lib, bc	Salzburg, 1776	I:3	offertory
277	Alma Dei creatoris	F	S, A, T, B, SATB, 2 vn, bc	[Salzburg, summer/autumn 1777]	I:3	offertory
273	Sancta Maria, mater Dei	F	SATB, str, bc	Salzburg, 9 Sept. 1777	I:3	gradual for feast of BVM, 12 Sept.; possibly composed for St Peter, Salzburg
A1	Miserere		SATB, orch	Paris, Mar.–Apr. 1778	—	lost; eight movts for work by I. Holzbauer
146	Kommet her, ihr frechen Sünder	B♭	S, str, bc	[Salzburg, 1770s]	I:4/4	aria
276	Regina coeli	C	S, A, T, B, SATB, 2 ob, 2 tpt, timp, 2 vn, b, bc	Salzburg, late 1770s	I:3	lacks authentic sources
343	O Gottes Lamm; Als aus Aegypten	F; C	S, bc	[Vienna or Prague, early 1787–8]	III:8	German sacred songs
618	Ave verum corpus	D	SATB, str, bc	Baden, 17 June 1791	I:3	motet

Traditionally thought to be by Mozart but lacking authentic sources: K34, Scande coeli limina, offertory, C, [? Kloster Seeon, Bavaria, early 1767], NMA, I:3; K276, Regina Coeli, C, [Salzburg, 1770s], NMA I:3

Spurious: K44, *Musica super cantum gregorianum*, by J. Stadlmayr; K142 and K197, Tantum ergo, by J. Zach, NMA I:3; K177, Offertory, by L. Mozart; K326, Hymn, by E. Eberlin; Anh A2, Lacrimosa, by E. Eberlin; Anh A17, Stabat mater, by P. Ligniville

CHURCH SONATAS

K	Key	Scoring	Place, date	NMA
67	E♭	2 vn, bc	[Salzburg, 1771–2]	VI:16
68	B♭	2 vn, bc	[Salzburg, 1771–2]	VI:16
69	D	2 vn, bc	[Salzburg, 1771–2]	VI:16
144	D	2 vn, bc	[Salzburg, early 1774]	VI:16
145	F	2 vn, bc	[Salzburg, early 1774]	VI:16
212	B♭	2 vn, bc	Salzburg, July 1775	VI:16
241	G	2 vn, bc	Salzburg, Jan. 1776	VI:16
224	F	2 vn, bc	[Salzburg, 1779–80]	VI:16
225	A	2 vn, bc	[Salzburg, 1779–80]	VI:16
244	F	2 vn, bc [org solo]	Salzburg, Apr. 1776	VI:16
245	D	2 vn, bc [org solo]	Salzburg, Apr. 1776	VI:16
263	C	2 tpt, 2 vn, bc [org solo]	[Salzburg, late 1776]	VI:16
274	G	2 vn, bc	Salzburg, 1777	VI:16
278	C	2 ob, 2 tpt, timp, 2 vn, bc	[Salzburg, Mar.–Apr. 1777]	VI:16
329	C	2 ob, 2 hn, 2 tpt, timp, 2 vn, bc [org solo]	[Salzburg, early 1779]	VI:16
328	C	2 vn, bc [org solo]	[Salzburg, 1777–9]	VI:16
336	C	2 vn, bc [org solo]	Salzburg, March 1780	VI:16

Spurious: K124A, by L. Mozart

ORATORIOS, SACRED DRAMAS, CANTATAS

K	Title (libretto)	Scoring	Composition	NMA	Remarks
35	Die Schuldigkeit des ersten und Fürnehmsten Gebots (I. A. Weiser)	3 S, 2 T, 2 ob/fl, 2 bn, 2 hn, trbn, str	Salzburg, 1766–7	I:4/i	oratorio, perf. Salzburg, 12 Mar. 1767; part 2 by J. M. Haydn, part 3 by A. C. Adlgasser
42	Grabmusik (?J. A. Wimmer, ?J. A. Schachtner)	S, B, SATB, 2 ob, 2 hn, str	Salzburg, 1767	I:4/iv	cantata; final recit and chorus c.1774–5
118	La Betulia liberata (P. Metastasio)	4 S, T, B, SATB, 2 ob/fl, 2 bn, 4 hn, 2 tpt, str	Italy and Salzburg, Mar.–July 1771	I:4/ii	oratorio, commissioned for Padua, apparently unperformed
469	Davidde penitente (?L. Da Ponte)	2 S, T, SATB, 2 fl, 2 ob, 2 cl, 2 bn, 2 hn, 3 trbn, timp, str	Vienna, Mar. 1785	I:4/iii	oratorio, arr. from Mass K427 with additional arias (nos. 6 and 11); perf. Vienna, Burgtheater, 13 Mar.
471	Die Maurerfreude (F. Petran)	T, TTB, 2 ob, cl, 2 hn, str	Vienna, 20 Apr. 1785	I:4/iv	cantata, perf. Vienna, lodge 'Zur gekrönten Hoffnung', 24 Apr. 1785; pub. Vienna, 1785
619	Die ihr des unermesslichen Weltalls Schöpfer ehrt (F. H. Ziegenhagen)	S, pf	Vienna, July 1791	I:4/iv	cantata
623	Laut verkünde unsre Freude (E. Schikaneder)	TT, B, fl, 2 ob, 2 hn, str	Vienna, 15 Nov. 1791	I:4/iv	cantata, perf. Vienna, lodge 'Zur neugekrönten Hoffnung', 17 Nov. 1791

Incomplete: K429, Dir, Seele des Weltalls (L.L. Haschka), T, TTB, fl, 2 ob, cl, 2 hn, bn, str, Vienna, 1785–6, NMA, I:4/iv, cantata partly completed by M. Stadler

Spurious: K623a, *Lasst uns mit geschlungnen Händen*, appended to 1st edn of K623 (Vienna, 1792)

OPERAS, MUSICAL PLAYS, DRAMATIC CANTATAS

K	Title (libretto)	Scoring	First performance	NMA	Remarks
38	Apollo et Hyacinthus (R. Widl)	2 S, 2 A, T, B, 2 ob, 2 hn, str	Salzburg, Benedictine University, 13 May 1767	II:5/i	Latin intermedio, perf. with Widl's Latin play, *Clementia Croesi*
51	La finta semplice (C. Goldoni, rev. M. Coltellini)	3 S, 2 T, 2 B, 2 fl, 2 ob/cor ang, 2 bn, 2 hn, str	unknown	II:5/ii	opera buffa, composed Vienna, mid-1768
50	Bastien und Bastienne (F. W. Weiskern, J. Müller and J. A. Schachtner, after M.-J.-B. Favart and H. de Guerville, *Les Amours de Bastien et Bastienne*)	S, T, B, 2 ob/fl, 2 hn, str	[?Vienna, F. A. Mesmer's house, ?Sept.–Oct. 1768]	II:5/iii	singpiel
87	Mitridate, re di Ponto (V. A. Cigna-Santi after G. Parini's Italian trans. of J. Racine, *Mithridate*)	4 S, A, 2 T, 2 fl, 2 ob, 2 bn, 4 hn, str	Milan, Teatro Regio Ducale, 26 Dec. 1770	II:5/iv	*dramma per musica*; aria 'Vado incontro al fato estremo' (III/3) Q. Gasparini; sketches survive
111	Ascanio in Alba (G. Parini)	4 S, T, SATB, 2 fl, 2 ob/cor ang, 2 bn, 4 hn, 2 tpt/hn, timp, str	Milan, Teatro Regio Ducale, 17 Oct. 1771	II:5/v	*festa teatrale*, for wedding of Archduke Ferdinand of Austria and Maria Beatrice Ricciarda of Modena; with ballet Anh C27.06
126	Il sogno di Scipione (P. Metastasio)	2 S, 3 T, SATB, 2 fl, 2 ob, 2 bn, 2 hn, 2 tpt, timp, str	Salzburg, Residenz, 29 Apr. 1772	II:5/vi	*azione teatrale*, composed Apr.–Aug. 1771, given as serenata at instalment of H. Colloredo as Prince-Archbishop of Salzburg
135	Lucio Silla (G. De Gamerra)	4 S, 2 T, SATB, 2 ob/fl, 2 bn, 2 hn, 2 tpt, timp, str	Milan, Teatro Regio Ducale, 26 Dec. 1772	II:5/vii	*dramma per musica*

196	La finta giardiniera (? G. Petrosellini)	4 S, 2 T, B, 2 fl, 2 ob, 2 bn, 2 hn, 2 tpt, timp, str	Munich, Salvatortheater, 13 Jan. 1775	II:5/vii	*dramma giocoso*; perf. as singspiel Die verstellte Gärtnerin, Augsburg, 1 May 1780
208	Il re pastore (P. Metastasio)	3 S, 2 T, 2 fl, 2 ob/cor ang, 2 bn, 4 hn, 2 tpt, str	Salzburg, Residenz, 23 Apr. 1775	II:5/ix	serenata, composed for visit of Archduke Maximilian
315e	Semiramis (O. von Gemmingen)	2 hn, 2 tpt/hn, str		—	duodrama, lost (? never begun), mooted as compositional project, Mannheim, Nov. 1778
345	Thamos, König in Ägypten (T. P. Gebler)	B, SATB, 2 fl, 2 ob, 2 bn, 2 hn, 2 tpt, 3 trbn, timp, str	?	II:6/i	incidental music; 2 choruses composed 1779–80
344	Zaide (Das Serail) (J. A. Schachtner after F. J. Sebastiani, *Das Serail*)	S, 2/3 T, 2 B, 2 fl, 2 ob, 2 bn, 2 hn, 2 tpt, timp, str	Frankfurt, 27 Jan. 1866	II:5/x	singspiel; composed Salzburg, 1780, incomplete; sketches survive
366	Idomeneo, re di Creta (G. B. Varesco after A. Danchet, *Idoménée*)	3 S, 3 T, B, SATB, 2 fl/picc, 2 ob, 2 cl, 2 bn, 4 hn, 2 tpt, 3 trbn, timp, str	(i) Munich, Residenz, 29 Jan. 1781; (ii) Vienna, Palais Auersperg, 13 Mar. 1786	II:5/xi	*dramma per musica*; (i) with ballet, K367; (ii) perf. with K489, 490, both composed by 10 Mar. 1786
384	Die Entführung aus dem Serail (G. Stephanie the younger after C. F. Bretzner, *Belmont und Constanze*)	2 S, 2 T, B, SATB, 2 fl/pic, 2 ob, 2 cl/basset hn, 2 bn, 2 hn, 2 tpt, timp, Turkish music, str	Vienna, Burgtheater, 16 July 1782	II:5/xii	singspiel; sketches survive; fragment K389, 'Welch ängstliches Beben', T, T, fl, ob, bn, 2 hn, str, Vienna, Apr.–May 1782, intended for *Die Entführung*
422	L'oca del Cairo (G. B. Varesco)	3 S, 2 T, 2 B, SATB, 2 ob, 2 bn, 2 hn, str		II:5/xiii	?*dramma giocoso*, composed Salzburg and Vienna, late 1783; incomplete: 1 trio finished, 6 nos. sketched
430	Lo sposo deluso (?P. Petrosellini, after *Le donne rivali*)	2 S, 2 T, 2 fl, 2 ob, 2 bn, 2 hn, 2 tpt, timp, str		II:5/xiv	?*dramma giocoso*, begun 1784–5; only ov., trio and qt completed; sketches survive

(*cont.*)

(cont.)

K	Title (libretto)	Scoring	First performance	NMA	Remarks
486	Der Schauspieldirektor (G. Stephanie the younger)	2 S, T, B, 2 fl, 2 ob, 2 cl, 2 bn, 2 hn, 2 tpt, timp, str	Vienna, Schloss Schönbrunn, 7 Feb. 1786	II:5/xv	singspiel, completed Vienna, 3 Feb. 1786; perf. with A. Salieri Prima la musica; sketches survive
492	Le nozze di Figaro (L. Da Ponte, after P.-A. Beaumarchais, *La Folle Journée, ou Le Mariage de Figaro*)	5 S, 1 T, 4 B, SATB, 2 fl, 2 ob, 2 cl, 2 bn, 2 hn, 2 tpt, timp, str	(i) Vienna, Burgtheater, 1 May 1786; (ii) Vienna, Burgtheater, 29 Aug. 1789	II:5/xvi	opera buffa; sketches survive; (ii) with arias K577, 579
527	Il dissoluto punito, ossia Il Don Giovanni (L. Da Ponte)	3 S, T, 4 B, SATB, 2 fl, 2 ob, 2 cl, 2 bn, 2 hn, 2 tpt, 3 trbn, timp, mand, str	(i) Prague, Nationaltheater, 29 Oct. 1787; (ii) Vienna, Burgtheater, 7 May 1788	II:5/xvii	*dramma giocoso*; sketches survive; (ii) with K540a–c
588	Così fan tutte, ossia La scuola degli amanti (L. Da Ponte)	3 S, T, 2 B, SATB, 2 fl, 2 ob, 2 cl, 2 bn, 2 hn, 2 tpt, timp, str	Vienna, Burgtheater, 26 Jan. 1790	II:5/xviii	*dramma giocoso*; sketches survive
620	Die Zauberflöte (E. Schikaneder)	7 S, 2 A, 4 T, 5 B, SATB, 2 fl/pic, 2 ob, 2 cl/basset hn, 2 bn, 2 hn, 2 tpt, 3 trbn, timp, glock, str	Vienna, Theater auf der Wieden, 30 Sept. 1791	II:5/xix	singspiel, mostly composed by July 1791; ov. and march completed 28 Sept. 1791; sketches survive
621	La clemenza di Tito (Metastasio, rev. C. Mazzolà)	4 S, T, B, SATB, 2 fl, 2 ob, 2 cl/basset hn, 2 bn, 2 hn, 2 tpt, timp, str	Prague, Nationaltheater, 6 Sept. 1791	II:5/xx	opera seria for Prague coronation of Leopold II; plain recits not by Mozart; sketches survive

Music in: P. Anfossi: Il curioso indiscreto, Vienna, 1783; F. Bianchi: La villanella rapita, Vienna, 1785; Anfossi: Le gelosie fortunate, Vienna, 1788; D. Cimarosa: I due baroni, Vienna, 1789; Martín y Soler: Il burbero di buon cuore, Vienna, 1789; see arias, ensembles

BALLET MUSIC

K	Title	Scoring	Place, date	NMA	Remarks
299b	Les petits riens	2 fl, 2 ob, 2 cl, 2 bn, 2 hn, 2 tpt, timp, str	Paris, May–early June 1778	II:6/2	perf. 11 June 1778, Paris, Opéra, after N. Piccinni, *Le finte gemelle*
300	[Gavotte]	2 ob, 2 bn, 2 hn, str	[Paris, early 1778]	II:6/2	?discarded movt of *Les petits riens*
367	[ballet]				for *Idomeneo*
446	[pantomime]	str	Vienna, Feb. 1783	II:6/2	perf. Vienna, Hofburg, 3 Mar. 1783; only 5 of at least 15 nos. extant
Anh C27.06	[ballet]		[Milan, late 1771]		presumably for *Ascanio in Alba*; only 9 nos. extant, arr. kbd

Sketches: K299c., for a ballet of 27 nos., [Paris, early 1778], NMA II:6/2 and X:30/3

Traditionally attributed to Mozart but lacking authentic sources: K135*a*, *Le gelosie del serraglio* (for Lucio Silla), [Milan, late 1772], autograph incipits for ballet of 32 nos., 6 from J. Starzer, *Les cinque soltanes*, NMA X:30/3

DUETS AND ENSEMBLES FOR SOLO VOICES AND ORCHESTRA

K	First words (author)	Voices	Accompaniment	Place, date	NMA	Remarks
479	Dite almeno in che mancai (G. Bertati)	S, T, B, B	2 ob, 2 cl, 2 bn, 2 hn, str	Vienna, 5 Nov. 1785	II:7/3	for Bianchi, *La villanella rapita*, perf. Vienna, Burgtheater, 28 Nov. 1785
480	Mandina amabile (Bertati)	S, T, B	2 fl, 2 ob, 2 cl, 2 bn, 2 hn, str	Vienna, 21 Nov. 1785	II:7/3	as K479; pub. Paris, 1789–90
489	Spiegarti non poss'io	S, T	2 ob, 2 bn, 2 hn, str	Vienna, 10 Mar. 1786	II:5/11	for *Idomeneo*, K366
540b	Per queste tue manine (Da Ponte)	S, B	2 fl, 2 ob, 2 bn, 2 tpt, str	Vienna, 28 April 1788	II:5/17	for *Don Giovanni*, K527
625	Nun liebes Weibchen	S, B	fl, 2 ob, 2 bn, 2 hn, str	Vienna, Aug./Sept. 1790	VI/2	for ?Schack, *Der Stein der Weisen*, Vienna, Theater auf der Wieden, 11 Sept. 1790; possibly only partly original
615	Viviamo felici (T. Grandi, *Le gelosie villane*)	S, A, T, B		Vienna, 20 Apr. 1791	—	lost

VOCAL ENSEMBLES WITH PIANO OR INSTRUMENTAL ENSEMBLE

K	First words (author)	Voices	Accompaniment	Place, date	NMA	Remarks
436	Ecco quel fiero istante (Metastasio, *Canzonette*)	S, S, B	3 basset hn	[Vienna, 1787 or later]	III:9	Notturno; ?partly by G. von Jacquin
437	Mi lagnerò tacendo (Metastasio, *Siroe*)	S, S, B	2 cl, basset hn	[Vienna, 1787 or later]	III:9	as K436
438	Se lontan ben mio (Metastasio, *Strofe per musica*)	S, S, B	2 cl, basset hn	[Vienna, 1787 or later]	III:9	as K436
439	Due pupille amabili	S, S, B	3 basset hn	[Vienna, 1787 or later]	III:9	as K436
346	Luci care, luci belle	S, S, B	3 basset hn	[Vienna, 1787 or later]	III:9	as K436
441	Liebes Mandel, wo is's Bandel	S, T, B	str	[Vienna, [1786–7]	III:9, X:30/4	incomplete
32	[Grazie agl'inganni tuoi] (Metastasio, *La libertà di Nice*)	S, T, B	fl, cl, 2 hn, 2 bn, b	[Vienna, 1784–8]	III:9, X:30/4	26 bars without words based on M. Kelly's duet 'Grazie agl'inganni tuoi'
549	Più non si trovano (Metastasio, *L'olimpiade*)	S, S, B	3 basset hn	Vienna, 16 July 1788	III:9	authenticity of acc. doubtful

Spurious: K43a, 'Ach, was müssen wir erfahren', duet by L. Mozart; K441c, 'Liebes Mädchen', trio M. Haydn

ARIAS AND SCENES FOR VOICE AND ORCHESTRA

K	First words (author)	Accompaniment	Place, date	NMA	Remarks
			For soprano		
23	Conservati fedele (Metastasio, *Artaserse*)	str	The Hague, Oct. 1765	II:7/1	rev. Jan. 1766
70	A Berenice – Sol nascente	2 ob, 2 hn, str	[Salzburg, early 1766]	II:7/1	?for Sarti, *Vologeso*, Salzburg, 28 Feb. 1767, or for perf. Mar. 1769
78	Per pietà, bell'idol mio (Metastasio, *Artaserse*)	2 ob, 2 hn, str	[Holland or Paris, c.1766]	II:7/1	
73A	Misero tu non sei (Metastasio, *Demetrio*)		Milan, 26 Jan. 1770	—	lost
88	Fra cento affanni (Metastasio, *Artaserse*)	2 ob, 2 hn, 2 tpt, str	[Milan, early 1770]	II:7/1	
79	O temerario Arbace – Per quel paterno amplesso (Metastasio, *Artaserse*)	2 ob, 2 bn, 2 hn, str	[Holland or Paris, c.1766]	II:7/1	
77	Misero me – Misero pargoletto (Metastasio, *Demofoonte*)	2 ob, 2 bn, 2 hn, str	[Milan, 1770]	II:7/1	
82	Se ardire, e speranza (Metastasio, *Demofoonte*)	2 fl, 2 hn, str	Rome, 25 Apr. 1770	II:7/1	
83	Se tutti i mali miei (Metastasio, *Demofoonte*)	2 ob, 2 hn, str	[Rome, Apr.–May 1770]	II:7/i	2 versions
217	Voi avete un cor fedele (after Goldoni, *Le nozze di Dorina*)	2 ob, 2 hn, str	Salzburg, 26 Oct. 1775	II:7/1	?for B. Galuppi, *Le nozze di Dorina*

272	Ah, lo previdi – Ah, t'invola agl'occhi miei (Cigna-Santi, *Andromeda*)	2 ob, 2 hn, str	Salzburg, Aug. 1777	II:7/2	composed for J. Duschek
294	Alcandro lo confesso – Non sò d'onde viene (Metastasio, *L'olimpiade*)	2 fl, 2 cl, 2 bn, 2 hn, str	Mannheim, 24 Feb. 1778	II:7/2	composed for A. Weber; 2 versions; sketches survive
295a	Basta vincesti – Ah, non lasciarmi (Metastasio, *Didone abbandonata*)	2 fl, 2 bn, 2 hn, str	Mannheim, 27 Feb. 1778	II:7/2	composed for D. Wendling; incomplete, possibly never finished
316	Popoli di Tessaglia – lo non chiedo (R. de' Calzabigi, *Alceste*)	ob, bn, 2 hn, str	Munich, 8 Jan. 1779	II:7/2	composed for A. Weber
351b	[*scena*]	ob, 2 cl, 3 hn, pf, str	St Germain, Aug. 1778	—	lost; composed for G. F. Tenducci
365a	Warum, o Liebe – Zittre, töricht Herz (J. G. Dyck, after C. Gozzi, *Le due notti affannase*)		Munich, Nov. 1780	—	partly lost; sung in Gozzi, trans. F. A. C. Werther, *Wie man sich die Sache denkt!*, Salzburg, 1 Dec. 1780
368	Ma che vi fece – Sperai vicino (Metastasio, *Demofoonte*)	2 fl, 2 bn, 2 hn, str	[Salzburg, 1779–80]	II:7/2	
369	Misera! dove son – Ah! non son io (Metastasio, *Ezio*)	2 fl, 2 hn, str	Munich, 8 Mar. 1781	II:7/2	composed for Countess J. Paumgarten
374	A questo seno – Or che il cielo (G. De Gamerra, *Sismano nel Mogol*)	2 ob, 2 hn, str	Vienna, Apr. 1781	II:7/ii	composed for F. Ceccarelli, perf. 8 Apr. 1781
383	Nehmt meinen Dank	fl, ob, bn, str	Vienna, 10 Apr. 1782	II:7/3	?composed for A. Weber

(*cont.*)

(cont.)

K	First words (author)	Accompaniment	Place, date	NMA	Remarks
416	Mia speranza adorata – Ah, non sai qual pena (G. Sertor, *Zemira*)	2 ob, 2 bn, 2 hn, str	Vienna, 8 Jan. 1783	II:7/3	composed for A. Lange, perf. 11 Jan. and 23 Mar. 1783
178	Ah, spiegarti, oh Dio		[Vienna, June 1783]	II:7/3	accompaniment extant only in kbd arr.; possibly an earlier version of K418
418	Vorrei spiegarvi, oh Dio	ob, 2 bn, 2 hn, str	Vienna, 20 June 1783	II:7/3	composed for A. Lange, for Anfossi, *Il curioso indiscreto*, Vienna, Burgtheater, 30 June 1783; sketches survive
419	No, che non sei capace	2 ob, 2 hn, 2 tpt, timp, str	Vienna, June 1783	II:7/3	as K418; sketches survive
490	Non più, tutto ascoltai – Non temer, amato bene	2 cl, 2 bn, 2 hn, vn solo, str	Vienna, 10 Mar. 1786	II:5/11	for *Idomeneo*, K366
505	Ch'io mi scordi di te – Non temer, amato bene	2 cl, 2 bn, 2 hn, pf, str	Vienna, 26/27 Dec. 1786	II:7/3	composed for N. Storace; text from 1786 *Idomeneo*
528	Bella mia fiamma – Resta, o cara (D. M. Scarcone, *Cerere placata*)	fl, 2 ob, 2 bn, 2 hn, str	Prague, 3 Nov. 1787	II:7/4	composed for J. Duschek
538	Ah se in ciel, benigne stelle (Metastasio, *L'eroe cinese*)	2 ob, 2 bn, 2 hn, str	Vienna, 4 Mar. 1788	II:7/4	composed for A. Lange; vocal part drafted 1778
540c	In quali eccessi – Mi tradì (Da Ponte)	fl, 2 cl, bn, 2 hn, str	Vienna, 30 Apr. 1788	II:5/17i	for *Don Giovanni*
569	Ohne Zwang, aus eignem Triebe	2 ob, 2 bn, 2 hn, str	Vienna, Jan. 1789	—	lost
577	Al desio di chi t'adora (?Da Ponte)	2 basset hn, 2 bn, 2 hn, str	Vienna, July 1789	II:5/16	A. Ferrarese del Bene, for 1789 version of *Le nozze di Figaro*; sketches survive

578	Alma grande e nobil core (G. Palomba)	2 ob, 2 bn, 2 hn, str	Vienna, Aug. 1789	II:7/4	for Cimarosa, *I due baroni*, Vienna, Burgtheater, Sept. 1789
579	Un moto di gioia (?Da Ponte)	fl, ob, bn, 2 hn, str	Vienna, summer 1789 (by 19 Aug.)	II:5/16	1789 for *Le nozze di Figaro*
580	Schon lacht der holde Frühling	2 cl, 2 bn, 2 hn, str	Vienna, 17 Sept. 1789	II:7/4	for Ger. version of G. Paisiello, *Il barbiere di Siviglia*, not used; orch incomplete
582	Chi sa qual sia (?Da Ponte)	2 cl, 2 bn, 2 hn, str	Vienna, Oct. 1789	II:7/4	for L. Villeneuve, for Martín y Soler, *Il burbero di buon cuore*, Vienna, Burgtheater, 9 Nov. 1789
583	Vado, ma dove? (?Da Ponte)	2 cl, 2 bn, 2 hn, str	Vienna, Oct. 1789	II:7/4	as K582
—	Quel destrier (Metastasio, *L'olimpiade*)		[1760s, early 1770s]		lost, see letter of Constanze Mozart, 13 Feb. 1799
—	Cara se le mie pene (?Metastasio, *Alessandro nell'Indie*)	2 hn, vn, va, b	?, by mid-1772	II:7/1	
—	?	?	Olmütz, Dec 1767	—	lost, see letter 28 May 1778
—	?	?	Vienna, late summmer–autumn 1768	—	lost, described in letters
—	—	?	various, by Dec. 1768	—	L. Mozart's catalogue describes '15 Italian arias', 10 or 11 of which seem to be lost; not necessarily for S
—	No caro fà corragio	str	[Vienna, Aug. 1790]	—	acc. recit for aria by Cimarosa in P. A. Guglielmi, *La Quakera spiritosa*, perf. Vienna, Burgtheater, 13 Aug. 1790

Traditionally attributed to Mozart but lacking authentic sources: K74b, Non curo l'affetto (Metastasio, *Demofoonte*, 2 ob, 2 hn, str, [Milan or Pavia, early 1771], NMA II:7/1; K119, Der Liebe himmlisches Gefühl, ?, NMA II:7/3, accompaniment extant only in kbd arrangement

(cont.)

(cont.)

K	First words (author)	Accompaniment	Place, date	NMA	Remarks
			for alto		
255	Ombra felice – Io ti lascio (G. de Gramera)	2 ob, 2 hn, str	Salzburg, Sept. 1776	II:7/ii	text from M. Mortellari, *Arsace* (Padua, 1775)
			for tenor		
21	Va dal furor portata (Metastasio, *Ezio*)	2 ob, 2 bn, 2 hn, str	(i) London, 1765; (ii) Paris, 1766	II:7/1	(ii) rev. L. Mozart
36	Or che il dover – Tali e cotanti sono	2 ob, 2 bn, 2 hn, 2 tpt, timp, str	[Salzburg, late 1766]	II:7/1	probably licenza perf. anniversary of Archbishop Sigismund's consecration, 21 Dec. 1766
71	Ah più tremar non voglio (Metastasio, *Demofoonte*)	2 ob, 2 hn, str	[Salzburg, early 1769]	II:7/1	only 48 bars extant, continuation lost?
209	Si mostra la sorte	2 fl, 2 hn, str	Salzburg, 19 May 1775	II:7/1	
210	Con ossequio, con rispetto (Petrosellini, *L'astratto, ovvero Il giocator fortunato*)	2 ob, 2 hn, str	Salzburg, May 1775	II:7/1	
256	Clarice cara (Petrosellini, *L'astratto, ovvero Il giocator fortunato*)	2 ob, 2 hn, str	Salzburg, Sept. 1776	II:7/2	sketches survive
295	Se al labbro mio non credi (?A. Salvi, *Artaserse*)	2 fl, 2 ob, 2 bn, 2 hn, str	Mannheim, 27 Feb. 1778	II:7/2	composed for A. Raaff
435	Müsst'ich auch durch tausend Drachen	fl, ob, cl, 2 bn, 2 hn, 2 tpt, timp, str	[Vienna, 1783]	II:7/4	orch incomplete; sketches survive
420	Per pietà, non ricercate	2 cl, 2 bn, 2 hn, str	Vienna, 21 June 1783	II:7/3	composed for J. V. Adamberger, for Anfossi, *Il curioso indiscreto*, not perf.; sketches survive

431	Misero! o sogno – Aura che intorni spiri (Mazzolà, *L'isola capricciosa*)	2 fl, 2 bn, 2 hn, str	[Vienna, 1783]	II:7/3	composed for J. V. Adamberger
540*a*	Dalla sua pace (Da Ponte)	fl, 2 ob, 2 bn, 2 hn, str	Vienna, 24 Apr. 1788	II:5/xviii	composed for F. Morella, for 1788 version of *Don Giovanni*
			for bass		
432	Cosi dunque tradisci – Aspri rimorsi atroci (Metastasio, *Temistocle*)	2 fl, 2 ob, 2 bn, 2 hn, str	[Vienna, 1782–3]	II:7/3	
512	Alcandro, lo confesso – Non sò d'onde viene (Metastasio, *L'olimpiade*)	fl, 2 ob, 2 bn, 2 hn, str	Vienna, 19 Mar. 1787	II:7/4	
513	Mentre ti lascio (Angioli-Morbilli, *La disfatta di Dario*)	fl, 2 cl, 2 bn, 2 hn, str	Vienna, 23 Mar. 1787	II:7/4	composed for G. v. Jacquin
539	Ich möchte wohl der Kaiser sein (J. W. L. Gleim)	pic, 2 ob, 2 bn, 2 hn, perc, str	Vienna, 5 Mar. 1788	II:7/4	German war song composed for F. Baumann, perf. Vienna, Leopoldstadttheater, 7 Mar. 1788
541	Un bacio di mano (?Da Ponte)	fl, 2 ob, 2 bn, 2 hn, str	Vienna, May 1788	II:7/4	composed for F. Albertarelli, for Anfossi, *Le gelosie fortunate*, Vienna, Burgtheater, 2 June 1788
584	Rivolgete a lui lo sguardo (Da Ponte)	2 ob, 2 bn, 2 tpt, timp, str	Vienna, Dec. 1789	II:5/18/2	for *Così fan tutte*, replaced by 'Non siate ritrosi'
612	Per questa bella mano	fl, 2 ob, 2 bn, 2 hn, db solo, str	Vienna, 8 Mar. 1791	II:7/4	composed for F. X. Gerl and F. Pischelberger
621a	Io ti lascio	str	[Prague or Vienna, 1788–9]	II:7/4	possibly only vn parts by Mozart, rest by G. v. Jacquin

SONGS (*with piano accompaniment unless otherwise stated*)

K	Title	First words	Author	Place, date	NMA	Remarks
53	An die Freude	Freude, Königin der Weisen	J. P. Uz	Vienna, autumn 1768	III:8	pub. Vienna, 1768
147		Wie unglücklich bin ich nit		[Salzburg, 1774–6]	III:8	Masonic
148	Lobegesang auf die feierliche Johannisloge	O heiliges Band der Freundschaft	L. F. Lenz	[Salzburg, 1774–6]	III:8	Masonic
307	Ariette	Oiseaux, si tous les ans	A. Ferrand	Mannheim, winter 1777–8	III:8	composed for E. A. Wendling
308	Ariette	Dans un bois solitaire	A. H. de la Motte	Mannheim, winter 1777–8	III:8	for E. A. Wendling
343	[2 Ger. sacred songs]	O Gotteslamm, Als Ägypten Israel	?	[Vienna or Prague, 1787–8]		
392		Verdankt sei es dem Glanz	J. T. Hermes	[Salzburg, c.1780]	III:8	
391	[An die Einsamkeit]	Sei du mein Trost	J. T. Hermes	[Salzburg, c.1780]	III:8	
390	[An die Hoffnung]	Ich würd' auf meinem Pfad	J. T. Hermes	[Salzburg, c.1780]	III:8	
349	Die Zufriedenheit	Was frag ich viel	J. M. Miller	[Munich, winter 1780–1]	III:8	
351		Komm, liebe Zither	?	[Munich, winter 1780–1]	III:8	
468	Lied zur Gesellenreise	Die ihr einem neuen Grade	J. F. von Ratschky	Vienna, 26 Mar. 1785	III:8	Masonic; ? perf. Vienna, 16 Apr. 1785; accompaniment.: org in autograph, pf in Mozart's catalogue

472	Der Zauberer	Ihr Mädchen, flieht Damöten ja!	C. F. Weisse	Vienna, 7 May 1785	III:8	pub. Vienna, 1788
473	Die Zufriedenheit	Wie sanft, wie ruhig	C. F. Weisse	Vienna, 7 May 1785	III:8	
474	Die betrogene Welt	Der reiche Tor	C. F. Weisse	Vienna, 7 May 1785	III:8	pub. Vienna, 1788
476	Das Veilchen	Ein Veilchen	J. W. von Goethe	Vienna, 8 June 1785	III:8	pub. Vienna, 1789
477a	Per la ricuperta salute di Ophelia		Da Ponte	Vienna, c.Sept. 1785		lost, set by Mozart, Salieri and 'Cornetti', advertised in *Wienerblättchen*, 26 Sept. 1785
483		Zerfliesset heut', geliebte Brüder	A. V. von Schlittersberg	[Vienna, late 1785–early 1786]	III:9	Masonic song, with male chorus
484		Ihr unsre neuen Leiter	A. V. von Schlittersberg	[Vienna, late 1785–early 1786]	III:9	Masonic song, with male chorus
506	Lied der Freiheit	Wer unter eines Mädchens Hand	J. A. Blumauer	[Vienna, late 1785–early 1786]	III:8	pub. Vienna, 1786
517	Die Alte	Zu meiner Zeit	F. von Hagedom	Vienna, 18 May 1787	III:8	pub. Vienna, 1788
518	Die Verschweigung	Sobald Damötas Chloen sieht	C. F. Weisse	Vienna, 20 May 1787	III:8	incomplete but pub. Vienna, 1788, lost
519	Das Lied der Trennung	Die Engel Gottes weinen	K. E. K. Schmidt	Vienna, 23 May 1787	III:8	pub. Vienna, 1789
520	Als Luise die Briefe	Erzeugt von heisser Phantasie	G. von Baumberg	Vienna, 26 May 1787	III:8	
523	Abendempfindung	Abend ist's	J. H. Campe	Vienna, 24 June 1787	III:8	pub. Vienna, 1789
524	An Chloe	Wenn die Lieb' aus deinen blauen	J. G. Jacobi	Vienna, 24 June 1787	III:8	pub. Vienna, 1789
529	Des kleinen Friedrichs Geburtstag	Es war einmal, ihr Leutchen	J. E. F. Schall	Prague, 6 Nov. 1787	III:8	pub. Vienna, 1788

(cont.)

(cont.)

K	Title	First words	Author	Place, date	NMA	Remarks
530	Das Traumbild	Wo bist du, Bild	L. H. C. Hölty	Prague, 6 Nov. 1787	III:8	circulated as work by G. v. Jacquin
531	Die kleine Spinnerin	Was spinnst du	?	Vienna, 11 Dec. 1787	III:8	pub. Vienna, 1787
552	Beim Auszug in das Feld	Dem hohen Kaiserworte treu	?	Vienna, 11 Aug. 1788	III:8	pub. Vienna, 1788
596	Sehnsucht nach dem Frühlinge	Komm, lieber Mai	C. A. Overbeck	Vienna, 14 Jan. 1791	III:8	pub. Vienna, 1791
597	Im Frühlingsanfang	Erwacht zum neuen Leben	C. C. Sturm	Vienna, 14 Jan. 1791	III:8	pub. Vienna, 1791
598	Das Kinderspiel	Wir Kinder	C. A. Overbeck	Vienna, 14 Jan. 1791	III:8	pub. Vienna, 1791
—	Zur Eröffnung der Meisterloge, Zum Schluss der Meisterarbeit	Des Todes Werk, der Faulniss Grauen; Vollbracht is die Arbeit der Meister	A. Veit von Schittlersberg	[Vienna, c.Aug 1785]	III:8	Masonic, ?perf. 12 Aug. 1785; lost, only texts survive
—	Bey Eröffnung der Tafelloge, Kettenlied, Lied in Nahmen der Armen	Legt für heut das werkzeug nieder, Wir singen, und schlingen zur Wette, Brüder! der blinde Greis am Stabe	G. Leon	[Vienna, June–July 1790]		Masonic, ?perf. 6 July 1790; lost, only texts survive

Spurious: K52, 'Daphne deine Rosenwangen', arr. by L. Mozart of 'Meiner liebsten schöne Wangen' from *Bastien und Bastienne* K51 with new text, *NMA* II:5/3; K149, Ich hab' es längst gesagt ('Die grossmütige Gelassenheit', Günther), by L. Mozart; K150, Was ich in Gedanken küsse ('Geheime Liebe', Günther), by L. Mozart; K151, Ich trachte nicht nach solchen Dugen ('Die Zufriedenheit', F. R. L. von Canitz), by L. Mozart; K152, Ridente la calma, by J. Mysliveček, *NMA* III:8; K350, Wiegenlied, by B. Flies

CANONS

K	Work and type	Place, date	NMA	Remarks, alternative texts
89aI	canon 4 in 1	[Salzburg, c.1772]	III:10	
89	Kyrie, 5 in 1	[Salzburg, c.1772]	III:10, I:1/1/6	
89aII	(i) Incipe Menalios, 3 in 1; (ii) Cantate Domino, 8 in 1; (iii) Confitebor, 2 in 1 (+ 1); (iv) Thebana bella cantus, 6 in 2	[Salzburg, c.1772]	III:10, X:30/3	
347	canon 6 in 1	[Vienna, c.1785]	III:10	pub. with text Wo der perlende Wein (Breitkopf)
348	V'amo di core teneramente, 12 in 3	[Vienna, 1782–5]	III:10	
507	canon 3 in 1	Vienna, c.3 June 1786	III:10	pub. with text Heiterkeit und leichtes Blut (Härtel)
508	canon 3 in 1	Vienna, c.3 June 1786	III:10	pub. with text Auf das Wohl aller Freunde (Härtel)
508a	2 canons 3 in 1, 6 canons 2 in 1	[Vienna, after 3 June 1786]	III:10	
232	Lieber Freistädtler, lieber Gaulimauli (Mozart), 4 in 1	Vienna, after 4 July 1787	III:10	pub. with text Wer nicht liebt Wein (Härtel)
228	canon 4 in 2	Vienna, before 24 Apr. 1787	III:10	pub. with text Ach! zu kurz (Härtel)
553	Alleluia, 3 in 1	Vienna, 2 Sept. 1788	III:10	
554	Ave Maria, 4 in 1	Vienna, 2 Sept. 1788	III:10	
555	Lacrimoso son'io, 4 in 1	Vienna, 2 Sept. 1788	III:10	pub. with text Ach zum Jammer (Breitkopf)
556	Grechtelt's enk (Mozart), 4 in 1	Vienna, 2 Sept. 1788	III:10	pub. with text Alles Fleisch (Breitkopf)

(cont.)

(cont.)

K	Work and type	Place, date	NMA	Remarks, alternative texts
557	Nascoso e il mio sol, 4 in 1	Vienna, 2 Sept. 1788	III:10	
558	Gehn wir im Prater (Mozart), 4 in 1	Vienna, 2 Sept. 1788	III:10	pub. with text Alles ist eitel hier (Breitkopf)
559	Difficile lectu mihi mars (Mozart), 3 in 1	Vienna, 2 Sept. 1788	III:10	pub. with text Nimm, ist's gleich warm (Breitkopf)
560, 560a	O du eselhafter Peierl/Martin (Jakob)! (Mozart), 4 in 1	Vienna, 2 Sept. 1788	III:10	
561	Bona nox! Bist a rechta Ox (Mozart), 4 in 1	Vienna, 2 Sept. 1788	III:10	pub. with text Gute Nacht (Breitkopf)
562	Caro bell'idol mio, 3 in 1	Vienna, 2 Sept. 1788	III:10	pub. with text Ach süsses teures Leben (Breitkopf)
562c	[?2 vn, va, b] 4 in 1	[Vienna, 1780s]	III:10	
—	8 canons 2 in 1	[Vienna, c.3 June 1786]	III:10	
—	canon 4 in 1	[Vienna, c.1786]	III:10	

Traditionally attributed to Mozart but lacking authentic sources: K229, 3 in 1, [Vienna, c.1782], NMA III:10, pub. with text Sie ist dahin (Hölty); K230, 2 in 1, [Vienna, c.1782], NMA III:10, pub. with text Selig, selig (Hölty); K231, Leck mich im Arsch, 6 in 1, [Vienna, c.1782], NMA III:10, pub. with text Lasst froh uns sein (Breitkopf)

Spurious: K73x, canonic studies from G. B. Martini; *Storia della musica*; K233, by W. Trnka, NMA III:10; K234, by W. Trnka, NMA III:10; K562a, by Michael Haydn, NMA III:10

SYMPHONIES, SYMPHONY MOVEMENTS

K	Key	Movts	Scoring	Place, date	NMA	Remarks
16	E♭	3	2 ob, 2 hn, str	[London, 1764–5]	IV:11/1	no. 1
19	D	3	2 ob, 2 hn, str	[London, 1765]	IV:11/1	no. 4
19a	F	3	2 ob, 2 hn, str	[London or Paris, 1765–6]	IV:11/1	
22	B♭	3	2 ob, 2 hn, str	The Hague, Dec. 1765	IV:11/1	no. 5
43	F	4	2 ob/fl, 2 hn, str	[Salzburg or Vienna, 1767]	IV:11/1	no. 6
45	D	4	2 ob, 2 hn, 2 tpt, timp, str	Vienna, 16 Jan. 1768	IV:11/1	no. 7; adapted as ov. to *La finta semplice*
45a	G	3	2 ob, 2 hn, str	[The Hague, 1766]	IV:11/1	Lambach, rev. c.1767
48	D	4	2 ob, 2 hn, 2 tpt, timp, str	Vienna, 13 Dec. 1768	IV:11/1	no. 8
73	C	4	2 ob/fl, 2 hn, 2 tpt, timp, str	Salzburg or Italy, 1769–70	IV:11/1	no. 9
74	G	3	2 ob, 2 hn, str	[Milan, 1770]	IV:11/2	no. 10
110	G	4	2 ob/fl, 2 bn, 2 hn, str	Salzburg, July 1771	IV:11/2	no. 12
120	D	1	2 fl, 2 ob, 2 hn, 2 tpt, timp, str	[Milan, Oct.–Nov. 1771]	IV:11/2	finale, to form sym. with ov. to *Ascanio in Alba*, K111
112	F	4	2 ob, 2 hn, str	Milan, 2 Nov. 1771	IV:11/2i	no. 13
114	A	4	2 fl/ob, 2 hn, str	Salzburg, 30 Dec. 1771	IV:11/2	no. 14
124	G	4	2 ob, 2 hn, str	Salzburg, 21 Feb. 1772	IV:11/2	no. 15
128	C	3	2 ob, 2 hn, str	Salzburg, May 1772	IV:11/3	no. 16
129	G	3	2 ob, 2 hn, str	Salzburg, May 1772	IV:11/3	no. 17
130	F	4	2 fl, 4 hn, str	Salzburg, May 1772	IV:11/3	no. 18

(*cont.*)

(cont.)

K	Key	Movts	Scoring	Place, date	NMA	Remarks
132	E♭	4	2 ob, 4 hn, str	Salzburg, July 1772	IV:11/3	no. 19; alternative slow movts
133	D	4	fl, 2 ob, 2 hn, 2 tpt, str	Salzburg, July 1772	IV:11/3	no. 20
134	A	4	2 fl, 2 hn, str	Salzburg, Aug. 1772	IV:11/3	no. 21
161, 163	D	3	2 fl, 2 ob, 2 hn, 2 tpt, timp, str	Salzburg, 1773–4	IV:11/3	movts K161 from ov. to *Il sogno di Scipione* K126; K163 finale to form sym. with *Il sogno di Scipione*
184	E♭	3	2 fl, 2 ob, 2 bn, 2 hn, 2 tpt, str	Salzburg, 30 Mar. 1773	IV:11/4	no. 26
199	G	3	2 fl, 2 hn, str	Salzburg, ?10 Apr. 1773	IV:11/4	no. 27; date on MS possibly 16 Apr.
162	C	3	2 ob, 2 hn, 2 tpt, str	Salzburg, ?19 Apr. 1773	IV:11/4	no. 22; date on MS possibly 29 Apr.
181	D	3	2 ob, 2 hn, 2 tpt, str	Salzburg, 19 May 1773	IV:11/4	no. 23
182	B♭	3	2 ob/fl, 2 hn, str	Salzburg, 3 Oct. 1773	IV:11/4	no. 24
183	g	4	2 ob, 2 bn, 4 hn, str	Salzburg, 5 Oct. 1773	IV:11/4	no. 25
201	A	4	2 ob, 2 hn, str	Salzburg, 6 Apr. 1774	IV:11/5	no. 29
202	D	4	2 ob, 2 hn, 2 tpt, str	Salzburg, 5 May 1774	IV:11/5	no. 30
200	C	4	2 ob, 2 hn, 2 tpt, timp, str	Salzburg, 17 [?12] Nov. 1774 [?1773]	IV:11/4	no. 28
121	D	1	2 ob, 2 hn, str	[Salzburg, end 1774–early 1775]	IV:11/5	finale, to form sym. with ov. to La finta giardiniera K196
204	D	4	2 ob, 2 bn, 2 hn, 2 tpt, str	after 5 Aug. 1775	IV:11/7	redacted from Serenade K204
102	D	1	2 ob/fl, 2 hn, 2 tpt, str	[Salzburg, Apr. and Aug. 1775]	IV:11/5	finale, to form sym. with versions of ov. and 1st aria of *Il re pastore*, K208
250	D	4	2 ob, 2 bn, 2 hn, 2 tpt, timp, str	Salzburg, after June 1776	IV:11/7	redacted from Serenade K250 with new timp part and other revs.
297	D	3	2 fl, 2 ob, 2 cl, 2 bn, 2 hn, 2 tpt, timp, str	Paris, June 1778	IV:11/5	no. 31, 'Paris'; 2 slow movts, probable original in 1st edn. (Paris, 1788); sketches survive

318	G	1	2 fl, 2 ob, 2 bn, 4 hn, (2 tpt), timp, str	Salzburg, 26 Apr. 1779	IV:11/6	no. 32; tpt part added 1782–3
319	B♭	4	2 ob, 2 bn, 2 hn, str	Salzburg, 9 July 1779	IV:11/6	no. 33; third movt (minuet) added c.1784–5
320	D	3	2 ob, 2 bn, 2 hn, 2 tpt, timp, str	[Salzburg or Vienna], after 3 Aug. 1779	IV:11/8	redacted from Serenade K320 with added timp
338	C	3	2 ob, 2 bn, 2 hn, 2 tpt, timp, str	Salzburg, 29 Aug. 1780	IV:11/6	no. 34; frag. minuet (? originally complete) after 1st movt cancelled in autograph
409	C	1	2 fl, 2 ob, 2 bn, 2 hn, 2 tpt, timp, str	Vienna, May 1782	IV:11/10	minuet mooted as intended for K338 although scoring differs
385	D	4	2 fl, 2 ob, 2 cl, 2 bn, 2 hn, 2 tpt, timp, str	Vienna, July 1782	IV:11/6	no. 35, 'Haffner'; orig. intended as serenade, possibly with another minuet (lost) and March K408/2a; fls and cls later addns
425	C	4	2 ob, 2 bn, 2 hn, 2 tpt, timp, str	Linz, Oct.–Nov. 1783	IV:11/8	no. 36, 'Linz'; rev. Vienna, c.1784–5
444	G	1	2 ob, 2 hn, str	[Vienna, late 1783 or 1784]		no. 37; introduction for symphony by M. Haydn
504	D	3	2 fl, 2 ob, 2 bn, 2 hn, 2 tpt, timp, str	Vienna, 6 Dec. 1786	IV:11/8	no. 38, 'Prague', last movt probably composed first; sketches survive
543	E♭	4	fl, 2 cl, 2 bn, 2 hn, 2 tpt, timp, str	Vienna, 26 June 1788	IV:11/9	no. 39
550	g	4	fl, 2 ob, [2 cl], 2 bn, 2 hn, str	Vienna, 25 July 1788	IV:11/ix	no. 40; 2 versions, 1st without cls
551	C	4	fl, 2 ob, 2 bn, 2 hn, 2 tpt, timp, str	Vienna, 10 Aug. 1788	IV:11/ix	no. 41, 'Jupiter'

Traditionally thought to be by Mozart but lacking authentic sources: K45b, B♭, 2 ob, 2 hn, str, [Vienna, 1768], NMA IV:11/1; K75, F, 2 ob, 2 hn, str, [Salzburg, 1771], NMA IV:11/2; K81, D, 2 ob, 2 hn, str, [Rome, Apr. 1770], NMA IV:11/2; K84, D, 2 ob, 2 hn, str, [Milan/Bologna, 1770], also attr. L. Mozart, C. D. von Dittersdorf, NMA IV:11/2; K95, D, 2 fl, 2 tpt, str, [Rome, Apr. 1770], NMA IV:11/2; K96, C, 2 ob, 2 hn, 2 tpt, timp, str, [Milan, Oct.–Nov. 1771], NMA IV:11/2; K97, D, 2 b, 2 hn, 2 tpt, timp, str, [Rome, Apil 1770], NMA IV:11/2; Anh C11.03, B♭, 2 ob, 2 hn, str, date uncertain

Spurious: K16a, a, author unknown but not Mozart; K17, B♭, by L. Mozart; K18, Eb, by C. F. Abel (see Arrangements); K98, F, also attr. 'Haydn'

CASSATIONS, SERENADES, DIVERTIMENTI, MISCELLANEOUS WORKS

K	Title	Key, movts	Scoring	Place, date	NMA	Remarks
32	Gallimathias musicum		hpd, 2 ob, 2 hn, 2 bn, str	The Hague, Mar. 1766	IV:12/1	
100	Cassation	D, 8	2 ob/fl, 2 hn, 2 tpt, str	[Salzburg, 1769]	IV:12/1	with March K62
63	Cassation	G, 7	2 ob, 2 hn, str	[Salzburg, 1769]	IV:12/1	
99	Cassation	B♭, 7	2 ob, 2 hn, str	[Salzburg, 1769]	IV:12/1	
113	Divertimento	E♭, 4	(i) 2 cl, 2 hn, str; (ii) 2 ob, 2 cl, 2 hn, 2 cor ang, 2 bn, str	(i) Milan, Nov. 1771; (ii) [Salzburg, early 1773]	IV:12/2	'Concerto ò sia Divertimento'
131	Divertimento	D, 7	fl, ob, bn, 4 hn, str	Salzburg, June 1772	IV:12/ii	
185	Serenade	D, 7	2 ob/fl, 2 hn, 2 tpt, vn solo, str	Vienna, July–Aug. 1773	IV:12/2	with March K189
203	Serenade	D, 8	2 ob/fl, bn, 2 hn, 2 tpt, vn solo, str	Salzburg, Aug. 1774	IV:12/3	with March K237
204	Serenade	D, 7	2 ob/fl, bn, 2 hn, 2 tpt, vn solo, str	Salzburg, 5 Aug. 1775	IV:12/3	with March K215
239	Serenata notturna	D, 3	2 vn, va, db (solo); str, timp	Salzburg, Jan. 1776	IV:12/3	
250	Serenade	D, 8	2 ob/fl, 2 bn, 2 hn, 2 tpt, vn solo, str	Salzburg, June 1776	IV:12/4	'Haffner'; with March K249
251	Divertimento	D, 6	ob, 2 hn, str	Salzburg, July 1776	VII:18	possibly soloistic
286	Notturno	D, 3	4 groups, each 2 hn, str (solo)	[Salzburg, Dec. 1776–Jan. 1777]	IV:12/5	possibly soloistic
320	Serenade	D, 7	2 fl/pic, 2 ob, 2 bn, 2 hn/posthorn, 2 tpt, timp, str	Salzburg, 3 Aug. 1779	IV:12/5	'Posthorn', with marches K335
477	Maurerische Trauermusik	c	2 ob, cl, 3 basset hn, dbn, 2 hn, str	Vienna, 1785	IV:11/10	dated July 1785 in Mozart's catalogue but performed at memorial service in November; date of composition uncertain
522	Ein musikalischer Spass	F, 4	2 hn, str	Vienna, 14 June 1787	VII:18	possibly soloistic
525	Eine kleine Nachtmusik	G, 4	2 vn, va, vc, b	Vienna, 10 Aug. 1787	IV:12/6	orig. 5 movts, 2nd lost

WIND ENSEMBLE

K	Title	Key	Scoring	Place, date	NMA	Remarks
33*a*	Solos		fl, bc	Lausanne, Sept. 1766	—	lost
33*h*	Piece		hn, bc	Salzburg, ?	—	lost, mentioned in L. Mozart's letter, 16 Feb. 1778
41*b*	Pieces		2 tpt, 2 hn, 2 basset hn	?, by late 1768	—	lost
186	Divertimento	B♭	2 ob, 2 cl, 2 cor ang, 2 hn, 2 bn	Milan, [Mar.] 1773	VII:17/1	
166	Divertimento	E♭	2 ob, 2 cl, 2 cor ang, 2 hn, 2 bn	Salzburg, 24 Mar. 1773	VII:17/1	
213	Divertimento	F	2 ob, 2 bn, 2 hn	Salzburg, July 1775	VII:17/1	
240	Divertimento	B♭	2 ob, 2 bn, 2 hn	Salzburg, Jan. 1776	VII:17/1	
252	Divertimento	E♭	2 ob, 2 bn, 2 hn	[Salzburg, early 1776]	VII:17/1	
188	Divertimento	C	2 fl, 5 tpt, timp	[Salzburg, mid-1773]	VII:17/1	
253	Divertimento	F	2 ob, 2 bn, 2 hn	Salzburg, Aug. 1776	VII:17/1	
270	Divertimento	B♭	2 ob, 2 bn, 2 hn	Salzburg, Jan. 1777	VII:17/1	
361	Serenade	B♭	2 ob, 2 cl, 2 basset hn, 2 bn, 4 hn, db	Vienna [1783–4]	VII:17/2	perf. Vienna, Burgtheater, 23 Mar. 1784
375	Serenade	E♭	[2 ob,] 2 cl, 2 bn, 2 hn	(i) Vienna, Oct. 1781; (ii) [Vienna, late July 1782]	VII:17/2	obs added in 2nd version
388	Serenade	c	2 ob, 2 cl, 2 bn, 2 hn	[Vienna, July 1782]	VII:17/2	arr. as str qnt K406
411	Adagio	B♭	2 cl, 3 basset hn	[Vienna, 1782–3]	VII:17/2	
410	Adagio	F	2 basset hn, bn	[Vienna, 1784–5]	VIII:21	
487	12 Duos		2 hn	Vienna, 27 July 1786	VIII:21	

Traditionally attributed to Mozart but lacking authentic sources: K289, Divertimento, E♭, 2 ob, 2 bn, 2 hn, [Salzburg, late 1770s], NMA, VII:7/1

Spurious: K187, Divertimento, C, 2 fl, 5 tpt, timp, arr. by L. Mozart of dances by Starzer and Gluck; see also 'Arrangements', K626b/28

MARCHES

K	Key	Scoring	Composition	NMA	Remarks
41c	—	2 ob, bn, 2 hn, 2 vn, b	?, by late 1768	—	lost
62	D	2 ob, 2 hn, 2 tpt, str	[Salzburg, 1769]	IV:12/1	used in *Mitridate* K87, possibly for Cassation K100
290	D	2 hn, str	Salzburg, summer 1772	VII:18, IV:/13/2	with Divertimento K205
189	D	2 fl, 2 hn, 2 tpt, 2 vn, b	Vienna, July–Aug. 1773	IV:12/2, IV:13/2	with Serenade K185
237	D	2 ob, 2 bn, 2 hn, 2 tpt, 2 vn, b	[Salzburg, summer 1774]	IV:12/3, IV:13/2	with Serenade K203
215	D	2 ob, 2 hn, 2 tpt, str	Salzburg, Aug. 1775	IV:12/3	with Serenade K204
214	C	2 ob, 2 hn, 2 tpt, str	Salzburg, 20 Aug. 1775	IV:13/2	
248	F	2 hn, str	Salzburg, June 1776	VII:18, 23, IV:13/2	with Divertimento K247
249	D	2 ob, 2 bn, 2 hn, 2 tpt, str	Salzburg, 20 July 1776	IV:13/2	with Serenade K250
335	D, D	(i) 2 ob, 2 hn, 2 tpt, str; (ii) same but 2 fl	[Salzburg, Aug. 1779]	IV:13/2, IV:12/5	2 marches, with Serenade K320
445	D	2 hn, str	[Salzburg, summer 1780]	VII:18	?with Divertimento K344
408/1	C	2 ob, 2 hn, 2 tpt, timp, str	[Vienna, 1782]	IV:13/2	
408/3	C	2 fl, 2 bn, 2 hn, 2 tpt, timp, str	[Vienna, 1782–3]	IV:13/2	
408/2	D	2 ob, 2 bn, 2 hn, 2 tpt, timp, str	[Vienna, 1782]	IV:13/2	
544	D	fl, hn, str	Vienna, June 1788	—	lost

DANCE MUSIC

K	No.	Keys	Scoring	Place, date	NMA	Remarks
			Minuets with and without trios			
41d			various	?, by late 1768	—	lost
65a	7	G, D, A, F, C, G, D	2 vn, b	Salzburg, 26 Jan. 1769	IV:13/1/1	
103	19	C, G, D, F, C, A, D, F, C, G, F, C, G, B♭, E♭, E♭, A♭, D, G	2 ob/fl, 2 hn/tpt, 2 vn, b	[Salzburg, spring–summer 1772]	IV:13/1/1	originally 20, rearranged by Mozart as 19; 12 arr. keyboard, early 1770s
61lg			2 fl			see 'Arrangements etc.'
122	1	E♭	2 ob, 2 hn, 2 vn, b	[Italy, early 1770]	IV:13/1/1	possibly an arrangement of a minuet by another composer
164	6	D, D, D, G, G, G	fl, 2 ob, 2 hn/tpt, 2 vn, b	Salzburg, June 1772	IV:13/1/	
176	16	C, G, E♭, B♭, F, D, A, C, G, B♭, F, D, G, C, F, D	2 ob/fl, bn, 2 hn/tpt, 2 vn, b	Salzburg, Dec. 1773	IV:13/1/i	alternative versions of trios 1 and 2 also known; minuet 2, 3, trio 2, 6 also arr. keyboard
363	3	D, B♭, D	2 ob, 2 bn, 2 hn, 2 tpt, timp, 2 vn, b	[Vienna, 1782–3]	IV:13/1/2	
461	6	C, E♭, G, B♭, F, D	2 ob/fl, 2 bn, 2 hn, 2 vn, b	Vienna, 1784	IV:13/1/2	no. 6 incomplete
463	2	F, B♭	2 ob, bn, 2 hn, 2 vn, b	[Vienna, 1784]	IV:13/1/2	quadrilles
568	12	C, F, B♭, E♭, G, D, A, F, B♭, D, G, C	2 fl/pic, 2 ob/cl, 2 bn, 2 hn, 2 tpt, timp, 2 vn, b	Vienna, 24 Dec. 1788	IV:13/1/2i	pub. Vienna, 1789
585	12	D, F, B♭, E♭, G, C, A, F, B♭, E♭, G, D	2 fl/pic, 2 ob/cl, 2 bn, 2 hn, 2 tpt, timp, 2 vn, b	Vienna, Dec. 1789	IV:13/1/2	only nos. 1–4 survive in autograph score; others from kbd arr. pub. Vienna, 1791
599	6	C, G, E♭, B♭, F, D	2 fl/pic, 2 ob/cl, 2 bn, 2 hn, 2 tpt, timp, 2 vn, b	Vienna, 23 Jan. 1791	IV:13/1/2	

(cont.)

(*cont.*)

K	No.	Keys	Scoring	Place, date	NMA	Remarks
601	4	A, C, G, D	2 fl/pic, hurdy-gurdy, 2 ob, 2 cl, 2 bn, 2 hn, 2 tpt, timp, 2 vn, b	Vienna, 5 Feb. 1791	IV:13/1/2	
604	2	B♭, E♭	2 fl, 2 cl, 2 bn, 2 hn/tpt, timp, 2 vn, b	Vienna, 12 Feb. 1791	IV:13/1/2	
Spurious: K104, by Michael Haydn, *NMA* IV: 13/1/1; K105, by Michael Haydn, *NMA* IV:13/1/1; K61h, by Michael Haydn, *NMA*, IV:13/1/1; K315*a*, by J. C. Bach, *NMA* IV:13/1/1						
				German dances, ländler		
509	6	D, G, E♭, F, A, C	2 fl/pic, 2 ob, 2 cl, 2 bn, 2 hn, 2 tpt, timp, 2 vn, b	Prague, 6 Feb. 1787	IV:13/1/2	kbd. arr. pub. Vienna, 1791 differs from autograph; possibly authentic
536	6	C, G, B♭, D, F, F	pic, 2 fl, 2 ob/cl, 2 bn, 2 hn/tpt, timp, 2 vn, b	Vienna, 27 Jan. 1788	IV:13/1/2	pub. Vienna, 1789
567	6	B♭, E♭, G, D, A, C	pic, 2 fl, 2 ob/cl, 2 bn, 2 hn, 2 tpt, timp, 2 vn, b	Vienna, 6 Dec. 1788	IV:13/1/2	pub. Vienna, 1789
571	6	D, A, C, G, B♭, D	2 fl/pic, 2 ob/cl, 2 bn, 2 hn/tpt, timp, Turkish music, 2 vn, b	Vienna, 21 Feb. 1789	IV:13/1/2	
586	12	C, G, B♭, F, A, D, G, E♭, B♭, F, A, C	2 fl/pic, 2 ob/cl, 2 bn, 2 hn, 2 tpt, timp, tamb, 2 vn, b	Vienna, Dec. 1789	IV:13/1/2	
600	6	C, F, B♭, E♭, G, D	pic, 2 fl, 2 ob/cl, 2 bn, 2 hn, 2 tpt, timp, 2 vn, b	Vienna, 29 Jan. 1791	IV:13/1/2	
602	4	B♭, F, C, A	2 fl/pic, 2 ob/cl, 2 bn, 2 hn/tpt, timp, hurdy-gurdy, 2 vn, b	Vienna, 5 Feb. 1791	IV:13/1/2	
605	2	D, G	2 fl/pic, 2 ob, 2 bn, 2 hn/tpt, 2 posthorns, timp, 2 vn, b	Vienna, 12 Feb. 1791	IV:13/1/2	manuscript Vienna, Gesellschaft der Musikfreunde, with third dance, 'Die Schlittenfahrt', authorship uncertain

606	6	all B♭	2 vn, b, winds	Vienna, 28 Feb. 1791	IV:13/1/2	'Ländlerische', wind parts lost
611	1	C	2 fl, 2 ob, 2 bn, 2 tpt, timp, hurdy-gurdy, 2 vn, b	Vienna, 6 Mar. 1791	IV:13/1/2	'Die Leyerer', identical with K602, no. 3
			Contredanses			
123	1	B♭	2 ob, 2 hn, 2 vn, b	Rome, 13/14 Apr. 1770	IV:13/1/1	
101	4	F, G, D, F	2 ob/fl, bn, 2 hn, 2 vn, b	[Salzburg, early 1776]	IV:13/1/1	
267	4	G, E♭, A, D	2 ob/fl, bn, 2 hn, 2 vn, b	[Salzburg, early 1777]	IV:13/1/2	
462	6	C, E♭, B♭, D, B♭, F	2 ob, 2 hn, 2 vn, b	[Vienna, 1781–7]	IV:13/1/2	wind parts possibly added later
463	2	F, B♭	2 ob, bn, 2 hn, 2 vn, b	[Vienna, 1781–7]	IV:13/1/2	each preceeded by a minuet
534	1	D	pic, 2 ob, 2 hn, side drum, 2 vn, b	Vienna, 14 Jan. 1788	IV:13/1/2	'Das Donnerwetter', extant only in pf arr. and incomplete orch parts
535	1	C	pic, 2 ob/cl, bn, tpt, side drum, 2 vn, b	Vienna, 23 Jan. 1788	IV:13/1/2	'La bataille'
565	2	B♭, D	2 ob, 2 hn, bn, 2 vn, b	Vienna, 30 Oct. 1788	—	lost
587	1	C	fl, ob, bn, tpt, 2 vn, b	Vienna, Dec. 1789	IV:13/1/2	'Der Sieg vom Helden Koburg'
106	3	D, A, B♭	2 ob, 2 bn, 2 hn, 2 vn, b	Vienna, Jan. 1790	IV:13/1/2	
603	2	D, B♭	pic, 2 ob, 2 bn, 2 hn, 2 tpt, timp, 2 vn, b	Vienna, 5 Feb. 1791	IV:13/1/2	
607	1	E♭	fl, ob, bn, 2 hn, 2 vn, b	Vienna, 28 Feb. 1791	IV:13/1/2	'Il trionfo delle dame'
609	5	C, E♭, D, C, G	fl, side drum, 2 vn, b	Vienna, Mar. 1791	IV:13/1/2	
610	1	G	2 fl, 2 hn, 2 vn, b	Vienna, 6 Mar. 1791	IV:13/1/2	'Les filles malicieuses'; identical to K609 no. 5 but different scoring

Traditionally attributed to Mozart but lacking authentic sources: K269b, [Salzburg, ?early 1776], nos. 2, 12 identical to K101 nos. 2, 3 NMA IX: 272; K510, [?Prague, 1787], NMA IV:13/1/2; K535a, [Vienna, c.1789], only kbd version extant, NMA IV:13/1/2

CONCERTOS, CONCERTO MOVEMENTS *piano (all entitled 'Concerto')*

K	Key	Scoring	Place, date	Cadenzas K624	NMA	Remarks
			piano			
37, 39–41						nos. 1–4, see 'Arrangements'
107/1–3						see 'Arrangements'
175	D	pf, 2 ob, 2 hn, 2 tpt, timp, str	Salzburg, Dec. 1773	1–4	V:15/1	no. 5, possibly for org; obs, 1st hn rev. 1777–8; pub. Vienna, 1785
238	B♭	pf, 2 ob/fl, 2 hn, str	Salzburg, Jan. 1776	5–7	V:15/1	no. 6
242	F	3 pf, 2 ob, 2 hn, str	Salzburg, Feb. 1776	—	V:15/1	no. 7, 'Lodron'; also version for 2 pf
246	C	pf, 2 ob, 2 hn, str	Salzburg, Apr. 1776	8–14	V:15/2	no. 8, 'Lützow'
271	E♭	pf, 2 ob, 2 hn, str	Salzburg, Jan. 1777	15–22	V:15/2	no. 9, 'Jeunehomme'
365	E♭	2 pf, 2 ob, 2 bn, 2 hn, str	[Salzburg, 1779–80]	23–4	V:15/2	no. 10
382	D	pf, fl, 2 ob, 2 hn, 2 tpt, timp, str	Vienna, Mar. 1782	25–6	V:15/1	new finale for K175
386	A	pf, 2 ob, 2 hn, str	Vienna, 19 Oct. 1782	—	V:15/8	rondo, incomplete; possibly intended as finale for K414
413	F	pf, 2 ob, 2 bn, 2 hn, str	Vienna, late 1782–early 1783	37–8	V:15/3	no. 11; pub. Vienna, 1785
414	A	pf, 2 ob, 2 hn, str	Vienna, late 1782–early 1783	27–36	V:15/3	no. 12; pub. Vienna, 1785; sketches survive
415	C	pf, 2 ob, 2 bn, 2 hn, 2 tpt, timp, str	Vienna, late 1782–early 1783	39–41	V:15/3	no. 13; pub. Vienna, 1785
449	E♭	pf, 2 ob, 2 hn, str	Vienna, 9 Feb. 1784	42	V:15/4	no. 14; composed for Barbara Ployer; probably begun 1782–3

450	B♭	pf, fl, 2 ob, 2 bn, 2 hn, str	Vienna, 15 Mar. 1784	43–5	V:15/4	no. 15
451	D	pf, fl, 2 ob, 2 bn, 2 hn, 2 tpt, timp, str	Vienna, 22 Mar. 1784	46–7	V:15/4	no. 16; pub. Paris, c.1785
453	G	pf, fl, 2 ob, 2 bn, 2 hn, str	Vienna, 12 Apr. 1784	48–51	V:15/5	no. 17; composed for Barbara Ployer; pub. Speyer, 1789
456	B♭	pf, fl, 2 ob, 2 bn, 2 hn, str	Vienna, 30 Sept. 1784	52–7	V:15/5	'Paradies'
459	F	pf, fl, 2 ob, 2 bn, 2 hn, str	Vienna, 11 Dec. 1784	58–60	V:15/5	no. 19
466	d	pf, fl, 2 ob, 2 bn, 2 hn, 2 tpt, timp, str	Vienna, 10 Feb. 1785	—	V:15/6	no. 20
467	C	pf, fl, 2 ob, 2 bn, 2 hn, 2 tpt, timp, str	Vienna, 9 Mar. 1785	—	V:15/6	no. 21
482	E♭	pf, fl, 2 cl, 2 bn, 2 hn, 2 tpt, timp, str	Vienna, 16 Dec. 1785	—	V:15/6	no. 22
488	A	pf, fl, 2 cl, 2 bn, 2 hn, str	Vienna, 2 Mar. 1786	61	V:15/7	no. 23
491	c	pf, fl, 2 ob, 2 cl, 2 bn, 2 hn, 2 tpt, timp, str	Vienna, 24 Mar. 1786	—	V:15/7	no. 24
503	C	pf, fl, 2 ob, 2 bn, 2 hn, 2 tpt, timp, str	Vienna, 4 Dec. 1786	—	V:15/7	no. 25; sketches survive
537	D	pf, fl, 2 ob, 2 bn, 2 hn, 2 tpt, timp, str	Vienna, 24 Feb. 1788	—	V:15/8	no. 26, 'Coronation', pf part incomplete; sketches survive
595	B♭	pf, fl, 2 ob, 2 bn, 2 hn, str	Vienna, 5 Jan. 1791	62–4	V:15/8	no. 27; possibly begun 1788; pub. Vienna, 1791

(cont.)

K	Title	Key	Solo	Accompaniment	Place, date	NMA	Remarks
					strings		
190	Concertone	C	2 vn	solo ob, vc; 2 ob, 2 hn, 2 tpt, str	Salzburg, 31 May 1774	V:14/2	
207	Concerto	B♭	vn	2 ob, 2 hn, str	Salzburg, 1773	V:14/1	date on autograph 14 April 1775, but originally '1773'
211	Concerto	D	vn	2 ob, 2 hn, str	Salzburg, 14 June 1775	V:14/1	
216	Concerto	G	vn	2 ob, 2 hn, str	Salzburg, 12 Sept. 1775	V:14/1	
218	Concerto	D	vn	2 ob, 2 hn, str	Salzburg, Oct. 1775	V:14/1	
219	Concerto	A	vn	2 ob, 2 hn, str	Salzburg, 20 Dec. 1775	V:14/1	
261	Adagio	E	vn	2 fl, 2 hn, str	Salzburg, 1776	V:14/1	possibly for K219
269	Rondo	B♭	vn	2 ob, 2 hn, str	Salzburg, 1776	V:14/1	possibly for K207
364	Sinfonia concertante	E♭	vn, va	2 ob, 2 hn, str	[Salzburg, 1779–80]	V:14/2	sketches survive
373	Rondo	C	vn	2 ob, 2 hn, str	Vienna, 2 Apr. 1781	V:14/1	
470	Andante	A	vn	2 ob, 2 hn, str	Vienna, 1 Apr. 1785	—	lost

Traditionally attributed to Mozart but lacking authentic sources: K206a, F, vc, lost; K271i, D, vn, NMA, X:29/1

Spurious: K268, E♭, vn, possibly by J. F. Eck; KAnh C14.05, 'Adelaide Concerto', D, vn, by H. Casadesus, pub. Mainz, 1930 wind

47c	Concerto		tpt	?	Vienna, c.Nov. 1768	—	lost, perf. Vienna, Waisenhauskirche, 7 Dec. 1768
191	Concerto	B	bn	2 ob, 2 hn, str	Salzburg, 4 June 1774	V:14/3	
271k	Concerto	C	ob	2 ob, 2hn, str	Salzburg, 1777	V:14/3	identical to K314
313	Concerto	G	fl	2 ob, 2 hn, str	Mannheim, early 1778	V:14/iii	lacks authentic sources
314	Concerto	C	ob	2 ob, 2 hn, str	Salzburg, 1777	V:14/3	arr. for flute not authentic; sketches survive
315	Andante	C	fl	2 ob, 2 hn, str	[Mannheim, early 1780]	V:14/3	
A9	Sinfonia concertante		fl, ob, bn, hn	?	Paris, c.Apr. 1778	—	lost; possibly partly transmitted by KAnh C14.01, E♭, ob, cl, bn, hn solos, acc. 2 ob, 2 hn, str, NMA, X:29/1
299	Concerto	C	fl, hp	2 ob, 2 hn, str	Paris, Apr. c.1778	V:14/6	
320	Sinfonia concertante	G	2 fl, 2 ob, 2 bn				movts iii and iv of Serenade K320, perf. as independent Sinfonia concertante (see letter of 29 Mar. 1783)
412+514	Concerto	D	hn	2 ob, 2 hn, str	[Vienna, 1791]	V:14/5	movt ii incomplete; commonly performed version of K514a 1792 completion by F. X. Süssmayr
417	Concerto	E♭	hn	2 ob, 2 hn, str	Vienna, 27 May 1783	V:14/5	
447	Concerto	E♭	hn	2 cl, 2 bn, str	[Vienna, 1787]	V:14/5	
495	Concerto	E♭	hn	2 ob, 2 hn, str	Vienna, 26 June 1786	V:14/5	
622	Concerto	A	cl	2 fl, 2 bn, 2 hn, str	Vienna, Oct. 1791	V:14/5	draft of movt I, G, for basset hn (K584b)

CHAMBER

Strings and wind, miscellaneous

K	Title	Key	Scoring	Place, date	NMA	Remarks
41a	Divertimenti	?	fl, hn, tpt, trbn, vn, va, vc	?, by late 1768		lost
205	Divertimento	D	2 hn, bn, str	[Salzburg, summer 1772]	VII:18	with March K290
247	Divertimento	F	2 hn, str	Salzburg, June 1776	VII:18	with March K248
285	Quartet	D	fl, vn, va, vc	Mannheim, 25 Dec. 1777	VIII:20/2	for F. Dejean
285a	Quartet	G	fl, vn, va, vc	Mannheim, Jan.–Feb. 1778	VIII:20/2	
287	Divertimento	B♭	2hn, str	[Salzburg, summer 1777]	VII:18	
298	Quartet	A	fl, vn, va, vc	[Vienna, 1786–7]	VIII:20/2	
334	Divertimento	D	2 hn, str	[Salzburg, 1779–80]	VI:18	?with march K445
370	Quartet	F	ob, vn, va, vc	[Munich, early 1781]	VIII:20/2	
407	Quintet	E♭	hn, vn, 2 va, vc	[Vienna, late 1782]	VIII:19/2	
581	Quintet	A	cl, 2 vn, va, vc	Vienna, 29 Sept. 1789	VIII:19/2	

Traditionally attributed to Mozart but lacking authentic sources: K285a, Quartet, G, fl, vn, va, vc, [Mannheim, early 1778], NMA VIII:20/2; K285b, Quartet, C, fl, vn, va, vc, only sketch survives, pub. Speyer, 1788, movt ii arr. from Serenade K361; K292, Duo, B, bn, vc, pub. Leipzig, 1805, NMA, VIII:21

String quintets: 2 violins, 2 violas, cello

K	Key	Composition	NMA	Remarks
174	B♭	Salzburg, Dec. 1773	VIII:19/1	
515	C	Vienna, 19 Apr. 1787	VIII:19/1	pub. Vienna, 1789
516	g	Vienna, 16 May 1787	VIII:19/1	pub. Vienna, 1790
406	c	[Vienna, 1788]	VIII:19/1	arr. from Serenade K388
593	D	Vienna, Dec. 1790	VIII:19/1	
614	E♭	Vienna, 12 Apr. 1791	VIII:19/1	

Spurious: K46, arr. of movts from Serenade K361

String quartets

K	Key	Place, date	NMA	Remarks
80	G	Lodi, 15 Mar. 1770	VIII:20/1/1	movt iv added Vienna, late 1773 or Salzburg, early 1774
136	D	[Salzburg, early 1772]	IV:12/6	Divertimento
137	B♭	[Salzburg, early 1772]	IV:12/6	Divertimento
138	F	[Salzburg, early 1772]	IV:12/6	Divertimento
155	D	[Italy, 1772–3]	VIII:20/1/1	
156	G	[Italy, 1772–3]	VIII:20/1/1	
157	C	[Italy, 1772–3]	VIII:20/1/1	
158	F	[Italy, 1772–3]	VIII:20/1/1	
159	B♭	[Italy, 1772–3]	VIII:20/1/1	
160	E♭	[Italy, 1772–3]	VIII:20/1/1	
168	F	Vienna, Aug. 1773	VIII:20/1/1	
169	A	Vienna, Aug. 1773	VIII:20/1/1	
170	C	Vienna, Aug. 1773	VIII:20/1/1	
171	E♭	Vienna, Aug. 1773	VIII:20/1/1	
172	B♭	[Vienna, Aug.–Sept. 1773]	VIII:20/1/1	
173	D	Vienna, [Sept.] 1773	VIII:20/1/1	
387	G	Vienna, 31 Dec. 1782	VIII:20/1/2	pub. Vienna, 1785, together with K421, 428, 458, 464, 465, ded. J. Haydn
421	d	[Vienna, June 1783]	VIII:20/1/2	
428	E♭	[Vienna, June–July 1783]	VIII:20/1/2	
458	B♭	[Vienna, 9 Nov. 1784]	VIII:20/1/2	'Hunt'
464	A	Vienna, 10 Jan. 1785	VIII:20/1/2	
465	C	Vienna, 14 Jan. 1785	VIII:20/1/2	'Dissonance'
499	D	Vienna, 19 Aug. 1786	VIII:20/1/3	'Hoffmeister', pub. Vienna, 1786
546	c	Vienna, 26 June 1788	IV:11/10	Adagio and fugue, possibly for string orch; fugue arr. from K426 (piano)
575	D	Vienna, June 1789	VIII:20/1/3	'Prussian'
589	B♭	Vienna, May 1790	VIII:20/1/3	'Prussian'
590	F	Vienna, June 1790	VIII:20/1/3	'Prussian'

String sonatas, duos, trios

K	Title	Key	Scoring	Place, date	NMA	Remarks
33b	Solos	—	vc, b	Donaueschingen, Oct. 1766	—	lost
41g	Nachtmusik		vn, b	[?Salzburg, 1760s]	—	lost
46d	Sonata	C	vn, b	Vienna, 1 Sept. 1768	VIII:21	
46e	Sonata	F	vn, b	Vienna, 1 Sept. 1768	VIII:21	
266	Trio	B♭	vn, b	[Salzburg, early 1777]	VIII:21	
404a	6 preludes		vn, va, vc	Vienna, 1782	—	doubtful; for fugues by J. S. and W. F. Bach; see 'Arrangements'
423	Duo	G	vn, va	Salzburg or Vienna, 1783	VIII:21	
424	Duo	B♭	vn, va	Salzburg or Vienna, 1783	VIII:21	
563	Trio	E♭	vn, va, vc	Vienna, 27 Sept. 1788	VIII:21	'Ein Divertimento . . . di sei pezzi'
—		—	b viol, b	? by late 1768	—	lost
—	6 trios		2 vn, vc	? by late 1768	—	lost

Traditionally attributed to Mozart but lacking authentic sources: K404a, 6 preludes for fugues by J. S. and W. F. Bach, [Vienna, 1782], doubtful

Keyboard and two or more instruments

K	Title	Key	Scoring	Place, date	NMA	Remarks
254	Divertimento	B♭	pf, vn, vc	Salzburg, Aug. 1776	VIII:22/2	pub. Paris, c.1782
452	Quintet	E♭	pf, ob, cl, bn, hn	Vienna, 30 Mar. 1784	VIII:22/1	sketches survive
478	Quartet	g	pf, vn, va, vc	Vienna, 16 Oct. 1785	VIII:22/1	pub. Vienna, 1785–6
493	Quartet	E♭	pf, vn, va, vc	Vienna, 3 June 1786	VIII:22/1	pub. Vienna, 1787; sketches survive
496	Trio	G	pf, vn, vc	Vienna, 8 July 1786	VIII:22/2	pub. Vienna, 1786; sketches survive
498	Trio	E♭	pf, cl, va	Vienna, 5 Aug. 1786	VIII:22/2	pub. Vienna, 1788
502	Trio	B♭	pf, vn, vc	Vienna, 18 Nov. 1786	VIII:22/2	pub. Vienna, 1788
542	Trio	E	pf, vn, vc	Vienna, 22 June 1788	VIII:22/2	pub. Vienna, 1788
548	Trio	C	pf, vn, vc	Vienna, 14 July 1788	VIII:22/2	pub. Vienna, 1788
564	Trio	G	pf, vn, vc	Vienna, 27 Oct. 1788	VIII:22/2	pub. London, 1789
617	Adagio and Rondo	c	armonica, fl, ob, va, vc	Vienna, 23 May 1791	VIII:22/1	

Keyboard and violin (sonatas unless noted otherwise)

K	Key(s)	Place, date	NMA	Remarks
6–7	C, D	Salzburg, Paris, 1762–4	VIII:23/1	pub. Paris, 1764, ded. Marie-Thérèse de Bourbon
8–9	B♭, G	Paris, 1763–4	VIII:23/1	pub. Paris, 1764, ded. Adrienne-Catherine de Thesée
10–15	B♭, G, A, F, C, B♭	London, 1764	VIII:22/2	pub. London, 1765. ded. Queen Charlotte of Mecklenburg-Strelitz; vc ad lib
26–31	E♭, G, C, D, F, B♭	The Hague, [Feb.] 1766	VIII:23/1	pub. The Hague and Amsterdam, 1766, ded. Princess Caroline of Nassau-Weilburg
301	G	[Mannheim, early 1778]	VIII:23/1	K301–6 pub. Paris, 1778, ded. Elisabeth Maria Aloysia Auguste, Electress of the Pfalz
302	E♭	[Mannheim, early 1778]	VIII:23/1	
303	C	[Mannheim, early 1778]	VIII:23/1	
305	A	[Mannheim, early 1778]	VIII:23/1	
296	C	Mannheim, 11 Mar. 1778	VIII:23/1	K296, 376–380 pub. Vienna, 1781
304	e	Paris, summer 1778	VIII:23/1	
306	D	[Paris, summer 1778]	VIII:23/1	
378	B♭	[Salzburg, 1779–80]	VIII:23/1	
372	B♭	Vienna, 24 Mar. 1781	VIII:23/2	Allegro only, incomplete; completed by M. Stadler
379	G	[Vienna, probably Apr. 1781]	VIII:23/2	
359	G	[Vienna, summer 1781]	VIII:23/2	variations on French song, 'La bergère Célimène', pub. Vienna, 1786
360	g	[Vienna, summer 1781]	VIII:23/2	variations on French song, 'Hélas, j'ai perdu mon amant', pub. Vienna, 1786
376	F	[Vienna, summer 1781]	VIII:23/2	
377	F	[Vienna, summer 1781]	VIII:23/2	
380	E♭	[Vienna, summer 1781]	VIII:23/2	
454	B♭	Vienna, 21 Apr. 1784	VIII:23/2	for Regina Strinasacchi; pub. Vienna, 1784
481	E♭	Vienna, 12 Dec. 1785	VIII:23/2	pub. Vienna, 1786
526	A	Vienna, 24 Aug. 1787	VIII:23/2	pub. Vienna, 1787
547	F	Vienna, 10 July 1788	VIII:23/2	'for beginners'

Spurious: K55–60, 'Romantic', by ?, *NMA* X:29/2; K61, by H. F. Raupach

KEYBOARD

Sonatas

K	Key	Place, date	NMA	Remarks
		Solo keyboard		
279–83	C, F, B♭, E♭, G	[Salzburg or Munich, late 1774–early 1775]	IX:25/1	
284	D	[Munich, Feb.–Mar. 1775]	IX:25/1	pub. Vienna, 1784
309	C	Mannheim, Nov.–Dec. 1777	IX:25/1	K309–11 pub. Paris, 1782
311	D	[Mannheim, Oct.–Nov. 1777]	IX:25/1	
310	a	Paris, 1778	IX:25/1	
330	C	[Vienna, 1783]	IX:25/2	K330–2 pub. Vienna, 1784
331	A	[Vienna, 1783]	IX:25/2	
332	F	[Salzburg or Munich, 1780]	IX:25/2	
333	B♭	[Linz or Vienna, 1783]	IX:25/2	pub. Vienna, 1784
457	c	Vienna, 14 Oct. 1784	IX:25/2	pub. with Fantasia K475, Vienna, 1785
533	F	Vienna, 3 Jan. 1788	IX:25/2	pub. with rev. version of Rondo K494, Vienna, 1788
545	C	Vienna, 26 June 1788	IX:25/2	'for beginners'
570	B♭	Vienna, Feb. 1789	IX:25/2	
576	D	Vienna, July 1789	IX:25/2	

Traditionally attributed to Mozart but lacking authentic sources: K33d–g, [1766], lost, listed in catalogue of publisher Breitkopf (1803); 547a, F, [Vienna, 1788], includes arrangements from K547 and K545, NMA IX:26, doubtful

K	Key	Place, date	NMA	Remarks
		Keyboard duet		
381	D	[Salzburg, mid-1772]	IX:24/2	K381, K358 pub. Vienna, 1783
358	B♭	[Salzburg, late 1773–early 1774]	IX:24/2	
497	F	Vienna, 1 Aug. 1786	IX:24/2	pub. Vienna, 1787
521	C	Vienna, 29 May 1787	IX:24/2	pub. Vienna, 1787
		for 2 keyboards		
448	D	Vienna, Nov. 1781	IX:24/1	

Traditionally attributed to Mozart but lacking authentic sources: K19d, C, [London, 1765], NMA IX: 24/2, doubtful, KA43/375c, B?, 2 kbd, 1782–3

Variations

K	Theme	Key	Place, date	NMA	Remarks
			Solo keyboard		
24	Dutch song, 'Laat ons juichen', by C. E. Graaf	G	Amsterdam or The Hague, by 7 Mar. 1766	IX:26	pub. The Hague, 1766
25	Dutch national song, 'Willem van Nassau'	D	Amsterdam or The Hague, by 7 Mar. 1766	IX:26	pub. The Hague, 1766
180	'Mio caro Adone' from Salieri, *La fiera di Venezia*, Vienna, 1772	G	[?Vienna, autumn 1773 or later]	IX:26	pub. Paris, 1778
179	Minuet, finale of ob conc. no.1, 1768, by J. C. Fischer	C	[Salzburg, by Dec. 1774]	IX:26	pub. Paris, 1778
354	'Je suis Lindor', song in Beaumarchais, *Le Barbier de Séville*, by A. L. Baudron	E♭	Paris, early 1778	IX:26	pub. Paris, 1778
265	French song 'Ah vous dirai-je, maman'	C	[Vienna, 1781–3]	IX:26	pub. Vienna, 1785
353	French song, *La Belle Françoise* ('Adieu donc, dame françoise)	E♭	[Vienna, 1781–3]	IX:26	pub. Vienna, 1786
264	'Lison dormait' from N. Dezède, *Julie*, Paris, 1772	C	[Vienna, 1781–6]	IX:26	shortened version pub. Paris, 1786; complete version pub. Vienna, 1786
352	'Dieu d'amour' from A.-E.-M. Grétry, *Les Mariages samnites*, Paris, 1776	F	[Vienna, 1781–6]	IX:26	pub. Vienna, 1786
398	'Salve tu, Domine' from G. Paisiello, *I filosofi immaginari*, Vienna, 1781	F	[Vienna, Mar. 1783–6]	IX:26	pub. Vienna, 1786

460	'Come un agnello' from Sarti, *Fra i due litiganti*, Milan, 1782	A	[Vienna, 1783–4]	IX:26	autograph has 2 variations; version with 8 variations pub. Vienna, 1784 possibly by Sardi
455	'Les hommes pieusement (Unser dummer Pöbel meint)' from Gluck, *La rencontre imprévue*	G	Vienna, 25 Aug. 1784	IX:26	pub. Vienna, 1785; possibly earlier version, 1781–2
500	?original	B♭	Vienna, 12 Sept. 1786	IX:26	
54	probably orig.	F	Vienna, July 1788	IX:26	1st edn. (1785) has spurious 4th variation; reused by Mozart, with vn, K547
573	Minuet from vc sonata op. 4 no. 6 by J. P. Duport	D	Potsdam, 29 Apr. 1789	IX:26	pub. Berlin, 1791
613	'Ein Weib ist das herrlichste Ding', by B. Schack or F. X. Gerl for E. Schikaneder, *Der dumme Gärtner aus dem Gebirge*, Vienna, 1789	F	Vienna, Mar.–Apr. 1791	IX:26	

Traditionally attributed to Mozart but lacking authentic sources: K21a, C, ?original theme, [London, 1764–5], lost, listed in catalogue of publisher Breitkopf (1803); K54, F, July 1788, surviving autograph probably piano part to sonata for kbd, vn, K547

piano duet

501	probably original	G	Vienna, 4 Nov. 1786	IX:24/ii

Miscellaneous

K	Title	Key	Composition	NMA	Remarks
			solo keyboard or 2 keyboards		
1a	Andante	C	Salzburg, early 1761	IX:27/1	
1b	Allegro	C	Salzburg, early 1761	IX:27/1	
1c	Allegro	F	Salzburg, 11 Dec. 1761	IX:27/1	
1d	Minuet	F	Salzburg, 16 Dec. 1761	IX:27/1	
1	Minuets	G, C	Salzburg, early 1760s	IX:27/1	
2	Minuet	F	Salzburg, Jan. 1762	IX:27/1	
3	Allegro	B♭	Salzburg, 4 Mar. 1762	IX:27/1	
4	Minuet	F	Salzburg, 11 May 1762	IX:27/1	
5	Minuet	F	Salzburg, 5 July 1762	IX:27/1	
5aa	Allegro	C	[?, c.1764]	IX:27/1	
95b	Andante	B♭	[?, c.1764]	IX:27/1	
33B	[without title]	F	Zurich, Oct. 1766	X:30/4	
41e	Fugue		?, by late 1768	IX:27/1	lost
72a	Allegro	G	[Verona, Jan. 1770]	IX:27/2	incomplete, known only from portrait by S. dalla Rosa
94	Minuet	D	[Salzburg, 1769]	IV:13/1	
284f	Rondo		Mannheim, Nov. 1777	—	lost, mentioned in letter of 29 Nov. 1777
395	Capriccio	C	Munich, Oct. 1777	—	identical with K284a
315a	8 minuets, 7 trios		[Salzburg, late 1773]	IV:13/1, IX:27/2	

400	Allegro	B♭	[Vienna, 1782 or later]	IX:25/2	incomplete, finished by M. Stadler
401	Fugue	g	[Salzburg, early 1770s]	IX:27/2	incomplete, finished by M. Stadler
153	Fugue	E♭	[Vienna, 1782]	IX:27/2	incomplete, finished by S. Sechter
394	Prelude and fugue	C	[Vienna, early 1782]	IX:27/2	
396	Fantasia	c	[Vienna, early 1782]	IX:27/2	incomplete
397	Fantasia	d	[Vienna, 1780s]	IX:27/2	last 10 bars probably spurious
399	Suite	C	[Vienna, 1782]	IX:27/2	Sarabande incomplete
154	Fugue	g	[Vienna, 1782]	IX:27/2	incomplete, finished by S. Sechter
453a	Funeral March	c	Vienna, c.1784	IX:27/2	from musical notebook of B. Ployer
475	Fantasia	c	Vienna, 20 May 1785	IX:25/2	pub. with Sonata K457 (Vienna, 1785)
485	Rondo	D	Vienna, 10 Jan. 1786	IX:27/2	pub. Vienna, c.1786
494	Rondo	F	Vienna, 10 June 1786	IX:25/2	pub. London and Speyer, 1788; rev. version in sonata K533
511	Rondo	a	Vienna, 11 Mar. 1787	IX:27/2	pub. Vienna, 1787
540	Adagio	b	Vienna, 19 Mar. 1788	IX:27/2	
574	Gigue	G	Leipzig, 16 or 17 May 1789	IX:27/2	
355	Minuet	D	[Vienna, 1780s]	IX:27/2, X:30/4	trio by M. Stadler
236	Andantino			—	see 'Arrangements'
312	Allegro	g	[Vienna, 1790–1]	IX:25/2	incomplete
426	Fugue	c	Vienna, 29 Dec. 1783	IX:24/1	for 2 kbd, pub. Vienna, 1788; arr., with new introduction, for str qnt, K546
—	Larghetto and Allegro	E♭	[Vienna, 1782–3]	IX:24/1, suppl.	for 2 kbd; incomplete, finished by M. Stadler

(cont.)

K	Title	Instrument	Key	Place, date	NMA	Remarks
		for mechanical organ or glass harmonica				
594	Adagio and Allegro	Mechanical org	f	[Vienna, late 1790]	IX:27/2	
608	Allegro and Andante	Mechanical org	f	Vienna, 3 Mar. 1791	IX:27/2	
616	Andante	Mechanical org	F	Vienna, 4 May 1791	IX:27/2	
356	Adagio	glass harmonica	C	[Vienna, 1791]	IX:27/2	

miscellaneous

K	Title	Key	Place, date	NMA	Remarks
15a–ss	London Sketchbook		London, 1764–5	IX:27/1	short pieces for kbd
32a	Capricci		[?1764–6]	—	lost
41f	Fugue a 4		?, by late 1768	—	lost
Anh. A65	Adagio	F	[Salzburg, early 1770s]	ed. N. Zaslaw in *Haydn, Mozart and Beethoven: Essays in Honour of Alan Tyson*, ed. S. Brandenburg (Oxford, 1998), 101–14	
393	Solfeggios for voice		[Salzburg and Vienna, 1781–5]	I:1/1/5 (no. 2 only)	
453b	Exercise book for Barbara Ployer		Vienna, c.1784	X:30/2	
506a	Attwood Studies		Vienna, 1785–6	X:30/1	
516f	Musikalisches Würfelspiel	C	[Vienna, 1787]	H. Nouchi, 'Mozart: Musical Game in C major K. 516f', *Mitteilungen der Internationalen Stiftung Mozarteum* 38 (1990), 89–101	

ARRANGEMENTS OF WORKS BY OTHER COMPOSERS

K	Orig. composer, work	Orig. scoring	Mozart's scoring	Date of arr.	NMA	Remarks
37	(i) Raupach, op. 1 no. 5, (ii) ?, (iii) L. Honauer, op. 2 no. 3	kbd	kbd, 2 ob, 2 hn, str	Salzburg, Apr. 1767	X:28/2	
39	(i) Raupach, op. 1 no. 1; (ii) J. Schobert, op. 17 no. 2; (iii) Raupach, op. 1 no. 1	kbd	kbd, 2 ob, 2 hn, str	Salzburg, June 1767	X:28/2	
40	(i) Honauer, op. 2 no. 1; (ii) J. G. Eckard, op. 1 no. 4; (iii) C. P. E. Bach, Wq117	kbd	kbd, 2 ob, 2 hn, str	Salzburg, July 1767	X:28/2	
41	(i) Honauer, op. 1 no. 1; (ii) Raupach, op. 1, no. 1; (iii) Honauer, op. 1 no. 1	kbd	kbd, 2 ob, 2 hn, str	Salzburg, July 1767	X:28/2	
61gII	M. Haydn, minuet	kbd	orch	[Salzburg, c.1771]	IV:13/1/1	
122	M. Haydn, minuet	orch	orch	Bologna, c.Aug. 1770	IV:13/1/1	
44	J. Stadlmayr, Musica super cantum gregorianum	5vv	SATB	[Salzburg, c.1768–9]	—	
107/1	J. C. Bach, op. 5 no. 2	kbd	kbd, 2 vn, b	[Salzburg, c.1772]	X:28/2	
107/2	J. C. Bach, op. 5 no. 3	kbd	kbd, 2 vn, b	[Salzburg, c.1772]	X:28/2	
107/3	J. C. Bach, op. 5 no. 4	kbd	kbd, 2 vn, b	[Sazburg, c.1772]	X:28/2	
236	C. W. Gluck, 'Non vi turbate, no' from *Alceste*		kbd	Vienna, 1782–3	XVIII:3–5/2	20 bars only

(cont.)

(cont.)

K	Orig. composer, work	Orig. scoring	Mozart's scoring	Date of arr.	NMA	Remarks
284*e*	J. B. Wendling, concerto	fl, str	?addl wind	Mannheim, Nov. 1777	—	lost
405	J. S. Bach, *Well-Tempered Clavier*	kbd	str	Vienna, 1782	—	Ed. in *Mozart-Jahrbuch* 1962–3, 144–55
470a	G. B. Viotti, Vn Concerto no.16		added tpt, timp	[Vienna, c.1789–90]	—	
506a	J. Haydn, duet 'Cara, sarò fedele', from *Armida*			[Vienna, c.1786–91]	—	formerly considered part of Attwood exercises
537d	C. P. E. Bach, 'Ich folge dir', from *Auferstehung und Himmelfahrt Jesu*	T, tpt, str	added fl, ob, tpt	[Vienna, Feb. 1788]	—	
566	G. F. Handel, *Acis and Galatea*	S, T, T, T, B, rec, 2 ob, bn, 2 vn, va, bc	added 2 fl, 2 cl, bn, 2 hn	[Vienna, Nov. 1788]	X:28/1/1	
572	Handel, *Messiah*	S, A, T, B, SATB, 2 ob, 2 tpt, timp, str	added 2 fl, 2 cl, 2 bn, 2 hn, 3 trbn, rev. tpt parts	Vienna, Mar. 1789	X:28/1/2	
591	Handel, *Alexander's Feast*	S, T, B, SATB, 2 rec, 2 ob, 3 bn, 2 hn, 2 tpt, timp, str	added 2 fl, 2 cl, rev. tpt parts	[Vienna, July 1790]	X:28/1/3	
592	Handel, *Ode for St Cecilia's Day*	S, T, SATB, fl, 2 ob, 2 tpt, timp, lute, str	added fl, 2 cl, 2 bn, 2 hn, rev. tpt parts	[Vienna, July 1790]	X:28/1/4	

624	cadenzas	—	kbd	various	—	for J. S. Schroeter op. 3 nos. 1, 4, 6; unidentified concerto by I. v. Beecke; and unidentified composers
626b/28	Gluck, Gavotte from *Paride ed Elena*	orch	2 fl, 5 tpt, timp		—	
18	C. F. Abel, symphony op.7 no.6	orch	added cls	London, 1764–5	—	
—	L. Mozart, Litaniae de venerabili altaris sacramento	S, A, T, B, SATB, 2 hn, str	various changes		X:28/3–5/1	
—	L. Mozart, Litany	SATB, orch	trbn/va solo arr. for ob	[Salzburg, c.1774]	X:28/3–5/2	

Attributed to Mozart but lacking authentic sources: K404, preludes to fugues by J. S. Bach

Appendix 2
Mozart movies (theatrical releases)

La Mort de Mozart (France, 1909, dir. Louis Feuillade; released in the United States as *Mozart's Last Requiem*)

Footprints of Mozart (United States, 1914, dir. Thomas Ricketts)

Mozarts Leben, Lieben und Leiden (Austria, 1921, dir. Otto Kreisler and Karl Toma)

Whom the Gods Love (UK, 1936, dir. Basil Dean; re-released in 1949 as *Mozart*)

Eine kleine Nachtmusik (Germany, 1939, dir. Leopold Hainisch)

Melodie Eterne (Italy, 1940, dir. Carmine Gallone; released in English as *Eternal Melodies*, 1948)

Wen die Götter lieben (Austria, 1942, dir. Karl Hartl; see *The Mozart Story*, 1948)

The Mozart Story (United States, 1948, dir. Karl Hartl and Frank Wisbar; an expanded version *Wen die Götter lieben*, 1942, with twenty-two additional minutes)

Unsterblicher Mozart (Germany, 1954, dir. Alfred Stöger)

Reich mir die Hand, mein Leben (Austria, 1955, dir. Karl Hartl; released in the United States as *The Life and Loves of Mozart*)

Motsart i Salieri (USSR, 1962, dir. Vladimir Gorikker; released internationally as *A Requiem for Mozart* and *Mozart and Salieri*)

Das Leben Mozarts (Austria, 1967, dir. Hans Conrad Fischer)

Mozart in Prag – Don Giovanni 67 (Germany, 1968, dir. Wolfgang Esterer)

Mozart in Love (United States, 1975, dir. Mark Rappaport)

Mozart. Aufzeichnungen einer Jugend (Germany, 1976, dir. Klaus Kirschner; also released as *Vorname Mozart*)

Noi Tre (Italy, 1984, dir. Pupi Avati)

Amadeus (United States, 1984, dir. Miloš Forman)

Vergesst Mozart (Germany, 1985, dir. Slavo Luther; released in the United States as *Forget Mozart* and in Czechoslovakia as *Zabudnite na Mozarta*)

Mozart (Canada and Hungary, 1987, dir. Nicholas Vazsonyi)

Mozart und Da Ponte (Austria, 1989, dir. Gernot Friedel)

Wolfgang A. Mozart (Austria, 1991, dir. Juraj Herz; also released as *Wolfgang – Mehr als ein Prinz*)

In Search of Mozart (England, 2005, dir. Phil Grabsky; www.insearchofMozart.com)

Further reading

W. Freitag, *Wolfgang Amadeus & Co: Mozart in Film* (Mödling, 1991)
H. Green, 'Celluloid Mozart', *Opera News* 23 (9 Feb. 1959), 31
M. Ulmer and J. Wittwer, 'Die Ikonographie des Mozart-Mythos im Film', in *Mozart: Mythos, Markt und Medien. Ein Komponist zwischen Kunst und Kommerz 1791–1991*, ed. T. Hickl, S. Sprick-Schütte and M. Halusa (Anif/Salzburg, 1995), 41–59

Appendix 3
Mozart operas on DVD and video

This list of important video recordings of Mozart operas is selective; it includes the majority of productions from major opera houses and festivals, made-for-TV productions and theatrical releases but is by no means complete. Most of these recordings are readily available from a variety of sources including major record stores, opera houses and, in particular, from online dealers in opera video. Given the vagaries of cataloguing and the lack of a standardized format for describing the details of video productions, only the basic information is given here. Nevertheless, individual productions can easily be found from the sources mentioned above.

Apollo et Hyacinthus

1983, dir. Claus Helmut Drese, cond. Helmut Müller-Brühl, Cappella Clementina; singers include Manfred Hohenleitner, Cedric Rossdeutscher, Allan Bergius, Panito Iconomou, Michel Lecocq (recorded at Schloss Augustusburg, Brühl)

1991, dir. Vittorio Patané, cond. Peter Schneider, Münchner Rundfunkorchester; singers include Claes H. Ahnsjö, Caroline Maria Petrig, Julie Kaufmann, Daphne Evangelatos, Birgit Calm (recorded at the Cuvilliestheater, München)

Bastien und Bastienne

1954, dir. ?, cond. Albert Kaiser, Collegium Musicum Basel; singers include Hans Jonelli, Heidi Bumbrunn, Mogens Wedel

1963, dir. Christopher Muir, cond. Clive Douglas; singers include George Hegan, Eunice McGowan, Keithe Neilson

1989, dir. Walter Berry, cond. Niksa Bareza, Haydn-Sinfonietta Wien; singers include Rhonda Ingle, Franz Supper, Johannes Jokel (recorded at the Gmundner Festpiele, 1989)

La clemenza di Tito

1987, dir Göram Järvefelt, cond. Arnold Östmann; singers include Stefan Dahlberg, Anita Soldh, Lani Poulson, Jerker Arvidson, Maria Höglind, Pia-Marie Nilsson (recorded at the Drottningholm Court Theatre)

1991, dir. Nicholas Hytner, cond. Andrew Davis, London Philharmonic Orchestra; singers include Philip Langridge, Ashley Putnam, Diana Montague (recorded live at the Glyndebourne Festival, with new recitatives by Stephen Oliver)

Così fan tutte

1957, dir. Roger Burckhardt, cond. Albert E. Kaiser, Collegium Musicum Basel; singers include Ingeborg Wieser, Charlote Sender, Hedda Heusser, Hans Jonelli, Franz Lindauer, Derrik Olsen

1959, dir. Marcello Cortis, cond. Alberto Erede, Société des Concerts du Conservatoire; singers include Teresa Stich-Randall, Nan Merriman, Mariella Adani, Luigi Alva, Heinz Blankenburg, Marcello Cortis (recorded live at the Festival d'Aix-en-Provence)

1965, dir. Marcello Cortis, cond. Serge Baudo, Société des Concerts du Conservatoire; singers include Teresa Stich-Randall, Teresa Berganza, Mariella Adani, Michel Sénéchal, Wladimiro Ganzarolli, Gabriel Bacquier (recorded live at the Festival d'Aix-en-Provence)

1968, dir. John Copley, cond. Georg Solti; singers include Pilar Lorengar, Josephine Veasey, Lucia Popp, Donald Grobe, Wladimiro Ganzarolli, Kieth Engen (recorded live at the Royal Opera, Covent Garden)

1975, dir. Adrian Slack, cond. John Pritchard, London Philharmonic Orchestra; singers include Helena Dose, Sylvia Lindenstrand, Daniele Perriers, Anson Austin, Thomas Allen, Grantz Petri (recorded at the Glyndebourne Festival)

1984, dir. Thomas Olofsson, cond. Arnold Östmann, Drottningholm Court Theatre Orchestra; singers include Ann Christine Biel, Maria Höglind, Ulla Severin, Lars Tibell, Magus Lindén, Enzo Florimo

1987, dir. Marco Arturo Marelli, cond. Bruno Weil, Wiener Volksoper; singers include Gunnel Bohman, Thomas Lander, Ulrike Steinsky, Martina Borst, Bruce Ford, Jürgen Freier (German version by Richard Bletschacher)

1989, dir. Jean-Pierre Ponnelle, cond. Nikolaus Harnoncourt, Wiener Philharmoniker; singers include Edita Gruberova, Dolores Ziegler, Teresa Stratas, Luis Lima, Ferruccio Fulanetto, Paolo Montarsolo

1989, dir. Ilio Catani, cond. Riccardo Muti; singers include Daniella Dessi, Dolores Ziegler, Alessandro Corbelli, Jozef Kundlak, Adelina Scarabelli, Claudio Desderi

1989, dir. Peter Sellars cond. Craig Smith, Wiener Symphoniker; singers include Susan Larson, Janice Felty, James Maddalena, Frank Kelly, Sue Ellen Kuzman, Sanford Sylvan

1989, dir. Johannes Schaaf, cond. Jeffrey Tate; singers include Hans Peter Blochwitz, Andreas Schmidt, Claudio Desderi, Margaret Marshall, Susanne Mentzer, Anne Howells (recorded at the Royal Opera, Covent Garden)

1992, dir. Peter Mumford, cond. John Eliot Gardiner; singers include Amanda Roocroft, Rosa Mannion, Elmore James, Rodney Gilfry, Claudio Nicolai

1996, dir. Brian Large, cond. Riccardo Muti; singers include Barbara Frittoli, Angelika Kirchschlager, Bo Skovhus, Michael Schade, Monica Bacelli, Alessandro Corbelli

2000, dir. Brian Large, cond. Nikolaus Harnoncourt, Opernhaus Zürich; singers include Cecilia Bartoli, Agnes Baltsa, Liliana Nikiteanu, Roberto Sacca, Oliver Widmer, Carlos Chausson

2000, dir. Yves-André Hubert, cond. René Jacobs; singers include Alexandra Deshorties, Liliana Nikiteanu, Stephan Genz, Jeremy Ovenden, Graciela Oddene, Pietro Spagnoli

Don Giovanni

1916, dir. Edoardo Bencivenga; cast includes Mario Bonnard, Alfredo De Antoni, Camillo De Riso, Lea Giunchi, Matilde Guillaume (silent)

1955, dir. Paul Czinner and Alfred Travers, cond. Wilhelm Furtwängler, Wiener Staatsoper; singers include Otto Edelmann, Elisabeth Grümmer, Cesare Siepi, Dezsö Ernster, Anton Dermota, Lisa della Casa, Erna Berger, Walter Berry (Salzburg Festival production)

1964, dir. Jean Meyer, cond. Peter Maag, Société des Concerts du Conservatoire; singers include Gabriel Bacquier, Giorgio Tadeo, Teresa Stich-Randall, Luigi Alva, Ilva Ligabue, Wladimiro Ganzaroli, Mariella Adani, Theodor Uppman (recorded live at the Festival d'Aix-en-Provence)

1967, dir. Jean Meyer, cond. Serge Baudo; singers include Gabriel Bacquier, Gundula Janowitz, William Blankenship, Sylvia Stahlmann, Mariella Adani, Heinz Blankenburg, Jacques Mars, Roger Soyer (recorded live at the Festival d'Aix-en-Provence)

1977, dir. Dave Heahe, cond. Bernard Haitink, London Philharmonic Orchestra; singers include Benjamin Luxon, Stafford Dean, Leo Goeke, Rachel Yakar, Horiana Branisteanu, Elizabeth Gale, John Rawnsley, Pierre Thau (Glyndebourne Festival production)

1979, dir. Joseph Losey, cond. Lorin Maazel, orchestra of the Théâtre National de l'Opéra de Paris; singers include Ruggero Raimondi, John Macurdy, Edda Moser, Kiri Te Kanawa, Kenneth Riegel, José van Dam, Teresa Berganza, Malcolm King

1983, dir. Adrian Noble, cond. Peter Robinson, Kent Opera; singers include Peter Knapp, Thomas Lawlor, Janice Cairns, Mark Curtis, Jan Mackenzie, Geoffrey Moses, Roger Bryson, Meryl Drower

1987, dir. Václav Kaslik, cond. Zdenek Kosler, orchestra of the National Theatre, Prague; singers include Pavel Horácek, Eva Depoltová, Daniela Sounová-Brouková, Jirina Marková, Miroslav Kopp, Ludek Velo, Bohuslav Marsik, Karel Prusa (recorded live at the National Theatre, Prague)

1987, dir. Claus Viller, cond. Herbert von Karajan; singers include Samuel Ramey, Anna Tomowa-Sintow, Gösta Winbergh, Paata Burchuladze, Julia Varady, Ferruccio Furlanetto, Alexander Malta, Kathleen Battle (recorded at the Salzburg Festival)

1987, dir. Giorgio Strehler, cond. Riccardo Muti, La Scala; singers include Thomas Allen, Sergej Koptchak, Edita Gruberova, Francisco Araiza, Ann Murray, Claudio Desderi, Natale de Carolis, Susanne Mentzer

1987, dir. Thomas Olofsson, cond. Arnold Östmann, orchestra of the Drottningholm Court Theatre; singers include Håkan Hagegård, Bengt Rundgren, Erik Saedén, Helena Dose, Gösta Winbergh, Birgit Nordin, Tord Wallström, Anita Soldh

1989, dir. Carlo Battistoni, cond. Riccardo Muti, orchestra of the Teatro all Scala; singers include Thomas Allen, Sergei Koptchak, Edita Gruberova, Francisco Araiza, Ann Murray, Claudio Desderi, Natale De Carolis, Susanne Mentzer

1990, dir. Brian Large, cond. James Levine, orchestra of the Metropolitan Opera, New York; singers include Samuel Ramey, Ferruccio Furlanetto, Carol Vaness, Karita Mattila, Jerry Hadley, Dawn Upshaw, Philip Cokorinos, Kurt Moll

1990, dir. Peter Sellars, cond. Craig Smith, Wiener Symphoniker; singers include Herbert Perry, Eugene Perry, Dominique Labelle, Lorraine Hunt Lieberson, Carroll Freeman, James Patterson, Ai Lan Zhu, Elmore James

1990, dir. Luca Ronconi, cond. Riccardo Chailly, Teatro Comunale di Bologna; singers include Ruggero Raimondi, Jane Eaglen, Rockwell Blaxe, Daniella Dessi, Alessandro Corbelli, Giovanni Furlanetto, Adelina Scarabelli, Andrea Silvestrelli

1991, dir. José Montes-Baquer, cond. James Conlon; singers include Thomas Allen, Carolyn James, Carol Vaness, Ferruccio Furlanetto, Kjel Magnus Sandvé, Andrea Rost, Reinhard Dorn, Matthias Hölle (produced at the Opernhaus Köln)

1997, dir. Manuela Crivelli, cond. Claudio Abbado, Chamber Orchestra of Europe; singers include Simon Keenleyside, Matti Salminen, Carmela Remigio, Bruno Lazzaretti, Anna Caterina Antonacci, Bryn Terfel, Ildebrando d'Arcangelo, Patrizia Pace

2000, dir. Gary Halvorson, cond. James Levine; singers include Renée Fleming, Ferruccio Furlanetto, Paul Groves, Hei-Kyung Hong, Sergei Koptchak, Solveig Kringelborn, Rohn Relyea, Bryn Terfel

Die Entführung aus dem Serail

1990, dir. Thomas Olofsson, cond. Georg Solti, Orchestra of the Royal Opera House; singers include Aga Winska, Marianne Hellström, Richard Croft, Bengt-Ola Morgny, Tamás Szüle, Emmerich Schäffer (made for TV, BBC)

2003, dir. Chloé Perlemuter, cond. Franz Welser-Möst; singers include Klaus Maria Brandauer, Malin Hartelius, Patricia Petibon, Piotr Beczala, Boguslaw Bidzinski, Alfred Muff (made for TV)

La finta giardiniera

1957, dir. and cond. Sarah Caldwell, Boston University Symphony Orchestra; singers include James Billings, Plyna Bagaretou, Merle Puffer, Lesli Loosli, Rosalind Hupp, Rolanda Ringo, Richard Christopher (recorded for Public Television, sung in English)

1960, dir. Willi Pribil, cond. Hans Gabor, Wiener Kammeroper orchestra; singers include Hermine Biedermann, Ursula Wendt, Ruth Rohner, Helga Wangen, Herbert Prikopa, Hans Krämmer, Hano Werner (recorded at the Schlosstheater, Schönbrunn)

1964, dir. Roy Bosier, cond. Armin Brunner, Zürcher Kammeroper orchestra; singers include Hans Jonelli, Elfriede Pfleger, Madeleine Baer, Fritz Peter, Linda Trotter, Franz Lindauer, Ruth Rohner (recorded live at the Zürcher Kammeroper)

1979, dir. Filippo Crivelli, cond. Marc Andreae, RTSI; singers include Tullio Pane, Valeria Mariconda, Ernesto Palacio, Romana Righetti, Benedetta Pecchioli, Carmen Lavani, Mario Chiappa

1985, dir. ?, cond. Adam Medveczky, Magyar Állami Operaház (Hungarian State Opera); singers include Julia Kukely, Margit Laszlo, Marta Szücs, Andras Molnar, Janos Bandi, Peter Korcsmaros, Istvan Gati, Jozsef Lukacsi

1988, dir. Göran Järvefelt and Thomas Olofsson, cond. Arnold Östman, Drottningholm Theatre orchestra; singers include Britt-Marie Aruhn, Stuart Kale, Richard Croft, Annika Skoglund, Petteri Salomaa (recorded at the Drottningholm Court Theatre)

1989, dir. Karl Ernst Herrmann, cond. Sylvain Cambreling; singers include Ugo Benelli, Joanna Kozlowska, Marek Torzewski, Malvina Major, Elzbieta Szmytka, Russell Smythe, Lani Poulson (recorded at the Théâtre de la Monnaie, Brussels)

1990, dir. Karl-Ernst and Ursel Herr, cond. Sylvain Cambreling, Monnaie Symphony Orchestra; singers include Ugo Benelli, Joanna Kozlowska, Marek Torzewski, Malvina Major, Elzbieta Szmytka, Russell Smythe, Lani Poulson, Mireille Mossé (recorded live at the Monnaie de Munt, Brussels)

La finta semplice

1962, dir. Gottlieb Zeithammer, cond. Armin Brunner, Zürcher Kammeroper orchestra; singers include Slata Ognjanovic, Ernst-August Steinhoff, Ruth Rohner, Ursula Sutter, Giacomo Tavoli, Franz Lindauer, Gottlieb Zeithammer

1991, dir. Christian Gagneron, cond. René Jacobs, Concerto Köln; singers include Lena Lootens, François Harismendy, Guy de Mey, Jennifer Larmore, Isabelle Poulenard

Idomeneo

1963, dir. Michel Crochot, cond. Peter Maag, Konzertvereinigung Köln; singers include Teresa Stich-Randall, Enriqueta Tarres, Ronald Down, William

MacAlpine, Giogio Tadeo, Jacques Villisech, Antoine Selva (Festival d'Aix-en-Provence)

1974, dir. John Cox, cond. John Pritchard, London Philharmonic Orchestra; singers include Richard Lewis, Leo Goeke, Alexander Oliver, Josephine Barstow, Bozena Betley, Dennis Wicks, John Fryatt (Glyndebourne Festival Opera House)

1983, dir. Brian Large and Jean-Pierre Ponnelle, cond. James Levine, Orchestra of the Metropolitan Opera; singers include Luciano Pavarotti, Ileana Cotrubas, Hildegard Behrens, Frederica von Stade, John Alexander, Timothy Jenkins

1983, dir. Christopher Swann, cond. Bernard Haitink; singers include Philip Langridge, Jerry Hadley, Yvonne Kenny, Carol Vaness, Thomas Hemsley, Anthony Roden, Roderick Kennedy (Glyndebourne Festival production)

1989, dir. Johannes Schaaf, cond. Jeffrey Tate, Royal Opera orchestra; singers include Philip Langridge, Marie McLaughlin, Elizabeth Connell, Ann Murray, Robert Tear, Stuart Kale, Mark Beesley

1991, dir. Thomas Olofsson and Michael Hampe, cond. Arnold Östman, Drottningholm Theatre orchestra; singers include Stuart Kale, David Kuebler, Ann Christine Biel, Anita Soldh, Jan-Erik Jakobsson (recorded at the Drottningholm Court Theatre)

Mitridate, re di Ponto

1987, dir. Jean-Pierre Ponnelle, cond. Nikolaus Harnoncourt, Concentus Musicus; singers include Gösta Winbergh, Ann Murray, Joan Rodgers, Peter Straka, Massimiliano Roncato, John Fisher (recorded at the Teatro Olimpico, Vicenza)

Le nozze di Figaro

1949, dir. Georg Wildhagen, cond. ?, Staatsoper Berlin; singers include Mathieu Ahlersmeyer, Tiana Lemnitz, Erna Berger, Willi Domgraf-Fassbaender (in German)

1960, dir. Alan Burke, cond. Georg Tintner, Sydney Symphony Orchestra; singers include Russell Smith, Heather McMillan, Valda Bagnall, Geoffrey Chard, Marie Tysoe, Noel Melvin, Ereach Riley, John Probyn, Raymond McDonald

1963, dir. Gustav Rudolf Sellner, cond. Lorin Maazel, Wiener Philharmoniker; singers include Dietrich Fischer-Dieskau, Hilde Güden, Graziella Sciutti, Geraint Evans, Jan van Kesteren, Peter Lagger, Patricia Johnson, Evelyn Lear, Barbara Vogel (recorded at the Kleines Festspielhaus, Salzburg)

1963, dir. Peter Ebert, cond. Silvio Varviso, Glyndebourne Festival Orchestra; singers include Heinz Blankenburg, Liliane Berton, Carlo Cava, Rosa Laghezza, Edith Mathis, Michel Roux, Hugues Cuenod, Leyla Gencer, Derick Davies, Maria Zeri, John Kentish (Glyndebourne Festival Opera House)

1966, dir Günther Rennert, cond. Karl Böhm, Wiener Philharmoniker; singers include Ingvar Wixell, Claire Watson, Reri Grist, Edith Mathis, Walter Berry, Margaret Bence, Zoltan Kelemen, David Thaw, Klaus Hirte, Deirdre Aselford, Hans Pfeifle (Salzburg Festival)

1973, dir. Peter Hall, cond. John Pritchard, London Philharmonic Orchestra; singers include Knut Skram, Ileana Cotrubas, Kiri Te Kanawa, Benjamin Luxon, Marius Rintzler, Nucci Condo, Frederica von Stade (Glyndebourne Festival production)

1975, dir. Jean-Pierre Ponnelle, cond. Karl Böhm, Wiener Philharmoniker; singers include Hermann Prey, Mirella Freni, Dietrich Fischer-Dieskau, Kiri Te Kanawa, Maria Weing, Paolo Montarsolo, Heather Begg, John van Kesteren, Hans Kraemer, Janet Perry, Willy Caron

1980, dir. Helge Toma, cond. Karl Böhm, Wiener Staatsoper; singers include Hermann Prey, Lucia Popp, Gundula Janowitz, Bernd Weikl, Agnes Baltsa, Margarita Lilova, Kurt Rydl, Heinz Zednik, Kurt Equiluz, Maria Venuti, Edith Schteininger (recorded live, Tokyo-Bunkakaikan)

1980, dir. Giorgio Strehler, cond. Georg Solti, Opéra de Paris; singers include: José van Dam, Lucia Popp, Gabriel Baquier, Gundula Janowitz, Frederica von Stade, Kurt Moll

1981, dir. Adrian Kiernander, cond. Emily Mair, Orchestra Sinfonia Wellington; singers include Roger Creagh, Lynne Cantlon, Louise Malloy, Timothy Hawley, Wendy Dixon, Linda Shearer, Roger Wilson, Anthony Benfell, Leslie Corizac, Patricia Aldersley, Leo Barnett, Greta Bently, Gillian Stier (in English)

1981, dir. Göan Järvefelt, cond. Arnold Östman, Drottningholm Baroque Orchestra; singers includ Sylvia Lindenstrand, Per-Arne Wahlgren, Georgine Resick, Mikael Samuelsson, Anne Christine Biel (recorded at the Schlosstheater Drottningholm)

1983, dir. Peter Hall, cond. Jeffrey Tate, Orchestre de la Suisse Romande; singers include Ruggero Raimondi, Anna Tomowa-Sintow, Claudio Desderi, Maria Ewing, Jolanta Radek, Marijke Hendriks, Patriia Kern, Jules Bastin, Michael Cousins, Francoi Loup, Hugues Cuenod

1985, dir. Jean-Pierre Ponnelle, cond. James Levine, Metropolitan Opera Orchestra; singers include Kathleen Batle, Carol Vaness, Frederica von Stade, Ruggero Raimondi, Thomas Allen (recorded live, Metropolitan Opera)

1985, dir. ?, cond. Mario Bernardi, Montreal Opera Company; singers include Allan Monk, Claude Corbeil, Anne Marie Roddi, Benito Arnould (Canadian Broadcasting Corporation)

1989, dir. Johannes Schaaf, cond. Bernard Haitink, Royal Opera orchestra; singers include Claudio Desderi, Marie McLaughlin, Thomas Allen, Carol Vaness, Stella Kleindienst, Sarah Walker, Richard Van Allan, Judith Howarth, Robert Tear, Alexander Oliver, Federico Davia (recorded at the Royal Opera House, Covent Garden)

1989, dir. Peter Sellars, cond. Craig Smith, Wiener Symphoniker; singers include Jayne West, Jeanne Ommerlé, Susan Larson, Sue Ellen Kuzma, James Maddalena, Stanford Sylvan, David Eviths, Frank Kelley, Herman Hildebrand, William Cotton, Lynn Torgove

1989, dir. Peter Hall, cond. Simon Rattle, Orchestra of the Age of Enlightenment; singers include Joan Rodgers, Marianna Rorholm, William Shimell, Felicity Palmer, Alison Hagley, Donald Adams, Dale Duesing, Gunnel Bohman, John Graham Hall, Francois Loup, Mario Bolognesi (Glyndebourne Festival)

1989, dir. Michael Hampe, cond. Bernard Haitink; singers include Thomas Allen, Ljuba Kazarnovskaya, Dawn Upshaw, Susanna Mentzer, Ferruccio Furlanetto, Klara Tackacs, John Tomlinson, Ugo Benelli (recorded live, Festspielhaus Salzburg)

1990, dir. Marco-Arturo Marelli, cond. Bruno Weil, Volksoper Wien; singers include Boje Skovhus, Gunnel Bohman, Chrsitane Böiger, Hedwig Fassbender, Gertrud Jahn, Lotte Leitner, Sten Byriel, Alfred Sramek, Volker Vogel (recorded at the Volksoper Wien, in German)

1991, dir. Jonathan Miller, cond. Claudio Abbado, Wiener Philharmoniker; singers include Cheryl Studer, Marie McLaughlin, Gabriele Sima, Ruggero Raimondi, Lucio Gallo, Margarita Lilowa, Heinz Zednik (recorded live at the Theater an der Wien)

1991, dir. Peter Hall, John Bury, cond. Andrew Davis, Lyric Opera of Chicago; singers include Samuel Ramey, Felicity Lott, Maria Ewing, Frederica von Stade, Thomas Hampson, Marie McLaughlin

1991, dir. John Copley, cond. Scott Bergeson; singers include Dean Peterson, Maureen O'Flynn, Joseph McKee, Susanne Marsee, Kathryn Gamberoni, William Stone, Jonathan Green, Elizabeth Hunes, Don Yule, Peter Blanchet, Michele McBride (New York City Opera)

1991, dir. Claus Viller and Michael Hampe, cond. Bernard Haitink; singers include Thomas Allen, Dawn Upshaw, Ferruccio Furlanetto, Susanne Mentzer, Klara Takacs, John Tomlinson, Ugo Benelli, Alexander Oliver, Machiko Obata, Alfred Kuhn Kedwig Witte (Salzburger Festspiel production)

1993, dir. Olivier Mille and Jean-Louis Thamin, cond. John Eliot Gardiner; singers include Rodney Gilfry, Hillevi Martinpelto, Bryn Terfel, Alison Hagley, Pamela Helen Stephen, Susan McCulloch, Francis Egerton, Julian Clarkson, Carlos Feller, Constanze Backes

1994, dir. Derek Bailey and Stephen Medcalf, cond. Bernard Haitink; singers include Gerald Finley, Alison Hagley, Renée Fleming, Andreas Schmidt, Manfred Röhrl, Wendy Hillhouse, Marie-Ange Todorovitch, Robert Tear, Donald Adams, John Graham-Hall, Susan Gritton (Glyndebourne Festival production)

1994, dir. Maté Rabinovski and Jean-Pierre Vincent, cond. Paolo Olmi, Orchestre de l'Opéra Nationale de Lyon; singers include Giovanni Furlanetto, Elzbieta

Szmytka, Janice Watson, Ludovic Tézier, Francesca Provvisionato, Rebecca Hoffman, Tiziana Tramonti, Marcello Lippi, Sergio Bertocchi, Gérard Théruel, Jorge Anton

1999, dir. Alexandre Tarta, cond. Daniel Barenboim, Orchestra of the Staatskapelle Berlin; singers include Roman Trekel, Emily Magee, Dorothea Röschmann, René Pape, Patricia Risley, Rosemarie Lang, Peter Schreier, Peter Menzel, Kwangchul Youn, Bernd Zettisch, Yvonne Zeuge

2004, dir. Pierre Barret, cond. René Jacobs, Concerto Köln; singers include Pietro Sagnoli, Rosemary Joshua, Angelika Kirchschlager, Alessandro Svab, Antonio Abete, Enrico Facini, Serge Goubioud

L'oca del Cairo

1958, dir. Harmut Rötting, cond. Hans Gabor, Wiener Kammeroper; singers include Bengt Wiksten, Kage Jehrlander, Kurt Equiluz, Edda Mittermayer, Franz Wyzner, Gertraud Matuschka (recorded live, Schlosstheater Schönbrunn)

1991, dir. ?, cond. Hans Rotman, Kammerorchester Transparant/Flämische Oper; singers include Rolande van der Paal, Greetje Anthoni, Leonie Schoon, Herman Bekaert, Bernard Loonen, Romain Bischoff, Ioan Micu, Cox Habbema, Eddy Habbema (recorded for ZDF Television)

Il re pastore

1989, dir. Brian Large and John Cox, cond. Neville Marriner, Academy of St Martin in the Fields; singers include Angela Maria Blasi, Sylvia McNair, Iris Vermillion, Jerry Hadley, Claes H. Ahnsjö (recorded at the Landestheater, Salzburg)

1989, dir. Eberhard Harnoncourt, cond. Wim van Zutphen; singers include Arno Raunig, Elisabeth Schoex, Monika Meergraf, Robert Schindler, Zeeger Vandersteen (recorded at Schloss Eggenberg, Graz)

1989, dir. Brian Large and John Cox, cond. Neville Marriner; singers include Angela Maria Blasi, Sylvia McNair, Iris Vermillion, Claes H. Ahnsjö, Jerry Hadley

Il sogno di Scipione

1991, dir. Peter Schneider, cond. Vittorio Patané, Münchner Rundfunkorchester; singers include Robert Swenson, Julie Kaufmann, Caroline Maria Petrig, Claes H. Ahnsjö, Hermann Winkler

Der Schauspieldirektor

1954, dir. Ludwig Berger, cond. Walter Martin, RSO Hamburg; singers include Willy Maertens, Valerie Bak, Rosl Schwaiger

1964, dir. Guy Hoffman, cond. Alexander Prott; singers include Pierrette Alarie, Claire Gagnier, Jean-Paul Jeannotte, Paul Berval, Guy Hoffman (Canadian Broadcasting Corporation)

1990, dir. ?, cond. Gerard Schwartz, Mostly Mozart Festival Orchestra; singers include Werner Klemperer, Frances Ginsberg, Sally Wolf, Vinson Cole (concert version, Lincoln Center)

Zaide

1953, dir. Erwin Euller, cond. Heinz Norfolk, Niederösterreichisches Tonkünstlerorchester; singers include Kurt Dieman, Wilhelm Leitner, Liane Dubin, Erich Zur Eck, Hans Peter Krasa, Erwin Euller (live recording, Sommerarena Baden)

1989, dir. Ryszard Peryt, cond. Ruben Silva, Sinfonieta/Warszawsk Opera Karerlana (Warsaw Chamber Opera); singers include Jolanta Zmurko, Jerzy Knetig, Adam Kruszewski, Zdzislaw Nikodem, Andreij Klimczak

Die Zauberflöte

1975, dir. Ingmar Bergman, cond. Eric Ericson; singers include Britt-Marie Aruhn, Gösta Bäckelin, Ulrik Cold, Elisabeth Erikson, Håkan Kagegård, Josef Köstlinger, Birgit Nordin, Erik Saedén, Ragnar Ulfung, Irma Urrila (in Swedish as *Trollflöjten*)

1978, dir. Dave Heather, cond. Bernard Haitink, London Philharmonic Orchestra; singers include Leo Goeke, Felicity Lott, Benjamin Luxon, Elisabeth Conquet, May Sandoz, Thomas Thomaschke, Willard White, John Fryatt (Glyndebourne Festival production)

1983, dir. Peter Windgassen and August Everding, cond. Wolfgang Sawallisch, Orchestra of the Bayerische Staatsoper; singers include Kurt Moll, Francisco Araiza, Jan-Hendrik Rootering, Edita Gruberova, Lucia Popp, Wolfgang Brendel, Gudrun Sieber, Norbert Orth

1986, dir. Henry Prokop and Göran Järvefelt, cond. Richard Bonynge, Orchestra of the Australian Opera; singers include Grant Wilson, Yvonne Kenny, John Fulford, Donald Shanks, Christa Leahmann, Graeme Ewer, John Pringle, Peta Blyth

1991, dir. Brian Large and John Cox, cond. James Levine, Orchestra of the Metropolitan Opera; singers include Kathleen Battle, Francisco Araiza, Manfred Hemm, Kurt Moll, Lucianna Serra, Barbara Kilduff, Andreas Schmidt, Heinz Zednik (sets designed by David Hockney)

1992, dir. Roberto de Simone, cond. Alain Lombard, Orchestre Nationale de Bordeaux; singers include Erich Knodt, Patrick Tower, Roderick Kennedy, Helena Vink, Charlotte Margiono, Karsten Mewes, Gaele Le Roi, Uwe Peper, Gillian Webster, Béatrice Uria-Monzon, Yvonne Lea (recorded at the Grand Théâtre de Bordeaux)

1994, dir. Robert Carsen, cond. William Christie; singers include Hans Peter Blochwitz, Rosa Mannton, Nathalie Dessay, Reinhard Hagen, Linda Kitchen, Anton Scharinger (recorded live at the Festival d'Aix-en-Provence)

1995, cond. John Eliot Gardiner, English Baroque Soloists; singers include Michael Shade, Gerald Finley, Cyndia Sieden, Uwe Peper, Christiane Oelze, Detlef Roth, Harry Peeters, Constanze Backes

2003, dir. Sue Judd, cond. Colin Davis, Orchestra of the Royal Opera House; singers include Willi Hartmann, Dorothea Röschmann, Diana Damrau, Franz-Josef Selig, Simon Keenlyside, Ailish Tynan, Adrian Thompson (television production for BBC)

Appendix 4
Mozart organizations

Austria

Internationale Stiftung Mozarteum, Schwarzstrasse 26, A-5020 Salzburg; telephone 662 88 940 13, fax 662 88 24 19, website: www.mozarteum.at
In addition to a list of concerts and details on museums, this site includes a useful online bibliography of writings about Mozart, especially from the 1990s on; the bibliography can be searched by author, topic or Köchel number.

Mozart-Gemeinde Niederösterreich, Stuwer-Str. 1-3/1/1, A-1020 Wien

Mozartgemeinde Wien, Amalien-Str. 29a, A-11300 Wien; telephone 43 1 876 7201

Neue Mozart-Ausgabe; website www.nma.at
The official website of the Neue Mozart-Ausgabe. In addition to brief news items, the site includes a database that lists the locations of Mozart's autographs, a summary of the edition and information on Mozart librettos as well as links to other sites.

France

Cercle Mozart Strasbourg, 5, rue de Londres, F-67000 Strasbourg

Germany

Deutsche Mozart-Gesellschaft, Frauentorstrasse 30, D-86152 Augsburg; telephone 49 0821 518588, fax 49 0821 157228, email: info@Deutsche-Mozart-Gesellschaft.de, website: www.mozartgesellschaft.de
The Deutsche Mozart-Gesellschaft sponsors concerts and lectures and, additionally, published a useful but accessible scholarly periodical, *Acta Mozartiana*.

Mozartgemeinde Arnsberg, Kettelburgstr. 23, 59759 Arnsberg; telephone 49 02932 35254, fax 49 02932 52187

Mozart Gemeinde Augsburg e.V., Musikalienhandlung A. Böhm & Sohn, Ludwigstr. 15, 86152 Augsburg; telephone 49 5 02 84-25

Bamberger Mozartgesellschaft, Accademia mozartiana, Hornthalstr. 38, D-96047 Bamberg; telephone/fax 49 0911 55 68 86

Mozartgemeinde Bayreuth, Habichtweg 32, 95445 Bayreuth; telephone 49 09 21 41 46 5, fax 49 09 21 74 54 75 3

Mozartgesellschaft Berlin-Brandenburg e.V., Unter den Eichen 42, 12203 Berlin; telephone 49 030 8314169, fax 49 030 8312463

Mozart-Gesellschaft Dortmund e. V., Ruhrallee 9, 44139 Dortmund; telephone 49 0231 42 74 335, fax 49 0231 42 74 385, website: www.mozart-gesellschaft-dortmund.de

Mozartverein zu Dresden e.V., Ermelstrasse 21, 01277 Dresden

Mozartgesellschaft Frankfurt a. M. e.V., Donnersbergstr. 3a, 55129 Mainz; telephone 49 069 590701, fax 49 069 5961576

Mozartgemeinde Hildesheim e.V., Adolf-Kolping-Str. 67, 31139 Hildesheim; telephone 49 05121 26 16 71

Mozartgemeinde Koblenz u. Umgebung e.V., Arenberger Str. 212, 56077 Koblenz; telephone 49 0261 65336

Mozart-Gesellschaft Kurpfalz e.V., Leistadter Str. 14, 67273 Weisenheim am Berg; telephone/fax 49 06353 8833

Mozartgemeinde Regensburg e.V., Am Stahlzwingerweg 23, 93047 Regensburg

Mozartgesellschaft Schwetzingen e.V., Angela Bräunig Uhlandstr. 4, 68723 Schwetzingen; telephone 49 06202 33 64, fax 49 06202 12 79 77

Mozart-Gesellschaft Stuttgart e.V., Kernerstrasse 2 A, 70182 Stuttgart; telephone 49 0711 2237126, fax 39 0711 2237331, website: www.deutsche-mozart-gesellschaft.de

Mozartgemeinde Südostbayern e.V., Mallinger Strasse 12, 83043 Bad Aibling; telephone 49 08061 7714

Mozartgesellschaft Zweibrücken-Bitche-Pirmasens, Kreuzbergstr. 7, 66482 Zweibrücken; telephone 49 41 332 / 41 991

Italy

Associazione Mozart Italia; website: www.mozartitalia.org
In addition to details about the Associazione Mozart Italia, this website includes links to other sites as well as considerable useful information and a picture gallery.

Netherlands

Mozartkring Gelre-Niederrhein, Peter Cornelius Hoofstraat 8, NL-6573 CE Beek-Ubbergen; telephone 31 2468 41914

Romania

Societatea Romana Mozart, cp. 218, RO-3400 Clug (Ro); telephone 40 95 119 488

Switzerland

Mozart Gesellschaft Luzern, Obergrundstraase 13, 6003 Luzern; telephone 041 241 01 60, fax 041 240 14 53, email: cdillier@mhs.fhz.ch

Mozart-Gesellaschaft Zürich, Girhaldenweg 10, CH-8148 Zürich; telephone 41 12157599, fax 41 1215715

United States of America

Mozart Society of America, Department of Music, University of Nevada Las Vegas, Las Vegas, NV, USA 89154-5025; telephone: 702 895 3114, fax 702 895-4239, email: msa@nevada.edu website: www.nulv.edu/mozart

Friends of Mozart, Inc., PO Box 24, FDR Station, NY 10150; telephone 212 832 9420

Mozart Society of California. PO Box 221351, Carmel, CA 93922; telephone 831 625 3637, website: www.mozart-society.com

Appendix 5
Mozart websites

Associazione Mozart Itali www.mozartitalia.org

A useful and attractive site including accounts of the association's activities, information about Mozart, sound clips, a picture gallery and general Mozart news. Email: AMI@MozartItalia.org

Mozart 2006 www.mozart2006.at

A site sponsored by the city of Salzburg to promote Mozart celebrations during the year marking the 250th anniversary of his birth. A monthly calendar describes a series of events planned for 2006 and a forum is available for those who register.

The Mozart Project www.frontiernet.net/tilde'sboerner/mozart/index.html

An extensive site with information on Mozart's works, a biography, selected essays and a bibliography as well as a list of links. The information is sometimes dated, relying on older scholarship; nevertheless it gives a great deal of useful information.

Openmozart.net www.openmozart.net

Another extensive site with a catalogue, notes on Mozart's works, a biography, a list of Mozart books, images and links to other sites. It also includes a message board where Mozart scholars and aficionados can post and reply to messages of common interest.

OperaGlass Mozart http://rick.stanford.edu/opera/Mozart/main.html

This site includes a complete list of Mozart's operas with detailed information and librettos for selected works.

Patterns of Mozart Reception in the Nineteenth Century www.soton.ac.uk/~me/pmr/pmr.html

This interesting website documents a research project by Mark Everist, University of Southampton, to catalogue nineteenth-century arrangements, for a variety of ensembles and solo instruments, of Mozart's works. At present it includes lists of instrumental works based on *La clemenza di Tito*, *Così fan tutte*, *Don Giovanni*, *Le nozze di Figaro* and *Die Zauberflöte*, as well as a bibliography.

Salzburg Festival www.salzburgfestival.com

Includes the full programmes for the current and next year with information on artists, venues, history and publications as well as press releases and details on ticket purchase.

Index of Mozart's works by Köchel number

This index includes only works mentioned in the main text. For further details on all of Mozart's works, see Appendix 1.

Index of Mozart's works by genre

This index includes only works mentioned in the main text. For further details on all of Mozart's works, see Appendix 1.

Masses, mass movements

Litanies, Vespers

Shorter church works

Oratorios, sacred singspiels, cantatas

Operas

Music for plays, pantomimes and ballets

Scenes, arias and chorus with orchestra

Songs with keyboard (or mandoline) accompaniment

Songs for several voices

Canons

Symphonies

Cassations, serenades, divertimentos and other movements for strings and winds

Marches and dances for orchestra

Concertos for one or more solo instrument (excluding keyboard concertos)

Concertos for one or more keyboards

Church sonatas

Divertimentos, serenades and other movements for winds

Divertimenti and other movements for strings

String quintets and quintets for strings and winds

String quartets and quartets for strings and winds

Trios and duos for strings and winds

Quintets, quartets and trios with keyboard or glass harmonica

Sonatas, variations and other works for keyboard and violin

Works for two keyboards or keyboard four hands

Sonatas and fantasies for keyboard

Variations, rondos and other works for keyboard or mechanical clock

Arrangements of works by other composers

Copies of works by other composers

General index